CHILD DEVELOPMENT
An Introduction

THIRD EDITION

CHILD DEVELOPMENT
An Introduction

JOHN W. SANTROCK
University of Texas at Dallas

STEVEN R. YUSSEN
University of Wisconsin–Madison

wcb
WM. C. BROWN PUBLISHERS
DUBUQUE, IOWA

BOOK TEAM

John Stout *Executive Editor*
James M. McNeil *Editor*
Sandra E. Schmidt *Senior Developmental Editor*
Mary K. Sailer *Designer*
Kathy Loewenberg *Art Production Assistant*
Karen Slaght *Senior Production Editor*
Shirley M. Charley *Photo Research Editor*
Vicki Krug *Permissions Editor*

wcb group

Wm. C. Brown *Chairman of the Board*
Mark C. Falb *President and Chief Executive Officer*

wcb

WM. C. BROWN PUBLISHERS, COLLEGE DIVISION

G. Franklin Lewis *Executive Vice-President, General Manager*
E. F. Jogerst *Vice-President, Cost Analyst*
Chris C. Guzzardo *Vice-President, Director of Marketing*
George Wm. Bergquist *Editor in Chief*
Bob McLaughlin *National Sales Manager*
Catherine M. Faduska *Director of Marketing Services*
Craig S. Marty *Director of Marketing Research*
Eugenia M. Collins *Production Editorial Manager*
Marilyn A. Phelps *Manager of Design*
Faye M. Schilling *Photo Research Manager*

Cover photo by Kathleen Loewenberg

The credits section for this book begins on page 629, and is considered an extension of the copyright page.

With special appreciation to our wives
Mary Jo and Suzann and to our children
Jennifer and Tracy, David and Elayna

"Thinking it should be taught
as a course -
Homespun - manu - apart for
Instihution criteria.
When I cut it cuts two way
" " " " " one way.
Preowned - forused.

BRIEF CONTENTS

CONTENTS

S E C T I O N

PERSPECTIVES ON CHILD DEVELOPMENT

S E C T I O N

2

BIOLOGICAL PROCESSES AND PHYSICAL DEVELOPMENT

2 BIOLOGICAL PROCESSES, GENETICS, AND NEUROLOGICAL DEVELOPMENT   37

PROLOGUE The Child's Mission Control   38
PREVIEW   39

EVOLUTION, ETHOLOGY, AND GENERAL BIOLOGICAL PRINCIPLES OF DEVELOPMENT   39

3   PHYSICAL DEVELOPMENT 71

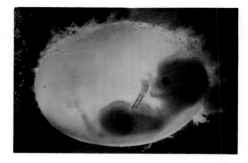

SECTION

3

COGNITIVE PROCESSES AND DEVELOPMENT

8 LANGUAGE DEVELOPMENT 229

SECTION

4

SOCIAL AND PERSONALITY PROCESSES AND DEVELOPMENT

14 SEX-ROLE DEVELOPMENT 487

SECTION

PROBLEMS AND DISTURBANCES

CONCEPT TABLES

PERSPECTIVE ON CHILD DEVELOPMENT BOXES

PREFACE

Some eleven years ago we agreed to write the first edition of *Child Development*. We wanted to provide a book for undergraduate students that would portray the scientific study of child development in a lively and enthusiastic manner. Six years ago, the second edition of *Child Development* appeared. Because ours is a field of rapidly developing knowledge with extensive research on children being conducted throughout the world, the second edition represented a substantial revision of the first edition. While capturing the changing scientific base of information about children, the second edition also was written in a manner designed to be enjoyable for students as well.

The third edition of *Child Development* continues the tradition of the first and second editions of *Child Development,* but with some significant changes that we believe will make the book even more attractive to you and your students. First, we have retained the topical approach so popular in the first and second editions. Second, we have culled the recent research literature on child development and provided leading examples of quality studies. Every effort also has been made to describe the breadth of research in the field of child development. Third, we have added extensive, unique pedagogy that is considerably expanded over the previous editions.

Why is *Child Development* written from a topical perspective? By means of this process-oriented perspective, your students will be able to see how developmental processes reflect fundamental changes in the childhood years. To this end, separate sections focus on biological processes and physical development; cognitive processes and development; and social/personality processes and development. In addition, the first section of the text provides a very comprehensive, comprehensible discussion of history, issues, and methods.

Our final section on problems and disturbances gives special attention to the abnormal aspects of development.

The research included in the core of the text—research focused on biological, cognitive, and social/personality processes—includes basic ideas about child development, as well as "leading edge" research that helps students sense where the field is headed. Later in the preface, when we discuss major changes from the second edition, a number of highlights of these topics will be mentioned.

Another important ingredient of the third edition *Child Development* is the breadth and uniqueness of the pedagogy. An important feature of pedagogy is organization. Each of the 16 chapters of this book has been carefully constructed to provide a very organized presentation of material. Such organization is critical for students when they are reading a text that includes such an extensive amount of research information, and should greatly enhance your students' ability to comprehend and remember research information.

How did we accomplish this important task of organization? Each chapter begins with an outline, then a preview of major topics to be discussed appears. As each major topic is described, the student is given a "road map" telling what will follow. Then, even within major topics, students will encounter "mini-road maps," giving a sense of organization to what is about to be read. Also, two or three times in each chapter students will come across a *Concept Table,* an organizational device that activates memory of major topics and key concepts discussed to that point, and shows students how complex themes and concepts are related. Students can get overwhelmed as they proceed through such chapters as "Biological Processes, Genetics, and Neurological Development," and "Information Processing." The organizational tables help students get a handle on large blocks of information before they reach the end of the chapter. Then, at the end of the chapter, students are provided a functional outline that stimulates them to review the main ideas and key concepts discussed in the entire chapter, and shows the hierarchical organization of chapter material.

Each chapter begins with an easy-to-read, enjoyable *Prologue* related to that particular chapter. For example, chapter 2 opens with "The Child's Mission Control," and chapter 7 begins with "Strange Games with Strange Creatures." In addition to the prologues, each chapter has several boxes called *Perspective on Child Development,* which provide the student with a detailed discussion of research on child development or other points of interest. By reading these boxes students gain a better sense of how research in the field of child development is carried out. Students also find that key terms are in bold face within the chapter, are listed at the end of the chapter, and are defined at the end of the book. A list of suggested readings also appears at the end of the chapter.

CHANGES IN THE THIRD EDITION OF CHILD DEVELOPMENT

The major changes in the new edition include both organizational and content revisions. We will consider each section and chapter in turn.

Section 1: Perspective on Child Development

The second edition of *Child Development* included an opening section on the foundations of development. The third edition divides this section into two parts. The first section now includes only one chapter and provides an overview of the history, issues, and methods of child development. A major addition to this first chapter is the inclusion of a section on issues in child development, which emphasizes qualitative change, stages, continuity-discontinuity, and individual differences. The scientific orientation section provides a much more organized format for understanding measures, strategies of research design, and the time span inquiry. Theories no longer are discussed in chapter 1 but are described in greater detail where appropriate at different points in the text.

Section 2: Biological Processes and Physical Development

The second section now includes two chapters, "Biological Processes, Genetics, and Neurological Development" and "Physical Development." Chapter 2 includes much more developmental information on the brain than appeared in the second edition, as well as greater consideration of psychobiological principles of development. And chapter 3 houses much more information about physical development throughout the childhood years than was present in the second edition. While infancy now does not have a separate chapter title, by looking at chapters 2 and 3 you can see the detailed attention given to foundations of development in the infant years through a complete discussion of ethology, genetics, neurological development, prenatal development, birth, and the first two years of life.

Among the highlights of research on biological processes and physical development are:

A thorough discussion of evolution and ethology

General psychobiological principles, such as forward reference

Extensive information about genetic-environmental interaction, including the concepts of canalization and reaction range

Elegant portrayal of the brain at both cellular and anatomical levels

The ontogeny of neurotransmitters, such as dopamine

The processes of neural development

The integration of function in the brain

Overview of prenatal development, including the effects of nicotine, alcohol, and caffeine on the fetus and infant

Section 3: Cognitive Processes and Development

An entire chapter has now been devoted to sensory and perceptual development and can be found in the section on cognitive processes and development. Now learning, like sensory/perceptual development, is housed in the section on cognitive processes and development, and the discussion of perceptual learning has been placed in the chapter on sensory/perceptual development. Discussion of both perceptual development and learning includes considerable information on how children interpret their world and the cognitive factors in learning. The increased cognitive orientation of the discussion of perception and learning led to their inclusion in the section on cognitive processes and development. Also, each of these topics—learning and sensory/perceptual development—now is given separate chapter treatment. This decision allows the chapters on learning and sensory/perceptual development to be understood more clearly by students because the chapters are more cohesive wholes.

The chapter on Piaget and the cognitive developmental view was a popular part of the second edition of *Child Development*. This chapter has been retained, but we think you will find the chapter has been nicely updated and organized more coherently. The chapter on information processing in the second edition also was liked by many professors, although there were some complaints that it could have been organized more clearly for the benefit of students. We have spent considerable time providing a sensible, easy-to-follow overview of the dynamic field of information processing. And, because of the extensive research attention given to information processing, you will find an extensive amount of updating in this chapter. Language development continues to have its own chapter as does intelligence. You will find both of these chapters to be better organized than in the second edition and you will discover that each topic has benefitted from the inclusion of contemporary research. In particular, a modern information-processing interpretation has been added to the intelligence chapter with particular attention given to the distinction between knowledge and process in cognition.

Among the research topics given special attention in the area of cognitive processes and development are:

The constructivist and ecological perspectives on perception

Details of the imaginative manner in which researchers study infant perception

Spelke's intriguing research on bimodal perception

New and old models of information processing—Broadbent's and Klatsky's

Strengths and weaknesses of information-processing perspective

An innovative approach to reading involving the role of writing

A stimulating discussion of schools and information processing

Extensive coverage of milestones of language, including Eve Clark's theory of meaning

Section 4: Social/Personality Processes and Development

The section on social/personality processes again opens with a chapter on socialization theories and processes. However, the third edition provides much more information about the cognitive and ethological perspectives on socialization than appeared in the second edition. And the first chapter in this section includes a valuable outline and analyses of the child's social environment, including information about culture, social contexts, and relationships. A full chapter is now devoted to families and includes the discussion of attachment. A contemporary view of family processes emphasizes ideas about the way children construct relationships, carry these relationships forward in time, and are influenced by intergenerational relationships. Our discussion of peers is no longer in the families chapter, but begins the next chapter: now the important extrafamilial settings of peers and school are housed in the same chapter. The discussion of peer relations includes new ideas about social information processing and social knowledge as well as the development of friendships. Further, the topic of play has been given greatly expanded treatment in this chapter. The overview of schools focuses on new data about day care and early childhood education, the school as a social context for development, and ethnic considerations. The two chapters on personality development contain much more information about the important issue of stability and change than appeared in the second edition. New information emphasizes trait x situation interaction and Mischel's recent longitudinal data on delay of gratification. And the increasingly important topic of social competence is dealt with at length. The development of the self continues to be presented in a manner that allows students to see its sequential unfolding. The discussion of sex roles and moral development is retained in a single section and includes Gilligan's recent ideas about differing male and female perspectives on moral development.

Among the research highlights of the section on social and personality development are:

Application of Neisser's perceptual model to children's socialization

Hinde's ethological ideas on relationships

Emphasis throughout on how children construct relationships

Stress on how children carry relationships forward

A developmental focus to personality development

The new look in play research

Gilligan's recent ideas on moral development

Evaluation of the nature of social competence and its assessment

Sex roles and computers

Section 5: Problems and Disturbances

The description of problems and disturbances has its own section in the new edition. This section, containing one chapter, has been rewritten with a stronger developmental stance. New information focuses on the nature of the science of developmental psychopathology, childhood depression, school related problems, and the issue of continuity-discontinuity in understanding problems and disturbances in development.

TO THE STUDENT: HOW TO PROFIT FROM THE PEDAGOGY

You already have read about some of the pedagogical, or learning, devices that appear in this book to make your learning more effective. Start with the chapter outline that organizes the most important ideas of the chapter. By studying this outline for a few minutes before beginning each chapter you get an advanced look at the content of the chapter and at what the main, as well as secondary, topics are. Then read the Prologue section that begins each chapter. This brief essay is designed to heighten your interest in the subject matter of the chapter and should motivate you to read further. The final introductory part of each chapter is called the Preview. Read this useful brief section to further see what the major topics of the chapter will be.

As you move into the interior of each of the chapters, you will discover that each major heading is introduced by a very brief description of what will be discussed within that heading. These "road maps," like the Preview and Outline, provide you with an organization of what you will be reading in the next few pages. On virtually every page or two you will encounter boldfaced terms, which should alert you to the fact that you should learn the definition of the boldfaced words. It also signals that the term is defined for you in the glossary at the end of the book. Two or three times in each chapter you will come across Concept Table. Go through each of these tables to review the major features and concepts of the material that you have just read. If some of these concepts still seem fuzzy to you, it suggests you should return to their location in the chapter and review the information about the concept. The Concept Tables are a detailed check on the material you have read, and should help you to understand how different themes and concepts are related.

At the end of the chapter read the Summary, which appears in outline form. The Summary provides a review of the major topics and concepts of the entire chapter. By the time you have read the Summary, the overall outline of the entire chapter should fall into place for you, and you should have a good sense of how the material of the chapter fits together. You also will find the Key Terms listed at the end of the chapter. Go down the list and try to define each of the terms. If a term is foreign to you, go back to its appearance in the chapter and review the term. Finally, read the Suggestions for Further Reading. You will find a combination of articles and books suggested, some of which are more detailed scientific reading than appears in this text, others that are lighter, more personal pieces. Both types of reading should further your knowledge about the exciting field of child development.

INSTRUCTIONAL AND LEARNING AIDS

Melvyn B. King and Debra E. Clark, State University of New York–Cortland, have provided a helpful Instructor's Manual for use with *Child Development* that will save you time in preparing for this course. For each chapter, the manual includes a Chapter Summary, Learning Objectives, List of Key Terms (referenced to learning objectives and text page), Research Project (with complete instructions and data collection forms), Classroom Activities, and Essay Questions. A comprehensive Test-Item File is also included in the Instructor's Manual. It contains multiple-choice, true-false, and fill-in-the-blank questions, each referenced to text page and learning objective. The Instructor's Manual also contains a brief essay on "Ethics, Human Subjects, and Informed Consent."

The Student Study Guide, also written by Melvyn B. King and Debra E. Clark, contains the following elements for each chapter: Learning Objectives, Chapter Overview, Guided Review, Key Terms Matching Exercise, Evaluate Your Progress (two twenty-question practice tests), Questions to Stimulate Thought, and a Student Research Project (with complete instructions and data collection forms). A brief essay on "Ethics, Human Subjects, and Informed Consent" is also included to familiarize your students with the research process. Each item in the Guided Review, Key Terms Exercises, and student self-tests is referenced to the appropriate text page and learning objective.

All questions are available on TestPak, a free, computerized testing service available to adopters of *Child Development*. The call-in/mail-in service offers a test master, a student answer sheet, and an answer key within two working days of receipt of the instructor's request.

TestPak is also available for instructors who want to use their Apple®*IIe*, Apple®*IIc*, or IBM®PC microcomputer system to create their own tests. Upon adoption of *Child Development* and upon request, the instructor will receive the Test-Item File, program diskettes, and user's guide. With these, the instructor will be able to create tests, answer sheets, and answer keys. The program allows for adding, deleting, or modifying test questions. No programming experience is necessary.

Also free to adopters of *Child Development* is **wcb** QuizPak, the interactive self-testing, self-scoring quiz program. Your students can review text material from any chapter by testing themselves on an Apple®*IIe*, *IIc*, or IBM®PC. Adopters will receive the QuizPak program, question disks, and an easy-to-follow User's Guide. You may modify or delete the questions we provide or add your own. No programming experience is necessary.

wcb StudyPak is a computerized Study Guide to help your students master the material in *Child Development*. StudyPak includes guided reviews with fill-in-the-blank, short answer, multiple-choice, and matching items; quizzes; and games. The easy-to-use program includes a built-in diagnostic scoring system that identifies the learning objectives the student has not mastered. StudyPak is available on the IBM®PC, Apple®*IIe*, and *IIc*.

ACKNOWLEDGEMENTS

The history of *Child Development* is now eleven years of age. We agreed to write the first edition of *Child Development* at SRCD in 1975. The first edition was published in 1978 and the second edition in 1981. We are deeply grateful to our publisher, William C. Brown, for the continuing support of our writing. In particular, we are thankful for the early support of two young developmental psychologists not long out of graduate school at the University of Minnesota Institute of Child Development. The staff at William C. Brown has provided very competent support through all three editions of *Child Development,* from editorial advice, through the production of a beautiful book, to the enthusiastic sales representatives who market the text.

There are many people who spent long hours on this project. We benefited considerably from the competent editorial support of James McNeil, Social Sciences Editor, and Sandy Schmidt, Senior Developmental Editor. They form a great team—intelligent, supportive, and hard-working. Karen Slaght deserves mention for her work as Production Editor, making our words and concepts more sensible. Mary Sailor, Designer, has provided creative touches to make the book more attractive. Shirley Charley, Photo Research Editor, has made special efforts at tracking down suggested photographs. Vicki Krug, Permissions Editor, has efficiently obtained permissions.

The reviewers of the third edition of *Child Development* have provided constructive criticism that has made the book a much better one than otherwise would have been possible. We are deeply indebted to the following individuals in this regard:

Ruth L. Ault
Davidson College

Debra E. Clark
SUNY–Cortland

Roger W. Coulson
Iowa State University

Dennis T. Farrell
Luzerne County Community College

Robert A. Haaf
University of Toledo

Daniel W. Kee
California State University at Fullerton

Melvyn B. King
SUNY–Cortland

Daniel K. Lapsley
University of Notre Dame

Jose E. Nanez
University of Minnesota

Daniel J. O'Neill
Bristol Community College

Ed Scholwinski
Southwest Texas State University

Matthew J. Sharps
University of Colorado

Mark S. Strauss
University of Pittsburgh

Very special thanks go to an outstanding cognitive psychologist, trained at Yale University, who recently has become interested in developmental processes. James C. Bartlett, University of Texas at Dallas contributed information to, and even wrote large blocks of, Section III on cognitive processes and development. We deeply appreciate his willingness to participate in *Child Development III*. His ideas and work have done much to enable the book to be published in 1986. Special thanks also go to Melvyn B. King and Debra E. Clark of SUNY–Cortland, who have prepared an excellent Instructor's Manual and Student Study Guide and to Nancie Martens for writing the glossary.

A final note of thanks goes to our families. Mary Jo Santrock and Suzanne Yussen have lived through three editions of *Child Development*. We appreciate their support and encouragement of our writing careers. Our children, Tracy and Jennifer Santrock and Elayna and David Yussen, have provided us with firsthand experiences at watching children develop. Tracy was 7, Jennifer was 5, Elayna was just being born, and David had not yet been born when the first edition of *Child Development* was published. Now Tracy is 18, Jennifer 16, Elayna 11, and David 7. Through these eleven years they have helped us render a treatment of child development that captures the complexity, subtlety, and humanness of it.

John W. Santrock
Steven R. Yussen

CHILD DEVELOPMENT
An Introduction

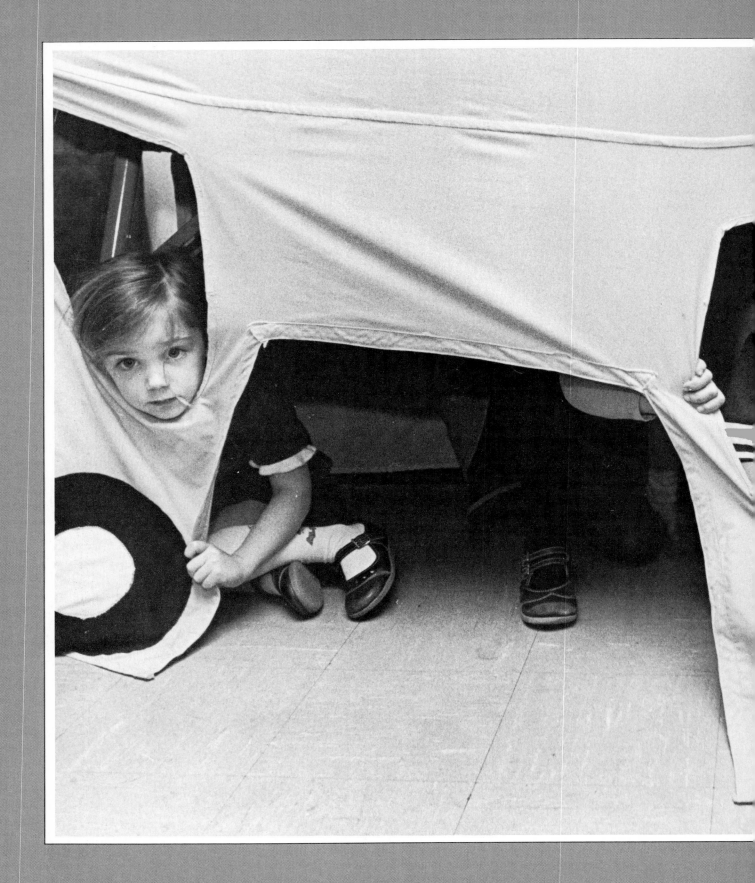

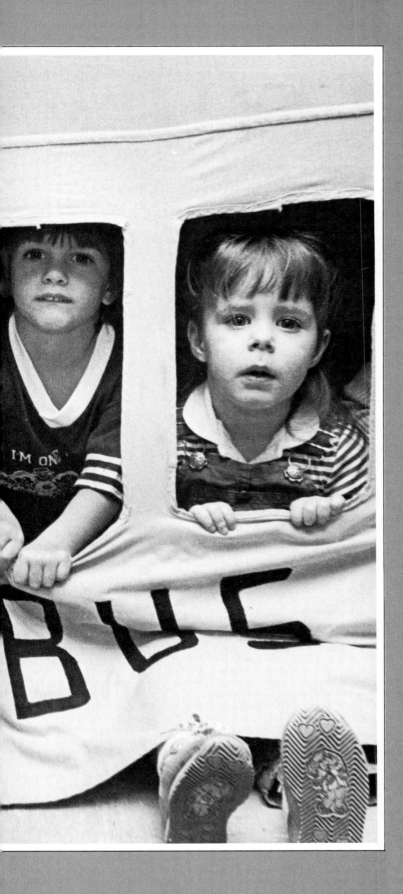

PERSPECTIVES ON CHILD DEVELOPMENT

CHAPTER

1

INTRODUCTION, HISTORY, ISSUES, AND SCIENTIFIC ORIENTATION

PROLOGUE

THE DISAPPEARING RABBIT, SEX-TYPED MONSTERS, ALBERT AND THE WORM, AND THE DEPLETED CAN OF HAIR SPRAY

I t's there. Now it's gone. What happened? It just disappeared under the blanket. So Chip doesn't lift the blanket off the stuffed rabbit he loves so much. Four months later the same sequence happens again. Chip's stuffed rabbit is lying in the playpen, and his mother drops a blanket over the rabbit. It was there. Now it's gone. But now Chip knows it is not really gone, so he lifts up the blanket and recovers his rabbit. Chip was six months and ten months of age, respectively, when these situations occurred. In the first six months of life most infants have not developed object permanency, but in the second six months most infants begin to acquire the sense that objects continue to exist even though they cannot be immediately perceived.

We move forward to the preschool years and overhear a conversation between two girls at a nursery school. Angie says to Donna, ''Boys are mean. Girls are nice.'' Donna replies, ''Yeah, Bobby is mean. You are nice.'' Donna continues, ''I'm afraid of monsters. Are you afraid of monsters?'' Angie responds, ''I am afraid of monsters. I saw one in my room last night.'' Donna says, ''Monsters are boys. Girls are nice.'' Preschool-aged children already have developed ideas about sex differences and often make grand generalizations about what boys are like and what girls are like.

Continuing on to the elementary school years, we observe Tracy, a fifth grade girl whose teacher has presented her with the following information:

Albert spotted a worm in the water. He swam over to the worm and bit into him. Albert was caught and pulled through the water.

The teacher asks, ''Who was Albert? Why did he bite the worm? Who caught him and how?'' While the paragraph provides no answers to these questions, Tracy's prior knowledge and own experiences offer her some clues. Tracy thinks for a moment and then responds that Albert is probably a fish who was hungry and was caught on the hook of a fisherman. Such inferences are part of the way children process and interpret information they encounter in their world. As they mature, children improve dramatically in their abilities to draw such inferences.

''Oh my gosh. I can't believe it. Help. I can't stand it,'' Robert desperately exclaims. His mother responds, ''What is wrong? What is the matter?'' Robert says, ''Everyone in here is looking at me!'' The mother queries, ''Why?'' Robert says, ''Look, this one piece of hair just won't stay in place,'' as he rushes to the rest room in the restaurant. Five minutes later he returns to the table after depleting a can of hair spray. Robert has just turned thirteen and shows a great deal of concern about his physical development. His natural curiosity is understandable since during the last six months his body has been changing rapidly after undergoing only gradual change during his elementary school years. His egocentric sense that everyone was looking at him in the restaurant also is a common occurrence during the early adolescent years.

We have chosen four circumstances to introduce you to the field of child development. Infants develop a sense of object permanency, preschool children develop grand generalizations about sex differences, elementary school children improve in the ability to make inferences, and early adolescents show a heightened concern about their changing body. These are but a few of the many fascinating unfoldings of development you will read about in this book.

PREVIEW

In this chapter we initially describe some contemporary concerns about children. Then we turn our attention to the historical background of interest in childhood and chart the processes and nature of development. Subsequently, we explore a number of issues raised by an interest in the child's development. And, finally, we portray the scientific orientation necessary to acquire valid knowledge about children.

Research on child development can be used to devise better education curricula.

CHILD DEVELOPMENT AND CONTEMPORARY SOCIETY

Everywhere a person turns in contemporary society, the development and well-being of children capture public attention, the interest of scientists, and the concern of policymakers. Consider some of the topics you read about in newspapers and magazines every day: genetic research, child abuse, homosexuality, mental retardation, parenting, IQ, effects of divorce on children, working mothers, and the use of computers to teach children. What the experts are discovering in each of these areas has direct and significant consequences for understanding children and how they are to be treated. Let's examine some of these issues.

During the past several years, our educational system has come under attack. A national commission, appointed by the Office of Education, concluded that our children are being more and more poorly prepared for the increasingly complex future they will be asked to face in our society. The problems are legion—declining skills of those entering the teaching profession, adolescents graduating from high school with primary grade level reading and mathematics skills, a shortage of qualified mathematics and science teachers, less and less time being spent by students in engaging academic work in their classrooms, an absence of any real signs of challenge and thinking required by the school curriculum, and an unfortunately high drop-out rate across the four years of high school. The solutions to these difficulties will not be easy. However, in searching for solutions, policymakers will repeatedly find themselves turning to experts in the field of child development, for to design an engaging curriculum, a planner must know what engages and motivates children. To improve our national effort in teaching thinking skills, the planner

must understand what thinking is and how it changes across the school years. And to understand the roots of the social difficulties encountered by so many of today's adolescents, difficulties that lead them to drop out of school in droves, the planner needs to understand the nature of the socialization processes involved in the transition to adolescence and the ways in which schools fail to address them.

We hear a great deal from experts and popular writers about different pressures on the contemporary family. Mothers and fathers are increasingly becoming two-worker families, while at the same time the number of one-parent families has increased over the past two decades as a result of a climbing rate of divorce. With more children being raised by single parents or by parents who are both working, the time parents have to spend with their children is being squeezed and the quality of child care is of concern to many. Are working parents better using the decreased time with their children? Are day-care arrangements being worked out to provide quality alternatives for parents? How troubled should we be about the increasing number of latchkey children—those at home alone after school, waiting for their parents to return from work? Answers to these questions can be formed by several different kinds of information obtained by experts in child development. These include studies of the way working parents use time with their children and the nature of their parenting approaches and behaviors, studies of the way various day-care arrangements influence children's social and intellectual growth in relation to home-care arrangements, and examination of the consequences of the child being without adult supervision for several hours every day after school.

We are now and for the foreseeable future will be in the information age. Increasingly, our economy and lives are becoming dependent upon the quality, speed, and availability of information. Advances in the field of computing have brought this about, and nowhere is the trend more apparent than in the explosion of purchasing and use of microcomputers in business, at home, and in schools. Computing power, available only to large corporations in the 1960s, is now in the hands of four- and five-year-olds sitting at their home or school microcomputer. How will this change the nature of children's learning and development in the future? Futurists have many ideas about this, but no one really knows. The nature of the change, however, must be reckoned with on several different fronts at once. From our perspective as developmentalists, the fronts to be considered are numerous. How do family members interact with one another now that extensive time is spent with the computer? How are television time and school work influenced? How do children's social interaction patterns with other children change because of exposure to computing, the tendency to associate with other "hackers," and the discovery of the computer as companion, babysitter, or mentor? Finally, how will exposure to computing and programming alter the very nature of thinking, learning, and reasoning, the way these activities must surely have been altered forever when humans learned to read and write and use mathematics to understand the world many years ago? Psychologists are beginning to address these questions now, but as you might expect, the evidence is still quite sketchy.

Parents and educators must face the challenging task of helping many mentally retarded children grow and adapt in a world that is beyond their easy comprehension and intellectual pace. How are they to do this most effectively? What experiences and social grouping arrangements will have the best payoff? Should the children be tracked separately in school or "mainstreamed,"

More children now are growing up in single-parent families than at any other time in history.

i.e., joined with their nonretarded age peers in school? The answers are not easy but surely depend upon the type of retardation, the knowledge we have acquired about the nature of children's learning and cognitive development, and practical attempts to train retarded children to master a number of intellectual and practical living skills.

This survey of contemporary social issues has purposefully been brief. You will hear more about them in later chapters of the book. In the meantime, we hope your appetite has been whetted for the exciting field of study that you have just begun. Now we turn back the clock and study the history of interest in child development.

(9-31)

THE HISTORY OF INTEREST IN CHILD DEVELOPMENT

Our conception of child development has changed dramatically in modern times from what it was in the not too distant past or in medieval and ancient societies. Let's move back through time and see how children have been perceived at different points in history. First, we consider historical accounts of childhood and their recent revision. Then we portray the lives of children in ancient Greece and Rome. Next, we discuss the way children were characterized in the Middle Ages and the philosophical views of the child generated during and after the Renaissance. To conclude our historical discussion, we briefly enumerate several changes in the way children are viewed today compared to earlier historical times.

Historical Accounts and Their Recent Revision

Childhood has become such a distinct period it is hard to imagine that it was not always thought to be that way. Philip Aries' (1962) account of the historical interest in childhood has served as a guide for many years in our efforts to understand how children were viewed and treated at different historical points. In his book *Centuries of Childhood,* Aries presented samples of art along with some publications from different eras to conclude that most societies divided development into infancy, which lasted for many years, and adulthood, which extended somewhere from what we call middle childhood today to postadolescence. (See figure 1.1 for the artistic representation of children two centuries ago.)

We should point out that a belief in the historical conception of childhood as a miniature adulthood has persisted for many years. However, there has been a lively reawakening of interest in the study of childhood from an historical perspective during the last decade (Borstelmann, 1983; Cairns, 1983; Kessen, 1979). This renewed study has cast some doubt on Aries' conclusions. They probably were overdrawn, reflecting artistic style, aristocratic subjects and artists, and an idealization of society at the time. For example, as we see next, as early as the existence of ancient Greece and Rome, rich conceptions of children were evident.

FIGURE 1.1
Paintings portraying the child as a miniature adult.

Ancient Greece and Rome

The children of antiquity are usually depicted as having been subject to great child abuse. Because our contemporary lens focuses on the child abuse of today, it is useful to consider just how extensive it was in the past. Writings suggest that in ancient Greece and Rome, for example, adults regularly abandoned infants, abused them sexually, disfigured them, and regularly murdered unwanted infants (infanticide). Horrible as these acts sound to us, however, they must be placed alongside the generally higher level of brutality that existed for all members of society and the lower level of value or worth placed on human life in general at that time.

Along with reports of brutality, it is possible to find historical writings suggesting that many ancient societies also treated children with special attention and concern. For example, in Egypt children were "seen as helpless and incapable of directing their own affairs, as having special physical needs in terms of feeding and mobility, as needing and desiring to play . . . there are many expressions of tenderness and affection toward children . . . Hammurabi's code included specific provisions for child maintenance" (Borstelmann, 1983, p. 4).

In ancient Greece the writings of the Athenians also suggest special attention to children and consideration of how they are related to deities, laws, and customs and of society's responsibility to train and educate them.

> . . . the Greeks viewed children as objects of affection, important family members, and symbols of their societies future. They placed much more stress on very early training to mold and shape children to cultural interests and took particular cognizance of age and individual differences. Although infanticide was both legally and culturally approved, there was considerable unease about such action and expression of compassion for abandoned newborns. Once accepted into a family, an infant's safety and place were secure; the child was usually seen as important and loved, as providing pleasure to the parents (Borstelmann, 1983, p. 5).

The children of Rome were viewed much like those of the Greeks. This is not surprising since Romans prized their Greek heritage and borrowed much from it. According to Lloyd Borstelmann, the Romans were unique, in relation to the Greeks, however, in that they accentuated the legal claim of fathers to have complete control over the lives and futures of their children and required unquestioning obedience and allegiance to themselves.

The Middle Ages

The medieval period of history began as the Roman empire declined in the second and third centuries A.D. and extended forward for almost a thousand years. Although it is easy to simplify history and believe that the whole period can be characterized in a particular way, such a simplification is foolish. A great many events of enormous magnitude and consequence took place, making any simple generalizations about attitudes toward children during the period highly suspect. However, it is possible to identify several important trends during the period, which give us some idea of the changes that probably occurred in attitudes and ideas about children. First, as the Roman empire collapsed, Christianity grew enormously in numbers of followers and in influence. Christianity preached ideas about the soul, developed competing notions about the pureness and innocence of each soul born into the world on the one hand and original sin on the other, and took a strong role in the religious and secular upbringing of children.

In the hands of Christianity, medieval medicine grew and flourished. Medieval medicine was characterized by a significant amount of philosophy, common sense, and faith. However, it also developed a number of ideas about the special medical treatment required by infants for their physical as well as psychological well-being. A number of major legal systems were developed during the Middle Ages, including the famous Magna Carta in England. Although the Romans' legal system had treated children strictly as property, the Magna Carta introduced a number of special additions, including rights of children to inheritance and the right of children with some major disabilities to receive special treatment by society (i.e., mainly special housing and custodial care in the case of, say, mental insanity, retardation, or leprosy).

The Renaissance and Beyond

The period between the fourteenth and the seventeenth centuries is often referred to as the Renaissance. During this time, there was a rejuvenation and rapid cultural advance in art, music, science, philosophy, and literature. Major changes in political alliances, economies, and religious denominations caused changes in everyday life, society, and the family. The church came to exert an even more powerful role in the lives of children, since with all of the transformation came much upheaval, and family kinship ties became weakened. The experience of children, as always in history, depended to a great extent on what social class they belonged to. (In Rome, of course, our examples were drawn from aristocratic society, and we know little about the experiences of the extensive number of slave children except that their lot was undoubtedly an unpleasant one.) During the Renaissance, schooling became available for many more children, and a relatively sophisticated field of pediatric medicine arose.

Philosophical Views of the Child

As an interest in childhood increased during the Renaissance, philosophers began to speculate about the nature of the developing child and how he or she should be reared. Such interest also was evident as early as the Greek society of Plato and Aristotle, but the interest in the well-being and nature of children at that time was not nearly as great as that sparked during the Renaissance.

During the Middle Ages, the goal of child rearing was salvation; that is, parenting was designed to remove the sin from children's lives. For example, Catholics and Puritans believed it was more important to rear a child who had been saved than a child who was happy. This concept of children, sometimes called the **original sin** view, reflected the philosophical perspective that children are basically evil, and only through the constraints of societal upbringing and/or salvation will they become mature adult beings.

By contrast, two other views about the nature of the child emerged during the Renaissance, the **tabula rasa** and **innate goodness** views. First, near the end of the seventeenth century, John Locke argued that children are not innately evil but instead are like a blank slate (tabula rasa), becoming a particular kind of child or adult because of the experiences they have in life. Locke believed that childhood experiences were important in determining adult characteristics. Thus, he advised parents to spend time with their children, helping them learn to become contributing members of society. Second, during the eighteenth century, Jean Jacques Rousseau agreed with Locke that children are not basically evil. However, Rousseau stressed that rather than being like a blank slate (that is, neither good nor evil), children are innately good. Since he believed children are basically good, Rousseau reasoned that they should be permitted to grow naturally with little monitoring or constraint from parents. With the unveiling of the original sin, tabula rasa, and innate goodness views of children, the crucible of the nature–nurture debate of development emerged. The original sin and innate goodness views place a premium on the importance of nature in development, while the tabula rasa perspective emphasizes the significance of nurturing. More about the nature–nurture argument appears later in the chapter, where we describe the issues of development. Next we look briefly at how we view children today.

Child Development in Contemporary Times

We now conceive of childhood as a highly eventful and unique period of life that lays an important foundation for the adult years and is highly differentiated from them. Most social science approaches to childhood identify a large number of distinct periods in which special skills are mastered and new life tasks are confronted. Childhood is not seen as an inconvenient "waiting" period during which adults must suffer the incompetencies of the young. We value it as a special time for growth and change, and we invest great resources in caring for and educating our children. We protect them from the excesses of the adult work world through tough child labor laws; we treat their crimes against society under a special system of juvenile justice; and we have governmental provisions for helping children when ordinary family support systems fail or when families seriously interfere with the children's well-being.

Thus far we have studied the historical background of interest in children. Now we turn our attention to the important processes involved in children's development.

THE PROCESSES OF DEVELOPMENT

You are a unique individual. Your thoughts, feelings, and behaviors are not like anyone else's, yet you are much like other people your age. You have the same biological equipment everyone else has—a brain, eyes, a heart, and so forth. You, like everyone else, have a mind as well, one that thinks and reasons and remembers. You also have some similar social experiences with others. All of us have grown up in some form of family and have relationships with peers and friends, and most of us have spent many years in school.

How have you become simultaneously unique and yet similar to others of your generation? What processes have contributed to this outcome? These are the questions posed by developmental psychologists, who attempt to understand the processes of change that contribute to the commonality and distinctiveness of children. These processes include those that are biological and physical in nature, those that are cognitive, and those that are social and/or involve personality.

Biological and Physical Processes

Biological and physical processes that influence development include evolution, ethology, genetics, neurological development, and physical growth. The theory of evolution proposed by Charles Darwin rests on the

Child developmentalists are interested in charting children's physical growth.

principle of natural selection. This principle emphasizes considerable genetic diversity in a species. As part of this diversity some organisms have more beneficial characteristics that help them adapt to their environment. These beneficial characteristics are likely to be perpetuated. This view emphasizes a strong continuity between humans and lower animals. Ethology is a modified instinctual view of the organism, stressing the release of unlearned patterns of behavior by certain environmental circumstances. Ethologists use careful observation to study the organism in its natural habitat. The field of genetics emphasizes that genes are the basic building blocks of living organisms. Neurological development focuses on the nature of the brain and its development.

The emphasis in developmental psychology on evolution, ethology, genetics, and neurological development reveals its strong ties to biology. Not only have developmental psychologists looked to biological processes for explanation of physical growth and development, but cognitive processes have a strong biological flavor. Recently there has been considerable interest in the biological basis of social development as well. Much more information about the nature of these biological processes appears in chapter 2, where we discuss genetics and neurological development.

Physical growth and development involves the changes in physical and anatomical features that can be detected. Weight gain, overall height changes, growth of head and limbs, and the changing size of the brain, heart, and lungs are all part of this process. Patterns of physical growth are an important part of development. We discuss these patterns in chapter 3, beginning with prenatal development and the birth process and continuing through pubertal processes. Throughout our discussion of physical growth and development will be a concern for the biological foundations that account for such growth and development, as well as the experiences that might modify the biological forces.

Cognitive Processes

A second set of processes that account for developmental change are cognitive in nature. **Cognitive processes** are mental activities—thought, perception, attention, problem solving, language, and the like. These processes, like physical growth processes, have strong biological foundations. The predominant cognitive theory of development in the twentieth century, that of Jean Piaget, stresses a biological unfolding of cognitive structures. Cognitive activities are seen as strong, often causal influences on how we behave in various life circumstances. The cognitive theorists stress that it is not so much what children experience in their lives that accounts for an understanding of development, but how they use cognitive activities to modify and understand such experiences. Our discussion of cognitive processes in development focuses on such topics as sensory and perceptual development (chapter 4), learning (chapter 5), cognitive development and Piaget's theory (chapter 6), information processing (chapter 7), language (chapter 8), and intelligence (chapter 9).

Social and Personality Processes

One of the major issues that has characterized developmental psychology throughout its existence is the degree to which development is based on unlearned, biological processes and the degree to which it is based on social, experiential matters. We explore this issue, known as the nature–nurture, or genetic–environmental, question in some detail in chapter 2. **Social processes** refer to a child's interactions with other individuals in the environment. Two children consoling each other, a mother hugging her daughter, a father spanking his son, and a teacher warmly greeting a student in a classroom are all aspects of social processes in development. Our discussion of social processes focuses on a number of socialization perspectives and the nature of relationships (chapter 10), family processes (chapter 11), and peers, play, schools, and the media (chapter 12).

Personality processes traditionally have referred more to a property of the individual child than have social processes. Yet it is very difficult to present meaningfully the aspects of the child's personality, such as self, sex roles, and morality, without frequently referring to the child's thoughts and actions about the social world. For example, our discussion of socialization perspectives in chapter 10 is as much an overview of theories of personality as it is a presentation of different ideas on how children are socialized. In chapter 13 a brief overview of personality theories is followed by a discussion of social competence and a developmental portrayal of the unfolding of the self. Then in chapters 14 and 15 we chart two of the most important aspects of personality—sex roles and moral development. Finally, in chapter 16 we describe problems and disturbances in personality.

How do children use their cognitive abilities to modify and understand experiences?

While it is helpful to study the different processes of development in different sections and chapters, keep in mind while reading this text that the child is an integrated human being with only one mind and one body. Biological and physical, cognitive, and social and personality processes are inextricably woven together. In many chapters, you will read how social experiences shape cognitive development, how cognitive processes restrict or promote social development, and how cognitive processes are tied to biological development.

The major sections of this book emphasize a process orientation. For example, you will study biological development throughout childhood in section 2. Within each section, or in some cases each chapter, you will learn about the unique features of such processes as they change through each developmental period.

We have discussed many aspects of childhood and contemporary society, historical background, and processes of development. A summary of these ideas is

	CONCEPT TABLE 1.1	
	Childhood and Contemporary Society, Historical Background, Processes of Development	
Concept	**Processes/Related Ideas**	**Characteristics/Description**
Childhood and contemporary society	Nature of concerns about children	Everywhere a person turns in contemporary society the development and well-being of children have captured public attention. Among the interests are educational reform, contemporary family issues, the information age and computers, and mental retardation.
Historical background	Historical accounts and their recent revision	Aries' historical accounts of children suggested little concern about children's developmental status apart from adults except for the infancy period. The recent revival of historical interest in childhood indicates that Aries' view probably was stereotypical and that greater concern for children's status was present than previously thought.
	Children of antiquity	The children of antiquity usually are described as having been subjected to considerable abuse. However, there is evidence that in Egypt, Greece, and Rome children did have a special place in society.
	The Middle Ages	Christianity had a profound impact on how children were viewed in the Middle Ages.
	The Renaissance and beyond	In the Renaissance and later, philosophical views of children were prominent. Three such views were original sin, tabula rasa, and innate goodness.
	Contemporary times	In contemporary times we view childhood as a highly eventful and unique period of life that provides an important foundation for adult development and maturity. Considerable effort is spent promoting the physical and psychological well-being of children.
Processes of development	Biological, physical	Include evolution, ethology, genetics, neurological development, and physical growth and development.
	Cognitive	Focus on perception, cognitive factors in learning, cognitive developmental changes and Piaget's theory, information processing, language, and intelligence.
	Social, personality	Emphasize socialization perspectives and the nature of relationships; family processes; peers, play, schools, and the media; personality, social competence, and the development of the self; sex roles and moral development; and problems and disturbances.

presented in Concept Table 1.1. Next we outline the complex issues that confront child development researchers as they study various processes.

ISSUES IN DEVELOPMENT

A developmental perspective on children raises certain important questions that often guide research on children. These include the question of qualitative change during childhood, the issue of stages of child development, the concern about continuity and discontinuity in development, and the existence of differences among children in the progress and nature of development.

Qualitative Change

Jean Piaget, a pioneer in developmental psychology, made many important claims about the development of intellectual functioning in children. Among those claims, perhaps none is more provocative than his claim of **qualitative change** in intelligence. That is, a child's intelligence is not simply less than an adult's, but it is intelligence of a qualitatively different kind. For example, Piaget argued that very young children (one-year-olds) lack a fully developed object concept (Flavell, 1977) in that they do not conceive of objects as existing independently of themselves. According to Piaget, this object concept is something that must develop over the first two years of life and represents an outstanding intellectual achievement of this period. Before the object concept is fully developed, the child may not realize that an object continues to exist when his or her back is turned or when the object itself has disappeared behind another object. Inferences of object permanence appear intuitive and transparently obvious to adults and, indeed, to three-year-old children. Thus it is clearly arguable that a shift from one type of thinking to another, not simply an accumulation of mental power, has taken place. The development of the object concept represents a prototype of what qualitative change in development can mean.

Does development involve qualitative changes of the sort that Piaget claimed? The answer is not obvious, but a developmental perspective suggests that qualitative changes are possible. For example, there may be qualitative changes in personality, although not necessarily for all children and not necessarily in intellectual or biological processes. These are empirical issues that must be resolved on the basis of intensive research in specific problem areas of development. The developmental perspective simply raises the question of qualitative change; it does not answer the question.

Stages of Development

Piaget went further than simply proposing qualitative changes in childhood intelligence. He also proposed that there are identifiable stages of intellectual development in childhood. The notion of stages is a controversial one within psychology; not only do researchers disagree about the existence of developmental stages, they also argue about the characteristics of such stages.

Any conceptualization of developmental **stages** must incorporate the notion of qualitative change. Beyond this, the stages-of-development concept implies that qualitative changes must occur in certain sequences (stage 2 must be preceded by stage 1 and not vice versa). Many developmental psychologists (Flavell, 1977) would go still further to claim that the idea of stages implies (1) a certain degree of abruptness of transition from one stage to another and (2) concurrence in the appearance of behaviors or competencies that characterize a given stage. That is, if an entire set of organized behaviors appeared rather suddenly in the course of development and did so for most if not all individuals at a certain point in the life span, we would have clear evidence for a developmental stage of some sort. Unfortunately, evidence for such occurrences is quite rare

and unconvincing, leading some investigators to doubt the stage concept (Flavell, 1977) and others to redefine the concept (Wohlwill, 1973). Despite these problems, the concept of stages has an enduring appeal for developmental psychologists. We will return to this concept repeatedly throughout this text.

Continuity Versus Discontinuity in Development

The issue of **continuity versus discontinuity** in child development is not simple. It has at least three dimensions. First, stage theories imply abruptness of change from one stage to the next, suggesting a discontinuity from one stage to the next. At another level, however, stage theories imply clear continuity. This is because such theories suggest psychological functioning at a later stage is dependent upon functioning at an earlier stage. Put simply, stage theories imply that achievement of one stage is dependent upon achievement of all prior stages; an individual cannot achieve stage 3 without going through stage 2. Though change from one stage to the next may be abrupt, stage theories assume a connectivity between what occurs before and after the change (Kagan, 1980). Such connectivity is a form of continuity. Thus, the second and most widely discussed dimension of the continuity–discontinuity issue is the extent to which later development is dependent on earlier development.

For many years it was believed that early experience, particularly within the family during the first five years of life, determines development later in life, even during the adult years. This view initially was proposed by Freudian psychoanalytic theorists and has continued to have an important impact on developmental thinking for many years. Such a view represents a strong form of the continuity argument. In recent years psychologists questioned whether early experience is the sole determinant of later development. While they agree that early experiences represent important prototypical models for how later experiences will be dealt with, many developmental psychologists argue that early experience does not have irreversible effects. These psychologists take a discontinuity stance in the sense that they emphasize the individual's capacity for change throughout the life cycle rather than later development being determined by early experience alone. Thus, from this perspective, while infant experiences have important ramifications for development in later childhood and adolescence, experiences during later

There is a connectivity between earlier and later development.

To what extent do studies of nonhumans generalize to humans?

childhood and adolescence also contribute to the nature of child and adolescent development. Arguments about the relative importance of early experience and the degree to which development is continuous or discontinuous are still very much a part of developmental psychology.

Yet a third dimension of the continuity–discontinuity issue pertains to the extent to which development in humans is continuous with development in lower animals. That is, do the same principles that explain development and behavior in rats and monkeys also account for the human child's development, or is there more of a discontinuity between the nature of development in lower animals and children? Many cognitive theorists believe in the discontinuity side of this argument—namely, that there are qualitative differences between the development of children and that of lower animals—while many behaviorists and ethologists argue for continuity. A summary of the three dimensions of the continuity–discontinuity issue are presented in table 1.1.

TABLE 1.1
The Dimensions of Continuity Versus Discontinuity

Dimension	Characteristics
Stages versus nonstages	Stages imply an abrupt, discontinuous relation between one stage and the next; nonstage views imply a smoother course of development.
Degree to which later development is related to earlier development	The view that later development is related to earlier development represents continuity; the less that later development is tied to earlier development represents discontinuity.
Extent to which development in children is related to development in lower animals	The view that development in children is similar to development in lower animals represents continuity; the view that development in children is dissimilar to development in lower animals represents discontinuity.

Poor nutrition in infancy is associated with negative emotional characteristics in middle childhood.

Now that we have discussed a number of important dimensions of the continuity–discontinuity issue, we turn our attention to a summary of the factors that may produce discontinuity or continuity in development.

Factors That May Promote Discontinuity in Development

What are some of the factors that may lead to discontinuous change in development? Four such factors follow (Bee & Mitchell, 1980).

1. Changes in broad expectations at different historical eras. For instance, males may be more nurturant and females more assertive because of changes in sex roles linked with the women's movement. Furthermore, historical changes in an individual's lifetime may produce discontinuous changes in personality, cognition, or even health (for example, because of exercise).
2. Changes in specific life experiences of the child. Social learning and contextual theorists argue that changes in behavior will occur whenever a child's environment changes significantly.
3. Regular changes in life tasks at different ages, consisting of different demands. For example, is independence a crisis only in infancy and adolescence?

4. Biological changes, such as hormone changes, that affect both behavior and attitudes. The hormone alterations that are related to puberty exemplify this kind of change.

Factors That May Generate Continuity in Development

In contrast, there are reasons why stability, or consistency, in development may occur.

1. Biological processes. An individual may inherit certain tendencies and characteristics. There is some indication, for example, that certain forms of mental illness, such as schizophrenia, are strongly influenced by inheritance. Similarly, intelligence and certain aspects of personality, such as introversion or extraversion, have genetic ties.
2. The continuing influence of early experiences. If early experiences are more important in development than later experiences, then the tendencies and characteristics we develop in infancy and childhood may persist through adolescence and adulthood. Both Freud and Piaget have taken this position. One aspect of early experience that researchers have only recently explored is the role of infant nutrition in

PERSPECTIVE ON CHILD DEVELOPMENT 1.1

THE LINK BETWEEN NUTRITION IN INFANCY AND SOCIAL DEVELOPMENT IN CHILDHOOD

David Barrett, Marian Radke-Yarrow, and Robert Klein (1982) have conducted investigations that suggest the infant's diet may be linked with emotional characteristics at the time the child enters elementary school. The first investigation, a five-year longitudinal study, focused on 148 boys and girls in three rural Guatemalan villages. The second study was a survey of 65 six- to eight-year-old children from low-income families in San Diego.

In the Guatemalan research, children who had received supplemental high-calorie drinks in addition to their regular diets from birth to age four, and whose mothers had received supplements during pregnancy, were studied. The average child in the three villages was not grossly underfed; for example, a typical four-year-old weighing thirty-five pounds was estimated to be living on about 1,300 calories a day, while standards established by the World Health Organization call for such a child to receive about 1,600 calories. To study the effects of the nutrition supplements on emotional characteristics of the children, the researchers administered a battery of psychological tests and observed the children during various play, competitive, and problem-solving situations.

The results: Children who had nutritional supplements prenatally and for the first two years after birth were consistently more active, involved, and helpful and less anxious than their peers; they also were more likely

social and emotional development. In Perspective on Child Development 1.1, you will discover how even mild caloric deficiencies in the diets of infants may be linked with social and emotional characteristics in middle childhood.

3. Early experience plus consistent later experience. Many of us choose life courses that are compatible with the way we think about ourselves. Consequently, we may continue to show consistency over our life course not necessarily because early experience predominates but because the early patterns continue to be rewarded in the circumstances we choose later in our development. Social learning theory accepts this scenario as a major reason why individuals show stability and consistency in their lives.

Individual Differences in Intraindividual Change

Developmental changes in a given type of functioning (say, creative thought) may follow a declining course of development in some children, a stable course of development in others, and an increasing course of development in still others. This possibility is not inconsistent with impressions we form from everyday experience. We may be impressed by someone who was a problem child but by the end of adolescence had shown signs of maturity. We may know someone else who was socially competent as a child, but who made life miserable for everyone involved during adolescence. Such everyday impressions do not constitute scientific evidence. However, a developmental perspective suggests that individual differences in the course to express happy or sad emotions than were others in the group, who often appeared withdrawn or uninterested. Whether children received food supplements from two to four years of age, however, did not seem to influence their behavior when they were six to eight years old.

In the second investigation, conducted with low-income families in San Diego, children whose mothers were undernourished during pregnancy and whose weight was low at birth were compared with children whose mothers had better diets. The undernourished group interacted less with their school-age peers, were more dependent on adults, and appeared to be sadder and less friendly than the nourished group.

According to the researchers, these results suggest a cycle in which subtle alterations of the central nervous system and lack of energy often combine with a poor home environment to stunt the child's emotional growth. The result may be withdrawal on the part of the child and neglect or rejection on the part of the care giver. It seems that the child attempts to adapt to the physiological stress of nutritional deficit by developing behaviors that remove him or her from the environment and inhibit the later development of appropriate patterns of social interaction. The researchers believe that nutrition may be critical in the first years of life because during the period of infancy the child is beginning to develop patterns of dealing with the world and responding to other people.

of development—*intraindividual change*—may be critically important for an understanding of biological, cognitive, and social functioning.

Attempts to understand the various processes of development and to generate more valid conclusions about the issues we have been discussing have led to an increased scientific orientation in the field of child development. Next we outline this scientific orientation.

SCIENTIFIC ORIENTATION

First we explore what we mean by assuming a scientific orientation in our study of child development. Then we describe three world views as well as a number of methods used by child psychologists in their scientific study of children.

What Do We Mean When We Refer To the Science of Child Development?

The **science** of child development is characterized by theories that can be verified or proved false on the basis of actual evidence collected about children. The science of child development also includes a number of methods of collecting information. These theories and methods are at the heart of understanding how we acquire accurate information about children. Without them the study of child development might well be classified as art or religion. With them we are able to describe, predict, understand, and change the development of children. The theories of child development are many. To do justice to these theories we have woven our discussion of them into various chapters of the book.

For example, psychoanalytic theory is discussed in chapters 10 and 13, ethological theory is described in chapters 2 and 10, social learning theory is outlined in chapters 5 and 10, and cognitive developmental theory is evaluated in chapters 6 and 10. Before we discuss the methods child development researchers use, however, the world views of scientists who study children deserve mention.

World Views

World views are grand models that transcend more precise, specific, testable models. World views are highly abstract, containing ideas that cannot be directly proved or disproved scientifically. Nevertheless, while the world views themselves are not testable, they do serve to stimulate ideas, issues, and questions that can be tested. Three prominent world views have characterized inquiry about children: mechanistic, organismic, and contextual.

The Mechanistic World View

A good way to contrast the mechanistic, organismic, and contextual world views is in terms of the assumptions they make about children's development. The **mechanistic world view** assumes a vision of the child as a passive machine that reacts to events in the environment but does not actively anticipate events or formulate its own goals and in most instances does not engage in complex internal activity of any kind. For the most part, the mechanistic world view also assumes that social, environmental experiences are more important determinants of development than are biological foundations. Furthermore, analysis of the child's development is carried out in a fine-grained molecular manner.

Consider a child named Robert who is six years old and having difficulty with his peers. The scientist with a mechanistic world view would say that Robert's peer-related behavior is due to his experiences with the environment. This scientist would view Robert as a child who responds to his environment but does not create his environment. The scientist would not be interested in studying Robert's cognitive or mental activity as a possible determinant of his peer-related problems. This scientist would take a very careful, detailed look at Robert's environment to discover the causes of his problems.

The Organismic World View

The **organismic world view** assumes that the child is active and mindful with goals and plans and uses complex strategies to attain his or her ends. For the most part the organismic world view assumes a strong biological foundation of development. Experiences with the social world primarily provide the setting for the unfolding of development rather than being the causes of it. This view typically is more global than the fine-grained analysis of the mechanistic world view. Although most organismic perspectives stress the maturational unfolding of cognition, this view is not confined to cognitive matters alone but includes biological and personality considerations as well. In studying Robert's peer-related difficulties, the scientist with an organismic perspective would view Robert as active and mindful with a long biological, maturational history. This scientist would be interested in talking with Robert about his interpretation of his world.

The Contextual World View

The **contextual world view** is neither a purely passive nor a purely active view of the child but an interactive one. Its basic concept is that the child continuously responds to and acts on the contexts in which he or she lives. There are many such contexts in the child's life—environmental, sociohistorical, and biological contexts, for example. Environmental contexts pertain to such settings as family, school, and peer groups. Sociohistorical contexts refer to such matters as social norms in society and how historical conditions may influence the child's behavior. Biological contexts involve health and physical skills. In regard to all of these contexts, we can speak not only of the contexts influencing the child but of the child influencing the contexts as well. For example, the child's family might make unreasonable demands that he or she begins to refuse more often; this might alter the family's subsequent behavior, which in turn alters the child's behavior, and so forth.

Some developmental psychologists have preferred to describe the contextual world view as **dialectical** in nature (Lerner, 1982). This means the child is constantly changing and contexts are changing as well rather than an equilibrium being achieved. For instance, Klaus Riegel (1975) has argued that too much of our theorizing about children's development has consisted of efforts to portray the child as an organism

How would your world view influence your interpretation of a
child's disruptive peer behavior?

striving for balance or equilibrium. In contrast, Riegel believes that a better understanding of development will take place if we study disequilibrium and change. For Riegel, development always is in a state of flux. Balance and equilibrium, while strived for, are never attained. Developing children are changing organisms in a changing world. At the moment completion and equilibrium seem to be reached, new questions and doubts arise in the child and in society. While the dialectical approach has been embraced by a number of developmental psychologists (e.g., Lerner, 1982), others (e.g., Lapsley, 1985) argue that the abstractness of the approach should not substitute for the solution of specific scientific problems.

The scientist with a contextual world view looking at Robert's peer-related behavior would study the many different contexts in Robert's life, such as the environmental, sociohistorical, cognitive, and biological. This scientist would study how Robert influences these contexts and how such contexts influence him. The scientist would view Robert as a changing child in a changing world.

As you read about theories of development at different points in other chapters, keep in mind how the world views we have discussed here share some important assumptions with those theories. Although theories are also abstract in nature, they generally are not as broad and abstract as world views. A brief survey of world views is presented in table 1.2. Now we turn our attention to the methods child development researchers use in scientifically studying children.

Methods

What are some ways of collecting information about children's development? That is, what measures are used? What are the strategies child developmentalists follow in designing research studies? And what is the time span of inquiry used in the study of children's lives? Let's explore the answers to these three important research questions.

Ways of Collecting Information about Children

There are many different ways to conduct systematic observations of children under controlled conditions. We can watch the behavior of infants and children in a laboratory or in the natural setting in which they live, give questions to children in the form of interviews or surveys, develop and administer standardized tests, and conduct a case study or use the clinical method.

Systematic Observation
We watch things all the time, but this does not usually constitute what we would call scientific observation or research. If we are not trained as an observer and do not practice our skills on a regular basis, we are not quite sure what to look for, may not remember what we have seen, may change what we look for from one moment to the next, and often communicate our observations ineffectively.

For observations to be effective, we have to know what we are looking for, whom we are going to observe, when and where we are going to observe, how the observations are going to be made, and in what form they are going to be recorded. This is the process of **systematic observation.**

The most common way of recording what we see is to write it down, using shorthand or symbols. Tape recorders, cameras, special coding sheets, and one-way windows have all been used to make observations more efficient.

When we observe, it frequently is necessary to control certain factors that determine development but are not the focus of our inquiry. For this reason much of

TABLE 1.2
Mechanistic, Organismic, and Contextual
World Views

World View	Characteristics/Description
Mechanistic	1. Organism is viewed as passive, machinelike. 2. Social, environmental experiences are very important. 3. Psychological phenomena are analyzed in fine-grained, molecular fashion.
Organismic	1. Organism is viewed as active, mindful. 2. Strong biological foundation is stressed. 3. More global approach to psychological phenomena than mechanistic view.
Contextual	1. Organism is neither purely active nor purely passive but interactive. 2. Organism is continually responding to and acting on contexts. 3. Important to consider variety of contexts and possibly dialectical nature of development.

the research conducted in child psychology has been in a laboratory, a controlled setting in which much of the real world, with its complex factors, is removed. However, there are costs involved in conducting laboratory research. First, it is virtually impossible to conduct research in a laboratory without the participants knowing they are in an experiment. Second, the laboratory setting may be "unnatural" and cause "unnatural" behavior on the part of the participants. Third, some aspects of development are difficult if not impossible to produce in the laboratory. Certain types of stress, for example, might be difficult (and unethical) to investigate in the laboratory. Thus, matters pertaining to the impact of marital discord and the physical use of punishment on children's development would not be viable candidates for laboratory observation. While laboratory research remains an extremely valuable tool for developmental psychologists, naturalistic observation or field studies have sometimes been called on when information about development in real-world settings is necessary. Observations have been made in homes, at work, and in schools, parks, shopping malls and other places where people commonly go. Piaget's observations of his children at home were naturalistic observations. Jane Goodall (1972) spent months living in the

While laboratories are often controlled settings with much of the "real world" removed, this particular laboratory includes some naturalistic characteristics, such as books and learning materials, to make it more like a school setting.

open in Africa with chimps to observe their behavior in a natural setting. Roger Barker wrote *One Boy's Day* after he had followed a young boy around for an entire day and observed his behavior in a variety of natural settings (Barker & Wright, 1951).

Though often presented as a dichotomy, laboratory and field research are really two points on a continuum ranging from naturalism to control. For example, we can conduct laboratory studies with a decidedly "natural" character. Thus, instead of studying memory for some unknown combination of letters like *isz, bkd,* and so on, we might investigate the memory of autobiographical events. We can also carry out naturalistic studies under controlled conditions. For example, we might observe the behavior of children at school after we had created two decidedly different teaching styles, one a high degree of verbal interaction and question asking with students and the other a low degree of verbal interaction and question asking.

Interviews and Surveys   An **interview** is a set of questions put to someone and the responses that person makes. The interview can range from very unstructured to very structured. For example, a very unstructured interview might include questions such as, "Tell me about some of the things you do with your friends" or "Tell me about yourself." A very structured interview might question whether the respondent highly approves, moderately approves, moderately disapproves, or highly disapproves of his friends using drugs.

Researchers also are able to question children through surveys, or questionnaires. A **questionnaire** is similar to a highly structured interview, except that respondent reads the question and marks his or her answer on a sheet of paper rather than verbally responding to the interviewer. One major advantage of questionnaires is that they can easily be given to a very large number of people, sometimes as many as 10,000 people. Questions on surveys should be concrete, specific, and unambiguous, but often they are not. And some assessment of the authenticity of the replies should be made, but often it is not.

Structured interviews conducted by an experienced psychologist can produce more detailed responses than are possible with a questionnaire and can help eliminate careless responses. A good interviewer can encourage the respondent to open up as well. But interviews are not without problems. Perhaps the most critical of these problems involves the response set of "social desirability," in which the person tells the interviewer what he or she thinks is socially most acceptable or desirable rather than how he or she truly feels or thinks. When asked about her sexual relationships, for example, a female may not want to admit having had sexual intercourse on a casual basis. Skilled interviewing techniques and built-in questions to help eliminate such defenses are critical in getting accurate information from an interview.

Another problem with both interviews and surveys or questionnaires is that some questions may be retrospective in nature; that is, they may require the participant to recall events or feelings that occurred at some point in the past. Unfortunately, retrospective interviews are seriously affected by distortions in memory. It is exceedingly difficult to glean accurate information about the past from verbal reports. However, because of the importance of understanding retrospective verbal reports, 1978 Nobel prizewinner Herbert Simon and cognitive psychologist Ulric Neisser have investigated better ways to gain more accurate verbal assessments of the past (Ericsson & Simon, 1978; Neisser, 1982). This study focuses on the information-processing aspects of cognition, such as short- and long-term memory and incomplete and inconsistent verbalized information, as well as the intensity and frequency of past experience.

Standardized Tests **Standardized tests** actually can be questionnaires, structured interviews, or behavioral in nature. Their distinctive feature is that they are developed to identify an individual's characteristics or abilities, relative to those of a large group of similar individuals. The individual's score is compared to the scores of large numbers of people to see how he or she compares with them. Children are usually given a percentile score on such tests. For example, we say a child

scored in the 92 percentile on the Stanford-Binet Intelligence Test. This tells how much higher or lower the child scored than the large group of children who initially were given the test. Among the standardized tests widely used are intelligence tests like the Stanford-Binet and Wechsler Scales and personality tests like the Harter Perceived Competence Scale for Children.

The main advantage of standardized tests is their ability to provide a comparison of one child's score with large numbers of other children's scores. In other words, standardized tests provide information about individual differences among children. However, information obtained on standardized tests does not always successfully predict behavior in nontest situations. Standardized tests are based on the belief that a child's behavior is consistent and stable, varying little from one context to the next. However, while personality and intelligence, two of the primary targets of standardized tests, have some stability, they sometimes vary, depending on the situation in which a child is evaluated. Thus, a child may perform poorly on a standardized test of intelligence but when observed in a less anxious context, such as the natural surroundings of his or her home, the child may perform much better. This drawback is particularly relevant to minority group children, some of whom have been inappropriately classified as mentally retarded on the basis of their scores on an intelligence test. More information about standardized intelligence tests appears in chapter 9.

Case Study and Clinical Method **A case study** is an in-depth look at a single individual and is used mainly by clinical psychologists. In some instances the unique aspects of a child's life cannot be duplicated, either for practical or ethical reasons, yet has implications for our understanding of the mind and behavior. Traumatic experiences, emotional and physical, have led to some fascinating case studies in psychology. For example, Genie, a child who was reared in almost complete isolation from the age of twenty months to the age of thirteen years is proof of human resilience, although she never learned to ask questions and did not understand much grammar.

The case study or clinical method actually can be viewed as a variation of naturalistic observation. However, in many instances we can only look at the unique aspects of a particular person when we use the case study or clinical method, whereas when we use naturalistic observation we may look at large numbers of children in search of some general principles about the development of the mind and behavior.

The **clinical method** involves sophisticated observation and interviewing skills that have been developed through experiences with many children, often those who have psychological problems. Piaget relied heavily on the clinical method with his three children to discover the structure of their thought.

Both the case study and clinical method have some disadvantages. Usually only a single individual is involved in the case study format, and usually only a small sample is included in the clinical method. Both often involve judgments of unknown reliability in the sense that no check is made to see if other psychologists or observers agree with the observations being made. Thus, how well such observations generalize to large numbers of children can be questioned, as can the accuracy of the judgments.

An overview of the measures used to assess information about children's development is presented in table 1.3.

Strategies of Research Design

In addition to the selection of measures to use in studying development and behavior, another important methodological decision involves the strategy for setting up a research study. There are three main ways a research study can be set up: experimental, quasi-experimental, and correlational.

Experimental Strategy Ideally, we would like for our research in child development to be conducted in an experimental way because, more than other strategies, this one allows us to determine more precisely whether something is causing a child to act, feel, or think in a particular way. An **experiment** is a carefully controlled context in which the factors that are believed to influence the mind or behavior are controlled. The experimenter manipulates the "influential" factors, called **independent variables,** and measures the **dependent variables,** which are the measures or behaviors examined for any change resulting from the influence of the independent variables.

TABLE 1.3
Methods Used to Obtain Information about Children's Development

Method	Main Characteristics	Advantages	Disadvantages
Systematic observation	Controlled conditions in laboratory or naturalistic setting; involves careful watching of behavior.	Precise control over what is being studied.	In laboratory, subject awareness, unnatural aspects; in natural setting, less control.
Interviews and questionnaires	Questions put to someone and the responses he or she makes. Range from structured to unstructured. Interviews involve verbal responses to interviewer, whereas questionnaires involve paper-and-pencil responses.	Allow person's perceptions to be assessed, which may give important information beyond observed behavior. Questionnaires can be given to very large samples.	Assess person's perception, which may not tell much about his or her behavior. Social desirability can influence respondent.
Standardized tests	Questionnaires, structured interviews, or behavior designed to identify an individual's characteristics relative to those of a large group of similar individuals.	Ability to provide a comparison of one individual's score with large numbers of other people's scores.	Based on belief that behavior is stable; yet behavior may be different outside of test situation.
Case study and clinical method	Case study is in-depth look at a single individual; clinical method involves sophisticated observation and interviewing skills developed through many experiences.	Provide a very detailed look at a single individual's mind and behavior.	May not generalize to large numbers of people, and their accuracy may be questioned.

What are some different ways we could use to study the effects of exercise in pregnant women on their offspring?

In an experiment, we randomly assign subjects to the treatments or experiences. If the assignment is truly random, then there is only a slim chance that the two groups will differ from each other on some particular characteristic since any extraneous factor will have been randomly distributed in the groups. The following experiment should help you understand the importance of the experiment in the study of children.

The problem to be investigated is how aerobic activity on the part of a pregnant woman affects the development of her infant. First, in order to clearly define our independent variable, we need to decide the nature and frequency of the aerobic activity. We decide to have the pregnant woman perform the aerobic activity four times per week (one hour per session) under the direction of a trained instructor.

We also give careful consideration to what our dependent variables will be. We choose to use two measures: breathing and sleeping patterns. We decide that not only do we need to have a group of pregnant women who exercise aerobically, but we also need a group of subjects who do not. We randomly assign the subjects to the two treatments, one in which they get the aerobic exercise, the other in which they do not. The group that gets the exercise is called the **experimental group,** and the group that gets zero level of the independent variable (in this case, aerobic exercise) is referred to as the **control group.** The control group is the comparison or baseline group. After the experimental group has exercised aerobically four times a week during their pregnancy and the other group has abstained from aerobic exercise during the same time period, the two sets of offspring are tested during the first week of life on the dependent variables. When we compare the results

of the two groups, we find that the experimental group infants have more regular breathing and sleeping patterns than the control group infants. We conclude that aerobic exercise by pregnant women promotes more regular breathing and sleeping patterns in the newborn.

We should make a final comment about the random assignment of the subjects to the experimental and control groups. By randomly assigning the pregnant women to the two treatments, we greatly reduced the likelihood that the two groups differed on some relevant subject variable such as the mother's exercise history, health problems, intelligence, and so forth. Why? Because every subject with any particular degree of a specific characteristic was equally likely to end up in either the experimental group or the control group. How did we make the random assignment? We consulted a table of random numbers in a statistics book, but we could have accomplished the same result by flipping a coin.

Quasi-Experimental Strategy Often researchers use a technique that resembles the experiment in all important respects except one—the degree of prior control exercised over the independent variable. In such a pseudoexperiment, sometimes called a quasi-experiment, we acknowledge that we cannot randomly assign our subjects to experiences or conditions. In such investigations, participants determine which group they will be in because of the experiences in their lives. Thus, we might study the self-esteem of working women versus homemakers, the coping skills of divorced women as compared to married women, and social skills of children attending day-care centers compared with those staying with their mothers at home. Quasi-experiments are useful in gathering information about social matters that create tricky problems for exercising tight experimental control, although they are not true experiments since we cannot randomly assign the participants to the categories of the investigation. Therefore, causation cannot be inferred from quasi-experiments.

To further understand the principle of **quasi-experimental strategy,** let's consider another investigation involving aerobic exercise. In this study we decide to study aerobic exercisers as they actually exist in society rather than randomly having one set of subjects exercise and another not. We might decide that to be included in the aerobic exercise group, pregnant women will have said they exercise aerobically on a regular basis, defined as three or more 45-minute aerobic classes per week. We also believe it is important to have a control group of individuals who have not exercised aerobically at all during their pregnancy. Since we do not randomly assign subjects to a group in a quasi-experimental strategy, it is very important to match the subjects in the groups on certain characteristics (Cook & Campbell, 1979), such as age, social class (e.g., education and occupation), and sex. We are still interested in finding out the relationship of aerobic activity by pregnant women to the breathing and sleeping patterns of the newborn.

In the quasi-experiment we find no differences between the infants whose mothers are aerobic exercisers and those whose mothers are nonexercisers. This may have happened because of our failure to match the subjects on certain variables, such as intelligence or health. Or, it may have occurred because the aerobic exercisers did not exercise as regularly as they said they did, while the nonexercisers may have exercised more than they indicated.

Correlational Strategy   Often it is of interest to know how one measured characteristic is associated with another—height with weight, intelligence with motivation, self-esteem with social class, drug use with parental upbringing, and so forth. One measure of such associations is the **correlation coefficient.**

The correlation coefficient ranges from -1.00 to $+1.00$. A negative number indicates an inverse relation. For example, a frequent finding is that individuals with high IQs are reasonably rapid learners, which would indicate a high positive correlation. By contrast, we usually find a negative correlation between permissive parenting and a child's self-control. The higher the number in the index (whether positive or negative), the stronger the association between the variables. An index of 0 indicates that there is no association between the variables.

A correlation alone cannot be used to support the argument that one event causes another. We cannot argue, for example, that because height and weight are positively correlated, we grow tall because we gain weight (or vice versa). It is always possible that some unnoticed third factor is the causal agent linking these two events together. See figure 1.2 for an example of the subtle but critical distinction between correlation and causation.

The fact that one variable increases as another increases (or decreases as another decreases) does not necessarily mean the first causes the second. For instance, if we find that as parents use more permissive-indifferent ways to deal with their children the children's self-control decreases, it does not necessarily mean that the parenting style caused the children's behavior. Rather the link between these variables might be due to other factors, such as genetic background, poverty, and sociohistorical conditions.

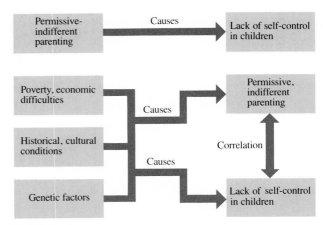

FIGURE 1.2
Evaluating the correlation between parenting and children's behavior.

To further understand the principle of correlation, let's consider another example related to aerobic activity. In this case we are interested in the correlation between the aerobic activity of adolescent females and whether their best friends and their parents exercise aerobically. We find a positive correlation between the adolescent's frequency of aerobic exercise and that displayed by either parents or peers.

To conclude our discussion of correlation, it is helpful to consider the circumstances under which a correlational strategy might be chosen over an experimental one: (1) The focus of inquiry is so new we have little knowledge of which variables to manipulate. (2) It is physically impossible to manipulate the variables. (3) It is unethical to manipulate the variables.

We have discussed a number of issues in development, scientific orientation and world views, methods, and research strategies. A summary of these ideas is presented in Concept Table 1.2.

The Time Span of Inquiry

Discussion of research designs can be complicated, especially when issues of development are involved. Our approach here is to start with the simplest designs. These are the simple cross-sectional and simple longitudinal designs, which are the basis for all developmental research. Next we describe the sequential designs, which are the most complex, although they are actually only further elaborations of simple cross-sectional and simple longitudinal designs. We will discuss the advantages and disadvantages of each design.

CONCEPT TABLE 1.2
Issues in Development, the Science of Child Development and World Views, Methods, and Research Strategies

Concept	Processes/Related Ideas	Characteristics/Description
Issues in development	Qualitative change	The issue of qualitative change focuses on whether the child's development is different from one point to another point rather than being more or less.
	Developmental stages	The issue of developmental stages emphasizes whether qualitative changes occur in sequences. This controversial issue has endured in the study of children's development.
	Continuity–discontinuity	The issue of continuity–discontinuity has three dimensions: abruptness in stage change, the degree to which later development is dependent on earlier experiences and/or development, and whether there is continuity between human children and lower animals. There are a number of reasons why children's development will reveal continuity or discontinuity.
	Individual differences	It is widely accepted that individual differences occur although the nature and cause of such differences is widely debated.
Scientific orientation and world views	Scientific orientation	When we talk about taking a scientific orientation, we are referring to a number of theories and methods involved in the collection of information about children.
	World views	World views, which are even more abstract than theories, influence the scientific study of children. Three such world views are: mechanistic, organismic, and contextual.
Methods	Systematic observation	Systematic observation involves controlled conditions in a laboratory or naturalistic setting. It involves careful watching of behavior.
	Interviews and questionnaires	Questions put to someone and the responses he or she makes are involved in interviews and questionnaires, or surveys. These questions range from structured to unstructured. An interview involves verbal responses, whereas a questionnaire involves paper-and-pencil responses.
	Standardized tests	Questionnaires, structured interviews, or behavior designed to identify a child's characteristics relative to those of a large group of similar children are involved in standardized tests.
	Case study and clinical method	The case study is an in-depth look at a single child; the clinical method involves sophisticated observation and interviewing skills developed through many experiences.
Research strategies	Experimental	The experimental strategy involves the random assignment of subjects to treatments or experiences. An experiment is a carefully controlled situation in which the factors believed to influence the child's mind and behavior are controlled.
	Quasi-experimental	The quasi-experimental technique resembles an experiment in important ways except that we cannot randomly assign the subjects to experiences or conditions.
	Correlational	The correlational technique investigates the association of two or more variables. It cannot be used to infer that one event caused another event.

Cross-Sectional and Longitudinal Designs Consider two different ways in which we might attempt to examine effects related to age. First, we might perform a cross-sectional study, comparing groups of children in different age ranges. A typical **cross-sectional study** might include groups of five-year-olds, eight-year-olds, and eleven-year-olds. The different groups could be compared with respect to a variety of dependent variables, such as IQ performance, memory, independent behavior, and conformity to peers. All of this could be accomplished in a very short time; even a large study can be completed within a month or so.

Second, we might perform a **longitudinal study** to examine effects related to age. In this case, we would take a single group of children, all of approximately the same age, and test them today and on one or more occasions in the future. For example, we might decide to examine attachment to parents at ages six months, one year, and three years.

Longitudinal studies take a long time to complete. An advantage of cross-sectional designs is that they are very efficient in terms of time. However, a major disadvantage of cross-sectional designs is their inability to

PERSPECTIVE ON CHILD DEVELOPMENT 1.2

THE EFFECTS OF TELEVISION ON CHILDREN'S IMAGERY AND LEARNING

One of the major changes in the lives of children and adults in the last fifty years has been the increased exposure to television. While television has not always been viewed as a positive influence on children's development, there are instances when it may have a beneficial effect. One such case is the exposure of preschool children to the television show "Sesame Street." This program, designed to enhance the cognitive skills of young children, began in November 1969 and has had a large viewing audience since its inception. It is the rare child who has not spent many memorable hours prior to the first grade watching the characters of "Sesame Street" provide an enjoyable context for learning letters, numbers, words, and other cognitive as well as social tasks.

Between July 1969 and July 1970, Hayne Reese (1974) collected data from 49 children ranging in age from twenty-seven to seventy-five months. His interest was in the role of age and imagery in children's learning. Approximately 40 percent of the data were collected prior to the time that "Sesame Street' was introduced in November 1969, and about 60 percent after. This provided a serendipitous opportunity to study cohort effects on children's learning.

As shown in the figure opposite there appears to have been a cohort change around November 1969. Prior to that time, preschool children failed to experience any benefit from an imagery strategy in learning. After that time, the young preschool children benefited as much as the older children, who were almost six years of age. The results of this investigation suggest that changing sociocultural conditions were able to decrease substantially the age at which children effectively use imagery in learning.

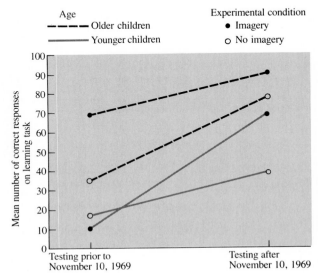

Cohort effects on children's learning: the effects of "Sesame Street."
From Reese, H. W., "Cohort, age, and imagery in children's paired associate learning," in Child Development, 45, pp. 1176–1178. Copyright © 1974 by The Society for Research in Child Development, Inc. Reprinted by permission.

control for **cohort effects,** that is, effects that are due to a subject's time of birth or generation but not actually to her or his age. For example, cohorts can differ with respect to years of education, child-rearing practices, health, and attitudes on topics such as sex and religion. These cohort effects are important because they can powerfully affect the dependent measures in a study ostensibly concerned with age. Cohort effects can look like age effects, but they are not. An example of a cohort effect can be found in Perspective on Child Development 1.2, which portrays the role of the television show "Sesame Street" on children's learning.

Cohort			
Time of testing	**1982**	**1984**	**1986**
1986	4 years old	2 years old	Newborn
1988	6 years old	4 years old	2 years old
1990	8 years old	6 years old	4 years old

FIGURE 1.3
Example of a sequential design. This design includes three cohorts (born in 1982, 1984, and 1986) tested at three different times (1986, 1988, and 1990) plus new independent samples of cohorts.

Although longitudinal studies are time-consuming, they are valuable in allowing us to track changes in individual children over time. If our concern is with individual differences in the course of development, longitudinal designs are indispensible. Unfortunately, the problems of testing and history are especially troublesome in longitudinal studies.

Sequential Designs In recent years developmental psychologists have constructed **sequential designs** (e.g., Baltes, 1973; Baltes, Reese & Lipsitt, 1980; Schaie, 1965). These designs allow us to see whether the same pattern of development is produced by each of the research strategies. In particular, sequential designs are adept at providing insight about possible cohort effects that might be responsible for research findings. A sequential design has at least two cohorts, two age groups, and two times of measurement. (See figure 1.3 for an example of a sequential design.) Keep in mind that while sequential designs provide a wealth of data about age changes, cohort differences, and history effects, we should be mindful of the tremendous difficulty of collecting data that permit such analyses.

Ethical Standards in Working with Children

Child psychologists subscribe to the code of ethics of the American Psychological Association and the Society for Research in Child Development. Most training programs require their graduate students to learn these codes. To be licensed to practice psychology in most states, prospective psychologists must pass a formal test on ethical standards. Among the most important concepts in working with children are the following ethical imperatives:

1. Always obtain informed consent from parents or legal guardians if children are to be tested in any way or are to be the objects of research. Parents have the right to a complete and accurate description of what will be done with their children and may refuse to let their charges participate.
2. Children have rights, too. The psychologist is obliged to explain precisely what the child will experience. Children may refuse to participate, even after parental permission has been given. If so, the investigator must not test the child. Similarly, if a child becomes upset during some professional interaction, it is the psychologist's obligation to calm down the youngster. Failing to do so, the activity must be discontinued.
3. The psychologist must always weigh the potential for harming children against the prospects of contributing some clear benefits to them. If there is the chance of any harm—such as when drugs are to be used, social deception is to take place, or the child is to be treated aversively (e.g., punished or reprimanded)—the psychologist must be able to convince a group of impartial peers that the benefits of the experience for the child clearly outweigh any chance of harm.
4. The psychologist must always adhere to accepted standards of practice, using techniques and procedures that treat children courteously and respectfully. Since children are in a vulnerable position and lack power and control when facing an adult, the psychologist should always strive to make the professional encounter a positive and supportive experience.

SUMMARY

I. We began the chapter by thinking about child development and contemporary issues. Then we studied the history of interest in child development, focusing on historical accounts and their recent revision, ancient Greece and Rome, the Middle Ages, the Renaissance and beyond, and child development today.

   A. Aries' historical accounts of children suggested little concern about children's developmental status apart from adults, except for the infancy period. The recent revival of historical interest in childhood indicates that Aries' view was probably stereotypical and that greater concern for children's status was present than previously believed.

   B. The children of antiquity usually are described as having been subjected to considerable abuse, although there is evidence that in Egypt, Greece, and Rome children had a special place in society.

   C. Christianity had a profound impact on how children were viewed in the Middle Ages.

   D. In the Renaissance, philosophical views of childhood were prominent, with three competing views being the original sin, tabula rasa, and innate goodness perspectives.

   E. In contemporary times, we view childhood as a highly eventful and unique period of life that provides an important foundation for the development of adult maturity. Considerable effort is expended to promote the physical and psychological well-being of children.

II. This book takes a process orientation in the study of children's development. The major processes are biological, physical; cognitive; and social, personality. Remember that while we often will be studying these processes separately, the child is an integrated human being and these processes are intricately interwoven. Child developmentalists are interested in discovering the nature of change that contributes to the commonalities and distinctiveness of children.

III. Among the important issues in the study of children's development are qualitative change, stages of development, continuity versus discontinuity, and individual differences in intraindividual change.

   A. The issue of qualitative change focuses on whether the child's development is different from one point to another point rather than being more or less. Such changes are difficult to document.

   B. The issue of developmental stages emphasizes whether qualitative changes occur in sequences. This controversial issue has endured in the study of children's development.

   C. The issue of continuity versus discontinuity has three dimensions: abruptness in stage change, the degree to which later development is dependent on earlier experiences and/or development, and the extent to which there is continuity between human children and lower animals. There are a number of reasons why children will show either continuity or discontinuity in their development.

   D. With regard to the issue of individual differences in intraindividual change, it is widely accepted that such differences occur but the nature and causes of such differences are widely debated.

IV. When we talk about taking a scientific orientation in the study of children's development, we are referring to a number of theories and methods involved in the collection of information about children. The theories are described in different sections of this book and the methods include measures, strategies of research design, and the time span of inquiry. World views, which are even more abstract than theories, also influence the scientific study of children. Three such world views are the mechanistic, organismic, and contextual.

   A. Methods include systematic observation, interviews and questionnaires, standardized tests, and the case study and clinical method. Each of these methods has strengths and weaknesses.

   B. Three strategies for setting up a study of children's development are experimental, quasi-experimental, and correlational strategies.

   C. Three research designs characterize the time span of inquiry about children's development: cross-sectional, longitudinal, and sequential.

   D. Child psychologists subscribe to a code of ethics when conducting research with children.

KEY TERMS

biological and physical processes 11
case study 24
clinical method 25
cognitive processes 12
cohort effects 30
contextual world view 20
continuity versus discontinuity 15
control group 26
correlation coefficient 28
cross-sectional study 29
dependent variables 25
dialectical 20
experiment 25
experimental group 26
independent variables 25
innate goodness 11

interview 23
longitudinal study 29
mechanistic world view 20
organismic world view 20
original sin 11
personality processes 13
qualitative change 14
quasi-experimental strategy 27
questionnaire 23
science 19
sequential designs 31
social processes 13
stages 15
standardized tests 24
systematic observation 22
tabula rasa 11
world views 20

REVIEW QUESTIONS

1. Provide an outline of the history of interest in children's development. Be sure to include information about recent revisions of earlier historical accounts.
2. What are the major processes of development? Include in your answer examples of each process.
3. Evaluate the nature of the following issues in the study of children's development: qualitative change and stages of development.
4. What are the considerations in the issue of continuity versus discontinuity of development? What do we mean when we talk about individual differences in intraindividual change?
5. Discuss the world views of scientists who study children.
6. Provide an overview of the measures used to study children's development.
7. Discuss the three major types of research design in child development.
8. Evaluate how we study the time span of children's development.

SUGGESTED READINGS

Appelbaum, M. I., & McCall, R. B. (1983). Design and analysis in developmental psychology. In W. Kessen (Ed.), *Handbook of child psychology* (4th ed., Vol. 1).
A comprehensive and authoritative treatment of methodology, techniques for designing developmental research, and approaches to handling special research problems such as social interaction and field research. An excellent reference source.

Borstelmann, L. J. (1983). Children before psychology: Ideas about children from antiquity to the late 1800s. In W. Kessen (Ed.), *Handbook of child psychology* (4th ed., Vol. 1).
A comprehensive treatment of the historical conception of children from ancient times until the eighteenth century. Offers a good picture of many different historical societies and influential philosophers who wrote about children.

Child Development and *Developmental Psychology*
These two research journals are highly respected sources of scientific information about children's development. Go to your library and leaf through the last several years of these journals to get a sense of what researchers in child development are interested in.

Kessen, W. (1979). The American child and other cultural inventions. *American Psychologist, 34,* 815–820.
An entertaining essay describing how childhood has come to be understood and viewed in contemporary America. Contrasts this conception with conceptions of children at other times in history.

BIOLOGICAL PROCESSES AND PHYSICAL DEVELOPMENT

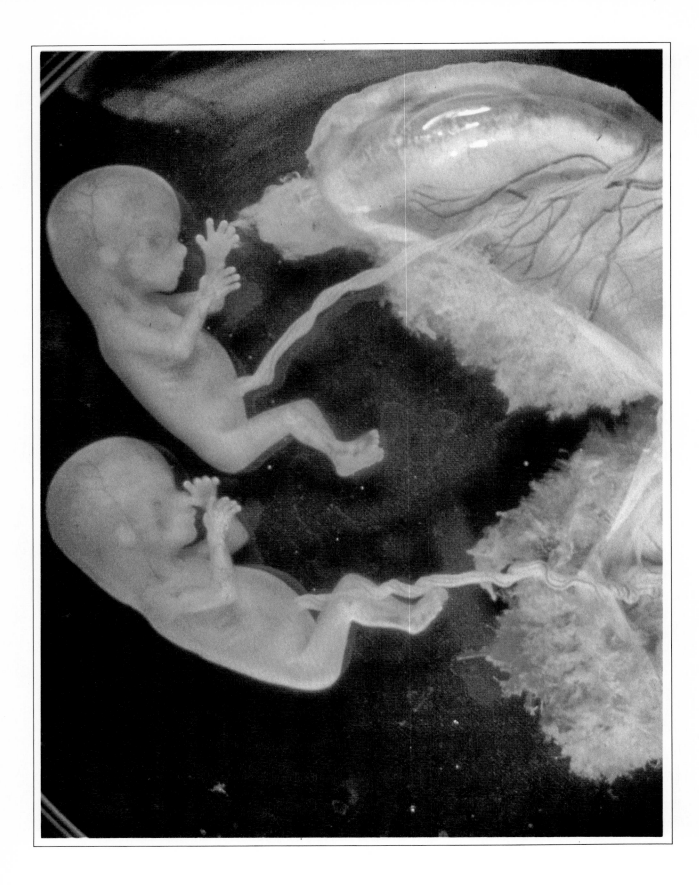

BIOLOGICAL PROCESSES, GENETICS, AND NEUROLOGICAL DEVELOPMENT

PROLOGUE

THE CHILD'S MISSION CONTROL

I magine a child walking along a sidewalk careful not to step on the cracks that separate the concrete squares. Someone yells, "Get out of the way," as another boy comes zeroing in fast on a skateboard. The child responds:

His eyes grow wider.

His muscles tense up.

He gasps.

His heart skips a beat.

And very rapidly his brain processes all of the information in this perilous circumstance, sending a message down to his muscles, which send him flying into a bush, safe but scratched up.

Looking up from the bush with a trickle of blood dripping down his face, the boy gets an angry look—it was his older brother on the skateboard! "You idiot," he yells at his brother, "I am not going to let you forget this!" His mind is already putting together plans to get even.

Such rapid reactions were the work of the nervous system, the body's mission control. In less than a second, hundreds of thousands of nerve cells relayed all kinds of information to move the boy out of his brother's path.

When the child's nervous system is not responding to emergencies, it is monitoring and coordinating the normal work of trillions of cells in the body. It keeps track of all of the child's internal operations, such as heart rate, breathing regularity, and water level, and it senses environmental changes, making necessary adjustments. This wondrous system keeps the child's life running smoothly and on course.

The nerve cells in a canary's brain are exactly the same as those in a frog's brain. The reason frogs croak and canaries sing is that the nerve cells are organized differently in the two brains. The nerve cells in the frog's vocalization system are connected together in such a way that they produce croaking, the canary's singing. The human child's own gift of speech is present because human nerve cells are organized in ways that permit language processing. This is why the study of brain functioning—of the anatomy and fine structure of the brain—is so important. It is the key to understanding all of the complex and marvelous things that the child's brain can do.

PREVIEW

The child is a biological being. Whether we are studying a newborn, a preschool child, or an adolescent, always remember that the biological heritage of the child is involved in determining the child's thoughts and behaviors. Take away the child's genes and we have no child. Remove the child's brain, and thought, as well as behavior, ceases. Three main themes characterize our portrayal of biological influences. First, you will gain a sense of the child's biological heritage by reading about evolution, ethology, and other biological principles of development. Second, you will learn about the critical importance of genetic influences on development. And, third, you will read about the incredible advances being made in understanding the development of the child's brain and nervous system.

EVOLUTION, ETHOLOGY, AND GENERAL BIOLOGICAL PRINCIPLES OF DEVELOPMENT

The fascinating story of evolution has been unfolding for millions of years. We trace its course and then turn to a view with close ties to evolution, that of ethology. You will discover that ethology has become an increasingly prominent view in the field of child development in recent years.

Evolution

In evolutionary terms, humans are relative newcomers to earth, but in a short time they have established themselves as the most successful and dominant species. As Carl Sagan (1980) has commented, humans arrived late in December if we consider evolutionary time in terms of a calendar year. As our earliest ancestors left the forest to feed in the savannahs and finally to form hunting societies on the open plains, their minds and behavior changed.

Our journey through evolution begins with a description of an erroneous portrayal of evolution, continues with the story of natural selection, and concludes with some provocative comments about the pace of evolution.

An Erroneous Conception: Ontogeny Recapitulates Phylogeny

The statement "ontogeny recapitulates phylogeny" refers to the belief that as an individual goes through different stages of development he or she repeats some characteristics of the adult forms of lower life forms on the phylogenetic scale (e.g., amoeba, flatworm, fish, monkey, and the like). **Ontogeny** is the developmental history of an organism. **Phylogeny** is the evolutionary history of a group of organisms. Initially, E. Haeckel (1891) advanced this principle to explain why structures appear in a specific sequence during embryological development (for example, gills showing up in the human embryo). Early in the history of developmental psychology, G. Stanley Hall (1904) called on this principle to explain the nature of human development as well. This notion has been discarded in modern evolutionary theory because observations reveal that embryos do not, in fact, pass through stages that resemble adult ancestors. Instead, developing embryos of each major vertebrate group pass through some stages resembling embryos of other vertebrates. While today we no longer believe in Haeckel's view, the principle of natural selection, described next, remains an important evolutionary concept.

The Principle of Natural Selection

The principle of **natural selection** provides an explanation of the evolutionary process. This principle is based on Charles Darwin's observations of many animal species around the world. Darwin pointed out that organisms reproduce at rates that could lead to enormous increases in population sizes of most species. However, despite these massive reproductive capacities, population size tends to remain fairly constant.

Darwin stressed that there is extensive variability— sometimes referred to as genetic diversity—among individuals in a species. Some of these variations appear to be advantageous for survival. Darwin argued that individuals characterized by these beneficial characteristics would be more likely to survive and succeed in reproducing themselves. In this way their characteristics would be perpetuated to a greater degree than the less advantageous characteristics of other individuals.

FIGURE 2.1
Think about how the adaptive characteristics of humans, such as eating, have evolved.

Gradually, the organisms with the favorable characteristics would comprise a greater proportion of the population, and over a long period of time, the reproductive advantage could produce a gradual modification of the whole population. However, if environmental conditions change, new sets of characteristics might be favored and the whole process could move off in a different direction. Darwin emphasized that these processes have guided the evolution of living things. Figure 2.1 portrays some of the adaptive characteristics of humans that have evolved.

The Pace of Evolution

Evolution proceeds at a very slow pace, indeed. For example, the lines leading to the emergence of human beings and the great apes began to diverge about fourteen million years ago! Modern man, *Homo sapiens,* came into existence about 50,000 years ago. By looking at figure 2.2, you can see the evolution of the human brain. Civilization as we know it began about 10,000 years ago. In the ensuing 10,000 years there have been no sweeping evolutionary changes in humans: our brain is not ten times as big, we do not have a third eye in the back of our head, and we cannot fly. This is not surprising because we have existed for only about 50,000 years, and historically it has taken much longer for mammalian species to develop.

Brain evolution

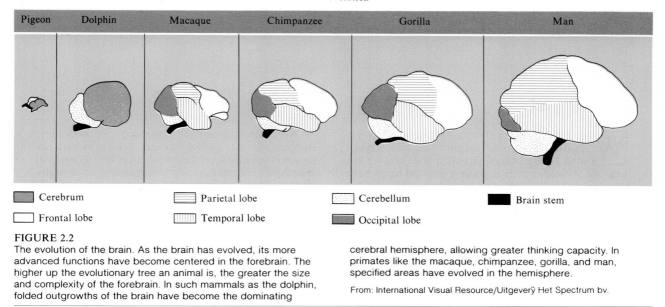

| Pigeon | Dolphin | Macaque | Chimpanzee | Gorilla | Man |

Cerebrum Parietal lobe Cerebellum Brain stem

Frontal lobe Temporal lobe Occipital lobe

FIGURE 2.2
The evolution of the brain. As the brain has evolved, its more advanced functions have become centered in the forebrain. The higher up the evolutionary tree an animal is, the greater the size and complexity of the forebrain. In such mammals as the dolphin, folded outgrowths of the brain have become the dominating cerebral hemisphere, allowing greater thinking capacity. In primates like the macaque, chimpanzee, gorilla, and man, specified areas have evolved in the hemisphere.

From: International Visual Resource/Uitgeverÿ Het Spectrum bv.

Ethology

The key to ethology is evolution. Ethologists believe that we can only fully appreciate the origin of behavior if we recognize that many patterns of behavior are transmitted by means of evolution. To learn more about ethology we evaluate one of the most important concepts in the ethological view—critical periods—and study the fascinating research of two European zoologists.

Critical Periods

Ethologists believe certain periods of time in development are critical. These time frames are called **critical periods** because it is believed they represent an optimal time for the emergence of certain behaviors. Specific forms of stimulation are required during the critical period for normal development to proceed. Examples of such critical periods and stimulation are presented in Perspective on Child Development 2.1, where the classical studies of Konrad Lorenz (1965) with graylag geese and Niko Tinbergen (1969) with stickleback fish are described. For instance, in the work of Lorenz, the critical period for attachment for goslings is a very short, rigid period from the time of hatching to about thirty-six hours later.

It is not easy to find examples of critical periods in human development, particularly of the short duration suggested by experiments such as those of Lorenz. The development of language in early childhood may to some degree involve a critical period. Nonetheless, the capacity for development of spoken language continues into adulthood, although it is much more difficult to learn at that time. Developmental research in vision also reveals that deprivation early in development often produces some form of deficit (Aslin, 1981).

However, the concept of critical period actually originated in the study of embryology, and the same rigidity should not be expected in postnatal development, particularly in humans. While humans simply do not seem to experience the short, rigid sensitive periods for learning seen in lower animals, we may have some very long, reasonably flexible sensitive periods, during which we are particularly skilled at certain kinds of behaviors. Attachment, language, and vision are examples of three such human systems that may have lengthy, somewhat flexible sensitive periods.

PERSPECTIVE ON CHILD DEVELOPMENT 2.1

THE ATTACHMENT OF GRAYLAG GEESE AND THE MATING BEHAVIOR OF STICKLEBACK FISH

Working mostly with graylag geese, Lorenz studied a behavior pattern that was considered to be programmed within the genes of the animals. A newly hatched gosling seemed to be born with the instinct for following its mother. Observations showed that the gosling was capable of such behavior as soon as it was hatched from the egg. Lorenz proved that it was incorrect to assume that such behavior was programmed in the animal.

In a remarkable series of experiments, Lorenz separated the eggs laid by one female goose into two groups. One group he returned to the female goose to be hatched by her; the other group was hatched in an incubator. The goslings in the first group performed as predicted; they followed their mother as soon as they were hatched. But those in the second group, who saw Lorenz when they were first hatched, followed him everywhere, just as though he were their mother. Lorenz marked the goslings and then placed both groups under a box. Mother goose and "mother" Lorenz stood aside as the box was lifted. Each group of goslings went directly to its "mother." (See figure top right.)

Lorenz used the word *imprinting* to describe this early modification of behavior. A number of interesting facts have evolved from imprinting experiments. In every case in which imprinting is observed, there is a critical period of time during which the individual will respond to the imprinting experience. For chicks and ducklings this critical period lasts from the time of hatching to about thirty-six hours thereafter. Peak sensitivity usually occurs at thirteen and sixteen hours. After the critical period, young animals can still be taught to follow an object, but the nature of the learning experience is distinctly different from the imprinting experience. Experiments with young rodents, dogs, and monkeys show that imprinting also takes place in mammals.

While Lorenz was busy observing and conducting experiments with graylag geese, Tinbergen was observing the behavior of the stickleback fish, a small fish that lives in North European freshwaters. (See figure bottom right.) Early in the spring, both sexes are ready to mate. Through an intricate system each member of the pair engages in certain behaviors that serve as a stimulus for the behavior of the other member. First, the male stickleback marks off a territory and forms a nest at the bottom of the water. Then his belly changes color, becoming bright red. The bright red color signals the female stickleback that he is ready to mate. At some point a female stickleback swims into his territory with her abdomen swollen by the presence of eggs and her head in an upward position. Her abdomen and posture signal the male's next behavior, an impressive zigzag dance. The dance stimulates the female to approach the male. As she does so, the male turns and swims toward the nest. The female follows and the male puts his head in the nest opening. He subsequently withdraws his head indicating to the female that she should now place her entire body in the nest. Once the female is in the nest, the male begins shaking and taps her in a rhythmic manner at the base of her tail. This tapping signals her to lay the eggs, after which she abruptly leaves the nest. Then the male enters the nest and deposits his sperm, thus fertilizing the eggs.

Tinbergen's work with the stickleback fish illustrated an important idea in ethology—the fixed-action pattern, which means nearly the same thing as instinct, being defined as unlearned behavior that is universal in a species. The unlearned behavior is triggered by the presence of naturally occurring stimuli, referred to as sign stimuli.

Konrad Lorenz, a pioneering
student of animal behavior,
is followed by three
imprinted graylag geese.

Tinbergen's research with the
stickleback fish suggests the
importance of sequence of actions
and of signals between partners.

General Biological Principles of Development

We have seen that evolution is an important biological foundation of development. Here we look at two additional biological principles of development—forward reference and differentiation/hierarchical organization.

Forward Reference

Newborns in virtually all species of animals have a number of behavioral capabilities. In this sense, at birth the organism is **preadapted.** Studies of prenatal development suggest that many of the behavioral competencies of the newborn actually arise prior to birth. For example, the sucking reflex in mammals appears during the prenatal period. The appearance of such behaviors is preparatory or anticipatory. Put another way, early neurological maturation has a **forward reference.**

Differentiation and Hierarchical Organization

The principles of **differentiation** and **hierarchical organization** in biological development emerged in the study of embryology. As an individual's development unfolds, behavior becomes more differentiated. This suggests that as the individual's range of behaviors increases with age, so does the perceptual ability to analyze stimuli in more precise ways, to interpret the world in a more complex manner, and to socially interact in more intricate patterns. Since it is believed that later neural and behavioral differentiation builds on earlier more simple forms of development, it is argued that integrated hierarchies are formed.

Hierarchical organization is particularly salient at the neurological level. For example, during the prenatal period the brain develops from a central core outward such that the last layers to appear are the outer cortical layers. Later in the chapter, when we discuss neurological development, such hierarchical organization will become readily apparent.

GENES AND THE NATURE OF HEREDITY–ENVIRONMENT INTERACTION

In addition to evolution, forward reference, and differentiation and hierarchical organization, there is another very important psychobiological principle in development: the nature of heredity-environment interaction. The role of genes in development is complex so we will spend considerable time outlining what genes are, some basic genetic principles, the distinction between genotype and phenotype, the study of behavior genetics, and some conclusions about the nature of heredity-environment interaction.

Genes

Each of us still carries around the genetic code we inherited from our parents. Physically, this code is carried by biochemical agents called genes and chromosomes, which are located within the cells of our body. The genes and chromosomes that all people have inherited are alike in one very important respect: they all contain human genetic codes. A fertilized human egg cannot develop into a dog, a cat, or an aardvark.

Each of us begins life as a single cell weighing about one twenty-millionth of an ounce! This tiny piece of matter houses an individual's entire complement of genes and chromosomes. Encoded in the genes and chromosomes is a set of information or instructions that orchestrates development from a single cell into an adult made of trillions of cells, each containing a perfect replica of the original genes and chromosomes.

Each human cell consists of forty-six chromosomes and probably as many as 50,000 genes. **Chromosomes** are threadlike structures that come in structurally similar pairs (twenty-three of them in humans). **Genes** are segments of chromosomes. Genes are comprised of **DNA** (deoxyribonucleic acid), a long molecule that runs along the length of each chromosome. The discovery of DNA by the British scientists James Watson and Frances Crick was a dramatic breakthrough in understanding genetic transmission. As shown in figure 2.3, each DNA molecule consists of two long strands arranged in a spiral staircase. Just before a cell divides, the two strands unzip down the middle and a new second strand emerges next to the original one. The new DNA molecules are exact replicas of the old one. In this manner, genes are precisely copied.

Genes are transmitted from parents to offspring by means of **gametes,** or sex cells, which are created in the testes of males and the ovaries of females. Gametes are formed by the splitting of cells; this process is called **meiosis.** In meiosis, each pair of chromosomes in the cell separates, and one member of each pair goes into each gamete, or daughter cell. Thus, each human gamete has twenty-three unpaired chromosomes. **Reproduction** takes place when a female gamete (ovum) is

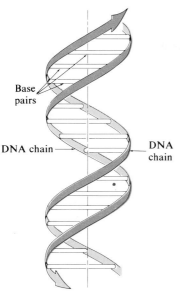

FIGURE 2.3
The double helix: the DNA molecule.

fertilized by a male gamete (sperm) to create a single-celled **zygote.** In the zygote, two sets of unpaired chromosomes combine to form one set of paired chromosomes, one member of each pair being from the mother and the other member from the father. In this manner, each parent contributes 50 percent of the heredity to the offspring.

None of us possesses all of the characteristics that our genetic structure makes possible. The actual combination of genes makes possible what is known as the **genotype.** However, not all of this genetic material will be manifested in our observed and measurable characteristics. These observed and measurable characteristics are referred to as **phenotypes** and include physical characteristics such as height, weight, eye color, and skin pigmentation, and psychological characteristics such as intelligence, creativity, personality, and social tendencies.

Some Genetic Principles

Genetic determination is a very complex affair, and many principles have been discovered that govern this complexity; on the other hand, some aspects of genetics are still unexplored. Let's look at the factors involved in five of the principles that we do know are an important part of our genetic life; **dominant–recessive genes,** sex-linked genes, polygenically inherited characteristics, reaction range, and canalization.

Dominant–Recessive Genes

Some important principles of genetics that were worked out in experiments with garden peas by Gregor Mendel have implications for the way in which inheritance works in human beings as well. Mendel found that when he combined round pea plants with wrinkled pea plants, the next generation of pea plants consistently came out round. He determined that the gene for round pea plants was *dominant,* and the one for wrinkled plants was *recessive* (tending to go backward or recede).

What is the color of your parents' hair? If they both have brown hair, you probably have brown hair. If one of your parents has brown hair and the other blond hair, you are still likely to have brown hair because brown hair is controlled by a dominant gene. Blond hair, by contrast, is based on a recessive gene. If both of your parents have blond hair, then you are likely to have blond hair because there is no dominant gene to interfere with the appearance of blond hair. Examples of other dominant gene-linked traits include brown eyes, farsightedness, and dimples; examples of recessive gene-linked traits are blue eyes, normal vision, and freckles.

Sex-Linked Genes

Another important genetic principle involves sex-linked traits. Some characteristics are determined by genes carried on the twenty-third chromosome pair—the one that determines the sex of the offspring—with the result that these characteristics are more or less likely to appear in members of one sex. The sex-linked chromosomes are referred to as X and Y. The female has two X chromosomes, whereas the male has one X and one Y chromosome. Females, then, always contribute an X chromosome to the offspring, so it is the male who determines the sex of the offspring because he contributes either an X (a girl) or a Y (a boy).

Let's look at one sex-linked human characteristic—color blindness. The gene for color blindness is recessive and appears only on the X chromosome. Most females with this recessive gene also have a dominant gene for normal vision on their second X chromosome. For a female to be color blind, she has to have a recessive gene on both her X chromosomes. By contrast, because males have only one X chromosome, when the recessive gene for color blindness shows up there, the male will be color blind because he does not have a second X chromosome to cancel out the recessive gene. In other words, if a female inherits the recessive gene

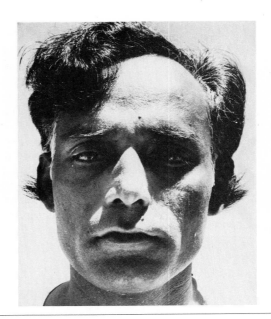

FIGURE 2.4
Hairy ear rims represent a sex-linked characteristic. The gene for this condition is located on the Y chromosome.

it may not show, but if a male inherits it the trait will be apparent. Another sex-linked characteristic is illustrated in figure 2.4.

Polygenic Inheritance

Another very important genetic principle is that of **polygenic inheritance.** Genetic transmission is usually more complex than the rather simple examples we have just examined. Few psychological characteristics are the result of the actions of single gene pairs. Most are actually determined by the interaction of many different genes (remember that there are as many as 50,000 of these) in the chromosomes. Traits produced by the mixing of genes are said to be polygenically determined.

Reaction Range

Given any individual genotype, there is a range of phenotypes that could be expressed (see figure 2.5). Suppose, for example, that we could identify all the genetic loci that can contribute to intelligence in the embryo. Would measured intelligence during adulthood

be directly predictable from knowledge about the specific **alleles** (two or more alternative forms of a gene that can occur at a particular chromosomal locus) at all of these loci? That is, would we know, from the genetic codes at each of the loci, precisely how bright the individual would be? No, we would not. This is because even if we had a good enough genetic model (and, of course, we do not), intelligence is a characteristic that is continuously shaped by the experiences a person has throughout life. Let us suppose, for simplicity sake, that intelligence is a measure of how efficiently and rapidly individuals learn and store new information. Genetically, individuals may be predisposed to learn faster or slower, to package certain kinds of information (e.g., sounds) relatively more effectively than other kinds (e.g., sights), to take in information optimally during different lengths of time, and so on. The learning environment created for the individual throughout infancy and childhood will determine how much this individual genotype can maximize opportunities to acquire and store information. Suppose a "visual" learner predisposed to focus on new experiences over short periods of time is exposed mostly to new auditory (sound) experiences over long periods of time during formative periods of childhood. She or he is not being provided

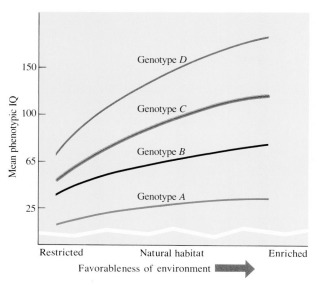

FIGURE 2.5
Hypothetical set of reaction ranges of intellectual development of several genotypes under environmental conditions that range from poor to good. Although each genotype responds favorably to improved environments, some are more responsive to environmental deprivation and enrichment than others (Gottesman, 1963).

optimal stimulation, may learn little, and most importantly, may through "disuse," become an inactive and inefficient "visual" learner.

For most characteristics, like intelligence, it is useful to think about a collection of genetic codes that predispose a person to develop in a certain way and environments that are more or less responsive to this development. The environment may be highly supportive of the expression of the characteristic or it may be highly stultifying. It is also useful to think about the genetic codes as setting broad limits on the range of outcomes that may be possible. For example, there may be a number of individuals whose genotype would predispose them to be geniuses in the right environment or mentally retarded under extremely impoverished conditions. By contrast, other individuals in the same range of environmental conditions, would not have the capability of expressing "genius," but only moderate "brightness"; still others would express only "average" or "slightly retarded" status in the same circumstances.

Reaction range, then, suggests a limit on how much environmental change can mold intelligence. Sandra Scarr (1984) explains reaction range this way. Each of us has a range of potential. For example, a person with "medium-tall" genes for height who grows up in a poor environment may be shorter than average. But in an excellent nutritional environment, the person may grow up taller than average. However, no matter how well fed the person is, an individual with "short" genes will never be taller than average. Scarr believes intelligence works in the same manner. That is, there is a range within which environment can modify intelligence, but intelligence is not completely malleable. Reaction range gives us an estimate of how modifiable intelligence is. The idea of reaction range is compatible with the view that intelligence is influenced by genetic–environmental interaction.

Canalization

Some experts argue that genotypes, in addition to yielding a range of phenotypical outcomes, also experience just the opposite phenomenon for many human characteristics. That is to say, many human characteristics seem to be immune to vast changes in environmental events and seem to stay on track regardless of what assaults are made on their expression by the environment. Proposals such as this have been made by Waddington (1957). **Canalization** refers to the narrow path or track that marks the development of some characteristic. It is clear that in human development a variety of conserving and preserving forces seems to protect an individual from changing much, even in the face of drastic environmental inputs. Jerome Kagan (1984), for example, has repeatedly reminded us of the Guatemalan children he studied, who, though many had undergone extreme malnourishment as infants, seemed to experience normal social and cognitive development. Also, many children who are exposed to clinically pathological parenting or child abuse, do not grow up to be pathological parents or child abusers themselves. However, the concept of canalization has not been explained with respect to any particular genetic mechanisms; this has led some recent critics to wonder about its scientific usefulness (Gottlieb, 1983).

CONCEPT TABLE 2.1
Biological Foundations of Development, Genes, and Genetic Principles

Concept	Processes/Related Ideas	Characteristics/Description
Biological foundations	Evolution	Evolution involves ideas about ontogeny recapitulating phylogeny, natural selection, and the pace of evolution. "Ontogeny recapitulates phylogeny" refers to the belief that as an individual goes through stages of development he or she repeats some of the characteristics of the adult forms of lower animals. It is an outmoded conception. Natural selection emphasizes that organisms with beneficial characteristics are more likely to adapt and survive, so their characteristics are perpetuated. Evolution proceeds at an incredibly slow pace.
	Ethology	Ethology refers to the modified instinct view of the organism that stresses the release of unlearned patterns of behavior by certain environmental circumstances. Ethologists stress the importance of critical periods of development.
	Biological principles	Two important biological principles are forward reference, the concept that behaviors are preadapted, and differential, hierarchical organization.
Genes	Genes	Genes are biochemical agents that are the basic building blocks of heredity.
	Chromosomes	Chromosomes are threadlike structures that come in structurally similar pairs (twenty-three in humans). Genes are segments of chromosomes.
	DNA	Deoxyribonucleic acid is a long molecule that runs along the length of each chromosome. DNA is the key chemical substance in genetic makeup.
	Genotype and phenotype	The actual combination of genes is genotype; the observed and measurable characteristics of the genetic material is phenotype.
Genetic principles	Dominant–recessive genes	A dominant gene exerts its full effect regardless of its genetic partner. A recessive gene's code is masked by a dominant gene and will only be expressed when paired with another recessive gene.
	Sex-linked genes	Some characteristics are determined by genes located on the twenty-third chromosome pair—the one that determines the sex of the offspring—with the result that these characteristics are more or less likely to appear in members of one sex.
	Polygenic inheritance	Few psychological characteristics are the result of the action of a single gene. This principle refers to the determination of a phenotype by some combination of genes.
	Reaction range	Given any individual genotype, a range of phenotypes can be expressed.
	Canalization	Canalization is the narrow path or track that marks the development of some characteristic.

So far we have discussed information about biological foundations, genes, and genetic principles. A summary of these ideas is presented in Concept Table 2.1.

Behavior Genetics

A field of inquiry in psychology and biology that has received considerable attention in recent years is called **behavior genetics,** the discipline that is concerned with the degree and nature of the hereditary basis of behavior. Workers in this field assume that behaviors are jointly determined by the interaction of hereditary and environmental factors.

First, we study the methods used by behavior geneticists, second, we look at some aspects of development influenced by genetic factors, and third, we draw some conclusions about genetic–environmental interaction and its effects on development.

The Methods of Behavior Geneticists

The first set of methods of behavior geneticists, selective breeding and inbreeding, has been used with animals. The second set, the twin study, family of twins design, kinship studies, and adoption studies, has been used with humans. A concept called heritability often is used to mathematically estimate the degree of genetic influence.

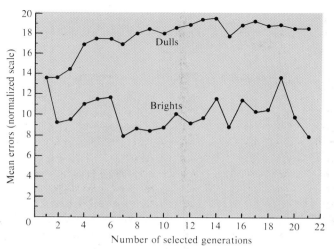

FIGURE 2.6
The results of Tryon's selective breeding experiment performed over twenty-one generations. The results are plotted in terms of mean number of errors made by the animals as a function of number of selected generations (Postman, 1962).

Identical, or monozygotic, twins come from the same egg and are genetically more similar than fraternal twins.

Selective Breeding and Inbreeding An investigation that reveals the procedure of inbreeding was conducted by Robert Tryon (1940). Basically, the procedure of **selective breeding** involves the mating of organisms of like characteristics. Tyron selectively bred for "maze-bright" and "maze-dull" rats. As suggested in figure 2.6 Tryon's experiment was highly successful. He produced two lines of rats that differed in their ability to learn mazes. In just seven generations, the dullest animal in the bright line was making fewer errors than the brightest animal in the dull line. Since the strains were called "maze-bright" and "maze-dull," it would seem that substantial differences in the behavior of the two strains would emerge in a variety of learning circumstances. In mazes similar to the one used for selecting the two strains the "maze-bright" rats were clearly superior, but in other, different learning contexts the "maze-bright" rats did not outperform their "duller" counterparts. Nonetheless, that organisms could be selected for maze behavior suggests learning is to some degree influenced by heredity.

Inbreeding occurs when brothers and sisters are mated with each other. When their offspring, their offspring's offspring, and so forth are mated, the result is a homogeneous strain of organisms after several generations. When different animal families are kept distinct and inbred over several generations, a number of genetically determined characteristics should appear.

One classic example of inbreeding involved the trait of aggression (Ginsburg & Allee, 1942). Three different inbred strains of mice were observed. There were highly significant differences in the tendencies of one of the strains to initiate more fights than the other two strains did, suggesting that aggression is determined at least in part by genetic factors.

Twin Study, Family of Twins Design, Kinship Study, and Adoption Study Of course we cannot conduct selective breeding and inbreeding experiments with humans. So what are we to do? Several strategies are now used more than others by behavior geneticists to investigate the role of genetics in human behavior: the twin study, family of twins design, kinship studies, and adoption studies.

These strategies focus on the genetic relationship of an individual to members of his or her family. In the twin study and family of twins design the focus is on the genetic relationship between twins. In the **twin study** the comparison is between identical twins (**monozygotic**, meaning they come from the same egg) and fraternal twins (**dyzygotic**, meaning they come from two different eggs and are therefore genetically more distant than identical twins). In the **family of twins design**, monozygotic twins, siblings, half-siblings, and parent and offspring are compared. **Kinship studies** of the role of heredity in behavior include other family members as well, members such as uncles, cousins, grandparents, and so forth.

By means of **adoption studies** we can study individuals who are genetically more similar or more dissimilar from each other. An adopted child is genetically closer to her biological parents than to the caregivers who have reared her. Investigators look to see if the child's characteristics are more similar to those of her biological parents or those of her adopted parents.

Heritability   Estimates often vary widely as to the heritability of a particular characteristic. **Heritability** is a mathematical estimate, which is often computed with a standard heritability quotient. It compares, for a population, the amount of variation in genetic material to the total amount of variation among people. Similarity is measured by use of the correlation coefficient *r*. The highest degree of heritability is 1.00. A heritability quotient of .80 suggests a strong genetic influence, one of .50 a moderate genetic influence, and one of .20 a much weaker, but nonetheless perceptible, genetic influence.

Although heritability values may vary considerably from one study to the next, it is often possible to determine the average magnitude of the quotient for a particular characteristic. For some kinds of physical characteristics and mental retardation, the heritability quotient approaches 1.00. That is, the environment makes almost no contribution to variation in the characteristic. This is not the same as saying the environment has no influence; the characteristic could not be expressed without it.

The heritability index is by no means a flawless technique for assessing the contribution of genetic factors to development. It is only as good as the data to which it is applied and the assumptions the investigator is willing to make about the nature of genetic–environmental interactions. As Sandra Scarr and Kenneth Kidd (1983) have explained, there are at least three limitations to be kept in mind. First, there is the issue of how varied the environments are in the sample tested. The narrower the range of environmental differences represented in the sample, the higher the heritability quotients will be. The opposite will be true if a broader range of environmental differences are present. Second, there is the question of how reliable and valid the measures of the underlying characteristic being investigated in the study are (e.g., IQ, temperament). The weaker the measure, the less confidence

Separated at birth, the Mallifert twins meet accidentally.

Drawing by Chas. Addams; © 1981 The New Yorker Magazine, Inc.

we may place in the heritability quotient, which is likely to be falsely low because of the poor measurement. Finally, the heritability quotient assumes that we can treat inheritance and environmental influences as factors to be quantitatively added together, with each part contributing a distinct amount of influence. In reality, of course, these two factors must interact. The role and nature of the interaction is lost in the heritability computation.

Some Aspects of Development Influenced by Genetic Factors

What aspects of development are influenced by genetic factors? Quite clearly they all are. However, behavior geneticists have been interested in more precise estimates of the variation in a characteristic accounted for by genetic factors. Most of the conclusions from such research efforts are imprecise. Nonetheless, many different aspects of development, including intelligence and temperament, have been evaluated with respect to the degree to which they are related to genetic factors.

Intelligence What do we know about the role of genetics in intelligence? First, we consider some estimates and difficulties in predicting the role of genetics in intelligence; second, we consider the role of genetics in mental retardation.

The family of twins design has helped to provide a more accurate estimate of the heritability of intelligence. It consists of studies of monozygotic (MZ) twins, siblings, half-siblings, and parent and offspring. In one investigation that used this strategy, the estimate of heritability for half-siblings was .40, whereas for parent and offspring it was .56 (Rose, Harris & Christian, 1979).

Earlier studies of the heritability of intelligence placed the figure at approximately .80 (for example, Loehlin & Nichols, 1976), a figure that is now disputed and thought to be too high. In a recent review of human behavior genetics, Norman Henderson (1982) argued that a figure of .50 seems more appropriate. In keeping with the trend of providing a range rather than a point estimate of heritability, intelligence is given a range of from .30 to .60. Clearly, then, intelligence is not totally malleable. By the same token, although genetic inheritance makes an important contribution to intelligence, environmental factors can modify intelligence substantially.

We already have seen that there are difficulties inherent in the heritability concept, and as we now see there are other difficulties with predicting the genetic contribution to intelligence as well. First, although there has been a long history of testing for some ability called "intelligence," there is by no means agreement on what it is. One provocative proposal is that human beings really have eight or nine highly developed and divergent cognitive skills (Gardner, 1982), very few of which have been sampled on standard intelligence tests. Another view (Sternberg, 1982) is that intelligence consists of a number of basic cognitive operations that manifest themselves in different arrangements, depending upon the problem or task that is confronted. In this latter view, it could also be argued that our existing tests do not do a good job of measuring individual differences in intelligence. Second, intelligence is perhaps the most widely researched topic in all of behavioral genetics, so there is more information available on the question but less agreement on how to synthesize it or interpret what it means. Third, the question

asked above, about the role of genetics in intelligence, to be a manageable one, must be broken down into more modest queries. For example, it would be more fruitful to ask about the role of genetics in phenomena that are logical subsets of the larger domain—e.g., spatial reasoning, numerical reasoning, short-term memory—than to focus on the whole domain at once. Fourth, there are really separate questions to ask, which are not all the same and for which our science has progressed to different levels of elegance. The nuts-and-bolts analysis of how particular genetic loci cause what chemical reactions to occur to produce what differences in brain and central nervous system development is very far removed from a tractable solution. We do not have the foggiest notion of which brain functions might discriminate among different levels of intelligence, let alone which genetic loci, in combination, might contribute to such differences. However, we have a much greater likelihood of success if the question is: What do we know about current factors contributing to individual differences in large populations of individuals in society?

Geneticists and psychologists have identified a range of types of mental retardation. Some are part of a pattern in which some *major gene defect* or *damage to a chromosome* is present, leading to a biochemical error in brain and central nervous system development or functioning. Scarr and Kidd (1983) indicate that there are more than 150 known types of retardation that seem to be associated with single-gene defects and many more that are the product of chromosomal abnormalities. Typically, these forms of retardation result in severe intellectual deficits if they cannot be corrected.

Another type has been referred to as **cultural familial retardation.** Typically, this type of retardation is part of a pattern in which other members of the child's family also have below average intellectual capabilities and there is a family history extending across more than one generation of others in the family having the same profile. Cultural familial retardation is harder to diagnose and treat than other kinds, because it is subtle, and one has a difficult time disentangling environmental and genetic contributions to it. Often children with cultural familial retardation have very boring and impoverished intellectual environments. In comparison with the retardation caused by single-gene defects or chromosomal abnormalities, the degree of intellectual deficit is often less severe.

A child with Down's syndrome.

Children differ in their temperament—Thomas and Chess have classified children as "easy," "difficult," or "slow-to-warm-up."

Let's look now at two different types of retardation that seem to have a clear genetic defect surrounding them. The **PKU syndrome** (phenylketonuria) is one such type of retardation. Here the problem resides in a genetic code that fails to produce an enzyme necessary for metabolism. In the absence of this enzyme, the cells fail to break down an amino acid, phenylalanine, interfering with metabolic processes and generating a poisonous substance that enters the nervous system. Mental functioning deteriorates rapidly if the enzyme deficiency is not treated shortly after birth. Fortunately, the absence of this enzyme can be detected early and treated by diet to keep phenylalanine at a very low level so that normal metabolism can proceed and the poisonous substance is not generated. A recessive gene is responsible for this disorder.

Perhaps the most common genetically transmitted form of retardation is **Down's syndrome.** The Down's child has a flattened skull, an extra fold of skin over the eyelid, and a protruding tongue. Among other characteristics are a short, thin body frame and extreme retardation of motor abilities. The cause of Down's syndrome is an extra chromosome—Down's children have forty-seven chromosomes instead of the usual forty-six. It is not known why the extra chromosome occurs, but it may have to do with the health of the female ovum or the male sperm.

Temperament At birth, newborn infants do not all have the same temperament. Some infants are extremely active, moving their arms, legs, and mouths incessantly; others are very tranquil. Some children explore their environment eagerly for great lengths of time; others do not. Some older infants respond warmly and openly to people; others fuss and fret. All of these characteristics are believed to be part of a child's inborn emotional temperament.

Individual temperaments can vary so widely that some parents have an easy time dealing with children, while others seem unable to cope with them. A mother who is quiet and inactive can easily adjust to a quiet and inactive baby, but imagine her difficulty in dealing with an active and easily agitated newborn. A father who does not need much face-to-face social interaction

TABLE 2.1
Dimensions of Temperament in the Chess and Thomas Research

Dimension	Description	Easy child	Difficult child	Slow-to-warm-up child
Activity level	Degree of energy movement		High	Low
Rhythmicity	Regularity of eating, sleeping, toileting	Regular	Irregular	
Approach–withdrawal	Ease of approaching new people and situations	Positive	Negative	Negative
Adaptability	Ease of tolerating change in routines, plans	Positive	Negative	Negative
Intensity of reactions	Degree of affect when pleased, displeased, happy, sad	Low to moderate	High	Low
Threshold of responsiveness	Amount of stimulation required for responding			
Quality of mood	Degree of positive or negative affect	Positive	Negative	
Distractibility	Ease of being distracted			
Attention span, persistence	Length of time focused on an event, activity			

will find it easy to manage a similarly introverted baby, but he may not be able to provide an extraverted baby with sufficient stimulation.

In the classic longitudinal study by Alexander Chess and Stella Thomas (Chess & Thomas, 1977; Thomas, Chess & Birch, 1970), temperament was defined as broadly as possible and a great deal of information was collected on individuals from birth onward.

Table 2.1 lists the different dimensions of the infants' behavior that Chess and Thomas identified in their original sample of infants. On the basis of the degree of the babies' responsiveness for each dimension, the authors were able to identify three different profiles of children. These profiles seemed to be moderately stable across the childhood years. The groups were referred to, respectively, as the "easy" child, the "difficult" child and the "slow-to-warm-up" child. The adjectives appearing in the table indicate which of the nine dimensions were critical in spotting a profile and what the level of responsiveness was for a critical feature. Those entries where a blank appears are indicative of dimensions of temperament that seemed to be uncorrelated with the other cluster of characteristics for the given type of child (i.e., easy, difficult, slow-to-warm-up).

A number of scholars, including Chess and Thomas themselves, conceive of temperament as a stable characteristic of newborns that comes to be shaped and modified by the later experiences of the child. This raises the question of whether some genetic role can be found in one or more of the dimensions of temperament listed in the table. A number of twin studies have recently been conducted to answer this question (e.g., DeFries, Plomin, Vandenberg & Kuse, 1981; Goldsmith & Gottesman, 1981; Matheny, Dolan & Wilson, 1976). Not all of them have examined each of the dimensions listed in the table, nor have all of them operationalized the construct of "temperament" in precisely the same way. In each case investigators did find differences in the similarity among identical versus fraternal twins. Using the correlations reported in these studies, a simple calculation of heritability would place the quotient in the range of .50 to .60 across the different sets of results. Thus, there is some evidence that genetic variation in the group is associated with behavioral variation in temperament. Interestingly, however, the strength of this association seemed to decline as the infants became older (Goldsmith & Gottesman, 1981). This finding offers support for the idea that temperament becomes more malleable with experience. Alternatively, it may be that as the child becomes older, it becomes harder to identify behavioral manifestations of the same aspects of temperament seen earlier. The temperament differences may still be present; psychologists, however, may not know how to spot the relevant patterns in children.

Some Conclusions about Genetic–Environmental Interaction and Its Effects on Development

Both genes and an environment are necessary for an organism to exist. In an article entitled "Calling All Camps! The War Is Over," Sandra Scarr and Richard Weinberg (1980) summarized this often repeated point:

> One cannot assess the relative impact of heredity and environment on intelligence per se, because everyone must have both a viable gene complement and an environment in which the genes can be expressed over development. No genes, no organism; no environment, no organism. Behavioral differences among individuals, on the other hand, can arise in any population from genetic differences, from variation among their environments, or both. (p. 860)

What do we know and what do we need to know about the role of genetic–environmental interaction in development? Scarr and Kidd (1983) provided some answers to these important questions in developmental psychology. In answering the question "What do we know?" they concluded the following:

1. Literally hundreds of disorders appear because of miscodings in such genetic material as DNA. Normal development clearly is inhibited by these defects in genetic material.
2. Abnormalities in chromosome number adversely influence the development of physical, intellectual, and behavioral features of individuals, usually in a severe manner.
3. There is no one-to-one relation between genotype and phenotype.
4. It is very difficult to distinguish between genetic and cultural transmission. There usually is a familial concentration of a particular behavioral disorder, but most familial patterns are considerably different from what would be precisely predicted from simple modes of inheritance.
5. When we consider the normal range of variation, the stronger the genetic resemblance, the stronger the behavioral resemblance. This holds more strongly for intelligence than personality or interests. The influence of genes on intelligence is present in early child development and continues through the late childhood years.
6. Being raised in the same family accounts for some portion of intellectual differences among individuals, but common rearing accounts for little variation in personality or interests. One reason for this discrepancy may be that families place similar pressures on their children for intellectual development in the sense that the push is clearly toward a higher level, while they do not direct their children toward similar personalities or interests, in which extremes are not particularly desirable. That is, virtually all parents would like for their children to have above average intellect, but there is much less agreement about whether a child should be encouraged to be highly extraverted.

In answering the question "What do we need to know?" Scarr and Kidd commented that it is very beneficial to know the pathways by which genetic abnormalities influence development. The PKU success story is but one such example in which scientists discovered the genetic linkage of the disorder and subsequently how the environment could be changed to reduce the damage to development.

Understanding variation in the normal range of development is much more complicated in most instances than revealing the genetic path of a specific disorder. For example, to understand the differences between two brothers, one with an IQ of 95 and the other with an IQ of 125, requires a polygenic perspective. Models of cultural and genetic inheritance, and their complex interactions, are more likely to explain behavioral variation than more molecular models of gene pathways, at least in the foreseeable future.

Developmental models of genetic influence across the entire life cycle are critical to understanding development. While developmental psychologists are very familiar with the species-specific patterns of development described by Piaget and Erikson, few of us attribute these patterns to evolutionary, genetic factors. Rather, developmental psychologists have tended to search for the proximal, immediate causes of these patterns. However, there may be some more distal reasons for such patterns of development, namely, causes that have evolved over the course of millions of years. For instance, puberty is not an environmentally produced accident of development; rather, it is heavily influenced

CONCEPT TABLE 2.2
The Methods of Behavior Geneticists, Influence of Heredity on Development,
and Genetic–Environmental Interaction

Concept	Processes/Related Ideas	Characteristics/Description
Methods of behavior geneticists	Selective breeding and inbreeding	Selective breeding involves the mating of organisms with like characteristics. Inbreeding occurs when brothers and sisters are mated with each other.
	Twin study, family of twins design, kinship study, and adoption studies	Since selective breeding and inbreeding cannot be used with humans, behavior geneticists rely on these other methods to study the effects of genes on children's behavior.
	Heritability	Heritability is a mathematical estimate of the degree to which a characteristic is inherited. It is by no means flawless, and unfortunately the nature of genetic–environmental interaction is lost in heritability computation.
Influence of heredity on development	Range	All behaviors are in some way influenced by heredity.
	Intelligence	Early estimates placed the heritability index for intelligence at about .80. More recent estimates are in the range of .30 to .60. It is important to remember that intelligence is a global construct with issues about its measurement still being widely debated. Further, there are probably many intelligences, and there are different forms of mental retardation as well. This suggests that rather than estimating the extent to which general intelligence and general retardation are due to heredity, we should be focusing on more precise forms of these constructs.
	Temperament	Temperament has been studied by Chess and Thomas. They view temperament as a rather stable characteristic of infants but one that is influenced by environmental experiences to a greater degree later in development.
Genetic–environmental interaction	General conclusions	No genes, no organism; no environment, no organism. Both genes and environment are necessary for an organism even to exist.
	What we know	Literally hundreds of disorders appear because of miscodings in genetic material like DNA. Abnormalities in chromosomes influence development. There is no one-to-one correspondence between genotype and phenotype. It is very difficult to distinguish genetic and cultural transmission. In the normal range, the stronger the genetic resemblance, the stronger the behavioral resemblance. Being raised in the same family accounts for some portion of intellectual differences among individuals, but common rearing accounts for much less variation in personality or interests.
	What we need to know	We need to know the pathways by which genetic abnormalities influence development. We also need to unravel the complicated nature of genetic transmission in normal development. Developmental models of genetic influence across the entire life cycle are needed.

by evolutionary and genetic programming. While puberty can be affected by such environmental influences as nutrition, social interaction, exercise, and the like, the basic evolutionary and genetic program is wired into the species. It cannot be eliminated, and it should not be ignored. Such an evolutionary perspective is becoming an important facet of developmental psychology and in the process is directing attention to new forms of analysis, raising new questions, and providing a more complete account of the nature of development.

So far, the story of biological foundations of development has taken us through the ethological and evolutionary perspectives, provided a look at several biological principles, and documented the importance of genes in development. A summary of main ideas about methods of behavior geneticists, influence of heredity on development, and genetic–environmental interaction is presented in Concept Table 2.2. But the story would be far from complete without consideration of the most important physical structure in development—the brain (see figure 2.7), which we describe next.

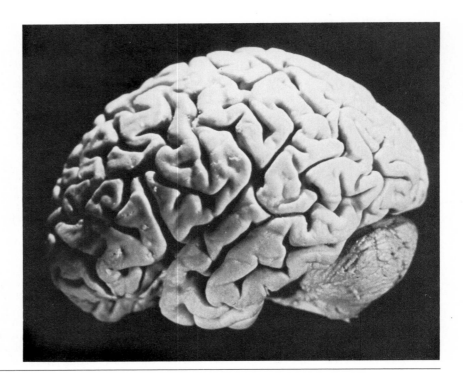

FIGURE 2.7
Photograph of the human brain showing the many convolutions of the cerebral cortex. Each ridge is a gyrus. Each groove is a sulcus. The surface area of the cortex is greatly increased by such folding.

THE BRAIN AND NEUROLOGICAL DEVELOPMENT

Understanding the nature of the brain and neurological development requires information about the brain as a processor of information, the neuron itself, processes involved in the development of neurons, the evolution of the brain, and the integration of function in the brain.

The Brain as a Processor of Information

The nervous system does many different information-processing jobs. Indeed, the most basic function of the brain is the processing of information. The flow of information to the brain, in the brain, and out of the brain can be described in terms of three components: afferent nerves, efferent nerves, and interneurons. The cells that carry the input are called **afferent nerves** (from the Latin for "bring to"), and the nerves that carry output are the **efferent nerves** (meaning, "bring forth").

Any complex information processing is accomplished by passing the information through systems of **interneurons,** which make up most of the brain. For example, as you read this page the afferent input from your eye is transmitted to your brain, then passed through many interneuron systems, which translate (process) the patterns of black and white into neural codes for letters, words, associations, and meanings. Some of the information is stored in the interneuron systems for future associations, some (if you read aloud) will be output as efferent messages to your lips and tongue.

The Neuron and Its Organization

Two things need to be considered further if we are to understand how the nervous system works: the **neuron** (the basic cell in the brain that processes information) and what we have been calling interneuron systems. Fortunately, all neurons—afferents, efferents, and interneurons–are essentially identical, and the basic operations of the neuron are well understood. Thus, we

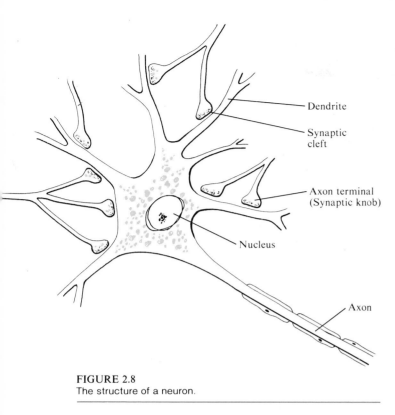

FIGURE 2.8
The structure of a neuron.

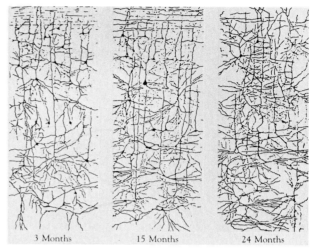

FIGURE 2.9
The development of dendritic spreading in human infants at three, fifteen, and twenty-four months of age.

can get a good notion of how the basic brain unit, the neuron, works. The key concept in the workings of interneuron processing systems is organization.

The neuron is the basic cell that handles information processing in the brain. There are some 10 to 20 billion neurons in the human brain. The average neuron has been described as being as complex as a small computer, each one having as many as 15,000 physical connections with other cells (Kolb & Whishaw, 1980). At times the brain may be lit up with as many as a quadrillion connections. The three basic parts of the neuron are the soma, dendrites, and axon.

The neuron's cell body, or **soma,** contains the nucleus (see figure 2.8), which directs the manufacture of all of the substances the neuron uses for growing and maintaining all of its processes. Most neurons are created very early in life and will not be replaced if they are destroyed. Interestingly, though, some types of neurons continue to multiply in adults, and most neurons seem to remain capable of changing their shapes

and sizes and connections throughout the life span (Frederickson, 1985).

The part of the neuron that extends away from the soma is called the **dendrite** (see figure 2.8). Most nerve cells have a number of dendrites that radiate outward from the cell body. The dendrites are the receiving part of the neuron, serving the important function of collecting information and orienting it toward the cell body. The receptive surface area of dendrites may be increased by the sprouting of spines on the dendritic branches. As shown in figure 2.9, when the developing brain is viewed under microscopic conditions, there is evidence of tremendous growth of these dendritic branches and spines in the first years of life. The absence of these branches and spines has been documented in the brains of some severely retarded children (Purpura, 1974).

Although many dendrites often radiate from the cell body of the neuron, there is only one axon. The **axon** is much thinner than a dendrite and looks like an ultrathin cylindrical tube. It may also be a lot longer than a dendrite. The axon of a single cell may extend all the way from the top of the brain to the base of the spinal cord, a distance of over three feet. The function of the axon is to carry information away from the cell body to other cells.

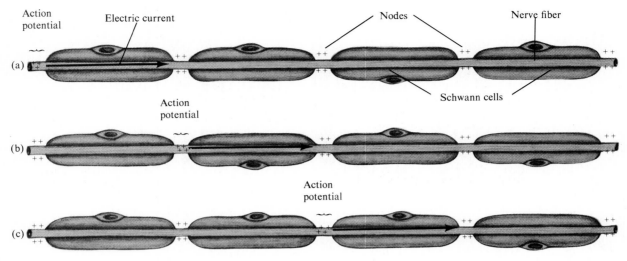

FIGURE 2.10
In myelinated nerve fibers, the action potential jumps from one node to the next greatly increasing the speed of propagation (Hole, 1984).

Neurons send information down their axons in the form of brief impulses, or "waves" of electricity. Perhaps in the movies you have seen a telegraph operator sending out single clicks that go down a telegraph wire to the next station. That is what neurons do. To send information to other neurons, they send single, electrical clicks called **action potentials** down their axons. By changing the rate and timing of the clicks, the neuron can vary the nature of the message it sends. As you reach out to turn this page, hundreds of such clicks will be streaming down the axons in your arm to tell your muscles just when to flex and how vigorously.

Whether an axon is myelinated is particularly important in how fast information travels. **Myelin** is a substance that wraps around the axon. Some axons have this sheath while others do not. By wrapping around the axon, myelin improves the spread of the electrical charge so that the action potential "jumps" from one set of gaps in the sheath to the next. These gaps are called the **nodes of Ranvier** (see figure 2.10).

Though neurons have an unbelievable network of connections, the neurons themselves do not directly touch one another. The story of such connections between one neuron and another is one of the most intriguing and highly researched in contemporary neuroscience. The story focuses on the **synapse,** which is the functional connection between neurons. When an axon gets to its destination, it usually branches out into a number of fibers that end in **synaptic knobs** (see figure 2.11). The cell that is sending the information is called the presynaptic cell and the one that is receiving the message is labeled the postsynaptic cell.

How does the functional connection of the synapse take place? The answer lies in chemical substances called **neurotransmitters,** which can be found in tiny synaptic vesicles in the synaptic knobs. The molecules are stored in the vesicles, waiting for an action potential to come down through the axon. Once the action potential reaches the synaptic knobs, the electrical signal causes miniature springlike molecules to contract, pulling the vesicles out to the edge of the synaptic knob. At the edge, the vesicles burst open, and the neurotransmitter molecules spew forth into the space between the two cells. In the space (called the synaptic cleft), the molecules bump about randomly and some of them land on postsynaptic receptors, where they fit like small keys in equally small locks. Look at figure 2.11 to see how synaptic transmission works. A summary of the basic features of the structure, type, and electrochemical activity of neurons is presented in table 2.2.

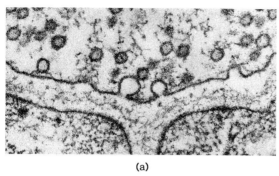

(a)

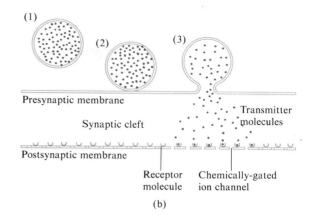

(b)

FIGURE 2.11
Synaptic transmission. (a) Electron photograph showing synaptic vesicles apparently opening into the synaptic cleft. (Magnification × 104,000) (b) Proposed interpretation of (a). A synaptic vesicle (1) fuses with the presynaptic membrane of the synaptic knob (2) and releases its contents into synaptic cleft (3). Neurotransmitter molecules fuse with receptor molecules in the postsynaptic membrane. This causes a change in membrane potential.

TABLE 2.2
The Neuron

		Description
Structure	Axon	Thin, long cylindrical tube that carries information away from the cell body to other cells.
	Dendrite	The receiving part of the neuron that collects information and orients it toward the cell body.
	Soma	The cell body that contains the nucleus; manufactures all of the substances the neuron uses for growth and maintenance.
Types	Afferent	Neurons responsible for the flow of information to the brain.
	Efferent	Neurons involved in the flow of information away from the brain.
	Interneurons	Neurons that participate in any complex processing of information—they make up much of the brain.
Electrochemical Activity	Axon potential	The brain impulses or waves of electricity that move down the axon.
	Myelin sheath and nodes of Ranvier	The myelin sheath wraps around the outside of many neurons; gaps in the sheath from one neuron to the next are the nodes of Ranvier. Myelination makes the transmission of the action potential more efficient.
	Synaptic Transmission	
	Synapse	Functional connection between neurons.
	Synaptic knobs	End point of axon that forms a bulblike structure.
	Synaptic cleft	Actual physical space between neurons.
	Presynaptic cell	Cell that sends information.
	Postsynaptic cell	Cell that receives information.
	Synaptic vesicles	Where neurotransmitters are housed in synaptic knobs.
	Neurotransmitters	Chemical substances that respond to the electrical nature of the action potential and carry information from the presynaptic to postsynaptic cell.

Myelin.

FIGURE 2.12
The nerve impulse, conducted down a
nerve fiber that ends in skeletal muscle,
releases a small amount of the chemical
acetylcholine. The action of acetylcholine
at the motor endplate initiates the
chemical changes that cause the muscle
to contract. The photo shows a number of
nerve fibers leading to and crossing
several striated muscle cells.

More than thirty neurotransmitters have been discovered, and it is likely that the list will grow to one
hundred or more in the near future. One neurotransmitter is **acetylcholine,** which is used at synapses between nerves and muscles (see figure 2.12). Every
voluntary movement made by the developing child is
mediated by acetylcholine. Acetylcholine is involved in
learning and memory. Drugs that increase it can enhance learning, whereas drugs that interfere with acetylcholine appear to impede learning (Drachman,
1978). Two additional neurotransmitters with interesting roles in development are dopamine and norepinephrine. **Dopamine** may be involved in the serious
mental disturbance of schizophrenia (Meltzer & Stahl,
1976). Too much dopamine seems to produce schizophrenic symptoms, such as a difficulty in maintaining
contact with reality. And as we soon will see, this neurotransmitter may also play a key role in development.
Norepinephrine appears to be associated with mood. Too
much norepinephrine may produce a manic state and

PERSPECTIVE ON CHILD DEVELOPMENT 2.2

THE ONTOGENY OF THE NEUROTRANSMITTERS NOREPINEPHRINE AND DOPAMINE

We know little about the ontogeny of neurotransmitters in human prenatal and infant development, but neurobiologists have studied their development in nonhuman species (Parmelee & Sigman, 1983). It is commonly known that neurotransmitters usually are more concentrated in some parts of the brain than in others. For example, in both young and adult monkeys norepinephrine and dopamine have their highest concentrations in the prefrontal regions of the neocortex and the lowest in the occipital cortex. However, the relative concentrations of these neurotransmitters varies with age. Norepinephrine shows a progressive increase from birth through two to three years of age. The increase between the neonatal and young adulthood period (two to three years in monkeys) has been found to range from 171 percent to 719 percent.

The developmental changes for dopamine are more complex and erratic, but in general dopamine reaches peak concentration earlier in development than norepinephrine, usually by five months of age. However, in the prefrontal cortex dopamine concentrations decline over the first eighteen months before increasing again at two to three years. Some neurobiologists (e.g., Goldman-Rakic, Isseroff, Schwartz, & Bugbee, 1983) speculate that in terms of frontal-lobe functioning, the early postnatal decline in dopamine and later increase at two to three years may reflect a change from trophic (growth, nutritional) to transmitter function for this substance.

too little seems to lead to depression (Schildkraut & Kety, 1967). Further information about neurotransmitters is found in Perspective on Child Development 2.2, where the ontogeny of norepinephrine and dopamine is portrayed.

Now that we have studied the basic nature of the neuron, we turn our attention to some of the processes that seem to be involved in the development of neurons.

Processes of Neural Development

Five important processes involving neurons have implications for understanding development: proliferation, growth, differentiation, migration, and myelination (Cowan, 1979; Tanner, 1978).

Proliferation refers to the generation of new cells through the process of cell division. This process is prolific during prenatal development, and virtually all of the proliferation process has taken place by birth. Consider how rapidly such cell division must be taking place

during prenatal development if the newborn human infant has some 10 to 100 billion neurons. At the minimum, neurons are probably being produced on the average of about 25,000 per minute.

Not only does the proliferation of neurons occur during prenatal development, but neurons also grow in *size* as well, both in terms of the soma and the axons and dendrites that connect neurons. The most rapid period of increase in the size of neurons seems to occur from the sixth month of the prenatal period through the first year of life. The growth of the brain is particularly rapid at about the time of birth (Goldman-Rakic et al., 1983). As brain development proceeds through the childhood years, some scientists (e.g., Epstein, 1978) argue there are alternations between rapid and slow growth. For example, sometime between the ages of five and seven the child's brain may undergo a growth spurt. This has been documented by the use of an **electroencephalogram,** a device to measure the electrical output of the brain. Brain waves seem to show a sharp increase to a higher level of maturity at this point in development (Epstein, 1980). Growth spurts in the brain also seem to occur at about the time the transition from infancy to early childhood is made and also at about the time adolescence is entered, although these spurts are not as well documented as the one occurring at about five or seven years of age. Other prominent neuroscientists (e.g., Conel & Dekaban), however, dispute the conclusion that there are major shifts in brain activity so late in development. They emphasize major maturational changes in the brain at eight months in the fetus and three and nine months in the infant.

A third process of neural development is **differentiation,** the process by which primitive nerve cells take on properties that allow them to function in specialized ways in different parts of the nervous system. Thus some neurons become sensory neurons, others motor neurons, and yet others interneurons.

A fourth process involving the development of neurons is **migration.** That is, nerve cells have to be in the right place at the right time in development. This process occurs on a very large scale and is incredibly orderly. Just exactly how this migration process works is still unknown, although some neurobiologists have argued that glial cells, nonneural cells, probably play a part (Cowan, 1979).

A fifth process in the development of neurons is myelination, which continues through adolescence and adulthood and, in some areas of the brain, even into very old age. By studying many prenatal and postnatal brains, researchers have been able to determine when myelination is most likely to occur in development (Lecours, 1975; Yakovlev & Lecours, 1967). The ages at which myelination begins and ends seem to vary from one brain structure to another, as does the time required for the myelination itself.

The myelination of auditory pathways begins as early as the fifth month of prenatal development, while the myelination of visual pathways does not start until near the end of fetal development. However, once the myelination of visual pathways begins, it proceeds very rapidly, being completed sometime during the first six months of the infant's life. However, while the myelination process for auditory pathways begins earlier in

prenatal development, its cycle of completion does not occur until some time later, even as late as four to five years of age.

For the most part, neural pathways that transmit information from the senses to the higher levels of the brain, such as the cerebral cortex, complete their myelination reasonably early in development, as do neural pathways from the cerebral cortex to muscles. However, pathways that connect different regions of the cerebral cortex seem to be myelinated later. For instance, the myelination of some of the large nerve fiber bundles that connect the two hemispheres of the brain may continue to occur after the first decade of life.

Thus far in our survey of the brain we have focused on development at the cellular level. It also is very important to consider the brain at more molar levels as well. As we follow the evolution of the brain, we now give more attention to the development of larger brain structures and their functions.

The Evolution of the Brain

First, we outline the embryological development of the brain and then provide information about the brain structure that more than any other distinguishes human development from the development of the lower animals: the neocortex. Our discussion conforms to the framework of the evolutionary development of the brain—hindbrain, midbrain, and forebrain.

Embryological Development

During the development of the embryo, the nervous system begins as a long, hollow tube on the back of the embryo. With further development of the nervous system, the brain develops into a large mass of neurons, losing its primitive tubular appearance. By the time of birth the initial primitive organization of the brain is hardly recognizable because such tremendous growth and differentiation has taken place. Figure 2.13 dramatically reveals the prominence of the tubular shape of the nervous system at six weeks in the human embryo. The elongated tube changes shape and develops into three major divisions: the **hindbrain,** the portion of the brain that will be adjacent to the spinal cord; the

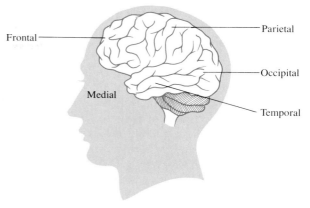

FIGURE 2.14
The location of the four lobes of the human brain.

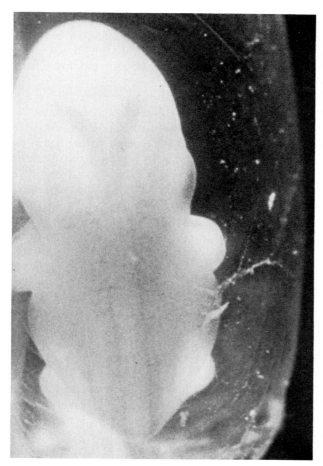

FIGURE 2.13
The tubular shape of the nervous system at six weeks in the human embryo.

midbrain, which is above the hindbrain; and the **forebrain,** which in humans and other higher mammals produces the neocortex of the mature brain.

The Neocortex

The **neocortex** is the most recently developed part of the brain in the evolutionary scheme. It is the largest part of the human brain in terms of volume (about 80 percent) and covers the lower portions of the brain almost like a large cap.

The neocortex is made up of two nearly symmetrical hemispheres, the left and the right, divided by a fissure. Each of the two hemispheres is subdivided into four lobes: frontal, parietal, temporal, and occipital (see figure 2.14). It is important to note that the lobes are not strictly functional regions but rather convenient anatomical regions. Nonetheless, there are functional differences among the lobes, and they are often used in a somewhat loose and descriptive manner to describe functions. For example, the correspondence between lobes and functioning is most clear in the **occipital lobe,** where visual functioning occurs. The **temporal lobe** is associated with hearing. The **frontal lobe** is thought to be involved in the control of voluntary muscles as well as being the seat of higher intelligence. The **parietal lobe** is involved in body sensation.

More than 75 percent of the neocortex is made up of areas referred to as association areas, or the association cortex. These many large areas are not directly related to sensory or motor processes. It is believed that the association areas are responsible for many of our highest human accomplishments, such as thinking and problem solving.

Of special interest is the finding that damage to a specific part of the cortex often does not result in a specific loss of function. With the exception of language areas (which are localized), loss of function seems to depend more on the extent of damage to the association areas than to the specific location of the damage. By observing brain-damaged individuals and using mapping techniques, scientists have found that the association cortex is involved in linguistic and perceptual functioning. The largest portion of association areas is located in the frontal lobe, directly under the forehead. Damage to this area does not lead to sensory or motor loss. Indeed, it is this area that may be most directly related to thinking and problem solving. Early experimentation even referred to the frontal lobe as the center of intelligence, but more recent research suggests that damage to the frontal lobe may not result in a lowering of intelligence (Gross & Weiskrantz, 1964). Planning and judgment are characteristics often associated with the frontal lobe (e.g., Milner, 1963), and personality may also be linked with the frontal lobe.

Split-Brain Research and the Cerebral Hemispheres

One of the most fascinating areas of brain research involves the study of split brains. This research focuses on the functions of the left and right hemispheres of the brain and the role the fibers that connect these hemispheres play. In this section you will read about Roger Sperry's pioneering split-brain research, the functions of the right hemisphere, and the role of the hemispheres in development.

Roger Sperry's Split-Brain Research

The two hemispheres of the brain are connected by a large bundle of axons called the **corpus callosum.** For many years scientists were unaware of the function of this bundle, although they speculated that it was involved in the communication of information between the two hemispheres. The corpus callosum of an epileptic patient known as W. J. was deliberately severed in an operation performed in the 1960s. Neurosurgeons thought the surgery might reduce the unbearable seizures he was experiencing by limiting them to only one side of his brain. Roger Sperry (1968) examined W. J. to see how information comes into and goes out of the left and right hemispheres of the brain. Put briefly, the right hemisphere receives information only from the left side of the body, and the left hemisphere gets information only from the right side of the body. Consequently, if you hold an object in your left hand, only the right hemisphere of your brain can detect this. If you see an object, say, a car, in the right side of your visual field, only the left hemisphere of your brain registers this event (see figure 2.15). For people with a corpus callosum that has not been severed, both hemispheres of the brain detect such information because it can be communicated from one hemisphere to the other via the corpus callosum. But what happens to individuals when their corpus callosum is cut?

The left hemisphere is sometimes called the major hemisphere because it seems to control the ability to use language. The right, or so-called minor hemisphere, does not seem to be able to transform sensations into words. Patients in Sperry's experiments (Sperry, 1974; Sperry & Gazzaniga, 1967) such as W. J. whose hemispheres had been severed could describe in words sensations that were received by the left hemisphere (a stimulus in the right visual field). However, the patients were unable to describe in words sensations that were received by the right hemisphere (a stimulus in the left visual field). As more split-brain patients are evaluated, more recent evidence suggests that language is indeed a very infrequent occurrence in the right hemisphere (Gazzaniga, 1983).

The Right Hemisphere

Although the right hemisphere does not control language, it is involved in some types of abstract thinking and the formation of simple concepts. Some experts feel that it is a misnomer to call the right hemisphere minor, because it actually controls some important nonlinguistic activities better than the left hemisphere does. The right hemisphere seems to have more control over perceptual responses based on touch than does the left hemisphere (Levy & Sperry, 1972). Furthermore, emotional reactions may be more related to the right hemisphere than to the left (Leg & Bryden, 1979).

The Role of the Cerebral Hemispheres in Development

As yet we do not have a clear development timetable for the growth of the cerebral hemispheres. Electrical recordings of the brain suggest that by several months after birth the hemispheres already show

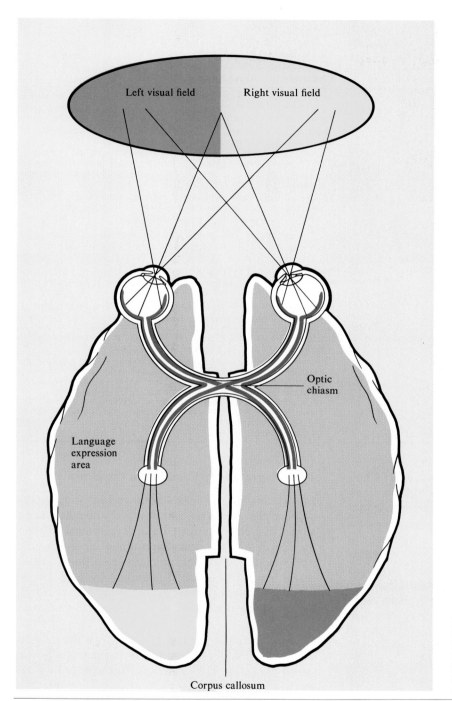

FIGURE 2.15
Pathways traveled by information from the left and right visual fields of the eyes to the left and right cerebral hemispheres

CONCEPT TABLE 2.3 The Brain as a Processor of Information, Processes of Neural Development, and the Evolution of the Brain		
Concept	**Processes/Related Ideas**	**Characteristics/Description**
The brain as a processor of information	Basic ideas	Above all else, the main function of the child's brain is to process information. This processing involves receiving, connecting/integrating, and reacting.
	Organization	The child's brain is elegantly organized in terms of structure and function at both the cellular and anatomical levels.
	The neuron	The neuron is made up of three parts—soma, dendrites, and axon. Information in the neural system is transmitted electrochemically. The action potential and myelination are important aspects of this transmission, as are synapses and neurotransmitters.
	Neurotransmitters	Information about the development of neurotransmitters comes almost exclusively from research with lower animals. Three important neurotransmitters are acetylcholine, norepinephrine, and dopamine.
Processes of neural development	Proliferation	The generation of new cells through cell division.
	Growth	The increase in size of neurons.
	Differentiation	The change from primitive nerve cells to specialized cells with varying functions.
	Migration	The movement of cells to various locations in the nervous system.
	Myelination	The development of a sheath around an axon.
Evolution of the brain	Embryological development	The lowest level of the brain is the hindbrain, the midlevel is the midbrain, and the highest level is the forebrain.
	Neocortex	The neocortex is the highest level of the forebrain, and it is here that much of what makes us human resides. The neocortex includes the left and right hemispheres and four lobes—occipital (vision), temporal (hearing), frontal (intelligence), and parietal (body sensation). Split-brain research involves severing the corpus callosum, the bundle of fibers that connects the two hemispheres. This research has led to the conclusion that language is controlled by the left hemisphere.

definite specialization (Shucard, Shucard & Cummins, 1979). Investigation of the effects of brain damage on children, however, reveals that hemispheric specialization is not completed until at least the adolescent years. The area of language development has been the focus of the most interest in hemispheric specialization. Children who experience brain damage to the left hemisphere under the age of two typically have no problems in developing language ability, and when similar damage occurs between the preschool years and adolescence, there seems only to be a temporary language loss. By the middle of adolescent development, however, if brain damage to the left hemisphere occurs, there usually is not a full recoupment of language ability (Kinsbourne & Hiscock, 1983).

We have evaluated the brain as a processor of information, processes of neural development, and the evolution of the brain. A summary of these ideas is presented in Concept Table 2.3. Now we consider one final key concept in understanding how the child's brain works—the integration of function.

The Integration of Function in the Brain

How do all of the various brain regions cooperate to produce the wondrous complexity of thought and behavior that characterize human development? Part of the answer to this question, such as how the child's brain works in solving a math problem or writing an essay, is still beyond the grasp of neurobiology. Still, we can get a sense of integrative brain function by considering something like the act of a child escaping from an angry, barking dog.

Imagine a child playing in a sandbox when a vicious dog comes running up and begins barking loudly. The sound of the barking is relayed from the child's ear, through the thalamus in the lower portion of the forebrain, to her auditory cortex, and on to the auditory association cortex. At each stage the stimulus energy has been processed to extract information, and at some stage, probably at the association cortex level, the sounds are finally matched with something like a neural memory representing previous sounds of dogs she has heard. The association to "dogs" sets new machinery

How could this child's brain integrate information about a barking dog?

in motion. The child's attention (guided by a part of the brain called the reticular formation) swings to the auditory signal being held in her association cortex, and simultaneously her head turns toward the noise. Now her visual association cortex reports in: "objects matching barks are present." In other association regions, the visual and auditory reports are synthesized ("we have things that look and sound like dogs"), and neural associations representing potential actions ("flee") are activated. But firing the neurons that code the plan to flee will not get her out of the sandbox. Her cortex must engage the basal ganglia of the brain, and from there the commands will arise to set the brain stem, motor cortex, and cerebellum (a lower brain-stem structure involved in movement) to the actual task of transporting the child out of the sandbox.

Which part of her brain did the child use to escape? Virtually all systems had some role; each was quite specific, and together they generated the behavior. By the way, the child will probably remember an event such as that involving the vicious, barking dog. That is because her limbic circuitry probably issued the "start print" command when the significant association "dogs" was first triggered. The next time the sounds of loud barking reach her auditory cortex, the associations triggered will include those of this recent escape (Frederickson, 1985).

SUMMARY

I. Evolution, ethology, and biological principles reflect the biological foundations of development.
 A. Evolution involves ideas about the notion that ontogeny recapitulates phylogeny, natural selection, and the pace of evolution.
  1. The statement "ontogeny recapitulates phylogeny" refers to the belief that as an individual goes through stages of development, some of the adult forms of lower animals on the phylogenetic scale are repeated. While fascinating, it is an outmoded conception.
  2. Natural selection argues that organisms with beneficial characteristics are more likely to adapt and survive, so their characteristics are perpetuated.
  3. Evolution proceeds at an incredibly slow pace.
 B. Ethology is a modified instinct view of the organisms that stresses the release of unlearned patterns of behavior by certain environmental circumstances. Ethologists stress the importance of critical periods of development.
 C. Two important biological principles of development are forward reference, the concept that behaviors are preadapted, and differentiation and hierarchical organization.

II. An understanding of genetics focuses on genes, genetic principles, behavior genetics, and the nature of heredity–environment interaction.
   A. Knowing about genes includes understanding just what genes are and the related concepts of chromosomes, DNA, genotype, and phenotype.
      1. Genes are segments of chromosomes. Genes are the basic building block of heredity.
      2. Chromosomes are threadlike structures that come in structurally similar pairs (twenty-three in humans).
      3. DNA, or deoxyribonucleic acid, is the key chemical substance, running the length of each chromosome, in genetic makeup.
      4. The actual combination of genes is genotype; the observed and measurable characteristics of the genetic material is phenotype.
   B. Five important genetic principles involve dominant–recessive genes, sex-linked genes, polygenic inheritance (few psychological characteristics are the result of single-gene action, and phenotypes are invariably produced by a combination of genes), reaction range, and canalization.
   C. Behavior genetics is a field concerned with the degree and nature of the hereditary basis of behavior. Behavior geneticists call on a number of methods to study genetic influences and evaluate a wide range of human characteristics in terms of genetic influences.
      1. Among the methods used by behavior geneticists are selective breeding, inbreeding, twin study, family of twins design, kinship study, adoption study, and the concept of heritability. Recent evaluation of the heritability index suggests that it is open to multiple interpretations.
      2. Among the wide range of characteristics shown to be influenced by heredity are intelligence and temperament.
   D. Conclusions about the interaction of heredity and environment suggest that the issue of heredity versus environment is somewhat misleading, since both genes and environment are necessary even for an organism to exist. However, we do know that genes set some limits on development and the genes of a particular species increase the likelihood that certain forms of behavior will emerge at a particular point in development.

III. Understanding the nature of the brain and neurological development focuses on information about the brain as a processor of information, the neuron itself, processes involved in the development of neurons, the evolution of the brain, and the integration of function in the brain.
   A. Above all else, the main function of the brain is to process information. This processing involves receiving, connecting/integrating, and reacting.
   B. The brain is elegantly organized in terms of structure and function at the cellular and anatomical levels. At the cellular level the basic structure is the neuron.
      1. The neuron is made up of three parts: the soma, dendrites, and axon. Information in the neural system is transmitted electrochemically. The action potential and myelination are important aspects of this transmission, as are synapses and neurotransmitters.
      2. Information about the development of neurotransmitters comes almost exclusively from research with lower animals. Three important neurotransmitters are acetylcholine, norepinephrine, and dopamine.
   C. The processes of neural development include proliferation, growth, differentiation, migration, and myelination.
   D. Information about the evolution of the brain focuses on embryological development and the neocortex.
      1. The lowest level of the brain is the hindbrain, the midlevel is the midbrain, and the highest level is the forebrain.
      2. The neocortex is the highest level of the forebrain, and it is here that much of what makes us human resides.
      3. The neocortex includes the left and right hemispheres and four lobes—occipital (vision), temporal (hearing), frontal (intelligence), and parietal (body sensation).
      4. Split-brain research involves severing the corpus callosum, the bundle of fibers that connects the two hemispheres. This research has led to the conclusion that language is controlled by the left hemisphere.
   E. For the most part, psychological functions do not involve a single structure in the brain but rather the integration of function by a number of structures.

KEY TERMS

acetylcholine 60

action potentials 58

adoption studies 50

afferent nerves 56

alleles 46

axon 57

behavior genetics 48

canalization 47

chromosomes 44

corpus callosum 64

critical periods 41

cultural familial retardation 51

dendrite 57

differentiation 44, 62

DNA 44

dominant–recessive genes 45

dopamine 60

Down's syndrome 52

dyzygotic 49

efferent nerves 56

electroencephalogram (EEG) 61

family of twins design 49

forebrain 63

forward reference 44

frontal lobe 63

gametes 44

genes 44

genotype 45

heritability 50

hierarchical organization 44

hindbrain 62

inbreeding 49

interneurons 56

kinship studies 49

meiosis 44

midbrian 63

migration 62

monozygotic 49

myelin 58

natural selection 39

neocortex 63

neuron 56

neurotransmitters 58

nodes of Ranvier 58

norepinephrine 60

occipital lobe 63

ontogeny 39

parietal lobe 63

phenotype 45

phylogeny 39

PKU syndrome 52

polygenic inheritance 46

preadapted 44

proliferation 61

reaction range 47

reproduction 44

selective breeding 49

soma 57

synapse 58

synaptic knobs 58

temporal lobe 63

twin study 49

zygote 45

REVIEW QUESTIONS

1. Describe the nature of evolution and its importance for understanding development.
2. What is ethology? Include in your overview the research of Lorenz and Tinbergen.
3. Define the general biological principles of forward reference and of differentiation and hierarchical organization.
4. Outline the important structures involved in genetic transmission.
5. Explain the genetic principles of dominant–recessive genes, sex-linked genes, polygenic inheritance, reaction range, and canalization.
6. Describe the methods used by behavior geneticists and the extent to which heredity influences intelligence and temperament.
7. What conclusions can we make about heredity–environment interaction?
8. Outline the basic structures and functions of the brain.
9. Describe the processes of neural development.
10. Discuss the evolution of the brain, the neocortex, split-brain research, and the integration of function in the brain.

SUGGESTED READINGS

Gottlieb, G. (1983). The psychobiological approach to developmental issues. In P. H. Mussen (Ed.), *Handbook of child psychology* (4th ed., Vol. II). New York: John Wiley.

This chapter provides an excellent overview of important psychobiological principles involved in development. This volume also contains other detailed reviews of research focused on the biological basis of development.

Gould, S. (1983). *Hen's teeth and horse's toes: Reflections on natural history*. New York: Norton.

This book is a collection of fascinating articles by a biologist interested in evolution. The essays originally were published in the magazine *Natural History*.

Lorenz, K. Z. (1965). *Evolution and the modification of behavior*. Chicago: University of Chicago Press.

Provides details about Lorenz's work with graylag geese and extensive discussion of the principles of ethology, particularly critical periods.

Watson, J. D. (1968). *The double helix*. New York: New American Library.

A personalized account of the research leading up to one of the most provocative discoveries of the twentieth century—the discovery of the DNA molecule. Reading like a mystery novel, it illustrates the exciting discovery process in science.

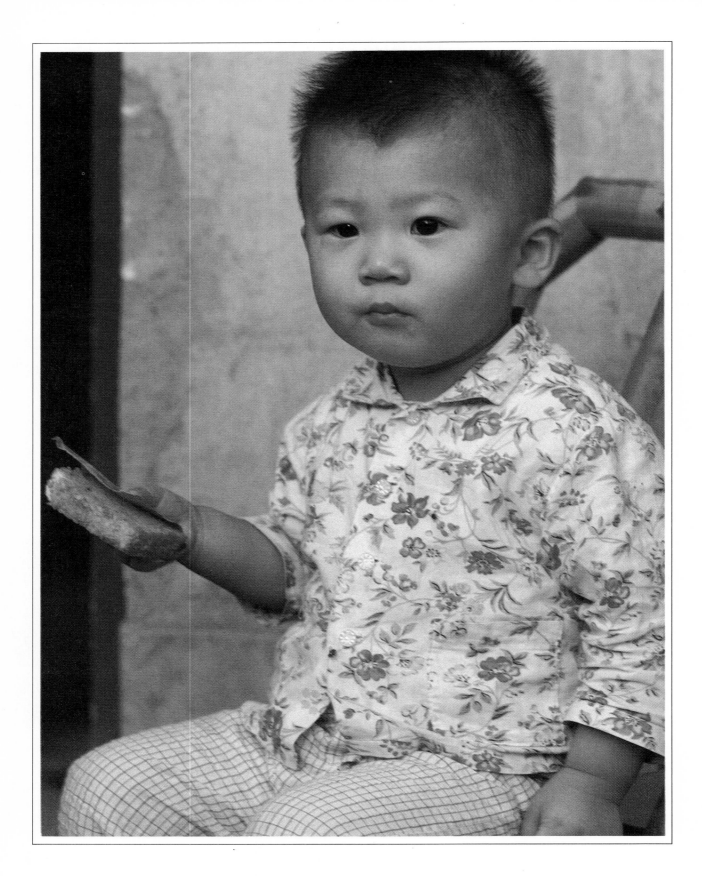

CHAPTER

3

PHYSICAL DEVELOPMENT

PROLOGUE

LOUISE, CONCEPTION IN A TEST TUBE

The year is 1978. One of the most dazzling occurrences in the past decade is about to unfold. Mrs. Brown is infertile, but her physician informs her about the development of a new procedure. The procedure is to remove the mother's ovum surgically, fertilize it in a laboratory medium with live sperm cells obtained from a male donor, store the fertilized egg in a laboratory solution that substitutes for the uterine environment, and finally implant the egg in the mother's uterus.

Mrs. Brown wants a baby very much so she decides to become a candidate for the procedure, which is known as **in vitro fertilization.** Her hormone levels are monitored, and when she is about to ovulate, she enters the hospital where the egg is removed in the following way: The doctor makes a small incision in her abdomen and inserts a metal tube with an optical arrangement that allows the doctor to see the ovaries. The doctor also inserts a micropipette, a narrow tube, through the incision and removes the egg shortly before it would normally have been shed from the ovary.

Mrs. Brown's egg was placed in a solution that kept it alive and nourished. The solution with the egg in it was then mixed with the sperm. Once the egg was fertilized, it was permitted to go through several cell divisions, and embryological development began. The embryo was then picked up with another fine tube, inserted in Mrs. Brown's cervix, and flushed to the uterus. Mrs. Brown went home about eight hours thereafter.

The in vitro fertilization was successful. The life that began in the test tube flourished, and Mr. and Mrs. Brown named their daughter, who was born some nine months later, Louise.

Neither Louise nor other test-tube babies seem to have any physical problems. There may even be a slight decrease of birth defects when this procedure is used. Similarly, there is no evidence of long-term psychological harm. Most children who are test-tube babies do not know their backgrounds, and no systematic records have been kept.

As with many other remarkable breakthroughs in biology and medicine, in vitro fertilization is not without ethical concerns. For example, Ruth Hubbard (1980), a Harvard biologist, wonders whether it is better to expend our effort in providing each woman (and man) with the opportunity of having her own "biological child" or to focus more on the many children in the world who need parents by concentrating on foster care and adoption.

P R E V I E W

We begin the study of physical development by outlining the course of prenatal development and the birth process. Then we portray infant development, with a particular interest in growth and motor milestones. Next we turn to the continued growth that characterizes the childhood years, and finally we consider the explosive physical changes that characterize adolescence.

PRENATAL DEVELOPMENT

Prenatal development includes conception and three periods—germinal, embryological, and fetal. We consider each of these in turn and also evaluate the extensive interest generated about environmental influences on prenatal development.

Conception

Life processes begin when a single sperm cell from the male unites with the ovum (egg) in the female's Fallopian tube in a process called fertilization or **conception.** The ovum is produced in the ovaries at about midpoint in the female's menstrual cycle. Fertilization takes place within several days after the ovum begins its journey from the ovaries through the Fallopian tubes to the uterus. If the ovum travels to the uterus without being fertilized, it disintegrates within several days, making conception impossible until the next menstrual cycle.

Germinal Period

The **germinal period** lasts for two weeks after conception. Almost immediately, twenty-three chromosomes from the sperm cell and twenty-three from the ovum cell pair off, producing twenty-three pairs, or forty-six chromosomes. Within one to two days the chromosome pairs double and split, with half of them gravitating to each side of the cell. Then the fertilized ovum divides into two cells. These cells and their daughter cells continue dividing at regular intervals, eventually forming a round structure called the **blastula.** This is made up of approximately 100 to 150 cells and is formed within one week after conception. The differentiation of cells already has commenced, with the inner layer of the blastula, called the **blastocyst,** later becoming the embryo and the outer layer of cells, called the **trophoblast,** later making up the tissues that provide nutrition and protection for the embryo. During the next week, a major milestone involves the blastula's firm attachment to the wall of the uterus. This process is called **implantation** and usually occurs seventeen days after fertilization.

Embryological Period

Once the blastula has become implanted in the wall of the uterus, the inner cells (blastocyst) quickly become differentiated into three layers. The outer layer, called the **ectoderm,** eventually becomes the child's hair, skin, nails, and nervous system. The middle layer, called the **mesoderm,** later becomes the muscles and bones, as well as the circulatory and excretory systems. The inner layer, referred to as the **endoderm,** subsequently develops into the digestive system, lungs, pancreas, and liver.

The development of the ectoderm, mesoderm, and endoderm occurs during the **embryological period,** a period lasting from about two to eight weeks after conception. It is during this period that a primitive human form takes shape. The basic parts of the body—head, trunk, arms, legs—can be identified. Some finer features, such as eyes and ears, fingers and toes, are also discernible. Internal organs have begun to develop, and some of these are functioning, at least to some degree. A primitive heartbeat, circulatory activity, liver and kidney function, and some nervous system action can be distinguished.

It is also during this period that the life-support system for the embryo is formed. The part of the embryo attached to the uterine wall becomes the placenta, the meeting ground for the circulatory system of both

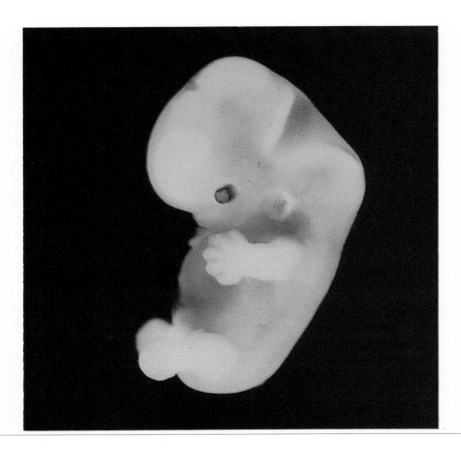

left: The embryo at five weeks. The arms and legs are becoming more differentiated and the face starts to form. right: The fetus at ten weeks. Basic organ systems have now been formed— during the fetal period from two months to conception, the organ systems mature rapidly.

embryo and mother. Semipermeable membranes keep their bloodstreams separate but allow such substances as oxygen, drugs, vitamins, and some nutrients (sugar and protein) to pass through to nourish the embryo. The umbilical cord transports waste substances from the embryo to the placental barrier; the cord also has membranes that allow for the passage of only certain substances. Blood cells are too large to pass through the membranes of the placenta, so there is no direct link between the circulatory system of the mother and that of the embryo. By the end of this period the embryo is about one inch (2.5 cm) long and weighs about half an ounce (14 g). The end of the embryological period is marked by the beginning of the ossification of bones at about eight weeks after conception.

Fetal Period

The **fetal period** lasts from about eight weeks after conception until birth—a total of about seven months in full-term babies. At twelve weeks of age the fetus is about three inches (7.5 cm) long and weighs approximately one ounce (28 g). It has become active, moving its arms and legs vigorously, opening and closing its mouth, and moving its head. A number of physical and anatomical features become well differentiated. On the face, for example, forehead, eyelids, nose, and chin can be distinguished; the upper arms, lower arms, and hands are clearly distinguishable, as are the lower limbs. The genitals can be identified as male or female. Further progress is noted on a month-by-month basis.

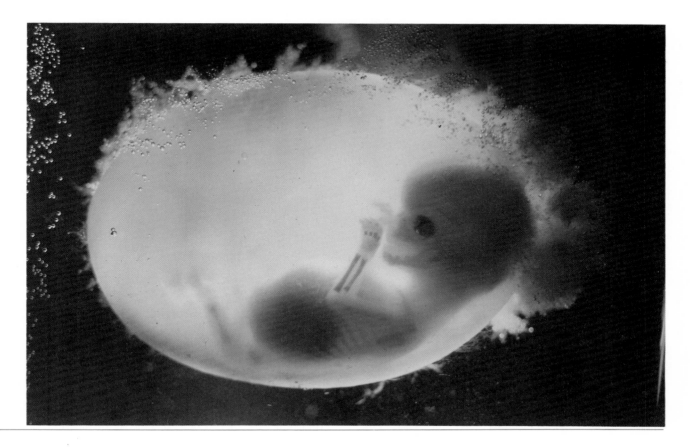

By the end of the fourth month, the fetus is about six inches (15 cm) long and weighs about four ounces (110 g). Whereas a great deal of growth has already occurred in the head and facial structures, there is now an increased growth spurt in the lower parts of the body. A number of prenatal reflexes (automatic responses involving one part of the body), such as arm and leg movements, become stronger and can be felt by the mother for the first time.

By the end of the fifth month, the fetus is about twelve inches (30 cm) long and weighs about a pound (450 g). Structures of the skin have formed; there are fingernails and toenails; and the fetus is more active, exhibiting a preference for a particular position in the womb.

By the end of the sixth month, the fetus is about fourteen inches (36 cm) long and weighs about two pounds (900 g). The eyes and eyelids are completely formed; there is a fine layer of hair on the head of the fetus; it exhibits a grasping reflex; and there is evidence of irregular breathing movements.

By the end of the seventh month, the fetus is about sixteen inches (40 cm) long and weighs about three pounds (1.4 kg). At this time the chances of survival are good if the child is born prematurely. For this reason it is sometimes called the age of viability. If prematurely born, however, the infant is very sensitive to infection and must be cared for in a well-regulated environment provided by an incubator.

T A B L E 3 . 1
Summary of Major Changes from Conception to Birth

Period	Age	Height	Weight	Notable Changes
Germinal	(0–2 weeks)			Rapid cell division Ovum attaches to uterine wall Inner and outer mass formed
Embryonic	(2–8 weeks)	2.5 cm	14 g	Ectoderm, mesoderm, and endoderm differentiated Human form takes shape Internal organs begin to develop Placenta and umbilical cord form
Fetal	(8–37 weeks)	50 cm	3.2 kg	Growth and change to sustain independent life
Third Month	12 weeks	7.5 cm	28 g	Activity, movement Head growth, facial features
Fourth Month	16 weeks	15 cm	110 g	Reflexes become brisker Growth spurt in lower part of body Mother feels movement
Fifth Month	21 weeks	30 cm	450 g	Skin structures form Fetus has characteristic life
Sixth Month	26 weeks	36 cm	900 g	Eyes, eyelids formed Fine layer of hair on head Grasp reflex Irregular breathing
Seventh Month	30 weeks	40 cm	1.4 kg	"Age of viability"
Eighth–Ninth Months		50 cm	3.2 kg	Rapid weight gain Fatty tissues develop Organ system activity (e.g., heart, kidneys, step up)

During the eighth and ninth months, the fetus grows longer and gains substantial weight—about four pounds (1.8 kg). At birth, the average American baby is twenty inches (50 cm) long and weighs seven pounds (3.2 kg). During these months the fatty tissues develop and the functioning of various organ systems (e.g., heart and kidneys) is stepped up. See table 3.1 for a summary of these changes.

Environmental Influences on Prenatal Development

Some expectant mothers tiptoe about in the belief that everything they do and feel has a direct effect on their unborn child. Others behave more casually, assuming that their experiences have little impact on the unborn child. The truth lies somewhere between these extremes. Although living in a comfortable, well-protected environment, the fetus is not totally immune to the larger environment surrounding the mother. There are some well-documented ways in which this environment can affect the child. Thousands of babies every year are born deformed or mentally retarded or suffer from other congenital defects as a result of events as early as two months *prior* to conception.

Geneticists and specialists in fetal life are finding that the mother's physical and mental health are critical factors in the development of a healthy infant. Some researchers believe that the months before a woman gets pregnant determine the health of the fetus and newborn infant (Witherspoon, 1980). Emotional upset and poor diet of a woman before pregnancy are implicated as possible problems that may alter the course of her infant's health. Environmental factors, such as the time of year the baby is born, also are associated with birth characteristics. For example, children conceived in the summer are about 20 percent heavier than those conceived in the winter, and about 10 percent heavier than those conceived in spring and fall. The rate of fetal malformations is one-third higher among children conceived in spring and fall than those conceived in the summer. Why this is so remains to be explained.

Weeks of prenatal development

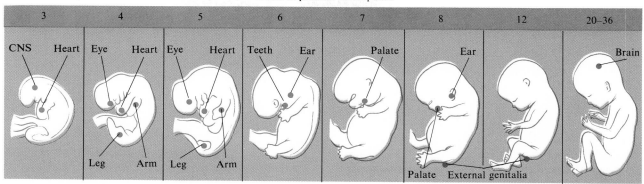

● Part of fetus where damage is greatest

FIGURE 3.1
The effects of teratogens at specific points in prenatal development.

For many years, scientists believed that almost all birth defects were genetically triggered. Now we know that many abnormalities are also due to such factors as maternal diseases and blood disorders, diet, irradiation, drugs, temperature, and oxygen level. Maternal characteristics such as age and emotional well-being can influence the health of the newborn as well.

Scientists now label any agent that causes birth defects a **teratogen,** which comes from the Greek word *tera,* meaning "monster," and the field of study that focuses on birth defects is called **teratology.** Some general conclusions from research in this embryonic field follow. Rarely is there a consistent link between specific teratogens (e.g., drugs) and specific birth defects (e.g., malformation of the legs). There are so many different teratogens that virtually every fetus is exposed to at least several of them. Consequently, it often is difficult to determine which teratogen causes a particular birth defect. In addition, it sometimes takes a long time for the effects of some teratogens to show up—only about half are present at birth.

Despite the uncertainties about teratology, scientists have been able to discover the identity of some teratogens and the particular point of fetal development

at which they do their greatest damage. Figure 3.1 reveals the particular points in prenatal development at which teratogens do the most harm. The most damaging effects occur in the first eight weeks of prenatal development, but damage to the brain can occur in the last months of pregnancy as well. Because the various organ systems begin and end their prenatal development at different times, their sensitivity to teratogens varies over time. Vulnerability to damage from teratogens for the brain is highest at fifteen to twenty-five days into prenatal development, for the eye from twenty-four to forty days, for the heart from twenty to forty days, and for the legs from twenty-four to thirty-six days (Tuchmann-Duplessis, 1975).

Fetuses are also adversely affected when mothers drink alcohol, smoke cigarettes, and ingest caffeine. It is yet to be determined just how much of these commonly used drugs is required before the adverse effect on the fetus takes place, but researchers are increasingly aware that even small doses taken on a regular basis may affect the fetus. For more information about the effects of alcohol, cigarettes, and caffeine on the fetus and infant, read Perspective on Child Development 3.1.

PERSPECTIVE ON CHILD DEVELOPMENT 3.1

PROSPECTIVE MOTHERS: THEIR NICOTINE, ALCOHOL, AND CAFFEINE INTAKE—EFFECTS ON THE FETUS AND INFANT

Infants seem to be adversely affected when their mothers smoke heavily. For example, women who smoke heavily during pregnancy have offspring who weigh less than normal for a number of months, which may make them susceptible to several health problems (Willemsen, 1979). In one recent short-term longitudinal investigation (Landesman-Dwyer & Sackett, 1983), 271 infant–mother pairs were studied during the infants' eighth, twelfth, and sixteenth weeks of life by having mothers keep diaries of their infants' and their own activity patterns. Previously, information had been collected about the mothers' smoking patterns during pregnancy. Mothers who smoked spent less time feeding their infants by an average of 20 to 30 minutes per day, and their infants were awake on a more consistent basis than infants whose mothers did not smoke during pregnancy.

Infants born to alcoholic mothers tend to have more problems adapting to sights, sounds, temperature changes, and other demands of the environment than those born to mothers who drink moderately or not at all (Willemsen, 1979). **Fetal alcohol syndrome (FAS)** affects the offspring of many alcoholic mothers (Jones, Smith, Ulleland, & Streissguth, 1973). It is characterized by microencephaly (small head) and defective limbs, joints, face, and heart. Children with FAS may show abnormal behavior such as hyperactivity and seizures. The majority of FAS children score below average on intelligence tests (Abel, 1981).

Even moderate alcohol use during pregnancy may cause significant long-term effects on the offspring. In one investigation (Streissguth, Barr, & Martin, 1983), 417 mothers were queried about their use of alcohol during the fifth month of pregnancy. An "AA" score (average alcohol consumed per day) was obtained at this time. Then at nine to thirty-five hours after birth, infants were individually administered the Brazelton Neonatal Assessment Scale. On the basis of this assessment, the mother's use of alcohol during the fifth month of pregnancy was significantly negatively correlated to the infant's state of arousal—the more the mother drank, the less attentive and alert the infant was (see figure opposite). Further information from Streissguth's laboratory (Streissguth, Martin, Barr, Sandman, Kirchner & Darby, 1984) suggests that these attentional deficits are still present at four years of age. The average alcohol intake by the drinking mothers was only one drink per day. Such recent findings have led some women to forego all alcohol during pregnancy.

Many prospective mothers ingest large quantities of caffeine just before and during pregnancy. Recently, the possibility that caffeine use during early pregnancy may have harmful effects on the newborn has been documented (e.g., Jacobson, 1983). Just prior to pregnancy more than 300 prospective mothers were queried about their use of coffee, tea, and cola. Caffeine consumption prior to pregnancy was associated with greater arousal and irritability and poorer self-quieting ability in the newborn. The possibility exists, then, that the mother's caffeine intake during early pregnancy may have effects on the infant's behavior.

At this time, there is no clear consensus on how much nicotine, alcohol, and caffeine intake during or just prior to pregnancy is safe. Some researchers suggest that several glasses of wine daily will not harm the fetus, whereas others recommend total abstention several months before pregnancy is anticipated as well as during pregnancy. Some women who smoke heavily switch to filtered cigarettes when they become pregnant to lessen tar and nicotine intake. But the smoke that comes through a filtered cigarette has more carbon monoxide than a nonfiltered one, and the resulting decrease in oxygen in the blood may impair fetal brain development.

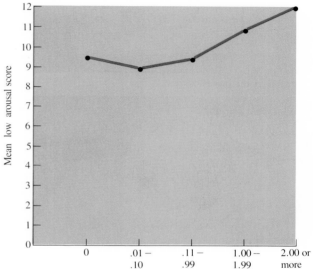

The effects of different levels of alcohol intake during pregnancy on the infant's level of arousal. A higher score indicates lower arousal. Examination of these scores indicated that the infant tended to swing back and forth between being awake and being drowsy when high scores were obtained, whereas the infant seemed to swing back and forth between being awake and crying more often when low scores were obtained.

Data from Streissguth, A. P., H. M. Barr, and D. C. Martin, "Maternal alcohol use and neonatal habituation assessed with the Brazelton Scale," in *Child Development*, 1983, 44, 1113. © The Society for Research in Child Development. Reprinted by permission.

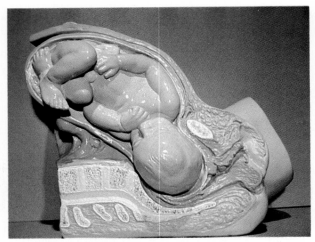

Cervix dilates as the uterus contracts.

Progress of the head to pelvic floor.

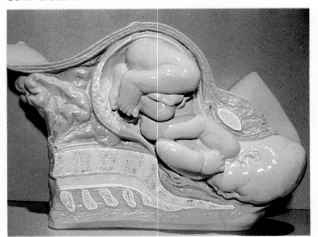

Emergence of the head as it rotates.

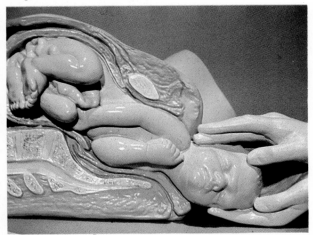

The shoulder begins to emerge.

FIGURE 3.2
Four stages of childbirth.

BIRTH—A DRAMATIC TRANSITION FOR THE FETUS

A few days or weeks before birth, the fetus usually becomes positioned head downward, with legs and feet extended upward. Labor, the activity by which the infant is pushed out of the mother's womb, is signaled by the onset of contractions in the uterus (see figure 3.2).

Birth marks a dramatic transition for the fetus. In the womb the fetus was in a dark, free-floating, low-gravity environment with a relatively warm, constant temperature. At birth the newborn must quickly adjust to light, gravity, cold, and a buzzing array of changing stimuli. In addition, the very process of being pushed out of the womb is physically strenuous and exhausting. Our discussion of birth focuses on the importance of birth date and weight, the issue of bonding, and the reflexes and skills of the newborn.

Birth Date and Weight

A full-term infant is one who has grown in the womb for the full thirty-seven to forty weeks between conception and delivery. Not all babies are born on schedule, however. In the past babies born after fewer than thirty-seven weeks in the womb were called premature. More recently the term **premature birth** has begun to lose favor with scientists because it has not sufficiently distinguished early birth from retarded prenatal growth (Kopp & Parmalee, 1979). Currently the trend is to refer to babies born after a briefer than regular time period in the womb as **short-gestation babies** (The term *gestation* refers to the length of time between conception and birth.) By contrast, infants born after a regular gestation period of thirty-seven to forty weeks, but who weigh less than five and a half pounds are called **low-birth-weight** or **high-risk infants.** In one investigation (Milham, Widmayer, Bauer & Peterson, 1983), children were assessed at least once per year through the first four years of life. The most severe cognitive deficits appeared among those who had been short-gestation or low-birth-weight babies and came from an impoverished rather than a middle-class family.

A short gestation period does not necessarily harm the infant. A short-gestation period can be distinguished from retarded prenatal growth, which suggests that the fetus has been damaged in some way (Kopp, 1983). The neurological development of the short-gestation infant continues after birth on approximately the same timetable as if the infant still were in the womb. For example, consider an infant born after a gestation period of thirty weeks. At thirty-eight weeks, approximately two months after birth, this infant will show the same level of brain development as a thirty-eight-week-old fetus who is yet to be born.

Preterm Infants

Claire Kopp (1983) recently summarized the converging results of a number of longitudinal studies focused on preterm infants. From this, we can draw four important conclusions about preterm infants: (1) There have been fewer and fewer serious consequences of preterm births as each advance in intensive-care technology has come along. Some of these advances are as follows: Between 1961 and 1965 changes occurred in how preterm infants were fed and intravenous fluid

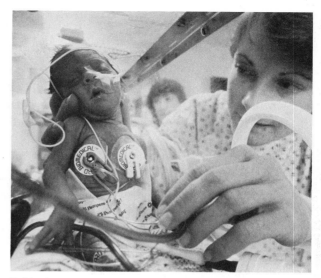

Babies born after a briefer than regular time in the womb are called short-gestation babies.

therapy was introduced. Between 1966 and 1968 better control of oxygen reaching bodily tissues occurred. In 1971 artificial ventilation began to be used. In the mid-1970s, neonatal procedures became less intrusive to the infant. (2) Outcomes for infants born with some already identified problem are likely to be worse than for infants who have no such problem. For example, statistics reported from medical centers caring for extremely sick or very tiny babies report disheartening survival rates for the infants. (3) Social class differences continue to be associated with the preterm infant's immediate outcomes. Broadly stated, the higher the social class, the more favorable are the outcome statistics. There is nothing exotic in this link. Social class differences are also associated with a host of other differences likely to have as much explanatory power as the class differences themselves. For example, quality of environment, cigarette and alcohol consumption, and IQ are all associated with social class differences in just the way you might expect. (4) There is no good evidence that preterm infants, as a rule, encounter difficulty in school several years later. Nor do these children perform more poorly on a variety of measures of intelligence or information-processing skill. Such claims

PERSPECTIVE ON CHILD DEVELOPMENT 3.2

PARENT–CHILD RELATIONSHIPS WITH PRETERM INFANTS

There is no question that preterm infants are thought of as different by all of the adults who surround them. Medical professionals know a host of things about what difficulties the infants might encounter, the infants are surrounded by an exotic environment of high-technology life-support equipment, and the staff-to-patient ratio is probably the most favorable one you will see in an entire hospital. Parents know these children are different too! They have understandable fears about their infant's health and chance of survival. Often the baby is kept in the hospital for some time, making the business of learning the new role of caregiver awkward and strained. And parents must deal with a considerable amount of uncertainty for a long time.

How do parents deal with preterm infants? In what ways do they treat them differently from full-term babies? In an authoritative survey of recent research on socioemotional development in infants, Campos, Barrett, Lamb, Goldsmith & Stenberg (1983) considered these questions and summarized the handful of research investigations that have shed some light on them.

Some studies have shown that before the newborn even goes home from the hospital, mothers of preterm infants express less confidence in their ability to parent and care for the newcomer as compared with parents of full-term babies. Their behavior is also different. They tend to do less of the "hold close, cuddle, and smile" routine. Maybe they feel awkward or see the infant as more fragile than a full-term baby.

Susan Goldberg (Goldberg, 1977; Goldberg, Brachfield & DiVitto, 1980), who has studied many preterm babies and their mothers, speculated that mothers of these children may develop a sense of inadequacy because the anticipated interaction with their infants is frustrated and because the close, postnatal bond is shut off. As the infants go home, differences in the handling of preterm and full-term babies continue. In early infancy, one group of investigators found that mothers of preterm infants are more intrusive with their infants. The mothers in their study actively intervened and tried to make things happen with their babies and to keep the interaction moving along more than other mothers did.

Although it is intuitively appealing to identify difference in interactions between mothers and their babies as due to the mothers, it is equally plausible that differences in the preterm babies' behaviors and responsiveness, as compared with full-term infants, may account for why their mothers treat them differently. In at least some of the longitudinal studies surveyed by Kopp (1983), there was evidence, after all, that preterm babies do have a profile different from full-term babies. For example, one investigator (Field, 1979) found that four-month-old preterm babies had a lower score on a widely used infant development measure, the Denver Developmental Screening Test, talked (vocalized) less, were fussier, and tended to avoid eye contact with their mothers, as compared with full-term infants. Thus, in the face of having to deal with infants who actually are different from full-term babies, perhaps the differences in the way mothers handle preterm babies are based on the mothers' sincere efforts to negotiate this "infant difference."

to the contrary had been made from early research findings just one or two generations ago. More information about parent–child relationships with preterm infants appears in Perspective on Child Development 3.2.

The majority of infants, both full-term and short-gestation, do not show serious impairments at birth. Less than 10 percent have any abnormality, and most abnormalities disappear during later development. One method that is frequently used to assess the health of the newborn is the **Apgar Scale,** which is shown in table

TABLE 3.2
The Apgar Scale

	Score		
	0	1	2
Heart rate	Absent	Slow—less than 100 beats per minute	Fast—100–140 beats per minute
Respiratory effort	No breathing for more than one minute	Irregular and slow	Good breathing with normal crying
Muscle tone	Limp and flaccid	Weak, inactive, but some flexion of extremities	Strong, active motion
Body color	Blue and pale	Body pink, but extremities blue	Entire body pink
Reflex irritability	No response	Grimace	Coughing, sneezing, and crying

From Apgar, V. A., "A proposal for a new method of evaluation of a newborn infant," in *Anesthesia and Analgesia . . . Current Researches*, 32, pp. 260–267. © 1953 International Anesthesia Research Society.

3.2. One minute and five minutes after birth the obstetrician or nurse gives the newborn a rating of 0, 1, or 2 on each of five signs: heart rate, respiratory effort, muscle tone, body color, and reflex irritability. A high total score is favorable—7 to 10 suggests the newborn's condition is good, 5 indicates there may be developmental difficulties, and 3 or below signals an emergency and indicates that survival may be in doubt.

A test that is more subtle than the Apgar in detecting an infant's neurological integrity is the **Brazelton Neonatal Assessment Scale.** It includes an evaluation of the infant's reaction to people. The Brazelton test is usually given on the third day of life and then repeated two to three days later. Twenty reflexes are assessed along with reactions to twenty-six circumstances, such as the infant's response to a rattle. A very low Brazelton score can indicate brain damage. But if the infant merely seems sluggish in responding to social circumstances, it is often recommended that parents of the unresponsive infant make a special effort to observe and provide attention to the infant (Brazelton, 1979). For sluggish infants, "Brazelton training" usually is recommended. Brazelton training involves using the Brazelton Scale to show parents how their newborn responds to people. As part of the training, parents are shown how the neonate can respond positively to people and how such responses can be stimulated. The Brazelton training has been shown to improve the social interaction of high-risk infants as well as the social skills of healthy, responsive infants (Brazelton, 1979; Myers, 1982; Widmayer & Field, 1980; Worobey & Belsky, 1982).

Bonding

Perhaps the most controversial strategy focused on the role of the mother in the neonate's life involves what has been referred to as **bonding.** It has been argued that long-term consequences for the child's development are set in motion during the first hours, days, or weeks of the neonate's interaction with his or her social world. Situations surrounding delivery may prevent or make difficult the occurrence of an emotional bond between the neonate and the mother. This view particularly has been made in the case of preterm infants who often are isolated from their mothers to an even greater degree than are full-term infants. In many hospitals it also has been common to give the mother sufficient drugs to make the delivery of the child less painful. Such drugs often make the mother drowsy and less responsive to the neonate.

Pediatricians have been the most adamant about the importance of bonding during the initial hours and days of the neonate's life. In particular, Marshall Klaus and John Kennell (1976) have been influential in introducing bonding to many hospital settings. They argue that the first few days of life represent a critical period in development. During this time close contact, particularly physical contact, between the neonate and the mother creates an important emotional attachment that provides a foundation for optimal development for years to come. Is there evidence that such close contact between the mother and neonate is absolutely critical for optimal development later in life? While some research has been offered in support of the bonding hypothesis (e.g., Carlson, et al., 1978; Klaus et al., 1972;

How important is bonding in the first few days of the infant's life?

Klaus & Kennell, 1976; Leifer, Leiderman, Barnett & Williams, 1972), a growing body of research challenges the significance of the first few days of life as a critical period (e.g., Bakeman & Brown, 1980; Brown & Bakeman, 1980; Campbell, 1977; Crawford, 1982; Field, 1977; Rode, Chang, Fisch & Sroufe, 1981; Zeskind, 1980). Quite clearly, strong conclusions about the positive effects of bonding are not merited at this time. Indeed the strong form of the bonding hypothesis, namely, that the neonate must have close contact with the mother in the first few days of life to develop optimally, is incorrect.

A climate of fear has emerged on the part of some expectant parents that if bonding does not occur their neonate will later develop problems adjusting to the world and will likely never form a close emotional attachment with the mother. And parents with infants or children may look back to when their child was born and note that mother–infant bonding was not implemented in their case. Such parents should not worry. Most mother–infant pairs seem to compensate for any negative effects that might have occurred during their separation in the postpartum period (Grossman, Thane & Grossman, 1981). Nonetheless, the weakness of the maternal–infant bonding research should not be used as an excuse to keep motivated mothers from interacting with their infants in the postpartum period because such contact brings pleasure to many mothers

(McCall, 1982; Rosenblith & Sims-Knight, 1985). In the case of some infant–mother pairs, such as those involving preterm infants, adolescent mothers, or mothers from disadvantaged backgrounds, the practice of bonding may set in motion a climate for improved mother–infant interaction after the mother and infant leave the hospital (Maccoby & Martin, 1983).

The Newborn's Reflexes and Skills

Because the newborn is capable of very few responses, for a long time it was difficult to assess what the infant sensed, perceived, or learned. In the past two decades scientists have developed sophisticated techniques to make inferences about these matters. The view used to be that the newborn is a passive, empty-headed organism that perceives nothing, does nothing, and learns nothing. New evidence, however, has reversed this notion. The neonate is now regarded as an active individual exploring the environment and picking up information through primitive but nonetheless effective perceptual apparatus, that is, the eyes, ears, nose, mouth, and skin.

Newborns are not as helpless as they look. First of all, the activities needed to sustain life functions are present at birth. The newborn can breathe, suck, swallow, and get rid of wastes. It can look, hear, smell, feel, turn its head, and signal for help from the first minute after birth. Right from the start, the newborn's

Concept	Processes/Related Ideas	Characteristics/Description
	CONCEPT TABLE 3.1 **Prenatal Development and Birth**	
Prenatal development	Conception	Occurs when a single sperm cell from the male unites with the ovum of the female.
	Germinal period	Lasts for two weeks after conception. Cell division, formation of the blastula, and implantation are important in this period.
	Embryological period	Differentiation continues with the formation of the ectoderm, mesoderm, and endoderm. Period lasts from about two to eight weeks after conception. Ossification of bones at about eight weeks ends this period.
	Fetal period	Lasts from about eight weeks after conception until birth. Growth and change to sustain independent life occurs. Fetus can be identified as male or female by three months, and by seven months chances have greatly improved that if born the infant will survive.
	Environmental influences	Teratology is the field of study that focuses on birth defects. There are many different teratogens, and rarely is there a consistent link between a specific teratogen and a specific birth defect. Research now indicates that the fetus is adversely affected when pregnant women drink alcohol, smoke cigarettes, and ingest caffeine.
Birth	Birth date and weight	Short-gestation babies are those born after a briefer time in the womb than is regularly the case. Infants born after a regular gestation period of thirty-seven to forty weeks but who weigh less than five and a half pounds are called low-birth-weight or high-risk infants. As intensive-care technology has improved, preterm infants have benefited considerably. Social class differences are associated with preterm infants. There is no good evidence that preterm infants perform more poorly in school than full-term infants.
	Bonding	There is no evidence that bonding during the first few days of life is a critical period, although bonding may set in motion positive mother–infant interaction that will continue later.
	The newborn's reflexes and skills	Newborns are not as helpless as they look. Reflexes do govern movements in an automatic fashion. The Apgar and Brazelton scales often are used to screen neonatal problems.

attention can be captured by sharply contoured or circular shapes. This indicates that mental curiosity is not entirely swamped by needs for food and comfort.

For the neonate, reflexes govern movements in an automatic fashion. One of the most frequent and dramatic reflexes shown by the neonate is the **Moro reflex,** a vestige from our ape ancestry. When a neonate is handled roughly, hears a loud noise, sees a bright light, or feels a sudden change of position, it becomes startled, arches its back, and throws its head back. At the same time, the neonate flings out its arms and legs, then rapidly closes them to the center of the body, now flexing the body as if falling. This reflex occurs in all newborns but disappears by about three to four months of age.

We have discussed many important ideas about prenatal development and the birth process. A summary of these ideas is presented in Concept Table 3.1. Now we turn our attention to the infant's physical development.

INFANT PHYSICAL DEVELOPMENT

The infant's pattern of physical development during the first two years of life is exciting. At birth, the neonate has a gigantic head (relative to the rest of its body) that flops around in an uncontrollable fashion and possesses reflexes that are dominated by evolutionary movements. In the span of twelve months, the infant becomes capable of sitting anywhere, standing, stooping, climbing, and probably walking. During the second year growth decelerates, but rapid increases in such activities as running and climbing occur.

The First Year

During the infant's first year, there are periods of relative quiet in growth and development and periods bursting with rapid change. At birth the infant has no

TABLE 3.3
Milestones of Motor Development in Three Areas, Reflecting Cephalo-Caudal Sequence

Age in Months	Control of		
	Head	*Trunk and Arms*	*Legs*
Birth			
1	Side-to side-movement		Limited support stepping reflex
2	Hold head and chin up		
3		Hold chest up in face-down position	
4		Reach for objects in sight (without success)	
5	Head erect in sitting position		
6		Sit up with some support	
7		Roll over in prone position	
8			Walk with assistance
9			
10			Support self alone
11			Pull self up in standing position
12			
13			Walk alone
14			

appreciable coordination of the chest or arms. By three or four months, however, two striking accomplishments take place. The first is the infant's ability to hold the chest up while in a face-down position. The other is the ability to reach for objects placed within the infant's direct line of vision. By five months, the infant can sit up with some support and grasp objects. Further indications of the dramatic increase in motor development during the first year of life are shown in table 3.3. Note the significant lag time from control of head and trunk to control of arms and legs indicated in the table. As we see next, this lag time reflects an important principle of growth called the cephalo-caudal pattern.

Cephalo-Caudal Pattern

The **cephalo-caudal pattern** suggests that the greatest growth always occurs at the top of the person—the head—with physical growth in size, weight, and feature differentiation gradually working its way down from top to bottom (e.g., neck, shoulders, middle trunk, and so on). This same pattern is manifested within the head area because the top parts of the head—the eyes and brain, for example—grow faster than the lower portions—such as the jaw. An illustration of this type of growth pattern can be seen in figure 3.3, indicating

the prominence of the head area. Notice that an extraordinary proportion of the total body is occupied by the head at birth but that by the time the individual reaches maturity this proportion is almost cut in half.

Proximodistal Pattern

In addition to the cephalo-caudal pattern of development, there is a second pattern called the **proximodistal pattern.** Simply put, this refers to the pattern of growth starting at the center of the body and moving toward the extremities. An example of this is the early maturation of muscular control of the trunk and arms as compared with that of the hands and fingers.

Rhythmic Behavior

Another important characteristic of the first year of life is the common appearance of rapid, repetitious movements of limbs, torso, and head. Such **rhythmic motor behavior**—kicking, rocking, waving, bouncing, banging, rubbing, scratching, swaying—has intrigued scientists for many years. These infant motor behaviors stand out not only because they occur frequently, but because of the pleasure infants seem to derive from performing the acts as well.

Explanations of rhythmic motor behavior have been numerous. Arnold Gesell (1954) saw rocking as a specific stage in development, but warned (Gesell & Amatruda, 1941) that persistent rhythmic motor behavior

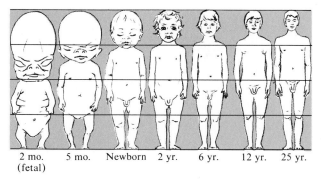

FIGURE 3.3
Changes in body form and proportion during prenatal and postnatal growth (Patten, 1933).

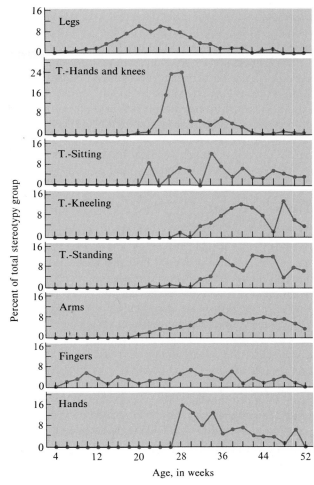

FIGURE 3.4
Frequency of rhythmic motor behavior in the first year of life. (Frequencies have been expressed at each age as a percentage of the total bouts of the stereotypy group seen at that age. Vertical scale indicated on the left is the same for each horizontal axis. Data have been pooled for the sample, N = 20, T = torso.) (Thelen, 1981.)

was a sign of developmental delay or impoverished environment. Jean Piaget (1952) referred to kicking and waving as "circular reactions," a stage of sensorimotor development when infants attempt to repeat a behavior that has an interesting effect on their environment. Psychoanalysts have interpreted rocking as the infant's attempt to establish relations with an "aloof" mother (Brody & Axelrad, 1970). And pediatricians have suggested that head banging is due to a bad temper (Levy & Patrick, 1928). In one investigation (Kravitz & Boehm, 1971), mothers of 200 infants were questioned about their infants' rhythmic behavior. It was concluded that rhythmic behavior has no neurological explanation, a conclusion similar to that reached in a review of the functions of rhythmic behavior (Mitchell & Etches, 1977).

Esther Thelen (1981), however, believes that rhythmic behavior in infancy serves a more important developmental function than it has been ascribed in the past. She believes that rhythmic motor cycles serve an important adaptive function for infants in their first year of life; namely, they represent an important transition between uncoordinated activity and complex, coordinated motor behavior. She conducted extraordinarily detailed observations of twenty normal infants from the time they were four weeks old until they were one year old. More than 16,000 bouts of rhythmical behavior were observed. Infants generally spent about 5 percent of their time performing this type of behavior, but some infants at some ages performed rhythmic movements as much as 40 percent of the time they were being observed. The forty-seven distinct movements observed included variations of kicking, waving, bouncing,

scratching, banging, rubbing, thrusting, swaying, and twisting. When stereotyped movements were grouped by body part and posture, their frequencies showed characteristic developmental profiles over the first year, as shown in figure 3.4. Rhythmic leg behavior, for example, gradually increased at about one month, peaked at five to six months, and then declined. Rhythmic arm movements also gradually increased, but their first occurrence and peak frequency were later than for rhythmic leg movements. If all rhythmic cycles are

(88-93)

summed, the age of peak frequency is six to seven months, with a small but real decline in the last few months of the first year (Thelen, 1979).

Rhythmical stereotypies do seem to represent an important transition between uncoordinated activity and complex, coordinated, voluntary motor control. For example, kicking movements peaked just before the onset of locomotion and declined dramatically in the last third of the year. Rocking on hands and knees appeared just before crawling, and rhythmical hand and arm movements appeared before complex manual skills.

The Second Year

There is a deceleration in growth during the second year of the infant's life. The average infant gains approximately five inches in height and five to six pounds in weight. Somewhere around the last few months of the first year of life, and extending well into the second year, the infant begins to eat less. The plump infant gradually changes into a leaner, more muscular child during the second year. The brain also grows more slowly now. Head circumference, which increased by approximately four inches during the first year, increases only by about two inches this year. By the end of the first year, the brain has attained approximately two-thirds of its adult size, and by the end of the second year, about four-fifths of its adult size. During the second year, eight more teeth erupt to go along with the six to eight that appeared during the first year. By their first birthday, most infants have moved from an awkward, upright standing position to walking without support. Refinement of **gross motor skills,** such as walking, make significant strides during the second year. Let's look more closely at such gross motor skills as well as fine motor skills.

Gross Motor Skills

Several months into the second year the infant may be able to run and can sit down on a chair unassisted if the chair is short (when the seat is about ten inches off the floor). At about eighteen months, the infant can climb stairs, by twenty months walk downstairs with one hand held, and by twenty-four months run efficiently without falling very often. At between eighteen and twenty-four months, the toddler (the name often given to the infant who is in the second year of life) enters the "runabout age"—scurrying from place to place, throwing caution to the wind, and evidencing no concern for the danger of his or her ventures.

Gross motor skills develop significantly during the second year.

The development of walking and running skills is important for the infant's emotional as well as physical development. They provide infants with a sense of mastery of their world. Initially, the infant performs very poorly at walking and running, but during the course of the second year will pick himself or herself up time and time again to face the world and test reality.

Fine Motor Skills

Frank and Theresa Caplan (1981) describe the development of fine motor skills during the second year of life.

> The way she handles objects that go together is a good illustration of the halfway state the baby has reached. She puts her doll's sock next to its foot, for example, but cannot carry the operation further. She does the same thing with her own shoe, indicating that she knows where it belongs by holding it against her foot. She recognizes that her action is incomplete, gestures to any nearby adult for help, and gives a grunt of satisfaction when the task is performed for her. Her intentions clearly outrace her abilities at this point, a most frustrating state of affairs.
>
> From the baby's point of view, unfamiliar objects are expressly made to be investigated, usually by being pulled apart. Doors that open and shut and drawers that pull out are much more interesting than his own small toys. If he can reach nothing else, his clothing will do. A period of silence in the playpen can often mean that he is busily pulling his garments off. Mothers who do not look on this particular activity with favor may come to tolerate it more easily if they regard it as an important prelude to their child's learning to dress himself. (p. 7)

TABLE 3.4
Gross and Fine Motor Development During the Second Year

Gross Motor	Fine Motor
Visually monitors walking, watching placement of feet in order to be able to deal with obstacles in path by avoiding them	Turns pages of a book, one at a time
Runs, but generally lacks ability to start efficiently or stop quickly	Manipulates more freely with one hand; alternates from one hand to the other
Jumps crudely with two-foot takeoff	Has fully developed right- or left-handedness
Walking rhythm stabilizes and becomes even	Increased smoothness of coordination in fine-motor movements
Goes up and down stairs alone without alternating feet	
Can walk approximately on line	
Likes to walk on low walls with one hand held	
Can walk a few steps on tiptoe	
Can be trusted alone on stairs	
Can walk backwards ten feet	
Can quickly alternate between sitting and standing	
Tries to balance self on either foot, not yet successfully	
Is sturdy on feet; less likely to fall	
Still geared to gross-motor activity	

2d year Growth Table reprinted by permission of Grosset & Dunlap from *The Second Twelve Months of Life* by Frank and Theresa Caplan, copyright © 1977 by Frank and Theresa Caplan.

Year-and-a-half-olds begin to show preference for one hand, either right or left. This tendency shows up in their play, holding of spoon or cup, handling of a crayon or pencil in scribbling. Fine-motor improvement is reflected, too, in the child's ability to dump raisins from a bottle (a test used by child psychologists to appraise the manual dexterity and thinking ability of very young children). (p. 219)

A summary of gross and fine motor skills during the second year of life appears in table 3.4.

PHYSICAL DEVELOPMENT IN CHILDHOOD

Now we turn our attention to physical development in early childhood and subsequently in middle and late childhood.

Early Childhood

Our discussion of physical development in early childhood focuses on physical growth, nutrition, and motor development.

Physical Growth

We first discuss information about height, weight, fat, muscles, and other bodily parts and then consider individual variation and growth problems.

The average child grows two and one-half inches in height and gains between five and seven pounds a year during early childhood. As the preschool child grows

TABLE 3.5
Physical Growth, Ages Three to Six
(Fiftieth Percentile)

	Height (inches)		Weight (pounds)	
Age	Boys	Girls	Boys	Girls
3	37.9	37.7	32.2	31.8
3½	39.3	39.2	34.3	33.9
4	40.7	40.6	36.4	36.2
4½	42.0	42.0	38.4	38.5
5	42.8	42.9	40.5	40.5
5½	45.0	44.4	45.6	44.0
6	46.3	45.6	48.3	46.5

Source: From *Growth and Development of Children*, 7th edition, by George H. Lowrey. Copyright © 1978 by Year Book Medical Publishers, Inc., Chicago.

older, the percentage increase in height and weight is less with each additional year of age. Table 3.5 shows the averge height and weight of children as they age from three to six years. Girls are only slightly smaller and lighter than boys during this age frame, a difference that continues until puberty. During the preschool years both boys and girls slim down as the trunk of their bodies becomes longer. Although their heads are still somewhat large for their bodies, by the end of the preschool years most children have lost the look that makes them seem topheavy. Body fat also shows a slow, steady decline during the preschool years, sometimes allowing the chubby baby to look much leaner by the end of early childhood. As you might expect, girls have more fatty tissue than do boys, and boys have more muscle tissue than girls do.

As preschool children grow older, the percentage of increase in height and weight is less with each additional year of age.

Some body systems show signs of maturing—for instance, the child's heart rate slows down and becomes more stable (Eichorn, 1970). Nonetheless, there still are signs of immaturity in many body systems, including bones, joints, and muscles, which are much more susceptible to injury than those of children in middle and late childhood (Lundsteen & Bernstein-Tarrow, 1981).

Clearly, there is a great deal of individual variation in our growth patterns. Think back to your preschool years. Although it is not easy to remember that far back, you may recall that the preschool years were the first time you started noticing that some other children were taller than you, some were shorter, some were fatter, some thinner, some were stronger, some weaker.

Much of the variation in height is due to genetic factors, but there is evidence that environmental experiences contribute as well. In reviewing more than 200 studies of the heights of preschool children around the world, researchers concluded that two very important contributors to height differences are ethnic origin and nutrition (Meredith, 1978). Urban, middle-class, and firstborn children were taller than rural, lower-class, and later-born children, possibly because the former experience better health care and nutrition. The researchers also noted that children at the age of five were approximately one-half inch shorter if their mother smoked during pregnancy. In the United States height differences among preschool children are mainly due to genetic inheritance because most children receive enough food for their bodies to grow appropriately. On the average, black children are taller than white children in the United States (Krogman, 1970).

Children who experience growth problems, being unusually short or unusually tall (which is less frequent), usually do so for one of three reasons: a congenital reason, a physical problem that develops during childhood, or an emotional difficulty. In many instances individuals with congenital growth problems (those due to genetic conditions or prenatal difficulties) can be treated with hormones. Usually such treatment is directed at a master gland, the **pituitary,** located at the base of the brain. This gland secretes hormones that control growth. With regard to physical problems that develop during childhood, malnutrition and chronic infections can stunt growth although if they are properly treated, normal growth usually is achieved (Lowrey, 1978). Finally, some psychologists believe that emotional problems can produce growth abnormalities. For instance, Lita Gardner (1972) argues that children who are deprived of affection may experience alterations in the release of hormones by the pituitary gland. This type of growth retardation is called **deprivation dwarfism.** Some children who are small and weak but are not dwarfs also may show the effects of an impoverished emotional environment—although most parents of such children generally say they are small and weak because they have a poor body structure or constitution.

Nutrition

Early feeding and eating habits are important aspects of development. Here we look at the role of nutrition in physical development and intelligence.

It is widely recognized that what we eat affects our skeletal growth, body shape, and susceptibility to disease. Recognizing that nutrition is important for the child's growth and development, the federal government provides money for school lunch programs. On the average, the preschool child requires approximately 1,400 to 1,800 calories a day. Children with unbalanced or malnourished diets show below average physical development by the third year of life. Some evidence suggests that when the appropriate nutrients are introduced into the diet of the malnourished child, physical development will improve. For instance, when provided milk supplements over a twenty-month period, deprived children between the ages of four and fifteen showed gains of 3.6 percent in height and 29 percent in weight. More information about the role of nutrition in physical development appears in Perspective on Child Development 3.3.

MALNUTRITION IN THE PHILIPPINES

I magine you are five years old and live in the Bayambang area of the Philippines. Your parents are very poor. They do not get enough food to eat, and what they are able to afford does not constitute a well-balanced diet. There is a limited amount of protein in the Philippines; only the wealthy people get enough. Even if protein were plentiful, the price would probably be too high for your parents.

Compare yourself to a five-year-old growing up in Des Moines, Iowa. The five-year-old in Des Moines lives in a land where protein is plentiful. It is so plentiful that the five-year-old in Iowa has no worry about protein intake. Even if he comes from a lower-class family in the United States, he will get far more protein than the average five-year-old in the Philippines. Indeed, one of the major problems the five-year-old in Iowa may be facing is that he is getting too much fat in his diet—more about this appears later in the chapter.

The table at bottom right presents a comparison of the malnutrition in the Bayambang area of the Philippines with nutrition in Iowa. Note that at all ages of childhood malnutrition in the Philippines is apparent.

Socioeconomic status within a culture is also linked with the nutrition and physical development of young children. The curves of body weight shown in the figure opposite reveal the average weights of young children from three different social classes in Manila (upper income, middle income, and lower income) along with young children living in Bayambang and Iowa (Bailey, 1970).

Note that the upper-income children from Manila approach their counterparts from Iowa, while those from middle- and lower-income families have much lower body weights. Also note the average weight of young children from the Bayambang area of the Philippines, an impoverished area.

Where growth retardation is apparent, there is generally some inadequacy of many nutrients in the common diet, and caloric deficiency may also occur. It appears that protein, vitamin A, and iron deficiencies are the most common problems. These deficiencies are particularly acute in impoverished areas when children are under the age of five.

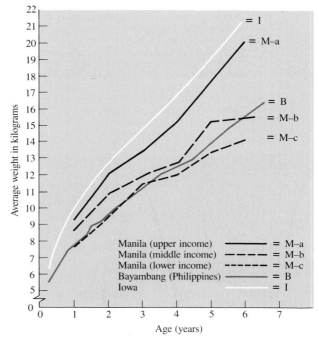

Average weight of infants and toddlers of different socioeconomic groups (males and females combined).

Malnutrition Scores in Bayambang Area, Philippines, 1964 (Based on Two-thirds of Iowa Standard)

Age Group	% Below Malnutrition on Line
Infants 0–5 months	5.7
Infants 6–11 months	17.8
Toddlers 1–3 years	24.0
Preschool 4–6 years	13.4
School age 7–9 years	16.7
School age 10–12 years	18.7

Table and figure from Bailey, K. V. A., "A study of human growth in the framework of applied nutrition and public health nutrition programs in the Western Pacific region," in J. Brozek, editor, *Monographs of The Society for Research in Child Development,* 35, serial no. 140. © 1970 The Society for Research in Child Development. Reprinted by permission.

TABLE 3.6
Fat and Calorie Intake of Selected Fast-Food Meals

Selected Meal	Calories	Percent of Calories from Fat
Burger King Whopper, fries, vanilla shake	1250	43
Big Mac, fries, chocolate shake	1100	41
McDonald's Quarter-Pounder with cheese	418	52
McDonald's Filet O'Fish sandwich	402	56
Pizza Hut ten-inch pizza with sausage, mushrooms, pepperoni, and green pepper	1035	35
Arby's roast beef plate (roast beef sandwich, two potato patties and cole slaw), chocolate shake	1200	30
Kentucky Fried Chicken dinner (three pieces chicken, mashed potatoes and gravy, cole slaw, roll)	830	50
Arthur Treacher's fish and chips (two pieces breaded, fried fish, french fries, cola drink)	900	42
Typical restaurant "diet plate" (hamburger patty, cottage cheese, etc.)	638	63

Reprinted by permission of Rodale's *Runner's World* Magazine, Copyright 1980.

Eating habits develop early in life—too many children are being brought up on high-fat-content meals.

What is an appropriate diet for a preschool child? Clearly there is individual variation, and experts may disagree on detail, but in general the diet should include fats, carbohydrates, protein, vitamins, and minerals.

A particular concern in our culture is the amount of fat in our diet, and as we emphasized earlier, eating habits get ingrained very early in life. In table 3.6 you will find the number of calories and the percentage of fat in the offerings of a number of fast-food restaurants. Most fast-food meals are high in protein, especially meat and dairy products. But the average American has no need to be concerned about obtaining protein. What must be of concern is the vast number of young children who are being weaned on fast foods that are not only high in protein but also have a high fat content. (It is during the preschool years that many individuals get their first taste of fast foods.) The American Heart Association recommends that the daily limit for calories from fat should be approximately 35 percent. Compare this figure with the higher figures in table 3.6. Clearly, many fast-food meals contribute to excessive fat intake by young children.

Perhaps the most direct evidence of the effects of nutrition on development is provided by animal studies, which have shown that the development of the brain is related to protein intake. In one study (Zamenhof, van Marthens, & Margolis, 1968), one month before impregnation one group of female rats was placed on a high-protein diet, and a similar group was placed on a low-protein diet. When the brain and body weights of

TABLE 3.7
Perceptual-Motor Behaviors Checklist

The following tasks are reasonable to expect in 75 to 80 percent of the children of the indicated ages. Children should be tested individually.

The data upon which this is based have been collected from children in white middle-class neighborhoods.

A child failing to master four to six of the tasks for his or her age probably needs (a) a more thorough evaluation and (b) some kind of remedial help.

Various sex differences are indicated.

Two to Three Years

	Yes	No
1. Displays a variety of scribbling behavior.	_____	_____
2. Can walk rhythmically at an even pace.	_____	_____
3. Can step off low object, one foot ahead of the other.	_____	_____
4. Can name hands, feet, head, and some face parts.	_____	_____
5. Opposes thumb to fingers when grasping objects and releases objects smoothly from finger-thumb grasp.	_____	_____
6. Can walk a two-inch wide line placed on ground, for ten feet.	_____	_____

Four to Four and a Half

	Yes	No
1. Forward broad jump, both feet together and clear of ground at the same time.	_____	_____
2. Can hop two or three times on one foot without precision or rhythm.	_____	_____
3. Walks and runs with arm action coordinated with leg action.	_____	_____
4. Can walk a circular line a short distance.	_____	_____
5. Can draw a crude circle.	_____	_____
6. Can imitate a simple line cross using a vertical and horizontal line.	_____	_____

Five to Five and a Half

	Yes	No
1. Runs thirty yards in just over eight seconds.	_____	_____
2. Balances on one foot (girls 6–8 seconds) (boys 4–6 seconds).	_____	_____
3. Child catches large playground ball bounced to him chest-high from fifteen feet away; four to five times out of five.	_____	_____
4. Rectangle and square drawn differently (one side at a time).	_____	_____
5. Can high jump eight inches or higher over bar with simultaneous two-foot takeoff.	_____	_____
6. Bounces playground ball, using one or two hands, a distance of three to four feet.	_____	_____

Six to Six and a Half

	Yes	No
1. Can block print first name in letters 1½ to 2 inches high.	_____	_____
2. Can gallop, if it is demonstrated.	_____	_____
3. Can exert six pounds or more of pressure in grip strength measure.	_____	_____
4. Can walk balance beam 2 inches wide, 6 inches high, and 10 to 12 inches long.	_____	_____
5. Can run sixty feet in about five seconds.	_____	_____
6. Can arise from ground from back lying position, when asked to do so as fast as he can, in two seconds or under.	_____	_____

From Cratty, J., *Psychomotor Behavior in Education and Sport*, pp. 61–63, 1974. Courtesy of Charles C Thomas, Publisher, Springfield, Illinois.

the offspring were measured, the weights of the off-spring of mothers on the high-protein diet were greater than those of the offspring of mothers on the low-protein diet. The brains of the mothers themselves were subsequently analyzed: the brains of the mothers on the high-protein diet had more cells than did those of the mothers on the low-protein diet. Thus, we may conclude that the nutrition of the mother may affect not only the development of her own brain but the development of her offspring's brain as well.

In another study, two groups of black South African infants, all one year old, were extremely malnourished. The children in one group were given adequate nourishment during the next six years; there was no intervention in the poor nutrition of the other group. After the seventh year, the poorly nourished group of children had significantly lower IQs than the adequately nourished group did (Bayley, 1970).

Motor Development

Building towers with blocks . . . running as fast you could, falling down, getting right back up, and running just as fast again . . . scribbling, scribbling, and then scribbling some more on lots of pieces of paper . . . cutting paper with scissors—during your preschool years, you probably developed the ability to perform all of these motor activities. A summary of the manner in which a number of gross and fine motor skills change during the course of early childhood is outlined in table 3.7.

Three- to five-year-olds often experience considerable large-muscle development, particularly in the arms and legs. Thus daily forms of exercise are recommended because of this considerable increase in gross motor skills during early childhood. It is also important that sedentary periods be kept brief and few. Although fine motor skills also are increasing during this period, they seem to show more growth during the beginning of middle childhood than during early childhood (Robinson, 1977).

How is motor development assessed? The Bayley Motor Scale can be used for children through the age of two and a half; the Gesell Developmental Schedules and the Denver Developmental Screening Test can be used for those through the age of six. The Bayley test was designed primarily for very young children, mainly infants, so it is not surprising that postural control, locomotion, and prehensile activity are emphasized and that there is an absence of attention to such important aspects of movement as striking, catching, throwing, jumping, running, and kicking behaviors, which are included on the Gesell and Denver tests.

The Denver Developmental Screening Test deserves further mention because it was created as a simple, inexpensive, and fast way to diagnose delayed development in children from birth through six years of age. The test is individually administered and includes an evaluation of language and personal–social ability in addition to separate assessments of gross and fine motor skills. Gross motor skills that are evaluated include the child's ability to sit, walk, broad jump, pedal a tricycle, throw a ball overhand, catch a bounced ball, hop on one foot, and balance on one foot. Fine motor-adaptive skills that are evaluated include the child's ability to stack cubes, reach for objects, and draw a man.

One promising test that provides a more detailed assessment of gross motor skills is the DeOreo Fundamental Motor Skills Inventory (DeOreo, 1976). Performance is evaluated in eleven categories: striking, balancing, skipping, jumping, galloping, hopping, catching, running, climbing, throwing, and kicking. Items are divided into product components, such as "Can the child run thirty-five yards in less than ten seconds?" and process components, such as "While running does the child keep his body erect or inclined backwards?"

Middle and Late Childhood

The period of middle and late childhood involves slow, consistent growth—the calm before the rapid growth spurt that will appear during adolescence. During the elementary school years, children grow an average of two to three inches per year until at the age of eleven,

the average girl is four feet, ten inches tall, and the average boy is four feet, nine and one-half inches tall. Weight increases range from three to five pounds per year until at the age of eleven, the average girl weighs eighty-eight and one-half pounds, and the average boy weighs eighty-five and one-half pounds (Krogman, 1970).

During middle and late childhood, children's legs become longer and their trunks slimmer, and they are steadier on their feet. Fat tissue tends to develop more rapidly than muscle tissue (which increases substantially in adolescence). Children who had a rounded, somewhat chubby body build (sometimes referred to as **endomorphic**) have noticeably more fat tissue than muscle tissue, while the reverse is true of children with **mesomorphic** body builds (athletic, muscular). **Ectomorphy** (skinny, thin body build) characterizes those who do not have a predominance of fat or muscle, which accounts for their tendency to appear somewhat scrawny (Hurlock, 1980).

During middle and late childhood, motor development of children becomes much smoother and more coordinated than was the case in early childhood. For

The motor development of children becomes much smoother and more coordinated in the middle and late childhood years.

example, only one child in a thousand can even hit a tennis ball over the net at the age of four, yet by the age of eleven, most children can learn to play tennis. In the early elementary school years, children can become competent at running, climbing, throwing and catching a ball, skipping rope, swimming, bicycle riding, and skating, to name just some of the many physical skills that, when mastered, provide a considerable source of pleasure and accomplishment. Developing competence in these physical skills indicates increases in children's strength, speed, flexibility, and precision, including steadiness, balance, and aiming (Lundsteen & Bernstein-Tarrow, 1981). There usually are marked sex differences in these gross motor skills, with boys outperforming girls rather handily. However, in fine motor skills, girls generally outperform boys.

During middle and late childhood, sensory mechanisms continue to mature. Early farsightedness is overcome, binocular vision becomes well-developed, and hearing acuity increases. Children of this age have fewer illnesses than younger children, particularly fewer respiratory and gastrointestinal problems. Widespread immunization has considerably reduced the incidence of disease, and many illnesses can be prevented by practicing habits of good health, safety, and nutrition (Lundsteen & Bernstein-Tarrow, 1981).

We have considered a number of physical developments in the first year, second year, early childhood, and middle and late childhood. A summary of these ideas is presented in Concept Table 3.2. Now we turn to physical development during adolescence.

CONCEPT TABLE 3.2
Physical Development in Infancy and Childhood

Concept	Processes/Related Ideas	Characteristics/Description
First year	General growth pattern	There are periods of relative quiet in growth and periods bursting with change.
	Cephalo-caudal pattern	Greatest growth always occurs at the top of the person.
	Proximodistal pattern	Pattern of growth beginning at center of body and moving outward toward extremities.
	Rhythmic behavior	Rapid, repetitious movement of limbs, torso, and head that may serve important adaptive functions for infants, representing the transition between uncoordinated activity and complex, coordinated motor behavior.
Second year	General growth pattern	There is a deceleration of growth in the second year.
	Gross motor skills	Refinement of gross motor skills, such as walking, is significant in the second year.
	Fine motor skills	There is an increased smoothness in fine motor skills, such as turning the pages of a book one at a time.
Early childhood	General growth pattern	Percentage increase in height and weight is less as preschool child ages. There is a great deal of individual variation in growth patterns during the preschool years. Problems with the pituitary gland can trigger growth abnormalities.
	Nutrition	Nutrition influences both physical development and intelligence.
	Motor development	Three- to five-year-olds experience considerable large-muscle development, and their fine motor skills improve markedly. A number of tests have been devised to assess motor development.
Middle and late childhood	General growth pattern	Slow consistent growth occurs. Sensorimotor coordination continues to improve. Children often can be classified as endomorphs, ectomorphs, or mesomorphs.

ADOLESCENCE

Dramatic biological changes characterize development during early adolescence, but such changes slow down during late adolescence. To understand these changes we study the concept of puberty, sexual maturation, changes in height and weight, and psychological adaptation to physical change.

Puberty

Puberty often is used as the most important marker for the beginning of adolescence. However, major pubertal changes have taken place long before adolescence ends. For the most part, then, puberty coincides with early rather than late adolescence.

What is **puberty**? It usually is thought of as a period of rapid change to physical maturation. Sexual maturation is one of the most prominent aspects of the pubertal process. In figure 3.5, a rough representation of sexual maturation and decline is presented in terms of sex-hormone levels (Petersen & Taylor, 1980). Our further discussion of the pubertal process focuses on the endocrine system, height and weight, and sexual maturation.

The Endocrine System

Before we describe the physical changes that characterize puberty, such as sexual maturation and gains in height and weight, it is important to know something about the hormonal system that stimulates these physical changes. Endocrinology, or the study of the endocrine system, is highly complex. Here we will outline several basic ideas that help us understand how the endocrine system works.

The endocrine system is made up of endocrine glands and their secretions. The **endocrine glands** are often less noticeable than other glands because their secretions are carried in the blood stream instead of through ducts. Glands with ducts are called exocrine glands and secrete such substances as saliva, sweat, and breast milk. The secretions of endocrine glands are hormones, which are powerful chemical substances that regulate organs. These organs are often far from the endocrine glands where the secretions are first emitted.

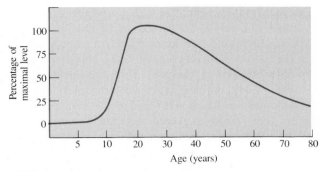

FIGURE 3.5

Hypothetical representation of sexual development in terms of sex-hormone levels (Peterson and Taylor, 1980).

The aspects of the endocrine system that are most important in puberty involve the **hypothalamic–pituitary–gonadal axis** (Nottelmann et al., 1985; Nottelmann et al., in press). The **hypothalamus** is a structure in the higher portion of the brain. The pituitary gland, often referred to as a master gland, is located at the base of the brain. Its reference as a master gland comes from its regulation of a number of other glands. The term **gonadal** refers to the sex glands—the testes in males and the ovaries in females. The hormonal system involving the hypothalamus, pituitary gland, and gonads works like this. While the pituitary monitors endocrine levels, it is regulated by the hypothalamus. The pituitary sends a signal via a **gonadotropin** (a hormone that stimulates the testes or ovaries) to the appropriate gland to manufacture the hormone. Then the pituitary, through interaction with the hypothalamus, detects when the optimal level is reached and responds by maintaining gonadotropin and sex-hormone secretion (Petersen & Taylor, 1980).

Two main general classes of sex hormones are important in understanding pubertal development: androgens and estrogens. **Androgens** mature primarily in males, and **estrogens** mature mainly in females. Current research, however, has been able to pinpoint more precisely which androgens and estrogens seem to play the most important roles in pubertal development. For example, **testosterone** appears to assume an important role in the pubertal development of males. Throughout puberty, increasing testosterone levels are clearly linked with a number of physical changes in boys: development of external genitals, increase in height, and voice changes (Fregly & Luttge, 1982). In females, **estradiol** is probably the most important hormone responsible for

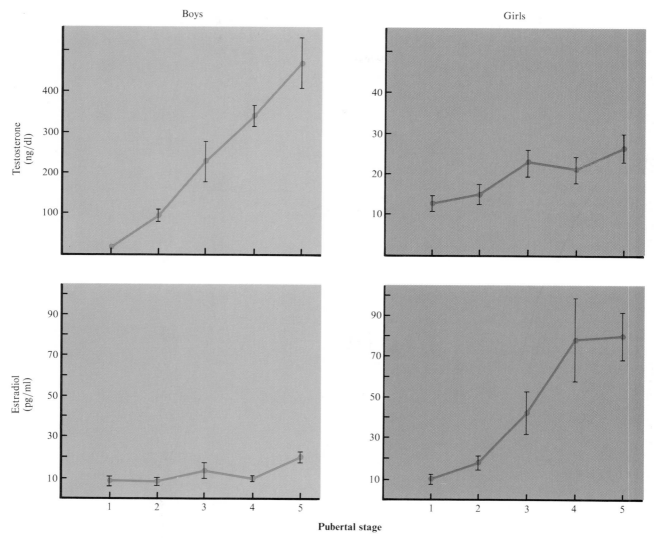

FIGURE 3.6
Hormone levels by sex and pubertal stage for testosterone and
estradiol (Nottelmann et al., 1985).

pubertal development. The level of estradiol increases throughout puberty and then varies in women across their menstrual cycle. As the estradiol level rises, breast and uterine development occur and skeletal changes appear as well (Dillon, 1980; Fregly & Luttge, 1982). As shown in figure 3.6, in one study (Nottelmann et al., 1985) testosterone levels were found to increase eighteenfold in boys but only twofold in girls across the pubertal period. In the same study there was an eight-fold increase in estradiol levels in girls but only a two-fold increase in boys. Note that both testosterone and estradiol are present in the hormonal makeup of both boys and girls but that testosterone is dominant for boys while estradiol is stronger in girls. It should be mentioned that testosterone and estradiol are part of a complex hormonal system and that alone each hormone is not solely responsible for pubertal change. Nonetheless, their strong association with the physical changes of puberty suggests that they clearly play a very important role in the pubertal process.

Height and Weight

As boys and girls undergo the adolescent growth spurt, they make rapid gains in height and weight. However, as is indicated in figure 3.7 the growth spurt for girls occurs approximately two years earlier than that for boys. The growth spurt in girls begins at approximately age ten and one-half and lasts for about two years. During this time period, girls increase in height by about three and one-half inches per year. The growth spurt for boys usually begins at about twelve and one-half years of age and also lasts for approximately two years. Boys usually grow about four inches per year in height during this growth spurt (Faust, 1977; Tanner, 1966, 1970). These averages do not reflect the fairly wide range of time within which the adolescent growth spurt begins. Girls may start the growth spurt as early as age seven and one-half or as late as age eleven and one-half, while boys may begin as early as age ten and one-half or as late as age sixteen (Faust, 1977; Tanner, 1970).

Boys and girls who are shorter or taller than their peers before adolescence are likely to remain so during adolescence (e.g., Tanner, 1970). At the beginning of the adolescent period, girls tend to be as tall or taller than boys their age, but by the end of the junior high years most boys have caught up or, in many cases, even surpassed girls in height. Even though height in the elementary school years is a good predictor of height later in adolescence, there is still room for the individual's height to change in relation to the height of his or her peers. As much as 30 percent of the height of late adolescents is unexplained by height in the elementary school years (Tanner, 1970).

The rate at which adolescents gain weight follows approximately the same developmental timetable as the rate at which they gain height. Marked weight gains coincide with the onset of puberty. During early adolescence girls tend to outweigh boys, but by about age fourteen, just as with height, boys begin to surpass girls (e.g., Faust, 1977; Tanner, 1970).

Now let's turn our attention to the hallmark of pubertal development—sexual maturation.

Sexual Maturation

Think back to your last few years of childhood and then to your first years of adolescence. Probably nothing comes to mind more strikingly than the sexual maturation that began to occur during the first two years of

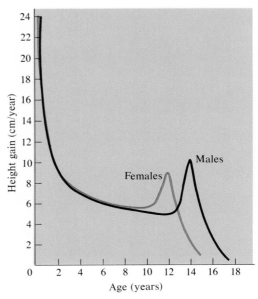

FIGURE 3.7
Typical individual growth curves for height in boys and girls. These curves represent the height of the typical boy and girl at any given age (Tanner, Whitehouse, and Takaishi, 1966).

adolescence. You also probably recall that during the last few years of childhood your interest in sexual activity and sexual relationships was near the level it reached during the first several years of adolescence. Few aspects of development throughout the life cycle attract more curiosity and mystery than the onset of sexual maturation during early adolescence. Let's look at the sexual maturation of boys and then girls.

Researchers have found that male sexual characteristics develop in the following order: increase in size of testicles and penis, appearance of straight pubic hair, minor voice changes, first ejaculation (the first ejaculation usually occurs through masturbation or during sleep—the so-called wet dream), appearance of kinky pubic hair, onset of maximum growth, growth of axillary hair (in armpits), more detectable voice changes, and growth of facial hair (e.g., Faust, 1977; Garrison, 1968).

Three of the most noticeable areas of sexual maturation in boys are penis elongation, testes development, and the growth of pubic hair. The normal range and average age of development for these sexual characteristics, as well as for the height spurt, is shown in figure 3.8.

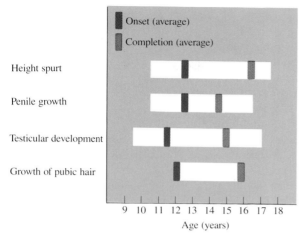

FIGURE 3.8
Normal range and average age of height spurt and development of sexual characteristics in males.

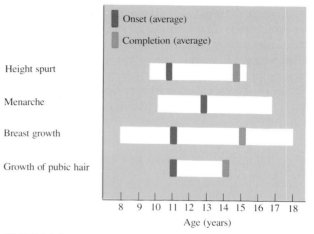

FIGURE 3.9
Normal range and average age of height spurt and development of sexual characteristics in females.

Adolescent females experience the following sequence of physical changes in puberty. First, either the breasts enlarge or pubic hair appears. Later some hair will appear in the armpits. As these changes occur, the female grows in height, and her hips become wider than her shoulders. Fatty tissue in and encircling the breasts, shoulders, and hips creates a more rounded appearance in the adolescent female. Her first menstruation, referred to as menarche, indicates that sexual maturity is near. Initially, her menstrual cycles may be very irregular, and even for the first several years she may not be ovulating in every cycle. In other words, she may not become fertile until several years after her period begins. There is no exaggerated enlargement of the larynx in females during puberty and, hence, no voice change comparable to that occurring in adolescent males (e.g., Faust, 1977; Haeberle, 1978).

Two of the most noticeable aspects of the female's sexual maturation are pubic hair and breast development. Figure 3.9 illustrates the normal range and average age of development of these sexual characteristics, as well as information about menarche and height gain.

Individual Variation

The pubertal sequence may begin as early as ten and as late as thirteen and one-half years of age for most boys, at which time there is an acceleration in the

The pubertal sequence may begin as early as 10 years of age and as late as 13½ for boys.

growth of the testes. If this sequence terminates at the time of the first ejaculation, the average age of termination is thirteen and one-half to fourteen (although ejaculation could occur much earlier or later depending upon when the process started). However, the average range is wide enough that if we have two boys of the same chronological age, one may complete the pubertal sequence before the other has begun it. In girls the age range of the first menstrual period is even wider—it may occur at age ten or it may not happen until age fifteen and one-half (Hill, 1980b).

In some cases puberty may be delayed until very late in adolescence. In the United States, if puberty has not been reached by the age of fifteen or sixteen for boys, it represents a serious lag in the development of sex organs and hormones. Today there is an increasing tendency to administer sex-hormone treatment to boys and girls who have not reached puberty by age fourteen or fifteen.

Psychological Adaptation to Changes in Physical Development

A host of psychological and social consequences accompany changes in the adolescent's physical development. Think about yourself as you began puberty. Not only did you probably begin to think in different ways about yourself, but important individuals, such as peers and parents, probably began acting differently toward you. Maybe you were proud of your changing body even though you may have been perplexed about what was going on. Or possibly you felt embarrassed about the changes that were taking place and experienced a lot of anxiety. Perhaps you looked in the mirror on a daily or sometimes even an hourly basis to see if you were maturing physically and to see if you could detect anything different about your changing body. Possibly you were no longer treated as the little boy or the little girl and instead were perceived by peers in terms of your sexual attractiveness. Perhaps your parents no longer perceived you as someone they could sit in bed and watch television with or as someone who should be kissed good night. One of the major ways in which psychological aspects of pubertal change have been investigated is by studying adolescents who are early or late maturers. This topic is explored in Perspective on Child Development 3.4.

PERSPECTIVE ON CHILD DEVELOPMENT 3.4

THE EFFECTS OF EARLY AND LATE MATURATION ON DEVELOPMENT

If you are a female, imagine that you are ten years old and already well on the road to "developing." You had your first period last month, and you are already buying bras. If you are a male, imagine that you are eleven years old and already shaving and have pubic hair and broad shoulders. What effects are the early development of these sexual characteristics likely to have on such matters as your self-esteem, body image, and peer relations?

The majority of research that has addressed the issue of early and late maturation in adolescence has been collected as part of a longitudinal growth study at the University of California. The upshot of the California investigations concerning early and late maturation is that boys who mature early in adolescence (as measured by their skeletal growth) perceive themselves more positively and are more successful in peer relations than their late-maturing counterparts. The findings for early-maturing girls are also positive but not as strongly as for boys (Mussen & Jones, 1958).

Another longitudinal investigation of early and late maturation was conducted by Dale Blyth and his colleagues (Blyth, Bulcroft & Simmons, 1981). Presence or absence of menstruation and relative onset of menses were used to classify girls as early, middle, and late maturers. For boys, the classification was made on the basis of the peak rate of height growth. More than 450 individuals were followed for five years beginning in the sixth grade and continuing through the tenth grade in Milwaukee, Wisconsin, from 1974 through 1979. Students were individually interviewed and achievement-test scores and grade-point averages were obtained.

The findings for early-maturing boys confirmed the California results, whereas the data for early-maturing girls were mixed. Early maturation in girls seemed to be disadvantageous for grades and achievement-test performance at school. Early-maturing girls also were more likely to show problem behavior at school such as skipping classes. However, early maturation was advantageous for girls in terms of independence and opposite-sex relationships. Some of the most intriguing findings, though, pertained to the girls' body image.

One of the most important tasks of adolescence is to incorporate dramatic physical changes into a positive body image. With regard to satisfaction with one's figure, a complex pattern developed for adolescent girls. (See the figure opposite). More developed, menstruating girls showed greater satisfaction with their figures in the sixth grade than did late-maturing girls.

"Well, whatever it is we change into, it can't come soon enough for me."

Drawing by D. Reilly; © 1973 The New Yorker Magazine, Inc.

But by the ninth and tenth grades, the pattern was reversed. When all girls were developed, it was the late maturers who were more satisfied with their figures. One reason for this pattern of findings is that by the ninth and tenth grades, early maturers are usually shorter and stockier and late maturers are often taller and thinner. Possibly the late maturing female in the ninth and tenth grades more closely approximates the American ideal of feminine beauty—tall and slim.

In the longitudinal investigation by Dale Blyth and his colleagues, early maturation for girls seemed to have mixed effects, whereas early maturation for boys seemed to have an overall positive effect. However, it is important to examine the particular dimension of psychological and social development in question. In one study (Peskin, 1967), early maturing boys had fewer commitments and less successful identities in their 30's. Possibly they reached a false identity too early in development. And, although early maturation seemed to be disadvantageous for a girl's body image, school performance, and school behavior, it appeared to be an advantage in opposite-sex relationships and independence. Nonetheless, when we piece together the many findings of the California Longitudinal Study and the Milwaukee Project, early maturation favors boys but has more mixed blessings for girls.

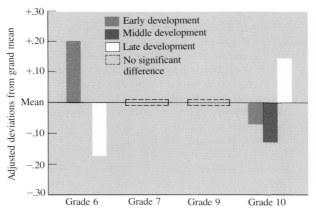

Female pubertal development and satisfaction with figure (Simmons, Blyth, and McKinney, 1983).

SUMMARY

I. Information about prenatal development focuses on conception, the germinal period, the embryological period, the fetal period, and environmental influences.
   A. Conception occurs when a single sperm cell unites with an ovum.
   B. The germinal period lasts for two weeks after conception. Cell division, formation of the blastula, and implantation are important in this period.
   C. The embryological period lasts from about two to eight weeks after conception. Differentiation continues with the formation of the ectoderm, mesoderm, and endoderm. The ossification of bones at about eight weeks ends this period.
   D. The fetal period lasts from about eight weeks to birth. Growth and change to sustain independent life occurs. The fetus can be identified as male or female at about three months, and by seven months chances have improved markedly that if born the infant will survive.
   E. There has been a dramatic increase in the study of environmental influences on prenatal development. Teratology is the label given to the field that focuses on birth defects. There are many different teratogens, and rarely is there a consistent link between a specific teratogen and a specific birth defect. Research now indicates that the fetus is adversely affected when pregnant women drink alcohol, smoke cigarettes, or ingest caffeine.
II. The study of birth has emphasized birth date and weight, as well as the matter of bonding and the newborn's reflexes and skills.
   A. Short-gestation babies are those born after a briefer than regular time. Infants who are born after a regular gestation period of thirty-seven to forty weeks but who weight less than five and one-half pounds are called low-birth-weight or high-risk infants. As intensive-care technology has improved, preterm babies have benefited considerably. Social class differences are associated with preterm babies. There is no solid evidence that preterm infants perform more poorly than regular term infants years later in school.
   B. There also is no evidence that bonding during the first few days of life is critical for development, although bonding may stimulate positive mother–infant interaction after leaving the hospital.
   C. Newborns are not as helpless as they look. Reflexes do govern movements in an automatic fashion. The Apgar and Brazelton scales often are called on to screen developmental problems in the neonate.
III. During the first year of infancy there are periods of relative quiet in growth and periods bursting with change. The cephalo-caudal and proximodistal patterns characterize growth. Rhythmic behavior may serve an important adaptive function by representing the transition between uncoordinated and highly coordinated motor behavior.
IV. During the second year of infancy there is a deceleration in growth. Gross and fine motor skills improve considerably.
V. During the early childhood years, the percentage increase in height and weight is less as the preschool child ages. There is a great deal of individual variation in growth patterns. Problems with the pituitary can trigger growth abnormalities. Nutrition influences both physical development and intelligence. And gross and fine motor skills continue to improve during early, middle, and late childhood. Slow, consistent growth characterizes middle and late childhood. Children often can be classified as ectomorphs, endomorphs, and mesomorphs.
VI. Dramatic biological changes characterize development during early adolescence, but such changes slow down during late adolescence. To understand these changes information about puberty, sexual maturation, changes in height and weight, and the psychological adaptation to physical change is crucial.
   A. Puberty is a period of rapid change to physical maturation. It is characterized by sexual maturation, gains in height and weight, and endocrine system changes. There can be considerable individual variation in pubertal timing.
   B. Puberty instigates considerable psychological adaptation. The young adolescent spends an extensive amount of time being concerned about his or her body image. The effects of early and late maturation on a number of characteristics have been studied. Generally the findings are more positive for early-maturing adolescents, particularly boys, although the results may vary with the characteristics being studied.

KEY TERMS

androgens 96
Apgar Scale 83
blastocyst 73
blastula 73
bonding 83
Brazelton Neonatal Assessment Scale 83
cephalo-caudal pattern 86
conception 73
deprivation dwarfism 90
ectoderm 73
ectomorphy 94
embryological period 73
endocrine glands 96
endoderm 73
endomorphic 94
estradiol 96
estrogens 96
fetal alcohol syndrome (FAS) 78
fetal period 74
germinal period 73
gonadal 96
gonadotropin 96

gross motor skills 88
high-risk infants 81
hypothalamic–pituitary–gonadal axis 96
hypothalamus 96
implantation 73
in vitro fertilization 72
low-birth-weight infants 81
mesoderm 73
mesomorphic 94
Moro reflex 85
pituitary gland 90
premature birth 81
proximodistal pattern 86
puberty 96
rhythmic motor behavior 86
rhythmical stereotypies 88
short-gestation babies 81
teratogen 77
teratology 77
testosterone 96
trophoblast 73

REVIEW QUESTIONS

1. Discuss the nature of conception, the germinal period, the embryological period, and the fetal period.
2. Describe the environmental influences on prenatal development.
3. Evaluate the importance of birth date and weight on the infant's development.
4. Discuss the reflexes and skills of the newborn.
5. Describe physical development in infancy.
6. Describe physical development in childhood.
7. Discuss the effects of pubertal development.

SUGGESTED READINGS

Brazelton, T. B. and Lester, B. M. (Eds.). (1982). *New approaches to developmental screenings of infants.* New York: Elsevier.
Information by a group of experts on infant development focused on such topics as the assessment of newborns and interventions with handicapped infants.
Brooks-Gunn, J., and Petersen, A. C. (Eds.). (1982). *Girls at puberty: Biological and psychological perspectives.* New York: Plenum.
A series of articles by leading scholars that present relatively recent information about how females experience puberty.
Caplan, F. (1981). *The first twelve months of life.* New York: Bantam.
An easy-to-read, well-written account of each of the first twelve months of life. One of the best of the books for prospective parents or the parents of a newborn.
Cratty, B. (1974). *Psychomotor behavior in education and sport.* Springfield, IL: Chas. C. Thomas.
Bryant Cratty is Director of the Perceptual-Motor Learning Laboratory at UCLA. He has spent considerable time researching better ways to enhance the physical development of children. This book presents a number of articles by Cratty, including discussions of the clumsy child, movement abilities in early childhood, and early childhood education.
Rosenblith, J. F., and Sims-Knight, J. E. (1985). *In the beginning.* Monterey, CA: Brooks/Cole.
An excellent portrayal of the course of growth in infancy. Extensive discussions of bonding, genetic abnormalities, prenatal environment, and developmental milestones.

COGNITIVE PROCESSES AND DEVELOPMENT

SENSORY AND PERCEPTUAL DEVELOPMENT

PROLOGUE

APPARENTLY THE CREATURE
CAN PERCEIVE PEOPLE

You are a scientist studying the visual perception of one of the most helpless creatures on earth. This creature has very poor motor coordination and can move itself only with great difficulty. Its behavior in general appears unorganized, and though it cries when uncomfortable, it has few other vocalizations. In fact, it sleeps most of the time. You are curious about this creature and want to know what it can see.

Your problem is one of communication. You must give this creature a way to tell you about its visual world. But how can you do this?

While examining this creature one day, you make an interesting discovery—when you rapidly move a large object toward it, it moves its head backwards, as if to avoid a collision. The head-movement reaction suggests some sort of vision, and you begin to examine the visual information that will induce this natural reaction regularly. Does the creature actually perceive an approaching object? Or does it simply respond to changes in the height or width of an object? You launch a series of inquiries to find out.

You soon discover another method for studying the creature's visual perception. You notice that it looks at some objects for fairly extensive periods and at others hardly at all. There is little apparent rhyme or reason to these preferences, but this gives you a powerful tool—you can present the creature with pairs of objects, carefully controlling the differences between them. By studying the minimum differences necessary for the creature to show a preference, you can make an estimate of its visual acuity. And by presenting the objects at different distances from the creature, you can examine its focusing ability.

The preference method is useful, but limited to cases where one object is preferred over another. How can you test discrimination between objects that are equally preferred? This has you stumped for a while, but then you think of a phenomenon you can exploit, a phenomenon that psychologists call habituation (commonly known as boredom). If you put an object in front of the creature, it is likely to spend time looking at it. But after a while it will habituate or get bored, and looking time will drop. Now you can present a subtly different object, perhaps one of a slightly different color. Will looking time or interest increase? If it does, the creature has communicated to you that it sees the two objects differently. Using this technique with colored chips, you discover the creature has color vision. And using the technique with pictures of faces, you discover it can tell faces apart. Apparently, the creature can recognize people. This creature is beginning to appear much more competent than you originally thought. Although its motor abilities may be limited, it can see a great deal!

In case you haven't guessed already, your creature is a human infant. And the natural reaction, preference, and habituation techniques all can be used to study how infants see.

P R E V I E W

Sensation and perception are the processes we use to gather and interpret information from the world. A major interest is when and in what ways these processes change during the course of children's development. Does a newborn infant see? Can a fetus hear? Can a newborn experience pain? Can an infant piece together auditory and visual information? These are among the intriguing questions we evaluate in this chapter. We begin, however, by simply exploring why it is important to study sensory and perceptual development, then turn to theories of perceptual development and techniques used to study perceptual development. Next we enter the exciting world of the infant's visual perception, move on to auditory perception, and then consider the topic of bimodal perception. We conclude the chapter with an overview of what is known about the other senses in children's development.

WHY STUDY SENSORY AND PERCEPTUAL DEVELOPMENT?

There are three basic answers to the question of why we study sensory and perceptual development. The first is simply that our sensory and perceptual experiences raise a number of fascinating questions any naturally curious person would want to answer if possible (Bornstein, 1984). How accurately do we perceive—is the world actually similar to the way that we experience it? How is it possible that the world appears stable when we are constantly moving our eyes and head? Given that perception is based on two-dimensional images projected on our retinas, how can we perceive three-dimensional space? Why does a siren get higher in pitch as a fire engine comes toward us? How does one explain individual differences in people's tolerance for pain?

A second answer has its roots in philosophy, specifically in epistemology. **Epistemology** is concerned with the origins of human knowledge, with how a person comes to know the world. Two traditional approaches to epistemological questions involve the **nativist** answer, which appeals to "prewired" genetic knowledge and processes, and the **empiricist** answer, which appeals to the process of learning through experience. Today we recognize that neither the nativist nor the empiricist answer can account for acquisition of knowledge; prewired structures and learning experiences must interact in the course of development. Still, there remains the crucial problem of determining just how nature and nurture interact. The study of perceptual development is central to this problem (Hochberg, 1978).

A third answer is that perceptual development is relevant to a host of practical problems of great relevance in our lives. For example, learning to read is partly a problem of learning and differentiating the letters of the alphabet. That this is not an easy task is revealed by childrens' frequent left-right-reversal errors in writing (writing *d* instead of *b,* for example) (Bornstein, Gross & Wolf, 1978). If we had better knowledge of perception in young children, we might be able to speed this process of letter learning, and also help dyslexic children, who have special problems with it (Gibson & Levin, 1975).

THEORETICAL AND METHODOLOGICAL APPROACHES TO PERCEPTION

Given that perceptual development in infants and young children is an important area of study, we need theories to guide our research. We also need methods to investigate sensory and perceptual development.

Theories of Perception

Today two theoretical frameworks are more dominant than others: the **constructivist viewpoint** of Jean Piaget and information-processing psychologists and the **ecological framework** of Eleanor and James Gibson and their followers. We briefly discuss each framework in turn.

The Constructivist Framework

Sit up and look about the room that surrounds you. Although you may not realize it, as you take in the room your eyes are almost constantly moving. They move two or three times a second, and they provide visual data only when they pause between movements. Moreover, the angle of highest-acuity (foveal) vision is extremely small—about two degrees. Thus, each fixation is giving you high-resolution information of a very limited slice of space. It is as if you were trying to examine a totally dark room armed only with a narrow-beam flashlight that you could move around. Yet rapid fixations are not what you experience. What you experience is a stable

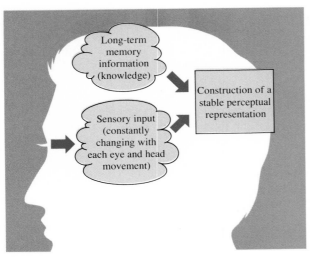

FIGURE 4.1
According to the constructivist, experience is a construction based on visual sensory input plus information retrieved from memory.

FIGURE 4.2
An example of invariants in the ecological framework. The telephone poles in this display are all cut by the horizon in the same ratio. The proportion differs for objects of different heights. The line where the horizon cuts the tree is just as high above the ground as the point of observation, that is, the height of the observer's eye. Hence everyone can see his own *eye-height* on the standing objects of the terrain (Gibson, 1979).

room extended in space around you—you even experience the room behind your head, where you cannot visually sense it. What is the basis for such experience? The constructivist has a provocative answer. What you experience is a construction based on the sensory input from your eyes *plus* information retrieved from memory. It is a kind of *representation* of the world that you build up in your mind. Figure 4.1 illustrates this conceptualization.

A constructivist viewpoint has important implications for the study of perception across the life span. It suggests that many changes in perception reflect changes in constructive activities and/or changes in long-term memory knowledge on which constructive activities are based. That is, changes in perception are bound up with changes in our internal representations of reality.

The great Swiss theoretician Jean Piaget is best known for his constructivist views on the development of intelligence (chapter 6). However, he also viewed perception in constructivist terms. Information-processing psychologists (chapter 7) take a constructivist approach to perception as well (Neisser, 1967). However, another group of ecologically oriented thinkers take issue with the idea that perception is constructive. They argue that we can directly perceive information existing in the environment around us. We need not build representations of the world within our heads; information about the world is available "out there."

The Ecological Framework

Look at figure 4.2 and ask yourself whether the telephone poles are of equal height. If you answered yes, you are correct (assuming the ground in the picture is flat), but how did you know? James Gibson points out that there is an **invariant** in the visual information that specifies the constancy in height. Indeed, it specifies your own height relative to the telephone poles. Note the point at which the horizon line intersects each of the poles. There is a constant ratio between the length of the pole above this point and the length of the pole below it (the ratio is about 2:1 in the drawing). This ratio is an invariant that tells you that the height of the poles is constant. Further, the point of intersection on each pole shows the height of your eyes above the ground (the point would be even with your eyes if you were standing right next to the pole). If you do not believe this, try the experiment in the real world. Find some level ground with telephone poles and look at the point at which the horizon intersects each pole. Then stand on something (e.g., your car) and look at the poles again. The point of intersection will be noticeably higher.

Eleanor Gibson (1969), James Gibson (1979), and other ecological theorists argue that the invariants in stimulation to our sensory receptors provide rich information about many aspects of the world. These aspects pertain to events (e.g., one billiard ball hitting another and setting it in motion), objects (the face of

The spatial layout of a neighborhood or city is an example of a perceptual invariant.

a friend), places (the spatial layout of your neighborhood or your entire city), and pictures (your favorite painting at the museum). Since these things are actually in the world and since perceptual invariants specify their properties, you need not build up internal representations in order to perceive them. You need only attend to the appropriate information.

A notable feature of the ecological approach is its assumption that even complex things (e.g., spatial layout) may be perceived directly (i.e., through picking up invariants), without complicated constructive activity. If complex things can be directly perceived, perhaps they can be perceived at young ages—perhaps even by very young infants. Thus, the ecological framework has inspired investigators to search for the competencies that very young infants possess (Bower, 1982). Of course, ecological theorists do not deny that perception develops as infants and children grow up. In fact, it is assumed that as perceptual processes mature, a child grows more efficient at discovering invariant properties of the information available to his or her senses.

Techniques for Studying Infant Sensation and Perception

Partly because of the ecological framework, there has been a tremendous surge of interest in studying perception in infants. But how does one examine what an infant can perceive? Since an infant is preverbal and has limited motor skills, it is a daunting challenge to explore his or her perceptual world. However, in recent years, we have seen the invention of many clever techniques that make it possible for psychologists to meet this challenge. Since we will be covering material on infant perception at various points throughout this chapter, it is useful to get an overview of how some of these techniques work. Although there has been much use of psychophysiological techniques, of greater relevance to the present chapter are the behavioral techniques of natural responses, preferences, habituation, and conditioned head rotation. We now briefly describe these four techniques.

Natural Responses

Observing natural responses is probably the simplest way to study an infant's perception. Present the infant with a stimulus, and observe how he or she responds. Some types of responses can tell us a good deal about what the infant perceives. For example, if we give a baby something sour to taste and see that she purses her lips, we have good evidence for a sense of taste (Steiner, 1979)! The problem, of course, is that some natural responses may be subtle or ambiguous. Indeed, some of an infant's perceptions just might not lead to any naturally observable response.

Preferences

Another simple method involves the **preference technique,** looking for evidence that an infant prefers one stimulus to another. If it is visual perception you are interested in, you can place two visual stimuli in front of an infant and determine which stimulus the infant looks at more (Fantz, 1958). If you have a question about sense of smell, you can place an odorous substance on each side of an infant's head, and see if the infant turns toward one more than the other. If sense of taste is your concern, you can give an infant the opportunity to suck at two nipples, one with substance A (e.g., sweetened water) and the other with substance B (e.g., unsweetened water). If the infant sucks at one nipple more than the other, evidence for a preference exists (Desor, Maller & Greene, 1977).

Data on preferences are important in themselves. We need to know what infants like and do not like. However, observations of preferences have also been valuable in showing infants' ability to distinguish between things. In order to prefer one stimulus to another, an infant must be able to tell them apart. Unfortunately, the converse does not hold. An infant may be able to distinguish two stimuli but find them equally interesting. If so, he or she will show no preference.

Habituation

Habituation is perhaps the most popular technique for studying infants' perceptual worlds. You present an infant with a stimulus (say, a colored circle). You monitor her interest in this stimulus (perhaps you measure the percentage of time she spends fixating it with her eyes). You repeat the stimulus and monitor her interest again. And again . . . and again. With repeated presentation of the very same stimulus, the infant's interest drops off (as would anyone's).

After habituation has occurred, you present a different stimulus (perhaps a different-colored circle). If the infant can distinguish this new stimulus from the original stimulus, she is likely to show **dishabituation,** that is, renewed interest. The occurrence of habituation and dishabituation shows that the infant can discriminate between the two stimuli (it can show evidence for color vision). Further, the technique can be adapted to study memory and formation of concepts. It is truly a powerful tool. To learn in more detail how an actual research study involving habituation and dishabituation is conducted, read Perspective on Child Development 4.1.

PERSPECTIVE ON CHILD DEVELOPMENT 4.1

DO INFANTS PERCEIVE NUMBER?

Recently the popular press has drawn our attention to the possibility of teaching basic concepts in mathematics to very young children and even infants. A few programs have sprung up to teach infants and toddlers to count, discriminate forms, and even understand abstract algebraic relations. It is too soon to tell whether these programs will be successful or have a substantial impact on children's later development. One thing is certain, though. Before we invest much effort in trying to teach such skills to infants, we must determine first what their basic capacities are. What evidence do we have, for example, that infants can work with numerical concepts?

A rather dramatic demonstration of one important competency has been offered by Mark Strauss and Susan Curtis (1982). Utilizing an habituation procedure, they demonstrated that infants as young as ten to twelve months are able to discriminate between a complex stimulus containing three items and one containing either four or two items. These same children, however, are not able to discriminate between four and five items. This is a startling discovery. One possible conclusion is that year-old infants can count as high as three or four items but no higher. This interpretation is probably false. More likely, infants are able to notice in a single perceptual act up to five variations in the number of objects. Among older children, such implicit sensitivity to number without recourse to counting is

Conditioned Head Turning

The technique of **conditioned head turning** is reliable and has grown in popularity. An infant sits on her mother's lap. A sound comes from a speaker. If the infant turns toward the speaker, she sees a colorful mechanical toy in motion (the toy is turned on by the experimenter). This is rewarding, and the infant soon learns to look toward the speaker whenever she hears a sound coming from it. It is possible to manipulate the loudness of the sound, determining the infant's threshold for hearing (Schneider, Trehub & Bull, 1980). The technique can also be used to test discrimination between two different sounds (e.g., two different melodies).

In the following sections, we first explore visual perception in infancy and childhood. Then we turn to auditory perception and finally to the other senses.

VISUAL PERCEPTION

How do we see? Anyone who has ever taken photographs on vacation can appreciate the miracle of vision. The camera is no match for it. Consider a favorite scenic spot that you have visited and photographed sometime in the past. Compare your memory of this spot to the photo that you took. Although your memory may be faulty, there can be very little doubt that the richness of your perceptual experience is not captured in the photo. The sense of depth that you felt at this spot probably is not conveyed by the photo either. Nor is the subtlety of the colors you perceived, or the intricacies of textures and shapes. Human vision is highly complex, and its development is complex as well. But this complexity should not deter us. Each step in understanding how visual perception develops is well worth the effort.

---

referred to as **subitizing.** Some critical details of Strauss' and Curtis's demonstration are presented next.

Ninety-six infants between ten and twelve months of age were presented with a series of slides to examine. The slides showed pictures of common objects such as dogs, houses, and dolls. In one critical manipulation, the slides varied in several respects on each presentation (e.g., the size of the picture, its relative placement in the visual field) but always contained the same number of objects (e.g., three things). After a series of presentations, the infants gradually spent less time looking at each slide, displaying the phenomenon we have described as habituation, that is, the gradual decrease of response intensity after repeated presentation of an event perceived as identical.

Following habituation, the critical test trials were presented. In these trials, the infants were presented with two slides containing the same number of items as in the habituation series (familiar number) and two slides containing one more or one less than the preceding number (new number). In all cases the depicted objects in the slides were similar. Children showed greater interest in the slides with the new number than with the familiar number of objects. That is, they attended more to the new items; in technical terms, dishabituation occurred. Since there were no other characteristics infants could use to discriminate between the familiar and new slides, the inescapable conclusion is that they discriminated between the *familiar* and *new* number of things.

We owe many provocative statements to the psychologist William James. Among the most quoted of all his remarks is one concerning the perceptual world of the newborn: "a great blooming, buzzing confusion" (James, 1890, p. 488). Is the visual perception of newborn infants actually consistent with this quote? Almost one hundred years later, we have learned that the answer is no. There recently has been a great burst of research on the visual perception of infants, including newborn infants only minutes or hours old. To sum up this research with one simple statement, infants' perception of visual information is *much* more advanced than we previously had thought.

In the pages that follow we first treat visual preferences in infancy, describing an important line of research that was pioneered by Robert Fantz (1958, 1961). Then we turn to studies of a similar nature on perceiving simple, "lower-order" types of visual information, including detail (visual acuity) and color. We will see that perception of these lower-order variables develops rather rapidly, sometimes maturing by two months of age. The section continues with research on perception of "higher-order" information, information such as that for depth and for the unity of objects, information about distinguishing different faces, and information about spatial relations among things in the environment.

Visual Preferences

Our tour of infant visual perception begins with the studies of Robert Fantz (1958, 1961), a true pioneer in this area. Fantz's technique was to place his infant subjects in a "looking chamber" (see figure 4.3) and to attach two visual displays at the ceiling of the chamber above the infant's head. An experimenter viewed the infant's eyes by looking through a peephole. If the infant was fixating on one of the displays, the experimenter was able to see its reflection in the infant's eyes, as shown in figure 4.4. Thus, it was possible for the experimenter to monitor the duration of looking at each display. The basic result is simple: When presented with a pair of visual displays, an infant will typically look longer at one than at the other. For example, infants look longer at a display of stripes than at a display of a solid gray patch. Even newborn infants will show such preferences in looking time. This indicates that they

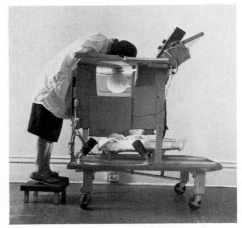

FIGURE 4.3
The looking chamber used to study visual preferences.

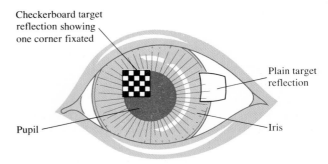

FIGURE 4.4
Schematic drawing of an infant's eye as seen in the looking chamber by the experimenter when checked and plain squares are exposed. This illustrates the limiting condition for satisfying the criterion of fixation. More generally the target reflection would overlap the pupil to a greater degree (Fantz, 1966).

can *see,* and more importantly that they can **discriminate** differing visual stimuli. Thus, human newborns are not blind, and their visual world is not just a "confusion." It is sufficiently coherent to allow for visual preferences.

In the years since Fantz's original discoveries, infants' visual preferences have been heavily researched. We have learned not only that infants have visual preferences but also that these preferences change as infants grow older. For example, figure 4.5 shows the results of a study on preferences for a bull's-eye versus

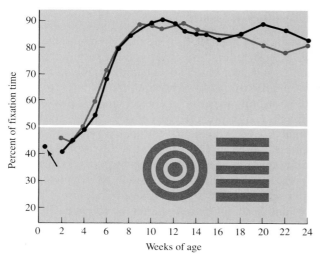

FIGURE 4.5
Relative preference for a bull's-eye versus a grating at different ages (Banks and Salapatek).

"What you're looking at could make you a very rich man."

a grating (Fantz & Nevis, 1967). While newborn infants showed a slight preference for the grating, by eight weeks of age they preferred the bull's-eye. Subsequent research showed that the bull's-eye preference in infants two months and older is due to more than one factor. In other research infants preferred curved over straight-line patterns (Fantz, Fagan & Miranda, 1975). Infants' preference for stimuli with multiple line orientations and concentric patterns also has been documented (Ruff & Birch, 1974). Thus, the attractiveness of the bull's-eye pattern reflects infants' preferences for curves, concentric shapes, and lines in many directions. Although we do not yet fully understand infants' preferences, several researchers have speculated that the visual patterns infants prefer are those that stimulate greater neural activity in the infant's cortex (Bornstein, 1978; Haith, 1980; Karmel & Maisel, 1975). Such activity is believed to be helpful for the neurological development of the brain.

Visual Acuity and Accommodation in Infancy

Given that infants are not blind at birth, we are led to ask just how well they can see. Extensions of Fantz's preference method have been used to measure infants' visual acuity. A careful review of this literature (Banks

& Salapatek, 1983) suggests that visual acuity in newborn infants is about 20/600 in Snellen notation (the kind of notation used by your optometrist). This is about thirty times lower than adult visual acuity (20/20). But by six months of age acuity appears to be 20/100 or higher. To appreciate what 20/100 means, remember having your vision tested with an old-style Snellen chart. The single large E at the top of such charts requires 20/200 vision. The next row of such charts requires 20/100.

A question related to visual acuity is the effectiveness of **accommodation,** that is, maintenance of high visual acuity over a range of viewing distances. It was once believed that infant acuity was best for objects about eight inches away, and became much worse for objects nearer or farther away. You may have read in books or magazines that a newborn baby may not see your face clearly unless it is positioned about eight inches away. Indeed, focusing errors by the eye of a newborn are much greater than those of a three-month-old. Surprisingly, however, this has little direct impact on infants' perception of near and far objects. A number of studies show that visual acuity in one-month-olds does not vary as a function of viewing distance (Fantz, Ordy & Udelf, 1962; Salapatek, Bechtold & Bushnell, 1976). Although this sounds paradoxical, it can be explained by the limited acuity of young infants' vision, as well as considerations of depth of focus. In regard to visual acuity, the limited resolution of vision in infants makes extremely sharp focusing simply unnecessary. In regard to depth of focus, one relevant factor is the diameter of the pupils (the openings in the irises) of a young infant's eyes. This diameter is relatively small. Because it is small, an external object can be moved through a large range of distances while remaining in fairly good focus. Near-sighted people who squint to see clearly reveal this same principle.

Perception of Color

For the majority of us who have full color vision, it is difficult to imagine what monochromatic (noncolor) vision would be like. Certainly, a "color-blind" person can perceive most of what is important as he or she moves around the world. However, the mere fact of our preference for color photographs, color TV, and color computer monitors illustrates that color is something we use and/or prefer in vision. But what about infants? Do they see colors as well as normal adults see them? Or do infants resemble adults who are partially or totally color-blind?

Color vision in infants has been tested with the habituation technique. A colored light is shown repeatedly to an infant, and—after he or she habituates—an uncolored white light is shown. Using such a technique with three-month-olds, Mark Bornstein (1976) demonstrated dishabituation with a number of colors that adult dichromats are unable to see. His results suggested that three-month-old infants are in command of full color vision. Research with younger infants is not entirely consistent (Pulos, Teller & Buck, 1980). However, one recent study (Maurer, Lewis, Cavanagh & Anstis, 1985) suggests adultlike functioning in all three types of color-sensitive receptors (cones) in one- to two-month-old infants.

Perception of Depth

You may not find it surprising that young infants show visual preferences and that visual acuity, accommodation, and color vision develop quite rapidly in the first few months of infancy. However, we turn now to some truly amazing experiments on infants' "higher-order" perception of depth, the unity of objects, the subtle differences among faces, and the spatial relations among objects. Much of this provocative research has been stimulated by the ecological approach (e.g., Gibson & Spelke, 1983), which stresses that even higher-order information is directly available to the sensory receptors and need not be constructed by the mind. If such information need not be constructed, it might be perceived very early in life. And a good deal of research suggests that it is.

Since an image on the retina has only two dimensions, our perception of depth—the third dimension—is a very clear case of higher-order perception. The classic study of depth perception in infants was conducted by Eleanor Gibson and Richard Walk (1960) using the **visual cliff.** (See figure 4.6.) A central board above two checkerboard floors forms a high "cliff" on one side and a shallow "cliff" on the other. But a sheet of glass is above both checkerboard floors, at roughly the same level as the central board. Thus, an infant can crawl all over the apparatus and never suffer a fall. Yet crawling on the high side *appears* to be dangerous. An infant between six and fourteen months old is less likely to crawl on this deep side than on the shallow side. Apparently, then, six- to fourteen-month-old infants have some ability to see the depth of surfaces, as well as many other aspects of surfaces (Gibson, 1985).

Exactly how early in life does depth perception develop? Since younger infants do not crawl, this question has proven difficult to answer. Research with two- to four-month-olds has shown differences in heart rate when the infants are placed directly on the deep side of the cliff versus the shallow side of the cliff (Campos, Langer & Krowitz, 1970). These heart-rate differences might imply depth perception at two to four months. However, an alternative interpretation is that young infants are responding to differences in some visual characteristic of the deep and shallow cliffs, with no actual knowledge of depth. Thus, although infants

FIGURE 4.6
A child's depth perception is tested on the visual cliff. The apparatus consists of a board laid across a sheet of heavy glass, with a patterned material directly beneath the glass on one side and several feet below it on the other. Placed on the center board, the child crawls to his mother across the "shallow side." Called from the "deep" side, he pats the glass (see left), but despite this tactual evidence that the "cliff" is in fact a solid surface, he refuses to cross over to the mother.

see depth by the time that they can crawl, precisely when they see depth has not yet been determined.

Fortunately, there are alternative techniques that may reveal information about the depth-perception abilities of very young infants. For example, some recent studies by Albert Yonas, Carl Granrud, and their colleagues have taken advantage of the fact that infants tend to reach toward the *nearer* of two objects that they see. In one of their studies (Yonas, Granrud & Pettersen, 1985), the researchers found that five-and-a-half- and seven-month-olds also reach toward the *larger* of two objects, *if* these objects are viewed through one eye. This finding suggests that in the absence of binocular (two-eye) information, infants as young as five-and-a-half-months (a) perceive depth and (b) use size as a cue for depth. Although infants under five-and-a-half-months did not use size as a depth cue, they apparently can use other types of cues for depth (Granrud, Yonas, Smith, Arterberry, Glicksman & Sorknes, 1984). Moreover, research using the habituation technique suggests that even twelve-week-old infants can perceive size independent of distance when viewing moving objects (Granrud, Arterberry & Yonas, 1985).

Perception of Objects

The objects in our visual world maintain a kind of unity even when partially hidden from view. For example, if a chair in your living room is partly occluded by the coffee table in front of it, you still see the chair as complete. It does not look like *part* of a chair but like a *whole* chair that is only partly visible from where you stand (J. J. Gibson, 1979). Imagine what our visual worlds would be like if we did not see objects as wholes—a constantly changing mishmash of colors? An abstract–expressionist motion picture? Perhaps the best answer is that it is impossible to imagine such visual worlds, since even our imagery is composed of perceptual objects (Kosslyn, 1980). In any event, if we want to understand how we see objects as wholes, we must explore the emergence of this ability in infants.

Some important work by Elizabeth Spelke (Kellman & Spelke, 1979, 1981; Spelke & Born, 1982) has clarified this issue of when infants perceive objects as unitary. In one condition of the Kellman and Spelke experiment, a four-month-old infant viewed a rod with a block placed in front of it. The rod moved slightly to the left and to the right during viewing. After the first viewing episode, two test stimuli were shown to the infant. These were (a) a complete rod with nothing in front of it, and (b) a rod with a gap and nothing in front of it. The result was that the infant looked longer at the rod with the gap than at the complete rod. This suggests that the first phase of the experiment produced habituation. More importantly, habituation apparently was to the complete rod, even though only part of the rod was seen. Thus, the Kellman and Spelke experiment showed that partly occluded objects are perceived as wholes by infants only four months old. Future research must determine whether two-month-olds, or even newborns, also perceive objects as units.

Face Perception

If there is any object that should be perceived as a unit, it is the face of another person. In an early study of perception of faces, Robert Fantz (1961) found that two-month-old infants showed a preference for viewing a normal versus a rearranged drawing of a face (see figure 4.7). Further, even newborns show differences in visual tracking when a moving face is shown as opposed to when a moving rearranged face is shown (Goren, Sarty & Wu, 1975). Thus, there is evidence suggesting that even newborn infants are sensitive to properties of faces. But this does not mean that they can recognize individual faces.

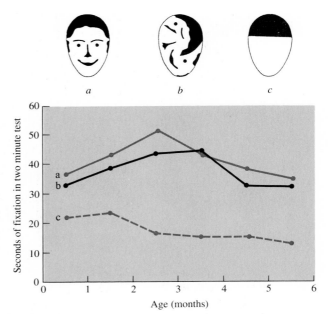

FIGURE 4.7

Adaptive signficance of form perception was indicated by the preference that infants showed for a "real" face (*a*) over a scrambled face (*b*), and for both over a control (*c*). The results charted here show the average time scores for infants of various ages when presented with the three face-shaped objects paired in all the possible combinations.

The adaptable preference and habituation techniques can be applied to the problem of face perception. Infants are shown one face, and then their responses to that same face versus a new face are compared. If the infants have habituated to the first face and if they have the ability to distinguish this face from the new face, they will show more attention to the new face than the old face. For example, in one study five-and-a-half-month-old infants showed a visual preference for looking at a new face, as compared to an habituated face (Fagen, 1972). Other studies have suggested such discrimination as early as three months of age (Gibson & Spelke, 1983), but no younger. Although a younger infant may seem to visually recognize his or her mother, the infant probably is relying on hearing, smell, and/or touch information, not visual face recognition.

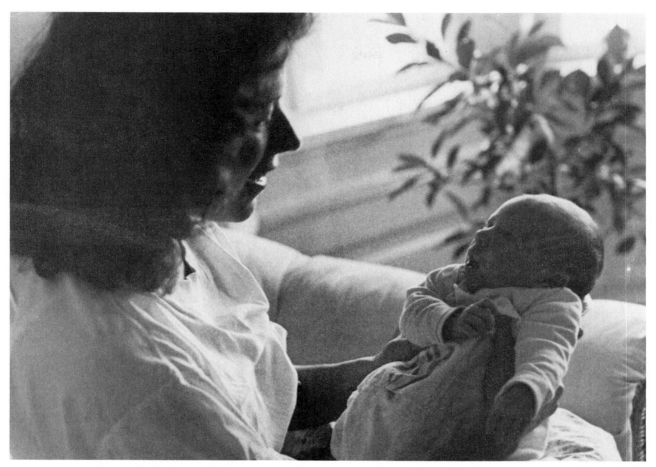

While infants younger than 3 months of age may recognize their mother, they likely are relying on sensory information other than visual recognition.

Although perceptual identification of individual faces emerges in infancy, it continues developing throughout childhood. One method of studying face perception in childhood is the **simultaneous comparison method,** which is illustrated in figure 4.8. A child looks at the top face and attempts to decide which (if any) of the comparison faces represents the same person. A second method is that of **face recognition.** After viewing a number of photographs of faces, subjects take a test in which they try to distinguish copies of these photographs from photographs of entirely new people. Although the face recognition depends on memory, it provides results that are similar to those of the simultaneous comparison task. Both tasks show that face perception improves until about sixteen years of age. This extended period of development is puzzling in itself. But contained within this puzzle is a still deeper puzzle: The development of face perception does not follow a straightforward and gradual increase. Rather, face perception improves through young childhood, then stops improving or even declines in the years after puberty, and finally does not begin improving again until late adolescence, as indicated in figure 4.9 (Benton & Van Allen, 1973; Carey, Diamond & Woods, 1981).

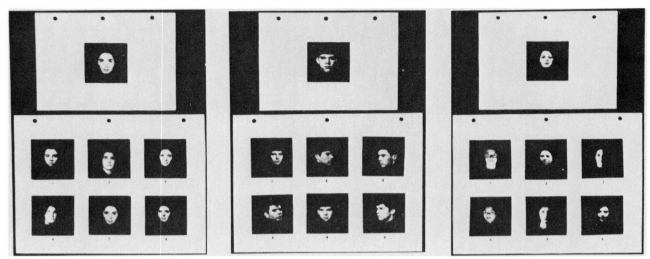

FIGURE 4.3
Left: Test item calling for matching of identical front views.
Center: Test item calling for matching of frontal view with three-quarter views. Right: Test item calling for matching of frontal views under different lighting conditions.

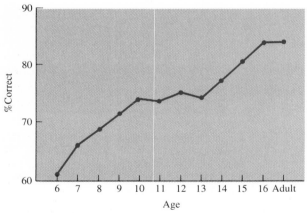

FIGURE 4.9
Performance on Benton and Van Allen's task of facial recognition. Data for ages six and seven and for adults from Benton & Van Allen (1973); data for ages eight to eleven from Benton & Van Allen (1973) and from Experiment 3 of Carey, Diamond, & Woods (1980); data for ages twelve to sixteen from Experiment 3 of Carey, Diamond & Woods (1980).

One interpretation of this fascinating finding is that maturational events associated with the onset of puberty actually disrupt, temporarily, face encoding processes (Carey, 1981). In any event, our abilities to visually recognize people apparently are based on very complex processes. Unraveling these processes is a challenge for future research.

Perception of Spatial Relations

As we move around through a new environment, we develop a sense of where things are located. But when we have learned where something is located, just what exactly have we learned? What *frame of reference* have we used in learning the locations of objects? We might learn the location of a building relative to ourselves ("the shopping center is to my right"). This is an example of using an **egocentric frame of reference.** Alternatively, we might learn the location of this same building relative to various landmarks in the area (we might have the same sort of information that a map conveys). This is an example of using a nonegocentric or **objective frame of reference.** Jean Mandler (1983) argues that adults use both egocentric and objective frames of reference, depending on the situation. For example, many of us learn the routes to new places in an egocentric way ("Go to main street, turn right, and then go straight ahead until you get to the shopping mall . . . then turn right at the first light, and left at the light after that, and you will see my house on the corner on your right"). Yet in other situations an objective framework dominates (we realize there must be a shortcut to a place we have visited before, and then discover this shortcut by using "sense of direction"). In general, egocentric representations appear to be associated with knowledge of "routes" and objective representations with "map" or "survey" type knowledge allowing shortcuts and sense of direction. A recent study by Sally Doherty and James Pellegrino (1985) suggests that route knowledge of one's own neighborhood is better for nine- to twelve-year-old children than seven- to eight-year-old children. And fifteen-year-old children appear to have not only good knowledge of routes through their neighborhoods but good survey knowledge of these neighborhoods as well.

If adults can use both egocentric and objective frames of reference, what about young infants? Jean Piaget (1971) argued that in the first year of life infants are restricted to egocentric orientation. Indeed, a number of recent empirical studies lend some support to this claim. For example, in a study conducted by Linda Acredolo (1978), infants six, eleven, and sixteen months old were placed at one end of a room, from which position they could view two windows (see figure 4.10). A buzzer sounded and three seconds later an experimenter appeared in one of the two windows, calling the infant's name and entertaining her with toys. This procedure continued until the infant learned which window to look toward. After this, the infant was moved (by her mother) to the opposite side of the room (from S_1 to S_2 in figure 4.10) and testing resumed. The finding was that six- and eleven-month-old infants responded egocentrically, looking in the same direction—relative to their bodies–that they had looked in before (this meant they looked toward the wrong window). Only

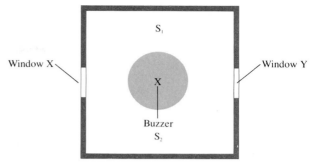

FIGURE 4.10
The experimental space used by Acredolo (1978).

the sixteen-month-old infants consistently responded with an objective frame of reference (looked in a new direction but toward the correct window). In other research with a similar technique, Acredolo (1977) found a continuing drop in using egocentric reference from three to five years of age. She also found that the provision of landmarks (e.g., a star painted around one of the windows) and a familiar environment (the child's own home) increase objective responding by younger children (Acredolo, 1978, 1979; Acredolo & Evans, 1978).

The early emergence of objective frames of reference may derive from infants' body movements. As an infant starts to crawl around, the changing (egocentric) directions of stationary objects may become quite noticeable (what was on the right is now on the left after turning around). This may lead the infant to start attending to landmarks, and this puts him or her on the road to establishing true objective reference frames (Bremner, 1985; Bryant, 1985). In any event, objective frames of reference are clearly in evidence by the end of the infancy period (two years). Indeed, there appear to be cases in which preschoolers find it difficult to use an egocentric frame of reference (Allen, Kirasic & King, 1985).

Another aspect of spatial perception is acquiring knowledge of large-scale spaces, spaces too large to be seen all at once. If you are sitting in your bedroom and

One aspect of spatial perception is acquiring knowledge of large-scale spaces.

the door is shut, can you identify what lies beyond each wall? Can you point toward the TV in the living area, or the stove in the kitchen? And what about the spatial locations of your house, your school, and the downtown area of the city where you live? Can you sketch a map showing all of these locations? Chances are you can perform all of these tasks with some degree of accuracy. But some of us—those with a "good sense of direction"—are much better at such tasks than others (Kozlowski & Bryant, 1977). The rest of us—those with a mediocre or poor sense of direction—generally regard this as a significant failing. The study of development of "mapping" in young children may help us

discover why individual differences in sense of direction occur. Further, mapping in children is important in its own right. How many cases of children getting lost are due to their difficulties in mapping large-scale space?

In an experiment on the development of mapping ability (Hazen, Lockman & Pick, 1978), three- to five-year-old children were led on a route through four rooms, each containing a toy. After training in identifying which doors to use and which toys would be encountered in successive rooms, the children were given a reversed-route test. All of the children showed some ability to choose which doors to go through and to identify toys that would be encountered when they took the

CONCEPT TABLE 4.1
Visual Perception in Infancy and Childhood

Concept	Important Methodological Technique(s)	Development
Preferences	Preferential looking	Preferences for some patterns are present at birth, but preferred patterns change because of maturation of the visual system.
Visual acuity	Preferential looking and others	Visual acuity is about 20/600 at birth, but it rapidly improves up to six months of age.
Accommodation	Preferential looking and others	Although focusing errors decrease with age, accommodation is constant over a range of distances.
Color	Habituation	Adultlike trichromatic vision is present by three months; younger infants may be partially color-blind.
Depth	Visual cliff (natural response) and others	Perception of depth is present by approximately six months (crawling age) and possibly sooner.
Objects	Habituation and others	The unity of objects is perceived by four months.
Faces	Habituation, simultaneous comparison, and recognition	Recognition of individual faces is present as early as three months, but face recognition continues to develop in childhood and adolescence.
Spatial relations	Conditioned head turning (in infants), object search, and others	Egocentric reference is present in the first year, depending on landmarks and familiarity of the context. However, spatial perception—especially that of large-scale space—continues to develop in childhood.

reverse route. However, younger children made more errors. Furthermore, all of the children were relatively poor at making inference judgments—that is, judgments of the toy behind a door that they had not traveled through during training. Thus, there are deficiencies in young childrens' learning of large-scale layouts, though what perhaps is more surprising is that children as young as three years old learn such layouts as well as they do. An important next step is to determine why some children are better at mapping than others.

We have discussed many different aspects of visual perception so far. A summary of these ideas is presented in Concept Table 4.1.

HEARING AND SPEECH PERCEPTION

In this section we first consider sensitivity to simple sounds, localization of sounds, and voice perception and recognition. Then we turn to "higher-order" skills of speech and music perception. We will see that even these higher-order skills develop quite early.

Sensitivity to Simple Sounds

Is there hearing prior to birth? Can a fetus in the womb hear his or her mother's voice and other auditory stimuli? If you ask this question of an expectant mother in her eighth or ninth month of pregnancy, you are likely to get an answer of yes. Pregnant mothers have reported movements by their babies in response to loud noises (Forbes & Forbes, 1927). More careful investigations have documented fetal movement (Sontag & Wallace, 1935) and heart-rate changes (Bernard & Sontag, 1947) in response to auditory stimuli. Unfortunately, the auditory stimuli used in these early studies produced vibrations that might have created tactile sensations. Thus, the infants might have not have heard the stimuli but rather felt them through sense of touch (Aslin, Pison & Jusczyk, 1983). Although more recent studies have used more refined methods, prenatal hearing remains an open question. We do know, however, that when an auditory stimulus is presented to a fetus several weeks before birth, there is an electrophysiological response in the fetus's auditory system

(Sakabe, Arayama & Suzuki, 1969). This does not prove that the fetus can hear, but it certainly suggests that possibility.

Hearing in infants immediately after birth is much less controversial. There is agreement that newborns can hear but that their sensory thresholds are somewhat higher than those of adults. That is, a stimulus must be louder to be heard by newborns than to be heard by adults. However, the locations of these thresholds for sounds of different frequencies (pitches) have not been firmly established (Aslin et al., 1983). One problem has been a lack of control over the auditory stimuli themselves. Another problem has been the identification of a behavioral response that reliably indicates that a stimulus was heard. For example, auditory thresholds in infants have been assessed by examining startle reactions (Suzuki, Kamijo & Kiuchi, 1964), changes in respiration rate (Barnet & Goodwin, 1965), and changes in heart rate (Steinschneider, Lipton & Richmond, 1966). While these studies agree that infants' thresholds are higher than those of adults, they do not agree on the extent of this difference (Hecox, 1975). Measures of electrophysiological responses provide clearer evidence on auditory thresholds in infants. Consistent with the behavioral data, thresholds for the electrophysiological responses are higher in infants than in adults, and the difference is at least ten decibels (Aslin et al., 1983).

Given that hearing is less sensitive in infants than adults, when and at what rate does it improve? Some research on this topic has used the technique of conditioned ("visually reinforced") head turning (Liden & Kankkunen, 1969; Moore, Thompson & Thompson, 1975; Schneider, Trehub & Bull, 1980; Trehub, Schneider & Endman, 1980). The data have shown that thresholds get lower (sensitivity improves) between infancy and adulthood but that infants as young as six months of age are relatively more sensitive to high frequency sounds (i.e., sounds at 10,000 Hz or higher, Aslin et al., 1983). Indeed, sensitivity to sounds of very high frequency (19,000 Hz) might be adultlike by twenty-four months (Schneider et al., 1980). (A 10,000-Hz tone is about one octave higher than the highest note on a piano—a 19,000-Hz tone is almost one octave higher still.)

Localization of Sounds

Studies using visually reinforced head turning are based on an interesting fact: Six-month-old infants can perceive where sounds are located in space. That is, the auditory world at six months of age consists not simply of sounds with different frequencies but of sounds that come from different places. It was traditionally believed that localization of sounds is not possible for newborns and emerges only at four or five months of age. But then a clever investigator (Wertheimer, 1961) presented click sounds to the right and left sides of newborn infants' heads. The infants showed an observable tendency to look right or left in the direction of the clicks! More recent studies have substantiated these findings of sound localization in newborns (e.g., Muir, Campbell, Low, Killen, Galbraith & Karchmar, 1978). However, there is some fascinating evidence that whereas newborn infants will look in the direction of sounds, infants forty to one hundred days old show a marked decrement in this behavior. Then, at around one hundred days of age, the behavior emerges again (Muir, Abraham, Forbes & Harris, 1979). Thus, while auditory space is present at birth, it may subsequently be lost for a period. Alternatively, sound localization may remain stable, while looking behavior temporarily declines.

Voice Perception and Recognition

Although it is impressive that newborns have a sense of *where* sounds are, do they also have a sense of *what* sounds are? Research suggests that one type of sound can be identified early—this is the sound of one's mother.

The **nonnutritive sucking technique** (Eimas, Sigueland, Jusczyk & Vigorito, 1971)—a variant of the habituation technique—was applied to the problem of voice recognition in infants (Mehler, Bertoncini, Barriere & Jassik-Gerschenfeld, 1978; Mills & Melhuish, 1974). One-month-old infants were given a nipple to suck, and strong sucks were rewarded with the sound of a stranger's voice. Infants initially showed a high rate of sucking. However, after a period in which the voice was not changed, sucking rate declined, showing habituation. At this point, the stranger's voice was replaced by either (a) a new stranger's voice or (b) the

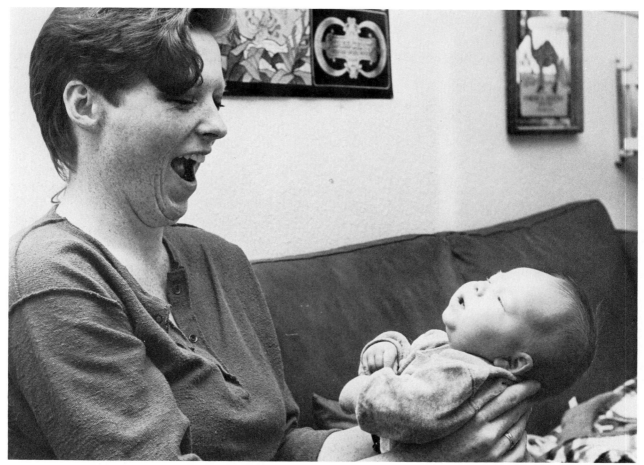

The sound of one's mother can be recognized very early in infancy.

voice of the infant's own mother. The infants sucked more to their mother's voice, showing that they could recognize it. Indeed, even three-day-old infants will show this effect (DeCasper & Fifer, 1980).

You might marvel that infants could learn their mother's voice in only three days. Perhaps they don't. Perhaps they start learning it when still in the womb (Aslin et al., 1983)! At any rate, if you enjoy talking to your newborn son or daughter, your efforts are not wasted. Although your little one does not understand the content of your speech, he or she may have a sense that it is you who are speaking. He or she probably also is sensitive to some basic speech sounds.

Perception of Speech

There are many puzzles in the literature on perceptual development, but none are deeper than those involving speech perception. Some of the most exciting research addressing this puzzle was initiated by Peter Eimas (Eimas et al., 1971), who studied infants' perception of simple stop consonants, such as *b, d, g, p, t, k*. These stop consonants can be classified in terms of several dimensions or features, one of which is **voicing**. You can experience for yourself the feature of voicing by putting your palm in front of your mouth while saying, "pa," "ta," "ka," and then "ba," "da," "ga." You should

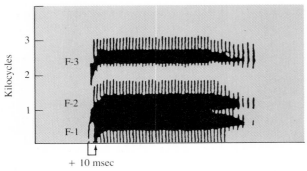

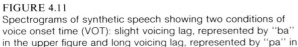

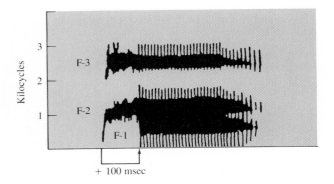

FIGURE 4.11
Spectrograms of synthetic speech showing two conditions of voice onset time (VOT): slight voicing lag, represented by "ba" in the upper figure and long voicing lag, represented by "pa" in the lower figure. The symbols F–1, F–2, and F–3 represent the first three formats, that is, the relatively intense bands of energy in the speech spectrum (Eimas et al., 1971).

feel an abrupt burst of air when uttering the first three syllables but not when uttering the final three syllables. The consonants of the first three syllables are *voiceless*, whereas the consonants of the final three syllables are *voiced*.

Features such as voicing are critically important for the perception of speech. However, the acoustic information that specifies such features can be incredibly subtle, as revealed by **sound spectrograms.** A spectrogram displays the intensity of sound as a function of both time and frequency. Figure 4.11 shows two sound spectrograms, one for "ba" and one for "pa." The difference—one of voicing—primarily concerns the lowest band of energy, that labeled F–1 in the graph. This F–1 band begins earlier for "ba" than for "pa," but the difference is the barest fraction of a second, about 90 milliseconds. Yet we perceive the difference between "ba" and "pa" effortlessly. You might think that such a subtle distinction might take years for a child to learn. In fact, it does not. Research conducted by Eimas and his colleagues used a variant of the nonnutritive sucking technique (described in the last section). They found that even one-month-old infants can tell "ba" from "pa." Additional studies showed perception of voicing with other stimulus pairs ("da" versus "ta"), and also perception of other speech features (e.g., place of articulation—e.g., "da" versus "ga"). Finally, there is

evidence that infants actually are sensitive to categories of speech—they respond to various examples of "pa" as being different from various examples of "ba." (Eimas, 1975; Morse, 1972.)

These amazing findings of speech perception by infants raise many questions about both perception and language. One of these questions is whether learning is necessary for performing subtle speech discriminations. Cross-language studies suggest the answer is not always. Infants make some discriminations that are not required in the language of their parents (Werker, Gilbert, Humphrey & Tees, 1981). Indeed, they appear to be better at some discriminations than are adults of their culture (Aslin et al., 1983)!

Although subtle discriminations between different speech sounds do not always depend on learning, there are ways in which speech perception develops with age. One way in which it develops concerns *awareness* of speech sounds, which is not the same thing as *discrimination* among speech sounds. Have you ever played the child's game of pig Latin? (Aveha ouya verea layedpa heta amega foa igpa atinla?) It is based on the simple rule of taking the first sound of a word, moving it to the end of this word, and adding an "a" sound. Although this game can be simple, it depends upon a type of awareness that not all children have. Further, this type of awareness is apparently related to childrens' ability to read (Crowder, 1982).

Nonreading children have trouble with pig Latin (Gleitman & Rozin, 1973). Further, other tests of awareness of speech sounds show marked improvements from about four years of age to about six years of age (Liberman, Shankweiler, Liberman & Fowler, 1977; Rozin, Bressman & Taft, 1974)—the period of time in which training in reading begins. In the Liberman et al. experiment, children indicated the number of speech sounds in words such as *eye* (one phoneme), *pie* (two phonemes), and *boat* (three phonemes). The four-year-old children could not perform the task, while the five-year-old children scored 17 percent correct, and the six-year-old children scored 70 percent correct. The low performance of the younger children was not due to an inability to count—they performed much better when the task was that of counting syllables instead of speech sounds. These data suggest that awareness of speech sounds is difficult for children to acquire. The data also imply that awareness of speech sounds may be a critical component of learning to read. Indeed, there is evidence that without training in reading, awareness of speech sounds may remain quite meager throughout a person's life (Morais, Cary, Alegria & Bertelson, 1979).

Perception of Melodies

If infants can identify voices and discriminate among speech sounds, can they hear music? Consider a mother singing a lullabye to her baby. The song may be soothing, but does the infant actually hear the melody? Or does the infant hear only a sequence of sounds?

The evidence favors the former possibility. Infants have been shown to detect changes in the tones of a multitone sequence (Chang & Trehub, 1977), changes in the ordering of tones within a sequence (Demany, 1982), and changes in the rhythm of a sequence of tones (Chang & Trehub, 1977), as well as other attributes.

An illustrative study (Trehub, Bull & Thorpe, 1984) used the method of visually reinforced head turning with eight- to eleven-month-olds. The infants heard many repetitions of a six-note melody. They were trained to turn their heads when a new melody was presented (if an infant turned his or her head when the new melody was played, a "reinforcer toy" was presented for the infant to see). The question was: What sorts of changes from the standard melody would be noticed by the infants? The results showed that infants were especially sensitive to changes in **melodic contour**—the sequences of ups and downs in pitch—and also to changes in the octaves of the individual notes. However, the infants were relatively insensitive to the precise intervals between successive notes.

The early sensitivity of infants to contour may be relevant to "motherese," a pervasive style in which adults in many cultures speak to their infants. Motherese appears to be characterized by an exaggeration of the pitch contours in speech (Fernald & Simon, 1981; Stern, Spieker & McKain, 1982). Further, such exaggerated contours appear to be preferred by four-month-old infants (Fernald & Kuhl, 1981). Infants' preference for exaggerated over nonexaggerated contours may not be present in all situations, particularly when the auditory stimuli consist of tones instead of voices (Colombo, 1985). However, there is no question that even four-month-old infants can discriminate among sounds with different pitch contours. This ability may be a building block for language as well as music cognition.

Of course, the development of music perception does not stop with detection of contour and other primitive features. Walter Dowling (1982) has recently reviewed what we know about such development throughout the childhood years. He notes that his own daughter at eighteen months appeared to recognize the "Sesame Street" theme. She would run to the television upon hearing this theme but not upon hearing other melodies. This observation converges with the fact that children of about this age often begin singing recognizable songs. Such songs are not adultlike; they do not stay within a key. But childrens' singing and their song recognition suggest an emerging ability to perceive and remember the intervals between notes.

The perception of music continues to develop long after the age of two. One extensive study focused on the perception and memory of very brief melodies by adults and children aged five years and up (Zenatti, 1969). There was improvement in performance with age, and with subjects aged six years and over, "tonal" melodies were remembered better than "atonal" melodies. These findings suggest that even six-year-old children perceive music with reference to musical scales (Bartlett & Dowling, 1980).

Children's singing and their song recognition reveal an emerging ability to perceive and remember the intervals between notes.

BIMODAL PERCEPTION

It may be somewhat misleading to discuss auditory perception as if it were completely separate from visual perception or from perception in any other modality. As Elizabeth Spelke (1979) points out, humans live in a world of objects and events that are heard, seen, and felt. When individuals look and listen to an event simultaneously, they experience a unitary episode, not one that is visually and auditorially separated. Spelke (1979) has conducted research demonstrating that infants only four months old have **bimodal perception,** the ability to perceive auditory and visual events in a related, unified manner. We do not know if the human newborn has bimodal perception, but the finding that newborns make eye movements toward sounds (Wertheimer, 1961) does suggest this. Additional information about Spelke's research on bimodal perception is presented in Perspective on Child Development 4.2.

PERSPECTIVE ON CHILD DEVELOPMENT 4.2

BIMODAL PERCEPTION OF VISUAL AND AUDITORY INFORMATION

Imagine yourself playing basketball or tennis. There are obviously many visual inputs: the ball coming and going, other players moving around, etc. But there also are many auditory inputs: the sound of the ball bouncing or being hit and the grunts, groans, and curses emitted by yourself and others. There is also good correspondence between much of the visual and auditory information: when you see the ball bounce, you also hear a bouncing sound; when a player leaps, you hear her groan.

As Elizabeth Spelke (1979) has pointed out: "Humans live in a world of objects and events that can be seen, heard, and felt. When mature perceivers look and listen to an event simultaneously, they experience a unitary episode" (p. 626).

All of this is so commonplace, it scarcely seems worth mentioning. But consider the task of a very young infant with little practice at perceiving. Can he or she put vision and sound together as precisely as adults? Jean Piaget (1952), along with earlier thinkers (Berkeley, 1709; Mill, 1829), believed that the answer is no. His claim was that bimodal perception is achieved only after a considerable period of learning to piece together visual and auditory information. However, the ecological approach of James J. Gibson (1979) and Eleanor J. Gibson (1969; Gibson & Spelke, 1983) suggests an alternative view: Perhaps there is higher-order information that is *invariant* over the auditory or visual modalities. If so, it is possible that even young infants can perceive such information. Recall the discussion at the start of this chapter on direct perception of higher-order information in infancy. Bimodal information might simply be another type of higher-order information that is readily perceived in infancy.

To test bimodal perception, Spelke (1979) performed three experiments with the following structure: Two simple films were shown side-by-side in front of a four-month-old infant. One film showed a yellow kangaroo bouncing up and down, and the other showed a gray donkey bouncing up and down. There also was an auditory sound track—a repeating thump or gong sound. A variety of measures assessed the tendency of the infant to look at one film versus the other.

In Experiment 1, the animal in one of the films bounced at a slower rate than the animal in the other. And the sound track was in synchrony either with the film of the slow-bouncing animal or with the film of the fast-bouncing animal. Infants' first looks were more frequently toward the film that was "specified" by the sound track.

Experiments 2 and 3 explored two components of the relationship between the sound track and the matching film: common tempo and simultaneity of sounds and bounces. The findings showed that infants are sensitive to both of these components.

Spelke's clever demonstration suggests that infants only four months old "do not appear to experience a world of unrelated visual and auditory sensations. They can perceive unitary audible and visible events" (p. 636). However, a cautionary note comes from David Lewkowicz (1985), who failed to find evidence that four-month-old infants have bisensory perception of frequency of events. As Lewkowicz points out, the problem may have been that his procedure, which involved flashing checks and simple tones, was less naturalistic than Spelke's. On the positive side, Arlene Walker–Andrews and Elizabeth Lennon (1985) have recently reported evidence that five-month-olds have bisensory perception of information concerning changing distance of objects. Faced with a film of an approaching car and another film of a car driving away, a five-month-old will tend to look at the film that corresponds to a sound track (if the sound track is of a car sound getting louder, the infant tends to look more at the film of an approaching car).

CONCEPT TABLE 4.2
Auditory and Speech Perception in Infancy and Childhood

Concept	Important Methodological Technique(s) Used with Infants	Development
Auditory sensitivity	Startle reactions, changes in heart and respiration rate (natural responses), and visually reinforced head turning	There is hearing at birth, but sensory thresholds are elevated. Infants appear relatively more sensitive to high-frequency sounds.
Localization of sounds	Presentation of sounds to an infant's right and left, with monitoring of head or eye movements (natural responses)	While newborns look in the direction of sounds, this looking shows a decrement between forty and one hundred days of age. Then it reemerges.
Voice perception	Nonnutritive sucking technique (habituation)	Infants appear sensitive to their mother's voice by three days of age. This suggests the possibility of prenatal learning.
Speech perception	Nonnutritive sucking technique (habituation)	Perception of some phonetic contrasts is present by one month; perception of others is present by one year. Speech perception can be categorical and probably is based on general properties of the auditory system. Despite these feats by infants, linguistic awareness of speech sounds is difficult for older children to achieve.
Perception of sound sequences	Visually reinforced head turning	There is sensitivity to melodic contour by eight to eleven months. Sense of tonality appears to emerge in childhood, perhaps by age six.

We have discussed a number of aspects of auditory and speech perception. A summary of these ideas is presented in Concept Table 4.2.

THE OTHER SENSES

We human beings not only see and hear, we smell, taste, and touch things, and we certainly feel pain. These other modalities have not been explored to the extent of vision and hearing, but we have learned some things about their emergence in infancy. In this section we review what is known about the senses of smell, taste, touch, and pain early in the child's development. We will see that there is evidence that all of these senses develop quite early in life.

Smell

Asafetida is a substance obtained from the roots of plants from the *Ferula* genus. Once used in medicine, it is bitter and extremely offensive to the adult nose. If you were forced to smell this substance, you would be likely to grimace and move away. Apparently, one-day-old infants have a similar reaction. An important study by Trygg Engen and his colleagues (Lipsett, Engen &

Kaye, 1963) showed that infants less than twenty-four-hours of age will make body and leg movements and show changes in respiration (breathing) when exposed to asafetida. Further, the concentration of asafetida needed to produce these responses drops markedly over the first four days of life. Thus, the sense of smell is present at birth, and it appears to develop in the days immediately afterward. Other research by the same group of scientists (Engen & Lipsett, 1965) showed that very young infants (thirty-two to sixty-eight hours of age) are not only sensitive to unpleasant odors, they can discriminate between two different unpleasant odors.

Infants' sense of smell is fortunately not only for unpleasant odors. They apparently can recognize the smell of their mother's breasts (presumably pleasant). One study used the following procedure (McFarlane, 1975): A two- to seven-day-old infant was exposed to two breast pads, one to her right and one to her left. One of these breast pads had been used by her mother, while the other was clean. The finding was that infants spent more time turned toward their mother's pad than toward the clean pad, clearly demonstrating some sense of smell. However, it has not been shown that infants this young can actually recognize the smell of their own mother as opposed to that of other mothers. To test for

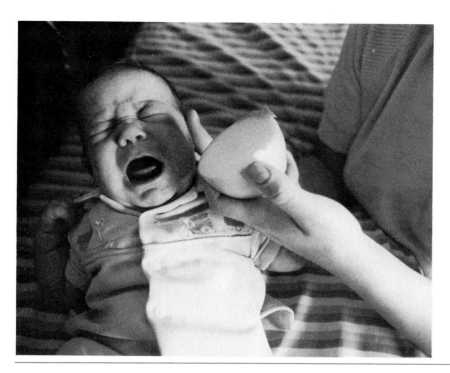

Infants have a sense of smell.

such refined discrimination, McFarlane (1975) conducted a study in which the clean breast pad was replaced by another mother's breast pad. Two-day-old infants showed no difference in turning to the breast pad of their own mother versus pads of other infants' mothers. It may not be until two weeks of age that infants can recognize their own mother's smell.

Taste

Anatomical studies of the taste buds in fetuses (Bradley & Stern, 1967) suggest there may be taste sensitivity prior to birth (Acredolo & Hake, 1982). Indeed, when saccharin is added to the amniotic fluid of a near-term fetus, increased swallowing is observed (Windle, 1940). In any event, sensitivity to sweetness is very well demonstrated in the sucking behavior of newborn infants (Crook & Lipsett, 1976; Lipsett, Reilly, Butcher & Greenwood, 1976). When sucks on a nipple are rewarded with a water and sweetener (sucrose) solution, the amount of sucking will increase. Yet within a "burst" of sucking, the rate of sucking is slower for more-sweetened solutions than for less-sweetened solutions. This pattern suggests a form of "savoring" of sweet tastes by young infants (note that when you savor

a taste you swallow slowly, not quickly). Thus, it appears that newborns can taste sweet substances and apparently enjoy such substances. Our "sweet tooth" comes early.

Taste in newborns also can be demonstrated by movements of muscles in the face. In one study, sweet stimulation was followed by movements resulting in a smilelike expression, while sour stimulation caused a pursing of the lips (Steiner, 1979). And this was with infants only a few hours old! Indeed, similar facial responses to tastes were observed in premature infants, as well as in developmentally malformed neonates who lacked an intact cortex. Thus, distinguishing some tastes may not require much in the way of "higher mental processes." Tell this to one of your gourmet friends.

Touch

Just as newborns make reflexive movements to tastes, they also make reflexive movements to touch. A touch to the cheek can produce a head-turning response, while a touch to the lips can produce sucking movements (Acredolo & Hake, 1982). Further, even mild tactile stimuli can produce changes in heart rate and motor behavior (Wolff, 1967; Yang & Douthitt, 1974).

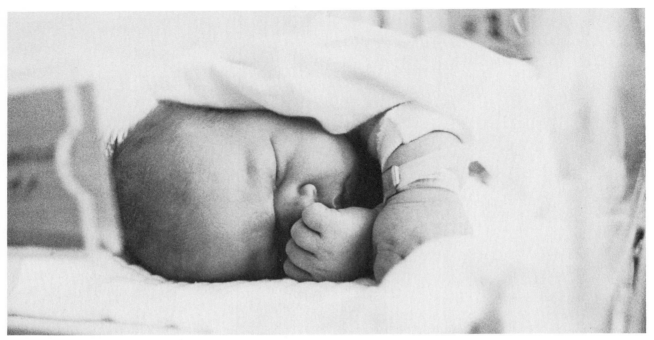

If allowed, the male infant drifts into a deep sleep after being circumcised.

Pain

If and when you have a son and consider whether he should be circumcised, the issue of infants' pain perception will probably become important to you. Circumcision is usually performed on young boys about the third day of life. Will your young son be uncomfortable if circumcised at three days? Megan Gunnar, Steven Malone, and Robert Fisch (in press) have conducted a number of studies of circumcision. Because the neonate can be immobilized by restraining him on a "circumstraint" board, this surgery usually is performed without anesthesia. Routine circumcision provides an opportunity to evaluate how the newborn copes with an apparently intense stressor in the absence of drugs or illness.

The results indicated that the surgical techniques are clearly stressful. Intense crying occurs, and massive productions of adrenocortical steroids, as well as other biochemical changes associated with stress, appear. It actually is somewhat remarkable that this newly born infant does not suffer serious consequences from the circumcision. Instead, the circumcised infant displays remarkable resiliency and ability to cope. Even during the aversive surgery, the soothing given by care givers seems to help calm the infant. And within several minutes after the surgery, he can nurse and interact in a normal manner with his mother (Marshall et al., 1982). If allowed, the newly circumcised neonate drifts into a deep state of sleep that seems to serve as a coping mechanism.

In sum, there is every indication that the neonate senses pain (Anders & Chalemian, 1974; Emde, Harmon, Metcalf, Koenig & Wagonfeld, 1971; Gunnar, Malone & Fisch, in press). Furthermore, the healthy neonate does seem to be very adapted to cope with environmental stressors that cause pain.

SUMMARY

I. Perceptual development, particularly in the infant years, is currently a very active research area in child development. Perception is important to study because it raises some intrinsically interesting questions, because it is relevant to the theoretical question of how we come to know the world, and because there are practical problems involving perception.

II. Research on perceptual development involves theories as well as a number of innovative research techniques.
  A. Two dominant theoretical perspectives are the constructivist and ecological frameworks.
     1. The constructivist approach holds that children construct representations or models of the world in their minds.
     2. The ecological approach stresses the richness of perceptual information and the child's ability to extract invariants from this richness. The ecological approach has stimulated researchers to examine perceptual development in young infants.
  B. Among the important techniques for studying perceptual development are natural responses, preferences, habituation, and conditioned head turning.

III. An understanding of visual perception in infancy and childhood focuses on visual preferences, visual acuity, and accommodation, perception of color, perception of depth, perception of objects, face perception, and perception of spatial relations.
  A. Visual acuity in newborn infants has been measured by using visual preferences, as well as other strategies. Infants' visual acuity initially is quite low (20/600) but improves markedly over the first six months of life. Accommodation also improves as infants grow older. However, because of limited acuity and depth of field, acuity remains constant over a range of distances, even in newborns.
  B. The perception of color develops quite early. Studies using the habituation technique suggest that full color vision is present by three months of age. However, younger infants may be partially color-blind.
  C. Perception of objects and individual faces also is present by three months of age.
     1. Habituation techniques have indicated that infants at about three months of age perceive that objects are unitary.
     2. Other research using the habituation technique supports recognition of individual faces by three-month-old infants. Still younger infants show more interest in face than nonface stimuli.
     3. The development of face perception in childhood shows a puzzling trend of gradual improvement until about ten years of age, no improvement or even decline until about thirteen to fourteen years of age, and then improvement until about sixteen years of age.
  D. Perception of depth clearly is present by the time infants can crawl (six to fourteen months), as shown by the visual cliff experiments. Depth perception at earlier ages remains open to question.
  E. Knowledge of spatial location of objects often is based on an egocentric frame of reference, particularly in infants under one year of age. The use of an egocentric reference begins to decline after one year of age. The mapping of large-scale space is impressive in three-year-olds, though it does improve thereafter.

IV. Information about hearing and speech perception emphasizes sensitivity to simple sounds, localization of sounds, voice perception and recognition, perception of speech, perception of melodies, and bimodal perception.
  A. Newborn infants are responsive to sounds, which suggests that they can hear. However, newborns apparently have heightened thresholds for hearing, especially with low-frequency sounds.
  B. Newborn infants not only can hear, they look to the right or left in accordance with a sound's location. Although present in newborns, looking toward sounds disappears temporarily in infants between forty and one hundred days old.

C. Discrimination among different voices also is impressive in newborns. Three-day-old newborns apparently can recognize their own mother's voice.

D. Research with the nonnutritive sucking technique shows discrimination of subtle speech features in infants only one month old. However, speech perception improves with age, and conscious awareness of phonemes in language improves from four to six years of age, possibly because of reading training.

E. Infants six months and older also are sensitive to properties of sequences of sounds (melodies), including the property of contour. As children get older, they develop a sense of tonality and become more sensitive to the precise intervals of a melody.

F. Bimodal perception refers to the ability to perceive auditory and visual events in related, unified ways. This higher-order form of perception may be present by 4–5 months of age.

V. The development of the other senses—smell, taste, touch, and pain—have not been thoroughly investigated. However, we do know that these four senses are present in newborns. Research investigations focused on circumcision reveal the presence of the sense of pain in neonates as well as the fact that the healthy newborn is very adapted to cope with stress.

KEY TERMS

accommodation 115
bimodal perception 128
conditioned head turning 113
constructivist viewpoint 109
discriminate 114
dishabituation 112
ecological framework 109
egocentric frame of reference 120
empiricist 109
epistemology 109
face recognition 119
habituation 112
invariant 110

melodic contour 127
nativist 109
nonnutritive sucking technique 124
objective frame of reference 121
preference technique 111
sensation and perception 109
simultaneous comparison method 119
sound spectrogram 126
subitizing 113
visual cliff 116
voicing 125

REVIEW QUESTIONS

1. Discuss why sensory and perceptual development is an important area of inquiry in the study of children.
2. Contrast the constructivist and ecological frameworks.
3. Describe the main techniques for studying infant perception.
4. Discuss what we know about visual preferences, acuity, and accommodation in infancy.
5. Outline the perception of color, depth, objects, and faces in infancy.
6. What do we know about the development of spatial relations?
7. Evaluate the nature of hearing and speech perception in infants and children.
8. What is known about the development of the senses of smell, taste, touch, and pain?

SUGGESTED READINGS

Acredolo, L. P., & Hake, J. L. (1982). Infant perception. In B. B. Wolman (Ed.), *Handbook of developmental psychology*. Engelwood Cliffs, NJ: Prentice-Hall.
A comprehensive overview of perception in infancy.

Aslin, R. N., Pisoni, D. B., & Jusczyk, P. W. (1983). Auditory development and speech perception in infancy. In P. H. Mussen (Ed.), *Handbook of child psychology* (4th ed., Vol. 2). New York: John Wiley.
Explores in an extensive manner what is known about auditory perception in infants.

Banks, M. S. (In collaboration with Salapatek, P.). (1983). Infant visual perception. In P. H. Mussen (Ed.), *Handbook of child psychology* (4th ed., Vol. 2). New York: John Wiley.
Presents a wealth of research on visual perception in infants. Provides considerable detail about the intriguing experiments designed by developmental psychologists to enter the world of the infant's perception.

Bornstein, M. H. (1984). Perceptual development. In M. H. Bornstein & M. E. Lamb (Eds.), *Developmental psychology: An advanced textbook*. Hillsdale, NJ: Lawrence Erlbaum.
An advanced introduction to theory and research on perceptual development, with an emphasis on infancy.

CHAPTER

LEARNING

PROLOGUE

JESS, CONTROLLER OF HIS TEACHER'S BEHAVIOR

Jess is an eighth-grader at a junior high school in California. Only fourteen years old, he already weighs 185 pounds. He is the school's best athlete, but he used to get some of his biggest thrills out of fighting. He knocked out several fellow students with bottles and chairs. He once hit the principal with a stick, for which he received a forty-day suspension from school.

Jess's teachers unanimously agree that he was an "impossible" case; no one seemed to be able to control him. But one week, his teachers began to notice an almost complete turnabout in Jess's behavior. His math teacher was one of the first to notice the "strange" but improved behavior. He looked at her and said, "When you are nice you help me learn a lot." The teacher almost fell off her chair. Not knowing quite what to say, she finally smiled. Jess continued, "I feel really good when you praise me." Jess continued a consistent pattern of such statements to his teachers and even came to class early or sometimes stayed late just to chat with them.

What was responsible for Jess's turnaround? Some teachers said he was attending a mysterious class every day and maybe what went on in it might provide some clues to his change in behavior. In that "mysterious" class a teacher was training students in behavior modification, which emphasizes that behavior is determined by its consequences. Those consequences weaken some behaviors and strengthen others.

As an experiment, Paul Graubard and Harry Rosenberg (1974), selected seven of the most incorrigible students in a junior high school—Jess was one of them—and had a teacher give the seven students instruction and practice in behavior modification in one forty-three-minute class period a day.

In their daily training sessions the students were taught a number of rewards to use to shape a teacher's behavior. Rewards included eye contact, smiling, and sitting up straight and being attentive. The students also practiced ways to praise the teacher, saying such things as, "I like working in this class where there is a good teacher." Furthermore, they worked on ways to discourage certain teacher behaviors by saying such things as, "I just have a rough time working well when you get mad at me." Jess had the hardest time learning how to smile. He was shown a videotape of his behavior and observed that he actually leered at people when he was told to smile. Although it was a somewhat hilarious process, Jess practiced smiling in front of a camera until he got it down. Eventually he developed a charming smile.

The experiment was divided into three phases. During the first phase students did not try to change their regular teachers' behavior. This first phase was reserved for establishing a norm of the teachers' behavior, or what is called a **baseline.** During the second phase, the students worked at changing the teachers' behavior. This is usually referred to as the **acquisition phase,** or in this experiment, the **intervention phase.** Finally, the students entered the last phase of the experiment, in which they were not to use any of the techniques they had learned to change the teachers' behavior. This last phase is referred to as **extinction** because the consequences for behavior are removed. The students were taught to keep accurate records for the experiment, and they kept daily tallies of the number of positive and negative contacts they had with their teachers.

By looking at figure 5.1 you can see the number of positive and negative behaviors shown by Jess and his six classmates during interaction with their teachers. During the five weeks in which the students implemented their behavior change tactics, the average number of positive teacher–student interchanges improved dramatically and the number of negative contacts dropped substantially. Then several weeks after

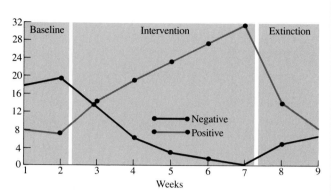

FIGURE 5.1
Average number of positive and negative teacher–student contacts.

Reprinted from *Psychology Today* Magazine. Copyright © 1974 American Psychological Association.

the students stopped using the behavior change tactics (extinction), the number of positive contacts nose-dived and the number of negative interchanges increased slightly.

When the experiment was over the students resumed their use of behavior change strategies, but no formal records were kept. Informal comments and observations suggested that the students were having more positive relationships with their teachers after the program had formally ended than before it had begun.

But what happened in the long run, one year, two years later? In the case of the experiment by Graubard and Rosenberg (1974) we do not know, but in many cases such behavior modification interventions do not result in long-lasting changes once the consequences for behavior are removed. More about behavior modification appears in this chapter.

PREVIEW

In this chapter we explore the world of children's learning, first asking the question, "What is learning?" Then we evaluate the nature of classical conditioning and operant conditioning. The chapter concludes with an overview of cognitive factors involved in learning.

WHAT IS LEARNING?

To understand what learning is we initially try to pin down the elusive definition of learning. Then we look at several views on different kinds of learning and how to evaluate them.

Defining Learning

First, learning anything new involves a *change*. For instance, when a child is learning how to use a computer, he or she will probably make some mistakes along the way, but at some point the child's mind and behavior are likely to change enough so that he or she attains an understanding of how to use the computer. In other words, the child changes from someone who could not operate a computer to someone who can.

Second, learning has a *relatively permanent* influence on the child's mind and behavior. Thus once the child learns how to use the computer, the skill does not usually go away. Once the child has learned how to add and subtract, this ability becomes a relatively permanent part of the mind and behavior.

Third, learning involves *experience*. Through experiences with other people, children learn how to behave mannerly or not so mannerly. Through experiences, children learn positive or negative attitudes toward studying. On the other hand, behavior and thought due to maturation, reflexes, and instincts or to the influence of fatigue, injury, disease, or drugs does not involve learning.

Thus, *learning* can be defined as a relatively permanent change in the mind or behavior that occurs through experience and cannot be accounted for by reflexes, instincts, and maturation or the influence of fatigue, injury, disease, or drugs. Now that we have defined learning, let's look at the different kinds of learning.

Different Kinds of Learning

In this section we look at learning in terms of the different behaviors and thoughts involved, and then we study the way most psychologists differentiate types of learning—in terms of experience.

Behaviors and Thoughts

Because learning involves a change in behavior through experience, we might ask how many different kinds of behavior can be changed and come up with that many forms of learning. In this sense we might include motor learning, learning mathematical concepts, learning to read, learning to solve problems, perceptual learning, and so forth. These kinds of learning might be broken down into smaller subcategories. For example, motor learning might be divided into fine and gross motor skills. In that sense learning to throw a ball would be in a different category from learning to write—the former being a gross motor skill, the latter a fine motor skill.

One view of learning based on the idea of describing it in terms of behavior and thoughts has been developed by Robert Gagne (1977). He describes five major outcomes of learning. These five outcomes along with examples of performance made possible by each are presented in table 5.1. You will notice a heavy cognitive flavor in Gagne's categories of learning. Indeed, many of the forms of learning described by Gagne will not be described in this chapter but rather in chapter 7, where information processing is discussed, and in chapter 9, where intelligence is evaluated. There are times in this chapter when cognitive processes are emphasized, but the primary interest here is the nature of experiences, which we describe next.

TABLE 5.1
Five Major Categories of Learned Capabilities, Including Subordinate Types and Examples of Each

Capability (Learning Outcome)	Examples of Performance Made Possible
Intellectual skill	Demonstrating symbol use, as in the following:
Discrimination	Distinguishing printed *m*'s and *n*'s.
Concrete concept	Identifying the spatial relation "underneath"; identifying a "side" of an object.
Defined concept rule	Classifying a "family," using a definition. Demonstrating the agreement in number of subject and verb in sentences.
Higher-order rule	Generating a rule for predicting the size of an image, given the distance of a light source and the curvature of a lens.
Cognitive strategy	Using an efficient method for recalling names; originating a solution for the problem of conserving gasoline.
Verbal information	Stating the provisions of the First Amendment to the U.S. Constitution.
Motor skill	Printing the letter *R*. Skating a figure eight.
Attitude	Choosing to listen to classical music.

From *The Conditions of Learning*, 3/e by Robert M. Gagne. Copyright © 1977 by Holt, Rinehart & Winston. Copyright © 1965, 1970 by Holt, Rinehart & Winston, Inc. Reprinted by permission of CBS College Publishing.

Experiences

Because there seem to be fewer experience categories than behavior and thought categories and because experiences are such a key ingredient of learning, classification in terms of experience has been more popular than classification in terms of thought and behavior.

Psychologists have been ingenious at reducing the myriad experiences we have to a small number of basic forms of learning. We briefly consider how many forms of learning three well-known learning theorists believe exist. First, Ivan Pavlov (1927) argued that there is basically one type of learning: Organisms learn to associate biological stimuli, biological responses, learned stimuli, and learned responses in a complex manner. This type of learning emphasizes how the organism responds to the environment. For example, a child may respond to a person in a particular way because the child has previously associated that person with the eating of food.

Second, B. F. Skinner (1938) argues that there are two kinds of learning. Skinner agrees with Pavlov that one of the types of learning involves responding to the environment as Pavlov outlined, but Skinner believes there is a second very important form of learning, which focuses more on how the child operates on the environment to produce a change in behavior. For example, Skinner stresses that the child actively moves around in the environment and experiences consequences for his or her actions. Thus the child may learn to work hard in school by spending long hours studying and being rewarded for the effort.

Third, Albert Bandura (1977) believes that in addition to responding to and operating on the environment, children learn extensively by observing the behavior of other people. For example, the adolescent learns how to drive a car by observing the behavior of other skilled drivers. Thus Bandura believes there are three basic learning processes.

Now that we have a feel for some of the different forms of learning, let's turn our attention in more detailed ways to these types of learning. First, we evaluate the learning process of classical conditioning.

CLASSICAL CONDITIONING

In this section we study the basic classical conditioning experiment and its elements; discuss compound stimuli; explore why classical conditioning works; cover phobias, counterconditioning, and systematic desensitization; and evaluate the contributions and limitations of classical conditioning.

The Basic Classical Conditioning Experiment and Its Elements

An understanding of classical conditioning can be gleaned from a description of the basic classical conditioning experiment and an overview of its elements.

The Basic Classical Conditioning Experiment

Ivan Pavlov's (1927) experiments with salivating dogs are among the best-known studies in psychology. In his original experiment, Pavlov discovered that he could change behavior by presenting stimuli to an organism.

Ivan Pavlov

FIGURE 5.2
Surgical preparation for studying the salivary reflex. When the dog salivated, the saliva would collect in a glass funnel attached to the dog's cheek. This way the strength of the salivary response could be precisely measured (Chance, 1979).

Let's look more closely at the nature of these stimuli and how they were arranged to get the organism to respond differently. Before an experimental session began, Pavlov had a dog's cheek surgically treated so that its saliva could be measured (see figure 5.2). While the experiment was going on, the dog was restrained in a

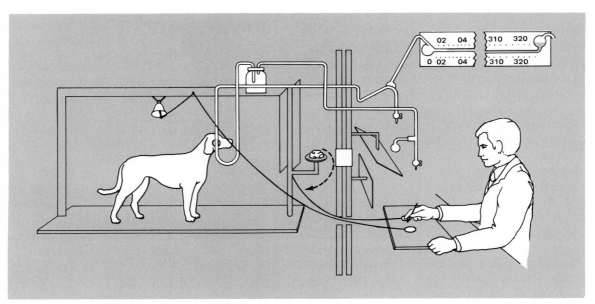

FIGURE 5.3
A modern apparatus for Pavlov's experiment in classical
conditioning (Morgan and King, 1971).

harness (see figure 5.3). Next Pavlov sounded a tuning fork. (At this point in the experiment the dog did not salivate.) Soon after, while the tuning fork was still being sounded, Pavlov gave the dog some meat powder. As the dog ate the meat powder, it salivated. By repeatedly pairing the sound of the tuning fork with the meat powder, Pavlov soon discovered that the dog began to salivate at the appearance of the sound alone. Prior to this the dog had only salivated when the food was presented. Through the association of the meat powder and the sound, the dog learned to salivate to the sound of the tuning fork alone. This process of association is called **classical conditioning.**

The Elements of Classical Conditioning

There are four important elements in the classical conditioning experiment: the unconditioned stimulus, the unconditioned response, the conditioned stimulus, and the conditioned response.

An **unconditioned stimulus (UCS)** can elicit a response before learning occurs, usually through a reflex. In Pavlov's experiment the meat powder was the unconditioned stimulus. Because the tuning fork was not able to produce salivation before it was paired with the food, the tuning fork was the **conditioned stimulus (CS),**

which acquires the ability to elicit a response by being associated with an unconditioned stimulus. Again in Pavlov's experiment, the dog's salivating was the **unconditioned response (UCR),** behavior that is unlearned and occurs in response to an unconditioned stimulus. When the dog began salivating to the tuning fork, the salivating became a **conditioned response (CR)** rather than an unconditioned response. Thus the conditioned response was learned through a pairing of the tuning fork and the food.

In order to keep these terms straight it is a good idea to go over them several times. Also, the diagram in figure 5.4 should provide further help in your understanding of the terms and procedures of classical conditioning.

Compound Stimuli

In reality the world of children's experiences is a world with many stimuli. Recent research on classical conditioning has stressed competition for associative strength among all stimuli present in the context in which learning takes place (Rescorla & Wagner, 1972). For example, when the researcher manipulates a specific CS (e.g., a light), there are other stimuli in the situation that can function as conditioned stimuli as

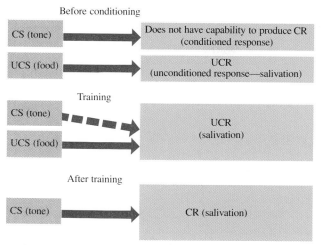

Before conditioning

| CS (tone) | → | Does not have capability to produce CR (conditioned response) |

| UCS (food) | → | UCR (unconditioned response—salivation) |

Training

| CS (tone) | ⇢ | |
| UCS (food) | → | UCR (salivation) |

After training

| CS (tone) | → | CR (salivation) |

FIGURE 5.4
Diagram of the classical conditioning procedure. At the start of training, the UCS will evoke the UCR, but the CS does not have the capacity to evoke the appropriate response. During training the CS and the UCS are presented such that the CS comes to evoke the response. The key learning ingredient in classical conditioning is the association of the UCS and CS.

well. A number of investigators are now studying compound stimuli in an effort to isolate effective conditioned stimuli. A **compound stimulus** is made up of two or more discrete components. A compound stimulus might consist of a light and a bell, or a light, a bell, and a shock. Three examples of how such compound stimuli are studied in classical conditioning are higher order conditioning, overshadowing, and blocking (Houston, 1981).

After the link between the CS and UCS is firmly developed, the CS can be used to condition other stimuli, a process that is called **higher order conditioning.** In this type of conditioning there is a second conditioned stimulus, which never comes into direct contact with the unconditioned stimulus. For example, after a number of pairings of a light and meat powder, the light (the first CS) elicits a conditioned response, in this case the salivation of a dog. Then the sound of a tuning fork (the second CS) is paired with the light but never with the meat powder itself. Higher order conditioning then occurs when the sound alone elicits the CR. This example illustrates second order conditioning. Pavlov revealed that the strength of a second order response was approximately one-half of a first order response. While third order and fourth order responses have been conditioned, their strength is greatly diminished and they are very difficult to establish.

In **overshadowing,** two conditioned stimuli, such as a bell and a light, are presented together and paired with a UCS. Then the experimenter tests for the effectiveness of the bell and the light alone in eliciting the CR. If one CS is more effective than the other in producing the CR, then overshadowing has been demonstrated (Odling-Smee, 1978).

In **blocking,** one CS, such as a light, is paired with a UCS. Then the light and a bell (another CS) are paired with the same UCS. Next, the experimenter tests the effectiveness of the bell in producing the CR. The bell characteristically is less effective in producing the CR than it would have been if the light had not originally been paired with the UCS. The fact that the light already produced the CR in some way *blocks* the establishment of a strong bell–CR connection during the pairing of the light/bell and CR (Kamin, 1969).

Research into such processes as overshadowing and blocking demonstrates that the contiguity of the CS and UCS does not always produce conditioning (Dickinson, 1980; Mackintosh, 1983). In these experiments, even though the CS and UCS are paired, one CS can be blocked or overshadowed by another CS. The trend in classical conditioning research is to study multiple determinants of behavior and to reveal the organism's ability to learn the predictive relation between stimuli (Mackintosh, 1983). In such experimentation the pairing of a single CS with a UCS may not be sufficient to produce a CR—it may be necessary to inspect other stimuli in the learning situation that provide information about the predictability of the UCS–CS relation (Dickinson, 1980).

Why Does Classical Conditioning Work?

The two reasons given to explain why classical conditioning works involve stimulus substitution and information theory (Tarpy & Mayer, 1978). The traditional explanation of classical conditioning is based on **stimulus substitution theory.** Pavlov himself subscribed to this theory, arguing that the nervous system is structured in such a manner that the contiguity between the CS and the UCS creates a bond between them and eventually the CS substitutes for the UCS. If indeed the CS can substitute for the UCS, then the two stimuli should evoke very similar responses. However, researchers have found that the CS and UCS are not as similar as Pavlov believed. For example, a shock UCS produces flinching and jumping in rats (that is, highly activated behavior), whereas a CS paired with shock invariably elicits freezing and immobility (Bindra & Palfai, 1967; Blanchard & Blanchard, 1969).

A second explanation of why classical conditioning works is based on **information theory** (Rescorla, 1967). This view stresses that the CS acquires information value, meaning the child learns information about whatever event follows it in time. Put another way, the child uses the CS as a sign or expectancy that a UCS will follow (Tolman, 1932). The view of the CS as having informational value goes beyond the original meaning of Pavlov's classical conditioning, but as we will see later in the chapter, the concept of expectancy has an important role in our understanding of children's learning.

Emphasis on the information the child processes in a classically conditioned context is reflected in many contemporary learning studies (Dickinson, 1980; Mackintosh, 1983). Rather than viewing a classical conditioning context in the manner of Pavlov, such studies have taken on a cognitive flavor, as classical conditioning researchers describe the child's memory or image of past events and how the child has processed these events.

Phobias and Counterconditioning

Phobias are irrational fears, which many psychologists believe are generated by classical conditioning. The famous behaviorist John Watson and Rosalie Raynor (1920) conducted an experiment to demonstrate this. A little boy named Albert was shown a white laboratory rat to see if he was afraid of it. He was not. Subsequently, as he played with the rat a loud noise was sounded behind Albert's head. As you might imagine, the loud noise caused little Albert to cry loud and long. After only seven pairings of the loud noise with the white rat, Albert began to fear the rat even when the noise was not sounded. Through stimulus generalization, Albert's fear was also produced by objects similar to the white rat—a rabbit, a dog, and a sealskin coat. You should be aware that today we could not ethically conduct this experiment in the manner that Watson and Raynor did. Particularly noteworthy is the fact that they did not remove Albert's fear of rats, so presumably this phobia remained with him after the experiment.

If we can produce fears by means of classical conditioning, we should also be able to eliminate them as well. **Counterconditioning** is a procedure for weakening a classically conditioned CR by associating the stimuli that currently elicit it to a new response incompatible with the CR. Watson (with Mary Cover Jones, 1924) used a counterconditioning procedure to eliminate fear in a three-year-old boy named Peter. Peter had many of the same fears Albert had, but they were not produced by Watson. Peter was afraid of white rats, fur coats, frogs, fish, and mechanical toys, to name just a few of the many objects that scared him. To get rid of these fears, a rabbit was brought into Peter's view but far enough away that it would not upset him. At the same time Peter was fed crackers and milk. On each successive day the rabbit was moved closer and closer to Peter as he was simultaneously given food. Eventually Peter reached the point where he would eat with one hand and pet the rabbit with the other.

YOU'VE GOT TO STOP RINGING THAT BELL EVERY TIME YOU FEED HIM, DR. PAVLOV... YESTERDAY HE ATE THE AVON LADY

Evaluation of Classical Conditioning

Since Pavlov's original experiments with dogs, researchers have made rabbits blink and children jerk to the sound of a buzzer, a glimpse of light, or the touch of a hand. The adaptability that classical conditioning brings has a great deal of survival value for the child. Through the process of classical conditioning, children jerk their hands away before they are burned by fire and the child becomes frightened by the appearance of a rapidly approaching truck before it hits the child. As children acquire language, the words that stand for objects also serve as important signals for classical conditioning. A peer yells, "Snake," and a little girl runs crying to her mother, for example. To learn about other examples of classical conditioning with young children, read Perspective on Child Development 5.1.

PERSPECTIVE ON CHILD DEVELOPMENT 5.1

CLASSICAL CONDITIONING AND AFFECTIVE BEHAVIOR

Once upon a time a young psychologist wanted to train his small son to the potty. Since children don't ordinarily find the seat too comfortable or stimulating, he decided to change its image by introducing an element of pleasure. He obtained a circus poster of a clown—colorful, smiling, with a big nose. He then placed a red light bulb on the nose and switched it on while the child was on the potty. The child was entranced and often wanted to go to the bathroom. Later, it wasn't difficult to rig an electrical circuit so that when the child urinated, a connection was made, and there was the lighted red nose.

But conditioning processes often produce **stimulus generalization,** which means that stimuli like the original, specific stimulus can evoke a similar response.

As you might anticipate, father and son went for a car ride one day and were stopped by a big red traffic light. Guess what happened!

Some conditioning isn't funny. Most teachers have experienced one or more of the following:

Four-year-old Mary comes to nursery school with her mother, but when Mother leaves, Mary cries and carries on, with strong emotional behavior. Only when mother promises to stay does Mary quiet down again. She continues to watch fearfully lest mother show some signs of abandoning her.

Peter becomes slightly nauseated whenever a test is announced. Sometimes he becomes actively sick and has to go home.

And Monday depresses us—that's why it's "Blue Monday." But we enjoy Friday—it is T.G.I.F. (Thank God It's Friday).

If you asked Mary, Peter, or yourself why these feelings occurred, you would probably get an answer, but it might well be a rationalization rather than the truth. That is because we frequently don't know enough about

our real reasons for feeling as we do, although we can call upon our intellect for an explanation that may satisfy us. The behaviors described above can be considered examples of classical conditioning, in which form of learning we are frequently unaware that we are learning, and are certainly not motivated to try (Ringness, 1975).

From Thomas A. Ringness, *The Affective Domain in Education,* pp. 41–42. Copyright © 1975 by Little, Brown and Company (Inc.). Reprinted by permission.

CONCEPT TABLE 5.1
Classical Conditioning

Concept	Components	Functions/Characteristics
Basic experiment and its elements	Unconditioned stimulus (UCS)	A stimulus that can elicit a response before learning occurs.
	Conditioned stimulus (CS)	A stimulus that acquires the ability to elicit a response after being associated with a UCS.
	Unconditioned response (UCR)	Behavior that is unlearned and occurs in response to UCS.
	Conditioned response (CR)	A learned response that follows UCS–CS pairing.
Compound stimuli	Higher order conditioning	Condition in which a new stimulus comes to elicit the CR by being paired with a CS.
	Overshadowing	Two CS paired together, then with UCS; see if one CS is more effective than another.
	Blocking	One CS paired with UCS, then this CS and another CS paired with same UCS; see if pairing of first CS and UCS blocks effectiveness of second CS.
Explanations	Stimulus substitution theory	Pavlov's explanation: Bond forms between UCS and CS, then CS takes place of (substitutes for) UCS.
	Information theory	CS acquires information value or expectancy of what is going to follow it in time; emphasis on processing information in a learning context.
Other processes	Counterconditioning	CS is associated with a stimulus that produces a response incompatible with unwanted CR. At same time, the important stimulus associated with CS is withheld if possible.

Although Pavlov described all learning in terms of classical conditioning, it has become apparent that classical conditioning is a simple type of learning and that we learn in a number of other ways. Nonetheless, classical conditioning does help a child learn about his or her environment, and as we have just seen it has successfully been used in the elimination of fears. However, a view of learning that only describes the child's responding to the environment fails to capture the active nature of the child in influencing the environment.

So far we have considered a number of ideas about classical conditioning. A summary of these ideas is presented in Concept Table 5.1. Next we study the nature of operant conditioning.

OPERANT CONDITIONING

In reviewing the many dimensions of operant conditioning, we look first at the operant view of B. F. Skinner, then at various aspects of positive reinforcement, next at the principle of punishment, and finally at some applications of operant conditioning.

Skinner's Operant Conditioning

B. F. Skinner (1938, 1957) believes it is important to distinguish between classical and operant conditioning. In classical conditioning, behavior is elicited by the conditioned stimulus (CS). Thus in Pavlov's experiments the dog's salivation seems to be triggered by external stimulation. Skinner refers to such events, as when salivation is elicited by food, as **respondents.** However, in **operant conditioning** the organism *operates* on the environment to produce a change that will lead to reward (Skinner, 1938). Skinner describes **operants** as responses that are actively emitted in relation to specific consequences. For example, a simple operant is pressing a lever that leads to the delivery of food. Although Skinner believes that operant behavior is not elicited by external events, he clearly thinks that behavior is controlled by external forces. In Skinner's operant conditioning, the reinforcement does not establish an association between the response and the stimulus. What is strengthened, from Skinner's perspective, is the operant behavior itself, which is more likely to occur.

One of the basic beliefs of Skinner, as well as other behaviorists, is that the mechanisms of learning are the same for all species. This belief led to an extensive study of lower animals in the hope that with more simple organisms than humans the basic mechanisms of learning could be fleshed out. Skinner and other behaviorists made every effort to study the organism under precisely controlled conditions so that the connection between the operant and the specific consequences that follow it could be examined in minute detail. One of the ways in which Skinner attempted to achieve such control was the development in the 1930s of a piece of apparatus that became known as the Skinner box (see figure 5.5). The box was designed so that every once in awhile a magazine would deliver food pellets into a tray. After a rat became accustomed to the box, Skinner installed a lever and observed the rat's behavior. As the hungry rat explored the box, it would occasionally press the lever and a food pellet would come out. Soon after, the rat learned that the consequences of pressing the lever were positive—it could eat. Further control in such experimental situations was achieved by soundproofing the box and making sure the experimenter only handled the animal when it was placed in the cage at the beginning of the experiment and taken out when the trials were over. Furthermore, in many such experiments the responses of the organism were mechanically recorded by such devices as a cumulative recorder, and the stimuli were mechanically dispensed through some form of automatic programming. Such precautions were made in an attempt to avoid human error.

Positive Reinforcement

The use of **positive reinforcement** is believed to be a powerful determinant of behavior when it follows the behavior. We study the following aspects of positive reinforcement to understand some of the varied ways in which stimuli are experienced: time interval, shaping, primary and secondary reinforcement, schedules of reinforcement, extinction, generalization, and discrimination, reinforcement history, reinforcement in natural settings, and extrinsic and intrinsic motivation.

FIGURE 5.5
A rat in a Skinner box

Time Interval

As is true in classical conditioning, learning seems to be more efficient in operant conditioning when the interval between stimuli and responses is on the order of seconds rather than minutes or hours. In general, then, the shorter the interval between the child's response and its consequences, the more effectively learning will proceed (Johnson, 1972; Logan, 1960). In operant conditioning a distinction is often made between the immediate consequences of behavior and delayed consequences. Learning may be more efficient under immediate consequences because delayed consequences allow other responses to occur, and thus undesired rather than desired behaviors may be reinforced.

Shaping

A child who enters a new learning situation may not have the slightest inclination to behave in a way that is appropriate for the setting. On the first day of school she may walk around the room and talk incessantly, not realizing that generally one of the first requirements in school is to sit quietly at one's desk. A boy whose mother asks for some help in baking a cake hasn't the slightest inkling of what to do first. An autistic child initially does not speak at all. In each case **shaping** is required to develop the desired response.

Skinner first showed that such zero-level entry behavior can be shaped gradually through *successive approximations* to produce the final, desired response (Skinner, 1938). The child may gradually learn to sit quietly at her desk by first being reinforced for a distantly related response, such as approaching the desk to sit down, and then a closer response, such as sitting down for a moment, and so on, until the final behavior appears. The boy's mother may first reward him for selecting a baking utensil, then for mixing some ingredients, and so on, until all components of the task have been mastered. A therapist may first reward the autistic child for a sound faintly resembling speech, then for a word, a phrase, and finally, whole sentences. O. Ivar Lovaas (1977; Lovaas, Koegel & Schreibman, 1979) has had some success with this procedure.

Primary and Secondary Reinforcement

In a consideration of the nature of reinforcement it is important to distinguish between primary and secondary reinforcers. If an infant's vocalizing is increased by tactile stimulation, the tactile stimulation is a **primary reinforcer.** Later the infant may vocalize in the mere presence of the person who provided the stimulation. The sight of the person is a **secondary reinforcer.** It gained its functional effect by first being associated with the primary (original) reinforcer. In this fashion money, grades on a report card, social praise, and public recognition may become secondary reinforcers. Secondary reinforcers may not be as effective as primary reinforcers if the association between the two is lost. For example, money may lose its influence if it is no longer associated with such primary reinforcing events as eating, warmth, shelter, and stimulating experiences.

Schedules of Reinforcement

The consequences of a certain behavior for a child may be governed by different **schedules of reinforcement** or **punishment.** A schedule is a rule that explains when the consequence occurs in relation to the behavior. The relation may be determined by time (**interval schedule**)

If an infant's vocalization is increased by tactile stimulation, the tactile stimulation is a primary reinforcer.

or by the frequency of the specific behaviors (**ratio schedule**). First, let's consider an example of an interval schedule. A boy's mother complains to her husband that their son is developing a bad habit of leaving his dirty clothes on the floor. The father decides to reward the son for putting his dirty clothes in the hamper by using an interval schedule, in which he rewards the son the first time he puts the clothes in the hamper in a two-hour time period. Then the father continues using this interval schedule, based on rewarding the son the first time he engages in the positive behavior during the time period specified.

Now let us modify the example given above to explain the concept of ratio schedule. Suppose that on one occasion our hypothetical child disposed of a single article of soiled clothing and was praised by his parent, while on another occasion he disposed of five articles of clothing and was then praised. In the former case we have an example of a ratio schedule of one; one response elicits one reinforcement. In the latter case we have a ratio schedule of five; five responses of a particular kind produce one reinforcement. The numbers chosen are, of course, arbitrary. Any number of responses might be required of the child before a reinforcer is given, and hence the ratio schedule has an

infinite range of possible values. Just as time is a factor in the way behavior is reinforced, so is the nature of the response itself. Sometimes a single behavior will garner a reinforcement. Other times, we will have to respond repeatedly before a reward is forthcoming. Unlike time, however, the relationship between the type of ratio schedule governing our behavior and the rate with which we learn and unlearn responses is more complicated (e.g., Platt & Day, 1979). The larger the ratio schedule, the longer it will take the child to learn the response in question, but the longer it will take for the response to be forgotten. For example, the child asked to clean his room may take longer (presumably several responses) to master the habit of picking up all soiled clothing on the floor for a single reward, than he would if every single pickup elicited a word of praise. But having learned the response under the larger ratio schedule, he will be more likely to continue picking up clothing, if his father later discontinues the praise, than he would under the ratio schedule of one.

The complexities of scheduling reinforcement are numerous (e.g., Schaeffer, 1979; Wurster & Griffiths, 1979). This brief survey touches only the surface of the many kinds of existing schedules that are studied in the experimental laboratory. There are, for example, combined schedules in which both the time (interval) and number of responses (ratio) together serve as criteria for the reward contingency, **variable schedules** in which the interval or ratio contingency changes value from one occasion to the next, and a variety of *partial* schedules in which one is sometimes rewarded and sometimes not for a particular response. These subtle schedules permit us both to explain a wide range of learned behaviors that might not be obvious to the novice student of operant theory and to develop highly individual programs for modifying children's behaviors.

Extinction, Stimulus Generalization, and Stimulus Discrimination

In operant conditioning, **extinction** occurs when the consequences of a response are removed, as when a reward that normally follows a behavior is withheld. **Spontaneous recovery** characterizes extinction. This means that even though the reward continues to be withheld after the response has been extinguished, the conditioned response reappears, although in a diminished fashion. As the reward continues to be absent, the degree of spontaneous recovery lessens until it eventually disappears altogether.

Stimulus generalization in operant conditioning refers to the tendency of a response that has been rewarded in the presence of one stimulus to occur in the presence of another stimulus similar to the first. For example, the infant who has been rewarded for smiling by her mother may also smile in the presence of other social figures who look like her mother (an aunt, a neighbor).

Stimulus discrimination in operant conditioning refers to the tendency of the conditioned response to occur in the presence of one stimulus but not another. For example, the child may learn to smile at her aunt but not at her uncle, who has a menacing look.

Be aware that these processes—extinction, generalization, and discrimination—can occur in classical conditioning as well as operant conditioning. In classical conditioning, extinction occurs when the CS is given alone and is no longer paired with the UCS. In classical conditioning, stimulus generalization results when a stimulus similar to the CS elicits the CR. Also in classical conditioning, stimulus discrimination refers to the tendency of the CR to occur in the presence of the CS but not in the presence of other stimuli.

Reinforcement History

Each child has a unique history of previous reinforcement; an event that is reinforcing for one child may well not be reinforcing for another. A child who works to learn a response for the reward of a toy may not work for the reward of new clothes or social praise. Some children are more likely to learn a response when the event that follows the response is social in nature, for example, verbal praise and social attention. Other children are more likely to work for material rewards like toys, candies, and treats.

One way to find out what is the most effective reinforcing event for a child is by scaling the value of different objects. For example, Sam Witryol and his colleagues developed a technique whereby young children are asked to judge which of two objects they prefer. The objects were drawn from toys, edibles, and other attractive objects, and all possible pairs were presented to the children. From the pattern of preferences that emerged, Witryol was able to describe a hierarchy of incentive values for the items. For example, most children preferred a piece of bubble gum to a marble and a marble to a paper clip. Other objects shown to them included a penny, a toy cow, an M&M candy, and a metal washer (Witryol, 1971).

Recently, Jeffrey Fagen, Carolyn Rovee-Collier, and their associates (Fagen, 1980; Rovee-Collier, Sullivan, Enright, Lucas & Fagen, 1980) have also demonstrated the importance of reinforcement history in infants. Using infants as young as three or four months, they measured infants' foot kicks in the presence of an attractive mobile secured to the babies' cribs. During conditioning phases of the experiments, the infant's right ankle was secured to a ribbon that was connected to the mobile. By kicking, the infant made the mobile move, an event that was highly interesting. The movement of the mobile was construed as the reinforcer. In the experiments it was shown that the type of mobile used influenced the infant's later tendency to kick. For example, in one study the infants were trained to kick with mobiles that had from six to ten moving elements and were later switched to a mobile with only two moving elements. After the switch, these infants kicked more vigorously and showed more distress in their vocalizations (even after twenty-four hours) than did a group of infants who had seen only the less elaborate

Peer reinforcement can dramatically alter a child's behavior.

mobile. Apparently, the trained infants remembered the specific characteristics of their reinforcers and were upset when the reinforcer changed. In other words, the infants had acquired specific expectations for reinforcement, based on their specific history of reinforcement with a type of mobile.

Reinforcement in Natural Settings

An important question in reinforcement is the degree to which the processes of learning we have been describing apply in the natural world of the child (Schwartz, 1981). Many psychologists have shown that young children frequently can and do reward one another in the preschool setting (Fagot, 1977; Hartup, 1983; Lamb & Roopnarine, 1979). By doing so, children dramatically alter one another's behavior. The demonstration has proven particularly powerful in increasing or decreasing the likelihood children will engage in sex-stereotyped behaviors and activities. Little girls, for instance, will be more likely to engage in artistic activities if their friends applaud their efforts. Little boys will be more likely to perform high-energy, physical activities if their peers praise them for doing so. To learn more about reinforcement in naturalistic settings, read Perspective on Child Development 5.2.

PERSPECTIVE ON CHILD DEVELOPMENT 5.2

REINFORCEMENT OF SEX-TYPED
BEHAVIOR BY PEERS

Michael Lamb and his associates (Lamb, Easterbrooks & Holden, 1980) investigated some important features of the naturalistic interaction among children. The investigators selected forty-nine middle-class children who attended a combined nursery school and kindergarten program. The youngsters ranged in age from about three to six years of age. Each child was observed over nine weeks for twelve ten-minute periods of free play. During these periods observers recorded the children's sex-stereotyped activities and the reactions of their peers. These peer reactions were described in seven different categories of reinforcement (to praise, join play, imitate, approve, observe, comply, and covet toy); five different categories of punishment (to criticize, divert, abandon play, disapprove, and disrupt activity); and a category of neutral responses. In some of the sessions observers also attempted to gauge the children's competence in interacting with others their age.

The results of the study are fascinating. About two-thirds of the time the children's behaviors did receive reinforcement or punishment, with reinforcement much more likely for "sex-typical" behaviors than for others. Children of the same sex generally tended to interact most often, and most of the behavior focused on sex-typical activities. For example, boys were more likely to play with transport toys or to engage in strenuous physical activity such as climbing, whereas girls were more likely to do art work or engage in female role play.

The ways in which children reinforced and punished each other differed according to their age. The younger preschoolers were more likely than older ones to reinforce the actions of their age-mates by joining them in play, imitating their behavior, or coveting a friend's toy. By comparison, the older children were more likely to influence a peer by complying with the friend's wishes or by simply observing—that is, paying attention to—the friend. The older children tended more than the younger ones to punish their age-mates by acting in apparently conscious ways intended to change the friend's behavior. For example, they criticized, disapproved, diverted, or disrupted the friend's actions.

Perhaps most important for the concepts of reinforcement and punishment, the peer reactions had their intended effect. Reinforcers did increase the occurrence of the behaviors to which they were directed, and punishers decreased the behaviors in question. The children were also remarkably consistent throughout the sessions in the individual way in which they chose to reinforce and punish others.

In summary, then, children quite frequently reinforce and punish one another's behavior. The peer reaction tends to sustain gender-typical behaviors; younger children reinforce and punish differently from older children; and there is some consistency in the style in which individual children dispense rewards and punishment.

Intrinsic and Extrinsic Motivation

The concept of intrinsic motivation is closely linked with competence motivation. **Intrinsic motivation** refers to behavior that is motivated by an underlying need for competence and self-determination (Deci & Ryan, 1980). By contrast, **extrinsic motivation** refers to behavior that is influenced by external rewards. If a child works at a job because it will earn him or her money, then extrinsic motivation is behind the child's behavior. However, if the child is working because he or she is genuinely interested in doing a competent job, then intrinsic motivation is involved.

A dilemma faced by many parents and teachers is when to allow a child's intrinsic motivation to go to work and when to use incentives to motivate the child. **Incentives** are external cues that stimulate motivation. They can be positive in the sense of a father paying his son $100 for an A, or they can be negative in the sense of something that is painful, such as the father telling his son that if he doesn't get a B average he is going to have to start providing his own gas money for his car.

Though it is often difficult to decide on whether to introduce incentives to motivate a child, several guidelines are available. If a child is not doing competent work, seems bored with what he or she is doing, and has a negative attitude, then it may be an appropriate time to think about introducing incentives to improve performance. Sometimes extrinsic rewards may get in the way of intrinsic motivation, however, particularly if the child is already doing excellent work. One investigation with children is instructive (Lepper, Green & Nisbett, 1973). Baseline observations of children's initial intrinsic interest in a drawing activity were collected. Children with a high interest in the drawing activity were exposed to one of three conditions. In the expected-reward condition, children agreed to engage in the drawing activity to obtain a reward. In the unexpected-reward condition, the children had no knowledge of a reward until they had finished their play. And in the no-reward condition, children neither expected nor received a reward. As shown in figure 5.6, the children in the expected-reward condition showed less subsequent intrinsic interest in the drawing activity than did children in either of the other two conditions, apparently because their intrinsic motivation was detracted by the extrinsic motives.

Punishment

The process of **punishment** decreases the occurrence of a behavior. That is, if a punishing stimulus follows a behavior, the behavior is less likely to recur. The use of punishment is pervasive in our world. Consider Mark, who asks Valerie for a date and hears, "Are you kidding? Me go out with you!" Mark does not ask Valerie out again. Also consider a one-year-old whose mother spanks him for playing with an electrical socket. After the spanking, the infant does not go near the socket again. For ethical reasons, psychologists do not go around spanking infants to see whether such a stimulus decreases behavior. However, a number of laboratory experiments on punishment have been conducted with lower animals, and some modified versions of punishment experiments with animals have been conducted with humans. Psychologists have made recommendations about the effective use of punishment and decisions about when it might be called for in human behavior.

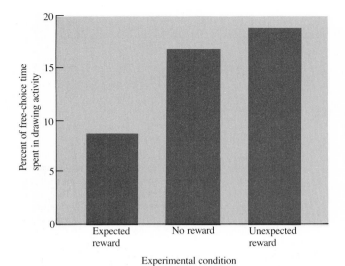

FIGURE 5.6
Children's choice of time spent in a drawing activity after extrinsic reward, no reward, and unexpected reward (Lepper, Greene, and Nisbett, 1973).

Laboratory studies of punishment with animals typically involve having a rat press a bar to obtain food. Once the rat consistently presses the bar, a shock is delivered to the rat when it presses the bar. The experimenter then notes how rapidly the rat's bar pressing decreases. In animal studies, it has been found that punishment is most effective when the punishing stimulus is delivered as soon after the response as possible and when it is administered at a high rather than a low level of intensity.

Do studies with children support the belief that an immediate, intense punishment is effective? In several investigations the use of reasoning has been more effective in controlling children's behavior than physical punishment or the timing of punishment (e.g., Parke, 1974). Why is reasoning effective in decreasing behavior? First, reasoning provides the child with an explanation of why he or she should not engage in a certain behavior and often includes information about the consequences of the child's actions for others. Second, the parent who uses reasoning provides the child with a nonaggressive model whom the child can imitate. It should be mentioned that the effectiveness of various punishment strategies depends on the age of the child, the relationship with the parent, and the nature of the deviant behavior (Grusec & Kuczynski, 1980).

Even though punishment has many side effects there are circumstances when it is beneficial.

When punishment is used with humans, there may be a number of negative side effects (Newsom, Favell & Rincover, 1983). First, punishment may lead to escape or avoidance. Second, when a response is successfully reduced or eliminated by punishment and no appropriate alternative behavior is strengthened, other undesirable behaviors may take the place of the punished behavior. Third, a person who administers punishment is serving as an aggressive model, possibly inadvertently modeling how to behave in an aggressive, punishing manner. Fourth, desirable behaviors may be eliminated along with undesirable ones. For example, a child may stop interacting with other children altogether when he is slapped for biting another child. Because punishment has so many side effects, are there circumstances when it is called for? There may be some circumstances when punishment is beneficial. For example, when positive reinforcement has not been found to work, punishment can be considered. And when the behavior that is being punished is considered more destructive than the punishment itself, the process may

be justified. For example, some children engage in behavior that is very dangerous to their well-being, such as head banging. In such cases, the use of punishment, even electric shock, may reduce the injurious behavior. Nonetheless, as punishment is reduced, it is always wise to reinforce an alternative behavior so that undesirable behavior does not replace the punished response.

Applications of Operant Conditioning

Just as counterconditioning has been developed as an application of classical conditioning to eliminate fears, there has been a widespread attempt to use the principles of operant conditioning to help children live better-adjusted lives. The applications of classical and operant conditioning to changing behavior in the everyday course of children's lives are referred to as behavior modification. Behavior modification based on operant conditioning emphasizes changing behavior by following behavior with reinforcement. In clinical psychology, behavior modification is often referred to as behavior therapy. Let's now examine the applications of operant conditioning in the form of behavior modification by describing its themes as well as its contributions and limitations.

Themes

Behavior modification, sometimes nicknamed B-Mod, simply refers to the use of learning principles, most often those involving classical and operant conditioning, to change maladaptive or abnormal behavior. The term *behavior modification* has sometimes been associated with authoritarian, manipulative control, and even linked with brainwashing and psychosurgery. In a number of instances, however, behavior modification, of which operant conditioning is the primary form of learning, has been successful in changing behaviors so that an individual can lead a more adaptive, pleasant life.

Briefly, the principle of behavior modification is to replace unacceptable, maladaptive responses with acceptable, adaptive ones. In operant behavior modification, consequences for behavior are set up to ensure that an acceptable response is being reinforced and that unacceptable ones are not. Advocates of this approach argue that many emotional and mental health problems result from inadequate response consequences in which, unwittingly, unacceptable behaviors are reinforced. For example, a child who cries or acts aggressively may be receiving too much attention from a parent or teacher when the crying or aggression is displayed. In such instances, the parent or teacher would be instructed to remove his or her attention to see if the behaviors are reduced or eliminated. An example of a successful behavior modification program is presented in Perspective on Child Development 5.3, where behavior modification in the classroom is described.

BEHAVIOR MODIFICATION IN THE CLASSROOM

One vast arena for the application of operant principles to the solution of practical problems has been the public school classroom. Perhaps foremost among the problems addressed has been the management of behavior in unruly or out-of-control children. School psychologists, for example, have had great success in showing teachers and parents how to alter contingencies so that their impulsive, hyperactive, or inattentive charges become more focused and successful learners.

In the 1980 issue of *Behavioural Analysis and Modification,* one such effort, undertaken with great success, was described. Let us examine it in some detail since it nicely illustrates the power of behavior modification techniques. It also has an interesting twist from the typical demonstration since the agents of change were the children themselves.

Allen Israel, Masha Pravder, and Sheila Knights set up a peer-administered program to eliminate disruptive behavior in a fifth-grade classroom. Two disruptive children were identified in a classroom of twenty-two. One child was targeted for behavior modification since his behavior was particularly unacceptable and disruptive; the other child was not targeted directly. The teacher and a graduate student taught each of the other twenty children a system for modifying the target child's behavior.

Through use of didactic instructions, role plays, and discussion, the class was taught the procedures that they would follow during all sessions of this phase.

The children were told that, during each session, they would be recording the frequency of hand raising and calling out exhibited by the target child. The children were then taught to rate the target child on a scale from 1–5 based on his behavior during the session. A 5 indicated that the target always raised his hand and never spoke without permission. A 1 indicated that the child never raised his hand and always spoke

without permission. The peers were told that at the end of each day, the coordinator would randomly choose one of them to serve as the leader. The leader's job was to announce the number of points (s)he awarded to the target child, record them on a chart in front of the room, praise the child, and place a star on his chart if he earned a minimum of three points. The color of the star differentiated level of target performance. Peers also would give the child feedback if his performance did not meet criteria. The entire class was given the option of applauding if the target child earned the maximum number of points.

The coordinator would then indicate how many points she awarded to the target child. If the number of points she awarded was within one point of the number awarded by the leader, the leader would receive a star placed next to his/her name on a separate chart in front of the room. The class as a unit would also be able to earn a star based on the coordinator's evaluation of how well they continued at their task without attending to the target child's inappropriate vocalizations. The criterion for earning a star was receiving a rating of at least 3 on a scale of 1–5.

On the day following the training session during which the above procedures were taught, they were implemented. This phase was in effect for 8 days. (p. 226)*

The results were that the target child decreased his inappropriate behavior, even after the peer reward system faded several days later and the focus shifted from the individual child to the class as a whole. In addition, the second disruptive child, who had not directly participated either as target or "control agent," also became less disruptive. He had benefited from observational learning—a topic in the next major section of this chapter.

*Behavioural Analysis and Modification 4/3 (1980) by Urban & Schwarzenberg, Munich.

Evaluation of Operant Behavior Modification

It is important to point out that some behavior modification programs work and others do not. For example, in an attempt to improve the socially competent behavior of juvenile delinquents (Fixsen, Phillips, Phillips & Wolf, 1976), an extensive behavior modification program worked quite well in a community-based center but not in traditional juvenile institutions. Similarly, operant behavior modification may be effective in helping one child develop adaptive behavior but not another. For example, in the investigation of behavior modification programs with juvenile delinquents (Fixsen, Phillips, Phillips & Wolf, 1976), the main focus involved a **token economy.** A token economy is a system, based on operant conditioning, in which an individual in a clinical setting is given artificial rewards such as poker chips for socially constructive behavior. The tokens themselves can be exchanged for desirable items and privileges. A child may use the tokens to use the telephone or go to the playground; for snacks, television time, and home time, such as a weekend pass to go home. However, one child may become so wedded to the tokens that eventually when they are removed, the positive behaviors that were associated with the tokens may disappear. Yet for another child, when the tokens are removed, the practice of positive behavior engendered by the tokens may continue.

We have discussed a number of ideas about operant conditioning. A summary of these ideas is presented in Concept Table 5.2. Next we study cognitive factors in children's learning.

CONCEPT TABLE 5.2
Operant Conditioning

Concept	Processes/Related Ideas	Characteristics/Description
Skinner's view of operant conditioning	Operant	Response is actively emitted after specific consequences; operant behavior is what is strengthened.
Positive reinforcement	Time interval	Immediate consequences are more effective than delayed consequences.
	Shaping	Shaping is the process of rewarding closer and closer approximations to desired behavior.
	Primary and secondary reinforcement	Primary refers to innate reinforcers such as food and water, while secondary refers to the acquisition of a positive value—money, smiles—through experience.
	Schedules of reinforcement	A schedule is the rule that explains when the consequence occurs in relation to the behavior; includes ratio and variable schedules.
	Extinction, stimulus generalization, and stimulus discrimination	Extinction refers to the situation when the consequences of a response are removed; it is characterized by spontaneous recovery. Stimulus generalization refers to the tendency of a response that has been rewarded in the presence of one stimulus to occur in the presence of another stimulus similar to the first. Stimulus discrimination indicates the tendency of the conditioned response to occur in the presence of one stimulus but not another.
	Reinforcement history	The child's reinforcement history is an important determinant of whether a reinforcer will be effective; sets up expectations.
	Reinforcement in natural settings	Psychologists are interested in the extent to which reinforcement works in nonlaboratory situations. Studies with children suggest that peer reinforcement of sex-typed behavior is prevalent.
	Intrinsic and extrinsic motivation	At times external rewards can interfere with learning, particularly when the child already is motivated to learn.
Punishment	Definition	Punishment is the process that results in a decrease in the occurrence of a behavior.
	Research with children	Suggests that reasoning is often more effective than high-intensity punishment. Researchers recommend that alternatives to punishment be fully explored before punishment is used.
Applications of operant conditioning	Theme	Behavior modification refers to the use of learning principles to change maladaptive behavior.
	Evaluation	Some behavior modification programs work; others do not.

COGNITIVE FACTORS IN LEARNING

Both classical and operant conditioning emphasize the association or connection between specific stimuli in the environment and specific responses on the part of the organism. This view of learning has been called S–R theory. (Actually in the case of classical conditioning the process is S–S learning rather than S–R learning because the key connection is between the UCS and CS.) No room is given to the possibility that cognitive factors such as thinking, memory, plans, expectancies, and the like might be involved in the learning process. Many Skinnerians point out that they are not denying the existence of thinking processes, rather that they cannot be observed and that attention to them may interfere with discovering the important environmental conditions that govern behavior.

However, many psychologists believe that learning involves much more than stimulus–response connections. A view of learning that gives some importance to the role of cognitive factors in learning is the **S–O–R model,** in which *S* stands for stimulus, *O* for the organism, and *R* for response. The *O* is sometimes referred to as the black box because the mental activities of the organism cannot be seen but rather must be inferred (Ault, 1977). Some of the cognitive activities that psychologists believe mediate or modify incoming stimuli before they connect up with actual behavior include expectancies, insight, attention, memory, and plans. In the next sections we look at some of the most influential cognitive views of learning: expectancies, insight, observational learning and imitation, concept learning, and cognitive behavior modification. It is important to remember that while these views argue that learning involves some cognitive mediation, they still assign a very important role in the learning process to the environment.

Expectancies

Some years ago Edward Chase Tolman (Tolman, Ritchie & Kalish, 1946) argued that when classical and operant conditioning are occurring, the child acquires certain expectations. In classical conditioning, the boy fears the rabbit because he expects it will hurt him. In operant conditioning, a child works hard all semester in school because she expects to get a good grade at the end of the semester.

More recently social learning theorists have stressed that **expectancies** are an important aspect of learning (Bandura, 1977; Mischel, 1973). For example, Albert Bandura (1977) has distinguished between outcome expectancies ("This is what I expect to happen to me if I take this course of action") and efficacy expectancies ("I am/am not a skillful/capable person"). Such expectancies can mediate the link between the experiences the child has in the environment and subsequent behavior. The child, for example, who believes he is a skillful, competent person may not be as deterred from a goal when he fails once or twice along the way as a child who has less positive expectations for his success. And remember from our discussion of the reinforcement history of the child earlier in the chapter that past experiences with reinforcement establish expectations on the part of the child.

Insight Learning

Wolfgang Kohler, a German psychologist, spent four years in the Canary Islands during World War I observing the behavior of apes. While there he developed two fascinating experiments. One is called the "stick" problem, the other the "box" problem. Though the two experiments are basically the same, the solutions to the problems are different. In both dilemmas, the ape discovers that it cannot reach an alluring piece of fruit, either because the fruit is too high or it is outside of the ape's cage beyond its reach. To solve the stick problem, the ape has to insert a small stick inside a larger stick to reach the fruit. To master the box problem, the ape must place several boxes on top of one another to get high enough to reach the fruit (see figure 5.7).

According to Kohler (1925), solving these problems does not involve trial and error and mere connections between stimuli and responses. Rather, when the ape realizes that his customary actions are not likely to get the fruit, he often sits for some time and pensively seems to ponder how he is going to solve the problem. Then he often pops up, as if he has had a sudden flash of insight, and either puts the sticks together or piles the

FIGURE 5.7
This chimp has developed the insight to stack boxes on top of one another in order to reach the fruit (Kirk, 1975).

Albert Bandura

boxes on top of one another and gets the fruit. Kohler called this kind of learning **insight learning,** which can be defined as the sudden reorganization or reconceptualization of a problem that leads to immediate recognition of the solution. Insight does occur in children's learning. A child may stare at a difficult math problem for an hour, and all of a sudden the solution will pop into the child's head. Another child may try for two days to fix her bicycle, and suddenly a way to handle the problem will emerge.

Observational Learning, Imitation

Albert Bandura (1977) believes that if learning worked in a trial-and-error fashion, in many instances it would be very laborious and sometimes hazardous. Thus it would not make much sense to put a fifteen-year-old boy with no driver's training or experience in an automobile, have him drive down the road, and reward the positive responses he makes. Not many of us would want to be near the road. Instead, many of the complex things we do in life are due to our exposure to competent models who display appropriate behavior in solving problems and coping with their world.

Observational learning, also referred to as imitation and modeling, involves a reinterpretation of learning. For example, though a cat may learn to press a bar to obtain a piece of liver (operant conditioning), the cat may learn to press the bar much more quickly if it simply observes another cat being rewarded for bar pressing. Thus in many instances observational learning may be more economical than operant conditioning in terms of time. Experiments by Bandura and his colleagues (e.g., Bandura, Ross & Ross, 1963) demonstrated that observational learning often occurs when a modeled response is not rewarded. In other words, we learn a great deal of information about the environment simply by watching and listening to a model, even if the model has not been reinforced. The following experiment illustrates this point, as well as the distinction between learning and performance.

One experiment conducted by Bandura (1965) involved an equal number of boys and girls of nursery school age watching a filmed model beat up an adult-sized plastic Bobo doll under one of three conditions. In the first condition, an aggressor was rewarded with candy, soft drinks, and praise for aggressive behavior; in the second condition, the aggressor was criticized and even spanked (this was simulated) for the aggressive behavior; and in the third condition, the filmed aggressor received no consequences for the behavior. Subsequently, each child was left alone in a room filled

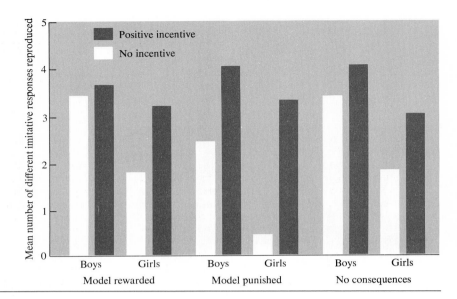

FIGURE 5.8
Results of Bandura's experiments with
children and aggression (Bandura, 1965).

with toys, including a Bobo doll, where he or she was observed through a one-way mirror. As shown in figure 5.8, children who watched the aggressor being rewarded or receiving no consequences for aggressive behavior imitated the aggressive behavior to a much greater degree than the children who watched the aggressor being punished for the aggressive behavior. As might be expected, boys showed more aggressive behavior than girls. The important point about the results described thus far is that observational learning occurred just as extensively when modeled aggressive behavior was not rewarded as when it was rewarded.

A second important point about the results shown in figure 5.8 focuses on the distinction between learning and performance. Just because an organism does not perform a response does not mean it has not learned. As shown in figure 5.8, when children were offered rewards (in the form of decals and fruit juice) for imitating the model's behavior, the differences in imitative behavior among children in the three conditions disappeared. In this experiment, the children in all three conditions had learned about the model's behaviors, but the performance of those behaviors did not occur for some children until reinforcement was presented. Bandura argues that when a person observes a model's behavior and makes no observable response, the individual may still have acquired the modeled responses in cognitive form.

In some imitative learning the child tries to reproduce faithfully someone else's responses—copying a design, mimicking a gesture, repeating verbatim what has been heard. However, imitation would be limited if this were the only form it took. A child may produce a response similar to one witnessed, although not exactly the same. For example, a child may learn to produce sentences containing a specific grammatical form (e.g., the passive construction) without repeating the same sentences that were heard. In this way children have learned to produce sentences with passive verbs, prepositional phrases, adverbs, correct verb tenses, and conjunctions (Heward & Eachus, 1979; Moerk & Moerk, 1979; Sherman, 1971; Zimmerman & Rosenthal, 1974). A child can also learn moral arguments, abstract concepts, and strategies for solving problems through simple observation (Rosenthal & Zimmerman, 1978; Zimmerman & Rosenthal, 1974). Again, the child is learning some behavior consistent with a pattern present in the modeled acts rather than merely mimicking the responses of others.

Clearly, observational learning or imitation is involved in a great deal of children's learning, and when a child is being imitated, a reciprocal process may be occurring. The child who is being imitated may be influenced by the fact that his or her behavior is being copied. To learn more about this intriguing possibility, read Perspective on Child Development 5.4.

PERSPECTIVE ON CHILD DEVELOPMENT 5.4

THE EFFECT OF BEING IMITATED

We usually think of imitation as a one-way process. An adult or child model acts in a given way, and the child observer learns to imitate the action. A number of recent investigations, however, have shown that the act of imitation also has consequences for the *model*. Thus, the process is a two-way street—that is, it is reciprocal. Some of this work has been done by Mark Thelen and his associates (e.g., 1976, 1978, 1980).

In one investigation, Thelen and his associates (1980) demonstrated that young elementary school children are more attracted to an adult who imitates them than to an adult who does not. First- and second-grade children performed a series of idiosyncratic behaviors in a game and then were imitated by one adult and not imitated by a second adult. The two adults were participants in the experiment and had been carefully coached on imitating or not imitating the child's idiosyncratic behaviors. While the modeling and imitation took place, another child stood by and simply observed the whole procedure. Results showed that the children who modeled the game were more attracted to the adult participant who imitated them than to the adult who did not. Interestingly, the child observers who did not participate in the procedure were also attracted more to the adult who had imitated the other child. Apparently, a child enjoys being imitated and tends to like the imitator. It may also make an uninvolved observer like the imitator as well. The reason for this effect is not altogether clear. It is generally thought, however, that the child perceives the adult imitator as similar to him- or herself and that the identification triggers a bond of affection. However, it may also be that the act of imitation signals the importance of one's own behavior and that the child is in some sense grateful to the "messenger" of this news. The two explanations are difficult to untangle experimentally, but this does not detract from the vitality of the basic phenomenon.

Thelen and his colleagues have also shown that young children are quite savvy about the fact that imitating someone can ingratiate one with them (1978, 1980). They demonstrated that, when consciously motivated to influence another child, a child may use imitation as a means of ingratiating him- or herself.

In one investigation (1980), fifty-seven children in the fourth, fifth, and sixth grades were each paired off with another child of the same sex but one grade lower whom they did not know well. The younger child was designated as the model and played a game of ball, having been coached to play with several idiosyncratic behaviors; for example, the child was coached to verbalize the choice of one of several available balls, to always choose a green ball, to blow on the ball, to bounce the ball on the floor once, and finally to roll the ball on the floor to the experimenter. Prior to the game, the older child was given either an *incentive* to influence the younger child or no incentive at all. The experimenter told the older children in the incentive group to encourage the younger models to eat some crackers that tasted terrible. It was explained that the crackers were a health food and that the health food company would pay twenty-five cents to the older child for each cracker the younger child could be induced to eat after the ball game.

In the ball game each child's goal was to get a ball across a room to the experimenter. The model (younger child) took a turn before the older child played. This alternation continued for ten turns. The measure of imitation was the number of idiosyncratic responses by the older child that mimicked the special ways in which the younger child had been coached to play the game (e.g., blowing on the ball). Results showed that older children in the incentive group imitated several of the idiosyncratic modeled behaviors more frequently than older children in the no-incentive group. Thus, the older children had probably used imitation as a way of ingratiating themselves with the younger ones, in hopes of eventually coaxing the younger children to eat a few of the unsavory but lucrative crackers.

(A footnote: Since the relevant data in the experiment were gathered during the ball game itself, the older children did not have to follow through with a sales pitch nor were the terrible-tasting crackers ever eaten. This part of the procedure was dismissed by explaining that the cracker company had stopped manufacturing the crackers. All children were given a small prize for their help.)

The child who is being imitated may be influenced by his/her behavior being copied.

Concept Learning

It is useful to be able to respond to all events in the same class in a consistent manner. In the presence of friends, for example, the child behaves differently from the way he behaves in the presence of adults. The child's friends are a class of events whose characteristics are different from those of adults. He learns to react one way at school, regardless of the specific classroom or teacher, and another way at home or at play. These are examples of **concept learning:** the same response is learned for an entire class of situations or events. (Concept learning can also refer to a large class of responses that are similar in the sense that they occur in the same stimulus situations. In this discussion, the *stimulus class* concept is highlighted.)

There are a number of different views about how concepts are learned. One (Harlow, 1949) is that the learner acquires *sets,* or a tendency to notice that certain responses inherently belong with certain kinds of events. Harry Harlow developed an experimental procedure for studying the acquisition of learning sets that has been used in many studies with children (Brown, 1970; Cameron, 1979). The child is presented with a learning problem, such as which of three objects in a game leads to reinforcement. Once he has learned this, many similar problems are presented, each made different from the last through use of different kinds of objects. Given enough problems to work with, the child may learn certain "tricks," such as avoiding all the items in a particular location or of a particular color. In other words, he has formed a *response set* for dealing with this class of situations. The set enables him to master each new problem quickly.

The learning of sets does not seem to be haphazard. Children gradually develop strategies for handling each new problem that appears. The correct strategy is usually learned suddenly, not gradually, and differs according to the child's age and intelligence and the nature of the task. Preschool children take longer to get the idea of the set and retain primitive strategies, such as position habits and preferences for specific objects, longer than elementary school children do. Children with higher IQs learn the sets faster than do children with lower IQs. Problems that contain more irrelevant information are more difficult than those with less irrelevant information (Stevenson, 1972).

A second view is that children develop *mediators,* or mental steps that intervene between the presentation of a stimulus and the response made to it. The mediator is viewed as an internalized stimulus, that is, a response association that guides behavior directed toward external events. In an early view the mediator was viewed as a linguistic unit, a word or phrase (Kendler & Kendler, 1962). It was thought that the preschool child lacked mediators and rather learned concepts through trial and error. The older child was thought to have mediators, learning concepts in a streamlined, shortcut fashion. In recent formulations this view has changed. Some scholars still believe that mediators exist but that these may take many forms—general symbols (Kendler & Hynds, 1974) or perceptual or attentional preferences (Gollin & Garrison, 1980; Odom, 1977). Changes in concept learning are seen as more gradual, with children moving from a lesser efficiency in producing and using mediators to a greater efficiency as they grow older (Kendler & Hynds, 1974; Watanabe, 1979).

One extensively studied problem is children's ability to control themselves and wait patiently when faced with an attractive toy or possible prize (e.g., Mischel, in press; Toner, Holstein & Hetherington, 1977). Often experimenters help the child by encouraging the youngster to conjure up an image or to recite a helpful phrase. These mediating events often help children to wait longer.

Yet another view of concept learning is that children approach a task with a number of **hypotheses** about what properties are part of the stimulus class in question. They must sift through hypotheses by taking stock of those which lead to correct response choices and those which do not. Eventually, they may be able to reject all the incorrect ones and discover the correct one. Marvin Levine (1975) has developed one influential theory based on this view. Suppose, for example, that a child is to learn to respond to large objects. In various learning trials, he or she may be exposed to objects varying in size (large, medium, small), color (red, green, blue), and form (circular, rectangular, triangular). Among the hypotheses entertained by the child may be: (a) large is correct, (b) small is correct, (c) red is correct, (d) green is correct, (e) circular is correct. (There are nine variables in all in this example.) The child's abilities to simply grapple with a large number of hypotheses and to keep track of which hypotheses are wrong (because they lead to no reward) are themselves among the variables that influence performance (e.g., Levine, 1975; Offenbach, 1980).

As we can see, cognitive factors have become a prevalent part of trying to understand the nature of children's learning. So far we have seen the importance of expectancies, insight, imitation, and concept learning. Now we return to a discussion of behavior modification, showing how cognitive factors have been called on to improve the likelihood that behavior modification will improve the child's maladaptive behavior.

Cognitive Behavior Modification

The belief that cognitive factors mediate the relation between environment and behavior has spawned a form of behavior modification known as **cognitive behavior modification.** From this perspective, the child's cognitive processes play a key role in modifying his or her behavior. The therapist uses rehearsal, homework assignments, self-monitoring, and rewarding feedback to improve the child's behavior.

One of the most promising results of the cognitive behavior modification approach centers on **self-instructional methods** (Meichenbaum, 1975, 1977). Donald Meichenbaum, a pioneer in this approach, emphasizes the importance of getting children to change what they are saying to themselves. The therapist often models appropriate self-statements, has the child role play these statements, and uses reinforcements to strengthen the new self-dialogue.

In one investigation (Meichenbaum & Goodman, 1971), a procedure was developed to train children to use self-talk to control their impulsiveness. In this strategy, the therapist first performed some task, describing each important part of the task. The child was then asked to do what the therapist had done. The child was encouraged to do the task a second time, in this instance whispering the description to himself. Examples of the content and sequence of self-instructional procedures with impulsive children are shown in table 5.2. Compared with groups of impulsive children who did not receive such training, the ability of these second-grade children to handle a number of learning problems showed marked improvement. Furthermore, the improvement was still evident one month after the training sessions had ended.

Conclusions about the Role of Cognitive Factors in Learning

In this section we have seen how important cognitive factors are in the learning process. We have seen that even in classical conditioning, a process that

TABLE 5.2
Content and Sequence of Self-Instructional Procedures with Impulsive Children

Content of Self-Instructions

Type of Self-Statement	Sample Self-Statement
Problem definition	"Let's see, what am I supposed to do?"
Problem approach	"Well, I should look this over and try to figure out how to get to the center of the maze."
Focusing of attention	"I better look ahead so I don't get trapped."
Coping statements	"Oh, that path isn't right. If I go that way I'll get stuck. I'll just go back here and try another way."
Self-reinforcement	"Hey, not bad. I really did a good job!"

Sequence of Self-Instructions

- The therapist models task performance and talks out loud while the child observes.
- The child performs the task, instructing himself or herself out loud.
- The therapist models task performance while whispering the self-instructions.
- The child performs the task, whispering to himself or herself.
- The therapist performs the task using covert self-instructions with pauses and behavioral signs of thinking (e.g., stroking beard or chin, raising eyes briefly).

From Kendall, P. C., and J. D. Norton-Ford, *Clinical Psychology.* Copyright © 1982 John Wiley & Sons, Inc. Reprinted by permission of John Wiley & Sons, Inc.

historically has been viewed as very reflexive, cognitive factors such as imagery and memory are being investigated. And we have observed that in the area of behavior modification, cognitive factors are being called on as mediators linking environment to behavior. In chapter 10, where we discuss perspectives on how children are socialized, we will discuss further the importance of cognitive factors in children's social learning. In the next four chapters we continue our exploration of the child's cognitive world, first focusing on the well-known views of cognitive developmental psychologist Jean Piaget.

SUMMARY

I. Learning is a relatively permanent change in behavior resulting from experience. Learning can be classified in terms of thoughts and behaviors or experiences.

II. Classical conditioning is a procedure by which a neutral stimulus comes to elicit a response by being paired with a stimulus that regularly evokes the response. It is also called respondent conditioning.

A. The basic classical conditioning experiment was first conducted by Ivan Pavlov and involved the association of an unconditioned stimulus, unconditioned response, conditioned stimulus, and conditioned response.

B. Researchers increasingly study compound stimuli in the investigation of classical conditioning. Three forms of classical conditioning that involve compound stimuli are higher order conditioning, overshadowing, and blocking.

C. Explanations of how classical conditioning works focus on stimulus substitution and information theories.

D. Children's fears may develop through the classical conditioning process. Not only can such fears be acquired through classical conditioning, but research indicates they may be eliminated through the counterconditioning process.

E. An evaluation of classical conditioning suggests its importance in learning but reveals that it misses the significance of the active nature of children in the learning process.

III. An understanding of operant conditioning involves B. F. Skinner's approach, positive reinforcement, punishment, and applications of operant conditioning.

A. Operant conditioning, as described by Skinner, emphasizes the child's acting (operating) on the environment with behavior being controlled by the consequences of the behavior. The operant is a response actively emitted by the child in relation to consequences.

B. Information about positive reinforcement focuses on time interval, shaping, primary and secondary reinforcement, schedules of reinforcement, extinction, stimulus generalization and stimulus discrimination, reinforcement history, and reinforcement in natural settings.

1. Immediate consequences are more effective than delayed consequences.

2. Shaping refers to the process of rewarding closer and closer approximations to desired behavior.

3. Primary reinforcement is due to innate factors while secondary reinforcement occurs through experience.

4. Schedules of reinforcement, such as variable and ratio, are rules that explain when the consequence occurs in relation to behavior.

5. Extinction refers to the situation in which the consequences of a response are removed; it is characterized by spontaneous recovery. Stimulus generalization refers to the tendency of a response that has been rewarded in the presence of one stimulus to occur in the presence of another stimulus similar to the first. Stimulus discrimination indicates the tendency of the conditioned response to occur in the presence of one stimulus but not another.

6. The child's reinforcement history is important in determining whether a reinforcer will be effective; it sets up expectancies on the part of the child.

7. Psychologists are interested in the extent to which reinforcement works in nonlaboratory situations. Studies with children suggest that peer reinforcement of sex-typed behavior is prevalent.

8. At times external rewards can interfere with learning, particularly when the child already is motivated to learn.

C. Punishment is the process that results in a decrease in the occurrence of a behavior. Research with children suggests that reasoning often is more effective than high-intensity punishment. Researchers recommend that alternatives to punishment always be fully explored before punishment is used.

D. Behavior modification refers to the use of learning principles to change maladaptive behavior. Some behavior modification programs work; others do not.

IV. Interest in cognitive factors involved in learning has increased. Among the influential cognitive views of learning are those focused on expectancies, insight, observational learning and imitation, and concept learning.

A. Tolman and Bandura argue that expectancies are a critical part of the learning process, mediating the link between environment and behavior.

B. Kohler demonstrated the importance of insight learning, a sudden reorganization of a problem that leads to an immediate solution.

C. Children learn extensively through observation and imitation. An important distinction in imitation involves acquisition performance.

D. Concept learning involves learning the same response for an entire class of situations or events. Three views of concept learning are those focusing on learning sets, mediators, and hypotheses.

E. From the perspective of cognitive behavior modification, the child's cognitive processes play a key role in linking environment to behavior. Self-instructional methods have shown promising results in this regard.

F. The cognitive approach to learning has been an important contribution to understanding the relation between environmental experiences and children's behavior.

KEY TERMS

acquisition phase 138
baseline 138
behavior modification 153
blocking 143
classical conditioning 142
cognitive behavior modification 162
compound stimulus 143
concept learning 160
conditioned response (CR) 142
conditioned stimulus (CS) 142
counterconditioning 144
expectancies 156
extinction (classical and operant) 138, 149
extrinsic motivation 151
higher order conditioning 143
hypotheses 161
incentives 151
information theory 144
insight learning 157
interval schedule 148
intervention phase 138
intrinsic motivation 151
observational learning 157
operant conditioning 146

operants 146
overshadowing 143
phobias 144
positive reinforcement 147
primary reinforcer 148
punishment 152
ratio schedule 148
respondents 146
schedules of reinforcement (or punishment) 148
secondary reinforcer 148
self-instructional methods 162
shaping 148
S–O–R model 156
spontaneous recovery 149
stimulus discrimination (classical and operant) 149
stimulus generalization (classical and operant) 145, 149
stimulus substitution theory 143
token economy 155
unconditioned response (UCR) 142
unconditioned stimulus (UCS) 142
variable schedules 149

REVIEW QUESTIONS

1. What is learning?
2. Describe the nature of classical conditioning.
3. Discuss the many facets of operant conditioning.
4. How does punishment work in changing the child's behavior?
5. Discuss intrinsic and extrinsic reinforcement.
6. Outline the role of expectancies, insight, and imitation in learning.
7. What are some conclusions about the role of cognition in learning?

SUGGESTED READINGS

Axelrod, S., & Apsche, J. (Eds.). (1983). *The effects of punishment on human behavior*. New York: Academic Press.
An up-to-date authoritative volume on how punishment can be used effectively to control behavior. Considerable detail about reducing the negative side effects of punishment and a full consideration of the ethical issues involved in the use of punishment.

Bandura, A. (1977). *Social learning theory*. Englewood Cliffs, NJ: Prentice-Hall.
A full description of Bandura's ideas about observational learning, as well as a number of other cognitive processes that mediate the relation between the environment and behavior.

Chance, P. (1979). *Learning and behavior*. Belmont, CA: Wadsworth.
An excellent, well-written paperback on the processes of learning described in this chapter. Emphasizes that observational learning should be given equal status with classical and operant conditioning as a key learning process.

Kalish, H. I. (1981). *From behavioral science to behavior modification*. New York: McGraw-Hill.
An excellent overview of the successes and failures of behavior modification, including both classical and operant conditioning. Also includes excellent overviews of the basic learning processes described in this chapter.

Skinner, B. F. *Walden two*. (1960). New York: Macmillan.
Skinner once entertained the possibility of a career as a writer. In this interesting and provocative book, he outlines his ideas on how a more complete understanding of the principles of instrumental conditioning can lead to a happier life. Critics argue that his approach is far too manipulative.

(167-196)

COGNITIVE DEVELOPMENT AND PIAGET'S THEORY

PROLOGUE

THE TEN-YEAR-OLD BOY AND
THE RARE ALBINO SPARROW

An amazing thing happened when Jean was only ten years old. He wrote an article about the rare albino sparrow, an article that was published in the *Journal of the Natural History of Neuchâtel*. The article was so brilliant that the curators of the Geneva Museum of Natural History, who had no idea the article had been written by a ten-year-old, offered the preadolescent boy a job as a curator of the museum. The heads of the museum quickly withdrew their offer when they found out that Jean was only ten years old.

Jean is Jean Piaget, born August 9, 1896, in Neuchâtel, Switzerland. His father was an intellectual who taught young Jean to think systematically. Jean's mother also was very bright and strongly religious as well. His father seemed to maintain an air of detachment from his mother, who has been described by Piaget as prone to frequent outbursts of neurotic behavior.

In his autobiography, Piaget (1952a) detailed why he chose to pursue the study of cognitive development rather than emotional development.

> I started to forego playing for serious work very early. Indeed, I have always detested any departure from reality, an attitude which I relate to . . . my mother's poor mental health. It was this disturbing factor which at the beginning of my studies in psychology made me keenly interested in psychoanalytic and pathological psychology. Though this interest helped me to achieve independence and to widen my cultural background, I have never since felt any desire to involve myself deeper in that particular direction, always much preferring the study of normalcy and of the workings of the intellect to that of the tricks of the unconscious. (p. 238)

Piaget's interest in zoology continued through his adolescent years and culminated in his doctoral dissertation on the behavior of mollusks in 1918 at the University of Neuchâtel. During his adolescence, though, Piaget was not just interested in zoology. Philosophy and psychology books filled his room, and he spent much of his spare time reading Kant, Durkheim, and James (philosopher, sociologist, and psychologist, respectively).

While his studies had taken him in the direction of biology and other intellectual pursuits, the deteriorating health of Piaget's mother had an important impact on his first job after he completed his doctorate degree. In 1918 Piaget took a position at Bleuler's psychiatric clinic in Zurich, where he learned about clinical techniques for interviewing children. Then, still at the young age of twenty-two, he went to work in the psychology laboratory at the University of Zurich, where he was exposed to the insights of Alfred Binet, who developed the first intelligence test. By the time Piaget was twenty-five, his experience in varied disciplines had helped him see important links between philosophy, psychology, and biology.

PREVIEW

Our study of the cognitive developmental view begins with an overview of Jean Piaget's place in child psychology. Then we focus on the basic nature of cognitive developmental theory and the processes responsible for cognitive change. Next we turn our attention to the nature of cognitive stages in Piaget's theory. Finally, we evaluate Piaget's theory, including contributions and criticisms.

JEAN PIAGET AND HIS PLACE IN CHILD PSYCHOLOGY

In discussing Sigmund Freud's contribution to psychology, Edwin Boring (1950) remarked that "It is not likely that the history of experimental psychology can be written in the next three centuries without mention of Freud's name and still claim to be a general history of psychology. And there you have the best criterion of greatness: posthumous fame" (p. 707). More than thirty-five years after Boring published his book, it seems quite likely that his judgment was correct—Freud is still a dominating presence in our field. It is interesting to speculate that Piaget's contribution to cognitive psychology is as important as Freud's contribution to personality and psychopathology. With Piaget's death being a rather recent event (he died in 1980), it may be too early to judge. But certainly for the foreseeable future Piaget's contributions will be strongly felt. He was truly a great man of psychology.

Shortly after Piaget's death, John Flavell, a leading Piagetian scholar, described what we owe Piaget:

> Jean Piaget died in Geneva, Switzerland, on September 16, 1980. He was eighty-four years old. It is hard to think of anything important to say about this great scientist that is not already well known to readers of this Newsletter—so truly outstanding and widely recognized were his contributions to our field. A long and detailed obituary for such a figure would certainly be richly deserved, but it would hardly be needed in present company. So let us, instead, honor his memory by briefly reminding ourselves of some of the many things child developmentalists owe him.
>
> First, we owe him a host of insightful concepts of enduring power and fascination—both mundane concepts that children acquire and theoretical concepts

Jean Piaget

> that illuminate their acquisition. My favorites include the childhood concepts of object permanence, perspective, conservation, and measurement, and the theoretical concepts of scheme, assimilation, accommodation, decentration, and invariance.
>
> Second, we owe him a vast conceptual framework which has highlighted key issues and problems in human cognitive development and has informed and guided the efforts of nearly a generation of researchers in this area. This framework is the now-familiar vision of the developing child, who, through its own active and creative commerce with its environment, builds an orderly succession of cognitive structures enroute to intellectual maturity.
>
> These two debts add up to a third, more general one: We owe him the present field of cognitive development—that is, we owe him a wide field of scientific inquiry. What would exist in its place today had Piaget never lived is anyone's guess, of course, but there are those of us who remember well what it was—and especially wasn't—before his influence was felt. Our task is now to extend and go beyond what he began so well (*SRCD Newsletter,* Fall 1980, p. 1).

From Flavell, J. H., "A Tribute to Piaget," in *Society for Research in Child Development Newsletter,* Fall 1980, p. 1, The Society for Research in Child Development.

COGNITIVE DEVELOPMENTAL THEORY AND PROCESSES OF CHANGE

Initially we describe the nature of cognitive developmental theory and briefly discuss how it differs from a cognitive learning view. Then we turn our attention to the processes Piaget believed are responsible for cognitive changes.

The Basic Nature of Cognitive Developmental Theory

Cognitive developmental theory focuses on the rational thinking of the developing child. It also stresses that cognitive development unfolds in a stagelike sequence, whose stages are ordered and uniform for all children. Cognitive developmental theory emphasizes the biological maturation of the child and how such maturation underlies the child's cognitive stage of development. Environmental experiences are important in the cognitive developmental view, but from Piaget's perspective are primarily the "food" for the child's cognitive machinery. Whereas in the learning perspective described in chapter 5 cognitive processes were seen as important mediators in linking environmental experiences to behavior, from Piaget's perspective such cognitive processes are more than mediators. Rather cognitions are the central focus of development, causing the child's behavior rather than just mediating the environment's effect on the child's behavior. A large portion of this chapter will be devoted to a discussion of Piaget's stages of cognitive development. Before we discuss these stages, however, we describe the processes Piaget believed are responsible for changes in children's thought.

Processes Responsible for Cognitive Changes

The processes Piaget offered to explain cognitive changes are adaptation, assimiliation, and accommodation; organization; and equilibration. We consider each of these in turn.

Adaptation, Assimilation, and Accommodation

If children are to develop normally, they have to interact effectively with the environment. Effective interaction is called **adaptation.** For Piaget the interaction is a cognitive one. It involves the child's use of thinking skills. Adaptation is subdivided into **assimilation** and **accommodation,** which usually occur together. In assimilation, the child tries to incorporate features of the environment into already existing ways of thinking about them. In accommodation, the child tries to incorporate new features of the environment into his or her thinking by slightly modifying existing modes of thought. An example may help to clarify these terms.

A young girl is presented with a hammer and nails to use in hanging a picture on her bedroom wall. She has never had the opportunity to use a hammer before. From experience and observation, however, she realizes that a hammer is an object to be held, that it is swung by the handle to strike the nail, and that it is swung repeatedly. Realizing each of these things, she incorporates her behavior into a conceptual framework that already exists (assimilation). But the hammer is heavy, so she must hold it near the top. As she swings too hard, the nail bends, so she must adjust the pressure of her taps. These adjustments show her sensitivity to the need to alter the concept slightly (accommodation).

Another example involves a young infant who discovers a small wood chip in her bath (Flavell, 1977). The infant might play with the chip as if it were a boat—she is assimilating the chip to her category of boats. Yet she also learns some things about wood chips—that they float, for instance, and can be tipped over if there is a collision. Thus, the infant is learning some things about wood chips—she is accommodating. In assimilating and accommodating she is growing intellectually.

Organization

A second mechanism of change is **organization,** that is, the tendency of isolated behaviors or thoughts to be grouped into a higher-order, more smoothly functioning system. Every level of thought is organized in some fashion. Continual refinement of this organization is an inherent part of development. The girl who has only a vague idea about how to use a hammer may also have a vague idea about how to use other tools. After learning how to use each one, she must interrelate these uses, or organize her knowledge, if she is to become skilled in using tools. In the same way, the child continually integrates and coordinates the many other branches of knowledge that often develop independently. Organization occurs within stages of development as well as across them.

Equilibration

Equilibration is a third mechanism invoked to explain how a child shifts from one stage to the next. The goal of better organization is to reach a more lasting state of balance in thought. This goal is achieved as thought becomes more logical and abstract. But before a new stage of thought can be reached, the child must face the inadequacy of the current one. He or she must experience cognitive conflict, or uncertainty. If a child believes that the amount of liquid is changed simply because it was poured into a container with a different shape, he or she might be puzzled by such issues as where the extra liquid came from and whether there is actually more liquid to drink. These puzzles will eventually be resolved as thought becomes concrete. In the everyday world the child is constantly faced with such counterexamples and inconsistencies. Let's now look at these stages of cognitive development that we have been mentioning.

PIAGET'S STAGES OF COGNITIVE DEVELOPMENT

Piaget postulated that the child passes through a series of stages of thought from infancy to adolescence. Passage through the stages is the result of biological pressures to *adapt* to the environment (assimilation and accommodation) and to *organize* structures of thinking. These stages of thought are described as qualitatively different from one another, which means that the way a child reasons at one stage is very different from the way a child reasons at another. This contrasts with the quantitative assessments of intellect made in standard intelligence tests, where the focus is on how much the child knows, or how many questions the child answers correctly. Thought development is landmarked by the following major stages: sensorimotor, preoperations, concrete operations, and formal operations. We consider each of these in turn and then conclude with an overview of Piaget's stages and the concept of egocentrism.

Sensorimotor Thought

To learn more about the **sensorimotor stage** we first describe its basic nature and features, then turn to the many aspects of infant development to which it applies. Finally, we examine the six substages of sensorimotor development, giving considerable attention to object permanence.

Basic Features of Sensorimotor Thought

Two of the most important features of sensorimotor thought involve the coordination of sensation and action and nonsymbolic aspects of the period.

The sensorimotor stage lasts from birth to about two years of age, corresponding to the period known as infancy. During this time the infant develops the ability to organize and coordinate his or her sensations and perceptions with his or her physical movements and actions. This coordination of sensation with action is the source of the term *sensorimotor*. The stage begins with the newborn, who has little more than reflexes to coordinate his or her senses with actions. The stage ends with the two-year-old, who has complex sensorimotor patterns and is beginning to adopt a primitive symbol system. For example, the two-year-old can imagine looking at a toy and manipulating it with his or her hands before he or she actually does so. The child can also use simple sentences—for example, "Mommy, jump"—to represent a sensorimotor event that has just occurred.

Think about your dog or cat and the kind of intelligence that the animal possesses. Although many of us brag about the intelligence of our pets, realistically we realize that their cognitive abilities are limited. Piaget would argue that their abilities are limited in a quite specific way: they are bound up with the animal's behavior; they are not reflective or contemplative abilities, and they do not provide for conscious thinking about things that are not perceptually available. In a word, these abilities are not symbolic.

Think about your own cognition when you are engaged in behavior that is well-practiced—something such as driving home from work or mowing your lawn. There is a kind of intelligence in such behavior. You show tremendous physical coordination and timing and must continuously monitor perceptual information. You also must make many small adjustments and compensations, even some low-level decisions (e.g., to change lanes in preparation for an upcoming turn, or to stop when the light turns yellow). Yet, while accomplishing all of these complex behaviors, you may have been thinking about entirely different things (problems at work or with a personal relationship). And your subsequent ability to remember these behaviors probably is quite meager. Piaget would argue that the intelligence you use in such well-practiced behaviors is similar to that of your dog or cat—it is a nonsymbolic sensorimotor intelligence.

Piaget argued that deferred imitation does not occur until 1½–2 years of age. Recent research suggests it may come earlier, however.

Nonsymbolic, sensorimotor intelligence is what Piaget claimed for the very young infant, up until about one and a half years or so. Thus, the most critical aspect of Piaget's sensorimotor stage is that it is nonsymbolic throughout most of its duration (Flavell, 1977; Piaget, 1970).

Support for the nonsymbolic nature of thought in early infancy comes from the observation of **deferred imitation,** that is, imitation of a behavior observed some time ago. While a two-year-old might see Daddy exercising in the morning and then try to imitate the movements later that evening, a one-year old is unlikely to do so. According to Piaget, only at the end of the sensorimotor period, when the child is approximately one and a half to two years old, does deferred imitation emerge. This claim may need adjusting because Andrew Meltzoff (1985) has recently found evidence for deferred imitation in infants only fourteen months old.

Additional arguments for the nonsymbolic nature of thought in early infancy concerns the solving of problems through internal reflection or insight. Problem solving occurs quite early in life, perhaps by twelve

TABLE 6.1

Multidimensional View of Development During the Sensorimotor Period

Stage	Developmental Unit	Intention and Means—End Relations	Meaning	Object Permanence
1	Exercising the ready-made sensorimotor schemes (0–1 mo.)			
2	Primary circular reactions (1–4 mo.)		Different responses to different objects	
3	Secondary circular reactions (4–8 mo.)	Acts upon objects	"Motor meaning"	Brief single-modality search for absent object
4	Coordination of secondary schemes (8–12 mo.)	Attacks barrier to reach goal	Symbolic meaning	Prolonged, multimodality search
5	Tertiary circular reactions (12–18 mo.)	"Experiments in order to see"; discovery of new means through "groping accommodation"	Elaboration through action and feedback	Follows sequential displacements if object in sight
6	Invention of new means through mental combinations (18–24 mo.)	Invention of new means through reciprocal assimilation of schemes	Further elaboration; symbols increasingly covert	Follows sequential displacements with object hidden; symbolic representation of object, mostly internal

From The Origins of Intellect: Piaget's Theory, 2d ed. by J. L. Phillips, Jr. W. H. Freeman and Company. Copyright © 1975.

Schema.

months of age. But Piaget claimed that until about one and a half to two years of age, this problem solving is of the trial-and-error variety, devoid of an internal, symbolic component. For example, one of Piaget's daughters insightfully discovered how to get a matchbox open; looking at the slightly opened matchbox, she began opening and closing her mouth. Only after making a few such movements did she reach for the matchbox and pull out its drawer with her hands. Piaget interpreted the moving-mouth behavior as reflecting internal, symbolic operations, which emerge only at the end of the sensorimotor stage.

The Far-Ranging Implications of Sensorimotor Thought

Sensorimotor development is studied on a number of fronts. Investigators note the way the infant coordinates the different perceptual modalities, such as looking at objects and touching them; the manner in which the child imitates actions and sounds; the way the child plays; and the way the child seems to represent basic categories of experience, such as spatial relations, time, and causality. These categories of sensorimotor concepts or schemes are listed in table 6.1. In the section that follows, we will discuss the general characteristics of the sensorimotor stage and then offer a more detailed account of how one important sensorimotor characteristic develops—the infant's sense of object permanence. Object permanence is perhaps the most widely discussed and researched concept in the sensorimotor period. Unlike other stages, the sensorimotor stage is subdivided into six substages, which demarcate qualitative changes in the nature of sensorimotor organization. The term *scheme,* or *schema,* is used to refer to the basic unit for an organized pattern of sensorimotor functioning. Within a given substage, there may be many different schemes—for example, sucking, rooting, and blinking in substage 1—but all have the same organization. In stage 1 they are basically reflexive in nature. From substage to substage, the schemes change in organization. This change in organization is at the heart of Piaget's descriptions of the substages.

Space	Time	Causality	Imitation	Play
			Pseudo imitation begins	Apparent functional autonomy of some acts
All modalities focus on single object	Brief search for absent object	Acts, then waits for effect to occur	Pseudo imitation quicker, more precise. True imitation of acts already in repertoire and visible on own body	More acts done for their own sake
Turns bottle to reach nipple	Prolonged search for absent object	Attacks barrier to reach goal; waits for adults to serve him	True imitation of novel acts not visible on own body	Means often become ends; ritualization begins
Follows sequential displacements if object in sight	Follows sequential displacements if object in sight	Discovers new means; solicits help from adults	True imitation quicker, more precise	Quicker conversion of means to end; elaboration of ritualization
Solves detour problem; symbolic representation of spatial relationships, mostly internal	Both anticipation and memory	Infers causes from observing effects; predicts effects from observing causes	Imitates (1) complex, (2) nonhuman, (3) absent modules	Treats inadequate stimuli as if adequate to imitate an enactment, i.e., symbolic ritualization or "pretending"

Simple reflexes

Primary

The Substages of Sensorimotor Development

Piaget portrayed sensorimotor development as having six substages: simple reflexes; first habits and primary circular reactions; secondary circular reactions; coordination of secondary circular reactions; tertiary circular reactions, novelty, and curiosity; and internalization of schemes.

Simple Reflexes (Birth to One Month)

In the substage of **simple reflexes** the basic means of coordinating sensation and action is through reflexive behaviors, such as sucking and rooting, that the newborn has brought into the world. During this period the infant engages in practice or exercise of these reflexes. More importantly, he or she develops an ability and penchant for producing behaviors that resemble reflexes in the absence of obvious reflex stimuli. For example, the newborn may suck when a bottle or nipple is only nearby. At birth, the bottle or nipple would have produced the sucking pattern only when placed directly in the newborn's mouth or touched to the newborn's lips. This reflexlike action in the absence of a triggering stimulus is evidence that the infant is initiating action and actively structuring experiences, even shortly after birth.

First Habits and Primary Circular Reactions (One to Four Months)

The infant learns to coordinate sensation and action with two related types of schemes or structures, habits and primary circular reactions. A *habit* is a scheme based upon simple reflexes, such as sucking, which has become completely divorced from its eliciting stimulus. For example, an infant in the first substage might suck when orally stimulated by a bottle or when visually shown it, but an infant in the second substage may exercise the sucking scheme even when no bottle is present.

A **primary circular reaction** is a scheme based upon the infant's attempt to reproduce an interesting or pleasurable event that initially occurred by chance. In a popular Piagetian example, a child accidentally sucks his fingers when they are placed near his mouth; later he searches for the fingers to suck them again, but the fingers do not cooperate in the search because he cannot coordinate visual and manual actions.

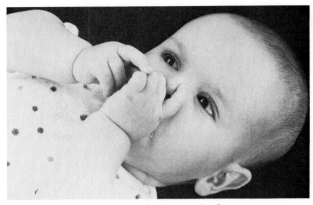

How might this be a primary circular reaction?

The habits and circular reactions are stereotyped—that is, the infant repeats them the same way each time. The infant's own body remains the center of attention; there is no outward pull by environmental events.

Secondary Circular Reactions (Four to Eight Months)

In the substage of **secondary circular reactions** the infant becomes more object oriented, or focused on the world around him, and moves beyond preoccupation with the self in sensation interactions. The chance shaking of a rattle, for example, may produce a fascination with the result, and the child repeats this action for the sake of experiencing the objective result. The infant imitates some simple actions of others, like the baby talk or burbling of adults, and some physical gestures, but his imitations are limited to actions he is already able to produce himself. Although directed toward objects in the world, the infant's schemes lack an intentional, goal-directed quality.

Coordination of Secondary Reactions (Eight to Twelve Months)

Several significant changes take place at this stage. The infant readily combines and recombines previously learned schemes in a *coordinated* fashion. He or she may look at an object and grasp it simultaneously, or visually inspect a toy, such as a rattle, and finger it simultaneously in obvious tactual exploration. Actions are even more outward-directed than before.

Related to this coordination is the second achievement—the presence of *intentionality,* the separation of means and goals in accomplishing simple feats. For example, the infant may manipulate a stick (the means)

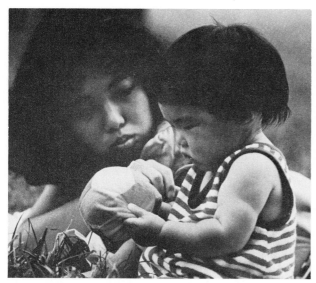

How does this involve the coordination of secondary circular reactions?

means, goal.

to bring a desired toy within reach (the goal). He or she may knock over one block to reach and play with another one.

As we will see later, this substage has generated a great deal of interest on the part of investigators who wish to examine the logic and validity of the infant stages (e.g., Fischer, 1980; Gratch, 1977).

Tertiary Circular Reactions, Novelty, and Curiosity (Twelve to Eighteen Months)

In **tertiary circular reactions** the infant becomes intrigued by the variety of properties that objects possess and by the multiplicity of things he or she can make happen to objects. A block can be made to fall, spin, hit another object, slide across the ground, and so on. Tertiary circular reactions are schemes in which the infant purposefully explores new possibilities with objects, continuously changing what is done to them and exploring the results. Piaget speaks of this period as marking the developmental starting point for human curiosity and interest in novelty. Previous circular reactions have been devoted exclusively to reproducing former events (with the exception of imitation of novel acts, which occurs as early as substage 4). The tertiary reaction is the first to be concerned with novel ones. As such, it is the mechanism par excellence for trial-and-error learning.

How does this involve Piaget's tertiary circular reactions substage of infancy?

Symbol

Internalization of Schemes (Eighteen to Twenty-Four Months)

In the substage of **internalization of schemes** the infant's mental functioning shifts from a purely sensorimotor plane to a symbolic plane; the infant develops the ability to use primitive symbols. For Piaget, a **symbol** is an internalized sensory image or word that represents an event. Primitive symbols permit the child to think about concrete events without directly acting or perceiving. Moreover, symbols allow the child to manipulate and transform the represented events in simple ways. In one example, a child opened a door slowly to avoid disturbing a piece of paper lying on the floor on the other side. Clearly, the child had an image of the unseen paper and what would happen to it if the door were opened quickly. More recent scholars have debated whether two-year-olds really have such representations of action sequences at their command (Corrigan, 1981; Fischer & Jennings, 1981).

Object Permanence

Before turning to the next period in cognitive development, we must consider one of the infant's most significant sensorimotor accomplishments—the understanding of **object permanence** (Bower, 1974; Fischer, 1980; Flavell, 1977).

To think logically about themselves and the world around them, children must grasp some simple ideas. One is that the self is physically separate, or distinct, from surrounding objects and events—a self–world differentiation. Another is that objects and events continue to exist even though the child is not in direct perceptual contact with them ("Mother is still around even though I can't see her," "My pet turtle is still in the bedroom even though I'm in the kitchen").

Imagine what thought would be like if people could not distinguish between themselves and other events in the world, or if events were believed to last only as long as the person has direct contact with them. Highly chaotic, disorderly, and unpredictable, no doubt. This is what the mental life of the newborn infant is like; there is no self–world differentiation and no sense of object permanence (Piaget, 1952b). By the end of the sensorimotor period, however, both are clearly understood. The transition between these extreme states is not abrupt; rather, it is marked by qualitative changes that reflect movement through each of the substages of sensorimotor thought.

The principal way object permanence is studied is by watching the infant's reaction when an attractive object or event disappears. If the infant shows no reaction, it is assumed that he or she has no belief in its

continued existence. On the other hand, if the infant is surprised at the disappearance and searches for the object, it is assumed that he or she has a belief in its continued existence. According to Piaget, the distinct stages described in table 6.2 exist in the development of object permanence. However, as discussed in Perspective on Child Development 6.1, other views of object permanence have been developed.

T A B L E   6 . 2

Piaget's Description of the Six Substages
of Object Permanence

Stage	General Description
Sensorimotor 1	There is no apparent object permanence. When a spot of light moves across the visual field, the infant follows it but quickly ignores its disappearance.
Sensorimotor 2	A primitive form of object permanence develops. Given the same experience, the infant looks briefly at the spot where the light disappeared, with an expression of passive expectancy.
Sensorimotor 3	The infant's sense of object permanence undergoes further development. With the newfound ability to coordinate simple schemes, the infant shows clear patterns of searching for a missing object, with sustained visual and manual examination of the spot where the object apparently disappeared.
Sensorimotor 4	The infant actively searches for a missing object in the spot where it disappeared, with new actions to achieve the goal of searching effectively. For example, if an attractive toy has been hidden behind a screen, the child may look at the screen and try to push it away with a hand. If the screen is too heavy to move or is permanently fixed, the child readily substitutes a secondary scheme—for example, crawling around it or kicking it. The new actions signal that the infant's knowledge or belief in the continued existence of the missing object is stronger than it was in the previous substage.
Sensorimotor 5	The infant now is able to track an object that disappears and reappears in several locations in rapid succession. For example, a toy may be hidden under different boxes in succession in front of the infant, who succeeds in finding it. The infant is apparently able to hold an image of the missing object in mind longer than before.
Sensorimotor 6	The infant can search for a missing object that disappeared and reappeared in several locations in succession, as before. In addition, the infant searches in the appropriate place even when the object has been hidden from view as it is being moved. This activity indicates that the infant is able to "image" the missing object and to manipulate the image (follow it) from one location to the next.

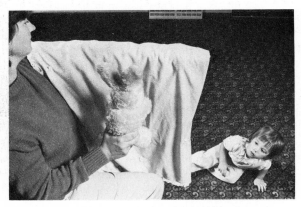

To know the rabbit exists even though it is hidden from view signifies object permanence.

PERSPECTIVE ON CHILD DEVELOPMENT 6.1

OTHER VIEWS OF OBJECT PERMANENCE

Although Piaget's stage sequence is a neat summary of what might happen as the infant comes to fathom the *permanence* of things in the world, it cannot adequately handle the weight of many contradictory findings in the research that has accumulated in the past twenty years. His stages broadly describe the interesting changes fairly well, but the infant's life is not so neatly compartmentalized into six distinct organizations as Piaget supposed. As well, some of Piaget's explanations for the causes of change are simply wrong. In the spirit of constructive criticism, consider the following major shortcomings of his account.

1. Ina Uzgiris and J. M. Hunt (1972, 1975; Hunt, 1976) have offered convincing evidence that there are more than six landmarks in the general course of sensorimotor growth and in the development of object permanence in particular. These authors have identified a dozen or more behavioral accomplishments that the infant masters in a given developmental sequence. In their view infant change is more gradual and continuous than Piaget's description implies.

2. Piaget's account ignores the many psychological "performance variables" that influence what the child might do. The manner in which an object is hidden, the amount of time it is hidden, the way in which the adult alternates hiding places, as well as yet other variables, all influence how the child performs (e.g., Bower, 1974; Corrigan, 1981; Harris, 1975).

3. Piaget claimed that certain processes are crucial in stage transitions. The data do not always support his explanations, however. For example, according to Piaget, the critical requirement for the infant to progress into sensorimotor substage 4 is the coordination of vision and the sense of touch, or hand–eye coordination.

   According to Piaget, another important feature of progress into substage 4 is the infant's inclination to search for an object hidden in a familiar location rather than looking for the object in a new location. If new locations serve as hiding places, the infant progressing into

substage 4 should make frequent mistakes, selecting the familiar hiding place (A) instead of the new location (B). This phenomenon is sometimes called the A-B error of substage 4, or perseveration. Unfortunately, perseveration does not occur consistently in an infant's behavior (Corrigan, 1981; Harris, 1975; Sophian, 1985). Sometimes it occurs and sometimes it doesn't. Further, there is accumulating evidence that the A-B errors are sensitive to the delay between the hiding of an object at B and the infant's attempt to find it (e.g., Diamond, 1985). Thus, the A-B error might be partly due to memory failures.

4. Finally, for the purposes of our discussion, there is the problem that infant *competencies* may sometimes be described incorrectly by Piaget. According to him, for example, the infant in substage 6 is able mentally to conceive of a series of actions and operate with this mental conception over time. Thus, suppose an object is made invisible by placing it inside a covered container. Then the object is moved from one hiding place to another so the infant cannot see it directly. The infant should be able to follow the unseen object's movement, since he supposedly has the object in mind. A close look at such tasks (Corrigan, 1981) reveals that the sensorimotor stage 6 infant may succeed at finding objects without using a specific image or memory of the object coordination. But several facts argue that the infant at substage 4 is oblivious to his tactile experiences (e.g., Gratch, 1977; Harris, 1975). For example, if an object is covered while it is still in the infant's hands, a six-month-old infant does not look for it (Gratch, 1972). Instead he may rely on understanding what the person hiding the objects is doing and simply look in those locations where that adult has been. Such performances, then, depend on learning "how to search," not on where the invisible thing is. Fischer and Jennings (1981) go so far as to argue that two-year-olds probably do not readily utilize mental images of absent events at all.

N.B
Cognitive

ego cen trism
animism

CONCEPT TABLE 6.1 Cognitive Developmental Theory, Processes of Change, and Sensorimotor Development		
Concept	**Processes/Related Ideas**	**Description/Characteristics**
Nature of cognitive developmental theory	Thought, biological maturation, and stages	Cognitive developmental theory stresses that thought or cognition is the central focus if we are to understand children's development. It emphasizes biological maturation and unfolding of cognitive stages.
Processes responsible for changes in thought	Adaptation, assimilation, and accommodation	Effective interaction with the environment is called adaptation. According to Piaget, the interaction is a cognitive one. Adaptation is subdivided into assimilation and accommodation, which usually occur together.
	Organization	Every level of thought is organized, from sensorimotor in infancy to formal operational in adolescence.
	Equilibration	The mechanism by which the child resolves cognitive conflict and attains a balance in thought is equilibration.
Sensorimotor thought	Basic features	Sensorimotor thought essentially involves the infant's ability to organize and coordinate his or her sensations with his or her physical movements. The stage lasts from birth to about two years of age and is nonsymbolic throughout most of its duration.
	Far-ranging implications	There are many dimensions to sensorimotor thought. Perceptual modalities, imitation, play, and basic categories of experience, such as time and causality, are included.
	Substages of sensorimotor thought	Six substages were proposed by Piaget: simple reflexes; first habits and primary circular reactions; secondary circular reactions; coordination of secondary reactions; tertiary circular reactions, novelty, and curiosity; and internalization of schemes.
	Object permanence	Object permanence is one of the infant's most significant accomplishments. Piaget described six substages of developing object permanence. Views other than Piaget's have been offered to account for object permanence.

We have discussed many ideas about cognitive developmental theory, processes of change, and sensorimotor development. A summary of these ideas is described in Concept Table 6.1. Next we study the nature of preoperational thought.

Preoperational Thought

To understand preoperational thought we focus on the general nature of preoperational thought, its early and late phases, egocentrism, and animism.

What Is Preoperational Thought?

Since the second stage of thought is called preoperational, it would seem that not much of importance is occurring until full-fledged operational thought appears. The **preoperational stage** spans the period from approximately two to seven years of age, and it is a time when stable concepts are formed, mental reasoning emerges, egocentrism is stronger in the beginning but eventually decreases, and magical belief systems are constructed. Thus, preoperational thought is anything but a convenient waiting period for concrete operational thought, even though the label *preoperational* does suggest that between two and seven years of age the child does not yet think in an operational manner.

Symbolic function.
intuitive thory

The symbolic world of the young child's scribbles and drawings.

Operations are internalized sets of actions that allow the child to do mentally what before was done physically. They are highly organized and conform to certain rules and principles of logic. The operations appear in one form in the concrete operational period and in another form in the formal operational period. In sum, while stable concepts are formed, mental reasoning emerges, and magical belief systems are constructed during the preoperational stage, these thoughts are still flawed and not well organized. Thus, the preoperational stage should be viewed as the beginning of the ability to reconstruct at the level of thought what has been established in behavior and a transition from a primitive to a more sophisticated use of symbols.

Two Phases of Preoperational Thought

Preoperational thought can be divided into two phases or substages: the symbolic function substage and the intuitive substage. The **symbolic function substage** of preoperational thought exists roughly between the ages of two and four years. By two years of age the child has the ability to develop a mental representation of an object in his or her head. The child at this point has begun to use symbols to represent objects that are not present. The ability to engage in such symbolic thought is sometimes referred to as symbolic function, and it greatly broadens the child's mental world during this

age period. This symbolic world is reflected in young children's drawings. Think about the manner in which young children use shapes and scribbles to represent people, houses, and so forth. Such scribbling and drawing can be viewed as an example of how symbolic function develops during the preschool years. For example, for the three-year-old a primitive circle may represent a person and a line a house. Other examples of the use of symbolism in the early childhood years are the prevalence of pretend play, which is discussed in chapter 12, and language, which is described in chapter 8. Thus during this early portion of preoperational thought, the ability to think in symbolic ways and represent the world mentally predominates.

The preoperational stage of thought continues from four to seven years of age for most children but a new substage, called **intuitive thought,** emerges. During this time frame the child begins to reason about various matters and wants to know the answers to all sorts of questions. Children's thinking in this substage is viewed as prelogical. While reasoning and a search for answers to many questions are prevalent, such reasoning is very imperfect compared to adult standards. We should point out that Piaget referred to this time period as intuitive because on the one hand young children seem so sure about their knowledge and understanding, yet on the

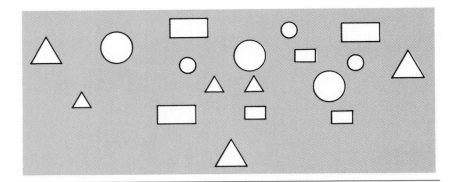

FIGURE 6.1
A random array of objects.

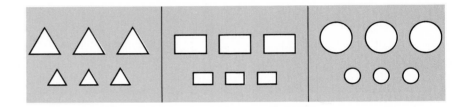

FIGURE 6.2
An ordered array of objects.

other are so unaware of how they know what they know. Let's look further at young children's inaccurate reasoning and why questions.

An important limitation of the young child's reasoning ability is the difficulties he or she has putting things into their correct classes. Faced with a random collection of objects that can be grouped together on the basis of two or more properties, the preoperational child is seldom capable of using these properties consistently to sort the objects into what you would refer to as competent classification.

For example, look at the collection of objects shown in figure 6.1. You would respond to the direction "Put the things together you believe belong together" by sorting the characteristics of size and shape together. Your sorting might look something like that shown in figure 6.2. In the social realm, a five-year-old girl might be given the task of dividing her peers into groups according to whether they are friends and whether they are boys or girls. She would be unlikely to arrive at the following classification: friendly boys, friendly girls, unfriendly boys, and unfriendly girls. Another such example, one developed by David Elkind (1976), illustrates the preoperational child's shortcomings in reasoning in terms of understanding religious concepts.

When asked the question "Can you be a Protestant and an American at the same time?" six- and seven-year-olds usually said no, while nine-year-olds were much more likely to say yes, understanding that objects can be cross-classified simultaneously.

The child's earliest questions begin to occur around the age of three, and by the age of five or six he or she has just about exhausted the adults around with persistent inquiries, particularly with questions involving "why?" The child's questions provide clues to mental development and reflect his or her intellectual curiosity. Such questions indicate an emergence of the child's interest in reasoning and figuring out why things are the way they are. A sample of the kinds of questions children ask during this question-asking period of four to six years of age follow (Elkind, 1976):

"What makes you grow up?"
"What makes you stop growing up?"
"Why does a lady have to be married to have a baby?"
"Who was the mother when everybody was a baby?"
"Why do leaves fall?"
"Why does the sun shine?"

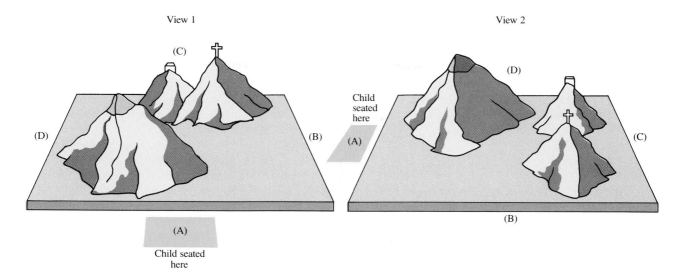

View 1

(C)

(D) (B)

(A)

Child seated here

View 2

Child seated here

(A)

(D)

(C)

(B)

FIGURE 6.3

The three mountains task devised by Piaget and Inhelder (1967). View 1 shows the child's perspective from where he or she is sitting. View 2 is an example of the photograph the child would be shown mixed in with others from different perspectives. For the child to correctly identify this view, he or she has to take the perspective of a person sitting at spot (B). Invariably the preschool child who thinks in a preoperational way cannot perform this task. When asked what the perspective or view of the mountains will look like from position (B), the child selects a photograph taken from location (A), the view he or she has at the time.

Egocentrism

One of the most salient features of preoperational thought is **egocentrism,** the inability to distinguish between one's own perspective and the perspective of someone else. The following telephone conversation between four-year-old Mary, who is at home, and her father, who is at work, typifies Mary's egocentric thought:

> *Father:* Mary, is Mommy there?
> *Mary:* (Silently nods)
> *Father:* Mary, may I speak to Mommy?
> *Mary:* (Nods again silently)

Mary's response is egocentric in the sense that she fails to consider her father's perspective before replying. A nonegocentric thinker would have responded verbally.

Piaget and Barbara Inhelder (1969) initially studied young children's egocentrism by devising the three mountains task (see figure 6.3). The child walks around the mountains and becomes familiar with what the mountains look like from different perspectives. The child can see that there are different objects on the

"Look what I can do, Grandma!"

mountains as well. The child then is seated on one side of the table on which the mountains are placed. The experimenter takes a doll and moves it to different locations around the table, at each location asking the child to pick one photo from a series of photos that most accurately reflects the view the doll is seeing. Children in the preoperational stage almost always pick the view they have from where they are sitting rather than the view the doll has.

Animism

Another facet of preoperational thought is **animism,** the belief that inanimate objects have human qualities and are capable of human action. Remarks like "That tree pushed the leaf off and it fell down" or "The sidewalk was angry with me. It made me fall down" reveal this notion. Animism is a failure to distinguish the appropriate occasions for employing human and the nonhuman perspectives. However, we should note that several recent investigations have questioned the pervasiveness of the animism phenomenon. In many cases, animistic statements may reflect children's incomplete knowledge of the objects referred to (Dolgin & Behrend, 1984), their incomplete knowledge of how animate and inanimate things differ (Bullock, 1985), or their assumption that they are playing a game when an adult questioner wants them to be serious (Gelman & Spelke, 1981). Perhaps animism should be viewed as incomplete knowledge and understanding, not as a child's general conception of the world in which he or she lives.

We have discussed a number of ideas about preoperational thought. A summary of these ideas is provided in Concept Table 6.2. Next, we study the nature of concrete operational thought.

CONCEPT TABLE 6.2 Preoperational Thought		
Concept	**Processes/Related Ideas**	**Characteristics/Description**
Basic nature	Time frame	Roughly spans the ages of two to seven years.
	Cognitive processes	This period is a time when stable concepts are formed, mental reasoning emerges, egocentrism is prominent, and magical belief systems are constructed. The child does not yet think in an operational manner. Thought is still flawed and not well organized. This period also is characterized by a shift from primitive to more sophisticated symbol use.
Phases or substages of preoperational thought	Symbolic function substage	The symbolic function substage occurs between two and four years of age. At this time symbolic thought occurs on a regular basis in the form of language, pretend play, scribbling and drawing. Symbols are frequently used to represent objects not present.
	Intuitive substage	The intuitive substage lasts from approximately four to seven years of age. Reasoning is present but in a prelogical form. Question asking is prevalent. Children seem sure about their knowledge and understanding but are unaware of how they know what they know. Children in this substage have difficulty classifying objects into classes simultaneously.
Other processes	Egocentrism	Children in the preoperational thought stage have difficulty taking the perspective of another person. Piaget and Inhelder investigated such perspective-taking problems with the three mountains task.
	Animism	Animism is a characteristic of preoperational thought that refers to the belief that inanimate objects have human qualities.

Concrete Operational Thought

As the child enters the **concrete operational stage** of thought, he or she is not as egocentric as earlier, does not show animistic thought, reveals conservation skills, and is characterized by decentered and reversible thought. In our discussion of concrete operational thought we look first at a task that has been widely used to study such thought—the beaker task. Then we focus on the processes of decentering and reversibility as we describe what a concrete operation is. Next we describe the classification skills of the concrete operational thinker. Finally, we outline the constraints of concrete operational thought.

The Beaker Task—Studying the Conservation of Liquid

Perhaps the most famous of all Piaget's tasks are those of conservation, the hallmark of concrete operations. Of these conservation tasks, that of the conservation of liquid quantity is perhaps the most researched. In this task, which is illustrated in figure 6.4, the child is presented with two identical beakers, each filled to the same level with liquid (often, the liquid is milk). The child is asked whether these beakers have the same amount of liquid; the child usually says yes. Then the liquid from one beaker is poured into a third beaker, which is taller and thinner than the first two (see figure).

Which beaker holds more liquid? The preoperational thinker is unable to conserve properties of objects that have been superficially changed.

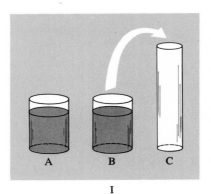 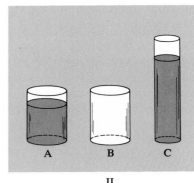

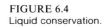

FIGURE 6.4
Liquid conservation.

I   II

The child is asked if the amount of liquid in the tall, thin beaker is equal to that which remains in one of the original beakers. If the child is less than seven or eight years old, he or she is likely to say no and to justify his or her answer in terms of the differing height or width of the beakers. Older children usually answer yes and can justify their answers appropriately (e.g., "if you poured the milk back, it would show that the amount is the same").

In Piaget's theory, failing the conservation-of-liquid-quantity task is a sign that a child is at the preoperational stage of development. Passing the test is a sign that the child has reached the concrete operational stage. However, this interpretation has been subject to dispute, and it has been compromised by a number of findings. Despite such problems of interpretation, the conservation tasks that Piaget developed have had a dramatic impact on the field of cognitive development. These tasks are ingenious and have produced some highly provocative findings. One wonders what the field would be like today if Piaget had not invented these tasks.

Decentering, Reversibility, and the Nature of a Concrete Operation

According to Piaget, concrete operational thought is made up of operations, that is, mental actions or representations that are reversible (Piaget, 1967). A critical feature of the concrete operational stage is the child's ability to pass tests such as the conservation of liquid quantity. Other such tests include the conservation of weight (testing knowledge that weight is unaffected by changing the physical shape of material)

and number (testing knowledge that number is unaffected by spreading out stimuli or massing them together). For example, a well-known test of reversibility of thought involving the conservation of weight focuses on two identical balls of clay. The experimenter rolls one ball into a long, thin shape, and the other remains in its original ball shape. The child is then asked if there is more clay in the ball or the long, thin piece of clay. By the time children reach the age of seven or eight, most answer that the amount of clay is the same. In order to answer this problem correctly, children have to be able to imagine that the clay ball is rolled out into a long, thin strip and then returned to its original round shape. Such imagination involves a reversible mental action. Thus a **concrete operation** is a reversible mental action on real, concrete objects. Such concrete operations allow the child to decenter and to coordinate several characteristics rather than focusing on a single property of an object. In the clay example, the preoperational child likely focuses on height *or* width, and the concrete operational child coordinates information about both dimensions.

Classification

Many of the concrete operations identified by Piaget focus on the way children reason about the properties of objects. One important skill that characterizes the concrete operational thinker is the ability to classify or divide things into different sets and subsets and to consider their interrelationships. An example of the concrete operational child's classification skills involves a

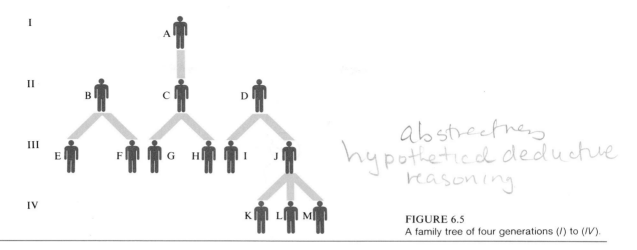

abstractness
hypothetical deductive reasoning

FIGURE 6.5
A family tree of four generations (*I*) to (*IV*).

family tree of four generations (see figure 6.5; Furth & Wachs, 1975). This family tree suggests that the grandfather (A) has three children (B, C, and D), each of whom has two children (E through J), and finally one of these children (J) has three children (K, L, and M). A child who comprehends the classification system can move up or down a level (vertically), across a given level (horizontally), and up and down and across (obliquely) within the system. He or she understands that person J can at the same time be father, brother, son, and grandson, for example.

Some Constraints of Concrete Operational Thought

Reference to the *concrete* nature of thought in the middle and late childhood years suggests that there is a limitation to concrete operational thought in that the child needs to have clearly available perceptual physical supports. That is, the child needs to have objects and events present in order to think about them. The concrete operational thinker is not capable of imagining the necessary steps to complete an algebraic equation, for example.

During the concrete operational stage most children are in elementary school. Piaget's ideas have been widely applied to education, although Piaget himself was not an educator. Perspective on Child Development 6.2 describes why Piaget's ideas were welcomed by educators and provides information about thinking games for children based on Piaget's theory.

Formal Operational Thought

First we describe the major characteristics of formal operational thought and then evaluate individual variation in this form of thought.

The Characteristics of Formal Operational Thought

Formal operational thought involves abstractness and hypothetical deductive reasoning, contrary-to-fact reasoning, idealism, and an understanding of metaphor. Most significantly, it is abstract. The adolescent is no longer limited to actual, concrete experience as an anchor for thought. Instead, he or she may conjure make-believe situations, events that are strictly hypothetical possibilities, or purely abstract propositions and proceed to reason logically with them.

The abstract quality of thought at the formal operational stage is evidenced primarily in the adolescent's verbal problem solving. While the concrete thinker would need to *see* the concrete elements A, B, and C to be able to make the logical inference that if A>B and B>C, then A>C, the formal operational thinker can solve this problem merely through verbal presentation.

On the social plane, one important implication of this theory is that the formal thinker no longer need rely on concrete experiences with people to form complex judgments about them. The formal thinker may make such judgments largely on the basis of verbal description, speculation, or gossip.

PERSPECTIVE ON CHILD DEVELOPMENT 6.2

PIAGET, EDUCATION, AND THINKING GAMES FOR CHILDREN

Hardly a day passes without the appearance of a new article applying the principles of Piaget's theory of cognitive development to the education of American children. Frank Murray (1978) describes why Americans have moved so swiftly to embrace Piaget. Two social crises, the proliferation of behaviorism and the dominance of the psychometric approach to intelligence (IQ testing), have made the adoption of Piagetian theory inevitable, he says. The first social crisis was the post-Sputnik concern of a country preoccupied with its deteriorating position as the engineering and scientific leader in the world, and the second was the need for compensatory education for minority groups and the poor. Curriculum projects that soon came into being after these social crises include the "new math," Science Curriculum Improvement Study, Project Physics, "discovery learning," and Man: A Course of Study. All of these projects have been based upon Piaget's notion of cognitive developmental changes in thought structure. Piaget's theory contains a great deal of information about the young person's reasoning in the areas of math, science, and logic—material not found anywhere else in the literature of developmental psychology.

Piaget was not an educator, nor was he principally concerned with problems of education. However, he provided a scientifically sound conceptual framework from which to view educational problems. In summarizing the general principles of education implicit in Piaget's image of the child, David Elkind (1976) concluded:

First of all . . . the foremost problem of education is *communication*. According to the Piaget image, the child's mind is not an empty slate. Quite the contrary, the child has a host of ideas about the physical and natural world, but these ideas differ from those of adults and are expressed in a different linguistic mode. . . . We must learn to comprehend what children are saying and to respond in the same mode of discourse.

A second implication is that the child is always unlearning and relearning as well as acquiring entirely new knowledge. The child comes to school with his own ideas about space, time, causality, quantity, and number. . . .

Still a third implication for educational philosophy . . . is that the child is by nature a knowing creature. If the child has ideas about the world which he has not been taught (because they are foreign to adults) and which he has not inherited (because they change with age) then he must have acquired these notions through his spontaneous interactions with the environment . . . . education needs to insure that it does not dull this eagerness to know by overly rigid curricula that disrupt the child's own rhythm and pace of learning. (pp. 108–9)*

An application of Piaget's ideas to education that is particularly creative and innovative is the elementary school program of Hans Furth and Harry Wachs (1975, p. 171). They seemed to take the following comment by Piaget seriously:

Whenever anyone can succeed in transforming their first steps in reading, or arithmetic, or spelling into a *game* [emphasis added], you will see children become passionately absorbed in those occupations, which are ordinarily presented as dreary chores. (Piaget, 1970, p. 155)

Furth and Wachs developed 179 thinking games that were to be incorporated into the day-to-day learning of children in the primary grades. They tried out this method for two years in an experimental school in Charleston, West Virginia—the Tyler Thinking School.

One of the games they developed is called Overlaps. This game works on several different properties of thought at the same time—ordering things, seeing different perspectives, and working with combinations.

This game demonstrates for children that an outline of overlapping forms does not always make clear which piece has been placed first. It emphasizes the importance of temporal ordering.

How does this reflect concrete operational thought?

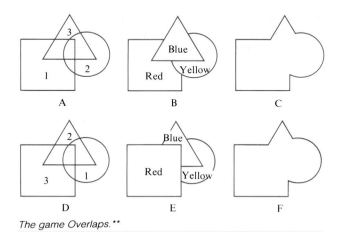

The game Overlaps.**

In a variation, a concrete pattern constructed from the cutout forms becomes the model, and the child selects the proper card to match it. Later the child may construct and draw his own patterns. The game can be varied by asking the child to transpose the parts of the pattern or attempt to think of how it would look from different positions.**

Some of the games were specifically directed toward such basic skills as reading and mathematics. Other games were directed to more general knowledge about the world—the typical preoccupation of Piagetians. This general knowledge is a foundation on which school learning builds.

A series of overlapping forms (triangles, circles, squares) is drawn on a card. Each form bears a number which indicates whether it was drawn first, second, third, and so on. The child is given similar forms cut out of cardboard or plastic. He follows the instruction of the model to discover that the pieces can be arranged in various orders of overlap to create entirely new patterns which retain the original outline (see the figure above right).

*From *Child Development and Education: A Piagetian Perspective* by David Elkind. Copyright © 1976 Oxford University Press.

**From *Thinking Goes to School: Piaget's Theory in Practice* by Hans G. Furth and Harry Wachs. Copyright © 1974, 1975 by Oxford University Press.

Adolescents often engage in flights of fantasy.

Adolescents' ability to work with conjured-up possibilities is easily seen in the way they approach problem solving. The style of problem solving used has often been referred to as **deductive hypothesis testing.** Consider a modification of the familiar game Twenty Questions that Jerome Bruner (1966) and his associates used in extensive research with children of varying ages. The person is shown a set of forty-two colorful pictures displayed in a rectangular array (six rows of seven pictures each) and is asked to determine which picture the experimenter has in mind (that is, which is "correct"). The person is allowed to ask only questions to which the experimenter can reply yes or no. The object of the game is to select the correct picture by asking as few questions as possible. The person who is a deductive hypothesis tester formulates a plan to propose and test a series of hypotheses, each of which narrows the field of choices considerably. The most effective plan consists in a "halving" strategy. (*Q*: Is it in the right half of the array? *A*: No. *Q*: Okay; is it in the top half? And so on.) Used correctly, the halving strategy guarantees the questioner the correct solution in seven questions

or less, no matter where the correct picture is located in the array. Even if he or she is using a less elegant strategy than the optimal "halving" one, the deductive hypothesis tester understands that when the experimenter answers no to one of his or her guesses, several possibilities are immediately eliminated.

By contrast, the concrete thinker may persist with questions that continue to test some of the same possibilities that previous questions should have eliminated. For example, the child may have asked whether the correct picture was in row 1 and received the answer no but later asks whether the correct picture is *x*, which is in row 1.

Thus, the formal operational thinker tests his or her hypotheses with judiciously chosen questions and tests. Often a single question or test will help him or her to eliminate an untenable hypothesis. By contrast, the concrete thinker often fails to understand the relation between a hypothesis and a well-chosen test of the hypothesis.

The make-believe nature of formal operational thought can be seen in **contrary-to-fact reasoning.** Suppose, for example, that an adolescent is asked to

"Reprinted by permission: Tribune Media Services."

imagine that the room in which she is sitting suddenly has no walls and to describe what she now sees. The adolescent can easily perform such mental gymnastics (e.g., Elkind, 1976). The important point is that this mental feat involves representing an imaginary event that counters the concrete reality of the moment.

The adolescent who is a formal operational thinker begins to show an enthusiasm for what is ideal rather than only what is real. Adolescents often engage in extended speculation about ideal characteristics, qualities they desire in themselves and also in others. During adolescence such thoughts often lead adolescents to compare themselves and others in regard to such ideal standards. And rather than seeing their world as one of limits, adolescents view their world with limitless possibilities, frequently engaging in fantasy flights into the future. It is not unusual for the adolescent to become impatient with these newfound ideals and to be perplexed over which of the many ideal selves to adopt.

Finally, let's consider one last property of formal thinking, the ability of the adolescent to appreciate metaphorical meaning. A **metaphor** is an implied comparison between two ideas that is conveyed by the abstract meanings contained in the words used to make the comparison. A person's faith and a piece of glass may be alike in that both can be shattered easily. A runner's performance and a politician's speech may be alike in that both are predictable. Concrete thinkers find it difficult to understand such metaphorical relations. Consequently, many elementary school children are puzzled by the meanings of parables and fables (Elkind, 1976).

The social implications of the use of metaphors are obvious. Metaphor greatly extends the network of symbols and meaning that the adolescent is able to use in thinking about people. It makes possible a host of abstract comparisons between people and nonliving things, people and animals, and people and plants, among others.

Individual Variation

For the most part Piaget emphasizes universal and consistent patterns of formal operational thought. Piaget's theory does not adequately account for the unique, individual differences that characterize the cognitive development of adolescents. These differences have been documented in a far-ranging set of research studies, meaning that certain modifications in Piaget's theory of formal operational thought need to be pursued (e.g., Bart, 1971; Berzonsky, Weiner, & Raphael, 1975; Neimark, 1982; Overton & Meehan, 1982).

The studies suggest that formal operational thought does develop during early adolescence for many boys and girls, but that this stage of thinking is far from pervasive. Instead, early adolescence is more likely to be characterized by a consolidation of concrete operational thought (Hill, 1983). One limitation of formal reasoning may involve the content of the reasoning; while the fourteen-year-old may reason at the formal operational level when it comes to analyzing algebraic equations, he or she may not be able to do so with verbal problem-solving tasks or when reasoning about interpersonal relations.

	CONCEPT TABLE 6.3 Concrete Operational and Formal Operational Thought	
Stage	**Process/Related Ideas**	**Characteristics/Description**
Concrete operational	Beaker task	The beaker task is one of the most famous of all Piagetian tasks; it is widely used to assess concrete operational thought through its measurement of conservation of liquid.
	Decentering, reversibility, and the nature of a concrete operation	For Piaget, concrete operational thought is made up of operations—mental actions or representations that are reversible. Concrete operations allow the child to decenter and coordinate several characteristics rather than focusing on a single property.
	Classification	One important skill that characterizes the concrete operational child is the ability to classify or divide things into different sets and to consider their interrelationships.
	Some constraints	The child needs to have clearly available perceptual physical supports—that is, the child has to have objects and events present to think about them.
Formal operational	Piaget's adolescence stage	Piaget believed formal operational thought is the fourth and final stage of development, being entered during early adolescence
	Abstractness and hypothetical deductive reasoning	Most significantly, formal operational thought is abstract and involves make-believe situations and events that are hypothetical possibilities. Purely abstract propositions are made and then reasoned about in a logical way to deduce a solution to a problem. The formal operational thinker tests hypotheses, trying to discover which one is correct.
	Contrary-to-fact reasoning	The adolescent can represent an imaginary event counter to the concrete reality of the moment.
	Idealism	The adolescent shows enthusiasm for what is ideal rather than only what is real. The adolescent engages in extended speculation about the ideal characteristics of others as well as himself or herself.
	Metaphor	Formal operational thinkers understand metaphor; concrete operational thinkers do not.
	Individual variation	Most adolescents do not engage in logical thinking in the formal way Piaget envisioned, although other aspects of formal operational thought, such as idealism and abstractness, do characterize the thoughts of most adolescents. There is a considerable amount of individual variation in adolescent thought.

We have discussed many aspects of concrete and formal operational thought. A summary of these ideas is provided in Concept Table 6.3. Next, the nature of egocentrism at different stages of thought is evaluated.

Egocentrism and the Piagetian Stages

Just as you were taken on a journey through sensorimotor development in terms of the transformation of the infant's thoughts about object permanence to help you understand sensorimotor development, we now consider the important Piagetian concept of egocentrism and how it is transformed as the child moves through the four main Piagetian stages. Reviewing the transformations in egocentric thought should help to ingrain the main Piagetian stages in your memory.

In everyday speech we use the term *egocentrism* to mean thinking only of oneself, that is, failing to realize that one's own needs and wishes may not be consistent with the needs and wishes of others. The Piagetian concept is somewhat broader, referring to a lack of differentiation between a subject and an object of some type (Elkind, 1976). In addition, each successive cognitive stage has its own unique brand of egocentric thought.

In the sensorimotor stage, egocentrism reveals itself in a failure of the infant to distinguish between a "real" external object and his or her sense impression of this object. This early form of egocentrism is part of the infant's lack of object permanence, and it disappears with the achievement of object permanence.

In the preoperational stage, there is a failure to distinguish between internal symbols—one's own thoughts and words—and external things that can be perceived by others. This type of egocentrism can make nightmares more frightening because the child may not differentiate the symbolic content of the dream from a real event. It also may explain why children at this age believe that words are inseparable from their referents, that one sort of object (a chair) could not possibly be called by another name (rose). Preoperational children are famous for their tendency to let egocentrism interfere with effective communication.

Egocentrism in the concrete operational stage involves a failure to differentiate between what one perceives and what one believes. That is, one's own assumptions are treated like facts. This may explain why concrete operational children are sometimes slow to give up a mistaken idea or fruitless strategy. It may also explain why they sometimes tell lies to their parents. As David Elkind (1976) notes:

> This frequently occurs when the child does something he knows to be wrong. Although the child may be aware that he has committed a wrong he may also make some assumption about his behavior that excuses or exonerates his act so that he feels genuinely innocent. When he denies the action on the basis of this assumptive reality he is more than likely to infuriate the adult. Many toe-to-toe shouting matches between parent and child follow upon the child's denial of guilt and the parent's adamant demand that the child confess his misdeed. At such times the parent fails to appreciate that for the child an assumptive reality is the *truth*. (p. 86)*

A young adolescent in the formal operational stage is highly sophisticated at distinguishing facts from assumptions. However, he or she is susceptible to a type of naive idealism that can be viewed as egocentric. As Piaget (1967) himself remarked:

> With the advent of formal intelligence, thinking takes wings and it is not surprising that at first this unexpected power is both used and abused. . . . Each new mental ability starts off by incorporating the world in a process of egocentric assimilation. Adolescent egocentricity is manifested by a belief in the omnipotence of reflection, as though the world should submit itself to idealistic schemes rather than to systems of reality. (pp. 63–64)

A less attractive form of adolescent egocentrism is a young person's belief that others are often thinking about him or her. According to Elkind (1976):

> [T]he adolescent is continually constructing, or reacting to, an **imaginary audience.** It is an audience because the adolescent believes that he will be the focus of attention, and it is imaginary because, in actual social situations, this is not usually the case (unless he contrives to make it so). The construction of imaginary audiences would seem to account, in part at least, for a wide variety of typical adolescent behaviors and experiences.
>
> The imaginary audience, for example, probably plays a role in the self-consciousness which is so characteristic of early adolescence. When the young person is feeling critical of himself, he anticipates that the audience—of which he is necessarily a part—will be critical too. And, since the audience is his own construction and privy to his own knowledge of himself, it knows just what to look for in the way of cosmetic and behavioral sensitivities. The adolescent's wish for privacy and his reluctance to reveal himself may, to some extent, be a reaction to the feeling of being under the constant critical scrutiny of other people. The notion of an imaginary audience also helps to explain the observation that the affect which most concerns adolescents is not guilt but, rather, shame, i.e., the reaction to an audience. (pp. 91–92)*

Fortunately, the imaginary audience and other forms of adolescent egocentrism do not last forever. Through education, hypothesis testing and the growth of interpersonal skills, the adolescent eventually overcomes these tendencies, though of course perhaps none of us ever sheds them entirely. Some researchers also believe that the development of social perspective taking rather than egocentric thought provides a better explanation of the imaginary audience (Lapsley & Murphy, 1985).

In summary, egocentrism in the sensorimotor stage leads to a confusion of objects with their sensory impressions. In the preoperational stage, it reveals itself in failure to differentiate between names and their referents, and between one's own thoughts and what others can perceive. In the concrete operational stage, there is a tendency to confuse one's beliefs and assumptions with fact. And in the formal operational stage, there is a feeling that one's idealistic constructions can change the world for the better. There also is the notion that everyone else is paying attention to you.

EVALUATION OF PIAGET'S THEORY

In the mid-1970s Piaget's theory was very much the central focus of attention in the field of cognitive development. There were skeptics even then (e.g., Brainerd, 1972, 1976), but the attitude seemed to be one of wait and see. That is, Piaget's theory has served us well; it seems to be wrong in places but let's see how we can shore it up. Now in the 1980s a new feeling has caught up with many cognitive scholars (e.g., Fischer, 1980; Flavell, 1985; Gelman, 1982; Gelman & Baillargeon, 1983; Kuhn, 1980; Mandler, 1983). The last line in John Flavell's eulogy to Piaget stated that our main task is to extend and go beyond what Piaget began so well. Let's now consider what Piaget began so well as well as what some of the current misgivings are in regard to Piaget's view.

Piaget's Major Contributions

Four major contributions of Piaget are (1) his brilliant observations of children, (2) his ideas of what to look for in development, (3) the qualitative nature of children's mental life, and (4) his imaginative ideas about how children's thought changes.

Brilliant Observations of Children

To begin with, Piaget was a brilliant observer of children. He collected thousands of firsthand observations of what children do and how they seem to think that have withstood the scrutiny of time (in some cases thirty to fifty years). There are many reasons for crediting Piaget with genius, but this accomplishment alone would be sufficient. The more we (the authors of this text) attempt to verify Piaget's observations with our own children and those that we encounter professionally, the more impressed we are. The insights are easily and often surprisingly verified. The young infant really does fail to search for an object when it is hidden. The four-year-old who watches a liquid poured from one container into another differently shaped actually says that there is now "more" or "less" liquid than before. The nine-year-old really does get stuck in hypothetico-deductive problem solving. And the list goes on. There are literally hundreds of such observations, first made by Piaget, that accurately describe how children generally reason in these situations.

Ideas about What to Look For in Development

A second contribution is that Piaget has given us many good ideas about what to look for in development. For example, he has shown us that infants are very complex and subtle creatures whose seemingly chaotic patterns of response are actually highly organized and structured. Contemporary experts on infancy have benefited to an extraordinary degree by his suggestions and descriptions of this organization. Or, as another example, he has shown us that the major change from childhood to adolescence involves a shift from the world of concrete and narrow logic to the plane of verbal reasoning and broad generalization. This insight has had a widely felt influence on educators and those who work with adolescents.

Qualitative Nature of Children's Mental Life

A third contribution is Piaget's focus on the qualitative nature of mental life. By always directing us to think of what the child's "mental environment looks like," he has served up a forceful argument for adults to learn how to deal with children on their own intellectual terms. This qualitative focus has also been a refreshing antidote to the behavioral psychologist's lack of concern for the subject's mental life and the psychometric expert's preoccupation with attaching numbers to intellectual performance.

Imaginative Ideas about Children's Cognitive Changes

A final contribution is the host of imaginative ideas that Piaget has offered about how the child changes. The concepts of *assimilation* and *accommodation,* for example, are now well-rehearsed terms in the vocabulary of most psychologists. The concepts remind us of the double-sided nature of each of our exchanges with the environment. We must make the experience fit our cognitive framework (schemas, operations), yet simultaneously adjust our cognitive framework to the experience. The concept of *equilibration* offers an elegant view of developmental pacing. According to this idea, significant cognitive change comes only when our cognitive frameworks (schemas, operations) are clearly shown to be inconsistent with each other or the environment. And then change will only be likely if the situation is structured to permit gradual movement to the very next higher level of cognition.

The Criticisms of Piaget's Theory

Piaget (1970) once remarked that he always considered himself one of the chief "revisionists of Piaget" (p. 103). But there are quite a few others, and some of them feel his theory is fundamentally wrong. Five sorts of research findings are troublesome for the Piagetian perspective (Gelman & Baillargeon, 1983; Kuhn 1984; Mandler, 1983). These findings focus on stages, the nature of concepts, procedures involving Piagetian problems, training studies, and the timing involved in the emergence of cognitive abilities.

Stages

Perhaps the broadest criticism concerns Piaget's claim for stages of development (Brainerd, 1978; Flavell, 1985). To claim that a child is in a particular stage of development is to claim that he or she possesses a universally characteristic, prototypical system by which he or she approaches many different tasks. It should be possible to detect many similarities in the quality of thinking in a variety of tasks, and there should be clear links between stages of development such that successful attainment of one conceptual understanding predicts successful attainment of another. For example, we might expect children to learn how to conserve at about the same time that they learn how to cross-classify or seriate items. All three capabilities are supposed to provide evidence of concrete operational thought. As several critics have noted, however, lack of similarity, lack of cross-linkages, and lack of predictability seem to be present everywhere (Fischer, 1980; Flavell, 1985; Kuhn, 1980). As Kurt Fischer (1980) puts it, unevenness seems to be the rule in cognitive development rather than the exception.

Fuzziness of Concepts

Another problem is that the most interesting concepts in the theory—assimilation, accommodation, and equilibration—which are used to explain how progress is made in development, are tricky to pin down operationally, despite their theoretical glitter. That is, unlike concepts such as reinforcement and imitation, these Piagetian concepts have very loose ties to experimental procedures and manipulations. They sound nice, but it is not always clear to what they refer. Despite work over the years to flesh out these concepts and anchor them in concrete procedures, not much progress has been made.

Procedural Changes in Piagetian Problems

Very small changes in the procedures involving a Piagetian problem have significant effects on a child's cognition. To some degree this is due to the fact that such matters as remembering the various parts of a task can determine the likelihood that it will be completed correctly (Trabasso, 1977). Thus, a child's stage is at best one of several factors involved in solving Piagetian tasks.

Training Studies

It has been possible to take a child who seems to be at one Piagetian stage, such as preoperational thought, and train the child to pass tasks at the concrete operational level (Gelman, 1969). Such findings pose problems for Piaget, who argued that such training only works at a superficial level and is ineffective unless the child is at a transitional point from one stage to the next.

Timing of Emerging Cognitive Abilities

Recent studies of infants and young children show how certain cognitive abilities emerge earlier than Piaget believed, and their subsequent development may be more prolonged than he thought (Gelman & Baillargeon, 1983; Mandler, 1983). One example is symbolic thought, as indicated by the ability to think about objects in their absence. Thinking about objects in their absence seems to appear prior to twelve months of age, not by eighteen to twenty-four months as Piaget believed. For example, infants under one year of age can recall the locations of previously viewed objects (Ashmead & Perlmutter, 1980). Another example is conservation of number. Piaget claimed that conservation of number (like conservation of liquid) does not appear until about seven to eight years of age. Yet we have evidence of number conservation by children three years of age (Gelman, 1979). Not only do such cognitive skills appear earlier than Piaget believed, but several cognitive developmental experts (Gelman & Baillargeon, 1983; Mandler, 1983) argue that their development is spread out in time much longer than Piaget believed. That is, the younger child can do more and the older child less than should be possible according to the Piagetian stages.

In the next chapter we will study the view adopted by researchers who have primarily been responsible for the revision of Piaget's theory. This view, called the information-processing approach, has received increased attention in recent years as researchers probe the nature of children's thought.

SUMMARY

I. The field of cognitive development has been dominated by the ideas of one man—Jean Piaget. Understanding Piaget's theory requires information about the basic features of the cognitive developmental view as well as the processes thought to be responsible for cognitive changes in children.

   A. The cognitive developmental view stresses that cognition is central to understanding children's development. This view emphasizes biological maturation and the unfolding of cognitive stages.

   B. Processes believed to be responsible for cognitive change include adaptation, assimilation, and accommodation; organization; and equilibration.

II. Information about sensorimotor thought focuses on its basic features, its far-ranging implications, the substages of sensorimotor thought, and object permanence.

   A. Sensorimotor thought involves the infant's ability to organize and coordinate his or her sensations with physical movements. The stage lasts from birth to approximately two years of age and is nonsymbolic through most of its duration.

   B. There are many dimensions to sensorimotor thought: perceptual modalities, imitation, play, and basic categories of experience, such as time and causality.

   C. The substages of sensorimotor thought are simple reflexes; first habits and primary circular reactions; secondary circular reactions; coordination of secondary circular reactions; tertiary circular reactions, novelty, and curiosity; and internalization of schemes.

   D. Object permanence is one of the infant's most significant accomplishments. Piaget described six stages of object permanence although other views of object permanence have been proposed.

III. Preoperational thought roughly spans the age of two to seven years. It is a time when stable concepts are formed, mental reasoning emerges, egocentrism is prominent, and magical belief systems are constructed. Transformation from primitive to more sophisticated symbol use occurs. Two substages are the symbolic function substage, between two and four years, and the intuitive substage, between four and seven years. The egocentric thought of the preoperational child suggests that he or she has difficulty taking the perspective of another. Animism also characterizes preoperational thought.

IV. Concrete operational thought and formal operational thought are the third and fourth Piagetian stages.

   A. According to Piaget, concrete operational thought is made up of operations—mental actions or representations that are reversible. Concrete operations allow the child to decenter and coordinate several different sets rather than focusing on a single characteristic. The beaker task has been widely used to assess concrete operational thought through its measurement of the conservation of liquid. One important skill that characterizes concrete operational thought is classification, the ability to classify or divide things into different sets and to consider their relationship to one another. A constraint of the concrete operational stage is that the child has to have objects and events present to think about them.

   B. Piaget believed formal operational thought is the fourth and final stage of development, being entered in early adolescence. Most significantly, formal operational thought is abstract and involves make-believe situations and events that are hypothetical possibilities. Contrary-to-fact reasoning, idealism, and metaphor are other characteristics of formal operational thought. There is considerable individual variation in formal operational thought.

V. At the sensorimotor stage, egocentrism produces a confusion of objects with their sensory impressions. In the preoperational stage, egocentrism is revealed in the failure to differentiate names and their referents and to differentiate between one's own thoughts and what others can perceive. In the concrete operational stage, there is a tendency to confuse one's beliefs with facts. In the formal operational stage, there is a sense that one's idealistic construction can change the world for the better, as well as the notion that everyone else is paying attention to you.

VI. Piaget has made a number of very important contributions to the field of child development, but his theory has been criticized as well.

   A. Among the most important contributions of Piaget are his brilliant observations of children, his ideas about what to look for in development, his view of the qualitative nature of children's mental life, and his imaginative ideas about how children's thought changes.

   B. The criticisms of Piaget's theory focus on stages, fuzziness of concepts, procedural changes in tasks that produce different results, training studies that speed up the development of cognitive abilities, and the timing of emerging cognitive abilities.

KEY TERMS

accommodation 170
adaptation 170
animism 182
assimilation 170
cognitive developmental
theory 170
concrete operation 184
concrete operational
stage 183
contrary-to-fact
reasoning 188
deductive hypothesis
testing 188
deferred imitation 172
egocentrism 181
equilibration 171
formal operational
thought 185
imaginary audience 191

internalization of
schemes 175
intuitive thought 179
metaphor 189
object permanence 176
operations 179
organization 170
preoperational stage 178
primary circular
reactions 174
secondary circular
reactions 174
sensorimotor stage 171
simple reflexes 174
symbol 175
symbolic function
substage 179
tertiary circular
reactions 175

REVIEW QUESTIONS

1. Who is Jean Piaget and what is his place in child development?
2. Discuss the basic nature of cognitive developmental theory and the processes responsible for cognitive changes in children.
3. Outline the most important features of sensorimotor thought.
4. Describe the nature of preoperational thought.
5. Provide an overview of concrete operational thought.
6. Evaluate the stage of formal operational thought.
7. Discuss the developmental course of egocentrism.
8. What are the contributions and criticisms of Piaget's theory?

SUGGESTED READINGS

Cowan, P. A. (1978). *Piaget with feeling: Cognitive, social, and emotional dimensions.* New York: Holt, Rinehart & Winston.
Philip Cowan is head of the clinical psychology program at the University of California at Berkeley. He, like many clinicians, believes Piaget has more to tell us about social and emotional development than Piaget himself thought.

Ginsberg, H., & Opper, S. (1979). *Piaget's theory of intellectual development* (2nd ed.). Englewood Cliffs, NJ: Prentice-Hall.
One of the best explanations and descriptions of Piaget's theory of development.

Flavell, J. H. (1985). *Cognitive development* (2nd ed.). Englewood Cliffs, NJ: Prentice-Hall.
An outstanding statement of the major contemporary ideas about cognitive development by one of the leading scholars in the field. Although inspired by Piaget's work, the author goes well beyond it, offering new insights, critical evaluation, and reflections about his own research.

Furth, H. G., & Wachs, H. (1975). *Thinking goes to school.* New York: Oxford University Press.
An intriguing application of Piaget's ideas to education. Includes 179 thinking games that can be incorporated into the everyday teaching of children.

INFORMATION PROCESSING

PROLOGUE

MIND AND SUPERMIND

Bobby: "Hi, how are you?"
Robert: "I'm fine thank you. What can I do for you today?"
Bobby: "I'm in a big hurry. My math answers are due tomorrow, and I don't have time to finish them. Do you think you can help me with them?"
Robert: "Yes. Math is no problem for me."
Bobby: "O.K. I'll give you the problems and come back for them later."

T his conversation was between eleven-year-old Bobby and his computer, which he named Robert. Unlikely? Well, human beings have been enthralled by the idea that they might in some way construct lifelike mechanisms in their own image—robots, androids, thinking machines. The plots of various movies often go something like this: The machine at first obeys its human creator, then becomes sophisticated and outgrows its maker, becoming more impudent and dangerous, but in the end is defeated by the wisdom of the human being.

Until recently this scenario was science fiction, but today an electronic network can come precariously close to having power over us. Computer scientists have created programs that mimic human intelligence in a number of ways and even outdo human intellect in certain areas. We know that computers can calculate numbers much faster and more accurately than we could ever hope to do (note Bobby and his math homework dilemma). Some computers can summarize news stories, comprehend spoken sentences, follow orders, and play games.

Artificial intelligence (AI) refers to the field of inquiry involved with developing computers and robots that perform intellectual tasks we commonly think of as characterizing human thought. Are child and adult minds likely to be taken over by the superminds of computers and robots? Edward Fredkin, Professor of Electrical Engineering and Computer Science at MIT comments:

Eventually, no matter what we do there will be artificial intelligences with independent goals. It's very hard to imagine a machine that's a million times smarter than you as your slave. Once artificial intelligences start getting smart, their smartness will grow with explosive speed. If that happens at Stanford, say, the Stanford AI lab may have immense power all of a sudden. It's not that the United States might take over the world, it's that the Stanford AI lab might. (1982, p. 318)

The computer should in theory be able to translate verbal and other symbols into its own kind of symbols, rework them according to its own programmed instructions, and thus process information in ways that are said to be intelligent and to be called thinking. However, there are some things children's minds can do that computers cannot. First, it is important to recognize that all artificial intelligence works toward known end states, goals defined by their creators, you and me. A machine can learn and improve on its own program, but it does not have any means of developing a new goal for itself. Second, computers seem to be better at simulating the logical processes of our mind than the nonlogical, intuitive, and possibly unconscious aspects of our mind. Many of our most creative efforts seem to be based on such nonlogical intuitive mental processes. Third, the extraordinary multiple pathways in the brain probably produce thinking that cannot be mimicked by a computer. A computer can be made to look like it is performing **parallel processing,** the simultaneous consideration of a number of lines of thought, as it pursues one line of thought for a millisecond and then switches to another point and considers it for another several milliseconds. But the computer really is not engaging in parallel processing. We do much of this processing at a nonconscious level, and multiple simultaneous considerations seem to be responsible for many of the new ideas children and adults develop. Donald Norman (1982), cognitive psychologist at the University of California at San Diego, also points out that we do not have any programs that are self-aware or that begin to approach the consciousness that even children have. The child's mind can examine its own ideas and react to them—not just with thoughts about the ideas but with emotions as well. We are not even close to simulating consciousness on a computer and possibly never will.

PREVIEW

In this chapter we study the information-processing perspective on children's cognition. We begin with an overview of the information-processing approach and then turn to two very important aspects of information processing—attention and memory. Then we consider children's ability to understand and draw inferences. Next we turn to an evaluation of the value of the information-processing perspective for education. Finally, we examine the strengths and weaknesses of the information-processing approach.

THE INFORMATION-PROCESSING APPROACH

Our tour through the information-processing approach begins with its early history, then considers the importance of the computer metaphor in understanding information processing, and subsequently evaluates important questions raised by an information-processing approach to cognition.

Early History

Debate and theorizing on the topic of cognition has been occurring in psychology for over a hundred years, and in philosophy for much longer than that. The Greek philosophers Plato and Aristotle had many interesting views on the nature of cognition (Anderson & Bower, 1973; Boring, 1950). And experimental research on cognitive functions—especially the function of memory—is approximately as old as the field of psychology itself (Ebbinghaus, 1985).

Unfortunately, scientific progress in the study of cognition was initially quite slow, and indeed research on cognition almost dropped out of sight from the 1920s until World War II, especially in the United States. What caused this was the rise of a behavioristic doctrine (Watson, 1913) that had no use for "mentalistic" concepts such as attention, memory, comprehension, and the like. The consequence was that for about three decades the field of attention lay dormant, and the field of memory suffered a similar fate. There was much research on learning—often conducted with animal subjects—but memory as an aspect of human cognition received little investigation. Thought and problem

solving were addressed, but they were viewed as phenomena of behavioral learning—the formation of stimulus–response associations—rather than as cognitive processes.

To be sure there were exceptions to the general dominance of behaviorism in the early part of this century. The 1930s saw the publication of Sir Frederick Bartlett's *Remembering* (1932), a decidedly contemporary treatment of memory that anticipated many recent developments. Further, the brilliant contribution of Jean Piaget had its start at about this time (e.g., Piaget, 1960). Nonetheless, not until the 1950s did truly cognitive approaches begin to gain momentum. One of these approaches was of singular importance and is the topic of this chapter. It is the information-processing approach.

The Computer Metaphor—Old and New Models

The information-processing approach focuses on the elementary processes of cognition and relies on a computer metaphor: The human mind is viewed as a type of computational device in some ways similar to man-made computers (see figure 7.1). Because information-processing psychologists view the mind as a computational device, their theories and models can often be pictured in the form of computer programs or flowcharts. We now turn our attention to one rather old and

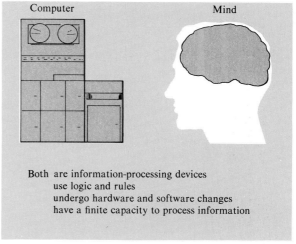

Both are information-processing devices
    use logic and rules
        undergo hardware and software changes
        have a finite capacity to process information

FIGURE 7.1
Computers and the mind: an analogy.

one relatively new model of information processing. These two models span the development of information-processing theory from the 1950s to the present.

Broadbent's Model

Donald Broadbent's model of information processing (1958)—with some of the terms modified to make the model more understandable—is shown in figure 7.2. Notice that his model has three memory "stores," a sensory store, which holds sensory features of stimuli for very short periods of time; a short-term store, which holds stimuli in consciousness once they have been recognized; and a long-term store, which is the repository of all of our permanent knowledge. Note that at the level of sensory memory, the system can process information in a parallel manner; that is, several different messages can be processed and remembered at once. But at the level of short-term memory there is a type of bottleneck—the limited capacity of short-term memory makes it difficult to handle more than one message at any one time. A filter serves the function of selective attention. It protects short-term memory from becoming overloaded.

Although you may not realize it, you have probably had experiences that support Broadbent's model. Consider the experience of standing by yourself, and listening in on some of the conversations going on around you (fig. 7.3). It is amazing how easy this is to do. Without moving your head or using your eyes, you can "tune in" one conversation, then "switch" to another, then move to a third, and so on. It is almost like changing channels on the radio. However, when you switch from conversation 1 to conversation 2, what exactly happens? Do you actually stop hearing conversation 1? Not really. You still are aware of the sounds being made. What happens is that you stop "following" the content of conversation 1 and begin following the content of conversation 2. This is consistent with the idea of a filter between sensory memory, which holds only sensory features such as sounds, and short-term memory, which holds the recognized content of what you have attended to.

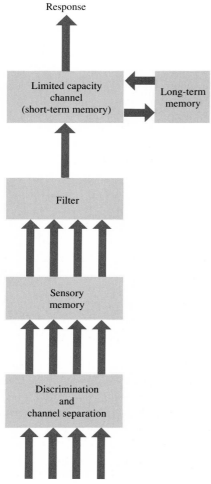

FIGURE 7.2
Broadbent's information-processing model developed in the 1950s (Wingfield and Sandoval, 1980).

FIGURE 7.3
How is information processing at work here?

Klatzky's Model

Broadbent's model was very influential for a time, but today our conceptions of information processing have become more complex and flexible. This is illustrated by Roberta Klatzky's model (1984) shown in figure 7.4. Comparing this model to Broadbent's earlier effort, we note a major change in emphasis: Whereas Broadbent's model stressed the importance of memory stores (sensory, short-term, and long-term), Klatzky's model emphasizes processes. Instead of information being transferred from one store to the next, information is processed along a continuum of levels: "shallow" sensory analysis of stimuli (activate sensory knowledge), "deeper" processes of categorization and naming of stimuli (activate concepts, labels), and still "deeper" processes of thinking and making inferences about stimuli (reason, compare). For example, in reading a word, your system might first process the visual features, its letters, then recognize the word and "look up" its meaning, and finally relate this word to other words you have read in order to understand a whole sentence.

Of course, memories are not absent from Klatzky's model. It is just that their functions have been changed to an extent. Long-term memory is not something reached only at the end of processing. It is involved in processing virtually from the start. Sensory analysis, categorization, naming and thinking and inferencing all involve communication with appropriate types of long-term memory knowledge. (This makes good sense when you think about it. Reading depends on long-term memory codes that allow recognition of individual letters and words, as well as on codes that support understanding.) Further, all types of analysis can leave new memory records in long-term memory (so we can remember what we have done). However, in most situations, the "deeper" sorts of analysis support better long-term memory.

Sensory and short-term memory also are present. The former is associated with processing at more "shallow" levels and the latter with processing at somewhat "deeper" levels. There currently is some disagreement on the nature and importance of sensory memory. Some investigators argue this sort of "memory" is simply activation in the sense organs or in closely connected nerves—hardly what most of us mean by the term *memory* (Klatzky, 1984). However, short-term memory is viewed by almost all investigators as critically important for processing. Note that in Klatzky's model—as well as in Broadbent's earlier model—short-term memory and focal attention are

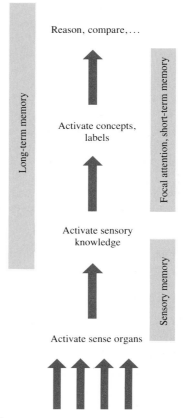

FIGURE 7.4
Klatzky's information-processing model developed in the 1980s (Klatzky, 1984).

viewed as closely connected if not the same thing. And in both of these models focal attention is thought to be limited in capacity.

A final point about Klatzky's model concerns parallel versus serial processing. In Broadbent's model, there is parallel processing of sensory features, but only serial processing at the level of contact with long-term memory knowledge. In contrast, contemporary models such as Klatzky's have a more flexible view; some highly practiced processes become automatic, even though they involve long-term memory contact. A critical feature of **automatic processes** is that they can proceed outside of focal attention—and they do not draw on processing capacity. Hence, such processes can be performed in parallel fashion. In contrast, nonautomatic processes, referred to as **controlled** (or effortful) **processes,** are demanding of focal attention (capacity). Hence, they often proceed serially.

To get a feeling for the distinction between automatic and controlled processes, consider walking while chewing gum simultaneously (in parallel). This is easy for most of us since both walking and chewing gum are "automatized" activities (although President Lyndon Johnson reportedly once said of another politician, "He couldn't walk down the street and chew bubble gum at the same time"). But what about doing complicated mental arithmetic while skiing down a steep mountain slope? You might be able to perform these two tasks serially, but to perform them in parallel might be a bit risky.

In summary, Broadbent's classic model and Klatzky's more contemporary model agree on the distinctions between short-term memory and long-term memory and on the fundamental notion of limited processing capacity. However, Klatzky's model has a more fluid view of levels of processing (Craik & Lockhart, 1972) and introduces a distinction between automatic and controlled processes.

Questions about Children's Cognition Raised by the Information-Processing Approach

The information-processing approach raises important questions about the nature of children's cognition: Does processing speed increase as children grow older? Does processing capacity increase as children grow older? What is the role of knowledge in accounting for developments in cognitive processing? Are there differences in development pertaining to controlled versus automatic processes?

Processing Speed

Implicit in information-processing models is the idea that speed is an important factor. First, many cognitive tasks, both in the laboratory and in real life, are performed under time pressure. For example, when driving, it is important that you be able to read signs quickly so that you will not miss your exit or make a much more serious error. Second, speed is an advantage even in tasks without time pressure. Consider memorizing foreign language vocabulary: Although you might have all semester to learn a set of words, obviously it is preferable to be able to learn these words quickly.

There is a good deal of evidence that processing speed is slower in younger children than older children.

But the causes of this difference have not been determined. Although some may be biological in origin, they may in some cases reflect differences in knowledge about and/or practice on a task.

Processing Capacity

Information-processing capacity can be viewed as a type of mental energy needed to perform mental work. The difficulty we have in dividing attention to two things at once is attributed to limits on capacity. So also is the trouble we have performing complex tasks (such as mentally working complicated arithmetic problems). Although capacity is thought to be limited at all ages, there is no generally accepted measure of a child's capacity, and thus findings are ambiguous. For example, it is possible that capacity does not change with age but that young children must spend more capacity on lower-level processes (such as identifying stimuli), leaving less capacity for higher-level processes (such as dividing attention or performing complex computations).

Role of Knowledge

If one has knowledge that is relevant to a task, information processing is generally more efficient. It is known for example that "masters" at chess are much better than novices at remembering the details of chessboard displays (Chase & Simon, 1973). It is obvious that older children know more than younger children. Could it be that age differences in information processing are entirely attributable to age differences in

Processing speed is slower in younger than in older children.

knowledge? This seems unlikely, but the role of knowledge in cognitive development is a current research topic (Flavell, 1985).

Controlled Versus Automatic Processes

The essential difference between controlled and automatic processes is twofold: First, controlled processes are assumed to draw heavily on information-processing capacity; this is why they are called effortful. Automatic processes draw minimally on such capacity. Second, controlled processes are intentional, that is, done on purpose. Automatic processes are more difficult to control; once initiated, they tend to "run off" on their own.

Many findings suggest that age differences in cognition frequently involve controlled processes. In contrast, at least some automatic processes appear to be age-invariant. This pattern fits well with the hypothesis that amount of capacity is relatively low in early childhood. Unfortunately, various authors disagree on how best to define controlled and automatic processes (Hasher & Zacks, 1979; Shiffrin & Schneider, 1978). Another complication is that a process that is controlled at one age may be automatic at another.

So far we have discussed a number of ideas about the features of the information-processing approach. A summary of these ideas is presented in Concept Table 7.1.

CONCEPT TABLE 7.1 Features of the Information-Processing Approach		
Concept	**Related Ideas/Processes**	**Characteristics/Description**
Early history	Philosophy, early psychology	Debate and theorizing about information processing have been occurring in psychology for over a hundred years and much longer in philosophy.
	1950s	It was not until the 1950s that truly cognitive approaches to development began to gain momentum.
Two information-processing models	Broadbent's model	Broadbent's model is a classical model of information processing that emphasizes distinctions between short-term and long-term memory and the fundamental notion of limited processing capacity.
	Klatzky's model	Klatzky's model has the same features as Broadbent's model but provides a more fluid view of levels of processing and introduces a distinction between automatic and controlled processes.
Questions about children's cognition raised by an information-processing approach	Processing speed	Speed of processing is an important factor in understanding the nature of children's information processing. Processing speed is slower in younger children than older children, but the causes of the difference have not been documented.
	Processing capacity	Information processing can be viewed as a type of mental energy needed to perform mental work. Capacity is limited at all ages although no accepted measure of capacity has been developed.
	Role of knowledge	Could all age differences in information processing be due to age differences in knowledge? This seems unlikely, but age changes in cognitive development related to knowledge are currently a focus of research.
	Controlled versus automatic processes	Controlled processes are assumed to draw heavily on information-processing capacity while automatic processes draw minimally on such capacity. Controlled processes are intentional while automatic processes are not. There are many age differences in controlled processes, but there seem to be few such differences in automatic processes.

ATTENTION

Children often hear the phrase "Pay attention!" as they are growing up. **Attention** can be defined as the focusing of perception to produce increased awareness of a stimulus. Our discussion of attention emphasizes the orienting reflex, the scanning of visual patterns, advances in attention during early childhood, and changes in attention in the elementary school years.

The Orienting Reflex

Besides the rather obvious signs of attention, such as turning the head, a number of physiological responses accompany increased attention to a stimulus. Collectively, these physiological changes are referred to as the **orienting reflex (OR)** (e.g., Sokolov, 1976). Among these physiological changes are dilation of the pupils of the eyes, an increase in muscle tone, changes in electrical activity of the brain, perspiration, constriction of blood vessels in the limbs and dilation of blood vessels in the head, which produce increased blood flow to the brain and a change in heart rate. Such physiological changes seem to increase the organism's ability to perceive and respond to a stimulus. For instance, dilated pupils allow more light to come into the eyes, enhancing visual sensitivity.

Scanning Visual Patterns

Much of what we know about attention in infancy comes from the study of how infants scan visual patterns. When we look at a complex pattern, our eyes do not stay still. Rather they make what are called **saccadic movements,** fixating first on one part of the pattern, then on another, then another, and so on. The locations of these eye fixations provide clues to the way in which a pattern is processed.

How do infants scan patterns? Three conclusions stand out (Banks & Salapatek, 1983): First, even newborns can detect a contour and fixate it. Second, both the orientation and size of the stimulus affect fixation. Third, as infants get older, they scan a pattern more thoroughly, fixating on internal parts as well as external parts. Up to one month of age, infants tend to fixate on the external parts of a pattern and exclude the internal parts. This has been called the **externality effect,** which has been demonstrated with stimuli as meaningful as the mother's face. For example, in one investigation (Maurer & Salapatek, 1976) one- and two-month-old infants were exposed to the faces of their mothers while the mothers maintained a stationary and expressionless pose. With both the faces of the mother and a stranger, the one-month-olds concentrated on the external details such as the hairline and chin. By contrast, the two-month-olds looked more at the internal features such as the eyes (see figure 7.5).

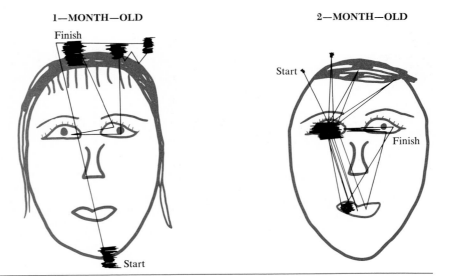

FIGURE 7.5
How one- and two-month-old infants scan the human face (Salapatek, 1975).

Advances in Attention during Early Childhood

There seem to be great changes in a child's ability to pay attention during the early childhood years. The toddler, for example, wanders around a good deal, shifts attention from one activity to another, and generally seems to spend very little time focused on any one object or event. The preschooler, by comparison, is often seen playing a game or watching a television program for a half hour. A number of people researching the impact of educational television on young children have combined an interest in measuring the child's television viewing behavior with an interest in measuring the child's learning of television material.

In one study the attention of children from two to four years of age to an episode of "Sesame Street" was examined (Anderson & Levin, 1976). The children watched the program with their mothers in a setting resembling a living room. The youngest children often got up to play with toys or turned and talked to other people in the room. These patterns of distraction declined among the older children.

Attentional Changes in the Elementary School Years

The changes in ability to pay attention continue beyond the preschool years into the first or second year of school. In the classroom children are able to observe the teacher for extended periods of time, and they can pore over their books in long periods of independent

study. These demands on attention exceed what was required of the preschooler, who is generally free to move about in various play activities. These apparent changes in attention have a dramatic influence on the child's learning (Stevenson, 1972).

The development of strategic use of attention is aptly shown in a study of visual scanning (Vurpillot, 1968). Children were shown two similar pictures and asked to judge whether the two were identical (see figure 7.6). To perform well on this task, the child has to systematically scan the pictures, comparing them feature by feature. Observation of the eye movement patterns of six- and nine-year-old children suggested they were engaging in systematic scanning of the pictures but four-year-old children were not.

FIGURE 7.6
Sample of the stimuli: a pair of identical houses and a pair of different houses (Vurpillot, 1968).

Elementary school aged children attend to stimulus features that are relevant and scan information more systematically than preschool children.

It appears that after the age of six or seven there is a shift to cognitive control of attention so that children act less precipitously and reflect more (Paris & Lindauer, 1982). In other words, older children attend to stimulus features that are relevant to a particular task and scan information in a more systematic and organized manner than preschool children. Preschool children, by contrast, are more influenced by features that stand out or are *salient* than those that are relevant to solving a problem or performing well at a task. The development of such attentional strategies is important for practical reasons—low-achieving students often are deficient in attentional skills (Piontkowski & Calfee, 1979; Zelniker & Jeffrey, 1979).

Divided and Selective Attention

Children are constantly bombarded by a tremendous number of stimuli. Although they usually cannot possibly handle all of these stimuli, children often are interested in handling more than just one. Thus, there are two different types of attention tasks that children must frequently face: selective attention tasks and divided attention tasks. In a **selective attention task,** the child has the problem of ignoring some stimuli while focusing on others more relevant to his or her interests and goals. For example, the child may need to ignore the blaring of a television set while studying for a test. A number of clever experiments have shown that as children get older they become more efficient at performing selective attention tasks.

One relevant developmental study of selective attention was reported by Anne Higgins and James Turnure (1984). Preschool, second, and sixth grade children performed either an easy or a difficult visual perception task under three conditions: quiet, continuous soft music, and continuous loud music. The "irrelevant" music was found to impair the younger children's performance. In contrast, the music actually improved the older childrens' performance (perhaps because it increased alertness). Furthermore, irrelevant music caused the younger children to frequently glance away from their visual perception task. It did not have this effect on the older children. Of course, depending on the particular situation, even adults have great problems in selectively attending. However, the Higgins and Turnure study shows that as children get older, they also get better at handling selective attention tasks. Indeed, development of selective attention continues improving after the elementary school years—adults exceed twelve-year-olds in selective attention tasks (Sexton & Geffen, 1979).

In a **divided attention task,** the child has the problem of handling two or more information "channels" at once. For example, the child might be listening to what the teacher is saying while also listening to what a friend is whispering to him or her. Following the content of both of these messages is bound to be difficult. In one interesting investigation (Schiff & Knopf, 1985) nine- and thirteen-year-old children viewed displays showing a set of visual symbols (e.g., *, &, =, %, $) in the center and some letters (e.g., A, G, M, S, T) in the corners. The older children were considerably better at the divided attention task of (a) detecting whether the symbols at the center included a certain target symbol and (b) remembering the letters shown in the corners. Other types of divided attention tasks show developmental improvements as well (Guttentag, 1984).

MEMORY

Memory is a central feature of cognitive development that pertains to all situations in which we retain information over time. Sometimes information is retained for only a few seconds or less, whereas at other times it is retained for a lifetime. Memory is involved when we look up a telephone number and dial it. Memory also is involved when we remember the name of our best friend from elementary school. Our overview of memory in children's development begins with the fascinating topic of infant memory. Then we consider one of the most basic distinctions in memory, that between short-term and long-term memory. Next we focus on memory span and speed of processing and subsequently turn our attention to a number of control processes that help improve children's memory. To conclude the discussion we consider memory characteristics of the child and the context in which memory occurs.

Infant Memory

Since memory abilities are usually assessed by examining some type of verbal response, you can imagine that it is not an easy task to study infant memory. First, we provide information about a procedure called conjugate reinforcement that has been used to investigate infant memory. Second, we study the extent to which infants have conscious memory.

Conjugate Reinforcement

In the **conjugate reinforcement technique,** which is illustrated in figure 7.7, one end of a ribbon is tied to an infant's ankle and the other end to a mobile (Rovee-Collier, 1984). When the infant kicks, the mobile moves. This is rewarding for the infant—who soon doubles his or her kicking rate after the ribbon is tied to the mobile and the infant's ankle. After the infant's kicking behavior has been increased, the mobile is removed from the crib for some period of time. Later the mobile is reattached to the crib, the infant's ankle and mobile are ribboned once again, and the infant's kicking behavior is again observed. If the infant "remembers" that his or her kicks in this situation were enjoyable, the infant should immediately increase his or her rate of kicking. This is what three-month-olds do even up to an interval of one week of remembering. Use of the conjugate reinforcement technique to investigate memory has indicated that infants as young as two months of age can remember for as long as three days (Earley, Griesler & Rovee-Collier, 1985). And the duration of remembering can be extended through the use of a reactivation technique. If the mobile is reexposed to the infant twenty-four hours before the test (it is reattached to the crib but not tied to the infant's ankle), retention over four or five weeks can be demonstrated (Earley et al., 1985; Fagan, Ohr & Fleckenstein, 1985; Hayne & Rovee-Collier, 1985). Apparently, if a twelve-week-old views a mobile that he or she played with four weeks earlier, the infant can be "reminded" of the kicking responses he or she learned through such playing.

Conscious Memory

Although it is interesting to show that infants "remember" in the conjugate reinforcement setting, you may suspect that certain key aspects of adult-type memory are not really demonstrated by this technique. John Flavell (1985) and others (Lockhart, 1984) argue that memory in children and adults involves conscious feelings of "I have seen that before" and additional retrieval ability (such as, "where have I seen that before—was it at the zoo?") that are not present in young infants. And while recall in children may entail a conscious representation or image of something not present ("I recall our first meeting as if it were yesterday"), recall in young infants may not. Flavell argues—as did Jean Piaget—that young infants do not have this ability to consciously recall or reflect on objects when they are not perceptually available.

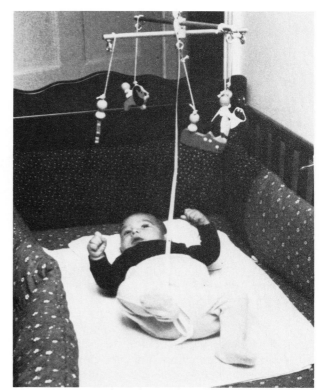

FIGURE 7.7
The conjugate reinforcement situation.

Just when do infants acquire the ability to consciously remember the past? In one investigation (Ashmead & Perlmutter, 1980) parents kept diaries of memory behavior in their seven- to eleven-month-old infants. An entry in one of the diaries describes the behavior of a nine-month-old girl who was looking for ribbons that had been removed from the drawer where they had been kept. She first looked in the "old" drawer. Failing to find the ribbons, she searched other drawers until she found them. The next day the young girl went directly to the "new" drawer to find the ribbons. More formal experiments support the existence of such memory in infants over six months of age (Fox, Kagan & Weiskopf, 1979). For example, when an object is shown to an infant and then subsequently removed, the infant of seven months or older will search for the object but younger infants will not (Kail, 1984). Thus, the data suggest that the memory of infants in the first six months of life is not what adults usually mean by memory, that is, a conscious recollection of prior events.

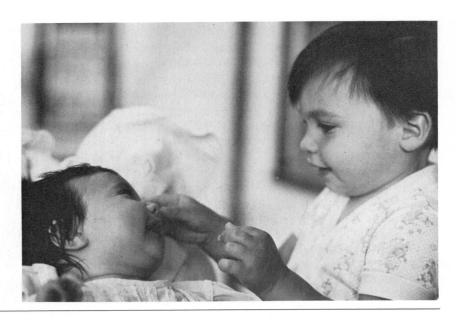

Conscious memory remains minimal until the child is about three years old.

The type of memory evidenced in the conjugate reinforcement technique with two-month-olds is referred to as learning adaptive responses or skills rather than the conscious recollection of specific past episodes.

Some psychologists, Piaget himself, for instance, refer to the learning of adaptive responses or skills as memory in the broad sense while reserving the label memory in the strict sense to the conscious recollection of past episodes. Piaget believed that memory in the broad sense may be present quite early but that memory in the strict sense is not in place until one and a half to two years of age. As we have seen, though, memory in the strict sense probably is in place earlier than Piaget believed.

It is interesting to speculate about why memory in the strict sense, or conscious memory, develops later than other learning and memory skills. One possibility is that conscious memory must await the maturation of certain brain structures, such as the hippocampus (Schacter & Moscovitch, 1984). Another possibility is that conscious memory may depend on the development of structures of knowledge called schemata (Mandler, 1983; Olson & Strauss, 1984), a view in the spirit of Piaget's theory of cognitive structure.

Despite evidence of conscious memory within the first year of life, there is a sense that such recall remains minimal until the child is about three years old. Think about your own infancy. Try to think about a specific episode, like the birth of a sibling. Can you remember anything about such an event in your first two years of life? For more information about the possibility that you have infantile amnesia read Perspective on Child Development 7.1.

Short-Term and Long-Term Memory

Short-term memory appears to retain information for up to twenty to thirty seconds, assuming no rehearsal is used. With rehearsal, short-term memory can retain information for considerably longer periods. As an example of short-term memory, consider what happens when you try to remember a telephone number you just heard. If you attempt to remember the number five seconds after hearing it, you probably will be successful. But what occurs if you try to do the same thing four to five minutes later? Unless you have been rehearsing the phone number, your memory is likely to fail. This is because short-term memory for unrehearsed information does not exceed twenty to thirty seconds, and the processes needed for long-term retention, what psychologists refer to as encoding information into **long-term memory,** are difficult and often error prone.

PERSPECTIVE ON CHILD DEVELOPMENT 7.1

INFANTILE AMNESIA

As children and adults, we have little or no memory for events we experienced before three years of age. This is the phenomenon of **infantile amnesia.** It is not a simple matter to examine how well a child or an adult remembers events from infancy—some events may be reported, but they may or may not be remembered accurately. The clever technique used in one investigation involved asking children and adults whether they remembered information of a very specific type—information surrounding the birth of a younger sibling (Sheingold & Tenney, 1982). Each of the subjects had at least one younger sibling. Here are some examples of the questions they were asked: Who told you your mother was leaving to go to the hospital? What time of day was it when she left to go to the hospital? Did you visit your mother while she was in the hospital?

Both children and adults were tested, and the reports of the children were checked against their mothers' recall. Fortunately, there was good agreement between children and their mothers, supporting true memory for the type of information tested. The information from the adults involved siblings who were one year and three months to seventeen years and five months younger than they were. Recall by these subjects is shown in the figure opposite: It was virtually zero unless their siblings were three or more years younger. This finding suggests that if a child is less than three when a certain event occurs, he or she will be unlikely to remember it as an adult.

Infantile amnesia may not be restricted to humans. For example, in one investigation (Feigley & Spear, 1970) young and old rats were trained to jump across a barrier to avoid an electric shock. Twenty-eight days

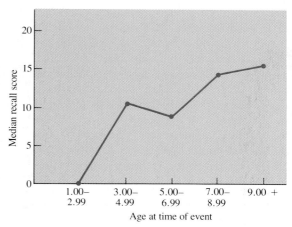

Median recall scores as a function of age for sibling births reported by college students.
From Sheingold, K., and Y. J. Tenney, "Memory for a salient childhood event," in U. Neisser (ed.), *Memory Observed.* W. H. Freeman and Company. Copyright © 1984.

later, the older rats demonstrated memory of the training but the younger rats did not. This and other studies using nonhuman subjects may help us determine the mechanisms responsible for infantile amnesia, but the phenomenon at present remains unexplained (Kail, 1984). Although Sigmund Freud (1953) thought that infantile amnesia is the result of repressing memories of sexual feelings experienced early in life, it is unlikely that this explanation could be applied to rats.

Although we are capable of memorizing a number in a more-or-less permanent way (many people claim they can recall their own telephone numbers from three or more previous residences), this generally is not accomplished easily or quickly. Thus while short-term retention of information seems to be somewhat effortless, encoding information for long-term retention is much more difficult. Long-term memory involves more effortful use of retrieval as well. We often struggle to recall information that (we think) is in long-term memory but that for some reason cannot be "found." In sum, there seem to be adequate reasons for making a distinction between short-term and long-term memory.

Memory Span and Speed of Processing

One task that has been devised to assess short-term memory is the **memory span task.** If you have ever taken an IQ test, you undoubtedly have taken a memory span test. You simply hear a short list of stimuli, usually digits, presented at a rapid pace (typically one per second). Then you are asked to repeat the digits back. On the basis of research with the memory span test, there is good evidence that short-term memory increases during early childhood. For example, as shown in figure 7.8, memory span increases from about two digits in two- to three-year-olds to about five digits in seven-year-olds. Yet between seven and thirteen years of age memory span only increases by one and a half digits (Dempster, 1981). Keep in mind though that there are individual differences in memory span and this is why IQ tests and various aptitude tests are used. In addition, as an indication of the importance of memory span, research with young adults suggests that performance on a memory span test is strongly linked to performance on the Scholastic Aptitude Test (SAT), accounting for about 50 percent of the predictability of scores on both the math and verbal sections of this test (Dempster, 1985).

It is important for us to ask why there are age differences in memory span. It turns out that although many factors are involved, including rehearsal of information, what seems to be most important in these age changes is the speed and efficiency of information processing, particularly the speed with which memory items can be identified. For example, in one investigation (Case, Kurland & Goldberg, 1982), children were tested on their speed at repeating auditorially presented words. Speed of repetition was highly predictive of memory span using these same words. Indeed when speed of repetition was controlled, the memory spans of the six-year-olds were equal to those of young adults (the adults were tested with nonsense words so their repetition times equaled those of the children).

A converging source of evidence that development of memory span is linked to speed of perceptual identification is neurobiological in origin. Lawrence Howard and John Polich (1985) measured the latency of the P300 component of the event-related brain potential. The **P300** is part of the electrical activity in the brain that is initiated by processing a stimulus. It can be measured noninvasively by attaching electrodes to a

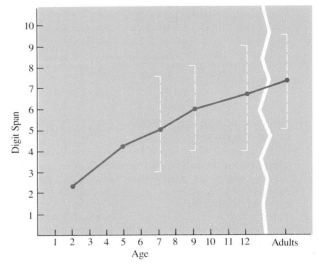

FIGURE 7.8
Developmental differences (solid line) and individual differences, expressed as ranges (dashed lines), in digit span (Dempster, 1981).

person's head and recording the electrical activity—including the waveform called the P300—in response to simple stimuli. Howard and Polich argue that the latency of the P300 is a measure of speed of categorizing or evaluating stimuli. Their findings show that P300 latencies in response to simple tones grow shorter from five to fourteen years of age. Further, P300 latencies predict memory span—children showing shorter latencies show larger memory spans (interestingly, adult subjects do not show this relationship).

Speed of processes other than perceptual identification may be linked to short-term memory development. For example, the rate of internally rehearsing items (covered in the next section) may become faster as children grow older (Hulme, 1984). Further, it is not just processes affecting short-term memory that appear to get faster with age. The speed of naming a stimulus or imagining it rotating also increases with age (Kail, 1985).

Control Processes

If we know anything at all about long-term memory, it is that such memory depends on the learning activities that people engage in when learning and remembering information. Most learning activities that have been studied to date fit under the category of effortful, control processes. Such activities are under the learner's conscious control and are appropriately referred to as strategies. Five such control processes involved in memory are rehearsal, organization, semantic elaboration, imagery, and retrieval or search processes.

Rehearsal

What all **rehearsal** has in common is extended processing of material to be remembered after it has been presented. If someone tells you his or her phone number and you run through it in your mind while frantically searching for a pencil, you are using rehearsal. If after hearing the number you notice it includes the year that Columbus discovered America (1492 in 690–1492), you also are rehearsing. In the first instance—with no association involving 1492 and Columbus—you are engaging in what is called **maintenance rehearsal;** in the second instance—in which you do make the association with Columbus—you are performing **elaborative rehearsal** (Craik & Lockhart, 1972). Maintenance rehearsal simply involves a rote restatement, as in repeating items, while elaborative rehearsal can include organizational, elaborative, and imaginative activities.

A classic study of the development of rehearsal was conducted by John Flavell and his colleagues (Flavell, Beach & Chinsky, 1966). Children from five to ten years old were given the task of remembering a set of from two to five pictures of nameable objects for a short (fifteen-second) retention interval. The novel feature of the experiment was that the experimenter was a trained lip reader. The critical result was that some of the children made lip movements that evidenced rehearsal of the names of the pictures. Further, the percentage of children making such movements increased with age—10 percent of the five-year-olds, 60 percent of the seven-year-olds, and 85 percent of the ten-year-olds made lip movements suggesting rehearsal. Finally, in a subsequent study of six-year-olds (Keeney, Cannizzo & Flavell, 1967), researchers found that those children who engaged in rehearsal showed better recall than those who did not. And if nonrehearsers were taught to rehearse, their performance rose to that of the spontaneous rehearsers.

Some more recent studies (DeLoache, Cassidy & Brown, 1985; Wellman, Ritter & Flavell, 1985) make the interesting point that rudimentary, rehearsal-like processes begin to appear at very young ages. In one

study, three- and four-year-old children watched a toy dog being hidden under one of three cups. Instructed to remember where the dog was hidden, the children engaged in behaviors such as looking at, pointing to, and touching the "baited" cup over a forty-second interval. Such behaviors were related to accuracy of remembering, and they were engaged in less frequently by children not given a memory instruction but told simply to "wait" for a period (Wellman et al., 1985). Another study showed that even two-year-olds will engage in such rehearsal-like behavior, under simplified conditions (DeLoache et al., 1985). These findings are "evidence of an early natural propensity to keep alive what must be remembered, a rudimentary and imperfect version of what will later become more elaborate and planful mnemonic strategies" (DeLoache et al., 1985, p. 125).

Organization

The use of organization improves long-term memory. Do children show increased **organizational processing** in middle and late childhood? In one investigation (Moely, Olson, Halwes & Flavell, 1969), children were presented with a circular array of pictures from four different categories: clothing, furniture, animals, and vehicles. The children were told to study the pictures so that later they could say their names back to the experimenter. They also were told they could move the pictures around in order to remember them better. The results showed that while ten- and eleven-year-olds performed such grouping, younger children did not. Importantly, when younger children were put through a brief training procedure that encouraged semantic grouping, they were able to follow this strategy. And their memory for the pictures improved.

Semantic Elaboration

Semantic elaboration is a process in which information is encoded in a form that preserves the meaning of words and sounds. Semantic elaboration increases during middle and late childhood and is an important factor in long-term memory. Research on memory for meaningful sentences is instructive. In experiments by Scott Paris and his colleagues (Paris & Lindauer, 1976; Paris, Lindauer & Cox, 1977) children heard sentences that implied but did not actually mention certain tools or instruments. One of their sentences was "Her friend swept the floor." It clearly implies but does not actually mention the instrument "broom". The critical question asked by Paris and Lindauer was this: If a child hears a sentence such as "Her friend swept the floor" will the child spontaneously infer that a broom was used? If so, we can make a prediction about recall performance in a subsequent test. Specifically, we can make the prediction that a word like *broom* should be a good cue for reminding the child of the sentence. In fact, the results obtained by Paris and Lindauer supported the prediction for eleven-year-olds but not for seven-year-olds. This suggests that spontaneous inferential processing increases from seven to eleven years of age.

Imagery

Another control process that develops as children move through the middle and late childhood years is **mental imagery.** However, imagery is a process that even adults sometimes fail to use spontaneously (Paivio, 1971). A typical experiment that examined this process (Pressley & Levin, 1977) used the paired-associates recall procedure. A list of eighteen pairs of words was presented to second graders and sixth graders. Half of the children were told to construct mental images for each of the pairs, as this would help their learning (they were given practice at image construction and were shown drawings of the types of images most helpful to paired-associates recall). These are images in which two objects interact in some way (e.g., an image of a dog with a kite in his mouth). The older children benefited from the imagery instructions. So did the younger children in most of the experimental conditions. However, when the pairs were difficult to image and the presentation rate was fast (six seconds per pair), the younger children showed little or no benefit from imagery. Apparently, seven- and eight-year-old children can sometimes use imagery strategies but not with difficult pairs and fast presentation. Children four or five years old appear to have still greater difficulties in using an imagery strategy. For more information about the effectiveness of imagery in promoting children's memory, read Perspective on Child Development 7.2.

Retrieval/Search Processes

Not all learning activities take place at the time of presentation of material to be remembered. Some occur at the time of testing. There are also developmental differences in such **retrieval** activities, as evidenced by another investigation of imagery and memory (Pressley

& Levin, 1980). Younger (first grade) and older (sixth grade) children were tested on paired-associates recall. However, there actually were two different imagery groups. In one group, the children were instructed to use imagery not only when they were learning the pairs but also when they were recalling the pairs. In the other group, the children were instructed to use imagery when learning, but they were not instructed to use imagery when recalling. Older children performed identically in the two imagery groups. But younger children showed better recall in the first than in the second group. Apparently, the younger children engaged in imagery-based learning and yet failed to capitalize on such learning unless instructed to use imagery in recall. They suffered a deficit in spontaneous use of an effective retrieval strategy.

Retrieval strategies are not limited to situations involving mental imagery. For example, Kobasigawa (1974) has shown that as children get older, they make more and better use of category information in the process of remembering. Children from six to eleven years old were shown three different pictures from each of eight different categories (e.g., three zoo animals, three fruits, etc.). There followed a test in which the children attempted to recall the pictures. In one condition, they were given a deck containing category cues (e.g., a picture of a zoo was the cue for the animals—these category cues had also been shown during learning). They were used by only 33 percent of the six-year-old subjects but by 75 percent of the eight-year-old subjects and by over 90 percent of the eleven-year-old subjects.

Characteristics of the Learner

Apart from the obvious variable of age, many characteristics of a learner can determine the level of his or her memory performance. These characteristics include attitudes, motivations, and health-related factors. However, the characteristic that has been examined most thoroughly is the previously acquired knowledge of the learner.

The knowledge that a learner possesses probably contributes to most memory tasks. And since knowledge is something that increases with age, it clearly should contribute to development of memory. In support of this reasoning, Jean Mandler (Mandler & Robinson, 1978) compared memory for meaningful scenes and disorganized arrays of objects in first, third, and

PERSPECTIVE ON CHILD DEVELOPMENT 7.2

PLACES, KEYWORDS, AND IMAGERY

A number of devices, called **mnemonics,** can be employed to help us remember. An ancient mnemonic attributed to the Greek poet Simonides, who lived in the fifth century B.C., uses the method of places, or "loci." Simonides was able to use this method to identify all the guests who had been at a banquet with him and were maimed beyond recognition when the building collapsed and crushed them. (Fortuitously, Simonides had not been present when the building collapsed.) He was able to accomplish this great feat by generating vivid images of each individual and mentally picturing where they had sat at the banquet table.

This is a mnemonic device that you can apply to memory problems of your own. Suppose you have a list of chores to do. To make sure you remember them all, here is what to do. First associate a concrete object with each chore. A trip to the store becomes a dollar bill, a telephone call to a friend becomes a telephone, clean-up duty becomes a broom, and so on. Then create an image for each "object" so that you imagine it in a particular room or location in a familiar building, such as your house. You might imagine the dollar bill in the kitchen, the telephone in the dining room, and so forth. The vividness of the image and the unique placement of it virtually guarantee recollection. It helps to move mentally through the house in some logical way as the images are "placed."

A very powerful imagery mnemonic, first suggested by Richard Atkinson (1975), is the *Keyword Method.* It has been used to great practical advantage by one of our University of Wisconsin colleagues, Joel Levin. Professor Levin and his associates have shown the technique to be an efficient procedure for teaching school-aged children how to rapidly master new information such as foreign vocabulary words, the states and capitals in the United States, and the names of U.S. presidents. In one recent study, for example, fourth- and fifth-grade children learned the capital cities of each of the fifty states. Here, in Professor Levin's own words, is how the instruction was done.

> Let me illustrate using one of my favorites, Annapolis, Maryland. In the first of a three-stage process, students were taught keywords for the

Dual keyword illustration for learning the states and capitals.

> states, such that when a state was given (*Maryland*) they could supply the keyword (*marry*). Then, since the criterion task required that the student supply the capital in response to a state name, in the second stage we gave students the reverse type of keyword practice with the capitals. That is, they had to respond with the capital (*Annapolis*) when given a keyword (*apple*). Finally, in the third stage, an illustration . . . (see figure above) was provided. In comparison to a very liberal control condition that allowed unrestricted study and self-testing, keyword subjects were better at remembering the capitals. This was true on an immediate test, but especially so on a surprise retest three days later. (Levin, 1980, p. 20)

From Levin, Joel, et al., "The Keyword Method in the Classroom: How to Remember the States and Their Capitals," in *Elementary School Journal* 80, (4). © 1980 by The University of Chicago Press. Reprinted by permission.

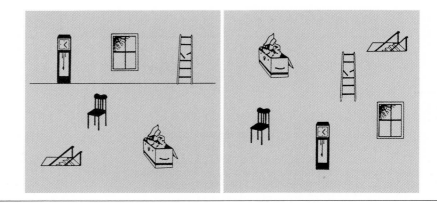

FIGURE 7.9
An example of an organized and unorganized version of a picture (Mandler and Robinson, 1978).

fifth graders. Figure 7.9 shows an example of a scene and a meaningless array. One interesting finding was that the scenes were recognized better than the arrays and that this difference grew larger with age. That is, the benefit of viewing organized scenes was less for the first graders than for the older children. This suggests that a child's growing knowledge of scenes can be beneficial to his or her memory for scenes.

The effects that knowledge can have upon memory are impressively strong. In one study (Chi, 1978), a group of children and a group of adults were tested on memory for chessboard displays. After viewing a chessboard, all subjects attempted to recall the locations of pieces. The results should strike you as quite unusual, given the research we have covered thus far in the chapter: The children were better, and by a substantial margin. How could this be so? The answer is simple: The children were all skilled chess players, whereas the adults were novices. What this study shows is that when childrens' knowledge of stimuli to be remembered exceeds that of adults, children's memory for the stimuli can be superior. Such is the power of the effects of knowledge on memory.

Given the strength of knowledge effects, one might ask whether the learner's knowledge is a more important determinant of memory than the control processes (e.g., organization, imagery) he or she employs. Although this question sounds reasonable, it probably is unanswerable. The reason is that the subject's knowledge and his or her control processes do not function independently. They interact with each other and together determine efficiency of learning and memory. Some support for interactions between knowledge and control processes comes from a study by Mary Zembar and Mary Naus (1985). They tested recall memory in third and sixth graders, and used three different types of materials: "kiddie" materials, consisting of very common words; "typical experimental" materials, consisting of nouns of intermediate difficulty; and "advanced adult" materials, consisting of very difficult words. Their results showed that children in both age groups showed good recall and used efficient memory strategies when given materials that were easy for them but not when given materials that were difficult for them. That is, subjects' knowledge of the materials affected their use of efficient memory strategies.

The two factors of knowledge and control processes are tightly intertwined. Indeed, one important type of memory knowledge actually concerns control processes. Such knowledge is that of **metamemory** (Brown et al., 1983; Flavell, 1985; Flavell & Wellman, 1977), which can be loosely defined as knowledge about one's own memory. More specifically, metamemory comprises (1) knowledge that learning information is different from simply perceiving information, in that specific memory strategies are sometimes necessary for the former, (2) diagnostic knowledge of the various factors (e.g., rehearsal, recall versus recognition testing) contributing to performance of different memory tasks, and (3) knowledge of how to monitor memory during

How can this circumstance suggest the importance of knowledge in memory?

the course of learning (e.g., the ability to tell when one has studied sufficiently to pass an exam).

The sophistication of childrens' metamemory—as assessed through their answers on verbal test batteries—improves from the preschool years through adolescence and beyond (Brown et al., 1983; Flavell, 1985). However, a basic question has been raised: Does children's metamemorial knowledge of memory strategies actually predict their use of such strategies and their level of performance in learning and remembering tasks? The answer appears to be yes. Although the relationship of metamemory to memory performance is often weak or absent in younger children (e.g., second graders), it appears to grow stronger in older children (sixth graders) (Ledger & Groff, 1985; Short, 1985). Moreover, the weak associations that are found with younger children may reflect difficulties of measuring metamemory rather than a true absence of metamemory–memory connections. If metamemory questions are carefully worded and given after children have had some exposure to a task, the answers to these questions may be more valid. For example, in one study of first and second graders, it was shown that children's causal attributions regarding organizational processing—that is, their ideas about whether organizing information improves its memorability—was related to organizational processing in a subsequent memory task (Fabricius & Hagen, 1984). An important feature

of this experiment is that children were asked about the effects of organization on memory only after some experience in tasks requiring both organization and memory.

Of the three different types of metamemorial functioning, perhaps the most crucial from a practical standpoint is that of memory monitoring. Whether or not one knows the most efficient memory strategies, it is crucial to be able to tell when one has finally mastered a body of information, so that it is possible to safely stop studying. Yet memory monitoring appears deficient in young children, as shown by another of John Flavell's studies (Flavell, Friedrichs & Hoyt, 1970). In the first phase of the experiment, the investigators determined the *memory spans* of children in nursery school through fourth grade. Then, in the second phase, each child was given a new set of pictures equal in length to his or her predetermined span. The child was told to study this list of items as long as was necessary to recall it perfectly. When the child signaled that he or she was ready to recall, his or her recall was tested.

The results were straightforward; older children recalled more pictures than younger children, despite the fact that all of the children had lists that were equal to their predetermined spans. Apparently, the younger children were deficient at monitoring their recall readiness—they usually stopped studying before they actually were ready to recall. Younger children are also deficient at other aspects of metamemory (Flavell, 1985; Kail, 1984).

The Context of Memory

Memory is involved in an extraordinary range of children's activities. Children make a plan, remember it, and carry it out. They put something down and then later remember where it is. Children encounter someone they know and try to remember their conversation with him or her the last time they saw the person. However, for many years the vast majority of our research information about memory has come from testing in laboratory situations and in most instances testing children's remembrances of familiar verbal materials, particularly words. In considering the importance of context in children's memory, we should be concerned not only about the physical context in which memory is encoded, stored, and retrieved but also about the nature of the materials to be remembered.

Ulric Neisser (1982) has described two important features of naturalistic memory. First, in most cases of daily remembering, it is meanings and not surface details that children need to remember. Just as an oral historian recalls what has happened rather than remembering some formula of words that characterizes it, children also must recall the substance of what they hear and read rather than its verbatim form.

Second, children use the past to define themselves. Bobby asks who he is. He has a name, a family, a place to stay. He knows a great deal about himself—what he has done, how he feels, where he has been, the people he knows, how he has been treated. His past, together with his present and the future that past leads him to expect, defines Bobby. What would Bobby be without his memory of his past? Many of the specifics of his past are beyond recall. Some things, though, he can remember very well, either when he chooses to or when someone provides him with cues.

Neisser (1982) goes on to talk more about the substance of what is recalled. He believes that the single clear memories children recall so vividly actually stand for something else—they are like "screen memories." Their real basis is often a series of repeated experiences, a sequence of related events that the single recollection simply typifies or represents. For example, a characteristic finding in memory study is that individuals cannot recall specific sentences but easily can recall the theme or general idea represented by the sentences (Bransford & Franks, 1971). Neisser prefers to call such memories **repisodic** rather than episodic, because what seems to be an episode actually reflects a repetition. For example, in the Watergate scenario John Dean remembered the themes of many conversations with President Nixon, but according to the presidential tapes Dean actually assigned the comments to the wrong day and put them in the wrong conversations. Dean's memory, then, was not like a tape recorder, but it seemed to receive the general message of what was going on.

Children often use more sophisticated memory strategies in naturalistic settings, such as their home, than in university laboratories.

As suggested earlier, much research on children's memory has been conducted in laboratory situations. We have little information about children's memory in naturalistic circumstances—about remembering to take vitamins, turning off the iron, studying in the bedroom for a test, and retrieving a book that had been put away a year earlier. One investigation (Ceci & Bronfenbrenner, 1985) revealed that children often use more sophisticated memory strategies in the naturalistic context of their own homes than in a university laboratory.

So far we have discussed many ideas about attention and memory. A summary of these ideas is presented in Concept Table 7.2.

CONCEPT TABLE 7.2 Attention and Memory		
Concept	**Processes/Related Ideas**	**Characteristics/Description**
Attention	Basic nature	Attention plays an important role in processing information. It involves focusing perception to produce increased awareness of stimuli.
	Orienting reflex	Attentional changes are accompanied by such physiological changes as pupil dilation, increased muscle tone, brain electrical activity, perspiration, constriction of blood vessels, and heart rate. Collectively these physiological changes are called the orienting reflex, or OR.
	Scanning visual patterns	When we look at patterns, our eyes make saccadic movements. Infants' pattern scanning involves an externality effect up to one month of age, with two-month-olds being more likely to focus on internal features.
	Advances in attention in early childhood	The child's attention increases substantially during early childhood. Distraction decreases through the early childhood period.
	Attentional changes in elementary school children	After the age of six or seven there is a shift to cognitive control of attention. While preschool children focus more on salient features, elementary school children are more likely to attend to task relevant features. An important distinction can be made between selective and divided attention.
Memory	Basic nature	Memory is a central process in cognitive development and information processing that involves the retention of information over time.
	Infant memory	Infant memory involves conjugate reinforcement, conscious memory, and infantile amnesia. Infants as young as two months of age remember as long as three days or less. However, when memory in the strict sense—conscious memory—is considered, we have to wait until the age of seven months or older. As children and adults, we have little or no memory for events experienced before the age of three—the process of infantile amnesia.
	Short- and long-term memory	Short-term memory involves retention for up to twenty or thirty seconds and is more effortless than long-term memory. Long-term memory involves more effortful use of retrieval.
	Memory span and speed of processing	Memory span tests have been used to assess short-term memory. Memory span increases substantially during childhood and is related to speed of processing information.
	Control processes	Long-term memory depends on the learning activities people engage in when learning and remembering information. Most learning activities fall under the category of control processes, five important ones being rehearsal, organization, semantic elaboration, imagery, and retrieval/search processes.
	Characteristics of the learner	Apart from the obvious variable of age, many characteristics of the learner can determine the level of memory performance—attitudes, health, motivation. Knowledge that a learner has also seems to contribute to memory performance. An important type of memory knowledge is metamemory—knowledge about one's own memory.
	Context of memory	Most research on memory has been conducted in laboratories. A current research interest is the study of children's memory in more naturalistic contexts. Neisser argues that two important features of memory in such contexts is meaning and the repisodic nature of memory.

UNDERSTANDING AND INFERENCING

Our discussion of attention and memory has led us to consider some rather complex types of processes. But still more complex processes are to be found in the domain we call thinking. *Thinking* refers to a great many activities including problem solving, understanding, and making inferences. Problem solving is central to the study of intelligence, which we cover in chapter 9. Understanding and inferencing are more naturally covered here. To learn more about understanding and inferencing we revisit Roberta Klatzky's model of information processing, discuss the concept of deep processing, describe schemata and scripts, and then consider the development of scripts in children.

Klatzky's Model Revisited, Deep Processing, Schemata, and Scripts

In the context of information-processing models—for example, the model shown in figure 7.4—we can conceptualize comprehension and inferencing as the end point of the continuum of levels of processing (what Klatzky referred to as "reason, compare"). As information enters the system, it is processed for its sensory features (shallow processing), it activates its name and associated concepts in long-term memory (deeper processing), and finally it is understood and thought about, which usually involves inferring things not explicitly stated. To see better the nature of understanding and inferencing, consider this paragraph from a study by John Bransford and Marcia Johnson (1972):

> The procedure is actually quite simple. First you arrange things into different groups depending on their makeup. Of course, one pile may be sufficient depending on how much there is to do. If you have to go somewhere else due to lack of facilities that is the next step, otherwise you are pretty well set. It is important not to overdo any particular endeavor. That is, it is better to do too few things at once than too many. In the short run this may not seem important, but complications from doing too many can easily arise. A mistake can be expensive as well. The manipulation of the appropriate mechanisms should be self-explanatory, and we need not dwell on it here. At first the whole procedure will seem complicated. Soon, however, it will become just another facet of life. It is difficult to foresee any end to the necessity for this task in the immediate future, but then one never can tell. (p. 722)

There is no real problem in processing the words and phrases of this passage, but did you understand it? Unless you are very clever indeed (or have encountered this paragraph before in another course), you probably did not. Despite the familiar words and good syntax, the passage as a whole appears incomprehensible.

But is it truly incomprehensible? No it is not. Read the paragraph one more time, this time with the knowledge of what it is about: washing clothes. Given the topic, the initially bizarre-sounding paragraph suddenly becomes coherent. All the sentences link together, and the meaning becomes concrete. What has happened?

One thing that has happened is that learning of the topic allowed you to activate appropriate knowledge from long-term memory. You probably know a good many things about washing clothes—the reason one does it, the places in which one does it, the sequence of operations one is likely to follow, and so on. If such knowledge is activated when you read the washing-clothes paragraph, it becomes easy to interpret the various words and sentences in a way that makes good sense. And this brings us to a second thing that happened after you learned the topic of the paragraph. After activating your knowledge of washing clothes and then reading the paragraph a second time, you suddenly were able to make good inferences about how to interpret each word and phrase. Words such as *pile, endeavor,* and *mechanism* are highly abstract and ambiguous. But knowing the passage is about washing clothes and having read other parts of the passage, you can easily guess what these and other words mean. Good guesses lead to good comprehension.

In summary, comprehension and inferencing are **deep processes** that depend on activating appropriate long-term memory knowledge. Many psychologists argue that such knowledge is organized in structures they refer to as **schemata** (Bartlett, 1932; Mandler, 1983). There are schemata for scenes or spatial layouts (you may have a schema for a typical kitchen), as well as schemata for common events (you may have a schema for going to a restaurant, playing baseball, and writing a term paper). Schemata for events are often called **scripts** (Schank & Abelson, 1977), and these have been the focus of some interesting research. An example of a "restaurant" script is shown in figure 7.10 (Bower, Black & Turner, 1979). Notice that this script has information about physical features, people, and typical happenings. This type of generalized knowledge should be useful to people when they are in a situation and trying to interpret what is going on around

Name:	Restaurant		**Roles:**	Customer
Props:	Tables			Waiter
	Menu			Cook
	Food			Cashier
	Bill			Owner
	Money			
	Tip			
Entry Conditions:	Customer is hungry.		**Results:**	Customer has less money.
	Customer has money.			Owner has more money.
				Customer is not hungry.

Scene 1: *Entering*
Customer enters restaurant.
Customer looks for table.
Customer decides where to sit.
Customer goes to table.
Customer sits down.

Scene 2: *Ordering*
Customer picks up menu.
Customer looks at menu.
Customer decides on food.
Customer signals waitress.
Waitress comes to table.
Customer orders food.
Waitress goes to cook.
Waitress gives food order to cook.
Cook prepares food.

Scene 3: *Eating*
Cook gives food to waitress.
Waitress brings food to customer.
Customer eats food.

Scene 4: *Exiting*
Waitress writes bill.
Waitress goes over to customer.
Waitress gives bill to customer.
Customer gives tip to waitress.
Customer goes to cashier.
Customer gives money to cashier.
Customer leaves restaurant.

FIGURE 7.10
A simplified version of Schank and Abelson's (1976) schematic representation of our organized knowledge of activities involved in going to a restaurant (Bower, Black, and Turner, 1979).

What is the likely nature of this child's script for a restaurant?

them. For example, if you are in a restaurant and a man comes over and lays a piece of paper on your table, your script can tell you he is probably a waiter who is giving you a check (of course, he might be a spy leaving a secret message, but your script lets you make a good first guess).

The Development of Scripts in Children

What have we learned about the development of scripts in childhood? The evidence that is currently available suggests that scripts emerge quite early in life, perhaps by one year of age if not sooner (Nelson, 1977; Schank & Abelson, 1977). Scripts may explain why young infants grow distressed when there is a change in their daily routine (Mandler, 1983). And certainly there is very clear evidence that children have scripts and other types of schemata by the time they start school. In one study (Nelson, 1978) four- and five-year-old children were asked to describe what happens when eating in different locations (at home, in a day-care center, and at McDonald's). The descriptions they gave were impressively detailed and in good correspondence with those given by adults in other studies (Bower, Black & Turner, 1979). The children showed knowledge of the beginnings and endings of the various types of eating episodes and of events that were central versus optional in an episode.

Not only can children describe their scripts, they spontaneously make inferences based on those scripts. For example, if children hear a story that conforms to a script and later are given a recognition test, they will falsely recognize objects and actions that are typical of the script, even though these items were not actually presented in the story (Brown, 1976; Rabinowitz, Valentine & Mandler, 1981). Apparently, children infer from their scripts that the typical actions occurred, and this leads them to judge that the actions were actually part of the story. For example, after hearing a story about lunchtime at school, a child may think that she heard something about opening a lunch box, even though she did not. Adults show this same sort of error, and so it appears that scripts govern inferencing at all phases of development. Of course, scripts and other types of schemata can grow more complex and differentiated as children learn more about their world (Gruendel, 1980). As adults we may have separate scripts for Chinese and French restaurants and for fancy restaurants versus diners. A young child who has not experienced many restaurants obviously would lack such detailed scripts.

We previously discussed the fact that the knowledge of the world children carry in their minds increases dramatically throughout the preschool and elementary school years. Recent research suggests that schemata and scripts are intimately involved in this development of knowledge. Specifically, some provocative new findings support the conclusion that a child's world knowledge initially is organized in terms of schemata and scripts for familiar events and activities. Only later do taxonomic categories emerge (Lucariello & Nelson, 1985; Mandler, 1979; Nelson, 1982).

An example helps to clarify the distinction between schematic/scriptal categories and taxonomic categories. As adults, we realize that elephant, dog, and cow

all fit within the taxonomic category of animals. However, they do not fit naturally within the same script—whereas elephant fits within a visiting-the-zoo script, dog fits more naturally within a playing-with-pets script, and cow within an on-the-farm script. In contrast, elephant, tiger, and camel all fit within a visiting-the-zoo script. Now if preschool children rely primarily on schematic and scriptal categories, as opposed to taxonomic categories, they might fail to recognize that elephant, dog, and cow all are examples of a single category (animals). Yet they should have no difficulty in recognizing that elephant, tiger, and camel all fit together (zoo animals). In fact, Joan Lucariello and Katherine Nelson (1985) have provided evidence for this line of reasoning. They presented three- and four-year-olds with a nine-word list containing three members of each of three taxonomic categories (animals, clothes, and foods) or a list containing three members of each of three scriptal categories (zoo animals, clothes to put on in the morning, and lunch foods). Recall was higher in the scriptal condition than in the taxonomic condition. Further, children in the scriptal condition showed more "clustering"—a stronger tendency to recall the three words of a category together. Research conducted with older children shows that script-based categorization continues into the childhood years (Mistry & Lange, 1985).

Having considered many different aspects of information processing, we turn to a discussion of how the information-processing perspective provides a framework for educating children.

INFORMATION PROCESSING AND EDUCATION

Elementary and secondary schools in the United States are in serious need of reform. This point has been recognized by a number of states in which educational reform movements are already underway or at least in the planning stages. But just what sort of reform is needed? The main thrust of many current proposals is that there is a great deal of wasted time and fluff in our school curricula; children need to work more on the "basics," such as English and math, instead of the "frills," such as athletics, band, etc. Many such proposals call for extensions in the school day and school year, as well as more homework. Many also argue that teachers should be given more power and prestige to

enforce a rigorous regimen of study (though these teachers also should be tested to ensure that they are competent and worthy of the prestige they are given). The essential notion seems to be that more time and work—enforced by tough and competent teachers—is a large part of the answer to our problems in educating children.

But these proposals are not novel. As Patricia Cross (1984) points out in a provocative article:

> . . . similar recommendations in the recent wave of reports on school reform foster a sense of déjà vu.
>
> Our collective memories are short. Yet we have only to look back one decade to find a school reform movement of today; more than a dozen books and reports calling for the reform of education were published between 1970 and 1976. Why can't we find excellence in education and then hang onto it? The pattern of educational reform has been to generate a lot of enthusiasm, reform the curriculum, raise the standards, restore prestige to teaching—and then somehow have improvements swept away again by the rising tide of mediocrity. (p. 168)

Later in her provocative article, Cross calls this the "swinging pendulum solution": We "get tough" in education, then grow lax in our enforcement of standards, then grow alarmed and "get tough" again ad infinitum. Clearly this is not satisfactory, so what *really* is the problem? Why can't we aim for a "spiral staircase solution" (figure 7.11)? If we must discard and then return to old issues and approaches—and probably we must in a democratic society in which fads come and go—can't we at least have a more advanced perspective on each "return trip"? With all of the advances in science and technology in other areas of our life, why have we failed to find lasting improvements in how we educate our children?

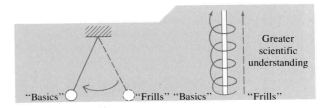

FIGURE 7.11
The spiral staircase solution.

An answer to this rather depressing question is suggested by Robert Glaser (1982) in his article "Instructional Psychology." Glaser points out that since the early part of this century the fields of education and psychology have not interacted as much as they might. The consequence has been that educational policy, unlike policy in many other areas of life, has been affected only slightly by scientific and technological advances. Without the influence of such advances, the swinging pendulum solution is about all that is possible in changing educational curricula. On the bright side, however, there have been many recent advances in our understanding of human cognition and information processing, and the time seems ripe to exploit these advances by applying them to education. In fact, Glaser describes a number of ways in which information-processing research can aid the teaching process. To learn more about Glaser's ideas as well as the role of schools in improving cognition see Perspective on Child Development 7.3.

Our journey through the information-processing approach has been a rather long one. However, one final consideration merits attention: the strengths and weaknesses of the approach.

PERSPECTIVE ON CHILD DEVELOPMENT 7.3

SCHOOLS, COGNITION, AND INFORMATION PROCESSING

One example cited by Robert Glaser (1982) of how the information-processing approach can be applied to improving the education of children involves geometry. Information-processing research suggests that solving problems in geometry benefits from three separate types of knowledge: (1) knowledge of different geometric "objects" such as points, line segments, and angles, (2) knowledge of facts and rules for making inferences and proving theorems (e.g., the sum of the angles of a triangle is 180 degrees), and (3) knowledge of strategies for carrying out proofs (e.g., knowledge that one should set goals, form plans, and organize one's attacks on a problem) (Greeno, 1978). Interestingly, while the first two types of knowledge are specifically taught in school, the third is not; it is simply left up to the individual student to divine the appropriate strategies. Glaser argues that this probably is not what is best for the student, particularly the student having trouble with geometry. Instead of just ignoring the problem of strategies, we should further study such strategies and investigate ways to teach them to students having problems.

A meaningful type of educational reform can do more than simply help students learn their subjects; it should improve their basic information-processing skills. In these days of rapidly changing technology and knowledge, the goal of schooling more than ever before must be that of creating a lifetime learner (Cross, 1984) with the processing skills to acquire new knowledge throughout a long life. This goal seems reachable in view of some recent cross-cultural research. Several studies have shown that children from rural or isolated communities are not as advanced cognitively as city dwellers (Meacham, 1975; Wagner, 1974). One source of these differences appears to be schooling. For example, Harold Stevenson (1982) and his colleagues found that Peruvian children enrolled in school exceeded Peruvian children not in school on tests of contextual memory, spatial representation, serial memory, and visual analysis and conceptualization. However, these effects though reliable were quite small in size.

It may not be too much to hope that schooling can become a truly powerful factor in improving cognition in young people. Perhaps, for example, we can improve our ways of testing intelligence to do more than

STRENGTHS AND WEAKNESSES OF THE INFORMATION-PROCESSING APPROACH

Like all major approaches to the study of children, the information-processing approach has its weaknesses as well as its strengths. First, we report on its strengths and then on its weaknesses.

Strengths

There are two major strengths of the information-processing approach: theoretical precision and the generation of interesting and informative research.

Theoretical Precision

One major strength of the information-processing approach is increased theoretical precision. Some recent theories are sufficiently clear to be couched in formal terms, such as those of production systems (Klahr, 1984). Theories with this degree of precision must be logically sound, and thus at least possibly true, and they also are capable of quantitative predictions for childrens' performance.

predict who will succeed and who will fail. Appropriate types of intelligence tests—based on information-processing models—might be used to determine what needs to be done to improve a child's chances of success in the classroom (Hunt, Frost & Lunneberg, 1973). And difficult subjects might be made much easier if we determine the processing that these subjects demand and then work on ways in which this processing can be taught.

In summarizing his article Glaser delineates five important principles for research on improving the educational process. First, we need more knowledge of learning over substantial periods of time, weeks and months or even years. Such long-term learning is at the very core of education, but psychologists have been negligent in addressing it. Second, psychologists must examine domains of knowledge that are taught in school, domains such as geometry and reading. Restricting research to artificial laboratory tasks will limit the generalizability of our findings. Third, we must go beyond describing how people learn and address the crucial issue of how they might learn better. That is, we

must take a prescriptive as well as a descriptive approach. Fourth, we must increase our attention to individual differences in the way that children learn. Many problems of education concern how to deal with the diversity of talents and styles of individual students. We need better solutions to these problems. Finally, we need better information on how new learning depends on old learning. The best way to teach a child depends on what that child already knows. We need more information on how to assess a child's current state of knowledge and how to make the transition from one state to the next.

There may always be tension between two functions of schooling—true cognitive development and more socially relevant enterprises, such as athletics, band, and even drivers' education. No doubt this tension will produce shifts of emphasis, as with a swinging pendulum. But if we are successful in developing an instructional psychology, we may achieve something similar to a spiral staircase. That is, we may continually develop more sophisticated ways of fulfilling the varied and changing functions of schooling.

Interesting and Informative Research

An even greater strength of the information-processing approach is the wealth of interesting research it has generated. The types of questions raised by this approach have a way of suggesting clever experiments that may well outlast the approach itself. A good example of such research is that of Robert Siegler (1984), who has investigated the rules that children use to solve Piaget's balance scale task. A child is shown a balance scale (see figure 7.12) with some weights on both sides. The scale is locked in the horizontal position, but the child must judge if it will tilt, and if so which way it will tilt, when it is free to move. In a systematic series of experiments, Siegler has manipulated both the number of weights on each side of the scale and the distance of the weights from the fulcrum of the scale. He has found that while five-year-olds consider only the number of weights, older children are more sophisticated at taking distance from the fulcrum into account. Indeed, Siegler has been able to specify the rules on which different-aged children are basing their judgments. He has also begun to uncover the steps through which these rules are learned.

Weaknesses

The two main weaknesses of the information processing approach are the questionable testability of models and the few insights that have been made about the mechanisms of developmental change.

Questionable Testability of Models

The information-processing approach is characterized by a large number of specific theories or models. Some of these models are so limited in scope that it is simply impossible to relate them to larger issues of development. Other models—especially the more recent ones—are tackling the "big picture" of cognitive development. But it is not yet clear that we will be able to test these models against one another and determine which is most accurate or useful.

Consider Frank Keil's (1984) argument that changes in knowledge are what are fundamental to the growth of intelligence in children. He conceives of children as being genetically programmed to acquire knowledge in certain "natural" domains (language, for instance) but also equipped with some all-purpose processes for

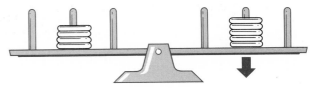

FIGURE 7.12
A balance beam locked in place with stacks of weights on each side. (When the lock is released, the right-hand arm will fall.)

learning in "nonnatural" domains (chess, for example). Thus, from Keil's perspective, children's development of intelligence is simply a matter of growing expertise in a number of domains.

By contrast, while Robbie Case (1984) recognizes that knowledge is a critical factor in the development of children's intelligence, he believes the more fundamental mechanism of cognitive development is that of increasing short-term storage space—itself reflecting increased efficiency, or automaticity—of mental operations.

As we can see, these two prominent cognitive psychologists have developed very different models to explain the growth of children's intelligence. Keil emphasizes growth in knowledge, whereas Case stresses short-term memory processes. Will it be possible to accept one and reject the other on the basis of experimental research? Maybe, but some psychologists are skeptical.

Few Insights about the Mechanisms of Developmental Change

A second weakness of the information-processing approach is that it has offered few insights into a very basic question: How do cognitive changes in young children differ from cognitive changes in older children? Much of the research conducted by information-processing investigators often seems as applicable to one age segment of the population as another. Yet many prominent developmental psychologists, such as John Flavell (1985), believe there are age-related constraints on development, constraints with roots in biological maturation. Case's (1984) view of growth in short-term memory storage begins to capture the idea of age-related constraints, but much more research information is needed along such age-related lines.

In sum, information-processing models appear to show considerable promise for increasing our understanding of children's cognition. However, they do have weaknesses, as well as strengths.

SUMMARY

I. Among the important features of the information-processing approach are its early history, information-processing models, and questions it raises about children's cognition.
   A. Debate and theorizing about information processing have been occurring in psychology for over a hundred years and much longer in philosophy.
   B. Broadbent's model is a classical model that emphasizes distinctions between short-term and long-term memory and the notion of limited processing capacity. Klatzky's more recent model includes Broadbent's features but also provides a more fluid view of levels of processing and introduces a distinction between automatic and controlled processes.
   C. Four issues raised by the information-processing approach involve processing speed, processing capacity, role of knowledge, and controlled versus automatic processes.
      1. Speed of processing is an important factor in cognition and is faster for older children than younger children.
      2. Information processing can be viewed as a type of mental energy needed to perform mental work. Capacity is limited at all ages.
      3. It has been speculated that age differences in capacity are due to knowledge.
      4. Controlled processes are assumed to draw heavily on capacity while automatic processes do not. Controlled processes are intentional; automatic processes are not. There are many age differences in controlled processes but there appear to be few age differences in automatic processes.
II. Information about attention emphasizes its basic nature, the orienting reflex, scanning visual patterns, advances in attention in early childhood, and further changes in the elementary school years.
   A. Attention plays an important role in information processing. Attention involves the focusing of perception to produce increased awareness of stimuli.
   B. Attentional changes are accompanied by many physiological changes, such as dilation of pupils. Collectively these physiological changes are known as the orienting reflex (OR).
   C. When we look at patterns, our eyes make saccadic movements. The pattern scanning of infants up to one month of age involves an externality effect, while two-month-olds are more likely to focus on internal features.

   D. Children's attention increases substantially in early childhood. Distraction decreases as children move through the early childhood years.
   E. After age six to seven there is a shift to cognitive control of attention. While preschool children focus on more salient features, elementary school children are more likely to attend to task relevant features. An important distinction can be made between selective and divided attention.
III. An understanding of memory in children involves its basic nature, infant memory, short- and long-term memory, memory span and speed of processing, control processes, characteristics of the learner, and the context of memory.
   A. Memory is a central process in children's cognitive development and information processing. Memory refers to the retention of information over time.
   B. Information about infant memory focuses on conjugate reinforcement, conscious memory, and infantile amnesia.
   C. Short-term memory involves retention for up to twenty or thirty seconds and is more effortless than long-term memory. Long-term memory involves more effortful use of retrieval.
   D. Memory span tests have been used to assess short-term memory. Memory span increases substantially in childhood and is related to speed of processing.
   E. Long-term memory depends on the learning activities people engage in when learning and remembering information. Most learning activities fall under the heading control processes. Five important control processes are rehearsal, organization, semantic elaboration, imagery, and retrieval/search processes.
   F. Apart from the obvious variable of age, many characteristics of the learner can determine the level of memory performance. Knowledge that a learner has also seems to contribute to memory. An important type of memory knowledge is metamemory—knowledge about one's own memory.
   G. Most research on children's memory has been conducted in laboratories; a current research interest is the study of children's memory in naturalistic contexts. Neisser argues that two important features of naturalistic memory are meaning and repisodic memory.

IV. Understanding and inferencing are complex information-processing activities. Klatzky's model of information processing, the concept of deep processing, schemata and scripts, and the development of scripts in children provide us with information about understanding and inferencing.

V. Elementary and secondary schools in the United States are in need of reform. One important reform focuses on training children to become more efficient in processing information rather than merely pouring knowledge into their heads. Schools have been shown to influence the cognition of children to some degree, but with an increased emphasis on improving children's information-processing skills, the effects could become more pronounced.

VI. There are both strengths and weaknesses in the information-processing approach.
   A. Two strengths are theoretical precision and the generation of interesting and informative research.
   B. Two weaknesses involve the questionable testability of models and the few insights uncovered about developmental change.

KEY TERMS

artificial intelligence (AI) 198
attention 204
automatic processes 201
conjugate reinforcement technique 207
controlled processes 201
deep processes 218
divided attention task 206
elaborative rehearsal 211
externality effect 204
infantile amnesia 209
long-term memory 208
maintenance rehearsal 211
memory 206
memory span task 210
mental imagery 212

metamemory 214
mnemonics 213
organizational processing 211
orienting reflex (OR) 204
P300 210
parallel processing 198
rehearsal 211
repisodic 216
retrieval 212
saccadic movements 204
schemata 218
scripts 218
selective attention task 206
semantic elaboration 211
short-term memory 208

REVIEW QUESTIONS

1. Discuss the basic features of the information-processing approach, including its early history, models, and questions it raises about the nature of children's cognition.
2. Outline the important aspects of attention in children.
3. Discuss the nature of infant memory.
4. What do we know about short- and long-term memory, memory span, and speed of processing in memory?
5. Describe the important control processes involved in children's memory.
6. How do characteristics of the learner and the context of memory affect memory performance?
7. Evaluate the nature of understanding and inferencing in children's cognition.
8. How can the information-processing perspective be applied to education?
9. Discuss the strengths and weaknesses of the information-processing approach.

SUGGESTED READINGS

Hunt, M. (1982). *The universe within.* New York: Simon & Schuster.
Hunt traveled to many universities and talked to top scholars in the cognitive area; this book represents his distillation of their ideas. The outcome is an extraordinarily insightful and well-written overview of the current state of knowledge on cognition. Includes many intriguing comments about the relation of the mind to a computer.

Kail, R. (1984). *The development of memory in children.* San Francisco: W. H. Freeman.
A readable overview of developmental changes in children's memory. Includes information about many of the aspects of memory considered in this chapter, such as metamemory, control processes, and short-term, long-term memory distinctions.

Klatzky, R. (1984). *Memory and awareness.* San Francisco: W. H. Freeman.
An up-to-date and provocative thesis on theoretical developments in attention and memory. Stimulates considerable thought about the nature of children's thought processes.

Matlin, M. (1983). *Cognition.* New York: Holt, Rinehart & Winston.
Covers a wide-ranging set of ideas about cognition, from memory to decision making and problem solving.

Siegler, R. S. (1983). Information-processing approaches to development. In P. H. Mussen (Ed.), *Handbook of child psychology* (4th ed., Vol. 1). New York: John Wiley.
Siegler, one of the leading figures in the information-processing movement, provides a detailed look at the nature of information processing and its application to children's cognition.

CHAPTER 8

LANGUAGE DEVELOPMENT

PROLOGUE

STRANGE GAMES WITH STRANGE CREATURES

Y ou are an intelligent young girl who has been captured by a group of some rather bizarre creatures, members of a highly advanced species who interact with all sorts of complex devices, drape unusual garments all over themselves, frequently emit long sequences of sound, and in general behave in complex and mysterious ways. You have no idea where these creatures came from or what they want with you. On the bright side, they appear to be friendly, even affectionate, and give you plenty of good food, including lots of chocolate, which you love. But they won't let you go. And they insist on you playing some sort of weird game they have invented.

They started the game one day at your snack time. You expected some fruit, and one of your captors came with a banana. However, instead of giving the banana to you, he placed it where you could see it but could not get to it. Then he gave you a small plastic object, a pink square to be exact, and a small board. Not knowing what else to do, you took the pink square and placed it on the board. It stuck in place. Your captor then made some very strange, excited sounds and gave you the banana.

Your captors repeated this game again and again. After a time they started using fruits other than just bananas. It soon became obvious that for you to get different fruits, you had to put different pieces of plastic on the board. For example, to get an apple that had been brought, you had to put a blue triangle on the board. If you put the pink square on the board, your captors made some of their very strange sounds, but the apple stayed where it was—out of reach.

Different chips for different foods was only the start of the complexity that followed. Before long, getting some food depended not only on you sticking the corresponding chip on the board; in addition, you had to put a special chip above it. This chip was a funny-looking six-sided thing. And the order was important. If you put the six-sided shape below the chip instead of above it, you did not get your food.

After awhile the captors taught you a plastic "name" for yourself, as well as a name for each of them and for each of your fellow prisoners (you were not the only prisoner they had). If you wanted one of your captors to give you an apple, you had to put his plastic name at the top of the board, put the six-sided chip below it, put the blue-triangle chip (for apple) below that, and finally, put your own plastic name at the bottom. So much work for an apple?

Later, your captors taught you ways of asking and answering questions and of making strange deals. For example, one of your captors wrote to you on the board, "If you pick up the apple, you will get some chocolate; if you pick up the banana, you will get no chocolate." You picked up the apple, and sure enough, they gave you chocolate!

What could this game be about? Who are these creatures and why are they interested in you? These creatures are psychologists who are studying language. You are one of their nonhuman subjects, a chimpanzee named Sarah. They are interested in you because they want to find out if nonhuman species can learn simple languages.

PREVIEW

In this chapter the incredible, elegant story of language is told. We first consider the characteristics of language that make it human and the functions of language. Then we turn to a number of theories that have been offered to explain language, showing particular interest in the role of biology. Next we consider milestones in the development of language as we move from preverbal developments to the completed language system. Finally, we discuss intriguing information about bilingualism and evaluate reading and writing systems.

CHARACTERISTICS OF HUMAN LANGUAGE AND THE FUNCTIONS OF LANGUAGE

To begin the story of language we first investigate the characteristics of language that make it human. Then we turn to the important functions language serves.

Characteristics of Human Language

Every human society has language. There are thousands of human languages, and they differ so drastically that many people despair of ever mastering more than one. Yet all human languages have some things in common; if they did not, we would not call them all language. What are these characteristics that all human languages share?

George Miller's (1981) succinct definition of language provides a good place to begin: "A language is a set of sequences of words" (p. 73). With this definition, Miller is referring to two different characteristics that all languages share: the presence of words and sequencing. We start by discussing these two characteristics and then consider three more: infinite generativity, displacement, and multiple levels of rule systems.

Words with Conventional Meanings

It might seem obvious that all languages have *words,* but think for a minute about what words are. We produce and perceive words every day—yet words have an almost magical property: They stand for or symbolize things other than themselves. We use our words to refer to things, things like objects, people, actions, events, and even abstract ideas. What a word refers to is arbitrary in the sense that it is based on convention—a word refers to something commonly agreed upon by a group of language users. To understand this point, consider the fact that different languages have different names for the same thing. What we call a house is also called *casa* (in Spanish) and *maison* (in French). Since different languages have different words, we are forced to conclude that words are linked arbitrarily and by convention to their referents.

Sequencing

Although words are a critical ingredient of language, the mere presence of words is not enough to make a language. **Sequencing** of these words also is required. Can you imagine a language with only one-word utterances? True, a thirteen-month-old baby may use one-word utterances, but some people will argue that the baby actually has whole sentences (holophrases) in mind. In any case, adults the world over speak in sequences of words called sentences.

Infinite Generativity

Why is sequencing important for language? The answer brings up a third characteristic, the **infinite generativity** of language. George Miller (1981) points out that sequencing allows a finite number of individual words to combine together in an infinite number of sentences. Of course, there are some sequences of words that speakers do not use. There are rules of syntax that distinguish grammatical from ungrammatical sequences. Nonetheless, the total number of grammatical sequences is theoretically infinite (de Villiers & de Villiers, 1978). Thus, language has a creative aspect. We can say things never said before.

Displacement

Displacement refers to the power of language to communicate knowledge across time and space. With language it is possible to have second-hand experience of things not available perceptually. There may be some things that cannot be imagined or understood unless directly experienced (e.g., the feeling of one's arm—or heart—being broken). Even so, anyone hooked on reading light fiction can attest to the power of displacement in language. But reading light fiction is just one example of how language gives second-hand experience. Language contributes in a most profound way to the transmission of knowledge from one person to another and from one generation to the next (Brown, 1973).

Levels of Rule Systems

A final aspect of language is that it has different **levels of rule systems,** including those of phonology, morphology, syntax, semantics, and pragmatics. We discuss these five levels of rule systems next.

Phonology **Phonology** pertains to the basic speech sounds, or **phonemes,** of language. So a first step is to ask just what a phoneme is.

Pronounce the word *peep* aloud. Does it begin and end with the same speech sound? Most adult English speakers would say that it does. They would do so because the first and last sounds are the same phoneme in English. But these two sounds would not be the same in other languages, and indeed the two *p*'s are produced somewhat differently and are acoustically discrepant (Miller, 1981). Specifically, they differ in aspiration, a feature of speech that is distinctive in some languages but not in English. To prove to yourself that the two *p*'s are different, say, "Don't peep now" while holding your palm in front of your mouth. You can feel the aspiration—as a puff of air—accompanying the first *p* but not the second. If you can only feel the difference, and do not actually hear it, that is perfectly all right. In English you do not need to hear it. However, speakers of Chinese must attend to this difference, as the aspiration feature is distinctive in that language.

The point we are making is really twofold. First, phonemes differ from one another with respect to distinctive features. Each phoneme can be viewed as a combination of features (see table 8.1). Second, different languages use different distinctive features. Thus, different languages have different phonemes.

TABLE 8.1
Distinctive Features for Six Common Phonemes

Distinctive Feature	Consonants					
	p	*b*	*f*	*v*	*m*	*n*
Consonantal	+	+	+	+	+	+
Vocalic	−	−	−	−	−	−
Anterior	+	+	+	+	+	+
Coronal	−	−	−	−	−	+
Voice	−	+	−	+	+	+
Nasal	−	−	−	−	+	+
Strident	−	−	+	+	−	−
Continuent	−	−	+	+	−	−

Note: All six phonemes are consonants (+ consontal, − vocalic) made at the front of the mouth (+ anterior). However, only four are made with vibration of the vocal chords (+ voicing), only two are produced with a buzzing quality (+ strident) and a continuous sound (+ continuent), only two have a nasal quality (+ nasal), and only one (*n*) is made with the tongue at the top-center of the mouth (+ coronal).

TABLE 8.2
A Phonetic Alphabet for English Phonemes: The Major Consonants and Vowels of English and Their Phonetic Symbols

Consonants				Vowels	
p	**p**ill	*o*	**th**igh	i	b**ee**t
b	**b**ill	ð	**th**y	ɪ	b**i**t
m	**m**ill	š	**sh**allow	e	b**ai**t
t	**t**ill	ž	mea**s**ure	ɛ	b**e**t
d	**d**ill	č	**ch**ip	æ	b**a**t
n	**n**il	ǰ	**g**y**p**	u	b**oo**t
k	**k**ill	l	**l**ip	ʊ	p**u**t
g	**g**ill	r	**r**ip	ʌ	b**u**t
ŋ	si**ng**	y	**y**et	o	b**oa**t
f	**f**ill	w	**w**et	ɔ	b**ough**t
v	**v**at	ʍ	**wh**et	a	p**o**t
s	**s**ip	h	**h**at	ə	sof**a**
z	**z**ip			ɨ	m**a**rry

In English there are about thirty-eight phonemes, including thirteen vowels and twenty-five consonants. When each phoneme is given a written symbol, we have what is called a **phonetic alphabet.** A useful phonetic alphabet is shown in table 8.2. Some of the symbols are written as are letters of the alphabet (e.g., *k*). However, phonemes are not the same as letters, and this is what we mean when we say that spelling is irregular. For example, the *k* phoneme occurs in *kill,* but it also occurs in *cat.* For quite a long time some people have argued that we should reform our system of spelling in English, using a truly phonetic alphabet, such as that shown in table 8.2. If such arguments were followed, we might have to give up spelling bees.

After all this talk of phonemes, it is time to return to phonology: Phonology is the study of rules that govern the sequencing of phonemes in a language. Phonological rules ensure that certain sound sequences occur (e.g., *sp, ar, ba*) and others do not (e.g., *zx, qp*). A good example of how such rules operate can be found in the study of how we pronounce plurals. Take the three words, *rope, robe,* and *rose.* Pronounce them in the singular and then in the plural (*ropes, robes,* and *roses*). If you listen to yourself, you will discover that you make different sounds in pluralizing these three words. Specifically, you probably said something like *rowps, rowbz,* and *rowzəz* (look at table 8.2 again). This is because of phonological rules that govern the way you speak. You may not be aware that you know these rules, but your speech obeys them nonetheless.

Morphology A phoneme like *p* need not have meaning. The smallest units of language that do carry meaning are **morphemes.** Some morphemes can function by themselves as words, (e.g., *open, walk, crash, pick*). However, other morphemes cannot stand by themselves but must be combined with other morphemes (e.g., *ed* as in *opened, walked, crashed,* and *picked*). Although morphemes of the latter type cannot function independently, they have meaning in the sense that they systematically alter what other morphemes mean. For example, when the morpheme *ed* is added to a verb, it conveys information that something happened in the past (when *ed* is added to *open,* we get *opened*). Many words are composed of two or more morphemes (e.g., *helper* consists of *help* and *er, chemist* consists of *chem* and *ist*). However, many other words consist of only one morpheme (e.g., *kangaroo* has three syllables but only one morpheme—no part of *kangaroo* carries meaning).

Morphology refers to the rules involved in the combining and sequencing of morphemes. These rules ensure that some sequences of morphemes appear in words whereas others do not (e.g., *re* and *turn* can be sequenced as *return* but not as *turnre*). Again, you may not be aware that you know such rules, but your language obeys them anyway.

Noam Chomsky, a pioneer in the development of ideas about linguistic grammars.

Syntax Another set of language rules involves the combining of words into acceptable phrases and sentences. Because you and I share the same rules of **syntax,** if I say to you, "Bob slugged Tom" and "Bob was slugged by Tom," you know who did the slugging in each case. You also understand that the sentence "You didn't say that, did you?" is syntactically correct, but that "You didn't say that, didn't you?" is unacceptable English.

A concept closely related to syntax is **grammar,** which refers to the formal description of syntactical rules. In school most of us learned rules of grammar about how sentences are structured. Linguists devise grammatical rules that are similar in some ways to those you learned in school but that are much more complex and powerful. Many contemporary linguists (e.g., Chomsky, 1965) distinguish between the deep structure and the surface structure of sentences. **Surface structure** is the actual order of words in a spoken sentence. **Deep structure** concerns the syntactic relations

The rules:
1. S ⟹ NP + VP
2. NP ⟹ T + N
3. VP ⟹ V + NP

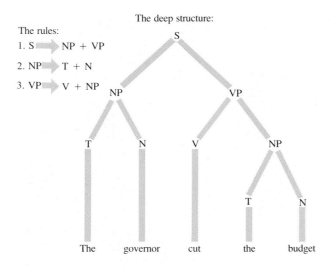

The deep structure:

Terms:
S = sentence
NP = noun phrase
VP = verb phrase
T = article (e.g., "the")
N = noun (e.g., "governor," "budget")
V = verb (e.g., "cut")

FIGURE 8.1
Some deep structure rules for a simple sentence.

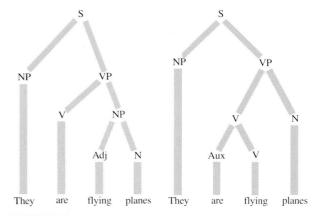

FIGURE 8.2
Two deep structures for a single ambiguous sentence ("Adj"
stands for adjective and "Aux" stands for auxilary verb).

among the words in a sentence. Deep structure employs syntactic categories such as noun phrase, verb phrase, noun, verb, and article (see figure 8.1).

By applying syntactic rules in different ways, one and the same sentence (or surface structure) can have two different deep structures, and this is one reason why sentences can be ambiguous in meaning. Consider the following fictional headline (it was the winner of a contest for ambiguous headlines): "Mrs. Nixon found drunk on White House lawn." Was Mrs. Nixon intoxicated or did she spot a drunk on the lawn? Either interpretation can fit the sentence, depending upon the deep structure applied. Other examples of deep-structured ambiguity can be found in the sentences "Visiting relatives can be boring" and "They are flying planes." The two deep structures for this last sentence are shown in figure 8.2.

Semantics Yet another set of language rules, **semantics,** pertains to the meaning of words and sentences. Semantic rules proposed by some linguists place restrictions on how words can be used in sentences. For example, "The bicycle talked to the boy" may be syntactically correct, but it is semantically nonsensical in

that it breaks semantic restrictions—bicycles are inanimate things and thus they cannot talk. Of course, when we speak metaphorically we can break semantic restrictions and yet still get our meaning across. For example, "Sally is a block of ice" is not so hard to understand (Ortony, 1979).

Pragmatics Rules of **pragmatics** pertain to the social context of language and to how people use language in conversation. Such rules allow us both to convey intended meanings and to understand those with whom we are talking. The domain of pragmatics is broad indeed. It covers such things as (a) taking turns in discussions (instead of everyone talking at once), (b) using questions to convey commands ("Why is it so noisy in here?" "What is this, Grand Central Station?"), (c) using words like *the* and *a* in a way that enhances understanding ("I read *a* book last night. *The* plot was boring."), (d) using polite language in appropriate situations (e.g., when talking to one's boss), and (e) telling stories that are interesting, jokes that are funny, and lies that convince. Pragmatic rules differ among languages. If you ever study the Japanese language, you will come face to face with countless pragmatic rules about conversing with people with various levels of social status holding various relationships with you. Some of these pragmatic rules concern ways of saying thank you (see table 8.3). Indeed, the pragmatics of saying thank you are complex even in our own culture. Preschoolers' use of this term varies with sex, socioeconomic status, and the age of the person they are addressing (Becker & Smenner, 1985).

LANGUAGE DEVELOPMENT

What kind of pragmatic rules might be involved in this communication?

pragmatics

TABLE 8.3
Different ways of Saying "Thank You" in Japanese (with Romanized Spelling)

Expression	Context	Expression	Context
Dōmo	Used with a social "inferior" who has served you in some way (e.g., a servant who has brought some tea).	Dōmo arigatō	Used with a social "equal" who has done a small favor for you (e.g., held open a door).
Arigatō	A more formal expression used in similar situations as *Dōmo* (tourists are advised to use this word after being served in a store or shop).	Arigatō gozaimasu	Used with a social "superior" in a polite or a formal situation (e.g., a "greeter" in a department store might say this as you leave the store with packages).
		Dōmo arigatō gozaimasu	Used with a "superior" in a very formal situation (e.g., your boss has just given you a gift).

What does the Whorf/Sapir hypothesis suggest about the role of
culture in language?

The Functions of Language

In this section we study the role of language in perception, cognition, and communication.

Perception

Language influences how we see things in our world.
Though we have stressed the universal aspects of language in our presentation of the psycholinguistic view,
there may be some cultural differences in language. For
example, some words may have a different meaning for
you than for me because of the different experiences
we have had. Similarly, your experiences differ a great
deal from those of people growing up in other countries
or areas of the world. Consider the Eskimo, who has a
dozen or more words to describe the various textures,
colors, and physical states of snow, whereas in English
we only have a few. As we see next, the issue of cultural
variation in language has focused on the Whorf/Sapir
hypothesis.

The **Whorf/Sapir hypothesis** stresses that the more
vocabulary or categories we have, the more our perceptions will be differentiated. Thus the Eskimo may
see more variations of snow than you or I (Whorf, 1956;
Sapir, 1958). However, other interpretations are possible. The speakers of two languages may have the same
perceptions but not be able to code or work with them
efficiently (Cole & Scribner, 1974). Furthermore, certain categories, such as color, may be universal and independent of language (Heider, 1972).

Eleanor Heider (1972) argues that color systems are
universal and there is not as much cultural variation in
language as the Whorf/Sapir hypothesis suggests. In
her experiment, Heider selected eight colors considered to be prototypes (best examples) by English
speakers, as well as thirteen colors believed to be non-
prototypes by English speakers. The subjects were
twenty-three speakers of twenty-three languages other
than English. The results indicated that the prototype
colors were more easily coded (named) by all twenty-
three speakers in the twenty-three different languages

than were the nonprototype colors. Thus people from all cultures were more likely to have a name for red than for chartreuse. The importance of Heider's research is that it suggests thought is not always based on language, as the Whorf/Sapir hypothesis has argued.

Nonetheless, there are instances in which language does influence perception and thought. Though there appear to be universal prototypes for colors, other concepts may not be as universal. Consider the perception of birds. Your prototype for bird may be parakeet, whereas to a South American it is probably some other bird that is much larger, more exotic, and more colorful. In addition, the nature of our experiences builds up a lexicon rich in names or poor in names for a particular concept, whether it be birds, cards, or sports. For example, if you have a library of names in your head that has been built up through your years of experience in attending antique automobile shows, you are much more likely to "see" fine gradations among such cars than someone who has not had such experiences and who does not have such a library of coded names and their descriptions. In this manner, language can operate as a window that acts as a sort of filtering system in contributing to the amount and nature of information passed on for further processing (Solso, 1979).

Cognition

In chapter 7 we saw that in short-term memory, information not only can be coded in auditory and visual forms but in a semantic manner as well. And semantic coding is even more important in long-term memory. Recall the idea of depth of processing, suggesting that semantic elaboration produces deeper processing of information in long-term memory.

Language not only is very important in memory, but it helps us to think, make inferences, tackle difficult decisions, and solve problems. Language can also be thought of as a tool for representing ideas. Some psychologists have even argued that we cannot think without language, a proposition that has produced heated controversy. Is thought dependent on language, or is language dependent on thought? Language does provide the medium for representing abstract experiences. Language rules clearly are more sophisticated at an earlier point in our infancy and childhood than

How does research on deaf and/or hearing-impaired children improve our understanding of language development?

thought is (Bruner, 1964). Moreover, L. Vygotsky (1962) posited that children's "private speech"—utterances they speak aloud while working on a task—can help them guide or direct their own thought processes. In support of this view, the overall incidence of private speech by children is greater when they are performing more cognitively demanding academic tasks than when they are performing less demanding nonacademic tasks. Further, private speech diminishes when an adult is present to impose structure on the task and direct the child's activity (Berk & Garvin, 1984). However, while private speech and other uses of language may facilitate cognition in some situations, cognition serves as an important foundation for language as well.

Evidence that cognition is an important foundation of language development comes from studies of deaf children. On a variety of thinking and problem-solving tasks, deaf children performed at the same level as children of the same age who had no hearing problems. Some of the deaf children did not even have command of written or sign language (Furth, 1973). In summary, then, it appears that thought can direct language and that language can direct thought.

Communication

We hear it all the time—"He just can't communicate with me" and "I can't communicate with him." We have become a culture in which communication is essential to success and happiness, and language certainly helps us to communicate. It seems that from early infancy onward we have a strong motivation to communicate with other people (Brown, 1973). Animals, however, often do not show such strong motivation. Chimpanzees, for example, often have to be coerced into communicating with an experimenter. Language makes it possible for our communication to occur in a much more abstract and complex manner than that of lower animals.

So far we have discussed a number of ideas about human language, levels of rule system, and functions of language. A summary of these ideas is presented in Concept Table 8.1.

THEORIES OF LANGUAGE

No mystery is deeper than how a child learns language. The mystery lies not in the fact that there is a good deal to learn but that there is an infinity to learn! The language characteristic of infinite generativity has an important implication for what the child must do. Simply memorizing utterances will not work. Since the number of meaningful utterances is infinite, no child could possibly memorize them all. Instead the child must do

CONCEPT TABLE 8.1
Characteristics of Human Language, Levels of Rule Systems, and Functions of Language

Concept	Processes/Related Ideas	Characteristics/Description
Language rules	Words with conventional meanings	Human languages have words that refer to common agreement by a group of language users.
	Sequencing	The utterances found in human languages consist of sequences of words forming phrases and sentences.
	Infinite generativity	Because of the creative and rule-governed nature of language, the number of grammatical sequences is infinite.
	Displacement	Languages communicate across time and space, giving second-hand experience of many things.
Levels of rule systems	Phonology	Phonology refers to rules that govern the sequencing of phonemes (basic sounds that differ in their distinctive features).
	Morphology	Morphology refers to rules that govern the sequencing of morphemes (the smallest units of language that carry meaning).
	Syntax	Syntax refers to rules that govern the ordering of words within sentences or phrases. These rules apply to deep structure as well as surface structure.
	Semantics	Semantics refers to rules that place restrictions on how words must be used to make meaningful sentences.
	Pragmatics	Pragmatics refers to rules for facilitating good communication and good social relations among language users.
Functions of language	Perception	Language does influence how we perceive the world, although not to the extent argued by the Whorf/Sapir hypothesis.
	Cognition	Language directs cognition, and cognition directs language; language helps us to think, and semantic coding is a prominent way in which information is stored in long-term memory.
	Communication	Language makes it possible for communication to occur in a much more abstract and complex manner than it otherwise would.

something much more amazing—build in his or her head a kind of "language engine" (Miller, 1981) that can generate the infinity of admissible sound sequences of language. How a child manages to construct this engine is a question researchers are trying to answer.

Historically, there are three main theories of language: behaviorist learning, nativist, and cognitive. We consider each of these three theories in some detail.

Behaviorist Learning Theories

Initially, we study the basic theoretical orientation behaviorists take when analyzing the nature of language. Then we turn to a number of environmental processes believed to be important in the learning of language.

The Behavioral View

Imagine that you are a pigeon or some other simple creature and that you have been placed in a small wooden box. At one end of the box is a small circular disk. You do not know why you have been placed there, but you do know you are hungry. Simply by chance you turn your head toward the disk, and some food pellets fall out of a hole below the disk. You eat the pellets.

This event repeats itself again and again. However, at a certain point in the process, your turning toward the disk will no longer cause the food to appear. You must also take a step or two toward the disk. Obligingly, you begin to produce this behavior to obtain the food pellets. At a still later point, it becomes necessary for you to come right up to the disk. Still later, you must actually peck at the disk in order to get some food. You learn all of these behaviors.

What has happened? In terms of the learning theory developed by B. F. Skinner, your behavior has been "shaped." You have been trained to make a certain response to obtain a reward.

Would it be possible for you to learn language in this way? Well, probably not if you were a pigeon. Pigeons' brains are very small, and their vocal tracts are unsuited to produce the sounds of human language. But suppose you were a human infant. Could you first be shaped to produce the words of a language and later shaped to produce appropriate sequences of words, and in this way learn to speak and understand? According to behaviorist learning theory (Skinner, 1957), the answer is yes. However, many scientific findings as well as what we know about the structure of language suggest strongly that the answer is no.

Learning Processes

What are the learning processes likely to account for the role of the environment in learning language? We look at shaping and reinforcement, imitation, and other aspects of environmental influences such as "motherese."

Shaping and Reinforcement   To begin with the findings, a landmark experiment by Roger Brown (Brown & Hanlon, 1970) is telling. The interchanges between mothers and their children in the early stages of learning to speak were tape-recorded. Although the speech of the children included many ungrammatical sequences, the mothers appeared to understand them quite well. In addition, the mothers responded to most of these ill-formed utterances in a positive (reinforcing) manner. In short, there was no evidence for shaping in the direction of good grammar.

Can we rule out **shaping** and **reinforcement** as factors affecting a child's language learning? Not entirely. The available evidence does not span all ages or all types of linguistic construction. Further, some types of reinforcers—as yet undiscovered—may be quite subtle (for example, a quick smile, or signs of attentiveness) and may change as children grow older (de Villiers & de Villiers, 1978). Yet they may have effects. Despite these considerations, it presently seems clear that shaping and reinforcement are at best a small part of language acquisition in childhood. A good deal of language acquisition must occur in other ways (de Villiers & de Villiers, 1978).

Imitation   Other relevant research has focused on **imitation,** another important process in learning theory (Bandura, 1971). On the surface, it is plausible that young children learn language by imitating the speech of their parents. Indeed, there is no question that young children sometimes imitate. We even have evidence that if children practice imitating certain sentence structures—that of the passive voice, for example—they increase their spontaneous use of such structures and grow more proficient at comprehending such structures when spoken by others (Whitehurst, Ironsmith & Goldfien, 1974; Whitehurst & Vasta, 1975). More recent evidence suggests that there are different forms of imitation, ranging from rote repetition of a parent's speech production to more creative forms of modeling and rehearsal (Moerk, 1985). Further, whereas some instances of imitation may have a "consolidation" function—facilitating the storage of particular words or expressions in memory—others may have a "looped replay" function, providing more time for the child to analyze and understand an utterance (Snow, 1985). Some promising findings indicate that children's tendencies to imitate language can be exploited to facilitate the process of learning a language. Specifically, a child who is delayed in his or her expressive language ability can be helped if the parents start using carefully selected lists of words and grammatical constructions in their speech to the child (Whitehurst, 1985).

Although imitation may contribute to the acquisition of language, there are individual differences in its nature and extent (Bloom, Hood & Lightbown, 1973). In fact, Eric Lenneberg (1962) described a case of a child who was physically unable to speak, and therefore unable to engage in imitation, but who nonetheless learned language. Thus, although imitation can help in language learning, its role appears facilitative, not absolutely necessary (de Villiers & de Villiers, 1978).

Creative Generalization of Rules

Another problem with the behavioral learning approach is based more on theory than on empirical fact; it pertains to the claim that language has infinite generativity. Such generativity is difficult to handle with the concepts of shaping and reinforcement. Furthermore, it seems unlikely that the generativity of language could arise through imitation. For a child to produce truly novel utterances, utterances that he or she has never heard, generalization of complex rules appears necessary. For example, a child might hear the sentence "The plate fell on the floor" and later might spontaneously remark, "My mirror fell on the blanket." Many theorists argue that generalization of rules, not shaping or imitation, is involved in such instances.

"Motherese"

Although learning theory mechanisms are inadequate by themselves to explain language learning, they may be involved to some degree. Furthermore, the learning theory perspective deserves much credit for highlighting the role of *environmental factors* in a child's acquisition of language. Perhaps the most fascinating of these factors is known as **motherese,** a characteristic way in which mothers, fathers, and people in general talk to young language learners. If you pay attention to your behavior when talking to a two-year-old, you will notice some interesting things.

Your sentences will be simple and short, you will use exaggerated intonation contours (speaking with great ups and downs in pitch), you will pause for long periods between sentences, and you will place great stress on the more important words. You also will probably repeat yourself frequently and engage in the behaviors of **prompting** (rephrasing a sentence you have spoken if it appears that the child has not understood), **echoing** (repeating what the child says to you, especially if it is an incomplete phrase or sentence), and **expanding** (restating what the child has said in a more linguistically sophisticated form). The term *motherese* is a misnomer in that you need not be a mother to speak in this way. Fathers' and mothers' speech to their three- to nine-month-old children has been found to be quite similar (Kruper, 1985). Even four-year-olds will speak differently to two-year-olds than to children their own age (Shatz & Gelman, 1973).

Two prosodic characteristics of motherese, exaggerated intonation contours and the occurrence of whispering, have been extensively examined by Anne Fernald (Fernald, 1983; Fernald & Simon, 1984). She has performed highly sophisticated acoustic analyses of mothers' speech to their three- to five-day-old babies versus other adults. According to these analyses, mothers' speech to infants has higher pitch, wider pitch excursions, longer pauses, shorter utterance lengths, and more repetitions of pitch contours and whispering than does their speech to other adults. Most remarkably, 77 percent of mothers' utterances to their babies involved expanded pitch contours and/or whispering, while almost none of their utterances to other adults contained these features. When mothers simply imagine that they are talking to their babies, their speech resembles that of true motherese, but only to an extent. Thus, the reactions of a physically present baby apparently contribute to motherese-type speech.

What might be the functions of the exaggerated contour and other features of mothers' speech to infants? In general, there can be no question that these aspects of motherese help get messages across. For example, Fernald (1985) has documented that the intonation contours in motherese provide clues concerning the emotional content of what a mother is saying. Further, James Morgan (1985) has found that exaggerated contours tend to occur at syntactical phrase boundaries. Thus, pitch contours offer clues about the syntax as well as the meaning of the message.

MARVIN by Tom Armstrong. © by and permission of News America Syndicate.

The functions of prompting, echoing, and expanding have also been examined. Expansion in particular has been extensively discussed. When a young child utters a short, primitive sentence, such as "Brush teeth" or "Dog bark," an adult is quite likely to expand it syntactically. She might say: "Oh, you want to brush your teeth" or "Yes, the dog is barking." It would seem on the surface that this technique of expansion could not help but improve the child's knowledge of syntax. However, research on this question has not been encouraging (de Villiers & de Villiers, 1978), and some researchers wonder if expansion helps at all (Flavell, 1985).

A positive role for a type of echoing was suggested by a study of communicative competence of adopted and nonadopted one-year-olds (Hardy-Brown & Plomin, 1985). Communicative competence of one-year-olds was assessed by (a) analyzing video recordings of the infants interacting with their mothers, (b) examining productive vocabulary of the infants as reported by their mothers, and (c) evaluating infants' performance on eight language-relevant items from the Bayley scale of infant intelligence (see chapter 9). It was found that the mothers' tendency to imitate (echo) the vocalizations of their babies was positively correlated with the communicative competence of these babies. That is, mothers who tended to imitate more were likely to have babies who were advanced in their language. Of course, future research must address the issue of whether mothers' echoing actually causes improvements in language acquisition or whether mothers of more linguistically competent infants tend to imitate more.

Recasting appears to be a promising technique for speeding language learning (Nelson, 1975; Nelson, Carskaddon & Bonvillian, 1973). In response to a sentence uttered by a young child, an adult can recast the

What are the characteristics of "motherese"?

sentence, phrasing the same or a similar meaning in a different way, perhaps turning it into a question. For example, if a child says "The dog was barking," one can respond by asking, "When was the dog barking?" Recasting has had some positive effects on children's use of linguistic structures, and—interestingly—parents do not spontaneously use it as much as they use expansion (Flavell, 1985). Perhaps recasting might be used in programs for improving "motherese" of parents of slow language learners. Indeed, the effects of recasting fit with suggestions that "following in order to lead" a child helps him or her learn language (Schaffer, 1977). That is, letting a child initially indicate an interest and then proceeding to elaborate that

interest—commenting, demonstrating, and explaining—may enhance communication and help language acquisition. In contrast, an overly active, directive approach to communicating with the child may be harmful (Schaffer, 1977).

To conclude our discussion of the many aspects of the environment that can influence language learning, we consider the process of **labeling.** Young children are forever being asked to identify the names of objects. Roger Brown once called this the great word game and claimed that much of the early vocabulary acquired by children is motived by this adult pressure to identify the words associated with objects. As described in Perspective on Child Development 8.1, there often is a highly ritualized nature to this great word game, a ritual involving mother–child labeling activity.

PERSPECTIVE ON CHILD DEVELOPMENT 8.1

PICTURE BOOKS, FIRST WORDS, AND LABELING

A nat Ninio and Jerome Bruner (1978) took a close look at the subtle interplay between a mother and her infant son as the two performed the great word game in its quintessential setting—reading picture books and playing with objects. The mother and child were part of a longitudinal study that covered the period of eight months to eighteen months in the child's life. The child was firstborn, and his parents were white, English, and middle-class. Labeling was part of the filmed play activity captured in the videotape records, made every two to three weeks in the infant's home.

The investigators uncovered some remarkable findings. Chief among these was the ritualized nature of mother–child labeling activity. It seemed as though labeling of pictures was a highly structured activity that obeyed clear rules and had the texture of a dialogue. A number of scholars have described conversations as having fairly tight patterns in ascribing roles, turn-taking, imitating, and responding (e.g., Bruner, 1975; Cherry-Wilkinson, Clevenger & Dolloghan, 1981; Snow, 1977). So did the labeling activity. Each time mother and child interacted over a picture name, for example, they took about the same number of turns, lasting about the same length of time. And the linguistic forms of the mother's utterances in book reading were very limited. She made repeated use of four key types of statements: (1) "Look!" (to get the child's attention); (2) "What's that?"; (3) "It's an X!" (labeling the picture for the child); and (4) "Yes!" (giving the child feedback on his utterance). These types of statements accounted for virtually all of the language the mother directed toward the child while reading books during the entire period of the study, and they obeyed some simple rules of occurrence. For example, the attention getter "Look!" always preceded the query, "What's that?" or the labeling phrase, "It's an X!" Similarly, the query always proceded the labeling phrase.

At the outset of the study, of course, few of the child's verbal responses to the mother's queries were distinguishable words. At best, the child produced consistent babble. By the end of the period, however, words were present. Associated with this change, the mother dropped the question "What's that?" from the ritual since the child now could produce a word for the picture.

Summarizing key points of the study, in the author's own words:

> The book reading dialogue seems . . . to be a format well suited to the teaching of labeling. It has few elements and strict ordering rules between them. It is flexible in the sense of accepting a great variety of responses by the child. It is highly repetitive. Not only do the fixed elements ["Look," "What's that?" and "It's a (*label*)"] appear over and over again, with minimal changes in the wording, but the variable elements, the labels themselves, appear repeatedly as well. (Ninio & Bruner, 1978, p. 12)

Nativist Theories

If language is impossible to acquire through learning theory mechanisms such as shaping and reinforcement, perhaps it is simply innate, that is, inherited as part of our genetic makeup. Of course, no specific language such as English is innate. Still, human infants may come equipped with a prewired "language acquisition device" (McNeill, 1970) that helps them learn the language around them. The famous linguist Noam Chomsky (1957) has been a foremost advocate of this nativist idea. He claims that young children acquire language very quickly and that they do so under learning conditions that are much less than ideal (there is no effective shaping, for example). How can this occur unless children are born with a good deal of language-related machinery already in place in their brain? Aside from the rapidity with which children learn language, four compelling arguments favor Chomsky's nativist view: language universals, lateralization of brain function, critical periods, and communication in nonhuman species.

Argument 1: Language Universals

One type of argument for the nativist position is that there are **language universals.** These universals include certain phonological categories (consonants, vowels, syllables), syntactic categories (sentences, noun phrases, verb phrases, and so on), and even semantic categories (number, animacy). All human languages appear to have such categories (Maratsos, 1983), and they are therefore good candidates for what might be found in a young child's "language acquisition device."

Argument 2: Lateralization of Language Function

A second argument for the nativist position concerns **lateralization of language** in the human brain, which we discussed in chapter 2. Current evidence suggests that language processing in the vast majority of people is controlled by the left hemisphere of the brain. Indeed, studies of language in brain-damaged individuals have pinpointed two specific areas of the left hemisphere that are especially critical. One of these, called Broca's area, is important for speech production, whereas the other, called Wernicke's area, is more heavily involved in speech comprehension (see figure 8.3). Thus, depending on where brain damage has occurred (as a result of a stroke, for example), a patient may be more likely to suffer from impairments in speaking or from difficulties in understanding the speech of others.

As we pointed out in chapter 2, lateralization of language in the human brain is detectable several months after birth, perhaps even earlier (Entus, 1975; Molfese, 1972, 1973). These developmental findings, together with the discoveries of Broca's and Wernicke's areas, suggest some inborn capacity to construct linguistic mechanisms in certain parts of the brain (Miller, 1981).

Argument 3: Critical Periods

A third type of evidence for a nativist position concerns the concept of **critical periods** for acquiring language (Lenneberg, 1967). If you have ever listened to Henry Kissinger speak, you have some evidence for critical periods. If a person over twelve years old emigrates to a new country and starts to learn its language, it is likely that for the rest of that person's life he or she will speak the language with a foreign "accent." This is not true of those who emigrate as young children (Asher &

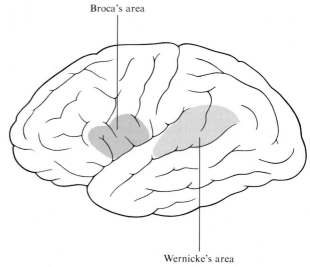

FIGURE 8.3
Speech and language functions are localized in Broca's and Wernicke's areas in the left hemisphere of the human brain. Broca's area plays a role in the production of speech, translating information from other speech areas of the brain into actual speech. Wernicke's area is involved in the comprehension of the auditory input and the monitoring of speech output. Damage to these regions can seriously interfere with the ability either to produce or understand speech (Miller, 1981).

Garcia, 1969; Oyama, 1973). Similarly, speaking like a native New Yorker is less related to how long you have lived in the city than to the age at which you moved there. Speaking with a New York "dialect" is more likely if you moved there at an age of less than twelve (Labov, 1970). Apparently, puberty marks the close of a critical period for fully acquiring the phonological rules of different languages and dialects. Eric Lenneberg (1962) has speculated that lateralization of language in the brain is subject to a similar critical period. Up until twelve years or so, a child who has suffered left-hemisphere damage may be able to shift language to the right side of the brain. But after this point, such a shift becomes impossible. Unfortunately, a critical period for shifting lateralization of language is quite controversial and is not so well supported as a critical period for phonological rules (de Villiers & de Villiers, 1978). The experiences of a girl named Genie add further support to the critical period notion. Her case is reviewed in Perspective on Child Development 8.2.

THE CURIOUS CASE OF GENIE

Until she was thirteen and a half years old, Genie was raised with virtually no linguistic (or any other) input. Her prior life has been vividly described by Jill and Peter de Villiers (1978).

Genie's first months seemed to have been medically unremarkable, at least as revealed by scanty pediatric records. However, from the age of about twenty months until she was discovered, Genie was kept in a small closed and curtained room, either tied to a pottychair or laid in a covered infant crib, confined from the waist down. Her mother, who was almost blind, visited her for only a few minutes each day to feed her with soft infant food. There was no opportunity for Genie to hear television or radio, for there was neither in the house. If she made noises she was liable to be beaten by her father, who could not tolerate noise. The father and elder brother of Genie did not speak to her but were wont to bark at her like dogs. It was the father's belief that Genie was hopelessly retarded, based on the fact that she was delayed in starting to walk because of a congenital hip dislocation that was treated during her first year.

It is unnecessary to explain that such circumstances did not leave Genie intact in body and mind. However, although she was malnourished, there was no evidence of physical abnormalities sufficient to account for her behavior, for she had adequate hearing, vision, and eye-hand coordination. She was severely disturbed emotionally, having frequent but silent tantrums, yet there were no other symptoms of childhood autism. The most likely explanation of her behavior was the chronic social deprivation she had suffered for those twelve years (Fromkin, Krashen, Curtiss, Rigler & Rigler, 1974).

Shortly after her rescue, Genie was tested on a series of language comprehension tests. Although within a very short time she began imitating words and learning names, her comprehension of grammar was completely absent. So Genie qualifies as the most satisfactory case to date to test Lenneberg's critical age hypothesis for first-language acquisition.

After her emergence into the world, Genie was placed in a foster home, where she began to acquire a first language primarily by exposure rather than training, like a normal child. (de Villiers & de Villiers, 1978, pp. 215–216)

Genie's linguistic progress over a five-year period occurred at phonological, morphological, syntactic, and semantic levels (Curtiss, Fromkin, Rigler, Rigler & Krashen, 1975). Her progress at the phonological level was similar to that of young normal children, and eventually she was able to produce all of the phonemes of English. However, her speech remained difficult for others to understand, apparently because of articulatory difficulties—she perceived phonemes better than she produced them.

With respect to the morphological level, Genie learned to use word endings to put words in the plural (s) or progressive (ing) forms, and she also mastered articles such as *a* and *the*. However, she had trouble with word endings for the past tense (*ed*). Genie's knowledge of syntax advanced her as far as the production of three-word utterances. However, it is unclear that her knowledge of syntactical rules surpassed that of Sarah, a chimpanzee trained to talk with colored plastic shapes (Premack & Premack, 1972). Genie's achievements at the semantic level were by far her most impressive. She showed good knowledge of how to classify words (e.g., she needed no training to know that things like shirt and pants are clothes), and she was advanced compared to young normal children in her knowledge of color and number concepts. Apparently, she was more advanced conceptually than linguistically (de Villiers & de Villiers, 1978).

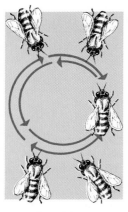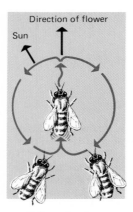

Round dance   Tail-wagging dance

FIGURE 8.4
The language dances of honey bees. The round dance indicates that nectar is within 100 meters of the hive. The tail-wagging dance points in the direction of the nectar when it is more than 200 meters away. Distances between 100 and 200 meters are signalled by a third dance (Nobel Foundation, 1974).

FIGURE 8.5
Sarah, a female chimpanzee, was trained to communicate by placing plastic tokens in sequence. She arranged tokens for "Mary give chocolate Sarah" on a magnetic board. Mary was the experimenter; the vertical order was Sarah's own idea (Miller, 1981).

Argument 4: Communication in Nonhuman Species

A fourth sort of nativist argument is that communication systems found in other species of animals do not approach in richness and complexity the languages of human beings. Nonhuman primates gesture at each other, cats meow and purr, birds have songs and various calls, and bees perform elaborate ritualistic dances. While some of these systems might be called languages—this has been debated—not one of them has all five characteristics of human language that we described at the start of the chapter.

Consider, for example, the lowly bee (von Frisch, 1974). After a worker bee has gone hunting for nectar and comes back to the hive, she goes through a highly intricate dance to communicate the location of the nectar to the other bees (see figure 8.4). The dance of the bees is certainly intriguing, and perhaps it possesses the language characteristics of sequencing (the dances are extended in time) and displacement (the dances are removed in time and place from the nectar). However, there is no evidence for different *levels* of communication, there is no learning of *words* with conventional relations to their referents, and it is doubtful whether there is infinite generativity (bees do not vary the order of their symbols to generate different meanings). Clearly, bee talk is very different from human talk.

But what about animals higher on the evolutionary scale, such as chimpanzees? Do chimpanzees have languages that are more like humans'? (See figure 8.5). Apparently they do not, at least not when one focuses on their natural way of life. Certainly chimpanzees in the wild have identifiable calls: various hoots, howls, grunts, etc. However, there are not very many of these— about two dozen, in fact—and they are unlike human words in that they simply express emotions and are probably instinctive responses, not learned utterances with conventional relations to their referents. Other characteristics of language, such as infinite generativity and multiple levels, are also apparently lacking in chimpanzee communication.

The absence of language in chimpanzees is striking, especially in view of their high level of intelligence (Miller, 1981). However, their intelligence raises an interesting question: Although chimpanzees in the wild do not have advanced language, could chimpanzees be taught an advanced form of language? To learn about research on this intriguing question, see Perspective on Child Development 8.3.

PERSPECTIVE ON CHILD DEVELOPMENT 8.3

APE TALK

A number of psychologists have spent years trying to teach language to apes. For example, the Kelloggs (Kellogg & Kellogg, 1933) adopted a seven-month-old chimpanzee and named her Gua. They tried to rear her alongside their ten-month-old-son, Donald. Gua was treated very much the way we rear infants and young children—she was dressed, talked with, and played with. Nine months after she was adopted, Gua knew ninety-five words and Donald only a few more. The Kelloggs discontinued the project because they were afraid Gua's talents were slowing down Donald's progress!

The Hayeses (Hayes & Hayes, 1951) adopted a chimpanzee named Viki when she was only a few days old. Their goal was to teach Viki to speak. They eventually taught her to say "Mama," but it was a painstaking effort. The Hayeses would sit day after day holding and shaping Viki's mouth to make the desired sounds. She eventually learned three other words—*Papa, cup,* and *up*—but she never learned the meanings of these words, and her speech was not very clear.

Another famous chimpanzee named Washoe was adopted by the Gardners when she was ten months old (Gardner & Gardner, 1971). Having recognized that

Washoe using American Sign Language: "sweet" for a lollipop.

the Kelloggs and the Hayeses had not really been able to demonstrate that chimpanzees have language with human qualities, they tried to teach Washoe the American Sign Language, which is the sign language of the deaf. People conversed with Washoe only with the manual gestures of American Sign Language. The events of the daily routine, such as meals and wash-ups, household chores, play with toys, and car rides to interesting places provided many opportunities for the use of sign language. (See figure below.)

There is yet another way to teach "language" to chimpanzees. The Premacks (Premack & Premack, 1972) constructed a set of plastic shapes that symbolized different objects and were able to teach the meanings of the shapes to a six-year-old chimpanzee, Sarah. She was able to respond correctly using such abstract symbols as "same as" or "different from." For example, she could tell you that "banana is yellow" is the same as "yellow color of banana." Sarah eventually was able to "name" objects, respond "yes," "no," "same as," and "different from" and tell you about certain events by using symbols (such as putting a banana on a tray). Did Sarah learn a generative language capable of productivity? Did the signs Washoe learned have an underlying system of language rules?

Herbert Terrace (1979) doubts that these apes have been taught language. Terrace was part of a research project focused on teaching language to an ape by the name of Nim Chimpsky (named for Noam Chomsky). Initially, Terrace was optimistic about Nim's ability to use language as humans use it, but after further evaluation he concluded that Nim really did not have language in the sense that humans do. Terrace argues that apes do not spontaneously expand on a trainer's statements like humans do; rather, the apes essentially *imitate* their trainer. Terrace also believes that apes do not understand what they are saying when they speak; instead, they are responding to cues from the trainer that he or she is unaware of.

In sum, it seems that chimpanzees can learn to use signs to communicate meanings. This used to be the old boundary for language. However, the question of whether chimpanzees can use ordered grammars that have significant characteristics of human grammar is more problematic. Thus, the capacity for infinite generativity of language has not yet been demonstrated in chimpanzees.

Cognitive Theories

Noam Chomsky's idea of the young language learner as richly endowed with prewired equipment is widely accepted today. However, there is a question about the type of equipment that the young learner possesses. Is such equipment specifically linguistic, such as a specialized "language acquisition device" (McNeill, 1970), or is it more generally cognitive, deriving from humans' generally high level of intelligence (Maratsos, 1983)? A growing group of language researchers is beginning to argue that language derives less from specifically linguistic abilities than from more general cognitive abilities (e.g., Anderson, 1976, 1980; Bates & McWhinney, 1978; Maratsos & Chalkey, 1980; Slobin, 1973). The basic claim is that a child's growing intelligence and his or her desire to express meanings, together with language input provided by the parents, are what "drive" the acquisition of language. Thus, the focus is on the semantic and pragmatic levels of language as opposed to the syntactic, morphological, or phonological levels.

One type of evidence for the cognitive view is that a child's early utterances seem to indicate knowledge of semantic categories, such as agent and action, rather than linguistic categories, such as noun and verb (Maratsos, 1983). For example, Daniel Slobin (1972) analyzed the early speech productions of children learning eighteen different languages in countries all over the world. He found that all of these children started with one-word utterances and then advanced to two-word utterances. Further, the two-word utterances consistently fell into the categories of meaning that are listed in table 8.4.

Slobin concluded from his research that "A child easily figures out that the speech he hears around him contains discrete, meaningful elements, and that these elements can be combined." According to Slobin, the child is concerned with how combining known words can convey certain meanings—syntactic rules and categories are not yet important to him. Indeed, rules that are purely syntactic in nature, such as rules for noun gender that exist in some languages, are mastered by children relatively late in their development (Slobin, 1973).

TABLE 8.4
Fourteen Meanings of Childrens'
Two-Word Utterances

Meaning	Example of utterance
Identification	"See doggie"
Location	"Book there"
Repetition	"More milk"
Nonexistence	"Allgone thing"
Negation	"Not wolf"
Possession	"My candy"
Attribution	"Big car"
Agent-action	"Mama walk"
Agent-object	"Mama book" (meaning, "Mama read book")
Action-location	"Sit chair"
Action-direct object	"Hit you"
Action-indirect object	"Give papa"
Action-instrument	"Cut knife"
Question	"Where ball?"

Reprinted with permission from *Psychology Today* Magazine. Copyright © 1972 American Psychological Association.

In support of Slobin's views of semantics-before-syntax, there is evidence that children can tell that semantically deviant sentences are wrong before they can tell that syntactically deviant sentences are wrong (Washburn & Hakes, 1985). This evidence implies that a five-and-one-half-year-old might detect the unacceptability of "The bicycle talked to the boy" (semantically deviant) and yet fail to reject sentences such as, "The boy ride the bicycle" and "What you are doing today?" (syntactically deviant).

Another sort of argument for a cognitive theory, and against a nativistic theory, concerns what we have learned about how language has evolved. Since a spoken language leaves no physical trace, the age of human language is difficult to determine. However, according to some estimates, language evolved as recently as 10,000 to 100,000 years ago (Swadesh, 1971). This is indeed quite recent in evolutionary time, perhaps too recent for a large amount of purely linguistic machinery to have evolved in the brain. From an evolutionary perspective, cognition is much older than human language. For example, tool-making activity—clearly a sign of high intellectual functioning—is at least two million years old (Miller, 1981). Considerations like these tend to favor the view that language is at least partly a product of rather general cognitive abilities, not just specific linguistic abilities.

babbling.   ✓

CONCEPT TABLE 8.2 — Theories of Language Acquisition		
Theory	**Processes/Related Ideas**	**Characteristics/Descriptions**
Behavioral learning	Children learn language through imitation, shaping, and reinforcement.	Some learning through imitation almost certainly occurs. However, problems for this theory are that (1) shaping of grammatically correct utterances is not evident in parent–child interactions, (2) some children seldom imitate, and (3) all children show creative generalization of rules.
Nativistic	Children have substantial prewired machinery for the acquisition of human language.	This theory is supported by evidence for language universals, lateralization of language function, critical periods in phonological development, and the absence of humanlike language learning in other species.
Cognitive	Although children have prewired machinery, much of it is cognitive rather than strictly linguistic.	Young children's speech shows more evidence of semantic than syntactic categories. Further, language may be recent in evolutionary time. Both observations suggest that general cognitive machinery is used for learning language.

Conclusions about Theories of Language

To conclude our discussion of theories of language learning, we should note that they all probably carry some truth. Imitation and reinforcement occur to an extent and probably have important functions (e.g., learning of words and expressions). Further, the evidence on lateralization and critical periods supports some prewired linguistic machinery, especially for the phonological, morphological, and syntactic levels of language. Finally, cognitive learning strategies are also quite likely to facilitate language learning, especially learning of semantic and pragmatic rules. Moreover, since none of these theories is by itself adequate to handle all aspects of language acquisition, we might do well to keep all three.

Concept Table 8.2 provides a summary of the major points made about theories of language acquisition. Next we turn our attention to some of the major discoveries involving the course of language development.

MILESTONES IN THE DEVELOPMENT OF LANGUAGE

In this section we examine some early developments in language and then turn our attention to later developments.

Early Developments

The early development of language focuses on preverbal developments, one-word utterances, and two-word utterances.

Preverbal Developments

It is a happy event for a young child's parents when the child utters his or her first word. The event usually occurs when the child is about ten to thirteen months old (de Villiers & de Villiers, 1978), though some children take longer. Although some parents view the onset of language as coincident with this first word, a number of highly significant accomplishments precede this dramatic event. These preverbal accomplishments fall into three main areas: vocalization, communication, and cognition (Flavell, 1985).

Babbling   Vocalization begins with the infant's **babbling,** somewhere between three and six months of age. The onset of babbling is controlled by biological maturation, not reinforcement or even the ability to hear. Even deaf babies will babble for a time (Lenneberg, Rebelsky & Nichols, 1965).

It once was assumed that all possible phonemes in all the world's languages were produced by babies in the babbling stage. However, we now know that this is

What kind of pragmatic communication skills are involved in this situation?

not true (Flavell, 1985). Perhaps the best guess about the function of babbling is that it exercises the child's vocal apparatus and helps the child to develop articulatory skills that later will be useful to produce words and sentences (Clark, 1983).

Pragmatic Skills of Communication A baby's earliest communication skills have little to do with the baby's babbling. Instead, they consist of a number of interesting pragmatic skills that support communication (Flavell, 1985). Some of these skills pertain to *attracting attention* from parents and other people in the environment. Infants can engage the attention of others through their looking behavior, specifically their ability

to make and break eye contact with others, and also through vocalizing sounds and making manual actions such as pointing. One fourteen-month-old displayed—even flaunted—his knowledge of using eye contact for attention. At a family gathering of several adult relatives, he picked out one adult, established eye contact with her, and then ran over for a hug. Then he chose another adult and repeated the procedure. This went on for several minutes, and he eventually engaged every adult in the room, *except* for his grandfather. This avoidance of Grandpa was apparently deliberate, because despite repeated entreaties from Grandpa, little David avoided making eye contact with him. And he never ran over to Grandpa for a hug (this apparently was a kind of game on David's part, as he is very fond of his grandfather). David's skill at avoiding eye contact with Grandpa reminded David's father of an overworked waiter who skillfully avoids eye contact with customers who are waiting for their checks. Both overworked waiters and fourteen-month-old babies appear to have knowledge of how eye contact establishes reciprocal attention between two people.

Another type of pragmatic knowledge is revealed by the ability to *request* and *assert*. Before the age of about nine months, a child who wants a toy may look toward it while reaching and fussing. But an older child is likely to establish eye contact with a nearby adult and begin alternating eye contact between the adult and the toy while fussing (Bates, 1979). Such behavior is easily understood as a request to bring the object. Assertions are a bit harder to identify (Flavell, 1985). However, babies frequently will point toward an object while showing no particular interest in picking it up or playing with it. This sort of behavior may be an invitation for another person simply to look at the thing pointed to. It appears to be an early form of asserting—communicating about things in the world.

Cognitive Development

For a child to master his or her language, some achievements in the cognitive area probably are required. A likely candidate for such a required achievement is the ability to use and comprehend symbols, that is, to have knowledge that one thing can stand for another. Recall our earlier discussion that words are symbols having arbitrary relations to their referents. Unless a child can think symbolically, he or she is unlikely to learn this sort of relation and should not advance far in his or her language. As we learned in chapter 6, Jean Piaget theorized that capacity for symbolic thought is not present at birth but must develop over the first two years of life. Thus, it may be no coincidence that a child's language competence begins to develop quite rapidly around the end of the child's second year.

One-Word Utterances

A child's first words include important people ("Dada," "Mama"), familiar animals (e.g., "dog," "kittie"), vehicles (e.g., "car," "boat"), toys (e.g., "ball," "doll"), foods (e.g., "milk," "cookies"), body parts (e.g., "eye," "nose"), clothes (e.g., "hat"), household items (e.g., "clock"), greeting terms (e.g., "bye"), and others. The first words of babies born fifty years ago are similar to those of babies born recently (Clark, 1979, 1983). Babies seem to differ in that some use more referential terms (i.e., object names) while others use more expressive terms (e.g., "bye-bye," "naughty") (Nelson, 1973). Although "referential babies" appear initially to learn new words faster, they are no more advanced than "expressive babies" in their knowledge of linguistic rules (de Villiers & de Villiers, 1978). Our further discussion of the one-word utterance focuses on the holophrase hypothesis, Eve Clark's theory of meaning, and the overextensions and underextensions of words.

The Holophrase Hypothesis

During the stage of one-word utterances, it can be difficult to determine what a particular utterance means. One possibility is that the single word stands for a complete sentence in the young child's mind; the child thinks a complete sentence but, because of limited cognitive or linguistic skills, can only produce one word at a time. According to this view, the one-word utterance is a **holophrase,** a single word that implies a whole sentence (Dale, 1976; de Villiers & de Villiers, 1978).

The holophrase idea represents one hypothesis about the meaning of one-word utterances. An alternative hypothesis is that a one-word utterance really is what it appears to be: a thought corresponding to just one word. Consider a case in which a young child hears a footstep in the hall and utters "Mama." According to the holophrase hypothesis, the child may actually mean "Here comes Mama" or "That's the sound of Mama coming" or even "I'm glad Mama is coming because I'm starting to get hungry." However, an alternative interpretation is that the sound of the footstep made the child think of his or her mother and that the thought of the mother evoked the corresponding word (Flavell, 1985).

Eve Clark's Theory of Meaning

It seems likely that the truth about one-word utterances does not fit either the holophrase hypothesis or the one-word/one-idea hypothesis. Consider a child who shoves a glass in your face and cries "milk" (Flavell, 1985). She clearly means more than the simple word milk, but has she actually formulated a sentence in her mind? Eve Clark (1983) has formulated a theory that offers some insight into the meaning of one-word utterances.

According to Clark, it is important to distinguish between *words* on the one hand and *concepts* on the other. Beginning around nine months of age or even earlier, children begin acquiring concepts. They learn that sets of physically different stimuli (e.g., different views of their mother's face) can be the same person or thing (mother). Children acquire more and more new concepts in succeeding months, while they are learning words. When they are learning words, children are learning how different sequences of phonemes map onto their store of concepts. Of course, learning words may help children add to their store of concepts. The processes of learning words and learning concepts are highly intertwined (Kuczaj, 1985). Nonetheless, there will be many concepts—perhaps especially when the language learning process has only just begun—that a child has not yet associated with words.

So what happens when children want to say something? They have some concepts in mind—perhaps quite a few—and try to choose some word to express them. The children do the best that they can in choosing a word, but probably the word does not capture all of their concepts. Although they are thinking about more than just one word, they may not have a full sentence in mind. What they have in mind are concepts, some of them concepts that the children have not verbalized to themselves. Figure 8.6 illustrates this state of affairs.

Overextensions and Underextensions of Words

Clark's theory is also useful for explaining how children can "know" a word and yet use it incorrectly. One way that children can misuse words is by **overextending** their meaning. For example, they may use the word *ball* not only for balls but also for other toys, radishes, and stone spheres on park gates; they may use the word *watch* for a clock, a gas meter, a fire hose wound on a spool, and a bathroom scale with a round dial (Clark, 1973). In both of these cases, a word's meaning has been overextended to include a set of objects that (according to adults) do not fit within it. Another way of misusing a word is by **underextending** its meaning. For example, a child may use the word *car* when she is looking out the window and a car goes by, but not when she is on the street and a car goes by (Bloom, 1973). Apparently, her use of *car* has been underextended to cases in which cars are seen from windows.

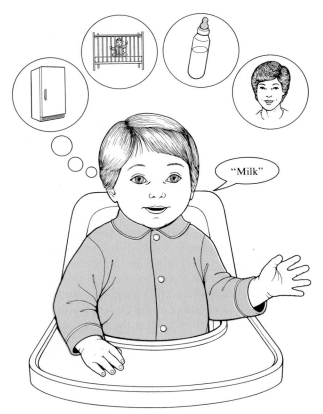

FIGURE 8.6
A young child who has many concepts in mind may utter one word in an attempt to communicate them.

Overextensions and underextensions are more prevalent in childrens' *production* of words than in their *comprehension* of words. For example, a child may call many round objects *ball*. Yet, if you put her in front of several round objects, including a ball, a clock, and a Frisbee, she may be able to tell you which one is the *ball* (Clark, 1983). This finding seems puzzling at first—does the child know the extension of *ball* or does she not? However, if we remember the distinction between concepts and words, the finding can be understood. The child probably has the concept of ball, as well as the concept of clock and Frisbee. However, she may have learned the word *ball* much better than *clock* or *Frisbee*. Hence, when she wants to name a clock or Frisbee, she may not recall their proper (adult) names, and so she settles for *ball,* a term she knows well that maps onto similar concepts. Although the child may know that clocks and Frisbees are not balls, she also wants to communicate; hence she overextends a little. From this analysis, we see how children's "misuses" of words arise from their active attempts to communicate.

Two-Word Utterances

By the time children are eighteen to twenty-four months old, they usually begin uttering two-word statements. During this two-word stage, they quickly grasp the importance of expressing concepts and the role language plays in communicating with others. It is not unusual for as many as a thousand two-word utterances to appear on a monthly basis at this point in development (Braine, 1963). These two-word utterances can convey a wealth of meaning, as we discussed earlier (table 8.4). However, they differ substantially from adult word combinations. Language usage at this time has been referred to as **telegraphic speech.** Articles, auxiliary verbs, and other connectives are usually omitted. When we send telegrams to people we try to be short and precise, excluding any unnecessary words. Children in the two-word stage are doing something quite similar. Of course, telegraphic speech is not limited to two-word utterances; three- and four-word utterances can also be telegraphic (e.g., "Mommy give ice cream," "Mommy give Tommy ice cream").

A question that has not yet been answered is whether children at the two-word-utterance stage have a grasp of syntactical rules. On the positive side, some children appear to use word order to help them communicate and interpret different meanings. For example, a child may say, "Daddy pat" when her father is patting her, and "pat Daddy" when she is patting her father (de Villiers & de Villiers, 1978; Flavell, 1985). However, not all children appear to use word order in this way. Thus, we simply do not know how much syntactical knowledge to attribute to children in the two-word stage.

Later Developments

The two-word utterances that we have been considering are an important first step toward the long, complex utterances we adults are fond of speaking. Psychologist Roger Brown (1973) has developed a way

What spatial adjective is being demonstrated by this child?

to chart a child's progress from this first step onward. Brown's technique is to measure the **mean length of utterance (MLU)** in the everyday speech of a child. To compute MLU, you simply tape-record a sample of speech (say, fifty to one hundred utterances), count the number of morphemes in each utterance, and then calculate the average. MLU has turned out to be useful in measuring the progress of language development. It

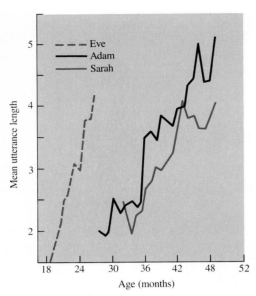

FIGURE 8.7
The average length of utterances generated by three children who ranged in age from one and one-half to just over four years (Brown, Cazden, and Bellugi-Klima, 1969).

works much better than chronological age, for example. Figure 8.7 shows MLU as a function of age for three different children studied by Brown and his colleagues (Brown, Cazden & Bellugi-Klima, 1969). Note that Eve attained an MLU of 3 when she was only two years old. In contrast, Adam and Sarah attained this same MLU when they were around three years old. Thus, there are large individual differences in attaining later stages of language development. We now consider some specific accomplishments in the child's later knowledge of phonology, morphology, syntax, semantics, and pragmatics.

Phonology

Although a good deal of phonological development has occurred by the time that MLU reaches 3, there is still some way to go. Some children have problems speaking consonant clusters (e.g., *str* as in *string*) throughout the preschool years. Furthermore, pronouncing some of the more difficult phonemes (such as *r*, for example) can cause problems even into the school-age years. Finally, some of the phonological rules for pronouncing word endings of words (for the past tense, for example) are not mastered until children are six to eight years old.

Morphology

As children advance beyond two-word utterances, there is very clear evidence that they know morphological rules. Children begin using the plural and possessive forms of nouns (e.g., *dogs* and *dog's*), putting appropriate endings on verbs (e.g., *s* when the subject is third-person singular, *ed* for the past tense, and *ing* for the present progressive tense), using prepositions (*in* and *on*), articles (e.g., *a* and *the*), and using various forms of the verb *to be* (e.g., "I was going to the store"). In a classic study of these and other grammatical morphemes, Roger Brown (1973) found evidence for a consistent pattern of development. One of his findings was that children learn to make nouns plural (e.g., *dogs*) before they learn to make nouns possessive (e.g., *dog's*). And only after this do children learn to put verbs in the third-person singular form (e.g., *runs* in the sentence "He runs fast"). What makes this pattern intriguing is that the same basic word ending (*s*) is involved in all three cases. We can therefore see that it is not the ending that is learned. Rather, it is rules for applying the ending that are learned.

Some of the most important evidence for morphological rules comes from overgeneralizations of these rules. Have you ever heard a preschool child say "foots" instead of "feet," or "goed" instead of "went"? If you do not remember having heard such things, talk to some parents who have young children; you will hear about some interesting examples of errors in the use of morphological word endings. Moreover, you will see that these errors frequently follow from rules. More information about such errors and the rules they follow is presented in Perspective on Child Development 8.4.

Syntax

Similar evidence that children learn and actively apply rules can be found at the level of syntax. After advancing beyond two-word utterances, children utter word sequences that display a growing mastery of complex rules for how words should be ordered. Consider, for example, the case of *wh-* questions, questions such as "Where is Daddy going?" and "What is that boy doing?" To ask these questions properly, it is necessary to know two important differences between *wh-* questions and simple affirmative statements (e.g., "Daddy is going to work" and "That boy is waiting for the school

---

PERSPECTIVE ON CHILD DEVELOPMENT 8.4

FOOTS, FEETS, AND WUGS

In considering the type of "error" made by a child who uses *foots*, note that the *s* ending is appropriate for pluralizing a great many English words. When a child says "foots," the child is demonstrating knowledge of a rule; the "error" lies in failing to honor one of this rule's exceptions. Interestingly, overgeneralization often follows a three-stage sequence: First, the child correctly produces an irregular form (says "feet"). Then, after learning a general rule, the child overgeneralizes this rule (e.g., says "foots" or "feets"). Finally, the child produces the appropriate forms, having learned the rule as well as its exceptions (e.g., says "feet" but also "fingers" and "toes") (Flavell, 1985).

If you still doubt that children learn morphological rules, consider a classic experiment performed by Jean Berko (1958). She presented preschool and first grade children with cards such as the one shown in the figure at right. A child was asked to look at a card while the experimenter read the words aloud. Then the child was asked to supply the missing word. This might sound easy, but Berko was interested not just in the child's ability to recall the right word but with his or her ability to say it "correctly" (with the ending that was dictated by morphological rules). "Wugs" would be the correct response for the card in the figure opposite. Although the children were not perfectly accurate, they were certainly much better than chance. Moreover, they showed their knowledge of morphological rules not only with plural forms of nouns ("There are two wugs") but also with the possessive forms of nouns and with the third-person singular and past-tense forms of verbs.

What makes this study by Berko impressive is that most of the "words" were fictional. They were created especially for the experiment. Thus, the children could not base their responses on remembering past instances of hearing the words. It seems they were forced to rely upon *rules*. Their performance suggests that they did so successfully.

This is a wug.

Now there is another one.
There are two of them.
There are two _____ .

The plural allomorph /-z/.
From Berko, J., "The Child's Learning of English Morphology," in *Word*, 1958, 14, 150–177, 361. © 1958 International Linguistic Association. Reprinted by permission.

---

bus"). First, a *wh-* word must be added at the beginning of the sentence. Second, the auxiliary verb (*is*) must be inverted, that is, exchanged with the subject of the sentence. Young children appear to learn quite early where to put the *wh-* word, but they take much longer to learn the auxiliary-inversion rule. Hence, it is common to hear preschool children asking questions such as "Where daddy is going?" and "What that boy is doing?"

Interestingly, once children have mastered the auxiliary-inversion rule, they sometimes overgeneralize it to "how come" questions (Kuczaj & Brannick, 1979). Although it is correct to ask "How come that boy is running?" children will sometimes ask "How come is that boy running?" The sequence "is that boy running" would be correct if it came after "why." But following "how come," it is a highly intelligent, rule-governed error.

Smithereens

"If you don't mind my asking, about how much does a sentence diagrammer pull down a year?"

Copyright © United Feature Syndicate, Inc.

Some interesting recent cross-cultural findings suggest that how children learn syntactical rules depends upon their language. For example, Michael Akiyami (1984) showed that English-speaking preschoolers find it more difficult to understand true-negative statements ("You are not a baby") than false-negative statements ("You are not a child"). However, Japanese-speaking children showed the opposite pattern. The differing results suggest different strategies for processing the sentences, which in turn reflect subtle differences in syntactic rules for negation in English versus Japanese. Akiyami concluded: "It seems that children are so sensitive to fine differences in languages that they do develop strategies best suited for their language. The belief that children all over the world learn their language the same way needs to be corrected" (p. 227).

As children advance into the school-age years, they become incredibly skilled at using syntactical rules to construct lengthy and complex sentences. Sentences such as "The man who fixed the fence went home" and "I don't want you to use my bike" are impressive demonstrations of how children can use syntax to combine two ideas into a single sentence (Flavell, 1985). Just how a young child achieves such mastery of complex

syntactial rules, while at the same time possibly struggling over relatively simple arithmetic rules, is a mystery we have yet to solve.

Semantics

As children advance beyond the two-word stage, not just morphology and syntax improve. Knowledge of meanings is rapidly advancing as well. In the first place, the number of word meanings that children know is increasing. The speaking vocabulary of a six-year-old has been estimated as ranging from 8,000 to 14,000 words (Carey, 1977). Assuming that the learning of words starts when a child is twelve months old, this translates into five to eight words a day between ages one and six (de Villiers & de Villiers, 1978). After five years of work the six-year-old child is not slowing down. According to some estimates the average child of this age is moving along at the awe-inspiring rate of twenty-two words per day (Miller, 1981)! How would you fare if you were given the task of learning twenty-two new words per day? It truly is miraculous how quickly children learn language.

One way that children achieve such rapid new-word learning is through a "fast mapping" process (Carey, 1977). Hearing a new word being used in a sentence can provide many clues as to what the word means, and young children apparently make use of these cues effectively. For example, consider a child who is entirely unfamiliar with the color term *chartreuse*. Suppose you say to this child, in the course of some activity, "Bring me the chartreuse one, not the red one." The child might figure out which one you mean, particularly if there are only two objects present and only one of them is red. At the same time, the child might start to learn the meaning of *chartreuse* (Heibeck & Markman, 1985).

Despite the rapid course of new-word learning, some classes of words are not fully understood until well into the childhood years. One such class is relational words. **Relational words** are words that specify relationships. The relationships can be among objects (e.g., *more* as in "The piano weighs more than the table"), events (e.g., *longer* as in "Today's game went longer than the one last week"), or people (e.g., *borrowed* as in "The lady borrowed her friend's new Porsche"). One important subset of relational words is that of *spatial adjectives,* including *big* and *small, thick* and *thin.* Studies have shown that while some of these adjectives are well understood by preschool children, others are not. For example, Eve Clark (1972) examined how well four-year-old children could supply opposites for words like *big* (*small*) and *deep* (*shallow*). Her results showed an excellent understanding of the *big–small* pair (all of her subjects could supply *small* as the opposite of *big* and vice versa). Furthermore, there was weaker but still good understanding of the pairs *long–short* and *tall–short*. However, there was only moderate understanding of *high–low,* poorer understanding of *thick–thin* and *wide–narrow,* and almost no understanding of *deep–shallow*.

Why are spatial adjectives such as *thick, wide,* and *deep* so difficult for preschoolers to understand? One popular view is that such terms are sematically complex in their internal representations. An alternative view is that they simply are used less frequently than other spatial adjectives, so children have less experience with them. In any case, some spatial adjectives take a long time to master (Clark, 1983). The same conclusion holds for "possessive verbs," verbs that offer or imply transfer of possession (e.g., *trade, spend, buy,* and *sell*), another type of relational word (Gentner, 1975). Do not be surprised if a preschooler talks of buying something when he or she really is thinking of getting something for free.

Pragmatics

Although there are many great differences between a two-year-old's language and a six-year-old's language, none are more important than those pertaining to pragmatics, that is, rules of conversation. There is no question that apart from many differences at phonological, morphological, syntactical, and semantic levels of language, a six-year-old is simply a much better conversationalist than is a two-year-old. The development of this conversational skill occurs in several areas (de Villiers & de Villiers, 1978): At around three years of age children show an improved ability to talk about things not physically present. Thus they improve their command of the characteristic of language we have referred to as displacement. One way in which such displacement is revealed is in games of pretend. Although two-year-olds may know the word *table,* they

are unlikely to use this word to refer to an imaginary table that they pretend is standing in front of them. However, most children over three have this ability, even if they do not always use it. (There are large individual differences in preschoolers' talk of imaginary people and things.)

Somewhat later in the preschool years, at around age four, children show remarkable sensitivity to the needs of others in conversation. One way in which they show such sensitivity is in their use of the articles *the* and *an* (or *a*). When adults are telling a story or describing an event, they generally use *an* (or *a*) when they first refer to an object or animal, and then use *the* when referring to it later (e.g., "Two boys were walking through the jungle when *a* fierce lion appeared. *The* lion lunged at one boy while the other ran for cover"). Even three-year-olds follow part of this rule (they consistently use *the* when referring to previously mentioned things). However, using the word *a* when something is initially mentioned develops much more slowly. Although five-year-olds follow this rule on some occasions, they fail to follow it on others (Warden, 1976).

Another important pragmatic ability that emerges around four or five years of age has to do with speech style. As adults, we have an excellent ability to change our speech style in accordance with the social situation and the person with whom we are speaking. An obvious example is that adults speak in a simpler way to a two-year-old than to an older child or an adult. Interestingly, even four-year-olds speak differently to a two-year-old than to a same-aged peer. They "talk down" to the two-year-old, using shorter utterance lengths (Shatz & Gelman, 1973). However, children in this age range do show some deficiencies in communicating with one- and two-year-olds (Tomasello & Mannle, 1985). For example, they appear less adept than adults at providing an infant with nonverbal cues (gestures) to the meaning of what they are saying. They also use fewer conversational devices to keep a dialog with an infant running smoothly. For example, children will frequently ignore an infant's most recent utterance or at least fail to continue conversing about the topic of this utterance.

The adaptiveness of speech to social situations.

Although pragmatic abilities develop quite rapidly during the preschool years, they continue developing in later years as well. One interesting set of late-developing abilities are those pertaining to making requests. Although five-year-olds can comprehend requests, they are unlikely themselves to generate requests, particularly politely worded requests for someone to help them with some difficulty they face. However, older children show developing knowledge of the pragmatics of making requests. By the time that children are nine years old, they show an impressive ability to take into account both the difficulty of satisfying the request and the status of the person of whom they are making the request (Axia & Baroni, 1985; Wilkinson, Wilkinson, Spinelli & Chiang, 1984).

Another set of pragmatic abilities that develop during the elementary school years are those pertaining to lying. School-age children are much more

CONCEPT TABLE 8.3
Milestones in Language Acquisition

Time Period	Processes/Related Ideas	Characteristics/Description
Early accomplishments	Preverbal	Babbling may help to develop articulatory skills. Pragmatic skills of gaining attention and requesting/asserting emerge. Symbolic abilities are acquired.
	One-word utterances	Rapid acquisition of new words takes place. Refinements in knowledge of meaning of words and a reduction in overextensions and underextensions emerge.
	Two-word utterances	Expression of multiple meanings through telegraphic speech emerges. Some use of word order to express different meanings is possible.
Later accomplishments	Phonology	Ability to pronounce consonant clusters, as well as difficult phonemes and word endings, improves.
	Morphology	Rules for combining morphemes together (e.g., correct word endings for plural, possessive, and third-person singular forms of words) are acquired. Overgeneralizations of rules appear and are corrected.
	Syntax	Mastery of *wh-* questions and other complex syntactic forms is attained. There is a growing ability to produce complex sentences containing multiple ideas.
	Semantics	Learning of the complex meanings of relational terms such as spatial adjectives (e.g., *thick-thin*) takes place.
	Pragmatics	Improvements in displacement (talking about things not physically present, as in "pretend" games) are evident. Knowledge of using articles (*the, a*) to enhance communication increases. Modifications of speech style depending on age and status of listener are evident.

accomplished at convincing other people of things, including things that are not true. Although lying is certainly not admirable, to do it successfully requires much skill: If you want to tell a believable lie, you must be aware of what your listener already knows and of what information and style of language will convince him or her of something else. It is no wonder that parents find it easy to catch their five- and six-year-olds in lies but have increasing difficulty as these children grow up (de Villiers & de Villiers, 1978).

Just as children get better at lying effectively, they also get better at distinguishing lies from sincere statements made by others. An interesting study conducted at Harvard Project Zero (Demorest, Meyer, Phelps, Gardner & Winner, 1984) examined children's interpretations of stories containing sincere versus deceptive statements made by one character to another. For example, one of the stories involved a character telling another character that his hair looked terrific when (a) the second character had just received an excellent haircut (sincere statement condition) or (b) the second

character had just received a very poor haircut (deceptive statement condition). Although six-, nine-, and thirteen-year-olds all performed well at judging that sincere statements actually were sincere, the younger children performed much more poorly at detecting that deceptive statements actually were lies.

Demorest and his colleagues also examined the ability to detect sarcastic statements (the first character points and laughs when saying, "That new haircut you got looks terrific"). All of the children were quite poor at this task; only adults showed significant skill at distinguishing lies from sarcastic remarks. This finding suggests that while we learn to detect lies in the elementary school years, we learn about sarcasm only later in life, at some point during the adolescent years.

We have covered much ground in our survey of the milestones of language development. Concept Table 8.3 is a useful summary of the major points we have considered. It will be helpful for you to review this table before proceeding further.

BILINGUALISM

Learning a first language is, for the vast majority of humanity, an affair of infancy and childhood. Although some unfortunates like Genie start to learn their first language in adolescence or later, they do not get very far. However, learning a second language is a very different matter. This can occur at any time of life from young childhood through old age. Though learning a new language is difficult for most of us, it is hardly impossible. We may never shake our first-language accents, but we can grow fluent nonetheless.

Just how is it possible to attain great proficiency in more than one language? We now turn to a discussion of two different types of bilingual individuals: (1) those who learn two languages simultaneously in young childhood and (2) those who learn two languages successively in time.

Simultaneous Acquisition of Two Languages

An excellent analysis of the simultaneous acquisition of two languages has been provided by Virginia Volterra and Traute Taeschner (1978). They considered the language development of three children, each of whom acquired mastery of two languages from one to four years of age. The goal was to identify "stages" in the children's early usage and mastery. One child grew up in an English-speaking environment where her mother spoke to her mostly in English and her father spoke to her only in German. The other children were two sisters, living in Rome, who had been immersed in two languages since birth. Their father spoke Italian exclusively, while their mother spoke only German to them. The data used in the study consisted of extensive tape recordings of the two sisters and a detailed diary of the first girl made by her father. Volterra and Taeschner (1978) believe there are three distinct stages in learning two languages.

In the first stage, the child seems to have one mixed vocabulary, or lexicon. Words from the two languages are often used together in short phrases, and for any single word in one language, there is not always a corresponding word in the other. The child seems to move freely among the two languages without clearly discriminating between them.

In the second stage, the child has separate vocabularies for the two languages and does not mix them. Phrases contain words from only one language, and for any single word in one language, there is a corresponding one in the other language. Generally, one child uses the same syntactic rules for both languages.

In the third stage, the child advances significantly in syntax. Different rules for producing utterances in the two languages emerge and there is a differentiation between the languages in all other ways. To help keep the languages distinct, the child only speaks the language associated with the person being addressed.

Successive Acquisition of Two Languages

Although simultaneous acquisition of two different languages is undeniably fascinating, successive acquisition is at the heart of some pressing educational problems. Consider the case of a hypothetical but quite typical young boy named Octavio. Octavio's Mexican parents moved to the United States one year before Octavio was born. They do not speak English fluently and have always spoken to Octavio in Spanish. At six years of age Octavio has just entered the first grade at an elementary school in San Antonio, Texas, and does not speak English.

What is the best way to teach Octavio? How much easier would elementary school be for Octavio if his parents had been able to speak to him in Spanish and English when he was an infant?

According to the 1980 census, well over six million children in the United States come from homes where the primary language is not English. Often, like Octavio, they live in a community where this same non-English language is the major means of communication. These children face a more difficult task than most of us—they must master the native tongue of their family to be effective at home and in their own community, and they must also master English to make their way in and contribute to the larger society. The number of bilingual children is expanding at such a rapid rate in our country (some experts, for example, predict a tripling in their numbers by early in the twenty-first century) that they constitute an important subgroup of language learners to be dealt with by society. Although the education of such children in the public schools has a long history, only recently has a national policy evolved to guarantee a quality language experience for them.

What is the best way to teach children whose first language is not English?

Widespread efforts in the early 1960s to incorporate bilingual education components into the American school curricula resulted in the enactment by Congress in 1967 of the Bilingual Education Act (as title VII of the Elementary and Secondary Education Act). The Educational Amendments Act of 1974 revised and strengthened the 1967 statute: in federal fiscal year (FY) 1975, congressional appropriations for bilingual education were 85 million dollars. This figure nearly doubled within three to four years.

Great debates have raged concerning how best to conduct this bilingual education. Does one teach English as a foreign language, adopting the child's native tongue as the language of the classroom, or does one treat English as a second, equal language and strive for balance in usage of English and the native tongue? The answer to this has important consequences for the way school curricula and texts are written in cities with large concentrations of Spanish-speaking children (e.g., New York, Miami, San Antonio, and Los Angeles).

Practical educational decisions about bilingual education ideally should rest on a sound understanding of how second-language learning comes about. Research in this area is only beginning, but already we have learned enough to question a good many previously held beliefs. Barry McLaughlin (1978) considers several popular notions about second-language learning, including the three following:

1. The young child acquires a language more quickly and easily than an adult because the child is biologically programmed to acquire languages, whereas the adult is not.
2. The younger the child, the more skilled in acquiring a second language.
3. Second-language acquisition is a qualitatively different process than first-language acquisition. (pp. 197–200)

Although these ideas sound plausible, it may surprise you to learn that the bulk of research evidence weighs against all three! It certainly is true that young children are impressive at the task of language learning. But so are adults who are highly motivated and are also extensively exposed to a new language. Although a college student might feel quite the moron when trying to learn French, consider the number of hours per day (or week) he or she actually spends with this language. In contrast, a young child learning his or her first language is almost literally immersed in it, hearing it and trying to use it to communicate every day. Motivation is probably also involved. Although a college student might have difficulty actually opening up that French book, there can be no doubt that a young child is simply driven to learn his or her first language. When studies have controlled these critical variables of exposure time and motivation and have measured language competence by objective criteria, the evidence does not favor a superiority of younger children over older children and adults but rather the reverse. Furthermore, there has been no strong evidence that the basic mechanisms of language learning are different in young children than in older children and adults.

Of course, the foregoing is not meant to deny that there are benefits to beginning second-language learning early. As McLaughlin (1978) remarks:

The success of young children in acquiring two languages under such conditions need not be attributed to superior language learning skills. Given the same amount and quality of exposure, an older child (or an adult) would presumably do just as well, most likely better. This, of course, is not to denigrate the young child's achievement or to downgrade the advantages of early introduction to a second language. Older children and adults do not have the amount of time at their disposal for learning a second language that the young child does. There is no reason not to utilize this advantage and to begin language instruction early. The practice of total immersion programs of introducing children to a second language in kindergarten through games, songs, rhymes, and so forth, has produced extremely favorable results and is in all likelihood a more pleasant way to acquire a second language for the child than the repetitious drills that often characterize later classroom instruction. (p. 200)

A qualification on McLaughlin's conclusions concerns the phonological level of language. As we mentioned earlier, it appears to be difficult to acquire new accents after the time of puberty. Thus, the learning of phonemes may indeed be better in young children than in the rest of us, perhaps because of a critical period tied to biological maturation.

WRITING AND READING

There is an important language-related task the child must tackle in the preschool and elementary school years: the task of learning to read. First, we consider writing systems, which differ in how visual symbols map onto different levels of language, and then we turn to some methods for teaching our own alphabetic writing system to children. Subsequently, we discover that writing may have important implications for teaching children to read, we describe the major ways children are taught to read, and finally we evaluate the role or speech in reading.

Writing Systems

Robert Crowder (1982) has summarized a good deal of what is known about the variety and evolution of writing systems. According to the best archeological evidence, making visual marks to represent experiences has been occuring for some 50,000 years. However, the appearance of writing, as opposed to art, probably is much more recent. At least five major writing systems have been invented, but the current systems of the world have evolved from just two sources: the Egyptian system, which originated around 3500 B.C., and the Chinese system, which originated around 2000 B.C. Our own **alphabetic writing system** evolved from the Egyptian.

Our alphabetic system is one of three basic types of systems that are used in the world today. It is a system in which the visual symbols (letters) correspond—but only roughly—to the phonemes of our speech. That is, letters refer to phonemes, but with compromises and exceptions that we call spelling irregularities (see our earlier discussion of the phonological level of language).

Two alternatives to our alphabetic system are the **syllabic** and **logographic writing systems.** In a syllabic system, such as that of the Japanese Katakana, each written symbol corresponds to a spoken syllable. If we used such a system in English, we might have a letter for *bas* and another for *ket,* and we might spell *basket* by writing these two letters side by side. In a logographic system, which is found in Chinese, each visual symbol corresponds to a word, so that in such a system we might have a single visual symbol for *basket.*

It is interesting to note that in the evolution of writing there has been a trend to move downward from meaning to sound and from longer segments of sound (words) to shorter segments of sound (syllables, phonemes) in linking the language to visual symbols. In the earliest logographic systems the visual symbols looked like (were drawings of) what they represented. But these symbols often became streamlined and highly abstract, sometimes to the extent that they no longer resembled their referents at all. Figure 8.8 shows the evolution of some written symbols in Sumerian cuneiform writing.

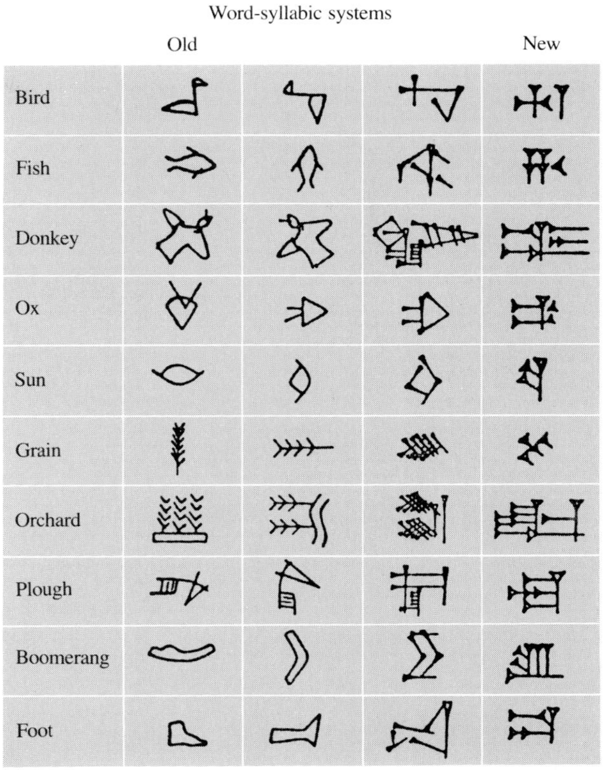

Word-syllabic systems

FIGURE 8.8
Pictorial origins of ten cuneiform signs (Gelb, 1952).

The evolution from a logographic to a syllabic writing system often involves a recognition of homophones (different-meaning words that sound alike). As a hypothetical example, a symbol for a word like *sun* might begin to be used for *son.* Another important evolutionary step is the taking of two word symbols and combining them to form a longer word (symbols for the words *sun* and *day* might be combined to make *sunday*). At this point, we have begun to form a syllabary. Apparently only once in ancient history—around 1000 B.C. in the Near East—was a transition made from a syllabic to an alphabetic system.

Logographic-stage sentence:

Phoneticization-stage sentence:

Syllabary-stage words:

Alphabet-stage words:

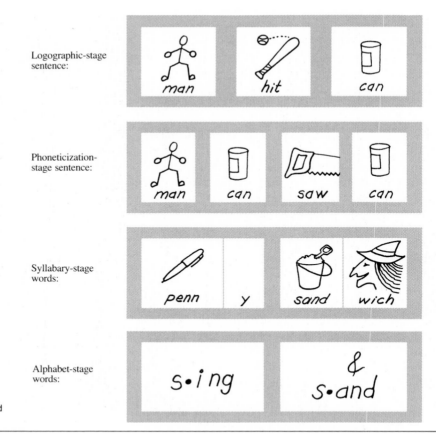

FIGURE 8.9
Examples of materials used by Rozin and Gleitman (Rozin and Gleitman, 1977).

Techniques for Teaching Reading

The evolution of writing is historically interesting, but it is also important for practical reasons: It may provide a clue to how best to teach reading to young children. This is the argument of Paul Rozin and Lila Gleitman (1977), two primary experts in the field of reading research. Rozin and Gleitman have developed a method for the teaching of reading in which children begin with pictographic representations, which they then learn to relate to sounds and subsequently to syllables. After this the children move to using the alphabetic system of spelling out words. There are five separate stages in all, and we outline these below (see figure 8.9 for examples of the Rozin and Gleitman materials).

In the first, "semasiographic" stage of the Rozin and Gleitman method, children are taught that meaning can be represented visually. They send and try to understand messages using only a pencil and paper or chalk and a chalkboard. Speaking in these "communication games" is strictly against the rules. Hence, children are trained to code and decode meaning using only visual markings. An example of a communication game is to "say" where an object is hidden in a room simply by drawing some sort of picture (e.g., a map). Such games are fun for five- and six-year-old children (and even for much older people).

In the second, "logographic" stage, children learn that certain pictures stand for certain words. Further, they practice reading and writing simple sentences made up of these pictures. Some example picture sentences are shown in figure 8.9. Note that each picture is printed on a card. Note also that the word is spelled out below each picture—this is to get the children familiar with the look of English orthography and perhaps to get them started in learning this orthography.

In the third, "phoneticization" stage, children are taught that written symbols can correspond to sounds, not just meanings. Specifically, they learn that if two

How might writing exercises help this child's reading development?

different words sound the same, they also may be written the same (e.g., a picture of a can is used to stand for *can,* even when *can* is used as a verb, as in "The man can saw the can" (see figure 8.9).

In the fourth, "syllabary" stage, children learn symbols that correspond to spoken syllables. In the course of such learning, children come to realize that two one-syllable words can be "put together" to form a completely new two-syllable word (e.g., *sand* and *witch* can combine to form *sandwich*; see figure 8.9). The children also learn to read and write some syllables that have no meaning by themselves, such as *y* and *er.* Pictures are not much use in representing such syllables. Hence, the children are taught adult-type spellings for them (see figure 8.9).

In the fifth, "alphabet" stage, children are taught that syllables can be broken down into phonemes and that alphabetic characters roughly correspond (with compromises and exceptions) to these phonemes. This

is done through various "blending" exercises, in which a given alphabetic symbol (e.g., *s*) is combined with different combinations of letters (*ing, and*) to produce different words (see figure 8.9).

An important aspect of this approach pertains to problems of linguistic awareness of phonemes. Awareness of the phonemes contained within syllables is difficult for children to attain and can be a serious stumbling block in reading. In the method proposed by Rozin and Gleitman, care is taken to instill in children four other aspects of reading before this final task is faced.

But does the method actually work? Some preliminary data are encouraging. Specifically, stages 1 through 4 appear to be learnable by first grade students, even those who have a poor prognosis for reading. Stage 5, however, causes more problems. Thus, it is not yet clear that the five-stage program actually facilitates the linguistic awareness that children need in order to learn our alphabetic system of reading. There is good reason for optimism, however. In the first place, the five-stage method has not yet been refined. Improvements in the materials and procedures may increase its effectiveness enormously. Second, a side benefit of the method is that it is fun for children and motivates them to read. Since motivation is doubtlessly important in overcoming reading difficulties, the motivational aspect of the five-stage method could be its strongest feature.

Rozin and Gleitman (1977) were hardly the first to devise a technique for the teaching of reading. In the history of learning-to-read techniques, three approaches have been dominant. These are the **ABC method,** which emphasizes memorization of the names of the letters of the alphabet, the **whole-word method,** which focuses on learning direct associations between whole words and their meanings, and the **phonics method,** which stresses the sounds that letters make when in words—such sounds can differ from the names of the letters (e.g., the sound of the name of the letter *c* is not to be found in *cat*). Today the ABC method is in ill repute; because of the imperfect relationship between the names of letters and their sounds in words, the technique is viewed as poor if not actually harmful to children. Despite its poor reputation, the ABC method was the method by which many children in past generations successfully learned to read.

Most disputes in recent times have centered on the merits of the whole-word and phonics methods. Although some research has compared these two types of techniques, the findings have not been conclusive (Crowder, 1982). However, there is evidence suggesting that drilling the sounds made by letters in words (part of some phonics methods) can be helpful to an extent in some aspects of reading—e.g., spelling and reading aloud (Chall, 1967; Williams, 1979). In any case, many current techniques of reading instruction incorporate both whole-word and phonics components.

If you review what we said about the Rozin and Gleitman technique, you will see that it too has both sorts of components. Children initially learn single symbols for words (clearly a whole-word approach) but later attend to the phonemes that make up words and learn to associate visual symbols with these phonemes (clearly a phonetics approach).

The Role of Speech in Reading

Do you hear yourself talking as you read these words? Many people will answer this question in the affirmative, even if they have been reading without making a sound. What such people (including your authors) hear is a kind of mental imagery of speech, imagery that is nonetheless real for the fact that a person's mouth is shut. Such imagery suggests that **speech coding** plays a role in the process of reading, even when reading is silent.

Not everyone reports speech imagery when they read. Further, many proponents of speed-reading techniques will tell you that such speech imagery can be prevented—indeed that it should be prevented if one wants to read efficiently. What can scientific research tell us about this matter?

One thing research tells us is that there are two possible uses of internal speech coding in reading. First, speech coding may contribute to interpreting the meaning of words on the page; that is, speech coding may facilitate a process called **lexical access.** When our eyes land on a particular word, we may first translate the visual information into a speech code and then look up the meaning of this speech code in our internal dictionary, or lexicon.

Second, speech may contribute to short-term memory for words we have recently read. Short-term memory is important in reading. We need it for "holding on to" early words in a sentence until we can get to the later words. In addition, speech coding is useful for short-term memory.

SUMMARY

I. There are a number of important characteristics of human language and functions of language.

  A. Human language shares five characteristics: words with conventional meanings, sequencing, infinite generativity, displacement, and multiple levels of rule systems (phonology, morphology, syntax, semantics, and pragmatics).

  B. Three very important functions of language are perception, cognition, and communication.

II. No mystery is deeper than how children learn language. Historically, three theories have attempted to explain how we acquire language: behaviorist learning, nativist, and cognitive.

  A. The behavioral learning position argues that children learn language through imitation, shaping, and reinforcement. Other aspects of the environment that are important in language learning are "motherese," prompting, echoing, expanding, recasting, following in order to lead, and labeling.

  B. The nativist position emphasizes the biological basis of language. It maintains that children have substantial prewired machinery for the acquisition of language. The nativist position is supported by evidence related to language universals, lateralization of language function, critical periods, and the absence of humanlike language in other species.

  C. The cognitive position suggests that although children have prewired machinery, much of it is cognitive rather than strictly linguistic.

  D. All theories probably carry some truth, but it is impossible to ignore the strong role of biology in understanding language.

III. Milestones in the development of language focus on early accomplishments and later developments.

  A. Early accomplishments include preverbal matters, one-word utterances, and two-word utterances.

    1. Preverbal influences include babbling, pragmatic skills, and symbolic abilities.

    2. One-word utterances focus on the holophrase hypothesis, Eve Clark's theory of meaning, and underextensions and overextensions.

    3. Two-word utterances involve expression of multiple meanings through telegraphic speech.

  B. Later developments in language involve phonology, morphology, syntax, semantics, and pragmatics.

    1. Morphological development involves the acquisition of rules for combining morphemes, and an overgeneralization of rules appears and is then corrected.

    2. The development of syntax involves the mastery of *wh-* questions and the ability to produce complex sentences with multiple ideas.

    3. Semantic development focuses on learning the complex meanings of relational terms.

    4. Pragmatics includes improvements in displacement, knowledge of using articles, and modifications of speech style depending on the age and status of the listener.

IV. Information about bilingualism focuses on simultaneous acquisition of languages and successive acquisition of languages. There is no evidence that second-language learning is better in younger children than in older children or adults.

V. Writing and reading are also important aspects of language development.

  A. Our alphabetic writing system is one of three basic kinds, the other two being syllabic and logographic. The evolution of writing has followed the trend of moving from meaning to sound and from longer to shorter segments of sound.

  B. One technique of reading follows the same progression as the evolution of writing. Other techniques are the (now ill-favored) ABC method, the whole-word method, and the phonics method. Research suggests that speech coding is not necessary for lexical access, but it may improve short-term memory while one is reading.

KEY TERMS

ABC method 266
alphabetic writing system 263
babbling 249
critical periods 244
deep structure 233
displacement 232
echoing 240
expanding 240
grammar 233
holophrase 251
imitation 239
infinite generativity 231
labeling 242
language universals 244
lateralization of language 244
levels of rule systems 232
lexical access 266
logographic writing systems 263
mean length of utterance (MLU) 253
morphemes 233

morphology 233
motherese 240
overextending 252
phonemes 232
phonetic alphabet 232
phonics method 266
phonology 232
pragmatics 234
prompting 240
recasting 241
reinforcement 239
relational words 256
semantics 234
sequencing 231
shaping 239
speech coding 266
surface structure 233
syllabic writing systems 263
syntax 233
telegraphic speech 253
underextending 252
whole-word method 266
Whorf/Sapir hypothesis 236

REVIEW QUESTIONS

1. What makes language human?
2. Outline the multiple levels of rules involved in language.
3. What are the main functions of language?
4. Provide an overview of the theories of language, provide some conclusions about the theories, and describe the role of the environment in language development.
5. What are the early developments in language acquisition?
6. Outline the later developments in language acquisition.
7. Discuss simultaneous and successive acquisition of languages.
8. What do we know about writing and reading systems?

SUGGESTED READINGS

Bruner, J. (1983). *Child talk*. New York: Norton.
 A fascinating view of the child's language by a leading cognitive theorist.
Clark, E. (1983). Meanings and concepts. In P. H. Mussen (Ed.), *Handbook of child psychology* (4th ed., Vol. 3). New York: John Wiley.
 An excellent review of conceptual and semantic development.
Crowder, R. G. (1982). *The psychology of reading*. New York: Oxford University Press.
 A thorough and highly readable introduction to reading processes.
Maratsos, M. (1983). Some current issues in the study of the acquisition of grammar. In P. H. Mussen (Ed.), *Handbook of child psychology* (4th ed., Vol. 3). New York: John Wiley.
 A very thorough, informative, up-to-date overview of what is known about language development.
Slobin, S. I. (1979). *Psycholinguistics* (2nd ed.). Glenview, IL: Scott, Foresman.
 An excellent, comprehensive treatment of the field of the psychology of language.
Terrace, H. (1979). *Nim*. New York: Knopf.
 An intriguing commentary about the ape language controversy.

CHAPTER

INTELLIGENCE

LARRY P., INTELLIGENT, BUT NOT IN CERTAIN INTELLIGENCE-TESTING CONTEXTS

L arry is black and comes from an impoverished background. When he was six years old he was placed in a class for the educable mentally retarded (EMR). The primary reason Larry was placed in an EMR class was his score of 64 on an intelligence test.

Is there a possibility that the intelligence test Larry was given is culturally biased? Psychologists still debate this issue. The controversy has been the target of a major class action challenging the use of standardized IQ tests to place black elementary school students in classes for the educable mentally retarded. The initial lawsuit, filed on behalf of Larry P., claimed that the IQ test he took underestimated his learning ability. The lawyers for Larry P. argued that IQ tests place too much emphasis on verbal skills and fail to account for the background of black children. Therefore, it was argued, Larry was incorrectly labeled mentally retarded and may forever be saddled with the stigma of being called retarded.

As part of the lengthy court battle involving Larry P., six black EMR students were independently retested by members of the Bay Area Association of Black Psychologists in California. The psychologists made sure they established good rapport with the students and made special efforts to overcome defeatism and distraction on the part of the students. Certain items were reworded in terms more consistent with the children's social background, and recognition was given to nonstandard answers that showed a logical, intelligent approach to problems. The retesting produced scores of 79 to 104—17 to 38 points higher than the scores the students received when initially tested by school psychologists. The retest scores were above the ceiling for placement in an EMR class.

In the case of Larry P., it was ruled that IQ tests are biased and their use discriminates against blacks and other ethnic minorities. The ruling continued the moratorium on the use of IQ tests in decisions about placement of a child in an EMR class. In the Larry P. trial it was revealed that 66 percent of elementary school students in EMR classes in San Francisco were black, whereas blacks only make up 28.5 percent of the San Francisco school population.

What was the state's argument for using intelligence tests as part of the criteria for placing children in EMR classes? At one point the state suggested that because blacks tend to be poor and poor pregnant women tend to suffer from inadequate nutrition, it is possible that the brain development of many black children has been retarded by their mothers' poor diets during pregnancy. However, from the beginning of the trial, a basic point made by the state was that blacks are genetically inferior to whites intellectually. The decision in favor of Larry P. is currently being appealed.

In another court case, this one in Illinois, it was ruled that IQ tests are not culturally biased (Armstrong, 1980). Many psychologists continue to take exception to the ruling in the Larry P. case, arguing that the evidence does not suggest the tests are biased and that informed consent procedures and regular review of children's progress in special education would protect rights to equal protection under the law, as well as rights to special education services when needed.

It should be pointed out that before intelligence tests were available, teachers relied on their own biases in assigning students. Thus intelligence tests, by themselves, are not to blame. Rather, such tests can be misused by people who lack competent psychological training.

Alfred Binet

THEORIES, DEFINITIONS, AND MEASUREMENTS: MORE THAN IQ

In everyday conversation we often equate intelligence with IQ. When asked what IQ and intelligence are, many of us respond, "That's how smart you are." But intelligence must be more than IQ (an abbreviation for the intelligence quotient derived from performance on intelligence tests). Although most of us have some idea of what intelligence is, not everybody defines it in the same way. For many years psychologists have been trying to pin down a definition of intelligence and also to find better ways to measure it.

Our discussion of theories, definitions, and measurement emphasizes the pioneering work of Alfred Binet and the concept of general intelligence, the more recent efforts of David Wechsler, who has developed several widely used tests of intelligence, the factor analytic approach, and the modern information-processing approach.

Binet and the Concept of General Intelligence

We now examine the development of the first intelligence test and Binet's concept of *g*, which stands for general intelligence; the standardization of the Binet test; and what the Binet test is like today.

The Development of the First Intelligence Test

Alfred Binet and Theodore Simon devised the first intelligence test in 1905 to determine which students in the schools of Paris would not benefit from regular classes and consequently should be placed in special classes. Binet and Simon did not work from a basic definition of intelligence but proceeded in a trial-and-error fashion, simply relying on the test's ability to discriminate between children who were successful in school and those who were not. On this basis they found that "higher" mental abilities (memory, attention, and comprehension) were better means for making this distinction than "lower" mental abilities (reaction time, speed of hand movement in a specified amount of space, and the like). The latter measures had been used by the American psychologist James McKeen Cattell as indicators of intelligence, but Binet found that they were not very good at predicting which children would succeed in French schools.

Although the Binet test was made up of items that tested several different mental capacities (including memory, comprehension, attention, moral judgment, and aesthetic appreciation), Binet was primarily concerned with the child's general intelligence, which he noted simply as the letter *g,* rather than the child's specific mental abilities.

Binet developed the concept of **mental age (MA)** to describe the general level of the child's intellectual functioning. This term was devised to refer to the number of items a child of a given age answered correctly. It was believed that an IQ, or intelligence quotient, could be calculated by using the concept of mental age and comparing it with the child's chronological age. The formula for calculating IQ became

$$IQ = \frac{\text{Mental Age}}{\text{Chronological Age}} \times 100$$

A child of six with a mental age of six would, therefore, have an IQ of 100, a six-year-old with a mental age of eight an IQ of 133, and a six-year-old with a mental age of five an IQ of 83. By comparing a child's general level of intellectual functioning with that of the average child of the same age, Binet had a means of predicting how dull or bright the child would be in the classroom.

Standardization of the Binet

Over the years extensive effort has been expended to standardize the Binet test, which has been given to thousands of children and adults of different ages, selected at random from different parts of the United States. By administering the test to large numbers of people and recording the results, it has been found that intelligence as measured by the Binet has an almost **normal distribution** (see figure 9.1). This type of distribution is reflected in a frequency distribution that is very symmetrical, with a majority of the cases falling in the middle of the possible range of scores and fewer scores appearing toward the ends of the range.

The revisions of the Binet test have resulted in what are now called the Stanford-Binet tests (Stanford for Stanford University, where the revisions were done). The Stanford-Binet has a mean of 100 and a standard deviation of 16. The **mean** is the average score, and the **standard deviation** is how much the scores vary. As you can see by looking at figure 9.1, about 68 percent of the scores fall within what is called the average range: 84–116.

In the 1972 revision of the Stanford-Binet, preschool children scored an average of about 110 on the test, compared with a mean of 100. The 1972 sampling included more children from minority groups than was true of earlier samplings. What could explain the 1972 increase? Preschool children today are experiencing more visual and verbal stimulation from books, television, toys, and other educational materials, and their parents average two to three more years of education than was true of earlier generations.

Historically, labels have been used to reflect how far away from the mean a person scored on the IQ test. One who scored 102 was labeled "average"; one who scored 60 was labeled "mentally retarded"; and one who scored 156 was labeled "genius." The evaluation of intelligence is rapidly moving away from such categorization. Many experts believe that an intelligence quotient based on the results of a single intelligence test should not be the basis for so classifying a child. Such labels have often remained with the child for many years even though circumstances of the testing may have led to inappropriate measurement.

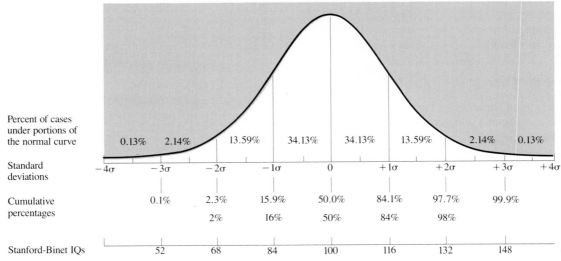

FIGURE 9.1
The normal curve and Stanford-Binet IQ scores (Sattler, 1982).

The Binet Today

The current Stanford-Binet test can be given to individuals from the age of two years through adulthood. It includes many different types of items, some requiring verbal responses and some calling for nonverbal performance. For example, items that characterize the six-year-old's performance on the test include the verbal ability to define at least six words, such as *orange* and *envelope,* and the nonverbal ability to trace a path through a maze. Items that reflect an average adult's intelligence include defining such words as *regard* and *disproportionate,* explaining a proverb, and comparing idleness and laziness. The fourth edition of the Stanford-Binet was published in 1985 (Thorndike, Hagan & Sattler). One important addition to the latest edition is the analysis of the individual's responses into four separate area scores: verbal reasoning, quantitative reasoning, abstract/visual reasoning, and short-term memory. In addition, a composite score is also computed.

The Wechsler Scales

Like Binet, David Wechsler subscribes to a view of intelligence that emphasizes its general nature. Wechsler has defined intelligence as "the global capacity of the individual to act purposefully, to think rationally, and to deal effectively with the environment" (1958, p. 7). In using the term *global* capacity Wechsler was referring to the general structure of intelligence. Like the Binet, the Wechsler scales provide a score that reflects general intelligence. However, Wechsler was more systematic than Binet in organizing the component parts of intelligence. Unlike the Binet, which is organized by age levels, the Wechsler scales are divided into verbal and nonverbal categories, which in turn are further subdivided to reflect specific aspects of intelligence. In table 9.1 examples of the various subtests of the Wechsler Intelligence Scale for Children are presented, along with examples of items used to measure each type of intellectual functioning. Remember that even though the Wechsler provides an evaluation of specific mental abilities, it also provides a general score for overall intelligence. Currently three main versions of the Wechsler tests are being used: the Wechsler Adult Intelligence Scale (WAIS), used for adults; the Wechsler Intelligence Scale for Children (WISC-R), used for those ages five to eighteen; and the Wechsler Preschool and Primary Intelligence Scale (WPPIS), devised for children ages four to six and a half.

TABLE 9.1
Examples of Subtests of the Wechsler Intelligence Scale for Children

Verbal	Performance
Similarities: The child must think abstractly and logically to answer sixteen questions. Example: "How are a skunk and a rabbit the same?"	*Picture Arrangement:* With each of eleven items the child is to rearrange parts of a figure or picture to make it complete or to tell a meaningful story. This test of nonverbal reasoning requires that the child understand how parts of a picture or a story go together. The pictures are shown to the child, who manually arranges the pieces in the right order.
Vocabulary: Forty words are used to test word knowledge. This subtest is thought to be an excellent indicator of general intelligence, measuring a variety of cognitive functions including concept formation, memory, and language development. Example: "Tell me what the word *cabinet* means."	*Block Design:* The child must put together a set of different-colored blocks ten times to match each of ten designs the examiner shows. Visual-motor coordination, perceptual organization, and an ability to visualize spatially are among the cognitive functions measured. This subtest is one of the best for measuring general intelligence.

The Factor Analytic Approach

The **factor analytic approach** is similar to the Wechsler in its emphasis on specific components of intelligence. It differs from the Wechsler in that it involves a mathematical analysis of large numbers of responses to test items in an attempt to come up with the basic common factors in intelligence.

A General and a Specific Factor

Many years before Wechsler began analyzing intelligence in terms of its general and specific nature, C. E. Spearman (1927) had proposed that intelligence has two factors. His was called a **two-factor theory** and suggested that intelligence consists of *g*, standing for general intelligence, and *s*, standing for specific factor. Spearman believed that these two factors could explain an individual's performance on an intelligence test. However, some factor approaches abandoned the idea of a general structure for intelligence and instead searched for specific factors only.

Multiple-Factor Theory

L. L. Thurstone (1938) developed an elaborate framework for understanding the idea that there are many specific types of intelligence. This view that a number of specific factors rather than one general and one specific factor make up intelligence is called **multiple-factor theory.** Thurstone consistently discovered six to twelve abilities that he called primary mental abilities. The seven that appeared most consistently when Thurstone analyzed people's test responses were (1) verbal comprehension, (2) number ability, (3) word fluency, (4) spatial visualization, (5) associative memory, (6) reasoning, and (7) perceptual speed. Figure 9.2 provides examples of the types of items that are included on tests designed to assess specific factors.

VERBAL REASONING
Choose the correct pair of words to fill the blanks. The first word of the pair goes in the blank space at the beginning of the sentence; the second word of the pair goes in the blank at the end of the sentence.

...... is to night as breakfast is to ......

A. supper — corner
B. gentle — morning
C. door — corner
D. flow — enjoy
E. supper — morning

The correct answer is E.

NUMERICAL ABILITY
Choose the correct answer for each problem.

Add 13	A 14		Subtract 30	A 15
12	B 25		20	B 26
	C 16			C 16
	D 59			D 8
	E none of these			E none of these

The correct answer for the first problem is B; for the second, E.

ABSTRACT REASONING
The four "problem figures" in each row make a series. Find the one among the "answer figures" that would be next in the series.

Problem figures   Answer figures

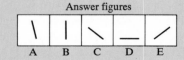

The correct answer is D.

A   B   C   D   E

CLERICAL SPEED AND ACCURACY
In each test item, one of the five combinations is underlined. Find the same combination on the answer sheet and mark it.

V. <u>AB</u> AC AD AE AF

W. aA aB BA Ba <u>Bb</u>

X. A7 7A B7 <u>7B</u> AB

Y. Aa Ba <u>bA</u> BA bB

Z. 3A 3B <u>33</u> B3 BB

| | AC | AE | AF | AB | AD |
| V. | | | | ∎ | |

| | BA | Ba | Bb | aA | aB |
| W. | | | ∎ | | |

| | 7B | B7 | AB | 7A | A7 |
| X. | ∎ | | | | |

| | Aa | bA | bB | Ba | BA |
| Y. | | ∎ | | | |

| | BB | 3B | B3 | 3A | 33 |
| Z. | | | | | ∎ |

FIGURE 9.2
Sample items from the Differential Aptitude Tests, which seek to measure intelligence through analysis of individual factors of intelligence (The Psychological Corporation, 1972).

Today we still believe it is important to look at the different aspects of intelligence rather than general intelligence alone. From time to time, psychologists have attempted to distinguish academic from nonacademic intelligence, social from nonsocial (abstract) intelligence, and so on. (Many people who do very well when it comes to verbal reasoning may not be able to replace a fuse. Others can take one look at an automobile engine and tell what is wrong with it but are not able to make verbal analogies.) The factor analytic approach to intelligence has fostered the belief that we should be searching for different kinds of intelligence rather than one general intelligence.

Fluid and Crystallized Intelligence

Yet another entrant in the search for the structure of intelligence is the theory of fluid and crystallized intelligence proposed by Raymond Cattell. Cattell (1963) proposed that two forms of intelligence act to influence the primary mental abilities described by Thurstone. Cattell labeled the two forms fluid and crystallized. **Fluid intelligence** focuses on the individual's adaptability and capacity to perceive things and integrate them mentally. It appears to be independent of education and experience. For example, some individuals seem to intuitively think through problems with strategies they have never been taught. In comparison, schooling and environment are said to determine **crystallized intelligence,** which involves skills, abilities, and understanding. Instruction and observation are thought to enhance such skills. For example, an individual may learn how to play a particular game only after he or she has seen someone else do it or has been given instructions on how to proceed.

The Structure of Intellect

If Thurstone's seven primary mental abilities were not enough, consider that J. P. Guilford (1967) proposed 120 mental abilities, calling his perspective the **structure of intellect.** As shown in figure 9.3, the 120 mental abilities are made up of all the possible combinations of five operations, four contents, and six products (5 $\times$ 4 $\times$ 6 = 120).

Operations are intellectual activities or processes, that is, what one does with information. Guilford's five cognitive operations focus on cognition (such as discovery, recognition, and awareness), memory, divergent production (generation of many different ideas), convergent production (finding a single best answer), and evaluation. **Contents** can be figural (such as visual or spatial), symbolic (e.g., letters, numbers, or words), semantic (word meanings), or behavioral (nonverbal performance). **Products** index the form in which information occurs—units, classes, relations, systems,

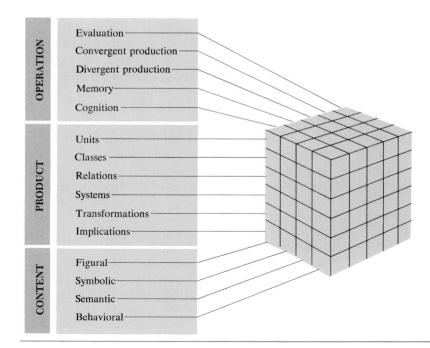

FIGURE 9.3
The three-dimensional structure of intellect proposed by J. P. Guilford (Guilford, 1967).

	CONCEPT TABLE 9.1 Traditional Theories, Definitions, and Measurements of Intelligence	
Theories/Measures	**Representatives/Examples**	**Characteristics/Explanations**
General	Binet	Emphasized assessment of general intelligence; conceived of intelligence as a general ability.
	Wechsler	While assessing intelligence at both general and specific levels, Wechsler defined intelligence as a general, global property of the person.
Specific	Spearman	Believed intelligence consists of a general and a specific factor.
	Thurstone	Argued that intelligence is made up of a number of specific primary mental abilities.
	Cattell	Suggested that there are basically two types of intelligence—fluid and crystallized.
	Guilford	Envisioned an intellect model of 120 mental abilities made up of all combinations of operations, contents, and products.
Measures	Stanford-Binet	Widely used intelligence test organized according to age levels; produces an IQ, a general index of intelligence. The 1985 edition also provides for an analysis of different aspects of intelligence.
	Wechsler scales	Another widely used set of intelligence measures; provides scores for overall intelligence, verbal and performance intelligence, and a number of specific aspects of intelligence.

transformations, or implications. The products dimension is hierarchical in that units combine into classes, classes form relations, relations comprise systems, and so on.

We have discussed a number of theories of intelligence and a number of measures that have been devised to assess intelligence. To help you remember some of the main points about such theories and measures, read Concept Table 9.1.

The Information-Processing Approach to Intelligence

We have already seen in chapter 7 that the information-processing perspective has become prominent in the study of children's cognition. Our treatment of information processing here focuses on how this perspective views intelligence. First, we examine the distinction between knowledge and process in intellectual development, then we discuss Robert Sternberg's componential analysis of intelligence.

Knowledge Versus Process in Intelligence

The information-processing approach raises two very important questions about intelligence: (1) What are the information-processing abilities that occur in development? and (2) What are the changes in world knowledge or "expertise" that occur in development?

Few would deny that both changes in processing and changes in knowledge occur in development. However, there is disagreement about which is more fundamental. For example, though there is accumulation of knowledge in childhood, this accumulation may simply be the consequence of a growing reserve of "processing capacity." That is, the older child's greater capacity may be what allows him or her to learn more sophisticated knowledge. Alternatively, though processing efficiency clearly goes up as children get older, perhaps this reflects older children's greater knowledge and the fact that greater knowledge allows more efficient information-processing activities. It has been difficult to decide between these two possibilities, creating what Frank Keil (1984) calls the structure/process dilemma of cognitive development. The dilemma concerns the basic issue of what the "mechanisms" of intellectual development are (Sternberg, 1984). Are they those of changing information-processing abilities? Are they those of changing knowledge and expertise? Or are they both?

To make the structure/process dilemma somewhat more concrete, consider a simple computer metaphor. Suppose that we have two computers and that each is capable of solving multiplication problems (e.g., 13×24, 45×21). However, one computer works much faster than the other. What could be the explanation? One possibility is that the "faster" computer

Sternberg ✓

truly is faster—it has faster subroutines for performing arithmetic computations, or more core (i.e., short-term memory), allowing two or more computations to proceed at once. Alternatively, the "faster" computer might have a greater store of relevant knowledge; perhaps it has in its data bank (long-term memory) a complete multiplication table going up to 99 × 99. The "slower" computer might be forced to get by (as do most humans) with a smaller table going up to only 12 × 12. In this case the "faster" computer need not be fundamentally faster—its subroutines may be relatively slow—but it is able to perform the multiplication task relying on knowledge instead of computation. The issue we face in the development of intelligence is similar to that of explaining the difference between the "fast" and "slow" computers. Is it processing or knowledge that is responsible for how intelligence changes with age? Based on some recent research on memory—reviewed in chapter 7—(Zembar & Naus, 1985), it seems likely that the answer may be both. If so, the essential task for researchers is to determine the ways that processing and knowledge interact in the course of intellectual development.

R. J. Sternberg's Componential Analysis

R. J. Sternberg (1982) has proposed that we might better understand intelligence if it were viewed in terms of information-processing components. His view, called **componential analysis,** attempts to understand the availability, accessibility, and ease of execution of a number of information-processing components. The basic concept in this approach is the **component,** an elementary information process that operates on internal representations of objects (Newell & Simon, 1972; Sternberg, 1977). A component may translate sensory input into conceptual representation, transform one conceptual representation into another, or translate conceptual representation into some form of motor output. Once again, in Sternberg's perspective we see the familiar model of receiving, processing, and reacting that initially was used to describe how the brain processes information (chapter 2). According to Sternberg, a component can be classified according to function (what it does) and level (whether it has a higher-level function in terms of planning and decision making or a lower-level, more precise function).

Sternberg has identified five such information-processing components, each performing a different function: metacomponents, performance, acquisition (or storage), retention (or retrieval), and transfer components.

R. J. Sternberg, whose information-processing view of intelligence has gained considerable recognition in recent years.

R.J. Sternberg — inform. process. compon.

1. **Metacomponents** are higher-order control processes used for executive planning and decision making when problem solving is called for. The decisions of which problem to solve and how to solve it are metacomponential decisions.
2. **Performance components** are processes used to carry out a problem-solving strategy. A set of performance components involves the actual working through of a problem.
3. **Acquisition (or storage) components** are processes used in learning new information. For example, this might involve rehearsing new information to transfer a trace of it into long-term memory.
4. **Retention (or retrieval) components** index processes involved in accessing previously stored information. For example, you might search through your long-term memory store in an organized manner to find a fact you need at a particular moment.
5. **Transfer components** are processes used in generalization, such as using information learned on one task to help solve another task. For example, having learned how to use a typewriter should expedite your ability to use a computer.

PERSPECTIVE ON CHILD DEVELOPMENT 9.1

THE MECHANICS OF VERBAL ABILITY

Earl Hunt and his colleagues (Hunt, 1978; Hunt, Frost, & Lunneborg, 1973; Hunt & Lansman, 1975) have described the mechanics of information processing that underlie performance on tests of verbal ability. Hunt (1978) says that tests of verbal ability reflect two kinds of processes: (1) those related to knowledge acquired through experience, and (2) pure mechanical processes whose operations are independent of the specific information that is processed. One such mechanical process is decoding. **Decoding** is the process in which an external stimulus activates overlearned information in long-term memory, such as when you have to retrieve the name of a familiar word after you have been given a printed word related to the familiar word.

The measure Hunt used to study decoding was devised by Michael Posner (1970). Two letters are flashed on a screen next to each other. The subject has to indicate as rapidly as possible whether the letters are the same or different. In the Hunt (1978) experiment, one condition involved giving the subjects instructions to respond "same" only if the two letters were physically identical to each other (such as AA). In the second condition, a name identity judgment was required in that the subjects were to respond "same" if the letters had the same name (AA or Aa). The college population that served as the subjects typically took about 75 to 80 milliseconds longer in the name identity than in the physical identity condition. Physical identity can be directly compared, but name identity requires decoding to determine the name of the two symbols.

Using the information-processing task of decoding, Hunt (1978) found differences between the name and physical identity reaction times of a number of groups,

How much do we need to sample behavior outside of IQ testing to get a true picture of the child's intelligence?

In addition to Sternberg's componential analysis, Earl Hunt (1978) has focused on describing the mechanics of information processing that might undergird performance on tests of verbal ability. More about Hunt's ideas on this matter appears in Perspective on Child Development 9.1.

The shift in interest to information processing and away from products as measured by intelligence tests does not mean that information-processing theorists are uninterested in products (Sternberg, 1982). Rather, these theorists are suggesting that attention should be given to the knowledge base generated by the processes.

Concept Table 9.2 provides a summary of the information-processing approach to intelligence. Our discussion of this approach suggests that traditional standardized IQ tests will require some revision before we can truly assess the construct of intelligence accurately. As we see in the next section, other proposals to revise the assessment of intelligence through standardized IQ tests have been made as well.

ranging from high-verbal university students to mentally retarded school children (see table at right). Of particular interest are the three university groups. The high-verbal group had scored in the top 25 percent of a standardized test of verbal ability, the low-verbal group in the bottom 25 percent, and the normal group in between. As can be seen, the low-verbal college students had longer decoding times than the high-verbal students. Hunt argues that the slower decoding times are due to slower activation of long-term memory, more precisely, the slower activation of correct names stored there. Though there is more to verbal ability than decoding, the evidence provided by Hunt suggests that decoding is one important component of verbal ability. Other research indicates that the ability to maintain ordered information in short-term memory for a brief time is also more evident in the way high-verbal students process information than the way low-verbal students do (Hunt, Lunneborg, & Lewis, 1975).

Verbal Ability and Decoding

Group	Difference Between Name Identity and Physical Identity (msec)
High-verbal university students	64
Normal university students	75–80
Low-verbal university students	89
Young adults not in a university	110
Severe epileptic adults	140
Adults past 60 years of age	170
10-year-old children	190
Mildly retarded schoolchildren	310

Average differences in response time between name identity and physical identity conditions in a letter-matching task for various groups of subjects.

From Hunt, Earl, "Mechanics of Verbal Ability," in *Psychological Review*, pp. 85, 109–130. Copyright 1978 by the American Psychological Association. Reprinted by permission.

CONCEPT TABLE 9.2
The Information-Processing Approach to Intelligence

Concept	Processes/Related Ideas	Characteristics/Description
Questions raised about intelligence by an information-processing approach	Knowledge/Process distinction	The information-processing approach raises the important question of whether the older child's greater capacity is due to more processing capacity and efficiency rather than just an accumulation of knowledge.
R. J. Sternberg's componential analysis	The nature of componential analysis	Componential analysis refers to attempts to understand intelligence by viewing it in terms of information-processing components. Availability, accessibility, and ease of execution of components are thought to be important.
	Components	A component is an elementary information process that operates on internal representations of objects. Sternberg has outlined five components: metacomponents, performance components, acquisition (or storage) components, retention (or retrieval) components, and transfer components.

ALTERNATIVES AND SUPPLEMENTS TO STANDARDIZED INTELLIGENCE TESTS

A number of psychologists either believe the standardized tests of intelligence do not do a good job of assessing intelligence and should be replaced or they argue that such tests only partially evaluate intelligence and should be supplemented by other measures. Initially we look at the concept of validity in intelligence testing and then describe two strategies designed to replace intelligence tests and two strategies to supplement them. We conclude with a final note about intelligence tests and a comparison of Piagetian and psychometric approaches.

Validity

Many of the critics of standardized intelligence tests believe the tests are not valid. **Validity** means that a measure should measure what it is intended to measure. Thus a test for anxiety should measure anxiety, a test for attention should measure attention, and a test for intelligence should measure intelligence. The validity problem is compounded by the fact that intelligence may be defined in different ways, as we have seen. Nonetheless, psychologists have set out to establish the validity of intelligence tests. One form of validity that has been given considerable attention in the domain of intelligence is **criterion validity.** To assess validity we have to measure intelligence and then relate that measure to some other measure. The second measure, or criterion, varies in how closely it is related to the first measure, in our case the intelligence test we have decided to study. It is not unusual for validity studies to include other tests of intelligence as the second or third measures to relate the first measure to. For example, a study might try to show how people's scores on the Stanford-Binet are positively related to the same people's scores on the Wechsler and the Primary Mental Abilities tests. In most instances, these measures are very positively correlated to each other. (This is not surprising because many of the items are similar from test to test.)

However, many psychologists have shown an interest in whether intelligence tests can accurately predict a criterion that is very different from the intelligence measure itself, such as grades in school, occupational success, ability to get along with people, creativity, and so forth. To make a long story short, intelligence tests are reasonably good at predicting grades in school (Stevenson, Hale, Klein & Miller, 1968) and not bad at predicting occupational success (Cronbach, 1970). There is much less evidence that they can predict the ability to get along with people or predict creativity, although intelligence and creativity are positively related (Richards, 1976).

Nonetheless, there have been a number of efforts to replace standardized intelligence tests with other measures and to develop additional tests that supplement the standardized tests.

Measures Designed to Replace Standardized Intelligence Tests

Two types of assessment have been devised to replace standardized intelligence tests: competence tests and culture-fair tests.

Testing for Competence

In an article called "Testing for Competence Rather Than for Intelligence," David McClelland (1973) argued that although intelligence tests do a reasonably good job of predicting school performance, they often do not fare as well in predicting occupational success. Most standardized intelligence tests are heavily weighted with verbal items, in particular those requiring verbal reasoning or knowledge. McClelland's argument is that such verbal reasoning and knowledge may not always be efficient at predicting how competent someone will be at a particular job. It has been found, for instance, that intelligence test scores predict performance more reliably for jobs requiring abstract, symbolic thinking than for jobs that are less dependent on these skills (Ghiselli, 1966). For example, they are better at predicting job success as a stockbroker, an occupation that requires the ability to make financial analyses and projections, than success as a police officer, an occupation that calls for extensive person-to-person contact and routine reports. Even for jobs requiring abstract, symbolic thought, however, IQ tests are not as reliable in predicting success as they are in predicting performance in school.

If we do not use intelligence tests to predict competence in an occupation, then what will we use? McClelland (1973) makes three recommendations. First, **criterion sampling** should be called on. If one wants to find out whether a senior graduating from high school can expect to be successful as a police officer, one would start by defining what a police officer does. Certainly one of the criteria would have to be communication skills and the type of vocabulary used by a

How might we test for the skills required to be a competent policeman?

police officer on the job. In criteria testing, then, the first step is to define the criteria for success at what you are trying to predict. Testers must rely less on paper-and-pencil measures, like IQ tests and abstract word games; instead, they should go out into the real world and watch what successful people do in specific occupations. For example, Jacob Kounin (1971) attempted to define the criteria for good teaching by going into classrooms and videotaping the performance of "good" and "bad" teachers.

The second recommendation McClelland makes is that tests should be designed to reflect changes in what the individual has learned. Intelligence tests have been designed to measure intellectual skills that were thought to be stable. In other words, if a person's scores on tests administered at different times and under approximately the same circumstances vary greatly, the tests are generally thought to be unreliable. McClelland believes that instead of developing tests that measure stability, we should be attempting to measure criteria that

reflect areas in which people can improve. For example, if it is found that teaching in elementary school requires a great deal of patience and highly developed communication skills, ways to measure these skills should be designed. It should be expected that individuals who initially do poorly on these criteria can improve and perform better on later tests.

This leads to McClelland's third recommendation for improving assessment: Ways to improve the characteristic tested should be made public and explicit. How to do well on important tests has often been viewed as a deep, dark secret. McClelland stresses that we should be as open as possible about the criteria that are evaluated by a test and state in a simple way how to improve on the test. Thus, if an important test measures reading comprehension and arithmetic skills, an individual should be aware of exactly how he or she is going to be tested, how to best prepare for the test, and how the test will be scored. Some tests follow this procedure, but many do not.

Most experts find merit in McClelland's recommendations, but some do not agree that intelligence testing should be eliminated completely. Intelligence tests are often efficient in predicting such significant outcomes as success in school subjects, different aspects of reading ability, and some aspects of job success. Again, however, it is important to remember that intelligence tests are invariably most effective when used in conjunction with the types of criterion testing McClelland recommends.

Culture-Fair Intelligence Tests

A second set of measures designed to replace traditional standardized intelligence tests are called **culture-fair tests.** These tests have been developed in an attempt to eliminate cultural bias. Recall our discussion of Larry P. in the prologue. It was argued that traditional standardized intelligence tests, such as the Binet and Wechsler scales, favor individuals from white, middle-class backgrounds more than individuals from lower-class, minority backgrounds. The argument is that the standardized tests are not culturally fair to the latter individuals because they have not had the same experience and exposure to information that the tests measure as have middle-class whites. For example, individuals with greater exposure to verbal knowledge and verbal reasoning are likely to perform better on such tests.

Two types of culture-fair tests have been developed. In the first, verbal items are removed (e.g., Raven, 1960). Figure 9.4 shows one kind of item on this type of test. However, while tests such as the Raven Progressive Matrices are designed to be culture-fair, there is evidence that individuals with more education do better on them than individuals with less education (Anastasi, 1976). A second type of culture-fair test focuses on the development of items that are familiar to people from all socioeconomic and ethnic backgrounds, or items that are at least familiar to the people who are taking the test. For example, a child might be asked how a bird and a dog are different—on the assumption that virtually all children have had exposure to birds and dogs.

In the United States particular concern has been voiced about the lack of intelligence tests that are culturally fair to blacks. The Dove Counterbalance General Intelligence Test (see table 9.2), sometimes referred to as the Chitling Test, was developed by a black sociologist, Adrian Dove, as a sarcastic rejoinder to the middle-class bias of most intelligence tests. Dove's test

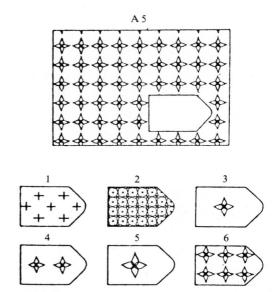

FIGURE 9.4
Sample item from the Raven Progressive Matrices Test. The individual is presented with a matrix arrangement of symbols, such as the one at the top of this figure, and must then complete the matrix by selecting the appropriate missing symbol from a group of symbols (J. C. Raven Limited).

was not presented as a serious effort to develop a culture-free test for blacks; it was designed to illustrate how the language used by many blacks differs from that of middle-class whites.

The Kaufman Assessment Battery for Children (K-ABC) has been promoted as an improvement over past culture-fair tests (Kaufman & Kaufman, 1983). It can be administered to children aged two and a half to twelve and a half. This test has been standardized on a more representative sample than most tests, including more minority and handicapped children. The intelligence portion of the test focuses less on language than the Stanford-Binet, and the test includes an achievement section involving such subtests as arithmetic and reading. Nevertheless, like other culture-fair intelligence tests, the K-ABC test has already found some detractors (Bracken, 1985; Keith, 1985).

Although the development of culture-fair tests has served to remind us that cultural bias exists in intelligence testing, the available culture-fair tests have not provided a satisfactory alternative. Crafting a truly culture-fair test, one that rules out the role of experiences resulting from socioeconomic and ethnic background, not only has been elusive, but it may be impossible.

TABLE 9.2
The Chitling Intelligence Test

1. A "gas head" is a person who has a:
   (a) fast-moving car
   (b) stable of "lace"
   (c) "process"
   (d) habit of stealing cars
   (e) long jail record for arson

2. "Bo Diddley" is a:
   (a) game for children
   (b) down-home cheap wine
   (c) down-home singer
   (d) new dance
   (e) Moejoe call

3. If a pimp is uptight with a woman who gets state aid, what does he mean when he talks about "Mother's day"?
   (a) second Sunday in May
   (b) third Sunday in June
   (c) first of every month
   (d) none of these
   (e) first and fifteenth of every month

4. A "handkerchief head" is
   (a) a cool cat
   (b) a porter
   (c) an Uncle Tom
   (d) a hoddi
   (e) a preacher

5. If a man is called a "blood," then he is a:
   (a) fighter
   (b) Mexican-American
   (c) Negro
   (d) hungry hemophile
   (e) red man, or Indian

6. Cheap chitlings (not the kind you purchase at a frozen-food counter) will taste rubbery unless they are cooked long enough. How soon can you quit cooking them to eat and enjoy them?
   (a) forty-five minutes
   (b) two hours
   (c) twenty-four hours
   (d) one week (on a low flame)
   (e) one hour

Answers: 1. c 2. c 3. e 4. c 5. c 6. c

Measures Designed to Supplement Standardized Intelligence Tests

Other measures have been developed to supplement standardized intelligence tests rather than replace them. Two such efforts focus on social intelligence and creativity. We now look at an attempt to measure social intelligence; and later in the chapter we discuss creativity when we study special cases of intelligence.

Social Intelligence

Life is more than solving verbal and numerical problems; we also need to get along with people. Thus some psychologists believe that intelligence should be construed to involve interpersonal skills as well. Jane Mercer (e.g., Mercer & Lewis, 1978) has put together

What is social intelligence?

a battery of measures she believes provides a more complete assessment of intelligence than a single traditional intelligence test. Her battery of tests is called **SOMPA,** which stands for System of Multicultural Pluralistic Assessment. It can be given to children from five to eleven years of age. SOMPA was particularly designed for use with children from an impoverished background. Instead of relying on a single test, SOMPA includes information about the child's intellectual functioning in four main areas: (1) verbal and nonverbal intelligence in the traditional intelligence test vein, assessed by the WISC-R; (2) social and economic background of family, obtained via a one-hour parental interview; (3) social adjustment to school, evaluated by an adaptive behavior inventory filled out by parents; and (4) physical health, ascertained by a medical examination. Thus Mercer hopes to obtain a more complete picture of the experiences and environmental background of the child than would be possible from giving the WISC-R alone. She also shows a concern for assessing the child's health, which might interfere with intellectual performance.

A Final Note about Intelligence Tests

Although intelligence tests have been widely criticized, they are still used pervasively in our society. At some point in your life you have had or may have some experience with intelligence tests, perhaps in elementary school or as part of a battery of tests for prospective employment. A child of yours may be given some type of intelligence test. If you become a teacher, you may receive reports from school psychologists telling you about your students' performances on the WISC-R or the Stanford-Binet. As a teacher or counselor, you may even administer intelligence tests.

Because intelligence tests are so widely used and misused, we have chosen to present extensive information about different kinds of intelligence tests. Authors of other child development texts do not present much information of this sort; they prefer to rely almost exclusively on Piaget's theories and the cognitive-developmental emphasis on qualitative changes in intelligence. Indeed, many Piagetians are among the most vocal critics of the use of IQ tests to measure intelligence. We now explore the similarities and differences between Piaget's view and the views presented so far in this chapter.

Comparison of Piagetian and Psychometric Approaches to Intelligence

By now you probably have guessed that Piaget's views about intelligence differ from the views of Binet, Wechsler, and Thurstone. The approach of the latter views is called the **psychometric approach,** referring to an emphasis on measurement-based tests. A professional who administers tests is sometimes referred to as a psychometrist, or psychometrician. Although there are differences, however, there are similarities as well. David Elkind (1969) has described some of these similarities and differences, which are discussed briefly here.

Piaget began his career as a developmental psychologist by working in Binet's laboratory, but he was more intrigued by the errors children made on the tests than by their correct answers. Piaget and the psychometricians agree that intelligence has a genetic component and that the maturation of thought processes is critical to understanding intelligence. The two views also agree that the most important aspect of intelligence is reasoning.

The most obvious difference between Piaget and the psychometric theorists lies in their views on the course of mental growth. The psychometric theorists are interested in quantifying mental growth, which often produces a number to describe the person's general level of intellectual functioning and to predict intelligence from one age to other ages, since it is argued that IQ is reasonably stable. The psychometric approach, then, maximizes individual differences and seeks to measure them. The Piagetian approach essentially ignores individual differences. Piaget emphasized the dynamic nature of intelligence and how it qualitatively changes. He was particularly concerned with how new cognitive structures emerge.

Despite Piaget's disinterest in individual differences, you might well wonder whether it is possible to construct a test of intelligence based on Piagetian tasks. Indeed, Lloyd Humphreys and his colleagues (Humphreys, Rich & Davey, 1985) have constructed such a test and have assessed its relation to the Wechsler verbal and performance intelligence scales. Their Piagetian Test of General Intelligence includes such problems as conservation of volume, classification, and changing perspectives, and it provides a score that correlates quite highly with both the Wechsler verbal and performance components (r's = .76 and .80, respectively). This finding indicates that the psychometric and Piagetian approaches might be fruitfully combined.

Another difference between the two approaches is evident in a comparison of their views on genetics. While both approaches stress the importance of genes in determining intelligence, the psychometric theorists are interested in differences across individuals—for example, they are very interested in how scores from a random sample of 5,000 children fall into place on a distribution of scores. Piagetians, on the other hand, focus more on changes within the individual that shape the organization of intelligence—for example, they are interested in how egocentrism constrains the way the preschool child organizes information about the world.

In this comparison of Piaget and the psychometric approach, we have stressed the fact that the psychometric approach emphasizes the utility of IQ in predicting intelligence at a later point in development. Earlier we also mentioned that the first intelligence tests were designed to predict whether a child would benefit from education. Now we consider whether IQ tests are accurate predictors of school performance and how stable intelligence is over a period of time.

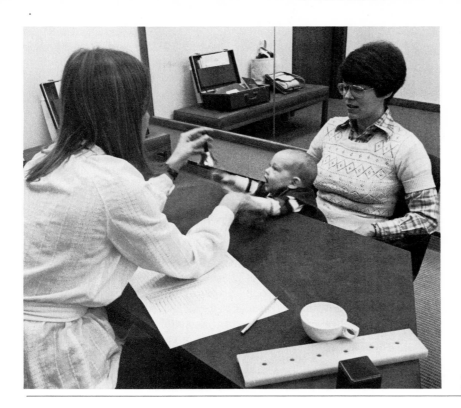

The Bayley Mental and Motor Scales being administered by a psychologist to a six-month-old infant.

INFANT INTELLIGENCE AND THE STABILITY OF INTELLIGENCE THROUGH DIFFERENT PERIODS OF DEVELOPMENT

Many of the standardized intelligence tests we have discussed so far do not assess infant intelligence. Intelligence tests that have been created for infants are often referred to as **developmental scales.** Let's now look at such infant intelligence tests and then chart the degree to which intelligence is stable through different time periods of development.

Infant Intelligence Tests

It is advantageous to know whether an infant is advancing at a slow, normal, or fast rate of cognitive development. If the infant is advancing at a particularly slow rate, for example, environmental enrichment may be called for. If an infant is progressing at an advanced rate, parents may be advised to provide toys that are designed to stimulate cognitive development in slightly older infants.

One of the most widely used developmental scales is the Bayley Mental and Motor Scales, consisting of a series of items to measure mental skills and to evaluate motor skills. The components of the Bayley Mental Scale were designed to measure the infant's adaptive responses to the environment. They include attention to visual and auditory stimuli; grasping, manipulating, and combining objects; shaking a rattle; and ringing a bell. Items that measure the infant's social and cognitive skills also are included: smiling, cooing, babbling, imitating, and following directions. Showing memory and being aware of object constancy (looking for a hidden toy) are part of the Bayley Mental Scale, as is beginning to understand language. The language items include following directions that involve the use of object names, prepositions, and the concept of "one." The Bayley Motor Scale tests the infant's ability to hold up his or her head, turn over, sit, creep, stand, walk, and go up and down stairs. It also tests manual skills, such as grasping small objects and throwing a ball

(Bayley, 1970). According to the Bayley scales, at approximately six months of age the average baby should be able to (Kessen, Haith & Salapatek, 1970):

1. accept a second cube—baby holds first cube, while examiner takes second cube and places it within easy reach of the infant;
2. grasp the edge of a piece of paper when it is presented;
3. vocalize pleasure and displeasure;
4. persistently reach for objects placed just out of immediate reach;
5. turn his or her head after a spoon the experimenter suddenly drops on the floor; and
6. approach a mirror when the examiner places it in front of the infant.

At approximately twelve months of age the average baby should be able to

1. inhibit behavior when commanded to do so; for example, when the infant puts a block in his or her mouth and the examiner says, "no, no," then the infant should cease the activity;
2. repeat an action if he or she is laughed at;
3. imitate words the experimenter says, like "mama," and "dada";
4. imitate actions of the experimenter: for example, if the experimenter rattles a spoon in a cup, then the infant should imitate this action;
5. respond to simple requests, such as "take a drink."

The Stability of Intelligence

In one study conducted by Nancy Bayley, the developer of the Bayley scales, no relation was found between the scales and intelligence as measured by the Stanford-Binet at the ages of six and seven (Bayley, 1943). Another investigation found correlations of only .01 between intelligence measured at three months and intelligence measured at five years of age, and .05 between measurement at one year and measurement at five years (Anderson, 1939). These findings indicate virtually no relationship between infant development scales and intelligence at five years of age. Again, it should be remembered that one of the reasons for this finding is that the components of intelligence tested in infancy are not the same as the components of intelligence tested at the age of five.

Let's look at an example of the absence of a relation between intelligence in infancy and intelligence in later years for two children in the same family. The first child learned to speak at a very early age. She displayed the characteristics of an extravert, and her advanced motor coordination was indicated by her ability to walk at a very early age. The second child learned speech very late, saying very few words until she was two and one-half years old.

Both children were given standardized tests of intelligence during infancy and then later, during the elementary school years. In the earlier test the first child's scores were higher than her sister's. In the later test their scores were reversed. What are some of the possible reasons for the reversal in the IQ scores of the two girls? When the second child did begin to speak, she did so prolifically, and the complexity of her language increased rapidly, undoubtedly as a result of her biological readiness to talk. Her sensorimotor coordination had never been as competent as the first child's, perhaps also accounting in part for her lower scores on the infant intelligence tests. The parents recognized that they had initially given the first child extensive amounts of their time. They were not able to give the second child as much of their time as they had the first, but when the second child was about three years old, they made every opportunity to involve her in physical and academic activities. They put her in a Montessori preschool program, gave her dancing and swimming lessons, and frequently invited other children of her age in to play with her. There may have been other reasons as well for the changes in scores, but these do serve to demonstrate that infant intelligence tests may not be good predictors of intelligence in later years. However, as discussed in Perspective on Child Development 9.2, aspects of the infant's behavior other than performance on infant IQ tests may be linked to later intelligence.

Can you predict what a child's IQ will be when she is ten or eighteen years old from her scores on an IQ test administered when she is two, three, and four years old? IQ tests still do not provide very reliable predictions of this sort. Based on statistical techniques, IQ scores obtained at two and three years of age are related to the IQ scores of the same individuals even at ten and eighteen years, although they are not very strongly related. IQ scores obtained at the age of four are much better at predicting IQ at the age of ten than at the age of eighteen (Honzik, MacFarlane & Allen, 1948).

PERSPECTIVE ON CHILD DEVELOPMENT 9.2

RESPONSE TO NOVEL STIMULATION IN INFANCY AND INTELLIGENCE AT FIVE TO SIX YEARS OF AGE

I n contrast to the poor predictive power of infant IQ tests, other aspects of infants' behavior are linked to intelligence at five and six years of age. Specifically, a number of recent studies have suggested that an infant's response to novel stimulation—what we have referred to as dishabituation (chapter 4)—is significantly correlated with later IQ. One impressive study by Susan Rose and Ina Wallace (1985) assessed the amount of time that six-month-old infants spent looking at novel versus previously viewed visual stimuli. "Novelty scores," which measured the preference for viewing novel stimuli, predicted WISC-R IQ scores at six years of age ($r = .56$). Infant preferences for novel auditory stimuli are similarly predictive of later IQ. Mary O'Connor, Sarale Cohen, and Arthur Parmelee (1984) found that four-month-old infants' cardiac (heart rate) responses to repetitive versus novel sounds predicted Stanford-Binet IQ at five years ($r = .60$). These findings are provocative in supporting the claim that the nature of intelligence—if measured appropriately—is fundamentally continuous from infancy through childhood (Fagan, 1985). They also suggest that intelligence may be conceptualized as including the component of responsiveness to novelty (Berg & Sternberg, 1985), not only in infancy but in childhood as well (Marr & Sternberg, 1985). Although some loose ends remain in the data on novelty–intelligence associations (McCall, 1985), the emerging findings promise some important new insights on the emergence and development of intelligence.

The intelligence of these children at age six is related to their response to novel stimulation (dishabituation) when they were infants.

There is a strong relation between IQ scores obtained at the ages of six, eight, and nine and IQ scores obtained at the age of ten. For example, in one study the correlation between IQ at the age of eight and IQ at the age of ten was .88. The correlation between IQ at the age of nine and IQ at the age of ten was .90. These figures show a very high relation between IQ scores obtained in these years. The correlation of IQ in the preadolescent years and IQ at the age of eighteen

is slightly less, but still statistically significant. For example, the correlation between IQ at the age of ten and IQ at the age of eighteen was .70 in one study (Honzik et al., 1948).

What has been said so far about the stability of intelligence has been based on measures of groups of individuals. The stability of intelligence also can be evaluated through studies of individual persons. As we see next, there can be considerable variability in an individual's scores on IQ tests.

Patterns of Change in Intellectual Growth

Robert McCall and his associates (McCall, Applebaum & Hogarty, 1973) studied 140 individuals and found that between two and one-half and seventeen years of age the average range of IQ scores was more than 28 points. The scores of one out of three children changed by as much as 30 points, and one out of seven by as much as 40 points. When individuals are assessed over long periods of time, their scores on intelligence tests often fluctuate considerably. Some experts also point out that while intelligence tests (and virtually all psychological tests) were designed to measure stable attributes of the individual, data like those collected by McCall indicate that intelligence is not as stable as the original theories of intelligence had predicted.

We have described the course of the development of intelligence and the many different ways it can be measured. But so far we have said little about what influences the development of intelligence. We barely touched on this issue in mentioning different definitions of intelligence, some of which emphasize the innate basis of intelligence, others of which focus on its experiential base. We also described the cultural bias involved in testing intelligence. When intelligence tests are given, it generally is hoped that environmental influences will be minimized or eliminated. The tests were designed to be stable measures of intelligence; the more the environment influences test scores and the more inconsistent a person's scores are over a period of time, the less reliable the tests are as indicators of intelligence. Some genetic influences on intelligence were presented in chapter 2. The ideas presented there are important for you to remember. You may want to review them in detail before reading the next section, which focuses on influences on intelligence.

INFLUENCES ON INTELLIGENCE

Is intelligence due mainly to heredity or mainly to environment? The answer, of course, is that neither heredity nor environment acts alone; they interact to affect intelligence. The nature of this interaction is complex, and experts point out that unfortunately little is known about the specific input of genetics to intelligence (Scarr & Kidd, 1983). What is known, however, does suggest that heredity cannot be ignored as an important influence on intelligence.

Genetic Influences on Intelligence

What is the influence of heredity in the broad range of normal and superior intelligence? Arthur Jensen (1969) examined the research literature that addresses this question. The most compelling information concerns the similarity of IQ for individuals who vary on a dimension of genetic similarity. If hereditary variation among people contributes to differences in IQ, then individuals who have very similar genetic endowments should have very similar IQs, whereas individuals with very different endowments should have very different IQs. Identical twins have identical genetic endowments, so their IQs should be very similar. Nonidentical (fraternal) twins and ordinary siblings are less similar genetically and so should have less similar IQs. Children from different parents are the least similar genetically and should have the least similar IQs. If relevant groups existed in each of these categories, the correlation based on pairs of children should be high for identical twins, lower for fraternal twins and ordinary siblings, and lowest for unrelated children. The graph in figure 9.5 illustrates these correlations.

For each kind of group, Jensen was able to find some studies in which each member of the pair was reared in the same environment. These studies permit us to see how significant the environmental variation is in contributing to IQ variation at the same time. As figure 9.5 demonstrates, the differences in correlation levels are generally greater for genetic differences than for environmental differences. For example, studies with identical twins produced an average correlation of about .82, if information on twins reared together and information on twins reared separately are combined. Studies of ordinary siblings revealed an average correlation of .50, again combining data about those reared together with data about those reared separately. The difference in correlations is .32. The environmental contrast with twins, however, yields a difference of about .11 (twins reared together: .89; separately: .78) and with ordinary siblings, a difference of about .10 (siblings reared together: .55; separately: .45). So genetic differences seem to produce larger IQ variation than environmental differences do. Based on this kind of evidence and some complex calculations, Jensen places the heritability quotient at about .80 for intelligence. However, it must be noted that many scholars criticize Jensen's work, and few accept his estimate without qualification.

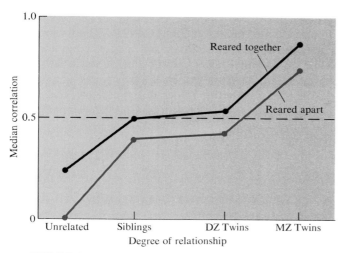

FIGURE 9.5
The influence of environmental similarity and biological relatedness on the similarity of IQ (Jensen, 1969).

now deceased) apparently fabricated the results that he reported in a classic study of IQ in twins (Burt, 1966).

Despite these criticisms of Jensen's work, more recent studies are adding to the evidence for a genetic contribution to IQ. Indeed, one recent study comparing identical and fraternal twins suggested that genetic factors contribute not only to general IQ but to the profile of specific abilities measured by the WISC-R. That is, the patterning of specific abilities, as well as the overall level of intelligence, may be genetically influenced (Segal, 1985).

Although there is indeed strong evidence for the heritability of IQ, there are also strong doubts that the actual figure is as high as Jensen claims. A more accurate estimate can be made only on the basis of future evidence that accepts a broader definition of intelligence, compares significantly dissimilar environments, and clarifies some of the technical problems with existing research literature.

Since heritability is an incomplete explanation of IQ, we have to look at environmental factors that can have influence on intelligence. In the next section we will explore in detail some of the most important environmental influences that interact with heredity to affect the child's intelligence.

Perhaps most important is the very definition of intelligence. Standard IQ tests tap a very narrow range of intellectual functioning, most of it based on specific things learned at school and at home. There are many facets of mental life related to everyday problem solving, work performance, and social adaptability that are not covered in IQ tests; at best, the genetic arguments apply only to a limited part of mental life (Kamin, 1974).

Second, there are substantive disagreements on just how much variation can be fairly attributed to the environment. Some critics claim that most heritability studies have not included environments that differ from one another in radical ways so it is not surprising that results support the interpretation that environment contributes little to variation. If studies were to include environments that differ significantly from one another, then greater variation would be attributable to the environment (Bronfenbrenner, 1972; Scarr & Weinberg, 1976).

A third argument is a somewhat technical one. Leon Kamin (1974) claims that much of the original evidence reviewed by Jensen is itself flawed. There are apparent errors in the reporting of results in research reports, flaws in the designs of studies, and inappropriate statistical procedures. Also, it has been learned that a world-renowned British psychologist (C. Burt,

Environmental Influences on Intelligence

The important environmental influences on intelligence include experiences at home, the effects of being institutionalized, school experiences, culture, race, and social class.

Home

Families influence their children's intellectual development both genetically and environmentally; untangling these two sources of influence is a formidable task. While we do not know how much of the variance in intellectual development is due to enriched surroundings provided by parents, family structure, and other environmental factors, we do know that these factors are significant. Recent efforts have focused on intervention with parents of children with low IQs to see whether working with the parents as well as the child can advance the child's intelligence. Other work has evaluated the influence of the size of the family and sibling order on the child's intelligence.

Parent–Child Development Centers The U.S. Office of Child Development has created what are called parent–child development centers in different parts of the United States. These centers have been developed to provide lower-class parents with information and insight into the processes of early child development. Three of the centers are the New Orleans Model (Andrews, Blumenthal, Bache & Weiner, 1975), the Birmingham Model (Lasater, Briggs, Malone, Gilliom & Weisburg, 1975), and the Houston Model (Leler, Johnson, Kahn, Hines & Torres, 1975). The projects assume that it is first necessary to change the mother's behavior and then after a time lag to see whether changes occur in the young child's behavior. For more details about the nature of one of the projects, that in New Orleans, read Perspective on Child Development 9.3.

PERSPECTIVE ON CHILD DEVELOPMENT 9.3

THE NEW ORLEANS PROJECT

For the New Orleans program, mothers and children were from low-income black families living in the central-city area. The program started when the infants were two months old and lasted until they were three years old. Two different models of parent education were tested: the *center-based model* and the *home-visit model*.

In the center-based model, mothers and their children came to the center two mornings a week for three hours. The basic format consisted of a small group discussion between a paraprofessional educator and the mothers. In the home-visit model, a paraprofessional educator from the center went to a participant's home twice a week for one and one-half hours, and the format was a one-to-one session between the paraprofessional educator and the mother. The paraprofessionals were women recruited from the community in which the program was conducted; they were not professional educators or college students. These two groups of mothers and their children were compared with a control group of mothers and children who did not participate in the center-based or home-visit program.

In the sessions with the mothers, information was presented that it was thought they needed to know to advance their child's development. To see whether the mothers and children were changing as a consequence of the sessions, they were observed in an unstructured waiting-room situation every six months. The criteria for evaluation reflect the content of the center-based and home-visit models. The table opposite indicates the aspects of positive and negative mothering considered by the program.

After all interactions between mother and child were coded, the mother's behavior was scored on a nine-point scale for insensitivity-sensitivity, rejection-acceptance, interference-cooperation, responsiveness, and verbal richness.

The children also were tested and observed periodically from two months to three years of age. An attempt was made to evaluate the child's competence by using many different measures of the child's intellectual functioning. The center used a very good individual measure of intelligence, the Stanford-Binet, but it employed many other measures as well. These included the Bayley Scales of Infant Development and other tests that involved measures of matching forms and colors, completing pictures, completing forms, a picture vocabulary test, a grammar test, and a test of familiarity with concepts.

The mother's behavior was observed in unstructured situations to see whether it actually was her behavior that produced changes in the young child's behavior. If the program was effective, differences in the mother's or the child's behavior would not be expected until late in the program.

The effects that were hoped for were demonstrated by the center-based model but not by the home-visit model. There were virtually no differences in the behaviors of mothers or children at the various measurement points throughout the home-visit model.

In the center-based model, the mother's competence in parenting was not changed when her child was four months old or twelve months old, but it was changed when the child was twenty-one and thirty-six months old. For example, when the children were three years old, the center-based mothers were more sensitive, accepting, cooperative, and responsive, and their

Not only have there been attempts to show that children's intelligence can be advanced by providing enrichment to the children and their mothers, but so too have there been efforts to document a relation between the family structure children are born into and their intelligence. Such studies focus on comparisons of children's intelligence in father-absent and father-present homes, on children growing up in small and large families, and on age spacing between siblings.

Family Structure, Family Size, and Sibling Order

Researchers have studied how various aspects of family structure influence the child's intelligence: whether the child lives in a single-parent or intact family, whether the child grows up in a large or a small family, and the child's location in sibling configuration. For example, children from father-absent families often score lower on IQ tests than children from intact families (Santrock, 1972), children from large families generally

Mother–Child Interaction Variables
(New Orleans Model)

Positive maternal techniques	Active participation in the child's activity	**Initiation of activity**	Activity initiated by the mother
			Activity initiated by the child
	General conversation with the child; includes labeling and giving information	**Child's use of language**	Number of units in which the child speaks
	Facilitation of the child's activity	**Mother's positive uses of language**	Elaboration or extension
	Positive control; includes giving suggestions and positive commands		Praise
			General conversation
			Positive verbal control
	Giving affection and praise		Asking the child a question
	Asking the child a question	**Mother's negative uses of language**	Correction
Negative maternal techniques	Negative nonverbal control of the child		Criticism
			Restriction, or negative control
	Negative nonphysical control of the child	**Mother's verbal behavior**	Number of units in which the mother addresses the child
	Negative reinforcement of the child or of the child's activity	**Maternal encouragement**	Scored if the mother actively encourages the child during the unit
	Ignoring a specific bid for attention by the child		

language was richer and more elaborate than was true of a group of control mothers. They encouraged more activities initiated by their children and used more positive techniques in their social interaction with them than the control-group mothers did. For example, they participated more actively in their children's activities; gave them more information; and were more positive in their use of control, affection, and praise.

What was the course of change in the child's competence? At two years of age there were no major changes, but at three years the children in the center-based group were more advanced on a number of items reflecting competence, such as matching forms and colors, completing patterns, completing forms, and completing pictures. Positive changes in the mother's behavior preceded positive changes in the child's competence. It is important to note that these changes occurred only when the training of the mothers took place in group settings. The enjoyment and friendship that evolved in these groups may be important social supports for developing new and better techniques for rearing children.

perform more poorly on intelligence tests than their counterparts from small families (Marjoribanks, Walberg & Bargen, 1975), and firstborn siblings often have higher IQs than siblings born later (Zajonc & Markus, 1975).

Some of the most provocative comments about such family configurations have been set forth by Robert Zajonc (Zajonc, Markus & Markus, 1979). Zajonc believes the child's intelligence depends on the average intelligence of all family members, including the child himself or herself. Zajonc would explain the finding that firstborn siblings have higher IQs than siblings born later by arguing that the firstborns are initially exposed only to adults, who have an intellectual level that is high. By contrast, a child born later may experience a lower intellectual atmosphere because she or he has to interact with parents and an intellectually inferior (to the parents) older sibling. With additional children, the family's intellectual climate weakens, according to Zajonc.

While Zajonc's proposal is intriguing, researchers have not always been able to find support for his beliefs (Rodgers, 1984). For example, one argument set forth by Zajonc is that when two siblings are spaced relatively far apart the configuration should be advantageous to both siblings. Why? Zajonc argues that the older sibling has spent more time alone with parents, and the younger sibling is interacting with an intellectually more mature individual in the form of the older sibling. Nonetheless, recent research investigations have failed to confirm the age-spacing argument (Brackbill & Nichols, 1982; Gailbraith, 1982).

We should note that while father absence, sibling order, and family size probably have some influence on intellectual functioning, it appears that the effects are not large. What is probably more important is the quality of the interaction among family members. Being born into a specific family structure does predispose the child to certain kinds of experiences, but many child developmentalists believe the quality of interaction among family members, regardless of family structure, is the most important consideration in the family's influence on children's intelligence.

Much earlier than the interest in providing stimulating environments for lower-class, impoverished children, such as in the New Orleans and Milwaukee projects, there was curiosity about the effects of institutionalization on children's intelligence (e.g., Spitz,

1945). The institutionalization studies are perhaps the most widely cited examples of the negative influence an impoverished environment can have on a child's intelligence.

Institutionalization

In one widely quoted study, Harold Skeels (1966) removed children from an unstimulating orphanage and placed them in an institution where they received individual attention. The change in institutions significantly raised their level of intellectual functioning. In the Skeels study children were assigned an "adoptive mother"—an older, mentally retarded girl—who was given the responsibility of caring for them. At the end of two and one-half years, the children with the mentally retarded "mother" showed an average gain of 32 points in IQ; the children who remained in the inferior institution dropped an average of 21 points in IQ.

Many studies of **institutionalization** have been criticized heavily on methodological grounds. For example, some of the early studies (e.g., Spitz, 1945) interpreted the negative effects on institutionalization in terms of the lack of mother love. Studies of institutionalization, however, do not provide accurate tests of the intrinsic importance of the mother or the family in the child's development. Multiple mothering in the institution, separation from the mother, and such distortions in mothering as rejection and overprotection are possible explanations for the observed effects of institutionalization (Yarrow, 1964).

The following study of institutionalization and children's intelligence illustrates the importance of the quality of caretaker's responsiveness in the child's social and cognitive development. The program also demonstrates how elderly people can be included in programs that attempt to help children.

Rosalyn Saltz (1973) evaluated two institutions described as good institutions (unlike those experienced by many orphaned children). The children were receiving extensive physical and perceptual stimulation at both. At one institution foster-grandparents were recruited to work part-time, giving their personal attention to the children. Forty-eight children, sixteen months to six years of age, were seen by the foster-grandparents for periods of up to four years. Each foster-grandparent was assigned to two children and worked with them four hours a day, five days a week. The type of interaction varied according to the age of

Quality of interaction in families is more important than family structure in predicting children's intelligence.

the children but always included pronounced affectional interchanges. Activities included rocking, eating (or feeding), taking walks, and playing games.

The results were impressive. Children in the foster-grandparent program had significantly higher IQ scores than the children in the other "good" institution, who were not in the foster-grandparent program. Furthermore, the children who were in the foster-grandparent program the longest showed the greatest gains, and average intellectual progress persisted for long periods of time. Finally, the effects were not confined to the children. The foster-grandparents also showed increases in self-esteem as a consequence of being able to work with institutionalized children. Prolonged social interaction, then, usually leads to changes in the behavior of the people involved. Saltz's study (1973) substantiates the theory that positive social experiences can modify intelligence. It is also an excellent example of how people who need others can help one another.

Descriptions of several institutions in the Soviet Union by Yvonne Brackbill (1962) and Urie Bronfenbrenner (1970) further support the belief that qualitative aspects of institutional care are important in

determining whether the child will show intellectual deficits. Where nurses give considerable individual attention to the infants and provide them with many visual-motor opportunities and where toddlers are trained to become self-reliant and to engage in appropriate peer interaction, institutionalized children show normal intellectual and personality patterns.

Children not only spend large chunks of their time at home, or in the case of the children just mentioned in an institution, but schooling also takes up a large portion of most American children's days. Psychologists and educators have been interested in whether the quality of schooling affects children's intelligence.

School

One of the most profound statements about the impact of schools on children's performance was made by James Coleman in *Equality of Educational Opportunity* (Coleman, Campbell, Hobson, et al., 1966). He stressed that variations in the quality of American schools do not account for variations in children's performance. This does not mean that individual schools cannot raise a child's intellectual performance. What it does mean is that in the Coleman report (1966) it could not be statistically proved that the type of schooling the average American child experiences has anything to do with his scores on measures of achievement. Several interpretations of these data are possible: (1) The quality of American schools is very high; thus, the quality of schooling would be expected not to vary much. (2) The quality of American schooling is uniformly low; this also assumes that the quality of schooling does not vary much. (3) The Coleman report was not a good study of the quality of schooling and had a number of faults. Which of these interpretations is chosen is a matter of taste (Hernstein, 1973). The Coleman report, however, did not prove that quality of schooling is unimportant to how well the child performs in school and on measures of intellectual functioning.

The Coleman report contradicts the belief that special educational programs can have a widespread effect in raising the intellectual level of disadvantaged children. Project Head Start and Project Follow Through (which are discussed in greater detail in chapter 12) are two programs that have attempted to raise the intelligence of disadvantaged children. The type of educational program they use to increase the IQs of disadvantaged children often varies greatly from school to school. Some programs have had considerable success in raising IQs through intervention in the preschool years. Other programs have intervened in infancy. Some of the programs have lasted only for several months, while others have been carried on into the elementary years.

Long-term follow-ups of compensatory education are revealing that such early interventions probably have long-term positive effects on children's intelligence (Collins, 1983; Lazar & Darlington, 1982). One evaluation of eleven early intervention programs initiated in the 1960s with disadvantaged preschool children involved the assessment of children at regular intervals during the elementary school years (Lazar & Darlington, 1982). School records were evaluated and IQ and achievement tests were given to the children. In addition, the children as well as their mothers were interviewed regarding such matters as self-worth, achievement aspirations, and attitudes toward school. A summary of the results from these long-term followups of compensatory education suggests that the early interventions do have long-term positive consequences for the children. For example, children participating in the compensatory education programs tend to perform better on achievement tests in math and reading than nonparticipants. Program participants are less likely to be placed in special education classes than nonparticipants and are also less likely to be held back a year in school. When asked to point out something that has made them proud of themselves, program children are more likely than nonprogram children to mention their school-related accomplishments.

In addition to family and school, the cultural and social contexts in which a child is reared influence his or her intelligence. In the next section we describe these influences by discussing cultural bias in testing, racial similarities and dissimilarities, and social class.

Culture, Race, and Social Class
Some experts believe it is virtually impossible to eliminate cultural bias in testing intelligence, even were it possible to develop a truly culture-free or culture-fair test.

Cultural Expectations in Intelligence Testing For one thing, the experiences of children taking intelligence tests vary extensively. For another, Japanese, Mexicans, Indians, and children of other ethnic groups are often given intelligence tests that have been developed—and usually administered—by middle-class Americans. Robert Thorndike, however, believes that cultural bias has been overstated in some cases. He points out that questions reflecting cultural bias are usually discovered when a subcultural group consistently performs more poorly than members of the majority culture. But if the test is "used to assess or predict accomplishments within the majority culture, there is a possibility that there are real and important differences in experience that result in lower scores for members of subcultural groups" (Thorndike, 1975, pp. 124–125).

Knowing different facts about a child may influence the way a child is treated. Let's say, for example, that you are a teacher and are in the teacher's lounge the day after school has started in the fall. You mention a student, Johnny Jones, by name. A fellow teacher remarks that she had Johnny in class last year. She comments that he was a real dunce, that she saw his IQ test scores once—78 on one test and 81 on the other. You cannot help but remember this information, and it may lead to thoughts that children like Johnny Jones just do not have much on the ball and that it is useless to spend much time trying to help them.

Consider another conversation you (a teacher) might have with a well-to-do family in the community during the first PTA meeting of the year. Jimmy Smith's mother mentions to you that he spent the summer in Paris, where he studied French. At the end of the conversation, she points out that just before school started he was given a battery of tests by a professional testing service, and his IQ was measured at 136. How will this kind of information influence the way you interact with Jimmy in school? Will it lead you to provide him with more challenging work and spend more time with him because you know he is able to learn the material?

Questions like these led Robert Rosenthal and Lenore Jacobsen (1968) to study self-fulfilling prophecies in the classroom. According to the theory of self-fulfilling prophecy, once teachers know the child's IQ, they adjust their teaching to a level they think is best suited to it and the child is thereby influenced to perform at that level, thus "fulfilling" their "prophecy." In *Pygmalion in the Classroom* (1968) Rosenthal and Jacobsen reported the findings of their study.

Here is the way they went about their investigation. Some teachers in a California elementary school were told at the beginning of the school year that some of their students had shown an outstanding potential for intellectual growth. This was actually not the case, however; the children who were labeled as "late bloomers" had been selected at random, and there was no evidence from intelligence test scores or other sources of information that they could improve their IQs any more than others could. Yet the children in the first and second grade who had been identified to the teacher as "late bloomers" made remarkable gains on IQ tests.

Other investigators have not found the dramatic changes that Rosenthal and Jacobsen did. Their study has also been criticized on methodological grounds (e.g., Elashoff & Snow, 1971; Thorndike, 1968). Yet its findings are impressive. Although the Rosenthal and Jacobsen study alone does not provide clear evidence for the expectancy effect, many educators and child-development specialists believe that expectancies do influence the way teachers, parents, and peers interact with children. The way they interact with children based on their expectancies probably influences the children's behavior, which, in turn, probably influences the teachers, parents, and peers to act accordingly. And so on.

Because of the effects of self-fulfilling prophecy, which stems from knowledge of a child's IQ, some states (e.g., New York, California, and Wisconsin) have stopped administering IQ tests to students. In these states tests are still given to individual students for special purposes, such as to determine whether or not a child should be placed in a learning disabilities program.

In addition to studying cultural bias in testing, psychologists also have been interested in charting cross-cultural similarities and differences in children's intelligence by comparing the intelligence of children from different countries and ethnic groups.

Cross-Cultural Comparisons Gerald Lesser and his colleagues (Lesser, Fifer & Clark, 1965) revealed that a child's culture does influence his or her mental abilities. They gave 320 Jewish, Chinese, black, and Puerto Rican children from New York City four tests that measured different aspects of intelligence. The following patterns of mental abilities were found: (1) The Jewish children scored higher on the verbal part, lower on reasoning and number, and lower still on space. (2) The black children scored higher on the verbal and lower in reasoning, space, and number. (3) The Puerto Rican children scored lower on the verbal part but higher on number, space, and reasoning. (4) The Chinese children scored low on the verbal part but

A child's culture is related to his or her mental abilities.

higher in number, space, and reasoning. In comparisons of the white and oriental children, the white children scored higher on the verbal part but lower on spatial orientation. In a more recent study Harold Stevenson and his colleagues (Stevenson, Stigler, Lee & Lucker, 1985) examined Chinese, Japanese, and American children from first through fifth grades on ten cognitive tests, a reading achievement test, and a mathematics achievement test. Although the data were voluminous and complex, it was very clear that the American children performed more poorly on mathematics achievement than both the Japanese and Chinese children. And the Chinese children were superior on reading achievement tests than their American and Japanese counterparts. While the achievement scores of the children from the cultures were significantly different, their general cognitive abilities were quite similar. Thus, the achievement differences do not seem to be due to general intellectual ability, but rather to such matters as instruction and practice in math and reading. Other studies support these claims as well (Song & Ginsburg, 1985; Uttal, Miller & Stevenson, 1985). A clear implication is that we Americans need to improve the level of math and reading instruction in our schools.

In conclusion, culture clearly plays an important role in the performance of a number of important achievement-related matters.

One of the hottest controversies in the search for influences on intelligence is the extent to which black and white children are intellectually different. Also controversial is the extent to which social-class differences influence children's intelligence.

Race and Social Class Do black children perform poorly on tests of intelligence in comparison with white children? Are the scores of children from lower-class homes lower than those from middle-class homes? The answer is yes to both questions. In a review of hundreds of studies, it was found that the mean IQ of blacks is 10 to 20 points below that of whites (Shuey, 1966). The average black child's IQ is 80 to 85. Also, lower-class children and adults score lower on measures of intelligence than middle-class children and adults do (e.g., Havighurst, Bowman, Liddle, Matthews & Pierce, 1962; McNemar, 1942).

In the cross-cultural study by Gerald Lesser and his colleagues (1965) comparisons of lower-class and middle-class children also were made. In all analyses the middle-class children scored higher on the IQ tests than the lower-class children did. The children of laborers averaged about 15 to 20 points lower than the children of professionals in these studies.

Arthur Jensen (1969, 1974) has made some provocative comments about the way children from lower- and middle-class society should be educated. He starts off with a basic idea that most would agree with: Children should be taught according to their individual needs and abilities; educational programs should not be administered uniformly to all children. So far, so good. But he goes further, arguing that whites and blacks and middle-class and lower-class children should be taught differently. He believes this policy should be carried out because the children themselves are genetically different: Jensen stresses that middle-class children essentially learn in a cognitive manner, while lower-class children learn in an associative way.

Associative learning, labeled by Jensen as Level I abilities, is S–R (stimulus-response) learning. It requires the child to make little or no cognitive transformation of the stimulus input but simply to make an association between two stimuli. **Cognitive learning,** called Level II abilities by Jensen, is a higher, more complex form of learning. The child who learns in a cognitive way must actively transform and change the stimulus input. With the cognitive learning task called anagrams, for example, the child must make as many new words as possible from the letters contained in a specific word. Jensen feels that one of the things wrong with schooling is that children from lower-class families have been taught in a cognitive manner.

Harold Stevenson (1973) disagrees with Jensen's assertion that lower-class children should be taught associatively and that middle-class children should be taught cognitively. Cognitive tasks and associative tasks cannot always be separated; items that supposedly measure associative learning are often related to items that apparently measure cognitive learning. It may therefore be impossible to separate cognitive and associative learning. Many experts believe that all children, other than perhaps infants or children living in highly controlled or deprived environments, learn primarily in a cognitive manner. The old view of the passive organism making stimulus-response connections seems to be on the way out.

Carl Bereiter (1975) has commented on Jensen's idea of fitting a specific educational curriculum to an individual child. Let's see how Jensen's idea of individualization might be applied to teaching children how to read. It could mean that some children should be given reading instruction at four years of age and that others should wait until they are ten or older.

> Consider the consequences if, as could easily happen, almost all the 4-year-old starters in a school system were white and well-to-do and almost all the 10-year-old starters were black and poor. No matter how well-intended the policy, and no matter how serious the effort to apply it without bias, there would be no escaping the charge that the school system had given up on black kids and was consigning them to the status of second-class citizens. The use of an open classroom would conceal the segregation to some extent, but it would not take a very astute observer to notice that the children in the "reading corner" [are] predominantly . . . white while the children in the "block play" and similar corners tended to be predominantly otherwise. (Bereiter, 1975, p. 456)

A summary of alternatives and supplements to standardized intelligence tests, infant intelligence and the stability of intelligence, and influences on intelligence appears in Concept Table 9.3.

	CONCEPT TABLE 9.3 Replacement and Supplementary Measures, Infant Intelligence and the Stability of Intelligence, and Influences on Intelligence	
Concept	**Processes/Related Ideas**	**Characteristics/Description**
Replacement and supplementary measures	Replacement measures include competence tests and culture-fair tests	Competence tests use criterion sampling to develop items that reflect competence. Culture-fair tests are designed with the belief that traditional measures are culturally biased. They use nonverbal items or items that are equally familiar to all cultures or at least to the culture of the children taking the test.
	Supplementary tests	SOMPA was designed for use with children from an impoverished background. It uses the WISC-R but supplements it with assessment of social and economic background, social adjustment, and health.
	A final note about intelligence tests	While intelligence tests have been heavily criticized, they still merit use in a number of contexts. Comparisons of the Piagetian and psychometric approaches reveal similarities as well as differences.
Infant intelligence tests and the stability of intelligence	Infant intelligence tests	Many standardized intelligence tests do not assess infant intelligence. Intelligence tests designed to measure infant intelligence are often referred to as developmental scales.
	Stability of intelligence	While intelligence is more stable across the childhood years than many other attributes, there is still considerable fluctuation in intelligence test scores for many children.
Influences on intelligence	Heredity	Heredity is a strong influence on intelligence, although it not as powerful as Jensen believed.
	Environment	Among the important environmental influences on intelligence that have been studied are home, institutionalization, school, and culture, race and social class.

SPECIAL CASES OF INTELLIGENCE

In this section we explore extremes in intelligence by evaluating the concepts of mental retardation and giftedness, provide further information about R. J. Sternberg's conception of intelligence, exploring what he has to say about mental retardation and giftedness, and discuss what we mean by creativity and attempt to distinguish between intelligence and creativity.

Mental Retardation

What is mental retardation? How is it determined that one child is mentally retarded and another is not? Not everyone agrees on this important matter. In 1977 the American Association on Mental Deficiency defined **mental retardation** as "significantly subaverage general intellectual functioning existing concurrently with deficits in adaptive behavior and manifested during the developmental period" (Grossman, 1977, p. 11). Traditionally, IQ has been the primary criterion for identifying a child as mentally retarded.

However, cultural and socioeconomic differences can influence performance on IQ tests. Such differences may result in the categorization of blacks, Mexican-Americans, and children from non-English-speaking backgrounds, for example, as mentally retarded even though they actually are not. Therefore, assessment for retardation should go beyond standardized IQ tests to include observations of children in everyday circumstances and environments—at home, in the community, in the classroom with an understanding teacher—to reveal whether or not they can follow instructions and handle problems successfully. Aspects of social competence should be considered in addition to intellectual competence.

Further consideration of mental retardation emphasizes the process of labeling and the causes of retardation.

Labeling

Mental retardation is not some kind of disease; it is a label that describes the child's position in relation to other children on the basis of some standard (or standards) of performance. Thus, if a child scores below 70 on the WISC–R, he or she is demonstrating less efficient performance than that of a large majority of same-age children who have taken the test. The child is likely to be labeled "mentally retarded," generating a number of inferences (Ross, 1974).

For example, the term *trainable* has been applied to children whose scores are between 25 and 45, and the term *educable* to those whose scores are between 55 and 69. An educable mentally retarded child is supposed to be able to successfully perform academic work at the third- to the sixth-grade level by the time he or she is sixteen years old. A trainable mentally retarded child is supposed to be unable to perform academic work at all; he or she is generally taught personal care and how to cope with some basic, simple routines in life. These children are not taught to read and write. Thus, a child's score on an IQ test has important implications for the type of treatment program to which he or she is assigned.

It is important to remember that an IQ score reflects a child's *current* performance; it does not always indicate academic *potential*. Therefore, the use of diagnostic labels that suggest assumptions about a child's potential can be dangerous. Remarkable strides are sometimes made in teaching retarded children to perform academic tasks that were thought to be impossible. Many experts believe the terms *trainable* and *educable,* as well as *mental retardation,* should always be thought of as labels that index only current performance. Because a child's level of performance may well change later, it may be wise to discard the label.

A score in the mentally retarded range on an IQ test reveals nothing about why the child is retarded. Next we will find that the most widely used classification of the causes of mental retardation distinguishes between organic and cultural-familial causes.

Causes of Retardation

Damage to the central nervous system, particularly to the brain, can produce mental retardation. Damage to the brain may occur during prenatal or postnatal development or as a result of an abnormal chromosome configuration. Down's syndrome is a well-known example of mental retardation that has an organic cause, the presence of an extra chromosome. Another type of organic disturbance that results in severe mental retardation is inadequate production of hormones, as in **cretinism.** Cretinism is caused by a hormone deficiency in the thyroid gland. When this deficiency is untreated, physical and mental development is stunted.

Many organic causes of mental retardation are linked to pregnancy and birth. For example, overdoses of radiation or the contraction of syphilis during pregnancy can cause retardation. Accidental injury to the brain of the fetus, as through a bad fall by the mother or the birth process itself, can cause mental retardation. Furthermore, although no clear link to mental retardation itself has been uncovered, inadequate protein intake on the part of the mother may be a contributing factor for mental retardation.

Most instances of mental retardation do not have a known organic cause. Such retardation is termed **cultural-familial.** For retardation to be considered cultural-familial, the following criteria must be met: there can be no detectable brain abnormality; the retardation must be mild; and at least one of the parents or one of the siblings must also be mentally retarded (Davison & Neale, 1975). It has been estimated that the number of people whose mental retardation is considered cultural-familial represents about 75 percent of the retarded population. Their intelligence test scores generally fall between 50 and 70, whereas the scores of those with organic retardation are likely to be much lower.

Both genetic and environmental factors contribute to the occurrence of cultural-familial retardation. For instance, parents who have low IQs not only are more likely to transmit genes for a lower intelligence to their offspring but also tend to provide them with a less enriched environment (Ross, 1974).

Some experts believe that replacing the impoverished environment of the cultural-familial retarded child with a more enriched one may stimulate normal

Skills in the visual and performing arts have usually not been included when criteria for admission to gifted classes in schools is at issue.

or even superior intellectual growth. Even though such children may make intellectual gains, however, the gains are usually limited. Of course, intensive effort at teaching mentally retarded children should not be abandoned. To the contrary, every effort should be made to encourage retarded children to learn and to achieve the best of their abilities. However, the process of change is usually an arduous one that requires great patience and commitment on the part of the teacher.

At the other end of the intelligence spectrum are those children with well-above-average intelligence, often referred to as gifted children. In the next section, we look at what it means for a child to be gifted and the educational programs that have been developed for such children.

Gifted Children

Many years ago the label "gifted" had a single meaning, namely high intelligence (White House Conference on Children, 1931). The **gifted child** still is described as an individual with well-above-average intellectual capacity (an IQ of 120 or more, for example), but he or

she may also be a child with a superior talent for something (Owen, Froman & Moscow, 1981). In their selection of children for gifted programs, most school systems still place the heaviest weight on intellectual superiority and academic aptitude and do not look as carefully at such areas of competence as the visual and performing arts, psychomotor abilities, and other specific aptitudes.

One classic study dominates our knowledge about gifted children, that of Lewis Terman (1925). In the 1920s Terman began to study approximately 1,500 children whose Stanford-Binet IQ scores averaged 150. Terman's research was designed to follow these children through their adulthood—it will not be complete until the year 2010.

The accomplishments of the 1,500 children in Terman's study are remarkable. Of the 800 males, seventy-eight have obtained Ph.D.s, forty-eight have earned M.D.s, and eighty-five have been granted law degrees. Nearly all of these figures are ten to thirty times greater than would have been found among 800 men of the same age chosen randomly (Getzels & Dillon, 1973).

Scrutiny of the gifted 1,500 continues. The most recent investigation focused on whether the gifted individuals had been satisfied with their lives (Sears, 1977). When the average age of the Terman gifted population was sixty-two, four target factors were assessed: life-cycle satisfaction with occupation; satisfaction with family life; degree of work persistence into their sixties; and unbroken marriage versus a history of divorce. The recorded events and expressions of feelings have been obtained at decade intervals since 1922. One of the most interesting findings of the study is that in spite of their autonomy and extensive success in their occupations, these men placed more importance on achieving satisfaction in their family life than in their work. Furthermore, the gifted individuals felt that they had found such satisfaction. As Terman suggested, they are not only superior intellectually but are physically, emotionally, morally, and socially more able as well.

Programs for gifted children usually follow one of three paths: enrichment, grouping, or acceleration. **Enrichment** focuses on special provisions for gifted children, including college-level courses in high school, advanced classes, independent study, and so forth. **Grouping** occurs when students with similar capacities are placed in a class together. **Acceleration** refers to any strategy that abbreviates the time required for a student to graduate, such as skipping a grade (Owen, Froman & Moscow, 1981).

Do such programs work? Julian Stanley (1977), widely known for his study of gifted children, has pointed out that most gifted children enrichment programs are comprised of busywork, are irrelevant, and in many instances are just plain boring. Research directed at assessing the impact of acceleration provides a more favorable picture; a summary of the acceleration studies suggests that, from first grade through college, acceleration seems to have a positive intellectual and emotional effect on gifted children (Laycock, 1979).

In the Terman study, for example, the individuals who had been accelerated in school were more successful in their jobs, education, and marriage and maintained better physical health than those who had not been accelerated (Terman & Oden, 1959). Grouping has been much more controversial than enrichment or acceleration. Research on grouping children into tracks has produced mixed results (Esposito, 1973), and many critics point out that it is unfair to poor children and ethnic minority groups.

Individuals who turn out to have exceptional talents as adults suggest that there is more to becoming a "star" in their respective fields than gifted programs. In one recent inquiry (Bloom, 1983), 120 individuals who had achieved stardom in six different areas—concert pianists and sculptors (Arts), Olympic swimmers and tennis champions (Psychomotor), and research mathematicians and research neurologists (Cognitive)—were interviewed to learn what they felt was responsible for their lofty accomplishments. It seems that exceptional accomplishments require particular kinds of environmental support, special experiences, excellent teaching, and motivational encouragement throughout development. Regardless of the quality of their gifts, each of the individuals experienced many years of special attention under the tutelage and supervision of a remarkable series of teachers and coaches. They also were given considerable support and attention by their parents. All of the "stars" devoted great amounts of time to practice and training, easily outrivaling the amount of time spent in other activities.

Sternberg's Dual-Faceted Model Applied to Mental Retardation and Giftedness

In addition to describing a number of components of intelligence, R. J. Sternberg (1984) has proposed a dual-facet conception of intelligence: skill at coping with novel tasks and situations and skill at "automatizing" information processing.

Coping with Novelty

The ability to cope with novelty can be tapped in tests of "insight problems" such as the following:

> Water lilies double in area every twenty-four hours. At the beginning of the summer there is one water lily on the lake. It takes sixty days for the lake to become covered with water lilies. On what day is the lake half covered? (Sternberg, 1984, p. 177)

Although this problem is difficult, a single insight provides you with the answer. You need only realize that twenty-four hours before the lake becomes fully covered, it must be only half covered (since water lilies double in area every twenty-four hours). Thus, the answer must be the fifty-ninth day. Presumably, intelligent behavior in everyday life sometimes involves the formulation of insights into novel situations or tasks.

Certainly all of us have some intuition of how good we are—compared to others—at dealing with the unexpected. Sternberg is suggesting that this is one basic type of intelligence.

Automatization

Automatization can be measured in tasks such as the "synonyms task." The subject takes a multiple-choice test in which each item consists of a word alongside some alternative words, one of which is its synonym. Some people can perform such tasks more quickly and accurately than others, presumably because they can automatize the processes of retrieving and comparing the meanings of the words. There may be different types of automatization, tapped by different types of tasks. In any event, Sternberg argues that automatization skills are an important facet of intelligence, not just in the laboratory but in real life. Presumably, individuals who quickly master complex tasks and learn information easily are good automatizers.

Giftedness and Mental Retardation

Sternberg's dual-facet view of intelligence has some important implications for thinking about giftedness and mental retardation. Sternberg and Davidson (1983) have argued that giftedness involves the ability of gifted children to think in novel ways and to do so in an insightful manner. Exceptional intellectual accomplishments—for example, major scientific discoveries, important inventions, and special literary and philosophical works—invariably involve major intellectual insights.

If gifted people are high in insightfulness, are the mentally retarded unusually low in this attribute? Sternberg argues that the answer is no. While the mentally retarded may not have many insights, neither do people of average intelligence. Thus Sternberg (1984) argues that retardation is not a failure to be insightful. It is better understood in terms of (a) inadequate automatization of processes (i.e., the second facet of intelligence) or (b) other deficits in the efficiency of information processing.

Closely related to the study of gifted children is creativity, an important aspect of mental functioning that is not measured by traditional IQ tests, a fact that has triggered considerable criticism of intelligence tests. As we see in the next section, children not only think, they think creatively.

Edison's creativity was not recognized by his teachers early in his schooling.

Creativity

Most of us would like to be creative, and parents and teachers would like to be able to develop situations that promote creative thinking in children. Why was Thomas Edison able to invent so many things? Was he simply more intelligent than most people? Did he spend long hours toiling away in private? Somewhat surprisingly, when Edison was a young boy his teacher told him he was too dumb to learn anything! There are other examples of famous individuals whose creative genius went unnoticed when they were younger (Larson, 1973): Walt Disney was fired from a newspaper because he did not have any good ideas; Enrico Caruso's music teacher informed him that he could not sing and that he didn't have any voice at all; Albert Einstein was four years old before he could speak and seven before he could read; and Winston Churchill failed one year of secondary school. Among the reasons such individuals are overlooked as youngsters is the difficulty we have in defining and measuring **creativity.** In this section we also will look at development changes in creativity, the role of imagery in creative thinking, and educational programs developed to promote creativity.

Definition and Measurement

The prevailing belief of experts who study creativity is that intelligence and creativity are not the same (Wallach, 1973). For example, scores on widely used tests of creativity developed by J. P. Guilford and by Michael Wallach and Nathan Kogan are only weakly related to intelligence scores (Richards, 1976). Yet it is as difficult to define creativity as it is to define intelligence. Just as intelligence consists of many disparate elements, so also is creativity a many-faceted phenomenon. An important question is whether measuring general creative functioning is appropriate or even possible.

David Ausubel (1968) emphasized that *creativity* is one of the most ambiguous and confusing terms in psychology and education. He believes that the term *creative* should not be applied to as many people as it is but should be reserved for describing people who make unique and original contributions to society.

The term *creativity* has been used in many ways. Following are the ways that some well-known figures define creativity and attempt to measure it in individuals.

Guilford's Concept of Divergent Thinking

Creative thinking is part of J. P. Guilford's model of intelligence (Guilford, 1967). The aspect of his theory of intelligence that is most closely related to creativity is what he called **divergent thinking,** a type of thinking that produces many different answers to a single question. Divergent thinking is distinguished from **convergent thinking,** a type of thinking that goes toward one correct answer. For example, there is one correct answer to this intellectual problem-solving task: "How many quarters can you get from sixty dimes?" It calls for convergent thinking. But there are many possible answers to this question: "What are some unique things a coat hanger can be used for?" This question requires divergent thinking. Going off in different directions may sometimes lead to more productive answers. Examples of what Guilford means by divergent thinking (his term for creativity) and ways of measuring it follow:

Word fluency: How facile are you with words? For example, name as many words as possible and as fast as possible that contain the letter *z*.

Ideational fluency: Here you have to name words that belong to a particular class. For example, name as many objects as you can that weigh less than one pound.

Adaptive flexibility: In this type of divergent thinking you must be able to vary your ideas widely when this is called for. For example, if you are shown a series of match sticks lined up on a table, you may be asked to put them together to form four triangles.

Originality: This time you would be required to name some unique ways to use an object. For example, what are some unusual ways to use hairpins?

Wallach and Kogan's Work   Michael Wallach and Nathan Kogan (1965) attempted to refine the ability to separate creativity from intelligence. Their work has included efforts to specify how creative people in the arts and sciences think. People who are rated as highly creative individuals are asked to probe introspectively into what it is that enables them to produce creative pieces of work. Two major factors evolve from this self-analysis by creative people. (1) They have what is called **associative flow.** That is, they can generate large amounts of associative content in their effort to attain novel solutions to problems. (2) They have the freedom to entertain a wide range of possible solutions in a playful manner. These responses led Wallach and Kogan to remove time limits from tests of creativity and to make sure that the tests were given in very relaxed, nonthreatening, informal situations.

Developmental Changes in Creativity

Some commonly held beliefs about developmental changes in creativity are (1) it begins to weaken around the age of five because of the societal pressure to conform; (2) serious drops in creativity occur at the age of nine and at the age of twelve; (3) adults are less creative than children (Dudek, 1974).

These stereotypes are not supported by good research data. Actually, a drop in creativity probably does not occur at the age of nine; what happens instead is that the child's form of expression changes. At about eight or nine years of age the child begins to develop a more differentiated view of reality compared to an earlier, more global view. The child is freer from perceptual dominance and clearly into the concrete operations stage. Consider the child's art, for example. The child now paints as he or she sees, not feels. Feeling does not entirely disappear from art, but it now is less important to the child than realistic detail.

According to Steven Dudek (1974) this change represents increased subtlety in thought and increased imagination, not less. Others may interpret the art as

less creative and less imaginative because surprise and vividness are missing. It has lost some of its spontaneity but not its complexity. At this point the child may require time to master the skills of the concrete operational period before he or she can use them spontaneously and freely.

The drop in creativity reported at about the age of twelve also occurs just after the child has entered a new stage in Piaget's theory. In the formal operations stage the child is learning how to develop hypotheses, how to combine ideas in complex ways, and how to think in more imaginative and abstract ways. Piaget pointed out that when children begin to develop new cognitive skills, egocentrism often results and pressures to conform are very strong. An increase in creativity might be expected during adolescence as the child gradually masters the use of these newly acquired cognitive skills. Evidence suggests that if repressive forces are not too strong, creativity does seem to increase in adolescence (Greenacre, 1971). Hence, neither adolescents nor adults are necessarily less creative than young children.

Encouraging Creativity

Let's look at ways creativity can be encouraged. You are an elementary school teacher. How might you go about fostering creativity on the part of your students? **Brainstorming** is one technique that has been effective in several programs developed to stimulate creativity in children. In brainstorming sessions a topic is presented for consideration and participants are encouraged to suggest ideas related to it. Criticism of ideas contributed must be withheld initially to prevent stopping the flow of ideas. The more freewheeling the ideas, the better. Participants are also encouraged to combine ideas that have already been suggested. Studies with children in regular classrooms (e.g., Torrance & Torrance, 1972) and in classrooms with educationally

handicapped children (e.g., Sharpe, 1976) indicate that brainstorming can be an effective strategy for increasing creative thinking.

Another useful technique is called **playing with improbabilities.** This method forces children to think about the events that might follow an unlikely occurrence. Torrance gave the following examples of questions that can be used to foster classroom discussion:

> What could happen if it always rained on Saturday?
> What could happen if it were against the law to sing?
> . . . Just suppose you could visit the prehistoric section
> of the museum and the animals could come alive? Just
> suppose you could enter into the life of a pond and
> become whatever you wanted to become? (pp. 436–437)

To answer these questions, the child must break out of conventional modes of thought and wander through fantasyland.

More important perhaps than any specific technique, however, is the need to foster a *creative atmosphere* in the classroom. Children need to feel that they can try out ideas, even if the ideas seem crazy or far-fetched, without being criticized by the teacher. The only way to produce a creative environment on a sustained basis is to *do* things creatively on a regular basis.

Creative thinking can be encouraged in any type of curriculum and in any kind of classroom situation; neither an open classroom nor progressive education is required. A word of caution, however: although experts believe that creative thinking exercises should be practiced in every classroom, they caution against spending too much time on creative activities at the expense of other equally important learning activities. Michael Wallach (1973), for one, has commented that many children do not need to read more creatively, they just need to learn how to read.

SUMMARY

I. Information about theories, definitions, and measurements of intelligence focuses on Binet and the general concept of intelligence, the Wechsler scales, the factor analytic approach, and the information-processing approach.

   A. Binet emphasized the assessment of general intelligence and conceived of intelligence as a general ability.

   B. Wechsler, while assessing intelligence at both the general and specific levels, nonetheless defined intelligence as a general, global property of a person.

   C. Spearman, Thurstone, Cattell, and Guilford all proposed factor analytic views of intelligence.

      1. Spearman argued that intelligence consists of a general and a specific factor.

      2. Thurstone emphasized that intelligence is made up of specific primary mental abilities.

      3. Cattell proposed that there are basically two kinds of intelligence: fluid and crystallized.

      4. Guilford developed the structure of intellect model, consisting of 120 mental abilities made up of all combinations of operations, contents, and products.

   D. The information-processing approach to intelligence requires consideration of the distinction between knowledge and process, as well as R. J. Sternberg's componential analysis.

      1. The information-processing perspective raises the important question of whether the older child's greater capacity may be due to more processing capacity and efficiency in information processing rather than to a mere accumulation of knowledge.

      2. Sternberg believes we might better understand intelligence if we viewed it in terms of components, elementary information processes such as metacomponents, performance components, acquisition components, retention components, and transfer components.

II. Replacement and supplementary measures for standardized intelligence tests have been proposed, and a final note about intelligence tests merits attention.

   A. There is concern about the validity of standardized intelligence tests.

   B. Tests of competency use criterion sampling to develop items that reflect competence. Culture-fair tests have been designed because it has been argued that many standardized intelligence tests are culturally biased. Culture-fair tests use either nonverbal items or items that are equally familiar to all cultures or at least to the culture taking the test.

   C. Social intelligence tests have been designed to supplement standardized intelligence tests. SOMPA is designed for use with people from impoverished backgrounds; it uses the WISC–R but supplements it with assessment of social and economic conditions, social adjustment, and health.

   D. While intelligence tests have been heavily criticized, they still merit use in a number of situations. Comparisons of the Piagetian and psychometric approaches reveal similarities as well as differences.

III. Many standardized intelligence tests do not assess infant intelligence. Intelligence tests that have been designed to evaluate infant intelligence are often referred to as developmental scales. While intelligence is more stable across the childhood years than many attributes of the individual, there still is considerable fluctuation in intelligence test scores of some individuals.

IV. Intelligence is influenced by both heredity and environment.

   A. Heredity is a strong influence on intelligence but not as strong as Jensen believed.

   B. Among the most important environmental influences on intelligence that have been studied are aspects of the home, such as intervention projects focused on children from impoverished families, and family structure, family size, and sibling order; institutionalization; school; and culture, race, and social class.

V. Information about special cases of intelligence emphasizes mental retardation, giftedness, R. J. Sternberg's dual-facet theory, and creativity.

   A. Mental retardation involves significantly subaverage intelligence existing concurrently with deficits in adaptive behavior and appearing during the developmental period. An important consideration in mental retardation is its status as a label. The causes of mental retardation are organic and cultural-familial.

   B. The gifted child is an individual who has above average intellectual capacity. Three programs for the gifted are enrichment, grouping, and acceleration.

   C. Sternberg has proposed a dual-facet conception of intelligence: skill at coping with novel tasks and situations and skill at "automatizing" information processing. Giftedness might be better understood in terms of thinking in novel ways, particularly thinking that is insightful. Sternberg nonetheless argues that neither the retarded nor average-IQ individuals are necessarily low on the attribute of insight. He believes that mental retardation can be better understood in terms of inadequate automatization of processes or other deficits in the efficiency of processing information.

   D. An important aspect of mental functioning not usually assessed by intelligence tests is creativity. Extensive efforts have been made to devise definitions and tests of creativity that are not measures of general intelligence. Originality and flexibility are two factors that tests of creativity try to measure. Developmental changes occur in creativity just as they do in general intelligence. These changes seem to coincide with Piaget's stages. Although some have argued that creativity decreases as children get older, it seems more accurate to say that creativity changes form through development. Most experts believe that creativity exercises should be practiced in every classroom but not to the detriment of developing sound academic skills.

KEY TERMS

acceleration 302

acquisition (or storage) components 279

associative flow 304

associative learning 298

brainstorming 305

cognitive learning 298

component 279

componential analysis 279

contents 277

convergent thinking 304

creativity 303

cretinism 300

criterion sampling 282

criterion validity 282

crystallized intelligence 277

cultural-familial 300

culture-fair tests 284

decoding 280

developmental scales 287

divergent thinking 304

enrichment 302

factor analytic approach 275

fluid intelligence 277

gifted child 301

grouping 302

institutionalization 294

mean 274

mental age (MA) 273

mental retardation 299

metacomponents 279

multiple-factor theory 276

normal distribution 274

operations 277

performance components 279

playing with improbabilities 305

products 277

psychometric approach 286

retention (or retrieval) components 279

SOMPA 285

standard deviation 274

structure of intellect model 277

transfer components 279

two-factor theory 275

validity 282

REVIEW QUESTIONS

1. Describe the Binet, Wechsler, and factor analytic approaches to intelligence.
2. Discuss the information-processing approach to intelligence.
3. What are some alternatives and supplements to standardized intelligence tests?
4. Describe how infant intelligence is measured and the degree to which intelligence is stable through the childhood years.
5. What are the influences of heredity and environment on intelligence?
6. Discuss the nature of mental retardation and giftedness.
7. Provide information about Sternberg's ideas on mental retardation and giftedness.
8. Outline the major ideas about the nature of creativity.

SUGGESTED READINGS

American Psychologist, vol. 36, no. 10, October, 1981. Special issue testing: concepts, policy, practice, and research.
American Psychologist is the Journal of the American Psychological Association. This entire issue is devoted to psychological testing and includes articles written by a number of experts.

Davis, G. A., and Scott, J. A. (Eds.). (1971). *Training creative thinking.* New York: Holt, Rinehart & Winston.
A collection of articles by several psychologists who study creativity, with practical suggestions on how to stimulate creativity in the classroom.

Gowan, J. C., Khatena, J., and Torrance, E. P. (Eds.). (1979). *Educating the ablest* (2d ed.). Itasca, IL: F. E. Peacock.
A selected book of readings on a variety of topics that relate to gifted children and the process of creativity. Includes sections on programs and curricula for gifted and creative children, the role of imagery, and developmental characteristics. Easy to read.

Sattler, J. (1980). *Assessment of children's intelligence* (2d ed.). Philadelphia: Saunders.
The author provides extensive information about the history of intelligence testing, with emphasis on the Binet and WISC–R tests. Extensive information is given about a variety of intelligence tests currently used with children.

Sternberg, R. J. (1984). Mechanisms of cognitive development: A componential approach. In R. J. Sternberg (Ed.), *Mechanisms of cognitive development.* San Francisco: W. H. Freeman.
Sternberg, one of the leading figures in the modern information-processing view of intelligence, describes in considerable detail the information-processing perspective on intelligence.

SOCIAL AND PERSONALITY PROCESSES AND DEVELOPMENT

CHAPTER

THE SOCIALIZATION PROCESS

PROLOGUE

THE WOLF GIRLS AND VICTOR

The year is 1940 and you are living in a rural village in India. You are walking in an isolated area and feeling very peaceful. But then you hear several howling sounds. You look behind the bushes and see two strange looking animals, or are they children? Their eyes glare like blue lights in the darkened area of the bushes.

One of the girls is about one and a half years old and the other about eight years old. They are the "wolf girls," so-called because it appears that they were reared by wolves. A missionary had heard reports of small, naked children running around on all fours and decided to go and observe the wolf children. In *Wolf Children and Feral Men* (*feral* means wild), the missionary Singh told the story of the two girls who had been reared by wolves.

The younger girl learned to walk upright, but she died about a year after she was taken to an orphanage. The older girl never learned to walk upright, although she eventually stopped howling like a wolf and learned to use about 50 words. She died after eight years at the orphanage.

Probably the most famous case of social isolation involves the Wild Boy of Aveyron (Lane, 1976). In 1799 a nude boy was observed running through the woods in France. The boy was eventually captured when he was believed to be about eleven years old. It was thought he had lived in the woods with no human contact for at least six years. Like the wolf girls, he seemed to be more animal than person. Experts examined the boy and proclaimed he was an incurable idiot. However, a young French physician, Jean Itard, believed differently, thinking that the bizarre behavior of the boy was

due to his social isolation. Itard named the boy Victor and over a period of five years tried to socialize him.

When Victor was first found he walked more like an animal than a human: when alone, he sat and rocked back and forth. He was unable to focus his eyes on anything for more than a few seconds, and he made no attempt to communicate. After five years with Itard, Victor had not changed very much. He did learn to eat with silverware and sleep in a bed, to wear clothes and focus his eyes, but he never learned to communicate effectively. His social development was very impoverished. Though he seemed to develop some affection for Itard and the woman who cared for him, he never learned to interact with others.

Psychologists have long wondered what people would be like if they were brought up in isolation from other people from the time they were born. Though circumstances such as those experienced by the wolf girls and Victor provide some indication of the outcome, to truly find the answers, we would have to randomly assign some children to live in isolation from other people for a number of years and other children to live a "normal" life with parents or caregivers. Of course, we cannot ethically do such a thing, so we try to get some sense of the importance of social experiences through such naturally occurring situations as those of the wolf girls and Victor.

The experiences of these children provide information about the importance of social conditions in understanding the nature of the mind and behavior. In the instances described here the children, through improved social conditions, were able to develop some human competencies, but their impoverished early experiences seemed to have lasting effects.

PREVIEW

In this chapter we study the nature of children's socialization. First, we focus on a number of theoretical
perspectives that have important implications for understanding how children are socialized. Second, we
provide an analysis of children's social environment.

THEORIES OF SOCIALIZATION

Historically, interest in the nature of children's socialization has been dominated by two theoretical perspectives: psychoanalytic and behavioral, social
learning. More recently, two other frameworks have
become prominent: those that emphasize cognitive factors and those that stress biological factors in socialization.

Psychoanalytic Theory

To learn about psychoanalytic theory we first study
some of the basic characteristics of the theory, then turn
to the two main representatives of the theory: classical
psychoanalytic theory, the view of Sigmund Freud, and
the views of revisionists of Freud's psychoanalytic
theory.

What Is Psychoanalytic Theory?

When we hear the term *psychoanalysis,* we usually
think of a bearded man pensively listening to a client
lying on a couch recount the early experiences of his or
her life. This stereotype has been prolonged by numerous cartoons that still proliferate in magazines (and
textbooks). The stereotype of the reclining patient on
a couch is not completely farfetched: The traditional
psychoanalysis practiced by Freud did have the client
lying on the couch looking away from him. One commentary indicated that Freud was somewhat shy and
didn't like having people staring at him all day. However, there were conceptual reasons for not having eye
contact as well. Freud said the therapist should be an
opaque mirror in which the client can see himself, and

Sigmund Freud, the architect of psychoanalytic theory.

the unobtrusive presence of the therapist is believed to
facilitate this. However, many contemporary psychoanalysts prefer a face-to-face conversation with their
clients.

Psychoanalytic theory is a view of personality that
emphasizes the private, unconscious aspects of a person's mind as the dominant feature of personality. Freud
believed that personality is like an iceberg, with the
conscious aspects of the mind being the tip of the iceberg above water and the unconscious aspects being the
bulk of the iceberg beneath the water (see figure 10.1).

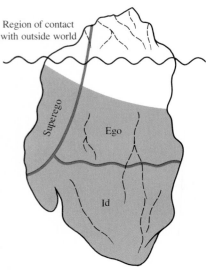

FIGURE 10.1
Conscious and unconscious processes. This rather odd-looking diagram illustrates Freud's belief that most of the important personality processes occur below the level of conscious awareness. In examining people's conscious thoughts and their behaviors, we can see some reflections of the ego and the superego. Whereas the ego and superego are partly conscious and partly unconscious, the primitive id is the unconscious, totally submerged part of the "iceberg" (Wrightsman, Sigelman, and Sanford, 1979).

Psychoanalytic theory is also a view of personality that stresses biological forces and the symbolic transformation of experience (Blos, 1985). In our description of Freud's theory we will see the strong emphasis on the biological determination of personality. But we also will discover that all psychoanalytic theorists focus on how we use symbols, many of which are beyond our conscious awareness, to represent experiences in our lives.

Freud's Theory

There are many details to Freud's theory, and his ideas have filled many volumes. Here we begin by touching on the nature of the man and then go on to describe his ideas about personality structures, defense mechanisms, personality development, and the status of Freud's theory today.

The Man Sigmund Freud was loved and hated, looked up to and looked down on. For many people he was a master, for others he was clearly wrong in his views on personality. Regardless of whether he is viewed as right or wrong in his assumptions about personality, Freud clearly must be regarded as one of the most influential thinkers of the twentieth century. Freud was a medical doctor who specialized in neurology. He developed his ideas about psychoanalysis from his work with patients who had mental problems. He was born in 1856 in Austria and died in London at the age of eighty-three. He spent most of his life as a physician in Vienna, Austria. He finally became convinced that he needed to leave Vienna toward the end of his life because of the anti-Semitism of the Nazis.

Freud was the firstborn child in his Jewish family. His mother saw him as very special, and his brothers and sisters treated him as a genius. One of Freud's main conceptions is that of the **Oedipus complex,** which consists of a child feeling a great deal of anxiety over sexual attraction to the parent of the opposite sex. It is very possible that this view arose from his own romantic attachment to his mother, who was young and beautiful.

The Structure of Personality One of the best-known aspects of Freud's theory is his division of personality into three structures: id, ego, and superego (Freud, 1935). According to Freud, at birth the mind houses only one personality structure, the id. Freud viewed the **id** as a bundle of sexual and aggressive instincts or drives that are primarily unconscious. From the time we are born, Freud believed, sexual and aggressive instincts dominate our life, always having to be kept in check. But because these instincts are primarily unconscious, said Freud, we are not aware of the underlying motivation of much of our behavior. By describing the newborn as a bundle of sexual and aggressive instincts Freud was taking a philosophical stance that suggests people are born into the world as basically evil or bad. Therefore, it is up to society to transform the bundle of evil into a socially acceptable creature. Freud was somewhat pessimistic about society's being able to accomplish this task. The reasons for his pessimism can probably be traced to two factors. First, the biological determinism of instinct theory was predominant at the time Freud was developing his views; second, Freud had experienced the horrors of World War I.

Freud believed not only that a dark, evil side of personality is within each of us, but that it is the controlling force in our lives. This id works according to the **pleasure principle,** always seeking pleasure and avoiding pain, regardless of what impact such pleasure seeking and pain avoiding will have on our life in the real world.

The thinking of the id was referred to by Freud as **primary process thinking,** which involves the effort on the part of the id to satisfy its wants and needs by simply forming a mental image of the object it desires. Thus we dream about sex, about food, and about how we would like to beat up the bully who keeps making us look bad. In some ways, then, the needs of the id can be satisfied through wish-fulfilling mental images as well as through actual behavior.

Clearly, it would be a chaotic and dangerous world if our personality were all id. However, in early childhood other aspects of personality develop.

As a child you learned that you could not always get what you wanted. You couldn't eat twenty-six Popsicles, and sometimes you weren't even allowed to eat one. Sometimes you had to gulp down spinach or peas, and you had to learn to use the potty rather than your diaper.

According to Freud, a new part of your personality was being formed—the **ego,** which is the side of your personality that considers the demands of reality. Just as the id obeys the pleasure principle, the ego abides by the **reality principle.** This principle suggests that children find ways to satisfy the wants and needs of the id within the boundaries of reality. Most of us are not cold-blooded killers or wheeler-dealers: we take into account obstacles to our satisfaction that exist in our external world. Children begin to adhere to the admonishments of their parents and realize they have to consider their peers and the fact that the world is not one in which sexual and aggressive impulses can go unrestrained. The ego helps children test reality—to see how far they can go without getting into trouble or hurting themselves.

The ego houses our higher mental functions such as reasoning, problem solving, and decision making, and for that reason it is sometimes referred to as the executive branch of personality. However, according to Freud, the ego develops out of the id and is forever wedded to it. Thus, although Freud recognized the importance of cognitive functions, such as problem-solving capabilities, he nonetheless believed that these always come into conflict with the wishes of the id; and in Freud's view the ego usually is the loser.

According to Freud, the id and the ego are void of any morality. They do not take into account whether something is right or wrong; This is left to the third branch, sometimes called the moral branch, of personality: the **superego.** It is mainly through interactions

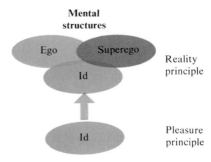

FIGURE 10.2
The development of personality structures according to Freud's theory.

with parents that the superego develops. By rewarding prosocial conduct and punishing antisocial behavior, parents teach children certain moral principles. Freud believed that the superego has two compartments, a **conscience,** which reflects our moral inhibitions that are the product of parents' punishments, and an **ego ideal,** which indicates our standards of perfection that are the result of parents' reward of good behavior. Freud believed that feelings or emotions are an important aspect of the superego. Guilt is a feeling that inhibits immoral behavior, and pride is an emotion that encourages it. In Freud's view, moral development is primarily a result of feelings of guilt that are instilled by punitive parents and such guilt is responsible for keeping id impulses in check. See figure 10.2 for a representation of the development of the id, ego, and superego.

At times the three different components of personality work in opposition to one another. Your id may want to have sex, but your ego says that you don't want the intrusion on the development of your career by having an unwanted child. And your superego says that it is morally wrong to have intercourse with someone on the first date. For the most part, though, the three components of personality work together. However, in working together, Freud always saw the id as a producer of conflict for the ego and superego. Regardless of how well we have adapted to reality and how well we have worked out an advanced moral system to live by, Freud believed that the impulses of the id will cause conflict. Indeed, Freud's view of the individual is one in which conflict is always a dominant characteristic.

Now we turn our attention to one of the most useful concepts in psychoanalytic theory—defense mechanisms. As you will see, these mechanisms help children adapt to the reality of the world.

Defense Mechanisms   The ego has a tendency to distort perceptions of reality in favor of the fantasy-oriented desires of the id. One way of reducing the conflict between the id and the ego is to express the desires of the id in a disguised manner. This is accomplished by means of defense mechanisms. **Defense mechanisms** are a powerful part of the symbolic transformation of experience. For example, a child may have a very strong aggressive drive, but it would not be safe for the child to express such desires of the id. Consequently, like a shield, the child may develop a defense mechanism that channels his or her aggressive impulses into socially acceptable activities like playing football or energetically pursuing a musical career (see figure 10.3). Now we turn our attention to six specific defense mechanisms: repression, reaction formation, regression, rationalization, displacement, and projection.

Freud believed that the most powerful and pervasive defense mechanism is **repression,** a tendency of the ego to push anxiety-producing information into the unconscious mind. For example, he thought that the Oedipus complex is solved through repression. As another example, a person may actually harbor the motive to brutally harm someone but repress the wish into the unconscious aspect of his mind because he knows it will lead to harmful consequences. It is important to distinguish between repression and suppression. In repression we are not aware of our harmful impulses, but in **suppression** we actively, consciously keep our impulses in check.

Reaction formation refers to the process by which repressed thoughts appear in the conscious part of the child's mind as mirror opposites of the repressed thoughts. When I was in elementary school I was asked whether I liked a particular girl. My response was, "Are you kidding, I hate her!" In truth I was embarrassed about the fact that I really liked her and had gotten to the point where I had repressed my puppy love for her. The repressed feeling of love had come out in its mirror opposite—hate.

The defense mechanism of **regression** is the tendency to return to an earlier stage of development. Under stress, we have a tendency to go back to patterns of behavior that brought us reward and security at an earlier age. Thus some people may eat a lot of food when they get frustrated. By eating a lot they satisfy their oral need, a regression to the satisfying feelings of their infant years. Similarly, some people cry like a baby when they get frustrated and can't seem to cope with their current problems.

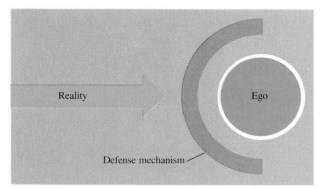

FIGURE 10.3
The function of an ego defense mechanism. Like a shield, the defense mechanism protects the ego from the harsher aspects of reality (Bruno, 1983).

How might regression be involved in this boy's behavior?

You are studying hard for an exam that is coming up tomorrow. You are really getting into the material when a friend calls up and says he has just set up a party that is going to start in an hour. He tells you that the certain person of the opposite sex you have been interested in but haven't had a date with yet is going to be there. You know that if you don't stay in your room and study that you probably will get a bad grade on the exam tomorrow. But you tell yourself, "Well, I did well on the first test in this class, and I have been studying hard all semester; it's time I had some fun." So you go to the party. You have engaged in the process of **rationalization,** a defense mechanism in which the real motive for your behavior is not accepted by your ego. The real motive is replaced by a sort of cover motive. The real motive is going to the party, having fun, and seeing the person you want a date with. But a little voice within you says that if that is the reason you are going then you should stay and study. Your ego now steps in and fixes up the motive so it looks better. Your ego says that you've worked hard all semester and you deserve a break and need to unwind, a rationale that is more acceptable than just going to have fun and meet a person you want to go out with.

Displacement is the process whereby a motive that is not acceptable in one form is acceptable in another or when an individual attributes an emotion to one person when it really is someone else's. In the first instance, recall our earlier example of aggression: Football is an acceptable form of aggression in our society whereas punching someone in the nose is not. In the second instance, consider the husband who is angry at his boss but comes home and within minutes has picked a fight with his wife and taken his anger out on her.

Projection occurs when we perceive our external world in terms of our own personal conflicts. We all have undesirable characteristics that we are not proud of and are distasteful to our ego. One way we cope with these undesirable traits it to project them onto someone else. The businesswoman, who is a real wheeler-dealer, taking advantage of everyone at the slightest opportunity to push herself up the corporate ladder, tells her associate, "Everybody around here is so manipulative. We have to watch out for these wheeler-dealers." In reality the speaker is the biggest manipulator in the company, but because it is distasteful to her, she paints everyone else as having her trait.

Freud believed that defense mechanisms are a prominent feature of our cognitive world, helping us adapt to the demands of reality. Next we see that another important feature of Freud's theory is its emphasis on the developmental unfolding of personality.

The Development of Personality Another important aspect of Freud's theory is that it is a **stage theory.** Freud argued that development involves distinct qualitative changes—changes that he called the stages of development. These stages, according to Freud, occur in a universal fashion and in a fixed sequence: the fact that they are qualitative means they are dramatic changes that significantly alter a person's life from one period of development to the next. Freud's is one of the most widely discussed stage theories in developmental psychology, as well as one of the most prominent theories of personality.

According to Freud, as the id, ego, and superego develop, we go through five clearly distinguishable stages. Each one can be defined in terms of an overriding theme that guides our life at that particular point in development. Freud's theory is said to be psychosexual because personality development is intertwined with the development of the sexual drive. As you will note Freud's stages are actually psychosexual stages: oral, anal, phallic, latency, and genital.

During the first twelve to eighteen months of life the activities of the infant that bring the greatest amount of pleasure center around the mouth: hence the infant is in the **oral stage** of development. The activities of chewing, sucking, and biting provide the chief sources of pleasure, reducing tension as they are engaged in.

The period lasting from about one and a half years to three years of life is called the **anal stage** in Freud's theory because the child's greatest pleasure surrounds the anus, or the eliminative functions associated with it. The shift to the anal stage is brought about by the maturation of the sphincter muscles and the child's ability to hold back or expel waste material at will. It is assumed that the exercise of the anal muscles reduces tension. This period is not easily forgotten by parents who typically experience considerable concern over their initially unsuccessful efforts at toilet training.

During the **phallic stage,** which lasts from about the third to the sixth year of life, the focus is on the child's genitals. It is during this period, according to Freud,

Which Freudian stage is this girl in?

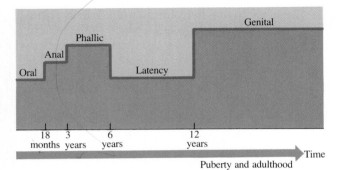

FIGURE 10.4
The five psychosexual stages proposed by Freud (Bruno, 1983).

that boys and girls become acutely aware of their sexual anatomy and the anatomical differences between the sexes. This awareness sets up a number of complex psychological problems. Working through these highly stressful conflicts about sexual matters may take a number of years and is said to form the basis for the mature adult's sexual identity.

During these early years the development of identification with parents is a central theme in Freud's view. The identification process proceeds differently for boys and girls. All children initially identify with their mother. However, during the phallic stage boys switch this identification to their father. This is a time when considerable conflict and psychosexual desires for the opposite-sexed parent need to be resolved. The sexual desire for the mother and rivalrous feelings toward the father on the part of boys is called the **Oedipus complex.** A girl's desire for her father and rivalrous feelings toward her mother are called the **Electra complex.** Freud actually pictured identification as a defense mechanism in which the child resolves inner conflict and sexual desires for the opposite-sexed parent by patterning himself or herself after the parent of the same sex.

But the child does not completely resolve the sexual conflicts experienced during the preschool years. Instead the troublesome feelings are repressed, driven from consciousness and locked away in the unconscious id. This repression marks the onset of the **latency stage,** the long period of middle and late childhood that lasts from about six years to eleven or twelve years of age. During the latency stage the child represses all interest in sexual matters, instead showing more intellectual interest and a desire to learn about the world. This activity channels ·much of the child's energy into emotionally safe areas and aids the child in forgetting the highly stressful problems of the previous stage. However, the latency stage is like the lull before the storm.

The **genital stage** begins with the onset of puberty and lasts throughout the adult years. At the beginning of the genital stage, sexual interest is reawakened. In the mature adult, Freud felt that the capacity to love and work are the two most important themes of life. It is during the adolescent years, Freud believed, that the individual feels strong sexual drives for someone other than his or her parents. Freud believed, however, that Oedipal sexual feelings may reemerge as the individual seeks a love object outside the family. More information about the genital stage and defense mechanisms in the adolescent years appears in Perspective on Child Development 10.1. Figure 10.4 reveals the fluctuations in sexual drive that Freud believed underlie personality development as well as the development of the psychosexual stages.

Before we go on to other psychoanalytic views, let's briefly evaluate the status of Freud's theory today, noting in particular the pervasive influence it has had on our pursuit of understanding the mind and behavior.

PERSPECTIVE ON CHILD DEVELOPMENT 10.1

THE ROLE OF DEFENSE MECHANISMS IN ADOLESCENT ADJUSTMENT: THE VIEWS OF PETER BLOS AND ANNA FREUD

For Peter Blos (1962, 1985), one of the most well accepted contemporary psychoanalytic theorists who studies adolescents, regression during adolescence is not defensive at all, but rather is an integral part of puberty. Such regression, according to Blos, is inevitable and universal. The nature of this regression may vary from one adolescent to the next. It may involve childhood autonomy, compliance, and cleanliness, or it may involve a sudden return to the passiveness that characterized the adolescent's behavior during infancy or early childhood. Blos believes that intrafamilial struggles during adolescence reflect the presence of unresolved conflicts from childhood.

An excellent example of how the psychoanalytic theorist works in tying together adolescent feelings with childhood experiences rests in the work of Joseph Adelson and Margery Doehrman (1980). When their patient, John, was sixteen he entered a group therapy session with other adolescents. At that time he was recovering from severe depression following the break-off of a serious relationship with a girlfriend. The girl's mother actually referred John to the clinic, sensing that John's depression was severe, just as she had earlier detected that his dependency on her daughter was acute. John was a handsome, intelligent, articulate adolescent and a leader at school, hardly the type of person you would think might be deeply and severely depressed.

After a series of sessions with John it became apparent that he kept most girls at a distance, particularly when they seemed to want to get seriously involved or to "mother" him. On the other hand, he was attracted to girls who were either aloof or tomboyish. It gradually became clear that John's relationships with girls were characterized by a wish to reestablish a union with his mother and that he had an intense fear of that wish. He was attracted to girls who were standoffish, but once he established a relationship with one of them, he would sink into an uncontrollable dependency upon her, to the point of being enthralled by such dependency.

To some degree, then, John's attachments to girls represented a wish to become reunited with his mother. What was John's relationship with his mother like in adolescence? He was often abusive toward her; he complained that she nagged at him all the time; but in truth he was frightened by his regressive feelings toward her,

according to Adelson. The regressive feelings came out clearly in group therapy when his intelligent participation would be replaced by sarcasm and then scorn whenever he seemed to be drawn to the "maternal" females in the group. This was particularly true with the woman therapist, who was seen as the group's "mother."

Although some psychoanalytic writers, like Blos, consider regression a normal part of adolescent development, for individuals like John the reappearance of unresolved conflicts from early childhood requires therapy. For most individuals, however, the conflicts are not so serious that therapy is warranted. Thus, the intensity and persistence of the regression determine whether it is a healthy or unhealthy part of adolescent development.

Anna Freud (1958, 1966) has developed the idea that defense mechanisms are the key to understanding adolescent adjustment. She believes that the problems of adolescence are not to be unlocked by understanding the id, or instinctual forces, but instead are to be discovered in the existence of "love objects" in the adolescent's past, both oedipal and preoedipal. She argues that the attachment to these love objects, usually parents, is carried forward from the infant years and merely toned down or inhibited during the latency years. During adolescence, these pregenital urges may be reawakened, or worse, newly acquired genital (adolescent) urges may combine with the urges that developed in early childhood.

Anna Freud goes on to describe how adolescent defense mechanisms are used to ward off these infantile intrusions. Youth may withdraw from their attachment and identification with their parents and suddenly transfer their love to others—to parent substitutes, to leaders who represent ideals, or to peers. Or, rather than transferring the attachment to someone else, adolescents may reverse their feelings toward the attachment figure—replacing love with hate or dependence with rebellion. Finally, the instinctual fears may even generate unhealthy defensive solutions. For example, the adolescent may withdraw within himself, which could lead to grandiose ideas of triumph or persecution; or regression could occur. Thus, from Anna Freud's perspective, a number of defense mechanisms are essential to the adolescent's handling of conflicts.

Freud's Theory Today   Few psychologists accept all of Freud's major theses today. His belief that virtually all of our behavior is motivated by unconscious desire seems too sweeping a statement. Many of the things that bother us are very well known to us. And sexual tension does not undergird all of our efforts to be competent in our world.

How then should we view the concepts in Freud's theory? Each idea should be evaluated for the broad insights it provides and not for its literal accuracy. For example, the concept of defense mechanisms was a major contribution to our understanding of personality, although such repression is not as pervasive as Freud believed. When we stop to think about our life it is not too difficult, if we are the least bit objective, to see how we are susceptible to using defense mechanisms in many stressful circumstances. It is also true that there is an unconscious aspect to our mind—we do many things for reasons unknown to us, yet we are more aware of the reasons for our behavior than Freud believed.

Freud's ideas opened many doors in psychology that had previously been ignored or considered too controversial for exploration. Current inquiries about sex roles, parent–child and parent–adolescent conflict, and aggression can all be traced to Freud's inquiries about personality. Next, however, we see that Freud has his dissenters as well.

The Freudian Revisionists

First we discuss some basic ideas of the Freudian revisionists and then outline the main points in Erik Erikson's well-known perspective on development.

The Main Themes   In the twentieth century there have been a host of scholars whose ideas fit within the framework of psychoanalytic theory but who nonetheless depart from Freud on at least one major point. For example, Erikson, like Freud, believes the unconscious mind is a significant aspect of personality, that early development is an important foundation for later development, and that we go through a series of stages in our development. However, Erikson believes we go through psychosocial stages of development rather than psychosexual ones, and he argues that we continue going through several stages during our adult years whereas Freud believed that one stage—the genital—characterizes all of adolescent and adult development.

Revised versions of Freud's psychoanalytic theory are often referred to as **neo-Freudian** (or **neopsychoanalytic**) theories of personality, although Carl Jung and Alfred Adler saw themselves as dissenters and preferred not to be associated with Freud's ideas. Consequently, some personality experts only refer to the later modifiers of psychoanalytic theory, such as Harry Stack Sullivan and Erik Erikson, as neo-Freudians.

Among the major trends apparent in the psychoanalytic revisionist views of personality (e.g., Adler, 1927; Erikson, 1968; Fromm, 1947; Horney, 1937; Jung, 1917; Rapaport, 1967; Sullivan, 1953) are the following:

1. Sexuality is not seen as the pervasive underlying force behind personality that Freud believed it to be.
2. The preeminence of the first five years of life in shaping adult personality is deemphasized, with later experiences in development being given at least some importance in the shaping of personality.
3. More emphasis is given to the social factors that influence personality. Harry Stack Sullivan (1953), in particular, has emphasized that personality cannot be studied apart from social circumstances. Sullivan pointed out that most personality characteristics actually describe an individual's ways of interacting with the social world—for example, nurturant, introverted, assertive, and so forth.
4. The ego and its conscious thought processes are given more strength in personality and are not always viewed as at the mercy of the id and its unconscious forces. In neopsychoanalytic theory this view is usually referred to as the autonomy of the ego, meaning that it has a separate line of development from biological instincts. Thus achievement, thinking, and reasoning are not necessarily tied to sexual and aggressive impulses.

Erik Erikson's Theory   One well-known contemporary neopsychoanalytic theorist is Erik Erikson. Like Freud, Erikson stresses the importance of early family experiences and unconscious thought. However, he believes Freud shortchanged the importance of culture in determining personality. For example, both Freud and

Erikson describe changes that take place during adolescence. For Freud these changes are primarily sexual in nature, but for Erikson they involve the development of an identity. Erikson believes it is during adolescence that individuals begin a thorough search for who they are, what they are all about, and where they are going in life. As part of this search for an identity, the adolescent often experiments with a variety of roles, some sexual, others ideological, and still others vocational.

Each of Erikson's eight ages (or stages) of development centers around a salient and distinct emotional concern stemming from biological pressures within the person and sociocultural expectations from outside the person. These concerns, or conflicts, may be resolved in a positive, healthy manner or in a pessimistic and unhealthy way (Erikson, 1968). Each conflict has a unique time period during which it ascends and overshadows all the others. For the later stages of development to proceed smoothly, each earlier stage conflict must be resolved satisfactorily. These stages are presented in figure 10.5. In the left-hand column are the major stages of development. The eight conflicts are listed diagonally, in order of their ascendancy.

Erik Erikson, the giant developmental theorist.

Phases of the life cycle	1	2	3	4	5	6	7	8
Late adulthood								Ego integrity vs. despair
Middle adulthood							Generativity vs. stagnation	
Young adulthood						Intimacy vs. isolation		
Adolescence					Identity vs. role confusion			
Middle and late childhood				Industry vs. inferiority				
Early childhood			Initiative vs. guilt					
Infancy		Autonomy vs. shame, doubt						
Infancy	Basic trust vs. mistrust							

FIGURE 10.5
Erikson's stages of development.

The first stage, **trust versus mistrust,** corresponds to the oral stage in Freudian theory. An infant is almost entirely dependent upon his or her mother for food, sustenance, and comfort. The mother is the primary representative of society to the child. If she discharges her infant-related duties with warmth, regularity, and affection, the infant will develop a feeling of trust toward the world. The infant's trust is a comfortable feeling that someone will always be around to care for his or her needs even though the mother occasionally disappears. Alternatively, a sense of mistrust or fearful uncertainty can develop if the mother fails to provide these needs in the caretaking setting. According to Erikson, she is setting up a distrusting attitude that will follow the child through life.

Autonomy versus shame and doubt is the second stage and corresponds to the anal stage in Freudian theory. The infant begins to gain control over the bowels and bladder. Parents begin imposing demands on the child to conform to socially acceptable forms and occasions for eliminating wastes. The child may develop the healthy attitude of being capable of independent or autonomous control of his or her own actions, or may develop the unhealthy attitude of shame or doubt because he or she is incapable of control.

Initiative versus guilt corresponds to the phallic period in Freudian theory. The child is caught in the midst of the Oedipus or Electra conflict, with its alternating love-hate feelings for the parent of the opposite sex and with fear of fulfilling the sexual fantasies that abound. The child may discover ways to overcome feelings of powerlessness by engaging in various activities. If this is done, then the basic healthy attitude of being the initiator of action will result. Alternatively, the child may fail to discover such outlets and feel guilt at being dominated by the environment.

Industry versus inferiority, coinciding with the Freudian period of latency, covers the years of middle childhood when the child is involved in expansive absorption of knowledge and the development of intellectual and physical skills. As the child is drawn into the social culture of peers, it is natural to evaluate accomplishments by comparing himself or herself with others. If the child views himself or herself as basically competent in these activities, feelings of productiveness and industriousness will result. On the other hand, if the child views himself or herself as incompetent, particularly in comparison with peers, then he or she will feel unproductive and inferior. This unhealthy attitude may negatively color the child's whole approach to life and learning, producing a tendency to withdraw from new and challenging situations rather than meet them with confidence and enthusiasm.

Identity versus identity confusion (diffusion) is roughly associated with Freud's genital stage, centering on the establishment of a stable personal identity. Whereas for Freud the important part of identity formation resides in the adolescent's resolution of sexual conflicts, for Erikson the central ingredient is the establishment of a clear path toward a vocation—selection of a job or an occupational role to aspire to. This allows the adolescent an objective that he or she and other members of society simultaneously acknowledge. If the adolescent comes through this period with a clearly selected role and the knowledge that others in society can clearly identify this role, feelings of confidence and purposefulness emerge. If not, the child may feel confused and troubled.

Erikson introduced the first of the post-Freudian stages, **intimacy versus isolation.** Early adulthood brings with it a job and the opportunity to form an intimate relationship with a member of the opposite sex. If the young adult forms friendships with others and a significant, intimate relationship with one individual in particular, then a basic feeling of closeness with others will result. A feeling of isolation may result from an inability to form friendships and an intimate relationship.

A chief concern of adults is to assist the younger generation in developing and leading useful lives. **Generativity versus stagnation** centers on successful rearing of children. Childless adults often need to find substitute young people through adoption, guardianship, or a close relationship with the children of friends and relatives. Generativity, or the feeling of helping to shape the next generation, is the positive outcome that may emerge. Stagnation, or the feeling of having done nothing for the next generation, is the unhealthy outcome.

In the later years we enter the period of **ego integrity versus despair,** a time for looking back at what we have done with our lives. Through many different routes, the older person may have developed a positive outlook in each of the preceding periods of emotional crises. If so, the retrospective glances will reveal a picture of life well spent, and the person will be satisfied (ego integrity).

However, the older person may have resolved one or more of the crises in a negative way. If so, the retrospective glances will yield doubt, gloom, and despair over the worth of one's life.

It should be noted that Erikson does not believe the proper solution to a stage crisis is always completely positive in nature. Some exposure and/or commitment to the negative end of the individual's bipolar conflict often is inevitable (for example, the individual cannot trust all people under all circumstances and survive). However, in a healthy solution to a stage crisis, the positive resolution of the conflict is dominant.

The Strengths and Weaknesses of the Psychoanalytic Theories

Like most grand theories of development, psychoanalytic theory has its strengths and weaknesses. First, we discuss some of its major contributions and strengths, and second, we look at some of its possible flaws and weaknesses.

Among the strengths of psychoanalytic theory are its focus on (1) the role of the past, (2) the developmental course of personality, (3) mental representation of the environment, and (4) the role of the unconscious mind; its emphasis on conflict; and its influence on developmental psychology as a discipline. Today we assume that past experiences influence our current thought and behavior. The psychoanalytic emphasis on the importance of early experience in influencing thought and behavior at later points in development has remained as an important part of developmental psychology. Also, the importance of viewing personality from a developmental stance continues as an important theme in the field. The psychoanalytic belief that environmental experiences are mentally transformed and represented in the mind likewise continues to be given considerable attention by psychologists. Psychoanalytic theorists forced psychologists to recognize that the mind is not all consciousness; some of what is in the mind is unconscious as well. Psychoanalytic theory has promoted the belief that conflict is one important ingredient of psychological problems and adjustment. Finally, psychoanalytic theory has continued to play an important role in forcing developmental psychologists to study the importance of personality and adjustment rather than being interested only in such experimentally oriented topics as sensation, perception, and learning.

Nevertheless, while psychoanalytic theory has made important contributions to psychology and has a number of strengths, it is not without its flaws and weaknesses. Some of its very strengths turn out to be some of its weaknesses as well, often because its orientations were stated in such an extreme manner. Five such prominent weaknesses are (1) the difficulty of testing psychoanalytic concepts, (2) lack of an empirical data base and overreliance on self-reports of the past, (3) overemphasis on the unconscious mind and sexuality, (4) a negative and pessimistic view of human nature, and (5) too much emphasis on early experience.

The main concepts of psychoanalytic theory have been very difficult to test scientifically. Researchers have tried to investigate concepts like repression in the laboratory, but their efforts have generally not met with a great deal of success. Much of the data used to support psychoanalytic theory come from patients' reconstruction of the past, often the distant past (adults perception of their infant and early childhood years), and thus may be of doubtful accuracy. Other data called on to support psychoanalytic theory come from the subjective evaluation of clinicians, and it is very easy for the clinicians to see what they expect to see because of theory they are used to. Freud and many other psychoanalytic theorists (though not Erikson) overemphasized the importance of sexuality in development. Most psychoanalysts also place too much faith in the power of the unconscious mind to control behavior, often to the point of ignoring the role of conscious thought processes. In addition, the psychoanalytic view provides a perspective on the individual that is too negative and pessimistic. We clearly are not born into the world only with a bundle of evil instincts and drives. Furthermore, psychoanalytic theory often places too much emphasis on the first five years of life as determinants of subsequent development. Personality development continues throughout the human life cycle and is influenced by past, present, and anticipated future circumstances, a point accurately captured by Erikson. Later experiences may be just as important as early experiences in determining development in many instances.

We have discussed a number of ideas about psychoanalytic theory. Concept Table 10.1 provides a summary of these ideas.

CONCEPT TABLE 10.1
Psychoanalytic Theories

Theorists and Features	Structures/Processes	Characteristics/Explanations
Freud	Structure of personality	
	Id	The instinctual, biological, unconscious aspect; location of sexual and aggressive impulses; pleasure principle and primary process thinking lie here.
	Ego	The rational part of personality that maintains contact with reality; reality principle here.
	Superego	Moral branch of personality, comprised of conscience and ego ideal.
	Defense mechanisms	Help reduce conflict between id and ego by means of disguise.
	Repression	Pushing anxiety-producing information into the unconscious.
	Reaction formation	Repressed thoughts appear as mirror opposites.
	Regression	Tendency to go back to an earlier stage of personality.
	Rationalization	Real motive for behavior is not accepted by ego.
	Displacement	Motive not acceptable in one form is acceptable in another form.
	Projection	Perceiving the external world in terms of one's own personal conflicts.
	Development of personality	Personality develops in psychosexual stages.
	Oral stage	Pleasure centers on mouth; first year of life.
	Anal stage	Pleasure focuses on anus; second year of life.
	Phallic stage	Pleasure involves child's genitals; third to sixth years.
	Latency stage	Interest in sexual matters repressed; sixth to eleventh or twelfth years.
	Genital stage	Sexual interest reawakened; strong sexual motivation; begins with puberty and lasts through remainder of life.
Freudian revisionists, neo-Freudian views	Basic themes	Less emphasis on sexuality; more life-cycle concerns; more stress on social factors; more interest in ego and conscious thought.
	Erikson's theory	Proposes eight stages of development throughout the human life cycle; stages are psychosocial rather than psychosexual; emphasizes interaction of biology and culture more than Freud did.
Strengths and weaknesses of psychoanalytic approach	Strengths	(1) Emphasis on past. (2) Development. (3) Mental representation and translation of environment. (4) Unconscious mind. (5) Conflict. (6) Impact on psychology in general.
	Weaknesses	(1) Concepts difficult to test. (2) Lack of empirical data base and overemphasis on past. (3) Overemphasis on unconscious mind and sexuality. (4) Negative and pessimistic view of human nature. (5) Too much emphasis on early experience.

While psychoanalytic theory continues to be one of the most prominent views of children's socialization, it has many competitors. One perspective, the behavioral, social learning view, which we describe next was for many years the major competitor of psychoanalytic theory in the field of children's socialization. As you read about the behavioral, social learning view, you will discover that many of the main points in psychoanalytic theory are totally unacceptable to the behavioral, social learning theorists.

The Behavioral and Social Learning Views

Behaviorism emerged as a prominent influence in psychology during the 1920s. Initially, we focus on the behavioral views of John Watson and B. F. Skinner and then turn our attention to the social learning perspective, a view that has played a strong role in socialization research. Next we outline important processes in the behavioral, social learning view. As we discuss this view it may be helpful for you to review the description of learning processes in chapter 5. Finally, we discuss the strengths and weaknesses of the behavioral, social learning approach.

The Behavioral View

Our discussion of the behavioral view begins with a journey back in time to the 1920s, where we encounter the strong influence of John Watson. Then we consider some of the basic points in B. F. Skinner's behavioral view.

John Watson's Views on Children

Unlike Freud, John Watson believed that the child's behavior can be shaped in an endless number of ways by parents, siblings, peers, teachers, and so forth. As you might expect, Watson's statements were critical of those who believed the child's behavior was dominated by instincts.

Watson, like Freud, did believe that parents play an important role in socializing the child. He argued that too often parents leave to chance stimulus–response connections between themselves and their children. In other words, parents may inadvertently be rewarding the wrong kind of behaviors and punishing desirable behaviors. Interestingly, Watson believed it was not a wise strategy for parents to hug, kiss, and pet their children. He felt that through such treatment children learned to become too dependent on their parents. Watson (1928) said that the right way to treat children is to deal with them as if they are young adults. Don't let them sit in your lap; and if you feel you have to kiss them, do it only once a day when you put them to bed at night. Don't be sentimental and soon you will see your child become more competent.

Child-rearing prescriptions, such as Watson's, have generated considerable debate about how children should be treated. The debate of how much attention, nurturance, and independence children should be given continues, as will be seen when we discuss this issue more extensively in chapter 11.

B. F. Skinner's Ideas

B. F. Skinner continued the behavioral emphasis of Watson. While a majority of Skinner's work has been with animals, he has liberally applied his behavioral ideas to human development. His view of how individuals should be socialized has probably created more controversy than any other view. The main theme of Skinner's work is that individuals are controlled by their environment. There is no room for the unconscious mind described by Freud in the behavioral view of personality advocated by Skinner and many other behaviorists. For Skinner, personality is simply learned behavior, behavior that is determined by its rewarding and punishing consequences. Thus for Skinner, children are likely to develop a healthy personality if they have been rewarded for appropriate behavior and they are likely to develop an inadequate personality if they have grown up in an environment where they have not been rewarded for appropriate behavior (Skinner, 1938, 1971). In Skinner's view, personality, like any behavior, is acquired and maintained through the principles of operant conditioning outlined in chapter 5.

Recall that Freud believed personality is comprised of three structures that interact with one another—id, ego, and superego. Neither these nor other personality structures exist within the child according to behaviorists. Indeed, behaviorists argue that searching for such structures is a mistake because it takes time away from discovering the environmental determinants of behavior, the true causes of personality. Behaviorists believe that personality must be studied by means of the method of observing behavior. Thus observations should be as precise as possible and should be directed at uncovering the controlling environmental conditions that determine a child's behavior.

Social Learning Theory

The social learning theorist shares the behaviorist's concern for studying the environment as an important determinant of social behavior, for the use of observation, and for the importance of reinforcement in influencing social behavior. However, social learning theorists believe behaviorists have missed much of the richness in social behavior by not studying how children process information about their social world. According to the social learning theorists, cognitive processes mediate the relation between the environment and behavior. To learn more about the social learning perspective, we study the views of the two most prominent social learning theorists, Albert Bandura and Walter Mischel.

Albert Bandura

In chapter 5 we highlighted Bandura's (1977a) ideas about the importance of observational learning in determining behavior. Here we provide an overview of his most important ideas about social behavior.

1. Personality is comprised of social behavior and cognitive processes such as memory and imagery.
2. The environment plays a powerful role in determining children's personality; biological processes are relatively unimportant.

3. Children's personality is learned through the processes of observational learning, instrumental conditioning, classical conditioning, and self-reinforcement.
4. Personality structures within the child probably do not exist—no one has ever observed them.
5. Social behavior, and hence personality, is reciprocally determined, suggesting that it is impossible to talk about the child's personality without reference to social interaction between children.
6. A child's social behavior often varies according to the situation or setting he or she is in. A child may show extraverted behavior with parents but reveal more introverted behavior at school.

Next we see that Walter Mischel, even more than Bandura, is responsible for putting the situation into personality.

Walter Mischel In his book *Personality and Assessment* (1968), Walter Mischel evaluated a massive amount of research to show how children's personality traits are not as consistent and stable as some personality theorists have portrayed them. At the time Mischel's book was published, another personality theory, trait theory, and psychoanalytic theory were (and still are) influential. Both place a heavy premium on the stability of a child's personality traits across time and situations. Thus, we consider a child to be either honest in nearly all situations and over time, or we consider him or her to be immoral. In reality, however, it is the very rare child who cheats, lies, and steals in nearly all contexts. And where is the child who does not at least engage in such inappropriate conduct occasionally (Hartshorne & May, 1928)?

The trait approach views personality as a bundle of personality traits housed somewhere in the child's mind and which when put together form the child's internal personality structure. As we just commented, however, behavioral and social learning theorists do not believe such an internal structure exists within the child.

Mischel was heavily criticized for taking the person out of personality (e.g., Bem & Allen, 1974) and replacing the person with situations. To some extent, his influential 1968 book reflected this heavy situational view of personality—that is, the child's personality is determined by the context the child is in. However, in

Walter Mischel, the creator of cognitive social learning theory.

a series of papers Mischel (1973, 1979) has pointed out that personality is determined by a number of characteristics and cognitive processes of the child, along with the situations or environmental settings in which the child lives. Following is a summary of the person variables Mischel says interact with environmental experiences to produce the child's personality:

1. Competencies. These include children's intellectual abilities, social and physical skills, and any special abilities children possess.
2. Expectancies. The expectancies children have for their own behavior and the behavior of others is an important influence on their behavior. The child's past history provides many expectations.
3. Encoding strategies and personal constructs. The way children process information in their world and cognitively transform that information influences their personality. Children use **personal constructs** to label stimuli they experience and to help make sense out of what they are like and what others are like. Children label and categorize themselves and others just like scientists do—calling themselves and others freaky, intolerable, honest, and the like. Being able to remember a construct over a long period of time and across many situations, as well as abstracting from past common elements about the self that are reasonably enduring, children develop a permanent sense of who they are.

4. Subjective stimulus values. The values children place on a stimulus are important determinants of their personality. These values require a great deal of specificity in that they often pertain only to certain situations and people. For example, children are often only anxious in certain situations, not all situations (Wolpe, 1963). Thus social learning theorists believe that personality often depends on the situation or context children are in, a concept called **situationism.**

5. Self-regulatory systems and plans. Like Bandura, Mischel believes that self-reinforcements, self-criticisms, and personal standards of conduct vary greatly; one behavior may be very important to one individual and totally disdained by another. For example, one student who gets a C throws his test paper into the wastebasket in a fit of anger because he feels he did not do well, while another student smiles and says, "Thank goodness I got a C. Now I don't think I'll flunk the class." The two students respond differently to the same stimulus because they do not have the same standards for their personal behavior. In addition, we can generate plans that can guide our life for years to come, such as deciding to get married, choosing to go to college, and opting to have a child.

In short, Mischel believes that both cognitive processes and experiences determine the child's personality, just as Bandura does. This view of personality has been called **cognitive social learning theory** because of its emphasis on cognitive processes and social experiences.

Some Important Behavioral and Social Learning Processes

Recall from chapter 5, where we discussed learning, that three very important processes in learning are reinforcement, punishment, and imitation. This holds true whether we are evaluating the nature of children's learning in intellectual domains, such as learning to read or learning math, or in social domains, as when children are learning manners, learning about parent–child relationships, or learning about peer relationships. Here we build on the basic ideas presented in chapter 5 and provide some additional information about learning processes involved in social circumstances.

Reinforcement Our description of reinforcement begins with some basic ideas about reinforcement and then covers information about the relative nature of reinforcement and self-reinforcement.

The saying "Behavior is determined by its consequences" is an important principle of social learning theory. When a person does or says something to you, you can react in one of three ways: positively, neutrally, or negatively. Consider the following interchange between two boys:

Carl: Where did you get that ice cream cone?
John: My mother gave it to me.
Carl: Why?
John: Because I was mad and started yelling.
Carl: You mean when you yell you get an ice cream cone?
John: I guess that's the way it works.

What is the likelihood that John will shout again? Right—greater than before. The basic point of reinforcement is that a behavior followed by a positive reward is likely to recur.

How might the mother have reacted to her son's yelling to decrease the chances of his yelling in later situations? She could have ignored the shouting (reacted neutrally), or sent him to his room or kept him from watching TV for some period of time (reacted negatively). Reacting neutrally or negatively to a person's behavior often decreases the likelihood of its recurrence.

Recall from chapter 5 our description of Jess and how he was trained to influence his teacher's behavior by rewarding certain things the teacher did. In our description of Jess we outlined three important aspects of studies that characterize many inquiries into the nature of children's reinforcement: baseline, acquisition, and extinction. We review these three steps here by providing another example of children's social behavior.

Some of the first studies of reinforcement with children were conducted with nursery school boys and girls who the teachers agreed needed some shaping up (Harris, Wolf & Baer, 1964). One boy repeatedly threw his glasses down and broke them; another loved to pinch adults, particularly the teacher. One girl spent over 80 percent of her time on the floor; another isolated herself from other children more than 85 percent of the time. It was decided that the teacher's attention might

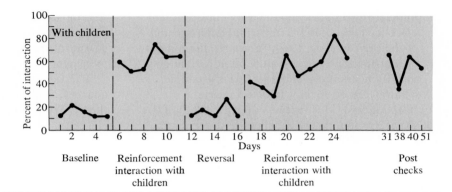

FIGURE 10.6
Daily percentages of time spent in social interaction with children during approximately two hours of each morning session (Harris, Wolf, and Baer, 1964).

serve as an important reinforcer to change the inappropriate behavior of the children.

The first step is to observe the child without making any changes. This procedure provides a baseline measure of the behavior that needs to be changed. The second step involves following the behavior to be changed with a positive consequence (a reinforcer)—in this case, the teacher's attention. This procedure is often called acquisition—a new response is being acquired or an old one is being strengthened. For example, when the girl isolated herself, the teacher simply gave no attention to her. However, an important part of this second step is for positive consequences to follow desirable behaviors. Thus, when the child was with one or more of the other children, the teacher provided positive reinforcement—the teacher smiled at her, patted her on the back, and commented on how nice it was that she was playing with the other children. As you can see in figure 10.6, this procedure was very effective in increasing the desired behavior.

In many of these studies a third step follows. It is called extinction and describes a decrease in performance when positive reinforcement is removed from the desired behavior. In the case of the child who isolated herself, the teacher initiated a phase in which the child was ignored when interacting with peers and was given attention when she isolated herself. In a fourth phase the teacher again reinforced peer interaction. The effects of reversal were evident, as you can see in the figure. Postchecks (phase 5) were made periodically to determine whether peer interaction was sustained even after the teacher's continued attention had been phased out. As the graph in figure 10.6 indicates, social interaction with peers remained at high levels during this last phase.

In most instances "acting out" types of behavior are more difficult to modify than such passive behavior as social isolation. Perhaps the more active behaviors have a payoff in terms of attention (it *is* hard not to say "ouch" when you are pinched). Peer attention to such behaviors is usually high, whereas most peers probably do not pay attention to passive behaviors.

We usually think about reinforcement in terms of whether people are rewarded for what they do, not in terms of their interpretation of the reinforcing stimulus. Even at an early age, however, the child is interpreting the meaning of reinforcements. Through a growing awareness of others, the child interprets reinforcement in a relative sense. One study showed that relative reinforcement, or **social comparison,** is important in determining whether children will behave aggressively or regressively (Santrock, Smith & Bourbeau, 1976). Children were placed in three-member, same-sex groups and given identical toys to play with. In one group, the target child received less reinforcement than the other two children (negative social comparison). In another group, the target child received the same amounts as the others (equal social comparison). In a third group, the target child received more reinforcement than the two other children (positive social comparison). Finally, in a fourth (control) group, the children were given no reinforcement as they played. Subsequently, the three children in each group went to another room where their social interaction with the other children was recorded by two concealed observers. After negative social comparison, children were more physically aggressive toward their peers, teased them more (e.g., holding up a toy and taunting them), and showed more regressive behavior (crying, self-stimulation, wanting to leave) than the others did.

Social comparison is a powerful force in motivating children's behavior.

These results suggest that people's actions may be influenced by a comparison they make between what has happened to somebody else and what has happened to them. For example, when you receive the results of a test, does it matter to you how others in your class did on the test? Do you sometimes ask a classmate, "What did you get?" If you are like almost everyone else, the performance of others probably matters to you. It can be expected to influence your study habits and possibly your performance on the next test.

According to Bandura (1977b), **self-reinforcement** is often just as important as reinforcement by others. Consider your attitude in writing a term paper for school. Although you may not ignore the prospect of getting a good grade, your striving for excellence probably also accounts for improved revisions of the paper; substandard performance would probably lead you to make self-critical remarks. In this sense, your achievement behavior is a function of what you do to yourself as much as what others do to you.

The existence of self-produced consequences and personal standards for performance suggests that reinforcement to control someone else's behavior will not always be successful. As Bandura (1977) has pointed out, if external reinforcement always worked, we would behave like weather vanes—in the presence of a Communist we would act like a Communist, and in the presence of a John Bircher we would act like a John Bircher.

Reciprocal Control Socialization is a reciprocal process. Consider the following excerpt from a conversation between husband and wife.

> *Wife:* Why haven't you fixed my screen door?
> *Husband: (Makes no observable response but sits huddled behind a newspaper)*
> *Wife: (Raises her voice)* A lot of thanks I get for all I do. You said three weeks ago . . .
> *Husband:* Stop nagging at me. As soon as I walk in here and try to read the paper, all I get is yelling.
> *Wife: (Shouting now)* You're so lazy, that's all I can do to get things done!
> *Husband:* All right, I'll fix it later. Now leave me alone!
> (Patterson & Hops, 1972, p. 424)

What have the participants learned in this interchange? The wife has learned that by yelling she can get her husband to make a promise; the husband, however, has also learned that a vague promise can turn off the yelling. This interaction is characterized by a coercive process in which each of them amplifies or increases the intensity of his or her behavior in order to control the other. Whenever one person is trying to control another, there usually is someone resisting control or attempting control in return. In this sense, Bandura (1977a) asserts, the Big Brother of George Orwell's *1984* and the manipulation and control of people suggested in Skinner's *Walden II* may never evolve.

Punishment Erma Bombeck has commented:

> I was raised on threats. . . . My mother had an inexhaustible supply of all-occasion intimidations. And I believed every one of them. . . . The other day I called Mother in desperation. "I need help," I said. "I've used every threat on my kids that you ever used on me and I've run out. Do you have anything stronger that you held out on me?" (Bombeck & Keane, 1971)

All children do some things wrong. In the eyes of their parents, many of them do many things wrong! How should parents deal with a child when he does something wrong?

One of the most frequent applications of punishment in behavior modification has been through the technique of **time-out.** Here is a concrete sample of how it works. A child who disrupts the classroom is immediately removed by the teacher to an isolated place where he cannot interact with anyone or engage in any rewarding activities. After a specified period of time (ten minutes, perhaps, for a young child), he is permitted to return to the classroom. The time-out technique has been used successfully in efforts to reduce tantrum behavior (Risley & Wolf, 1967); to eliminate dangerous climbing (Risley, 1978); and to extinguish destructive behavior of autistic children, such as self-slapping and hair pulling (Peterson & Peterson, 1968).

We should note that some psychologists do not like to refer to time-out as punishment since time-out involves simply removing the child from a pleasant situation. They feel the term *punishment* should be reserved for the presentation of an aversive stimulus that decreases behavior.

Most professionals who attempt behavioral change recommend the use of time-out over conventional punishment, which should be used as a last resort. They point out that when punishment is administered, the child often becomes so aroused that even when the parent provides reasons for his or her punishment, the child may not attend to them. The adult who uses punishment also exposes the child to a model who becomes aroused and outwardly expresses hostility when confronted with problems. Furthermore, desirable behaviors may be eliminated along with the undesirable behaviors when punishment is used. For example, the young child may stop interacting with other children altogether when he or she is slapped by his or her mother for biting them.

Even though there are legitimate reasons for not using punishment to change social behavior, punishment is used every day by parents, teachers, siblings, and peers. The one-year-old child who touches the burner on a stove may be admonished by a slap on the hand. The three-year-old child who wanders out into the street on a tricycle may be spanked and vehemently scolded as a way of underscoring the danger of cycling in the street.

Discipline Practices For many years punishment was analyzed in terms of its physical or psychological nature. More recently, different types of punishment have been identified: power assertion, induction, and love withdrawal (Hoffman, 1970). **Power assertion** refers to attempts to gain control over the child or the child's resources by such means as removing privileges, spanking, or threatening. **Induction** employs reasoning and explanation of the consequences of the child's actions for others. **Love withdrawal** often suggests the removal of the child from the parent; examples include such statements as "I'm going to leave you if you do that again" and "I don't like you when you do that."

Hoffman (1970) points out that all punishment leads to arousal. Power assertion produces a high level of arousal that involves hostility, and love withdrawal is likely to instill a high level of anxiety in the child. Furthermore, induction focuses the child's attention on the consequences of her or his actions, while power assertion and love withdrawal stress the child's own shortcomings. In studies of parent–child relations, it has been found that in middle-class families where mothers use inductive forms of discipline, the children are more advanced in the use of moral reasoning and are more likely to have guilt feelings than children whose mothers use power-assertive forms of discipline (Hoffman, 1970). At least with middle-class children, then, inductive discipline techniques are preferred over love-withdrawal and power-assertive techniques.

Might the effectiveness of different types of discipline vary with the age of the child? Mild forms of physical punishment may be the most effective method of disciplining infants and toddlers in some situations. Two-year-old children probably do not understand complex reasoning and have difficulty following verbal instruction; a light tap on their bottom may be effective in efforts to keep them from touching a hot stove, wandering into the street, or playing on the stairs.

Also, parents may vary the type of discipline technique according to the type and severity of a child's transgression, and they may use a combination of discipline techniques. Joan Grusec and Leon Kuczynski (1980) asked mothers of four- to five- and seven- to eight-year-olds to describe the discipline they would use in situations involving twelve different misdemeanors that included (a) simple disobedience (ignores request to stop making loud noise); (b) disobedience causing harm to physical objects (breaks vase while playing ball); (c) disobedience through which the child could hurt himself or herself (runs into street after ball and is almost hit by car); (d) disobedience leading to harm to others (fights—pushes peer off of tricycle); and (e) disobedience leading to psychological harm to others (makes fun of senile old man). Each mother's report of

Martin Hoffman argues that inductive discipline promotes moral development.

the discipline techniques she would use was determined more by what the child did than by some consistent child-rearing approach on the part of the mother. Two situations involving psychological harm to others elicited the use of reasoning, while other kinds of misdemeanors were more likely to trigger the use of some type of power assertion. Mothers frequently said they would use multiple techniques in handling the misdemeanor, usually power assertion combined with reasoning. In most cases mothers indicated they would use power assertion first and follow it with some type of reasoning.

Should the parent or teacher use punishment? Although reinforcement should almost always be the first choice, punishment is not always a bad choice. A frown, time-out, reasoning, and discipline during or shortly after bad behavior can all serve a positive socializing function. In most instances, however, the use of physical punishment is not a wise choice. Of course, any form of punishment used should reflect mature judgment on the user's part.

Imitation or Modeling Everyone learns extensively by example. Much of the learning for children at all age levels involves watching teachers, school officials, and peers doing or saying something. This form of social learning is called imitation, modeling, or vicarious learning. For example, a child who watches the teacher reward her best friend for cleaning up his work area may be induced (vicariously reinforced) to clean up her own work area.

According to Bandura (1977), most acquisitions in an observational setting occur merely through the proximity of the model and observer in time and space.

In other words, by his or her presence alone the child acquires a wide range of behaviors from teacher and classmates at school and from parents and siblings at home. As the child's perception and cognition mature, he or she learns more complex behaviors through modeling. The child's ability to imitate what someone else does or says, then, is related to age and intelligence (Mischel & Mischel, 1975).

Imitation is one of the major ways that emotional feelings and attitudes are learned and eliminated. Bandura (1977) has observed that many prejudices are acquired through imitation. For example, a young child who observes her parents' negative behavior about a person she has never met may also develop intensely negative emotions about that person.

Emotions and social stereotypes can be eliminated by the same process. In a classic study of children who were afraid of dogs, the use of a modeling procedure quickly eliminated the children's fear (Bandura, Grusec & Menlove, 1967). Children were shown a film in which a peer model first looks at a dog in a cage, then approaches the cage, and after several other steps, eventually acts very happy as he plays with the dog. The children who were afraid of dogs were later given opportunities to imitate the peer model's behavior. The group of children who had experienced this peer modeling engaged in considerably more activity with dogs than did a group of children who had not experienced the peer modeling.

Bandura (1977) believes that a number of psychological processes are involved in imitation. One of these is **attention.** Before the observer can reproduce the model's actions, he or she has to attend to what the model is doing or saying. The child may not hear the teacher present an idea in class if he or she is giving attention instead to the person sitting next to him or her. The child's attention to models in influenced by characteristics of the models themselves. Warm, powerful, atypical individuals command more attention than cold, weak, typical individuals do. The child pays closer attention when informed that he or she will be required to reproduce what the model does at a later time than he or she does when no such information is given.

The next consideration involves the child's **retention.** To reproduce a model's actions at a later time requires the child to code and store the information in his or her memory in order to recall it later. This process can be enhanced by verbal rehearsal of what the child has just seen or heard. A simple verbal description or vivid image of what the model did also assists retention.

A third process involved in modeling is **motoric reproduction.** Children may attend to the model and adequately code what they have seen, but because of limitations in motor development they may not be able to reproduce what the model has done. For example, hitting a tennis ball accurately or catching a football may involve motor coordination beyond that of a child, who is thus unable to reproduce that modeled behavior. Reproducing the letters a teacher has drawn may be difficult for some first graders because their hand–eye coordination may not have developed adequately. Therefore, having first graders spend long periods of time trying to print letters that exactly match the teacher's is not a wise strategy. This is not to say that children should not engage in activities, like printing, that call for fine hand–eye coordination. But they should not be expected to reproduce all written symbols exactly at such an early age.

One first grader recently brought home a printing exercise with a sad face drawn on it by the teacher. The sad face was placed on the paper because the child had tilted her letters more than the teacher liked. Can you guess what the child's least favorite activity at school is? This child is reasonably well coordinated for a six-year-old; think how damaging punishment of this nature can be for children whose motor development is below average or neurologically impaired. Failure to recognize the role of motor development in imitation may lead to emotional problems and difficulty in social interactions for the child.

A final process in Bandura's conception of modeling involves reinforcement or **incentive conditions.** In the example of modeling and aggression illustrated in figure 5.8 some children did not imitate the aggressive behavior they had seen until reinforcement conditions were appropriate. Once they were told that they would be rewarded for imitating the model's behavior, they readily imitated the model's aggressive actions. There are many situations in which people can easily do what they have seen a model do but may not be motivated to do so. A child who watches a teacher demonstrate lunchroom etiquette may not be motivated to imitate the teacher's actions unless appropriate incentives are provided—perhaps in the form of a special lunchroom treat. The appropriateness of the incentives, of course, will vary for individual children.

MISS PEACH

By Mell Lazarus

MISS PEACH by Mell Lazarus. Courtesy of Mell Lazarus and News America Syndicate.

Strengths and Weaknesses of the Behavioral and Social Learning Perspectives

Like psychoanalytic theory, the behavioral and social learning views have their strengths and weaknesses.

Strengths   Among the strengths and contributions of the behavioral and social learning views are the following:

1. The behavioral and social learning approaches have shown us that specific behaviors and environmental stimuli are important determinants of social behavior.
2. Both views have demonstrated the contribution of the observational method in learning about social behavior.
3. The rigorous experimental approach of the behavioral and social learning views has fostered a climate of scientific investigation in the field of socialization.
4. The social learning perspective has highlighted the tremendous importance of information processing in mediating the relation between behavior and environmental stimuli.
5. The social learning perspective has sensitized us to the importance of adapting to changing environmental circumstances, and both the behavioral and social learning perspectives have stressed how social behavior may vary from one context to another.

Weaknesses   Among the weaknesses of the behavioral and/or social learning perspectives are the following:

1. The behavioral view has been heavily criticized for believing that cognitive processes are not part of the socialization picture. This criticism of course does not apply to social learning theory.
2. Both the behavioral and social learning views are nondevelopmental views, believing that the processes that determine social behavior are essentially the same at all levels of development.
3. Both the behavioral and social learning perspectives are too reductionistic. That is, they reduce socialization to elements that are very fine-grained, possibly missing the Gestalt that may only be captured by looking at more global dimensions as well.
4. Critics have charged that the behavioral and social learning views are too mechanical. Jonas Langer (1969), a cognitive developmental psychologist, calls the behavioral perspective a mechanical mirror view, suggesting that behaviorists are arguing that an individual's social behavior merely mirrors or reflects his or her environment. This criticism does not apply to modern social learning theory, which stresses the cognitive transformation of environmental experiences. Critics also have said that the behavioral and social learning perspectives miss much of the richness of socialization because they ignore the creative, spontaneous aspects of socialization.

Concept Table 10.2 provides a summary of the behavioral and social learning views. In our discussion of cognitive learning, the importance of cognitive factors is clear. For example, reproducing the social actions of a model requires that children code the environmental stimuli that they see or hear and that they be able to retrieve the information later. In the next section we will look at other cognitive views and processes that have come to play such an important role in understanding children's socialization.

The Cognitive Perspective

We are in the midst of a cognitive revolution in psychology. Psychology is no longer defined as the scientific study of behavior but rather as the science of the mind and behavior (Santrock, 1986). This definition emphasizes that psychology consists of the study of such cognitive processes as thinking, memory, attention, reasoning, problem solving, and the like, as well as behavior. The cognitive revolution in psychology has not only infiltrated developmental psychology in general but

CONCEPT TABLE 10.2		
The Behavioral and Social Learning Views		
Concept	**Processes/Related Ideas**	**Characteristics/Description**
The behavioral view	John Watson's ideas	Watson believed the child can be shaped in an endless number of ways. He thought most parents are too easy on their children.
	B. F. Skinner's ideas	Skinner has continued the emphasis of Watson. He believes children should be rewarded for appropriate behavior. Operant conditioning is the major way children learn social behavior.
The social learning view	Albert Bandura's ideas	Bandura emphasizes the principle of reciprocal determinism and imitation; cognitive processes mediate the relation of environment to the child's social behavior.
	Walter Mischel's ideas	Mischel coined the term *cognitive social learning theory;* he believes, like Bandura, that cognitive processes mediate environment–behavior relations.
Processes in the behavioral and social learning views	Reinforcement	Reinforcement is a powerful determinant of children's social behavior; the principle that children's behavior is determined by the consequences of their behavior is important to consider in understanding children's social behavior. It is also important to consider the relative nature of reinforcement and self-reinforcement.
	Punishment	Most professionals recommend time-out over conventional punishment and also discuss punishment in the context of discipline. Hoffman proposed three types of discipline: power assertion, induction, and love withdrawal. Induction seems to be the wisest choice in most instances, although consideration of the nature of the deviation and the developmental status of the child should be taken into account.
	Imitation (modeling or vicarious learning)	Children learn social behavior extensively by observing models. Bandura argues that imitation consists of four processes: attention, retention, motoric reproduction, and incentive conditions.
Strengths and weaknesses of the behavioral and social learning views	Strengths	(1) Specific behaviors and environmental stimuli are important determinants of development. (2) Observational methods. (3) Rigorous experimental approach. (4) Social learning view emphasizes cognitive mediation. (5) Adaptation to changing social world and importance of context.
	Weaknesses	(1) Failure to recognize causative role of cognition. (2) Nonchronological view. (3) Too little attention to biological processes. (4) Too reductionistic. (5) Too mechanical.

has begun to influence the way we think about the socialization of children as well.

Awareness of the increased importance of cognitive processes in socialization represents a radical departure from the views of behaviorism and classical psychoanalytic theory that dominated thinking about socialization for many years. Socialization clearly is much more than the overt behavior of children being determined by environmental experiences in a very focused, narrow dimension of time. Socialization is also much more than unconscious thought, experiences with parents in the first five years of the child's life, and psychosexual stages. Our study of the important cognitive perspective on socialization focuses first on the applications of cognitive developmental theory to understanding socialization and then turns to the role of information processing in providing insight about socialization.

Cognitive Developmental Theory

In chapter 6 we spent considerable time describing the cognitive developmental theory of Jean Piaget. Here we focus on some of the implications of Piaget's theory for understanding socialization and then provide an overview of Lawrence Kohlberg's cognitive developmental perspective.

Jean Piaget   At this time it would be helpful for you to review some of the major points in Piaget's theory. Return to chapter 6 and reread the Piagetian perspective. In doing so, think about how Piaget's ideas can be applied to our understanding of children's social development as well as more pure dimensions of cognitive development such an understanding of numbers and geometric shapes. Recall that Piaget stressed the importance of maturation in explaining development. However, Piaget preferred to emphasize the adaptiveness and organization that occur in any biological system rather than the instincts Freud believed were at the heart of biological maturation. From the cognitive developmental perspective, socialization occurs as the child adapts to the experiences of a particular moment and reorganizes past ways of thinking. To help remember Piaget's main stages of cognitive development and how they compare with the stages proposed by Freud and Erikson, see figure 10.7.

An example of socialization research that has been heavily inspired by Piaget's theory is role taking (Flavell, 1974; Shantz, 1983). In many investigations the intent is not only to understand cognitive changes in role-taking ability but also to link these changes with empathy and moral judgment (e.g., Flavell, 1974; Rubin, 1973; Selman, 1976; Selman & Byrne, 1974).

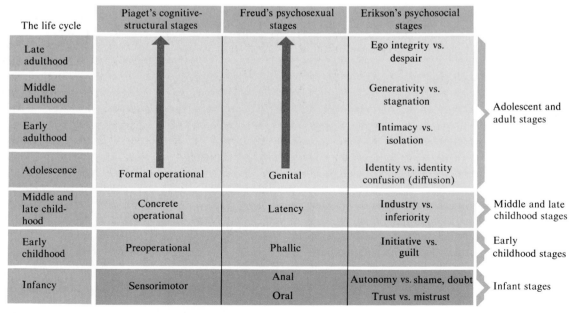

FIGURE 10.7
A comparison of the Piagetian, Freudian, and Eriksonian stages of development.

Interest in role-taking skills has been shown in young children as well as adolescents (Mussen & Eisenberg-Berg, 1977). One of the most thorough accounts of the development of role-taking skills has been proposed by Robert Selman (1976). From Selman's perspective, as children approach adolescence, they learn to reason in a complex manner, so that they are increasingly able to put together such complicated thoughts as "I think that you think that I think. . . ." Furthermore, adolescents discriminate more readily among alternative views of others than they did in the elementary years. Upon reaching early adolescence, they begin to be able to coordinate their various thoughts about others into a cohesive perspective on people in general, termed by Selman the "societal perspective." More information about Selman's views on role taking appears in chapter 13.

Lawrence Kohlberg   The application of cognitive developmental theory to socialization is quite recent. Lawrence Kohlberg (1969) believes that the American emphasis on behaviorism and social learning theory is a major reason our studies of socialization have not taken more of a developmental stance.

In addition to his contributions to understanding the development of moral thinking, Kohlberg (1969, 1976) has expanded Piaget's ideas on cognitive development to account for many social phenomena. For example, Kohlberg has applied the cognitive developmental perspective to sex-role development, role-taking abilities, peer relations, attachment-dependency relations, and the development of identity.

Like Piaget, Kohlberg believes that biological maturation and environmental experiences interact to produce the individual's state of thought, which in turn influences how the child interprets his or her social world. Kohlberg says that children attempt to attain a balance, or *equilibrium,* as they process incoming social information. Hence, adolescents who have achieved a stable sense of identity ("I know who I am and where I am going") can handle threats to their identity ("You aren't working hard enough—you play around too much") without being overwhelmed. Gradually, over a long time, the balance that has been achieved in a particular stage of thought is disrupted because maturing children gain cognitive abilities that enable them to perceive inconsistencies and inadequacies in their thinking about the social world. Just as a scientist who is confronted with unexplained events and outcomes must reformulate a theory to explain them, so too children must shift their former way of thinking to account

for new discrepancies. When children are able to balance the new information with past impressions, they have reached a new stage of thinking about social phenomena.

Hence, children in elementary school may categorize the identities of themselves and others along a limited number of dimensions, even just one or two, such as "He is a boy, and I am a girl." But as they grow into adolescence, such children begin to realize that different people are categorized by traits other than just gender. They recognize, for example, that individuals' style of interaction may shape their personal identity just as much as or more than their "maleness" or "femaleness."

Much of Kohlberg's focus is on children's interactions with other individuals, while Piaget's writings are mainly concerned with the individual's understanding of the physical world. Kohlberg, however, believes that these two parts of the environment, sometimes labeled respectively the "hot" and "cold" sides of cognition, are not independent. In his perspective, physical and social worlds show parallel development.

All the basic processes involved in physical conditions, and in stimulating developmental changes in these conditions, are also basic to social development. . . .

Lawrence Kohlberg has advanced our knowledge of the role cognition plays in social development.

Affective development and functioning and cognitive development and functioning are not distinct realms. "Affect" and "cognitive" development are *parallel;* they represent different perspectives and contexts in defining structural change. (Kohlberg, 1969, p. 349)

Kohlberg (1976) believes that personality develops within the framework of Piaget's stages of cognitive development. The concept of personality structure, then, is a part of rational thinking and the development of cognitive structures. The various strands of personality development (such as sex-role development, morality, identity, and so forth) are wired together by the child's developing sense of *self* and perceptions of the self in relation to other individuals (particularly in role-taking relationships). In Perspective on Child Development 10.2 Kohlberg's developmental view of the self is outlined.

PERSPECTIVE ON CHILD DEVELOPMENT 10.2

KOHLBERG'S VIEW ON THE DEVELOPMENT OF THE SELF

In Kohlberg's theory (1976) there are three major stages or perspectives of the self that each individual moves through. The first stage is called the **concrete-individual perspective** and is usually attained during early and middle childhood. During infancy, the individual discovers that he is distinct from the objects of his world. During the early and middle childhood years, he becomes preoccupied with the distinctiveness of himself and perceives the world as revolving around him. At this stage all social judgments and styles of interaction focus on the tangible feelings and needs of the self.

In late childhood and adolescence, a second stage of self-development appears, the **member-of-society perspective.** The individual at this stage sees herself as a member of a larger social unit—a family, a school, a city, culture, and so forth. Linked to such perceptions of self are judgments the individual makes to preserve the social order and fit each member of society into it.

The third and final level of self-development from Kohlberg's perspective is the **prior-to-society perspective.** At this stage, the self is perceived as a member of many different social units, each with an arbitrary membership determined by many uncontrollable factors. Social units are thought of as convenient and imperfect systems developed by people to assist them in getting along with one another. Consequently, the continued presence of these systems must be evaluated against the principles that all people share in common. Such universal principles are believed to be independent of a particular society or culture; instead, they rest in the mature structure of the individual's ego development.

As in other stage theories of development, Kohlberg's stages are considered fixed and invariable; everybody goes through them in the same order. However, not every person reaches the mature stage of the prior-to-society perspective.

Kohlberg's model of self-development is shown in the figure below. Notice the overlay of ego development on Piaget's stages of rational thinking and the separate strands of ego development linked with each other by virtue of being rooted in the ego structure.

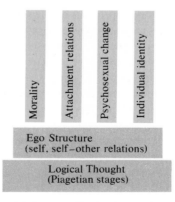

Kohlberg's model of personality development.
From *Childhood Socialization/Social and Personality Development* by John W. Santrock and Steven R. Yussen. Copyright © 1981 John Wiley and Sons, Inc. Reprinted by permission.

Information Processing

The cognitive approach to socialization is being influenced by the information-processing perspective as well as cognitive developmental theory. In this section we study the nature of social information processing and several examples of the importance of the information-processing perspective in understanding socialization. The examples include social memory, schemata, and social monitoring.

The Nature of Social Information Processing Recall our extensive discussion of information processing in chapter 7, where we observed how human beings attend to information, store information, retrieve information, reason about the information, and so forth. What is important for our interest here is that children process information about their social world just as they process information about a math problem or a sentence. We all remember information about our relationships with our parents and our peers just as we recall academic information. Our attention to what a peer is doing in a social situation can be as important to our understanding of peer relations as attention to a teacher's demonstration of solving a math problem is to learning about math. For example, in our discussion of peer relationships in chapter 12, we will see how intention cue detection skills, an aspect of processing information about social encounters, influence the popularity and rejection of children in the peer group (Dodge, Murphy & Buchsbaum, 1984).

Social Memory and Schemata A greatly understudied area of socialization is memory. There are two main reasons why memory of social relationships has not been a primary interest in socialization research. First, the behavioral view dominated empirical research on socialization for many years. This led to a focused effort to uncover the immediate environmental determinants of a child's behavior rather than on what the child had carried forward from past experiences in relationships. While psychoanalytic theory had emphasized the importance of the past (particularly the distant, early part of development) in determining current social relationships, the disenchantment with psychoanalytic theory by empirically oriented researchers led to an avoidance of the study of memory in social relationships. Second, several socialization studies demonstrated that mothers do a very poor job of remembering the precise details of how their children were reared (e.g., Becker & Krug,

1964; Yarrow, Campbell & Burton, 1968). Consequently, researchers assumed that such memories were so fraught with inaccuracies that they should be abandoned altogether in the search for empirical data about children's socialization.

By the time a child reaches the age of twelve, he or she has spent more than 70,000 hours in life. If we were to investigate the social relationships of twelve-year-olds without in some way accounting for their past experiences in relationships, would we not be likely to ignore some important aspects of development? While longitudinal studies that do not include retrospective information are clearly needed, cross-sectional studies that include memory of past social relationships and how they are carried forward in time are also clearly needed in our study of socialization.

Many questions about children's social memories need to be explored. Why do we remember some aspects of relationships and not others? When are memories trustworthy and when are they false? Why do we have so few memories from our early childhood? Do some individuals have more memories of childhood social relationships than others, and if so, why? What purpose do memories serve? How does the nature of social memory vary with age, culture, sex, and situation? And what happens when major sections of the past become inaccessible?

Recall from chapter 7 that Ulric Neisser (1982) has been one of the major proponents of an increase in the study of memory in ecologically valid circumstances. One of the most important aspects of Neisser's commentary about ecologically valid memory study is his belief that in most cases of remembering, it is meanings and not surface details that are the most important aspect of social memory. Children recall the substance of what went on in relationships rather than verbatim details about relationships. Neisser believes that it is not a single clear memory children carry forward but something like "screen memories." Often the basis of such screen memories is a series of repeated experiences, as in hundreds of encounters with a friend. Remember that Neisser calls such memories repisodic to capture the multiple encounters on which they are based. Thus, children's memories of social relationships are not like a tape recorder, but they may well get the general message or gist of what was going on.

Let's explore Neisser's (1967) description of a schema in greater detail to see how it may prove to be an important concept in understanding social memory.

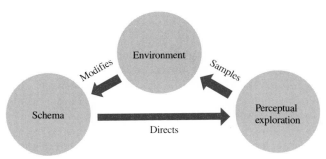

FIGURE 10.8
Neisser's ecological model of perception (Neisser, 1967).

How might a child's schemata for friendship develop?

Recall from chapter 7 that a schema is an organized structure of knowledge. As shown in figure 10.8, the schema is an important component in Neisser's ecological model of perception. Neisser emphasizes the role of schemata (plural of *schema*) in directing and exploring the social environment. For Neisser, social perception is a never-ending cycle in which schemata direct exploration of the environment and in which schemata themselves are being continually modified by information picked up in the course of exploring one's social world.

Let's consider the developing child's schemata for friendship. A child's first friendship develops as the child socially interacts with peers. As the child develops a closer relationship with one or more children, a schema of what friendship is about develops. This schema is an organized set of knowledge about what a friend is like. As the child continues the friendship, he or she picks up more information about what a friend is like and the schema becomes modified. The child may initially have a schema of friendship indicating that a friend is someone who always is nice; however, as the friendship develops, negative interchanges may lead to a change in the schema suggesting that the friend is nice most of the time but in some circumstances is not. Exploratory activities with other peers may continue to modify the child's schema for friendship. The schema will also be influenced by the child's own maturational development. In infancy no schema for friendship even exists. Then as the child's cognitive abilities mature, the schema becomes more detailed, organized, and abstract. While Neisser's cyclic model of perception and schemata has been applied primarily in the realm of cognitive development, as you can see, it also has important implications for understanding the nature of children's social development.

Examples of the increased willingness of some researchers to include memories of past social relationships in their attempt to understand current social relationships are beginning to appear. One area of social relationships in which social memories have begun to reveal some valuable data focuses on intergenerational relationships. In one investigation (Frommer & O'Shea, 1973) researchers discovered that mothers who have difficult relationships with their one-year-old infants were more likely to have had poor relationships with their own mothers than did mothers not reporting problems with their infants. In another study (Ricks, 1983) the mothers of securely attached infants had more positive recollections of their own childhood relationships with their mother, father, and peers than did the mothers of insecurely attached infants.

More information about social memory appears later in this chapter, where we describe the importance of carrying forward relationships in constructing current relationships; more information about intergenerational relationships appears in chapter 11 on the family. Keep in mind as you read the remainder of our discussion of socialization and personality development that the memory of social relationships is an impoverished area of inquiry and that such memory is important in how children construct their social relationships.

Social Monitoring John Flavell (1979) has described another important aspect of children's social information processing: children's ability to monitor their social thoughts and make sense of them. According to Flavell, children learn to evaluate the social behavior of others and its ties to social thoughts. Flavell argues that in the early years of development, the child attributes no social cognitions to others. Later on, the child may automatically assume that others' social thoughts always coincide with his or her social behavior. For example, the child may assume that helpful actions reflect an intent to help and that harmful actions reflect an intent to harm. Still later, the child may think that both types of actions portray either no intent at all or an incongruent one, such as a helpful action performed unintentionally for purely selfish reasons, or even an intent to achieve ultimate harm.

Flavell goes on to talk about the implications of childrens' and adolescents' ability to monitor their social cognitions as an indicator of their social maturity and competence.

> In many real life situations, the monitoring problem is not to determine how well you understand what a message means but rather to determine how much you ought to believe it or do what it says to do. I am thinking of the persuasive appeals the young receive from all quarters to smoke, drink, commit aggressive or criminal acts, have casual sex without contraceptives, have or not have the casual babies that often result, quit school, and become unthinking followers of this year's flaky cults, sects, and movements. (Feel free to revise this list in accordance with *your* values and prejudices.) Perhaps it is stretching the meanings of . . . cognitive monitoring too far to include the critical appraisal of message source, quality of appeal, and probable consequences needed to cope with these inputs sensibly, but I do not think so. It is at least conceivable that the ideas currently brewing in this area could some day be parlayed into a method of teaching children (and adults) to make wise and thoughtful life decisions as well as to comprehend and learn better in formal educational settings. (Flavell, 1979, p. 910)

The Biological Perspective

Not only are cognitive processes becoming much more prominent in the study of children's social and personality development, but there has been increased recognition of the child's biological heritage in understanding the socialization process. Thus, we no longer believe that children are simply socially molded in an infinite number of ways by environmental experiences. Rather, the trend in the study of children's socialization is to recognize the maturation of the child and its biological underpinnings and how biological forces interact with environmental experiences. It should be helpful for you to review some of the basic ideas described in chapters 2 and 3, where we provided details about biological processes and physical development. Return to those chapters and go over the basic ideas presented, in this instance thinking about how such biological processes might influence children's socialization. Now we consider the role of genetics in socialization, the theoretical view of ethology, and the link between biological maturation and the development of relationships.

Genetics and Socialization

It is instructive once again to think about the nature–nurture controversy that has existed for many years. Basically, it involves the extent to which the mind and behavior are influenced by innate (instinctive, genetically determined) factors and learned environmental factors. *Innate* refers to nature, *learned environmental* refers to nurture. It should be clear by now that nearly every aspect of the mind and behavior, including the child's social thoughts and behavior, is influenced by the interaction of nature and nurture rather than either acting alone. The expression of a given social behavior requires a proper environment and the existence of socialization objects, that is, people. Similarly, no social behavior can be attributed to environmental factors alone. At the very least, the child must have sensory receptors, motor nerve cells, and a brain that detects and processes the relevant social information, as well as muscles that actually perform the social behavior. Thus, the statement "No genes, no organism; no environment, no organism" bears repeating.

To what extent were you introverted or extraverted as a child? Do you think this was related to your genetic inheritance to some degree?

Consider the personality characteristic of introversion–extraversion, an often-studied aspect of both child and adult personality development. Introverted children have an inward orientation, while extraverted children have an outward, more gregarious orientation. The results of twin studies on the introversion–extraversion dimension of personality suggest a hereditability estimate in the range of .50 to .74 (Eaves, 1978; Floredus-Myrhed, Pedersen & Rasmussen, 1980; Koskenvuo, Langinvainia, Kaprio, Rantasalo & Sama, 1979), indicating a moderate to strong genetic influence on this aspect of personality. For more information on the role of genetic influences on socialization, read Perspective on Child Development 10.3.

PERSPECTIVE ON CHILD DEVELOPMENT 10.3

INFANT TEMPERAMENT AND SOCIALIZATION

Human beings are born into the world with different temperaments. They have different levels of activity, diverse reactions to novel events, varying degrees to which the rhythm of their daily lives is predictable, and different levels of intensity in their emotional peaks and valleys. One natural question to ask is: How does temperament influence the way infants are treated by their care givers? If temperament lays the foundation for the style of interaction an infant will have with his or her environment, how does the environment reciprocate? Care givers, of course, are an important part of the environment, and it would be instructive to know how they treat infants with different perceived temperaments. A recent study by Pnina Klein (1984) suggests some intriguing answers.

Dr. Klein interviewed the mothers of forty infants and observed them interacting with their infants. The infants were all born in 1980 in the primarily middle-class community of Pietach Tikva, Israel. Twenty-one of the infants were boys and nineteen were girls. The observations were made when the infants were six months of age and again when they were twelve months old. Klein used a time-sampling technique in which some sixty-two different behavioral categories were rated. These included (1) various kinds of stimulation directed toward the infant—touch, movement (kinesthesia), visual experience, and sounds; (2) responsiveness of the mother to infant vocalizing or signals of distress; (3) positive emotions displayed by the mother as in smiles and manipulation of the infant's body; and (4) a variety of objects displayed around the infant. The objects varied in complexity and in how much they could change when the infant acted upon them (note that this last category is not behavioral; rather, it describes stimuli).

After the first observation period (six months), each mother was also requested to complete a questionnaire designed to measure the infant's temperament, as perceived by the mother. The scale is named the Infant Temperament Questionnaire. The items on it are designed to assess the nine original dimensions in the Thomas and Chess (1977) research (see table 2.1,

chapter 2), which include activity level, approach-withdrawal, intensity, and distractibility.

The major results were as follows: (1) Infants with one profile of temperament received more stimulation from their mothers than did other infants. The infants in this profile were rated as more adaptable, approaching, intense in response, and positive in mood than other babies in the sample. (2) The stimulation difference held for both the six-month and the twelve-month observation periods. (3) Although the infants' profile included several elements, one element was more critical to the observed relation than others. Intensity of response was the most powerful link in the findings. In investigator Klein's own words:

> Of all temperament variables, intensity was found to relate to more observed variables of mothers' behavior than any of the other ITQ scales. Both at six and twelve months of age, infants rated by their mothers as more intense were found to receive more of almost all observed variables of sensory and social stimulation. Furthermore, it is interesting to note that even characteristics of the object environment, that is, its complexity, responsivity, and variety, related significantly to intensity. In other words, what mothers think of infants' temperament, especially what they perceive as level of intensity of an infant's response, predicts not only the mother's direct contact with the infant, but is also related to the choice of the type and number of objects mothers provide for their infants to play with. (p. 1216)

Of course, the findings from this study are correlational. We cannot speak very confidently in causal terms. Specifically, we cannot claim that the more responsive, joyous infants made their mothers, in turn, more responsive to them. Just the reverse may have been true. Or some other mechanism may have been operating to produce the correlation. Nevertheless, the findings are provocative and suggest a potentially important dimension for examining future patterns of mother–child interactions.

Ethology

We described the basic principles of ethology in chapter 2 as part of our discussion of biological influences on development. Here we review some of the basic ideas of ethology, emphasizing the importance of the ethological perspective in understanding social development. In following Robert Hinde's (1983) analysis, we consider some basic questions ethologists ask about social behavior and then turn to some important issues in the ethological approach to social development.

Three Questions Ethologists Ask In considering any social behavior, an ethologist is likely to ask three questions: Why did the organism behave in this way? How does the behavior change over time and why? What is the evolutionary origin of the behavior?

In order to answer the first question, the ethologist believes it is essential to provide an elaborate description and classification of behavioral events. An effort is made to specify the relations between the behavioral events and antecedent conditions. For example, if an observer discovers that a particular behavior is less likely to be elicited by familiar individuals than strangers, the observer infers that experience probably played a role in determining the behavior.

A second question the ethologist wants to answer involves delving further into the past. As an organism develops, its behavior changes. The course of such development requires analysis and explanation. After the ethologist asks the basic question of how the behavior changes, then he or she wants to know the extent to which such change is due to environmental influences, as well as how such influences produced their effects. For example, the ethologist studying delinquent behavior in adolescents is interested in knowing not only the immediate contextual influences on the behavior but the developmental course that preceded the behavior as well. Thus, from this perspective, delinquent behavior in adolescents may depend on propensities acquired in childhood that are carried forward to adolescence as well as such possible immediate determinants as recent frustrations (a long hot summer in a ghetto) and peer modeling.

A third question focuses on the evolutionary origin of the behavior under investigation. The ethologist believes that comparisons between closely related species provide information about the possible evolutionary course of a particular behavior. For example, John Bowlby's theory of attachment, which we will describe in chapter 11, was built upon the belief that a young primate depends on its mother for protection and food, and therefore it is biologically predisposed with a repertoire of behaviors for maintaining proximity to the mother.

Selected Issues of Interest to Ethologists Among the many issues in social development that are of interest to ethologists, the following are prominent: the role of observation, functional considerations, dichotomies in development and organism–environment interaction, sensitive periods, and relationships and personality.

With their interest in carefully describing behavior, ethologists have given considerable attention to how behavior should be assessed. Recall from chapter 2 that according to ethologists behavior should be studied by observing the organism in its natural habitat. Thus, you may remember the photograph of Niko Tinbergen in a marsh observing the behavior of the stickleback fish. Similarly, ethologists believe that to describe fully the social behavior of children they need to be observed in the naturalistic contexts of the home, playground, school, and so forth. A university laboratory is not regarded as natural because this setting is not a context in which relationships and social behavior develop.

A second issue ethologists are concerned about involves functional considerations of behavior. They point out that child development is studied by adults who see the end point of development as mature adulthood. But consider the behavior of an infant in terms of its natural selection. The behavior probably was not shaped because the child is a miniature adult but so the child will succeed at that particular point in development. For example, caterpillars are excellent leaf eaters, but they do not pretend to be butterflys. Ethologists argue that the word *development* too often diverts our attention from viewing each stage of development in its own right.

A third issue of interest to ethologists involves our now well-discussed ideas about the dichotomy between innate and learned behavior. Put succinctly, the ethologist argues, just as we have earlier, that such a dichotomy is inaccurate. Ethologists do believe it is important to consider the extent to which an individual is predisposed to learn something and that this consideration too often has been ignored. Comparative evidence suggests that what an individual learns and the situations in which an individual will learn vary among species.

A fourth issue ethologists study is that of sensitive periods. Robert Hinde (1983) makes a distinction between the concept of critical periods, discussed in chapter 2, and the concept of sensitive periods. Recall our discussion of Lorenz's ideas about imprinting's involving an irreversible critical period in geese. Ethologists now recognize that the critical period concept may have been too rigid. The more recently developed concept of **sensitive period** implies that a given effect can be produced more readily during one period than earlier or later. According to Hinde (1983), it does not, however, imply that the period is necessarily tied closely to chronological age or that the same effects cannot be obtained (although perhaps with more difficulty) later. Viewed in this manner, for example, the concept of sensitive period provides a useful label for suggesting that early infant–mother interaction is important in the development of attachment, a topic to be discussed in considerable detail in chapter 11.

A fifth issue ethologists study concerns relationships and personality. The ethological perspective on social behavior emphasizes that the child's relationships with other people form one of the most important aspects of the environment. If development is to be fully understood, the properties and dynamics of relationships must be charted. Hinde (1983) argues that certain properties of relationships are not descriptive of the behavior of the individuals in isolation. These include such features as synchrony, behavioral meshing, and competitiveness. Furthermore, relationships can have properties that emerge from the frequency and patterning of interactions over time. Thus, if we look at the relationship of a mother and infant at one point in time, we may not be able to describe it as rejecting, controlling, or permissive. However, through detailed observations over a prolonged time period, we may become more confident and accurate about such categorization. Hinde (1983) also believes we must pay attention to how relationships are influenced by the personality of the participants, as well as how relationships affect the personality of the participants.

Robert Hinde's views on ethology have made a strong impact on our thinking about the nature of the socialization process in recent years.

Biological Maturation and the Development of Relationships

We have already seen in the ethological perspective a strong concern about the role of biological maturation in the development of relationships. This perspective has begun to influence how we study children's socialization. Willard Hartup (1985) describes how such maturational changes in the child influence social interaction and relationships. The young infant has no rudimentary ability to coordinate his or her actions with the actions of other people, cannot use words, and has a very limited sense of self. Over time such conditions change, and the nature of the child's interactions with the caregiver change concomitantly. The sources of such change do not always depend heavily on experience, although the hundreds of hours spent with the infant in the early months of life probably contribute to the change.

Recent research on the development of close relationships reveals the prominent role of biological maturation. The visual stimuli infants find alluring change over the course of the first few months of life for reasons not likely due to social experiences. The infant's increasing interest in contour and complexity in visual stimulation is believed to be connected to the infant's preferences for looking at faces. The infant develops a preference for looking at familiar stimuli as well. This perceptual development closely parallels the infant's development of a preference for looking at familiar faces at about four to five months of age. At about this

CONCEPT TABLE 10.3		
Cognitive and Biological Perspectives on Socialization		
Perspective	**Processes/Related Ideas**	**Characteristics/Description**
Cognitive	Cognitive developmental theory	Piaget's ideas emphasize the adaptiveness and organization that occur in any biological system. Socialization occurs as the child adapts to the particular moment and reorganizes past ways of thinking. An example of Piagetian-inspired socialization research involves role taking. Kohlberg has expanded on Piaget's ideas and liberally applied cognitive developmental theory to many domains of socialization, particularly moral development and self-development.
	Information processing	Children process information about their social world just as they process information about a math problem. Discussion of social information processing focuses on social memory and schemata. There has been too little research on social memory and the cognitive organization of social matters. Neisser's ecological model of perception can be applied to schemata for social experiences. The development of social monitoring also affects social information processing.
Biological	Genetics and socialization	The expression of a given social behavior requires a proper environment and the existence of social objects, that is, people. However, no social behavior can be solely attributed to environmental experience. A genetic tie for the personality dimension of introversion–extraversion has been found, and research has shown how the infant's temperament contributes to socialization.
	Ethology	Hinde says ethologists ask three important questions about any social behavior: Why did the organism behave in this way? How does the behavior change over time and why? What is the evolutionary origin of the behavior? Among the important issues of interest to ethologists are the role of observation, functional considerations, dichotomies in development and organism–environment interactions, and relationships and personality.
	Biological maturation and the development of relationships	Recent research on close relationships suggests a prominent role for biological maturation.

time in infant development the child begins to show some discrimination in whom he or she responds to socially.

As the infant moves into the latter half of the first year of life, response to separation from the caregiver changes markedly. Crying and distress in reponse to separation from the mother are somewhat uncommon in the first four to five months of life, increase in the second half of the first year, then peak in the first half of the second year. Subsequently, these behaviors decline. Rearing conditions and cultural setting do not seem to influence the developmental unfolding of crying and distress to separation from the mother (Kagan, Kearsley & Zelazo, 1978).

Later on children expand the distance between themselves and their care giver as they explore their environment. Changes in the child are probably involved in this increased distancing. Children have come to understand that distance (distal) signals work in place of close (proximal) signals as a system for maintaining contact with the care giver. Thus at some point toward the end of the second year or the first half of the third year, young children sense that contact can be established from a considerable distance. This increased independence and transformation in the relationship of the young child and the mother also seem to be due in some degree to biological maturation and are not solely dependent upon experiences.

A summary of the main ideas pertaining to cognitive and biological perspectives on socialization is presented in Concept Table 10.3. Now that we have studied a number of theoretical perspectives on socialization, we turn our attention to an analysis of the child's social environment.

THE SOCIAL ENVIRONMENT OF CHILDREN

To conclude our introduction to the socialization of children, we consider the nature of the social environment children experience as they develop. First, we present information about the culture children are exposed to. Second, we describe four important contexts or settings in which socialization takes place. Third, we discuss the importance of close social relationships in children's development.

Culture

Culture is a very broad concept. It can be defined as the behavior patterns, beliefs, values, and any other products of humans that are learned and shared by a particular group of people and passed on from one generation to the next. Cultural groups can be as large as the population of the Soviet Union or the United States or as small as a group of South Sea islanders. How does this information get transmitted from one generation of people to the next? Through families, peers and friends, schools, community ties, the world of work, and television, to name some of the most important sources of cultural transmission. In this section we look at four important aspects of culture: its direct and indirect effects, cross-cultural comparisons, socioeconomic status, and the psychologist's evaluation of culture.

Direct and Indirect Effects

Direct effects of culture occur through immediate experience with the environment. Through interaction with parents at home, with colleagues at work, with peers and friends in the neighborhood, we experience the culture in which we live. Psychologists have proposed a number of processes involved in the direct experience of culture. In particular, the processes of social learning are thought to be an important part of cultural transmission. Two such important social learning processes are reinforcement and observational learning. Reinforcement is a complex concept. For our purposes here, we will simply refer to it as involving the presentation of a stimulus that increases the likelihood that a behavior will occur. Thus culture is directly experienced when a parent smiles at a child for showing consideration of another person's feelings. Subsequently, according to the principle of reinforcement, the child will have an increased likelihood of displaying consideration for others. Observational learning refers to the process of watching someone else engage in a behavior, and then subsequently performing the behavior yourself. For example, a person may watch a peer invest in the stock market and make a considerable amount of money. The observer subsequently invests in the stock market herself with the hope of making a lot of money. Observational learning theorists (e.g., Bandura, 1977) believe that much of observational learning occurs simply by being around someone else and does not have to involve watching someone else be rewarded for his or her behavior. We have all spent countless hours with parents, with peers, with colleagues at work, and with other people in other contexts. Through observational learning we absorb a phenomenal amount of information about our culture.

We also experience culture in an indirect manner (Bronfenbrenner, 1979). Indirect effects of culture occur when experiences in another social setting influence what is being experienced in an immediate context. For example, experiences at work may influence a woman's relationship with her husband. A child's experiences with his or her parents affect the child's behavior at school. With regard to the former example, consider the possibility that the woman shows a traditional sex-role orientation when she is married, believing that the husband should be dominant and the wife submissive. But after working several years and developing a number of friends in the job-related setting, she begins to question her traditional sex-role orientation and starts demanding more equal participation by her husband in household chores. In ways such as this, culture has indirect effects on an individual's behavior and mind.

Cross-Cultural Comparisons

In Brazil almost every middle-class family can afford a nanny, and there is no such thing as a baby-sitting problem. However, because many of the nannies believe in black magic, it is not beyond the realm of possibility for Brazilian parents to return home from a movie and find their infant screaming, presumably, according to the nanny, from a voodoo curse. Contrast the world of the middle-class Brazilian family with the world of the child in Thailand, where farm families are large and can only afford to educate their most promising child (determined by which child is most capable of learning English).

Phyllis Bronstein found that Mexican fathers were playful and companionable with their children.

It is very tempting to generalize, using information from a single culture, about the universal aspects of the mind and behavior. Such generalization was rampant earlier in this century. For example, it was believed that all adolescents the world over go through a period of storm and stress, characterized by plaguing self-doubt and conflict (Hall, 1904). Today, however, as much more substantial information has been collected about large numbers of adolescents in the United States (Dusek & Flaherty, 1981) and in other countries such as Italy (Young & Ferguson, 1981), we believe that the storm and stress view is incorrect. Some adolescents experience considerable turmoil of an enduring nature and others do not. Thus, as psychologists improved the quality of their controlled observations and began checking the universality of their findings across cultures, this view of adolescence was discarded.

Cross-cultural studies of sexual behavior indicate that culture and learning play a prominent role in shaping sexual conduct (Hyde, 1985b). For example, the inhabitants of the Ines Beag culture off the coast of Ireland are among the most sexually repressed in the world. The men believe that intercourse is bad for their health. They detest nudity—only babies can bathe nude. Premarital sex is taboo, and after marriage the partners keep their underwear on during sexual intercourse (Messinger, 1971). By contrast, in the South Pacific culture of Mangaia, sex for reproduction and pleasure is a major focus of life. Boys learn about masturbation as early as six or seven years of age. When a boy is thirteen, he undergoes a ritual in which an adult instructs him about sexual strategies and how to help his partner achieve orgasm. Two weeks after the ceremony the boy has sexual intercourse with an experienced woman. Soon after, the boy looks for girls with whom to practice his knowledge, or they search for him, knowing he is now a "man." Every woman in the Mangaian culture has orgasms, whereas women in the Ines Beag culture never have orgasms. The two sets of women have similarly constructed vaginas and clitorises—they are the same size and have the same nerve supply. Their different sexual responses, then, must be a consequence of social experiences such as those we have portrayed.

A recent investigation by Phyllis Bronstein (1984) provided information about maternal and paternal behaviors in Mexican families. Traditionally, it has been argued that Mexican fathers are more aloof and authoritarian, while mothers are warmer and more nurturant. However, Bronstein found that Mexican fathers were more playful and companionable with their children and mothers were more nurturant, but only in providing for the child's physical needs. When compared cross-culturally, the findings are similar to observations of parent–child interaction in the United States.

Thus we see that findings from cross-cultural comparisons are useful in confirming or refuting ideas about generalized principles based primarily on observations in only one culture. Moreover, as described in Perspective on Child Development 10.4, information about child-rearing practices across generations in different cultures sheds light on the contributions of heredity and environment to the socialization process. Keep in mind that both variation and congruence have been noted across cultures and that there are both genetic and environmental contributions to the socialization process. As we see next, there is also variation and congruence in subcultural comparisons of children from varying socioeconomic backgrounds within the same culture.

PERSPECTIVE ON CHILD DEVELOPMENT 10.4

MOTHER–INFANT BEHAVIOR ACROSS GENERATIONS AND ACROSS CULTURES

I n one set of cross-cultural observations William Caudill (Caudill, 1971; Caudill & Frost, 1972) compared the everday behavior of mothers and their three- and four-month-old infants in Japan and the United States. In 1971 he found that American mothers chatted more with their babies and that American babies talked more, displayed happier vocalizations, and engaged in more gross motor activity than the Japanese babies did. Japanese mothers took longer to respond to unhappy vocalizations by their infants and held them more than American mothers held their infants. The Japanese babies were more physically passive than American babies were. Caudill concluded that by three or four months of age Japanese and American babies had learned different behaviors as a direct result of the different caretaking behaviors of their mothers.

In an extension of this study William Caudill and Lois Frost (1972) observed a group of third- and fourth-generation Japanese-American mothers and their infants. The ancestors of the Japanese-Americans began coming to the United States at the end of the nineteenth century. By the end of World War II, this cultural group was firmly established in the middle-class society of the United States. By 1970 their children (Sansei, which means third generation) were also entrenched in middle-class society. The Sansei mothers and their children (Yonsei, meaning fourth generation) were the subjects of Caudill and Frost's study.

The researchers compared the data from the Japanese-American families with data from their earlier studies of Japanese and American families. Which group did the Japanese-American families more closely resemble? If the behavior of Japanese-American babies was more like that of the Japanese, a genetic interpretation would seem appropriate, even though it is well known that the caretaking ways of mothers in succeeding generations change and that these changes are reflected in their infants' behavior. (Indeed, many of the Sansei mothers did not like the fact that their mothers had reared them to conform to middle-class American society.)

The researchers found that the behavior of these mothers and their infants more closely resembled the American sample than the Japanese sample (see table at right). This resemblance was particularly evident in the mothers' chatting with their infants and the number of happy vocalizations by the infants. Caudill and Frost concluded that a genetic interpretation of these findings seemed inappropriate because the Japanese-American babies' behavior was like that of the American babies even though the Japanese-American babies are genetically Japanese.

In some respects, however, the data in the table at right also show that the Japanese-American mothers and infants have retained certain patterns of behavior from their Japanese cultural heritage. The Sansei mother is more like the Japanese mother in the greater amount of time she spends in playing with her baby, and this finding is probably related to the finding that the Yonsei baby is more like the Japanese baby in playing less by himself or herself. Also, the Yonsei and Japanese babies are alike in terms of nonnutritive sucking, and the Sansei mother is more like the Japanese mother in doing more carrying of the baby in her arms and lulling the baby.

Socioeconomic Status

You probably have some idea of what is meant by **social class.** We talk about it all the time: "He's lower class." "She's middle class." "They live in an upper-class neighborhood." In ways such as these we express our perceptions of socioeconomic status.

Social stratification in the United States carries with it certain inequalities. It is generally acknowledged that members of society have (1) occupations that vary in prestige, (2) different levels of power to influence the institutions of a community, (3) different economic resources, and (4) different educational and occupational opportunities. These differences in ability to

Paired Cultural Comparisons of Variables Related to Styles of Behaving

Dependent Variables	Mean Frequencies			Cultural Comparisons		
	Japanese (30 cases)	American (30 cases)	Japanese-American (21 cases)	Japanese and American p <	Japanese and Japanese-American p <	American and Japanese-American p <
Infant behavior						
Finger or pacifier	70	170	45	.001	...	.001
Total vocal	95	115	135	...	.05	...
Unhappy	67	44	27	.01	.001	.05
Happy	30	59	111	.001	.001	.001
Active	51	95	111	.001	.01	...
Baby plays	83	170	102	.001	...	.05
Caretaker behavior						
Positions	9	19	25	.001	.001	...
Plays with	40	23	71	.05	.05	.001
Talks to	104	121	214	...	.001	.001
Chats	80	119	205	.01	.001	.001
Lulls	23	2	14	.001	...	.01
In arms	204	132	193	.05	...	.05
Rocks	49	17	17	.01	.05	...

From Caudill, W., and L. A. Frost, "A comparison of maternal care and infant behavior in Japanese-American, American, and Japanese families," in U. Bronfenbrenner, (ed.), *Influences on Human Behavior.* © 1972, p. 339.

control resources and to participate in the rewards of society influence an individual's mind and behavior.

There is by no means total agreement on what the categories of social class should be and how they should be measured. However, the most common denominator of social class is occupation. According to one classification, upper-class individuals have professional and managerial positions, middle-class individuals work at lower-level white-collar and skilled blue-collar jobs, and lower-class individuals are semiskilled and unskilled workers. Most psychological research, however, focuses on comparisons of lower-class and middle-class individuals, it being argued that only a very small percentage of the population should be categorized as upper class. The following occupations help to define these two classes: lower class—factory workers, manual laborers, maintenance workers, welfare recipients; middle class—salespeople, managers, professionals (e.g., doctors, lawyers, teachers, accountants) (Hess, 1970).

Of course, the lower class is made up of a variety of individuals and is not a neat, homogeneous group; there are lower-class blacks, whites, Chicanos, people from rural Appalachia, and people from urban ghettos. There is also a wide range of income within the lower class; some lower-class families live in extreme poverty, whereas others may earn as much as $15,000 to $20,000 per year.

As an indication of some of the pervasive associations between social class and various aspects of the mind and behavior consider the following:

Lower-class children score substantially lower on intelligence tests than do middle-class individuals (Havighurst, Bowman, Liddle, Matthews & Pierce, 1962).

Anorexia nervosa, a disorder involving extreme weight loss, is much more characteristic of middle-class than lower-class females (Bruch, 1973).

The psychological problems of lower-class children are more likely to be externalizing (delinquency), whereas those of middle-class children are more often internalizing (anxiety disorder) (Achenbach & Edelbrock, 1981).

Middle-class mothers engage in more verbal interaction with their children than do lower-class mothers (Tulkin & Kagan, 1971).

Let's look in more detail at the last conclusion about verbal interaction. Steven Tulkin and Jerome Kagan (1971) observed thirty middle-class and twenty-six lower-class Caucasian mothers at home with their firstborn ten-month-old daughters. As shown in table 10.1, social class differences were minimal in areas of physical contact, prohibitions, and nonverbal interactions. In contrast, every verbal behavior observed was more frequent among middle-class mothers. The researchers concluded that lower-class mothers less frequently believed their infants were capable of communicating with other poeple and thus felt it was futile to interact with them verbally.

Of particular concern to social scientists in recent years has been the lower-class subculture of the poor. Although the most noticeable aspect of the working-class poor is their economic poverty, many other psychological and social characteristics of the lower-class poor have been outlined by Robert Hess (1970).

First, the poor are often powerless. In occupational circles they do not participate in the decision-making process; rules and regulations are usually handed down to them in an authoritarian way. They frequently feel that they cannot change their own plight; they perceive that even if they wanted to, they would not be able to deal more effectively with their world. Lower-class individuals may come to rely on luck, play the numbers games, and bet on the horses because of these helpless feelings.

Second, the poor are vulnerable to disaster. This vulnerability is closely related to their lack of power. They are likely not to be given advance notice when laid off from work, they usually do not have such financial resources as a savings account to fall back on when problems arise, and they usually have difficulty getting loans and credit.

Third, their range of alternatives is restricted. They do not have much mobility when it comes to deciding where to live, and a limited range of job opportunities is open to them. They have little leeway in choosing alternative medical services and are often at the mercy of governmental agencies who control welfare and health payments. Even when alternatives are available, they may not know about them or are not prepared to make a wise decision because of inadequate education and inability to read well.

TABLE 10.1
Maternal Behaviors Observed at Home

Variable	Working Class		Middle Class		
	Mean	SD	Mean	SD	p^a
Interaction:					
Interaction episodes	36.08	19.69	65.97	36.31	.001
Total interaction	132.50	83.44	251.83	144.46	.001
Location:					
Over 2 ft from child	1,402.73	536.38	1,243.27	488.03	.249
Within 2 ft	1,424.50	515.29	1,525.60	459.54	.441
Face to face	53.19	53.66	110.77	113.69	.022
Physical contact:					
Kiss	4.00	6.13	5.73	5.32	.262
Total holding	210.73	179.71	265.17	154.54	.228
Active physical contact	21.42	23.99	31.37	24.01	.128
Prohibitions:					
Verbal only	15.50	9.85	18.33	14.75	.409
Physical only	12.19	10.89	11.00	9.87	.669
Prohibitions ÷ time on floor	36.19	24.72	33.93	51.85	1.000
Prohibitions ÷ walk and crawl	19.04	13.69	16.50	15.20	.522
Responses to nonverbal behaviors:					
Positive response (%), child touches mother	56.36	22.50	63.89	21.03	.206
Positive response (%), child offers object to mother	90.65	15.44	86.40	16.22	.410
Maternal vocalization:					
Over 2 ft away	17.65	15.36	40.57	33.84	.002
Within 2 ft	148.77	73.92	329.37	183.81	.001
Face to face	19.00	15.97	38.20	28.48	.004
Total maternal vocalization	192.00	88.30	422.40	206.41	.001
Reciprocal vocalization (%)	11.27	6.12	20.70	10.19	.001
Keeping infant busy:					
Entertainment	54.65	40.46	99.13	62.08	.003
Give objects	26.23	19.72	38.53	14.76	.010
Response to spontaneous frets:					
Frets (%) to which mother responded	38.36	15.15	58.41	25.46	.001
Latency to respond (no. of 5-sec intervals)	1.98	0.70	1.62	0.54	.032

Note. All numbers (except percentages) refer to the number of 5-sec intervals in which the behavior occurred. The possible range is 0–2,880.

[a]Independent t tests; two-tailed.

From Tulkin, S. R., and J. Kagan, "Mother-child interaction in the first year of life," in *Child Development*, 45, pp. 31–41. Copyright © 1971 by The Society for Research in Child Development, Inc. Reprinted by permission.

Fourth, there is less prestige in being a poor member of the working class. This lack of prestige is transmitted to the child early in life; his or her observations of other children who wear nicer clothes and live in more attractive houses than he or she does tell the poor child that he or she has less than they do. Others also communicate information to the child about his or her relative position in the community; for example, the lower-class child learns that he or she is rarely asked to come over and play at the homes of middle-class children.

Finally, the experiences of the lower class do not overlap with those of the dominant middle class. Their conditions of work within the same company and the same community are not the same, nor are their recreational activities and travel the same.

Developmental Psychology and the Concept of Culture

Many developmental psychologists feel uncomfortable with terms like *culture* and *social class*. A major source of their uneasiness is the global nature of the concepts. Most psychologists like to analyze social conditions much more specifically. They like to look inside the family at the actual social exchanges taking place among family members, at the nature of communication in relationships, at a person's social attitudes and perceptions, and at his or her behavior in a group. Next we look at some of these social contexts and the importance of close relationships in development.

Social Contexts and Close Relationships

First, we examine four important social contexts in which many children spend their lives. Then we turn to the significance of close social relationships in the child's development.

Social Contexts

Four of the most important social contexts in a child's development are family, peers, school, and television. We briefly consider each of these contexts in turn.

Family Experiences within the family have an important influence on the mind and behavior. Interest in this influence grew out of Freudian theory. In particular, it was argued that experiences with parents during the first five years of life were critical for the development of social competencies throughout life. This view has been moderated substantially in recent years. It now is recognized that the mind and behavior are influenced by lifelong social conditions, not just those experienced in the first five years of life, and that many social conditions outside the family are also important influences on the mind and behavior. The nature of the family has also changed considerably in recent years, with far more individuals living in single-parent families than ever before in history. An entire chapter (11) is devoted to family processes in socialization.

Peers Peers are individuals who are about the same age or maturity as we are. Peers provide us with information about the world outside the family. From the peer group we receive feedback about our abilities. By comparing ourselves with peers we can determine whether we do things better than, as good as, or worse than others. It is hard for us to do this with parents or siblings because they are usually much older or younger. Much of chapter 12 is devoted to the powerful role of peers in the child's socialization.

School By the time children graduate from high school, they have spent more than 10,000 hours in the classroom. Experiences with teachers provide children with adult social encounters beyond their family. Such experiences provide children with feedback about their cognitive and social abilities. Schools are small societies with tasks to be accomplished and social experiences that are different from those children experience at home. Information on the school as an important socialization influence in the child's development appears in chapter 12.

Television Few social conditions in the last half of the twentieth century have had more of an impact on the mind and behavior than television. Children often spend more time in front of the television set than they do interacting with their parents, and adults frequently watch television more hours per week than they spend interacting with their spouse. Although only one of the vehicles of the mass media that affect the mind and behavior—radio, movies, books, newspapers, and magazines being others—television seems to have had the greatest impact. The role of television in children's socialization is also discussed in chapter 12.

Close Relationships

Willard Hartup (1985) recently called attention to three reasons why close relationships are important in the study of children's development.

Context First, as we have just seen, close relationships are the context in which much of socialization occurs. As you learned in the profile at the beginning of the chapter, communication skills are not acquired when children experience long bouts of social isolation. Mother–child, father–child, sibling, friendship, peer, teacher–child, dating, and intergenerational relationships are contexts providing meaningful socialization experiences that have an impact on development.

Bases or Resources for Functioning in the Wider Social World A second reason close relationships are important in development is because they serve as bases or resources that allow the child to function independently in the wider social world. For example, a secure attachment of the child to his or her parents is likely to promote exploration of the child's environment in healthy ways (Ainsworth & Bell, 1970), as well as a positive sense of self (Mahler, 1979a). In this manner, close relationships are more than just social contexts, they are gateways or channels for a widening range of social experiences.

A secure attachment to parents likely promotes the child's
healthy exploration of the social world.

Carrying Forward Relationships to Construct New Relationships A third reason close relationships are important in development is that those relationships in which the child participates and observes function as important models or templates—models or templates that often are carried forward to influence the construction of future relationships. Clearly close relationships do not merely repeat themselves in endless cycles over the course of the child's development. The quality of any relationship depends to some degree on the specific individual with whom the relationship is formed. However, the outcomes of previous relationships often can be detected in later ones.

These three themes of close relationships will reappear as you read the remaining chapters on children's social and personality development. Keep in mind as you read the remaining chapters that how children construct social relationships and the contexts in which they are socialized are key ingredients in understanding the socialization process.

SUMMARY

I. Historically, the two most prominent theories of socialization have been the psychoanalytic and behavioral, social learning.

   A. An understanding of psychoanalytic theory requires information about Sigmund Freud's classical theory, the Freudian revisionists and neo-Freudian views, and the strengths and weaknesses of the theory.

      1. Freud described the structure of personality in terms of the id, ego, and superego. He believed that children cope with the stress of reality by calling on defense mechanisms. He also argued that development is primarily psychosexual in nature. The stages are oral, anal, phallic, latency, and genital.

      2. The basic themes of the Freudian revisionists place less emphasis on sexuality and more stress on life-cycle concerns, social factors, and ego and conscious thought.

      3. Among the strengths of psychoanalytic theory are an emphasis on the past, interest in development, mental representation and translation of the environment, the unconscious mind, conflict, and its contribution to psychology in general. Among the weaknesses are the difficulty of testing its concepts, lack of an empirical data base and overemphasis of the past, overemphasis of the unconscious mind and sexuality, its negative and pessimistic view of development, and too much emphasis on early experience.

   B. Information about the behavioral and social learning views focuses on the behavioral view, the social learning view, the processes involved in each, and the strengths and weaknesses of each.

      1. The behavioral view involves John Watson's ideas and B. F. Skinner's theory.

      2. The social learning view emphasizes the cognitive social learning perspective of Albert Bandura and Walter Mischel.

      3. The processes emphasized in the behavioral and social learning views are reinforcement, punishment and the related topic of discipline, and imitation.

      4. The strengths of the behavioral and social learning views include their emphasis of specific behavioral and environmental stimuli, observational methods, rigorous experimental approach, cognitive social learning concern about cognitive mediation and adaptation to a changing social world, and the importance of context. The weaknesses of the views include their failure to recognize the causative role of cognition, the nonchronological nature of the views, too little attention to biological matters, too much reductionism, and too much emphasis on the mechanical nature of behavior.

II. The study of children's socialization has involved an increased interest in the role of cognitive and biological processes.

   A. The cognitive perspective is represented by two main approaches: cognitive developmental theory and information processing.

      1. Cognitive developmental theory includes the ideas of Piaget and Kohlberg. Piaget's ideas stress the adaptiveness and organization that occur in any biological system. Socialization occurs as the child adapts to the particular moment and reorganizes past ways of thinking. An example of Piagetian inspired socialization research involves role taking. Kohlberg has expanded Piaget's ideas and liberally applied cognitive developmental theory to many domains of socialization, particularly moral development and self-development.

      2. Children process information about their social world just as they process information about words and numbers. Social information processing involves social memory and schemata. There has been too little research on social memory and the cognitive organization of social matters. Neisser's ecological model of perception can be applied to schemata for social experiences. The development of social monitoring is another important aspect of children's social information processing.

B. The biological perspective on socialization includes information about genetics, ethology, and the role of biological maturation.
  1. The expression of a given social behavior requires a proper environment and the existence of social objects, that is, people. However, no social behavior can be solely attributed to environmental experience. A genetic tie for the personality dimension of introversion–extraversion has been documented through twin studies, and research has demonstrated how the infant's temperament contributes to socialization.
  2. Robert Hinde says ethologists ask three important questions about any given social behavior: Why did the organism behave in this manner? How does the organism change over time and why? And, what is the evolutionary origin of the behavior? Among the important issues of interest to ethologists are those pertaining to the role of observation, functional considerations, dichotomies in development and organism–environment interaction, sensitive periods, and relationships and personality.
  3. Study of the importance of biological maturation in socialization is beginning to reveal how close relationships are influenced by the child's biological maturation.
III. Information about the social environment children experience as they develop involves culture and social class, as well as social contexts and close relationships.
  A. An overview of culture and social class emphasizes the direct and indirect effects of culture, cross-cultural comparisons, the association of social class with social behavior, and how developmental psychologists view the role of culture in the empirical study of socialization.
  B. Four of the most important social contexts for children's socialization are the family, peers, school, and television. Close relationships are at the heart of understanding the socialization process. Close relationships are important in the study of development for three reasons: They are the context in which much of socialization occurs; they serve as bases or resources for independent functioning in a wider social world; and they are carried forward to influence the construction of new relationships.

KEY TERMS

anal stage 319
attention 334
autonomy versus shame and doubt 324
cognitive social learning theory 329
concrete-individual perspective 339
conscience 317
culture 348
defense mechanisms 318
displacement 319
ego 317
ego ideal 317
ego integrity versus despair 324
Electra complex 320
generativity versus stagnation 324
genital stage 320
id 316
identity versus identity confusion (diffusion) 324
incentive conditions 334
induction 332
industry versus inferiority 324
initiative versus guilt 324
intimacy versus isolation 324
latency stage 320
love withdrawal 332
member-of-society perspective 339

motoric reproduction 334
neo-Freudian (neopsychoanalytic) 322
Oedipus complex 316, 320
oral stage 319
personal constructs 328
phallic stage 319
pleasure principle 316
power assertion 332
primary process thinking 317
prior-to-society perspective 339
projection 319
psychoanalytic theory 315
rationalization 319
reaction formation 318
reality principle 317
regression 318
repression 318
retention 334
self-reinforcement 331
sensitive period 346
situationism 329
social class 351
social comparison 330
stage theory 319
superego 317
suppression 318
time-out 332
trust versus mistrust 324

REVIEW QUESTIONS

1. Discuss the main ideas of psychoanalytic theories and their strengths and weaknesses.
2. Describe the main ideas of the behavioral and social learning theorists and also report on their strengths and weaknesses. Be sure to document the distinction between the behavioral views of Watson and Skinner and the social learning perspectives of Bandura and Mischel.
3. Provide an overview of the cognitive perspective on socialization.
4. Describe the biological perspective on socialization.
5. How do culture and social class contribute to children's socialization?
6. What is the role of contexts and close relationships in children's socialization?

SUGGESTED READINGS

Bandura, A. (1977). *Social learning theory.* Englewood Cliffs, NJ: Prentice-Hall.

A comprehensive overview of Bandura's approach to development. Includes extensive information about the importance of observational learning.

Bronfenbrenner, U., & Crouter, A. C. (1983). The evolution of environmental models in developmental research. In P. H. Mussen (Ed.), *Handbook of child psychology* (4th ed., Vol. 1). New York: John Wiley.

Bronfenbrenner, a leading figure in the ecological approach, presents his views on how developmental psychology has been too constrained in its thinking and assessment regarding the contexts of development.

Cowan, P. A. (1978). *Piaget with feeling: Cognitive, social, and emotional dimensions.* New York: Holt, Rinehart & Winston.

Philip Cowan is head of the clinical psychology program at the University of California at Berkeley. He, like many other clinicians, believes Piaget has more to tell us about social and emotional development than Piaget himself thought.

Erikson, E. H. (1968). *Identity: Youth and crisis.* New York: Norton.

This book provides an excellent introduction to Erikson's life-cycle perspective, including fascinating stories about personal lives.

Hartup, W. W., & Rubin, Z. (Eds.). (1985). *Relationships and development.* Hillsdale, NJ: Lawrence Erlbaum.

This compendium of articles provides considerable insight into the new look in the study of children's relationships. Includes articles by Hartup, Hinde, Sroufe, and Weiss. Pays particular attention to the role of development in understanding relationships.

Hinde, R. (1983). Ethology and child development. In P. H. Mussen (Ed.), *Handbook of child psychology* (4th ed., Vol. 2). New York: John Wiley.

Robert Hinde's views have had a significant impact on the study of children's socialization. Here he outlines the basic questions ethologists ask when they study children's socialization and the research issues that interest ethologists. Extends the discussion of the ethological approach presented in this chapter.

Salkind, N. (1981). *Theories of development.* New York: Van Nostrand.

Includes more detailed information about Freud's, Erikson's, Skinner's, Bandura's, and Piaget's approaches than does this chapter. Also considers other theories of development as well.

THE FAMILY

PROLOGUE

WHY DON'T YOU GROW UP

Why don't you grow up? If I said it to them once I said it a million times. Is it my imagination, or have I spent a lifetime shutting refrigerator doors, emptying nose tissue from pants pockets before washing, writing checks for milk, picking up wet towels and finding library books in the clothes hamper?

Mr. Matterling said, "Parenting is loving." (What did he know? He was an old Child Psychology teacher who didn't have any children. He only had twenty-two guppies and two catfish to clean the bowl.) How I wish that for one day I could teach Mr. Matterling's class. How I would like to tell him it's more than loving. More than clean gravel. More than eating the ones you don't like.

Parenting is fearful, Mr. Matterling. You don't know how fearful until you sit next to your son on his maiden voyage behind the wheel of your car and hear him say, "My Driver's Ed teacher says I've got only one problem and that's every time I meet a car I pass over the center line."

And you worry. I worried when they stayed home. . . . I worried when they dated a lot. ("They're not meditating in the Christian Science reading room until 2 A.M., Ed.") I worried when they didn't date. ("Maybe we should try a sixteenth of an inch padding.")

I worried when their grades were bad. ("He won't be able to get into karate school with those marks.") I worried when their grades were good. ("So swing a little. You wanta spend the rest of your life reading William F. Buckley and basting your acne?")

I worried when they got a job. ("She looks so tired, and besides it could bring back her asthma attacks.") I worried when they didn't get a job. ("Mark my word, he'll take after your brother, Wesley, who didn't get a paper route until he was thirty-three.")

And a tired voice within me persisted, "Why don't you grow up?" . . .

This half-child, half-adult groping miserably to weigh life's inconsistencies, hypocrisy, instant independence, advice, rules, and responsibilities.

The blind date that never showed. The captaincy that went to the best friend. The college reject, the drill team have-nots, the class office also-rans, the honors that went to someone else. And they turned to me for an answer. . . .

And there were joys. Moments of closeness . . . an awkward hug; a look in the semidarkness as you turned off the test pattern as they slept. The pride of seeing them stand up when older people entered the room and saying, "Yes, sir," and "No, ma'am," without your holding a cue card in front of them. The strange, warm feeling of seeing them pick up a baby and seeing a wistfulness in their faces that I have never seen before. . . .

I shall never forgive Mr. Matterling for not warning me of the times of panic. It's not time yet. It can't be. I'm not finished. I had all the teaching and discipline and the socks to pick up and the buttons to sew on and those lousy meal worms to feed the lizard every day . . . there was no time for loving. That's what it's all about, isn't it? Did they ever know I smiled? Did they ever understand my tears? Did I talk too much? Did I say too little? Did I ever look at them and really see them? Do I know them at all? Or was it all a lifetime of "Why don't you grow up?" (Bombeck & Keane, 1971)

PREVIEW

In this chapter we begin the study of social processes and development. Our focus on the family begins with a consideration of important family processes and then moves to the study of children's development in families.

FAMILY PROCESSES

Five of the most important processes involved in the study of the family are reciprocal socialization and mutual regulation, the family as a system, the construction of relationships, the maturation of the child and the maturation of parents, and sociocultural and historical influences. Let's consider each of these in turn.

Reciprocal Socialization and Mutual Regulation

For many years the socialization process between parents and children was viewed as a one-way affair. Children were considered to be the products of their parents' socialization techniques. Willard Hartup (1985) refers to such perspectives as **social-mold theories** to describe the way the child is molded by his or her environment, particularly within the family. In such theories (the behavioral view of Skinner being the most prominent example), maturational processes have been given little attention. Instead, the child is looked upon as infinitely malleable; parents, as well as other adults, can shape children by effectively managing and manipulating their environments.

The socialization process between parents and their children is reciprocal—children socialize parents just as parents socialize children. For instance, the interaction of mothers and their infants has been symbolized as a dance or dialogue in which successive actions of the partners are closely coordinated (Lester, Hoffman & Brazelton, 1985). This coordinated dance or dialogue can assume the form of mutual contingency or synchrony (each person's behavior depends on the partner's previous behavior), or it can be reciprocal in a more precise sense (the actions of the partners can be matched, as when one partner imitates the other or there is mutual smiling). The exchange between a parent and an infant has been investigated in terms of specific behaviors as well as clusters of social behavior (at a more molar level).

Exchanging Specific Behaviors

One of the most frequently investigated aspects of reciprocal socialization in infancy is mutual gazing or eye contact. Microanalytic studies suggest that mutual visual regard is an important part of early social interaction. For example, in one investigation the mother and infant engaged in a variety of behavioral actions while they looked at each other. By contrast, when they looked away from each other, the rate of such behaviors was reduced considerably (Stern, Beebe, Jaffe & Bennett, 1977). These episodes of mutual gaze were referred to as "episodes of maintained engagement," a label reflecting how mutual gaze increases the variety of behaviors engaged in.

Molar Exchanges

Rather than studying specific behaviors in reciprocal interchanges between parents and infants, researchers have recently focused on clusters of responses. For example, rather than only observing smiles, an investigator may observe positive affective behavior of which smiles are only one component. In one investigation mothers and infants matched each other's affective tone (Lewis, 1972). For example, the amount of positive affective behavior on the part of the mother was correlated with the amount of such positive behavior on the part of the three-month-old infant. The same pattern of findings occurred for negative affective behavior (frowns and the like) as well.

Who Is "Driving" the Relationship?

We have seen that the behaviors of mothers and infants are interconnected. Behaviors such as gazing are synchronized, and affective states are reciprocal. The question arises as to which partner is driving the relationship. Is the mother doing most of the work in the partnership, being sensitive to the infant's states and changing her behavior according to her perception of the infant's needs?

Eleanor Maccoby and John Martin (1983), after reviewing a number of mother–infant studies, concluded that when the infant is very young, the mother is performing more work in facilitating interaction than the infant. Through all of the infant's first year and into the second, the mother is more likely to join the infant's nonsocial behavior than vice versa (Thomas & Martin, 1976). Over time, as the child becomes more capable

Who is "driving" the parent-child relationship?

of regulating his or her own behavior, the mother and the child interact with each other on more equal terms; that is, both "drive" or initiate the relationship.

In this section we have seen that socialization is a two-way process. However, so far we have only been considering socialization as a dyadic process, that it is between two people. Next we see that it is important to consider the entire family system in our study of social processes.

The Family as a System

As we have seen, the nature of parent–child relationships is very complex. Not only should we consider the reciprocal nature of parent–child relationships when we are interested in explaining the child's social behavior, but we should also look at the entire system of interacting individuals in the family. As a social system, the family can be thought of as a constellation of subsystems defined in terms of generation, gender, and role (Feiring & Lewis, 1978). Divisions of labor among family members define particular subunits and attachments define others, each family member being a participant in several subsystems, some dyadic, some polyadic.

As fathers become recognized as important socialization agents, it has become obvious that we should be studying more than two-party social interactions (Lamb, 1976). Children interact with more than one parent or adult most days of their lives, yet we know very little about how parents serve each other as sources of support as well as sources of dissatisfaction. One attempt to understand the link between spouse relationships and parent–infant relationships was conducted by Frank Pedersen and his colleagues (Pedersen, Anderson & Cain, 1980). They believe that the three dyadic units of interaction—mother–father, mother–child, and father–child—are interrelated. Using the husband–wife relationship as a point of reference, they set out to investigate the connections among family members. Forty-one families were observed on three separate occasions at home, with separate observations of husband–wife and parent–infant dyads. The infants were firstborn, five-month-old middle-class boys and girls.

The first hypothesis investigated was that positive interaction between the husband and wife, such as smiling and affection, would be positively linked with the expression of positive affect toward the infant by each parent. The results: There was little relationship between measures of positive husband–wife interaction and their positive interaction with the infant. However, when negative social interaction between the husband and wife was observed (e.g., verbal criticism, blame), it was strongly linked to the negative affect shown by the father toward the infant. These findings suggest that the family is a network of interacting individuals functioning as a system.

Preschool teachers are more likely to be drawn to and cuddle a child who has a history of seductive maternal behavior.

One subsystem of the family system that merits additional comment is the husband–wife support system. Since many mothers now work outside the home, the extent to which husbands share in what were once traditional female duties may go a long way toward developing a healthy family system. Husbands who adapt to such changes in the female role in our society reduce marital and family conflict and increase the likelihood that children will experience competent child rearing.

The Construction of Relationships

In our attempt to provide information about the contemporary flavor of scientific inquiry about families, we have talked about maturational processes, reciprocal socialization and mutual regulation, and the family as a system. Very recently a great deal of interest has been generated in understanding how relationships are constructed and carried forward in time. We no longer see socialization as a process through which parents simply mold children into mature beings. At the same time we do not believe the child constructs a vision of reality

ZIGGY, by Tom Wilson. Copyright 1972, Universal Press Syndicate. Reprinted with permission. All rights reserved.

The husband-wife support system has an important impact on parent-child relationships.

and social maturity apart from interactions with parents and other social agents. Rather, the contemporary view of socialization argues for adopting a view of the child emphasizing the transactions between a changing child and a changing social environment (Hartup, 1983).

One proposal for how we construct relationships and carry them forward in time was made by Alan Sroufe and June Fleeson (1985). They believe the following propositions describe relationships:

1. A continuity and coherence characterize close relationships over time.
2. Previous relationship patterns are carried forward to influence later relationships.

Continuity and Coherence

Changes in the child's behaviors are very extensive in the infant and early childhood years. Through all of this change, though, there is a remarkable coherence and system. There is a continuity to such close relationships as the mother–child relationship, over time. Some infants come to learn that their caregiver will be emotionally available; others expect their caregiver not to be available. What goes on in the relationship between caregivers and a child lead the child to construct a picture of relationships with social objects.

Carrying Forward Relationships

Relationships are carried forward to influence new relationships. For example, children who have a history of secure attachment have been observed to be more socially competent in preschool settings (Waters, Wippman & Sroufe, 1979). We do not know exactly how relationship histories are carried forward. It may be that an important part of this process is the motivation to maintain a consistency or coherence of self. An important part of this coherence may be continuing or reestablishing relationships that are similar to past relationship experiences.

For example, Sroufe and Fleeson (1985) point to observations of a teacher in a preschool classroom who became very upset and angry with several children in her classroom. Invariably these children had experienced chronic maternal rejection. When the teacher was observed to be strongly drawn to cuddle or caress a child, invariably the child came from a family with a history of seductive maternal behavior. Thus the rejected child misbehaves until he is punished, a situation that reproduces a familiar family relationship. By contrast, the seductive child has been treated as cute and charming; he or she knows how to elicit seductiveness from adults. When teachers were informed about their relationships with these children, they were able to modify their behavior toward them.

The Maturation of the Child and the Maturation of Parents

First, we consider the maturation of the child and the importance of parental adaptation to such changes. Second, we focus on the importance of the maturation of the parents themselves, in particular highlighting some of the interesting simultaneous changes that often characterize adolescent development and development in mid-life.

The Maturation of the Child

One factor that should not be overlooked in considering the parent's behavior toward the child is the child's maturation. Mothers and fathers obviously do not treat a thirteen-year-old in the same way as a two-year-old. The two-year-old and the thirteen-year-old have different needs and abilities, and the mother and father have different expectancies for the two children. Eleanor Maccoby (1980) has described how parents behave toward children of different ages.

> During the first year of a child's life, the parent-child interaction moves from a heavy focus on routine caretaking—feeding, changing, bathing, and soothing—and comes to include more noncaretaking activities like play and visual-vocal exchanges. During children's second and third years, parents often handle disciplinary issues by physical manipulation: They carry the child away from a mischievous activity to the place they want the child to go; they put fragile and dangerous objects out of reach; they sometimes spank. But as the child grows older, parents turn increasingly to reasoning, moral exhortation, and giving or withholding special privileges. As children move from infancy to middle childhood, parents show them less physical affection, become less protective, and spend less time with them.
>
> These changes in parental behavior seem clearly linked to the child's physical and mental growth—to changes in motor skill, language, judgment, and perspective-taking ability. It seems obvious that as the child grows larger and heavier, parents are less likely to resort to physical manipulation. And it seems almost equally obvious that parents are unlikely to reason with a child who doesn't yet talk and who seems to have a limited understanding of other people's speech. (pp. 395–396)

This brief look at maturational changes in the child and parenting suggests that successful parents do not maintain a static orientation toward the child throughout development. Rather, successful parenting often involves adaptive responses to the changing needs and emerging themes of the child's development.

The Maturation of Parents

First we consider how the age of parents may be linked to their child-rearing practices, and second, we focus on the maturing adolescent and maturing parents. Population statistics suggest that an increasing number of women are having babies at older ages than in the past. One investigation (Daniels & Weingarten, 1980) examined a group of "late-late" women who had their first children in their late thirties and early forties. These women said they were very satisfied about their mother role and ready to be parents. Overall it was concluded that there is no single perfect time to have children, although adolescence is not likely the best time. Still, recent studies of the relationships between adolescent mothers and their offspring suggest that even teenage mothers show a sensitive attachment relationship with the infant when appropriate social supports are available (Crockenberg, 1983). The father's role in the adolescent-parent family system is particularly important (Parke, Power & Fisher, 1980). For example, divorce rates among adolescent parents are much higher than in the general population (Furstenberg, 1976), a circumstance likely to increase the the amount of stress on the adolescent mother.

Information about the developmental status of the father and child-rearing practices, like that for the mother, is sparse. In one set of studies (Mitteness & Nydegger, 1982; Nydegger, 1975, 1981) younger and older fathers were compared. The older fathers seemed to fare better than younger fathers in some ways, being warmer, communicating better with their children, encouraging intellectual achievement more, and showing less rejection. However, the older fathers were less likely to place demands on their children and less likely to enforce rules.

Not only can we compare parents of different ages in relation to child-rearing practices, but it also is important to consider simultaneous changes in children and their parents. One time period in parent–child relationships that provides an intriguing comparison of

What are some developmental changes in the parents of adolescents that might be related to the nature of parent-adolescent relationships?

the developmental changes in children and parents is when children become adolescents and parents become middle-aged. Although many experts on adult development believe the mid-life crisis is not as pervasive as many writers have suggested (Neugarten, 1980), there are, nonetheless, some physical, cognitive, and social changes that do seem to characterize the middle-adulthood phase of the life cycle, the period many parents of adolescents are just entering.

Both mid-life and adolescence are transitional phases in the life cycle that involve coping with physical, cognitive, and social changes. What seems to make this a challenging time for the family is that the metamorphoses of parents and adolescents are taking place simultaneously. Laurence Steinberg (1980) comments further about these simultaneous changes in parents and adolescents:

> Ironically, early adolescents and mid-life parents seem simultaneously to be developing in opposite directions.

In order to cope with the changes, the family must understand this state of affairs. Consider the following facts:

1. Just as the adolescent enters puberty, approaching the peak strength and virility glorified in popular culture, the mid-life parent is beginning to worry about appearance, health, and sexual attractiveness.
2. Just as the adolescent finds a new way of looking at the world, a viewpoint that involves a broadening of possibilities and endless hypothetical situations to consider, the mid-life parent undergoes a shift in perspective, a shift toward limits and boundaries, toward the feeling that time is running out.
3. Just as the adolescent prepares for entrance into adult society and begins to consider seriously issues of work and career, the mid-life parent looks back—for better or worse—on his or her own occupational history and faces an occupational plateau. Whereas society recognizes that the adolescent is just starting out, it labels the mid-life adult as having already had a chance. (p. 10)

Sociocultural, Historical Influences on the Family

Family development does not occur in a social vacuum. Important sociocultural and historical influences have an impact on the development of the child in the family. Let's look more closely at how the family is embedded in sociocultural and historical contexts.

Changes in the family may be due to great upheavals in a nation, such as war, famine, or mass immigration, or to more subtle transitions in ways of life. The Great Depression in the early 1930s had some negative effects on families. During its height, the depression produced economic deprivation that seemed to heighten adult discontent, depression about living conditions, the likelihood of marital conflict, inconsistencies in relations with children, and risk of the father's impairment—heavy drinking, demoralization, and health disabilities (Elder, 1980).

More subtle changes in a culture that have significant influences on the family have been described by Margaret Mead (1978). These changes focus on the longevity of the elderly and their role in the family; the urban, suburban orientation of families and their mobility; television; and a general dissatisfaction and restlessness. Fifty years ago the older people who survived were usually hearty and still closely linked to the family, often helping to maintain its existence. As more people live to an older age, their middle-aged children have been pressed into a caretaking role for their parents, or the elderly parents may be placed in a nursing home. Elderly parents may have lost some of their socializing role in the family during the twentieth century as many of their children moved great distances away.

Many of these moves on the part of families have been away from farms and small towns to urban and suburban settings. In the small towns and farms individuals were surrounded by lifelong neighbors, relatives, and friends. Today, neighborhood and extended-family support systems are not nearly as prevalent. Families now move all over the country, often uprooting their children from a school and peer group they have known for considerable lengths of time. For many families it is not unusual for this type of move to occur every year or two, as one or both parents are transferred from job to job.

Television has played a major role in the changing family. Many children who watch television find that their parents are too busy working to share this experience with them. Children increasingly have experienced a world their parents are not a part of. Instead

of participating in neighborhood peer groups, children come home after school and plop down in front of the television set. Television has also allowed children and their families to see new ways of life. Lower-class families can look into the family lives of the middle-class more readily by simply pushing a button.

Another subtle change in families has been an increase in general dissatisfaction and restlessness. Women became increasingly dissatisfied with their way of life, placing great strain on marriages. With fewer elders and long-term friends close by to help and advise young people during the initial difficult years of marriage and childbearing, marriages began to fracture at the first signs of disagreement. Divorce has become epidemic in our culture. As women moved into the labor market, men simultaneously became restless and looked for stimulation outside of family life. The result of such restlessness and the tendency to divorce and remarry have produced a hodgepodge of family structures with far greater numbers of single-parent and stepparent families than ever before in history.

CHILDREN'S DEVELOPMENT AND FAMILY RELATIONSHIPS

To learn more about the role of family relationships in children's development, we study attachment in infancy, parenting styles, sibling relationships, the changing family in a changing society, parent–adolescent relationships, and intergenerational relationships.

Attachment in Infancy

Let's look at what attachment is, theories of attachment, how attachment develops, individual differences and situational variation in attachment, and the importance of attachment in the construction of relationships.

What Is Attachment?

In everyday language, an attachment refers to a relation between two individuals in which each person feels strongly about the other and does a number of things to ensure the continuation of the relationship. Many pairs of people are attached: relatives, lovers, a teacher and student. In the language of child psychology, however, **attachment** is often restricted to a relation between particular social figures and to a particular phenomenon thought to reflect unique characteristics of the relationship. The developmental period is infancy (roughly birth to two years), the social figures are the infant and one or more adult caregivers, and the phenomenon is a bond, which we now describe in greater detail.

Theories of Attachment

Attachment is a key ingredient of the socialization process. It is no surprise then that four of the theoretical perspectives we described in chapter 10—psychoanalytic, social learning, cognitive, and biological—have provided insights into the nature of the attachment process. We consider each of these contributions in turn and then draw some conclusions about the theories.

Psychoanalytic Theory   For Freud, the infant becomes attached to a person or object who provides oral satisfaction. Recall that Freud labeled the first stage of development the oral stage because he believed infants obtain considerable pleasure from sucking and biting objects. Freud argued that infants are likely to become attached to their mothers because it is mothers who are most likely to feed the infants. Erikson also emphasized the feeding situation as an important contributor to attachment but highlighted the development of trust on the part of the infant. Erikson (1968) stressed that mothers who are warmly involved in caregiving activities with their infants are likely to have infants who show trust rather than mistrust. Difficulties during these early infant years are believed by psychoanalytic theorists to often have life-long influences on relationships. Thus, the psychoanalytic theorists would predict that infants who have problems with the feeding situation and who have not developed a sense of trust may have difficulty establishing close relationships with others later in life.

Social Learning Theory   Learning theorists often call on the processes of primary and secondary reinforcement to explain attachment. Recall from chapter 5 that primary reinforcement is unlearned and that secondary reinforcement is learned. The feeding situation involves primary reinforcement since food is innately satisfying. By becoming associated with the feeding process, the caregiver becomes a secondary reinforcer for the infant. The caregiver's smiles, pats on the head, and mere presence become associated with the positive effect of food and satisfaction of the hunger drive in the infant. Now the infant will do what he or she can

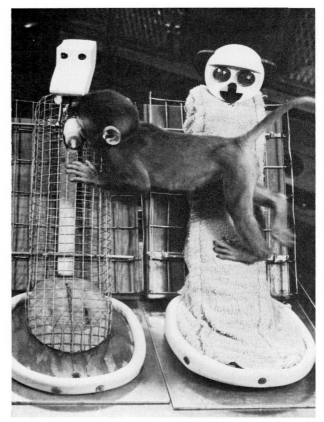

FIGURE 11.1
The classic Harlow infant monkey study revealed the importance of contact comfort in attachment. Here, the infant monkey clings to the cloth ''mother,'' but feeds from the wire ''mother.''

to maintain the mother's presence because she has become a rewarding individual.

As we can see, many learning theorists, like psychoanalytic theorists, place the feeding situation in a central role when attachment is at issue. Is feeding really such a critical factor in the development of attachment? Harry Harlow and Robert Zimmerman (1959) carried out a classic study to test the importance of feeding and **contact comfort** in the development of attachment. Infant monkeys were taken away from their mothers at birth and brought up during the next six months with surrogate (substitute) mothers. As shown in figure 11.1, one of the substitute mothers was made of wire while the other was covered with a soft cloth. Half of the infant monkeys were fed by the wire mother, half by the cloth mother. Periodically

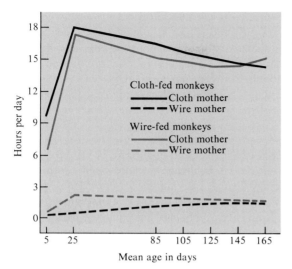

FIGURE 11.2
Harlow and Zimmerman's wire and cloth monkey study. The
average amount of time infant monkeys spent in contact with
their cloth and wire mothers is shown. The infant monkeys spent
most of their time with the cloth mother regardless of which
mother fed them (Harlow and Zimmerman, 1959).

during the study the amount of time the infant monkeys spent with either the wire or cloth mother was assessed. Also, the researchers created an experimental
situation in which they introduced a stressful circumstance by placing a strange looking creature in the area
where the monkeys were. This situation was designed
to see which mother the infant would prefer in a
stressful encounter. As shown in figure 11.2, regardless
of whether they were fed by the wire or the cloth
mother, the infant monkeys spent considerably more
time with the cloth mother. Furthermore, when they
were frightened by the strange creature, the infant
monkeys invariably ran to the cloth mother and clung
to her. Shortly thereafter, seeming to gain confidence,
they would approach the strange creature and explore
it. In sum, the Harlow monkey study provides strong
evidence that feeding is not the crucial factor in the
attachment process. Harlow and Zimmerman's research suggests that contact comfort, as they referred
to it, probably serves an important function in attachment. Most contemporary learning theorists now agree
that feeding is not the key variable in attachment.
Rather, they argue that there are many rewarding aspects of the interaction between infant and caregiver;
satisfying the infant's hunger is but one of a number

of behaviors the caregiver performs. Others include the
contact comfort, or tactile stimulation, described by
Harlow and Zimmerman, as well as visual and vocal
stimulation. Put together, all of these behaviors make
the caregiver a rewarding object to become attached to
(Gewirtz, 1969).

Cognitive Developmental Theory Some cognitive
psychologists (e.g., Kohlberg, 1969) have interpreted
attachment as a motivational system based on the need
to express competence (as opposed to achieving biological pleasure) in interpersonal exchanges. Attachment
from this perspective reflects the infant's intellectual
development. So, for example, the infant must first acquire the ability to appreciate objects as existing beyond momentary reach (object permanence), before
particular objects (e.g., a caregiver) can become part
of a stable motivational system.

To achieve a strong emotional bond with significant
caregivers, goes the argument, the infant must at least
first perceive *object permanence* with respect to those
people. That is, the infant must first perceive that people
are permanent fixtures in the world, existing beyond
the moments and places where they are encountered.
Some research suggests that an infant's general level
of cognitive development is correlated with the degree
of attachment (Clarke-Stewart, 1973; Stone &
Chesney, 1978). An interesting side issue has also
emerged. Since the time at which clear attachments
first emerge (about six to eight months) predates the
time at which object permanence is usually observed
with inanimate objects (e.g., Uzgiris & Hunt, 1975),
it has been speculated that the presence of attachment
reflects a special early case of object permanence (e.g.,
Bell, 1970). However, clever experiments have not consistently confirmed some of the implications of this notion.

Ethological Theory The most comprehensive account of attachment is that of John Bowlby. First presented in a paper in the *International Journal of
Psychoanalysis* in 1958 and more recently in a two-
volume work entitled *Attachment and Loss* (1969,
1973), Bowlby has set forth a theoretically elegant and
eclectic account of attachment based upon a synthesis
of ethology and several other traditions in psychology.
In his view, the infant and mother instinctively trigger
each other's behavior to form an attachment bond. The
neonate is biologically equipped with signals to elicit

responses from the mother; the neonate cries, clings, smiles, and coos, and later crawls, walks, and follows the mother. Such behavior is often elicited by the mother's specific action, such as leaving the room or putting the infant down. The infant's behavior is directed by the primary goal of maintaining the mother's proximity. The baby *processes information* about the mother's location, and his or her behavior changes on the basis of this feedback. Thus, as with other ethological explanations of behavior, *instinct* (or a fixed action pattern) is the primary force for developmental change; but it is transformed through social experience.

Bowlby has classified attachment into two main classes of action: executor and signaling responses. **Executor responses** include clinging, following, sucking, and physical approach; they bring the infant and mother in close contact and, functionally speaking, the infant is the main actor. **Signaling responses** refer to the infant's smiling, crying, and calling; they also bring the infant and mother together, but in this case the infant attempts to elicit (reciprocal) behaviors from the mother.

The development of attachment as an integrated system of behaviors occurs in four phases during the first year of life. During the first phase, extending from birth to two or three months, the infant directs his or her attachment to human figures on the basis of an instinctual bias; strangers, siblings, mothers, and fathers are equally likely to elicit smiling or crying since the infant is not yet discriminating. In phase two, from three to six months, attachment focuses on one figure, typically the primary caregiver (e.g., mother). In phase three, extending from six to nine months, the intensity of attachment to the mother increases; because of increased locomotor skills, the infant now more readily seeks proximity to the mother. Finally, in the fourth phase, which extends from nine months to a year, the elements of attachment listed above become integrated into a mutual system of attachment to which the infant and mother both contribute.

Evaluation of Attachment Theories   Our view is that each theoretical approach has provided a useful addition to the notion of attachment as a whole. From psychoanalysis has come the idea that the infant is born with a number of needs and that the individuals who help satisfy these needs will exert a powerful emotional pull on the child. From ethology we have learned that these needs are instincts obeying laws and principles much like the instincts in the nonhuman animal kingdom. Ethology has also taught us to examine instinctual response systems carefully, and to observe their naturalistic patterning over time. Learning theory has been useful in demonstrating that specific response categories (e.g., smiling, vocalizing) can be shaped between the caregiver and the infant, but its focus on specific classes of behavior has also been its theoretical undoing because attachment is a more global phenomenon, cutting across all behavioral categories. Finally, from cognitive psychology has come the notion that the emotional bond of attachment presupposes certain cognitive prerequisites in the infant (e.g., identification and discrimination of different people). However, this theory has not been particularly illuminating about how the specific course of cognitive growth is linked with the specific growth of attachment, and it also fails to account for the vast individual differences in attachment. In the final analysis, we think that the approach taken by Bowlby holds the most promise since it offers the most general and subtle account of the development of attachment.

How Does Attachment Develop?

The theories we have just reviewed offer some suggestions about how attachment develops. In the present section we will review some of the empirical sources of evidence about the development of attachment.

Perhaps the most widely cited longitudinal study of attachment is the one reported earlier by Schaffer and Emerson (1964). The investigators followed sixty Scottish infants from age five to twenty-three weeks old at the outset of the study until they were eighteen months old. The researchers periodically interviewed the mothers about the infants' responses to separation episodes and observed the infants' responses to several standardized situations in which the interviewer (a stranger) slowly approached the infant. Figure 11.3 depicts the course of infant attachment behavior over time. It indicates that the infants protested separation from anyone (indiscriminate attachment) during the first months of life. Beginning at about six months (twenty-five to twenty-eight weeks), attachment to the mother became more focused and remained strong from

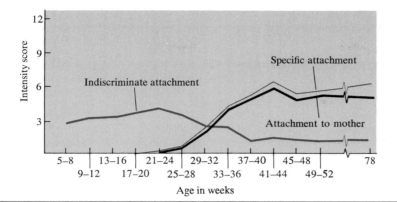

FIGURE 11.3
The developmental course of attachment
(Schaffer and Emerson, 1964).

ten months through the remainder of the eighteen-month period. Importantly, attachments to other specific caregivers were about as intense as attachment to the mother. Among the additional findings not shown in the figure, from seven months until almost the end of the first year, the specific attachment to the mother became more intense and fear of strangers generally occurred at about eight months, approximately one to two months after the onset of attachment to the mother.

In another well-known study of infant attachment, Mary Ainsworth (1967) observed twenty-nine infant–mother pairs in Uganda, Africa, for a period of nine months. The children ranged in age from two to fourteen months during the investigation. Her observations included, as indicators of attachment, smiling, crying, vocalization, separation protest, following, touching, greeting gestures, and using the mother as a base for exploration. As in the Schaffer and Emerson study, the Ugandan infants began to show the most intense signs of attachment to their mothers around seven months. However, there was evidence that the specific attachments began to develop earlier than in the Schaffer and Emerson sample; the Ugandan infants displayed the beginning of attachment to the mother by four months. Interestingly, there was also a time difference in the onset of fear of strangers, emerging later in the Ugandan infants.

There are reasons why we sometimes find differences across samples. The measures of attachment in the two studies just mentioned are not identical; that is, Ainsworth used a much larger number of measures, whereas much of Schaffer and Emerson's data were derived from maternal interviews. Nonetheless, there is good evidence that at about seven months of age most human infants develop a focused attachment to significant adults with whom they interact and that this bond becomes intensified in the next few months. And fear of strangers seems to be positively correlated with the onset of attachment to the caregiver, usually following it by several weeks to several months.

Individual Differences and Situational Influences
Let's now look at individual differences in attachment, particularly Mary Ainsworth's ideas about secure and insecure attachment, and let's also see how there is situational variation in attachment.

Individual Differences and Secure Attachment   To speak of attachment as experienced in the same way or to the same degree by all infant–caregiver pairs is, of course, a convenient fiction. There are striking individual differences among infants, and we would be surprised if it were otherwise.

To return to the Schaffer and Emerson (1964) investigation once more, for example, one-fourth of the infants showed fear of strangers before specific attachment to the mother. This is quite a striking and significant variation in the normal pattern of development. In Mary Ainsworth's (1967) early inquiry, five of the twenty-eight infants never did display positive affiliation (e.g., clinging, proximity seeking, visual contact) with their mothers. Other investigators have found similar patterns of individual variation (Main, 1973; Waters, 1978).

What does Ainsworth mean by secure and insecure attachment?

Ainsworth (1973, 1979) has offered a number of ideas about attachment, two of which we now explore. First, there are vast individual differences in the patterning of interactions between caregiver and infant that have profound consequences for the nature of the attachment that develops. Second, the resulting attachment seems to fall into distinct categories that are relatively enduring for the child. The two most important categories are **secure attachment** and **insecure attachment.** What does Ainsworth mean by "secure"? An infant who is securely attached uses the caregiver, or mother, as a secure base from which to explore the environment. He or she may move away from the mother freely but generally processes her location by occasionally glancing in her direction. The infant responds positively to being picked up; when put back down, the infant moves away freely to play. An insecurely attached infant, by contrast, shows ambivalent attachment behavior, particularly with regard to physical contact. The infant shows heightened separation anxiety in strange situations or in response to minor, everyday separations. He or she also tends to avoid proximity with the caregiver, a behavior that sometimes results in premature and inappropriate independence. Among those designated as insecurely attached, a further distinction is made: One subgroup exhibits insecurity by avoiding the mother, that is, for example, by ignoring her, averting her gaze, and failing to seek proximity; the other subgroup exhibits insecurity by resisting the mother, that is, clinging to her but at the same time fighting against the closeness by, for example, kicking and pushing away. Finer subdivisions of these three categories are possible as shown in Table 11.1. However, most investigators find the major subdivisions easier to work with and score reliably. In most groups of infants, it is assumed that the majority will be securely attached (two-thirds of Ainsworth's first sample of twenty-three babies were). It is the minority of infants who evidence some maladaptive attachment.

TABLE 11.1
Ainsworth's Classification of Attachment: Individual Differences

Characteristics	
Securely attached	
Group 1	Seeks interaction on reunion but not proximity. Does not resist when held. Little or no distress during separation episodes.
Group 2	Seeks interaction and more proximity on reunion. Does not resist when held. Little or no distress during separation episodes.
Group 3	Approaches mother on reunion. May also cry. Clutches when held, resists release. May or may not be distressed. Very active in seeking contact and resisting release.
Group 4	Greatest desire for proximity, interaction, and being held throughout. Distress evident in separation episodes.
Insecurely attached—avoidant	
Group 1	Infant fails to greet mother upon return. Fails to approach mother or attempt is abortive. If picked up, likely to squirm to get down and does not cling.
Group 2	Infant greets mother with mixed response, both approaching and turning and looking away. If picked up, always shows mixed response, momentarily clinging but also slipping away.
Insecurely attached—resistant	
Group 1	May reach or approach mother on reunion and seek contact. But great ambivalence shown, with hitting, kicking, and pushing.
Group 2	Fails even to contact mother. If approached or held, ambivalence shown.

Recently a number of researchers have argued that the classification differences in Ainsworth's categories (such as insecure versus secure attachment) are primarily due to temperamental characteristics of the infant (Campos, Barrett, Lamb, Goldsmith & Sternberg, 1983; Chess & Thomas, 1982; Kagan, 1982). Sroufe (1985) believes this is unfortunate because it promotes a stable-trait approach in understanding attachment rather than the qualitative-difference taxonomy of Ainsworth. Sroufe also believes the Ainsworth approach is superior to the infant temperament interpretation because Ainsworth's system captures the nature of the relationship between the caregiver and the infant, as derived from the history of their interaction. Nonetheless, the data on infant attachment are open to multiple interpretations.

Situational Variation in Attachment One-year-olds do not show as much distress toward a stranger when sitting on their mother's lap as they do when sitting on a table (Morgan & Ricciuti, 1969). Infants fuss less and explore their environment more when a novel toy is present (Rheingold & Samuels, 1969); the readiness of infants to explore an unfamiliar object depends in part on how closely the mother is positioned to the baby (Schwartz, 1978). Eye contact may also be important. Adults who maintain visual attention to the infant may give him or her a sense of security. For example, five-month-olds smile and vocalize more and cry less when their mother or a female stranger maintains direct eye contact with them (Lasky & Klein, 1979).

Alison Clarke-Stewart (1978) offered a penetrating analysis of the importance of situational variables. She focused on fear of the stranger and analyzed the factors that determine how much fear or wariness will surface in the stranger's presence. She examined the influence of the stranger's behavior in a longitudinal investigation of fourteen middle-class infants from one to two and one-half years old over a one-and-one-half-year period. In one brief interaction strangers behaved either in a hostile manner toward mothers by stomping into the room and launching into an angry, insulting dialogue with them, or in a pleasant manner by happily rushing into the room full of joyful, animated conversation. Infants maintained less physical contact with their mothers during and after hostile interactions than during and after the pleasant interactions. Interestingly, the child's behavior toward the stranger was not influenced by the tone of the interaction between the stranger and mother. By contrast, when strangers were either nice or nasty to the child himself or herself, there were clear effects on the child's interaction with the stranger but not on his or her behavior with the mother. "Nice" strangers briefly played with the child in a positive, friendly way with toys the child liked; "nasty" strangers acted unpleasantly and belligerently while playing with the child. The infants were more positive to the nice strangers (approaching, smiling, and touching) than to the nasty ones (avoiding, crying, and aggressing).

Attachment and the Construction of Relationships

In our discussion of the construction of relationships earlier in this chapter, we pointed out that relationships are carried forward to influence the development of new relationships. Work by Sroufe and his colleagues (Waters, Wippman & Sroufe, 1979), that supports this argument is presented in Perspective on Child Development 11.1.

Another investigation with older children also reveals how knowledge of the relationship history of each peer provides information that helps to predict the nature of peer interaction (Olweus, 1980). (See figure 11.4.) Some boys were typically aggressive and other boys were characteristically the recipients of aggression over a period of years. The "bullies" as well as the "whipping boys" had distinctive relationship histories. The bullies' parents had treated them with rejection and discord, power assertion, and permissiveness for aggression. By contrast, the whipping boys' mothers were anxious and overinvolved with their children and

PERSPECTIVE ON CHILD DEVELOPMENT 11.1

SECURE ATTACHMENT IN INFANCY AND SOCIAL COMPETENCE IN EARLY CHILDHOOD

I f, as the major theories claim, the first social bond(s) of attachment is critical for later development, it should be possible to determine a link between the degree or quality of attachment achieved in infancy and later social development. Such evidence is available from research conducted by Alan Sroufe.

In one investigation (Waters, Wippman & Sroufe, 1979), two such important links were established. First, eighteen-month-old infants who were or were not securely attached displayed different types of free play six months later. During a ten-minute free play period in which infants were placed in a room with their mothers and a number of toys, it was found that the secure infants showed and gave toys to their mothers—affectively shared—much more than either avoidant or resistant children did. Second, an independent group of fifteen-month-olds who were distinguished as securely or insecurely attached showed different levels of personal and interpersonal competence when they were three and one-half years old. Competence was assessed by means of a Q-sort technique in which a series of "descriptors" were evaluated by judges who observed children in preschool settings. Secure children received higher scores for "other children seek his or her company," "suggests activities," "peer leader," and "sympathetic to peer distress"; insecure children received higher scores for "basically withdrawn," "hesitates to engage," and "spectator (versus participant) in social activities." This link between attachment and later social competence has been verified by other investigators as well (Liebermann, 1977; Main & Londerville, 1977).

Other research from Sroufe's laboratory supports the link between attachment and other later behaviors. For example, in an investigation by Matas, Arend, and Sroufe (1978), a relation was shown wherein more securely attached infants at eighteen months of age were more capable of using specially designed tools and in solving simple problems six months later as shown in the figure opposite. Infants who had displayed secure attachment at eighteen months of age showed less frustration and were rated as happier at two years of age than their avoidant and ambivalent counterparts.

Van Pancake (1985) recently provided further evidence of the importance of secure attachment in infancy for the emergence of competent peer relations in early childhood. Twenty-four children (mean age four years, six months), for whom information about secure and insecure attachment had been obtained between twelve and eighteen months of age, were videotaped in a number of dyadic play sessions. Raters observed the videotape and coded the quality of the peer relationships. Children with a history of anxious-avoidant attachment were observed to have a less positive relationship with peers than their securely attached counterparts.

eschewed aggression. Bullying, then, is best described as a relational pattern and appears as a consequence of two relationship histories. It is interesting to note that well-adjusted boys were not the recipients of aggression by the bullies and that they were not involved in aggressive attacks on the whipping boys. The parents of the well-adjusted boys also did not sanction aggression, but their responsive involvement with their children apparently promoted the development of self-assertion as an adaptive pattern (Sroufe & Fleeson, 1985).

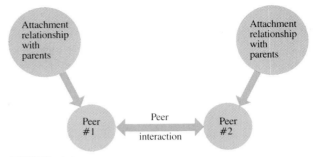

FIGURE 11.4
The construction of a peer relationship based on the attachment relationship history of each peer.

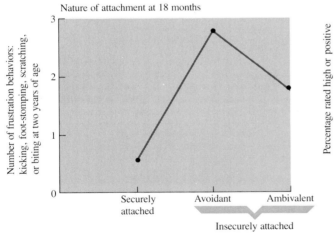

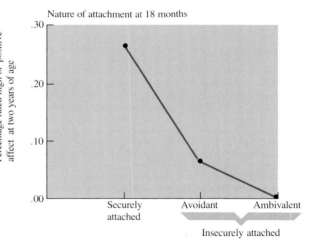

The effects of type of attachment on frustration behavior and positive affect.

From Matas, L., R. Arend, and A. Sroufe, "Continuity in adaptation in the second year: The relationships between quality of attachment and later competence," in *Child Development*, 49, pp. 547–556. Copyright © 1978 by The Society for Research in Child Development, Inc. Reprinted by permission.

Prediction of the nature of peer interaction is enhanced when we know the relationship history of both peers with their parents.

Thus as we construct relationships with others, how such relationships are pieced together depends on the relationship history of both members of the dyad. Here we have seen how the nature of peer interaction in children is influenced by the attachment relationship each peer member has experienced with his or her parents.

Issues in the Measurement of Attachment

Many different techniques have been used to measure attachment and related phenomena. These techniques range from asking mothers in an interview or questionnaire whether their infants do or do not exhibit particular behaviors (e.g., Ainsworth, 1967; Schaffer &

Emerson, 1964) to observing videotapes of infants interacting with an adult in a laboratory setting (e.g., Waters, Wippman & Sroufe, 1979). Generally, it is better to deal with firsthand observations of infants interacting with their caregivers, since interview data alone may be unreliable. The use of videotape in the past fifteen years has significantly improved observational techniques, since it allows for repeated scoring and checking of the adequacy of the behavioral categories selected for study and it also enables reexamination of the relatively permanent records in light of new developments in the field.

attachme[t]

Much of the early research on attachment relied on impressions of caregivers rather than on direct observation of caregivers interacting with their charges. However, interview data may be notably flawed and unreliably related to what actually takes place. To the extent that conclusions are based on interview data, they are highly suspect. But in the past decade much research has focused on observing infants with their care givers, and great strides have been made in improving observational techniques. Are the newer data trustworthy? They certainly are much better than the older work, but critics now worry about the lack of careful experimental control and design exhibited in the observational studies. For example, the Ainsworth Strange Situation Test, which has become a well-accepted procedure, requires that the child move through a series of introductions, separations, and reunions with mother and strangers in a prescribed order (see table 11.2 for a glimpse of a series of episodes in the Ainsworth situation). It sets up a highly complex series of social changes with somewhat arbitrary timing sequence regulations. How do we know if a child's responses in a particular episode reflect the isolated events of that episode or an arbitrary combination of factors in that and preceding episodes? In most studies using the Ainsworth procedure, we cannot answer this question satisfactorily. The point, then, is to not unduly criticize this one procedure but to indicate the general problem. When we observe infants in their natural environment and structure socially meaningful events, we often lose some degree of precise control over the situation. It is a common problem for most researchers working with attachment.

If the findings of contemporary research on attachment are accepted, some extreme critics (e.g., Maccoby & Masters, 1970; Masters & Wellman, 1974) have wondered whether the phenomenon of attachment even exists at all. That is, they wonder whether the evidence really supports the existence of a clear, underlying system that develops between an infant and its caregiver, as the ethological theories would have us believe. Critics point to the many ways that the intensity of such behaviors as crying and physical approach can be manipulated as the infant interacts with its caregiver. Situational variables, such as the child's preoccupation with another activity, playing in a familiar room, the presence of other social figures, and the physical similarity between stranger and mother, can all ameliorate distress and intense approach-and-contact behaviors. If "attachment" can disappear by manipulating such factors, how strong and real can this phenomenon be?

TABLE 11.2
Ainsworth's Strange Situation Test

The Ainsworth Strange Situation Test (Ainsworth & Bell, 1970) has been used in many studies of mother–infant attachment. The following episodes reveal how the Strange Situation Test is used to evaluate attachment.

Episode	Situation
"Episode 1" (M, B, O)	Mother (M), accompanied by an observer (O), carried the baby (B) into the room and then O left.
"Episode 2" (M, B)	M put B down in the specified place, then sat quietly in her chair, participating only if B sought her attention. Duration three minutes.
"Episode 3" (S, M, B)	A stranger (S) entered, sat quietly for one minute, conversed with M for one minute, and then gradually approached B, showing him a toy. At the end of the third minute, M quietly left the room.
"Episode 4" (S, B)	If B was happily engaged in play, S was nonparticipant. If he was inactive, she tried to interest him in the toys. If he was distressed, she tried to distract or comfort him. If he could not be comforted, the episode was curtailed; otherwise it lasted three minutes.
"Episode 5" (M, B)	M entered, paused in the doorway to give B an opportunity to respond spontaneously to her. S then left unobtrusively. What M did next was not specified—except that she was told that after B was again settled in play with the toys she was to leave again, after pausing to say "bye-bye." (Duration of episode undetermined.)
"Episode 6" (B alone)	The baby was left alone for three minutes, unless he was so distressed that the episode had to be curtailed.
"Episode 7" (S, B)	S entered and behaved as in episode four for three minutes, unless distress prompted curtailment.
"Episode 8" (M, B)	M returned, S left, and after the reunion had been observed, the situation was terminated.

From Mary Ainsworth and S. M. Bell, "Attachment Explorations, and Separation," *Child Development*, (1970): 49–67. © The Society for Research in Child Development, Inc. Reprinted by permission.

The critical problems in measuring attachment will never go away, nor will this very real phenomenon simply disappear because it is difficult to measure. There will have to be compromises in the views of attachment as a system until research can find reliable ways of documenting and measuring the phenomenon.

CONCEPT TABLE 11.1 Family Processes and Attachment		
Concept	**Processes/Related Ideas**	**Characteristics/Description**
Family processes	Reciprocal socialization and mutual regulation	Children socialize parents just as parents socialize children; parent–child relationships are mutually regulated by the parent and the child. In infancy, however, much of the relationship is driven by the parent; as the child develops self-regulation, the relationship is initiated on a more equal basis.
	The family as a system	The family is made up of a system of interacting individuals; some subsystems are dyadic, others are polyadic.
	The construction of relationships	Relationships are constructed through the child's interactions with parents. Such relationships reflect continuity and coherence and are carried forward to influence new relationships.
	The maturation of children and the maturation of parents	The nature of parent–child relationships is mediated by the maturation of both children and parents. A competent parent adapts to the maturational changes in the child.
	Sociocultural, historical contexts	The family is embedded in sociocultural, historical contexts that influence the nature of the child's and parents' development.
Attachment	Basic nature of attachment	In general attachment is a relationship between two people in which each person feels strongly about the other and does a number of things to ensure the continuation of the relationship. In infancy, attachment refers to a bond between the caregiver and the infant.
	Theories of attachment	Four main theories of attachment have been proposed: psychoanalytic, social learning, cognitive developmental, and ethological. Each has contributed in important ways to our understanding of attachment, although the ethological theory of Bowlby currently has been the most productive in promoting research on attachment. Research by Harlow and Zimmerman revealed the importance of contact comfort in attachment and documented the belief that feeding is not the crucial variable in attachment.
	Development of attachment	At about six to nine months of age infants focus their attachment on the primary caregiver.
	Individual differences	Ainsworth believes infants can be classified as insecurely or securely attached. Securely attached infants use the primary caregiver as a base from which to explore the environment.
	Situational variables	Situational variables are the environmental settings or circumstances that are capable of modifying the attachment bond. For example, by varying the social behavior of a stranger it was shown how the behavior of the infant changed.
	Construction of relationships	The attachment relationship is carried forward over time to influence the development of new relationships, such as peer relationships. By knowing the relationship history of both members of a peer interaction, we can more accurately predict the interaction.

To better appreciate the attachment researchers' difficulties, it may be useful to imagine the behaviors of audiences at two quite different musical events, a classical concert and a rock concert. Each occasion has its "scripted" events—entering the theater, being seated, greeting the performers, applauding when particular musical pieces are completed, and leaving when the performance is ended. But at a classical concert, each event is likely to be identified easily, clearly demarcated from the others, and fairly consistent from one performance to the next. At a rock concert, however, the less formal atmosphere and noise level, among other things, may often obscure the underlying scripted events. Infant attachment behavior is more like the events at a rock concert than those at a classical performance: there are certain scripted events, but the infant's changeable, fluid behavior creates considerable distraction for the observer.

A summary of the main ideas related to family processes and attachment appears in Concept Table 11.1. We have seen that attachment is an important aspect of early social development. In addition to attachment it also is wise to consider the type of parenting styles the child experiences as parents and children interact with each other. We consider these parenting styles next.

Parenting Styles

Parents want their children to grow into socially mature individuals, and they often feel a great deal of frustration in their role as parents. Child psychologists have long searched for ingredients of parenting that will promote competent social development in their children. For example, in the 1930s the behaviorist John Watson argued that parents were too affectionate with their children. Early research in child development focused on a distinction between physical and psychological discipline or between controlling and permissive parenting. More recently, greater precision in unraveling the dimensions of competent parenting has been accomplished.

Diana Baumrind's (1971) research has revealed that parents should be neither punitive toward their children nor aloof from them but rather should develop and enforce rules and regulations for their children. She emphasizes three types of parenting that are associated with different aspects of the child's social behavior: authoritarian, authoritative, and laissez-faire (permissive). More recently, developmental psychologists have argued that permissive parenting comes in two different forms. Thus in our overview of parenting styles we will focus on authoritarian, authoritative, and two forms of permissive parenting.

Authoritarian Parenting

Authoritarian parents are restrictive, have a punitive orientation, exhort the child to follow their directions, respect work and effort, place limits and controls on the child, with little verbal give-and-take between the child and the parent. **Authoritarian parenting** is linked with the following social behaviors of the child: an anxiety about social comparison, failure to initiate activity, and ineffective social interaction.

Authoritative Parenting

Authoritative parenting encourages the child to be independent but still places limits, demands, and controls on his or her actions. There is extensive verbal give-and-take, and parents demonstrate a high degree of warmth and nurturance toward the child. Authoritative parenting is associated with social competency on the part of the child, particularly self-reliance and social responsibility.

	Accepting Responsive Child-centered	Rejecting Unresponsive Parent-centered
Demanding controlling	Authoritative-reciprocal High in bidirectional communication	Authoritarian Power assertive
Undemanding low in control attempts	Indulgent	Neglecting, ignoring, indifferent, uninvolved

FIGURE 11.5
A two-dimensional classification of parenting patterns (Maccoby and Martin, 1983).

Eleanor Maccoby and John Martin (1983) revealed a scheme for categorizing parenting styles that involves various combinations of a demanding–undemanding dimension and an accepting–rejecting dimension. As shown in figure 11.5, an authoritarian parent (also called power assertive in the sense that the parent exercises considerable power over the child and/or the child's resources) is demanding and controlling as well as rejecting, unresponsive, and parent-centered. An authoritative parent is also demanding and controlling but is accepting, responsive, and child-centered. This parenting style is called authoritative-reciprocal by Maccoby and Martin.

Two Forms of Permissive Parenting

Notice in the fourfold scheme of parenting described by Maccoby and Martin that indulgent parents are undemanding but accepting and responsive, while neglecting parents are also undemanding but rejecting as well. The **permissive-indulgent pattern** on the whole seems to have more negative than positive effects on children. Consider the parents who are highly involved in their children's lives but allow them a great deal of freedom and do not control their negative behaviors. These children often grow up learning that they can get by with just about anything and often show a disregard for rules and regulations. Consider also the **permissive-indifferent parent,** who is very uninvolved in his or her children's lives. This type of parenting has consistently been linked to a lack of self-control on the part of the children. In sum, a lack of self-control seems to be one of the prominent results of children who experience permissive-indulgent or permissive-indifferent parenting.

Sibling Relationships

Sandra describes to her mother what happened in a conflict with her sister:

> We had just come home from the ball game. I sat down on the sofa next to the light so I could read. Sally [the sister] said, "Get up. I was sitting there first. I just got up for a second to get a drink." I told her that I was not going to get up, and that I didn't see her name on the chair. I got mad at her and started pushing her—her drink spilled all over her. Then she got really mad and started shoving me up against the wall and hitting me. I managed to grab her hair.

At this point Sally comes into the room and begins to tell her side of the story. Sandra interrupts, "Mother, you always take her side."

Competition among **siblings**—that is, brothers and/or sisters—along with concern about being treated fairly and equally by parents, are among the most pervasive characteristics of sibling relationships (Santrock, Smith & Bourbeau, 1976).

More than 80 percent of American children have one or more siblings. Because there are so many possible sibling combinations in a family, it is difficult to generalize about sibling influence and conflict. Among a variety of important factors to be considered in studying sibling relationships are birth order, sex of siblings, developmental status, and how siblings may function as models and teachers. We look at how these characteristics of sibling relationships are related to children's development, but first we consider how sibling relationships are possibly different from parent–child relationships, as well the parent's role in sibling relationships.

Sibling and Parent–Child Relationships

Is sibling interaction more influential than parent–child interaction? There is some evidence that it is. Linda Baskett (1974; Baskett & Johnson, 1982) observed the members of forty-seven families, each of which had two or three children. The siblings ranged from five to ten years of age. Observations were made for forty-five minutes on five different occasions. The children's observed behaviors included teasing, whining, yelling, commanding, talking, touching, nonverbal interacting, laughing, and complying. The interaction of the children with their parents was far more positive than their

Competitiveness among siblings is a frequent aspect of sibling life.

interaction with each other. Children and their parents had more varied and positive interchanges—they talked, laughed, and comforted one another more than siblings did. Children also tended to follow the dictates of their parents more than those of their siblings, and they behaved more negatively and punitively during interaction with their siblings than with their parents.

In some instances siblings are a stronger socializing influence on the child than parents are. Victor Cicirelli (1977) believes, in particular, that older siblings teach their younger siblings. Someone close in age to the child may understand his or her problems more readily and be able to communicate more effectively with the child than his or her parents can. In areas such as dealing with peers, coping with difficult teachers, and discussing taboo subjects, siblings often fare better than parents in the socialization process. Older siblings also may serve effectively in teaching younger siblings about identity problems, sexual behavior, and physical appearance—areas in which the parents may be unwilling or incapable of helping an adolescent.

An area of research attention in recent years involves the interaction of mothers with young siblings. Carol Kendrick and Judith Dunn (1980; Dunn & Kendrick, 1982) observed that older toddlers and preschool children were given less attention by their mothers after a younger sibling was born. They believe that the older sibling responds to such decreased attention by placing increased demands on the mother or by engaging in behavior that will attract the mother's attention. Toward the end of the first year of the younger sibling's life, the older sibling may sometimes begin to act aggressively toward the younger sibling, even hitting him or her on occasion. Arguments typically are triggered by the older sibling and are likely to increase as the younger sibling ages and is more likely to fend for himself or herself (Pepler, Ambramovitch & Corter, 1981).

In infancy and the toddler years there is evidence that more sibling rivalry appears between opposite-sex siblings than same-sex siblings (Dunn & Kendrick, 1981). It is argued that such differences are a consequence of the mother's behavior. Mothers were observed to spend considerably more time playing with the younger child when his or her sex was opposite that of the older sibling. However, one research investigation with siblings in the elementary school years revealed greater sibling rivalry between same-sex than opposite-sex siblings (Minnett, Vandell & Santrock, 1983). In this study more coercive interaction also appeared between eight- and twelve-year-old female siblings than between four- and eight-year-old female siblings, suggesting the possibility that same-sex sibling rivalry increases during the elementary school years.

Many parents of siblings who took part in this study (Minnett, Vandell & Santrock, 1983) expressed concern about their children's constant bickering and fighting, hoping that participation in the study would shed some light on sibling rivalry. Indeed, the process of social comparison is intensified in any sibling relationship. The child has a built-in need to know where he stands vis-à-vis his brother or sister: is he as strong, is he as smart, is he as worthwhile a person? All children are concerned about where they stand in these matters, but a sibling provides a more concrete reminder to the child to question his or her status in the family. Competitive sibling interaction, then, is a fact of sibling life, but so, too, are positive and neutral interactions. However, parents may overlook many of the positive and neutral sibling exchanges, responding instead to negative behaviors that require parental intervention.

Birth Order

Think about your birth order. Are you the eldest? the youngest? the middle child? Do you think being born in a particular sibling order has influenced your development? Birth order has been studied extensively over many years. To summarize some of the main conclusions about this large literature, it seems that firstborn children are more achievement oriented (Glass, Neulinger & Brim, 1974; Schachter, 1963) and more socially responsible than children born later. (Sutton-Smith & Rosenberg, 1970). It also seems that firstborns are more affiliative and sociable than children born later (Schachter, 1963). Nevertheless, there are some mixed findings in the sociability–affiliation domain since later-born children often have better peer relationships and in the case of boys may have fewer behavior problems (Lahey, Hammer, Crumine & Forehand, 1980; Miller & Maruyama, 1976). It is important to point out that birth order findings often account for a small percentage of variance when we are trying to predict the social competence of the child. Birth order, then, is best viewed as one of many variables that influence the child's development. It clearly is erroneous to conclude that because you are a firstborn you will be more achievement oriented than your friend who is a later-born child. Also remember that when differences between firstborn and later-born children are reported, they represent average differences. There clearly are many later-born children who are highly achievement oriented because their birth order did not produce a rigid social script that their parents followed.

Nevertheless, many mothers do seem to give different amounts of attention to firstborn siblings compared to later-born siblings, a finding that is often called on to explain firstborn findings. For example, in observations of mother–sibling interaction, mothers consistently gave more attention to their firstborn children than to children born later (Cushna, 1966; Gewirtz &

Gewirtz, 1965; Rothbart, 1967). This is perhaps explained by the fact that many mothers anxiously await the birth of their first child and that both parents often have high expectations for the child. By the time the second child is born, much of the novelty and intrigue of rearing a child probably has worn off.

Siblings as Models and Teachers

Older siblings are often effective models and teachers for their younger siblings. Helen Samuels (1977) observed the social interaction of infants (mean age, nineteen months) with their older preschool siblings (mean age, four and one-half years) in a twenty-minute play situation. She predicted that infants would find the older siblings attractive and treat them as models. A comparison of the siblings' behavior supported her prediction. The infant tended to look at, imitate, and follow the older sibling about, whereas the older sibling tended to show comparatively little interest of this sort in the infant.

In one investigation of siblings as teachers (Brody, Stoneman & MacKinnon, 1982), researchers found that older siblings were much more likely to assume a teaching role than were younger siblings. However, when these older siblings were studied in terms of their relationships with equal-status peers, the older siblings were much less likely to assume a stance of dominance toward the peers as they engaged in less teaching behavior. Other research on siblings as teachers (Cicirelli, 1972) has found that some siblings are better teachers than others. In particular, older sisters seem to be more competent than older brothers at teaching younger siblings. In the Cicirelli study the older sisters were more likely to demonstrate, explain, give feedback, and provide clues and hints when teaching a younger sibling how to solve a problem.

Dyadic Sibling Interaction and Development

When we study sibling interaction, it is important to consider the behavior of both members of the sibling dyad and their development. Judith Dunn and Carol Kendrick (1982, 1985) have followed this strategy by conducting highly detailed assessments of both siblings as they interact in naturalistic settings such as at home and at play. Their recent observations, in particular, reveal how the developmental status of a sibling is related to how siblings interact. Following young pairs of siblings over time suggested that at some point between the ages of one and two years younger siblings

began to initiate more sibling conflict than in their first year. During the second year of life they were physically more aggressive toward their older sibling and they showed anger in different ways, such as biting themselves and throwing things, actions that were not observed in the first year. The behavior of the older siblings changed as they developed as well. As they moved through the preschool years (being about two years older than their younger siblings), the older siblings expressed more concern about social rules and rationales, increased the number of their prohibitions and moral references toward the younger sibling, and voiced more interest in their own needs and feelings. This study is particularly important in signaling the manner in which detailed assessments of both members in close relationships over time provide insight into individual sources of change in the relationship.

The Changing Family in a Changing Society

The child's interaction with mother, father, and siblings provides the beginnings of the lifelong process of socialization. Thus far much of our discussion has focused on the mother's role in socialization, particularly in terms of attachment. Fathers, siblings, other relatives, peers, and teachers generally have not been given the credit that mothers have for influencing the child's social development. However, in recent years, there has been a trend toward studying the importance of multiple social agents and social settings on the child's development rather than relying solely on the mother's influence. In this section we look more closely at such family changes in a changing society, first focusing on the father's role in the child's development, second outlining in some detail the expanding interest in the effects of divorce on children, third providing recent information about children's development in stepparent families, and fourth describing the impact of working mothers on children.

The Father's Role in the Child's Development

Until the 1970s, the father was generally neglected in the study of parental influences on the child, although psychoanalytic theory places considerable importance on the father's role in socialization. Family sociologists have had the most to say about the importance of the father in the child's socialization; they believe the father has a low status in the American family, for the following reasons: (1) It is believed that the father's role

Many fathers can and do act sensitively with their infants.

has been much weaker than the mother's. (2) There is no biological basis for the father–child relationship, as there is for the mother–child relationship. (3) The father is poorly prepared for his parental role; as a boy he was not taught the duties and responsibilities of a father outside of his economic role as a provider.

Studies of fathers and their infants confirm that many fathers can and do act sensitively and responsively with their infants (Parke & Sawin, 1980) and that infants form attachments to both their mothers and fathers at roughly the same age (Lamb, 1977). In both humans and other primates, adult male behavior toward infants appears to be highly flexible and adaptive. Probably the strongest evidence of the plasticity of male caretaking abilities is derived from studies in which the males from primate species that are notoriously low in male interest in offspring are forced to live with infants whose female caretakers are absent; under these circumstances, the adult males show considerable competence in rearing the infants (Parke, 1981).

In virtually all of the investigations of fathers and infants (except for Field, 1978), mothers have been the primary caregivers, while fathers have had minimal

caregiving responsibilities. Field (1978) found that the primary caregiving fathers resembled the mothers in their tendencies to smile and vocalize imitatively but acted like secondary caregiving fathers in their tendency to play games and poke at the infants. In a more elaborate study of nontraditional families, Michael Lamb and his colleagues (Lamb, Frodi, Hwang, Frodi & Steinberg, 1983) interviewed fifty-one couples in Sweden during the period of pregnancy and later observed them interacting with their three-month-olds. Since 1974, Swedish parents have been given nine months (recently increased to twelve) of paid parental leave after delivery, and the government has gone to great lengths to encourage parents to take advantage of this arrangement. Half of the parents chose to follow the shared parenting arrangement (nontraditional parents), while the other half followed the traditional arrangement of the father working and the mother staying home and taking care of her infant. One of the most intriguing results in Lamb's Swedish study is the manner in which the parents differentiated between sons and daughters. Like traditional mothers and fathers studied in the United States (Hoffman, 1977; Lamb, 1977a, 1977b; Parke & Sawin, 1980), the traditional Swedish parents interacted preferentially with sons. By contrast, the nontraditional Swedish parents interacted preferentially with their daughters. Lamb suggests that possibly because of their concern that their daughters are traditionally accorded less attention than sons, the nontraditional parents not only eliminated but reversed this trend, with both mothers and fathers responsible for the change. Nonetheless, whether the parent was the mother or the father differentiated the behavior more noticeably than whether the family was traditional or nontraditional. For example, fathers were much less socially active with their infants than mothers were, regardless of family type.

While there has been a healthy increase in the participation of some fathers in the parenting process, for the most part the large majority of fathers still must be viewed as minimally involved in the child-rearing process. Time use studies of families confirm that most fathers spend very little time interacting with their children (Pleck, 1979).

Concept Table 11.2 summarizes our discussion of parenting styles, sibling relationships, and the father's role in the child's development. Next we turn our attention to a related aspect of the father's role: father absence and divorce.

CONCEPT TABLE 11.2
Parenting Styles, Sibling Relationships, and the Father's Role in the Child's Development

Concept	Processes/Related Ideas	Characteristics/Description
Parenting styles	Authoritarian	Authoritarian parents are restrictive, have a punitive orientation, exhort the child to follow their directions, respect work, place limits on the child, and are involved in little verbal give-and-take with child. Anxiety about social comparison, failure to initiate activity, and ineffective social interaction on the part of the child are often linked with authoritarian parenting.
	Authoritative	Authoritative parents encourage the child to be independent but still impose limits. There is extensive verbal give-and-take, and parents show a high degree of warmth. Social competency on the part of the child, particularly self-reliance and responsibility, is often associated with authoritative parenting.
	Permissive	The permissive-indulgent parent is undemanding but accepting and responsive. The permissive-indifferent parent is virtually uninvolved in the child's life. A lack of self-control on the part of the child is often linked with permissive parenting.
Sibling relationships	Sibling and parent–child relationships	Interaction of parents and children is often more positive and varied than interaction of siblings. Siblings may be better than parents in helping with peer relations and discussing taboo subjects. Mothers give more attention to firstborns.
	Birth order	Birth order has been studied extensively. As a rule, firstborns are more achievement oriented, socially responsible, and affiliative than later-born children, although many researchers believe that birth order accounts for only a small portion of the variance when the child's social competence is at issue.
	Siblings as models and teachers	Older siblings are often models and teachers for their younger siblings.
	Dyadic sibling interaction and development	Dunn and Kendrick argue that it is important to study the dyadic nature of sibling interaction in natural contexts and to consider the changing developmental characteristics of siblings as they age.
The father's role in the child's development	Fathers and infants	Many fathers can and do act sensitively and responsibly with their infants.
	Father's involvement	For the most part, the majority of fathers are still minimally involved with their infants and children.

Father Absence and Divorce

The increase in the number of children growing up in single-parent families is staggering. One estimate indicates that about 25 percent of the children born between 1910 and 1960 lived in a single-parent family sometime during their development. However, 40 to 50 percent of individuals born during the 1970s will spend some part of their childhood in a single-parent home (Bane, 1978).

The absence of the father from the home is an enormously complex topic. The degree to which fathers are away from home may fluctuate, even over relatively short periods. Social cataclysms, such as war, and more subtle societal changes, such as the increased demands of business on the middle-class father's time, are two examples of factors in father absence. Now we turn our attention to the predominant reason why fathers are away from their biological family—divorce—looking closely at its impact on children. Family conflict, the child's relationship with both parents, the availability of support systems, the age of the child, and the sex of the child and the custodial parent are important aspects of divorce that influence the child's behavior.

Family Conflict

Many separations and divorces are highly emotional affairs that immerse the child in conflict. Conflict is a critical aspect of family functioning that appears even to outweigh the influence of family

"Are you going to believe me, your own flesh and blood, or some stranger you married?"
Reproduced by permission of Jerry Marcus.

structure on the child's development. Children in single-parent families function better than those in conflict-ridden nuclear families (Hetherington, Cox & Cox, 1978; Rutter, 1983). Although escape from conflict may be a positive benefit of divorce for children, unfortunately, in the year immediately following the divorce, conflict does not decline but rather increases (Hetherington, Cox & Cox, 1978). At this time, children—particularly boys—in divorced families show more adjustment problems than children in homes in which both parents are present.

Parenting and Relationships with Ex-Spouse The child's relationship with both parents after the divorce influences his or her ability to cope with stress (Hetherington, Cox & Cox, 1978). During the first year after the divorce, the quality of parenting that the child experiences is often very poor; parents seem to be preoccupied with their own needs and adjustment, experiencing anger, depression, confusion, and emotional instability that inhibit their ability to respond sensitively to the child's needs. During this period, parents tend to discipline the child inconsistently, to be less affectionate, and to be ineffective in controlling the child.

Support Systems The majority of information we have about divorced families emphasizes the absent father or the relationship between the custodial parent and the child. However, child psychologists have become increasingly interested in the role of support systems available to the child and the family. Support systems for divorced families seem more important for low-income than for middle-income families (Colletta, 1978). The extended family and community services may play a critical role in the functioning of low-income families. Competent support systems may be particularly important for divorced parents with infant and preschool children because the majority of these parents must work full-time to make ends meet.

Age of the Child Another factor involving children of divorce focuses on the age of the child at the time of the divorce. Preschool children are not as accurate as elementary school children and adolescents in evaluating the cause of divorce, their own role in the divorce, and possible outcomes. Consequently, young children may blame themselves more for the divorce and distort the feelings and behavior of their parents, including hopes for their reconciliation (Wallerstein &

Kelly, 1980). Even adolescents experience a great deal of conflict and pain over their parents' divorce; but after the immediate impact of the divorce, they seem to be better than younger children at assigning responsibility for the divorce, resolving loyalty conflicts, and understanding the divorce process (Santrock & Madison, 1985; Wallerstein & Kelly, 1980). Young adults who experienced the divorce of parents during adolescence still look back and wonder if their life would have been better growing up with both parents in the home (Wallerstein, 1982). Additional information about the effects of divorce on adolescents and young adults is presented in Perspective on Child Development 11.2.

We know very little about the effects of divorce on infants. The early onset of divorce does seem to have a more negative effect on development than later onset.

PERSPECTIVE ON CHILD DEVELOPMENT 11.2

THE EFFECTS OF DIVORCE ON THE HETEROSEXUAL BEHAVIOR OF FEMALE ADOLESCENTS AND YOUNG ADULTS

Mavis Hetherington (1972) has shown that the heterosexual behavior of adolescent girls from father-absent and father-present homes is different. She studied three groups of twenty-four girls from homes where both parents were present, parents were divorced, or the father had died. The adolescent girls with absent fathers acted in one of two extreme ways. They were either very withdrawn, passive, and subdued around boys, or they were overly active, aggressive, and flirtatious. The girls who were inhibited, rigid, and restrained around males were more likely to have come from widowed homes. Those who sought the attention of males, who showed early heterosexual behavior, and who seemed more open and uninhibited were more likely to have come from homes in which the parents were divorced. In addition, early separation from fathers usually was associated with more profound effects, and the mothers' attitudes toward themselves and marriage differed according to whether they were widows or divorcées. Divorced women were more anxious, unhappy, and hostile toward males and more negative about marriage than were widows. Perhaps not surprisingly, daughters of divorcées had more negative attitudes about men than did daughters of widows.

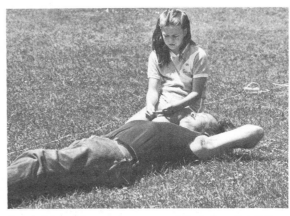

Even adolescents experience a great deal of conflict and stress over their parents' divorce.

Several examples of the actual behavior of the girls should provide a clearer picture of the study. One technique used to investigate the girls' behavior was to interview them sometimes with a male interviewer and sometimes with a female interviewer. Four chairs were placed in the room, including one for the interviewer. Daughters of widows most frequently chose the chair farthest from the male interviewer, while daughters of

During infancy, divorce may disrupt the attachment bond and many mothers have to go to work in order to provide support for the family. Strapped financially, many divorced mothers may not be able to afford quality day care. Thus many infants of divorced mothers are not being cared for by the mothers themselves during most of the day but are probably in day-care centers of questionable quality (Santrock & Sitterle, 1985).

The Sex of the Child and the Sex of the Custodial Parent One research study has directly compared children living in father-custody and mother-custody families (Santrock & Warshak, 1979, 1986). Children were videotaped during social interaction with their same-sex parent as the parent and child discussed a weekend plan and problems surfaced. The videotapes were rated by two people to ensure a high degree of

divorcées generally selected the chair closest to him. There were no differences when the interviewer was a female.

The interviewer also observed the girls at a dance and during activities at a recreational center. At the dance the daughters of widows often refused to dance when asked. One widow's daughter even spent the entire evening in the rest room. The daughters of the divorcées were more likely to accept the boys' invitations to dance. At the recreation center the daughters of divorcées were more frequently observed where boys were playing, while the daughters of the widows more often engaged in traditional "female" activities, like sewing and cooking (see table at right).

Hetherington (1977) continued to study these girls, following them into young adulthood to determine their sexual behavior, marital choices, and marital behavior. The daughters of divorcées tended to marry younger (eight of the daughters of widowed mothers were still not married at the time of the report) and tended to select marital partners who more frequently have drug problems and inconsistent work histories. In contrast, daughters of widows tended to marry men with a more puritanical makeup. In addition, both the daughters of the widows and the daughters of the divorcées reported more sexual adjustment problems than the daughters from intact homes. For example, the daughters from homes where the father was absent generally experienced fewer orgasms than daughters from in-

Group Means for Observational Variables in the Recreational Center

Observational variable	Group		
	Father absent		Father present
	Divorce	Death	
S-initiated physical contact and nearness with male peers	3.08	1.71	1.79
Male areas	7.75	2.25	4.71
Female areas	11.67	17.42	14.42

From Heatherington, E. M., "Effects of father absence on personality development in adolescent daughters," in *Developmental Psychology,* 7, pp. 313–326. Copyright 1972 by the American Psychological Association. Reprinted by permission of the publisher and author.

tact homes. The daughters from intact homes also showed more variation in their sexual role behavior and marital adjustment. They seemed to be more relaxed and dealt more competently with their roles as wives, suggesting that they had worked through their relationships with their fathers and were more psychologically free to deal successfully in their relationships with other males. On the other hand, the daughters of the divorcées and widows appeared to be marrying images of their fathers.

reliability. On a number of ratings of observed be-havior, children living with a same-sex parent were characterized by greater social competence than those living with an opposite-sex parent. For example, as shown in figure 11.6, father-custody boys and mother-custody girls were rated the highest in social maturity, and father-custody girls were rated the lowest. Possible explanations for this focus on the importance of the child's identification with the same-sex parent, the coercive interaction that may characterize mother–son relationships because boys are more aggressive than girls, and the possibility that the child in an opposite-sex custodial situation may be pushed into adult roles too soon by substituting for the absent spouse.

We have seen how extensive divorce has become in our society and observed its effects on children. Di-vorced parents often do not stay divorced very long, however. Next we look at children's lives in stepparent families.

Stepparent Families

The number of remarriages in which children are in-volved has been steadily growing. Projections into the 1990s estimate that approximately 25 to 30 percent of all children will be part of a stepfamily before their eighteenth birthday (Glick, 1980). Remarried families are usually referred to as stepfamilies, blended fami-lies, or reconstituted families.

When a remarriage occurs, adjustment to the new family may be overwhelming. The mother who remar-ries not only has to adjust to having another father for her children but also to being a wife again. There may not be much time for the husband–wife relationship to develop in stepfamilies. The children are a part of this new family from the beginning, a situation that leaves little time for the couple to be alone and to grow with each other (Visher & Visher, 1978).

We do not have nearly as much research informa-tion about stepparent families as divorced families, but recently attention has been given to the increasing number of children growing up in stepparent families. Researchers have found that children show more ad-justment problems when they are in a complex rather than a simple stepfamily (Hetherington, Cox & Cox, 1982). A **complex stepfamily** is one in which both the stepparent and the biological parent have brought chil-dren to the newly formed stepfamily; a **simple step-family** is one in which the stepparent has not brought children from a previous marriage to live in the newly

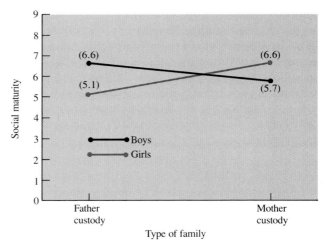

FIGURE 11.6
The child's rated social maturity observed during social interaction with the custodial parent in father-custody and mother-custody families.
Note: Data are based on sixty-four children six to eleven years old. The higher the score, the more favorable the rating.
From Santrock, John W., and Richard Warshak, "Father Custody and Social Development in Boys and Girls," *Journal of Social Issues,* 1979, 35, 112–125. Copyright © 1979 by the Society for the Psychological Study of Social Issues. Reprinted by permission.

formed stepfamily. In another investigation (Santrock, Warshak, Sitterle, Dozier & Stephens, 1985), children in stepfather, stepmother, and intact families were ob-served interacting with their parents, and both the par-ents and the children were interviewed about family relationships. When differences appeared they invari-ably suggested that the intact family atmosphere was more positive than in a stepparent family. Within the stepparent families, relationships between the child and the stepfather or stepmother were more strained than between the child and his or her biological parent. The relationship between the child and the stepfather was a very distant, somewhat unpleasant one, while the re-lationship betwen the child and the stepmother ap-peared to involve an extensive but sometimes abrasive set of interactions. In stepfather families the remarried mother was performing the bulk of the child-rearing duties, while in stepmother families the stepmother was receiving much more parenting support from the bio-logical father, who undoubtedly gained considerable parenting experience as a single father. The continuity of attachment to a biological, remarried parent was clearly evident in the child's life, as was the difficulty in establishing an attachment to the stepparent.

Working Mothers

Many divorced women with children are seeking employment to meet economic needs. Interestingly, indications are that divorced women with children are more productive and committed to their work than are married or single women (Feldman, 1973). Aletha Huston-Stein (Huston-Stein & Higgins-Trenk, 1978) believes that the divorced mother's orientation to the work ethic may be the product of a mid-life crisis not unlike that previously attributed only to men. Girls in the United States traditionally have been socialized under the aura of what Huston-Stein refers to as "the Cinderella myth." According to the myth, Prince Charming will sweep her away on his white stallion, and the two will have a few babies and live happily ever after. Of course, life is not this simple, and the reality of divorce has brought disillusionment.

While divorce is the most obvious example of the failure of the Cinderella myth, disillusionment also occurs for many married women as well. Mothers who choose to go to school or seek a job after marriage and childbearing probably do so in a more serious way and with more long-term commitment than women who believe their highest degree of satisfaction is to be found in the home.

Because household operations have become more efficient and family size has decreased in America, it is not certain that children with mothers who work outside the home actually receive less attention than children in the past whose mothers were not employed. Outside employment, at least for mothers with school-aged children and adolescents, may simply be filling time previously taken up by added household burdens and more children. Additionally, it cannot be assumed that if the mother did not go to work, the child or adolescent would benefit from the time freed up by streamlined household operations and smaller families.

According to Lois Hoffman (1979), who has studied working mothers for many years:

> Maternal employment is a part of modern life. It is not an aberrant aspect of it, but a response to other social changes and as such meets the needs that the previous family ideal of a full-time mother and homemaker cannot. Not only does it meet the parent's needs but in many ways it is a pattern better suited to socializing the child for the adult roles he or she will occupy. This is particularly true for the daughter, but for the son, too, the broader range of emotions and skills that each parent presents are more consistent with this adult role.

> Just as his father shares the breadwinning role and the child-rearing role with his mother, so the son, too, will be likely to share these roles. The rigid sex-role stereotyping perpetuated by the divisions of labor in the traditional family is not appropriate for the demands children of either sex will have made on them as adults. Furthermore, the needs of the growing child require the mother to loosen her hold on the child, and this task may be easier for the working woman whose job is an additional source of identity and self-esteem. (pp. 413–414)

While Hoffman and others conclude that the mother's working is not associated with negative child outcomes, a certain set of children from working-mother families bear further scrutiny; these are the so-called "latchkey" children. A very important point to consider when we study the effects of working mothers on children is what is happening to the children when they are away from their parents. During the course of the day, children of elementary school age and adolescents are at school. Infants are placed in some form of day care, and preschool-aged children usually attend nursery school or are in some form of day care. As we will see in chapter 12, the quality of day care many young children receive is far from optimal. Thus, negative effects on young children may not be due to the fact that their mothers are working per se but rather to the inferior quality of care the children are receiving when they are not with their parents.

Still, there is more to be said about latchkey children. These children typically do not see their parents from the time the children leave for school in the morning until about 6:00 or 7:00 P.M. They are called latchkey children because they are given the key to their home, take the key with them to school, and use it after school to let themselves into the home while their parents are still at work. Latchkey children are largely unsupervised for two to four hours a day during the school week. In addition, during the summer months, many children who only spent two to four hours each day unsupervised now spend whole days, five days a week unsupervised. We still know very little about the possible adverse effects of being a latchkey child, although interviews with latchkey children suggest some of the negative influences.

Thomas and Lynette Long (1983) conducted interviews with more than 1,500 latchkey children. They concluded that "a slight majority of these children have negative latchkey experiences." For example, some

The number of latchkey children has increased dramatically. A major concern is the unmonitored nature of these children's lives after school and during the summer months.

latchkey children may grow up too fast, hurried by the responsibility placed on them. David Elkind (1981) points out that latchkey children are stressed by taking on the psychological trappings of adulthood before they are prepared to deal with them. Still, some latchkey children may thrive on such responsibility, developing a mature sense of independence and accountability. One of the major problems for latchkey children is the lack of limits and structure in their lives during their latchkey hours. Without such limits and involvement of parents in their lives, it becomes easier for latchkey children to find their way into trouble—possibly abusing a sibling, stealing, or vandalizing. The Longs point out that 90 percent of the adjudicated juvenile delinquents in Montgomery County, Maryland, were latchkey children. All too often self-care is forced on children because of a divorce or death of a spouse. The custodial parent, now the main breadwinner, must work. Now the child, already having to deal with the stress of divorce or death, must also cope with further loss of time spent with the custodial parent.

CONCEPT TABLE 11.3
The Effects of Divorce on Children, Stepparent Families, and Working Mothers

Concept	Processes/Related Ideas	Characteristics/Description
Effects of divorce on children	Family conflict	Family conflict seems to affect children more adversely than divorce; nonetheless, in the first year after divorce, children (particularly boys) show adjustment difficulties.
	Parenting and relationships with ex-spouse	An on-going positive relationship with the ex-spouse on the part of both the mother and the child has a very positive effect on the child's adjustment to divorce. Parenting, particularly on the part of the mother, becomes less effective in the first year after the divorce, after which it improves.
	Support systems	Support systems are important for the adjustment of the single parent. Support systems are particularly salient in the lives of infants and young children from lower-class families.
	Age of child	Divorce is a highly stressful experience for a child of any age. The attachment bond may be disrupted in infancy and day care for the infant may be of poor quality. Young children blame themselves more for a divorce than older children. Even adolescents experience a great deal of stress when parents divorce.
	Sex of child and sex of custodial parent	In mother-custody families boys fare more poorly than girls; in father-custody families boys seem to show better adjustment than girls.
Stepparent families	Simple and complex stepfamilies	Children seem to have more difficulty adjusting in complex stepfamilies than in simple stepfamilies.
	Stepmother and stepfather families	Children show a stronger attachment to their biological custodial parent than to their stepparent. The child's relationship with the stepfather is often a distant, uninvolved one.
Working mothers	General effects	Most of the research on working mothers has not demonstrated negative effects on children although closer consideration of the nature of children's lives in day care and other contexts when their mothers are working is warranted.
	Latchkey children	One subset of working-mother children, latchkey children, may be particularly at risk for the development of self-control problems

It is very difficult to predict how a particular child will respond to the stress of divorce and simultaneously being pushed into self-care. The stress that promotes psychological disturbance in one child may strengthen the sense of competency in another child. Nevertheless, the huge number of latchkey children now present in the United States warrants further research attention.

Concept Table 11.3 summarizes our discussion of the effects of divorce on children, stepparent families, and working mothers. Thus far in our discussion of families and parent–child relationships we have focused primarily on the lives of infants and children. Next we continue the developmental story of families as we look more closely at the nature of parent–adolescent relationships and conflict.

Parent–Adolescent Relationships and Conflict

There appears to be some increase in conflict between parents and their children during early adolescence, although this conflict is often not as severe as many parents expect it to be and not as intense and pervasive as the media have sometimes pictured it. Many different reasons have been given for this. They include biological changes in levels of aggression, the appearance of adult sexuality, the push for independence, and the quest for identity. Other explanations focus on the difficulties parents may have as they enter mid-life and the mother's unwillingness to let her adolescent loose from the family circle. Still other explanations emphasize the disequilibrium that erupts in the family social

A moderate increase of conflict between adolescents and their parents during early adolescence may serve a positive developmental function.

system with the onset of adolescence, an upheaval that replaces the relatively smooth-functioning family system that existed during childhood. It also appears that the further along the adolescent moves toward adulthood, the less likely that conflict will characterize the parent–adolescent relationship (Montemayor, 1982).

Parent-adolescent conflict does not reach the proportions suggested by G. Stanley Hall's concept of sturm and drang. But as Raymond Montemayor suggests, it would be a mistake to go too far in the direction of thinking that parent–adolescent conflict is nonexistent. Indeed, the conflict that seems to characterize parent–adolescent relationships, particularly during early adolescence, is seen by many theorists as an important part of normal development. For example, in one recent investigation (Cooper, Grotevant,

Moore & Condon, 1982), adolescent identity exploration was positively related to frequency of expression of disagreement with parents during a family discussion task. Within some normal range, then, conflict with parents may be psychologically healthy for the adolescent's development. A virtually conflict-free relationship may suggest that an adolescent has a fear of separation, exploration, and independence.

Intergenerational Relationships

Intergenerational relationships can be comprised of many different age segments of child and adult development. First, we study social, historical forces in intergenerational relationships; second, we focus on some intriguing aspects of continuity in such relationships.

Social, Historical Forces

Among the social, historical forces that have influenced intergenerational relationships are population trends and period effects when social forces encourage intergenerational ties or when they are at odds between generations and discourage such ties.

Population Trends   During the last two centuries some rather dramatic changes have occurred in the population, changes that have important implications for intergenerational relationships. Prior to 1900, for instance, approximately 40 percent of American women moved through the so-called "ideal" life cycle of leaving home, marrying, bearing children, launching children, and living long enough to survive with their husbands through late adulthood. The remainder either never married, died before they reached a marriageable age, or were widowed when their children were young. In 1900 adults were also more likely to be of the same generation.

Today more people live to an older age and more parents are placing limits on the number of children they have. Today we are also more likely to see greater numbers of families of three or even four generations—parents, grandparents, and great-grandparents, for instance. And these generations are more likely to consist of one or more divorced or blended families. As the interest in the study of the entire life cycle has increased and a life-cycle perspective on development has gained popularity, the study of intergenerational relationships is becoming a logical place to study the transmission of socialization.

When Period Effects Encourage and Discourage Intergenerational Transmission

Social and historical forces—cohort or period effects—serve to moderate intergenerational relationships. Transmission is enhanced in areas where social forces encourage particular values or behavior. Thus, as the career identity of women continues to take hold, we would anticipate less intergenerational discontinuity in regard to sex-role attitudes in the future as increased numbers of mothers and their daughters subscribe to the importance of a woman's identity apart from a man's. Intergenerational transmission is probably reduced when social forces are at odds between generations. For example, in the late 1960s and 1970s, when the woman's role in society was emerging as a central social issue, it probably produced considerable splits among generations, with the late-adulthood generation (who grew up under a traditional sex-role orientation) being more at odds with younger generations, particularly the third generation of adolescents and young adults.

Continuity

Initially we chart some general conclusions about the existence of continuity in intergenerational relationships and then examine transmission across generations to infancy and adolescence.

The Degree of Intergenerational Continuity

As each new generation succeeds the preceding one, roles, positions, personality characteristics, attitudes, and values may be replicated or changed. As older family members die, their emotional, intellectual, personal, and genetic legacies are carried on by the next generation. Their children now become the first generation, and their grandchildren, the second generation. It appears that there is considerable contact among the generations (Leigh, 1982; Troll & Bengston, 1982). For example, Geoffrey Leigh (1982) interviewed 800 adults in 1964 and 500 adults in 1976, asking how often they saw, wrote to, or talked over the phone with parents and grown children. The link between frequency of contact with parents and children was charted according to stages of the family life cycle. There was a strong frequency of contact over the age groups, with almost all reporting contact with their parents at least once a month. A slight decline in weekly contacts with parents occurred during the early years of marriage, but overall the picture was one of maintenance of contact on a very regular basis. Other information also suggests that contact with family members continues in old age. In a national survey, 81 percent of adults over age sixty-five said they had seen one or more of their children in the last week and 73 percent said they had seen a grandchild.

As we continue to maintain contact with our parents and our children as we age, there is similarity in attitudes in some areas but discontinuity in others. For example, parent–child similarity is most noticeable in religious and political areas and least noticeable in sex roles, life-style, and work orientation. However, even when there are disagreements between generations on values, there seems to be a strong parent–child attachment, with parents and children often remaining close even in the face of little consensus on attitudes. Thus, parent–child attachments are exceptionally strong bonds throughout the life course.

Transmission across Generations to Infancy

We are beginning to accumulate evidence about the transmission of relationships across generations from middle-aged grandparents through their young adult children and then on to the offspring of the young adult parents (Hartup, 1985; Sroufe & Fleeson, 1985). For example, in one investigation (Frommer & O'Shea, 1973) mothers who had poor relationships with their own parents were more likely to have problems with their infant than mothers who reported good relationships with their own parents. In another study (Uddenberg, 1974) ninety-five mothers were interviewed four months after their babies were born and when the offspring reached four and one-half years of age. The maternal grandmothers were also interviewed with regard to parent–child relationships twenty years earlier. The nature of the new mother's relationship with her own mother was linked with psychiatric difficulties in the postpartum period, feelings of inadequacy as a parent, and ambivalent or negative feelings toward the infant. And such problems in relationships with her mother were associated with her own child's perception of her four years after delivery. In another investigation (Main, Kaplan & Cassidy, in press), an attachment interview was given to the mothers and fathers of infants whose own attachments had been classified according to Ainsworth's categories. The child's avoidance of the parent following separation in the Ainsworth Strange Situation was related to parental reports of rejection in their own childhood. Resistance of the infant toward the mother was associated with continuing anger and

Intergenerational relationships represent an increasing area of interest for developmental psychologists.

conflict in regard to the mother's own parents. And infants showing secure attachment had parents whose own relationships with their parents were described as secure. These results provide increasing evidence of the importance of studying relationships in an intergenerational manner.

Intergenerational Transmission to Adolescence In regard to intergenerational relationships, the age period that has received the most attention is middle adulthood, a time when adults often have adolescent offspring and parents who have entered, or are beginning to enter, late adulthood. In discussing the role of middle-aged parents, Erik Erikson (1968) believes it is important for parents at this point in the life cycle to assume responsibility for the new generation of adults that is about to emerge. Although Erikson does not argue that the transmission of values and attitudes to

the next generation has to occur through parent–child or parent–adolescent rearing, his major focus clearly is on the important role parents play in the generativity process.

At the same time that middle-aged parents may be working hard in trying to guide their adolescent offspring into mature youth or young adults capable of performing competently in a job and making autonomous decisions, they may also have to deal increasingly with the aging of their own parents. Adults at about the age of forty or fifty often reach a point at which they can no longer look upon their own parents as a secure base in times of emotional difficulties or financial problems. Instead, the parents themselves often need comfort, support, and affection from their middle-aged offspring (Lowy, 1981). Such simultaneous pressures from adolescents and aging parents probably contribute to stress during middle adulthood.

SUMMARY

I. Five important processes involved in family development are reciprocal socialization and mutual regulation, the family as a system, the construction of relationships, the maturation of children and parents, and sociocultural, historical contexts.

  A. Reciprocal socialization is the process whereby children socialize parents just as parents socialize children. Parent–child relationships are mutually regulated by the parent and the child, although in most of infancy the parent drives the relationship. As the child develops self-regulation, the relationship is initiated on a more equal basis.

  B. The family is made up of a system of interacting individuals; some of its subsystems are dyadic and others are polyadic. The mother (primary care giver)–child relationship is an important family subsystem.

  C. Relationships are constructed through the child's interaction with parents. Such relationships reflect continuity and coherence and are carried forward to influence new relationships.

  D. The nature of parent-child relationships is mediated by the maturation of both children and parents. A competent parent adapts to the maturational changes in the child.

  E. The family is embedded in sociocultural, historical contexts.

II. Information about attachment focuses on its basic nature, theories of attachment, the development of attachment, individual differences, situational variables, and the construction of relationships.

  A. Attachment refers to the relationship between two people in which one person feels strongly about the other and does things to ensure the continuation of the relationship. In infancy, attachment refers to the bond between the care giver and the infant.

  B. Four main theories of attachment exist: psychoanalytic, social learning, cognitive developmental, and ethological. Each has contributed to our understanding of attachment, although currently ethological theory has generated the most research interest, particularly the view of John Bowlby. Research by Harlow and Zimmerman suggests the importance of contact comfort in attachment and that feeding is not the crucial variable.

  C. When the infant is about six to nine months old, his or her attachment becomes focused on the primary caregiver.

  D. Ainsworth believes infants can be classified as insecurely or securely attached. Securely attached infants use the primary caregiver as a base from which to explore the environment.

  E. Situational variables refer to the environmental settings that are capable of modifying the attachment bond. For example, by varying the social behavior of a stranger, the infant's behavior changes.

  F. The attachment relationship is carried forward over time to influence new relationships, such as those with peers. By knowing the relationship history of both peers, the nature of a peer interaction can be predicted more accurately.

III. Parenting styles, sibling relationships, and the father's role are important aspects of family processes.

  A. Parenting styles include authoritarian, authoritative, permissive-indulgent, and permissive-indifferent. Authoritative parenting is most likely to be associated with socially competent behavior on the part of the child.

  B. Sibling relationships focus on the role of siblings compared to the role of parents in the child's development, birth order, siblings as models and teachers, and the nature of dyadic sibling relationships.

  C. Many fathers can and do act sensitively and responsibly with their infants, but for the most part fathers still are minimally involved with their infants and children.

IV. The effects of divorce and the mother's working have an impact on the child's development in a changing society.

  A. Information about the effects of divorce on children emphasizes family conflict, parenting and relationships with the ex-spouse, support systems, age of the child, and sex of the child and sex of the custodial parent.

  B. Research on stepfamilies has focused on simple and complex types and stepmother and stepfather families.

  C. In general, research on working mothers shows no negative effects on children, although a subset of children, called latchkey children, may be at risk for psychological problems.

V. Intense, prolonged conflict does not characterize the majority of parent–adolescent relationships. A moderate increase in conflict with parents does seem to characterize parent–adolescent relationships compared to parent–child relationships, and this moderate conflict probably serves the positive developmental function of promoting identity and independence.

VI. The study of intergenerational relationships focuses on social, historical forces and continuity.

   A. Population trends have increased the likelihood of intergenerational relationships over longer periods of time. Period effects can either enhance or discourage intergenerational transmission.

   B. There is generally a high degree of continuity between generations. The middle generation probably plays an important role in linking generations.

KEY TERMS

attachment 369
authoritarian parenting 381
authoritative parenting 381
complex stepfamily 390
contact comfort 370
executor responses 372
insecure attachment 374
intergenerational relationships 394

permissive-indifferent parent 381
permissive-indulgent pattern 381
secure attachment 374
siblings 382
signaling responses 372
simple stepfamily 390
social-mold theories 363

REVIEW QUESTIONS

1. Discuss the nature of reciprocal socialization and mutual regulation in families.
2. Why is it important to view the family as a system?
3. How do we construct relationships? Describe the importance of considering the maturation of both the child and the parents in understanding family relationships.
4. How do sociocultural, historical circumstances influence families?
5. Discuss the nature of attachment in infancy.
6. Provide an overview of parenting styles and their effectiveness in promoting social competence in children.
7. What is the nature of sibling relationships?
8. Discuss the father's role in children's development.
9. Describe the effects of divorce on children, the nature of stepparent families, and the impact of working mothers on children's development.
10. Outline the development of parent–adolescent conflict and its influence on adolescent development.
11. Discuss the development of intergenerational relationships.

SUGGESTED READINGS

Dunn, J., & Kendrick, C. (1982). *Siblings: Love, envy, and understanding.* Cambridge, MA: Harvard University Press.
Provides rich, detailed observations on the importance of development in understanding sibling relationships.

Maccoby, E. E., & Martin, J. A. (1983). Socialization in the context of the family: Parent-child interaction. In P. H. Mussen (Ed.), *Handbook of child psychology* (4th ed., Vol. 4). New York: John Wiley.
A very extensive, competent overview of what we know about children's socialization in families. Provides many new ideas about research on children and their families.

Sroufe, L. A., & Fleeson, J. (1985). Attachment and the construction of relationships. In W. W. Hartup and Z. Rubin (Eds.), *Relationships and development.* Hillsdale, NJ: Lawrence Erlbaum.
Presents the very important idea that to understand family development we need to study how people construct relationships. Provides details from research on child development, as well as clinical studies across generations.

Troll, L. E., & Bengston, V. L., (1982). Intergenerational relations throughout the life span. In B. B. Wolman (Ed.), *Handbook of developmental psychology.* Englewood Cliffs, NJ: Prentice-Hall.
A superb, well-written overview of the many complex aspects of intergenerational relations.

Wallerstein, J. S., & Kelly, J. B. (1980). *Surviving the breakup. How children and parents cope with divorce.* New York: Basic Books.
In addition to providing details of their extensive investigation of the effects of divorce on children, the authors present many suggestions for how parents should deal with children in a divorced family.

CHAPTER

12

PEERS, PLAY, SCHOOLS, AND THE MEDIA

PROLOGUE

YOU JERK

Y ou jerk, what are you trying to do to me," Jess yelled at his teacher. "I got no use for this school and people like you. Leave me alone and quit hassling me."

Jess is ten years old and has already had more than his share of confrontations with society. He has been arrested three times for stealing, been suspended from school twice, and has a great deal of difficulty getting along with people in social circumstances. He particularly has difficulty with authority figures. No longer able to cope with his outbursts in class, his teacher recommended that he be suspended from school once again. The principal was aware of a different kind of school she thought might help Jess.

Jess began attending the Manville School, a clinic in the Judge Baker Guidance Center in Boston for learning-disabled and emotionally disturbed children seven to fifteen years of age. Jess, like many other students at the Manville School, has shown considerable difficulty in interpersonal relationships. Since peer relationships become a crucial aspect of development during the elementary school years, Robert Selman (Selman, Newberger & Jacquette, 1977) has designed a peer therapy program at the Manville School to help students like Jess improve their peer relations in classroom settings, group activities, and sports. The staff at the Manville School has been trained to help peers provide support and encouragement to one another in such group settings, a process referred to as **peer sociotherapy.**

Structured programs at the Manville School are designed to help the children assist each other in such areas as cooperation, trust, leadership, and conformity. Four school activities were developed to improve the student's social reasoning skills in these areas.

First, there is a weekly peer problem-solving session in the classroom in which the peers work cooperatively to plan activities and relate problems. At the end of each week the peers evaluate their effectiveness in making improvements in areas like cooperation, conflict resolution, and so forth.

Second, the members of a class, numbering from six to eight students, plan a series of weekly field trips, for example, going to the movies or visiting historical sites. While the counselor provides some assistance, peer decision making dominates. When each activity is completed, the students discuss how things went and what might have been done to improve social relations with each other on the outings.

Third, Selman recognizes that there are times when the student has to get away from a setting where intense frustration occurs. When the student finds himself or herself in a highly frustrating situation (e.g., angry enough to strike out at a classmate), he or she is allowed to leave the room and go to a private "time-out" area of the school to regain composure. In time-out, the student also is given the opportunity to discuss the problems with a counselor who has been trained to help the child or adolescent improve social reasoning skills.

Fourth, during social studies and current events discussion sessions, the students evaluate a number of moral and societal issues that incorporate the thinking of theorists such as Lawrence Kohlberg.

PEERS AND FRIENDSHIPS

The story of peers and friendships includes information about the functions of the peer group, the development of peer relations, the impact of peer relations on social behavior, the coordinated worlds of peers and family, the importance of information processing and social knowledge in understanding peer relations, ways to improve children's social skills with peers, friendships, children's groups, and the role of peer relations in adolescent development.

Functions of the Peer Group

To learn more about the functions of the peer group, we study what the term *peers* means, the necessity of peers for competent social development, cross-cultural comparisons of peer relations, and the importance of peer relations in children's perspective taking.

The Meaning of the Term "Peers"

Children spend a great deal of time with their peers; many of their greatest frustrations and happiest moments come when they are with peers. The term **peers** usually refers to children who are about the same age, but children often interact with other children who are three or four years older or younger. Peers have also been described as children who interact at about the same behavioral level (Lewis & Rosenblum, 1977). Defining peers in terms of behavioral level places more emphasis on the maturity of the children than on their age. For example, consider the precociously developed thirteen-year-old female adolescent who feels very uncomfortable around underdeveloped girls her own age.

She may well find more satisfaction in spending time with seventeen- or eighteen-year-olds than with people her own age.

The influence of children who are the same age may be quite different from that of younger or older peers. For example, mixed-age groups often produce more dominant and altruistic behavior than do groups of children of the same age. Social contacts and aggression, however, are more characteristic of same-age peers. Willard Hartup (1976) has emphasized that same-age peer interaction serves a unique role in our culture:

> I am convinced that age grading would occur even if our schools were not age graded and children were left alone to determine the composition of their own societies. After all, one can only learn to be a good fighter among age-mates: the bigger guys will kill you, and the littler ones are no challenge.
>
> Perhaps one of the most important functions of the peer group is to provide a source of information and comparison about the world outside the family. From the peer group the child receives feedback about his or her abilities. The child evaluates what he or she does in terms of whether it is better than, as good as, or worse than what other children do. It is hard to do this at home because siblings are usually older or younger. (p. 10)

Peers and Competent Social Development

Studies about the necessity of peers for competent social development have been limited primarily to animals. For example, when peer monkeys who have been reared together are separated from one another, indications of depression and less advanced social development are observed (Suomi, Harlow & Domek, 1970). Attempts to use peer monkeys to counteract the effects of social isolation prove more beneficial when the deprived monkeys are placed with younger peers (Suomi & Harlow, 1972). Willard Hartup (Furman, Rahe & Hartup, 1979) is trying out the younger-peer therapeutic technique with human peer isolates in a nursery school. Initial reports indicate that the technique is as effective with humans as it has been with monkeys.

Regardless of the culture studied, there are often consistent differences between adult-child and peer interactions.

The human development literature contains a classic example of the importance of peers. Anna Freud (Freud & Dann, 1951) studied six children from different families who banded together after their parents were killed in World War II. Intensive peer attachment was observed; the children were a tightly knit group, dependent on one another and aloof with outsiders. Even though deprived of parental care, they became neither delinquent nor psychotic.

Cross-Cultural Comparisons of Peer Relations

Probably no other cross-cultural work with children is more widely cited than the work of Beatrice and John Whiting. In 1954 the Whitings and their colleagues began reporting their observations of children in six different cultures. The most recent publication of their work is the book *Children of Six Cultures: A Psychocultural Analysis.* For these observations the Whitings placed six teams of anthropologists in six different cultures, five of which were primarily farming communities: northern India; the Philippines; Okinawa, Japan; Oaxaca, Mexico; and western Kenya. The sixth setting was a small, nonfarming town in New England. The teams interviewed the mothers and conducted standardized observations of the children in the six cultures.

Among the most intriguing findings of the project were the consistent differences in adult–child and peer interactions across the cultures. Dependency, nurturance, and intimacy were rarely observed in peer relations but were frequently observed in adult–child

interaction. By contrast, aggressiveness, prosocial activity, and sociable behavior were the most frequently occurring behaviors in peer relations across the six cultures. Such findings support the belief that there may be universal differences between adult–child and peer interactions.

In other research the findings suggested that children in the United States seem to succumb to peer pressure more than children in many other countries (Bronfenbrenner, 1970). For example, Russian children, more than American children, resist peer pressure when peer norms conflict with adult standards (Devereaux, 1970). In the Russian culture, peer norms are much more likely to support adult norms than in the American culture. The reason for these findings becomes clearer when the Soviet socialization process is scrutinized. As soon as schooling begins in Russia, the peer group is assigned important duties in assisting the teacher. Conformity to group norms is stressed throughout education, and subordination of the individual to the group is omnipresent. Group competition between grades, schools, rooms, and rows within each room is emphasized. Although these practices are not foreign to schools in the United States, they are not as systematized as they are in the Soviet Union. In the United States the peer group may undermine the socialization practices of adults; in the Soviet Union, however, peer group norms even in adolescence support adult norms. Next, we see that other cross-cultural work has highlighted the importance of peer relations in the development of perspective-taking skills.

Peer Relations and Perspective Taking

A research investigation that took place in Norway and Hungary provides further support for the belief that peer relations serve important developmental functions. In this study (Hollis, 1975) the main interest focused on **perspective taking,** which can be defined as the ability to take someone else's point of view (perspective). The Norwegian and Hungarian children were seven to nine years old and lived in one of three settings in each country—an isolated, dispersed farm community, a village, or a town, which varied in terms of the relative physical isolation of the children from one another. The children were assessed on three measures of perspective taking: visual perspective taking, communication accuracy, and role taking. In the visual perspective-taking task, the children observed a three-dimensional display of buildings and were asked to tell

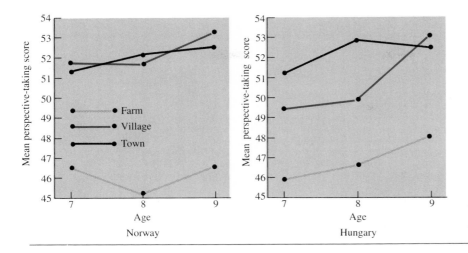

FIGURE 12.1
The perspective taking of rural farm, village, and town children in Norway and Hungary (Hollis, 1975).

what the view of the buildings would look like if they were seated at different locations around the table on which the buildings were placed. This is a widely used Piagetian task and provides an index of how egocentric a child is. The child who can decenter is able to provide a perspective of how the buildings look from other locations than where he or she is seated. Communication accuracy was assessed by telling each child a story and then having the child repeat the story to another person. Role taking was investigated by showing the child a seven-picture cartoon sequence that told an obvious story. Three pictures were then removed from the sequence and the child was told to tell the story to another person who had not seen all seven pictures. To analyze the results, the researchers combined the scores on these measures to obtain a total perspective-taking score. As shown in figure 12.1, in both Norway and Hungary, children from the isolated farm regions were much poorer at perspective taking than the children from the villages and towns.

The Development of Peer Relations

We generally do not think of infants and toddlers when considering peer relations, but now more than ever infants are being placed together in day-care centers as more mothers work outside the home. First, we study peer relations in infancy and then describe further development in early childhood and the elementary school years. Later in the chapter we will consider information about peer relations in adolescence.

Peer Relations in Infancy

Infants as young as six months of age do interact with each other when placed together (Vandell, Wilson & Buchanan, 1980). Six-month-old babies primarily interact by smiling, touching, and vocalizing; in the second year of life toys become a focus of peer interaction. In one investigation, observations of eight- to ten-month-old infants in a day-care center suggested that one infant seemed to be liked by her peers more than any others and that one boy was more likely to be avoided than the others (Lee, 1973). On close inspection some reasons for these individual differences appeared; the boy often initiated encounters with other infants by grabbing their toys, while the girl approached her peers in a positive way, by smiling, for example.

Toys seem to be very important in peer interaction during the second year of life (Mueller, 1979). Infants less than one year old seem not to use toys in peer interaction; at approximately twelve to fourteen months the presence of toys actually seems to decrease peer interaction; and at about fourteen months of age toddlers begin to use toys as a medium for play and peer involvement (Jacobson, 1981). It apparently takes time for the toddler to coordinate play that involves both an object (toy) and a person (peer).

When positive peer interaction begins to occur in the second year, it is likely to be accompanied by a display of affect, which is usually absent from peer exchanges in the first year (Mueller & Brenner, 1977). For example, when an eighteen-month-old touches another

What is the nature of peer interaction in infancy?

age-mate, he or she may smile. However, not only are positive interactions and affective displays more common in the second year but so are negative interchanges; that is, more fights over toys, hitting, biting, and hair pulling occur in the second year (Eckerman, Whatley & Kutz, 1975).

Recent research on early peer relationships has provided further support for the belief that rather than being merely a curious new phenomenon in human relationships, early peer relationships can be of enduring significance in the child's social and cognitive growth (Brownell & Brown, 1985; Hay, 1985; Mueller, 1985; Vandell, 1985). For example, in one investigation (Howes, 1985) early peer skills were related to sociometric status in the preschool years. Two three-year longitudinal studies were conducted. In both studies, positive affect during peer interaction in the toddler period predicted easy access to peer play groups and popularity with peers in the preschool period.

Peer Relations in Early Childhood and the Elementary School Years

The frequency of peer interaction, both positive and negative, picks up considerably during early childhood (Hartup, 1983). Although aggressive interaction and rough-and-tumble play increase, the *proportion* of aggressive exchanges to friendly interactions decreases,

especially among middle-class boys. Children tend to abandon this immature and inefficient social interaction with age and acquire more mature methods of relating to peers.

Socialization cannot be described solely in terms of the quality of social activity, however. Evidence suggests that social differentiation is also a major achievement of the maturing child. Children become more adept at using social skills, so that by the end of the preschool years, a rudimentary peer system has emerged.

Recall from our discussion earlier in this section how children from isolated farm regions in both Hungary and Norway were much poorer at perspective taking than children from villages and towns. As children enter elementary school they increase the amount of time they spend in peer interaction. At about this time children also increase their role-taking skills and improve their ability to take the perspective of a peer. During elementary school reciprocity is very important in many social interchanges—playing games, functioning in groups, and cultivating friendships. One of the increased skills that help elementary school children to develop their peer interaction is communication effectiveness. For example, in one investigation (Krauss & Glucksberg, 1969) the communication exchanges among peers at the kindergarten, first, third, and fifth

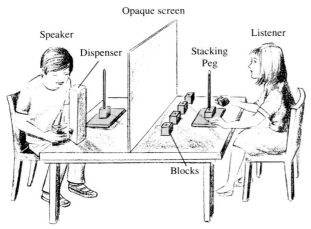

FIGURE 12.2
Experimental arrangement of speaker and listener to study the development of communication skills (Krauss and Glucksberg, 1969).

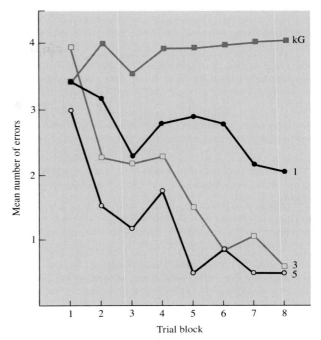

FIGURE 12.3
The development of communication skills for kindergarten, first, third, and fifth grade children: Number of errors in communicating information about a novel arrangement of blocks (Krauss and Glucksberg, 1969).

grade levels were evaluated. Children were asked to tell a peer about a new set of block designs. The peer sat behind a screen with similar blocks as the subject communicated to him or her. (See figure 12.2.) The kindergarten children made considerable mistakes in telling the peer how to duplicate the novel block stack. The older children were much more efficient in communicating to a peer how to construct the novel block stack, particularly the fifth graders, who were sensitive to the communication demands of the task and were far superior at perspective taking, figuring out how they had to talk for the peer to understand. (See figure 12.3.) We should also point out that during elementary school, children become more proficient at understanding complex messages, so the listening skills of the peer in the novel block-stacking experiment undoubtedly helped the communicating peer as well (Hartup, 1983).

Peer Relations and Social Behavior

Developmental psychologists have studied many different aspects of social behavior in peer relations. Here we focus on two of the most widely investigated areas of social behavior—popularity and conformity.

Popularity

Elementary and secondary school children often think, "What can I do to have all of the kids at school like me?" "How can I be popular with both girls and guys?" "What's wrong with me? There must be something wrong, or I'd be more popular." Sometimes children will go to great lengths to be popular; and in some cases parents will go to even greater lengths to try to insulate their offspring from rejection and to increase the likelihood that they will be popular.

What makes a child popular with peers? In one study children who gave the most reinforcements were found to gain popularity among their peers (e.g., Hartup, 1970). In coaching sessions designed to help children become better integrated in the peer group (Oden & Asher, 1975), students are encouraged to overcome their difficulty in interacting with their peers by listening carefully to their peers' conversation and by maintaining open lines of communication with their peers. And being oneself, being happy, showing enthusiasm and concern for others, and showing self-confidence but not conceit are among the characteristics that lead to popularity (Hartup, 1983). In many instances the opposites of these behaviors invite rejection from peers (Hollingshead, 1975).

Certain physical and cultural factors can also affect a child's popularity. Some research has shown that children who are physically attractive are more popular than those who are not; and contrary to what some believe, brighter children are more popular than less intelligent ones. Children growing up in middle-class surroundings tend to be more popular than those growing up in lower-class surroundings, presumably in part because they are more in control of establishing standards for popularity (e.g., Hollingshead, 1975). But remember that findings such as these reflect group averages; there are many physically attractive children who are unpopular and physically unattractive children who are very well liked. Furthermore, with the increased concern for equal treatment of minority groups, lower-class and ethnic group children can be expected to gain more influence in establishing the standards of popularity. Finally, popularity may fluctuate, and children sense the tenuous nature of popularity; even the child who is very popular with peers may have doubts about his or her ability to maintain that popularity.

Conformity

Do children conform more to the ideas and behaviors of their peers than to those advocated by parents? There are several ways to look at peer conformity. First, the influences that are exerted by parents and peers may be contradictory, and children may choose to conform to the perspectives of those they are with the most; or they may simply choose to rebel against parental authority. Second, children may become more responsible for themselves, seeing themselves as more independent of their parents and capable of making their own decisions. A third possibility is that a combination of both these perspectives may come into play.

In an effort to explore the developmental patterns of parental and peer conformity, Thomas Berndt (1979) studied 273 third through twelfth grade students. Hypothetical dilemmas were presented to the students, requiring them to make choices about conformity with friends on prosocial and antisocial behavior and conformity with parents on neutral and prosocial behaviors. For example, one prosocial item questioned whether students relied on their parents' advice in such situations as deciding about helping at the library or instructing another child to swim. An antisocial question asked a boy what he would do if one of his peers wanted him to help steal some candy. A neutral question asked a girl if she would follow peer suggestions to engage in an activity she wasn't interested in—for example, going to a movie she didn't want to see.

By the sixth grade, parent and peer influences are operating in different situations.

By the sixth grade, parent and peer influences were operating in different situations—parents had more impact in some situations, while peers had more clout in others. For example, it has been found that parents are more influential in a discussion of political parties but that peers seem to have more influence when sexual behavior and attitudes are at issue (Hyman, 1959; Vandiver, 1972).

By the ninth grade, parent and peer influences were in strong opposition to each other, probably because the increased conformity of adolescents to the social behavior of peers is much stronger at this grade level than at any other. Figure 12.4 displays the increased conformity to antisocial peer standards in the ninth grade. At this time adolescent adoption of antisocial standards endorsed by the peer group inevitably leads to conflict between adolescents and parents. Researchers have also found that the adolescent's attempt to gain independence meets with more parental opposition around the ninth grade than at any other time (Douvan & Adelson, 1966; Kandel & Lesser, 1969). As an indication of the importance of peers, consider the comments of one youth:

> I feel a lot of pressure from my friends to smoke and steal and things like that. My parents do not allow me to smoke, but my best friends are really pushing me to do it. They call me a pansy and a Momma's boy if I don't. I really don't like the idea of smoking, but my good friend Steve told me in front of some of our friends, "Kevin, you are an idiot and a chicken all wrapped up in one little body." I couldn't stand it any more, so I smoked with them. I was coughing and humped over, but I still said, "This is really fun—yeah, I like it." I felt like I was part of the group.

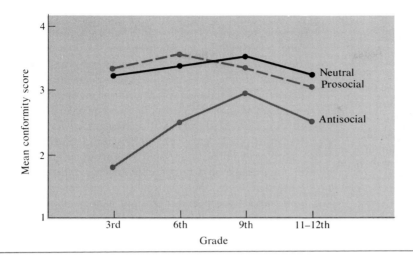

FIGURE 12.4
Mean scores for each grade on conformity for different types of behavior. Higher scores indicate greater conformity, and the neutral point is 3.5 (Berndt, 1979).

Youths engage in all sorts of negative conformity behavior. They may go places in cars with people they are afraid of, use vulgar language, steal, vandalize, and make fun of their parents and teachers. But many conformity behaviors are also positive. The majority of youth go to school and do not cause trouble for teachers; they may belong to clubs or groups that have prosocial functions; and they may belong to cliques that engage in constructive rather than destructive behaviors.

A stereotypical view of parent–child relationships suggests that parent–peer opposition continues into the years of late high school and college. But Berndt (1979) found that adolescent conformity to antisocial, peer-endorsed behavior decreases in the late high school years and that greater agreement between parents and peers begins to occur in some areas. In addition, by the eleventh and twelfth grades, students show signs of developing a decision-making style more independent of peer *and* parent influence.

The Coordinated Worlds of Peers and Family

Peer relations are both similar to and different from parent–child relations. For example, infants touch, smile, and vocalize when they interact with both parents and other children (Eckerman, Whatley & Kutz, 1975). However, rough-and-tumble play occurs mainly with other children and not with adults. Another difference in children's orientation toward peers and parents is that in times of stress, children usually move toward their parents rather than their peers (Maccoby & Masters, 1970). Willard Hartup (1979) described

some of the most important ideas about the interrelatedness of the worlds of child–child and parent–child relations:

As children grow older, their interactions with adult associates and with child associates become more extensively differentiated: (a) Different actions are used to express affection to child associates and to adults, and (b) dominance and nurturance are directed from adults to children, but appeals and submissions are directed more frequently by children to adults than vice versa.

Differentiation between the social worlds of the family and the peer culture continue through adolescence. In a study of "cross pressures," Brittain (1963) discovered that adult endorsement was sought more frequently when norms involving future aspirations or achievement were involved, whereas the reverse was true with status norms and identity issues.

The evidence, then, suggests that children live in distinctive, albeit coordinate, social worlds. Family relations and peer relations constitute similar sociobehavioral contexts in some ways and different ones in others. Children may not conceive of separate normative worlds until early adolescence, because child associates are not used extensively as normative models before that time (Emmerich, Goldman & Shore, 1971). But the family system and the peer system elicit distinctive socioemotional activity many years before these normative distinctions are made. The complex interrelations between the family and peer systems thus work themselves out over long periods of time (Hill, 1980a). (Hartup, 1979, pp. 947–948)

Social Information Processing and Social Knowledge

One of the major trends in the study of peer relationships in recent years has been an attempt to discover how children construct peer relationships. Recall from our discussion of the family in chapter 11 that children carry forward relationship histories that influence the nature of their peer interaction. Here we look at two important cognitive aspects of the construction of peer relationships: social information processing and social knowledge.

Social Information Processing

In processing information about their world children may go through a number of steps. This cognitive view has been applied to how children process information about social situations such as those involving peer interaction (Parke & Asher, 1983). An interesting application of the information-processing approach to social matters is the relation of processing style to aggressive behavior (Dodge, 1980; Dodge & Frame, 1982; Dodge, Murphy & Buchsbaum, 1984; Dodge & Newman, 1981). Kenneth Dodge believes that children go through five steps in processing social information: decoding of social cues, interpretation, response search, selection of an optimal response, and enactment. In one investigation Dodge (1980) demonstrated how distortions during the early phases possibly lead to aggression. For instance, aggressive boys are more likely than nonaggressive boys to perceive another child's actions as hostile when there is actually considerable ambiguity about the peer's intention. Moreover, when aggressive boys are allowed to search for cues to determine a peer's intention, they respond more rapidly and engage in a less efficient search than nonaggressive peers. Further information about children's skill in assessing intention by a peer is described in Perspective on Child Development 12.1.

PERSPECTIVE ON CHILD DEVELOPMENT 12.1

INTENTION-CUE DETECTION SKILLS IN CHILDREN

A peer accidentally trips and knocks a boy's soft drink out of his hand. The boy misinterprets the encounter as hostile, which leads him to retaliate aggressively against the peer. His aggression is viewed as inappropriate by other peers who observed the encounter. Through repeated encounters of this nature, peers come to perceive the boy as having a habit of acting inappropriately. In a recent investigation Kenneth Dodge and his colleagues (Dodge, Murphy & Buchsbaum, 1984) studied boys like the one just mentioned who misinterpreted social cues on a consistent basis. The researchers developed a measure to assess **intention-cue detection,** investigated whether this skill develops across the elementary school years, examined the relation between intention-cue detection and deviant behavior on the part of children, and described the role of intention-cue detection in developing a model of developmental psychopathology.

The measure of intention-cue detection skill was a discrimination task in which a child was presented with fourteen sets of three short videotaped vignettes, each showing social interaction between two children in which one child provokes the other. In two of the three vignettes the actor shows the same intention, but in the third he shows a different intention. The subject's task is to identify the different vignette. Intentions included those that were hostile, prosocial, accidental, and others.

This measure was given to 176 children in kindergarten, second, and fourth grades who were identified as having a peer status as popular, average, socially rejected, or socially neglected. Scores on the intention-cue measure increased with age, and normal children (popular and average) had higher scores than deviant children (neglected and rejected). The mistakes made by the deviant children consistently involved erroneously labeling prosocial intentions as hostile (see the figure opposite). A hostile intention was represented by a display of obviously purposeful destructive behavior accompanied by corresponding verbalizations and facial expressions. A prosocial intention was reflected in a purposeful destruction of a peer's play object, but in an effort to help someone else (such as destroying a block tower while cleaning up the room).

Thus children who are deficient (relative to their agemates) in intention-cue detection are likely to show behavior viewed as inappropriate by their peers. Since

Social Knowledge

The cognitive influence in research on social processes also involves information about social knowledge. As children become more cognitively advanced, they acquire more social knowledge. One of the most interesting aspects of social knowledge research involves the concept of scripts (Nelson, 1981), described in chapter 6. Children's scripts involve plans for particular goals (Renshaw & Asher, 1982). An important part of children's social life involves an assessment of what goals to pursue in poorly defined or ambiguous social situations. And social relationship goals, such as initiating or maintaining a social bond, are important. For example, does the child have the social knowledge to put together a script that will get a particular child to become his or her friend? As part of this script does the child know that saying nice things to the peer will make the peer like him or her more?

Other Ways to Improve the Social Skills of Children

We have studied the current interest in the role of cognition in understanding children's peer relations, and we have described several approaches to improving the social skills of children who have difficulty in peer relations. Other strategies are also being tried out in an effort to improve children's social skills; currently a great deal of thought is being devoted to how we should be constructing such interventions, as well as to how we can best assess such strategies and social skills (e.g., Asher, 1985; Dodge, 1985; Ladd & Mars, 1985; Rao, 1985). An example of a recent successful intervention designed to enhance children's peer skills follows.

Jacquelyn Mize (1985) assigned twenty-nine rejected and neglected preschool children to either a social skill training session or an attention control condition. Children to be trained in social skills participated in eight sessions designed to teach them skills in

children are capable of identifying hostile intentions at an earlier age than prosocial intentions, children deficient in intention-cue detection are likely to make errors in judging nonhostile actions as hostile. This error is likely to lead some children to act aggressively. Other children who make this attributional error may respond by withdrawing. Either response is likely to be judged by peers as inappropriate to the situation. Those who respond aggressively have a high probability of being rejected by peers, whereas those who withdraw have a high probability of being neglected by peers (Dodge, 1983).

In sum, Dodge and his colleagues believe that aggressive children show a systematic bias toward attributing hostile intentions to peers, even in situations when they are not warranted. This bias increases the likelihood that they will retaliate aggressively toward peers, behavior they sense is appropriate but behavior their peers view as inappropriate. The peer group likewise eventually comes to display a bias toward expecting that the agressive children will be hostile, justifying their rejection of them. An implication of these findings is that aggressive children perpetuate their deviant status and behavior through their biased patterns of perceiving the social world and thus may have difficulty changing their behavior.

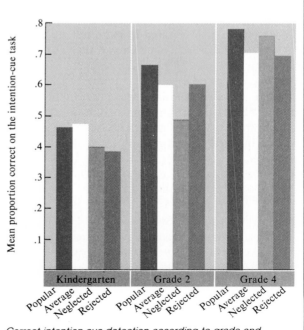

Correct intention-cue detection according to grade and status group (Dodge, Murphy, and Buchsbaum, 1984).

Around the ages of 8–10 children begin developing a real sensitivity to the feelings of another child according to Sullivan.

asking questions, leading, supporting, and commenting to peers. Previous assessment had revealed that popular and average children had used these skills more than neglected or rejected children. The children being trained improved significantly in the use of these skills, particularly those related to leading and commenting. These children also behaved in more socially competent ways in the preschool classroom than their counterparts in the control group, who only had been given attention.

While there is considerable interest in understanding the nature of children's social skills in peer relationships, as we see next, there is a corresponding increase in interest in the study of children's friendships.

Friendships

My best friend is nice. She's honest, and I can trust her. I can tell her my innermost secrets and know that nobody else will find out about them. I have other friends, too, but she is my best friend. We consider each other's feelings and don't want to hurt each other. We help each other out when we have problems. We make up funny names for people, and laugh ourselves silly. We make lists of which boys we think are the sexiest and which are the ugliest, which are the biggest jerks, and so on. Some of these things we share with other friends, some we don't.

This description of the nature of a friendship by a fourteen-year-old girl suggests the importance of intimacy in friendship—telling a friend innermost secrets. We will see that intimacy is one of the most important characteristics of friendships. Our overview of friendships focuses on cognitive factors, intimacy, similarity, shared support and knowledge, and conversational skills.

The Incidence of Friendship and Cognitive Factors

For many children, their most important encounters are with a friend or friends. While warm and trusting relationships may develop within large groups, friendships involve specific attachments that have several characteristics not unlike those found in parent–infant attachment (Hartup, 1983). For example, friends are a source of security in strange, upsetting circumstances, and separation from them arouses anxiety. Children enjoy being with their friends, develop a sense of trust in them, and derive a great deal of pleasure in being with them. Of course, unlike the parent–infant attachment system, friendship attachments are often not permanent. Despite their fragile nature, however, friendships can be as intense as attachments with parents and siblings.

While friendships exist in early childhood, they become much more predominant in the elementary school years and adolescence. Particularly around the ages of eight to ten, children begin developing a real sensitivity to the feelings of another child (Sullivan, 1953). Unfortunately, however, many children do not have a best friend, or even a circle of friends, in whom they can confide. One school psychologist always made a practice of asking children and adolescents about their friends. One eleven-year-old boy, when asked who his best friend was, replied, "My kite." Further discussion revealed that the boy's parents had rejected him and insulated him from the world of peers as well. This circumstance suggests how attachment histories and relationships are carried forward to influence friendship attachments. In one investigation of college-age youth as many as one of every three students surveyed said that they had not found or were not sure they had found a close, meaningful relationship with a same-sex peer (Katz, 1968).

The cognitive orientation in social processes has also begun to characterize the study of friendships. As children progress through middle and late childhood and adolescence, when they are asked about their friends they use more interpersonal constructs, are more flexible and precise in the use of these constructs, provide more complex and organized information about their friends, and understand that particular attributes characterize their friends as compared to their acquaintances. These changes undoubtedly are tied to general changes in cognitive and language development (Hartup, 1983; Shantz, 1983).

Intimacy in Friendships

Intimacy in friendships has been defined in different ways; for example, it has been broadly defined to include everything in a relationship that makes it seem close or intense (Huston & Burgess, 1979). But in most research studies, **intimacy in friendships** has been defined more narrowly in terms of intimate self-disclosure and the sharing of private thoughts. Another factor in intimacy is private and personal knowledge about a friend (Selman, 1980; Sullivan, 1953).

Most efforts to obtain information about friendships simply involve asking children such questions as "What is a friend?" or "How can you tell that someone is your best friend?" (Berndt, 1982). Researchers find that intimate friendships rarely appear during childhood but are most likely to arise first during early adolescence. For example, in one investigation (Diaz & Berndt, in press), fourth and eighth graders were asked about external or observable characteristics of their best friends, such as their friends' birth dates, and about more intimate information, such as their friends' preferences and personality characteristics (for example, what the friends worried about the most). To determine the accuracy of the reports, they were compared with their best friends' self-reports. Fourth and eighth graders did not differ in their knowledge of external or observable characteristics of their friends, but eighth graders knew more intimate things about their best friends than fourth graders did.

While an intimate relationship with a best friend seems to arise often in early adolescence, this period does not appear to be the time when adolescents rate their intimate friendships in the most positive light. Why might early adolescence be a time of less positive intimate relationships in friendship? The decline in positive ratings of friendship that seems to appear around the age of thirteen may be explained by the temporary period of conflict generated by an adolescent's opposite-sex interests (Sharabany, Gershoni & Hofman, 1981), or it may be due to the changes in friendships that accompany the transition to junior high school (Simmons, Rosenberg & Rosenberg, 1973).

It has been argued that girls have more intimate friendships than boys do (Douvan & Adelson, 1966). The assumption behind this suggested sex role difference is that girls are more oriented toward interpersonal relationships while boys are interested in assertiveness and achievement rather than warmth and empathy. Also, intimacy between boys may be discouraged because of the fear that it may lead to homosexuality. When children are asked to describe their best friends, girls refer more to intimate conversations and intimate knowledge and show more concern about faithfulness and rejection (Berndt, 1981; Bieglow & LaGaipa, 1980; Douvan & Adelson, 1966). Although some investigations have found no sex differences in the intimate aspects of friendships (e.g., Sharabany, Gershoni & Hofman, 1981), the weight of the evidence suggests that girls' friendships are characterized by more intimacy than boys' friendships are. For example, more girls than boys are likely to describe their best friend as "sensitive, just like me" or "trustworthy, just like me" (Duck, 1975).

Does intimate friendship have an effect on personality? There is some evidence that having a close and stable best friend is positively associated with self-esteem (Mannarino, 1978, 1979), but we do not know whether the differences between children are caused by self-esteem or intimacy in friendship. In other words, children with high self-esteem may be more likely to be able to develop a close, intimate friendship, just as easily as having a close friend may promote self-esteem.

Similarity in Friendships

The extent to which there is similarity between friends on a variety of characteristics has been of interest to psychologists for many years. Throughout the childhood and adolescent years, friends are generally similar in terms of age, sex, and race (Hallinan, 1979; Kandel, 1978; Tuma & Hallinan, 1979). Friends also usually have similar attitudes toward school, similar educational aspirations, and closely aligned achievement orientations (Ball, 1981; Epstein, 1983; Kandel, 1978). Such findings reveal the importance of schooling in children's lives and the tendency toward agreement between friends on this importance. As Thomas Berndt (1982) suggests, if friends have different attitudes about school, one of them may want to play basketball or go shopping rather than do homework. If one friend insists on completing homework while the other insists on playing basketball, conflicts are likely to weaken the friendship.

Friends also tend to be similar in their orientations toward teenage or youth culture. Friends generally like the same kinds of music, the same kinds of clothes, and the same kinds of leisure activities (Ball, 1981). However, some friendships are based on specific interests, such as horseback riding or playing golf. These types of friends often do not share as many similar ideas and attitudes.

Shared Support and Knowledge

Friendships involve a great deal of sharing. This shared support often appears very early in development. Friendships are also characterized by shared knowledge.

Shared Support John Gottman and Jennifer Parkhurst (1978) maintain that young children's ability to provide mutual support and ability to resolve conflict in imaginative fantasies is critical in establishing and maintaining intimacy among young friends. In coping with conflict young friends express considerable emotion, sympathy and support, and anguish. One excerpt from the fantasy play of two four-year-old best friends, Eric and Naomi, reveals extensive emotional support from Naomi.

Naomi: No, it's time for our birthday. We better clean up quickly.
Eric: Well, I'd rather play with my skeleton. Hold on there everyone. Snappers. I am the skeleton.
Eric: I'm the skeleton. Ooh, hee. Hugh, ha, ha. You're hiding.
Naomi: Hey, in the top drawer, there's the . . .
Eric: I am, the skeleton, whoa.
Naomi: There's the feet. (clattering)
Eric: (screams) A skeleton. Everyone a skeleton.
Naomi: I'm your friend. The dinosaur.
Eric: Oh, hi, dinosaur. You know, no one likes me.
Naomi: But I like you. I'm your friend.
Eric: But none of my other friends like me. They don't like my new suit. They don't like my skeleton suit. It's really just me. They think I'm a dumb-dumb.
Naomi: I know what. He's a good skeleton.
Eric: I am not a dumb-dumb.
Naomi: I'm not calling you a dumb-dumb. I'm calling you a friendly skeleton.

Shared Knowledge   By the middle of the elementary school years friendships involve a considerable amount of reciprocal information about each other's personal and social characteristics. One investigation by Gary Ladd and Elizabeth Emerson (1984) found that the friendships of first grade children were less likely to include a reciprocal awareness of their friend's differences from the self but by the fourth grade such awareness had developed. This suggests that the friendships of older children broaden to include characteristics that do not overlap with self-interests and coincide with the decrease in egocentrism that characterizes development during the elementary school years.

Conversational Skills

Yet another important factor in friendship is conversational skills. In one recent investigation (Parker & Gottman, 1985), the researchers devised a clever strategy for evaluating the role of conversational skills in friendship formation. Four- and five-year-old children were brought individually to a playroom where they played for thirty minutes with a talking doll that resembled a green human wearing silver clothes. The doll housed a wireless, hidden receiver/speaker that allowed a concealed assistant to act as its voice and converse with the subject. The assistant was trained to talk in age-appropriate ways while systematically varying the competence/incompetence of her speech with regard to a number of friendship skills. This strategy produced two experimental conditions—skilled and unskilled. Following the exposure of the children to the skilled and unskilled conversationalist from outer space (i.e., "the green extraterrestrial"), the experimenters evaluated the path of friendship formation. They found that children who met the skilled doll were more likely to "hit it off" and progress toward friendship, while those who met the unskilled doll tended not to hit it off. These findings provide evidence for the importance of conversational skills in friendship formation. Other research on communication skills and children's social relationships suggests that comforting and listening skills are key factors in peer popularity (Burleson, 1985).

We have been describing the nature of children's peer relationships as well as their more intimate interactions with friends. Children also spend time in larger assemblages as part of groups.

Children's Groups

Our discussion of children's groups focuses on the nature of children's groups, the naturalistic study of children's groups by the Sherifs, and a comparison of children's and adolescents' groups.

The Nature of Children's Groups

An assemblage of children is not necessarily a group or clique. A group exists when several children interact with one another on an ongoing basis, sharing values and goals. In addition to shared values and goals, norms and status positions are also important to the functioning of the group. Norms are the standards, rules, and guidelines by which the group abides; and status positions are positions of greater or lesser power and control within the group. Stable groups have values or norms that become established and maintained over time. And when leaders and followers become differentiated, an aggregation takes on the distinctive flavor of a group (Hartup, 1970).

The Naturalistic Study of Children's Group Formation

The most extensive work conducted on the formation of children's and adolescents' groups is that of Muzafer Sherif and his colleagues (Sherif, Harvey, White, Hood & Sherif, 1961). The Sherif naturalistic experiments often proceed according to a particular format. Middle-class white Protestant boys are recruited and removed

to a campsite during the summer. There they are exposed to an experiment in the natural setting of the camp. The observers are members of the camp staff.

In the first phase of the experiment in-group formation is established by placing two groups of boys who do not know one another together for a few days. In the second phase the two groups are brought together for the intergroup conflict phase. This conflict includes win–lose competition and planned frustration that is expected to increase the tension between the groups. In the third phase (e.g., Sherif et al., 1961), ways to reduce intergroup conflict are explored. The observers use strategies such as experiencing a common enemy or constructing superordinate goals that the two groups can only achieve together to reduce conflict.

Among the important findings to come out of Sherif's naturalistic experiments are the following: (1) Hierarchical structures invariably emerge within the groups. The top and bottom status positions are filled first, then the middle positions. (2) Norms develop in all groups. "We–they" talk is a frequent part of the groups' conversations. The groups often adopt nicknames, like the Bulldogs or the Sorcerers. (3) Frustration and competition contribute to hostility between the groups. (4) Intergroup hostility can often be reduced by setting up a superordinate goal that requires the mutual efforts of both groups. For example, Sherif's camp directors deliberately broke a water line so both groups of boys would have to pitch in together to help. Another time, the camp truck taking the boys to a movie in town was driven into a muddy ditch, requiring considerable team effort to get it out.

Children's Groups Compared to Adolescents' Groups

Children's groups differ from adolescents' groups in several important ways. The members of children's groups are often friends or neighborhood acquaintances. Their groups are usually not as formalized as many adolescent groups. During the adolescent years, groups tend to include a broader array of members— in other words, adolescents other than friends or neighborhood acquaintances. Try to recall the student council, honor society, or football team at your junior high school. If you were a member of any of these organizations, you probably recall that they were comprised of a number of individuals you had not met before and that they were a more heterogeneous group than your childhood peer groups. Rules and regulations were undoubtedly well defined, and captains or leaders were formally elected or appointed. Formalized structure and definition of status positions probably did not characterize many of your childhood peer groups.

In addition to more formalized structure and greater heterogeneity of members, adolescent peer groups also are more often made up of both sexes than children's peer groups (Dunphy, 1963). The increased frequency of formal groups in junior high, combined with the psychological changes of puberty, explain to some extent why adolescents' groups have mixtures of boys and girls more often than children's groups do.

So far we have seen the pervasive influence of peer relations and group behavior on children's development. The focus of a great deal of peer relations, particularly in early childhood, is play. Next we study the nature of children's play, discovering that while play is an important aspect of peer interaction, many other functions of play have been proposed as well. First, however, let's review our discussion of peer relations, friendships, and group behavior as summarized in Concept Table 12.1.

CONCEPT TABLE 12.1
Peers, Friendships, and Group Behavior

Concept	Processes/Related Ideas	Characteristics/Description
Peers	Function of the peer group	Social comparison and a source of information outside the family are two important functions of peer relations. Perspective taking is associated with peer relations. Peer relations are an important part of the development of social competence, and cross-cultural comparisons suggest similarities and differences in peer relations.
	Development	Peer relations are appearing more often in infancy because of the increased number of children in day care. Aggressive interaction increases in early childhood, although friendly interchanges increase as well. Children increase the amount of time they spend with peers in elementary school, a time at which role-taking and perspective-taking skills improve.
	Social behavior	Two important dimensions of social behavior in peer relations are popularity and conformity.
	Peers and family	The worlds of peers and the family are coordinated. In some ways peer relationships are similar to parent–child relationships, and in other ways they are different.
	Cognitive factors	There has been an increased interest in cognitive factors in peer relations; two such factors are social information-processing skills and social knowledge.
	Other ways to improve the social skills of children	There currently are a number of efforts underway to improve the social skills of isolated and rejected children. Such programs include strategies to improve children's ability to ask questions, comment, lead, and support.
Friendships	Incidence	Friendships become much more predominant in the elementary school years and adolescence. As they move through middle and late childhood, children describe their friends with more constructs and provide more complex and organized information about them.
	Intimacy	Intimacy in friendship involves self-disclosure and sharing private thoughts. Intimacy increases in the elementary school years and adolescence and is more characteristic of girls than boys.
	Similarity	Friends are similar on a number of dimensions, among them school-related matters.
	Shared support and knowledge	Friendships involve extensive sharing. Young children provide mutual support, and older children broaden the concept of friendship to include characteristics that do not overlap with self-interests.
	Conversational skills	Conversational skills are important in the formation of friendships.
Group Behavior	Nature of group formation	In addition to shared values and goals, norms and status positions are important in group functioning. When leaders and followers have been differentiated, an aggregation takes on the distinct flavor of a group.
	Naturalistic study of children's group formation	The Sherifs have studied children's group formation in natural settings, such as at a camp. Hierarchical structures emerge; there is considerable in-group, out-group comparison and talk; frustration and competition contribute to hostility between groups; and superordinate tasks can reduce intergroup hostility.
	Children's and adolescents' groups	Children's groups are not as formal, are less heterogeneous, and are less cross-sexed than adolescents' groups.

418

Psychoanalytic theorists believe that play relieves tension.

PLAY

An extensive amount of the time spent with peers in early childhood involves play, and play continues to be a common characteristic of the peer interaction of elementary school children as well. First, we study the functions of play, then look at the types of play, and finally examine the kind of play that often comes to mind when we think of young children—pretend play.

Functions of Play

The functions of play include affiliation with peers, tension release, advances in cognitive development, and exploration. Play increases the likelihood that children will affiliate with one another. During this interaction children practice the roles they will assume later in life.

Like Sigmund Freud, Erik Erikson (1950) believes that play permits the child to work off past emotions and to find imaginary relief for past frustrations. Because these tensions are relieved in play, the child (or adult) is better able to cope with problems in life and

to work efficiently. Thus, psychoanalytic theorists believe play permits an individual to let off excess physical energy and to release pent-up tensions that he or she has repressed. On the basis of this view of play, many psychologists and psychiatrists have children engage in **play therapy.** In their opinion, play therapy not only allows the child to work off his or her frustrations but also serves as a medium through which the therapist can analyze many of the child's conflicts and methods of coping with them. It is believed that the child feels less threatened and is more likely to display his or her true feelings in the context of play.

Jean Piaget (1962) saw play as a medium that helps advance the child's cognitive development. At the same time he stressed that the level of cognitive development the child has attained may constrain the way in which he or she plays. Play allows children to practice their competencies and acquired skills in a relaxed, pleasurable way. According to Piaget, cognitive structures need to be used and exercised, and play provides a perfect medium for such use. For example, a young child who has just learned how to add or multiply numbers begins to play with the numbers in different ways as she perfects these operations, laughing as she does so.

Daniel Berlyne (1960) sees play as exciting and pleasurable in itself because it satisfies the exploratory drive that each person has. This drive involves curiosity and a desire for information about something new or unusual. Play serves as a means whereby children can safely explore and seek out new information—something they might not otherwise do. Play promotes this exploratory behavior by offering children the possibilities of novelty, complexity, uncertainty, surprise, and incongruity. When these elements are components of play, children can be expected to engage in more exploratory behavior. Whether the objects or situations involved in play have these properties depends on the child's age and his or her prior experience with those objects. Play with a squeaking ball, for example, may hold the element of novelty for a four-month-old but not for a ten-month-old, who has played with such toys often.

Play is an elusive concept. It can range from an infant's simple exercise of a new-found sensorimotor talent to a preschool child's riding a tricycle to an older child's participation in organized games. One expert on play and games has observed that there is no universally accepted definition of play, probably because it can encompass so many different kinds of activities (Sutton-Smith, 1973).

Types of Play

One of the most elaborate attempts to examine developmental changes in children's social play was conducted many years ago by Mildred Parten (1932). Based on observations of children in free play at nursery school, she developed the following categories of play.

Unoccupied The child is not engaging in play as it is commonly understood. He or she may stand in one spot, look around the room, or perform random movements that seem to have no goal. In most nursery schools **unoccupied play** is less frequent than other types of play.

Solitary The child plays alone and independently of those around him or her. The child seems engrossed in what he or she is doing and does not care much about anything else that is going on. Parten found that two- and three-year-olds engage more frequently in **solitary play** than older preschoolers do.

In cooperative play, a group identity is present and activity is organized, according to Parten's classification.

Onlooker The child watches other children playing. He or she may talk with them or ask them questions but does not enter into their play behavior. The child's active interest in other children's play distinguishes this **onlooker play** from unoccupied play.

Parallel The child plays alone, but with toys like those that other children are using or in a manner that mimics the behavior of other playing children. The older the child, the less frequently he or she engages in this type of play; even older preschool children, however, engage in **parallel play** relatively often.

Associative Social interaction with little or no organization is involved in **associative play.** Children engage in play activities similar to those of other children; however, they appear to be more interested in being associated with one another than in the tasks they are involved with. Borrowing or lending toys and materials and following or leading one another in a line are examples of associative play. Each child plays as he or she wishes; there is no effort at placing the group first and himself or herself last.

Cooperative Social interaction in a group with a sense of group identity and organized activity characterizes **cooperative play.** Children's formal games, competition aimed at winning something, and groups formed by the teacher for doing things together usually are examples of this type of play. Cooperative play is the prototype for the games of middle childhood; little of it is seen in the preschool years.

Parten's research on developmental changes in play was conducted more than fifty years ago. To see whether her findings are now out-of-date, Keith Barnes (1971) observed a group of preschoolers, using Parten's categories of play. He watched the children's activities during an hour-long free-play period each school day for twelve weeks. He found that children in the 1970s did not engage in as much associative or cooperative play as they did in the 1930s. Barnes advanced several reasons to explain this difference: (1) Children have become more passive because of television viewing; (2) toys today are more abundant and attractive than they were forty years ago, so solitary play may be more natural; and (3) parents today may encourage children to play by themselves more than parents did years ago.

The developmental changes in social play that were observed by Parten were also observed by Barnes (Hartup, 1976). That is, three-year-old children engaged in solitary and parallel play more than five-year-old children did, and five-year-old children engaged more frequently in cooperative and associative play than in other kinds of play (see figure 12.5).

During the preschool years peer interaction may involve highly ritualized social interchanges. A **ritual** is a form of spontaneous play that involves controlled repetition. These interchanges have been referred to as *turns* and *rounds* by Catherine Garvey (1977). The contribution of each child is called a turn, while the

total sequence of alternating turns constitutes a round. Following is an example of a round between two five-year-olds:

Boy: Can you carry this?
Girl: Yeah, if I weighed fifty poinds.
Boy: You can't even carry it.
Ritual
Boy: Can you carry it by the string?
Girl: Yeah. Yes, I can. (lifts toy fish overhead by string)
Boy: Can you carry it by the eye?
Girl: (carries it by eye)
Boy: Can you carry it by the nose?
Girl: Where's the nose?
Boy: That yellow one.
Girl: This? (carries it by nose)
Ritual
Boy: Can you carry it by its tail?
Girl: Yeah. (carries it by tail)
Boy: Can you carry it by its fur?
Girl: (carries it by fur)
Boy: Can you carry it by its body?
Girl: (carries it by body)
Boy: Can you carry it like this? (shows how to carry it by fin)
Girl: (carries it by fin)
Boy: Right
Girl: I weigh fifty pounds almost, right?
(Garvey, 1977, pp. 118–19)

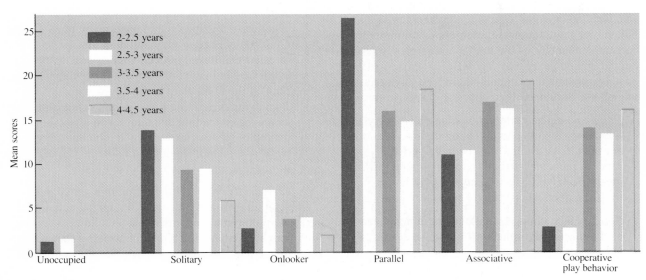

FIGURE 12.5
Mean unoccupied, solitary, onlooker, parallel, associative, and cooperative scores for three-, four-, and five-year-olds (Barnes, 1971).

In this ritual between a boy and girl, five years old, both language and motion were involved. The boy's turns were verbal; the girl's, mainly variations of picking up and carrying the object. In Garvey's (1977) work, there was a tendency for the five-year-old children to engage in more complex rituals than younger children, but three-year-old children were more likely to participate in longer rituals than their older counterparts. For example, a ritual between three-year-olds might involve the sequence "You're a girl."—"No, I'm not," repeated for as long as several minutes. As children become older and enter the elementary school years, rituals may become more formal and be found in games like Red Rover and London Bridge.

Pretend Play

When children engage in **pretend play** they have transformed the physical environment into a symbol (Fein, 1978). Make-believe play appears rather abruptly in the toddler's development, at about eighteen months of age, continues to develop between ages three and four, peaks between ages five and six, and then declines. In the early elementary school years, children's interests begin to shift to games.

In pretend play, children try out many different roles—they may be the mother, the father, the teacher, the next-door neighbor, and so forth. Sometimes their

Pretend play is a common form of play in early childhood.

pretend play reflects an adult role; at other times it may make fun of it. Here is one example of pretend play:

> Harvey was playing with Karen, his twin sister. Karen began to push the carriage. Harvey said, "Let me be the baby, Karen," and started to talk like a baby. He got into the carriage. Karen pushed him around the room as he squinted his eyes and cried. She stopped the carriage, patted his shoulder, saying, "Don't cry baby." He squirmed around, put his thumb in his mouth, and swayed his body.
>
> Josie came to the carriage and wanted to push Harvey. He jumped out and hit her in the face. She walked away almost crying. He went to her, put his arm around her and said, in a sympathetic manner, "Come, you be the baby, I'll push you in the carriage." She climbed in. He ran and got the dog and gave it to her saying, "Here, baby." She smiled and began to play with the dog. He went to the housekeeping corner, got a cup and held it to her mouth. He smacked his lips, looking at her, smiling. He pushed her around in the carriage. Karen ran to him and said, "Harvey, let me push the carriage, I'll be the mamma, you be the daddy." Harvey said, "O.K.," and reached his hand in his pocket and gave her money. He said, "Bye, baby," waving his hand (Hartley, Frank & Goldenson, 1952, pp. 70–72).

You probably can remember many episodes of pretend play from your own childhood—playing doctor, teacher, and so on. As you think about your early childhood years, play is probably one of the predominant things you remember. Further information about pretend play and the role of cognitive development in such play appears in Perspective on Child Development 12.2.

New Directions in Research on Play

In recent years play has been given considerable research attention in an effort to understand the nature of children's development. In particular, there has been a keen interest in how play is assessed as well as in the interface of cognition and play and language and play.

Play and Assessment

If norms for the development of play could be worked out and appropriate measures developed to assess those norms, an important addition to diagnosing normal and abnormal development could be achieved. If Piaget and Freud were correct, then play represents a window to the child's mind. Play may be an important index of the child's socioemotional and intellectual status. Thus, play can be an important addition or alternative to formal testing procedures administered to children, particularly those who are very young or severely impaired. Until recently, play assessment has been somewhat informal, lacking the rigor necessary for such evaluation. However, some signs of measures with psychometric respectability are emerging (e.g., Enslein & Fein, 1981; Roper & Hinde, 1978).

If we are to develop valid assessment measures of play, three problems must be solved. First, the elusive definition of play must be pinned down more precisely. Second, children's play is sensitive to ecological or contextual variation, thus, standardized settings need to be formulated to allow replication of assessment to be high. Third, interpretation of children's play content must be agreed upon by observers. For instance, when a child is aggressive while being observed during the assessment, does the aggression involve imitation, does it consist of a characteristic response style, or is it a cathartic release of inhibited impulses? Interpretation could be facilitated by supplementing standardized setting information with data from observations in natural settings, parental reports of play at home, and child interviews that probe for the child's motivation.

Play and Cognition

There are two main directions of contemporary research on play and cognition. The first concerns the extent to which play can be used as an index of the child's cognitive or intellectual status. The second concerns the nature of children's cognitions about play.

Several standardized procedures have been developed to measure the cognitive complexity of the child's play (Belsky & Most, 1981; Fein, 1975; Nicolich, 1977; Rosenblatt, 1977; Watson & Fischer, 1980). Such procedures permit the investigator to infer the cognitive competencies from observations of play. These procedures have also precipitated the reformulation of age norms for the onset of cognitive competencies associated with play (Rubin & Pepler, 1980). In particular, the assessment of cognitive competencies through play has underscored the importance of not overloading the child with complicated instructions and not relying too

PERSPECTIVE ON CHILD DEVELOPMENT 12.2

CHILDREN'S PRETEND PLAY AND COGNITIVE DEVELOPMENT

You may recall from our discussion in chapter 6 that Piaget believed play is an important aspect of sensorimotor development in infancy. For example, Piaget argued that play is evident when infants repeat acts that are satisfying. Acts such as banging, mouthing, and waving are examples of such play behaviors in infancy. During the second year of life, infants are more likely to play with objects in the manner in which the objects are used in daily life. Accompanying this play is an increase in the amount of pretense involved. For example, between fourteen and nineteen months of age there is an increase in the use of realistic objects in pretend play (Fein & Apfel, 1979); between nineteen and twenty-four months there is an increase in the use of a substitute object, such as a block for a doll (Ungerer, Zelazo, Kearsley & O'Leary, 1981). By twenty-four months, 75 percent of the infants in one investigation showed substitution behavior (Watson & Fischer, 1977).

During the preschool years most children become preoperational thinkers, according to Piaget's framework. It has been suggested that pretend play becomes more and more social with age, at least up to the elementary school years. For example, Piaget (1962) saw symbolic play as solitary through the first two years of life. He also indicated that by the concrete operational period, at about seven years of age, pretend play declines and is replaced by games with rules.

Research designed to evaluate such claims as those made by Piaget has often involved the observation of children during free play in familiar surroundings. A typical strategy was followed by Kenneth Rubin (1977, 1982), who coded play behavior in terms of the following categories: (1) functional or sensorimotor play (which includes simple, repetitive muscular activities with or without objects); (2) constructive play (the manipulation of objects to construct something); (3) dramatic or pretense play; and (4) games-with-rules (in which the child accepts prearranged rules and adjusts his or her behaviors to the rules). When these four categories were recorded, each was further subdivided in terms of social context. Did the play occur when the child was alone (solitary—functional play), when the child was in close proximity but not interacting with others (parallel—functional play), or when playing with others in joint activity (group—games-with-rules)?

For the most part, research following this strategy does document the belief that the portion of pretend play to other play types increases with age from three years up to approximately six to seven years of age (Rubin, Fein & Vandenberg, 1983). More precisely, interactive pretend play increases with age during the preschool years, then decreases somewhat at the beginning of the elementary school years. However, the frequency of solitary pretend play actually decreases during the preschool years, but then increases in the late preschool or early elementary school years. This increase in solitary pretend play may come about as a result of the practice of social games-with-rules, which often emerges at about six years of age. For example, when away from the group, the child may practice and consolidate the skills required to participate effectively in group game circumstances.

Several other comments about the increase in pretend play that characterizes the preschool years provide further illumination of the importance of cognitive development in play. The language development of preschool children undoubtedly is involved in their increase in pretend play. As they become more proficient at using language, preschool children use words in creative ways as they generate a world of fantasy. It is also at this time, the preschool period, that children often develop imaginary companions or playmates. As preschool children construct a play world that is highly symbolic in nature, from Piaget's perspective, they are practicing their cognitive skills in a relaxed, nonthreatening atmosphere. From the cognitive developmental perspective, then, play is an important context for the growth of cognitive skills.

heavily on verbal reports. For example, it has been found that children's conception of roles is more complex and is reasoned about at a higher level when assessed through formal, but simple, nonverbal play measures than when assessed via observations of spontaneous play (Watson & Fischer, 1980).

Researchers in child development have also become increasingly intrigued by children's thoughts about play. For example, in one investigation (Chaillé, 1978), children from five to eleven years of age were asked whether they could pretend to be a doctor, mother/father, teacher, friend, or the interviewer. At five years of age, virtually all of the children said they could enact the roles of doctor, parent, and teacher but could not be the friend or interviewer. Also, young children were found to comment about props (e.g., costumes) when enacting roles, while older children were more likely to refer to actions carried out by the pretense target. In addition, younger children were more likely to use toys as part of their description of pretend play than were older children. These findings suggest a move from material to nonmaterial or ideational conceptions of pretend play as children develop (see figure 12.6).

Play and Language

There has also been increased research interest in the interface of symbolic play and language. While theorists have stressed for some time that early pretend play and early language development have some common dimensions or have some influence on each other (Piaget, 1962; Vygotsky, 1978; Werner & Kaplan, 1963), only recently has this intersection been the focus of actual research. In particular, the research has been dominated by Piaget's belief that pretend play signals the beginning of representational thinking and the appearance of a special function (called the **semiotic function**) that overlays meaning on sound patterns, gestures, or images. For both Piaget and Vygotsky, the main issue focuses on the child's awareness that one thing can signify something else, even when the something else is not present. So far, researchers have not been able to provide convincing data that pretend play is either a prerequisite for language development or cognitive abilities, a concurrent achievement, or a consequence of having developed such abilities. It may be, as Kurt Fischer (1980) has noted, that precise correspondence between play and language and play and cognition is unlikely since development usually does not

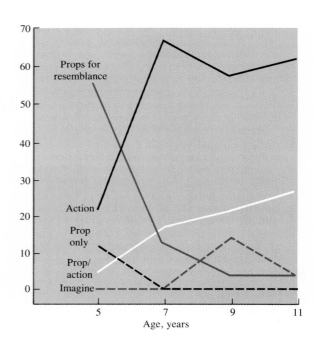

FIGURE 12.6
The graph on the left indicates affirmative responses to the question "Can you pretend to be *someone else*?" by age and item in percentages. The graph on the right indicates responses by category to the question "Can you pretend to be a *mother/father*?" by age, in percentages (Chaillé, 1978).

unfold evenly across different task domains. Future research in this area, however, should illuminate more precisely the line between play and language and play and cognition.

Thus far in this chapter we have examined the nature of children's peer relationships and their play. In both instances we have seen an increased interest in the role of cognition in understanding these important aspects of the child's social world outside the family. In the next section, we continue to investigate the child's world beyond the family by exploring yet another context intricately involved with the child's developing thoughts and social behaviors, the school.

SCHOOLS

Our overview of schools emphasizes the nature of the child's schooling, day care and early childhood education, classroom structure and climate, teachers, social class and ethnicity, and the transition to middle school or junior high school.

The Nature of the Child's Schooling

Information about the nature of the child's schooling focuses on two questions: (1) Does schooling influence the child's development? (2) What is the relation between school context and development?

The Impact of Schools
It is justifiable to be concerned about the impact of schools on children because of the degree of influence that schools have in children's lives. As noted earlier, by the time an individual has graduated from high school, he or she has spent 10,000 hours in the classroom (Kazalunas, 1978). School influences are more important today than in past generations because more children are in school longer. For example, in 1900, 11.4 percent of fourteen- to seventeen-year-olds were in school; today, 94 percent of the same age group are in school (Smith & Orlosky, 1975).

Children spend many years in schools as members of a small society in which there are tasks to be accomplished, people to be socialized and to be socialized by, and rules that define and limit behavior, feelings, and attitudes. The experiences children have in this society are likely to have a strong influence in areas such as identity development, belief in one's competence, images of life and career possibilities, social relationships, standards of right and wrong, and conceptions of how a social system beyond the family functions.

Researchers have found that academic and social patterns are intricately interwoven in the individual's schooling (Brookover, Beady, Flood, Schweitzer & Wisenbaker, 1979; Edmonds, 1979; Rutter, Maughan, Mortimore & Ouston, 1979). Schools that produced high achievement in lower-income students were identified not only by particular types of curriculum and time involved in teaching but by many features of the climate of the school, such as the nature of the teachers' expectations and the patterns of interaction between teachers and students. In other words, various aspects of the school as a social system contributed to the achievement of students in the school.

Additional research focusing on whether schools make a difference in a student's achievement suggests that this question cannot be appropriately addressed unless the extensive variation in schooling is taken into account. Schools vary even in similar neighborhoods serving similar populations. They may differ on such dimensions as whether they are integrated or segregated, coed or single-sex, parochial or secular, rural or urban, and large or small. Schools are also different in their social climates, educational ideologies, and their concepts of what constitutes the best way to promote the child's development.

Development and the Social Context at School
The social context differs at the preschool, elementary school, and secondary school levels.

The Preschool Setting
The preschool setting is a protected environment, whose boundary is the classroom. In this limited social setting, preschool children interact with one or two teachers, almost always female, who are very powerful figures in the young child's life. The preschool child also interacts with peers in a dyadic relationship or in small groups. It appears that preschool children have little concept of the classroom as an organized social system, although they are learning how to make and maintain social contacts and communicate their needs. The preschool serves to modify some patterns of behavior developed through family experiences. Greater self-control may be required in the preschool, and in many instances social patterns are mutually developed.

The Elementary School Setting
The classroom is still the major context for the elementary school child, although it is more likely to be experienced as a social unit than was true in the preschool. Further, the network of social expression is more complex now. Teachers

and peers have a prominent influence on the child during the middle childhood years, with teachers symbolizing authority in establishing the climate of the classroom, conditions of interaction with students, and the nature of group functioning. The peer group takes on a very prominent status in the lives of elementary school children. Not only is there interest in friendship, belonging, and status in peer groups at school, but the peer group also is a learning community in which social roles and standards related to work and achievement are formed.

The Secondary School Setting As children move into the junior high school years, the school environment increases in scope and complexity. The school as a whole, rather than the classroom, is now the social field. Adolescent students socially interact with many different teachers and peers from a range of social backgrounds. Students are often exposed to a greater mix of male and female teachers as well. Social behavior is heavily weighted toward peers, extracurricular activities and clubs, and the community. The student in secondary school is frequently aware of the school as a social organization and may be motivated to conform and adapt to the system or to challenge it.

Day Care and Early Childhood Education

We now explore in greater detail the early years of the child's contact with schooling. We first present information about day care and then evaluate the nature of early childhood education.

Day Care

Each weekday at 8:00 A.M., Ellen Smith takes her one-year-old daughter, Tanya, to the day-care center at Brookhaven College in Dallas. Then Mrs. Smith goes off to work and returns in the afternoon to take Tanya home. Tanya has excelled in day care, according to Mrs. Smith. Now, after three years at the center, Mrs. Smith reports that her daughter is very adventuresome and interacts confidently with peers and adults. Mrs. Smith believes that day care has been a wonderful way to raise Tanya.

In Los Angeles, however, day care has been a series of horror stories for Barbara Jones. After two years of unpleasant experiences with sitters, day-care centers, and day-care homes, Mrs. Jones has quit her job as a successful real estate agent to stay home and take care of her two-and-one-half-year-old daughter, Gretchen. "I didn't want to sacrifice my baby for my job," says Mrs. Jones, who was unable to find good substitute day

Students are often exposed to a greater mix of male and female teachers in secondary schools.

care. When she put Gretchen in a day-care center, Mrs. Jones says, she felt like her daughter was being treated like a piece of merchandise—dropped off and picked up.

Many mothers worry whether day care will adversely affect their children. They fear that day-care centers may lessen the emotional attachment of the infant to the mother, retard the infant's cognitive development, fail to teach the child how to control his or her anger, and allow the child to be unduly influenced by other children.

Traditionally, it has been argued that effective socialization of the child into a mature individual depends on the development of a strong attachment bond between the infant and his or her mother or primary caretaker. If this relationship is severed for a lengthy period of time on a daily basis, the child's attachment to the caretaker may be weakened. Selma Fraiberg (1977), in her book *Every Child's Birthright: In Defense of Mothering,* supports this traditional belief. Fraiberg says that she worries about babies and small children who are delivered like packages to neighbors, strangers, and storage houses. Fraiberg is not against all day care, though. She says that children between the ages of three and six can benefit from half-day nursery school programs that entail small groups and qualified teachers. The problem, according to Fraiberg, is that children in most day-care centers are there nine to eleven hours a day and are being cared for by poorly educated, unqualified personnel.

In our further examination of day care we look more closely at the nature of day care, including a description of the number of working mothers who require day care for their children and a survey of the variety of day care available. Then we look at an assessment of day-care effects on young children, in particular, the effects of day care on attachment.

The Nature of Day Care The number of women in the labor force with children under six and a spouse present in the home has increased from 2.5 million in 1960 to 4.4 million in 1975 to 6.2 million in 1984. The number of women in the labor force with children under six and no spouse present in the home has increased from .42 million in 1960 to .96 million in 1975 to 1.8 million in 1984. In the 1980s far more young children are being placed in day care than at any other time in history—about 2 million children currently receive

formal, licensed day care, and more than 5 million children attend nursery school or kindergarten. Additional uncounted millions of children are taken care of by unlicensed babysitters. Day care clearly is becoming a basic need of the American family.

Much of day care is informal and unregulated, consisting of whatever arrangements the harried parent can muster. For example, a mother may get a neighbor to babysit three afternoons a week and take the child to her mother's house two days a week. Formal day care is usually of one of two types: a center or a home. Centers invariably monitor large groups of young children and often have elaborate facilities. Some are commercial operations, others are nonprofit centers run by churches, civic groups, and employers. Day care may also be provided in private homes, sometimes by childcare professionals, sometimes by unlicensed mothers who want to earn extra money.

In the 1980s, more infants and young children are being placed in day care than at any point in history.

The Effects of Day Care on the Infant's Development
In reviewing the existing research on day care, Alison Clarke-Stewart and Greta Fein (1983) concluded that at this time it is virtually impossible to answer the question of whether day care has a positive or negative effect on young children's development. Some investigations show positive effects, others negative effects, and still others no effects at all. Trying to combine these results into an overall conclusion about day-care effects is problematic because of the different types of day care children experience and the different measures used to assess outcomes in different studies.

In many of the day-care/home-rearing comparisons, the day-care centers are university based or staffed. Such centers serve many different types of families, and while the programs differ, they do have some features in common. Babies are taken care of in small groups, and a caretaker is assigned to each infant who is younger than two years of age. The caretaker changes the infant's diapers and feeds the infant and is trained to enrich such routines by communicating with the infant. Periodically during the day, the caretaker seeks out the infant and engages him or her in some form of lively social interaction. The general conclusion from comparisons of children in high-quality university-staffed day-care centers and home-reared children is that there are few if any differences in the attachment behavior of the children (Belsky & Steinberg, 1978).

The day care that most babies receive, however, does not approach the quality of the university-based programs. Demonstration programs, such as Jerome Kagan's (Kagan, Kearsley & Zelazo, 1978), do show that it is possible to provide group care for infants that will not harm them and in some cases can actually aid their social development. Kagan's day-care center included a pediatrician, a nonteaching director, and an infant–teacher ratio of three to one. Teachers' aides also assisted at the center. The teachers and aides were trained to become competent caretakers of infants—to smile frequently, talk with the infants, and provide them with a safe environment that included many stimulating toys.

As an example of one of the many variables assessed by Kagan and his colleagues, we consider the results for peer play. To assess peer play, an unfamiliar peer of the same age, sex, and ethnicity of the child entered the room with the peer's mother, and a new set of toys was brought in. The child's behavior was observed for twenty-one minutes to assess such matters as the time spent in peer play and the duration of time spent looking at the peer. As shown in figure 12.7, particularly at twenty months of age, the home-reared children spent less time in play and more time looking at the peer (a likely indicator of wariness about the peer) than their day-care counterparts. However, at thirteen and twenty-nine months these differences did not appear. In looking

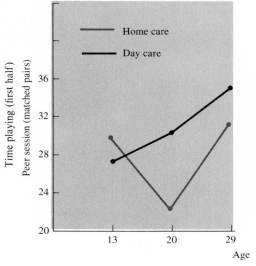
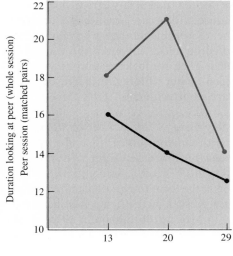

FIGURE 12.7
Absolute time spent playing (per minute) with the peer and duration of looking at peer (in seconds per minute), for matched pairs of day-care subjects and home controls (Kagan, Kearsley, and Zelazo, 1978).

at the overall indicators of social competence in children, Kagan and his colleagues (1978) concluded that there were few differences in any of the global measures of cognitive development or social development. Quality day care did not have any positive effects, but it did not have any negative effects either.

Early Childhood Education

Our discussion of early childhood education focuses initially on the overall effects of early childhood education, that is comparisons of children who go to nursery school and kindergarten with those who do not, and then we turn our attention to compensatory education and a description and results pertaining to Project Head Start and Project Follow Through.

The Effects of Early Childhood Education

The term **child-centered** has been used to describe the most popular form of education before the first grade. However, the term obscures the diversity of goals and curricula in the thousands of so-classified nursery schools. By child-centered is meant an emphasis on the individual child, providing the child with a number of experiences and making education a fun-filled adventure in exploration. However, some nursery schools emphasize social development, others cognitive development; some stress daily structured activities, others much more flexible activities. Nonetheless, some attempts have been made to come up with an answer to the question of whether attending kindergarten has a positive effect on young children's development.

The general conclusions about the effects of preschool education on children's development are as follows (Clarke-Stewart & Fein, 1983): (1) Children attending preschools interact more with peers—both positively and, often, negatively; (2) they are less cooperative and responsive with adults than home-reared children; (3) they are more socially competent and mature in that they are more confident and extraverted (Ramey, MacPhee & Yeates, 1982), more assertive (Rubenstein, Howes & Boyle, 1981), more self-sufficient and independent (Fowler, 1978), more helpful and cooperative with peers and adults (Sjolund, 1971), more verbally expressive and more knowledgeable about their social world (Clarke-Stewart & Fein, 1983), more comfortable in stressful circumstances (Kagan, Kearsley & Zelazo, 1978), and better adjusted when they go to school, for example, exhibiting more task persistence, leadership, and goal direction (Fowler & Kahn, 1974; Ramey, MacPhee & Yeates, 1982).

However, even though children attending early childhood education programs exhibit greater social competence, they also show some negative behaviors as well. While they are more independent, they also tend to be less polite and less compliant with teacher demands; while they are more assertive, they are also louder, more aggressive, and bossy, particularly if the school or family standards support such behavior (Lally & Honig, 1977; Ramey, MacPhee & Yeates, 1982). Although such behaviors are not positive, even these latter differences seem to be in a direction that shows greater developmental maturity, because the behaviors increase as the child ages through the preschool years (Clarke-Stewart & Fein, 1983).

Now that we have seen how early childhood education generally has a positive effect on children's development, we turn our attention to the nature of compensatory education and some more specific types of early childhood programs.

Compensatory Education

For many years children from low-income families did not receive any education before they entered the first grade. In the 1960s an effort was made to try to break the poverty/poor education cycle for young children in the United States through **compensatory education.** As part of this effort, **Project Head Start** began in the summer of 1965, funded by the Economic Opportunity Act. The program was designed to provide children from low-income families an opportunity to experience an enriched early environment. It was hoped that the early intervention might counteract the disadvantages these children had experienced and place them on an equal level with other children when they entered the first grade.

Head Start consisted of many different types of preschool programs in different parts of the country. Initially, little effort was made to find out whether some types of programs worked better than others. However, it soon became apparent that this was the case. Consequently, in 1967 **Project Follow Through** was established. A significant aspect of this program was planned variation, in which different kinds of educational programs were devised to see whether specific programs are effective. In the Follow Through programs the enriched planned variation was carried through the first few years of elementary school as well. Information about Project Follow Through is presented in Perspective on Child Development 12.3, including a description of five Follow Through models and research evaluation of the program.

PERSPECTIVE ON CHILD DEVELOPMENT 12.3

PROJECT FOLLOW THROUGH—MODELS AND RESEARCH EVALUATION

T he table opposite describes five Follow Through models. National research assessment of the effects of planned variation, such as that exhibited by the five models, supported the belief that such programs can enhance the child's social and cognitive development. Jane Stallings (1975) commented on how many of the different variations were able to obtain the desired effects on children. For example, children in the academically oriented, direct instruction approaches, such as the University of Oregon model, seemed to do better on achievement tests and were more persistent on tasks than children in other approaches that placed more emphasis on affective development. However, children in the affective education approaches, such as the Far West Laboratory model,

were absent from school less and showed more independence than children in other approaches, such as those that were highly structured. As shown in the figure below, children experiencing the highly structured academic orientation of the University of Kansas model (much like the University of Oregon model) persisted longer on tasks but were less independent than children involved in the Far West affective education program. Task persistence was defined as the child engaging in self-instruction over a specified period of time. Independence was defined as a child or a group of children engaging in any task without an adult. Thus Project Follow Through was important in demonstrating that variation in early education does have important effects on a wide range of social and cognitive behaviors.

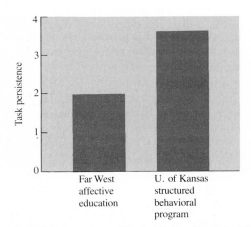

Task persistence scores of Project Follow Through children in the third grade.

From Stallings, J., "Implementations and child effects of teaching practices in follow-through classrooms," in *Monographs of the Society for Research in Child Development,* serial no. 163, p. 56. Copyright © 1975, The Society for Research in Child Development, Inc. Reprinted by permission.

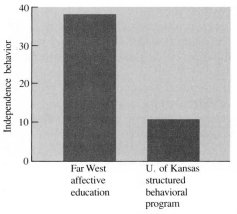

Independence behavior of Project Follow Through children in the third grade.

From Stallings, J., "Implementations and child effects of teaching practices in follow-through classrooms," in *Monographs of the Society for Research in Child Development,* serial no. 163, p. 56. Copyright © 1975, The Society for Research in Child Development, Inc. Reprinted by permission.

Five Project Follow Through Models

Model	Description
University of Oregon Engelmann/Becker Model for Direct Instruction	Emphasizes that children fail in school because they have not been instructed properly. Disadvantaged children lag behind other children in developing appropriate skills. It is a highly structured program, with sequentially programmed lessons. Teachers systematically reward children for success and monitor them closely so that learning failures do not build up. This program is based on learning theory and behavior modification.
High/Scope: Cognitively Oriented Curriculum Model	Developed by Dave Weikart, this model is based on Piaget's theory of cognitive development. The child is seen as an active learner who discovers things about the world. He or she should not be "taught," in the sense of being told information; rather, he or she should "learn" by planning, doing, experimenting, exploring, and talking about what he or she is doing. Communication and thinking skills are nurtured, and emphasis is placed on self-direction, not reliance on external reinforcement from others. Each child's level of development is continuously monitored so that appropriate materials can be used.
Florida Parent-Education Program	Places more direct importance on the role of parents than the first two models mentioned. This program was developed by Ira Gordon to involve parents in the emotional and intellectual growth of their children. It assumes that the child's learning habits and personality are formed primarily through experiences in the early home environment; thus parents are trained to supervise their child's learning at home. Parent educators work in the classroom and visit parents on a weekly basis.
Far West Laboratory Responsive Educational Program	Emphasizes the development of a healthy self-concept in the child and the freedom to decide his or her own course of learning. Teachers try to build up the child's confidence in ability to succeed and provide many different alternatives in the classroom so he or she can choose and direct activities. This program has much in common with a humanistic view of child development.
Bank Street College of Education Approach	An eclectic approach in which academic skills are seen as acquired within a broader context of planned activities. The program focuses on the child's interests at school, at home, and in the community, and views the child as an active learner seeking to become independent and to understand the world. To help the child in these efforts, he or she is encouraged to select from different alternatives, to make decisions, and to cope with the world. The individual nature of the child also is taken into account; learning experiences are constantly restructured to meet the needs of each child.

Classroom Structure and Climate

There has been a great deal of debate in educational circles on how classroom structure and climate influence development. Perhaps the most widely discussed aspect of this debate focuses on open versus traditional classrooms. The **open classroom** (or open education) concept has referred to many different dimensions (Giaconia & Hedges, 1982; Marshall, 1981):

Free choice by students of activities they will participate in

Space flexibility

Varied, enriched learning materials

Emphasis on individual and small-group instruction

The teacher as more of a facilitator than a director of learning

Students' learning to assume responsibility for their learning

Multiage grouping of children

Team teaching

Classrooms without walls, in which the physical nature of the school is more open

Some open classroom programs have more of these features than others. Thus research that compares open with traditional classrooms is difficult to interpret because there are so many variations of open classrooms.

Part of the problem with studies of open and traditional classrooms also is that these terms are not always reflected directly in the classroom. As a result, in some classrooms defined as open, the teachers may be using a teaching style more characteristic of traditional classrooms. One inadequate strategy that has been used too often is simply to ask teachers or school officials (who may have varying definitions of what constitutes open and traditional classrooms) to rate classroom climate.

In many instances, the measures that have been used to assess the effects of classroom climate have been standardized tests of intelligence and achievement. However, Rudolf Moos (Moos & Moos, 1978; Trickett & Moos, 1974) believes that it may be wise to assess educational effects other than those evaluated by standardized tests. Cognitive preferences, school satisfaction, and persistent motivation to learn are several other factors that children should be measured on as well.

Furthermore, experts believe that not only should different measures be used to assess the effects of classroom climate, but better instruments to evaluate classroom climate are needed. One such measure is the **Classroom Environment Scale (CES)** developed by Trickett and Moos (1974). The CES attempts to evaluate the social climate of classrooms. Teacher–student and peer relationships, as well as the organization of the classroom, are assessed. Students are asked to respond to a number of questions concerning nine different categories: teacher support, affiliation, task

TABLE 12.1
An Analysis of Studies Focused on the Dimensions of Open Classrooms
and Their Effects on the Child's Development

		Self-concept	Creativity	Favorable attitude toward school	Self-concept/ creativity average
Role of the Child	L	100			93.0
	S	50			58.5
Diagnostic Evaluation	L	100	100	73	100.0
	S	46	50	50	48.0
Materials to Manipulate	L	100	80	82	90.0
	S	27	50	56	38.5
Individualized Instruction	L	100			91.5
	S	44			55.5
Multiage Grouping	L		83		82.0
	S		33		54.0
Team Teaching	L			36	
	S			62	
Open Space	L			54	
	S			85	

Note: L refers to those studies having a larger or stronger effect on the child's development. S refers to those having a smaller or weaker effect on the child's development. The numbers are listed only in cells where there was a significant difference between whether a dimension of the open classroom had a stronger or a weaker effect on the child's development (such as self-concept).

orientation, competition, order and organization, rule clarity, involvement, teacher control, and innovation.

Because open classrooms have been defined in so many different ways some researchers have recommended that the concept of the open classroom be evaluated in terms of its components, or some combination of the components, rather than as a whole. In one evaluation of the components of open classrooms (Giaconia & Hedges, 1982), the researchers performed a meta-analysis of approximately 150 studies. A **meta-analysis** involves the application of statistical techniques to already existing research studies. The investigator sorts through the research literature looking for common results of many different studies to discover some consistent themes. The results indicated that the open classroom concept seems to have the following characteristics:

Lowered language achievement but by a very small amount

Little effect on math, reading, and other types of academic achievement

Moderately enhanced achievement motivation, cooperativeness, creativity, and independence

No effect on adjustment, anxiety, locus of control, or self-concept

Slightly improved student attitudes toward school, the teacher, curiosity, and general mental ability

However, the results tell us nothing about the particular dimensions of the open classroom concept. To identify these more precise effects, the following characteristics were investigated:

Role of the child (the degree of activity in learning)

Diagnostic evaluation (use of work samples and observations but rare use of tests to guide instruction)

Materials to manipulate

Individualized instruction (adjusting rate, methods, materials; calling on small-group methods)

Multiage grouping of students (two or more grades in the same area)

Open space (flexible use of areas, activity centers; no interior walls; flexible seating)

Team teaching (two or more teachers combining to plan and instruct the same students; use of parents as teaching aides)

In analyzing these aspects of classrooms, the researchers investigated the extent to which such features had larger effects or smaller effects on the students. Then, within those studies that had either larger effects or smaller effects of the open classroom concept, specific criteria of the open classroom were noted. Table 12.1 reveals the percentage of the studies

Non-achievement average	Reading achievement	Mathematics achievement	Language achievement	Achievement average
90.3				
62.0				
91.0				
44.3				
87.3	77			75.7
44.3	50			57.0
87.7				
62.0				
70.0		57	57	58.3
51.3		79	75	73.0
	73		71	68.7
	50		38	47.3

From Giaconia, R. M., and L. V. Hedges, "Identifying features of effective open education," in *Review of Educational Research*, 52, pp. 579–602. Copyright 1982. American Educational Research Association, Washington, D.C.

having either the larger or smaller effect in which a particular component was involved. For example, as can be seen, when open classrooms had a larger effect on self-concept, the role of the child was a criterion in all of the investigations, but when the studies only had a smaller effect, the role of the child was only a criterion of open classrooms in 50 percent of the investigations. Also, note that when the child's self-concept was linked to open education in the larger effect studies that diagnostic evaluation, materials to manipulate, and individualized instruction were included as components of open education. With regard to the average of non-achievement outcomes, all features except team teaching and open space were present in the larger effects of open classrooms. For the average of achievement outcomes, materials to manipulate and team teaching were involved in the larger effect studies while multiage grouping appeared less frequently in larger effect than smaller effect studies.

Enthusiasm is an important teacher characteristic.

Teachers

Virtually everyone's life is affected in one way or another by teachers: you were probably influenced by teachers as you grew up; you may become a teacher yourself or work with teachers in counseling or psychological services; and you may now or in the future have children whose education will be guided by many different teachers. How much influence do teachers really have on children? Try to think of some characteristics of the teachers you have liked or disliked, particularly their styles of communication and social interaction. You can probably remember several of your teachers vividly: Perhaps one never smiled, another required you to memorize everything in sight, and yet another always appeared happy and vibrant and encouraged verbal interaction. Our further discussion of teachers focuses on teaching styles and traits as well as Erik Erikson's criteria for a good teacher.

Teaching Styles and Traits

For many years psychologists and educators have been trying to create a profile of the personality traits of a good teacher. Because of the complexity of the task, a definitive profile may never be produced; yet several studies suggest that some traits are better for teachers than others. Teacher traits that relate positively to the student's intellectual development are enthusiasm, the ability to plan, poise, adaptability, and awareness of individual differences (Gage, 1965). Teachers who are

impulsive tend to produce more impulsive students who are less reflective in solving school tasks (Yando & Kagan, 1968). And teachers who are warm and flexible and encourage responsibility tend to produce students who respond constructively to failure and usually engage willingly in class activities (Thompson, 1944).

Erikson's Criteria for a Good Teacher

Erik Erikson (1968) believes that good teachers are able to produce a sense of industry rather than inferiority in their students. Good teachers are trusted and respected by the community and know how to alternate play and work, games and study. They know how to recognize special efforts and encourage special abilities. They also know how to give a child time and how to handle those children to whom school is not important.

Good teachers, in Erikson's view, allow a student to engage in peer interaction when academic work is getting to him or her and his or her interaction with the teacher seems to be deteriorating. At stake is the child's development of identification with those who know things and know how to do things. Time after time in interviews with talented and creative people, spontaneous comments reveal that one teacher helped to spark hidden talent. Without such teachers, many children never develop their abilities.

Erikson believes that many teachers emphasize self-restraint and a strict allegiance to duty as opposed to encouraging children to make discoveries on their own.

He remarks that either method may work well with some children but not with others. He also stresses that if the first method is carried to the extreme, children may develop too much self-restraint and sense of duty in conforming to what others do. If the opposite method is used in the extreme, Erikson believes that children should be "mildly but firmly coerced into the adventure of finding out that one can learn to accomplish things which one would never have thought of by oneself" (1968, p. 127).

There is another possible hazard in the child's development that Erikson feels teachers need to watch for. When the child conforms too much, he or she may view work as the only worthwhile activity in life. This type of child probably will not engage in imaginative activities and games to the extent that an individual with better identity development does. There are times when the grind of hard work should be left behind, and teachers can encourage students to do so.

Aptitude–Treatment Interaction

Some children may benefit from structure more than others, and some teachers may be able to handle a flexible curriculum better than others. As a result, a whole field of educational research has sprung up, referred to as **aptitude–treatment interaction (ATI)**. The term *aptitude* refers to academic potential and personality dimensions in which students differ; *treatment* refers to the educational technique (e.g., structured or flexible) adopted in the classroom. Lee Cronbach and Richard Snow (1977), as well as other education experts, argue that ATI is the best way to study teaching effectiveness.

Research has shown that a child's achievement level (aptitude) may interact directly with classroom structure (treatment) to produce the best learning and the most enjoyable learning environment (Peterson, 1977; Porteus, 1976). That is, students with a high achievement orientation often do well in a flexible classroom and enjoy it; students with a low achievement orientation do not usually do as well and dislike the flexibility. The reverse is true in a structured classroom. Many other ATI factors operate in the classroom. Education experts are just beginning to pin some of these down; further clarification of aptitude–treatment interaction should lead to useful information about how children can be taught more effectively. Richard Snow (1977) points out that individual differences (aptitudes) were ignored for many years in the design of instruction and curricula. Now individual differences

in student aptitudes, learning styles, cultural backgrounds, and so forth are forcing curriculum teams to consider more specific instructional situations and more specific groups of children.

Two ways in which the teacher's orientation can be classified are as challenging and demanding and as encouraging good performance. Jere Brophy (1979) reviewed several studies focused on these two types of teacher orientation. Teachers who work with high-socioeconomic status/high-ability students are usually more successful if they move at a quick pace, frequently communicating high expectations and enforcing high standards. These teachers try to keep students challenged, will not accept inferior work, and occasionally criticize the students' work when it does not meet their standards. Teachers who generally are successful with low-socioeconomic status/low-ability students are also interested in getting the most out of their students, but they usually do so by being warm and encouraging rather than demanding. They are friendly with their students, take more time out from academic subject matter to motivate the youth, praise and encourage more often, rarely criticize poor work, and move the curriculum along at a slower pace. When they call on individual students, they allow more time for the student to respond; they may provide hints to help the student get the correct answer (Brophy & Evertson, 1974, 1976). As we can readily see by this example, successful teaching varies according to the type of student being taught.

Social Class and Ethnicity

In this section we focus on the effects of social class and ethnicity on schooling.

Social Class

It often seems as though one of the major functions of schools in this country is to train children to function in and contribute to middle-class society, since politicians who vote on school funding are usually middle class, school-board members are predominantly middle class, and principals and teachers are often middle class. In fact, it has been stated many times that schools function in a middle-class society, and critics believe that the schools have not done a good job in educating lower-class children to overcome the cultural barriers that make it difficult to enhance their social position. This theme characterized the educational protest literature of the 1960s and early 1970s.

In *Dark Ghetto* Kenneth Clark (1965) described some of the ways in which lower- and middle-class children are treated differently in school. Teachers in the middle-class school spent more time in teaching their students and evaluated their work more than twice as often as teachers in the low-income school did. And teachers in the low-income school made three times as many negative comments to students as teachers in the middle-class school did; the latter made more positive than negative comments to their students.

Teachers have lower expectations for children from low-income families than for children from middle-income families. A teacher who knows that a child comes from a lower-class background may spend less time trying to help that child solve a problem and may anticipate that he or she will frequently get into trouble. The teacher may also perceive a gap between his or her own middle-class position and the lower-class status of the child's parents; as a result the teacher may believe that the parents are not interested in helping the child and may thus make fewer efforts to communicate with them.

The maturational experiences of teachers with a middle-class background are quite different from those of children or teachers with a lower-class background. A teacher from the middle class has probably not gone hungry for weeks at a time or experienced the conditions of an overcrowded apartment, perhaps without electricity or plumbing, where several children may sleep with one or two adults in one small room.

There is evidence from at least one study that teachers with lower-class origins may have different attitudes toward lower-class students than middle-class teachers have (Gottlieb, 1966). Perhaps because they have experienced many inequities themselves, they tend to be empathetic to the problems that lower-class children encounter. In this study, for example, the teachers were asked to indicate the most outstanding characteristics of their lower-class students. The middle-class teachers checked adjectives like "lazy," "rebellious," and "fun-loving"; the lower-class teachers, however, checked such adjectives as "happy," "cooperative," "energetic," and "ambitious." The teachers with lower-class backgrounds perceived the behaviors of the lower-class children as adaptive, whereas the middle-class teachers viewed the same behaviors as falling short of middle-class standards.

Ethnicity

Not only do students from lower-class backgrounds often experience discrimination in our schools; children from many different ethnic backgrounds do as well. In most American schools, blacks, Mexican-Americans, Puerto Ricans, Native Americans, Japanese, and Asian Indians are minorities. Teachers have often been ignorant of different cultural meanings that non-Anglo children have learned in their communities. The problems that boys and girls from non-Anglo backgrounds have had in conventional schools is well-documented (Casteñada, Ramirez, Cortes & Barrera, 1971; Minuchin & Shapiro, 1983).

The social and academic development of children from minority groups depends on such factors as teacher expectations; the teacher's preparation for working with children from different backgrounds; the nature of the curriculum; the presence of role models in the school for minority students; the quality of relations between school personnel and parents from different ethnic, economic, and educational backgrounds; and the relations between the school and the community (Minuchin & Shapiro, 1983).

By far the largest effort to study the role of ethnicity in schools has dealt with desegregation (Bell, 1980). The focus of desegregation has been on improving the proportions of black and white student populations in schools. Efforts to improve this ratio have typically involved busing students, usually the minority-group members, from their home neighborhoods to more distant schools. The underlying belief in such efforts is that bringing different groups together reduces stereotyped attitudes and improves intergroup relationships. But busing tells us nothing about what is going on inside the school. Black children bused to a predominantly white school are usually resegregated in the classroom. Segregation is frequently reinstituted by seating patterns, ability grouping, and tracking systems (Epstein, 1980).

In one comprehensive national study that focused on factors that contribute to positive interracial relations (Forehand, Ragosta & Rock, 1976), over 5,000 fifth grade students in more than ninety elementary schools and over 400 tenth graders in seventy-two high schools were evaluated. It was concluded that multiethnic curricula, projects focused on racial issues, and mixed work groups lead to positive changes, and that improved relationships are enhanced by the presence of supportive principals and teachers.

The attitude of school personnel toward ethnic pluralism is an important aspect of promoting the development of minority students.

Overall, however, the findings pertaining to desegregation have not been encouraging (Minuchin & Shapiro, 1983). Desegregation in itself does not necessarily improve race relations—positive consequences depend on what goes on in the classroom once children get there. School personnel who support the advancement of minority students, curricula that acknowledge ethnic pluralism, and the participation of students in cooperative activities and learning situations are likely to improve the minority student's development.

Transition to Middle School or Junior High School

The transition to middle school or junior high school from elementary school is of interest to developmental psychologists because even though it is a normative experience for virtually all children in our society, this transition can be stressful. The transition may be stressful because of the point in development at which it takes place (Hawkins & Berndt, 1985; Nottelmann, 1982). Transition to middle or junior high school occurs at a time in the development of children when a number of simultaneous changes are occurring, including changes in the individual, the family, and the school. These changes include the occurrence of puberty and related concerns about body image, the emergence of at least some aspects of formal operational thought, including accompanying changes in social cognition, increased responsibility and independence in association with decreased dependency on parents, change from a small, contained classroom

structure to a larger, more impersonal school structure, change from one teacher to many teachers and a small, homogeneous set of peers to a larger, more heterogeneous group of peers, and increased focus on achievement and performance (as well as assessment of such achievement and performance). While this list includes a number of negative features of the transition to middle school or junior high school, there are positive aspects to the change as well. Students are more likely to feel grown up, to have more subjects to select from, to have more opportunities to spend time with peers and more chances to locate compatible friends, and to enjoy increased independence from direct parental monitoring and teacher monitoring; they may also be more challenged intellectually by academic work (Hawkins & Berndt, 1985).

A number of research inquiries that chart children's development as they move from an elementary school into a middle or junior high school are beginning to appear (e.g., Blyth, Simmons & Bush, 1978; Douvan & Adelson, 1966; Felner, Ginter & Primavera, 1982; Goodlad, 1983; Gump, 1983; Hawkins & Berndt, 1985; Simmons, Rosenberg & Rosenberg, 1973). The upshot of these investigations is that the first year of a middle school or a junior high school can be very difficult for many students. One major reason for this difficulty is what is referred to as the **top-dog phenomenon** (Blyth, Simmons & Carleton-Ford, 1983). Moving from the top position (in elementary school, as the oldest, biggest, and most powerful students in the school) to the bottom or lowest position (in middle or junior high school, the youngest, smallest, and least powerful group of students) may create a number of difficulties for students. However, there is increased interest in the nature of schooling experiences that might produce better adjustment for children as they move from elementary school to middle or junior high school. It has been found that schools providing more supportiveness, less anonymity, more stability, and less complexity have a salutary effect on student adjustment in middle and junior high school transition.

Adjustment to the transition to middle or junior high school may be somewhat different for boys than for girls and for early-maturing versus late-maturing students. Recall from our discussion of physical development in chapter 3 that girls enter puberty on the average of about two years earlier than boys. Thus, a much larger percentage of girls in the first year of middle or junior

Sex and level of maturation may be important factors in understanding the transition from elementary to middle or junior high school.

high school have entered puberty than is the case for boys. These girls' sexual maturation and growth spurt may put them more on par with the older girls and boys in middle or junior high school. Moreover, since it is in middle and junior high school that pressures for dating begin to emerge, girls, many of whom are already moving well along the path to physical maturity, are likely to fare better than boys. It also is helpful to consider whether children making the transition to middle or junior high school are maturing early, on time, or late. Recall from our discussion of early and late maturation in chapter 3 that early-maturing girls, while they seem to get along better with male adolescents, nonetheless, seem to have more difficulty in achievement and academically related matters.

To provide more information about the nature of research on transition to middle or junior high school, we describe a recent investigation by Jacquelyn Hawkins and Thomas Berndt (1985). In this research inquiry, the investigators were interested in the transition from elementary to junior high school, focusing in particular on what the role of friendships might be in this transition. They studied 101 students at three points in time: the spring of the sixth grade (pretransition) and twice in the seventh grade (early and late posttransition). The sample consisted of students in two different kinds of schools, one being a traditional junior high school, the other being a school in which the students were grouped into small teams (one hundred students, four teachers). A number of different measures were called on to assess the students' adjustment, including self-reports,

peer ratings, and teacher ratings. The results indicated that adjustment dropped during posttransition, that is, during the seventh grade. For example, the self-esteem of students in both schools dropped in the seventh grade. However, the influence of the nature of the school environment appeared in the results. For instance, in the traditional junior high school students reported that they received less teacher support than in the sixth grade, but in the junior high with smaller classes more teacher support was reported during posttransition. Also, friendship (as measured by the quality of relationship and contact with friends) improved by late posttransition and influenced adjustment to junior high school. Students with higher scores on friendship measures had a more positive perception of themselves and more positive attitudes toward school in junior high school. These data show how a supportive, more intimate school environment and friendship formation and maintenance can ease the transition for students as they move from the elementary to middle or junior high school years.

This concludes our discussion of the school as a social context for development. So far in this chapter we have looked at three contexts beyond the family that are important in the child's development—peer relationships, play, and schools. (See Concept Table 12.2 for a summary of our discussion of play and schools.) Children spend large chunks of time in these contexts, as they also do in the final context we consider in this chapter, that of watching television, which is described next.

CONCEPT TABLE 12.2
Play and Schools

Concept	Processes/Related Ideas	Characteristics/Description
Play	Functions of play	The functions of play include affiliation with peers, tension release, advances in cognitive development, and exploration. Freud and Erikson describe play in terms of tension release. This view often encourages the use of play therapy with children who have problems. Piaget sees play as a medium that helps advance the child's cognitive development. Berlyne emphasizes the exploratory drive play satisfies. Play is an elusive concept that is difficult to define.
	Types of play	Parten describes five types of play: unoccupied, solitary onlooker, parallel, associative, and cooperative. During the preschool years the controlled repetition of ritual play often increases.
	Pretend play	When children engage in pretend play they have transformed the physical environment into a symbol. In pretend play children often try out many roles. There has been increased interest in the role of cognitive factors in pretend play.
	New directions in play research	Three important new directions of research on play are the assessment of play and the interface of play and cognition and play and language.
Schools	The nature of the child's schooling	Academic and social patterns are intricately interwoven. Various aspects of the school as a social system contribute to the achievement of students in the school. Preschool, elementary school, and secondary school settings vary considerably. While young children have no concept of the classroom as a social system, by adolescence students have developed a rather sophisticated view of the school as a social system.
	Day care and early childhood education	Many experts believe the child-centered approach of early childhood education represents the highest quality of education at any developmental level. Day care is an increasingly used context of infant development. Day care varies considerably, and the infant's social competence may vary according to the quality of day care. Children who attend preschool are more socially competent than those who do not, although they also show more negative behaviors. Compensatory education has attempted to break the poverty cycle through such programs as Project Head Start and Project Follow Through.
	Classroom structure and climate	The most widely discussed issue related to classroom structure and climate has been open versus traditional classrooms. The open classroom concept is multidimensional, and the criteria for its evaluation have often differed from one study to the next. The Classroom Environment Scale has improved assessment. Through meta-analysis, investigators have found that open classrooms are associated with lower language achievement and improved attitudes toward school, but they are not associated with many other aspects of achievement. What seems most important here is linking specific dimensions of open classrooms with specific dimensions of the child—in this regard individualized instruction and emphasis on the role of the child are positively linked with the child's positive self-evaluation.
	Teachers	A definitive profile of the competent teacher is difficult to formulate, although positive teacher traits include enthusiasm, planning, poise, adaptability, and awareness of individual differences. Erikson argues that good teachers promote a sense of industry in children. ATI refers to the importance of looking at the interaction of aptitude and treatment factors rather than at each factor alone.
	Social class and ethnicity	Schools have a stronger middle-class than lower-class bias, and teachers often have different expectations for middle- and lower-class children. Teachers from lower-class backgrounds often have a different orientation toward children than those from a middle-class background. A major result of the investigation of ethnicity and schooling has involved busing, a procedure that has not led to any consistent benefits for minority children. Rather than focusing on busing per se, schools and researchers need to stress what goes on in schools after children get there.
	Transition to middle school or junior high school	The transition from elementary school to middle school or junior high school coincides with a number of individual, familial, and social changes for the child. The transition is associated with adjustment difficulties for many children, although supportive, more intimate school settings, as well as friendships, seem to make the adjustment less difficult. Sex differences and early versus late maturation are other factors that appear to influence adjustment during this transition.

TELEVISION

Few developments in society over the last twenty-five years have had greater impact on children than television has. Many children spend more time in front of the television set than they do with their parents. Although only one of the vehicles of the mass media that affects children's behavior—books, comic books, movies, and newspapers also have some impact—television is the most influential.

To understand the effects of television on children, we study the functions of television, exposure to television, the role of television as a socialization agent, commercials, and the formal features of television.

The Functions of Television

Television has been called a lot of things, not all of them good; depending on one's point of view, it may be a "window on the world," "the one-eyed monster," or "the boob tube." Television has been attacked as one of the reasons that scores on national achievement tests in reading and mathematics are lower now than they have been in the past. Television, it is claimed, attracts children away from books and schoolwork. Furthermore, it is argued that television trains the child to become a passive learner; rarely, if ever, does television call for active responses from the observer.

To what extent do parents actively monitor their children's TV watching?

Television also is said to deceive; that is, it teaches children that problems are easily resolved and that everything always comes out right in the end. For example, it usually takes only from thirty to ninety minutes for detectives to sort through a complex array of clues and discover the killer—and they always find the killer. Violence is pictured as a way of life in many shows. It is all right for police to use violence and to break moral codes in their fight against evildoers. Moreover, the lasting results of violence are rarely brought home to the viewer. A person who is injured appears to suffer for only a few seconds, even though in real life a person with such an injury may not recover for several weeks or months or perhaps not at all. Yet one-half of all first grade children say that the adults on television are like adults in real life (Lyle & Hoffman, 1972).

The functions of television are to entertain and to communicate information. There has been little concern for the use of television in promoting healthy development in children. Television is a business; like all businesses, it is intended to make money, and making money takes precedence over public concern when television programming is planned.

However, there are some possible positive aspects to television's influences on children as well. For one, television presents the child with a world that is often different from the one he or she lives in. This means that through television the child is exposed to a wider variety of views and knowledge than may be the case when he or she is informed only by parents, teachers, and peers.

Aimee Leifer and her colleagues advocate production of more television shows for children that are entertaining but serve a socializing function as well (Leifer, Gordon & Graves, 1974). Examples of shows that already do this are "ZOOM," "Sesame Street," "Fat Albert," and "The Electric Company." "In the best of all worlds, which still recognizes the nature of the industry, there should be high quality television content presenting a wide diversity of characteristics, actions, and values, an increased number of shows devoted to children's programming, and adults who actively guide children in the use of television"(Leifer et al., 1974).

"Mrs. Horton, could you stop by school today?"
© 1981 Martha Campbell.

Children's Exposure to Television

Children watch a lot of television, and they seem to be watching more all the time. In the 1950s three-year-olds watched television for less than one hour a day, and five-year-olds watched for slightly over two hours a day (Schramm, Lyle & Parker, 1961), but in the 1970s preschool children watched television for an average of four hours a day, and elementary school children watched for as long as six hours a day (Friedrich & Stein, 1973).

Aletha Stein (1972) has described some of the different patterns of children's exposure to the media. Other than television, the only medium reaching large numbers of children in this country is books. Children also read comic books, magazines, and some newspaper comic strips; they go to movies; and they listen to the radio and to their records and tapes. Television, comic books, movies, and comic strips can be thought of as pictorial media; the children who use one of these pictorial media regularly tend to use the others also.

However, children who frequently use pictorial media are not necessarily frequent consumers of the printed media, such as books and the written, nonpictorial parts of newspapers and magazines (e.g., Greenberg & Domonick, 1969). Their use of the pictorial media increases until they are about twelve, after which time it declines. Children from low-income backgrounds use pictorial media more than children from middle-income homes do, and black children are exposed to pictorial media more than white children are (Schramm et al., 1961).

Of particular concern has been the extent to which children are exposed to violence and aggression on television. Up to 80 percent of the prime-time shows include such violent acts as beatings, shootings, and stabbings. There are usually about five of these violent acts per hour on prime-time shows. The frequency of violence is even greater on the Saturday morning cartoon shows, where there is an average of more than twenty-five violent episodes per hour (Friedrich & Stein, 1973).

The Role of Television as a Socialization Agent

Television can influence a wide range of children's social behavior. First, we look at the influence of television on aggression, second, at its effect on prosocial behavior, and third, at the social context in which children view television.

Aggression

Television violence contributes to antisocial behavior in children, particularly their aggression toward other children. Let's look at one example that demonstrates this fact clearly. One group of children was exposed to cartoons of the violent Saturday morning type; another group was shown the same cartoons with the violence removed. Children who saw the cartoons with the TV violence later kicked, choked, and pushed their friends more than did the children who saw the same cartoons without the violent acts (Steur, Applefield & Smith, 1974).

Prosocial Behavior

Television can also teach children that it is better to behave in prosocial rather than antisocial ways. Aimee Leifer (1973) has demonstrated how television can instill prosocial behaviors in young children. From the

television show "Sesame Street" she selected a number of episodes that reflected positive social interchanges. She was particularly interested in situations that teach children how to use their social skills. For example, in one exchange two men were fighting over the amount of space available to them; they gradually began to cooperate and to share the space. Children who watched these episodes copied the behaviors and in later social situations applied the lessons they had learned.

Television viewing may also influence the prosocial behavior of older children and adolescents. In an intriguing laboratory/field investigation of antisocial and prosocial television content, Ann McCabe and Richard Moriarity (1977) were able to demonstrate that observing prosocial activities portrayed in television sports shows was significantly related to the incidence of prosocial behavior that children and adolescents engaged in when they actually were observed playing hockey, baseball, and lacrosse. Television sports events were shown to ten- to thirteen-year-olds and fourteen- to seventeen-year-olds. The actual sports shows were edited to focus on prosocial or aggressive content. A third set of children, the control group, viewed sports shows with neutral content. Prosocial behavior was defined as any act, verbal or nonverbal, directed toward others that appeared to encourage, console, or otherwise enhance the well-being of that person or group. The effects of exposure to prosocial incidents on television sports shows were relatively long-lasting: present in the hockey group for as long as twenty-four hours following the sports shows, for as long as one week for the baseball group, and for as long as one to three weeks for the lacrosse group. In this particular study, viewing the antisocial, aggressive television sports shows did not influence the children's aggressive behavior.

The Social Context of Viewing Television

It is important to evaluate television-viewing patterns in the context of parental and peer influences. For example, one survey indicated that parents rarely discuss the content of TV shows with their children (e.g., Leifer et al., 1974). In studying the home environment of children's television viewing, the age period of two and one-half to six seems to be an important formative period for television-viewing habits. In one investigation (Huston, Seigle & Bremer, 1983), families kept a one-week diary of television viewing for each family member. A home interview was conducted prior to the

TABLE 12.2

Average Proportion of Snacks with Added Sugar Selected During Four Weeks of Experimental Intervention

Intervention Week	Condition				
	S–NC	NS–NC	S–C	NS–C	CT
3	.86	.88	.80	.71	.90
4	.74	.80	.73	.58	.84
5	.77	.86	.76	.68	.87
6	.83	.81	.83	.71	.88

Note: S–NC Commercials for food products with added sugar viewed without adult commentary
   NS–C No sugar added and public service announcement with adult commentary
   S–C Sugar added and adult commentary
   NS–NC No sugar added and pronutritional public service announcement with no adult commentary
   CT The control condition, in which children were given no television exposure

From Galst, J. P., "Television food commercials and pronutritional public service announcements as determinants of young children's snack choices," in *Child Development*, 51, pp. 935–938. Copyright © 1980 by The Society for Research in Child Development, Inc. Reprinted by permission.

diary week to obtain information about various child and family characteristics. Although parents with higher occupational status and more education had children who watched less television than their lower-socioeconomic counterparts, maternal employment was not linked with young children's television viewing. Low viewing was characteristic of children who attended preschool and day care. Further, children with younger siblings watched television more than those with older siblings, possibly because they were at home more. Mothers of high viewers reported more arguments about television rules and discussions about television content than did mothers of low viewers. Maternal regulation of television watching was only related to low viewing for the five-year-olds. At age five boys watched more television than girls, and children who used books and the printed media watched less than those who did not. Such looks into the social contexts of children's behavior provide a clearer picture of how social processes influence children's development.

Television Commercials

When we watch television we not only see regular programming, but we are exposed to commercials as well. For example, the average television-viewing child sees more than 20,000 commercials per year! A significant portion of the commercials shown during children's television shows involve food products that are high in sugar (Barcus, 1978). To investigate the effects of television food commercials and pronutritional public service announcements on children's snack choices, Joann Galst (1980) exposed three- to six-year-old children to

television cartoons over a four-week period. The advertising content of the shows consisted of either commercials for food products with added sugar, food products with no added sugar, or pronutritional public service announcements, with or without adult comments about the portrayed product. As shown in table 12.2, the most effective treatment in reducing the child's selection of snacks with added sugar was exposure to commercials for food products without added sugar and pronutritional public service announcements with accompanying positive comments by an adult. Other research (e.g., Peterson, Jeffrey, Bridgewater & Dawson, 1984) suggests that while some children attend to and remember pronutritional TV messages, they do not always change their preferences or consumption.

The Formal Features of Television

There is increasing interest in studying the formal features of television on children's understanding of the content of television shows (Calvert, Huston, Watkins & Wright, 1982; Wright & Huston, 1985). Such formal features include animation, movement, pace, visual techniques (such as fades and special effects), and auditory features (such as music and sound effects). In particular this research has been tied closely to the information-processing model of cognition. For example, initially research focused on the relation of form to children's attention but more recently has emphasized the informational functions of formal features. John Wright and Aletha Huston (1985) stress that form can affect what aspects of a content message are processed and can influence how actively the child engages in such processing.

Children learn rather early in their development that certain formal features of television programs index certain kinds of content. Animation, unusual voices, and sound effects are often associated with child-oriented content. Such features attempt to make the message funny and comprehensible. By contrast, adult male voices, low action, and talking heads are associated with adult-oriented content, which is uninteresting and incomprehensible. Dan Anderson (e.g., Anderson & Lorch, 1983) has argued that the association of specific formal features with comprehensible or incomprehensible content is one reason why children attend differently to these features. The research of Wright, Huston, and their colleagues has expanded Anderson's work to reveal how formal features index entertainment value, humor, and interest level, as well as comprehensibility.

Formal features of television programming that signal child-oriented content not only enhance children's attention, but they increase the likelihood that children will process the content more actively and it is hoped learn the content more thoroughly. One investigation (Campbell, Wright & Huston, 1983) clearly revealed this process. Two parallel sets of public service announcements containing nutritional information were developed. The content of the two announcements was virtually identical, but the forms were different. One set was produced with child-oriented forms—animation, character voices, and lively music. The second set was made with adult-oriented forms— live photography, adult male narration, and soft music. As shown in figure 12.8, five- and six-year-old children attended more to the child-oriented than the adult-oriented version. And children recalled more of the content of the child-oriented version regardless of how difficult the message was (see figure 12.9). The implication is that the form of television shows can lure children into doing some cognitive work when the forms signal that the content is age-appropriate, interesting, comprehensible, or in some other way worth some mental effort (Wright & Huston, 1985).

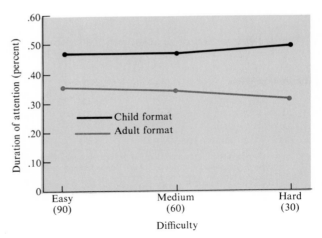

FIGURE 12.8
Mean attention to public service announcements made with child-format and adult-format features at three levels of difficulty (Campbell, Wright, and Huston, 1983).

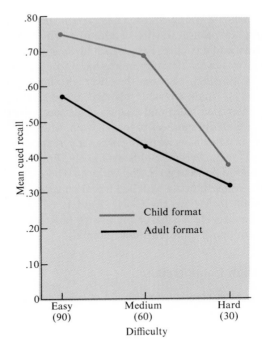

FIGURE 12.9
Mean cued recall for public service announcements made with child-format and adult-format features at three levels of difficulty (Campbell, Wright, and Huston, 1983).

SUMMARY

I. Understanding peers and friendship requires information about the functions of the peer group, the development of peer relations, peer relations and social behavior, the coordinated worlds of peers and families, social information processing and social knowledge, friendships, children's groups, and the role of peer relations in adolescent development.

  A. An understanding of the functions of the peer group requires information about the nature of peers, the role of peers in the development of social competence, cross-cultural comparisons, and the role of peer relations in perspective taking.

  B. Peer relations are now appearing more often in infancy because of the increased number of children in day-care centers. Aggressive interaction increases in early childhood, although friendly interchanges occur more often as well. Children increase the amount of time they spend with peers in elementary school, a time at which their role-taking skills improve.

  C. Two different aspects of social behavior in peer relations that have been studied are popularity and conformity.

  D. The worlds of peers and the family are coordinated; in some ways peer relationships are similar to parent–child relationships, and in others they are different.

  E. There has been increased interest in cognitive factors in peer relations. This interest includes social information processing and social knowledge. There is considerable interest in designing ways to improve children's social skills in peer relations.

  F. Findings about friendships include information on the incidence of friendship and cognitive factors, intimacy, similarity, and shared support and knowledge.

   1. Friendships become much more predominant in the elementary school years and adolescence. As children progress through middle and late childhood they describe their friends with more constructs and provide more complex and organized information about them.

   2. Intimacy in friendship involves self-disclosure and sharing private thoughts. Intimacy increases in the elementary school years and adolescence and is more characteristic of girls than of boys.

   3. Friends are similar on a number of dimensions, among them school-related characteristics.

   4. Friendships involve extensive sharing. Young children provide mutual support, and older children broaden the concept of friendship to include characteristics that do not overlap with self-interests.

   5. Conversational skills enhance friendship formation.

  G. Information about children's groups focuses on the nature of how such groups are formed, the naturalistic study of group formation, and children's groups compared to adolescent groups.

II. Play serves various functions, there are different styles of play, and pretend play is common among young children.

  A. The functions of play include affiliation with other children, the release of anxiety and tension, the advancement of cognitive development, and an increase in exploration of the environment.

  B. Styles of play include unoccupied, onlooker, parallel, associative, and cooperative. Rituals also are common in early childhood.

  C. Pretend play appears for the first time in infancy and seems to peak in the preschool years. Recent research has highlighted the importance of cognitive factors associated with pretend play.

  D. New directions in research on children's play focus on the assessment of play, play and cognition, and play and language.

III. Understanding the role of the school in children's development requires information about the nature of the child's schooling, as well as day care and early childhood education.

  A. Academic and social patterns are intricately interwoven. Various aspects of the school as a social system contribute to the achievement of students in the school.

  B. Preschool, elementary school, and secondary school settings vary considerably. Young children have little or no concept of the school as a social system, but by adolescence they begin to view the school as a sophisticated social setting.

C. Many experts believe the child-centered approach of early childhood education represents the highest quality of education at any developmental level. Day care has been an increasingly used setting for infant development.
   1. The nature of day care varies considerably. The infant's social competence may vary according to the quality of the day care.
   2. Children who attend preschool are more socially competent than those who do not attend, although they show more negative behaviors as well. Compensatory education has attempted to break the poverty cycle through such programs as Project Head Start and Project Follow Through.
D. The most widely studied aspect of classroom structure and climate has been open versus traditional classrooms. The open classroom concept is multidimensional, and the criteria for its evaluation have often differed from one study to the next. The Classroom Environment Scale has improved assessment of the open classroom concept. Through meta-analysis, investigators have discovered that open classrooms are associated with slightly lower language achievement and with more positive attitudes toward school, but they reveal no associations with other aspects of achievement. What seems to be most important here is linking specific dimensions of open classrooms with particular dimensions of the child. In this regard, individualized instruction and emphasis on the role of the child are positively linked with the child's positive self-evaluation.
E. A definitive profile of the competent teacher is difficult to create. However, positive teacher traits include enthusiasm, planning, poise, adaptability, and awareness of individual differences. Erikson argues that good teachers promote a sense of industry in children. ATI refers to the importance of looking at the interaction of aptitude and treatment factors rather than focusing on each factor alone when evaluating educational outcomes.
F. Schools have a stronger middle-class than lower-class bias, and teachers often have different expectations for middle- and lower-class children. Teachers from lower-class backgrounds often have a different orientation toward lower-class children than that of teachers from a middle-class background. The major investigation of ethnicity and schooling has involved busing, a procedure that has not led to any consistent benefits for minority children.
G. The transition to middle or junior high school coincides with a number of individual, familial, and social changes and is associated with adjustment difficulties for many children. However, aspects of the school environment, such as class size and support and friendship formation and maintenance, seem to make the adjustment less difficult. Sex differences and early versus late maturation also appear to be involved in this important transition.
IV. Information about the effects of television on children emphasizes the functions of television, children's exposure to television, the role of television as a social agent, commercials, and formal features.
A. The basic functions of television are to provide information and entertainment. Television provides a portrayal of a world beyond the family, teachers, and peers. However, television may train children to become passive learners, is often deceiving, and often takes children away from reading or studying.
B. Children watch huge amounts of television, with preschool children watching about four hours a day. Up to 80 percent of prime-time shows have violent episodes.
C. Television influences children's aggression and prosocial behavior. Parents rarely monitor or discuss the content of children's TV viewing. Children who read books watch less TV than those who do not read books.
D. Commercials seem to influence children's food preferences.
E. Children's attention and memory of the content of television programs are influenced by the formal features of the programming.

KEY TERMS

aptitude–treatment interaction (ATI) 435

associative play 419

child-centered 429

Classroom Environment Scale (CES) 432

compensatory education 429

cooperative play 419

intention-cue detection 410

intimacy in friendships 413

meta-analysis 433

onlooker play 419

open classroom 432

parallel play 419

peers 403

peer sociotherapy 402

perspective taking 404

play therapy 418

pretend play 421

Project Follow Through 429

Project Head Start 429

ritual 420

semiotic function 424

solitary play 419

top-dog phenomenon 437

unoccupied play 419

REVIEW QUESTIONS

1. Discuss the functions of the peer group and the development of peer relations.
2. What is the nature of popularity and conformity in the peer group?
3. Describe the coordinated world of the family and peers.
4. Discuss the role of cognitive factors in peer relations.
5. Outline the nature of children's friendships, children's groups, and relationships in adolescence.
6. Describe the functions of play, different types of play, and the nature of pretend play.
7. Describe the new directions in research on play.
8. Discuss the impact of schools on children and the nature of schools as a social setting. Also outline what we know about the influence of day care and early childhood education on children.
9. Evaluate what is known about classroom structure and climate, teachers, social class and ethnicity in the school setting, and the transition to middle or junior high school.
10. Describe the effects of television on children.

SUGGESTED READINGS

Garvey, C. (1977). *Play*. Cambridge, MA: Harvard University Press.
   This short book is an excellent overview of the most important aspects of children's play. Many examples reflecting the unique play experiences of children at different developmental levels are given.

Hartup, W. W. (1983). The peer system. In P. H. Mussen (Ed.), *Handbook of child psychology* (4th ed., Vol. 4). New York: John Wiley.
   A detailed look at the development of peer relations from infancy through adolescence by one of the leading researchers on peer relations.

Hartup, W. W., & Rubin, Z. (Eds.). (1985). *Relationships and development*. Hillsdale, NJ: Lawrence Erlbaum.
   Recent thinking about how we construct relationships and how they develop in childhood. Includes articles by many leading researchers.

Harvard Educational Review and/or *Journal of Educational Psychology*
   Go to your library and leaf through the issues of the last three to four years. They include a number of articles on school topics covered in this chapter.

Liebert, R. M., Neale, J. M., & Davidson, E. S. (1973). *The early window: Effects of television on children and youth*. Elmsford, NY: Pergamon Press.
   Excellent overview of the effects of television on youth. Provides ideas about the psychological processes underlying the influence of television as well as critical analysis of whether television has a positive or negative influence on children.

Minuchin, P. P., & Shapiro, E. K. (1983). The school as a context for social development. In P. H. Mussen (Ed.), *Handbook of child psychology* (4th ed., Vol. 4). New York: John Wiley.
   An authoritative, up-to-date review of the role of the school in the child's development.

Rubin, K. H., Gein, G. G., & Vandenberg, B. (1983). Play. In P. H. Mussen (Ed.), *Handbook of child psychology* (4th ed., Vol. 4). New York: John Wiley.
   A very thorough, detailed analysis of what is known about children's play provided by leading researchers in child development. Includes numerous insights into conducting research on children's play and the directions in which research on play is moving.

CHAPTER

13

PERSONALITY AND THE DEVELOPMENT OF THE SELF

PROLOGUE

WHEN I WAS YOUNGER, I USED TO TEASE VEGETABLES

Objective personality tests include questions about a wide array of beliefs, feelings, and experiences. At times certain questions may be perceived by the test taker as trivial or inconsequential. The apparent pointlessness of some test items has generated a parlor game of devising personality inventories composed of only facetious queries. One publicized true–false list, in part created by the humorist Art Buchwald, contains the following questions:

1. When I was younger, I used to tease vegetables.
2. Sometimes I am unable to prevent clean thoughts from entering my mind.
3. I am not unwilling to work for a jackass.
4. I would enjoy the work of a chicken flicker.
5. I think beavers work too hard.
6. It is important to wash your hands before washing your hands.
7. It is hard for me to say the right thing when I find myself in a room full of mice.
8. I use shoe polish to excess.
9. The sight of blood no longer excites me.
10. It makes me furious to see an innocent man escape the chair.
11. As a child, I used to wet the ceiling.
12. I am aroused by persons of the opposite sexes.
13. I believe I smell as good as most people.
14. When I was a child, I was an imaginary playmate.*

There is little doubt that objective personality tests often measure important aspects of personality. However, just what is being measured is sometimes unclear. Personality tests were designed primarily to measure traits that are stable over time and across different situations, that is, enduring characteristics of the person. Yet as we will see in this chapter, there are many contextual, situational influences on personality. Personality tests do a very poor job of measuring any contextual variation in personality. Thus, the personality characteristics measured by objective personality tests do not often generalize well to predict a person's behavior in a variety of situations and contexts. Later in the chapter, we will consider the difficulty of measuring such aspects of personality, self-concept, identity, and social competence.

*From Buchwald, Art, "Fun with personality test," in *American Psychologist*, 1965, 20, 990. Copyright © 1965 by the American Psychological Association. Reprinted by permission of the publisher.

PREVIEW

In this chapter we focus on the nature of children's personality. Initially, we study what personality is, then consider information about trait theory and the important issue of the interaction of traits and situations. Subsequently, we focus on stability and change in children's personality development, and finally we describe the developmental unfolding of the self, independence, and identity during the infant, childhood, and adolescent years.

WHAT IS PERSONALITY?

Psychologists have defined personality in various ways. Gordon Allport (1961) defined it as "the dynamic organization within the individual of those psychophysical systems that determine his characteristic behavior and thought" (p. 28). J. P. Guliford (1959) provided a more concise definition: "a person's unique pattern of traits" (p. 5). Another definition was proposed by David McClelland (1951): "the most adequate conceptualization of a person's behavior in all its detail" (p. 59).

As you can tell, personality has not been all that easy to define. But as Walter Mischel (1976) concludes, there are some common themes to most definitions of the word. **Personality** usually suggests distinctive patterns of behavior, thoughts, or feelings that characterize an individual and refers to the way these behaviors, thoughts, and feelings influence the individual's adaptation to the situations of his or her life.

Perhaps the most important aspect of our definition of personality is its emphasis on the individual. Personality psychology can best be described as the study of individuals—their characteristics and the manner in which they adapt to their environment. Sometimes this study has taken the form of evaluating common themes in the personality of many different individuals, whereas at other times it has been directed at revealing the uniqueness of an individual's adaptive behavior.

PERSONALITY THEORIES, TRAITS, AND TRAIT × SITUATION INTERACTION

In this section we provide a brief review of major personality theories, an examination of trait theory, and a description of the important issue of the interaction of traits and situations.

Review of Personality Theories

Just as we found that many theories have been developed to explain intelligence, so too have many theories been crafted to explain personality. Why do such phenomena as intelligence and personality promote the development of many theories? Intelligence and personality are very global constructs. Because they are broad concepts and include so much of the child's life, it is difficult to pin down their nature precisely. The result is the creation of a number of views that attempt to explain the development of intelligence and personality. We have already considered two of the most prominent theories of personality development in chapter 10—psychoanalytic and social learning. It also is important to consider the role that cognitive developmental theory may play in understanding personality development. Thus, views such as Lawrence Kohlberg's, also described in chapter 10, should be considered when the development of children's personality is at issue. At this time it would be helpful for you to review the main features of psychoanalytic, social learning, and cognitive developmental theories that have important implications for understanding children's personality development. It also is important to evaluate a fourth view of personality: trait theory. We describe this next.

Trait Theory

Our overview of trait theory emphasizes its nature, the study and analysis of traits, the basic themes of the trait approach, and some difficulties with this approach.

The Nature of Trait Theory

Trait theory begins with the commonsense belief that personality can be understood in trait terms. One of the best-known trait theorists was Gordon Allport (1937), who believed that personality traits have a very real existence, being the ultimate reality of personality organization. For Allport, personality traits are tendencies or predispositions to respond. They are not linked to specific situations or stimuli but are relatively general and enduring aspects of the person. Allport believed that the individual's pattern of personality traits determines his or her behavior. Thus, there is an emphasis in Allport's view on behavior's being determined by an internal personality structure rather than by external environmental conditions.

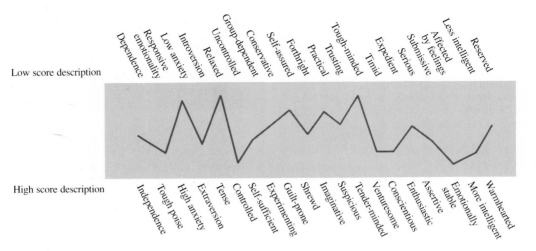

FIGURE 13.1
Sample profile from the Personality Factor Questionnaire (PFQ), a personality test that measures sixteen "personality factors" or traits.

The Study and Analysis of Traits

There are as many as 20,000 terms in the English language that we can legitimately say refer to possible trait differences among people. Quite obviously if we tried to describe or evaluate someone's personality using all or even half of these terms, we would be overwhelmed. Thus trait theorists have called on the technique of **factor analysis,** a complex statistical technique that informs us of the relationships among many different items. Using this technique we can reduce many different trait characteristics to a manageable bundle. Some trait theorists believe we can use this technique to uncover the basic dimensions of personality. For example, Raymond Cattell (1965) argues that there are sixteen such basic dimensions to personality. These are shown in figure 13.1. Another trait theorist, Hans Eysenck (e.g., Eysenck, 1967; Eysenck & Rachman, 1965), believes that there are two basic underlying dimensions to personality, those of introversion–extraversion and stability–instability (see figure 13.2).

The Basic Themes of the Trait Approach

Some of the basic assumptions that trait theorists adhere to are as follows:

1. Personality traits are underlying general dispositions that account for consistencies in children's behavior.
2. Some traits seem to be somewhat superficial and specific, and others are more generalized and basic—these latter traits probably account for the consistency in children's behavior.
3. The main objective of the trait approach is to identify underlying broad dispositions of the child. The trait approach emphasizes that these underlying dispositions can be measured through the use of objective personality tests.
4. The child's behavior, including what the child says about himself or herself is viewed as a sign of underlying traits.

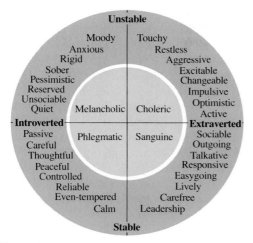

FIGURE 13.2
Eysenck's dimensions of personality. The inner ring shows the "four temperaments" of Hippocrates; the outer ring shows the results of modern factor analytic studies of the intercorrelations between traits by Eysenck and others (Mischel, 1971).

To understand the child's personality we need to study the interaction of traits and situations.

Some Difficulties with the Trait Approach

One of the major problems with the trait approach is that it does not give adequate attention to environmental influences on children's personality and the fact that children's personality is influenced by the contexts and situations in which they live. For example, would an adolescent describe herself as a dominant person or a submissive person? As she thinks about this question, she might say, "Well, I'm dominant with some people and in some situations, but with other people and in other situations I'm pretty submissive." As the situation changes, the individual's personality sometimes fluctuates with it—this is the view of situationism described in chapter 10 under social learning theory. Another major problem with the trait approach is that it does not explain how children's personality traits develop; it just describes those traits. And there is little in the trait approach to inform us of how the key traits of the child interact with one another. Clearly, there is more to the child's personality than just a list of autonomous traits.

The Interaction of Traits and Situations

In recent years even trait theorists have recognized that the study of children's personality traits must deal with how the qualities of the child and the situation influence each other (e.g., Bowers, 1973; Mischel, 1973, 1983). To evaluate the interaction of children's traits and situations we have to focus on how children's traits may vary according to the situation at the moment. Rather than being anxious everywhere, a child may only be anxious under some set of narrow circumstances, such as when she or he has to take a test in math (Endler, 1973).

Though recognizing that they need to account for situational differences in children's traits, trait theorists have criticized the situationism view of personality. They point out that in acknowledging the importance of the situation in determining children's personality we should not lose sight of the child. By combining some of the features of a trait approach and situationism, a view referred to as **trait × situation interaction** has developed (e.g., Mischel, 1979, 1983). This view recognizes the importance of characteristics of the child and the role of contexts and situations in modifying such characteristics in determining the child's personality. Mischel (1983) has argued that being aware of how the child's personality differs according to varied circumstances suggests that children are careful monitors of what they are like and that such information helps them to gain more control over their life rather than being controlled totally by situations. Mischel's (1973, 1983) view stresses that we can better understand the child's personality if we look at the child as an active aware problem solver who constructs and influences the world rather than responding passively to it. In sum, the trait × situation interaction view seems to have more to offer in our attempt to understand the child's personality than either a trait or a situationism view alone. One of the most accurate evaluations of the debate about the relative importance of traits and situations in determining the child's personality is that we should obtain a more accurate evaluation of the child's personality if we give more attention to the specific situations in which specific traits of the child appear. The following guidelines have been offered about the association of specific situations and specific traits of the child (Baron & Byrne, 1984):

1. The narrower and more limited a trait is, the more likely it is to predict the child's behavior. Rather than relying on broad characteristics, much of the current interest in traits is focused on rather specific aspects of the child's behavior. Though researchers may find it difficult to relate general, abstract traits like extraversion or self-concept to actual behavior in a given situation, they may not be as frustrated when they look at narrower traits. Consider the relatively narrow trait of energetic behavior. It has been found that people who actively participate in swimming, running, and other forms of exercise

are perceived by their friends, by experimental observers, and by themselves as energetic (McGowan & Gormly, 1976). As we become more precise about the traits we are describing, we find greater consistency across situations.

2. Some children are consistent on some traits, and other children are consistent on other traits. It may be wise to assume that not all children are equally consistent or inconsistent on the same characteristics. To investigate this possibility, Kendrick and Springfield (1980) asked people to decide on those traits they were the most and least consistent on across situations. In other words, people were asked how consistent they were on being anxious or self-assured, for example. Only on dimensions identified by the people as high-consistency traits in themselves across situations did their friends and parents agree with them. On the traits the individuals said they were not consistent on across situations, friends and parents' perceptions of the subject were more likely to disagree. It has also been argued that some children are just more consistent in their behavior than others, and consequently their behavior can be predicted better by personality measures (Bem & Allen, 1974).

3. Personality traits exert a stronger influence on a child's behavior when situational pressures are less powerful. Some situations, such as school, place considerable situational pressure on a child. Other settings, such as a playground or the child's bedroom, seem to place much less situational constraint on a child and probably allow a much wider range of behaviors to be exhibited. In these latter situations, knowledge of a child's personality traits should be of greater benefit in predicting his or her behavior than in situations where situational pressures are much greater (Monson, Hesley & Chernick, 1982).

As we have discussed personality, we often have talked about it in a general fashion. In reality, many personality researchers, particularly those of the social learning persuasion, study a particular apsect of personality. In the next section we look at several dimensions of the individual child that researchers in the personality field believe are important in understanding the child's development.

DELAY OF GRATIFICATION, EGO CONTROL/RESILIENCY, AND SOCIAL COMPETENCE

Three dimensions of the child that are important aspects of his or her personality development are (1) delay of gratification; (2) ego control/resiliency, and (3) social competence. We consider each of these in turn.

Delay of Gratification

Walter Mischel has intensively studied delay of gratification, a process he believes is an important dimension of the child's personality. **Delay of gratification** refers to the fundamental quality of purposefully deferring immediate gratification for delayed but more desired future gratification. The research focuses on the mechanisms that are involved in self-control (Mischel, 1974, 1984) in terms of both the child and the situation. An enduring concern of the research is how children can overcome stimulus control—the power of situations—and attain ever-increasing volitional control over their own behavior when faced with tempting situations.

Mischel's research has helped to specify how mental representations influence delay of gratification regardless of the power of the situation facing the child at the moment. In a typical experiment, children are given an opportunity to have a desired goal object now or wait until a later time and get an even more preferred object. For example, children may be told that they can have one marshmallow now or two marshmallows if they wait a specified amount of time (such as until the experimenter returns). The results of one experiment involving such delay of gratification are shown in figure 13.3. The data reported in this figure reflect how long the child (mean age of four years) was willing to wait by himself or herself for a preferred but delayed gratification (e.g., two marshmallows rather than one). When the rewards were unavailable for attention (obscured from view during the delay period), children waited more than ten times longer than when the rewards were exposed and could be observed. This suggests that children can gain control over their ability to delay gratification by keeping desired rewards out of sight.

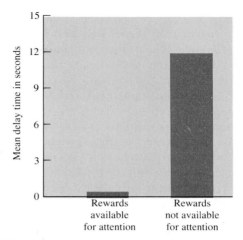

FIGURE 13.3
Delay of gratification as a function of the desired goal object's being available for attention (Mischel, Ebbesen, and Zeiss, 1972).

What might this girl do to improve her self-control and delay of gratification?

Further exploration of how children can control the situation involves their use of cognitive strategies to represent the environment. For example, Mischel's research has revealed that if children represent rewards mentally in consummatory or "hot" ways (such as focusing on their taste, thinking about how yummy, crunchy, and tasty pretzels are), they cannot delay gratification very long (Mischel & Baker, 1975). However, if they focus on their nonconsummatory or "cool" features, thinking of pretzels as if they were sticks or tiny logs, children can wait for them easily. How children mentally represent the outcomes of a situation is very important in determining their ability to delay gratification. In Perspective on Child Development 13.1, Mischel's recent research on delay of gratification is described. This research, which is longitudinal in nature, reveals the stability of delay of gratification over a number of years in children's development.

Mischel's research grew out of a social learning framework. Originally concerned with the situational and cognitive determinants of delay of gratification, only recently has his research looked at the stability of personality over long periods of time. The next dimension of children's personality that we consider did not grow out of the social learning tradition. Rather, interest in the child's ego development has its roots in psychoanalytic and trait theory, both views that stress stability of personality over long periods of time and emphasize the investigation of characteristics of the child rather than how the environment influences the child's behavior.

Ego Control and Ego Resiliency

An important contribution to our understanding of children's personality development is the research of Jack and Jeanne Block (Block, 1971; Block & Block, 1980). While being derived from a different theoretical background, their view of ego control and resiliency looks at some of the same dimensions of the child as Mischel's concept of delay of gratification. For example, the Blocks' conception of **ego control** has its roots in psychoanalytic theory and in particular the aspect of the ego known as the reality principle. Important aspects of ego control are delay of gratification, inhibition of aggression, anticipation of consequences, and caution in ambiguous circumstances. Each of these dimensions involves the child's control of impulses. **Ego resiliency** refers to the elasticity of the child. Elasticity is defined as the capacity of the boundary to change its characteristic of permeability–impermeability, depending on impinging psychological forces, and return to its original level after the forces no longer are pressing. The end points of this continuum are defined by resourceful adaptation to changing circumstances and flexible problem-solving strategies at one end and ego-brittleness on the other end. Ego-brittleness suggests there is little adaptive flexibility on the part of the child, often reflected in perseveration or disorganization of behavior when the child encounters stressful circumstances.

An important aspect of the Blocks' work on ego control and ego resiliency has been the identification of parenting characteristics and child-rearing strategies that predict a lack of impulse control. In one study, as children, undercontrollers tended to be neglected by parents. Mothers were often self-indulgent and narcissistic, while fathers frequently were self-absorbed and indifferent. The home situation often was unpredictable and at times frantic. There was little investment in parenting and typically little agreement about parenting. When parents were angry themselves, it was not unusual for them to displace the anger on their children.

The patterns for overcontrollers were clearer for males than females. The overcontrolling male often experienced parenting that was authoritarian in nature— joyless, constraining, and punitive. Parents usually were conservative and inhibited, with a brittle, controlling mother who ran the household and a father who pursued his own masculine interests. Compliance and responsibility for chores were imposed, and attempts to make the child feel guilty were not uncommon. Sons were often uncontrolled from an early part of their childhood and continued this personality pattern through their adult years, showing little expression of impulses.

With regard to ego resilient individuals, the family pattern involves mothers who are loving, patient, and competent and who encourage the discussion of feelings and problems. Parents of ego resilient individuals also seem to agree on child-rearing practices, are sexually compatible, and have similar moral philosophies. At the other end of the continuum, individuals who are ego-brittle tend to come from families that are conflicted and the mothers are anxious and ambivalent about their role as a mother. The mothers of ego-brittle individuals usually have few intellectual or philosophical interests.

PERSPECTIVE ON CHILD DEVELOPMENT 13.1

DELAY OF GRATIFICATION AND THE SEARCH FOR STABILITY AND ADAPTABILITY IN CHILDREN'S PERSONALITY DEVELOPMENT

T he personality research just described is what is known as process-oriented research. It focuses on the process of how personality can be changed, in this case, by varying how the environment is mentally represented or transformed. But as we saw earlier, a major focus of interest in the study of personality is the child, including the differences between one child and other children. Recently, Mischel has turned his attention to the stability of individual differences in delay of gratification over a number of years.

Mischel's research on the stability of individual differences (e.g., Mischel, 1983; Mischel, Peake & Zeiss, 1984) reveals impressive contiguity between a preschool child's delay of gratification for pretzels or marshmallows and independent ratings of the child's perceived cognitive and social competence made by his or her parents twelve years later. Mischel (1984) points out that while his research has shown that the preschool child who delays behavior in one situation may not do so in even slightly different contexts, he is now finding significant links between the preschool child's delay of gratification and cognitive and social competence in adolescence. As shown in the table opposite, the correlations between delay of gratification in early childhood and cognitive and social competence in adolescence suggest a general picture of a child who delayed gratification in the preschool years as developing into an adolescent who is seen as attentive and able to concentrate, able to express ideas well, responsive to reason, competent, skillful, able to plan ahead and think ahead, and able to cope and deal with stress in a mature way.

Mischel (1984) argues that taken together the results of the process-oriented experimental laboratory studies in conjunction with the investigations of individual differences over time portray personality as both adaptive to situations and consistent across time.

The Relation between Delay of Gratification in Early Childhood and Rated Cognitive and Social Competence During Adolescence

Items	Correlation
Positive	
Is attentive and able to concentrate	.49
Is verbally fluent, can express ideas well	.40
Uses and responds to reason	.38
Is competent, skillful	.38
Is planful, thinks ahead	.35
Is self-reliant, confident, trusts own judgment	.33
Is curious and exploring, eager to learn, open	.32
Is resourceful in initiating activities	.29
Is self-assertive	.29
Appears to have high intellectual capacity	.28
Has high standards of performance for self	.27
Can be trusted, is dependable	.25
Becomes strongly involved in what he does	.25
Is creative in perception, thought, work, or play	.24
Is persistent in his activities	.23
Negative	
Tends to go to pieces under stress, becomes rattled	−.49
Reverts to more immature behavior under stress	−.39
Appears to feel unworthy, thinks of himself as bad	−.33
Is restless and fidgety	−.32
Is shy and reserved, makes social contacts slowly	−.31
Tends to withdraw and disengage himself under stress	−.30
Shows specific mannerisms or behavioral rituals	−.27
Is stubborn	−.25
Turns anxious when his environment is unpredictable	−.25
Is unable to delay gratification	−.25
Attempts to transfer blame to others	−.24
Teases other children	−.22
Tends to be indecisive and vacillating	−.22

Note: The higher the positive number beside the item, the more likely the child was to delay gratification in childhood, while the higher the negative number beside an item, the less likely the child was to delay gratification in early childhood.

We have seen that delay of gratification and ego control/resiliency seem to be important dimensions of the child's personality. Clearly, there are many other dimensions that must be considered as well. As we saw in our discussion of traits, thousands of such characteristics can be used to describe children. For example, the child's sex-role orientation is an important dimension of personality. And so is the child's moral orientation. Indeed, these are such important dimensions of the child that we will deal with them in separate chapters (14 and 15). Now, however, we consider another important dimension of the child that has been given increased research attention in recent years—social competence.

Social Competence

It is the goal of most parents to rear a child who becomes socially competent. The concept of social competence has presented problems for conceptualization and assessment, however. In this section we follow the thinking of Everett Waters and Alan Sroufe (1983), first defining the socially competent child and then providing a developmental portrayal and assessment of **social competence.**

What Is Social Competence?

Waters and Sroufe (1983) define the socially competent child as "one who is able to make use of environmental resources to achieve a good developmental outcome" (p. 81). Resources in the environment are those things that can support or develop the ability to coordinate affect, cognition, and behavior in the service of short-term adaptation and long-term developmental progress. In infancy, adult social agents clearly are salient. In early childhood and beyond, play and peer relations may be very important. From early childhood on, the range of potential resources expands.

Resources within the individual are an important part of social competence as well. The possibilities range from specific skills and abilities to general constructs such as self-esteem. In our discussion of personality thus

Peer relations are an important aspect of social competence beginning early in development.

far in this chapter, we have encountered other important resources within the child. Delay of gratification, ego resiliency, and ego control are important strengths of the socially competent child. Need for the achievement, or the motivation to do something well, is also an important dimension of the socially competent child, particularly in an achievement-oriented society such as the United States (McClelland, 1955). In addition, the entire class of constructs labeled self, self-esteem, self-concept, and so on denote resources within the child, not in terms of stable traits but more in terms of theories the child has about his or her actions and abilities. It is important to remember that, as with resources in the environment, resources within the child usually have to be referenced to a particular point in development (for example, dependency is probably a positive characteristic in infancy but is more closely tied to a lack of social competence by adolescence).

Development and Assessment of Social Competence

First, we consider developmental aspects of social competence, then discuss some important assessment issues involved in social competence.

Developmental Considerations   Waters and Sroufe (1983) have attempted the difficult task of adapting the general definition of social competence, involving the effective tapping of resources, to each developmental period. This is accomplished for the early years of development by defining the salient issues of each period. From the developmental perspective, then, a key question becomes: What are the central issues or occupying tasks for twelve-month-olds, two-year-olds, the preschooler? And how well is the child doing in regard to these issues? In a general way we are trying to discover how well the child is adapting (drawing on environmental and personal resources) to the salient issues of a particular developmental period.

The key to age-appropriate assessment of social competence is to select the central issues for each developmental period. We should point out that child developmentalists do not always agree on what these issues are. However, those presented by Waters and Sroufe (1983) provide a good starting point and get us thinking developmentally about the unfolding of social competence. In table 13.1, a sequence of issues spanning the early years of development is presented. These issues

are not hurdles associated with one age; rather, they are issues that are involved to some extent in every phase of life. For instance, the infant is developing its sense of independence from birth, and individuation remains an important issue in adulthood. Still, it seems appropriate to conceive of issues as being relatively more salient at certain phases of the life cycle. Individuation, for instance, is an important issue for the toddler years. On the other hand, while infants can engage in peer interaction, peer relations seems more central to the child's adaptation in the preschool years and beyond.

Assessment   In describing the important features of assessing social competence, Waters and Sroufe (1983) point out four considerations: (1) broadband versus narrow assessments, (2) real behavior versus laboratory tasks, (3) assessments emphasizing the coordination of affect, cognition, and behavior, and (4) taxing behavioral and integrative/adaptive capacity.

Recall from our discussion of socialization in chapter 10 that it is important to assess both the global and more fine-grained aspects of the child's social behavior. Waters and Sroufe (1983) argue that, at least initially, it would be wise to understand broadly what the child's

TABLE 13.1
Issues in Early Development

Phase	Age (months)	Issue	Role for caregiver
1	0–3	Physiological regulation	Smooth routines
2	3–6	Management of tension	Sensitive, cooperative interaction
3	6–12	Establishing an effective attachment relationship	Responsive availability
4	12–18	Exploration and mastery	Secure base
5	18–30	Individuation (autonomy)	Firm support
6	30–54	Management of impulses, sex-role identification, peer relations	Clear roles and values, flexible self-control

From Sroufe, L. Alan, "The coherence of individual development: Early care, attachment, and subsequent developmental issues," in *American Psychologist*, 34, (10), pp. 834–841. Copyright © 1979 by the American Psychological Association. Reprinted by permission of the publisher and author.

social competence is like. For example, in studying toddler problem solving, the focus might be on enthusiasm, persistence, flexibility, and enjoyment in dealing with the problem rather than the part of the problem first addressed, the tool used first, or even the time required to solve the problem. In the attachment literature, researchers have often assessed the infant's tendency to stay close to its mother in terms of specific discrete behaviors. Often counts of touching the mother, looking at her, and the like are selected for measurement. However, such measures tend to be more situation specific than broad-based measures. An alternative approach is to select more broadly defined measures of proximity-seeking or contact-maintaining behaviors. Assessments of this nature usually do not involve frequency counts of behaviors but rather rating scales. Thus, in assessing attachment, Ainsworth, Sroufe, Waters, Main, and others have begun to use ratings of secure and insecure attachment rather than frequency counts of proximity seeking in their attempt to accurately capture the nature of social competence in infants. Keep in mind, however, that in our assessment of the child's development it is wise to consider both fine-grained, behavioral measures of the child and the more broadly based measures Waters and Sroufe recommend (e.g., Maccoby & Martin, 1983).

A second issue in assessment focuses on whether we should be assessing social competence through specific tasks in controlled laboratory contexts or designing more naturalistic and ecologically valid measures. As we discussed in chapter 1 in our description of methods, advantages and costs are associated with either choice. Developmental psychologists interested in assessing social competence are likely to find themselves going into and out of laboratory situations. However, Waters and Sroufe (1983) argue that early in the development of assessment devices for measuring social competence, it is particularly important to conduct ecologically valid assessment in real-life circumstances. They reason that laboratory measures often evaluate a narrow dimension of social competence whereas real-life, naturalistic assessments typically are more broadly based, which fits with their first assessment recommendation.

A third assessment issue in social competence focuses on the evaluation of how the child coordinates affect, cognition, and behavior. Waters and Sroufe believe that information about early social behavior (social attachment, problem solving, peer interaction, and self/behavior relationships) suggests we should be studying how affect, cognition, and behavior are coordinated. Assessing the coordination of these three dimensions rather than each dimension alone fits nicely with the belief that broad-based measures of social competence are needed. This also meshes with the belief that the affective world of the child is important, just as his or her cognitive and behavioral worlds are. Cognition and behavior are obviously important dimensions of the child's development, but in isolation they may not effectively reflect social competence. Social competence clearly is linked to motivation and control, and in circumstances where these are relevant, affect often is involved and frequently arises from either success or failure. As we see next, inclusion of affect in the assessment of social competence is important when critical events or transactions occur in the child's world.

Waters and Sroufe (1983) also believe that assessment of social competence needs to include measures that plug into the child's integrative/adaptive capacity in dealing with critical events or transactions in his or her world. Even within the range of typical behaviors, there are circumstances that challenge or tax the child's integrative capacity: for example, temperature change, sustained face-to-face interaction, response to separation and union, exploration of new environments, responses to success and failure, and sustained social play.

In sum, while the construct of social competence presents problems in conceptualization and assessment, the work of Waters and Sroufe (1983) is an important step toward defining the concept, describing its development, and providing ideas about how it should be assessed. In our discussion of different dimensions of the child in this section, we discovered that researchers are concerned with how stable personality is over time and across situations. Recall how carefully Mischel assessed delay of gratification from the time the child was in the preschool years until he or she reached the adolescent years. Remember that Mischel described how delay of gratification remained stable across the childhood years. Concept Table 13.1 summarizes our discussion of personality, traits, and social competence to this point. Next we focus in even greater detail on the issue of stability and change, one of the enduring concerns in the study of children's personality.

CONCEPT TABLE 13.1
Personality, Traits, and Social Competence

Concept	Processes/Related Ideas	Characteristics/Description
What is personality?	Individual, adaptation	Personality can be defined as the study of individuals and the manner in which they adapt to their environment.
Personality theories	Psychoanalytic, social learning, and cognitive developmental theories	These three theories, described in some detail in chapter 10, are very important theories of personality.
Trait theory	Its nature	Trait theory begins with the commonsense view that personality can be understood in trait terms and that the patterning of traits determines a child's behavior.
	The study and analysis of traits	Theorists and researchers vary in their views of which traits are central to understanding personality. Some study many traits; others focus only on one or two dimensions of personality, such as extraversion–introversion.
	Basic themes of the trait approach	Traits are underlying dispositions that account for consistency in children's behavior; some traits seem to be superficial while others are more basic. The main objective of the trait approach is to identify underlying broad dispositions; one's behavior is viewed as a sign of underlying traits.
	Difficulties with the trait approach	Trait theory does not give adequate attention to environmental influences on personality and the fact that children's personality may vary from one situation to another. Also, trait theory does not explain how personality develops in children. Further, there is little information about how key traits interact.
The interaction of traits and situations	Its nature	The characteristics of the child and the role of contexts and situations in modifying such characteristics are important in determining the child's personality.
	Some guidelines for the interaction of traits and situations	The more narrow and limited the trait is, the more likely it will predict the child's behavior. Some children are more consistent on certain traits than others, and other children are more consistent on other traits. Personality traits exert a stronger influence on a child's behavior when situational pressures are less powerful.
Delay of gratification, ego control/ resiliency, and social competence	Delay of gratification	Mischel's longitudinal work on delay of gratification in children reveals considerable stability over time, yet adaptation to different situations.
	Ego control/resiliency	The Blocks have studied ego control and ego resiliency and found that these important dimensions of personality development in children are related to a number of parental characteristics and parenting styles.
	Social competence	Waters and Sroufe describe social competence in terms of effective use of resources in the environment and resources in the individual. They evaluate different dimensions of social competence and discuss salient issues in social competence at different developmental levels. Waters and Sroufe also outline four assessment issues in social competence: global/fine-grained; naturalistic/ laboratory; coordination of cognition, affect, and behavior; and integrative/adaptive capacity in dealing with taxing circumstances.

STABILITY AND CHANGE IN PERSONALITY DEVELOPMENT

Our discussion of stability and change in children's personality development focuses first on some basic ideas about the nature of stability and change in personality development and second on some longitudinal studies of personality that have implications for understanding the stability–change issue.

The Issue of Stability and Change in Personality Development

The degree to which personality is stable or changes is a major issue in development. The issue may be approached in many different ways. We may wish to evaluate the extent to which early childhood personality characteristics predict personality characteristics in later childhood or even adulthood. For example, is the introverted young child also the introverted older child? Is the anxious child also the anxious adolescent? We may ask whether the achievement-oriented second grade girl is striving hard to be successful at the age of twelve, or to what extent the depressed three-year-old is still that way at the age of ten. Further, rather than looking only at the stability of a single personality characteristic, such as introversion, we may evaluate how one or several characteristics at one point in childhood predict another or several other characteristics at a later point in development. Or we may be interested in how social experiences, such as peer relationships, family experiences, and work experiences, can predict personality characteristics later in childhood or adolescence. And we may be concerned about whether such prediction is possible over a short period of time, such as several months or years, or over a longer period of time, such as ten to twenty years.

To the extent that there is consistency or continuity from one period of time to another in some attribute of the child's personality, we usually describe the child's personality as being stable. In contrast, to the extent that there is little consistency from one period of time to another in the child's personality, we refer to change or discontinuity in personality.

Personality theorists are often categorized on the basis of whether they stress stability and consistency in personality across time as well as across situations. Personality theorists called personologists or traditional trait theorists argue for consistency and stability, whereas contextual, situational theorists believe that

To what extent are personality characteristics, such as introversion and extraversion, stable?

there is little consistency and stability in personality but rather a great deal of change. The latter heavily stress the importance of studying the context in which behavior occurs because they believe the child's behavior often changes according to the context or situation in which the child is. We will discover the importance of studying the contextual aspects of the child's personality in combination with the characteristics a child brings to a situation as we survey some of the major efforts to evaluate the extent to which the child's personality remains stable through childhood and even into adulthood and the extent to which personality changes in the childhood years.

It is a common finding in the study of continuity and discontinuity in children's personality development that the closer in time we measure personality characteristics, the more stable a child's personality will appear. Thus, if we measure a child's self-concept at the age of five and then again at the age of seven, we are likely to find more stability than we would if we measured the child's self-concept at age five and then again at age ten. The task of evaluating continuity over long periods of time is a difficult one. Yet if we are to come up with even reasonable ideas about this issue, we need to follow children longitudinally rather than assess their lives in a cross-sectional manner.

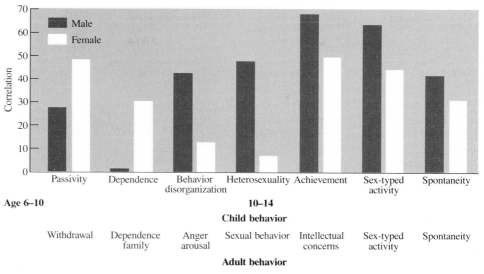

FIGURE 13.4
Summary of relations between selected child behaviors and
phenotypically similar adult behaviors (Kagan and Moss, 1960).

Two Longitudinal Studies of Personality in Children

To help you gain a sense of how longitudinal studies bear on the stability–change issue, we describe two well-known investigations. First, we consider the Fels Longitudinal Study, and then we evaluate the New York Longitudinal Study.

The Fels Longitudinal Study

In the **Fels Longitudinal Study,** Jerome Kagan and Howard Moss (1962) found that sex-typed characteristics tended to show some stability from the elementary school years through the end of the adolescent years. Investigating ratings of behavior in age periods birth to three, three to six, six to ten, ten to fourteen, and adulthood, Kagan and Moss (1962) found that the stability of the behaviors was linked to cultural sex-role standards. Mastery of intellectual tasks and sex-typed interests, which are reinforced for both boys and girls in our culture, were very consistent for both boys and girls from the ages of six to ten through early adulthood (age range nineteen to twenty-nine, mean twenty-four years). (See figure 13.4.) However, because in our culture males are more frequently rewarded for being aggressive and girls for being dependent, the Kagan and Moss study revealed consistency across these time periods for boys' aggressive behavior and for girls' dependency behavior.

The Kagan and Moss study, which was completed in the late 1950s, may not reflect our society's changing sex-role standards, when adolescence and adulthood may lead to more upheaval in commitment to sex-typed behaviors. Because distinctions in cultural standards for males and females are becoming more blurred, it is now easier for a female at eighteen to thirty years of age to choose a career once labeled "masculine" and not to show as much dependent behavior as was necessary at an earlier point in our history. Some would argue, however, that sex roles are more clearly defined for men than they are for women in our society. More will be said about changing sex roles in the next chapter.

The New York Longitudinal Study

An extensive longitudinal study conducted with a group of boys and girls in New York City provided some answers to the question of how various dimensions of personality change or remain stable (Thomas, Chess & Birch, 1970). The **New York Longitudinal Study** was begun in 1956, so the children are now adults. However, because of the inevitable lag between research and the public reports on it, information is available only from the subjects' birth to the beginning of their adult years. In chapter 2 we pointed out the existence of some stability of temperament in the infant and early childhood years. There we commented that while some stability of temperament occurs early in development through experiences, such temperament can be at least partly modified. Here we think about temperament once again, at this point in terms of stability and change in personality development.

Alexander Thomas and his associates set out to describe temperament as broadly as possible and to obtain as much information as they could. To this end, they interviewed the parents of 138 subjects from middle-class homes four times a year during the first year of life, twice a year for the next four years, and once a year after that. Interviews ranged over a wide variety of topics (eating, sleeping, playing, meeting new people, interacting with parents and siblings, and the like), with the goal of understanding the style of each individual's behavior across many situations. While temperament was rather stable in the early years of the child's development, the identification of temperament became more difficult as the child entered the adolescent period. Behavioral characteristics became increasingly influenced by the interaction of temperament, motivation, capability, and special events in life. The only predictable aspect of the period from infancy through adolescence was that the child would experience person–environment interaction. Consistency in development came from continuity over time in both the child and important aspects of his or her environment. And changes in development were produced by major changes in the child or in his or her environment.

In sum, the early years of child development are clearly an important element in predicting personality later in childhood, in adolescence, and even in adulthood. However, there is every reason to believe that later experiences in childhood are also important in determining what the older child's personality is like. And, in trying to predict the adolescent's personality development, experiences in infancy, childhood, and adolescence are important to consider. Thus, in trying to understand personality it would be misleading to look only at the child's life in the present tense ignoring the developmental unfolding of personality. So, too, would we be far off target if we only searched through the child's first five years of life in trying to predict the older child's or adolescent's personality. The truth about personality, then, lies somewhere between the infant determinism of Freud and a contextual approach that ignores the developmental unfolding of personality completely.

THE SELF, INDEPENDENCE, AND IDENTITY

Individuals carry with them a sense of who they are and what makes them different from everyone else. "I am male, bright, an athlete, a political liberal, an extravert, and a compassionate person," thinks one eighteen-year-old, taking comfort in his uniqueness. "There is no one quite like me. I am 5'9" tall and weigh 140 pounds. I grew up on a farm and attend the state university, where I take courses in secondary education. I am not married, but some of my friends are. I want to be a home economics teacher; I am expert at building canoes; and when I am not studying for exams, I write science fiction stories that I hope to publish some day." Real or imagined, the individual's developing sense of self and uniqueness is a strong motivating force in his or her life. But how early in development does the individual begin to sense his or her separate existence from others? Our further consideration of the self begins with a distinction between the "I" and "me" aspects of the self, then focuses on the development of the self and independence in infancy. Following this we chart the developmental unfolding of the self in the early childhood and elementary school years, examine adolescence and the developmental tasks of independence and identity, and consider the nature of self-concept and its measurement.

"I" and "Me": The Self as Knower and as Object

Most scholars who have devoted thoughtful attention to understanding the self have concluded that two distinct but closely intertwined aspects of self exist (Harter, 1983). Such a distinction was made very early in psychology by William James (1963), who described the "I" as knower in contrast to the "me" as aggregate of things objectively known. More recently, Ruth Wylie (1979) has continued the distinction between "I" and "me" in understanding the self. She contrasts the self as active agent or process with the self as the object of one's knowledge and evaluation. The "I," then, is the active observer, while the "me" is the observed (that is, the product of the observing process when attention to the self occurs). However, most research attention has been given to the self as an object of one's knowledge and evaluation as indicated by

© 1985 United Feature Syndicate, Inc.

the many studies of children's self-concept and self-esteem (Wylie, 1979). Self-concept and self-esteem are viewed as objects of one's knowledge in this categorization of the self. First, we focus on the topics of self-concept and self-esteem and then turn to the recent emphasis on the self as knower.

Self-Concept and Self-Esteem

While early in the history of psychology William James showed a strong interest in the self, during the twentieth century the psychologists most interested in the self have followed the tradition of **humanism,** which places a strong emphasis on the role of the self and self-concept as central to understanding the child's development (Gordon, 1975; Maslow, 1970; Rogers, 1951). The humanistic approaches have little scientific credibility. Indeed, the humanists believe scientific approaches keep the investigator from learning the most important facts about the child's existence—his or her uniqueness as a person and creative potential, for instance. In this regard, the humanists believe that science is too concerned with general principles that are common to all children rather than the unique nature of each child. Humanists also believe that to understand the child it is necessary to grasp the essence of the child's global self. In particular, they believe that the child's **global self-concept,** how he or she generally perceives himself or herself, is a key organizing principle of personality.

Theorists such as the humanists, who advocate the importance of perceptions such as self-concept, are taking a **phenomenological approach** to the study of children's development. That is, the child's perception

of the world is more important in understanding his or her development than is his or her actual behavior. From this view, reality exists in the perceptions of the child not in the actual behavior of the child. As you can readily anticipate, this approach to the child comes into direct conflict with the behavioral approach, which advocates that the key ingredients of the child's development are his or her behaviors, not perceptions of behavior.

One aspect of the child's self-perceptions that is closely linked to self-concept is self-esteem. Many theorists and researchers use the labels interchangeably while others believe a distinction can be made between self-concept and self-esteem. For example, one definition of self-esteem that places it in the same domain as self-concept is the value children place on themselves and their behavior, which would be investigated by finding out how good or bad children feel about themselves (McCandless & Evans, 1973). Other definitions of self-esteem only embrace the positive parts of self-concept, such as feeling proud about oneself or evaluating one's attributes highly.

One recent study of parenting practices and the self-esteem of preschool children revealed the importance of the consistency of parenting and the sensitivity of the parents to the young child's signals (Burkett, 1985). In particular the parents' respect for their children as individuals separate from them and as having their own needs were the best predictors of the preschool child's self-esteem. Another investigation by Stanley Coopersmith (1967) provided further information about the parenting factors that are important in the elementary school child's self-esteem. Coopersmith developed a

Parent-child connectedness is an important aspect of the child's self-esteem, and so is the parent's respect for the child's individuality.

self-esteem scale that involved asking the child to read a number of statements and check whether each of these is "like me" or "unlike me." The statements included the extent to which the child worries about himself or herself, the degree to which the child is proud of his or her school performance, how popular the child is with peers, how happy the child is, and so on. The following parental characteristics were significantly linked with the children's self-esteem: expression of affection, concern about the child's problems, harmony in the home, participation in friendly joint activities, availability to give competent, organized help when needed, setting clear and fair rules, abiding by these rules, and allowing the child freedom within well-prescribed limits.

The Self as Knower

A number of contemporary researchers are beginning to develop insight into the **self as knower** (Broughton, 1981; Dickstein, 1977; Gergen, in press; Greenwald & Pratkanis, in press; Harter, 1983; Lapsley & Quintana, 1985; Lewis & Brooks-Gunn, 1979). The interest is in crafting an account of the self that not only encompasses the self as object of knowledge, attention, and evaluation, but one that also includes the self as an active observing process. Thus, there is interest in combining "I" and "me" into a common theoretical account of the self. One of the first steps is to establish the domain of the self as knower. The approach in contemporary psychology that offers the most help in such a project is information processing (Lapsley & Quintana, 1985).

One area of interest that is emerging in the investigation of the self as knower is memory development. Two aspects of memory thought to reflect the self as knower are self-generation and self-reference. Self-generation describes instances when information that is self-generated is more easily retrieved and recalled than information that is passively encountered (Bobrow & Bower, 1969; Jacoby, 1978). For instance, individuals are more likely to recall their own contributions to discussion of a controversial topic than the inputs of others (Greenwald & Albert, 1968). Self-reference refers to the efficient retrieval of information encoded in terms of the self as opposed to information not self-encoded.

There is a clear indication in a number of memory studies that individuals are more likely to remember information that is encoded about the self than information that is not self-referenced (Markus, 1977; Rogers, 1981). For example, in one investigation (Rogers, Kuiper & Kirker, 1977), individuals were given either physical, acoustic, or semantic-meaning kinds of tasks. Another group of people were asked whether a particular word could be related to themselves. As suggested by figure 13.5, self-reference was the most effective strategy. For example, if the word *win* were on the list, they might think of the time they won a bicycle race, and if the word *cook* appeared, they might image the last time they cooked dinner.

An important developmental implication from research on memory for understanding the self as knower is the rather consistent finding that young children do not spontaneously use encoding and retrieval strategies (e.g., Flavell, Beach & Chinsky, 1966; Siegler, 1983). The weak performance of young children on memory tasks may be due to a production deficiency; that is, they may not know how or when to use appropriate memory strategies, although they often can be taught such strategies. Thus we would not anticipate that young children would encode to-be-remembered information with reference to the self (self-reference) or to construct information in a way that would help retrieval (self-generation). For instance, young children do not always produce their own elaborations of to-be-remembered information (Pressley, 1982). However, when the children are provided elaboration by the experimenter, or are given an encoding or retrieval strategy, their memory improves (Levin, 1976). Older children, however, are much better when they generate their own strategies than when they use strategies provided by the experimenter (Pressley, 1982; Siegler,

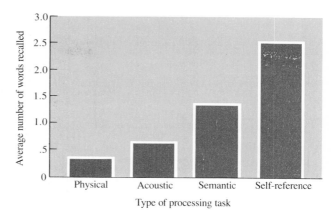

FIGURE 13.5
Number of words recalled as a function of level of processing (Rogers, Kueper, and Kirker, 1977).

1983). One possibility is that developmental differences in strategy use by children reflect the differential availability of a self schema for organizing memory input (Lapsley & Quintana, 1985).

We have only called attention to one general area of the self as knower—memory—to reveal the importance of information processing in understanding the active nature of the self. Two other examples suggest further ways in which the information-processing perspective might clarify our understanding of the self: At what point in development do children recall their successes and failures? When do children see the self as an important contributor to cause and effect in their world?

Now that we have studied the important distinction between the self as knower and the self as object, we turn our attention to the developmental unfolding of the self. In our developmental discussion, you will find information about the self as both knower and object.

The Development of the Self and Independence in Infancy

First we consider the emergence of the self in the first two years of life. Then we turn to the push for independence in the second year of life.

The Development of the Self in Infancy

In chapter 11 we saw the importance of attachment to a caregiver in the first year of life. But we soon will see that a true sense of self may not develop until the second year of life, at least in terms of consolidation of basic self categories.

TABLE 13.2
Development of Self-Knowledge, Emotional Experience, and Cognitive Growth

Age in Months	Self-Knowledge	Emotional Experience	Cognitive Growth
0–3	Interest in social objects; emergence of self–other distinction	Unconditioned responses to stimulus events (loud noise, hunger, etc.)	Reflexive period, primary circular reactions
3–8	Consolidation of self–other distinction, recognition of self through contingency	Conditioned responses (strangers, incongruity)	Primary and secondary circular reactions
8–12	Emergence of self-permanence and self categories; recognition of self through contingency and onset of feature recognition	Specific emotional experiences (fear, happiness, love, attachment)	Object permanence, means–ends, imitation
12–24	Consolidation of basic self categories (age, gender, emergence of efficacy); feature recognition without contingency	Development of empathy, guilt, embarrassment	Language growth; more complex means–ends; symbolic representations

Children begin the process of developing a sense of self by learning to distinguish themselves from others. To determine whether, in fact, infants are able to recognize themselves, psychologists have traditionally relied on mirrors. In the animal kingdom only the great apes can learn to recognize their reflection in a mirror, but human infants can accomplish this feat by approximately eighteen months of age. The ability of the toddler to recognize his or her mirrored reflection seems to be linked to the ability to form a mental image of his or her own face. This development of a sense of self does not occur in a single step but is rather the product of complex understanding that develops very gradually.

Michael Lewis and Jeanne Brooks-Gunn (1979) have conducted a number of studies of the development of the infant's ability to recognize the self. Lewis and his colleagues (e.g., Lewis & Cherry, 1977) believe that the process of self-development occurs at the same time as and parallels the more traditional cognitive and emotional aspects of development. In table 13.2 the parallel development of self-knowledge, emotional experience, and cognitive growth is shown (Lewis & Brooks-Gunn, 1979).

The mirror technique, initially used with animals, has been modified for use with human infants. The mother puts a dot of rouge on her infant's nose. During a pretest, an observer watches to see how frequently the infant touches his or her nose. Next the infant is

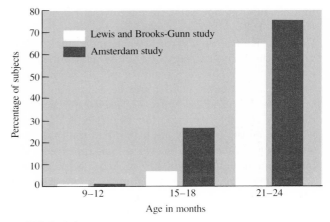

FIGURE 13.6
The development of self-recognition in infancy. Percentage of subjects showing recognition of the rouge by touching, wiping, or verbally referring to it in two different studies at different ages (Lewis and Brooks–Gunn, 1979).

placed in front of a mirror, and observers detect whether nose touching increases. Figure 13.6 presents the results of two separate investigations of self-recognition using the rouge and mirror technique. Thus in the second half of the second year of life there is good evidence that infants recognize their own image and coordinate the image they see with the actions of touching their own body (Amsterdam, 1968; Lewis & Brooks-Gunn, 1979).

The Development of Independence

Infants not only develop a sense of self, but they push for independence as well. Harriet Rheingold (1973), a prominent researcher in the area of independent behavior, describes her awareness of the infant's push for independence:

> Some eight years ago I began a series of studies designed to measure the effect of a strange environment on the behavior of infants at ten months of age. Only after the last sentence of the discussion of the study was written did I realize that it was not so much the strange environment that caused the distress of the children placed in it without their mothers, nor even the absence of their mothers, as it was being *placed* and *left alone* (Rheingold, 1969). That this was so was demonstrated in a later study in which infants the same age were given the opportunity to leave their mothers and enter that same strange environment by themselves (Rheingold & Eckerman, 1970). All the children did enter on their own initiative, even when the environment contained no toy. Not only did they enter, but they crept to places in the room from which they could not see the mother. They returned to the mother's room, left again, and returned again—some infants many times—but on a third of the returns they did not contact the mother. (Rheingold, 1973, pp. 182–183)

Rheingold (1973) indicated that in the process of investigating the influence of different environments, it became clear that she was seeing infants move away from their mothers. A review of the nonhuman primate research on independence (Rheingold & Eckerman, 1970) provided support for the belief that infants detach themselves from their mothers. As the nonhuman primates grow older, they leave their mothers more frequently, go farther, and stay away longer. To find out how far human children would stray from their mothers, Rheingold & Eckerman (1970) placed a mother and her child in a backyard, where the mother was seated and the child was left free to move around. They found a correlation between the age of the children (from one to five years) and the distance they traveled from their mothers. However, the continuing relationship to the mother was seen when older children were observed often bringing small items, such as pebbles and leaves, to their mothers. These observations are similar to the concept of emotional refueling described by Margaret Mahler (1979b).

Infants not only develop a sense of self, but they also push for independence.

Erik Erikson (1968) also believes independence is an important theme of infant development, particularly in the second year of life. Erikson calls the second stage in his eight-stage life-cycle theory autonomy versus shame and doubt. He believes this stage roughly corresponds to the second year of life. The major significance of this stage in the life cycle lies in rapid gains in muscular maturation, verbalization, and the coordination of a number of conflicting action patterns characterized by tendencies to "hold on" and "let go." Through such changes, the highly dependent child begins to experience his or her autonomous will, and the mutual regulation between adult and child faces a severe test. This stage becomes decisive in determining whether the child will feel comfortable in self-expression or feel anxious and show extensive self-restraint. Erikson believes that if the child does not develop a sense of self-control and free will at this point in development, he or she may become saddled with a lasting propensity for doubt and shame.

For the toddler to develop independence, a firmly developed early trust is necessary. The infant must have discovered that his faith in himself and his world are not going to be jeopardized if he is going to begin to "stand on his own two feet." The sense of autonomy that parents are able to grant to their small children depends on the dignity and sense of personal independence they experience in their own lives. In other words, the toddler's sense of autonomy is a reflection of the parents' dignity as autonomous beings. Erikson believes that much of the lasting sense of doubt developed in the toddler is a consequence of the parents' frustrations in marriage, in work, and in citizenship.

Erikson goes on to describe how the struggles and triumphs of this stage of development contribute to the identity crisis all adolescents undergo, either by supporting the formation of a healthy identity or by contributing to estrangement and confusion. The development of a sense of autonomy during the toddler years is critical for the development of identity during adolescence because out of the early childhood experience is born the courage to become an independent individual who can choose and shape his or her own future. The influence of the successful resolution of the autonomy–shame stage on the development of identity is reflected in one adolescent's statement, "I am what I can will freely."

The Development of the Self in Childhood

First we consider changes in the self during early childhood and then turn to further changes in the elementary school years. In particular, we call on Robert Selman's ideas on the development of the self and perspective taking.

Eleanor Maccoby (1980) concluded that initially children's self-definition focuses on external characteristics, such as how they look, where they live, and what activities they are involved in, but later—after about the age of six or seven—children begin to describe themselves more in terms of psychological traits (e.g., how they feel, their personality characteristics, and their relationships with others). With increasing age, group membership also assumes a more important status in self-definition. Maccoby (1980) also believes that another important part of the development of a self-concept is the child's increasing ability to understand how he or she is viewed by others. Very young children have difficulty in understanding other people's perspective of them, and they often are not aware of the impressions their behavior makes on others. Gradually, however, children begin to understand that their behavior will trigger reaction from others, and they begin to monitor their actions, acting differently depending on whom they are with and which aspect of their social self they want to be seen. This is a time at which children are more cautious about revealing themselves to others.

TABLE 13.3
Selman's Stages of Perspective Taking

Social Role-Taking Stage	Description
Stage 0—Egocentric Viewpoint (Age Range 3–6)[a]	Child has a sense of differentiation of self and other but fails to distinguish between the social perspective (thoughts, feelings) of other and self. Child can label other's overt feelings but does not see the cause and effect relation of reasons to social actions.
Stage 1—Social-Informational Role Taking (Age Range 6–8)	Child is aware that other has a social perspective based on other's own reasoning, which may or may not be similar to child's. However, child tends to focus on one perspective rather than coordinating viewpoints.
Stage 2—Self-Reflective Role Taking (Age Range 8–10)	Child is conscious that each individual is aware of the other's perspective and that this awareness influences self and other's view of each other. Putting self in other's place is a way of judging his intentions, purposes, and actions. Child can form a coordinated chain of perspectives, but cannot yet abstract from this process to the level of simultaneous mutuality.
Stage 3—Mutual Role Taking (Age Range 10–12)	Child realizes that both self and other can view each other mutually and simultaneously as subjects. Child can step outside the two-person dyad and view the interaction from a third-person perspective.
Stage 4—Social and Conventional System Role Taking (Age Range 12–15+)	Person realizes mutual perspective taking does not always lead to complete understanding. Social conventions are seen as necessary because they are understood by all members of the group (the generalized other) regardless of their position, role, or experience.

[a]Age ranges for all stages represent only an average approximation based on our studies to date.

From R. L. Selman, "Social-cognitive understanding," in T. Lickona, (Ed.), *Moral Development and Behavior*, 1976; reprinted by permission of the editor.

Selman's Ideas on the Development of the Self and Perspective Taking

Robert Selman (1976, 1980) has proposed a developmental sequence of perspective taking. He believes perspective taking moves through a series of five stages, ranging from three years of age through the adolescent years. As shown in table 13.3, these stages span the egocentric viewpoint of the preschool child to the in-depth societal perspective-taking view of the adolescent. Selman (1980) has shown how these stages of

An important aspect of the child's self-concept is the increasing ability to understand how he is viewed by others.

perspective taking can be applied to four dimensions of individual and social development: concepts of individuals, concepts of friendships, concepts of peers, and concepts of parent–child relationships. We consider the child's developing conception of individuals in greater detail. These concepts have often been assessed by Selman through individual interviews with the child based on the following dilemma:

> Eight-year-old Tom is trying to decide what to buy his best friend, Mike, for his birthday party. By chance, he meets Mike on the street and learns that Mike is extremely upset because his dog, Pepper, has been lost for two weeks. In fact, Mike is so upset he tells Tom, "I miss Pepper so much I never want to look at another dog again." Tom goes off, only to pass a store with a sale on puppies; only two are left and these soon will be gone. (Selman, 1980, p. 94)

The dilemma is whether to buy the puppy and how this will influence Mike psychologically.

To explore the issue of self-awareness the interviewer now begins with a general question such as, "Mike said he never wants to see another puppy again. Why did he say that?" Depending in part on the child's response, the interviewer subsequently chooses from a range of questions related to stages. Let's now look further at the stages of the child's conception of individual development.

Issues of interpersonal understanding related to concepts of the individual involve such matters as subjectivity (covert properties, such as people's thoughts, feelings, and motives), self-awareness (awareness of self's ability to observe its own thoughts and actions), personality (people's stable or predictable characteristics, e.g., shyness), and personality change (how and why people change). A description of the child's reasoning at different levels about the self and perspective taking is presented in Perspective on Child Development 13.2.

PERSPECTIVE ON CHILD DEVELOPMENT 13.2

CHILDREN'S LEVELS OF THINKING ABOUT THE SELF AND PERSPECTIVE TAKING

Level 0: Physicalistic Concepts of Self-Awareness

Two aspects of children's responses characterize the earliest reflective concept of self-awareness. First, when asked about the inner self, the child does not seem to view the nature of inner or psychological experiences as different from the material nature of outer experience. And, second, while very young children can describe a sense of being aware of a self, the nature of that self appears to have a quasi-physical air. Thus, a three-year-old child was asked,

Where does the rain come from?
I think from the clouds.

How do you know that?
I just told myself. That's how I knew.

What do you mean you told yourself?
My words told me.

When you think, where do you think?
In my mouth.

How do you think?
My words tell me.

And, in another comment by a three-year-old child, we see how the psychological self does not seem to be differentiated from the physical self in the early years of development:

I am the boss of myself.
How do you know?
My mouth told my arm and my arm does what my mouth tells it to do.

Level 1: Awareness of Distinctions Between Actions and Intentions

There are three intriguing aspects to the kind of thinking about self-awareness that characterizes level 1 thinking. First, young children are not aware that people can hide their inner or true feelings. For example, consider the following comments of a nine-year-old child:

Mike says he never wants to see another puppy again. Why did he say that?
Because he lost his dog Pepper.

Did he mean what he said?
Yes.

How do you know?
Because he said it.

Is it possible that Mike doesn't really know how he feels?
He said he was sad.

A second and related aspect of self-awareness at level 1 is that while covert attitudes and their overt actions are seen as separate, children using this level of reasoning seem to believe that the person's overt actions are the same as inner attitudes. For example, consider the comments of this eight-year-old child:

How does Mike feel inside?
Sad.

How do you know?
Because of the way he looks.

Could he look sad and be happy inside?
He could but you would be able to tell if you watched him long enough; he'd show you he was happy.

And, third, the young child's conception of fooling oneself or "awareness of unawareness" is different from that of older children and adults. Because level 1 perspective taking is yet actually self-reflective on the inner self, the young child seems to perceive fooling oneself as changing one's subjective beliefs and feelings rather than being unaware of such beliefs and feelings. For instance, an eight-year-old child was asked:

What does it mean to fool the self?
You do something and then you disagree with it. You find out you didn't want to do it.

Level 2: The Emergence of an Introspective Self and the Second-Person Perspective

Concepts at level 2 suggest a further understanding that the individual can take a clear perspective on the inner life that was separated from outer experiences at level 1. In social perspective-taking language, the self is now able to put itself in the place of the second person and look back toward the self's inner states. There are four aspects to this change in perspective taking and self-development. First, the ability to take a second-person perspective permits the child to rethink the relative significance of outer appearance and inner reality. There now appears to be a sense of greater importance attributed to inner experience and how one truly feels about social interactions beyond outward appearances. For instance, consider this ten-year-old's comments:

How is it you can hide the way you feel?
If you feel real sad and stuff, you put a smile on your face and you go with everyone else and try to be regular, but sometimes you can really be sad.

Is there a kind of inside and outside to a person?
Yes.

What would that mean?
If there was a brother and a sister, like the brother always says I can't stand you, but really inside, he really likes her.

Second, at level 2, perspective taking now involves a working belief in the self's ability to closely monitor the self's thoughts and actions. Consider the following excerpts from a twelve-year-old:

Is it possible to fool yourself?
Yes, sometimes.

How can you fool yourself?
You can say to yourself, I didn't really care and keep on saying you didn't care, and when someone brings up the subject, you say I didn't really care and sometimes it works and you don't really care about it.

Also at level 2, a third dimension arises. The child becomes reflectively aware that the individual, the self as well, can consciously and often deceptively put on a facade that is meant to mislead others with regard to what he or she thinks is going on internally. The concept of putting on a front is understood by the child as a useful strategy in covering up feelings. For instance, consider a twelve-year-old's comments:

Do you think there is a difference between fooling yourself and fooling somebody else?
Yes.

What is the difference?
It is easier to fool them because they don't have your mind.

A fourth and final dimension to level 2 thinking about perspective taking and self-development is the child's belief that one can attain an inner strength by gaining confidence in one's abilities. Self-awareness can now be related to the content of self-esteem. Inner awareness itself is now viewed as a confidence builder. For example, an eight-year-old commented:

Do you think there are any other reasons that Keith might have had for letting Jerry win?
Well, because he didn't want him to go off and start being a poor sport about it.

How would letting Jerry win stop him from being a poor sport?
Because it would let him think that Jerry did it by himself and so he is improving in playing Ping-Pong, so he will start playing a lot.

Why would he start playing a lot if he thought he won the game?
Because if he won the game he would think he would start getting better and play Ping-Pong more.

Do you think he might be trying to build up Jerry's confidence?
Yeah, he lets him win so he can make him think, "I am really better now. I can play better and sometimes win with Keith."

Continued on next page

Perspective on Child Development 13.2 (continued)

Level 3: Concepts of the Self as Observed and Observer, and Taking a Third-Person Perspective

George Herbert Mead (1934) believed that a mature concept of self comes from the child's cognitive capacity to take the perspective of another on one's own actions (Selman's level 2). Out of this self-as-action view emerges a self-as-entity phase that requires the ability to observe the self simultaneously as observed and observer. In Mead's terms, there evolves a concept of mind, or what Selman calls a third-person perspective on the self. This is the hallmark of Selman's level 3 thinking. Three aspects appear at level 3: the concept of the mind as the observer of a self-aware self, the idea of fooling the self through an act of will, and the notion that thoughts and feelings can appear even when opposed by mind and will. In the following comments of a twelve-year-old, we can see the depth of the young adolescent's thinking about the mind:

> *Is it possible to hide your feelings from yourself?*
> Yes, you just don't tell it to anybody. You put it out of your mind.

> *Is it possible to really succeed in hiding it from yourself?*
> Yeah, you just put it out of your mind; you don't want to know about it.

> *Do you then not know about it, or inside, do you still know about it?*
> You still know about it, but you don't think about it or talk about it.

Level 4: The Discovery of the True Self-Deception and the Unconscious as a Natural Explanatory Concept

The key theme of level 4 thinking is that no matter how vigilant the conscious mind is, and no matter how hard it works, there still are inner experiences that are not readily available to awareness. At this level, the adolescent sees that individuals can and do have thoughts, feelings, and motivations that are resistant to self-analysis by even the most introspective, probing thinker. Consider the thoughts of a sixteen-year-old:

> *If Mike says he never wants to see another puppy again, why does he say that?*
> Because he doesn't think that any puppy could take the place of Pepper.

> *Does he really mean that, that he never wants to see another puppy again?*
> No.

> *Can you say something and not mean it?*
> That is something right off the top of his head, like when you are really upset, you might say get out of here I never want to see you again. But you are really going to see them tomorrow and you are not going to be mad at them.

> *So Mike maybe doesn't know how he feels?*
> He is just talking out of emotions. He may think that at that instant he doesn't want to see another puppy, but he will grow over the initial loss.

> *If Mike thinks about what he said, will he realize that he really would like another dog?*
> Maybe, but maybe not. He might not be aware of his deeper feelings.

> *How is that possible?*
> He may not want to admit to himself that another dog could take Pepper's place. He might feel at some level that would be unloyal to Pepper to just go out and replace the dog. He may feel guilty about it. He doesn't want to face these feelings, so he says, no new dog.

> *Is he aware of this?*
> Probably not.

In our discussion of Selman's views, we have seen that the development of perspective-taking skills and self-understanding continues into the adolescent years. Next we take a comprehensive look at other aspects of self and personality development in adolescence.

Adolescence

First, we consider changes in the self during adolescence, then turn to the important adolescent theme of independence, and conclude with a discussion of identity development.

The Self

Among the most important features of self-development in adolescence are differentiation, individuation, stability, organization, idealism, abstractness, and the emergence of personality theory.

Differentiation, Individuation, and Stability First, adolescents have a more differentiated view of themselves than they did as children. As children they may simply have perceived themselves as "good" or "bad." As adolescents, they are likely to perceive themselves in more detailed ways, such as "I am a good person most of the time, except when my older sister bugs me, or when my father won't let me have the car, or when I have to study for an exam."

Second, adolescents develop what is called a more individuated view of themselves than they had as children. This indicates that adolescents have a more distinct view of themselves as unique people and more readily differentiate themselves from others than they did as children. Young children label themselves in terms of how they are similar to their peers, but as they approach adolescence, they tend to describe themselves more in terms of how they are different from their peers.

Third, the adolescent's self-concept is likely to be more stable than the child's. However, in an extreme form, stability can lead to rigidity and unrealistic self-appraisals. Even though we say that the self-concept of the adolescent becomes more stable as he or she grows older, this does not imply that self-concept does not change. It clearly does change, but as adolescents mature cognitively, they become more capable of integrating incoming information into a stable sense of who they are and where they are going.

Abstractness, Idealism, and Organization Three other distinct characteristics of the self in adolescents are abstractness, idealism, and organization. The adolescent begins to think in more abstract and ideal ways about the self—about what the self is capable of being. Such thoughts are often very elaborate, idealistic, and organized.

Becoming a Personality Theorist During adolescence the individual begins to think about the self more like many personality theorists think. The development of a personality theory during adolescence seems to consist of several elements that appear to be absent during the elementary school years. First, when adolescents are given information about themselves, they integrate this with previously acquired information about themselves relying solely on the concrete information at hand. Second, rather than thinking that they always behave consistently, adolescents are more likely than elementary school children to detect the contextual or situational variability in their own and others' behavior. Third, rather than merely accepting surface traits as a valid description of another person or themselves, adolescents begin to look for deeper, more complex—even hidden—causes of personality. These factors are not merely considered in isolation but as interacting forces that determine personality. This complex way of thinking about oneself and others does not appear in most individuals until adolescence. As is the case with formal operational thought, though, these implicit personality theories are not always employed; whether an adolescent uses such a strategy to understand himself or herself and others may depend upon a number of specific factors. It is important to note, however, that it does not seem that the individual is even capable of such thought until the beginning of adolescence (e.g., Barenboim, 1981; Livesley & Bromley, 1973; Stricker, Jacobs & Kogan, 1974).

Independence

Virtually all major developmentally focused theories consider independence to be an important aspect of adolescence (e.g., Ausubel, Sullivan & Ives, 1980; Erikson, 1968; Mahler, 1979b). First, we study the complexity of independence and then the link between parenting and independence in adolescence. Trying to define adolescent autonomy is more complex and elusive than it might seem at first. Think about autonomy for a moment. For most people, the term connotes self-direction and independence. But what does it really mean? Is it an internal personality trait that consistently characterizes the adolescent's immunity from parental influence? Is it the ability to make responsible decisions for oneself? Does autonomy imply consistent behavior in all areas of life, including school, finances, dating, and peer relations? What are the relative contributions of peers and other adults to the development of the adolescent's autonomy?

It is clear that adolescent autonomy is *not* a consistent and regular feature of all adolescent thought and behavior. For example, in one investigation (Psathas, 1957) high school students were asked twenty-five questions about their independence from their families. Four distinct patterns of adolescent autonomy emerged from analyses of the students' responses. One dimension, labeled "permissiveness in outside activities," was represented by questions such as, Do you have to account to parents for the way you spend your money? A second dimension, called "permissiveness in age-related activities," was reflected in questions such as, Do your parents help you to buy your clothes? A third independent aspect of adolescent autonomy, referred to as "parental regard for judgment," was indicated by responses to items such as, In family discussions, do your parents encourage you to give your opinion? And a fourth dimension, characterized as "activities with status implications," was indexed by parental influence on choice of occupation. Adolescent autonomy, then, is not a unified phenomenon but a summary label for a variety of adolescent interests, behaviors, thoughts, and feelings.

A number of investigations have focused on the relationship between parental attitudes and the adolescent's development of autonomy. Parents who adopt authoritarian decision-making strategies in dealing with their adolescent sons and daughters have adolescents who show little autonomy. Whether the adolescent's self-perceptions are sampled, whether confidence in decision making is evaluated, or whether initiative in joining parents in a mutual decision-making process is observed, the same conclusion about the relationship between adolescent autonomy and parenting strategies is evident (Hill & Steinberg, 1976).

While there is agreement that an authoritarian family structure restricts the adolescent's development of autonomy, there is not as much consistency in pinpointing the parenting practices that increase autonomy. Some investigations have found that a permissive parenting strategy allows the adolescent to

Adolescence is a time of increasing autonomy.

become more independent (Elder, 1968). Others suggest that a democratic parenting strategy is best (Kandel & Lesser, 1969).

While investigators vary in how they define permissive and democratic parenting techniques, in most instances a permissive strategy entails little parental involvement and few parental standards. By contrast, a democratic strategy usually consists of equal involvement on the part of parents and adolescents, with the parents having the final authority to set limits on their teenagers. When the overall competence and adjustment of the adolescent is evaluated (rather than just autonomy), an even more clear-cut advantage can be attributed to democratic over permissive strategies of parenting.

Adolescence is a period of development when the individual pushes for autonomy (or for the perception that he or she has control over behavior) and gradually develops the ability to take that control. This ability may be acquired through appropriate adult reactions to the adolescent's desire for control. At the onset of adolescence, the average person is not knowledgeable enough to make appropriate or mature decisions in all areas of life. As the adolescent pushes for autonomy, the wise adult will relinquish control in areas where the adolescent can make mature decisions and help the adolescent to make reasonable decisions in areas where his or her knowledge is more limited. Gradually, the adolescent will acquire the ability to make mature decisions.

Identity

According to Erikson (1968) the governing theme of self-development in adolescence is **identity:** Who am I? Where am I going? What kind of career will I pursue? How well do I relate to females and males? Am I able to make it on my own? These are questions that clamor for solutions in the adolescent years, all revolving around the development of an identity as a person. We described Erikson's ideas in Chapter 10 under our discussion of psychoanalytic theories. It may be helpful for you to review those ideas at this time. Here we focus further on his view of identity development and how he sees adolescence as a moratorium between childhood and adulthood. Then we turn to information about the four statuses of identity.

Erikson's Stage of Identity Versus Identity Confusion
During adolescence, world views become important to an individual who enters what Erikson terms a "psychological moratorium"—a gap between the security of childhood and the autonomy of approaching adulthood. Numerous identities can be drawn from the surrounding culture. Adolescents can experiment with different roles, trying them out and seeing which ones they like. The youth who successfully copes with these conflicting identities during adolescence emerges with a new sense of self that is both refreshing and acceptable. The adolescent who is not successful in resolving this identity crisis becomes confused, suffering from what Erikson refers to as *identity confusion.* This confusion may take one of two courses: the individual may withdraw, isolating himself or herself from peers and family or may lose his or her own identity in that of the crowd.

Identity confusion may account for the large number of adolescents who run away from home, drop out of school, quit their jobs, stay out all night, or assume bizarre behavior. Before Erikson's ideas became popular, these adolescents were often labeled delinquents and looked at with a disapproving eye. As a result of Erikson's writings and analyses, the problems these youths encounter are now viewed in a more positive light. Not

only do runaways, school dropouts, and those who quit jobs struggle with identity, virtually all adolescents go through an identity crisis, and some are simply able to resolve the crisis more easily than others.

One of the hallmarks of Erikson's view of identity development is the opportunity to explore and experiment with many different roles. Adolescents want to be able to decide freely for themselves such matters as what careers they will pursue, whether they will go to college or into military service, and whether or not they will marry. In other words, they want to free themselves from the shackles of their parents and other adults to make their own choices. At the same time, however, many adolescents have a deep fear of making the wrong decisions and of failing.

There are literally hundreds of roles for the adolescent to try out, and probably as many ways to pursue each role. Erikson believes that by late adolescence, occupational choices are central to the development of identity. Other important role choices involve sexuality (including decisions on dating, marriage, and sexual behavior), politics, religion, and moral values.

For example, many adolescents have been indoctrinated in the religious beliefs of their parents. By late adolescence, youth come to understand that they can make their own decisions about religion. The same can be said of political identity—most children report that they adopt their parents' political choices. But by late adolescence, youth make their own decisions. Unfortunately, some adolescents consistently and deliberately adopt choices that are opposite those of their parents as a means of attaining "independence." Such behavior does not meet the criteria for successful development of autonomy or identity but represents a negative identity.

Thus, the development of an integrated sense of identity is a complex and difficult task. Adolescents are expected to master many different roles in our culture. It is the rare, perhaps even nonexistent, adolescent who doesn't experience serious doubts about his or her capabilities in handling at least some of these roles competently.

In his effort to more fully understand the nature of identity development, Erikson has not only carefully observed and interviewed many adolescents in psychotherapy sessions, but he has analyzed the lives of famous individuals as well. For an insight into his analysis of the identity development of Adolf Hitler, Martin Luther, and Mahatma Gandhi, read Perspective on Child Development 13.3.

PERSPECTIVE ON CHILD DEVELOPMENT 13.3

ERIK ERIKSON'S ANALYSIS OF THE CHILDHOODS OF ADOLF HITLER, MARTIN LUTHER, AND MAHATMA GANDHI

In the following excerpts from Erikson's writings, the psychoanalytic method is used to analyze the youths of Adolf Hitler, Martin Luther, and Mahatma Gandhi. In one passage, Erikson (1962) describes the youth of Adolf Hitler:

I will not go into the symbolism of Hitler's urge to build except to say that his shiftless and brutal father had consistently denied the mother a steady residence; one must read how Adolf took care of his mother when she wasted away from breast cancer to get an inkling of this young man's desperate urge to cure. But it would take a very extensive analysis, indeed, to indicate in what way a single boy can daydream his way into history and emerge a sinister genius, and how a whole nation becomes ready to accept the emotive power of that genius as a hope of fulfillment for its national aspirations and as a warrant for national criminality. . . .

The memoirs of young Hitler's friend indicate an almost pitiful fear on the part of the future dictator that he might be nothing. He had to challenge this possibility by being deliberately and totally anonymous; and only out of this self-chosen nothingness could he become everything. (pp. 108–109)

But while the identity crisis of Adolf Hitler led him to turn toward politics in a pathological effort to create a world order, the identity crisis of Martin Luther in a different era led him to turn toward theology in an attempt to deal systematically with human nothingness or lack of identity.

In confession, for example, he was so meticulous in the attempt to be truthful that he spelled out every intention as well as every deed; he splintered relatively acceptable purities into smaller and smaller impurities; he reported temptations in historical sequence, starting back in childhood; and after having confessed for

hours, would ask for special appointments in order to correct previous statements. In doing this he was obviously both exceedingly compulsive and, at least unconsciously, rebellious.

At this point we must note a characteristic of great youth rebels; their inner split between the temptation to surrender and the need to dominate. A great young rebel is torn between, on the one hand, tendencies to give in and fantasies of defeat (Luther used to resign himself to an early death at times of impending success); and the absolute need, on the other hand, to take the lead, not only over himself but over all the forces and people who impinge on him. (pp. 155–157)

And in his Pulitzer Prize-winning book on Mahatma Gandhi's life, Erikson (1969) describes the personality formation of Gandhi during his youth.

Straight and yet not stiff; shy and yet not withdrawn; intelligent and yet not bookish; willful and yet not stubborn; sensual and yet not soft. . . . We must try to reflect on the relation of such a youth to his father, because the Mahatma places service to the father and the crushing guilt of failing in such service in the center of his adolescent turbulence. Some historians and political scientists seem to find it easy to interpret this account in psychoanalytic terms; I do not. For the question is not how a particular version of the Oedipal Complex "causes" a man to be both great and neurotic in a particular way, but rather how such a young person . . . manages the complexes which constrict other men. (p. 113)

In these passages, the workings of an insightful, sensitive mind is shown looking for a historical perspective on matters. Through analyses of the lives of famous individuals such as Hitler, Luther, and Gandhi, and through the thousands of youth he has talked with in person, Erikson has pieced together a descriptive picture of identity development.

In a Pulitzer Prize-winning book, Erikson analyzed the development of Mahatma Gandhi's identity.

The Four Statuses of Identity   James Marcia (1966) has analyzed Erikson's identity theory of adolescence and concluded that four identity statuses, or *modes of resolution,* can be applied to the theory—identity diffusion, foreclosure, moratorium, and identity achievement. The extent of an adolescent's commitment and crisis is used to classify him or her as having one of the four identity statuses. Marcia defines crisis as a period during which the adolescent is choosing among meaningful alternatives. He defines commitment as the extent to which an adolescent shows a personal investment in what he or she is doing or is going to do.

Adolescents classified as **identity diffused** (or **confused**) have not experienced any crisis (that is, they haven't explored meaningful alternatives) or made any commitments. Not only are they undecided upon occupational or ideological choices, they also are likely to show little or no interest in such matters.

The adolescent experiencing identity **foreclosure** has made a commitment but has not experienced a crisis. This occurs most often when parents simply hand down commitments to their adolescents, more often than not in an authoritarian manner. In such circumstances, adolescents may not have had enough opportunities to explore different approaches, ideologies, and vocations on their own. Some experts on adolescence, such as Kenneth Kenniston (1971), believe that experiencing a crisis is necessary for the development of a mature and self-integrated identity.

Marcia states that adolescents in the **moratorium** status are in the midst of a crisis but that their commitments are either absent or only vaguely defined. Such adolescents are searching for commitments by actively questioning alternatives.

Adolescents who have undergone a crisis and made a commitment are referred to as **identity achieved.** In other words, to reach the identity-achievement status, it is necessary for the adolescent to first experience a psychological moratorium, then make an enduring commitment.

In one investigation (Meilman, 1979) changes in identity status during the adolescent years were investigated. Each individual was given Marcia's identity status interview, designed to include questions about vocation (and for older subjects, questions about premarital sex as well). As indicated in table 13.4, there

TABLE 13.4
Percentages of Each Age Group in the Four Identity Statuses

Age Group[a]	Achievement	Moratorium	Foreclosure	Diffusion
12	0	0	32	68
15	4	0	32	64
18	20	4	24	48
21	40	12	16	28
24	56	12	8	24

[a]In years.

From Meilman, P. W., "Cross-sectional age changes in ego identity status during adolescence," in *Developmental Psychology*, 15, pp. 230–231. Copyright © 1981 by the American Psychological Association. Reprinted by permission of the publisher and author.

Identity development is an important concern during adolescence, but it should also be viewed as a process that continues through the college years and into adult life.

were substantial increases with age in the number of individuals who reached identity achievement status and a considerable decrease in the number of individuals who were in the foreclosure and diffusion statuses.

Some experts on adolescence argue that college experiences increase the likelihood that adolescents will enter a status of moratorium. The theory is that professors and peers stimulate older adolescents to rethink their vocational and ideological orientations. In one investigation, as many as four out of every five adolescents in a moratorium status switched their occupational orientation during their college years (Waterman & Waterman, 1972). As a rule, the incidence of successful resolution to the identity crisis and successful development of an identity commitment increases from the first year to the final year of college (Constantinople, 1969).

Nonetheless, in another investigation (Adams & Fitch, 1982), college students were discovered to regress to the moratorium status from an identity achievement status at some point in their college years. Clearly, then, college experiences stimulate the exploration of alternatives as individuals search for an identity. We believe that it is important to view identity development as a process that continues through the college years and beyond. While identity development seems to be a critical issue during the adolescent years, a concern with who one is, what one is all about, and where one is headed is a theme that is often reworked over and over again during the adult years.

So far we have discussed a number of important ideas about stability and change in personality and information about the self. A summary of these ideas is presented in Concept Table 13.2.

In our discussion of personality in this chapter we have encountered difficulties in measuring various aspects of personality. In the prologue we looked at the nature of so-called "objective" personality tests. In our description of social competence, we spent some time outlining Waters and Sroufes' arguments regarding issues surrounding the assessment of social competence. To close this chapter, we take a final look at the assessment of personality, in this instance at two constructs we have discussed often—self-concept and identity.

Measuring Self-Concept and Identity

Although it is widely accepted that a child has a self-concept and that an adolescent pursues an identity, psychologists have found the process of measuring self-concept and identity an arduous task. First we consider the measurement of self-concept and then of identity.

Self-Concept

One method that has frequently been used to measure children's self-concept is the Piers–Harris Scale (Piers & Harris, 1964), which consists of eighty items designed to measure the child's overall self-esteem. School psychologists often use the scale with boys and girls who have been referred to them for evaluation. By responding yes or no to such items as "I have good ideas," children reveal how they view themselves. The Piers–Harris Scale requires about fifteen to twenty minutes for completion and can be administered to groups as well as to individuals.

CONCEPT TABLE 13.2 Stability and Change in Personality and the Development of the Self		
Concept	**Processes/Related Ideas**	**Characteristics/Description**
Stability and change	Nature of the issue	Stability and change can be evaluated in a number of ways. We can study the extent to which early childhood characteristics predict later personality characteristics. We can evaluate aspects of the social environment early in development to see if they predict later personality development. We can study stability and change over short or long periods of time.
	Longitudinal studies	Sex-typed characteristics tended to be stable from the elementary school years through adolescence in the Fels Longitudinal Study. In the New York Longitudinal Study temperament in the early child years was somewhat stable; however, in the later childhood years and adolescence experiences were more likely to change temperament.
	Conclusions	The truth about stability and change in personality lies somewhere between the infant determinism of Freud and a contextualist view that ignores the developmental unfolding of personality completely.
Development of the self	"I" and "me"	An important distinction is made between the self as "I" (knower, active observer) and "me" (product of observing process, what is known).
	Infancy	By eighteen months of age infants can recognize themselves, indicating the rudimentary beginning of self-concept. Rheingold argues that independence is an important theme in infancy and that from the ages of one to five children increasingly move away from their mother to explore the environment. Erikson and other theorists view the second year of life as an important time in the development of independence. Erikson calls his second stage of development autonomy versus shame and doubt.
	Childhood	Initially, self-definition focuses on external characteristics. At around six to seven years of age, children describe themselves in terms of psychological traits. It is believed that during the elementary school years perspective taking also enhances the child's self-understanding. Robert Selman has developed a stage view of perspective taking, ranging from the egocentric view of the young child to the societal perspective taking of the adolescent. Selman has also described changes in perspective taking that are related to the child's conception of individuals. Young children have very physical conceptions of individuals. As children move through the childhood years, they increasingly consider the inner aspects of the individual and eventually in adolescence understand that individuals may have an unconscious mind that is hidden from awareness.
	Adolescence	Adolescents have a more differentiated, individuated, and stable view of themselves than they did when they were children. The adolescent's self-conceptions are more organized, abstract, and ideal than the child's. The adolescent begins to view the self not unlike a personality theorist, increasingly seeing the self in terms of a combination of the past and the present alone, in terms of contextual variation rather than global traits alone, and in terms of more complex, possibly even hidden reasons for one's own behavior.
		Most theorists agree that adolescence is an important period in terms of the development of independence. Independence is a global construct and includes a variety of behaviors and activities. Authoritarian parenting is associated with reduced independence, while democratic parenting is linked with increased independence.
		For Erikson, identity is the governing theme of self-development in adolescence. The adolescent asks: Who am I? Where am I going? What am I all about as a person? Erikson's fifth stage of development is identity versus identity confusion. One of the hallmarks of Erikson's view is the importance attached to the opportunity to explore and experiment with many different roles. According to Marcia the four statuses of identity are identity diffused (confused), foreclosure, moratorium, and identity achieved.

© 1959 United Feature Syndicate, Inc.

Children's self-perception often changes according to the situation, although self-concept measures like the Piers–Harris Scale are designed to measure a stable, consistent aspect of personality. Also, with self-reporting, it is difficult to determine whether children are telling about the way they really are or the way they want someone else to think they are. Even though the instructions on the Piers–Harris Scale and other measures of self-concept direct children to respond as they really are, there is no assurance that they will do so (Wylie, 1974).

A promising measure of self-concept has been developed by Susan Harter (1982). Her scale is called the **Perceived Competence Scale for Children.** Emphasis is placed on assessing the child's sense of competence across different domains rather than viewing perceived competence as a unitary concept. Three types of skills are assessed on separate subscales: cognitive (good at schoolwork; remember things easily); social (have a lot of friends; most kids like me); and physical (do well at sports; first chosen for games). A fourth subscale measures general self-worth (sure of myself; happy the way I am) independent of any particular skill domain. The importance of Harter's measure is that prior measures of self-concept, such as the Piers–Harris, lump together the child's perceptions of his or her competencies in a variety of domains in an effort to come up with an overall measure of the child's self-concept. Harter's scale does an excellent job of separating the child's self-perceptions of his or her abilities in different skill areas; and when general self-worth is assessed, questions that focus on overall perceptions of the self are used rather than questions that are directed at specific skill domains.

Recently, Susan Harter and Robin Pike (1984) developed the Pictorial Scale of Perceived Competence and Social Acceptance for Young Children, a downward extension of the Perceived Competence Scale for Children. There are two versions of the measure, one for preschool children and the other for first and second grade children. Each version taps four domains: cognitive competence, physical competence, peer acceptance, and maternal acceptance (See table 13.5). Analysis of preschool and early elementary school children's responses suggest that two factors are present: first, a general competence factor (physical and cognitive), and second, a general social acceptance factor (peer and maternal). The measure should not be viewed as a general self-concept scale but rather as a measure that evaluates perceived competence and social acceptance.

Identity

Identity is as difficult to measure, if not more difficult, than self-concept. John Hill (1973), while recognizing the importance of identity as an integrative concept in adolescence, indicated that there is little empirical information outside of clinical studies and psychobiographies (like that of Hitler) that would help in the evaluation of the concept of identity. There is even some question as to whether the process of identity formation is spelled out in sufficient detail to permit empirical studies derived from Erikson's explanation. While the developmental course of the theory remains mainly uncharted empirically, a number of current efforts are being directed at improved assessment of identity development (e.g., Craig-Bray & Adams, 1985; Grotevant & Adams, 1984). These criticisms of Erikson's theory are not unlike those leveled at Freud's theory over the years.

TABLE 13.5
Items Grouped According to Subscale for Each Form

Subscale and Item No.	Preschool–Kindergarten	First–Second Grades
Cognitive competence		
1	Good at puzzles	Good at numbers
5	Gets stars on paper	Knows a lot in school
9	Knows names of colors	Can read alone
13	Good at counting	Can write words
17	Knows alphabet	Good at spelling
21	Knows first letter of name	Good at adding
Physical competence		
3	Good at swinging	Good at swinging
7*	Good at climbing	Good at climbing
11	Can tie shoes	Good at bouncing ball
15*	Good at skipping	Good at skipping
19*	Good at running	Good at running
23	Good at hopping	Good at jump-roping
Peer acceptance		
2*	Has lots of friends	Has lots of friends
6	Stays overnight at friends'	Others share their toys
10*	Has friends to play with	Has friends to play with
14*	Has friends on playground	Has friends on playground
18*	Gets asked to play with others	Gets asked to play with others
22	Eats dinner at friends' house	Others sit next to you
Maternal acceptance		
4	Mom smiles	Mom lets you eat at friends'
8*	Mom takes you places you like	Mom takes you places you like
12*	Mom cooks favorite foods	Mom cooks favorite foods
16*	Mom reads to you	Mom reads to you
20	Mom plays with you	Mom plays with you
24*	Mom talks to you	Mom talks to you

Note. Item number refers to position of the item in the order administered to the child. Asterisk designates items common to both forms.

From Harter, S., and R. Pike, "The pictorial scale of perceived competence and social acceptance for young children, in *Child Development*, pp. 1969–1982. Copyright © 1984 by The Society for Research in Child Development, Inc. Reprinted by permission.

SUMMARY

I. Information about personality includes ideas about what personality is, personality theories and traits, and trait–situation interaction.

  A. Personality can be defined as the study of individuals and their adaptation to the environment.

  B. Psychoanalytic, social learning, and cognitive developmental theories have important implications for understanding personality development.

  C. Information about trait theory focuses on its nature, the study and analysis of traits, basic themes of the trait approach, and difficulties with this view.

  D. Study of the interaction of traits and situations recognizes the importance of characteristics of the child and the role of contexts and situations in modifying such characteristics in determining the child's personality. The more narrow and limited the trait is, the more likely it will predict the child's behavior. Some children are more consistent on some traits, and other children are more consistent on other traits. Personality traits exert a stronger influence on behavior when situational pressures are less powerful.

II. Three important aspects of personality development in children are delay of gratification, ego control/resiliency, and social competence.

  A. Mischel's longitudinal work on delay of gratification in children reveals considerable stability over time yet adaptation to different situations.

  B. The Blocks have studied ego control/resiliency and found these dimensions of personality to be related to a number of parental characteristics and child-rearing practices.

  C. Waters and Sroufe describe social competence in terms of effective use of resources in the environment and resources in the individual. They have evaluated different dimensions of social competence and discussed salient issues in social competence at different developmental levels. Waters and Sroufe have also outlined four assessment issues in social competence: global/fine grained; naturalistic/laboratory; coordination of cognition, affect, and behavior; and integrative/adaptive capacity in dealing with taxing circumstances.

III. Information about stability and change, an important issue in the study of personality development, focuses on the nature of the issue, longitudinal studies, and conclusions about the issue.
   A. Stability and change can be evaluated in a number of ways. We can study the extent to which early childhood characteristics predict later personality characteristics. We can evaluate aspects of the social environment early in development to see if they predict later personality development. We can study stability and change over short or long periods of time.
   B. Sex-typed characteristics tended to be stable from the elementary school years through adolescence in the Fels Longitudinal Study. In the New York Longitudinal Study temperament in the early childhood years was somewhat stable, but in the later childhood years and adolescence experiences were more likely to change temperament.
   C. The truth about stability and change in personality lies somewhere between the infant determinism of Freud and a contextualist view that ignores the developmental unfolding of personality completely.
IV. An overview of the development of the self emphasizes a distinction between "I" and "me", infancy, the childhood years, and adolescence.
   A. For many years psychologists have distinguished between "I" (knower, active observer) and "me" (product of observing process, what is known). While traditionally most research has focused on the self as object (self-concept), recently researchers have called on the information-processing perspective to guide research on the self as knower.
   B. Development of the self in infancy involves the emergence of the self and independence.
      1. By eighteen months of age infants can recognize themselves, indicating a rudimentary beginning of self-concept.
      2. Rheingold argues that independence is an important theme in infancy and that from one to five years of age children increasingly move away from their mother to explore the environment. Erikson and other theorists view the second year of life as an important time in the development of independence. Erikson calls the second stage of development autonomy versus shame and doubt.
   C. The development of the self in childhood involves some characteristics of self-definition and the development of perspective taking and the self.
      1. Initially, self-definition focuses on external characteristics. At around six to seven years of age, children describe themselves in terms of psychological traits.
      2. It is believed that during the elementary school years perspective taking also enhances the child's self-understanding. Robert Selman has crafted the most articulated view of the relation of self and perspective taking, describing a series of stages ranging from the egocentric view of the young child to the advanced societal perspective of the adolescent. Selman has also outlined changes in perspective-taking skills that focus on the child's conception of individuals. Young children have physicalistic conceptions of individuals. As they move through the elementary school years, children increasingly consider the inner aspects of the individual and eventually in adolescence become aware that the individual has an unconscious mind that is hidden from awareness.
   D. The development of the self in adolescence involves the characteristics of the adolescent's self-conceptions, the adolescent as a personality theorist, and the very important dimensions of independence and identity.
      1. Adolescents have a more differentiated, individuated, and stable view of themselves than children do, and adolescents' self-conceptions are more abstract, ideal, and organized than those of children.
      2. Adolescents begin perceiving themselves not unlike personality theorists who study personality.
      3. Independence is an important theme of adolescence as is identity development. Identity versus identity diffusion is the fifth stage of Erikson's developmental theory. An important aspect of identity development is the exploration of many different roles. Four statuses of identity, according to Marcia, are identity diffused (confused), foreclosure, moratorium, and identity achieved.
   E. There are many problems associated with the measurement of self-concept and identity. A promising measure of children's self-conceptions is the Perceived Competence Scale for Children.

KEY TERMS

delay of gratification 455
ego control 456
ego resiliency 456
factor analysis 452
Fels Longitudinal
Study 463
foreclosure 479
global self-concept 465
humanism 465
identity 477
identity achieved 479
identity diffused
(confused) 479

moratorium 479
New York Longitudinal
Study 463
Perceived Competence
Scale for Children 482
personality 451
phenomenological
approach 465
self as knower 466
social competence 458
trait theory 451
trait × situation interaction
454

REVIEW QUESTIONS

1. Discuss the nature of personality.
2. Review some basic points about psychoanalytic theory,
   social learning theory, and cognitive developmental
   theory (described in chapter 10) and their implications
   for understanding personality development.
3. Outline trait theory.
4. Describe the nature of the view known as trait ×
   situation interaction.
5. Discuss the nature of delay of gratification, ego
   control/resiliency, and social competence.
6. Distinguish between the self as knower and as object,
   and discuss the information-processing approach to the
   self as knower.
7. What do we know about the development of the self in
   infancy, childhood, and adolescence?
8. Discuss the development of independence.
9. Describe the nature of identity development as well as
   difficulties in measuring self-concept, identity, and
   social competence.

SUGGESTED READINGS

Brim, O. G., Jr., & Kagan, J. (Eds.). (1980). *Constancy
and change in human development*. Cambridge, MA:
Harvard University Press.
Includes detailed information about many different
aspects of the self and personality, including physical,
cognitive, and personality development. Provides
insight into some of the problems involved in
measuring constancy and change over long time
periods.

Erikson, E. H. (Ed.). (1965). *The challenge of youth*. New
York: Doubleday.
This excellent book of readings on youth includes
articles by Erikson on the fidelity and diversity of
youth, by Bruno Bettelheim on the problem of
generations, and by Kenneth Kenniston on social
change and youth in America. The focus of the
articles is the adolescent's development of identity.

Harter, S. (1983). Developmental perspectives on the self-
system. In P. H. Mussen (Ed.), *Handbook of child
psychology* (4th ed., Vol. 4). New York: John Wiley.
A thorough overview of the development of the self,
particularly in terms of its development during
childhood. Provides extensive information about self-
concept and self-esteem.

Lewis, M., & Brooks-Gunn, J. (1979). *Social cognition
and the acquisition of the self*. New York: Plenum.
An extensive overview of Lewis's work on the
development of the self in infancy. Chapters explore
the origin of the self, how to study the self in infancy,
and ideas about a unified theory of the self.

Mahler, M. S. (1979). *The selected papers of Margaret
Mahler (Vol. 2): Separation-individuation*. New York:
Jason Aronson.
A presentation of Margaret Mahler's insightful
writings about the separation–individuation process in
the first three years of life. Considerable information,
including case studies, of aberrant mother–child
relationships that restrict the development of
independence.

Selman, R. L. (1980). *The growth of interpersonal
understanding*. New York: Academic Press.
Presents considerable detail about Selman's
developmental theory of perspective taking and self-
development. Includes information about clinical
implications for helping children with problems.

Waters, E., & Sroufe, A. (1983). Social competence as a
developmental construct. *Developmental Review, 3*,
79–97.
Provides details about Waters and Sroufe's provocative
view of social competence.

14

SEX-ROLE DEVELOPMENT

PROLOGUE

"YOU STAY HERE WITH THE BABY WHILE I GO FISHING"

While observing the play activities of preschool boys and girls at a nursery school, a supervisor overheard the following conversation between a four-year-old boy and girl:

"You stay here with the baby while I go fishing," Shane said to Barbara as he walked away.

Barbara called to him, "I want to go fishing too."

Shane replied, "No. Girls don't go fishing. But I will take you out to a French restaurant when I get back."

Barbara returned to play with her dolls as Shane left. The supervisor talked with Shane's mother about whether Shane was merely mimicking his father's behavior. She said that he was not, because the entire family went fishing together. The sex roles children display, then, are not merely a replication of parental actions.

Another play scene observed by the supervisor focused on three boys sitting around a play table in a play kitchen. The boys began issuing orders like "I want a cup of coffee" or "Some more jelly for the toast over here." Girls were running back and forth between the stove and table as they cooked and served breakfast. In one scenario, the boys got out of hand, demanding cups of coffee one after another as the four-year-old girl, Ann, raced around in a dizzy state. Finally, she gained some control of the situation by announcing that the coffee was all gone. It didn't seem to occur to Ann to sit down at the table and demand coffee from the boys.

Sexist behavior from young children is nothing new, but viewing it as a problem is something that has occurred in recent years. Such behavior has become somewhat of an obsession with preschool teachers and directors, and it bothers many parents who are trying to rear their offspring free of sexual bias. They may carefully screen out books in which mothers primarily tie shoelaces and bake cookies, and they buy sports equipment for their daughters as well as (or in place of) dolls.

One of the main tasks facing the child is the development of a sense of self, and attaining a sexual identity is an important ingredient of such development. As children move from the toddler years into early childhood, they begin making generalizations about sex-related matters that may not be accurate. William, for instance, went with his mother to a doctor's office when he was two-and-a-half years old. As they sat in the waiting room, a man in a white coat walked by, and William commented, "Hi, Doc." Then a woman in a white coat walked by, and William said, "Hi, Nurse." His mother asked how he knew which person was a doctor and which was a nurse. William replied, "Doctors are daddies and nurses are mommies." However, William's own pediatrician was a female who had cared for him since birth. Many preschool children show some confusion about sex roles just as they reveal fuzzy, often inaccurate perceptions of their entire social world (Carper, 1978).

In this chapter we will study the role of children's development in obtaining a sexual identity, seeing that such identity is determined by an interaction of biological heritage and culture. Nowhere in the study of child development has there been greater cultural change in recent years than in the area of sex roles. Whereas at one time in history it was accepted that boys should grow up to be masculine and girls to be feminine and the many pieces of information they encountered from parents, teachers, siblings, and the media were consistent in portraying this course of development, today many boys and girls are likely to be getting more conflicting information about sex roles. A preschool girl may have a mother who is promoting her femininity yet become friends with a "tomboy" at her nursery school and have a teacher who is promoting assertiveness in young girls. The fascinating journey through the development of sex roles in this chapter provides much more information about the aspects of sex roles discussed so far.

PREVIEW

In this chapter we will examine information about androgyny and the components of sex-role development, biological and cognitive factors, environmental influences, sex differences and stereotypes, and sex-role development through infancy, childhood, and adolescence.

ANDROGYNY AND THE COMPONENTS OF SEX-ROLE DEVELOPMENT

All of us, particularly young children, are curious about our gender. Do you remember your childhood images of what girls and boys are like? Psychologists have come up with many different strategies to analyze sex roles. In particular, the concept of androgyny has dominated discussion of sex roles. We look at this concept and the degree to which androgynous individuals are more competent than individuals with a more traditional sex-role orientation.

The Concept of Androgyny

The label "sex role" has been used to describe the different characteristics children display because of their sex. However, some experts (e.g., Spence & Helmreich, 1978) define sex role as the behaviors that are expected of children because they are either male or female. Another important aspect of the child's sexual makeup is what is referred to as **sexual, or gender, identity.** We can define this as the extent to which individual children actually take on as part of their personalities the behaviors and attitudes associated with either the male or female role. In the United States and in most other countries, the well-adjusted child has traditionally been one who has developed a sex-appropriate sex role. That is, males are supposed to be "masculine" and females are supposed to be "feminine." In past years most research on children's sex roles was conducted along this line; researchers have traditionally assessed the concept of sex roles as a bipolar construct, with masculinity and femininity considered as opposites. Recently, however, an alternative view of children's sex roles has been developed and is based on the concept of androgyny.

TABLE 14.1
Examples of Masculine and Feminine Items
from Bem's Sex-Role Inventory

Masculine Items	Feminine Items
Acts as a leader	Affectionate
Analytical	Compassionate
Competitive	Feminine
Forceful	Gullible
Individualistic	Sensitive to the needs of others
Self-reliant	Sympathetic
Willing to take a stand	Warm

Psychologists began to suggest that the healthiest way to conceive of sex roles may be to view all children as having both masculine and feminine characteristics. **Androgyny** has become a byword in research on sex roles in the late 1970s and 1980s. What does it mean when we say twelve-year-old Bob is androgynous? It means that his psychological makeup includes both masculine and feminine aspects of behavior; some people say that people like Bob have an androgynous sex-role orientation. Sandra Bem (1974, 1977) and Janet Spence (Spence & Helmreich, 1978; Spence, Helmreich & Stapp, 1974) pioneered the notion that sex roles should not be looked at as bipolar sexual extremes but rather as dualistic dimensions within each sex. In other words, every male child has and should have some feminine attributes, and every female child has and should have some masculine attributes. Furthermore, both Bem and Spence believe that androgyny is not only natural but allows the child to adapt more competently to a wide variety of situations.

Sandra Bem created the Bem Sex Role Inventory (BSRI). See table 14.1 for examples of items on this inventory. Janet Spence developed the Personality Attributes Questionnaire (PAQ). Both of these measure androgyny. (To see whether you are androgynous or not rate yourself on the items in table 14.2.) The types of sex-role attributes that are tapped by these two increasingly used sex-role measures include dominance, independence, passivity, competitiveness, loyalty, aggressiveness, and forcefulness. Spence (Spence & Helmreich, 1978) has also developed the Child's Personal Attributes Questionnaire (Children's PAQ) to assess children's androgyny.

TABLE 14.2
Are You Androgynous?

The following items are from the Bem Sex-Role Inventory. To find out whether you score as androgynous on it, first rate yourself on each item, on a scale from 1 (never or almost never true) to 7 (always or almost always true).

1. self-reliant	16. strong personality	31. makes decisions easily	46. aggressive
2. yielding	17. loyal	32. compassionate	47. gullible
3. helpful	18. unpredictable	33. sincere	48. inefficient
4. defends own beliefs	19. forceful	34. self-sufficient	49. acts as a leader
5. cheerful	20. feminine	35. eager to soothe hurt feelings	50. childlike
6. moody	21. reliable	36. conceited	51. adaptable
7. independent	22. analytical	37. dominant	52. individualistic
8. shy	23. sympathetic	38. soft-spoken	53. does not use harsh language
9. conscientious	24. jealous	39. likable	54. unsystematic
10. athletic	25. has leadership abilities	40. masculine	55. competitive
11. affectionate	26. sensitive to the needs of others	41. warm	56. loves children
12. theatrical	27. truthful	42. solemn	57. tactful
13. assertive	28. willing to take risks	43. willing to take a stand	58. ambitious
14. flatterable	29. understanding	44. tender	59. gentle
15. happy	30. secretive	45. friendly	60. conventional

SCORING:

(a) Add up your ratings for items 1, 4, 7, 10, 13, 16, 19, 22, 25, 28, 31, 34, 37, 40, 43, 46, 49, 55, and 58. Divide the total by 20. That is your masculinity score.

(b) Add up your ratings for items 2, 5, 8, 11, 14, 17, 20, 23, 26, 29, 32, 35, 38, 41, 44, 47, 50, 53, 56, and 59. Divide the total by 20. That is your femininity score.

(c) If your masculinity score is above 4.9 (the approximate median for the masculinity scale) and your femininity score is above 4.9 (the approximate femininity median) then you would be classified as androgynous on Bem's scale.

From *Half the Human Experience: The Psychology of Women*, 3/e by Janet S. Hyde McKeachie. Copyright © 1985 by D. C. Heath and Company. Reprinted by permission of the publisher.

Androgyny involves a combination of masculine and feminine characteristics in the same individual.

Androgynous children are viewed positively for two reasons. First, the classification of a child as androgynous is based on the appearance of both masculine and feminine characteristics rather than the absence of both. Second, and more importantly, the attributes that comprise androgyny are those aspects of masculinity and femininity that are valued by our culture. The androgynous child is achievement oriented, shows high self-esteem, is a warm individual, and so on (Babladelis, 1979).

Are Androgynous Individuals More Competent Than People with a Traditional Sex-Role Orientation?

Though androgyny has many appealing qualities, some psychologists do not believe it provides the solution to determining which individuals have the best adjusted personality (Baumrind, 1982; Locksley & Colten, 1979). Diana Baumrind (1982) was not only interested in whether androgynous children are more competent but also in the kind of parenting styles that are associated with the development of androgyny. Furthermore, she was concerned about the extent to which androgynous parents are competent people. Baumrind's subjects were 9- and 10-year-old boys and girls and their parents. With regard to the parents, androgynous women did not differ in significant ways from other women. However, androgynous men were more like androgynous women than masculine men in their child-rearing practices, and they were more unconventional and autonomous in their personal lives. Sex-typed mothers were responsive and sex-typed fathers were firm in their child rearing. Androgynous parents were not more likely to be authoritative parents but rather were child-centered in their approach. Children of sex-typed parents were slightly more competent than children of androgynous parents, suggesting that androgyny may not be the American ideal we should be pushing children toward.

In another investigation (Jones, Chernovetz & Hansson, 1978), Bem's androgyny test was given to evaluate the degree to which adults show a traditional masculine or feminine versus an androgynous sex-role orientation. The adults were also given a number of other personality measures: self-esteem, helplessness, sexual maturity, and personal adjustment. The androgynous adults were not better adjusted. Indeed, for both sexes, a masculine orientation rather than androgyny was more likely to predict better flexibility and adjustment.

Where do you stand on this controversial issue? Who do you believe is better adjusted—androgynous, traditional female-oriented, or traditional male-oriented adults? It may be that for some people better adjustment is determined by the sociocultural context in which they live. Some women who are married, stay home most of the day, take care of their children, and have a traditionally oriented husband may be better adjusted by having a traditional female sex-role orientation. Other individuals who believe in change, and who think that both males and females should be characterized by personality characteristics of both sexes may be better adjusted with an androgynous sex-role orientation. None of the three sex-role orientations has exclusive rights to better adjustment as an adult.

BIOLOGICAL AND COGNITIVE FACTORS

First, we study the biological basis of sex-role development. Second, we focus on cognitive factors that are involved in sex-role development.

Biological Factors

Our overview of biological factors in sex-role development initially reviews psychoanalytic ideas, particularly Erik Erikson's view that anatomy is destiny. Then our attention turns to the role of hormones and eventually to John Money's belief that sex roles are invariably affected by biology and culture.

Freud and Erikson: Anatomy Is Destiny

One of Freud's basic assumptions was that human behavior and history are directly related to reproductive processes. From this assumption arises the belief that sexuality is essentially unlearned and instinctual. Erik Erikson (1968) has extended this argument, claiming that psychological differences in males and females stem from anatomical differences between the two groups. Erikson argues that because of genital structure, males are more intrusive and aggressive, while females are more inclusive and passive. Erikson's belief is sometimes referred to as the **anatomy is destiny** doctrine.

To support his ideas, Erikson designed and observed some play-building activities for eleven- to thirteen-year-old boys and girls. Erikson observed that the girls tended to construct low edifices that were almost always enclosed, while boys were more likely to build taller, elongated towers. According to Paula Caplan (1978), Erikson's conclusion that the differences in the play configurations of boys and girls are due to sexual anatomy seems to have been a matter of personal rather than scientific confirmation. When Erikson's data are scrutinized, his interpretation is further weakened. Erikson analyzed a total of 468 play configurations. Of these, only 39, or 8 percent, included any sort of tower structure.

Some psychoanalytic thinkers, however, protest that Erikson does not say that anatomy is destiny in an absolute sense; he simply argues that imagery is partly a function of body structure and that imagery provides a person with a unique perspective. Erikson also points out that women are transcending that perspective to correct our society's overemphasis on male intrusiveness and to arrive at a truly androgynous sexual orientation.

Hormones

Additional support for the importance of biological forces comes from the fact that the sexes differ genetically and biochemically. Much of the research used to support this belief has been conducted with animals because experimental manipulation of hormones is unethical with humans. Sex-related hormone levels in children are low and appear to be about the same for boys and girls, so it is unlikely that behavioral differences in boys and girls could be due to hormonal levels. However, with the onset of puberty, both boys' and girls' bodies are flooded with sex-related hormones. One review of the literature on sex hormones concluded that **testosterone** (male hormone) levels are related to aggression in adolescent males, but environmental influences can change hormonal levels drastically (Hoyenga & Hoyenga, 1979; Reinisch & Karrow, 1977).

In addition to the adolescent years, the period during which sex hormones are produced extensively is before birth. Anna Ehrhardt has studied the influence of prenatal hormonal changes on sex-role development (Ehrhardt & Baker, 1973). In the 1950s a number of expectant mothers were given doses of androgen (a male sex hormone); these women had a history of miscarriage, and the hormone is believed to ameliorate conditions that cause this problem. Six offspring of these mothers were studied; they ranged from four to twenty-six years of age. They were compared with siblings of the same sex who were unaffected by the hormonal treatment because their mothers had not been treated with androgen during the prenatal period. Results indicated that hormones are an important factor in sex-role development. The fetally androgenized girls expended comparatively more energy in their play and seemed to prefer boys over girls as playmates. Instead of dolls, they chose male sex-typed toys for play. They displayed little interest in future marriage and did not enjoy taking care of babies. They also preferred functional over attractive clothes and were generally unconcerned with their appearance. The boys whose mothers were treated with androgen engaged in rough-and-tumble play and outdoor sports to a greater extent than their unaffected brothers did.

Ehrhardt's work has been criticized for a number of reasons. For one, the inflated androgen levels require that these individuals be treated with cortisone for the remainder of their lives. One of the side effects of cortisone is a high activity level. The high energy and activity levels of the girls and boys, then, may be due to the cortisone treatment rather than to high levels of androgen (Quadagno, Briscoe & Quadagno, 1977). Second, "masculinized" girls may be perceived as deviant by their parents, siblings, and peers. Those around them may have thought of them as "boys" and treated them accordingly.

No one argues about the existence of genetic, biochemical, and anatomical differences between the sexes. Even strongly environmentally oriented psychologists acknowledge that boys and girls will be treated differently because of their physical differences and their different roles in reproduction. Consequently, the importance of biological factors is not at issue; what is at issue is the directness or indirectness of the effect of biological factors on social behavior. According to Aletha Huston (1983), if a high androgen level directly influences the central nervous system, which in turn produces a higher activity level, then the effect is reasonably direct. By contrast, if a high level of androgen produces strong muscle development, which in turn causes others to expect the child to be a good athlete and in turn leads her to participate in sports, then the biological effect is more indirect.

Biology × Culture

John Money is a well-known theorist and researcher who sees sex-role development as affected by both biology and culture (Money, 1973). His ideas are based on the notion of what he calls "critical periods," or brief times in the individual's life when biological changes combine with environmental events to produce a virtually irreversible sex-role patterning. These critical periods are crucial in the formation of the adolescent's sex role (Money, 1965).

In Money's view, there are two critical periods for sex-role development in youth: the first three years of life and puberty. During each of these periods, the young child or adolescent is confronted with rapid changes that influence his or her sex-role concept. One of several outcomes is possible: (1) The individual may form an adaptive concept of "maleness" or "femaleness" to fit his or her own physical category; (2) the individual may be confused about the psychological characteristics associated with his or her own physical category; or (3) the individual may settle on some mixed sex role (i.e., female role–male body, or male role–female body).

From the ages of one to three, children develop the ability to discriminate anatomical sex differences.

During the early critical period, from ages one to three, the child exercises his or her newly formed ability to discriminate anatomical sex differences and simple sex-role conventions (e.g., hair style, clothing) and to associate these with social attitudes about what boys and girls are like. During the critical adolescent period, sex-role identity once again is transformed, this time for different reasons. The adolescent experiences rapid physiological and anatomical changes and becomes able to deal with abstract social possibilities (e.g., what the ideal woman or man is like). These changes cause conflict and force the adolescent to reconsider ideas about sex roles.

Some of Money's research has focused on the earlier critical period. For example, Money has examined development in **hermaphrodites,** children born with abnormal sexual anatomies that make sex identification difficult (Money, 1965). In this way, he is able to see how biology and early socialization combine to influence sex-role development during later childhood, adolescence, and adulthood. At birth, hermaphrodites cannot be clearly identified as male or female on the basis of genital development. When such a child was nevertheless labeled a boy or a girl prior to the third or fourth birthday, later role development was consistent with the label. But when the label for the child was applied before the age of four and was later changed, severe maladjustment took place. The change in labeling usually was the result of extensive medical diagnosis, which revealed internal genital characteristics of the sex opposite to that formerly applied to the child. Boys and girls whose sex identification was changed before the age of three or four displayed relatively little maladjustment. These findings point up the importance of both biology and culture in the sex-role development of children.

Cognitive Factors

To explore the role of cognition in sex roles, the importance of self-categorization and language has been studied. First, we examine the idea of Lawrence Kohlberg and others that a stable gender identity must be reached before a sense of masculinity or femininity is achieved. Then we investigate the nature of sexism in language.

Self-Categorization and Stable Gender Identity

Lawrence Kohlberg (1966a) argued that to have an idea of what is masculine or feminine a child must be able to categorize objects into these two groups. According to Kohlberg, the categories become relatively stable for a child by the age of six. That is, by the age of six children have a fairly definite idea of which category they belong to. Further, they understand what is entailed by belonging to one category or the other and seldom fluctuate in their category judgments. This self-categorization is seen as the impetus for the unfolding of sex-role development according to Kohlberg.

Kohlberg reasons that sex-role development proceeds in this sequence: "I am a boy, I want to do boy things, therefore, the opportunity to do boy things is rewarding" (1966a, p. 89). The child, having acquired the ability to categorize, strives toward consistency between use of the categories and actual behavior. This striving for consistency forms the basis for the development of sex typing.

Others have expanded on Kohlberg's cognitive developmental theme (e.g. Block, 1973; Pleck, 1975; Rebecca, Hefner & Oleshansky, 1976). For example, one proposal suggests that initially there is a stage of undifferentiated sex-role concepts among very young children, then in the next stage (about the time of the preschool years) children adopt very rigid, conventional sex roles (Pleck, 1975). It is believed that this rigidity often peaks during the early adolescent years. Then at some point later in development, often not until the adult years, a stronger androgyny orientation emerges (e.g., Block, 1973; Pleck, 1975).

To investigate the cognitive developmental concepts of Kohlberg and others, Eileen O'Keefe and Janet Hyde (1983) studied the relation of cognitive developmental level to occupational choice and stereotyping. Two types of occupational attitudes were assessed: (1) personal aspirations and (2) ideas about jobs men and women do. Preschool, third grade, and sixth grade children were studied. Children chose stereotyped occupations for themselves even before they had developed a concept of gender stability. Boys' personal aspirations were

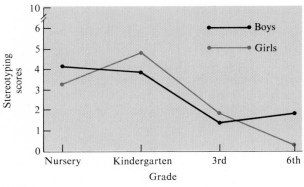

FIGURE 14.1
Stereotyping of adult occupations by children of different ages.
Note: 0 = no stereotyping; 10 = high stereotyping (O'Keefe and
Hyde, 1983).

more stereotyped than girls'. Gender-stable pre-schoolers gave more stereotyped responses than those not yet gender stable. And stereotyping decreased among the third and sixth graders (see figure 14.1). The results concerning the gender-stable preschoolers support Kohlberg's ideas about self-categorization; however, the early stereotyped responses of the nursery school children do not. The fact that young children already have stereotypes before they develop a stable gender identity is more compatible with the belief that environmental experiences contribute to sex-role development. We will discuss such environmental contributions shortly, but first we explore further information about the role of cognitive factors as we study language and sex roles.

PERSPECTIVE ON CHILD DEVELOPMENT 14.1

SEXISM IN CHILDREN'S THOUGHT AND LANGUAGE—HOW GOOD ARE GIRLS AT WUDGEMAKING IF THE WUDGEMAKER IS A "HE"?

One manner in which the role of language in sex-role development can be investigated is by studying children's interpretation of the "gender neutral" use of *he* and *his*. Janet Hyde (1984) investigated this issue by presenting cue sentences to first, third, and fifth graders, as well as college students. The individuals then told stories in response to a cue sentence containing *he, he or she,* or *they*. The individuals also supplied pronouns in a fill-in task and were questioned about their knowledge of the gender-neutral use of *he*. It was found that 12, 18, and 42 percent of the stories were about females when *he, she,* and *he or she* were used, respectively. Even first graders supplied *he* in gender-neutral fill-in sentences. Only 28 percent of the first graders, but 84 percent of the college students seemed to understand the grammatical rule for the gender use of *he*.

In a second experiment Hyde (1984) replicated some aspects of the first experiment and expanded the design to include third and fifth graders. *She* was included as a fourth pronoun condition in the storytelling and produced 77 percent female stories. The following description of a fictitious, gender-neutral occupation, wudgemaker, was read to the children, with repeated references either to *he, they, he or she,* or *she:*

Few people have heard of a job in factories, being a wudgemaker. Wudges are made of plastic, oddly shaped, and are an important part of video games. The wudgemaker works from a plan or pattern posted at eye level as *he or she* puts together the pieces at a table while *he or she* is sitting down. Eleven plastic pieces must be snapped together. Some of the pieces are tiny, so the *he or she* must have good coordination in *his or her* fingers. Once all eleven pieces are put together, *he or she* must test out the wudge to make sure that all of the moving pieces move properly. The wudgemaker is well paid, and must be a high school graduate, but *he or she* does not have to have gone to college to get the job.
(Hyde, 1984, p. 702)

One fourth of the children were given *he* as the pronoun, one fourth *they,* one fourth *he or she* (as shown above), and one fourth *she*. They were asked to rate how well women could do the job on a three-point scale and how well men could do the job. As shown in the figure at right, subject ratings of how well women could make wudges was influenced by pronoun, with ratings being lowest for *he,* intermediate for *they* and *he or she,* and highest for *she*. These data indicate that the use of gender-neutral *he,* compared to other pronouns, influences the formation of gender schema in children.

Language, Cognition, and Sex Roles

There is considerable interest in understanding the nature of sexism in language—the notion that the English language contains sex bias, particularly in terms of usages such as *he* and *man* to refer to everyone. To learn more about sexism in language, read Perspective on Child Development 14.1. Intriguing research on children's, adolescents', and adults' interpretations of various sex-related aspects of language is presented along with a discussion of whether sexist language produces sexist thought or vice versa.

Other research also suggests the importance of cognition in sex-role development. William Damon (1977) has conducted research revealing that the child's understanding of gender can influence his or her interpretation of **sex-role stereotypes** or expectations. In Damon's study, four- to nine-year-old children were told a story about George, a boy who persisted in playing with dolls, even after his parents informed him that boys should not play with dolls. The children subsequently were queried about the story in an effort to better understand their reasoning about sex roles. They were asked such questions as "Why do people tell George not to play with dolls? Is there a rule that boys should not play with dolls? What if George wanted to wear a dress to school?"

Damon found that four-year-olds consistently believed that doll play and cross-gender behavior is acceptable. But at about the age of six, children were vehement in their belief that doll play and cross-gender behavior were totally unacceptable. However, the nine-year-olds expressed less intense feelings about the doll

The research conducted by Janet Hyde (1984) touches on the important classic issue in developmental psychology first discussed in chapter 8 on language development. That is, to what extent does language influence thought or vice versa? In Hyde's research the issue is whether sexist language is primary and influences thought, or whether sexist thought is primary and produces sexist language. Stated in the language of schema theory, does sexist language produce the schema, or does the schema produce the sexist language? Hyde presented further data that address this issue. When the cue pronoun was *he,* the percentage of female stories was very low (12 percent in one experiment and 17 percent in another). However, when the truly neutral pronoun *they* was used, the percentage of female stories still was significantly below 50 percent (18 percent and 31 percent in the two experiments). Such results led Hyde to the conclusion that sexism in thought might be primary since an overwhelming majority of people think of males even when presented with the neutral pronoun *they.* However, it is important to note that even the youngest subjects had been exposed to sexist language for most of their lives, including hearing *he* and *they* used interchangeably in sentences. Thus, sexist thought may be the product of years of exposure to sexist language or other factors.

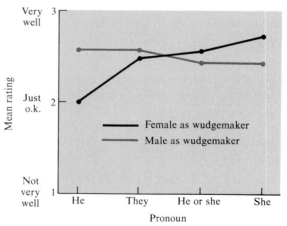

Mean ratings of how well women and men would do as wudgemakers, according to pronoun used in the description.

From Hyde, J. S., "Children's understanding of sexist language," in *Developmental Psychology,* 20, p. 703. Copyright © 1984 by the American Psychological Association. Reprinted by permission of the author.

Damon found nine-year-olds to be not that concerned about cross-gender behavior.

play and cross-gender behavior, becoming more flexible about sex roles. Damon's findings fit nicely with Lawrence Kohlberg's argument that until children recognize gender to be unchanging, they are likely to report that cross-gender behavior is reasonable behavior. However, when the child attains a sense of gender constancy, sex roles are more likely to be understood in terms of absolute standards or laws that every person should abide by. Subsequently, though, Kohlberg believes that as children's thought approaches and takes on more of a formal operational tone (more abstract and relative), they are more likely to reason in more flexible ways about sex-role standards.

While it is quite clear that cognitive factors are important in understanding the nature of children's sex-role development, this development has already started before children reach a stable sense of gender identity. For example, it has been found that two-year-old boys choose masculine toys even before they are aware such toys are more appropriate for them than for girls (Blakemore, LaRue & Olejnik, 1979). And three-year-old children have already acquired many sex-role stereotypes (e.g., Maccoby, 1980). Thus, while cognitive factors are important in understanding the manner in which children reason about sex roles, other factors must be contributing to sex-role development as well. As we see next, an important set of candidates for further understanding of sex-role development, in addition to biological and cognitive factors, are environmental influences.

ENVIRONMENTAL INFLUENCES

Cognitive capacities are extremely important in the child's development of sex-role identity, but these do not entirely explain the wide variation in behavior observed in members of the same sex. Although the child may have developed a clear idea of "male" and "female," the motivation for enacting appropriate behavior may be lacking. For example, a seven-year-old boy who knows he is a boy readily labels appropriate objects as male or female, but he has parents who support the women's liberation movement and stress equality between the sexes. His behavior will be less stereotyped along masculine lines than that of boys reared in more traditional homes.

One considerable change in the role of environmental influences on sex-role development in recent years has resulted in a deemphasis on parents as the critical socialization agents. There has been a corresponding increase in the belief that schools, peers, the media, and other family members should be given more attention when the child's sex-role development is at issue. Parents clearly are only one of many sources through which children learn about sex-role development. Yet it is important to guard against swinging too far in this direction because, particularly in the early years of life, parents do play a very important role in their child's sex-role development.

Our discussion of environmental influences on sex-role development emphasizes parent–child relationships, peers and teachers, media influences, and changing the sex-typed behavior of children.

Parent–Child Relationships

As already noted, Diana Baumrind (1982) has shown sex-typed mothers to be responsive and sex-typed fathers to be firm. Fathers and mothers both seem to be psychologically important for children even during infancy. Mothers are consistently given the responsibility for nurturance and physical child care, while fathers are more likely to engage in playful interaction with the child and be responsible for seeing that the child conforms to existing cultural norms. Fathers are more exacting and demanding with children than are mothers; and whether or not they have more influence on them, fathers are more involved in socializing their sons than their daughters (Lamb, 1981).

Parents often encourage girls to be more affectionate than boys.

Fathers seem to play an important role in the sex typing of both boys and girls. Reviews of sex-typing research indicate that fathers are more likely to act differently toward sons and daughters than mothers are (e.g., Huston, 1983). And most reviews of the father-absence literature (e.g., Lamb, 1981) conclude that boys show a more feminine patterning of behavior in father-absent than in father-present homes; however, close inspection of those studies suggests that this conclusion is more appropriate for young children, while the findings for elementary and secondary school children are mixed. For example, Hetherington, Cox, and Cox (1978) found that children's sex-typed behavior reflected more than the unavailability of a consistent adult male model. While many single-parent mothers were overprotective and apprehensive about their son's independence, when single parents encourage masculine and exploratory behavior and did not have a negative attitude toward the absent father, disruption in the son's sex-typed behavior did not occur.

Many parents encourage boys and girls to engage in different types of play activities even during infancy. In particular many parents emphasize that doll play is for girls only, while boys are more likely to be rewarded for engaging in gross motor activities. And often parents play more actively with male babies and respond more positively to physical activity by boys. There is also some evidence that parents encourage girls to be more dependent, more affectionate, and more emotional than boys; but there is no indication that parents show different reactions to aggression according to their child's sex. And with increasing age, boys are permitted more freedom by parents who allow them to be away from home without supervision than are girls (Huston, 1983).

Thus, we can see that parents, by action and example, influence their child's sex-role development. In the psychoanalytic view this influence stems principally from the child's identification with the parent of the same sex. The child develops a sense of likeness to the parent of the same sex and strives to emulate that parent. In social learning theory, the child acquires a motive to imitate the actions of the parent of the same sex.

Peers

Most children have already acquired a preference for sex-typed toys and activities before they are exposed to school. During the preschool and elementary school years, teachers and peers usually maintain these preferences through feedback to the boy or girl.

Children who play in sex-appropriate activities tend to be rewarded for doing so by their peers, while those who play in cross-sex activities tend to be criticized by their peers or left to play alone. Indeed, children seem to differentiate their peers very early on the basis of sex, with such patterns reflecting the preschool child's increasing awareness of culturally prescribed expectancies for males and females.

One of the most frequent observations of elementary school children's play groups is their gender segregation. Boys tend to play with boys, and girls are much more likely to play with girls. In one recent investigation (Luria & Herzog, 1985) children's free play was observed in several contexts—during lunch, on a museum trip, and at public and private schools, for example—and with different ages of children, three- and four-year-olds and fourth, fifth, and sixth graders. All-female, all-male, and cross-sexed groups of children were observed in all settings and at all ages. Interestingly, public school fourth through sixth graders showed much less cross-sex peer grouping than their private school counterparts. And it was only in the public school groupings that an overt ideology of cross-sex exclusion was ever heard. Overall, however, there appears to be an acceptance of cross-sex play in most children's peer groups, even though the majority of elementary school children express a same-sex play group preference.

Another set of recent observations from working-class elementary schools revealed considerable sex segregation that increased with age (Thorne, 1985). Somewhat separate girls' and boys' subcultures consolidated by about the third grade. However, the extent of sex segregation varied according to the context in which the children were observed and was experienced differently by some boys and girls than by others. Particular attention was given to tomboys in this investigation, those girls who cross gender lines to participate in the world of boys. Successful tomboys were observed to be gender bilinguals, switching patterns of touch, space use, talk, and naming as they crossed the gender divide. The daily interactions of a successful fifth grade tomboy showed that her access to boys' segregated activities depended on her specific athletic skills, verbal skills, and willingness to fight. She maintained access to the world of elementary school girls by claiming friendship with the most popular girl and by guarding girls' play from boys' invasions. Problems for the fifth grade girl emerged when she became involved in heterosexual atmospheres. To cope with this situation, the fifth grade tomboy used different strategies to avoid "going with" a boy and to maintain her "buddy" relationship with boys.

As we can see in such studies of children's peer groups, gender segregation and integration become an important aspect of sex-role development. And as we see next, not only peers, but teachers as well, contribute to children's sex-role development.

Teachers

Actual observations of teacher behavior in both preschool and elementary school classes suggest that boys are given more disapproval, scolding, and other forms of negative attention than girls (e.g., Cherry, 1975; Serbin, O'Leary, Kent & Tonick, 1973). However, the findings for positive teacher behavior are mixed; some investigators find that teachers give more positive attention to girls (Fagot, 1973), while others find that boys

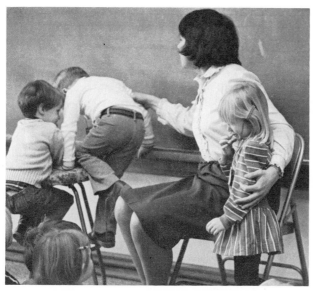

Preschool- and elementary-school female teachers are more likely to reward more traditional feminine than masculine characteristics, according to Fagot.

get more positive attention (e.g., Serbin et al., 1973). Similarly, there is no consistent evidence that teachers reward sex-typed social behaviors differently for boys and girls (Huston, 1983). Sometimes, however, the fact that boys do not do as well as girls in school early in their development is attributed to the fact that either female teachers treat boys differently from girls or that boys have few male models as teachers.

Female teachers are more likely to reward "feminine" behavior than "masculine" behavior. Beverly Fagot (1975) reasoned that teachers would most probably support student behaviors that were a part of their own behavioral system. Since most preschool and elementary school teachers are females, they would be expected to reward behaviors consistent with the feminine, or "good girl," stereotype. As expected, she found that teachers reinforced both boys' and girls' feminine behaviors 83 percent of the time. In a similar study Boyd McCandless (1973) found that female teachers rewarded feminine behaviors 51 percent of the time and masculine behaviors 49 percent of the time. Perhaps if more male adults were involved in early education, there would be more support of masculine behavior and activity.

It appears that by the time children have entered junior high school, they will have developed the expectancy that teachers are more likely to reward feminine than masculine behaviors. However, in the junior high school years a change in the mix of teachers young adolescents are exposed to occurs: During the junior high school years they are exposed to more equal numbers of male and female teachers. Unfortunately, few studies focus on how male and female teachers interact with male and female students during the adolescent years. A good guess is that some important cross-sex effects begin to emerge with the onset of puberty. For example, many young adolescent girls develop "crushes" on their male teachers. Also, some strong same-sex effects may result, one example being the adolescent male's identification with a male coach or teacher.

One study of junior high school students did reveal that teachers have reasonably strong stereotypes about male and female students (Buxton, 1973). "Good" male students were described by the junior high school teachers as active, adventurous, aggressive, assertive, curious, energetic, enterprising, frank, independent, and inventive. By contrast, "good" female students were depicted as appreciative, calm, conscientious, considerate, cooperative, mannerly, poised, sensitive, dependable, efficient, mature, obliging, and thorough. Such stereotypes may guide the way the teacher interacts with boys and girls and may influence the way boys and girls view their own sex role.

In sum, during the early years of schooling, teachers react more negatively to boys than to girls but do not necessarily give them less positive reinforcement or reward them differently for sex-typed behavior. However, teachers do have stereotypes about "good" masculine and "good" feminine behavior and are more likely to reward "feminine" behavior in boys and girls. Teachers, then, do exert a strong influence on children's sex typing, as do peers.

The Media

Children and adolescents watch an average of three to five hours of television every day of their lives. The programs they watch portray distinct male and female roles, and these portrayals can influence their concept of sex roles. Leading feminists argue that television teaches stereotyped values to children and does particular damage to girls (e.g., Deckhard, 1979; Hennessee & Nicholson, 1972). Perloff, Brown, and Miller (1978) have suggested that children see very different images of males and females on television. Males and females seem to appear with different frequency on television, occupational stereotypes are rampant, and these stereotypes appear not just on television but in movies, magazines, and books as well.

According to the more than twenty studies of male and female television exposure that have been conducted since the mid-1950s, males have outnumbered females in disproportionate numbers. About 70 percent of the characters on prime-time shows are male (Miller & Reeves, 1976; Tedesco, 1974).

In both television programs and commercials, men are portrayed as members of the work force more often than women are. For example, a woman in a leading role is often portrayed as a housewife or in some romantic capacity. In one investigation almost two of every three females were depicted as unemployed, but only one of three males was cast in this way (Tedesco, 1974). Men are also pictured in a greater variety of occupations than women are (e.g., Miller & Reeves, 1976), as well as having higher-status jobs (Downing, 1974).

Sex-role stereotypes also appear in the print media. In magazine advertising, females are generally portrayed as homemakers who are dependent on men for protection (Courtney & Lockeretz, 1971). Females usually appear in advertisements for beauty products, cleaning products, and home appliances, while males are usually in advertisements for cars, liquor, and travel.

In recent years the television networks have become more sensitive to how males and females are portrayed on television shows. Many programs now focus on divorced families, cohabitation, and women in high-status roles. But even with the onset of this type of programming, the overwhelming conclusion is that children are exposed to a sex-role stereotype that features males in dominant, assertive, high-status positions and females in submissive, nurturant, low-status positions.

To prove that television has an impact on sex-role development, it must be shown that children actually incorporate television's portrayals of males and females into their own sex-role values and identities. Unfortunately, there have been few investigations of this important matter. In one investigation children's imitation of mass media models was studied (Plost &

Rosen, 1974). Junior high school students were presented a slide show picturing a male and female in two occupations that career-development experts indicate are not sex typed: a systems analyst and a computer software designer. The students were shown two different tapes, one in which the computer designer was played by a male and the systems analyst by a female, and one in which the positions were reversed. In each case the students stated that they preferred the occupation depicted by the model of their sex. The important implication here is that youth may restrict their occupational aspirations to those careers portrayed as appropriate for their own sex.

Changing Sex-Typed Behavior

Efforts to change children's sex-typed behavior have taken two directions (Huston, 1983): "Gender-deviant" children are trained to show more appropriate sex-typed behavior, and attempts are made to free normal children from rigidly sex-typed patterns. Both types of intervention create ethical concerns; yet both produce valuable information about sex typing, that is, about psychological aspects of being male or female.

Most studies of gender deviance have included only boys, who are diagnosed as gender deviant when they play mostly with feminine sex-typed toys, dress up in female clothes, choose girls rather than boys as playmates, engage in female role playing, fantasize about being a girl, and express themselves with feminine gestures (Green, 1974; Rekers, 1979). In one investigation based on detailed observations, girls used very different gestural patterns than boys, such as hanging their wrists, limply holding books with their arms folded toward their body, and so forth (Rekers, 1979). Gender-deviant boys not only preferred feminine activities but also purposely avoided masculine activities. In particular, they indicated that the rough-and-tumble play of other boys either disinterested or frightened them (Green, 1974).

Gender deviance among girls has received less attention, possibly because our society allows girls more flexibility in their dress, play activities, and sex-typed interests than it does boys. For example, in one study a majority of junior high girls described themselves as "sort of tomboyish," and a majority of adult women indicated that they were tomboys during childhood

Our society allows more flexibility for female than male roles.

(Hyde, Rosenberg & Behrman, 1977). The characteristics used to describe gender-deviant girls are parallel to those used for boys—preferring masculine activities and boys as playmates, taking male roles in fantasy, fantasizing about being a boy, and dressing in male clothes. While masculine clothing and interests are commonplace among girls, gender-deviant girls also are characterized by strong avoidance of feminine clothing, activities, and playmates.

Both behavioral and psychoanalytic treatment procedures have been used in attempts to alter the sex-typed behavior of gender-deviant children. These treatment procedures have led to changes in children's play patterns but usually only in the situation where the treatment occurred. Consequently, clinical treatment has been augmented by direct interventions at home and at school. Parents and teachers have been taught behavior modification techniques, and young male adults have visited the children at home or at school, attempting to teach the gender-deviant boys athletic skills because feminine boys tend to perform very poorly in athletic skills. Indications are that such programs have led to more normal sex-typed behavior in boys, lasting for as long as one to three years after the intervention (Rekers, 1979).

PERSPECTIVE ON CHILD DEVELOPMENT 14.2

CAN AND SHOULD ANDROGYNY BE TAUGHT TO CHILDREN IN SCHOOL?

Believing that rigid sex roles may be detrimental to both males and females, a number of educators and social scientists have developed materials and created courses involving the teaching of androgyny to students. Among the curricula developed have been resource guides and examples of materials that can be used to study sex roles (Biemer, 1975; Hahn, 1975; Holman, 1975; Nickerson, 1975), as well as courses with outlines and lesson plans (Emma Willard Task Force on Education, 1971; Gaskell & Knapp, 1976; National Education Association, 1974; Stein, 1972).

In one study (Kahn & Richardson, 1983) tenth through twelfth grade students from three high schools in British Columbia were exposed to a twenty-unit course in sex roles. Students analyzed the history and modern development of male and female gender roles and evaluated the utility of traditionally accepted stereotypes of males and females. The course centered on student discussion supplemented by films, videotapes, and guest speakers. The materials included exercises to heighten awareness of one's own attitudes and beliefs, role reversal of typical sex-typed behaviors, role play of difficult work and family conflict circumstances, and assertiveness training for direct, honest communication.

A total of sixty-nine students participated in the sex-role courses. To determine whether the course changed the participants' sex-role orientation, these students were compared with fifty-nine students from the same schools who did not take the sex-role course. Prior to the start of the course, all students were given the Bem Sex Role Inventory. No differences between the two groups were found at that time. After the students completed the course, they and the control group were given the Attitudes Toward Women Scale (Spence & Helmreich, 1972) in an effort to determine their attitudes, either liberal or traditional, toward the changing roles of women in society. Scores on this measure can range from 25 (highly traditional) to 100 (highly liberal). As shown in the table at right, in schools 1 and 2, the students who took the sex-role course had more liberal attitudes about the female's role in society than students who did not take the course. In these schools, the students primarily were girls who chose to take the course as an elective. In school 3, students who took the sex-role class actually had more conservative attitudes toward the female's role in society than those who did not. The sex-role class in school 3 was required, and it was comprised almost equally of females and males.

While diagnosis and treatment of gender deviance have occurred, we have little knowledge of the origins of such patterns. One possibility is that many parents are indifferent to the occurrence of gender-deviant patterns of behavior in young children. Some parents think it is cute when little boys continue to dress up as females and play with dolls. Such children are often referred for treatment only after someone outside the family points out the child's effeminate characteristics. Other factors that show up in the case histories of some gender-deviant boys are maternal overprotection of boys and restrictions on rough-and-tumble play, absence of an adult male, weak father–son relationship, physical beauty of the small boy that leads to his being treated as a girl, absence of male playmates, and maternal dominance. In addition to attempting to change the sex-typed behavior of gender-deviant children, another effort has focused on teaching children about androgyny. An overview of research efforts designed to train children to become more androgynous is presented in Perspective on Child Development 14.2. And a summary of the information about sex roles considered thus far is provided in Concept Table 14.1.

Another attempt to induce a more androgynous sex-role orientation in students also met with mixed results when all students were considered (Guttentag & Bray, 1976). The curriculum lasted for one year and was implemented in the kindergarten, fifth, and ninth grade classes. It involved books, discussion materials, and classroom exercises. The program was most successful with the fifth graders and least successful with the ninth graders (who actually displayed a "boomerang effect" that produced even more rigid sex-typed behavior). The program's success varied from class to class, seeming to be most effective when the teacher produced sympathetic reaction in the peer group; however, some classes ridiculed and rejected the curriculum.

Ethical concerns are aroused when the issue is one of teaching children to depart from socially approved behavior patterns, particularly when there is no evidence of extreme sex typing in the groups of children to whom the interventions are applied. The advocates of androgyny programs believe that traditional sex typing is psychologically harmful for all children and that it has prevented many girls and women from experiencing equal opportunity. Huston (1983) concluded that while some people believe androgyny is more adaptive than either a traditional masculine or feminine pattern, it is not possible to ignore the imbalance within our culture that values masculinity more than femininity.

Sex-Role Attitudes Related to the Woman's Role in Society Following a High School Course on Sex Roles that Emphasized Androgyny

School	Groups	
	Experimental (Took sex-role course)	Control (Did not take course)
1	83.3	75.6
2	85.3	73.9
3	68.8	76.2

From Kahn, S. E., and A. Richardson, "Evaluation of a course in sex roles for secondary school students," in *Sex Roles*, 9, pp. 431–440. © 1983 Plenum Press, New York, NY.

CONCEPT TABLE 14.1 Androgyny, Sex Roles, Biological, Cognitive, and Environmental Factors		
Concept	**Processes/Related Ideas**	**Characteristics/Description**
Androgyny and the components of sex-role development	Sex roles	Sex role involves behaviors expected of individuals because they are male or female.
	Sexual or gender identity	Sexual identity involves the extent to which individuals take on as a part of their personality the behaviors and attitudes associated with male or female roles.
	Androgyny	Androgyny suggests that the most competent individuals have both masculine and feminine attributes. No consistent research evidence has been found that demonstrates androgynous individuals are more competent than others.
Biological and cognitive factors	Anatomy is destiny	Freud and Erikson argued that sex-role development is tied to anatomy and reproductive forces.
	Hormones	At two points in development hormones become critical— prenatally and during adolescence.
	Critical periods	Money argued that the first three years of life and puberty are critical periods but that sex-role development is always the result of the interaction of biology and culture.
	Cognitive factors	Kohlberg stressed that by age six the child's cognitive ability leads to categorization in sex-role terms. The cognitive developmental theory of Kohlberg has suggested that self-categorization and the development of a stable gender identity are precursors for sex-typed behavior. Others have expanded on this view and feel that a rigidity of sex roles often occurs during early adolescence. Research shows that this rigidity is stronger for boys than for girls. Damon's work suggests a cognitive developmental progression of sex roles. Hyde's research reveals links between language and thought in sex roles.
Environmental factors	Parent–child relationships	Parents by action and example influence children's sex-role development.
	Peers	Children tend to differentiate their peers very early on the basis of sex and continue to prefer same-sex peer groups throughout childhood. Nonetheless, cross-sex peer play is often acceptable.
	Teachers	Teachers react more negatively to boys than to girls in early schooling and are more likely to reward "feminine" behaviors in boys and girls.
	Media	The television shows children watch involve heavy sex-role stereotypes, as do the print media.
	Changing sex-typed behavior	Gender-deviant children are trained to show more appropriate sex-role behavior, and attempts are made to free children from rigid sex-typed patterns. Both interventions involve ethical considerations.

SEX DIFFERENCES AND STEREOTYPES

In this section we discuss the nature of sex-role stereotypes, provide a summary of sex differences, and focus more extensively on one possible sex difference that has been given increased research attention—achievement.

How Sex-Role Stereotypes Work

Sex-role stereotypes are broad categories that reflect our impressions about other people, events, and ourselves. The world is extremely complex; every day we are confronted with thousands of different stimuli. The use of stereotypes is one way in which we simplify this complexity. If we simply assign a label (e.g., the quality of "softness") to someone, we than have much less to

TABLE 14.3
Knowing the Sexes

How well do you know the sexes? For each of the adjectives listed below, indicate whether you think it better describes women or men in our society. Be honest with yourself, and follow your first impulse in responding.

a. verbal	g. mathematical
b. sensitive	h. suggestible
c. active	i. analytic
d. competitive	j. social
e. compliant	k. aggressive
f. dominant	

After recording your answers, continue reading this chapter for an interpretation of your responses.

Boys' superiority in math skills usually doesn't appear until the age of 12 or 13.

consider when we think about the person. However, once labels have been assigned, we find it remarkably difficult to abandon them, even in the face of contradictory evidence. Do you think you have a repertory of sex-role stereotypes? Table 14.3 provides a brief exercise in understanding sex-role behavior. Record your answers on a separate sheet of paper so you can check them later when they are discussed.

Many stereotypes are so general that they are extremely ambiguous. Take, for example, the stereotypes "masculine" and "feminine." Very diverse behaviors may be called up to support each stereotype, such as scoring a touchdown or growing facial hair. The stereotype, of course, may also be modified in the face of cultural change; whereas at one time muscular development may be thought masculine, at another time masculinity may be typified by a lithe, slender physique. The behaviors popularly agreed upon as reflecting the stereotype may fluctuate according to subculture.

Walter Mischel (1970) comments that even though the behaviors that are supposed to fit the stereotype often do not, the label itself may have significant consequences for the individual. Labeling a person "homosexual," "queer," or "sissy" can produce dire social consequences in terms of status and acceptance in groups, even when the person so labeled is not a homosexual, queer, or sissy. Regardless of their accuracy, stereotypes can cause tremendous emotional upheaval in individuals and undermine their own opinions about themselves and their status.

Sex Differences

How well did you do with the adjectives in table 14.3? According to Eleanor Maccoby and Carol Jacklin (1974), here are the facts: Women are more verbal (a); men are more mathematical (g) and aggressive (k).

With regard to verbal ability, girls tend to understand and produce language more competently than boys do. Girls are superior to boys in higher-order verbal tasks, such as making analogies, understanding difficult written material, and writing creatively, as well as on lower-order verbal tasks, such as spelling. Maccoby and Jacklin speculated that girls probably get an early start on boys in the use of language, but studies indicate that differences in the verbal abilities of boys and girls are not consistent until about the age of eleven. A similar developmental trend can be seen for mathematical skills, but this time in favor of boys. Boys' superiority in math skills does not usually appear until the age of twelve or thirteen and does not seem to be entirely influenced by the fact that boys take more math courses. Likewise, male superiority on visual-spatial tasks does not consistently appear until adolescence. However, sex differences in aggression appear early, by the age of two or three, and continue through adolescence. The differences are not confined to physical aggression—boys also show more verbal aggression as well as more fantasy aggression (imagining harm to someone or to some object rather than actually performing an aggressive act).

Closely related to ideas about math and visual-spatial abilities is whether there are differences in computer use, interest, and ability. Recent information suggests that as a society we are already beginning to define computers as predominantly male machines. Is this a stereotype or are there sex differences related to computers? To learn about the research done on this important topic in contemporary society, read Perspective on Child Development 14.3.

PERSPECTIVE ON CHILD DEVELOPMENT 14.3

GIRLS AND COMPUTERS

Marlaine Lockheed (1985) recently reviewed what we know about girls and computers. While girls and boys seem to show similar appreciation of the importance computers have for their personal futures, boys are more likely than girls to take computer courses in school, to report using computers in extracurricular settings, to indicate more frequent home use of computers, and to have more positive attitudes toward computers. For example, in computer courses offered in schools, male to female ratios range from 2:1 to 5:1, and boys have outnumbered girls at computer camps by approximately 3:1 (Hess & Miura, 1985). Further, a survey of home computer use found that 70 percent of the main users were male (*USA Today,* 1984). Several investigators have also found that males have more positive attitudes toward computers than do females (Chen, 1985; Collis, 1984).

While computers can be studied from the perspective of their function (such as object of study, recreation, tool), most research focused on sex differences has not made this distinction. It appears, however, that sex differences in computer usage emerge for some uses and not for others. Males use computers more than females for programming and game playing but not more for other computer applications, such as word processing. Moreover, sex differences seem to depend on the context in which the computer is used. For instance, computers in computer centers and arcades, which are often male "game preserves," are more frequently used by males, while computers in mixed-sex classrooms and offices are used equally by both sexes (Becker, 1985; Gutek & Bikson, 1985).

Let's look in greater detail at the use of computers for programming and why males outdistance females in this regard. Lockheed (1985) described six reasons why this may occur. First, both boys and girls are socialized to associate programming with math, mainly because programming courses are offered in conjunction with math courses or because math courses are prerequisites for programming courses. Math is perceived more as a masculine than a feminine domain. Second, the demands of programming, which emphasize rules and winning, are more compatible with male than female values (which emphasize relational ethics)(Gilligan, 1985). Third, boys are more likely than girls to possess the cognitive skills needed for programming, as noted in our emphasis on sex differences in math abilities. However, on many cognitive skills there are no sex differences. Fourth, the content and depth of introductory programming as taught in secondary schools is seen as irrelevant by girls to their academic objectives. Fifth, parental economic and personal support for computer programming is less positive for girls than boys—note the difference in sex enrollments in computer camps mentioned earlier. Sixth, teachers may unknowingly discriminate against girls in computer classes, providing a more positive climate for male use (McKelvey, 1984).

Undergirding much of the concern about sex differences in computer use is that if females fail to become involved with computers, they will be left behind males in an increasingly technological society. In two recent books, *Turing's Man* (Bolter, 1984) and *The Second Self* (Turkle, 1984), technology is portrayed as overwhelming humanity. In both books, females are not pictured in this technological, computer culture. One comment notes, "There are few women hackers. This is a male world" (Turkle, 1984, p. 210). As Marlaine Lockheed (1985) concludes, Turkle's computer hacker as a male should not serve as the model of computer users in the future.

Two myths about the sexes merit further examination: that girls are more social than boys, and that girls are more suggestible than boys. In many of the studies reviewed by Maccoby and Jacklin (1974), the measure of sociability was based upon diverse aspects of social interaction, which included interest in social events (e.g., faces and voices), responsiveness to social reward, dependence on caregivers, time spent with playmates, and understanding of the emotional needs of others. There simply was no evidence to suggest that girls engaged in these practices more than boys did. In some cases the reverse was observed; for example, boys spent more time with playmates than girls did. Suggestibility was indexed by children's spontaneous imitation of models, susceptibility to persuasive communication, and social conformity to group norms. There were no consistent sex differences in a large number of studies measuring these characteristics.

Even though we tell you straightforwardly that girls are not more social and not more suggestible than boys, do you believe us? If you do not, you have a firsthand example of how difficult it is to discard stereotypes.

Not everyone agrees with all of the conclusions of Maccoby and Jacklin's widely quoted work on sex differences. Jeanne Block (1976) acknowledges that Maccoby and Jacklin have made an important contribution to information about sex roles, but she also believes that some of their conclusions, and some of the data on which the conclusions are based, are shakier than Maccoby and Jacklin lead readers to believe. She argues that Maccoby and Jacklin did not differentiate between those studies that were methodologically sound and those that were not. She further criticizes the decisions they made about what kinds of studies should go into a particular category. For example, Maccoby and Jacklin lumped together many measures in their assessment of parental pressure on achievement motivation including the following: amount of praise or criticism for intellectual performance; parental standards for intellectual performance as expressed on a questionnaire item; expectations of household help from youth; the ages at which parents feel it is appropriate to teach a boy or girl more mature behaviors; number of anxious intrusions in the youth's task performance; pressure for success on memory tasks. While many of the measures are clearly linked with the achievement dimension, others may be more peripheral.

Although Block does commend Maccoby and Jacklin for their completion of the long, difficult task of organizing a sprawling, unruly body of information, she also suggests that such data are open to error and reasonable argument at virtually every step of the analysis. In other words, anyone attempting to impose structure and meaning on some 1,600 disparate studies of sex roles is bound to make a few questionable decisions. For those of you interested in reading more about sex differences in adolescence, both Maccoby and Jacklin's book (1974) and Block's critique (1976) are highly recommended.

Another critic of Maccoby and Jacklin (Tieger, 1980) argues that sex differences in aggression are not biologically based but are instead learned. Tieger argues that consistent sex differences do not emerge until about the age of six and that there are ample conditions in the first six years of the child's life for aggression to be learned. In a rejoinder to Tieger, Maccoby and Jacklin (1980) reviewed their data and conducted some further analyses. The reassessment supported their earlier claims that greater aggression by boys occurs well before the age of six, is present in studies of nonhuman primates, and appears in cross-cultural studies of children.

Achievement

Few topics have generated more controversy in the last decade than the belief that many women have been socialized to assume roles of incompetency rather than competency. Diana Baumrind (1972) has distinguished between instrumental competence and incompetence. Boys, she says, are trained to become instrumentally competent, while girls learn how to become instrumentally incompetent. By instrumental competence, Baumrind means behavior that is socially responsible and purposeful. **Instrumental incompetence** is generally aimless behavior.

The following is evidence offered by Baumrind (1972) in support of her argument: (1) Few women obtain jobs in science, and of those who do, few achieve high positions; (2) being a female is devalued by society; (3) being independent and achieving intellectual status causes the female to lose her "femininity" in society's eyes—both men and women devalue such behaviors in women; (4) parents usually have lower achievement aspirations for girls than boys (for example, parents expect their sons to become doctors and their daughters to become nurses); and (5) girls and women are more oriented toward expressive behavior than boys and men are.

When the total picture is considered, it does seem that girls have been socialized into roles of instrumental incompetence. There is reason to believe that differences in the achievement orientation of boys and girls are learned—not innately determined by sex. Stein and Bailey (1973) have listed several parental characteristics or attributes that are associated with the development of achievement orientation in girls. For example, achievement orientation can be encouraged through the modeling of a mother who has a career. In some instances, particularly when the mother assumes a traditional female role, the social interaction of the father takes on greater importance. Stein and Bailey also point out that socialization practices fostering so-called femininity in girls often run counter to those practices producing achievement orientation. Moderate parental permissiveness, coupled with attempts to accelerate achievement, is related to achievement orientation in girls. This kind of parenting is not compatible with what is usually prescribed for rearing a young woman.

A great deal of attention has been paid to expectancy for success, which seems to cross many areas of achievement. In general, girls tend to have a lower expectancy for success, lower levels of aspiration, more anxiety about failing, and a stronger tendency to avoid risking failure and to be more likely to accept failure than boys (Parsons, Ruble, Hodges & Small, 1976; Stein & Bailey, 1973). Girls are also more likely to attribute failure to their own inability, and success to external causes, while boys are more likely to assign success to ability, and failure to external causes. Findings such as these have led researchers such as Carol Dweck (Dweck & Elliot, 1983) to introduce the concept of learned helplessness as one explanation of the comparatively low achievement orientation of females.

Learned Helplessness A state of **learned helplessness** develops when a child believes that the rewards she or he receives are beyond personal control (Seligman, 1975). Two major systems of learned helplessness are a lack of motivation and negative affect. For example, if the child in a failure situation sees her behavior as irrelevant to the outcome, she is displaying

To what extent might some aspects of girls' achievement behavior be related to learned helplessness?

learned helplessness. Such perceptions lead to attributions that are seen as incontrollable or unchangeable, such as lack of ability, difficulty of the task, or presumably fixed attitudes of other people. In addition, attributions of failure to these factors are often linked with deterioration of performance in the face of failure. Individuals who attribute their failure to controllable or changeable factors, such as effort or luck, are more likely to show improvement in their performance (Dweck, 1975; Dweck & Reppucci, 1973; Weiner, 1974).

A number of investigations of achievement behavior suggest that girls are more likely to attribute failure to uncontrollable factors, like lack of ability, than boys (Dweck & Reppucci, 1973; Nicholls, 1975); to display disrupted performance or decreased effort under the pressure of impending failure or evaluation (Dweck & Gilliard, 1975); and to avoid situations in which failure is likely (Crandall & Rabson, 1960).

These sex differences in the effects of failure feedback on achievement behavior generally are attributed to girls' greater dependency on external social evaluation. However, some investigators believe that different evaluations of boys and girls by adults and peers may influence such sex differences. For example, Dweck and Bush (1976) found that when failure feedback for girls came from adults, little change in the girls' achievement behavior resulted; but when the feedback came from peers, the girls' achievement behavior increased substantially.

TABLE 14.4

Expectations of High-, Average-, and Low-Achieving Boys and Girls

Group	Initial Expectation		
	Grade 1	Grade 3	Total
Girls			
High achievers	6.2	2.6	4.4
Average achievers	6.6	7.8	7.2
Low achievers	6.6	8.2	7.4
Boys			
High achievers	7.6	6.6	7.1
Average achievers	8.8	6.4	7.6
Low achievers	4.6	4.8	4.7

From Stipek, D. J., and J. M. Hoffman, "Children's achievement-related experiences as a function of academic performance histories and sex," in *Journal of Educational Psychology*, 72, pp. 861–865. Copyright © 1980 by the American Psychological Association.

There does seem to be evidence that girls form lower expectancies for success than their past performance warrants (Dweck & Eliot, 1983). Girls, even when they outperform boys on a task, report that they do not feel they did as well when queried later. And it is often the *brightest* girls who underestimate their skills the most. For example, in one investigation (Stipek & Hoffman, 1980), the highest-achieving girls actually had lower expectancies for success than the average- or low-achieving girls. For boys, the expected results were obtained; that is, higher-achieving boys generated higher expectancies of success. (See table 14.4.)

SEX-ROLE DEVELOPMENT

Our overview of sex-role development focuses on the first three years of life, the third through the seventh years of life, middle childhood, and adolescence.

The First Three Years of Life

The majority of research studies focused on sex-role development have been conducted with children aged two to nine years. While some sex typing likely occurs during the first several years of life, it is difficult to assess. However, during the eighteen-month to three-year-old age period, children begin to show a great deal of interest in sex-typed play and activities. In home observations of toddlers, girls were more likely to play with soft toys, dolls, and dress-up clothes and to dance more, whereas boys were more likely to play with blocks and

transportation toys and to manipulate the objects (Fagot, 1974). During the one-and-one-half to three-year-old age period, children also begin to classify themselves and others according to gender (Marcus & Corsini, 1978; McConaghy, 1979). At this same time, young children interpret many of the activities and objects around them in culturally defined sex-appropriate ways. By the time children are three years of age, they know the sex stereotypes for toys, games, household objects, clothing, and work (Ruble & Ruble, 1980). Of all of these content areas of sex typing, sex-typed interests and activities appear earliest in the child's development (Huston, 1983).

Three to Seven Years of Age

During the three- to seven-year-old age period, children begin to acquire an understanding of gender constancy and increasingly enjoy being with same-sex peers (Hartup, 1983). At this time, they gain knowledge about stereotypes of sex-typed personal and social attributes. Masculine stereotypes include such traits as strength, robustness, aggression, adventurousness, and dominance; female stereotypes include such characteristics as the ability to express emotions, gentleness, submission, fretfulness, and coquetry (Best et al., 1977). Sex differences in responses to these stereotyped attributes begin to appear in this age range, and it has been found that boys consistently hold more stereotyped views than girls (Emmerich, 1979; Gold, Andres & Glorieux, 1979). During the three- to seven-year-old period, there is also evidence that children increasingly prefer same-sex models and attachment figures (Slaby & Frey, 1975).

Middle Childhood

In the middle childhood years, two divergent trends in sex typing occur. Children increase their understanding of culturally defined expectations for males and females, and simultaneously the behavior and attitude of boys increasingly reflect masculine sex typing. However, during the middle years of childhood girls do not show an increased interest in feminine activities. Actually, many girls begin to show a stronger preference for masculine interests and activities, a finding that has appeared in research studies conducted from the 1920s to the present. In one research study (Richardson & Simpson, 1982), the toy preferences of 750

TABLE 14.5
Proportions of Males and Females Requesting
Items in Each Category

	Male (%)	Female (%)
Classes of items requested by significantly more males:		
Vehicles	43.5	8.2
Sport	25.1	15.1
Spatial-temporal	24.5	15.6
Military toys	23.4	.8
Race cars	23.4	5.1
Doll (humanoid)	22.8	6.6
Real vehicles	15.3	9.7
Doll (male)	10.0	2.8
Outer space toys	7.5	.3
Depots	6.4	.5
Machines	4.5	.8
Classes of items requested by significantly more females:		
Doll (female)	.6	27.4
Doll (baby)	.6	23.0
Domestic	1.7	21.7
Educational-art	11.4	21.4
Clothes	11.1	18.9
Doll houses	1.9	16.1
Clothing accessories	2.2	15.3
Doll accessories	1.1	12.5
Stuffed animals	5.0	9.7
Furnishings	1.9	5.4

From Richardson, J. G., and C. H. Simpson, "Children, gender, and social
structure: An analysis of the contents of letters to Santa Claus," in *Child
Development*, 53, pp. 429–436. Copyright © 1982 by The Society for
Research in Child Development, Inc. Reprinted by permission.

children five to nine years old were assessed by evaluating their letters to Santa Claus. As shown in table 14.5, while such requests for toys were sex typed, more girls than boys asked for cross-sexed items. Boys and girls, though, do begin to show more flexibility in their understanding of sex-role stereotypes in the elementary school years, seeing that stereotypes are not absolute and that alternatives are feasible.

Huston (1983) calls attention to an additional developmental trend in sex typing. Interests, play activities, and social and occupational roles are sex typed earlier and in a more clearly defined way than are personality characteristics and social behaviors. Parents and other socialization agents also place more emphasis on sex-typed interests and activities than on personal–social sex differences.

Adolescence

During adolescence the individual's sex-role development becomes more wrapped up in matters of sexuality than was true during the infant and childhood years. As puberty proceeds, the boy's and girl's body becomes

BERRY'S WORLD

"Please don't bring me anything that requires my acting out traditional female roles!"

Reprinted by permission of Newspaper Enterprise Association, Inc.

flooded with sex hormones. The young adolescent increasingly thinks about himself or herself as a sexual being and views others as sexual beings as well. Such thoughts are often uncertain and may entail idealistic overtones. Recall from our discussion of cognitive development in chapter 6 that adolescent thought is more abstract and ideal than child thought. Thus, we would expect adolescents to engage in more abstract definitions of sex roles and render more symbolic interpretations of sex roles. Further, we would anticipate that adolescents become more flexible in their interpretation of sex roles because their increased reasoning powers enable them to see alternative ways in which matters can be handled. The idealism of adolescence may be manifested in thoughts of what an ideal male or female is like—the adolescent may think about what traits he or she prefers in such a person, whether the person is himself or herself, a friend, a boyfriend or girlfriend, or a potential marital partner. Inevitably, the adolescent compares himself or herself and others to

Sexual interest heightens dramatically in early adolescence.

this ideal standard, and also inevitably, no one the adolescent personally knows attains the high qualities of this ideal standard. However, people the adolescent does not know personally (and in whom he or she cannot see inadequacies), such as media stars (athletes, rock singers, movie stars), are more likely to meet the adolescent's quest for an ideal male or female and be retained as identification figures after whom the adolescent may try to model his or her behavior.

During adolescence males and females also focus more attention on the integration of vocational and lifestyle choices (Aneshenel & Rosen, 1980). For females, such choices have become more complicated because of conflicting norms and standards for females. Although it is now much more acceptable for females to simultaneously pursue career and family roles than in the past, this dual pursuit is still more consistently accepted for males than for females. Thus, more conflict seems to surround the pursuit of achievement and careers in the sex-role development of girls during adolescence than is true for boys.

SUMMARY

I. Information about androgyny and the components of sex roles focuses on the nature of sex roles, sexual or gender identity, and androgyny.
   A. Sex roles are behaviors expected of individuals because they are male or female.
   B. Sexual or gender identity refers to the extent to which individuals take on as part of their personality the behaviors and attitudes associated with male or female roles.
   C. Androgyny is a term reserved for the belief that the most competent individuals have both masculine and feminine attributes. No research evidence has been produced, however, that demonstrates the superiority of androgynous individuals in terms of competence.

II. Biological and cognitive factors are important contributors to sex-role development.
   A. Information about biological factors focuses on the concept of anatomy is destiny and on hormones and critical periods.
      1. Freud and Erikson argued that sex-role development is tied to anatomy and reproductive forces.
      2. At two points in development hormones become critical—the prenatal period and adolescence.
      3. Money argued that the first three years of life and puberty are critical periods but that sex-role development is always the result of the interaction of biology and culture rather than either acting alone.
   B. Among the cognitive factors important in sex-role development are the cognitive developmental views of Kohlberg and Damon and the link between language and cognition.
      1. Kohlberg argued that by the age of six the child's cognitive ability leads him or her to categorization in sex-role terms. Others have expanded on this view and feel that a rigidity of sex roles often occurs during early adolescence. Research shows that rigidity is stronger for boys than for girls. Damon's research has shown the existence of a cognitive developmental progression in sex roles that supports Kohlberg's ideas.
      2. Hyde's research on sexism demonstrated the importance of interface between cognition and language in sex-role development.

III. Environmental influences on sex-role development include parent–child relationships, peers, teachers, the media, and efforts to change the sex-typed behavior of children.

   A. Parent–child relationships have not been given as much attention in sex-role development in recent years as in the past. However, parents by action and example influence children's sex-role development.

   B. Children tend to differentiate their peers very early on the basis of sex and continue to prefer same-sex peer groups throughout childhood. Nonetheless, cross-sex peer play is often accepted.

   C. Teachers react more negatively to boys than to girls in early schooling and are more likely to reward "feminine" behaviors in boys and girls.

   D. The television shows children watch are heavily stereotyped in terms of sex roles, as are the print media.

   E. Attempts to change children's sex-typed behavior have focused on training gender-deviant children to show more appropriate sex-role behavior and teaching children to free themselves from rigid sex-typed programming. Both interventions involve ethical considerations.

IV. Sex-role stereotypes are pervasive in our culture, and psychologists have invested considerable time in trying to discover what truly are sex differences and what are sex-role stereotypes.

   A. A sex-role stereotype is a broad category that reflects our impressions about people, events, and ourselves.

   B. Maccoby and Jacklin concluded that there are four main sex differences: Boys are better at math, better at visual-spatial reasoning, and more aggressive, while girls are better at verbal activity. Some critics have faulted such conclusions.

   C. Baumrind argued that girls have been socialized to become instrumentally incompetent and boys to become instrumentally competent. Learned helplessness provides one explanation of lower achievement orientation on the part of females.

V. Information about sex-role development can be divided into the first three years of life, three to seven years of age, middle childhood, and adolescence.

   A. From eighteen months to three years of age, children start expressing considerable interest in sex-typed activities and classify themselves according to gender.

   B. From three to seven years of age, children begin to acquire an understanding of gender constancy and increasingly enjoy being with same-sex peers.

   C. During middle childhood, children understand more about culturally defined expectations for males and females, and the behavior of boys becomes increasingly masculine sex-typed.

   D. During adolescence, sexuality becomes a prominent aspect of sex-role development, interpretation of sex roles is more abstract and ideal, and there are greater achievement/career and life-style considerations.

KEY TERMS

anatomy is destiny 491
androgyny 489
hermaphrodites 493
instrumental incompetence
507

learned helplessness 508
sex-role stereotypes 504
sexual (gender) identity 489
testosterone 492

REVIEW QUESTIONS

1. Discuss the concepts of sex role, gender identity, and androgyny.
2. Are androgynous individuals necessarily more competent individuals?
3. Describe the biological and cognitive factors involved in sex roles.
4. What are the important environmental influences on sex-role development?
5. Discuss the nature of sex-role stereotypes.
6. What do we know about sex differences?
7. Outline the development of sex roles.

SUGGESTED READINGS

Bem, S. (1975). Androgyny vs. the tight little lives of fluffy women and chesty men. *Psychology Today, 9*(4), 58.
An entertaining and informative description of Bem's ideas about androgyny.
Block, J. (1976). Issues, problems, and pitfalls in assessing sex differences: A critical review of the psychology of sex differences. *Merrill-Palmer Quarterly, 22,* 283–308.
Huston, A. C. (1983). Sex-typing. In P. H. Mussen (Ed.), *Handbook of child psychology* (4th ed., Vol. 4). New York: John Wiley.
A lengthy, up-to-date overview of what we know about androgyny, and biological and cultural influences on sex-role development.
Hyde, J. S. (1985). *Half the human experience* (3rd ed.). Lexington, MA: D. C. Heath.
An excellent overview of sex roles related to the development of females.
Maccoby, E. E., and Jacklin, C. N. (1974). *The psychology of sex differences.* Stanford, CA: Stanford University Press.
This is an up-to-date review of the evidence on psychological differences between the sexes. It is fairly comprehensive and has carefully drawn conclusions. Moderately difficult reading.

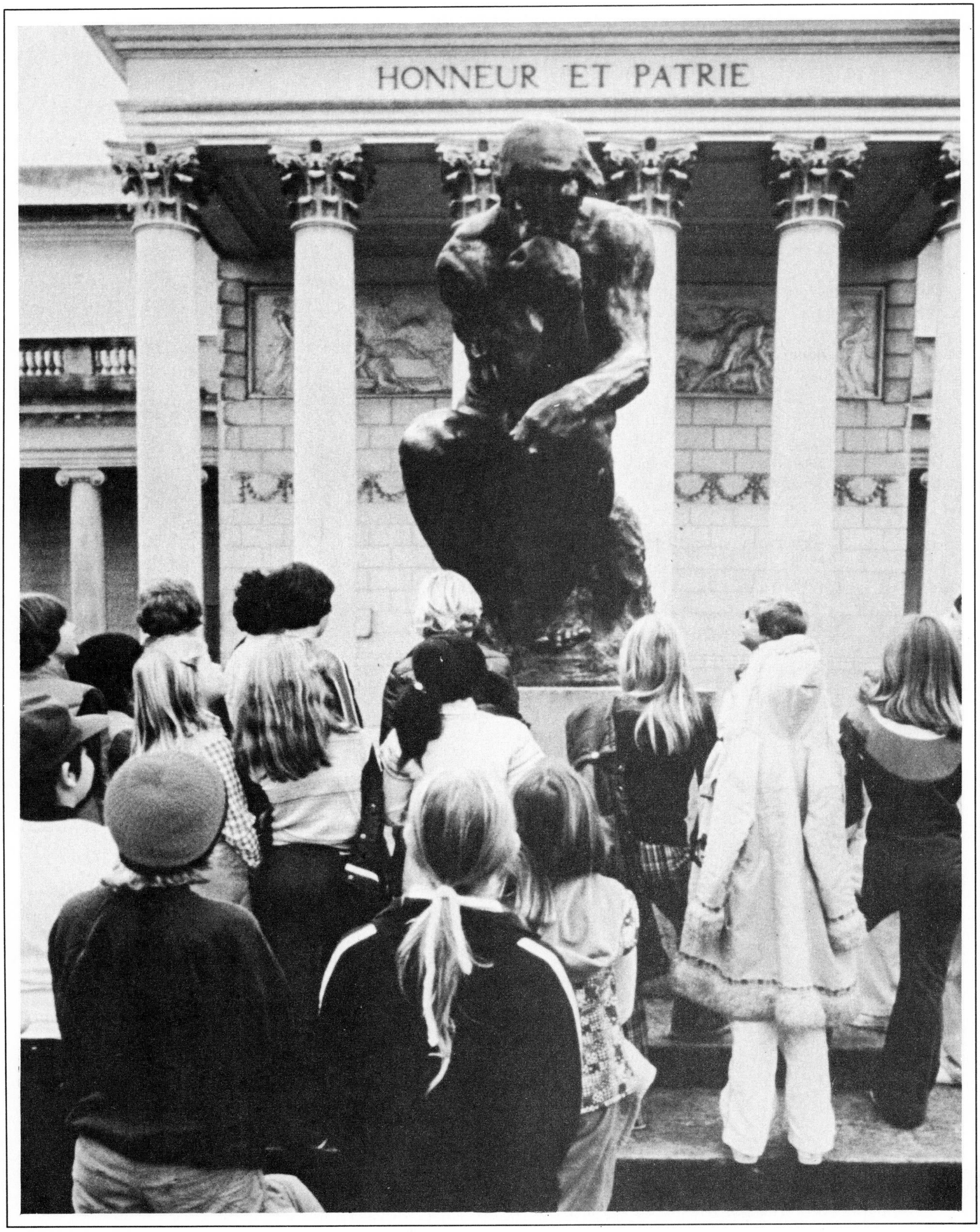
HONNEUR ET PATRIE

CHAPTER

15

MORAL DEVELOPMENT

PROLOGUE

OPERA GLASSES, THE NOMADIC TRIBE, AND A LIFEBOAT

In a theater in a small city in the English Midlands, attached to the backs of many of the seats is a small rack that once contained opera glasses. The racks were coin-operated: the insertion of a shilling released the opera glasses from their holder. At the end of a performance, the user would return the glasses to the rack, which locked automatically. The glasses would then be ready for a member of the next audience. The glasses were small, and in the darkness a user could easily slip them under a coat or into a pocket and carry them out of the theater without being seen. But for many years almost no one took them. The rate of theft was so low that the intake of shillings covered the losses and yielded a profit to the management. In the 1960s the rate of theft began to rise and reached the point where the management could no longer afford to replace the stolen glasses. So the system fell into disuse; only the empty racks remained to remind the theater-goer of a convenience made possible by the honesty of an earlier generation.

We may speculate about social changes in the Midlands (and elsewhere in the industrialized world) in the late 1960s. But more important for our present concerns is the fact that many social arrangements depend on the willing compliance of large numbers of people with social rules or customs that run counter to their immediate self-interest. The sight of the empty racks forcibly draws attention to the fragility of social arrangements fostering well-being or convenience. We can no longer take it for granted that these arrangements will be maintained.

In a sense the example of the opera glasses is trivial—a mere convenience that is easily dispensed with. But other arrangements can be vital to the survival of a group and its way of life, and these practices are less likely to be abandoned in a drift toward noncompliance. In a culture that depends upon both corn and cattle for its food supply, all members of the society must close the gate that keeps the cattle out of the corn patch. And in a nomadic desert tribe every member must cooperate in conserving and protecting the precious water supply. No child can

be allowed in a playful moment to pull the corks from the goatskins that carry the water. Social arrangements differ, then, in how vital they are to the survival and optimal functioning of the group and in the degree of compliance the society expects. A group adrift in a lifeboat cannot tolerate one single deviant who proposes to bore a hole in the bottom of the boat. A modern nation can tolerate a certain number of thieves or murderers, but it must keep theft and murder at a low rate or the social fabric will disintegrate.

Efforts by social scientists to examine human societies and to identify universal themes have a long and honorable history. Some problems seem to arise in all societies, and societies solve these problems in ways suited to their ecological niche. . . . All or nearly all societies have developed rules and norms to deal with these problems, applying socialization pressures as they teach them to their children. . . .

Such rules exist because human beings are social animals and each person's capacity to act—and indeed, each person's welfare and safety—depends upon the actions of other people. Each individual's behavior, then, must be integrated into a network of social arrangements. (Maccoby, 1980, pp. 296, 297, 299)*

While it seems probable that such rules and reasoning about the rules are embedded in the fabric of social relationships and cultural experiences, we will discover in this chapter that considerable controversy exists about the degree to which moral development is generated by societal and cultural experiences. Indeed, while virtually all theories accept the fact that social relationships are involved in moral development, the views vary in how much emphasis is placed on individualism and internalization of moral standards. We will discover that some social scientists believe morality is never completely internalized, always being wedded to the commerce of social relationships, while others argue that the most advanced level of moral development occurs when the individual has constructed his or her own individualistic standards that will guide moral behavior.

PREVIEW

Our interest in moral development focuses on what moral development is, moral reasoning, moral behavior, moral feelings and guilt, altruism, and the controversial topic of moral education.

WHAT IS MORAL DEVELOPMENT?

The study of moral development is one of the oldest topics of interest to those who are curious about human nature. As you may recall from reading in chapter 1, in prescientific periods philosophers and theologians heatedly debated the child's moral status at birth, which they felt had important implications for how the child was to be reared. Today people are hardly neutral about moral development; most have very strong opinions about acceptable and unacceptable behavior, ethical and unethical conduct, and the ways in which acceptable and ethical behaviors are to be fostered in children. We will discuss three important facets of moral development—thought, action, and feeling.

Moral development concerns rules and conventions about what people should do in their interaction with other people. In studying these rules, psychologists examine three different domains of moral development. The first domain concerns how children reason or think about rules for ethical conduct. For example, cheating is generally considered unacceptable. The child can be presented with a story in which someone has a conflict about whether or not to cheat in a specific situation. The child is asked to decide what is appropriate for the character to do, and why. The focus is thereby placed on the rationale, the type of reasoning the child uses to justify his or her moral decision. A second domain concerns how children actually behave in the face of rules for ethical conduct. Here, for example, the concern is whether the child himself or herself actually cheats in different situations and what factors influence this behavior. A third domain concerns how the child feels after making a moral decision. There has been more interest in a child's feelings after he or she has done something wrong than after he or she has done something right. Here the concern is whether a child feels guilty as the result of having cheated. We now consider moral thought, moral action, and moral feeling.

COGNITIVE DEVELOPMENTAL THEORY, MORAL REASONING, AND SOCIAL CONVENTIONAL REASONING

First we look at Piaget's cognitive developmental view of moral development, second we study Kohlberg's cognitive developmental perspective, and third we focus on the nature of social conventional reasoning.

Piaget's View

Piaget's ideas about the development of morality in childhood have been widely evaluated. We will discuss these ideas and also describe a cognitive disequilibrium view that emphasizes some basic ideas about the importance of formal operational thought in moral development.

Moral Reasoning in Childhood

Interest in how the child thinks about ethical issues has been stimulated by the work of Piaget (1932), who conducted extensive observations and interviews with children from four to twelve years of age. He watched them in natural play with marbles, trying to understand the manner in which they used and thought about the rules of the game. Later he asked them several questions about ethical concepts (e.g., theft, lies, punishment, justice) in order to arrive at a similar understanding of how children think about ethical rules. He concluded that there are two different modes (or stages) of moral thought. The more primitive one, **moral realism,** is associated with younger children (from four to seven years old); the more advanced one, **moral autonomy,** is associated with older children (ten years old and older). Children from seven to ten years of age are in a transition period between the two stages, evidencing some features of each stage.

What are some of the characteristics of these two stages? The moral realist judges the rightness or goodness of behavior by considering the consequences of the behavior, not the intentions of the actor. For example, a realist would say that breaking twelve cups accidentally is worse than breaking one cup intentionally while trying to steal a cookie. For the moral autonomist, the reverse is true; the intention of the actor becomes more important.

What might a Piagetian want to know about this moral situation?

The moral realist believes that all rules are unchangeable and are handed down by all-powerful authorities. When Piaget suggested that new rules be introduced into the game of marbles, the young children became troubled; they insisted that the rules had always existed as they were and could not be changed. The moral autonomist, by contrast, accepts change and recognizes that rules are merely convenient, socially agreed upon conventions, subject to change by consensus.

A third characteristic is the moral realist's belief in **immanent justice**—if a rule is broken, punishment will be meted out immediately. The realist believes that the violation is connected in some mechanical or reflexlike way to the punishment. Thus, young children often look around worriedly after committing a transgression, expecting inevitable punishment. Recent research (e.g., Jose, 1985) verifies that immanent justice responses decline during the latter part of the elementary school years. The moral autonomist recognizes that punishment is a socially mediated event occurring only if a relevant person witnesses the wrongdoing but that even then punishment is not inevitable.

Piaget's theory of moral judgment was crafted as a counterargument to the sociologist Émile Durkheim's view that the socialization process should instill respect in each individual for the social group. In Durkheim's view, each member of the group should accept its constraints and rules. Piaget's main thrust was to reveal the limitations of Durkheim's view (which was basically heteronomous in nature) by arguing that as the child develops, she or he becomes more sophisticated in thinking about social matters, particularly about the possibilities and conditions of cooperation. Piaget believed this social understanding comes about through the mutual give-and-take of peer relations. In the peer group, where others have similar status and power as the individual plans are negotiated and coordinated, disagreements are reasoned about and eventually settled. It is in the peer group that the child learns of the possibilities for cooperation not based on unilateral respect (as is typically the case in parent–child relationships, relationships in which the child simply acquiesces to the demands of more powerful social agents). In peer relationships, the child learns about cooperation through collaboration and commerce with others. Through such relationships, the fundamental nature of the child's moral development changes.

Cognitive Disequilibrium and Formal Operational Thought

Remember that Piaget believed adolescents usually become formal operational thinkers. Thus, they are no longer tied to immediate and concrete phenomena but are more logical, abstract, and deductive reasoners. Formal operational thinkers frequently compare the real to the ideal; create contrary-to-fact propositions; are cognitively capable of relating the distant past to the present; understand their roles in society, in history, and in the universe; and can conceptualize their own thoughts and think about their mental constructs as objects. For example, it usually is not until about the age of eleven or twelve that boys and girls spontaneously introduce concepts of belief, intelligence, and faith into their definitions of their religious identities. Thus, many of Piaget's tenets of cognitive developmental theory have significant implications for the moral development of the adolescent.

When children move from the relatively homogeneous grade school neighborhood to more heterogeneous high school and college environments, they are faced with contradictions between the moral concepts they have accepted and happenings in the world outside their family and neighborhood. Adolescents are ripe for recognizing that their beliefs are but one of many and that there often is a great deal of debate about right and wrong in ethical matters. Consequently, many adolescents may start to question and sometimes reject their former beliefs, and in the process they may develop their own moral system. Martin Hoffman (1980) refers to this Piagetian-related view of moral development as **cognitive-disequilibrium theory.**

Kohlberg's Theory

The most provocative view of moral development to come along in recent years was crafted by Lawrence Kohlberg (1958, 1976). Kohlberg believes that moral development is primarily based on moral reasoning and unfolds in a stagelike manner. Kohlberg arrived at this view after some twenty years of using a unique procedure in interviewing children, adolescents, and adults. In an interview the individual is presented with a series of stories in which characters face moral dilemmas. The following is one of the more popular Kohlberg dilemmas (Kohlberg, 1969):

It is not until 11–12 years of age that boys and girls begin to introduce concepts of faith into their religious identity.

In Europe a woman was near death from a special kind of cancer. There was one drug that the doctors thought might save her. It was a form of radium that a druggist in the same town had recently discovered. The drug was expensive to make, but the druggist was charging ten times what the drug cost him to make. He paid $200 for the radium and charged $2,000 for a small dose of the drug. The sick woman's husband, Heinz, went to everyone he knew to borrow the money, but he could only get together $1,000, which is half of what it cost. He told the druggist that his wife was dying and asked him to sell it cheaper or let him pay later. But the druggist said, "No, I discovered the drug, and I am going to make money from it." So Heinz got desperate and broke into the man's store to steal the drug for his wife. (p. 379)

TABLE 15.1
Kohlberg's Three Levels and Six Stages of Moral Development

Level and Stage	What Is Right	Reasons for Doing Right	Social Perspective of Stage
Level I: Preconventional Stage 1: Heteronomous morality	To avoid breaking rules backed by punishment, obedience for its own sake, and avoiding physical damage to persons and property.	To avoid punishment, and the superior power of authorities.	*Egocentric point of view.* Doesn't consider the interests of others or recognize that they differ from the actor's; doesn't relate two points of view. Actions are considered physically rather than in terms of psychological interests of others. Confusion of authority's perspective with one's own.
Stage 2: Individualism, instrumental purpose, and exchange	Following rules only when it is to someone's immediate interest; acting to meet one's own interests and needs and letting others do the same. Right is also what's fair, what's an equal exchange, a deal, an agreement.	To serve one's own needs or interests in a world where one has to recognize that other people have their interests, too.	*Concrete individualistic perspective.* Aware that everybody has his own interest to pursue and that these interests conflict, so that right is relative (in the concrete individualistic sense).
Level II: Conventional Stage 3: Mutual interpersonal expectations, relationships, and interpersonal conformity	Living up to what is expected by people close to one or what people generally expect of one's role as son, brother, friend, etc. "Being good" is important and means having good motives, showing concern about others. It also means keeping mutual relationships, such as trust, loyalty, respect, and gratitude.	The need to be a good person in one's own eyes and those of others. One's caring for others. Belief in the Golden Rule. Desire to maintain rules and authority which support stereotypical good behavior.	*Perspective of the individual in relationships with other individuals.* Aware of shared feelings, agreements, and expectations, which take primacy over individual interests. Relates points of view through the concrete Golden Rule, putting oneself in the other guy's shoes. Does not yet consider generalized system perspective.

From "Moral Stages and Moralization: The Cognitive-Developmental Approach," by Lawrence Kohlberg in *Moral Development and Behavior* edited by T. Lickona, Holt, Rinehart and Winston, 1975. Reprinted by permission of Lawrence Kohlberg.

The interviewee is then asked a series of questions about each dilemma. For the Heinz dilemma, Kohlberg asks such questions as these: Should Heinz have done that? Was it actually wrong or right? Why? Is it a husband's duty to steal the drug for his wife if he can get it no other way? Would a good husband do it? Did the druggist have the right to charge that much when there was no law actually setting a limit on the price? Why?

Based on the types of reasons individuals have given to this and other moral dilemmas, Kohlberg arrived at three levels of moral development, each of which is characterized by two stages. More details about the three levels and six stages in Kohlberg's theory are presented in table 15.1.

1. **The preconventional level.** At this low level the child shows no internalization of moral values; his or her moral thinking is based on the punishments (stage 1) and rewards (stage 2) he or she experiences in the environment.
2. **The conventional level.** At this level of morality the child's internalization of moral values is intermediate. He or she abides by certain standards of other people, such as parents (stage 3) or the rules of society (stage 4). While the moral standards are not generated by the child (externalized), the child does abide by standards rather than behaving according to the rewards and punishments in a given situation (internalized).

Level and Stage	What Is Right	Reasons for Doing Right	Social Perspective of Stage
Level II: continued Stage 4: Social system and conscience	Fulfilling the actual duties to which one has agreed. Laws are to be upheld except in extreme cases where they conflict with other fixed social duties. Right is also contributing to society, the group, or institution.	To keep the institution going as a whole, to avoid the breakdown in the system "if everyone did it," or the imperative of conscience to meet one's defined obligations (easily confused with stage 3 belief in rules and authority).	*Differentiates societal point of view from interpersonal agreement or motives.* Takes the point of view of the system that defines roles and rules. Considers individual relations in terms of place in the system.
Level III: Postconventional, or Principled Stage 5: Social contract or utility and individual rights	Being aware that people hold a variety of values and opinions, that most values and rules are relative to your group. These relative rules should usually be upheld, however, in the interest of impartiality and because they are the social contract. Some nonrelative values and rights like *life* and *liberty*, however, must be upheld in any society and regardless of majority opinion.	A sense of obligation to law because of one's social contract to make and abide by laws for the welfare of all and for the protection of all people's rights. A feeling of contractual commitment, freely entered upon, to family, friendship, trust, and work obligations. Concern that laws and duties be based on rational calculation of overall utility, "the greatest good for the greatest number."	*Prior-to society perspective.* Perspective of a rational individual aware of values and rights prior to social attachments and contracts. Integrates perspectives by formal mechanisms of agreement, contract, objective impartiality, and due process. Considers moral and legal points of view; recognizes that they sometimes conflict and finds it difficult to integrate them.
Stage 6: Universal ethical principles	Following self-chosen ethical principles. Particular laws or social agreements are usually valid because they rest on such principles. When laws violate these principles, one acts in accordance with the principle. Principles are universal principles of justice: the equality of human rights and respect for the dignity of human beings as individual people.	The belief as a rational person in the validity of universal moral principles, and a sense of personal commitment to them.	*Perspective of a moral point of view from which social arrangements derive.* Perspective is that of any rational individual recognizing the nature of morality or the fact that people are ends in themselves and must be treated as such.

3. **The postconventional level.** At the highest level morality is completely internalized and not based on the standards of others. The individual recognizes alternative moral courses, explores the options, and then develops a moral code that is his or hers. The code may be among the principles generally accepted by the community (stage 5) or it may be more individualized (stage 6).

Note that the more internalized the adolescent's moral judgments are, the more likely he or she is to be placed at a more advanced level by Kohlberg. *Internalization* refers to the extent to which the child either adopts the moral standards of others and abides by them or generates his or her own moral principles. The child who behaves or thinks in a particular moral way because of external pressures is not thought to have internalized moral standards. For an individual at the postconventional level, the rules of the society have to mesh with underlying moral principles. In cases where the rules of the society come into conflict with the individual's principles, the individual will follow his or her own principles rather than the conventions of the society. Some specific responses to the Heinz and the druggist dilemma are presented in table 15.2, which should provide you with a better sense of moral reasoning at the six stages in Kohlberg's theory.

TABLE 15.2
Examples of Kohlberg's Six Stages of Moral Development

Stage	Pro	Con
1	He should steal the drug. It is not really bad to take it. It is not like he did not ask to pay for it first. The drug he would take is only worth $200; he is not really taking a $2,000 drug.	He should not steal the drug; it is a big crime. He did not get permission; he used force and broke and entered. He did a lot of damage; stealing a very expensive drug and breaking up the store, too.
2	It is all right to steal the drug, because she needs it and he wants her to live. It is not that he wants to steal, but it is the way he has to use to get the drug to save her.	He should not steal it. The druggist is not wrong or bad; he just wants to make a profit. That is what you are in business for, to make money.
3	He should steal the drug. He was only doing something that was natural for a good husband to do. You cannot blame him for doing something out of love for his wife; you would blame him if he did not love his wife enough to save her.	He should not steal. If his wife dies he cannot be blamed. It is not because he is heartless or that he does not love her enough to do everything that he legally can. The druggist is the selfish or heartless one.
4	You should steal it. If you did nothing you would be letting your wife die; it is your responsibility if she dies. You have to take it with the idea of paying the druggist.	It is a natural thing for Heinz to want to save his wife, but is is still always wrong to steal. He still knows he is stealing and taking a valuable drug from the man who made it.
5	The law was not set up for these circumstances. Taking the drug in this situation is not really right, but it is justified to do it.	You cannot completely blame someone for stealing, but extreme circumstances do not really justify taking the law in your own hands. You cannot have everyone stealing whenever they get desperate. The end may be good, but the ends do not justify the means.
6	This is a situation which forces him to choose between stealing and letting his wife die. In a situation where the choice must be made, it is morally right to steal. He has to act in terms of the principle of preserving and respecting life.	Heinz is faced with the decision of whether to consider the other people who need the drug just as badly as his wife. Heinz ought to act not according to his particular feelings toward his wife, but considering the value of all the lives involved.

From Kohlberg, Lawrence, "Stage and sequence: The cognitive-developmental approach to socialization," in *Handbook of Socialization Theory and Research*, David A. Goslin, ed. © 1969 Houghton Mifflin Company, Boston, Massachusetts. Reprinted by permission.

Research on Kohlberg's Stages and Influences on the Stages

First, we review information about Kohlberg's own research and then turn to an overview of the three main influences that move children through the moral stages: cognitive development, modeling and cognitive conflict, and peer interaction and role/perspective-taking opportunities.

The Kohlberg Research

In his original work Kohlberg (1958) found that as the age of the child increased, his or her moral judgments become more advanced. Kohlberg also reported (1969) that age changes in children's responses to moral judgment items have been found in most industrialized Western countries, such as the United States, France, and Great Britain. And these changes occur regardless of the child's sex or social class. The stages are also significantly related to intelligence (Kohlberg, 1969). Kohlberg (1958) also found support for his belief that social participation in groups is one way to advance the moral judgment of children.

While Kohlberg's original research was conducted in 1958, he subsequently charted moral development in a longitudinal manner (Colby, Kohlberg, Gibbs & Lieberman, 1980). This twenty-year longitudinal study charted moral development from late childhood through the early adulthood years. The mean percentage of individuals reasoning at each of Kohlberg's stages at a given age is shown in figure 15.1.

The data show a clear relation between age and moral judgment. Over the twenty-year period, the use of stages 1 and 2 decreased. Stage 4, which did not appear at all in the moral reasoning of the ten-year-olds, was reflected in 62 percent of the moral thinking of the thirty-six-year-olds. Stage 5 did not appear until the age of twenty or twenty-two and never characterized more than about 10 percent of the individuals interviewed. Thus, just as formal operational thought does not always emerge in adolescence, neither do the higher stages of Kohlberg's theory of moral development. Reasoning about moral dilemmas does seem to change in adulthood—adults in their thirties reason at more advanced levels than adolescents or children.

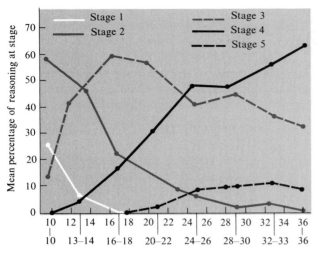

FIGURE 15.1
Mean percentage of reasoning at each stage for each age group (Colby, Kohlberg, Gibbs, and Lieberman, 1982).

Cognitive Development

Kohlberg believes that the adolescent's moral orientation unfolds as a consequence of cognitive development. As you will recall, cognitive development is dependent upon the interaction of genetic endowment and social experiences. The individual passes through the six stages in an invariant sequence, from less to more advanced. The individual acts constructively on the world as he or she proceeds from one stage to the next rather than passively accepting a cultural norm of morality.

Modeling and Cognitive Conflict

Several investigators have attempted to advance an individual's level of moral development by providing arguments that reflect moral thinking one stage above the individual's established level. These studies are based on the cognitive developmental concepts of equilibrium and conflict. By finding the correct environmental match slightly beyond the individual's cognitive level, a disequilibrium is created that motivates him or her to restructure his or her moral thought. The resolution of the disequilibrium and conflict should be toward increased competence, but the data are mixed on this question. In one of the pioneer studies on this topic, Eliot Turiel (1966) discovered that children preferred a response one stage above their current level over a response two stages above it. However, they actually

chose a response one stage below their level more often than a response one stage above it. Apparently the children were motivated more by security needs than by the need to reorganize thought to a higher level. Other studies indicate that children do prefer a more advanced stage over a less advanced stage (e.g., Rest, Turiel & Kohlberg, 1969).

Since the early studies of stage modeling, a number of investigations have attempted to more precisely determine the effectiveness of various forms of stage modeling and arguments (Lapsley & Quintana, in press). The upshot of these studies is that virtually any plus-stage discussion format, for any length of time, seems to promote more advanced moral reasoning. For example, in one investigation (Walker, 1982), exposure to plus-two stage reasoning (arguments two stages above the child's current stage of moral thought) was just as effective in advancing moral thought as plus-one stage reasoning. Exposure to plus-two stage reasoning did not produce more plus-two stage reasoning but rather, like exposure to plus-one stage reasoning, increased the likelihood that the child would reason one stage above his or her current stage. Other research has found that exposure to reasoning only one-third of a stage higher than the individual's current level of moral thought will advance moral thought (Berkowitz & Gibbs, 1983). In sum, current research on modeling and cognitive conflict reveals that moral thought can be moved to a higher level through exposure to models or discussion that is more advanced than the child's.

Peer Relations and Role/Perspective-Taking Opportunities

Kohlberg believes that peer interaction is a critical part of the social stimulation that challenges individuals to change their moral orientations. Whereas adults characteristically impose rules and regulations on children, the mutual give-and-take in peer interaction provides the child with an opportunity to take the role of another person and to generate rules democratically. Kohlberg stresses that role-taking opportunities can, in principle, be engendered by any peer group encounter. While Kohlberg believes that such role-taking opportunities are ideal for moral development, he also believes that certain types of parent–child experiences can induce the child to think at more advanced levels of moral thinking. In particular, parents who allow or encourage conversation about value-laden issues promote more

Kohlberg believes, as did Piaget, that the mutual give-and-take of peer relations is a key ingredient of moral development.

advanced moral thought in their children. Unfortunately, many parents do not systematically provide their children with such role-taking opportunities.

More information about the importance of peer relations, particularly the nature of peer discussion, is presented in Perspective on Child Development 15.1.

The Critics of Kohlberg

Kohlberg's theory has not gone unchallenged. Among the criticisms are those involving the link between moral thought, moral behavior, and moral feeling; the quality of the research; sex differences; and the care perspective and societal contributions. We consider each of these criticisms in turn.

Moral Thought, Moral Behavior, and Moral Feeling: Kohlberg and Cognitive Primacy

Moral reasons can always be a shelter for immoral behavior. That is, some critics believe Kohlberg has placed too much emphasis on moral thought and not paid

---

PERSPECTIVE ON CHILD DEVELOPMENT 15.1

PEER RELATIONS, TRANSACTIVE DISCUSSION, AND MORAL REASONING

Recall how researchers have found that modeling and discussion of moral matters above the child's moral stage often advance the child's moral reasoning. Research also suggests that an important factor in whether discussion of moral stages will advance children's moral reasoning is the quality of peer interaction and discussion involved (Berkowitz, 1981; Berkowitz & Gibbs, 1983; Berkowitz, Gibbs & Broughton, 1980). For example, in one investigation (Berkowitz & Gibbs, 1983) thirty dyads were observed and the nature of their discourse about moral issues assessed. The nature of the discourse focused on solutions to moral dilemmas in Kohlberg's moral judgment interview. Of the thirty dyads, sixteen showed stage change in moral development, while fourteen of the dyads did not. The researchers concluded that moral advances were made by certain dyads and not

others because of the style of reasoning of both members of the dyad. Such reasoning was termed **transactive discussion,** meaning reasoning that operates on the reasoning of another individual.

In the investigation of transactive discussion it was found that such discussion can follow one of two forms: representation of another's reasoning (such as feedback request, paraphrase, justification request, dyad paraphrase, and the like) or operation upon another's reasoning (such as clarification, contradiction, competitive extension, common ground/integration, comparative critique, and so on). Operational transactions are presumed to reflect more sophisticated discussion patterns than representation transactions. In this research effort operational transaction was observed to advance moral reasoning more than representation transaction (Berkowitz & Gibbs, 1983). (See the table opposite.)

enough attention to what children morally do or morally feel (Gibbs & Schnell, 1985). No one wants a nation of individuals who can reason at stages 5 and 6 of Kohlberg's model but who are liars, cheaters, and stealers lacking empathy. Thus, the critics stress that Kohlberg's view is too cognitive and too cold. Elizabeth Simpson (1976) captured this point nicely:

> Reasons can be a shelter, as we all know, especially when they are developed after the fact and are applied to our own behavior or to that of someone in whom we have an ego investment. In any case, reasons are inseparable from the personality of the reasoner, whether they apply to his own behavior or that of others. They are grounded not in the situation in which decisions are made, but in the reasoner's psychic definition of past experience, and that psychic definition frequently crosses all boundaries of rationality. Passionate irrationality in the name of impassioned reason occurs in the market, the classroom, and in science, as well as elsewhere, and often unconsciously. (pp. 162–163)

Quality of the Research

James Rest (1976, 1977, 1983) believes that more attention should be paid to the way moral judgment is assessed. Rest (1976) points out that alternative methods should be used to collect information about moral thinking rather than relying on a single method that requires individuals to reason about hypothetical moral dilemmas. Rest further points out that the Kohlberg stories are exceedingly difficult to score. To help remedy this problem, Rest (1976, 1977, 1983) has devised his own measure of moral development, called the Defining Issue Test, or the DIT.

In the DIT an attempt is made to determine which moral issues individuals feel are most crucial in a given situation by presenting them with a series of dilemmas and a list of definitions of the major issues involved (Kohlberg's procedure does not make use of such a list). In the dilemma of Heinz and the druggist, individuals might be asked whether a community's laws should be upheld or whether Heinz should be willing to risk being injured or caught as a burglar; they might also be asked

This investigation of transactional discussion was conducted with college students, but it is probable that such a strategy would be beneficial for children as well. The lesson to be learned here is the importance of communication in peer discussion. In particular, it appears that the language and listening skills of the peer discussants are important factors in whether the peer discussion promotes advances in moral judgment. Many children have substandard vocabularies, a fact that undoubtedly contributes to their lack of ability to engage in transactive discussion. Indeed, children and adolescents have been found to have difficulty conducting competent discussion in general (Danner, 1986). In sum, it appears that an important new avenue of inquiry in moral development has been unveiled, one that emphasizes the importance of children's communication skills in peer discussion aimed at advancing moral development (Lapsley, Enright & Serlin, 1986).

Percentages of Total Statements in Each Transact Category for Pre- to Posttest Moral Stage Changers and Nonchangers

Group	Transact Type			
	All Transacts	Representational Transacts	Operational Transacts	N
Nonchangers	19.9	7.2	12.9	14
Changers	26.6	8.8	17.8	16

Reprinted from "Measuring the Developmental Features of Moral Discussion," in the *Merrill-Palmer Quarterly*, Volume 29, No. 4, (1983) by Marvin W. Berkowitz and John C. Gibbs by permission of the Wayne State University Press. © 1983 The Wayne State University Press.

to list the most important values that govern human interaction. They are given six stories and asked to rate the importance of each issue involved in deciding what ought to be done. Then the subjects are asked to list what they believe are the four most important issues. Rest believes that this method provides a more consistent and accurate measurement of moral thinking than Kohlberg's system.

Another research investigation provides further criticism of the nature of the Kohlberg stories (Yussen, 1977). Most of the Kohlberg stories focus on the family and authority. However, when adolescents were invited to write stories about their own moral dilemmas, adolescents generated dilemmas that were broader in scope, focusing on such matters as friends, acquaintances, and other issues, as well as family and authority. The moral dilemmas were also analyzed in terms of the issues that concerned the adolescents the most. As shown in table 15.3, the moral issue that concerned adolescents more than any other was interpersonal relationships. As can be seen, there is reason to be concerned about the manner in which Kohlberg's data on moral development were collected.

Sex Differences and the Care Perspective

No other aspect of Kohlberg's theory has generated as much recent controversy as the extent to which Kohlberg's stages are more characteristic of the moral development of males than of females. Carol Gilligan (1982), writing in her book *In a Different Voice*, argues

that Kohlberg's theory and research are heavily sex-biased. She argues that females, because of their unique perspectives and concerns, should be included in the study of moral development. She reasons that their inclusion might produce a different perspective on moral development for both females and males. Gilligan thinks that individuals move from a level of selfishness focused on personal survival and practical needs to a level involving sacrificing one's own wishes for what other people want and then finally to the third and highest level, in which moral equality is sought between oneself and others. (See table 15.4 for a comparison of Gilligan's and Kohlberg's levels.) Woven

TABLE 15.3
Actual Moral Dilemmas Generated by Adolescents

Story Subject	Grade 7	Grade 9	Grade 12
	Percentage		
Alcohol	2	0	5
Civil rights	0	6	7
Drugs	7	10	5
Interpersonal relations	38	24	35
Physical safety	22	8	3
Sexual relations	2	20	10
Smoking	7	2	0
Stealing	9	2	0
Working	2	2	15
Other	11	26	20

From Yussen, Steven R., "Characteristics of moral dilemmas written by adolescents," in *Developmental Psychology*, 13, pp. 162–163. Copyright © 1977 by the American Psychological Association. Reprinted by permission of the publisher and author.

TABLE 15.4
Kohlberg's Versus Gilligan's Understanding of Moral Development

Kohlberg's Levels and Stages	Kohlberg's Definition	Gilligan's Levels
Level I. Preconventional morality		*Level I. Preconventional morality*
Stage 1. Punishment orientation	Obey rules to avoid punishment	Concern for the self and survival
Stage 2. Naive reward orientation	Obey rules to get rewards, share in order to get returns	
Level II. Conventional morality		*Level II. Conventional morality*
Stage 3. Good-boy/good-girl orientation	Conform to rules that are defined by others' approval/disapproval	Concern for being responsible, caring for others
Stage 4. Authority orientation	Rigid conformity to society's rules, law-and-order mentality, avoid censure for rule-breaking	
Level III. Postconventional morality		*Level III. Postconventional morality*
Stage 5. Social-contract orientation	More flexible understanding that we obey rules because they are necessary for social order, but the rules could be changed if there were better alternatives	Concern for self and others as interdependent
Stage 6. Morality of individual principles and conscience	Behavior conforms to internal principles (justice, equality) to avoid self-condemnation, and sometimes may violate society's rules	

From *Half the Human Experience: The Psychology of Women*, 3/e by Janet S. Hyde McKeachie. Copyright © 1985 by D. C. Heath and Company. Reprinted by permission of the publisher.

through Gilligan's concerns is her belief that Kohlberg has grossly underestimated the importance of interpersonal relationships and caring in moral development, regardless of whether males or females are under consideration. More details about Gilligan's view on the construction of moral thought is described in Perspective on Child Development 15.2.

Are there sex differences in moral development? A recent review of a large number of studies of sex differences in moral development by Lawrence Walker (1984) concluded that the overall pattern is one of nonsignificance. Of the 108 studies reviewed, only 8 revealed sex differences favoring males. Walker argues that rather than debating whether sex bias is inherent

---

PERSPECTIVE ON CHILD DEVELOPMENT 15.2

GILLIGAN'S VIEWS ON MORAL DEVELOPMENT— THE CARE PERSPECTIVE

Carol Gilligan (1982) notes that the main character in Kohlberg's dilemma is Heinz, a male. Possibly females have a difficult time identifying with him. While some of the other Kohlberg dilemmas are gender neutral, one is about the captain of a company of marines. Gilligan also points out that the subjects in Kohlberg's original research, those he has followed for twenty years, are all males. Gilligan also believes that Kohlberg's interpretations are flawed: The finding that females often only reach stage 3 is described as a defiency by Kohlberg, yet it easily could be analyzed as a defiency in Kohlberg's theory.

Going beyond her critique of Kohlberg's failure to consider females Gilligan has provided a reformulation of Kohlberg's theory based on the premise that an important voice is not present in his view. Following are two excerpts from her book, one from eleven-year-old Jake and one from eleven-year-old Amy, which reflect the importance of this voice. First, Jake's comments:

> For one thing, human life is worth more than money, and if the druggist only makes $1,000, he is still going to live, but if Heinz doesn't steal the drug, his wife is going to die. *(Why is life worth more than money?)* Because the druggist can get a thousand dollars later from rich people with cancer, but Heinz can't get his wife again. (Gilligan, 1982, p. 26)

Now Amy's comments:

> Well, I don't think so. I think there might be other ways besides stealing it, like if he could borrow the money or make a loan or something, but he really shouldn't steal the drug—but his wife

shouldn't die either. *(Why shouldn't he steal the drug?)* If he stole the drug, he might save his wife then, but if he did, he might have to go to jail, and then his wife might get sicker again, and he couldn't get more of the drug, and it might not be good. So, they should really just talk it out and find some other way to make the money. (Gilligan, 1982, p. 28)

Jake's comments would likely be scored as a mixture of stages 3 and 4, but also including some of the components of a mature level III moral thinker. Amy, by contrast, does not fit into the scoring system as well. Jake, like Kohlberg, sees the problem as one of rules and balancing the rights of people. However, Amy views the problem as one involving relationships—the druggist fails to live up to his relationship to the needy woman, the need to maintain the relationship between Heinz and his wife, and the hope that a bad relationship between Heinz and the druggist can be avoided. Amy concludes that the characters should talk it out and try to repair their relationships.

Gilligan (1982, 1985a, 1985b) concludes that there are two basic approaches to moral reasoning. In the **justice perspective,** people are differentiated and seen as standing alone—the focus is on the rights of the individual (i.e., on justice). In the **care perspective,** people are viewed in terms of their connectedness with other people, and the focus is on their communication with others. From Gilligan's view, Kohlberg has greatly underplayed the importance of the care perspective in the moral development of both females and males.

Carol Gilligan argues that the care perspective is underrepresented in most theories of moral development, particularly Kohlberg's.

in Kohlberg's theory, it might be more fruitful to ask why the myth that males are more advanced in moral development than females persists in light of so little evidence. Gilligan (1985a, 1985b) believes Walker has missed her main point. She states that her orientation focuses on the differences between two moral perspectives, one a justice perspective, the other a care perspective. She is quick to argue that her orientation does not stress whether males and females will differ on Kohlberg's stages of justice reasoning; that is, a feminine "voice" is not necessarily spoken more often by girls than boys (in a statistical sense). Rather, the feminine "voice" is associated with a feminine stereotype of caring and relationships. Gilligan fears that because so much empirical attention has been focused on sex

differences in the expression of the feminine "voice," her view that a concern for caring and relationships is a key ingredient of the moral development of both females and males will be lost (Gilligan, 1985b).

Thus we see that Gilligan senses Kohlberg's perspective does not pay adequate attention to the nature of attachment and relationships among people. Next we see that a related criticism of Kohlberg's theory, namely, that it is based too much on the individual, can be found in research and thinking about the role of culture and society in generating moral development.

Moral Development, Culture, and the Individual in Society

Many critics argue that moral development is more culture-specific than Kohlberg believes. As Urie Bronfenbrenner and James Garbarino (1976) have observed, moral standards in other cultures are not always consistent with the standards that children abide by in the United States. Bronfenbrenner and Garbarino believe that one of the key ingredients of moral development is the developmental unfolding of social relationships and cultural experiences. Bronfenbrenner and Garbarino (1976) created a model for understanding the link between developmental period, socialization experiences, and the extent to which individuals are exposed to different social agents and different sociopolitical views. A summary of this model is shown in table 15.5. The main theme of Bronfenbrenner and Garbarino's model is that the greater the exposure to multiple social agents and multiple sociopolitical views, the more advanced will be the child and adolescent's moral development. Their research suggests that individuals who grow up in a culture that is more sociopolitically plural (United States, West Germany) are less likely to be authority oriented and to have more plural ideas about moral dilemmas than their counterparts who grow up in less sociopolitically plural cultures (Poland, Hungary). Bronfenbrenner and Garbarino have also commented on the kinds of families children are likely to be exposed to in eastern European countries, which are less sociopolitically plural, and western European countries and the United States, which are more sociopolitically plural. In the former the family is expected to support the governmental regime, and families' styles are likely to be more monolithic. In the latter countries, where more individual freedom is allowed, more diverse family styles are common, and thus children are exposed to more varied cultural experiences.

TABLE 15.5
A Model for Studying the Relationship between Sociopsychological Pluralism and Moral Development

Developmental Level	Moral Socialization Outcome	Critical Pluralistic Variables
Infancy	Establishment of attachment, i.e., primary socialization.	Care-giving patterns, both behavioral and normative, contribute to progressively more complex systems of infant-adult interaction.
Early childhood	Expansion of primary attachment relationships into ever-widening circles.	Progressive expansion of patterns of attachment from primary caregiver to larger social systems. Initial pluralistic social settings, with several different persons serving as objects for the child's attention and affiliation and as sources of demands. Initial ability to respond to differential influences.
Later childhood	Development of relationships with social groups, particularly peer groups and children's institutions.	Development of multiple associations rather than complete immersion in one group.
Adolescence	Resolution of conflicting relationships to social groups so as to achieve both objective-principled moral orientation and social identity.	Integration of individual into adult roles and experiences. Relative congruence between goals and values of peer groups and adult institutions; neither "cultural warfare" of peer group against adult social structures nor domination of peer groups by adult authority. Pathways to adult activities consonant with previous socialization experiences.
Adulthood	Maintenance of creative tension between social identity and objective-principled moral orientation.	Systems of social support for alternative patterns of access to economic and social resources. Feedback to parental child rearing that supports encouragement of identity and diversity (i.e., neither authoritarian nor permissive, but authoritative child rearing). Pluralism in adults to encourage pluralism in children.

From J. Garbarino and U. Bronfenbrenner, "The socialization of moral judgement and behavior in cross-cultural perspective," in T. Lickona (Ed.), *Moral Development and Behavior*, reprinted by permission of the editor.

As part of the belief that culture contributes to moral development more than Kohlberg allows, some social scientists stress that Kohlberg's view is too individualistic. The social theorists argue that from Kohlberg's perspective morality is basically a property of the individual when in reality moral development more appropriately should be construed as a matter of the individual's accommodation to the values and requirements of society. This assumption basically argues that society is the source of all values, not the individual. This view of morality has been referred to as **societalism.** However, while Kohlberg's cognitive developmental view is more individualistic than traditional socialization views of morality that place a primary emphasis on social relationships and conventions, it is inappropriate to describe Kohlberg's theory as completely individualistic (Gibbs & Schnell, 1985). As we have seen, Kohlberg, while arguing about the importance of moral reasoning in understanding morality, nonetheless does not argue that social matters are unimportant in generating moral thought. As we will see later in the chapter, for example, in the section on moral education, Kohlberg has recently placed added emphasis on the social climate in which moral thought is produced.

Many social theorists believe that Kohlberg has not paid enough attention to the role of culture in understanding moral values.

In this section we have seen that one issue surrounding Kohlberg's theory of moral development is the extent to which moral reasoning is a property of the individual versus the degree to which it is generated by societal considerations. In the next section, we find that such considerations have led to attempts to distinguish moral reasoning and social conventional reasoning.

Moral Reasoning and Social Conventional Reasoning

In recent years considerable interest has been generated in whether reasoning about social matters is distinct from reasoning about moral matters (Nucci, 1982; Smetana, 1983, 1985; Turiel, 1977, 1978). Adherents of the belief that social reasoning is distinct from moral reasoning cast their thoughts within a cognitive developmental framework (Enright, Lapsley & Olson, 1984).

The architects of the social reasoning approach argue that conventional rules focus on behavioral irregularities. To control such behavioral improprieties, conventional rules are created. In this manner the actions of individuals can be controlled and the existing social system maintained. Such conventional rules are thought to be arbitrary, with no prescription necessary. For example, not eating food with our fingers is a social conventional rule, as is not talking before raising one's hand in class.

By contrast, it is argued that moral rules are not arbitrary and certainly do involve prescription. Furthermore, moral rules are not created through any social consensus but rather are obligatory, virtually universally applicable, and somewhat impersonal (Turiel, 1978). Thus, rules pertaining to lying, stealing, cheating, and physically harming another person are moral rules because violation of these rules confronts ethical standards that exist apart from social consensus and convention. In sum, moral judgments are constructed as concepts of justice, whereas social conventional judgments are structured as concepts of social organization (Lapsley, Enright & Serlin, 1986).

A review of research on **social conventional reasoning** suggests that the major thrust has been to demonstrate the independence of this form of reasoning apart from moral reasoning and to reveal how even young children make this distinction (Lapsley, Enright & Serlin, 1986). For example, in two studies children were queried about spontaneously occurring moral and social conventional transgressions (Nucci & Nucci, 1982; Nucci & Turiel, 1978). Children were asked, "If there was no rule in the school about (the observed event), would it be all right to do it?" Approximately 80 percent of the children at each grade level believed the social conventional act would be appropriate if no

Raising one's hand in class is an example of social conventional behavior.

rule existed to prohibit it. By contrast, more than 85 percent of the children at each grade level said that moral transgressions would not be appropriate even if there were no rules related to the transgressions. Other research suggests that children are more likely to evaluate actions in the moral domain on the basis of their intrinsic features (such as justice or harm), while social conventional actions are more likely to be interpreted in terms of their regulatory status in a social context (Nucci, 1982). Thus, it seems that actions in the social conventional area are judged wrong only if a social rule exists prohibiting them. By contrast, moral transgressions appear to be judged as universally wrong even in the absence of social consensus.

Researchers have also revealed that children's understanding of social rules unfolds in a stagelike fashion. The development of social conventional concepts seems to involve the progressive understanding that conventions involve shared knowledge of uniformities in the social system and further that such uniformities function to coordinate social interaction (Nucci, 1982).

An important contribution of research and thinking about social conventional reasoning is the recognition that complex social issues consist not only of moral components but of issues of social convention as well. While early research suggests that even young children distinguish moral and social conventional reasoning and that a cognitive development sequence of reasoning about social rules occurs, much additional research is required to spell out the empirical basis of this sequence, as well as the environmental experiences that might promote more advanced social conventional reasoning (Lapsley, Enright & Serlin, 1986).

For a summary of what we have learned about the nature of moral development and moral thought, read Concept Table 15.1.

In our discussion of the criticisms of Kohlberg's theory, we observed that moral thought does not always mesh with moral behavior. Next we consider the nature of moral actions as we explore environmental influences on moral behavior.

CONCEPT TABLE 15.1
The Nature of Moral Development and Moral Thought

Concept	Processes/Related Ideas	Characteristics/Description
The nature of moral development	Rules and regulations	Moral development concerns rules and conventions about what people should do in their interaction with other people.
	Components	There are three main domains of moral development: thought, behavior, and feelings.
Moral reasoning	Piaget's view	Piaget argued that children from four to seven years of age are in the stage of moral realism and from about the age of ten years move into the stage of moral autonomy. Formal operational thought may undergird changes in the moral reasoning of adolescents.
	Kohlberg's theory	Kohlberg proposed a provocative theory of moral development with three levels and six stages. As the individual develops through the levels, he or she shows increased internalization.
	Kohlberg's research and influences on the stages	Kohlberg's original research documented age changes in moral thought. His more recent longitudinal data continue to show a relation to age and the fact that the higher stages often do not emerge in adolescence. Among the most important influences on the stages are cognitive development, imitation, peer relations, and opportunities for role/perspective taking.
	Criticism of Kohlberg's theory	Kohlberg's views have been criticized on a number of grounds, including an overemphasis on cognition and an underemphasis on behavior and feeling, the quality of the research, failure to consider females and an underevaluation of a care perspective and relationships, and too much individualistic emphasis with too little attention given to cultural and societal matters.
Moral reasoning and social conventional reasoning	Distinction between moral and social conventional reasoning	Moral reasoning pertains to ethical matters, whereas social conventional reasoning refers to thoughts about social consensus and convention. Moral reasoning is prescriptive, whereas social conventional reasoning is more arbitrary. Moral reasoning places emphasis on justice, whereas social conventional reasoning focuses more on social regulation and the control of behavioral irregularities so that the social system can be maintained.

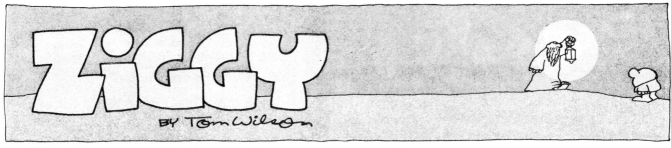

MORAL BEHAVIOR AND SOCIAL LEARNING THEORY

An understanding of moral behavior requires information about basic ideas involved in the study of moral behavior and the social learning approach, an evaluation of research on resistance to temptation and self-control, and cognitive social learning theory.

Basic Ideas about Moral Behavior and Social Learning Theory

The study of moral behavior has been influenced primarily by social learning theory. The familiar processes of reinforcement, punishment, and imitation have been invoked to explain how and why children learn certain responses and why their responses differ from one another; the general conclusions to be drawn are the same as elsewhere. When children are reinforced for behavior that is consistent with laws and social conventions, they are likely to repeat that behavior. When models who behave "morally" are provided, children are likely to adopt their actions. Finally, when children are punished for "immoral" or unacceptable behaviors, those behaviors can be eliminated, but at the expense of sanctioning punishment by its very use and of causing emotional side effects for the child.

To these general conclusions we add the usual qualifiers. The effectiveness of reward and punishment depends on the consistency with which they are administered and the schedule (e.g., continuous, partial) that is adopted. The effectiveness of modeling depends on the characteristics of the model (e.g., esteem, power) and the presence of symbolic codes to enhance retention of the modeled behavior.

TABLE 15.6
Adults as Moral Models for Children

Would you:	Percent who said yes, or probably:	Percent who said it is, or probably is, unethical:	Percent who would, or probably would, be more likely to if sure they wouldn't get caught:
Drive away after scratching a car without telling the owner?	44%	89%	52%
Cover for a friend's secret affair?	41%	66%	33%
Cheat on your spouse?	37%	68%	42%
Keep $10 extra change at a local supermarket?	26%	85%	33%
Knowingly buy a stolen color television set?	22%	87%	31%
Try to keep your neighborhood segregated?	13%	81%	8%
Drive while drunk?	11%	90%	24%
Accept praise for another's work?	4%	96%	8%

Reprinted from *Psychology Today* Magazine. Copyright © 1981 American Psychological Association.

What kind of adult moral models are children being exposed to in our society? Do such models usually do what they say? There is evidence that the adult models children are exposed to often display a double standard, with their moral thinking not always corresponding to their actions. A poll of 24,000 Americans sampled American views on a wide variety of moral issues. Eight detailed scenarios of everyday moral problems were developed to test moral decision making. A summary of the responses to these moral dilemmas is shown in table 15.6. Consider the example of whether the person queried would knowingly buy a stolen color television set. More than 20 percent of the respondents said they would, even though 87 percent said that such an act is probably morally wrong. Further, approximately 31 percent of the adults said that if they knew they would not get caught, they would be more likely to buy the stolen TV. While moral thought is a very important dimension of moral development, these data glaringly point out that what people believe about right and wrong does not always predict how they will act in moral situations.

Resistance to Temptation and Self-Control

A key ingredient of moral development from the social learning perspective is the child's ability to resist temptation and to develop self-control. When pressures mount for the child to cheat, to lie, or to steal, has he or she developed the ability to control himself or herself and resist such temptations?

Child developmentalists have invented a number of ways to investigate such temptations. In one procedure frequently employed, a child is shown an attractive set of toys and told that the toys belong to someone else, who has requested that they not be touched. The child then experiences some social influence, perhaps in the form of a discussion of the virtues of respecting other people's property or a model shown resisting or giving in to the temptation to play with prohibited objects. The child is left alone in the room to amuse himself or herself when the experimenter departs (under some pretext), announcing that he or she will return in ten or fifteen minutes. The experimenter then watches through a one-way mirror to see whether the child resists or gives in to the temptation to play with the toys.

In particular, there has been considerable interest in examining the effects of punishment on children's ability to resist temptation (Parke, 1972, 1977). For the most part, it has been found that a cognitive rationale enhances almost any form of punishment. Such rationales provide reasons as to why the child should not touch a forbidden toy, for example. In particular, such cognitive rationales have been more effective in getting children to resist temptation over a period of time than strategies that do not use such reasoning, such as when the parent puts the child in his or her room without explaining the consequences of the deviant behavior for others.

The ability to resist temptation is closely tied to delay of gratification. Recall from chapter 13 our belief that children's ability to delay gratification is an important

The social learning perspective argues that resistance to temptation and self-control are important aspects of moral development.

dimension of their personality development. Self-control is involved in both the ability to resist temptation and the ability to delay gratification. The child must overcome his or her impulses to get something that is desired but is known to be prohibitive in the case of resistance to temptation. Similarly, the child must exhibit a sense of patience and self-control in delaying gratification for something more desirable in the future rather than succumbing to the immediate pressures of pursuing a smaller reward now.

Considerable research has been conducted on children's self-control. Walter Mischel (1974) believes that self-control is strongly influenced by cognitive factors. Recall from our discussion of delay of gratification in chapter 13 how children's cognitive transformations of desired objects have a strong impact on how patient children are. Research has shown that children can instruct themselves to be more patient and in the process

exhibit more self-control. In one investigation (Mischel & Patterson, 1976) preschool children were asked to engage in a very dull task. Close by was a very enticing talking mechanical clown who tried to persuade the children to come play with him. The children who had been trained to say to themselves "I'm not going to look at Mr. Clown when Mr. Clown says to look at him" were much more likely to control their behavior and continue working on the dull task than children who were not given the self-instructional strategy.

Interest in cognitive factors in resistance to temptation, delay of gratification, and self-control reflect the increasing interest among social learning theorists in the manner in which such cognitions mediate the relation between environmental experiences and moral behavior. Next we consider the view that has captured this cognitive trend.

Cognitive Social Learning Theory

Combining elements of the cognitive development process with elements of the behavioral learning process highlights the cognitive social learning view of Walter and Harriet Mischel (1975). The Mischels distinguish between the child's **moral competence,** or ability to produce moral behaviors, and the child's **moral performance** of those behaviors in specific situations. In their view competence or acquisition depends primarily on cognitive-sensory processes; it is an outgrowth of these processes. Competencies include what children are able to do, what they know, their skills, their awareness of moral rules and regulations, their cognitive ability to construct behaviors. Children's moral performance, or behavior, however, is determined by their motivation and the rewards and incentives to act in a specific moral way.

In general, social learning theorists have been critical of Kohlberg's view. Among other reasons, they believe he places too little emphasis on moral behavior and the situational determinants of morality. However, while Kohlberg argues that moral judgment is an important determinant of moral behavior, he, like the Mischels, stresses that the individual's interpretation of both the moral and factual aspects of a situation leads him or her to a moral decision (Kohlberg & Candee, 1979). For example, Kohlberg mentions that "extramoral" factors, like the desire to avoid embarrassment, may cause the child to avoid doing what he or she believes to be morally right. In sum, both the Mischels and Kohlberg believe that moral action is influenced by a complex of factors. Overall, the findings are mixed with regard to the association of moral thought and behavior, although one recent investigation with college students found that individuals with both high principled moral reasoning and high ego strength were less likely to cheat in a resistance to temptation situation than their low-principled and low-ego strength counterparts (Hess, Lonky & Roodin, 1985).

So far we have seen that both the moral thought and the moral behavior of an individual are important components of moral development. Although psychoanalytic theory has always placed strong faith in the role of feelings in personality development, the emotional aspects of moral development were virtually ignored for many years. Now there seems to be a reemergence of interest in the affective aspects of moral development (Hoffman, 1979). Next we will explore this renewed interest in the emotional aspects of morality.

MORAL FEELINGS, GUILT, AND PSYCHOANALYTIC THEORY

First we consider information about the psychoanalytic account of guilt and describe Erik Erikson's ideas on moral development. Then we turn our attention to the increasing interest in guilt and empathetic affect.

Guilt and Psychoanalytic Theory

In psychoanalytic accounts the development of **guilt** occurs in the following way. Through identification with parents and their use of love withdrawal for disciplinary purposes, the child turns his or her hostility inward and experiences guilt. This guilt is primarily unconscious and reflects the structure of the personality known as the superego.

It is assumed that guilt-prone individuals avoid transgressing in order to avoid anxiety; on the other hand, the person with little guilt has little reason to resist temptation. Thus, in this view, guilt is responsible for harnessing the evil drives of the id and for maintaining the world as a safe place in which to live.

Remember from chapters 10 and 13 that Erik Erikson is a psychoanalytic theorist. Erikson's (1970) views are thus an example of a psychoanalytic view of the development of morality. Erikson believes there are three stages or moral development: specific moral learning in childhood, ideologies in adolescence, and ethical consolidation in adulthood. As we have seen, Erikson's main focus is on the adolescent's search for identity, which requires a sense of purpose. If the adolescent becomes disillusioned with the moral and religious beliefs that she acquired during childhood, she is likely to, at least temporarily, lose her sense of purpose and experience a vacuum in her life. This may lead to a search for an ideology that will give some purpose to the adolescent's life. For the ideology to be acceptable it must fit both the "evidence" and the adolescent's relatively high level of logical reasoning ability. If others share in this ideology, it promotes a sense of community in the adolescent as well. For Erikson, then, ideology emerges as the "guardian" of identity during adolescence because it provides a sense of purpose, assists in tying the present to the future, and contributes meaning to behavior (Hoffman, 1980).

Empathetic Affect and Guilt

Children as well as adults often try to make sense out of their world by attributing causes to their behavior and the events around them. When someone is in distress, then, we would expect the child to make inferences about the cause of the victim's distress. The child's ideas about the cause of the victim's distress probably combine with empathy, which is aroused because of the victim's suffering, to produce a feeling of guilt (not the Freudian type, which assumes repressed impulses).

Based on ideas such as these, Martin Hoffman has been constructing a developmental theory of guilt that highlights empathic distress and causal attribution. Summarizing his findings thus far, Hoffman (1979) concluded:

1. A full guilt response occurs in children as early as six years of age and a rudimentary response of guilt as early as two years of age (Radke-Yarrow, Zahn-Waxler & Chapman, 1983).
2. Discipline that involves pointing out the effects of the child's behavior on others contributes to the development of guilt.
3. Arousal of empathic distress seems to intensify guilt feelings (Thompson & Hoffman, in press).
4. The arousal of guilt is usually followed by some type of reparative act toward the victim or toward others (Regan, 1971), or if neither is possible, a prolongation of guilt.
5. Guilt sometimes sets off a process of self-examination and reordering of values, as well as a resolution not to act so selfishly in the future (Hoffman, 1975).

CONCEPT TABLE 15.2
Moral Behavior and Feelings

Concept	Processes/Related Ideas	Characteristics/Description
Moral behavior	Basic ideas	The study of moral behavior has been influenced primarily by social learning theory. The focus is on learned moral behavior, behavior learned through interaction with other people.
	Resistance to temptation and self-control	Two dimensions of moral behavior that social learning theorists often study are resistance to temptation and self-control. These aspects of moral behavior are closely tied to delay of gratification. Research has shown that cognitive factors are important determinants of resistance to temptation, self-control, and delay of gratification.
	Cognitive social learning theory	Cognitive social learning argues that cognitive processes mediate the influence of the environment on moral behavior. This theory also distinguishes moral competence from moral performance, suggesting that what a child morally knows does not always relate to what he or she morally does.
Moral feelings	Guilt and psychoanalytic theory	Psychoanalytic theorists have argued that guilt develops through identification with parents and their use of love withdrawal. Erikson stresses that identity is an important aspect of moral development in adolescence.
	Empathetic affect and guilt	Hoffman has proposed that guilt can be better understood by focusing on developmental concerns, empathy, and causal attributions.

For many years the study of moral development focused on its negative side through an interest in such behaviors as cheating, lying, and stealing. However, we can also study the positive side of moral development by examining a trait like altruism, or the selfless concern for the welfare of others. Altruism has been given considerable attention in recent years and, together with Kohlberg's theory, represents the area of greatest research in moral development. Before we move on to an examination of altruism, read Concept Table 15.2 for a summary of our discussion of moral behavior and moral feelings.

ALTRUISM

Altruistic behaviors include sharing possessions, contributing to worthy causes, and helping people in distress. In some studies children play games with the opportunity of sharing their winnings or prizes with others, either with their friends or with a charitable institution such as an orphanage. In other studies situations are created in which someone (actually a confederate of the experimenter) acts as if he or she is in need of help. The extent to which the child assists this person provides an index of altruistic or helping behavior. The conditions under which children will write letters to fictitious sick children in a hospital have also been studied. Staub (1971) has examined children's readiness to help a person in distress: Children were left alone or in pairs in a room and while there heard a chair crash to the floor in another room, followed by the cries and moans of a young girl.

In the following sections we will explore a number of different aspects of **altruism,** including its developmental course and the roles that empathy and perspective taking play in promoting altruism.

The Development of Altruism

In general, altruism increases as children develop (e.g., Underwood & Moore, 1980): Older children usually are more likely to be helpful or to share than are younger children, and older children show a greater variety of prosocial behaviors. However, as the following episode suggests, very young children, even as young as the second year of life, may display vividly altruistic behavior.

Today Jerry was kind of cranky; he just started completely bawling and he wouldn't stop. John kept coming over and handing Jerry toys, trying to cheer him up, so to speak. He'd say things like "Here, Jerry," and I said to John: "Jerry's sad; he doesn't feel good; he had a shot today." John would look at me with his eyebrows kind of wrinkled together like he really understood that Jerry was crying because he was unhappy, not that he was just being a crybaby. He went over and rubbed Jerry's arm and said "Nice Jerry" and continued to give him toys. (Zahn-Waxler, Radke-Yarrow & King, 1979, pp. 321–322)

In general, altruism increases as children develop.

Clearly, John was touched by his friend Jerry's disturbed state and acted in an altruistic manner toward him. Rather amazingly, John was not quite two years old when this incident occurred. Martin Hoffman (1975) agrees that toddlers less than two years of age show empathy toward individuals they perceive to be in distress. He believes that the initial stress the child senses involves his or her own primary discomforts—hunger, thirst, and pain. For example, the sight of an alarmed mother quickly becomes associated with feeling states in the infant that cause the infant primary discomfort. The infant cannot distinguish between "self" and "other" and so may produce a distress response when another person is distressed, as if it were happening to himself or herself. And as we saw in the interaction between Jerry and John, children also recognize noxious events experienced by others that they themselves have felt and likewise react to them with distress.

In Hoffman's view the classically conditioned empathic response to distress paves the way for the development of an altruistic motive. One of the earliest landmarks in this sequence is the appearance of person permanence (similar to Piaget's concept of object permanence), a sense that people exist independent of oneself. Once cognizant of this, children are able to convert their empathy into efforts to help another person in distress. However, young children are still egocentric and often confuse their own inner thoughts and feelings with those of another.

> This lack of understanding is often evidenced in the child's efforts to help, which consist chiefly of giving the other what he himself finds most comforting. Examples are . . . a thirteen-month-old who brought his own mother to comfort a crying friend even though the friend's mother was equally available, and . . . another child who offered his beloved doll to comfort an adult who looked sad. (Hoffman, 1975, p. 615)

It also has been speculated that internalized motives and self-rewards (intrinsic rewards such as increased self-esteem or feelings of satisfaction following an action) influence many prosocial actions. Moreover, it seems likely that as children become older, motives for assisting others become less dependent on external rewards, punishment, and the approval of authority. In this sense the development of altruism becomes more internalized with increasing age (Mussen & Eisenberg-Berg, 1977). Next we see that age differences probably also occur in empathic responding.

Altruism and Empathy

Empathic response is viewed as a critical building block in forming a basic motive to help others, hence its important role in moral development. Hoffman (1979) provided the following summary of research on empathy.

1. Very young children, approximately two to four years old, typically show empathy toward a hurt child, even though they sometimes do nothing or act inappropriately (e.g., Zahn-Waxler, Radke-Yarrow & King, 1979).
2. Older children and adults show empathy also, but usually their empathy is followed by some form of helpful behavior (e.g., Sawin, 1979).
3. The level at which empathy is aroused and the speed of the altruistic act increase in conjunction with the number and intensity of distress cues given by the victim (e.g., Geer & Jarmecky, 1973).
4. The level of empathic arousal drops after the helpful action but continues if there is no attempt to help (e.g., Darley & Latane, 1968).

In addition to **empathy,** another factor thought to be important in promoting altruistic tendencies in children is role taking or perspective taking.

Role-Taking and Perspective-Taking Skills

Role-taking and **perspective-taking skills** refer to the understanding that other people have feelings and perceptions different from one's own. By seven or eight years of age, the child has mastered complex role-taking skills (Flavell, Botkin, Fry, Wright & Jarvis, 1968; Selman, 1971), but others are mastered as early as the age of two or three (Flavell, 1985). Elementary school children's empathy is directed toward helping the other person, but they seek to find the true source of the other person's distress. And they are likely to discover the tentative and hypothetical nature of their inferences. Thus, their motivation to relieve the other's distress is less egocentric and based to a greater degree on the accurate assessment of the other's needs, trial and error, and response to corrective feedback (Hoffman, 1975).

Research on the link between role taking and altruism suggests that children who have well-developed role-taking skills show more kindness and helping behaviors toward other children (e.g., Rubin & Schneider, 1973). One investigator has successfully trained six-year-old children in role-taking skills and found that they subsequently have more altruistic tendencies than a nontrained group (Iannotti, 1978).

MORAL EDUCATION

Some years ago, John Dewey (1933) argued that the most important values taught in school focus on how the school is organized and governed. Educational experts sometimes refer to this as the "hidden curriculum." In the hidden curriculum, students learn about obedience and defiance of authority rather than about democratic principles. As Dewey suggested, schools were in the business of moral education long before the current "new morality" programs came on the scene. In the 1800s, youth who were exposed to McGuffey's Readers were taught how to behave as well as how to read.

Dewey was correct in arguing that the school is a moral system. Schools, like families, are settings for moral development. Teachers serve as models of ethical behavior. Classroom rules and peer relations transmit attitudes about cheating, lying, stealing, and

John Dewey was correct in arguing that every school has a moral atmosphere.

consideration of others. And the school administration, through its rules and regulations, represents a specific value system to children.

Some educational theorists believe that, while it is difficult to specify the appropriate moral virtues to instill in children, it is possible to identify generally accepted moral virtues and didactically inform students about them (e.g., Hamm, 1977). But other theorists believe that there are no universally agreed upon moral virtues and that "subjective" virtues should not be taught to children. Led by Lawrence Kohlberg, this group stresses that the moral-reasoning skills of children—rather than adherence to any value system—should be developed. While moral education programs embodying Kohlberg's beliefs vary from school to school, most have emphasized the role of the teacher

as a facilitator rather than a lecturer, the importance of discussing moral dilemmas, and the importance of give-and-take peer-group discussion.

By the late 1970s and the beginning of the 1980s Kohlberg had revised his views on moral education. A summary of his revisionist thinking on this subject appears in Perspective on Child Development 15.3.

Social Conventional Reasoning and Values Education

Recall that there has recently been increased interest in investigating the domain of social conventional reasoning to obtain a more complete picture of how children interpret complex social issues rather than relying only on their moral reasoning. Along this line it has been argued that contemporary values education is limited because of a failure to coordinate the teaching of social values with students' conceptions of morality. For example, it would seem inappropriate to discuss the morality of a particular dress code at a school because the issue of dress codes falls into the domain of social rather than moral convention (Nucci, in press). The implication is that students not only should be moved to a higher level of moral understanding but to a higher level of social conventional understanding as well.

One investigation reveals the importance of social conventional reasoning in education (Geiger & Turiel, 1983). The relation between disruptive school behavior (such as violations of classroom rules and defiance of school authorities) and social conventional reasoning was evaluated in a group of young adolescents. It was predicted that disruptive behavior by junior high school students would be related to the level of their social conventional reasoning. The findings revealed that virtually all of the nondisruptive students were at a higher level of social reasoning (an understanding that social convention is mediated by the social system), while three-fourths of the disruptive students reasoned at a lower level about social conventional matters. Thus, it may be possible to better understand the dynamics of school misbehavior when we investigate social conventional domains as well as moral domains (Lapsley, Enright & Serlin, 1986).

PERSPECTIVE ON CHILD DEVELOPMENT 15.3

KOHLBERG'S REVISIONIST THINKING ABOUT MORAL EDUCATION

I n 1974 Kohlberg established the "Just Community," a small school for black and white students from different socioeconomic backgrounds. In the Just Community emphasis was placed on considering realistic issues that arise in school, the nature of moral behavior as well as moral thought, and an active role for teachers as moral advocates.

The Just Community shared with other alternative schools a belief in self-governance, mutual caring, and group solidarity. The goal for moral development was geared toward increasing students' responsibility to the community (stage 4 in Kohlberg's theory) rather than self-principled reasoning. In a recent investigation of the effectiveness of the Just Community—actually named the Cluster School—(Power, 1984), it was found that a more positive orientation toward the community did develop and that students were likely to adhere to the rules they had established. However, although the moral reasoning of the students at the Cluster School did advance, students who simply participated in moral discussion programs advanced their moral reasoning, just as much as the students in the Cluster School.

The manner in which Kohlberg set up the Cluster School brings him closer to educators who are concerned with the moral "givens" in life. However, as indicated before, most programs that have included Kohlberg's ideas emphasize the process of moral reasoning rather than a specific moral content. The effectiveness of the programs often varies from school to school and from student to student. Success is usually better at the lower stages (2, 3, and 4) than at postconventional levels (5, 6) (Minuchin & Shapiro, 1983), and in open schools rather than traditional schools (Sullivan, 1975). There is also some question about the

persistence of the effects—how long lasting are the effects of such moral education programs? Usually, assessment takes place immediately after the semester in which moral education is taught, and rarely are there long-term followups.

With the development of the Cluster School in the middle 1970s Kohlberg himself seemed to change his ideas about moral education. Kohlberg (1981) reported that he was not satisfied with the discussion approach to moral education. He realized that attempts to instill principled reasoning about morality in adolescents may be unrealistic because most people do not reach this level of cognitive maturity even in adulthood. And he began to believe that the moral climate of the country was shifting to an emphasis on the self and away from a concern for others in the 1970s. As a consequence, Kohlberg began to show a stronger interest in the school as a social system and in creating moral school communities (Minuchin & Shapiro, 1983).

As a further indication of Kohlberg's belief in the importance of the moral atmosphere of the school, he has developed the Moral Atmosphere Interview. This interview poses dilemmas that deal with typically occurring problems in high schools, problems that are likely to involve social responsibility. In a recent investigation (Higgins, Power & Kohlberg, 1983), the Moral Atmosphere Interview was administered to samples of approximately twenty students from three democratic alternative high schools and three more traditional, authoritarian high schools. Students in the democratic schools perceived the rules of their schools to be more collective and described themselves and their peers as more willing to act responsibly than did students from the traditional schools.

SUMMARY

I. Moral development concerns rules and regulations about what people should do in their interaction with other people. There are three main domains of moral development: thought, behavior, and feelings.

II. Understanding moral thought requires information on Piaget's view, Kohlberg's theory, Kohlberg's research and influence on stages of thought, criticisms of Kohlberg's theory, and social conventional reasoning.

A. Piaget argued that children from four to seven years of age are in the stage of moral realism and that from about ten years of age on children move into the stage of moral autonomy. Formal operational thought may undergird the moral reasoning of adolescents.

B. Kohlberg proposed a provocative theory of moral development with three levels and six stages. As the individual develops through the levels, he or she shows increased internalization.

C. Kohlberg's original research documented age changes in moral thought. His more recent longitudinal data continue to show a relation with age and also the fact that the higher stages of moral thought do not usually appear in adolescence. Among the most important influences on the stages are cognitive development, modeling and cognitive conflict, peer relations, and role/perspective-taking opportunities. Transactional discussion in peer groups is a likely candidate for advancing moral reasoning.

D. Among the most vehement criticisms of Kohlberg's views are those related to the interface of moral thought, moral behavior and moral feeling; quality of the research; sex differences; the care perspective; and culture and societal considerations. In particular, considerable interest has focused on Gilligan's care perspective.

III. Information about moral behavior and social learning theory emphasizes basic ideas, resistance to temptation and self-control, and cognitive social learning theory.

A. The study of moral behavior has been influenced primarily by social learning theory. The focus is on learned behavior, behavior learned through interaction with other people.

B. Two dimensions of moral behavior that social learning theorists often study are resistance to temptation and self-control. These aspects of moral behavior are closely tied to a third dimension, delay of gratification. Research has shown that cognitive factors are important determinants of resistance to temptation, self-control, and delay of gratification.

C. Cognitive social learning theory argues that cognitive processes mediate the influence of the environment on children's moral behavior. Also stressed is a distinction between moral competence and moral performance, suggesting that what a child morally knows does not always predict what he or she will morally do.

IV. Information about moral feelings focuses on guilt and psychoanalytic theory as well as empathetic affect and guilt.

V. Altruism refers to a selfless concern about the welfare of others. Researchers have been interested in the development of altruism, the role of empathy in altruism, and the importance of role-taking and perspective-taking skills in altruism.

VI. Moral education has a long history. Some years ago John Dewey described the moral atmosphere of the school. More recently Kohlberg has proposed how children should be morally educated, revising his views within the last decade. Recently interest in enhancing students' social conventional reasoning in educational settings has developed.

KEY TERMS

altruism 536	moral development 517
care perspective 527	moral performance 534
cognitive-disequilibrium theory 519	moral realism 517
	perspective-taking skills 538
conventional level 520	postconventional level 521
empathy 538	preconventional level 520
guilt 535	role-taking skills 538
immanent justice 518	social conventional reasoning 530
justice perspective 527	
moral autonomy 517	societalism 529
moral competence 534	transactive discussion 524

REVIEW QUESTIONS

1. What is moral development?
2. Discuss the nature of cognitive developmental theory and the development of moral reasoning.
3. What is the nature of social conventional reasoning and how can it be distinguished from moral reasoning?
4. Describe in some detail the criticisms of Kohlberg's research and theory.
5. Discuss the care and justice perspectives of moral reasoning. To what extent do you believe there are sex differences in these forms of moral reasoning?
6. Outline the nature of moral behavior and social learning theory. Include in your discussion information about self-control and cognitive social learning theory.
7. Evaluate the basic ideas involved in the investigation of moral feelings, guilt, and altruism.
8. Discuss some different approaches to moral education and distinguish between them. Should schools be in the business of moral education?

SUGGESTED READINGS

Gilligan, C. (1982). *In a different voice*. Cambridge, MA: Harvard University Press.
This book advances Gilligan's provocative view that a care perspective is underrepresented in Kohlberg's theory and research.

Lapsley, D. K., Enright, R. D., and Serlin, R. C. (1986). Moral and social education. In J. Worrell and F. Danner (Eds.), *Adolescent development: Issues for education*. New York: Academic Press.
A thorough overview of what is known about moral education and the more recently developed field of social education. Includes thoughtful, detailed comments about the nature of moral and social conventional reasoning.

Lickona, T. (Ed.). (1976). *Moral development and behavior*. New York: Holt, Rinehart & Winston.
Contemporary essays outlining the major theories, research findings, and educational implications of moral development. Included are essays by Kohlberg, Hoffman, Mischel, Aronfreed, Bronfenbrenner, and Rest.

Radke-Yarrow, M., Zahn-Waxler, C., and Chapman, M. (1983). Children's prosocial dispositions and behaviors. In P. H. Mussen (Ed.), *Handbook of child psychology* (4th ed., Vol. 4). New York: John Wiley.
These prominent researchers in the field of children's prosocial development review what is known about children's altruism.

Rest, J. R. (1983). Morality. In P. H. Mussen (Ed.), *Handbook of child psychology* (4th ed., Vol. 3). New York: John Wiley.
Recent information about moral reasoning is evaluated, with considerable attention devoted to methodological issues in assessment. Valuable ideas about the importance of information processing in understanding moral reasoning are also offered.

PROBLEMS AND DISTURBANCES

PROBLEMS AND DISTURBANCES

PROLOGUE

LITTLE HANS, HIS WIDDLER, AND PHOBIA

At the age of three, Hans showed "a quite peculiarly lively interest in that portion of his body which he used to describe as his widdler." When he was three and a half, his mother caught him with his hand on it. She threatened him, "If you do that, I shall send for Dr. A. to cut off your widdler. And then what will you widdle with?" Hans replied, "With my bottom." Many other remarks about widdlers in animals and humans were made by Hans between the ages of three and four, including questions directed at his mother and father asking whether they had widdlers.

> *Mother:* What are you staring like that for?
> *Hans:* I was only looking to see if you've got a widdler, too.
> *Mother:* Of course. Didn't you know that?
> *Hans:* No, I thought you were so big you'd have a widdler like a horse.

Sigmund Freud, whose psychoanalytic theory was discussed earlier, believed that Little Hans, as the boy was called, was a classic example of the underlying sexual urges in our personality. One incident when the boy was four years old was given considerable importance by Freud, who believed that it suggested Hans was attempting to seduce his mother. As she was drying and powdering him after his bath, Hans asked if she would put her finger on his widdler. When she objected that such an act would be improper, Hans laughed and said, "But, it's great fun."

Hans's father wrote to Freud telling him that Hans had developed a nervous disorder. The symptoms reported were a fear of going into the streets, depression in the evening, and a fear that a horse would bite him. Hans's father pointed out that this sexual overexcitation was due to his mother's tenderness and that the fear of the horse was likely due to having been frightened by a large penis. Freud told Hans's father to tell the boy that all of this stuff about horses was nonsense and that the truth was he was very fond of his mother and wanted to be taken into her bed. The reason Hans was afraid of horses, said Freud, was that he had grown fascinated by their widdlers. Freud also said it was now time to tell Hans that women do not have widdlers at all.

After Hans had been enlightened, there was a fairly quiet period, but after an attack of flu, the phobia got worse. Conversations between Hans and his father

continued off and on, with his father telling Hans such things as his phobia would disappear if he would stop putting his hand on his widdler and reassuring him that females do not have widdlers. One day Hans and his father went to the zoo. Hans showed a fear of the giraffe, elephant, and all other large animals. Hans was informed by his father that he was afraid of big animals because they had big widdlers. Hans denied this.

Later Hans reported the following dream: "In the night there was a big giraffe in the room and a crumpled one; and the big one called out because I took the crumpled one away from it. Then it stopped calling out; and then I sat down on the top of the crumpled one."

After talking to the boy, the father informed Freud that the dream was a matrimonial scene transposed into the giraffe's life. Hans developed an urge for his mother and came into the room for that reason. The father believed the whole thing was a continuation of his fear of horses. The dream was thought to be related to Hans's habit of occasionally getting into his parents' bed in spite of his father's disapproval. Freud suggested that sitting down on the crumpled giraffe meant taking possession of the mother. Further support for this belief came when Hans called his mother a big giraffe the next day.

Freud believed that Hans wished to replace his father, whom he saw as a rival for his mother's affection, and desired to take possession of his mother. He thought that Hans transposed from his father onto the horses. The horses represented the father to Hans.

Joseph Wolpe and Stanley Rachman (1960) have criticized Freud's interpretation of Little Hans's phobia. They agree that Hans enjoyed being with his mother, but there is no evidence that he wanted to copulate with her. Hans kept being told that he was afraid of his father and that there was a relationship between the horses and his father, yet the boy repeatedly denied these things. Freud believed that Hans's phobia developed to keep him close to his mother, yet Hans still experienced anxiety when he went outside for walks with his mother. Freud also argued that the reason Hans's fear of horses eventually subsided is that he resolved the **Oedipus complex** (Freud's belief that in early childhood the young boy exhibits sexual desire for his mother and hostility toward and fear of his father). As Wolpe and Rachman have indicated, there was no evidence of an Oedipus complex in the first place. They believe that Hans's phobia can be explained by learning theory. Hans was a sensitive child who was always moved when people wept in his presence, and long before his phobia developed he became uneasy upon seeing the horses in a merry-go-round beaten. Wolpe and Rachman believe that an incident Freud referred to as a somewhat minor incident in the development of the phobia was indeed the cause of the entire disorder. This was an experience Hans had when a horse fell down in a bus:

> *Hans:* I'm most afraid too when a bus comes along.
> *Father:* Why? Because they are so big.
> *Hans:* No. Because once a horse in a bus fell.
> *Father:* When?

Hans then recounted the incident, which was confirmed by his mother.

> *Father:* What did you think when the horse fell down?
> *Hans:* Now it will always be like this. All horses in buses'll fall down.
> *Father:* In all buses?
> *Hans:* Yes. And in furniture vans too. Not often in furniture vans.
> *Father:* You had your nonsense already at that time?
> *Hans:* No. I only got it then. When the horse in the bus fell down, it gave me such a fright really: That was when I got the nonsense.

Hans (just like Little Albert in John Watson's conditioning experiment with rats) reacted with anxiety not only to the original conditioned stimulus (horses) but to other related objects (horse-drawn buses, vans, and features of horses). The main conclusion to be derived from the case of Little Hans is that it does not provide anything resembling direct support of such psychoanalytic views as the underlying sexual motivation of phobias and their ties to the Oedipus complex (Freud, 1959; Wolpe and Rachman, 1960).

Source: Based upon Freud, S., *Collected Papers*, Vol. 3. © 1959 Hogarth Press, London, England; and Wople, J., and S. Rachman, "Psychoanalytic 'evidence:' A critique based on Freud's case of Little Hans," in *Journal of Nervous and Mental Disease*, 130, pp. 135–148. © 1960 The Williams & Wilkins Company, Baltimore, MD.

PREVIEW

Throughout this book the focus has been on the development of children who are considered normal, although many examples of children with various behavioral problems have been discussed. This final chapter lends a closer eye to the major problems and disturbances of infants, children, and adolescents. First, different definitions of abnormality are evaluated, next the science of developmental psychopathology is described, and then an overview of the nature of problems and disturbances in infancy and early childhood, the elementary school-years, and adolescence is provided. The chapter concludes with a consideration of the important developmental issue of continuity–discontinuity as it pertains to understanding children's problems and disturbances.

DIFFERENT DEFINITIONS OF ABNORMALITY IN CHILDREN

Malevolent gods, demons, witches, vampires, and even the moon and planets have been called responsible for children's abnormal behavior. During the Middle Ages, Satan and Lucifer, as the devil was known, were seen as major provokers of madness in children. In such supernatural characterizations of abnormality the children who engaged in abnormal behavior were thought to be not only crazy but evil as well. Such interpretations have sometimes been referred to as the **religious** or **supernatural model** of abnormality. In this model the causes of the child's abnormal behavior are traced to sinfulness, demonic possession, or temptation by the devil. Some religious sects in the United States still hold to these beliefs. Intervention to try to remove or reduce the abnormal behavior comes in the form of exorcism, repentance, or confession. The goal is to save the child from eternal damnation.

Psychologists do not view the religious or supernatural model as a viable way to explain and understand children's abnormal behavior. Next we look at several models that have been given serious consideration by scientists interested in the nature of children's abnormality: the statistical model, the medical or disease model, the psychological and sociocultural model, and finally the interactionist model.

The Statistical Model

According to the **statistical model,** a statistical definition of abnormality emphasizes that a child is abnormal when he or she deviates from the average. But there are some problems with describing children this way. Shirley Temple, the famous child actress, would have been considered deviant according to this definition because she was far from average in terms of her acting ability. Yet we would not consider Shirley Temple a deviant actress or person. And all children are deviant from one another on certain dimensions. The fact that one child may like classical music even though none of his friends do does not make the musically inclined child deviant. It is primarily in the areas of social behavior and thought that we look for differences between children that might suggest abnormality. However, even in these areas averages often change from one time to another and from one culture to another. For example in the Mangain culture young adolescent males are trained in sexual techniques and then seek out or are sought out by young girls so the techniques can be practiced. In the United States, even though we have become a more sexually permissive culture, such behavior would be considered deviant for young adolescent males and females.

Similarly, behaviors that were considered abnormal early in the twentieth century are now viewed as normal. Think about the following comments on masturbation taken from a popular 1913 handbook called *What a Boy Should Know:*

> Whenever unnatural emissions are produced . . . he will be more easily tired. . . . He will probably look pale and pasty, and he is lucky if he escapes indigestion and getting his bowels confined, both of which will probably give him spots and pimples on his face. . . . The results on the mind are the more severe and more easily recognized. . . . His wits are not so sharp. . . . A boy like this is a poor thing to look at. (Schofield & Vaughan-Jackson, 1913, pp. 30–42)

In the past, masturbation was thought to cause everything from warts to insanity. But today, less than 15 percent of adolescents view masturbation as wrong (Hyde, 1979).

The Medical or Disease Model

Another model of abnormality is the **medical or disease model.** According to this view, a child is abnormal when there is some physical malfunctioning in his or her body. Thus psychological abnormality is believed to be some type of disease or illness precipitated by internal factors. Children's abnormalities are called "illnesses," and the children become "patients" in hospitals, where they are "treated" by doctors. The form of intervention in the medical model is usually some type of drug therapy or in rare instances removal of a portion of the brain. The goal of this treatment is to cure the illness.

There is clear evidence that biological factors play an important role in a number of forms of abnormality, and genetic inheritance has been linked to such debilitating psychological disorders as schizophrenia. Nonetheless, the medical model has underplayed the role of sociocultural factors and overemphasized the analogy between physical and mental disorders. If a child breaks her leg or contracts pneumonia, there is general agreement on the symptoms and treatments of the illness or disease. But psychologists and psychiatrists sometimes have a difficult time agreeing on the symptoms of a number of psychological abnormalities, such as anxiety and schizophrenia, much less on their treatments. For such reasons, the medical model has been subjected to strong attacks by some critics. Thomas Szasz (1961, 1977), one of the most vocal critics, goes so far as to say that the medical model of mental illness (which most psychiatrists, but not psychologists, follow) is a pseudoscience that should be placed in the same category as alchemy and astrology. However, although the analogy to disease and physical illness may not always be the best way to think of psychological abnormality, it is important that we recognize the significant role biological and genetic factors seem to play in a number of forms of abnormality.

Psychological and Sociocultural Approaches

Distorted views of reality and unusual behavior are two of the most common characteristics of serious mental disorders. One of the prominent theories we discussed earlier was the behavioral, social learning view. This perspective emphasizes that abnormality is heavily influenced by the sociocultural experiences we have and how those experiences influence our thoughts and behavior.

The behavioral, social learning perspective has much in common with the **sociocultural model** of abnormality. It seeks to determine the environmental factors that cause children to display unusual behavior and to understand why people in a society call such children sick, mentally ill, crazy, and so on. Thomas Scheff (1966) argues that mentally disturbed children are simply special representatives of social deviance. He points out that all cultures have norms, and if we violate those norms we will be labeled "deviant." If children steal, they are delinquents. Scheff says there are certain residual norms that are so widely adopted they are sometimes taken for granted as a part of nature. Thus normal children don't repeatedly steal things. Scheff feels that sociocultural factors are an important aspect of abnormality. He acknowledges that mental disorders do exist but feels they are not illnesses but rather problems in living. From Szasz's perspective, mental disorders reflect defective strategies children have adopted in trying to cope with difficult, stressful situations. Such ideas have much in common with Richard Lazarus's belief that to understand stress we need to look at how children cognitively interpret their self and their world (Lazarus & DeLongis, 1983).

The Interactionist Approach

We have looked at a number of ways to view abnormality. We can rule out the supernatural view, and the idea of abnormality as an illness or a disease may not be a very accurate course to follow either. But it would be wrong to go too far in the direction of the sociocultural model when we attempt to understand abnormality because we know that biological factors interact with sociocultural conditions to determine a child's behavior, thoughts, and feelings. Thus an **interactionist approach** to understanding abnormality seems to be the wisest choice. From this view, both biological factors and sociocultural conditions may produce a mental disturbance, and in most instances these factors interact with each other to produce the problem. We will call on our statement made earlier in the book to support this interpretation of abnormality: No genes, no organism; no environment, no organism. This orientation holds for both abnormal and normal behavior. As part of the environmental contribution, we need to consider what is acceptable and unacceptable behavior in a particular society.

One view of abnormality is the sociocultural model, arguing that sociocultural experiences determine what is abnormal or normal.

PROBLEMS AND DISTURBANCES THROUGH INFANCY, CHILDHOOD, AND ADOLESCENCE

Our overview of problems and disturbances through childhood begins with information about the domain of developmental psychopathology, then turns to a consideration of problems and disturbances in infancy and early childhood, the elementary school years, and adolescence.

The Science of Developmental Psychopathology

As its name indicates, **developmental psychopathology** has ties to many different areas of research, in particular developmental psychology, psychology in general, and the clinical sciences of psychiatry and clinical psychology (Cicchetti, 1984). While developmental psychopathology has historical roots that arise from psychoanalytic theory (e.g., Freud, 1955), not until the 1970s was it clearly mapped out as a separate field of research. Among the pioneers whose work helped pave the way for the emergence of this new discipline are E. James Anthony and Norman Garmezy (e.g., Anthony, 1956; Garmezy, 1978), whose studies of high-risk children revealed the strengths that make vulnerable children resilient to stress; Thomas Achenbach, (Achenbach, 1978) whose studies of problems and disturbances among children and adolescents have helped generate a topography and classification of developmental disturbances, showing which disturbances are more prevalent at particular ages; Alan Sroufe (Sroufe 1979), whose longitudinal studies of attachment patterns and the development of social competence have demonstrated the importance of early family patterns in pathology; Michael Rutter (Rutter, 1980), whose studies of maternal deprivation, autism, and childhood depression have sensitized researchers to important social processes involved in disturbances; Edward Zigler (1967), whose research on mental retardation has done much to foster our knowledge of developmental processes in psychopathology; and Stella Chess and Alexander Thomas (1977), who remind us that continuity and discontinuity are involved in the development of problems and disturbances.

Infancy and Early Childhood

As examples of some of the major problems and disturbances that surface in infancy and early childhood, we look first at sudden infant death syndrome, second at eating, sleeping, and elimination problems, third at infantile autism, and fourth at the abused child.

Sudden Infant Death Syndrome

Sudden infant death syndrome (SIDS) refers to the unexplained death of a child in the first year of life, usually between the ages of two and five months. *Unexplained* indicates that upon autopsy and review of the infant's pediatric history, no clear cause is found for the infant's death. The baby apparently just stops breathing, in most cases at night. There are approximately two crib deaths for every one thousand births, with about eight thousand crib deaths occurring in the United States each year. After the first ten days of life, infant crib death is responsible for more deaths in the first year of life than any other cause.

Lewis Lipsitt (1979) believes that while sudden infant death syndrome remains unexplained, there are some signs to suggest possible causes of sudden infant death syndrome.

Let us consider briefly what the mechanisms or processes might be like. Rapid myelinization and dendritic proliferation are characteristics of the period immediately following birth, which may be an especially important one for critical learning events. Very early unconditioned responses, such as the rooting, Babinski, Babkin, and grasping reflexes, undergo drastic alterations during the first four months of life. Vital responses with which the infant is biologically equipped at birth diminish drastically or become considerably altered over time. As McGraw (1943) demonstrated so well, many of these reflexes are supplanted by learned response systems, and the learned patterns of behavior become increasingly functional. . . . Innate response systems that are strikingly apparent at birth often diminish in frequency and intensity up to two or three months of age (McGraw, 1943) by which time these response propensities are displaced by "voluntary" or learned responses mediated by higher cortical centers. In consideration of the brain tissue maturation occurring during the first two or three months of life, it is not unthinkable that this period is quite critical for the development of certain behaviors which, if not adequately learned by the time that the unlearned protective reflexes have diminished, will place the organism in (even lethal) jeopardy. (pp. 976–977)

Eating, Sleeping, and Elimination Problems

During the first several years of life, eating, sleeping, and elimination problems may occur. We consider each of these in turn.

Eating Problems Sandy, a four-year-old girl, was referred to a pediatrician because she would not feed herself and would only eat strained foods that were restricted to oatmeal, cottage cheese, and an occasional fruit. Her feeding problem began early in her development, first appearing when she almost choked on a string bean at nine months of age. Her mother became frightened by the string bean event and refrained from giving her table foods for several weeks. Later when she tried to feed Sandy solid foods again, Sandy refused to eat them. An onslaught of battles over feeding ensued, with Sandy most often the victor (Bernal, 1972).

TABLE 16.1
The Problems of Obesity

Symptoms	Related Factors	Causal Factors	Treatment
Body weight greater than 20 percent of norm. Excessive body fat.	Fat infants tend to be obese later in childhood and in adulthood.	No single cause.	Difficult to treat.
Abnormal inactivity.	Pessimistic outlook.	Hereditary tendencies that may set weight boundaries.	Diet restrictions, increased physical exercise, and behavior modification (although no modification program available as yet for children).
Immature, dependent on mother, shy, fearful, timid, clumsy, slow, and apathetic.	Secondary effects of obesity are in damaging self-esteem, in peer relations, and social adjustment, as well as in health hazards.	Small percentage caused by endocrine disorders.	Individual psychotherapy not effective.
Most obese children are tall for their age, a factor that distinguishes their obesity from endocrine disease.	Tall for age rules out hormonal basis of obesity.	Psychogenic.	Group therapy and special group programs show promise but no follow-up data available yet.
	Below average in height as adults.	Rejecting mother tends to overfeed, which leads to child's failure to distinguish correct bodily sensations of hunger and satiation.	
		Modeling of obese parents.	

Eating is one of a baby's main activities, but it can be the source of problems, as in Sandy's case in which the eating context was used to show her mother who was boss. While there are many harmless minor variations in a baby's eating habits, there are other eating patterns that can be a source of stress between parents and infant and still others that may result in physiological damage to the young child.

For example, some evidence suggests that excessive weight gain in infancy is linked with a high incidence of **obesity** at six, seven, and eight years of age (Eid, 1970). And it is likely that fat babies will become fat adults, since overfed babies have a permanent increase in the total number of fat cells in the body (Brook, Lloyd & Wolf, 1972). Table 16.1 displays some of the symptoms, related factors, causes, and possible treatment of obesity.

Sleeping Problems In addition to food, another essential need of the human infant is sleep. Like eating problems, disruptions in sleep can occur early in childhood. Children may vary considerably with regard to their sleep requirements, but parents usually have some preconceived notion of how much sleep their children need. When the child's sleep patterns do not correspond to the parents' expectations, the parents are likely to intervene and contribute to a long battle over the regulation of the child's sleep. Sleep disturbances may originate in such parent–child conflict, or they may be related to other difficulties the child is experiencing. In either case, sleep problems fall into two categories: those related to falling asleep and those involving the disruption of sleep (Knopf, 1979).

Obese children and adolescents may have had excessive weight gain in infancy.

Some children dread going to sleep because they are afraid they will never wake up, while others are put to bed before they are ready to go to sleep. The possible causes of insomnia or unwillingness to go to sleep are numerous—parent–child conflict, sibling rivalry, child-rearing practices, as well as specific circumstances surrounding the sleep pattern. Parental inconsistency, failure to set limits, and reinforcement of behavior that tends to postpone going to sleep may be involved; or fear of separation from parents or guilt feelings about something may produce insomnia. Before looking for further cause of sleeping problems, parents should first check to see if they simply are requiring the child to get more sleep than he or she needs.

Most normal children occasionally experience fear during sleep; only when such fears persist and occur on a frequent basis is there cause for concern. Nightmares and night terrors are fear responses that disrupt sleep. Nightmares are reasonably common among children, occurring during the last third of the night in a stage of sleep called REM (rapid eye movement) when most dreams occur. By contrast, night terrors are much more infrequent and happen within the first two hours of night sleep in non-REM dreamless sleep.

Elimination Problems There are two major problems in the child's elimination: one is called enuresis, pertaining to urine, the other encopresis, relating to defecation. We will focus here on the more frequent problem of enuresis.

Enuresis is usually defined as the involuntary passing of urine, generally during nighttime sleep, in children older than three or four. Between eighteen and twenty-four months of age most children have developed the necessary physiological and social maturity to begin to control their bladders. Enuresis has been reported in as many as 26 percent of the children referred to psychiatric clinics for various problems (Kanner, 1972). In Leo Kanner's investigation, the children ranged from three to fourteen years of age, with children aged eight to eleven years showing the highest incidence. Of the enuretic children in this study 62 percent were boys and only 38 percent were girls.

Enuresis rarely occurs as an isolated symptom in children. Clinical observations suggest that it accompanies immature behaviors like whining, moodiness, irritability, restlessness, and disobedience, and such acting out behaviors as temper tantrums, nail biting, fear reactions, stuttering, and stealing (Kanner, 1972).

Irwin Knopf (1979) concluded that most instances of enuresis are the product of psychological and environmental conditions, mainly involving faulty habit training in which regulation is started too early, too late, or with training practices that are inconsistent and emotionally damaging.

Infantile Autism

Infantile autism, often diagnosed during infancy, may persist well into childhood. Probably the most distinguishing characteristic of autistic children is their inability to relate to other people. As babies, they require very little from their parents; they do not demand much attention; and they do not reach out (literally or figuratively) for their parents. They rarely smile. When someone attempts to hold them, they often try to withdraw by arching their backs and pushing away from the person. In their cribs or playpens they appear oblivious to what is going on around them, often sitting and staring into space for long periods of time.

In addition to deficits in attachment to others, autistic children often have speech problems. As many as one out of every two autistic children never learn to speak. Those who do may engage in a type of speech called **echolalia,** in which the child echos rather than responds to what he or she hears. Thus, if you ask, "How are you, Chuck?" Chuck will respond with "How are you, Chuck?" Autistic children also tend to confuse pronouns, inappropriately substituting *you* for *I,* for example.

A third major characteristic of autistic children is the degree to which they become upset over a change in their daily routine or their physical environment. Rearrangement of a sequence of events or even furniture in the course of their "normal" day often causes them to become extremely upset. Thus, autistic children are not flexible in adapting to new routines and changes in their daily life.

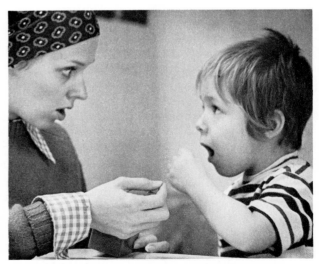

A psychologist applies Lovaa's linguistic approach to intensive one-to-one therapy to shape the behavior of this autistic child.

As can be seen, autism is a severe disorder. Michael Rutter and Norman Garmezy (1983) summarized some of the most important information we have developed in our search for the causes of autism. Autism seems to involve some form of organic brain dysfunction and possible genetic ties. No satisfactory evidence has been developed to suggest that family processes are linked to autism. Some of the frustrations a family with an autistic child experience are described in Perspective on Child Development 16.1.

PERSPECTIVE ON CHILD DEVELOPMENT 16.1

A CHILD CALLED NOAH

Noah was an autistic child. Following is an account by his father of the painful experience the Greenfields had in trying to help Noah (Greenfield, 1972).

4-16-67: We've decided to stop worrying about Noah. He isn't retarded, he's just pushing the clock hands about at his own slow speed. Yet. . . . (p. 22)

8-16-67: We took Noah to a pediatrician in the next town, who specializes in neurology. He said that since Noah is talking now there was little cause to worry; that Noah seemed "hypertonic," a floppy baby, a slow developer, but that time would be the maturing agent. We came away relieved. But I also have to admit that lately I haven't worried that much. (p. 26)

7-1-68: Noah is two. He still doesn't walk, but I do think he's trying to teach himself how to stand up. We're still concerned. And I guess we'll remain concerned until he stands up and walks like a boy. (p. 38)

6-6-69: Our fears about Noah continue to undergo dramatic ups and downs. Because of his increased opacity, the fact that he doesn't respond when we call his name and fails to relate completely to his immediate environment—a pattern of retardation or autism—we took him to a nearby hospital. I guess we both fear that what we dread is so, that Noah is not a normal child, that he is a freak, and his condition is getting worse. (pp. 51–52)

9-13-69: I'm a lousy father. I anger too easily. I get hot with Karl and take on a four-year-old kid. I shout at Noah and further upset an already disturbed one. Perhaps I am responsible for Noah's problems. (p. 71)

8-70: I also must note how very few people can actually understand our situation as a family, how they assume we are aloof when we tend not to accept or extend the usual social invitations. Nor have I mentioned the extra expenses a child like Noah entails—those expenses I keep in another book. (p. 90)

8-70: Even more heartbreaking has been the three-year period it has taken up to pierce the organized-medicine, institutionalized-mental-health gauze curtain. Most doctors, if they are unable to prescribe any form of curative aid, did their best to deter us from seeking it. Freudian-oriented psychiatrists and psychologists, if ill-equipped to deal with the problems of those not verbal, tried to inflict great feelings of guilt upon us as all-too-vulnerable parents. Neurologists and pediatricians, if not having the foggiest notions about the effects of diet and nutrition, vitamins and enzymes and their biochemical workings, would always suggest such forms of therapy are practiced only by quacks. And county mental-health boards, we discovered, who have charge of the moneys that might be spent helping children like Noah, usually tossed their skimpy fundings away through existing channels that do not offer proper treatment for children like Noah. (pp. 91–92)

The Abused Child

Unfortunately, parental hostility toward children in some families reaches the point where one or both parents abuse the child. Child abuse is an increasing problem in the United States (Parke & Lewis, 1980).

Estimates of its incidence vary according to different sources, but some authorities say that as many as half a million children are physically abused in the United States each year. Laws in many states now require doctors and even teachers to report suspected cases of child abuse. Yet many cases go unreported, particularly those of "battered" infants.

For several years it was believed that parents who commit child abuse are severely disturbed, "sick" individuals. However, parents who abuse their children are rarely psychotic. Ross Parke (1976; Parke & Collmer, 1976; Parke & Lewis, 1980) has developed a model for understanding child abuse that shifts the focus from the personality traits of the parents to analysis of three aspects of the social environment: cultural, familial, and community influences.

The extensive violence in the American culture is reflected in the occurrence of violence in the family. Violence occurs regularly on television, and parents frequently resort to power assertion as a disciplinary technique. Cross-cultural studies indicate that American television contains more violence than British television (Geis & Monahan, 1976) and that in China, where physical punishment is rarely used to discipline children, the incidence of child abuse is very low (Stevenson, 1974).

To understand child abuse in the family, the interaction of all family members should be considered, regardless of who actually performs the violent acts against the child. Even though the father, for example, may be the person who has physically abused the child, contributions of the mother, the father, and the child should be evaluated.

Many parents who abuse their children come from families in which physical punishment was used. They may view physical punishment as a legitimate way of controlling the children's behavior, and physical abuse may be a part of this sanctioning. Thus, the parents' experiences as children in their own families may contribute to their child-abuse punishment techniques.

Many aspects of the ongoing interaction among immediate family members also affect the incidence of child abuse. The child himself or herself may have some effect, for example, an unattractive child experiences

To understand child abuse, the entire family system needs to be studied.

more physical punishment than an attractive child does, and a child from an unwanted pregnancy may be especially vulnerable to abuse.

The interaction of the parents with each other may lead to child abuse as well. Dominant-submissive husband-wife pairs have been linked with child abuse (Terr, 1970). Husband-wife violence or such stressful family situations as those caused by financial problems, for example, may erupt in the form of aggression directed against the defenseless child. Such displaced aggression, whereby a person shifts an aggressive reaction from the original target person or situation to some other person or situation, is a common cause of child abuse.

Community-based support systems are extremely important in alleviating stressful family situations and thereby preventing child abuse. A study of the support systems in fifty-eight counties in New York State revealed a relationship between the incidence of child abuse and the presence of support systems available to the family. Both family resources—relatives and friends, for example—and such formal support systems of the community as crisis centers and child-abuse counseling were associated with a reduction in child abuse (Garbarino, 1976). Parke (1976) commented that "the family should not be treated as an independent social unit, but as embedded in a broader social network of informal and formal community-based support systems" (p. 14).

A summary of models of abnormality, the science of development psychopathology, and problems and disturbances in infancy and early childhood is presented in Concept Table 16.1.

CONCEPT TABLE 16.1
Models of Abnormality, the Science of Developmental Psychopathology, and Problems and Disturbances in Infancy and Early Childhood

Concept	Processes/Related Ideas	Characteristics/Description
Models of abnormality	Religious or supernatural model	Child is abnormal because of sinfulness, demonic possession, or temptation by the devil.
	Statistical model	Child is abnormal when he or she deviates too far from the average.
	Medical or disease model	Child is abnormal because of some physical malfunctioning of the body.
	Psychological and sociocultural models	Abnormality is due to defective strategies of coping with stressful circumstances and/or sociocultural conditions.
	Interactionist approach	The interaction of biological and sociocultural conditions can produce abnormality.
The science of developmental psychopathology	Ties to other disciplines	Developmental psychopathology has ties to developmental psychology, psychology in general, and the clinical sciences of psychiatry and clinical psychology.
	Pioneers	Pioneers in the field of developmental psychopathology include E. James Anthony and Norman Garmezy (high-risk children and strengths of vulnerable children); Thomas Achenbach (classification and topography of problems and disturbances); Alan Sroufe (early family patterns and problems); Michael Rutter (maternal deprivation, autism, and childhood depression); Edward Zigler (mental retardation); and Stella Chess and Alexander Thomas (longitudinal study revealing information about continuity-discontinuity).
Infancy and early childhood	Sudden infant death syndrome	SIDS is responsible for the deaths of more infants after the vulnerable first ten days of life than any other factor.
	Eating, sleeping, and elimination problems	Eating problems may entail failure to eat properly or at all, or involve obesity. Sleep problems are of two types: those related to going to sleep and those disrupting sleep. The latter can be subdivided into nightmares and night terrors. The major problem related to elimination is enuresis.
	Infantile autism	Infantile autism seems to involve some type of organic brain dysfunction, as well as heredity.
	Child abuse	Child abuse stems from cultural, familial, and community influences.

The Elementary School Years

Our overview of problems and disturbances in the elementary school years examines the wide spectrum of problems and disturbances that characterize not only the elementary school years but other points in child development as well, childhood schizophrenia, childhood depression, school-related problems, and the resilient child.

The Wide Spectrum of Problems and Disturbances

Thomas Achenbach and Craig Edelbrock (1981) investigated the prevalence of specific behavioral problems and competencies in children. Parents of 1,300 children being evaluated in 29 outpatient mental health settings and parents of 1,300 nonreferred children filled out the Child Behavior Checklist, which assesses behavioral problems and competencies. Problems and disturbances were evaluated in terms of the following ages of children: four to five, six to seven, eight to nine, ten to eleven, twelve to thirteen, fourteen to fifteen, and sixteen.

There was a general tendency for behavior problems to decline somewhat with age and for parents of lower socioeconomic status children to report more problems than parents of middle SES children, although there was no overall tendency for more problems to be reported for one gender than the other. Most of the problems reported for lower SES children and for boys were undercontrolled, externalizing behaviors (e.g., destroys others' things, fighting); the problems reported for girls tended to be either overcontrolled, internalizing behaviors (e.g., unhappiness, sadness, or depression) or not clearly classifiable as undercontrolled. Racial differences were few and small.

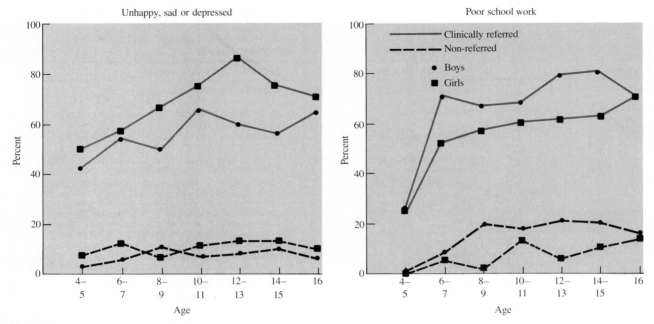

FIGURE 16.1
The two items most likely to differentiate clinically referred children from nonreferred children (Achenbach and Edelbrock, 1981).

The behavior problems that revealed the largest effects of clinical status across age and gender groups were unhappiness, sadness, or depression and poor school work (see figure 16.1). Both were reported by large proportions of the parents of referred children and very small proportions of the parents of nonreferred children. Certain problems that have been the subject of considerable interest by clinical psychologists, such as fears of certain animals, situations, or places and wetting the bed (see figure 16.2), showed very small differences between referred and nonreferred children.

Childhood Schizophrenia

Some children are afflicted by **childhood schizophrenia,** a condition that has many symptoms like infantile autism. Schizophrenic children, like autistic children, demand sameness in their environment. Another characteristic they share is distorted interpersonal relationships, often manifested in aloof and withdrawn behavior. One clinician (Goldfarb, 1970) has listed

several additional characteristics of childhood schizophrenia. Among them are poor coordination and disorientation, with schizophrenic children often acting in self-injurious ways. They often walk on the balls of the feet, and they will sit for long periods of time, tirelessly rocking the body. They may be insensitive to pain or be excessively sensitive to stimulation. They may have debilitating fears when no apparent danger is present or fail to show fear when fear is actually appropriate. The speech of schizophrenics is usually immature and meaningless; and frequently there is extensive retardation, yet the child may occasionally display normal or near-normal intellectual functioning. Another characteristic of schizophrenic children is their preoccupation with specific objects without regard for their specific function.

We have seen that autistic children and children with schizophrenia share some common problems. Table 16.2 displays some of these similarities, as well as some differences.

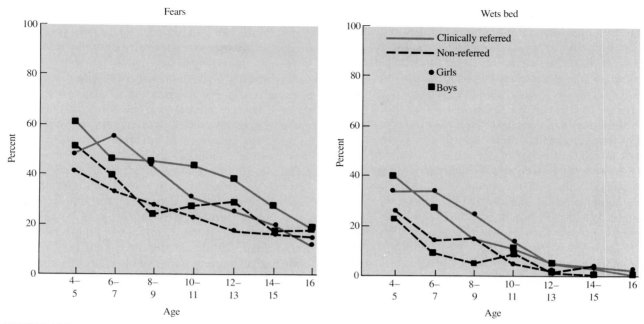

FIGURE 16.2
Two items that do not distinguish clinically referred children from nonreferred children (Achenbach and Edelbrock, 1981).

TABLE 16.2
Comparison of Autistic Children and Children with Schizophrenia

Clinical Picture	Childhood Schizophrenia	Infantile Autism
Onset	Gradual between ages two and eleven after period of normal development.	Gradual from birth.
Social and interpersonal	Decreased interest in external world, withdrawal, loss of contact, impaired relations with others.	Failure to show anticipatory postural movements; extreme aloneness; insistence on sameness.
Intellectual and cognitive	Thought disturbance; perceptual problems; distorted time and space orientation; below average IQ.	High spatial ability; good memory; low IQ but good intellectual potential.
Language	Disturbances in speech; mutism. If speech is present, it is not used for communication.	Disturbances in speech; mutism. If speech is present, it is not used for communication. Very literal; delayed echolalia; pronoun reversal; *I* and *yes* are absent till age six.
Affect	Defect in emotional responsiveness and rapport; decreased, distorted, and/or inappropriate affect.	Inaccessible and emotionally unresponsive to humans.
Motor	Bizarre body movements; repetitive and stereotyped motions; motor awkwardness; distortion in mobility.	Head banging and body rocking; remarkable agility and dexterity; preoccupation with mechanical objects.
Physical and developmental patterns	Unevenness of somatic growth; disturbances of normal rhythmic patterns; abnormal EEG.	Peculiar eating habits and food preferences; normal EEG.
Family	High incidence of mental illness.	Aloof, obsessive, and emotionally cold; high intelligence and educational and occupational levels; low divorce rate and incidence of mental illness.

Irwin Jay Knopf, *Childhood Psychopathology: A Developmental Approach*, © 1984, p. 240. Reprinted by permission of Prentice-Hall, Englewood Cliffs, New Jersey.

In addition to interest in childhood schizophrenia, there has also been considerable interest in the childhood precursors of adult schizophrenia (Rutter & Garmezy, 1983). First, abnormalities in interpersonal relationships, represented by oddities and isolation rather than shyness or timidity, are characteristic (Hanson, Gottesman & Heston, 1976). These social difficulties may be accompanied by antisocial behavior in boys that sometimes differs from that of juvenile delinquents in tending to be both solitary and confined to the home setting. Second, schizophrenia is sometimes associated with clumsiness and other indications of neurodevelopmental immaturity in childhood (Quitkin, Rifkin & Klein, 1976). Third, there may be an attentional deficiency that involves poor signal or noise discrimination (Garmezy, 1978). These findings point to the possibility of cognitive and attentional deficits in the genesis of schizophrenia.

In addition to studies of cognitive and attentional deficits in schizophrenics, there has been considerable interest in the extent to which having a schizophrenogenic mother predisposes an individual to develop schizophrenia. Clinicians report that schizophrenic individuals often have mothers with a high anxiety level who easily become upset. However, efforts to isolate the mother's behavior as the main cause of schizophrenia have not been very fruitful (e.g., Block, Patterson, Block & Jackson, 1958). Nevertheless, some clinicians believe that schizophrenia is linked with growing up in a "bad" family. For instance, in one investigation of a hundred families with schizophrenic children, seventy-five of the families were rated as pathological, with either the mother or the father (and in some cases both) being disturbed (Bender, 1974).

We should point out that as with all problems and disturbances, biological and experiential factors are probably involved in the development of schizophrenia. Drug therapy in particular has been effective in treating some instances of schizophrenia, suggesting the importance of biological factors (Alexander & Malouf, 1983). Though a number of drugs are used, the most widely used are the phenothiazines (Hogarty et al., in press). Questions still remain about the long-term effectiveness of such drugs, as well as their side effects. Moreover, extreme caution needs to be exercised with these drugs, and they should be discontinued if they interfere with educational opportunities and physical development (Campbell, 1976).

Childhood Depression

Alan Sroufe and Michael Rutter (1984) point to a number of reasons why depressive disorders reflect the importance of taking a developmental perspective in understanding psychopathology: (1) There are clear age-related changes in depression; (2) depression seems to have both biological and environmental determinants, calling for a developmental perspective possibly to integrate findings; and (3) while depressive disorders exist in childhood, they occur much more frequently in adulthood, suggesting there is no simple link between childhood and adult conditions. Among the age-related aspects of depression are the facts that (1) before the second half of the first year, infants show no grief reaction to loss; (2) infantile sequences of protest, despair, and detachment in the face of loss continue until about four or five years of age; (3) disorders with both cognitive and affective components of depression probably emerge after infancy; (4) the frequency of depression increases sharply during puberty, being more characteristic of girls than boys; and (5) depression becomes even more frequent during adulthood.

In childhood the features of depression are mixed with a broader array of behaviors than in adulthood. For example, during childhood, aggression, school failure, anxiety, antisocial behavior, and poor peer relations are often related to depression, which makes its diagnosis more difficult (Weiner, 1980). In the following example of an eleven-year-old girl, depression is mixed with anxiety and school-related matters.

Elizabeth is a pretty eleven-year-old black girl, who was brought to the hospital because she had thrown a book at the school principal. The principal had been trying to find out the reason Elizabeth was crying in the classroom. Elizabeth was restless and confused and could not concentrate for more than a few minutes. She said that people didn't like her, that everybody thought she was ugly. She believed that she had been justified in throwing the book at the principal: "He was bugging me; I was nervous." While Elizabeth's mother was interviewed in another room at the hospital, Elizabeth began to pace up and down, saying that she was feeling hot. She showed someone her clammy, perspiring hands, and began to cry, saying, "I'm dying. Something in my throat doesn't let me breathe. My stomach isn't pumping. People are trying to kill me. I'll die if I stay here. I was normal before I came. Now I am dying. . . ." During the next three days, Elizabeth had

Depression seems to have both biological and environmental determinants.

one or two severe anxiety attacks a day. Between the attacks, she was anxious, restless, and depressed. She did not show any signs of psychosis, in clinical or psychological testings.

The background history obtained on Elizabeth revealed that she had been an insecure, timid, and friendless child since entering school. When Elizabeth was seven years old, her father had been charged with attempting to seduce a thirteen-year-old female neighbor; and though the charges had been dismissed, the family was alienated and ostracized from the neighborhood. Elizabeth's father had then deserted the family, leaving Elizabeth, her thirteen-year-old brother, and her mother with no source of income. Elizabeth's mother was a tense, depressed woman, who felt harassed by the responsibilities of finding a job and caring for her children. Six months before Elizabeth's admission to the hospital, her mother had found a job that kept her away from home from 8:00 A.M. to 6:00 P.M. She had not had time to go over to school when Elizabeth brought a letter from her teacher reporting that Elizabeth seemed very unhappy, that her schoolwork had deteriorated, and that she was frequently absent. Elizabeth's mother was now extremely angry at Elizabeth. She explained, "I knew she was sad and hypersensitive, but it was not causing anybody else any problem. Now she has become violent and I can't take that" (Chess & Hassibi, 1978).

There has been considerable speculation about what causes depression to occur in children. To learn more about theories of childhood depression, read Perspective on Child Development 16.2.

PERSPECTIVE ON CHILD DEVELOPMENT 16.2

THEORIES OF CHILDHOOD DEPRESSION

Why does depression occur in childhood? A number of reasons have been offered. First, biological factors, such as heredity, neurotransmitters, and hormones, have been considered.

From the genetic studies of affective disorders, it appears that a genetic factor is involved to some degree in depression (Bertelsen, Harvald & Hauge, 1977). In the search for biochemical factors in depression, two neurotransmitters have been proposed as culprits: norepinephrine (Goodwin & Athanascious, 1979) and serotonin (Asberg, Thoren, Traskman, Bertilsson & Ringberger, 1976.)

As researchers explore the nature of depression in the childhood and adolescent years, they have also discovered that the greatest changes in depression seem to emerge during adolescence (Kendell, Rennie, Clarke & Dean, 1981). Because depression is more common in girls than boys, the question is raised as to whether depression is related to hormonal changes that accompany puberty. So far the findings on hormonal changes have not led to any clear conclusions about their role in depression during adolescence.

Psychoanalytic theories generally attribute the development of depression to early mother–child relationships, particularly oral difficulties or loss of a love object (Bowlby, 1980; Isenberg & Schatzberg, 1978). While positive evidence for the role of maternal loss or difficulties in oral matters during infancy is not available, the psychoanalytic emphasis on the importance of loss in the development of depression, regardless of the developmental time period, is an important contribution.

In recent years, cognitive theories have been crafted to provide a further understanding of depression. For example, Aaron Beck (1967, 1973) argues that people

School-Related Problems

Difficulties in school achievement, whether secondary to other kinds of disturbances or primary problems in themselves, seem to account for more referrals to clinical treatment than any other child problem (Weiner, 1980). This fact alone demonstrates the importance our society places on achievement. Because underachievement is so frequently associated with problems and disturbances, we will describe it further and also evaluate another school-related problem: school phobia.

Underachievement Underachievement in school refers to the child's failure to receive grades commensurate with his or her intellectual abilities. Unexpected poor school performance has been estimated to occur in 25 percent of school children. It also appears that approximately one-third of children and adolescents seen in psychiatric clinics are referred because of learning problems. Further, more than 50 percent of college students who request counseling and psychotherapy do so because of worries about studying and grades (Blaine & McArthur, 1971).

According to Irving Weiner (1980), school underachievement may occur because of sociocultural factors such as family and neighborhood value systems that minimize the importance of education and peer group attitudes that stamp academic success as unmanly for boys and unfeminine for girls. From Weiner's perspective, this type of underachievement does not constitute a psychological disturbance. Rather, school problems that do involve psychological disturbances can be traced to two circumstances. First, attention, concentration, and specific learning handicaps, often associated with neurological problems, usually are detected in the elementary school years. Second, neurotic patterns of family interaction may produce a pattern of what is referred to as passive–aggressive underachievement. A child who is passive–aggressive is purposefully inactive, working hard at making sure nothing happens that will raise his or her grades too far. It is the second pattern of underachievement that is more characteristic of children with achievement problems; this is the pattern we will focus on.

become depressed because early in their development they acquired cognitive schemata that are characterized by self-devaluation and lack of confidence about the future. Another view of depression suggests that it develops because the individual perceives that she or he cannot control undesirable events and attributes the causes of her or his depression to internal rather than external causes (Seligman & Peterson, in press).

Returning to the ideas of John Bowlby (1980), the argument is offered that insecure mother–infant attachment, a lack of love and affection in child rearing, or the actual loss of a parent during childhood leads to a negative cognitive set. This schema that is built up during the infant and/or childhood years causes the child to interpret later losses as yet other failures to create an enduring and close positive relationship. From Bowlby's perspective, then, early childhood experiences, particularly those involving loss, produce cognitive schemata that are carried forward to influence the way in which the child or adolescent interprets new experiences. When these new experiences involve further loss, the loss serves as the immediate precipitant of depression.

The theories suggest that vulnerabilities (genetic, biochemical, and earlier experiences), cognitive sets, and precipitating stress events, particularly those involving loss, are involved in understanding depression. We still know little about cognitive changes in childhood in terms of how they might influence the onset and development of depression. Nevertheless, the fact that depression in infancy is rare and increases considerably during adolescence indicates that cognitive developmental changes are likely candidates for further understanding of the developmental nature of depression (Rutter & Garmezy, 1983).

From Weiner's perspective, three factors usually contribute to the development of passive–aggressive underachievement:

1. Extensive hostility, usually toward parents, that cannot be expressed directly.
2. Worry about rivalry with parents and siblings that produces fear of failure or fear of success.
3. Adoption of a passive–aggressive pattern of behavior in coping with difficult, stressful situations.

Investigations of underachieving children frequently reveal that they are more likely than their achieving counterparts to feel hostility that they cannot express directly (Davids & Hainsworth, 1967). When parental demands include extraordinarily high standards for academic achievement, they are likely to trigger poor school performance (which may be an indirect retaliation toward the achievement-oriented parents).

Passive–aggressive underachieving children often either fear failure or fear success, which restricts their achievement. Children who fear failure usually have negative perceptions of their abilities and feel that they will never be able to equal the achievements of their parents or siblings. Such children usually have a very low tolerance for criticism; the more parents or teachers tell them they should be earning better grades, the more they withdraw from trying to compete in school. Children who fear success often set unrealistically high goals but rarely work hard in trying to achieve them. They are usually unwilling to risk making a mistake, and they often pride themselves on being able to accomplish something with a minimum of effort.

School Phobia School phobia in childhood may be traced to worries about exams, peer problems, teacher problems and real or imagined fear of parental desertion. In one investigation, it was reported that school phobia usually peaks around age eleven or twelve and occurs in as many as 2 to 8 percent of the children referred to child guidance clinics (Kahn & Nursten, 1962).

The following portrayal provides a clinical picture of a child experiencing school phobia (Chess & Hassibi, 1978). The child often begins to complain in a vague way at about breakfast time. She may feel nauseated, have a headache, or say her stomach feels funny. If forced to go to school, she may not be willing to enter the classroom or may feel sick while in class. She often worries about what is going on at home while she is away. She may even call home to see if everything is all right. At bedtime, she may begin to worry about the next morning.

In the majority of cases, the school-phobic child eventually refuses to go to school. The child may offer to study at home. However, if allowed to remain homebound, the child will isolate herself more and more from the outside world. Her parents may become angry about her behavior in such situations, openly displaying hostility toward her. When such children appear at a guidance clinic or in a psychiatrist's office, they usually appear anxious, depressed, angry, and lacking in self-esteem.

The Resilient Child

The ten-year-old child had everything against him: extreme poverty, an ex-convict father who was dying of chronic disease, an illiterate mother who sometimes abused him, two mentally retarded siblings. Yet his teachers described him as a charming boy, loved by everyone at school, a good student and a natural leader. How can we explain such outstanding resilience?

Norman Garmezy (1981; Garmezy, Masten & Tellegen, 1984) has been studying the competence and incompetence of children at risk for psychopathology for more than a decade. Approximately 200 children and their families have participated in the full project. Measures include six hours of parent interviews, two hours of interviews with the child, a variety of laboratory assessments of the child, and indices of stress and competence. The measures of stress include the Life Events Questionnaire, parent interview about stress-related circumstances, and socioeconomic status. Measures of school-based competence include two indices of academic achievement (e.g., grades and the Peabody Individual Achievement Test), classroom competence (teacher ratings), interpersonal competence (peer assessments), and a measure of general intellectual ability (the WISC-R). Further, both the parent and the child interviews contain extensive information about the child's competence.

The quality of the child's attention may be an important factor in understanding developmental psychopathology.

Garmezy is now studying these children in some depth, both in the classroom and through family interviews, in the hope of identifying the core variables. Among his early findings, much depends upon the quality of the child's attention. "Attentional dysfunction is the basic substrate out of which incompetence arises," Garmezy believes. The next question is How modifiable is this defect? at what age? and in what way?

Adolescence

Our overview of problems and disturbances in adolescence considers drugs and alcohol, delinquency, suicide, and eating disorders, particulary anorexia nervosa.

Drugs and Alcohol

In this section we look at the actual incidence of drug use by adolescents, at trends in drug use, and at several specific findings about alcohol.

The most extensive data about the use of drugs by adolescents comes from ongoing research by Lloyd Johnston, Jerald Bachman, and Patrick O'Malley at the Institute of Social Research, University of Michigan. For a number of years they have been charting

TABLE 16.3
Trends in Thirty-Day Prevalence of Sixteen Types of Drugs

	Percent Who Used in Last Thirty Days										
Approx. N =	Class of 1975	Class of 1976	Class of 1977	Class of 1978	Class of 1979	Class of 1980	Class of 1981	Class of 1982	Class of 1983	Class of 1984	'83–'84 change
	(9400)	(15400)	(17100)	(17800)	(15500)	(15900)	(17500)	(17700)	(16300)	(15900)	
Marijuana/Hashish	27.1	32.2	35.4	37.1	36.5	33.7	31.6	28.5	27.0	25.2	−1.8
Inhalants	NA	0.9	1.3	1.5	1.7	1.4	1.5	1.5	1.7	1.9	+0.2
Inhalants adjusted[a]	NA	NA	NA	NA	3.1	2.7	2.3	2.5	2.7	2.7	0.0
Amyl and butyl nitrites[c]	NA	NA	NA	NA	2.4	1.8	1.4	1.1	1.4	1.4	0.0
Hallucinogens	4.7	3.4	4.1	3.9	4.0	3.7	3.7	3.4	2.8	2.6	−0.2
LSD	2.3	1.9	2.1	2.1	2.4	2.3	2.5	2.4	1.9	1.5	−0.4
PCP	NA	NA	NA	NA	2.4	1.4	1.4	1.0	1.3	1.0	−0.3
Cocaine	1.9	2.0	2.9	3.9	5.7	5.2	5.8	5.0	4.9	5.8	+0.9
Heroin	0.4	0.2	0.3	0.3	0.2	0.2	0.2	0.2	0.2	0.3	+0.1
Stimulants[b]	8.5	7.7	8.8	8.7	9.9	12.1	15.8	13.7	12.4	NA	NA
Stimulants adjusted[b,c]	NA	NA	NA	NA	NA	NA	NA	10.7	8.9	8.3	−0.6
Sedatives[b]	5.4	4.5	5.1	4.2	4.4	4.8	4.6	3.4	3.0	2.3	−0.7
Barbituates[b]	4.7	3.9	4.3	3.2	3.2	2.9	2.6	2.0	2.1	1.7	−0.4
Methaqualone[b]	2.1	1.6	2.3	1.9	2.3	3.3	3.1	2.4	1.8	1.1	−0.7
Tranquilizers[b]	4.1	4.0	4.6	3.4	3.7	3.1	2.7	2.4	2.5	2.1	−0.4
Alcohol	68.2	68.3	71.2	72.1	71.8	72.0	70.7	69.7	69.4	67.2	−2.2
Cigarettes	36.7	38.8	38.4	36.7	34.4	30.5	29.4	30.0	30.3	29.3	−1.0

[a]Adjusted for underreporting of amyl and butyl nitrites.

[b]Only drug use that was not under a doctor's orders is included here.

[c]Adjusted for overreporting of the nonprescription stimulants.

From Johnston, L. D., J. G. Bachman, and P. M. O'Malley, *News and Information Services Release*, table 8, January 4, 1985. Institute of Social Research, The University of Michigan, Ann Arbor, MI.

the drug habits of very large numbers of randomly selected adolescents across the United States. Among their recent findings for 1984 high school seniors are the following (Johnston, Bachman & O'Malley, 1985):

1. Almost two-thirds of all seniors reported illicit drug use at some point in their lives. However, a substantial proportion have used only marijuana.
2. Marijuana is by far the most widely used illicit drug, with 54.9 percent saying they have used this drug at some point in their lives.
3. The most widely used class of other drugs is stimulants, with 27.9 percent of the students having used these at some point in their lives.
4. The most widely used licit (legal) drug is alcohol (92.6 percent have used it at some point), and the second most widely used is nicotine (69.7 percent have smoked cigarettes at some point in their lives).

A summary of these findings for 1984 high school seniors is presented in table 16.3 along with other information pertaining to drug use and nonuse.

The Institute of Social Research at the University of Michigan has been charting drug use of high school seniors since 1975. We will study the trends in drug use from 1975 through 1984 (Johnston, Bachman & O'Malley, 1985).

It appears that at some point near the end of the 1970s and the beginning of the 1980s a turning point in adolescents' use of illicit drugs occurred. Since that time illicit drug use by adolescents overall has gradually declined. Table 16.3 shows the percentage of high school seniors who used a particular drug in the last thirty days. Note that marijuana use peaked in 1978 and has continued to decline every year thereafter. Also notice that hallucinogen use peaked in 1979 and has declined each year since that time. With regard to licit drugs, alcohol use peaked in 1980 and has gradually declined thereafter. Cigarette smoking peaked in 1976 and has dropped considerably since that time.

Delinquents may drink for different reasons than nondelinquents.

With regard to alcohol use by adolescents, there has been only a slight decrease in use since 1979. The number of high school seniors reporting any occasions of heavy drinking (defined as five or more drinks in a row during the prior two weeks) has remained alarmingly high, although the percentage did drop from 41 to 39 percent from 1983 to 1984 (Johnston, Bachman & O'Malley, 1985).

The startling statistic that in the preceding two weeks 39 percent of the seniors in the United States in 1984 had five or more drinks on at least one occasion, combined with the increasing number of adolescents who drive, can only lead to one conclusion—too many alcohol-related adolescent driving accidents and deaths. In 1976 alone, for example, 8,000 adolescents died in alcohol-related car accidents, and most of the drunk drivers who caused those accidents were under twenty-five years of age.

Delinquents may drink for reasons different from those of nondelinquents. Delinquents seem to drink more for the effect than do nondelinquents, who are more likely to drink to help them socialize, celebrate, or simply "to have fun" (Barnes, 1977). At any rate, the relation between drinking and delinquency merits further study. Next we look in greater detail at the prevalent problem of junenile delinquency in our society.

Juvenile Delinquency

The term **juvenile delinquent** is applied to an adolescent who breaks the law or engages in behavior that is considered illegal. Like other categories of disturbance, juvenile delinquency is a broad concept; legal infractions may range from littering to murder. Because the youth technically becomes a juvenile delinquent only after

"I'll tell you one thing. As soon as I'm thirteen I'm gonna stop!"

Reprinted by permission: Tribune Media Services.

being judged guilty of a crime by a court of law, official records do not accurately reflect the number of illegal acts committed by adolescents.

Estimates regarding the number of juvenile delinquents in the United States are sketchy, although FBI statistics suggest that at least 2 percent of all youth are involved in juvenile court cases. The number of girls found guilty of juvenile delinquency has increased significantly in recent years. Delinquency rates among blacks, other minority groups, and the lower class are particularly high in relation to the overall populations of these groups. However, such groups have less influence than others over the judicial decision-making process in the United States and thus may be judged delinquent more readily than their white, middle-class counterparts.

The National Survey of Youth (Gold & Reimer, 1975) asked 1,395 adolescents about their delinquent behavior. As indicated in figure 16.3 the incidence of nontrivial delinquent acts rose between the early part of adolescence and the later part. For example, eighteen-year-olds confessed to about five times more nontrivial delinquent behavior than did eleven-year-olds. Note that there is an acceleration of delinquent acts around the age of fifteen.

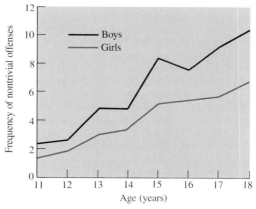

FIGURE 16.3
Mean frequency of nontrivial incidents committed by adolescents (Gold and Petronio, 1980).

There has been a longstanding interest in the role of family experiences in the development of delinquency (Glueck & Glueck, 1940; McCord & McCord, 1959; Rutter, in press). As you can see in Perspective on Child Development 16.3, while there is a clear association between family processes and delinquency, there are multiple interpretations of this association.

PERSPECTIVE ON CHILD DEVELOPMENT 16.3

FAMILY PROCESSES AND DELINQUENCY: CAUSE, CORRELATE, OR CONSEQUENCE?

Michael Rutter and Norman Garmezy (1983) raise the important question of whether research revealing an association of family experiences with delinquency involves family experiences as a cause, a correlate, or a consequence of delinquency. The associations may simply reflect some third factor, such as genetic influences; they may be a result of the disturbing effect of the child's behavior on family interaction; or they may indicate that family stress may lead to delinquency through some type of environmental effect.

The first possibility, whether some third factor is involved, can be examined by determining whether the association between family experiences and delinquency holds up when other significant variables are controlled. It has been found that even when social class and social atmosphere in the neighborhood are controlled, a link between family experiences and delinquency still holds (McCord, 1980; West & Farrington, 1977; Wilson, 1980). It also seems that early family stresses have long-term effects, mainly because they lead to forms of disturbance in the child that seem to persist rather than because a delayed or sleeper effect has occurred (Robins, 1978; West & Farrington, 1977). Further research also reveals that changes for the better in family relationships are linked with reduced conduct disturbances later in development (Rutter, 1971). With regard to the possibility that genetic mechanisms are involved in the association between family experience and delinquency, little research is available. However, several studies do suggest that genetic vulnerabilities on the part of the child may render the child more susceptible to environmental stress (Crowe, 1974; Hutchings & Mednick, 1974).

It is not only difficult to test the influence of genetic mechanisms, but it is also difficult to test the effects the child may have on the association between family processes and delinquency. Clearly, as we have argued throughout this book, socialization is a reciprocal process and one involving mutual regulation. There is evidence that parental child-rearing practices that seem to be effective with most children are not efficient in controlling delinquents (Patterson, 1982). Nevertheless, while causal influences are probably bidirectional, there are likely a number of circumstances in which the predominant influence is from parent to child.

Rutter and Garmezy (1983) conclude that family influences do have some kind of environmental influence on the development of delinquency or other conduct disturbances. The key family factors that seem to be involved in the emergence of conduct disturbances are family discord, deviant parental (and sibling) models, weak parent–child relationships, and poor discipline and monitoring of the child's activities. An example of research suggesting the importance of such family variables in the emergence of conduct disturbances is the work of Gerald Patterson (1977, 1979, 1981, 1982; Patterson & Stouthamer-Loeber, 1984).

In a study by Patterson and Stouthamer-Loeber (1984), family management practices were related to the delinquency of seventh and tenth grade boys. Delinquency was measured by police contacts and self-reports. The measures of family management skills involved monitoring, discipline, problem solving, and reinforcement. Monitoring was assessed through a series of interviews with the parents and the adolescent, basically trying to obtain an accurate account of parental supervision and knowledge of the adolescent's whereabouts. Discipline was assessed in terms of whether the mother followed up on her commands, the father's consistency in discipline style, and the mother's consistency in discipline style. Problem solving was based on videotaped observations of the quality of family interaction and problem resolution. Reinforcement was assessed through observation of parent–child interaction, a child interview, and interviewers' ratings filled out at the end of sessions with the family. In particular, the parent's reinforcement of prosocial behavior was of interest. As shown in the table at right, parental monitoring was much more strongly related to delinquency

The adolescent's self-image as an autonomous and effective individual can be important in avoiding or reducing delinquency.

Relation of Family Management Practices to Delinquency in Grades Seven and Ten

Family Management Practice	Police Contacts	Self-Reported Delinquent Life-Style
Monitoring	.55	.54
Discipline	.30	.35
Problem solving	−.03	.04
Reinforcement	−.09	−.24

From Patterson, G. R., and M. Stouthamer-Loeber, "The correlation of family management practices and delinquency," in *Child Development*, 55, pp. 1299–1307. Copyright © 1984 by The Society for Research in Child Development, Inc. Reprinted by permission.

than discipline, problem solving, or reinforcement, although discipline and, to a lesser degree, reinforcement also showed significant associations with delinquency. Further, it is important to note that parental monitoring also differentiated moderate offenders from persistent offenders. It seems that parents of delinquents are indifferent trackers of their sons' whereabouts, the type of companions they keep, and the kind of activities they engage in. When rule-breaking behavior occurs, such parents are less likely to provide punishment, such as loss of a privilege, work detail, or loss of allowance. If they react to such information at all, it often is in the form of lecturing, scolding, or barking out a threat, abrasive overtures usually not backed up by effective consequences. The significant association of discipline and delinquency suggested that consistent application of effective punishment such as time out, loss of privileges, and the like is necessary for long-term reduction in adolescents' antisocial behavior. Thus, from Patterson's perspective, both parental monitoring and discipline are key ingredients in determining whether an adolescent will engage in delinquent behavior.

A number of intervention studies also have been designed in an effort to reduce delinquency. One research review (Gold & Petronio, 1980) concluded that while the sources and styles of successful programs often vary, two themes seem to be dominant: (1) the support of warm, accepting relationships with adults, and (2) the enhancement of the adolescent's self-image as an autonomous and effective individual.

Suicide

Nationally, the suicide rate for adolescents suggests that suicide is the third major cause of death, after accidents and murder. Furthermore, the suicide rate for adolescents has increased 300 percent since 1950. On the average, each minute of the day an adolescent attempts suicide somewhere in the United States. Every day about fourteen succeed. (See figure 16.4.) The typical adolescent suicide victim is white, male, and from the middle class. Guns are the means most often used, and the most common reason is depression over the loss of a loved one or status.

Some experts predict that the adolescent suicide rate will go down in the 1980s as the population of the adolescent age-group declines. From this perspective, lessening competition for such important matters as jobs and college admission will mean that more adolescents will achieve their goals, and thus fewer will be pressured to commit suicide. However, other experts believe that the adolescent suicide rate will not decline until the incidence of violence and the pace of family

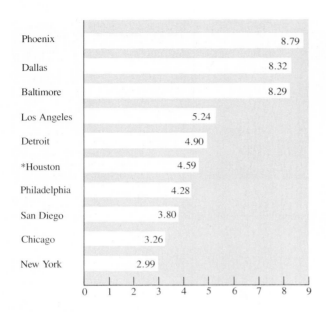

Phoenix	8.79
Dallas	8.32
Baltimore	8.29
Los Angeles	5.24
Detroit	4.90
*Houston	4.59
Philadelphia	4.28
San Diego	3.80
Chicago	3.26
New York	2.99

0 1 2 3 4 5 6 7 8 9

*Houston's rate is estimated

FIGURE 16.4
Suicide rates for people ten to nineteen years old in the ten
largest cities in 1981.

Eating disorders have become an increasing concern in the
world of adolescent females.

disintegration in our culture slow down. From this perspective, by the year 2000 the suicide rate for adolescent males will increase 120 percent, and the rate for
adolescent females will rise to 114 percent of its current level (Austin & Little, 1982).

Can we predict whether an adolescent will attempt
to commit suicide? It isn't easy, but there are some signs
that may serve as clues. For example, the adolescent
who talks about committing suicide often is serious.
And adolescents who attempt suicide once are likely to
try it again. Severe family problems, the loss of a loved
one, and other highly stressful events can signal an approaching suicide attempt.

The increase in adolescent suicide during the last
twenty-five years is a symptom of the stress that many
adolescents now experience as they try to grow from
dependent children to independent adults. But remember that while suicide attempts have increased,
suicidal adolescents represent a very small minority of
the adolescents in our culture. The large majority of
adolescents learn to deal effectively with stress and tension and never become so immersed in depression that
they consider taking their own lives.

Next we look at another problem that increases in
adolescence: eating disorders.

Eating Disorders

The ideal female in our culture today is characterized
by a thin, "perfect" body, whereas in past years a more
shapely, robust body was the ideal. As part of the search
for the ideal female figure, many girls and women constantly worry about their weight. Kim Chernin (1981)
has described two facts that make the current obsession with weight loss unusual. One is the scope of it.
Throughout history there have been dieters, including
Roman matrons who were willing to starve themselves.
But there has never been a period such as now, when
such large numbers of adolescents and adults have spent
so much money, time, and energy on their weight. The
second unusual aspect of the current concern about
weight loss is the degree to which it involves females
rather than males. Although our nation has its share
of adolescent and adult males who want to lose weight,
the truly excessively obsessive dieter is almost inevitably female. Females make up more than 90 percent
of the people who suffer from anorexia nervosa, a personality disorder that leads to self-starvation. Similarly, bulimia, a condition in which periods of heavy
eating are followed by self-induced vomiting, is almost
exclusively a female phenomenon. Along with obesity,
anorexia nervosa and bulimia are the major eating disorders in adolescence. Let's look in more detail at the
disturbance of anorexia nervosa.

CONCEPT TABLE 16.2
Problems and Disturbances in the Elementary School Years and Adolescence

Concept	Processes/Related Ideas	Characteristics/Description
Elementary school years	Overview of problems	Sadness, depression, and school-related problems are the most prominent disturbances of the elementary school years. Girls have more internalizing problems, boys more externalizing ones.
	Childhood schizophrenia	Childhood schizophrenia has many symptoms like infantile autism. It involves distorted interpersonal relationships, with behavior being aloof and withdrawn. There seem to be both cognitive and attentional deficits in schizophrenics.
	Childhood depression	Depression in childhood and adolescence is more difficult to diagnose than depression in adulthood. Girls are characterized by depression more than boys, particularly by the time puberty is reached. A number of theories of childhood depression have been set forth. They suggest that various vulnerabilities (genetic, biochemical, early experiences), cognitive sets, and precipitating experiences (particularly loss) contribute to depression.
	School-related problems	School-related problems include underachievement and school phobia.
	The resilient child	Garmezy and his associates have studied resilient or invulnerable children, who in particular seem to have more efficient attentional capabilities than their vulnerable counterparts.
Adolescence	Drugs and alcohol	National surveys of high school seniors suggest that illicit drug use began declining at some point around 1980. Alcohol is the most widely used licit drug and marijuana the most widely used illicit drug. While alcohol use has declined slightly, it still remains a major adolescent problem.
	Delinquency	There is an increase in delinquent acts between the beginning and the end of adolescence. Family processes seem to be implicated as important determinants of delinquency. Intervention programs that have been successful usually involve a warm, supportive relationship with an adult and enhancement of the adolescent's self-image.
	Suicide	Suicide is the third leading cause of adolescent death. It often occurs when adolescents lose someone they love and feel helpless about controlling that aspect of their lives.
	Eating problems	There seems to be an increase in eating problems in adolescence. Anorexia nervosa is an eating disorder that is almost exclusively female. The girl starves herself until she is emaciated.

Anorexia Nervosa Several physical and psychological features characterize **anorexia nervosa** in adolescence (Bruch, 1973). Severe malnutrition and emaciation are accompanied by amenorrhea (the cessation of menstrual periods as a result of a decrease in body fat). Often anorexic adolescents show an obsession with activity that they feel will peel off fat. Although anorexic adolescents avoid eating, the term *anorexia* is somewhat misleading. Actually, such adolescents have an intense interest in food, cook for others, talk about food, and insist on watching others eat. Usually when they begin dieting they are of average weight. However, many anorexic adolescents do not feel in control of their lives or useful. Many anorexics experience their bodies as something extra—not part of themselves.

They complain of feeling full after a few bites of food, which symbolizes a sense of control. (By contrast, the obese adolescent feels empty after a full meal and does not feel that he or she can control food.) The anorexic adolescent is also excessively preoccupied with body size, and a close look at the anorexic adolescent's family often reveals serious problems.

As anorexia progresses, abstinence from food alternates with uncontrollable eating binges during which the adolescent does not feel hungry. Many adolescents try to remove the food by forced vomiting, enemas, laxatives, or fasting. We have discussed a number of problems and disturbances in the elementary school years and adolescence. A summary of these ideas is presented in Concept Table 16.2.

CONTINUITY–DISCONTINUITY IN DEVELOPMENT AND DISORDERS

We conclude our discussion of problems and disturbances by considering some important aspects of continuity–discontinuity and how they are involved in the story of development and disorders. First we study some reasons why children's disturbances may be related to earlier circumstances. In a related matter we focus on why a child with a disorder may continue to have the disorder later in development. By contrast, we also discuss the reasons why some child disorders may not be linked to earlier circumstances, and the related matter of why children with a disorder may not have the disorder later in development.

Reasons for Continuity in Disorders

Three reasons why child disorders may be linked to earlier disorders or circumstances are biological processes, the continuing influence of early experience, and early experience plus consistent later experience.

Biological Processes and Prenatal Development

First, with regard to biological processes, a child may inherit certain disorders or tendencies that increase the likelihood of developing a disorder. Similarly, during prenatal development, a number of environmental experiences may lead to the development of abnormality. For example, a number of forms of mental retardation involve a major gene defect or damage to a chromosome, leading to a biochemical error in the development of the brain. Also recall from our discussion of prenatal development in chapter 3 that considerable interest has been generated in discovering the teratogens that underlie the development of problems and disturbances. These teratogens range from the mother's diet to the possible use of drugs and chemicals to the mother's emotional state. Developmental psychopathologists, in their effort to identify as early as possible children who have or will have psychological or learning handicaps, have coined the terms *at risk* and *perinatal stress*.

In one of the most comprehensive studies of children at risk, a variety of biological, social, and developmental characteristics were identified as predictors of serious coping problems at the age of eighteen (Werner & Smith, 1982). Among the factors were moderate to severe perinatal (at or near birth) stress and congenital defects, low socioeconomic status at two and ten years of age, level of maternal education below eight years, low family stability between two and eight years, very high or very low infant responsiveness at one year of age and low social responsiveness and a Cattell score below 80 at two years of age (the Cattell test is one of the early measures of infant intelligence—it was developed in 1940), and the need for long-term mental health services or placement in a learning disability class at ten years of age. When four or more of these variables were present, the stage was set for serious coping problems in the second decade of life.

In summarizing what we know about children at risk, Claire Kopp (1983) pointed out that a variety of biological risk conditions can impinge on the organism at the time of conception or during prenatal, perinatal, and postnatal life. The outcome of this assault varies and depends on the particular type and timing of the influence, but in general the earlier the assault, the greater the effects. The range of outcome for all perinatal and postnatal assaults is from severe impairment to normal development, although the processes accounting for variability are not fully documented. Factors in the environment act upon biological risk by heightening or attenuating effects. In some instances, as in perinatal stress, environmental influences may outweigh biological risk. Biological risk and adverse rearing conditions combine to have a more negative impact than either factor would alone.

Early Experience and Consistent Later Experience

Michael Rutter (1980) has listed a number of ways in which earlier experience may be connected to later disorders: (1) Experience produces the disorder at the time, and the disorder persists; (2) experience creates bodily changes that affect later functioning; (3) experience alters patterns of behavior at the time, which later take the form of a disorder; (4) early experiences can change family relationships and circumstances that over time lead to a disorder; (5) sensitivities to stress or coping strategies are changed and later predispose the person to disorder or buffer the person from stress; (6) experiences change the child's self-concept or attitudes, which in turn influence behavior in later circumstances; and (7) experience influences behavior by affecting the selection of environments or the opening or closing of opportunities.

Alan Sroufe (1979) has described a number of salient developmental issues that need to be considered when the study of developmental psychopathology is being planned (see table 16.4). As you can see from table 16.4, during the first year of life biological regulation, harmonious dyadic relationships, and the formation of an attachment relationship are central developmental tasks. As the infant progresses through

TABLE 16.4
Salient Developmental Issues

Age (Years)	Issues
0–1	Biological regulation; harmonious dyadic interaction; formation of an effective attachment relationship
1–2½	Exploration, experimentation, and mastery of the object world (caregiver as secure base); individuation and autonomy; responding to external control of impulses
3–5	Flexible self-control; self-reliance; initiative; identification and gender concept; establishing effective peer contacts (empathy)
6–12	Social understanding (equity, fairness); gender constancy; same-sex chumships; sense of "industry" (competence); school adjustment
13+	"Formal operations" (flexible perspective taking; "as if" thinking); loyal friendships (same sex); beginning heterosexual relationships; emancipation; identity

From Sroufe, L. A., and M. Rutter, "The domain of developmental psychopathology," in *Child Development*, 55, pp. 17–29. Copyright © 1984 by The Society for Research in Child Development, Inc. Reprinted by permission.

Individuality and self-control are likely important developmental tasks in understanding aspects of psychopathology pertaining to the second year of life.

the second year of life, exploration, experimentation, and mastery of the object world, as well as individuation and the development of self-control, become prominent developmental tasks. It is Sroufe's as well as Rutter's belief (Sroufe & Rutter, 1984) that issues at one developmental period lay the groundwork for subsequent issues, in much the same way as the life cycle framework proposed by Erik Erikson (1968).

Recall from chapters 2 and 13 our discussion of Chess and Thomas's New York Longitudinal Study beginning in infancy and continuing through the college years. We will draw from their vivid descriptions of the lives of several individuals to illustrate how early experiences and consistent later experiences can predict disorders. When we discuss discontinuity in disorders we will present information about another individual in Chess and Thomas's study.

In early childhood, David was one of the most active boys Chess and Thomas studied. He was always in motion and came across with a friendly and cheerful manner. Unfortunately, however, a considerable number of parental problems surfaced during David's childhood, including a growing sense of competitiveness in his parents. They continually bragged to others about what a superior child David was, although he did not have a superior IQ; any problems David had in school they attributed to poor teaching. As he developed in his elementary and secondary school years, his school performance and interest in other activities went downhill. The parents totally blamed the school and its teachers.

Picking up on his parents' cues that his failures were not his fault, David never developed a critical, evaluative approach to himself: when problems surfaced, he always put the blame—just as his parents did—on someone else. As David moved into the college years, apathy began to dominate his daily life, and, unfortunately, the attitudes of his parents as well as his own self-insulation and reluctance to take responsibility for his actions led to complete resistance to counseling that might have helped him out of his dilemma.

Further evidence of the importance of continuity in disorders comes from research on childhood experiences and depression in adolescence. As described in Perspective on Child Development 16.4, relationships of girls with their parents during childhood are better predictors of depression in adolescence than those of boys and their parents.

PERSPECTIVE ON CHILD DEVELOPMENT 16.4

THE CONTINUITY OF DEVELOPMENT: CHILDHOOD EXPERIENCES AND ADOLESCENT DEPRESSION

Recently Per Gjerde (1985) reported on data collected as part of an ongoing longitudinal investigation (Block & Block, 1980) that are germane to understanding childhood experiences in adolescent depression. Family functioning was assessed on numerous occasions when children were between the ages of three and thirteen and focused on 54 girls and 52 boys. Relations between parental socialization practices and depression in adolescence emerged primarily for girls. It may be that this sex difference is due to girls' socialization history since girls are socialized more toward compliance, passivity, and reliance on others (e.g., Block, 1983). Or it may be that by promoting personality characteristics such as dependency and helplessness parents are unwittingly encouraging a greater likelihood of depression. Or it also may be that by producing interpersonal orientations in girls, orientations characterized by a greater reliance on others, parents may be raising daughters who are more vulnerable to the lack of affection and deprivation that characterize the parenting style of depressed adolescents.

While the parenting practices of both mothers and fathers are related to depression in adolescent girls, the link seems stronger for fathers than mothers (see the table at right for information on some paternal child-rearing orientations when the child was three that were related to adolescent depression at age fourteen.). As indicated in the table, the paternal child-rearing practices that were implicated are lack of spontaneity and emotional support, emphasis on impulse control, absence of affection and positive reinforcement, concern about sexual matters, disappointment with a daughter, and failure to communicate both negative and positive feelings and opinions.

Maternal socialization practices were observed in a teaching situation at age four. Among the maternal teaching behaviors when the child was four that were related to depression in girls at age fourteen were authoritarian control, a strong achievement orientation, and absence of emotional support.

Parental socialization practices and quality of the home environment were also observed during early adolescence (ages twelve and thirteen). Relations with depression were, again, stronger for girls than boys. The aspect of the home environment at age twelve most likely to predict depression in girls two years later was the presence of a mother who was overcontrolled and unable to enjoy her relationship with her daughter. Observations of fathers with their daughters revealed a picture of conflict between the father and daughter in the case of depressed adolescent girls. When the girls were thirteen, the mothers of the depressed daughters were not very affiliative and the fathers were disregarding and ambivalent.

In sum, significant sex differences emerged in this research, with girls' patterns of depression more closely linked to parental socialization than those of boys. The adolescent depression of the girls was related to parental socialization practices extending all the way back to the preschool years. The fathers of the depressed girls were seen as controlling, withdrawn, and unexpressive individuals. In particular, they emphasized early attainment of self-control, deemphasized father–daughter communication, and avoided expression of affect. Mothers of subsequently depressed adolescent girls were authoritarian, achievement-oriented, and low in emotional support when the girls were four years old. Almost a decade later the mothers were observed to be overcontrolled and unaffectionate. Overall, then, a socialization pattern of early impulse control, achievement, and lack of affection and emotional support was linked with depression in adolescent girls.

Paternal Child-Rearing Orientations at Age Three That Predict Depression at Age Fourteen

Girls	Boys	Orientation
.46**	.05	Feels that the child is a bit disappointing
.35*	.25	Believes that children of different sexes should not see each other naked
.34*	.06	Teaches child always to control feelings
.38*	−.08	Believes that too much "TLC" can harm, weaken child
.60***	−.09	Gives sex information only when child can understand
−.21	.34*	Feels that long periods with child are interesting and educational
.06	.41*	Does not want child to be seen as different from others
−.35*	−.16	Puts wishes of mate before those of child
−.43**	−.10	Shows affection by hugging, kissing child
−.44**	.19	Believes that praising good is better than punishing bad
−.37*	.08	Lets child know attempts and accomplishments are appreciated
−.32*	−.05	Lets child know when angry with him or her
−.02	−.42*	Gives many duties, family chores to child

Note: *p < .05
       **p < .01
       ***p < .001

From Gjerde, Per F., Jack Block, and Jeanne Block, "Adolescent depression and parental socialization patterns: A prospective study," in a paper presented at the meeting of The Society for Research in Child Development, Inc., Toronto, April 1985.

Reasons for Discontinuity in Disorders

Possible reasons for discontinuity in disorders include changes in specific life experiences of the individual; regular changes in developmental tasks at different points in the life cycle that produce unique demands; and changes in society at different points in the development of the individual.

Changes in Specific Life Circumstances

Changes in specific life circumstances can diminish earlier disorders or they can produce disorders that were not present earlier in development. Consider first the example of Carl, one of Chess and Thomas's subjects.

He requested a discussion with Dr. Chess at the end of his first year in college because he felt depressed and was not coping very well with academic or social matters. He had few friends and said that he had difficulty studying, that he was unable to remember what he had read. By contrast, Carl had been a good student in high school, where he had had a number of friends and many interests. During his interview he did not appear depressed but expressed bewilderment at his situation, saying that it just wasn't like him to be doing so poorly socially and academically.

The background data indicated that during childhood Carl had been one of the most extreme "difficult child" types: he was intense, had negative reactions to new situations, and was slow to adapt to situations even after many exposures to them. This was true whether it was his first bath, his first day at elementary school, or his first shopping trip. Each of these experiences prompted Carl to stormy behavior, such as temper tantrums and shouting. The parents realized that Carl's reactions to his world were not due to their "bad parenting" but instead were part of his temperament. They were patient with him and often gave him considerable time and many opportunities to adapt to new situations that were frustrating to him. As a result, he did not become a behavior "problem," even through the "difficult group" has a higher risk for disturbed development (e.g., Thomas, Chess & Birch, 1970).

Later on in his elementary and secondary school years, Carl met up with few new situations and in the process was able to develop a positive view of himself. College, however, meant a lot of changes in his life. He now was away from home in unfamiliar situations, with new teachers who placed more complex demands on him, with new peers who were harder to get to know, and with a girl with whom he started living. According to Chess and Thomas, the radically different college experiences reawakened the "difficult child" behavioral reactions and brought Carl in for help.

After only one session, Carl began to get back on a more positive track. He discussed his temperamental pattern with Dr. Chess, including coping mechanisms that he might employ to help him out in social and academic situations. By the end of the academic year, his grades had improved, he broke off the living arrangement with the girl, and he started forcing himself to get more involved in peer group activities.

Regular Changes in Life Tasks at Different Ages

While adolescence sometimes had been incorrectly stereotyped as a time of stress for all adolescents, the developmental changes that characterize adolescence can trigger problems and disturbances in some individuals. We have seen that independence and identity are important themes of adolescent development. As the adolescent pushes for autonomy and searches for an identity, parents may adopt more stringent controls or become highly permissive in response to the changes going on with their adolescent. Such changes during adolescent development may precipitate problems and disturbances during adolescence that did not appear earlier in development.

Changes in Society at Different Points in the Individual's Development

A child may have developed a serious obesity problem, but when we look at the individual in adolescence we see that he no longer evidences any indication of the earlier problem. One reason this positive development may have occurred is changes in society over the years as he moved from childhood through adulthood. For example, the child with the serious obesity problem has been strongly influenced by the wave of media attention given to health and nutrition in recent years. Always made to clean his plate as a child, never involved in exercise, and filling his arteries full of sugar for a number of years, he looked in the mirror in adolescence and made the decision to do something about his life. For two years now he has eaten well-balanced but reduced-calorie meals, exercised regularly, and removed processed sugar from his diet. His psychological well-being has improved along with his physical fitness.

Conclusions about Continuity–Discontinuity and the Development of Disorders

For decades, we assumed considerable individual consistency in the development of disorders. More recently, this view has been questioned by the adult contextualists. The results of major studies, such as the New York Longitudinal Study and the California Longitudinal Study, that trace the lives of individuals across the childhood years and into the adult years suggest that either extreme in the continuity–discontinuity controversy is unsupported, although they give comfort to both. We reach the same conclusion, then, about the development of disorders as we did about the development of personality in chapter 13. The infant and early childhood years are far from meaningless in predicting later disorders, but later experiences are important as well. Thus, in trying to understand the development of disorders it would be a mistake to look only at the child or adolescents' life in the present tense, ignoring the unfolding of development. So too would it be an error if we only searched through the first two years of life in trying to predict why an individual has a disorder. The truth about disorders lies somewhere between the infant determinism of Freud and a contextual approach that ignores the developmental unfolding of disorders completely.

SUMMARY

I. Differentiating between what is normal and what is abnormal is not an easy task. Five different definitions or models of abnormality have been proposed: the religious or supernatural, statistical, medical or disease, sociocultural, and interactionist.

II. Understanding problems and disturbances from a developmental perspective requires information about the field of developmental psychopathology, infancy and early childhood, the elementary school years, and adolescence.

A. Not until the 1970s was research in the field of developmental psychopathology clearly mapped out, even though the field has historical ties that date to Freud.

B. Information about problems and disturbances in infancy and early childhood focuses on sudden infant death syndrome; eating, sleeping, and elimination problems; infantile autism; and the abused child.

1. Sudden infant death syndrome is responsible for the death of more infants after the vulnerable first ten days of life than any other factor. Why it occurs is still somewhat of a mystery.

2. Eating, sleeping, and elimination problems sometimes surface during the infant and early childhood years. Eating problems may focus on failure to eat properly or at all and on obesity. Sleep problems may involve going to sleep or disruptions in sleep. Nightmares or night terrors mark the latter problem. The major problem related to elimination involves enuresis.

3. Infantile autism seems to be related to some type of organic brain dysfunction, as well as heredity.

4. Understanding the nature of the abused child involves a knowledge of cultural, familial, and community influences.

C. The elementary school years include a variety of problems, with childhood depression and school-related problems being particularly prominent. The resilient child has been the focus of interesting research in this developmental period.

1. Sadness, depression, and school-related problems are most prominent. Girls have more internalizing problems, and boys and lower-class children have more externalizing problems.

2. Childhood schizophrenia has many symptoms that are similar to infantile autism. Childhood schizophrenia involves distorted interpersonal relationships and cognitive/attentional deficits.

3. Depression is more difficult to detect in childhood and adolescence than in adulthood. Girls are characterized by depression more than boys, particularly by the time they reach puberty.

4. School-related problems include underachievement, which is often tied to passive–aggressive behavior, and school phobia.

5. Garmezy and his associates have studied resilient or invulnerable children, who seem to have more efficient attention than their vulnerable counterparts.

D. Problems and disturbances in adolescence include the use of drugs and alcohol, delinquency, suicide, and eating disorders.

1. National surveys of high school seniors suggest that illicit drug use began declining at some point around 1980. Marijuana is the most widely used illicit drug, and alcohol is the most widely used licit drug. While alcohol use has declined slightly, it still remains a major adolescent problem.

2. There is an increase in delinquent acts between the beginning and the end of adolescence. Family processes seem to be implicated as determinants of delinquency. Intervention programs that have been successful involve a warm relationship with an adult and enhancement of the adolescent's self-image.

3. The third leading cause of death among adolescents is suicide. It often occurs when adolescents lose someone they love and feel helpless about controlling that aspect of their lives.

4. There seems to be an increase in adolescent eating disorders. In anorexia nervosa, an almost exclusively female disorder, the girl starves herself until she is emaciated.

III. An important issue in evaluating the development of disorders in childhood is continuity–discontinuity. There are reasons for both continuity and discontinuity in disorders.

A. Reasons for continuity include biological processes and prenatal development, as well as early experience and later consistent experience.

B. Reasons for discontinuity in disorders involve changes in specific life circumstances of the individual, regular changes in life tasks at different ages, and changes in society in different historical eras.

C. Conclusions about continuity–discontinuity in development suggest that both are likely to characterize the nature of how disorders develop.

KEY TERMS

anorexia nervosa 570

childhood schizophrenia 558

developmental psychopathology 551

echolalia 554

enuresis 554

infantile autism 554

interactionist approach 551

juvenile delinquent 566

medical or disease model 550

obesity 553

Oedipus complex 548

religious or supernatural model 549

sociocultural model 551

statistical model 550

sudden infant death syndrome (SIDS) 552

REVIEW QUESTIONS

1. Discuss the different definitions of abnormality.
2. Provide a glimpse of the science of developmental psychopathology, and outline some important problems in infancy and early childhood.
3. What are some major disturbances in the elementary school years?
4. What are resilient children, and what do we know about them?
5. Describe the main problems and disturbances of adolescence.
6. Provide an overview of the nature of continuity–discontinuity in disorders.

SUGGESTED READINGS

Child Development, February 1984.
This special issue is devoted to developmental psychopathology. Includes articles on stress, intervention, social skills, autism, child abuse, and many other topics.

Knopf, I. J. (1979). *Childhood psychopathology.* Englewood Cliffs, NJ: Prentice-Hall.
A thorough overview of the major disturbances in children. Includes information on conceptual models of psychopathology, the nature of psychopathology, the assessment of children with problems, and treatment approaches.

Lipsitt, L. P. (1979). Critical conditions in infancy: A psychological perspective. *American Psychologist, 34,* 973–980.
Lipsett is widely recognized for his contributions to our knowledge about infancy. In this article he writes about some of the abnormalities that develop in the infant years. Particular attention is given to crib death and the failure-to-thrive syndrome.

Rutter, M., and Garmezy, N. (1983). Developmental psychopathology. In P. H. Mussen (Ed.), *Handbook of child psychology* (4th ed., Vol. 4). New York: John Wiley.
This lengthy, highly detailed chapter spells out many important dimensions of the field of developmental psychopathology. Includes considerable discussion of Rutter's and Garmezy's important research.

Weiner, I. B. (1980). Psychopathology in adolescence. In J. Adelson (Ed.), *Handbook of adolescent psychology.* New York: John Wiley.
Weiner's chapter represents an excellent analysis of some of the major disturbances in schizophrenia, depression, and suicide.

GLOSSARY

A

ABC method A learning-to-read technique that emphasizes memorization of the names of the letters of the alphabet. p. 266

acceleration Any strategy that abbreviates the time required for a student to graduate, such as skipping a grade. p. 302

accommodation In Piaget's theory, the act of modifying a current mode or structure of thought to deal with new features of the environment; the converse of assimilation. In visual studies, the maintenance of high visual acuity over a range of viewing distances. pp. 115, 170

acetylcholine A special neurotransmitter used at synapses between nerves and muscles. Every voluntary movement made by the developing individual is mediated by acetylcholine. It is involved in learning and memory. p. 60

acquisition (or storage) components Also called storage components; processes used in learning new information. p. 279

acquisition phase Stage at which a new response is added to the individual's repertory of responses through learning. p. 138

action potentials Electrical clicks used by neurons to send information to other neurons down their axons. p. 58

adaptation In Piaget's theory, effective interaction with the environment necessary for normal development in children. Adaptation is subdivided into assimilation and accommodation. p. 170

adolescence The period of transition from childhood to early adulthood, entered at approximately eleven to thirteen years of age and ending at eighteen to twenty-one. This period is characterized by the onset of physical, cognitive, and social changes. p. 96

adoption studies A strategy of research used to assess the role of heredity in behavior by comparing an adopted child's similarity to his or her biological parents and to his or her adopted parents. p. 50

afferent nerves Neurons responsible for the flow of information to the brain. p. 56

alleles One of a pair of genes located at corresponding positions on a pair of chromosomes; alleles control or influence a specific trait, such as eye color. One is usually dominant and the other recessive. p. 46

alphabetic writing system One of the three basic writing systems used in the world today; a system in which the visual symbols (letters) correspond roughly to the phonemes of speech. p. 263

altruism The selfless concern for the welfare of others. p. 536

anal stage The second psychosexual stage in Freud's theory of development corresponding roughly to the second year of life; the period during which the child seeks pleasure through exercising the anus and eliminating waste. p. 319

anatomy is destiny Erikson's belief that psychological differences in males and females stem from anatomical differences between the two groups. p. 491

androgens Hormones produced by the sex glands which mature primarily in males. p. 96

androgyny Belief that an individual has both masculine and feminine characteristics of behavior. p. 489

animism The belief that inanimate objects have human qualities and are capable of human action. p. 182

anorexia nervosa A severe diminishment of appetite, particularly among adolescent females, characterized by an excessive preoccupation with body size, an intense fear of obesity, and an avoidance of eating even when emaciated. p. 570

Apgar scale Method used to assess the health of newborns one and five minutes after birth; evaluates heart rate, respiratory effort, muscle tone, body color, and reflex irritability. p. 83

aptitude Academic potential and personality dimensions in which students differ; characteristics of the learner. p. 435

aptitude–treatment interaction (ATI) Field of educational research that investigates the interaction between a child's achievement level (aptitude) and classroom structure for the purpose of producing the best learning and the most enjoyable learning environment. p. 435

artificial intelligence (AI) The field of inquiry involved with developing computers and robots that perform intellectual tasks we commonly think of as characterizing human thought. p. 198

assimilation In Piaget's theory, the incorporation of features of the environment into already existing ways of thinking. The converse of accommodation. p. 170

associative flow Factor that evolves from self analysis by creative people in which they can generate large amounts of associative content in their effort to attain novel solutions to problems. p. 304

associative learning Stimulus-response learning that requires the child to make an association between two stimuli with little or no cognitive transformation of the stimulus input. p. 298

associative play A type of play in which the children in a group are more interested in associating with each other than in the tasks they are involved with. There is little or no organization in this type of play. p. 419

579

attachment A relationship between an infant and one or more adult caregivers during the developmental period of birth to two years, which is characterized by a unique bonding between the two social figures involved. p. 369

attention Psychological process involved in imitation in which the observer must attend to what the model is doing or saying before he/she can reproduce the behavior; focusing perception to produce increased awareness of a stimulus. pp. 204, 334

authoritarian parenting A style of parenting having a restrictive, punitive orientation and placing limits and controls on the child with little verbal give and take between the child and the parent. p. 381

authoritative parenting A parenting style that places moderate restrictions on the child while maintaining considerable warmth and openness in communication. p. 381

automatic processes Processes that are independent of demands on limited attentional capacity, draw minimally on information-processing capacity, and are difficult to control once initiated. p. 201

autonomy versus shame and doubt The second stage in Erikson's eight-stage theory of development in which the child may develop the healthy attitude that he or she is capable of independent control of actions or may develop an unhealthy attitude of shame or doubt in that he or she is incapable of such control. p. 324

axon A thin, long cylindrical tube that carries information away from the cell body to other cells. p. 57

babbling Beginning of vocalization in an infant (3–6 mo.) that is controlled by biological maturation, not reinforcement or even the ability to hear. p. 249

baseline A characteristic level of performance that can be used to assess changes in behavior resulting from experimental conditions. p. 138

behavior genetics The discipline that is concerned with the degree and nature of the heredity basis of behavior. p. 48

behavior modification (B-MOD) The use of learning principles, most often those involving classical and operant conditioning, to change maladaptive or abnormal behavior. p. 153

behaviorist learning theory Learning through mechanisms such as imitation, shaping, and reinforcement. p. 239

bimodal perception The ability to perceive information from two senses in a unified manner; for example, visual and auditory information. p. 128

biological and physical processes The influences of evolution, genetics, neurological development, and physical growth on development. These factors contribute to the stability and continuity of the individual. p. 11

blastocyst The inner layer of the blastula. p. 73

blastula Round structure formed when the fertilized ovum divides into two cells and these two cells continue to divide at regular intervals. p. 73

blocking A form of compound stimuli in which, because one conditioned stimuli (CS) already elicits the conditioned response (CR), the formation of a strong connection between a second CS and the CR is prevented during its pairing with the unconditioned stimulus (UCS). p. 143

bonding Controversial strategy focusing on the mother's role during the first minutes, hours, or days of the neonate's interaction with his or her environment. Close contact, particularly physical contact, between mother and neonate during this critical period is believed to create an important emotional attachment that provides a foundation for optimal development for years to come. p. 83

brainstorming Technique for fostering creativity in which ideas flow free of criticism. All ideas, no matter how bizarre, are considered, and the combination of ideas previously suggested is encouraged. p. 305

Brazelton Neonatal Assessment Scale A more subtle test than the Apgar in detecting an infant's neurological integrity, it includes an evaluation of the infant's reaction to people along with assessment of twenty reflexes and the infant's reaction to various circumstances. p. 83

canalization A genetic principle that refers to the narrow path or track that marks the development of some characteristic. In other words, some human characteristics seem to be immune to vast changes in the environment and will stay on track even in the face of drastic environmental inputs. p. 47

care perspective Approach to moral reasoning in which people are viewed in terms of their connectedness with other people and the focus is on their communication with others. p. 527

case study An in-depth assessment of a particular individual used mainly by clinical psychologists. p. 24

cephalo-caudal pattern A general pattern of physical growth. The greatest growth in anatomical differentiation occurs first in the region of the head and later in lower regions in turn. p. 86

child-centered The most popular form of education before the first grade that emphasizes the individual child, providing the child with a number of experiences and making education a fun-filled adventure in exploration. p. 429

childhood schizophrenia Disorder with similar symptomatic behavior to autism but the onset is more gradual and occurs later, after a period of normal development. p. 558

chromosomes Threadlike structures contained in each human cell that come in structurally similar pairs (twenty three of them in humans). p. 44

classical conditioning Procedure by which a neutral stimulus comes to elicit a response by being paired with a stimulus that regularly evokes the response. Also called respondent conditioning. p. 142

Classroom Environment Scale (CES) Attempts to evaluate the social climate of classrooms through assessment of teacher-student and peer relationships, teacher support, affiliation, task orientation, competition, order and organization, rule clarity, teacher control, involvement, and innovation. p. 432

clinical method A method of study, usually with small samples, which involves sophisticated observation and interviewing skills on the part of the researcher. p. 25

cognitive behavior modification Method used to modify an individual's thoughts and images as an intermediary or mediating step in modifying the person's overt behavior. p. 162

cognitive developmental theory A theory that focuses on the rational thinking of the developing individual and stresses that cognitive development unfolds in stagelike sequence which is ordered and uniform for all individuals. Emphasizes biological maturation of the individual and how maturation underlies the individual's cognitive stage of development. p. 170

cognitive-disequilibrium theory Adolescents are faced with contradictions between the moral concepts they have accepted and happenings in the world outside their family and neighborhood. They begin to question and sometimes reject their former beliefs and may develop their own moral system. p. 519

cognitive learning A complex form of learning in which a child must actively transform and change the stimulus input. p. 298

cognitive processes Mental activities, such as thought, perception, attention, problem solving, and language, which influence development. p. 12

cognitive social learning theory Theory that both cognitive processes and experiences determine a child's personality; environment-behavior connections are mediated by cognitive and social factors. p. 329

cognitive theories The viewpoint that language derives less from linguistic abilities than from cognitive abilities. p. 248

cohort effects Effects that are due to a subject's time of birth or generation, but not actually to her or his age. p. 30

compensatory education Programs designed to provide children from low-income families an opportunity to experience an enriched early environment in an effort to place them on an equal level with other children who are not disadvantaged. p. 429

complex stepfamily Family in which both the stepparent and the biological parent have brought children to the newly formed stepfamily. p. 390

component A basic concept of componential analysis that operates on internal representations of objects. p. 279

componential analysis Sternberg's information-processing view, which attempts to understand the availability, accessibility, and ease of execution of a number of information-processing components. p. 279

compound stimulus A stimulus made up of two or more discrete components. p. 143

concept learning Generalization of a response or class of responses to an entire class of situations or events. p. 160

conception The moment at which a male sperm cell joins or fertilizes a female ovum in the female's fallopian tube, marking the beginning of prenatal development. p. 73

concrete-individual perspective First of three major stages in Kohlberg's theory of development of self; attained during early and middle childhood, all social judgments and styles of interaction focus on the tangible feelings and needs of the self during this stage. p. 339

concrete operation A reversible mental action on real, concrete objects. p. 184

concrete operational stage In Piagetian theory, the stage of thought that follows preoperations, lasting from about seven to eleven years of age and marked primarily by a need to anchor thought to concrete objects and events. This stage reveals conservation skills, and is characterized by decentered and reversible thought. p. 183

conditioned head turning Infant learns to turn his or her head toward the source of a sound as a result of being rewarded for this behavior. Reward may be the sight of a colorful mechanical toy in motion. p. 113

conditioned response (CR) The learned response to a conditioned stimulus. p. 142

conditioned stimulus (CS) An environmental event that elicits a response (CR) by being associated repeatedly with an unconditioned stimulus (UCS). p. 142

conjugate reinforcement technique A technique used to investigate infant memory which has indicated that infants as young as two months old can remember for as long as three days. p. 207

conscience Part of the superego which reflects child's moral inhibitions that are the product of parents' punishments. p. 317

constructivist viewpoint Belief that what you experience is a construction based on sensory input plus information retrieved from memory; a kind of representation of the world you build up in your mind. p. 109

contact comfort Tactile stimulation believed to serve an important function in attachment. p. 370

contents One component of Guilford's structure of intellect; contents can be figural, symbolic, semantic, or behavioral. p. 277

contextual world view A view of the individual as neither purely active nor purely passive but rather as an interactional role player with the environment, continuously responding to and acting on the contexts in which he or she lives. p. 20

continuity versus discontinuity A complex issue focused on at least three ideas: abruptness/smoothness of stage transition; connectivity of early and later development; and degree human development reflects development in lower animals. p. 15

contrary-to-fact reasoning In Piagetian theory, this mental feat, possible in the formal operational stage, involves representing an imaginary event that counters the concrete reality of the moment. p. 188

control group A group in psychological experiments exposed to all experimental conditions except the independent variable. The comparison or baseline group. p. 26

controlled processes Learning and memory strategies which draw heavily on information-processing capacities and are under the learner's conscious control. p. 201

conventional level Kohlberg's level of morality at which the child abides by certain standards of other people, such as parents or the rules of society. p. 520

convergent thinking A type of thinking that goes toward one correct answer; contrasts with divergent thinking. p. 304

cooperative play Play that is the prototype for the games of middle childhood in which a sense of group identity is present and activity is organized. p. 419

corpus callosum A large bundle of axons connecting the two hemispheres of the brain. p. 64

correlation coefficient A measure of degree of relationship between two distributions (samples) that ranges from $+1.00$ to -1.00. A positive coefficient means that the distributions increase together; a negative coefficient signifies an inverse relationship; a zero coefficient means no correlation. p. 28

counterconditioning The elimination of a response through conditioning an incompatible response to the same stimulus. p. 144

creative generalization of rules In language acquisition, the generalization of complex rules to produce novel utterances that have not been heard before. p. 240

creativity An important aspect of mental functioning not usually assessed by intelligence tests; finding a solution that is both unique and useful. p. 303

cretinism A severe form of mental retardation caused by a hormone deficiency in the thyroid gland. p. 300

criterion sampling A method of selecting a sample by first defining specific criteria for success at what the researcher wants to predict. p. 282

criterion validity The extent in which a measure of a test can be correlated to another measure or can accurately predict another measure or criterion. p. 282

critical periods Certain time frames in development that are optimal for the emergence of certain behaviors. Specific forms of stimulation are required during these periods for normal development to proceed. pp. 41, 214

cross-sectional study A method used to study a large number of representative persons or variables at a given period of time; frequently employed in the establishment of normative data. p. 29

crystallized intelligence Intelligence acquired through cultural contact, instruction, and observation; involves skills, abilities, and understanding. p. 277

cultural-familial retardation Type of retardation in which there is a family pattern of below-average intellectual capabilities and a family history extending across more than one generation with others in the family having the same profile. pp. 51, 300

culture The behavior patterns, beliefs, values, and any other products of humans that are learned and shared by a particular group or people and passed on from one generation to the next. p. 348

culture-fair tests Intelligence tests developed in an attempt to eliminate cultural bias. p. 284

D

decoding The process in which an external stimulus activates previously learned information in long-term memory. p. 280

deductive hypothesis testing In Piagetian theory, a characteristic of formal operational thought in which the adolescent is able to approach problem solving by formulating a plan to test a series of hypotheses, each of which narrows the field of choices considerably. p. 188

deep processes Information-processing technique that depends on activating appropriate long-term memory knowledge. p. 218

deep structure Concerns the syntactic relations among words in a sentence; employs syntactic categories, such as noun phrase, verb phrase, noun, verb, and article. p. 233

defense mechanisms Unconscious processes of the ego which keep disturbing and unacceptable impulses from being expressed directly. p. 318

deferred imitation Infant's ability to imitate a behavior observed some time ago. p. 172

delay of gratification Fundamental quality of purposefully deferring immediate gratification for delayed but more desired future gratification. p. 455

dendrite The part of the neuron that extends away from the soma. The receiving part of the neuron, serving the important function of collecting information and orienting it toward the cell body. p. 57

dependent variable Variable measured and recorded by experimenter. Changes in the dependent variable are presumed to be under the control of the independent or manipulated variable. p. 25

deprivation dwarfism A type of growth retardation caused by alterations in the release of hormones by the pituitary gland, which may result when children are deprived of affection. p. 90

developmental psychopathology A developmental perspective on problems and disturbances with ties to a number of disciplines. p. 551

developmental scales Intelligence tests that have been created for infants. p. 287

dialectical A term sometimes used to describe the contextual world view; assumes that both the individual and the contexts presented to him or her are continuously changing rather than being in equilibrium. p. 20

differentiation The neuronal process of development by which primitive nerve cells take on properties that allow them to function in specialized ways in different parts of the nervous system. pp. 44, 62

dishabituation Renewed interest shown by the infant when a new stimulus is presented and distinguished from the old stimulus after habituation has occurred. p. 112

discriminate The ability to distinguish among many stimuli and respond to only one. p. 114

displacement (defense mechanisms) Process whereby a motive that is not acceptable in one form is acceptable in another or when an individual attributes an emotion to one person when it really is someone else's. p. 319

displacement (language) Refers to the power of language to communicate knowledge across time and space giving us "second-hand experience" of things not available perceptually. p. 232

divergent thinking A type of thinking that produces many different answers to a single question. p. 304

divided attention task Individual is faced with the problem of handling two or more information "channels" at once. p. 206

DNA (deoxyribonucleic acid) A complex molecule running along the length of each chromosome that forms the basis for genetic structure in man. p. 44

dominant-recessive genes In the process of genetic transmission, a dominant gene is one that exerts its full characteristic effect regardless of its gene partner; a recessive gene is one whose code will be masked by a dominant gene and will only be expressed when paired with another recessive gene. p. 45

dopamine A neurotransmitter that may be involved in the serious mental disturbance of schizophrenia. p. 60

Down's syndrome A genetically transmitted form of retardation, which is caused by an extra chromosome and characterized by a flattened skull, an extra fold of skin over the eyelid, and a protruding tongue. p. 52

dyadic Having to do with two-person interaction between mother and child, father and child, or mother and father. p. 364

dyzygotic A term that refers to fraternal twins, meaning that they come from two different eggs and are therefore genetically more distant than identical twins. p. 49

echoing Repetition of what the child says to you, especially if it is an incomplete phrase or sentence. p. 240

echolalia A speech disorder, found in autistic children, in which the child echoes rather than responds to what he hears. p. 554

ecological framework Belief that we directly perceive information that exists in the environment around us; there is no need to build representations of the world within our heads—information about the world is available "out there." p. 109

ectoderm The outer layer of the differentiated blastocyst, which eventually becomes the child's hair, skin, nails, and nervous system. p. 73

ectomorphy Skinny, thin body build. p. 94

efferent nerves Neurons involved in the flow of information away from the brain. p. 56

ego Freudian part of the personality which tests reality and mediates between the demands of the id and the superego. p. 317

ego control Control of impulses through use of delay of gratification, inhibition of aggression, anticipation of consequences, and caution in ambiguous circumstances; based on psychoanalytic reality principle. p. 456

ego ideal Part of the superego which indicates child's standards of perfection that are the result of parents' reward of good behavior. p. 317

ego integrity versus despair The final conflict in Erikson's theory of development. This stage involves retrospective glances at and evaluations of life. p. 324

ego resiliency Refers to elasticity of the individual; the capacity of the boundary to change its characteristic of permeability-impermeability depending on impinging psychological forces, and return to its original level after the forces no longer are pressing. p. 456

egocentric frame of reference Developing a sense of where things are located in relation to ourselves. p. 120

egocentrism The inability to distinguish between one's own perspective and the perspective of someone else. p. 181

elaborative rehearsal Extended processing of to-be-remembered material utilizing organizational, elaborative, and imaginative activities. p. 211

Electra complex A Freudian conflict involving young girls that is parallel to the Oedipus complex in boys; the girl experiences sexual desire for her father accompanied by hostility toward her mother. p. 320

electroencephalogram (EEG) A device to measure the electrical output of the brain. p. 61

embryological period A period lasting from about two to eight weeks after conception during which the ectoderm, mesoderm, and endoderm develop, and primitive human form takes shape. p. 73

empathy The ability to understand the feelings or ideas of another person. p. 538

empiricist The view that all knowledge is derived from experience. p. 109

endocrine glands Secretes hormones, which are powerful chemical substances that regulate organs. These organs are often far from the endocrine glands where the secretions are first emitted. p. 96

endoderm The inner layer of the blastocyst, which develops into the digestive system, lungs, pancreas, and liver. p. 73

endomorphic A rounded, somewhat "chubby" body build. p. 94

enrichment Program for gifted children that includes college-level courses in high school, advanced classes, independent study, etc. p. 302

enuresis The involuntary passing of urine, generally during nighttime sleep, in children older than three or four. p. 554

epistemology The study of the origins of human knowledge. p. 109

equilibration In Piaget's theory, the mechanism by which the child resolves cognitive conflict and reaches a balance of thought. p. 171

estradiol Hormone responsible for a major portion of pubertal development in females. As estradiol level increases, breast and uterine development occur and skeletal changes appear as well. p. 96

estrogens Hormones produced by the sex glands which mature mainly in females. p. 96

ethology A biological approach to development. Ethologists believe that we can only truly appreciate the origin of behavior if we recognize that many patterns of behavior are transmitted by means of evolution. p. 41

executor responses Actions typical of attachment relationships including clinging, following, sucking, and physical approach; functionally the child is the main actor in this type of response. p. 372

expanding Restating what the child has said in a more linguistically sophisticated form. p. 240

expectancies Important aspect of learning, according to social learning theorists, which can mediate the links between the experiences the child has in the environment and subsequent behavior. p. 156

experiment A carefully controlled method of investigation in which the experimenter manipulates factors believed to be influential on a subject (independent variable) and measures any changes in the subject's behavior (dependent variable) that are presumably due to the influence of the independent variables. p. 25

experimental group The group of subjects in an experiment who are exposed to the independent variable. p. 26

externality effect Tendency of infants up to 1 month of age to fixate on the external parts of a pattern and exclude the internal parts. p. 204

extinction (classical conditioning) A process in which a conditioned response gradually disappears if the conditioned stimulus is repeatedly presented alone. p. 138

extinction (operant conditioning) The last phase of an experiment, following the conditioning trials, in which reinforcements are removed, and the conditioned behaviors gradually decrease or become extinct. p. 149

extrinsic motivation Behavior that is influenced by external rewards in contrast to internal, or self-motivated, action. p. 151

F

face recognition A test of the ability to judge familiarity of previously viewed faces. p. 119

factor analysis A statistical method used to derive common clusters or factors presumed to underlie a larger number of measures. p. 452.

factor analytic approach A type of intelligence testing that involves a mathematical analysis of large numbers of responses to test items in an attempt to come up with the basic common factors in intelligence. p. 275

family of twins design A strategy of research in which comparisons are made between monozygotic twins, siblings, half-siblings, parents, and offspring to assess the role of heredity in behavior. p. 49

Fels Longitudinal Study Study by Kagan and Moss finding that sex-typed characteristics tended to have some stability from the elementary school years through the end of the adolescent years and the stability was linked to cultural sex-role standards. p. 463

fetal alcohol syndrome (FAS) Syndrome affecting offspring of many alcoholic mothers; characterized by small head and defective limbs, joints, face, and heart. May also result in abnormal behavior and below-average intelligence. p. 78

fetal period The period of prenatal growth lasting from about the eighth week until birth, during which a number of physical and anatomical features become well differentiated, and the genitals can be identified as either male or female. p. 74

flexible classrooms The type of classroom setting that provides a wide variety of materials, involves many different planned activities, and allows students the freedom to choose their own groups and seating arrangements. Character-ized by one-to-one interaction between teacher and pupil and open-ended questions. p. 432

fluid intelligence The type of intelligence that involves the individual's adaptability and capacity to perceive things and integrate them mentally. This kind of intelligence appears to be intuitive or independent of education and experience. p. 277

forebrain The part of the immature brain in humans and other mammals that is the predecessor of the neocortex in the mature brain. p. 63

foreclosure Marcia's category of identity development in which the adolescent has made a commitment but has not experienced a crisis. p. 479

formal operational thought Piagetian concept which involves abstractness and hypothetical deductive reasoning, contrary-to-fact reasoning, idealism, and an understanding of the metaphor. p. 185

forward reference A principle of biological development which holds that early (prenatal) neurological maturation is preparatory or anticipatory for the acquisition of certain behaviors after birth. p. 44

frame of reference A system or framework in which spatial information can be represented in memory. Egocentric frames of reference are based on one's own body. Objective frames of reference are based on locations or directions external to one's own body. p. 120

frontal lobe A large section of the cerebrum, containing the motor projection areas and the centers for speech, problem solving, and reasoning. p. 63

G

gametes The sex cells; the means by which genes are transmitted from parents to offspring. p. 44

gender One's biological sex—male or female. p. 489

generativity versus stagnation The seventh conflict in Erikson's theory of development. This stage is positively resolved if an adult assists the younger generation in developing and leading useful lives. p. 324

genes Segments of chromosomes comprised of DNA. p. 44

genital stage The last of Freud's psychosexual stages during which sexual conflicts are resolved, a stable identity is reached, and personality reaches its highest form of organization. p. 320

genotype The unique combination of genes that forms the genetic structure of each individual. p. 45

germinal period The first two weeks of prenatal growth after fertilization, during which rapid cell division takes place. p. 73

gestation The length of time between conception and birth. p. 81

gifted child An individual with well-above-average intellectual capacity or a child with a superior talent for something. p. 301

global self-concept The sum total of an individual's feelings and perceptions about him/herself, including feelings about areas of competence, interests, uniqueness, etc.; key organizing principle of personality. p. 465

gonadal Refers to the sex glands, the testes in males and the ovaries in females. p. 96

gonadotropin A hormone that stimulates the testes and ovaries. p. 96

grammar The formal description of syntactical rules. p. 233

gross motor skills Large muscle activities such as walking, running, and jumping. p. 88

grouping Type of program for the gifted child in which students with similar capacities are placed in a class together. p. 302

guilt The affective state of psychological discomfort arising from a person's feeling of having done something morally wrong. p. 535

H

habituation Technique used to study infants' perceptual world. Repeated presentation of the very same stimulus causes a drop in the infant's interest. p. 112

heritability A mathematical estimate of the degree to which a particular characteristic is genetically determined. p. 50

hermaphrodites Persons born with the sexual anatomy of both male and female. p. 493

hierarchical organization A principle of biological development that describes how the individual's behavioral differentiation builds on earlier more simple forms of development; thus, integrated hierarchies are formed. p. 44

higher order conditioning A kind of classical conditioning, in which the conditioned stimulus (CS) in one series of trials is used as the unconditioned stimulus (UCS) in a second set of trials. p. 143

high-risk infants Infants born after a regular gestation period of 37 to 40 weeks, but who weigh less than five and one half pounds. Also called "low-birth-weight infants." p. 81

hindbrain The portion of the brain that will be adjacent to the spinal cord. p. 62

holophrase hypothesis Belief that, because of limited cognitive or linguistic skills, the child may use a single word to imply a whole sentence. p. 251

humanism School of psychology that places a strong emphasis on the role of self and self-concept as central to understanding the individual's development. p. 465

hypothalamic-pituitary-gonadal axis Interaction within the endocrine system involving the hypothalamus, pituitary gland, and gonads, which maintains optimal levels of hormone secretion. p. 96

hypothalamus A structure in the higher portion of the brain which regulates the pituitary gland. p. 96

hypothesis Learning concept where the child approaches a task with a number of ideas about the situation and must test alternative explanations in search of the correct answers. p. 161

I

id Freudian part of the personality governed by pleasure principle; contains all drives present at birth including sexual and aggressive instincts. p. 316

identity The individual's interest in who one is, what one is all about, and where one is going in life. An important ingredient in Erikson's theory; he believed that identity is a central concern during adolescence. p. 477

identity achieved Adolescent who has undergone a crisis and made a commitment according to Marcia's identity development theory. p. 479

identity confused (diffused) According to Marcia's theory, these are adolescents who have not experienced any crisis or made any commitment. Adolescent is undecided upon occupational or ideological choices and is apathetic about such matters. p. 479

identity versus identity confusion (diffusion) Erikson's fifth crisis of psychological development; the adolescent may become confident and purposeful or may develop an ill-defined identity. p. 324

imaginary audience A form of adolescent egocentrism where the adolescent believes he or she is the focus of attention in actual social situations. p. 191

imitation (modeling, vicarious learning) A form of learning in which new behaviors are acquired by observing others performing the behavior. p. 239

immanent justice Characteristic belief of the moral realist in which violation of a rule is connected in some mechanical or reflexlike way to the punishment. p. 518

implantation Firm attachment of the fertilized egg to the wall of the uterus. p. 73

inbreeding A procedure in which brothers and sisters are mated with each other, resulting in a homogeneous strain of organisms after several generations. p. 49

incentive conditions A final process in Bandura's conception of modeling in which reinforcement or incentive conditions increase the likelihood that a particular behavior modeled will be imitated. p. 334

incentives External cues that stimulate motivation and can be either positive or negative in nature. p. 151

independent variables The factors in an experiment that are manipulated or controlled by the experimenter to determine their impact on the subject's behavior. p. 25

induction Form of discipline that employs reasoning and explanation of the consequences of the child's actions for others. p. 332

industry versus inferiority Erikson's fourth crisis of psychological development; the school-aged child may develop a capacity for work and task directedness or he/she may view him/herself as inadequate. p. 324

infantile amnesia Phenomenon that as children and adults, humans have little or no memory for events we have experienced before three years of age. p. 209

infantile autism Childhood disorder characterized by aloofness, inability to relate to others, little or no need for physical contact or affection, absence of or severely restricted speech, active aversion to auditory stimuli, inflexibility to changes in routine, and self-stimulation through repetitive movements. p. 554

infinite generativity Characteristic of language that allows a finite number of individual words to combine together in an infinite number of sentences through sequencing. p. 231

information theory An explanation of classical conditioning that stresses the informational value of the conditioned stimulus (CS), i.e., the organism sees the CS as a sign of the unconditioned stimulus that follows. p. 144

initiative versus guilt Erikson's third crisis of psychological development, occurring during the preschool years; the child may develop a desire for achievement or he or she may be held back by self-criticism. p. 324

innate goodness Eighteenth-century belief that children are basically and inherently good and should be permitted to grow naturally with little monitoring or constraints from parents. p. 11

insecure attachment Pattern of attachment behavior characterized by ambivalence of infant to physical contact, heightened separation anxiety, and avoidance or resistance of caregiver. p. 374

insight learning A form of learning involving a sudden mental image of the solution to a problem. p. 157

instincts Innate biological forces that motivate a response. p. 342

institutionalization The process of placing a person in an institution for corrective or therapeutic purposes. p. 294

instrumental incompetence Ineffectiveness in dealing with other people and the environment, particularly inability to exhibit independence, self-initiated activities, and self-esteem about one's intellectual and physical abilities. p. 507

intention-cue detection Interpretation of social behaviors based on the perceived intent or purpose of the behavior. p. 410

interactionist approach View of understanding abnormalities that believes both biological factors and sociocultural conditions may produce a mental disturbance, and in most instances these factors interact with each other to produce the problem. p. 551

intergenerational relationships Relationships across generations, e.g., relationships involving children, parents, and grandparents. p. 394

internalization of schemes A substage of Piaget's sensorimotor development in which the infant (18–24 mo.) develops the ability to use primitive symbols. p. 175

interneurons Neurons participating in any complex processing of information and that make up much of the brain. p. 56

interval schedule Schedule of reinforcement (negative or positive) or punishment which is determined by time. p. 148

intervention phase Phase of behavior modification in which an attempt is made to alter or change the target behavior following the establishment of a baseline or norm. p. 138

interview A method of study in which the researcher asks questions of a person and records that person's responses. p. 23

intimacy in friendships Intimate self-disclosure and the sharing of private thoughts; private and personal knowledge about a friend. p. 413

intimacy versus isolation Erikson's sixth crisis of psychological development; the young adult may achieve a capacity for honest, close relationships or be unable to form these ties. p. 324

intraindividual change Developmental perspective which stresses individual differences as being critical to understanding biological, cognitive, and social functioning. p. 19

intrinsic motivation Behavior that is influenced by an underlying need for competence and self-determination. p. 151

intuitive thought A substage of Piaget's preoperational stage during which the child begins to reason about various matters and wants to know the answers to all sorts of questions. Child's thought is viewed as prelogical. p. 179

invariant An unchanging, internalized aspect of a stimulus that specifies constancy; e.g., assuming the ground is flat, a viewer knows that near and far telephone poles are of the same height, even though the far pole appears smaller. p. 110

in vitro fertilization Commonly referred to as "test-tube" fertilization, a process in which fertilization of an ovum occurs in a laboratory setting, outside the woman's body, and the egg is then later implanted in the woman's uterus. p. 72

J

justice perspective Approach to moral reasoning in which people are differentiated and seen as standing alone—the focus is on the rights of the individual. p. 527

juvenile delinquent Term applied to an adolescent who breaks the law or engages in behavior that is considered illegal. p. 566

K

kinship studies A strategy of research used to assess the role of heredity in behavior by comparing the genetic relationship between family members, including members such as uncles, cousins, grandparents, and other more distant relatives. p. 49

L

labeling The identification of words associated with objects. p. 242

language universals Certain features and consistancies that are shared by all or most languages. p. 244

latchkey Refers to children of working parents; children who are given the key to their home and take the key with them to school, using it in the evening to let themselves in the home while the parents are still at work. p. 391

latency stage Freud's fourth psychosexual stage (6–12 yrs. of age); the period during which the child's feelings and thoughts about sexual conflicts are actively repressed. p. 320

lateralization of language A concept referring to the evidence suggesting that language processing in the vast majority of people is controlled by the left hemisphere of the brain. p. 244

learned helplessness The attitude of an individual who believes that rewards are beyond personal control and that personal behavior will not affect the outcome of a situation. p. 508

learning A relatively permanent change in the mind or behavior that occurs through experience and cannot be accounted for by reflexes, instinct, maturation, or the influence of fatigue, injury, disease, or drugs. p. 140

learning sets Concept learning technique in which the learner acquires sets, or a tendency to notice that certain responses inherently belong with certain kinds of events. p. 161

levels of rule systems Rules that govern phonology, morphology, syntax, semantics, and pragmatics. p. 232

lexical access Internal speech coding process in which the visual information is translated into speech code, and then referenced in our internal dictionary or lexicon. p. 266

logographic writing systems Alternative to the alphabetic system; each visual symbol corresponds to a word. The Chinese writing system is logographic. p. 263

longitudinal study A method of study in which the same subject or group of subjects is repeatedly tested over a significant period of time. p. 29

long-term memory Memory for information that was, but is no longer, under attentional focus. p. 208

love withdrawal Disciplinary practice that often suggests or involves the removal of the child from the parent. p. 332

low-birth-weight infants Also known as "high-risk infants." Infants born after a regular gestation period of 37 to 40 weeks, but who weigh less than five and one half pounds. p. 81

M

maintenance rehearsal A controlled process that involves rote restatement or repetition of items. p. 211

mean The average score in a distribution of scores. p. 274

mechanistic world view Assumes a vision of the individual as a passive machine that reacts to events in the environment but does not actively anticipate events or formulate its own goals, and in most instances, does not engage in complex internal activity of any kind. p. 20

medical or disease model Model of abnormality in which a child is considered abnormal when there is some physical malfunctioning in his or her body. Psychological abnormality is believed to be some type of disease precipitated by internal factors. p. 550

meiosis The process by which gametes reproduce, which allows for the mixing of genetic material. p. 44

melodic contour The sequence of ups and downs in pitch of a melody. p. 127

member-of-society perspective Kohlberg's second stage of self-development in which the individual sees him/herself as a member of a larger social unit and makes judgments to preserve the social order and fit each member of society into it. p. 339

memory The retention of information over time. p. 206

memory span task Task that has been developed to assess short-term memory. Individual hears a short list of stimuli, usually digits, presented at a rapid pace and then is asked to repeat the digits back. p. 210

mental age (MA) Concept developed by Binet that describes the general level of a child's intellectual functioning. p. 273

mental imagery Control process which makes use of the construction of mental pictures or images to aid in memory recall. p. 212

mental retardation Significantly subaverage general intellectual functioning existing concurrently with deficits in adaptive behavior and manifested during the developmental period. p. 299

mesoderm The middle layer of the blastocyst, which later becomes the muscles and bones, as well as the circulatory and excretory systems. p. 73

mesomorphic Athletic, muscular body build. p. 94

meta-analysis Involves the application of statistical techniques to already existing research studies. p. 433

metacomponents High-order control processes used for executing planning and decision making when problem solving is called for. p. 279

metamemory Knowledge of one's own memory including knowledge that learning information is different from simply perceiving information, diagnostic knowledge of the various factors contributing to performance of different memory tasks, and knowledge of how to monitor memory during the course of learning. p. 214

metaphor An implied comparison between two ideas that is conveyed by the abstract meanings contained in the words used to make the comparison. p. 189

midbrain One of the three major divisions of the developing brain located above the hindbrain. p. 63

migration A process in neuronal development where the nerve cells are in the right place at the right time. p. 62

MLU (mean length of utterance) A measure developed by Roger Brown to chart a child's progress of language development using morphemes as the unit of analysis. p. 253

mnemonics The art of improving the memory with the aid of artificial systems. p. 213

monozygotic A term that refers to identical twins meaning that they come from the same egg. p. 49

moral autonomy The second stage of moral development in Piaget's theory; the child becomes aware that rules and laws are created by people, relative to social systems, and that in judging an action one should consider the actor's intentions as well as the act's consequences. p. 517

moral competence Knowledge of moral rules indicating that the person is capable of acting in appropriate moral ways. p. 534

moral development The acquisition of rules and conventions about what people should do in their interactions with others. p. 517

moral performance The carrying out of a particular moral behavior, dependent on factors of motivation as well as of moral understanding. p. 534

moral realism The first stage of moral development in Piaget's theory. Justice and rules are conceived of as unchangeable properties of the world, removed from the control of people. p. 517

moratorium Adolescents who are in the midst of a crisis, but their commitments are either absent or only vaguely defined. p. 479

Moro reflex An infantile startle response which is common to all neonates but disappears by about three to four months of age. When startled, the neonate arches its back, and throws its head back, flinging out its arms and legs. The neonate then rapidly closes arms and legs to the center of the body. p. 85

morphemes The smallest unit of language that carries meaning. p. 233

morphology The rules involved in the combining and sequencing of morphemes. p. 233

motherese A characteristic way in which mothers, fathers, and people in general talk to young language learners; uses short, simple statements; long pauses between statements; heavy stress on important words; and exaggerated intonation contours. p. 240

motoric reproduction A process involved in modeling in which the child may attend to the model and adequately code what he has seen but is unable to reproduce the behavior due to limitations in motor development. p. 334

multiple-factor theory View that a number of specific factors rather than one general and one specific factor make up intelligence. p. 276

myelin A substance that wraps around the axon and accelerates the transmission of electrical charges. p. 58

nativist Belief that proposes "prewired" genetic knowledge and processes. p. 109

nativist theories Theory that children have substantial prewired, innate machinery for the acquisition of human language. p. 243

natural selection A principle that provides an explanation of the evolutionary process; the belief that humans and other organisms whose characteristics are the most adaptive to the environment are more likely to survive; thus, the more favorable characteristics are perpetuated through reproduction. p. 39

neocortex The most recently developed part of the brain in the evolutionary scheme; it is the largest part of the human brain in terms of volume (about 80 percent) and covers the lower portions of the brain almost like a cap. p. 63

neo-Freudian (neopsychoanalytic) Revised versions of Freud's psychoanalytic theory, which place less emphasis on sexuality and the first five years of life, and place more emphasis on social factors and the autonomy of the ego. p. 322

neuron The basic cell that handles information processing in the brain. p. 56

neurotransmitters The chemical substances that respond to the electrical nature of the action potential and carry information from the presynaptic to postsynaptic cell. p. 58

New York Longitudinal Study Extensive study investigating the question of how various dimensions of personality change or remain stable; stressed the importance of the developmental unfolding of personality. p. 463

nodes of Ranvier Gaps in the myelin sheath from one neuron to the next. p. 58

nonnutritive sucking technique A variant of the habituation technique where the rate of the infant's sucking on a nipple is used to show habituition and dishabituation in voice recognition and perception. p. 124

norepinephrine Neurotransmitter apparently associated with mood. Too much may produce a manic state and too little seems to lead to depression. p. 60

normal distribution Frequency distribution that is very symmetrical, with a majority of the cases falling in the middle of the possible range of scores and fewer scores appearing toward the ends of the range. p. 274

nuclear family The basic unit in society, made up of at least two adults of the opposite sex, usually husband and wife, and their offspring. p. 364

obesity Weighing more than 20 percent over normal skeletal and physical requirements. p. 553

object permanence Significant sensorimotor accomplishment in which the infant grasps that objects and events continue to exist even though the child is not in direct perceptual contact with them. p. 176

objective frame of reference Developing a sense of where things are located in relation to other things; nonegocentric. p. 121

observational learning Learning that occurs as a result of watching or imitating others. p. 157

occipital lobe Portion of the brain where visual functioning occurs. p. 63

Oedipus complex A Freudian conflict beginning in early childhood in which the boy exhibits sexual desire for the mother and hostility toward and fear of the father. Eventually the boy renounces the mother and identifies with the father. pp. 316, 320, 548

onlooker play A type of play characterized by the child watching other children playing, but not joining with them in the activities. p. 419

ontogeny The developmental history of an organism. p. 39

ontogeny recapitulates phylogeny The belief that as an individual goes through stages of development the adult forms of human ancestors in the phylogenetic scale are repeated. p. 39

open classroom Classroom structure characterized by free choice of student activities, space flexibility, enriched learning materials, emphasis on the individual, team teaching, student self-responsibility, and/or classrooms without walls. p. 432

operant conditioning (instrumental learning) A form of learning advocated by Skinner in which the strength of a behavior is increased or decreased as a result of its consequences. p. 146

operants Responses that are actively emmited in relation to specific consequences. p. 146

operations Internalized sets of actions that allow the child to do mentally what before was done physically. Operations are highly organized and conform to certain rules and principles of logic. p. 179

operations (Guilford) Intellectual activities or processes; what one does with information. Guilford's five cognitive operations focus on cognition, memory, divergent production, convergent production, and evaluation. p. 277

oral stage The first psychosexual stage in Freud's theory (birth to one yr.) during which the child seeks pleasure by stimulating the mouth, lips, and gums. p. 319

organismic world view A view that assumes the individual is an active, mindful individual with goals and plans who uses complex strategies to attain ends; this world view also assumes a strong biological foundation of development, with the social world functioning primarily to provide the setting for the unfolding of development rather than being the cause of development. p. 20

organization The continuous process of refining and integrating every level of thought from sensorimotor to formal operation in Piagetian theory. p. 170

organizational processing The active grouping of input items into higher order units or "chunks" to aid recall. p. 211

orienting reflex (OR) Physiological changes that accompany increased attention to a stimulus. p. 204

original sin view Middle ages, Catholic and Puritan, concept of children, reflecting the philosophical perspective that children are basically evil. p. 11

overextension The tendency of children to misuse words by extending one word's meaning to include a whole set of objects that are not related to or are inappropriate for the word's meaning. p. 252

overshadowing In classical conditioning, when one of two conditioned stimuli (CS) that are paired with an unconditioned stimulus (UCS) is proved by testing to be the stronger elicitor of the conditioned response (CR). p. 143

P300 Waveform that is part of the electrical activity in the brain and is initiated by procesing a stimulus; P300 latencies predict memory span in children. p. 210

parallel play A type of play in which the child plays separately from the others, but with the same type of toys the other children are using or in a manner that mimics the behavior of the others. p. 419

parallel processing The simultaneous consideration of a number of lines of thought at a nonconscious level. p. 198

parietal lobe The portion of the brain associated with bodily sensations. p. 63

peer sociotherapy Therapy program in which peers provide support and encouragement to each other in a group setting. p. 402

peers Children who are about the same age, grade, status, or behavioral level. p. 403

Perceived Competence Scale for Children Measure of self-concept emphasizing the assessment of the child's sense of competence across different domains rather than viewing perceived competence as a unitary concept. p. 482

performance components Processes used to carry out a problem-solving strategy. A set of performance components involve the actual working through of a problem. p. 279

permissive-indifferent parent A parent who is very uninvolved in his or her children's lives. This type of parenting style consistently has been linked to a lack of self-control on the part of the child. p. 381

permissive-indulgent pattern Style of parenting in which parent is highly involved in the child's life but allows him/her considerable freedom and does not control negative behaviors; associated with impulsivity, aggressiveness, lack of independence, and inability to take responsibility. p. 381

personal constructs Representation of some event or relationship in the person's environment that is carried forward to influence the construction of future relationships and events. p. 328

personality Distinctive patterns of behavior, thoughts, and feelings influencing the individual's adaptation to the situations of his or her life. p. 451

personality processes The influences of aspects of individual personality on development. p. 13

perspective-taking skills The ability to take someone else's point of view. pp. 404, 538

phallic stage Freud's third psychosexual stage during which the child's (4–6 yrs.) genital area is the chief source of pleasure. p. 319

phenomenological approach A theoretical view which places greater emphasis on understanding the individual's perception of an event than on a factual account of the event or on the individual's behavior. p. 465

phenothiazines Most commonly used drug for the treatment of schizophrenia. p. 560

phenotype The observed and measurable characteristics of individuals, including physical characteristics such as height, weight, eye color, and skin pigmentation, and psychological characteristics, such as intelligence, creativity, personality, and social tendencies. p. 45

phobias A strong, persistent, and irrational fear which is elicited by a specific stimulus or situation. p. 144

phonemes The basic units of language; single speech sounds. Phonemes are void of meaning. p. 232

phonetic alphabet System giving each phoneme a written symbol. p. 232

phonics method Learning-to-read technique which stresses the sounds that letters make when in words. p. 266

phonology The study of rules that govern the sequencing of phonemes in a language. p. 232

phylogeny The evolutionary history of a group of organisms. p. 39

pituitary gland Often referred to as the "master gland." The pituitary gland is located at the base of the brain and secretes hormones that control growth. p. 90

PKU syndrome Genetically transmitted form of retardation in which a genetic code fails to produce an enzyme necessary for metabolism. p. 52

play therapy Therapy that allows the child to work off his frustrations and serves as a medium through which the therapist can analyze many of the child's conflicts and methods of coping with them. p. 418

playing with improbabilities Technique used to encourage creativity that forces children to think about the events that might follow an unlikely occurrence. p. 305

pleasure principle Principle governing the id to constantly seek pleasure and avoid pain, regardless of what impact such pleasure seeking and pain avoiding will have in the real world. p. 316

polyadic Social interactions of more than two people. p. 364

polygenic inheritance A complex form of genetic transmission involving the interaction of many different genes to produce certain traits. p. 46

positive reinforcement Pleasant or positive response to a behavior which increases the likelihood that the behavior will recur; a powerful determinant of behavior in operant conditioning. p. 147

postconventional level The highest level of morality in Kohlberg's theory of moral development in which moral values are completely internalized and not based on the standards of others. p. 521

power assertion Disciplinary practice that attempts to gain control over the child by such means as removing privileges, spanking, or threatening. p. 332

pragmatics Rules which pertain to the social context of language and how people use language in conversation. p. 234

preadapted A term used to describe newborns suggesting that many of the newborn's behavioral competencies actually arise during the prenatal developmental period. p. 44

preconventional level The first and lowest level in Kohlberg's theory of moral development. No internalization of morality occurs here; moral thought follows the belief that morality is determined by the external environment, particularly rewarding and punishing circumstances. p. 520

preference technique Technique used to determine an infant's ability to distinguish between things through his or her tendency to prefer one stimulus to another. p. 111

premature birth Term applied to babies born after less than 37 weeks in the womb. p. 81

preoperational stage In Piagetian theory, the stage of thought from about two to seven years of age when stable concepts are formed, mental reasoning emerges, egocentrism gradually decreases, and magical belief systems are constructed. p. 178

pretend play A type of play in which the child transforms the physical environment into a symbol by engaging in make-believe activities and playing out different roles. p. 421

primary circular reactions A scheme based upon the infant's attempt to reproduce an interesting or pleasurable event that initially occurred by chance (1–4 mo.). p. 174

primary process thinking The thinking of the id which involves the effort on the part of the id to satisfy its wants and needs by simply forming a mental image of the object it desires. p. 317

primary reinforcement Reinforcement due to innate factors rather than through experience. p. 148

prior-to-society perspective Kohlberg's third and final stage of self development in which the self is perceived as a member of many different social units, each with an arbitrary membership determined by many uncontrollable factors. p. 339

products In Guilford's structure of intellect, products index the form in which information occurs—units, classes, relations, systems, transformations, or implications. p. 277

Project Follow Through A program instituted in 1967 as an adjunct to Project Head Start. Under this program different kinds of educational programs were devised to see whether specific programs are effective. p. 429

Project Head Start Compensatory education program designed to provide the children from low-income families an opportunity to experience an enriched early environment and acquire the skills and experiences considered prerequisite for success in school. p. 429

projection Perception of our external world in terms of our own personal conflicts; attributing one's own unacceptable and disturbing impulses or wishes to someone or something else. p. 319

proliferation The generation of new cells through the process of cell division. p. 61

prompting Process of rephrasing a sentence you have spoken if it appears not to have been understood. p. 240

proximodistal pattern A general pattern of physical growth and development; the pattern of growth starting at the center of the body and moving toward the extremities. p. 86

psychoanalytic theory A view of personality that emphasizes the private, unconscious aspects of a person's mind as the dominant feature of personality. p. 315

psychometric approach Approach to intelligence that places its emphasis on measurement-based tests. p. 286

puberty The stage of development at which the individual becomes capable of reproduction; this stage is usually linked with the onset of adolescence, a rapid change to maturation. p. 96

punishment Refers to the situation in which a response is followed by an event which reduces the likelihood that the response will occur again. p. 152

qualitative change Piaget's view that a child's intelligence is not simply less than an adult's but it is intelligence of a qualitatively different kind. p. 14

quasi-experimental strategy An approximation to an experiment in which there is some loss of control over the independent variables due to the real-life manner in which they are defined. p. 27

questionnaire A method of study similar to a highly structured interview, except the subject reads the questions and marks the answers on a sheet of paper rather than verbally responding to the interviewer. p. 23

ratio schedule A schedule of reinforcement in which reinforcement is received after a number of responses. p. 148

rationalization After performing an unacceptable act or thinking a threatening thought, people frequently alleviate the anxiety or guilt that ensues by finding a perfectly reasonable excuse for their behavior. p. 319

reaction formation Defense mechanism which wards off an unacceptable impulse by over-emphasizing its opposite in thought and behavior. p. 318

reaction range A range of the potential phenotypical outcomes that are possible for an individual, given one's genotype and the influences of environmental conditions. The reaction range limits how much environmental change can modify an individual's behavioral characteristics. p. 47

reality principle Abiding principle of the ego that finds ways to satisfy the wants and needs of the id within the boundaries of reality. p. 317

recasting Responding to a child's utterance by expressing the same or a similar meaning in a different way, perhaps by turning it into a question. p. 241

regression Defense mechanism wherein during stress we have a tendency to go back to patterns of behavior that brought us reward and security at an earlier age. p. 318

rehearsal The extended processing of to-be-remembered material after it has been presented. A controlled process used to facilitate long-term memory. p. 211

reinforcement A mother's response to her child's ill-formed utterances in a positive manner. p. 239

relational words Words that specify relationships among objects, events, or people. p. 256

religious or supernatural model View in which the child's abnormalities in behavior are attributed to sinfulness, demonic possession, or temptation by the devil. p. 549

repisodic Characteristic in memory that individuals cannot recall specific sentences but can recall the theme or general idea represented by the sentence. p. 216

representation A model of the world built up in the mind based on sensory input plus information retrieved from memory. p. 110

repression A tendency of the ego to push anxiety-producing information into the unconscious mind. p. 318

reproduction A process that involves the fertilization of a female gamete (ovum) by a male gamete (sperm) to create a single-celled zygote. p. 44

respondents Event where behavior is elicited by some identifiable stimulus; subject responds to something. p. 146

retention Psychological process necessary in imitation; to produce a model's actions at a later time requires coding and storing the information in memory for later recall. p. 334

retention components (retrieval) Processes involved in accessing previously stored information. p. 279

retrieval A control process that involves the use of certain search strategies to recover items from memory. p. 212

rhythmic motor behavior Rapid, repetitious movements of limbs, torso, and head found in the first year of life. These motor behaviors occur frequently and appear to be a source of pleasure for the infant. p. 86

rhythmical stereotypies Common rhythmic motor behaviors occuring during the first year of life which seem to represent an important transition between uncoordinated activity and complex, coordinated, voluntary motor control. p. 88

ritual Form of spontaneous play that involves controlled repetition. These interchanges are sometimes referred to as "turns" or "rounds." p. 420

role-taking skills The ability to understand the feelings and perceptions that other people may be experiencing. p. 538

S–O–R model A view of learning that emphasizes the association between specific stimuli in the environment, cognitive activities of the organism involved, and responses of the organism. p. 156

saccadic movements Rapid movements of the eyes occuring three to four times per second. In infants, the method of scanning visual patterns where the eyes fixate on one part of the pattern, then another, then another, and so on. p. 204

schedules of reinforcement (or punishment) Rules that explain when the consequence occurs in relation to behavior; a statement of contingency on which reinforcement is received. p. 148

schemata (schema) A cognitive framework consisting of a number of organized ideas; a frame of reference for recording events or data. p. 218

scheme Refers to the basic unit for an organized pattern of sensorimotor functioning. p. 173

science Any discipline or field of study that is characterized by a systematic body of theories that can be verified or proved false on the basis of actual evidence collected. p. 19

scripts Schemata for events. p. 218

secondary circular reactions Infant (4–8 mo.) becomes more object oriented, or focused on the world around him, and moves beyond preoccupation with the self in sensitive action interactions. p. 174

secondary reinforcement Reinforcement which occurs through experience. Secondary reinforcement gains its functional effect by first being associated with the primary (original) reinforcer. p. 148

secure attachment Pattern of attachment behavior characterized by use of caregiver as a secure base from which to explore the environment and positive response to affection. p. 374

selective attention task Individual is faced with the problem of ignoring some stimuli, while focusing on others more relevant to his interests and goals. p. 206

selective breeding A procedure that involves the mating of organisms of like characteristics. p. 49

self as knower Account of self that not only encompasses the self as object of knowledge, attention, and evaluation, but one that includes the self as an active observing process. p. 466

self-instructional methods Strategy of cognitive behavior modification which emphasizes self talk as a means of behavior change. p. 162

self-reinforcement Self-produced consequences and personal standards that affect achievement behavior as much as external reinforcement and reward from others. p. 331

semantic elaboration The process in which information is encoded in a form that preserves the meaning of words and sounds. p. 211

semantics Language rules which pertain to the meaning of words and sentences. p. 234

semiotic function Piagetian belief that pretend play involves an overlay of meaning on sound patterns, images, or gestures. p. 424

sensation and perception Processes we use to gather and interpret information from the world. p. 109

sensitive period Less rigid interpretation of the critical period that implies that a given effect can be produced more readily during one period than earlier or later. p. 346

sensorimotor stage The earliest stage of thought in Piaget's model of cognitive development, lasting from birth to about two years of age; during this period the infant's ability extends from simple reflexes through the use of primitive symbols as the means of coordinating sensation and perceptions with physical movements and actions. p. 171

sequencing The utterances found in human languages consist of sequences of words forming phrases and sentences. p. 231

sequential designs Those designs that combine the features of cross-sectional and longitudinal designs in a search for more effective ways to study development. These designs allow us to see whether the same pattern of development is produced by each of the research strategies. p. 31

sex-role stereotypes Personality characteristics attributed to people on the basis of their sex without regard for their individuality. p. 504

sexual (gender) identity The extent to which the individual child takes on the behaviors and attitudes associated with the male or female role as a part of their personality. p. 489

shaping The process of rewarding closer and closer approximations to desired behavior. pp. 148, 239

short-gestation babies Refers to babies born after a briefer than regular time period in the womb. p. 81

short-term memory A level of memory storage where stimuli are stored and retrieved for up to thirty seconds, assuming no rehearsal is used. p. 208

siblings Brothers and/or sisters. p. 382

signaling responses Attachment behavior characterized by smiling, crying, and calling in which the infant attempts to elicit reciprocal behaviors from the mother. p. 372

simple reflexes Substage of Piaget's sensorimotor period in which the infant (0–1 mo.) practices or exercises reflexive behaviors as a means of coordinating sensation and action. The infant develops the ability to produce behaviors that resemble reflexes in the absence of obvious reflex stimuli. p. 174

simple stepfamily Family in which the stepparent has not brought children from a previous marriage to live in the newly formed stepfamily. p. 390

simultaneous comparison method A method for testing face perception in which a target face must be matched against one or more comparison faces. p. 119

situationism Social-learning belief that personality often depends on the situation or context in which the individual finds him/herself. p. 329

social class A grouping of people according to some combination of criteria, such as economic level, religion, education, or family background. p. 351

social comparison The child's interpretation of reinforcement in a relative sense that determines subsequent behavior. p. 330

social competence Ability to make use of environmental resources to achieve a good developmental outcome. p. 458

social conventional reasoning Refers to thoughts about social consensus and convention as opposed to moral reasoning, which stresses ethical matters. p. 530

social-mold theories Socialization process in which children are considered to be the products of their parents' socialization techniques and of their environment, particularly within the family. p. 363

social processes Refer to a child's interactions with other individuals in the environment and these interactions' effects on development. p. 13

societalism View of morality that argues that society is the source of all values, not the individual, and moral development should be construed as a matter of the individual's accommodation to the values and requirements of society. p. 529

sociocultural model Model of abnormality that seeks to determine the environmental factors that cause children to display unusual behavior and to understand why people in society call such children sick, mentally ill, or crazy. p. 551

solitary play A type of play in which the child plays alone and independently of those around him, with little or no concern for anything else that is going on. p. 419

soma The cell body that contains the nucleus; manufactures all the substances the neuron uses for growth and maintenance. p. 57

SOMPA (System of Multicultural Pluralistic Assessment) Battery of tests that includes information about the child's intellectual functioning in verbal and nonberbal areas, social and economic background, social adjustment, and physical health. p. 285

sound spectrogram A graph that is useful for representing speech and other acoustic stimuli. It represents frequency as a function of time. p. 126

spatial adjectives Adjectives that express spatial aspects of objects or spatial relationships among objects. p. 253

speech coding Encoding based on speech; a kind of mental imagery of speech that plays a role in the process of reading, even when the reading is silent. p. 266

speed-reading A technique emphasizing the number of words which can be read in a given period; this extremely fast reading is based on "skimming." p. 266

spontaneous recovery In conditioning, an increase in the tendency to perform an extinguished response after a time interval in which no additional stimulus or reinforcement is presented. p. 149

stage theory A concept that implies that qualitative changes in development occur in sequential phases which are universal and significantly alter a person's life from one period of development to the next. p. 319

stages Sequence of qualitative changes in development that are age related. p. 15

standard deviation A measure of scatter or dispersion of a distribution. p. 274

standardized tests Questionnaire, structured interview, or behavioral tests that are developed to identify an individual's characteristics or abilities, relative to those of a large group of similar individuals. p. 24

statistical model Model that defines abnormality as deviation from the average. p. 550

stimulus discrimination (classical conditioning) A process of learning to respond to certain stimuli that are reinforced and not to respond to others that are not. p. 149

stimulus discrimination (operant conditioning) The tendency of a response to occur in the presence of one stimulus but not another. p. 149

stimulus generalization (classical conditioning) A process occurring when a stimulus similar to the original conditioned stimulus also produces the conditioned response. p. 149

stimulus generalization (operant conditioning) The tendency of a response that has been reinforced in the presence of one stimulus to occur in the presence of another stimulus that is similar to the first. p. 145

stimulus substitution theory An explanation of classical conditioning arguing that the central nervous system is structured in such a way that the contiguity of the conditioned stimulus (CS) and the unconditioned stimulus (UCS) creates a bond between them that eventually allows the CS to substitute for the UCS. p. 143

structure of intellect model A concept referring to Guilford's perspective of intelligence which proposes that an individual's intellect is composed of 120 mental abilities formed by all the possible combinations of five operations, four contents, and six products. p. 277

subitizing Among older children, an implicit sensitivity to number without recourse to counting. p. 113

sudden infant death syndrome (SIDS) The unexplained death of a child in the first year of life, usually between the ages of two and five months. p. 552

superego Division of personality which serves as the internal representative of the values of one's parents and society; the moral branch of the personality. p. 317

suppression Defense mechanism in which we actively, consciously keep our impulses in check. p. 318

surface structure The actual order of words in a spoken sentence. p. 233

syllabic writing systems Writing system in which each written symbol corresponds to a spoken syllable. p. 263

symbol In Piagetian theory, an internalized sensory image or word that represents an event. p. 175

symbolic function substage Substage of Piaget's preoperational stage; child (2–4 yrs.) becomes able to develop a mental representation of an object in his or her head, and to use symbols to represent objects that are not present. p. 179

synapse Functional connection between neurons. p. 58

synaptic knobs End point of axon, which forms a bulblike structure. p. 58

syntax The rules that govern how words are combined into grammatically acceptable phrases and sentences. p. 233

systematic observation Method of data collection that is characterized by a well-defined set of objectives including what is to be observed, where and when the observation will take place, how the observation will be made, and in what form the data are to be reported. p. 22

tabula rasa Locke's view that children are not innately evil, but instead are like a blank tablet, becoming a particular kind of child or adult because of the experiences he or she has in life. p. 11

telegraphic speech Speech that includes content words, such as nouns and verbs, but omits the extra words that only serve a grammatical function, such as prepositions and articles. p. 253

temporal lobe The part of the brain associated with hearing. p. 63

teratogen Any agent that causes birth defects. p. 77

teratology The field of study that focuses on birth defects. p. 77

tertiary circular reactions Infant (12–18 mo.) purposefully explores new possibilities with objects, continuously changing what is done to them and exploring the results. p. 175

testosterone A hormone important in the pubertal development of males. Increasing testosterone levels are clearly linked with development of external genitals, increased weight, and voice change in boys. pp. 96, 492

time-out Strategy to change behavior based on removing the child from a rewarding situation. p. 332

token economy A system, based on operant conditioning, in which an individual in a clinical setting is given artificial rewards, such as poker chips, for socially constructive behavior. The tokens themselves can be exchanged for desirable items and privileges. p. 155

top-dog phenomenon Moving from the top position (in elementary school, as the oldest, biggest, and most powerful students in the school) to the bottom, or lowest, position (in middle, or junior high school, the youngest, smallest, and least powerful group of students). p. 437

trait × situation interaction Combination of the trait approach and situational approach of personality theory that recognizes the importance of characteristics of the child and the role of contexts and situations in modifying determining characteristics of a child's personality. p. 454

trait theory Personality theory based on tendencies or predispositions to respond not to specific situations or stimuli but through relatively general and enduring aspects of the person. p. 451

transactive discussion Reasoning that operates on the reasoning of another individual; of interest to researchers who study the role of communication among peers in moral development. p. 524

transfer components Processes used in generalization, such as using information learned on one task to help solve another task. p. 279

treatment In aptitude–treatment interaction, refers to the educational technique (e.g., structured class or flexible class) adopted in the classroom. p. 435

trophoblast In the differentiation of cells during the germinal period, the embryo and the outer layer of cells of the blastula. p. 73

trust versus mistrust Erikson's first stage of personality development in which the infant develops either the comfortable feeling that those around him care for his/her needs or the worry that his/her needs will not be taken care of. p. 324

twin study Strategies to focus on the genetic relationship between identical twins (monozygotic) and fraternal twins (dizygotic). p. 49

two-factor theory A theory of intelligence stressing that intelligence consists of g for general intelligence and s for specific intelligence. p. 275

unconditioned response (UCR) A reflex; an automatic response to an unconditioned stimulus (UCS). p. 142

unconditioned stimulus (UCS) An environmental event that automatically triggers a response (UCR) without learning having to take place. p. 142

underextension A tendency of children to misuse words by not extending one word's meaning to other appropriate contexts for the word. p. 252

unoccupied play A type of play in which the child is not engaged in activities that are normally regarded as play. The child may stand in one spot, look around the room, or perform random movements that seem to have no goal. p. 419

validity The extent to which a test evaluates what it purports to evaluate. p. 282

variable schedules A reinforcement schedule in which the first correct response after a variable length of time or a variable number of responses is rewarded. p. 149

visual accommodation Maintenance of high visual acuity over a range of viewing distances. p. 115

visual acuity A sensitivity to fine visual detail. p. 115

visual cliff A device used to determine depth perception. It consists of a central board above two checkerboard floors, forming the appearance of a high cliff on one side and a shallow one on the other. A sheet of glass is above both sides, so the deep side just "appears" to be dangerous. p. 116

voicing A way of classifying stop consonant sounds. For example, "ba" and "da" are voiced; "pa" and "ta" are voiceless. An abrupt burst of air accompanies the latter. p. 125

whole-word method A learn-to-read technique that focuses on learning direct associations between whole words and their meanings. p. 266

Whorf/Sapir hypothesis Hypothesis which stresses that the more vocabulary or categories we have, the more our perceptions will be differentiated. p. 236

world views Abstract models which, although untestable, serve to stimulate ideas, issues, and questions that can be tested. p. 20

zygote A single-celled fertilized ovum (egg) created in the reproductive process. p. 45

REFERENCES

Abel, E. L. (1981). Behavioral teratology of alcohol. *Psychological Bulletin, 90,* 564–581.

Achenbach, T. M. (1978). Developmental aspects of psychopathology in children and adolescents. In M. E. Lamb (Ed.), *Social and personality development.* New York: John Wiley.

Achenbach, T. M., & Edelbrock, C. S. (1981). Behavioral problems and competencies reported by parents of normal and clinic-referred children 4 to 16. *Monographs of the Society for Research in Child Development, 46,* (1, Serial No. 188).

Acredolo, L. P. (1977). Developmental changes in the ability to coordinate perspectives of a large-scale space. *Developmental Psychology, 13,* 1–8.

Acredolo, L. P. (1978). Development of spatial orientation in infancy. *Developmental Psychology, 14,* 224–234.

Acredolo, L. P. (1979). Laboratory versus home: The effect of the environment on the 9-month-old infant's choice of spatial reference system. *Developmental Psychology, 15,* 666–667.

Acredolo, L. P., & Evans, D. (1980). Developmental changes in the effects of landmarks on infant spatial behavior. *Developmental Psychology, 16,* 312–318.

Acredolo, L. P., & Hake, J. L. (1982). Infant perception. In B. B. Wolman (Ed.), *Handbook of developmental psychology.* Englewood Cliffs, NJ: Prentice-Hall.

Adams, G., & Fitch, S. A. (1982). Ego state and identity status development: A cross-sequential analysis. *Journal of Personality and Social Psychology, 43,* 574–583.

Adelson, J., & Doehrman, M. J. (1980). The psychodynamic approach to adolescence. In J. Adelson (Ed.), *Handbook of adolescent psychology.* New York: John Wiley.

Adler, A. (1927). *Practice and theory of individual psychology.* New York: Harcourt Brace Jovanovich.

Ainsworth, M. D. S. (1967). *Infancy in Uganda: Infant care and the growth of love.* Baltimore: Johns Hopkins University Press.

Ainsworth, M. D. S. (1973). The development of mother-infant attachment. In B. Caldwell & H. N. Riccuiti (Eds.), *Review of child development research* (Vol. 3). Chicago: University of Chicago Press.

Ainsworth, M. D. S. (1979). Infant-mother attachment. *American Psychologist, 34,* 932–937.

Ainsworth, M. D. S., & Bell, S. M. (1970). Attachment, exploration, and separation: Illustrated by the behavior of one-year-olds in a strange situation. *Child Development, 41,* 49–67.

Akiyami, M. M. (1984). Are language-acquisition strategies universal? *Developmental Psychology, 20,* 219–228.

Aldous, J. (1978, September 22). *Family careers over time.* Address given at the Department of Sociology, Notre Dame University, Notre Dame, IN.

Alexander, J. F., & Malouf, R. E. (1983). Intervention with children experiencing problems in personality and social development. In P. H. Mussen (Ed.), *Handbook of child psychology* (4th ed., Vol. 4). New York: John Wiley.

Allen, G. L., Kirasic, K. C., & King, S. (1985, April). *Preschool children's use of spatial frames of reference in seeking, finding, and remembering where.* Paper presented at the meeting of the Society for Research in Child Development, Toronto.

Allport, G. W. (1937). *Personality.* New York: Holt, Rinehart & Winston.

Allport, G. W. (1961). *Pattern and growth in personality.* New York: Holt, Rinehart & Winston.

Amsterdam, B. K. (1968). *Mirror behavior in children under two years of age.* Unpublished doctoral dissertation, University of North Carolina, Chapel Hill.

Anastasi, A. (1976). *Psychological testing* (2nd ed.). New York: Macmillan.

Anders, T. F., & Chalemian, R. J. (1974). The effect of circumcision on sleep-wake states in human neonates. *Psychosomatic Medicine, 36,* 174–179.

Anderson, D. R., & Levin, S. R. (1976). Young children's attention to "Sesame Street." *Child Development, 47,* 806–811.

Anderson, D. R., & Lorch, E. P. (1983). Looking at television: Action or reaction? In J. Bryant & D. R. Anderson (Eds.), *Children's understanding of television: Research on attention and comprehension.* New York: Academic Press.

Anderson, J. R. (1976). *Language, memory, and thought.* Hillsdale, NJ: Lawrence Erlbaum.

Anderson, J. R. (1980). *A theory of language acquisition based on general learning principles.* Unpublished manuscript, Carnegie–Mellon University, Pittsburgh.

Anderson, J. R., & Bower, G. H. (1973). *Human associative memory.* Washington, DC: Winston.

Anderson, L. D. (1939). The predictive value of infant tests in relation to intelligence at 5 years. *Child Development, 10,* 202–212.

Andrews, S. R., Blumenthal, J. M., Bache, W. L., & Weiner, G. (1975, April). *The New Orleans model: Parents as early childhood educators.* Paper presented at the meeting of the Society for Research in Child Development, Denver.

Aneshensel, C., & Rosen, B. (1980). Domestic roles and sex differences in occupational expectations. *Journal of Marriage and the Family, 42,* 121–131.

Anthony, E. J. (1956). The significance of Jean Piaget for child psychiatry. *British Journal of Medical Psychology, 29,* 20–34.

Apgar, V. A. (1953). A proposal for a new method of evaluation of a newborn infant. *Anesthesia and Analgesia: Current Research, 32,* 260–267.

Aries, P. (1962). *Centuries of childhood* (R. Baldrick, Trans.). New York: Knopf.

Armstrong, B. (1980, November). Illinois judge upholds IQ test use: Departs from Larry P. *APA Monitor,* pp. 6–7.

Asberg, M., Thoren, P., Traskman, L., Bertilsson, L., & Ringberger, V. (1976). Serotonin depression, a biochemical subgroup within the affective disorders. *Science, 191,* 478–480.

Asher, J., & Garcia, R. (1969). The optimal age to learn a foreign language. *Modern Language Journal, 53,* 334–341.

Asher, S. R. (1985, April). *Identification of socially rejected children.* Paper presented at the meeting of the Society for Research in Child Development, Toronto.

Ashmead, D. H., & Perlmutter, M. (1980). Infant memory in everyday life. In M. Perlmutter (Ed.), *New directions in child development, 10: Childrens' memory.* San Francisco: Jossey-Bass.

Aslin, R. N. (1981). Experiential influences and sensitive periods in development: A unified model. In R. N. Aslin, J. R. Alberts, & M. R. Petersen (Eds.), *Development of perception* (Vol. 2). New York: Academic Press.

Aslin, R. N., Pisoni, D. B., & Jusczyk, P. W. (1983). Auditory development and speech perception in infancy. In P. H. Mussen (Ed.), *Handbook of child psychology.* New York: John Wiley.

Atkinson, R. C. (1975). Mnemotechnics in second language learning. *American Psychologist, 30,* 821–828.

Ault, R. L. (1977). *Children's cognitive development.* New York: Oxford University Press.

Austin, L., & Little, L. (1982, April 18). Teen-age suicide: Dallas's growing tragedy. *Dallas Times Herald,* Sec. A, pp. 21–23.

Ausubel, D. P. (1968). *Educational Psychology.* New York: Holt, Rinehart & Winston.

Ausubel, D. P., Sullivan, E. V., & Ives, S. W. (1980). *Theory and problems of child development* (3rd. ed). New York: Grune & Stratton.

Axia, G., & Baroni, M. R. (1985). Linguistic politeness at different age levels. *Child Development, 56,* 918–927.

B

Babladelis, G. (1979). Accentuate the positive. *Contemporary Psychology, 24,* 3–4.

Bailey, K. V. (1970). A study of human growth in the framework of applied nutrition and public health nutrition programs in the Western Pacific region. In J. Brozek (Ed.), *Mongraphs of the Society for Research in Child Development, 35,* (Serial No. 140).

Bakeman, R., & Brown, J. V. (1980). Early interaction: Consequences for social and mental development at three years. *Child Development, 51,* 437–447.

Ball, S. J. (1981). *Beachside comprehensive.* Cambridge: Cambridge University Press.

Baltes, P. B. (1973). Prototypical paradigms and questions in life-span research on development and aging. *The Gerontologist, 13,* 458–467.

Baltes, P. B., Reese, H. W., & Lipsitt, L. P. (1980). Life-span developmental psychology. *Annual Review of Psychology, 31,* 65–110.

Bandura, A. (1965). Influence of models' reinforcement contingencies on the acquisition of imitative responses. *Journal of Personality and Social Psychology, 1,* 589–595.

Bandura, A. (1971). Analysis of modeling processes. In A. Bandura (Ed.), *Psychological modeling.* New York: Liebere-Atherton.

Bandura, A. (1977). *Social learning theory.* Englewood Cliffs, NJ: Prentice-Hall.

Bandura, A., Grusec, J. E., & Menlove, F. L. (1967). Vicarious extinction of avoidance behavior. *Journal of Personality and Social Psychology, 5,* 16–23.

Bandura, A., Ross, D., & Ross, S. A. (1963). Imitation of film-mediated aggressive models. *Journal of Abnormal and Social Psychology, 67,* 527–534.

Bane, M. (1978). *HEW policy toward children, youth, and families.* Discussion paper prepared under Order #SA–8139–77 for the Office of the Assistant Secretary for Planning and Evaluation, Cambridge, MA. (Mimeograph)

Banks, M. S., & Salapatek, P. (1983). Infant visual perception. In P. H. Mussen (Ed.), *Handbook of child psychology* (Vol. 2). New York: John Wiley.

Barcus, F. E. (1978). *Commercial children's television on weekends and weekday afternoons.* Newtonville, MA: Action for Children's Television.

Barenboim, C. (1981). The development of person perception in childhood and adolescence: From behavioral comparisons to psychological constructs to psychological comparisons. *Child Development, 52,* 129–144.

Barker, R., & Wright, H. F. (1951). *One boy's day.* New York: Harper & Row.

Barnes, G. M. (1977). The development of adolescent drinking behavior: An evaluative review of the impact of the socialization process within the family. *Adolescence, 13,* 571–591.

Barnes, K. E. (1971). Preschool play norms: A replication. *Developmental Psychology, 5,* 99–103.

Barnet, A., & Goodwin, R. (1965). Average evoked electroencephalic responses to clicks in the human newborn. *Electroencephalography and Clinical Neurophysiology, 18,* 441–450.

Baron, R. A., & Byrne, D. (1984). *Social psychology* (4th ed.). Boston: Allyn & Bacon.

Barrett, D. E., Radke-Yarrow, M., & Klein, R. E. (1982). Chronic malnutrition and child behavior: Effects of early caloric supplementation on social and emotional functioning at school age. *Developmental Psychology, 18,* 541–556.

Bart, W. M. (1971). The factor structure of formal operations. *The British Journal of Educational Psychology, 41,* 40–77.

Bartlett, F. C. (1932). *Remembering: A study in experimental and social psychology.* Cambridge: Cambridge University Press.

Bartlett, J. C., & Dowling, W. J. (1980). The recognition of transposed melodies: A key-distance effect in developmental perspective. *Journal of Experimental Psychology: Human Perception and Performance, 6,* 501–515.

Baskett, L. (1974). *The young child's interactions with parents and siblings: A behavioral analysis.* Unpublished doctoral dissertation, University of Oregon, Eugene.

Baskett, L. M., & Johnson, S. M. (1982). The young child's interaction with parents versus siblings. *Child Development, 53,* 643–650.

Bates, E. (1979). *The emergence of symbols: Cognition and communication in infancy.* New York: Academic Press.

Bates, E., & McWhinney, B. (1982). A functionalist approach to grammatical development. In L. Gleitman & H. E. Wanner (Eds.), *Language acquisition: The state of the art.* Cambridge: Cambridge University Press.

Baumrind, D. (1971). Current patterns of parental authority. *Developmental Psychology Monographs, 4* (I, Pt. 2).

Baumrind, D. (1972). Socialization and instrumental competence in young children. In W. W. Hartup (Ed.), *The young child* (Vol. 2). Washington, DC: National Association for the Education of Young Children.

Baumrind, D. (1982). Are androgynous individuals more effective persons and parents? *Child Development, 53,* 44–75.

Bayley, N. (1943). Mental growth during the first three years. In R. G. Barker, J. S. Kounin, & H. F. Wright (Eds.), *Child behavior and development.* New York: McGraw-Hill.

Bayley, N. (1965). Comparisons of mental and motor test scores for ages 1–15 months for sex, birth order, race, geographical location, and education of parents. *Child Development, 36,* 379–411.

Bayley, N. (1970). Development of mental abilities. In P. H. Mussen (Ed.), *Carmichael's manual of child psychology* (3rd ed., Vol. 1). New York: John Wiley.

Beck, A. T. (1967). *Depression.* New York: Harper & Row.

Beck, A. T. (1973). *The diagnosis and management of depression.* Philadelphia: University of Pennsylvania Press.

Becker, H. J. (1985). Men and women as computer-using teachers. *Sex Roles, 13,* 137–148.

Becker, J. A., & Smenner, P. C. (1985, April). *The spontaneous use of "thank you" by preschoolers.* Paper presented at the meeting of the Society for Research in Child Development, Toronto.

Becker, W. C., & Krug, R. S. (1964). *A comparison of the ability of the PAS, PARI, parent self-ratings and empirically eyed questionnaire scales to predict ratings of child behavior.* Mimeographed report, University of Illinois, Urbana.

Bee, H. L., & Mitchell, S. K. (1980). *The developing person.* New York: Harper & Row.

Bell, D. (Ed.). (1980). *Shades of brown: New perspectives on school desegregation.* New York: Teachers College Press.

Bell, S. M. (1970). The development of the concept of the object as related to infant-mother attachment. *Child Development, 41,* 291–311.

Belsky, J., & Most, R. (1981). From exploration to play: A cross-sectional study of infant free play behavior. *Developmental Psychology, 17,* 630–639.

Belsky, J., & Steinberg, L. D. (1978). The effects of day care: A critical review. *Child Development, 49,* 929–949.

Bem, D. J., & Allen, A. (1974). On predicting some of the people some of the time: The search for cross-situational consistencies in behavior. *Psychological Bulletin, 81,* 506–520.

Bem, S. L. (1974). The measurement of psychological androgyny. *Journal of Consulting and Clinical Psychology, 42,* 155–162.

Bem, S. L. (1977). On the utility of alternative procedures for assessing psychological androgyny. *Journal of Consulting and Clinical Psychology, 45,* 196–205.

Bender, L. (1974). The family patterns of 100 schizophrenic children observed at Bellevue, 1935–1972. *Journal of Autism and Childhood Schizophrenia, 4,* 279–282.

Benton, A. L., & van Allen, M. W. (1968). Impairment in facial recognition in patients with cerebral disease. *Cortex, 4,* 344–358.

Benton, A. L., & van Allen, M. W. (1973). *Manual: Test of facial recognition. Neurosensory Center Publication 287.* Department of Neurology, University Hospitals, Iowa City, IA.

Bereiter, C. (1975). Individualization and inequality. *Contemporary Psychology, 20,* 455–457.

Berg, C. A., & Sternberg, R. J. (1985, April). *Novelty as a component of intelligence throughout development.* Paper presented at the meeting of the Society for Research in Child Development, Toronto.

Berk, L. E., & Garvin, R. A. (1984). Development of private speech among low-income Appalachian children. *Developmental Psychology, 20,* 271–286.

Berkeley, G. (1709). *An essay towards a new theory of vision.*

Berko, J. (1958). The child's learning of English morphology. *Word, 14,* 150–177.

Berkowitz, M. (1981). A critical appraisal of the educational and psychological perspectives on moral discussion. *Journal of Educational Thought, 15,* 20–33.

Berkowitz, M., & Gibbs, J. (1983). Measuring the developmental features of moral discussion. *Merrill-Palmer Quarterly, 29,* 399–410.

Berkowitz, M., Gibbs, J., & Broughton, J. (1980). The relation of moral judgment stage disparity to development effects of peer dialogues. *Merrill-Palmer Quarterly, 26,* 341–357.

Berlyne, D. (1960). *Conflict, arousal, and curiosity.* New York: McGraw-Hill.

Bernal, M. E. (1972). Behavioral treatment of a child's eating problem. *Journal of Behavior Therapy and Experimental Psychiatry, 3,* 43–50.

Bernard, J., & Sontag, L. W. (1947). Fetal reactivity to tonal stimulation: A preliminary report. *Journal of Genetic Psychology, 70,* 205–210.

Berndt, T. J. (1979). Developmental changes in conformity to peers and parents. *Developmental Psychology, 15,* 608–616.

Berndt, T. J. (1981). Relations between social cognition, nonsocial cognition, and social behavior: The case of friendship. In J. H. Flavell & L. D. Ross (Eds.), *Social cognitive development.* Cambridge: Cambridge University Press.

Berndt, T. J. (1982). The features and effects of friendship in early adolescence. *Child Development, 53,* 1447–1460.

Bertelsen, A., Harvald, A., & Hauge, M. (1977). A Danish twin study of manic-depressive disorders. *British Journal of Psychiatry, 130,* 330–351.

Berzonsky, M. D., Weiner, A. S., & Raphael, D. (1975). Interdependence of formal reasoning. *Developmental Psychology, 11,* 258.

Best, D. L., Williams, J. E., Cloud, J. M., Davis, S. W., Robertson, L. S., Edwards, J. R., Giles, H., & Fowles, J. (1977). Development of sex-trait stereotypes among young children in the United States, England, and Ireland. *Child Development, 48,* 1375–1384.

Bieglow, B. J., & LaGaipa, J. J. (1980). The development of friendship values and choices. In H. C. Foot, A. J. Chapman, & J. R. Smith (Eds.), *Friendship and social relations in children.* New York: John Wiley.

Biemer, L. (1975). Female studies: The elective approach. *Social Science Record, 12,* 7–11.

Bindra, I., & Palfai, T. (1967). Nature of positive and negative incentive motivational effects on general activity. *Journal of Comparative and Physiological Psychology, 63,* 288–297.

Blaine, G. B., & McArthur, C. C. (1971). Problems connected with studying. In G. B. Blaine & C. C. McArthur (Eds.), *Emotional problems of the student* (2nd ed.). New York: Appelton-Century-Crofts.

Blakemore, J. E. O., LaRue, A. A., & Olejnik, A. B. (1979). Sex-appropriate toy preference and the ability to conceptualize toys as sex-role related. *Developmental Psychology, 15,* 339–340.

Blanchard, R. J., & Blanchard, D. C. (1969). Crouching as an index of fear. *Journal of Comparative and Physiological Psychology, 67,* 370–375.

Block, J. (1971). *Lives through time.* Berkeley, CA: Bancroft Books.

Block, J. (1976). Issues, problems, and pitfalls in assessing sex differences: A critical review of the psychology of sex differences. *Merrill-Palmer Quarterly, 22,* 283–308.

Block, J., Patterson, V., Block, J., & Jackson, D. D. (1958). A study of the parents of schizophrenic and neurotic children. *Psychiatry, 21,* 387–397.

Block, J. H. (1973). Conception of sex role: Some cross-cultural and longitudinal perspectives. *American Psychologist, 28,* 512–516.

Block, J. H. (1983). Differential premises arising from differential socialization patterns: Some conjectures. *Child Development, 54,* 1335–1354.

Block, J. H., & Block, J. (1980). The role of ego-control and ego-resiliency in the organization of behavior. In W. A. Collins (Ed.), *Minnesota Symposium on Child Psychology* (Vol. 13). Hillsdale, NJ: Lawrence Erlbaum.

Bloom, B. S. (1983, April). *The development of exceptional talent.* Paper presented at the meeting of the Society for Research in Child Development, Detroit.

Bloom, L. M. (1973). *One word at a time: The use of single-word utterances before syntax.* The Hague: Mouton.

Bloom, L. M., Hood, L., & Lightbown, P. (1974). Imitation in language development: If, when, and why. *Cognitive Psychology, 6,* 380–420.

Blos, P. (1962). *On adolescence.* New York: Free Press.

Blos, P. (1985). *Son and father.* New York: Free Press.

Blyth, D. A., Bulcroft, R., & Simmons, R. G. (1981, August 26). *The impact of puberty on adolescents: A longitudinal study.* Paper presented at the Annual Meeting of the American Psychological Association, Los Angeles.

Blyth, D. A., Simmons, R. G., & Bush, D. (1978). The transitions into early adolescence: A longitudinal comparison of youth in two educational contexts. *Sociology of Education, 51,* 149–162.

Blyth, D. A., Simmons, R. G., & Carlton-Ford, S. (1983). The adjustment of early adolescents to school transitions. *Journal of Early Adolescence, 3,* 105–120.

Bobrow, S., & Bower, G. (1969). Comprehension and recall of sentences. *Journal of Experimental Psychology, 80,* 455–461.

Bombeck, E., & Keane, B. (1971). *Just wait till you have children of your own.* New York: Fawcett/Crest.

Boring, E. G. (1950). *A history of experimental psychology.* New York: Appleton-Century-Crofts.

Bornstein, M. H. (1976). Infants are trichromats. *Journal of Experimental Child Psychology, 21,* 421–445.

Bornstein, M. H. (1978). Visual behavior of the young human infant: Relationships between chromatic and spatial perception and the activity of underlying brain mechanisms. *Journal of Experimental Child Psychology, 26,* 174–192.

Bornstein, M H. (1984). Perceptual development. In M. H. Bornstein & M. E. Lamb (Eds.), *Developmental psychology: An advanced textbook.* Hillsdale, NJ: Lawrence Erlbaum.

Bornstein, M. H., Gross, C., & Wolf, J. (1978). Perceptual similarity of mirror images in infancy. *Cognition, 6,* 89–116.

Borstelmann, L. J. (1983). Children before psychology: Ideas about children from antiquity to the late 1800s. In W. Kessen (Ed.), *Handbook of child psychology* (4th ed., Vol. 4). New York: John Wiley.

Bower, G. H., Black, J. B., & Turner, T. J. (1979). Scripts in memory for text. *Cognitive Psychology, 11,* 177–220.

Bower, T. G. R. (1974). *Development in infancy.* San Francisco: W. H. Freeman.

Bower, T. G. R. (1982). *Development in infancy* (2nd ed.). San Francisco: W. H. Freeman.

Bowers, K. (1973). Situationism in psychology: Analysis and a critique. *Psychological Review, 80,* 307–336.

Bowlby, J. (1958). The nature of the child's tie to his mother. *International Journal of Psychoanalysis, 39,* 35.

Bowlby, J. (1969). *Attachment and loss* (Vol. 1). London: Hogarth (New York: Basic Books).

Bowlby, J. (1973). *Attachment and loss* (Vol. 2). *Separation.* London: Hogarth Press.

Bowlby, J. (1980). *Attachment and loss* (Vol. 3). *Loss, sadness and depression.* New York: Basic Books.

Brackbill, Y. (1962). *Research and clinical work with children.* Washington, DC: American Psychological Association.

Brackbill, Y., & Nichols, P. L. (1982). A test of the confluence model of intellectual development. *Developmental Psychology, 18,* 192–198.

Bracken, B. A. (1985). A critical review of the Kaufman assessment battery for children (K-ABC). *School Psychology Review, 14,* 21–36.

Bradley, R. M., & Stern, I. B. (1977). The development of the human taste bud during the fetal period. *Journal of Anatomy, 101,* 743–752.

Braine, M. D. (1963). The ontogeny of English phrase structure: The first phase. *Language, 39,* 3–13.

Brainerd, C. J. (1972). The age/stage issue in conservation acquisition. *Psychonomic Science, 29,* 15–17.

Brainerd, C. J. (1976). "Stage," "structure," and developmental theory. In G. Steiner (Ed.), *The psychology of the twentieth century.* Munich: Kindler.

Brainerd, C. J. (1978). The stage question in cognitive-developmental theory. *The Behavioral and Brain Sciences, 1,* 173–182.

Bransford, J. D., & Franks, J. J. (1971). Abstraction of linguistic ideas. *Cognitive Psychology, 2,* 331–350.

Bransford, J. D., & Johnson, M. K. (1972). Contextual prerequisites for understanding: Some investigations of comprehension and recall. *Journal of Verbal Learning and Verbal Behavior, 11,* 717–726.

Brazelton, T. B. (1979). Behavioral competence of the newborn infant. *Seminars in Perinatology, 3,* 35–44.

Bremnar, J. G. (1985, April). *The role of active movement in the development of search in infancy.* Paper presented at the meeting of the Society for Research in Child Development, Toronto.

Brittain, C. V. (1963). Adolescent choices and parent-peer cross pressures. *American Sociological Review, 13,* 59–68.

Broadbent, D. E. (1958). *Perception and communication.* London: Pergamon Press.

Brody, G. H., Stoneman, Z., & MacKinnon, C. E. (1982). Role asymmetries in interactions among school-aged children, their younger siblings, and their friends. *Child Development, 53,* 1364–1370.

Brody, S., & Axelrad, S. (1970). *Anxiety and ego formation in infancy.* New York: International Universities Press.

Bronfenbrenner, U. (1970). *Two worlds of childhood: U.S. and U.S.S.R.* New York: Russell Sage Foundation.

Bronfenbrenner, U. (1972). Is 80% of intelligence genetically determined? In U. Bronfenbrenner (Ed.), *Influences on human development.* Hinsdale, IL: Dryden Press.

Bronfenbrenner, U. (1979). Contexts of child rearing: Problems and prospects. *American Psychologist, 34,* 844–850.

Bronfenbrenner, U., & Garbarino, J. (1976). The socialization of moral judgment and behavior in cross-sectional perspective. In T. Lickona (Ed.), *Moral development and behavior.* New York: Holt, Rinehart & Winston.

Bronstein, P. (1984). Differences in mothers' and fathers' behaviors toward children: A cross-cultural comparison. *Developmental Psychology, 20,* 995–1003.

Brook, C. G. D., Lloyd, J. K., & Wolf, O. H. (1972). Relation between age of onset of obesity and size of adipose cells. *British Medical Journal, 2,* 23–27.

Brookover, W., Beady, C., Flood, P., Schweitzer, J., & Wisenbaker, J. (1979). *School social systems and student achievement: Schools can make a difference.* New York: Praeger.

Brophy, J. (1979). Teacher behavior and its effects. *Journal of Educational Psychology, 71,* 733–750.

Brophy, J., & Everston, C. (1974). *The Texas teacher effectiveness project: Presentation of nonlinear relationships and summary discussion* (Report No. 74–6). Austin: University of Texas Research and Development Center for Teacher Education.

Brophy, J., & Everston, C. (1976). *Learning from teaching: A developmental perspective.* Boston: Allyn & Bacon.

Broughton, J. (1981). Piaget's structural developmental psychology IV. Knowledge without a self and without history. *Human Development, 24,* 320–346.

Brown, A. L. (1976). Semantic integration in childrens' reconstruction of narrative sequences. *Cognitive Psychology, 8,* 247–262.

Brown, A. L., Bransford, J. D., Ferrara, R. A., & Campione, J. C. (1983). Learning, remembering, and understanding. In P. H. Mussen (Ed.), *Handbook of child psychology* (4th ed., Vol. 3). New York: John Wiley.

Brown, J. V., & Bakeman, R. (1980). Relationships of human mothers with their infants during the first year of life. In R. W. Bell & W. P. Smotherman (Eds.), *Maternal influences and early behavior.* Jamaica, NY: Spectrum.

Brown, R. (1973). *A first language: The early stages.* Cambridge, MA: Harvard University Press.

Brown, R. (1979). *Psycholinguistics.* New York: Free Press.

Brown, R., Cazden, C. B., & Bellugi-Klima, U. (1969). The child's grammar from I to III. In J. P. Hill (Ed.), *Minnesota Symposia on Child Psychology* (Vol. 2). Minneapolis: University of Minnesota Press.

Brown, R., & Hanlon, C. (1970). Derivational complexity and order of acquisition in child speech. In J. R. Hayes (Ed.), *Cognition and the development of language.* New York: John Wiley.

Brownell, C. A., & Brown, E. (1985, April). *Toddler peer interactions in relation to cognitive development.* Paper presented at the meeting of the Society for Research in Child Development, Toronto.

Bruch, H. (1973). *Eating disorders.* New York: Basic Books.

Bruner, J. S. (1964). The course of cognitive growth. *American Psychologist, 19,* 1–15.

Bruner, J. S. (1966). *Toward a theory of instruction.* Cambridge, MA: Harvard University Press.

Bruner, J. S. (1975). From communication to language: A psychological perspective. *Cognition, 3,* 255–287.

Bruno, F. J. (1983). *Adjustment and growth.* New York: Wiley.

Bryant, P. (1985, April). *Discussion of papers on spatial problem solving and early cognitive development.* Paper presented at the meeting of the Society for Research in Child Development, Toronto.

Buchwald, A. (1965). Fun with personality test. *American Psychologist, 20,* 990.

Bullock, M. (1985). Animism in childhood thinking: A new look at an old question. *Developmental Psychology, 21,* 217–225.

Burkett, C. L. (1985, April). *Child-rearing behaviors and the self-esteem of preschool aged children.* Paper presented at the meeting of the Society for Research in Child Development, Toronto.

Burleson, B. R. (1985, April). *Communicative correlates of peer acceptance in childhood.* Paper presented at the meeting of the Society for Research in Child Development, Toronto.

Burt, C. (1966). The genetic determination of differences in intelligence: A study of monosygotic twins reared together and apart. *British Journal of Psychology, 57,* 137–153.

Buxton, C. (1973). *Adolescents in schools.* New Haven, CT: Yale University Press.

Cairns, R. (1983). The emergence of developmental psychology. In W. Kessen (Ed.), *Handbook of child psychology* (4th ed., Vol. 4). New York: John Wiley.

Calvert, S. L., Huston, A. C., Watkins, B. A., & Wright, J. C. (1982). The relation between selective attention to television forms and children's comprehension of content. *Child Development, 53,* 601–610.

Cameron, C. A. (1979). Trials per problem and age as factors in learning set formation of children. *Journal of Experimental Child Psychology, 27,* 410–422.

Campbell, B. K. (1977). An assessment of early mother–infant interaction and the subsequent development of the infant in the first two years of life. *Dissertation Abstracts International, 38,* 1856–1857.

Campbell, M. (1976). Biological intervention in psychosis of childhood. In E. Schopler & R. Reichler (Eds.), *Psychotherapy and child development.* New York: Plenum.

Campbell, T. A., Wright, J. C., & Huston, A. C. (1983, August). *Format cues and content difficulty as determinants of children's cognitive processing of televised educational messages.* Paper presented at the annual meeting of the American Psychological Association, Anaheim, CA.

Campos, J. J., Barrett, K. C., Lamb, M. E., Goldsmith, H. H., & Sternberg, C. (1983). Socioemotional development. In P. H. Mussen (Ed.), *Handbook of child psychology* (4th ed., Vol. 2). New York: John Wiley.

Campos, J. J., Langer, A., & Krowitz, A. (1970). Cardiac responses on the visual cliff in prelocomotor human infants. *Science, 170,* 196–197.

Caplan, F., & Caplan, T. (1981). *The second twelve months of life.* New York: Basic Books.

Caplan, P. (1978, August). *Erikson's concept of inner space: A data-based reevaluation.* Paper presented at the meeting of the American Psychological Association, Toronto.

Carey, S. (1977). The child as a word learner. In M. Halle, J. Bresnan, & G. A. Miller (Eds.), *Linguistic theory and psychological reality.* Cambridge, MA: MIT Press.

Carey, S. (1981). The development of face perception. In G. Davies, H. Ellis, & J. Shepherd (Eds.), *Perceiving and remembering faces.* New York: Academic Press.

Carey, S., Diamond, R., & Woods, B. (1980). The development of face recognition—A maturational component? *Developmental Psychology, 16,* 257–269.

Carlson, S. G., Fagerberg, H., Horneman, G., Hwang, C. P., Larsson, K., Rodlholm, M., Schaller, J., Danielsson, B., & Gundewall, C. (1979). Effects of various amounts of contact between mother and child on the mother's nursing behavior. *Developmental Psychobiology, 11,* 143–150.

Carper, L. (1978, April). Sex roles in the nursery. *Harper's.*

Case, R. (1984). The process of stage transition: A neo-Piagetian view. In R. J. Sternberg (Ed.), *Mechanisms of cognitive development.* San Francisco: W. H. Freeman.

Case, R., Kurland, D. M., & Goldberg, J. (1982). Operational efficiency and the growth of short-term memory span. *Journal of Experimental Child Psychology, 33,* 386–404.

Casteñada, A., Ramirez, M., Cortes, C. E., & Barrera, M. (Eds.) (1971). *Mexican-Americans and educational change.* Unpublished manuscript, University of California, Riverside.

Cattell, R. B. (1963). Theory of fluid and crystallized intelligence: A critical experiment. *Journal of Educational Psychology, 54,* 1–22.

Cattell, R. B. (1965). *The scientific analysis of personality.* Baltimore: Penguin Books.

Caudill, W. (1971). Tiny dramas: Vocal communication between mother and infant in Japanese and American families. In W. Lebra (Ed.), *Mental health research in Asia and the Pacific* (Vol. 2). Honolulu: East-West Center Press.

Caudill, W., & Frost, L. (1972). A comparison of maternal care and infant behavior in Japanese-American, American, and Japanese families. In U. Bronfenbrenner (Ed.), *Influences on human development.* Hinsdale, IL: Dryden Press.

Ceci, S. J., & Bronfenbrenner, V. (1985). "Don't forget to take the cupcakes out of the oven": Prospective memory, strategic time-monitoring, and context. *Child Development, 56,* 152–164.

Chaillé, C. (1978). The child's conceptions of play, pretending, and toys: Sequences and structural parallels. *Human Development, 21,* 201–210.

Chall, J. S. (1967). *Learning to read: The great debate.* New York: McGraw-Hill.

Chance, P. (1979). *Learning and behavior.* Belmont, CA: Wadsworth.

Chang, H. W., & Trehub, S.E. (1977). Auditory processing of relational information by young infants. *Journal of Experimental Child Psychology, 24,* 324-331.

Chase, W. G., & Simon, H. A. (1973). Perception in chess. *Cognitive Psychology, 4,* 55–81.

Chen, M. (1985). Gender differences in adolescents' uses of and attitudes toward computers. In M. McLaughlin (Ed.), *Communication Yearbook* (Vol. 10). Beverly Hills, CA: Sage Publications.

Chernin, K. (1981, November 22). Women and weight consciousness. *New York Times News Service.*

Cherry, L. (1975). The preschool teacher-child dyad: Sex differences in verbal interaction. *Child Development, 46,* 532–535.

Cherry-Wilkinson, L., Clevenger, M., & Dolloghan, C. (1981). Communication in small instructional groups: A sociolinguistic approach. In W. P. Dickson (Ed.), *Children's oral communication skills.* New York: Academic Press.

Chess, S., & Hassibi, M. (1978). *Principles and practice of child psychiatry.* New York: Plenum.

Chess, S., & Thomas, A. (1977). Temperamental individuality from childhood to adolescence. *Journal of Child Psychology and Psychiatry, 16,* 218–226.

Chess, S., & Thomas, A. (1982). Infant bonding: Mystique and reality. *American Journal of Orthopsychiatry, 52,* 213–222.

Chi, M. T. H. (1978). Knowledge structures and memory development. In R. Siegler (Ed.), *Childrens' thinking: What develops?* Hillsdale, NJ: Lawrence Erlbaum.

Chomsky, N. (1957). *Syntactic structures.* The Hague: Mouton.

Chomsky, N. (1965). *Aspects of the theory of syntax.* Cambridge, MA: MIT Press.

Cicchetti, D. (1984). The emergence of developmental psychopathology. *Child Development, 55,* 1–7.

Cicirelli, V. G. (1972). The effects of sibling relationship on concept learning of young children taught by child teachers. *Child Development, 43,* 282–287.

Cicirelli, V. G. (1977). Family structure and socialization: Sibling effects on socialization. In M. McMillan & M. Sergio (Eds.), *Child psychiatry: Treatment and research.* New York: Brunner/Mazel.

Clark, E. V. (1972). On the child's acquisition of antonyms in two semantic fields. *Journal of Verbal Learning and Verbal Behavior, 11,* 750–758.

Clark, E. V. (1973). What's in a word: On the child's acquisition of semantics in his first language. In T. E. Moore (Ed.), *Cognitive development and the acquisition of language.* New York: Academic Press.

Clark, E. V. (1979). Building a vocabulary: Words for objects, actions, and relations. In P. Fletcher & M. Garman (Eds.), *Language acquisition.* Cambridge: Cambridge University Press.

Clark, E. V. (1983). Meanings and concepts. In P. H. Mussen (Ed.), *Handbook of child psychology* (4th ed., Vol. 3). New York: John Wiley.

Clark, H. H., & Clark, E. V. (1977). *Psychology and language.* New York: Harcourt Brace Jovanovich.

Clark, K. (1965). *Dark ghetto.* New York: Harper & Row.

Clarke-Stewart, K. A. (1978). Recasting the lone stranger. In J. Glick & K. A. Clarke-Stewart (Eds.), *The development of social understanding.* New York: Gardner Press.

Clarke-Stewart, K. A., & Fein, G. G. (1983). Early childhood programs. In P. H. Mussen (Ed.), *Handbook of child psychology* (4th ed., Vol. 4). New York: John Wiley.

Colby, A., Kohlberg, L., Gibbs, J., & Lieberman, M. (1980). *A longitudinal study of moral judgment.* Unpublished manuscript, Harvard University, Cambridge, MA.

Cole, M., & Scribner, S. (1974). *Culture and thought: A psychological introduction.* New York: John Wiley.

Coleman, J. S., Campbell, E. Q., & Hobson, C. J. (1966). *Equality of educational opportunity* (2 vols.). Washington, DC: U.S. Government Printing Office.

Coletta, N. D. (1978). *Divorced mothers at two income levels: Stress, support, and child-rearing practices.* Unpublished thesis, Cornell University, Ithaca, NY.

Collins, R. C. (1983, Summer). Head Start: An update on program effects. *Newsletter of the Society for Research in Child Development,* pp. 1–2.

Collis, B. A. (1984). *The development of an instrument to measure attitudes of secondary school males.* Unpublished doctoral dissertation, University of Victoria, British Columbia.

Columbo, J. (1985, April). *Infant attention to FM sweeps.* Paper presented at the meeting of the Society for Research in Child Development, Toronto.

Constantinople, A. (1969). An Eriksonian measure of personality development in college students. *Developmental Psychology, 1,* 357–372.

Cook, T. D., & Campbell, D. T. (1979). *Quasi-experimentation.* Chicago: Rand McNally.

Coopersmith, S. (1967). *The antecedents of self-esteem.* San Francisco: W. H. Freeman.

Corrigan, R. (1981). The effects of task and practice on search for invisibly displaced objects. *Developmental Review, 1,* 1–17.

Courtney, A. E., & Lockeretz, S. W. (1971). Woman's place: An analysis of the roles portrayed by women in magazine advertisements. *Journal of Marketing Research, 8,* 92–95.

Cowan, M. (1979). The development of the brain. *Scientific American, 241,* 112–133.

Craig-Bray, L., & Adams, G. R. (1985, April). *Different methodologies in the assessment of identity: Congruence between self-report and interview techniques.* Paper presented at the meeting of the Society for Research in Child Development, Toronto.

Craik, F. I. M., & Lockhart, R. S. (1972). Levels of processing: A framework for memory research. *Journal of Verbal Learning and Verbal Behavior, 11,* 671–684.

Crandall, V. J., & Rabson, A. (1960). Children's repetition choices in an intellectual achievement situation following success and failure. *Journal of Genetic Psychology, 97,* 161–168.

Cratty, J. (1974). *Psychomotor behavior in education and sport.* Springfield, IL: Charles C Thomas.

Crawford, J. W. (1982). Mother–infant interaction in premature and full-term infants. *Child Development, 53,* 957–962.

Crockenberg, S. (1985, April). *Social support and the maternal behavior of adolescent mothers.* Paper presented at the meeting of the Society for Research in Child Development, Toronto.

Cronbach, L. J. (1970). *Essentials of psychological testing.* New York: Harper & Row.

Cronbach, L. J., & Snow, R. E. (1977). *Aptitudes and instructional methods.* New York: Irvington Books.

Crook, C. K., & Lipsett, L. P. (1976). Neonatal nutritive sucking: Effects of taste stimulation upon sucking rhythm and heart rate. *Child Development, 47,* 518–522.

Cross, K. P. (1984, November). The rising tide of school reform reports. *Phi Delta Kappan.*

Crowder, R. (1982). *The psychology of reading.* New York: Oxford University Press.

Crowe, R. R. (1974). An adoption study of antisocial personality. *Archives of General Psychiatry, 31,* 785–791.

Curtiss, S., Fromkin, V. A., Rigler, D., Rigler, M., & Krashen, S. (1975). An update on the linguistic development of Genie. In D. P. Dato (Ed.), *Georgetown University Round Table on Language and Linguistics.* Washington, DC: Georgetown University Press.

Cushna, B. (1966). *Agency and birth order differences in early childhood.* Paper presented at the meeting of the American Psychological Association, New York.

D

Dale, P. S. (1976). *Language development: Structure and function* (2nd ed.). New York: Holt, Rinehart & Winston.

Damon, W. (1977). *The social world of the child*. San Francisco: Jossey-Bass.

Daniels, P., & Weingarten, K. (1980). *Sooner or later: The timing of parenthood in adult lives*. New York: Norton.

Danner, F. (1986). Personal communication, quoted in Lapsley, D. K., Enright, R. D., & Serlin, R. C., Moral and social education. In J. Worrell & F. Danner (Eds.), *Adolescent development: Issues in education*. New York: Academic Press.

Darley, J. M., & Latane, B. (1968). Bystander intervention in emergencies: Diffusion of responsibility. *Journal of Personality and Social Psychology, 8,* 377–383.

Davids, A., & Hainsworth, P. K. (1967). Maternal attitudes about family life and child rearing as avowed by mothers and perceived by their underachieving and high achieving sons. *Journal of Consulting Psychology, 31,* 29–37.

Davison, G. C., & Neale, J. M. (1975). *Abnormal psychology*. New York: John Wiley.

de Villiers, J. G., & de Villiers, P. A. (1978). *Language acquisition*. Cambridge, MA: Harvard University Press.

DeCasper, A. J., & Fifer, W. P. (1980). Of human bonding: Newborns prefer their mothers' voices. *Science, 208,* 1174–1176.

Deci, E. L., & Ryan, R. M. (1980). The empirical exploration of intrinsic motivational processes. *Advances in Experimental Social Psychology, 13,* 39–80.

Deckhard, B. S. (1979). *The woman's movement*. New York: Harper & Row.

DeFries, J. C., Plomin, R., Vandenberg, S. G., & Kuse, A. R. (1981). Parent–offspring resemblance in cognitive abilities in the Colorado adoption project: Biological, adoption, and control parents and one-year-old children. *Intelligence, 5,* 245–277.

DeLoache, J. S., Cassidy, D. J., & Brown, A. L. (1985). Precursors of mnemonic strategies in very young children's memory. *Child Development, 56,* 125–137.

Demany, L. (1982). Auditory stream segregation in infancy. *Infant Behavior and Development, 5,* 215–226.

Demorest, A., Meyer, C., Phelps, E., Gardner, H., & Winner, E. (1984). Words speak louder than actions: Understanding deliberately false remarks. *Child Development, 55,* 1527–1534.

Demoss, V. (1980, June). Good, the bad, and the edible. *Runner's World*, p. 45.

Dempster, F. N. (1981). Memory span: Sources of individual and developmental differences. *Psychological Bulletin, 89,* 63–100.

Dempster, F. N. (1985). Short-term memory development in childhood and adolescence. In C. J. Brainerd & M. Pressley (Eds.), *Basic processes in memory development: Progress in cognitive development research*. New York: Springer-Verlag.

DeOreo, K. L. (1976). *Current work on the assessment of the development of gross motor skills*. Unpublished manuscript, Kent State University, Kent, OH.

Desor, J. A., Mallor, O., & Greene, L. S. (1977). Preference for sweet in humans: Infants, children and adults. In J. F. Weiffenbach (Ed.), *Taste and development*. Washington, DC: Department of Health, Education, and Welfare.

Devereaux, E. C. (1970). The role of peer-group experience in moral development. In J. P. Hill (Ed.), *Minnesota Symposium on Child Psychology* (Vol. 4). Minneapolis: University of Minnesota Press.

Dewey, J. (1933). *How we think: A restatement of the relation of reflective thinking to the educative process*. Lexington, MA: D. C. Heath.

Diamond, A. (1985). Development of the ability to use recall to guide action, as indicated by infants' performance on AB. *Child Development, 56,* 868–883.

Diaz, R. M., & Berndt, T. J. (1982). Children's knowledge of a best friend: Fact or fancy? *Developmental Psychology, 18,* 787–794.

Dickinson, A. (1980). *Contemporary animal learning theory*. Cambridge: Cambridge University Press.

Dickstein, E. (1977). Self and self-esteem: Theoretical functions and their implications for research. *Human Development, 20,* 219–240.

Dillon, R. S. (1980). *Diagnosis and management of endocrine and metabolic disorders*. (2nd ed.). Philadelphia: Lea & Febiger.

Dodge, K. A. (1980). Social cognition and children's aggressive behavior. *Child Development, 51,* 162–170.

Dodge, K. A. (1983). Behavioral antecedents of peer social status. *Child Development, 54,* 1386–1399.

Dodge, K. A. (1985, April). *Assessment and training of social skills*. Paper presented at the meeting of the Society for Research in Child Development, Toronto.

Dodge, K. A., & Frame, C. L. (1982). Social cognitive biases and deficits in aggressive boys. *Child Development, 53,* 620–635.

Dodge, K. A., Murphy, R. R., & Buchsbaum, K. (1984). The assessment of intention-cue detection skills: Implications for developmental psychopathology. *Child Development, 55,* 163–173.

Dodge, K. A., & Newmann, J. P. (1981). Biased decision-making processes in aggressive boys. *Journal of Abnormal Psychology, 90,* 375–379.

Doherty, S., & Pellegrino, J. W. (1985, April). *Developmental changes in neighborhood knowledge*. Paper presented at the meeting of the Society for Research in Child Development, Toronto.

Dolgin, K. G., & Behrend, D. A. (1984). Children's knowledge about animates and inanimates. *Child Development, 55,* 1646–1650.

Douvan, E., & Adelson, J. (1966). *The adolescent experience*. New York: John Wiley.

Dowling, W. J. (1982). Melodic information processing and its development. In D. Deutsch (Ed.), *The psychology of music*. New York: Academic Press.

Downing, M. (1974). Heroine of the daytime serial. *Journal of Communication, 24,* 130–137.

Drachman, D. A. (1978). Central cholinergic system and memory. In M. A. Lipton, A. DiMascio, & K. F. Killam (Eds.), *Psychopharmacology: A generation of progress*. New York: Raven Press.

Duck, S. W. (1975). Personality similarity and friendship choices by adolescents. *European Journal of Social Psychology, 5,* 351–365.

Dudek, S. Z. (1974). Creativity in young children—Attitude or ability? *Journal of Creative Behavior, 8,* 282–292.

Dunn, J., & Kendrick, C. (1981). Social behavior of young siblings in the family context: Differences between same-sex and different-sex dyads. *Child Development, 52,* 1265–1273.

Dunn, J., & Kendrick, C. (1982). *Siblings.* Cambridge, MA: Harvard University Press.

Dunn, J., & Kendrick, C. (1985). Siblings and development. In W. W. Hartup & Z. Rubin (Eds.), *Relationships and development.* Hillsdale, NJ: Lawrence Erlbaum.

Dunphy, D. C. (1963). The social structure of urban adolescent peer groups. *Society, 26,* 230–246.

Dusek, J. B., & Flaherty, J. F. (1981). The development of self-concept during the adolescent years. *Monographs of the Society for Research in Child Development, 46* (No. 4).

Dweck, C. S. (1975). The role of expectation and attribution in the alleviation of learned helplessness. *Journal of Personality and Social Psychology, 31,* 674–685.

Dweck, C. S., & Bush, E. S. (1976). Sex differences in learned helplessness: I. Differential debilitation with peer and adult evaluators. *Developmental Psychology, 12,* 147–156.

Dwek, C. S., & Elliot, E. S. (1983). Achievement motivation. In P. H. Mussen (Ed.), *Handbook of child psychology* (4th ed., Vol. 4). New York: John Wiley.

Dweck, C. S., & Gilliard, D. (1975). Expectancy statements as determinants of reactions to failure: Sex differences in persistence and expectancy change. *Journal of Personality and Social Psychology, 32,* 1077–1088.

Dweck, C. S., & Reppucci, N. D. (1973). Learned helplessness and reinforcement responsibility in children. *Journal of Personality and Social Psychology, 25,* 109–116.

Earley, L. A., Griesler, P. C., & Rovee-Collier, C. (1985, April). *Ontogenetic changes in retention in early infancy.* Paper presented at the meeting of the Society for Research in Child Development, Toronto.

Eaves, L. J. (1978). Twins as a basis for the causal analysis of human personality. In W. E. Nance (Ed.), *Twin research proceedings.* New York: Liss.

Ebbinghaus, H. D. (1964). *Memory: A contribution to experimental psychology.* New York: Dover. (Original work published 1885; translated 1913)

Eckerman, C. O., Whatley, J. L., & Kutz, S. L. (1975). The growth of social play with peers during the second year of life. *Developmental Psychology, 11,* 42–49.

Edmonds, R. (1979). Some schools work and more can. *Social Policy, 9,* 28–32.

Ehrhardt, A., & Baker, S. W. (1973, March). *Hormonal aberrations and their implications for understanding of normal sex differentiation.* Paper presented at the meeting of the Society for Research in Child Development, Philadelphia.

Eichorn, D. H. (1970). Physiological development. In P. H. Mussen (Ed.), *Manual of child psychology* (3rd ed., Vol. 1). New York: John Wiley.

Eid, E. E. (1970). Follow-up study of physical growth of children who had excessive weight gain in the first six months of life. *British Medical Journal, 2,* 74–76.

Eimas, P. D. (1975). Speech perception in early infancy. In L. B. Cohen & P. Salapatek (Eds.), *Infant perception: From sensation to cognition* (Vol. 2). New York: Academic Press.

Eimas, P. D., Siqueland, E. R., Jusczyk, P. W., & Vigorito, J. (1971). Speech perception in infants. *Science, 171,* 303–306.

Elashoff, J. D., & Snow, R. E. (1971). *Pygmalion reconsidered.* Worthington, OH: Charles A. Jones.

Elder, G. H. (1980). *Family structure and socialization.* New York: Arno Press.

Elder, G. H. (1968). Democratic parent-youth relationships in cross-national perspective. *Social Science Quarterly, 40,* 216–228.

Elkind, D. (1969). Piagetian and psychometric conceptions of intelligence. *Harvard Educational Review, 39,* 319–337.

Elkind, D. (1976). *Child development and education: A Piagetian perspective.* New York: Oxford University Press.

Elkind, D. (1981). *The hurried child.* Reading, MA: Addison-Wesley.

Emde, R., Harmon, R., Metcalf, D., Koenig, K., & Wagonfeld, S. (1971). Stress and neonatal sleep. *Psychosomatic Medicine, 33,* 491–497.

Emma Willard Task Force on Education. (1971). *Sexism in education.* Minneapolis, MN: Author.

Emmerich, W. (1979, March). *Developmental trends in sex-stereotyped values.* Paper presented at the meeting of the Society for Research in Child Development, San Francisco.

Emmerich, W., Goldman, K. S., & Shore, R. E. (1971). Differentiation and development of social norms. *Journal of Personality and Social Psychology, 18,* 323–353.

Endler, N. S. (1973). The person versus the situation—A pseudo issue? *Journal of Personality, 41,* 287–303.

Engen, T., & Lipsett, L. P. (1965). Decrement and recovery of responses to olfactory stimuli in the human neonate. *Journal of Comparative and Physiological Psychology, 59,* 312–316.

Enright, R., Lapsley, D., & Olson, L. (1984). Moral judgment and the social cognitive developmental research program. In S. Modgil & C. Modgil (Eds.), *Lawrence Kohlberg: Consensus and controversy.* Slough: NFER Press.

Enslein, J., & Fein, G. G. (1981). Temporal and cross-situational stability of children's social and play behavior. *Developmental Psychology, 17,* 760–761.

Entus, A. K. (1975). *Hemispheric asymmetry in processing of dichotically presented speech and nonspeech stimuli by infants.* Paper presented at the meeting of the Society for Research in Child Development, Denver.

Epstein, H. T. (1978). Growth spurts during brain development: Implications for educational policy and practice. In J. S. Chall & A. F. Mirsky (Eds.), *Education and the brain.* Chicago: University of Chicago Press.

Epstein, H. T. (1980). EEG developmental stages. *Developmental Psychobiology, 13,* 629–631.

Epstein, J. L. (1980). *After the bus arrives: Resegregation in desegregated schools.* Paper presented at the meeting of the American Educational Research Association, Boston.

Epstein, J. L. (1983). Selecting friends in contrasting secondary school environments. In J. L. Epstein & N. L. Karweit (Eds.), *Friends in school.* New York: Academic Press.

Ericsson, K. A., & Simon, H. A. (1978). *Retrospective verbal reports as data.* Unpublished manuscript, Carnegie-Mellon University, Pittsburgh.

Erikson, E. H. (1950). *Childhood and society.* New York: Norton.

Erikson, E. H. (1962). *Young man Luther.* New York: Norton.

Erikson, E. H. (1968). *Identity: Youth and Crisis.* New York: Norton.

Erikson, E. H. (1969). *Gandhi.* New York: Norton.

Erikson, E. H. (1970). Reflections on the dissent of contemporary youth. *International Journal of Psychoanalysis, 51,* 11–22.

Esposito, D. (1973). Homogeneous and heterogeneous ability grouping: Principal findings and implications for evaluating and designing more effective educational environments. *Review of Educational Research, 43,* 163–179.

Eysenck, H. J. (1967). *The biological basis of personality.* Springfield, IL: Charles C Thomas.

Eysenck, H. J., & Rachman, S. (1965). *The causes of and cures of neurosis.* San Diego: Knapp.

F

Fabricius, W. V., & Hagen, J. W. (1984). Use of causal attributions about recall performance to assess metamemory and predict strategic memory behavior in young children. *Developmental Psychology, 20,* 975–987.

Fagan, J. F., III. (1972). Infants' recognition memory for faces. *Journal of Experimental Child Psychology, 14,* 453–476.

Fagan, J. F., III. (1985, April). *Early novelty preferences and later intelligence.* Paper presented at the meeting of the Society for Research in Child Development, Toronto.

Fagen, J. W. (1980). Stimulus preference, reinforcer effectiveness, and relational responding in infants. *Child Development, 51,* 372–378.

Fagen, J. W., Ohr, P. S., & Fleckenstein, L. K. (1985, April). *A recency effect on the reactivation of infant memory.* Paper presented at the meeting of the Society for Research in Child Development, Toronto.

Fagot, B. I. (1973). Influence of teacher behavior in the preschool. *Developmental Psychology, 9,* 198–206.

Fagot, B. I. (1974). Sex differences in toddlers' behavior and parental reaction. *Developmental Psychology, 10,* 554–558.

Fagot, B. I. (1975, April). *Teacher reinforcement of feminine-preferred behavior revisited.* Paper presented at the meeting of the Society for Research in Child Development, Denver.

Fagot, B. I. (1977). Consequences of moderate cross-gender behavior in preschool children. *Child Development, 48,* 902–907.

Fantz, R. L. (1958). Pattern vision in young infants. *Psychological Record, 8,* 43–49.

Fantz, R. L. (1961). The origin of form perception. *Scientific Perception, 204,* 66–72.

Fantz, R. L. (1966). Pattern discrimination and selective attention as determinants in infancy. In A. H. Kidd & J. L. Rivoire (Eds.), *Perceptual development in children* (pp. 143–173). New York: International University Press.

Fantz, R. L., Fagan, R. F., & Miranda, S. (1975). Early visual selectivity. In L. Cohen & P. Salapatek (Eds.), *Infant perception: From sensation to cognition.* New York: Academic Press.

Fantz, R. L., & Nevis, S. (1967). Pattern preferences and perceptual-cognitive development in early infancy. *Merrill-Palmer Quarterly, 13,* 77–108.

Fantz, R. L., Ordy, J. M., & Udelf, M. S. (1962). Maturation of pattern vision in infants during the first six months. *Journal of Comparative and Physiological Psychology, 55,* 907–917.

Faust, M. S. (1960). Developmental maturity as a determinant in prestige of adolescent girls. *Child Development, 31,* 173–184.

Faust, M. S. (1977). Somatic development of adolescent girls. *Monographs of the Society for Research in Child Development, 42,* (1, Serial No. 169).

Feigley, D. A., & Spear, N. E. (1970). Effect of age and punishment condition on long-term retention by the rat in active- and passive-avoidance learning. *Journal of Comparative and Physiological Psychology, 73,* 515–526.

Fein, G. G. (1975). A transformational analysis of pretending. *Developmental Psychology, 11,* 291–296.

Fein, G. G. (1978). *Child development.* Englewood Cliffs, NJ: Prentice-Hall.

Fein, G. G., & Apfel, N. (1979). The development of play: Style, structure, and situation. *Genetic Psychology Monographs, 99,* 231–250.

Feiring, C., & Lewis, M. (1978). The child as a member of the family system. *Behavioral Science, 23,* 225–233.

Feldman, S. D. (1973). Impediment or stimulant? Marital status and graduate education. In J. Huber (Ed.), *Changing women in a changing society.* Chicago: University of Chicago Press.

Felner, R. D., Ginter, M., & Primavera, J. (1982). Primary prevention during school transitions: Social support and environmental structure. *American Journal of Community Psychology.*

Fernald, A. (1983). The perceptual and affective salience of mothers' speech to infants. In L. Feagans (Ed.), *The origins and growth of communication.* New Brunswick, NJ: Ablex.

Fernald, A. (1985, April). *Affect and intonation in mothers' speech.* Paper presented at the meeting of the Society for Research in Child Development, Toronto.

Fernald, A., & Kuhl, P. K. (1981, April). *Fundamental frequency as an acoustic determinant of infant preference for motherese.* Paper presented at the meeting of the Society for Research in Child Development, Boston.

Fernald, A., & Simon, T. (1984). Expanded intonation contours in mothers' speech to newborns. *Developmental Psychology, 20,* 104–113.

Field, T. M. (1977). Effects of early separation, interactive effects, and experimental manipulation on mother–infant face-to-face interaction. *Child Development, 48,* 763–771.

Field, T. M. (1978). Interaction patterns of primary versus secondary caretaker fathers. *Developmental Psychology, 14,* 183–185.

Field, T. M. (1979). Visual and cardiac responses to animate and inanimate faces by young term and preterm infants. *Child Development, 50,* 188–194.

Fischer, K. W. (1980). A theory of cognitive development: The control and construction of hierarchies of skills. *Psychological Review, 87,* 477–531.

Fischer, K. W., & Jennings, S. (1981). The emergence of representation in search: Understanding the hider as an independent agent. *Quarterly Review of Development, 1,* 18–30.

Fixsen, D. L., Phillips, E. L., Phillips, E. A., & Wolf, M. M. (1976). The teaching family model group home treatment. In W. E. Craighead, A. E. Kazdin, & M. J. Mahoney (Eds.), *Behavior modification, principles, issues, and applications.* Boston: Houghton Mifflin.

Flavell, J. H. (1974). The development of inferences about others. In T. Mischel (Ed.), *Understanding other persons.* Oxford: Blackwell, Basil, Mott.

Flavell, J. H. (1977). *Cognitive development.* Englewood Cliffs, NJ: Prentice-Hall.

Flavell, J. H. (1979). Metacognition and cognitive monitoring: A new area of psychological inquiry. *American Psychologist, 34,* 906–911.

Flavell, J. H. (1980, Fall). A tribute to Piaget. *Society for Research in Child Development Newsletter.*

Flavell, J. H. (1985). Cognitive development (2nd ed.). Englewood Cliffs, NJ: Prentice-Hall.

Flavell, J. H., Beach, D. R., & Chinsky, J. M. (1966). Spontaneous verbal rehearsal in a memory task as a function of age. *Child Development, 37,* 283–299.

Flavell, J. H., Botkin, P. T., Fry, C. L., Wright, J. W., & Jarvis, P. E. (1968). *The development of communication skills in children.* New York: John Wiley.

Flavell, J. H., Friedrichs, A. G., & Hoyt, J. D. (1970). Developmental changes in memorization processes. *Cognitive Psychology, 1,* 324–340.

Flavell, J. H., & Wellman, H. M. (1977). Metamemory. In R. V. Kail & J. W. Hagen (Eds.), *Perspectives on the development of memory and cognition.* Hillsdale, NJ: Lawrence Erlbaum.

Floredus-Myrhed, B., Pedersen, N., & Rasmussen, I. (1980). Assessment of heritability for personality based on a short form of the Eysenck Personality Inventory: A study of 12,898 twin pairs. *Behavior Genetics, 10,* 153–163.

Forbes, H. S., & Forbes, H. B. (1927). Fetal sense reaction: Hearing. *Journal of Comparative Psychology, 7,* 353–355.

Forehand, G., Ragosta, J., & Rock, D. (1976). *Conditions and processes of effective school desegregation. Final Report, U.S. Office of Education, Dept. of Health, Education, and Welfare.* Princeton, NJ: Educational Testing Service.

Fowler, W. (1978). *Day care and its effects on early development.* Toronto: The Ontario Institute for Studies in Education.

Fowler, W., & Khan, N. (1974). *The later effects of infant group care: A follow-up study.* Toronto: Ontario Institute for Studies in Education.

Fox, N., Kagan, J., & Weiskopf, F. (1979). The growth of memory during infancy. *Genetic Psychology Monographs, 99,* 91–130.

Fraiberg, S. (1971). *Every child's birthright: In defense of mothering.* New York: Basic Books.

Frederickson, C. J. (1985). *The brain.* Unpublished manuscript, University of Texas at Dallas, Richardson, TX.

Fredkin, E. (1982). Commentary. In M. Hunt (Ed.), *The universe within.* New York: Simon & Schuster.

Fregly, M. J., & Luttge, W. G. (1982). *Human endocrinology: An interactive text.* New York: Elsevier Science.

Freud, A. (1958). Adolescence. In R. S. Eissler (Ed.), *Psychoanalytic study of the child* (Vol. 13). New York: International Universities Press.

Freud, A. (1966). *The ego and the mechanisms of defense.* New York: International Universities Press.

Freud, A., & Dann, S. (1951). An experiment in group upbringing. In R. S. Eisler, A. Freud, H. Hartmann, & E. Kris (Eds.), *The psychoanalytic study of the child* (Vol. 6). New York: International Universities Press.

Freud, S. (1935). *A general introduction to psychoanalysis.* New York: Liveright.

Freud, S. (1953). Three essays on the theory of sexuality. In J. Strachey (Ed.), *The standard edition of the complete psychological works of Sigmund Freud* (Vol. 7). London: Hogarth. (Original work published 1905)

Freud, S. (1955). *Fetishism.* In J. Strachey (Ed.), *The standard edition of the complete psychological works of Sigmund Freud* (Vol. 21). London: Hogarth. (Original work published 1927.)

Freud, S. (1959). *Collected papers* (Vol. 3). London: Hogarth Press.

Friedrich, L. K., & Stein, A. H. (1973). Aggressive and prosocial TV programs and the natural behavior of preschool children. *Monographs of the Society for Research in Child Development, 38* (4, Serial No. 151).

Frisch, K. von (1974). Decoding the language of the bee. *Science, 185,* 663–668.

Fromkin, V. A., Krashen, S., Curtiss, S., Rigler, D., & Rigler, M. (1974). The development of language in Genie: A case of language acquisition beyond the "critical period." *Brain and Language, 1,* 81–107.

Fromm, E. (1947). *Man for himself.* New York: Holt, Rinehart & Winston.

Frommer, E., & O'Shea, G. (1973). Antenatal identification of women liable to have problems managing their infants. *British Journal of Psychiatry, 123,* 149–156.

Furman, W., Rahe, D. F., & Hartup, W. W. (1979). Rehabilitation of socially withdrawn preschool children through mixed-age and same-age socialization. *Child Development, 50,* 915–922.

Furstenberg F. F. (1976). *Unplanned parenthood.* New York: Free Press.

Furth, H. G. (1973). *Deafness and learning: A psychosocial approach.* Belmont, CA: Wadsworth.

Furth, H. G., & Wachs, H. (1975). *Thinking goes to school.* New York: Oxford University Press.

Gage, N. L. (1965). Desirable behaviors of teachers. *Urban Education, 1,* 85–96.

Gagne, R. M. (1977). *The conditions of learning* (3rd ed). New York: Holt, Rinehart & Winston.

Gailbraith, R. C. (1982). Sibling spacing and intellectual development: A closer look at the confluence models. *Developmental Psychology, 18,* 151–173.

Galst, J. P. (1980). Television food commercials and pro-nutritional public service announcements as determinants of young children's snack choices. *Child Development, 51,* 935–938.

Garbarino, J. (1976). The ecological correlates of child abuse: The impact of socioeconomic stress on mothers. *Child Development, 47,* 178–185.

Gardner, B. T., & Gardner, R. A. (1971). Two-way communication with an infant chimpanzee. In A. Schrier & F. Stollnitz (Eds.), *Behavior of nonhuman primates* (Vol. 4). New York: Academic Press.

Gardner, H. (1982). *Developmental psychology* (2nd ed.). Boston: Little, Brown.

Gardner, L. I. (1972). Deprivation dwarfism. *Scientific American, 227,* 76–82.

Garmezy, N. (1978). Attentional processes in adult schizophrenia and in children at risk. *Journal of Psychiatric Research, 14,* 3–34.

Garmezy, N. (1981). Children under stress: Perspectives on antecedents and correlates of vulnerability and resistance to psychopathology. In A. I. Rabin, J. Aronoff, A. M. Barclay, & R. A. Zucker (Eds.), *Further explorations in personality.* New York: John Wiley.

Garmezy, N., Masten, A. S., & Tellegen, A. (1984). The study of stress and competence in children: A building block for developmental psychopathology. *Child Development, 44,* 97–111.

Garrison, K. C. (1968). Physiological changes in adolescence. In J. F. Adams (Ed.), *Understanding adolescence: Current developments in adolescent psychology.* Boston: Allyn & Bacon.

Garvey, C. (1977). *Play.* Cambridge, MA: Harvard University Press.

Gaskell, J., & Knapp, H. (1976). *Resource guide for women's studies for high school students.* Victoria, BC: Department of Education.

Gazzaniga, M. S. (1967, August). The split brain in man. *Scientific American,* p. 25.

Gazzaniga, M. S. (1983). Right hemisphere language following brain bisection: A 20-year perspective. *American Psychologist, 38,* 525–537.

Geer, J. H., & Jarmecky, L. (1973). The effect of being responsible for reducing another's pain on subject's response and arousal. *Journal of Personality and Social Psychology, 27,* 232–237.

Geiger, K., & Turiel, E. (1983). Disruptive school behavior and concepts of social convention in early adolescence. *Journal of Educational Psychology, 75,* 677–685.

Geis, G., & Monahan, J. (1976). The social ecology of violence. In T. Lickona (Ed.), *Moral development and behavior.* New York: Holt, Rinehart & Winston.

Gelb, T. J. (1952). *A study of writing.* Chicago: University of Chicago Press.

Gelman, R. (1969). Conservation acquisition: A problem of learning to attend to relevant attributes. *Journal of Experimental Child Psychology, 7,* 167–187.

Gelman, R. (1979). Preschool thought. *American Psychologist, 34,* 900–904.

Gelman, R. (1982). Accessing one-to-one correspondence: Still another paper on conservation. *British Journal of Psychology, 73,* 209–220.

Gelman, R., & Baillargeon, R. (1983). A review of some Piagetian concepts. In P. H. Mussen (Ed.), *Handbook of child psychology.* New York: John Wiley.

Gelman, R., & Spelke, E. (1981). The development of thoughts about animate and inanimate objects: Implications for research. In J. H. Flavell & L. Ross (Eds.), *Social cognitive development: Frontiers and possible futures.* Cambridge: Cambridge University Press.

Gentner, D. (1975). Evidence for the psychological reality of semantic components: The verbal of possession. In D. A. Norman, D. E. Rumelhart, & The LNR research group (Eds.), *Explorations in cognition.* San Francisco: W. H. Freeman.

Gergen, K. J. (in press). Theory of the self: Impasse and evolution. In L. Berkowitz (Ed.), *Advances in experimental social psychology.* New York: Academic Press.

Gesell, A. (1954). The ontogenesis of infant behavior. In L. Carmichael (Ed.), *Manual of child psychology.* New York: John Wiley.

Gesell, A., & Amatruda, C. S. (1941). *Developmental diagnosis.* New York: Hoeber.

Getzels, J. W., & Dillon, T. J. (1973). The nature of giftedness and the education of the gifted. In R. M. W. Travers (Ed.), *Second handbook of research on teaching.* Chicago: Rand McNally.

Gewirtz, J. L. (1969). Mechanisms of social learning. In D. A. Goslin (Ed.), *Handbook of socialization theory and research.* Chicago: Rand McNally.

Gewirtz, J. L., & Gewirtz, H. B. (1965). Stimulus conditions, infant behaviors, and social learning in four Israeli child-rearing environments. In B. M. Foss (Ed.), *Determinants of infant behavior* (Vol. 3). New York: John Wiley.

Ghiselli, E. E. (1966). *The validity of occupational aptitude tests.* New York: John Wiley.

Giaconia, R. M., & Hedges, L. V. (1982). Identifying features of effective open education. *Review of Educational Research, 52,* 579–602.

Gibbs, J., & Schnell, S. V. (1985, April). *Moral development "versus" socialization: A critique of the controversy.* Paper presented at the meeting of the Society for Research in Child Development, Toronto.

Gibson, E. J. (1969). *The principles of perceptual learning and development.* New York: Appleton-Century-Crofts.

Gibson, E. J. (1985, April). *The concept of affordances in comparative development.* Paper presented at the meeting of the Society for Research in Child Development, Toronto.

Gibson, E. J., & Levin, H. (1975). *The psychology of reading.* Cambridge, MA: MIT Press.

Gibson, E. J., & Spelke, E. J. (1983). The development of perception. In P. H. Mussen (Ed.), *Handbook of child psychology.* New York: John Wiley.

Gibson, E. J., & Walk, R. D. (1960). The "visual cliff." *Scientific American, 202,* 64–71.

Gibson, J. J. (1979). *The ecological approach to visual perception.* Boston: Houghton Mifflin.

Gilligan, C. (1982). *In a different voice: Psychological theory and women's development.* Cambridge, MA: Harvard University Press.

Gilligan, C. (1985a). *Responses to critics.* Unpublished manuscript, Harvard University, Cambridge, MA.

Gilligan, C. (1985b, April). *Remapping development*. Paper presented at the meeting of the Society for Research in Child Development, Toronto.

Ginsburg, B., & Allee, W. C. (1942). Some effects of conditioning on social dominance and subordination in inbred strains of mice. *Physiological Zoology, 25*, 485–506.

Gjerde, P. (1985, April). *Adolescent depression and parental socialization patterns: A prospective study*. Paper presented at the meeting of the Society for Research in Child Development, Toronto.

Glaser, R. (1982). Instructional Psychology: Past, present, and future. *American Psychologist, 37*, 292–305.

Glass, D. C., Neulinger, J., & Brim, O. G. (1974). Birth order, verbal intelligence, and educational aspiration. *Child Development, 45*, 807–811.

Gleitman, L. R., & Rozin, P. (1973). Teaching reading by means of a syllabary. *Reading Research, 8*, 447–483.

Glick, P. C. (1977). Updating the life cycle of the family. *Journal of Marriage and the Family, 39*, 5–13.

Glueck, S., & Glueck, E. (1940). *Juvenile delinquents grown up*. New York: Commonwealth Fund.

Gold, D., Andres, D., & Glorieux, J. (1978). The development of Francophone nursery-school children with employed and nonemployed mothers. *Child Development, 49*, 75–84.

Gold, M., & Petronio, R. J. (1980). Delinquent behavior in adolescence. In J. Adelson (Ed.), *Handbook of adolescent psychology*. New York: John Wiley.

Gold, M., & Reimer, D. J. (1975). Changing patterns of delinquent behavior among Americans 13–16 years old, 1967–1972. *Crime and Delinquency Literature, 7*, 483–517.

Goldberg, S. (1977). Prematurity: Effects on parent-infant interaction. *Merrill-Palmer Quarterly, 23*, 163–177.

Goldberg, S., Brachfeld, S., & DiVitto, B. (1980). Feeding, fussing, and play. In T. M. Field, S. Goldberg, D. Stern, & A. M. Sostek (Eds.), *High-risk infants and children: Adult and peer interactions*. New York: Academic Press.

Goldfarb, W. (1970). Childhood psychosis. In P. H. Mussen (Ed.), *Carmichael's manual of child psychology* (3rd ed., Vol. 2). New York: John Wiley.

Goldman-Rakic, P. S., Isseroff, A., Schwartz, M. L., & Bugbee, N. M. (1983). The neurobiology of cognitive development. In P. H. Mussen (Ed.), *Handbook of child psychology* (4th ed., Vol. 2). New York: John Wiley.

Goldsmith, H. H., & Gottesman, I. I. (1981). Origins of variation in behavioral style: A longitudinal study of temperament in young twins. *Child Development, 52*, 91–103.

Gollin, E. S., & Garrison, A. (1980). Relationships between perceptual and conceptual mediational systems in young children. *Journal of Experimental Child Psychology, 30*, 325–335.

Good, T. L., Biddle, B., & Brophy, J. E. (1975). *Teachers make a difference*. New York: Holt, Rinehart & Winston.

Goodall, J. V. L. (1972). *In the shadow of man*. New York: Dell.

Goodlad, J. L. (1983). *A place called school*. New York: McGraw-Hill.

Goodwin, F. K., & Athanasious, P. Z. (1979). Lithium in the treatment of mania. *Archives of General Psychiatry, 36*, 840–844.

Gordon, I. J. (1975). *Human development: A transactional perspective*. New York: Harper & Row.

Goren, C. G., Sarty, M., & Wu, P. Y. K. (1975). Visual following and pattern discrimination of face-like stimuli by newborn infants. *Pediatrics, 56*, 544–549.

Gottesman, I. (1963). Genetic aspects of intellectual behavior. In N. R. Ellis (Ed.), *Handbook of mental deficiency*. New York: McGraw-Hill.

Gottlieb, D. (1966). Teaching and students: The views of negro and white teachers. *Sociology of Education, 37*, 345–353.

Gottlieb, G. (1983). The psychobiological approach to developmental issues. In P. H. Mussen (Ed.), *Handbook of child psychology* (4th ed., Vol. 2). New York: John Wiley.

Gottman, J. H., & Parkhurst, J. T. (1978, October). *A developmental theory of friendship and acquaintenceship processes*. Paper presented at the Minnesota Symposium of Child Psychology, Minneapolis.

Granrud, C. E., Arterberry, M., & Yonas, A. (1985, April). *Size constancy in 12-week-old infants*. Paper presented at the meeting of the Society for Research in Child Development, Toronto.

Granrud, C. E., Yonas, A., Smith, I. M., Arterberry, M. E., Glicksman, M. L., & Sorknes, A. C. (1984). Infants' sensitivity to accretion and deletion of texture as information for depth at an edge. *Child Development, 55*, 1630–1636.

Gratch, G. (1972). A study of the relative dominance of vision and touch in six-month-old infants. *Child Development, 43*, 615–623.

Gratch, G. (1977). Review of Piagetian infancy research: Object concept development. In W. F. Overton & J. M. Gallagher (Eds.), *Knowledge and development* (Vol. 1). New York: Plenum.

Graubard, P. S., & Rosenberg, H. (with F. Gray). (1974, March). Little brother is changing you. *Psychology Today*, pp. 42–46.

Green, R. (1974). One-hundred-ten feminine and masculine boys: Behavioral contrasts and demographic similarities. *Archives of Sexual Behavior, 5*, 425–446.

Greenacre, P. (1971). The childhood of the artist. In P. Greenacre (Ed.), *Emotional growth*. New York: International Universities Press.

Greenberg, B. S., & Domonick, J. R. (1969). *Television behavior among disadvantaged children*. Unpublished manuscript, Michigan State University, East Lansing.

Greenfield, J. (1972). *A child called Noah*. New York: Holt, Rinehart & Winston.

Greeno, J. G. (1978). A study of problem solving. In R. Glaser (Ed.), *Advances in instructional psychology* (Vol. 1). Hillsdale, NJ: Lawrence Erlbaum.

Greenwald, A., & Albert, R. (1968). Acceptance and recall of improvised arguments. *Journal of Personality and Social Psychology, 8*, 31–34.

Greenwald, A., & Pratkanis, A. (in press). The self. In R. Wyer & T. Srull (Eds.), *Handbook of social cognition*. Hillsdale, NJ: Lawrence Erlbaum.

Gross, C. G., & Weisenkrantz, L. (1964). Some changes in behavior produced by lateral frontal lesions in the macaque. In M. M. Warren & K. Akert (Eds.), *The frontal granular cortex and behavior*. New York: McGraw-Hill.

Grossman, H. J. (Ed.). (1977). *Manual on terminology and classification in mental retardation*. Washington, DC: American Association on Mental Deficiency.

Grossman, K., Thane, K., & Grossman, K. E. (1981). Maternal tactual contact of the newborn after various postpartum conditions of mother–infant contact. *Developmental Psychology, 17,* 158–169.

Grotevant, N. D., & Adams, G. R. (1984). Development of an objective measure to assess ego-identity in adolescence: Validation and replication. *Journal of Youth and Adolescence, 13,* 419–438.

Gruendel, J. (1980). *Scripts and stories: A study of childrens' event narratives.* Unpublished doctoral dissertation, Yale University, New Haven, CT.

Grusec, J. E., & Kuczynski, L. (1980). Direction of effects in socialization: A comparison of the parent's versus the child's behavior as determinants of disciplinary techniques. *Developmental Psychology, 16,* 1–9.

Guilford, J. P. (1959). *Personality.* New York: McGraw-Hill.

Guilford, J. P. (1967). *The nature of human intelligence.* New York: McGraw-Hill.

Gump, P. V. (1980). The school as a social situation. In M. R. Rosenzweig &. L. W. Porter (Eds.), *Annual review of psychology* (Vol. 31). Palo Alto: Annual Reviews.

Gunnar, M. R., Malone, S., & Fisch, R. O. (In press). The psychobiology of stress and coping in the human neonate: Studies of adrenocortical activity in response to stress in the first week of life. In T. Field, P. McCabe, & N. Schneidermann (Eds.), *Stress and coping* (Vol. 1). Hillsdale, NJ: Lawrence Erlbaum.

Gutek, B. A., & Bikson, T. K. (1985). Differential experiences of men and women in computerized offices. *Sex Roles, 13,* 123–136.

Guttentag, M., & Bray, H. (1976). *Undoing sex stereotypes: Research and resources for educators.* New York: McGraw-Hill.

Guttentag, R. E. (1984). The mental effort requirement of cumulative rehearsal: A developmental study. *Journal of Experimental Child Psychology, 37,* 92–106.

 H

Haeberle, E. J. (1978). *The sex atlas.* New York: Seabury Press.

Haeckel, E. (1891). *Anthropogenie oder Entwicklungsgeschichte des Menschen* (4th rev. and enl. ed.). Leipzig: Wilhelm Engelmann.

Hahn, C. L. (1975). Eliminating sexism from the schools: Implementing change. *Social Education, 39,* 140–143.

Haith, M. M. (1980). *Rules that babies look by.* Hillsdale, NJ: Lawrence Erlbaum.

Hall, G. S. (1904). *Adolescence* (Vols. 1 and 2). New York: Appleton.

Hallinan, M. T. (1979). Structural effects on children's friendships and cliques. *Social Psychology Quarterly, 42,* 43–54.

Hamm, C. M. (1977). The content of moral education, or in defense of the "bag of virtues." *School Review, 85,* 218–228.

Hanson, D. R., Gottesman, I. I., & Heston, L. L. (1976). Some possible childhood indicators of adult schizophrenia inferred from children of schizophrenics. *British Journal of Psychiatry, 129,* 142–154.

Hardy-Brown, K., & Plomin, R. (1985). Infant communicative development: Evidence from adoptive biological families for genetic and environmental influences on rate differences. *Developmental Psychology, 21,* 378–385.

Harlow, H. F. (1949). The formation of learning sets. *Psychological Review, 56,* 51–65.

Harlow, H. F., & Zimmerman, R. R. (1959). Affectional responses in the infant monkey. *Science, 130,* 421–432.

Harris, P. L. (1975). Development of search and object permanence during infancy. *Psychological Bulletin, 82,* 332–344.

Harris, R. F., Wolf, M. M., & Baer, D. M. (1964). Effects of adult social reinforcement on child behavior. *Young Children, 20,* 8–17.

Harter, S. (1982). The perceived competence scale for children. *Child Development, 53,* 87–97.

Harter, S. (1983). Developmental perspectives on the self system. In P. H. Mussen (Ed.), *Handbook of child psychology* (4th ed., Vol. 4). New York: John Wiley.

Harter, S., & Pike, R. (1984). The Pictorial Scale of Perceived Competence and Social Acceptance for Young Children. *Child Development, 55,* 1969–1982.

Hartley, R. E., Frank, L. K., & Goldenson, R. M. (1952). *Understanding children's play.* New York: Columbia University Press.

Hartshorne, H., & May, M. A. (1928). *Studies in deceit.* New York: Macmillan.

Hartup, W. W. (1970). Peer interaction and social organization. In P. H. Mussen (Ed.), *Carmichael's manual of child psychology* (3rd ed., Vol. 2). New York: John Wiley.

Hartup, W. W. (1976). Peer interaction and the development of the individual child. In E. Schopler & R. J. Reichler (Eds.), *Psychopathology and child development.* New York: Plenum.

Hartup, W. W. (1979). The social worlds of childhood. *American Psychologist, 34,* 944–950.

Hartup, W. W. (1983). Peer relations. In P. H. Mussen (Ed.), *Handbook of child psychology* (4th ed., Vol. 4). New York: John Wiley.

Hartup, W. W. (1985). On relationships and development. In W. W. Hartup & Z. Rubin (Eds.), *Relationships and development.* Hillsdale, NJ: Lawrence Erlbaum.

Hasher, L., & Zacks, R. T. (1979). Automatic and effortful processes in memory. *Journal of Experimental Psychology: General, 108,* 356–388.

Havighurst, R. J., Bowman, P. H., Liddle, G. P., Matthews, C. V., & Pierce, J. V. (1962). *Growing up in River City.* New York: John Wiley.

Hawkins, J. A., & Berndt, T. J. (1985, April). *Adjustment following the transition to junior high school.* Paper presented at the meeting of the Society for Research in Child Development, Toronto.

Hay, D. F. (1985, April). *The search for general principles in social life: Some lessons from young peers.* Paper presented at the meeting of the Society for Research in Child Development, Toronto.

Hayes, K. J., & Hayes, C. (1951). Picture perception in a home-raised chimpanzee. *Journal of Comparative and Physiological Psychology, 46,* 470–474.

Hayne, H., & Rovee-Collier, C. (1985, April). *Contextual determinants of reactivated memories in infants.* Paper presented at the meeting of the Society for Research in Child Development, Toronto.

Hazen, N. L., Lockman, J. J., & Pick, H. L., Jr. (1978). The development of childrens' representations of large-scale environments. *Child Development, 49,* 623–636.

Hecox, K. (1975). Electro-physiological correlates of human auditory development. In L. B. Cohen & P. Salapatek (Eds.), *Infant perception: From sensation to cognition* (Vol. 2). New York: Academic Press.

Heibeck, T. H., & Markman, E. (1985, April). *Word learning in children: An examination of fast mapping.* Paper presented at the meeting of the Society for Research in Child Development, Toronto.

Heider, E. R. (1972). Universals in color naming and memory. *Journal of Experimental Psychology, 93,* 10–20.

Henderson, N. (1982). Human behavior genetics. *Annual Review of Psychology, 33,* 403–440.

Hennessee, J. A., & Nicholson, J. (1972, May 28). NOW says: TV commercials insult women. *New York Times Magazine.*

Hernstein, R. J. (1973). Education, SES, IQ, and their effects. *Contemporary Psychology, 18,* 403–405.

Hess, L., Lonky, E., & Roodin, P. A. (1985, April). *The relationship of moral reasoning and ego strength to cheating behavior.* Paper presented at the meeting of the Society for Research in Child Development, Toronto.

Hess, R. D. (1970). Social class and ethnic influences on socialization. In P. H. Mussen (Ed.), *Carmichael's manual of child psychology* (3rd. ed., Vol. 2). New York: John Wiley.

Hess, R. D., & Miura, I. T. (1985). Gender differences in enrollment in computer camps and classes. *Sex Roles, 13,* 193–203.

Hetherington, E. M. (1972). Effects of father absence on personality development in adolescent daughters. *Developmental Psychology, 7,* 313–326.

Hetherington, E. M. (1977). *My heart belongs to Daddy: A study of the marriages of daughters of divorcées and widows.* Unpublished manuscript, University of Virginia, Charlottesville.

Hetherington, E. M., Cox, M., & Cox, R. (1978). The aftermath of divorce. In J. H. Stevens & M. Mathews (Eds.), *Mother-child/father-child relations.* Washington, DC: National Association for the Education of Young Children.

Hetherington, E. M., Cox, M., & Cox, R. (1982). Effects of divorce on parents and children. In M. E. Lamb (Ed.), *Nontraditional families.* Hillsdale, NJ: Lawrence Erlbaum.

Heward, W. L., & Eachus, H. T. (1979). Acquisition of adjectives and adverbs in sentences written by hearing impaired and aphasic children. *Journal of Applied Behavior Analysis, 12,* 391–400.

Higgins, A., Power, C., & Kohlberg, L. (1983, April). *Moral atmosphere and moral judgment.* Paper presented at the meeting of the Society for Research in Child Development, Detroit.

Higgins, A. T., & Turnure, J. E. (1984). Distractibility and concentration of attention in children's development. *Child Development, 55,* 1799–1810.

Hill, J. P. (1973). *Some perspectives on adolescence in American society.* Unpublished manuscript, Cornell University, Ithaca, NY.

Hill, J. P. (1980a). The early adolescent and the family. In *The seventy-ninth yearbook of the National Study of Education.* Chicago: University of Chicago Press.

Hill, J. P. (1980b). *Understanding early adolescence: A framework.* Carrboro, NC: Center for Early Adolescence.

Hill, J. P. (1983, April). *Adolescent development.* Invited presentation at the meeting of the Society for Research in Child Development, Detroit.

Hill, J. P., & Steinberg, L. (1976, April). *The development of autonomy in adolescence.* Paper presented at the symposium of research on youth problems, Madrid, Spain.

Hinde, R. A. (1983). Ethology and child development. In P. H. Mussen (Ed.), *Handbook of child psychology* (4th ed., Vol. 2). New York: John Wiley.

Hochberg, J. E. (1978). *Perception* (2nd ed.). Englewood Cliffs, NJ: Prentice-Hall.

Hoffman, L. W. (1977). Changes in family roles, socialization, and sex differences. *American Psychologist, 32,* 644-657.

Hoffman, L. W. (1979). Maternal employment: 1979. *American Psychologist, 34,* 859–865.

Hoffman, M. L. (1970). Moral development. In P. H. Mussen (Ed.), *Carmichael's manual of child psychology,* (3rd ed., Vol. 2). New York: John Wiley.

Hoffman, M. L. (1975). Developmental synthesis of affect and cognition and its implications for altruistic motivation. *Developmental Psychology, 11,* 607–622.

Hoffman, M. L. (1979). Development of moral thought, feeling, and behavior. *American Psychologist, 34,* 958–966.

Hoffman, M. L. (1980). Moral development in adolescence. In J. Adelson (Ed.), *Handbook of adolescent psychology.* New York: John Wiley.

Hogarty, G. E., Schooler, N., Ullrich, R., Mussare, F., Ferron, P., & Herron, E. (in press). Depot Fluphenazine and social therapy in the aftercare of schizophrenic patients: Relapse analysis of a two-year controlled trial. *Archives of General Psychiatry.*

Hole, J. W., Jr. (1984). *Human anatomy and physiology.* Dubuque, IA: Wm. C. Brown.

Hollingshead, A. B. (1975). *Elmtown's youth and Elmtown revisited.* New York: John Wiley.

Hollis, M. (1975). Logical operations and role-taking abilities in two cultures: Norway and Hungary. *Child Development, 46,* 638–649.

Holman, D. R. (1975). Teaching about women in secondary schools: Springboard for inquiry. *Social Education, 39,* 140–143.

Honzik, M. P., MacFarlane, J. W., & Allen, L. (1948). The stability of mental test performance between two and eighteen years. *Journal of Experimental Education, 17,* 309–324.

Horney, K. (1937). *The neurotic personality of our time.* New York: Norton.

Houston, J. P. (1981). *Fundamentals of learning and memory.* New York: Academic Press.

Howard, L., & Polich, J. (1985). P300 latency and memory span development. *Developmental Psychology, 21,* 283–289.

Howes, C. (1985, April). *Predicting preschool sociometric status from toddler peer interaction.* Paper presented at the meeting of the Society for Research in Child Development, Toronto.

Hoyenga, K. B., & Hoyenga, K. T. (1979). *The question of sex differences.* Boston: Little, Brown.

Hubbard, R. (1980). Test-tube babies: Solution or problem. *Technology Review, 85.*

Hulme, C. (1984). Developmental differences in the effects of acoustic similarity on memory span. *Developmental Psychology, 20,* 650–652.

Humphreys, L. G., Rich, S. A., & Davey, T. C. (1985). A Piagetian test of general intelligence. *Developmental Psychology, 21,* 872–877.

Hunt, E. (1978). Mechanics of verbal ability. *Psychological Review, 85,* 109–130.

Hunt, E., Frost, N., & Lunneborg, C. (1973). Individual differences in cognition: A new approach to intelligence. In G. H. Bower (Ed.), *The psychology of learning and motivation* (Vol. 7). New York: Academic Press.

Hunt, E., Lansman, M. (1975). Cognitive theory applied to individual differences. In W. K. Estes (Ed.). *Handbook of learning and cognitive processes* (Vol. 1) Hillsdale, NJ: Lawrence Erlbaum.

Hunt, E., Lunneborg, C., & Lewis, J. (1975). What does it mean to be high verbal? *Cognitive Psychology, 7,* 194–227.

Hunt, J. M. (1976). Ordinal scales of infant development and the nature of intelligence. In L. B. Resnick (Ed.), *The nature of intelligence.* Hillsdale, NJ: Lawrence Erlbaum.

Hurlock, E. B. (1980). *Developmental psychology* (5th ed.). New York: McGraw-Hill.

Huston, A. C. (1983). Sex-typing. In P. H. Mussen (Ed.), *Handbook of child psychology* (4th ed., Vol. 4). New York: John Wiley.

Huston, A. C., Siegle, J., & Bremer, M. (1983, April). *Family environment and television use by preschool children.* Paper presented at the meeting of the Society for Research in Child Development, Detroit.

Huston, T. L., & Burgess, R. L. (1980). Social exchange in developing relationships: An overview. In T. L. Huston & R. L. Burgess (Eds.), *Social exchange in developing relationships.* New York: Academic Press.

Huston-Stein, A., & Higgens-Trenk, A. (1978). Development of females from childhood through adulthood: Career and feminine role orientations. In P. Baltes (Ed.), *Life-span development and behavior* (Vol. 1). New York: Academic Press.

Hutchings, B., & Mednick, S. A. (1974). Registered criminality in the adoptive and biological parents of registered male adoptees. In S. A. Mednick, F. Schulsinger, J. Higgins, & B. Bell (Eds.), *Genetics, environment, and psychopathology.* Amsterdam: North Holland.

Hyde, J. S. (1979). *Human Sexuality.* New York: McGraw-Hill.

Hyde, J. S. (1984). Children's understanding of sexist language. *Developmental Psychology, 20* 697–706.

Hyde, J. S. (1985a). *Half the human experience.* Lexington, MA: D. C. Heath.

Hyde, J. S. (1985b). *Understanding human sexuality.* New York: McGraw-Hill.

Hyde, J. S., & Phillis, D. E. (1979). Androgyny across the life span. *Developmental Psychology, 15,* 334–336.

Hyde, J. S., Rosenberg, B. G., & Behrman, J. A. (1977). Tomboyism. *Psychology of Women Quarterly, 2,* 73–75.

Hyman, H. M. (1959). *Political socialization.* New York: Free Press.

Ianotti, R. J. (1978). Effect of role-taking experiences on role taking, altruism, and aggression. *Developmental Psychology, 14,* 119–124.

Isenberg, P. I., & Schatzberg, A. F. (1978). Psychoanalytic contributions to a theory of depression. In J. O. Cole, A. F. Schatzberg, & S. H. Frazier (Eds.), *Depression.* New York: Plenum.

Israel, A. C., Pravder, M. D., and Knights, S. A. (1980). A peer administered program for changing the classroom behavior of disruptive children. *Behavioral Analysis and Modification, 4,* 224–238.

Jacobson, J. L. (1981). The role of inanimate objects in early peer interaction. *Child Development, 52,* 618–626.

Jacobson, S. W. (1983, April). *Maternal caffeine consumption prior to pregnancy: Effects on the newborn.* Paper presented at the Biennial Meeting of the Society for Research in Child Development, Detroit.

Jacoby, L. (1978). On interpreting the effects of repetition: Solving a problem versus remembering a solution. *Journal of Verbal Learning and Verbal Behavior, 17,* 649–667.

James, W. (1950). *The principles of psychology.* New York: Dover. (Original work published 1890)

James, W. (1963). *Psychology.* New York: Fawcett. (Original work published 1890)

Jensen, A. R. (1969). How much can we boost IQ and scholastic achievement? *Harvard Educational Review, 39,* 1–123.

Jensen, A. R. (1974). *Educational differences.* New York: Barnes & Noble.

Johnson, D. M. (1972). *A systematic introduction to the psychology of thinking.* New York: Harper & Row.

Johnston, L. D., Bachman, J. G., & O'Malley, P. M. (1985, January 4). News and Information Services Release, Institute of Social Research, University of Michigan, Ann Arbor.

Jones, K. L., Smith, D. W., Ulleland, C. N., & Streissguth, A. P. (1973). Patterns of malformation in offspring of chronic alcoholic mothers. *Lancet, 1,* 1267–1271.

Jones, W., Chernovetz, M. E., & Hansson, R. O. (1978). The enigma of androgyny: Differential implications for males and females? *Journal of Consulting and Clinical Psychology, 46,* 298–313.

Jose, P. E. (1985, April). *Development of the immanent justice judgment in moral evaluation.* Paper presented at the meeting of the Society for Research in Child Development, Toronto.

Jung, C. G. (1917). *Analytical psychology.* New York: Moffat, Yard.

Kagan, J. (1980) Perspectives on continuity. In O. B. Brim & J. Kagan (Eds.), *Constancy and change in human development.* Cambridge, MA: Harvard University Press.

Kagan, J. (1982). *Psychological research on the human infant: An evaluative summary.* New York: W. T. Grant Foundation.

Kagan, J. (1984). *The nature of the child.* New York: Basic Books.

Kagan, J., Kearsley, R. B., & Zelaso, P. R. (1978). *Infancy: Its place in human development.* Cambridge, MA: Harvard University Press.

Kagan, J., & Moss, H. A. (1962). *Birth to maturity.* New York: John Wiley.

Kahn, J. H., & Nursten, J. P. (1962). School phobias: Refusal, a comprehensive view of school phobia, and other failures of school attendance. *American Journal of Orthopsychiatry, 32,* 707–718.

Kahn, S. E., & Richardson, A. (1983). Evaluation of a course in sex roles for secondary school students. *Sex Roles, 9,* 431–440.

Kail, R. (1984). *The development of memory in children.* San Francisco: W. H. Freeman.

Kail, R. (1985, April). *Development of mental rotation: A speed-accuracy study.* Paper presented at the meeting of the Society for Research in Child Development, Toronto.

Kamin, L. J. (1969). Predictability, surprise, attention, and conditioning. In B. A. Campbell & R. M. Curch (Eds.), *Punishment and aversive behavior.* New York: Appleton-Century-Crofts.

Kamin, L. J. (1974). *The science and politics of IQ.* New York: Halsted Press.

Kandel, D. B. (1978). Similarity in real-life adolescent friendship pairs. *Journal of Personality and Social Psychology, 36,* 306–312.

Kandel, D. B., & Lesser, G. S. (1969). Parent-adolescent relationships and adolescent independence in the United States and Denmark. *Journal of Marriage and the Family, 31,* 348–358.

Kanner, L. (1972). *Child psychiatry* (4th ed.). Springfield, IL: Charles C Thomas.

Karmel, B. Z., & Maisel, E. B. (1975). A neuronal activity model for infant visual attention. In L. B. Cohen & P. Salapatek (Eds.), *Infant perception: From sensation to cognition* (Vol. 1). New York: Academic Press.

Katz, P. A. (1968). *No time for youth: Growth and constraint in college.* San Francisco: Jossey-Bass.

Kaufman, A. S., & Kaufman, N. L. (1983). *Kaufman assessment battery for children: Interpretive manual.* Circle Pines, MN: American Guidance Service.

Kazalunas, J. R. (1978). Sexism in education. *Clearing House, 51,* 388–391.

Keeney, T. J., Cannizzo, S. R., & Flavell, J. H. (1967). Spontaneous and induced verbal rehearsal in a recall task. *Child Development, 38,* 953–966.

Keil, F. C. (1984). Mechanisms in cognitive development and the structure of knowledge. In R. J. Sternberg (Ed.), *Mechanisms of cognitive development.* San Francisco: W. H. Freeman.

Keith, T. Z. (1985). Questioning the K-ABC. What does it measure? *School Psychology Review, 14,* 9–20.

Kellman, P. J., & Spelke, E. S. (1979, March). *Perception of partly occluded objects in infancy.* Paper presented at the meeting of the Society for Research in Child Development, San Francisco.

Kellman, P. J., & Spelke, E. S. (1981, April). *Infant perception of partly occluded objects: Sensitivity of movement and configuration.* Paper presented at the meeting of the Society for Research in Child Development, Boston.

Kellogg, W. N., & Kellogg, C. A. (1983). *The ape and the child.* New York: McGraw-Hill.

Kendall, P. C., & Norton-Ford, J. D. (1982). *Clinical psychology: Scientific and professional dimensions.* New York: John Wiley.

Kendell, R. E., Rennie, D., Clarke, J. A., & Dean, C. (1981). The social and obstetric correlates of psychiatric admission in the puerperium. *Psychological Medicine, 11,* 341–350.

Kendler, H. H., & Kendler, T. S. (1962). Vertical and horizontal processes in problem solving. *Psychological Review, 69,* 1–16.

Kendler, T. S., & Hynds, L. T. (1974). A reply to Brier and Jacobs's criticism of the optional shift methodology. *Child Development, 45,* 208–212.

Kendrick, C., & Dunn, J. (1980). Caring for the second baby: Effects on interaction between mother and firstborn. *Developmental Psychology, 16,* 303–311.

Kendrick, D. T., & Springfield, D. O. (1980). Personality traits and the eye of the beholder: Crossing some traditional philosophical boundaries in the search for consistency in all the people. *Psychological Review, 87,* 88–104.

Kenniston, K. (1971). Youth: A "new" stage of life. *The American Scholar, 39,* 631–654.

Kessen, W. (1979). The American child and other cultural inventions. *American Psychologist, 34,* 815–820.

Kessen, W., Haith, M. H., & Salapatek, P. H. (1970). Infancy. In P. H. Mussen (Ed.), *Carmichael's manual of child psychology* (3d ed., Vol. 1). New York: John Wiley.

Kinsbourne, M., & Hiscock, M. (1983). The normal and deviant development of functional lateralization of the brain. In P. H. Mussen (Ed.), *Handbook of child psychology* (4th ed., Vol. 2). New York: John Wiley.

Kirk, D. L. (1975). *Biology today* (2d ed.). New York: Random House.

Klahr, D. (1984). Transition processes in quantitative development. In R. J. Sternberg (Ed.), *Mechanisms of cognitive development.* San Francisco: W. H. Freeman.

Klatzky, R. L. (1984). *Memory and awareness.* San Francisco: W. H. Freeman.

Klaus, M. H., & Kennell, J. H. (1976). *Maternal-infant bonding.* St. Louis, MO: Mosby.

Klaus, M. H., Jerauld, R., Kreger, N. C., McAlpine, W., Steffa, M., & Kennell, J. H. (1972). Maternal attachment: Importance of the first post-partum days. *New England Journal of Medicine, 286,* 460–463.

Klein, P. (1984). Behavior of Israeli mothers toward infants in relation to infants' perceived temperament. *Child Development, 55,* 1212–1218.

Knopf, I. J. (1979). *Childhood psychopathology*. Englewood Cliffs, NJ: Prentice-Hall.

Kobasigawa, A. (1974). Utilization of retrieval cues by children in recall. *Child Development, 45,* 127–134.

Kohlberg, L. (1966a). A cognitive-developmental analysis of children's sex-role concepts and attitudes. In E. E. Maccoby (Ed.), *The development of sex differences*. Stanford, CA: Stanford University Press.

Kohlberg, L. (1966b). *The development of modes of moral thinking and choice in the years 10 to 16*. Unpublished doctoral dissertation, University of Chicago, Chicago.

Kohlberg, L. (1969). Stage and sequence: The cognitive-developmental approach to socialization. In D. A. Goslin (Ed.), *Handbook of socialization theory and research*. Chicago: Rand McNally.

Kohlberg, L. (1976). Moral stages and moralization: The cognitive-developmental approach. In T. Lickona (Ed.), *Moral development and behavior*. New York: Holt, Rinehart & Winston.

Kohlberg, L. (Ed.). (1980). *Recent research in moral development*. New York: Holt, Rinehart & Winston.

Kohlberg, L. (1981). *The philosophy of moral development: Moral stages and the idea of justice*. New York: Harper & Row.

Kohlberg, L., & Candee, D. (1979). *Relationships between moral judgment and moral action*. Unpublished manuscript, Harvard University, Cambridge, MA.

Kohlberg, L., & Zigler, E. (1967). The impact of cognitive maturity on the development of sex role attitudes in the years 4 to 8. *Genetic Psychology Monographs, 75,* 84–165.

Kohler, W. (1925). *The mentality of apes*. New York: Harcourt Brace Jovanovich.

Kolb, B., & Whishaw, I. Q. (1980). *Fundamentals of human neuropsychology*. San Francisco: W. H. Freeman.

Kopp, C. B. (1983). Risk factors in development. In P. H. Mussen (Ed.), *Handbook of child psychology* (4th ed., Vol. 2). New York: John Wiley.

Kopp, C. B., & Parmelee, A. H. (1979). Prenatal and perinatal influences on behavior. In J. D. Osofsky (Ed.), *Handbook of infant development*. New York: John Wiley.

Koskenvuo, M., Langinvainia, H., Kaprio, J., Rantasalo, I., & Sama, S. (1979). *The Finnish twin registry: Baseline characteristics III. Occupational and social factors*. Helsinki: Department of Public Health and Science, University of Helsinki.

Kosslyn, S. M. (1980). *Image and mind*. Cambridge, MA: Harvard University Press.

Kounin, J. S. (1971). *Discipline and group management in classrooms*. New York: Holt, Rinehart & Winston.

Kozlowski, L. T., & Bryant, K. J. (1977). Sense of direction, spatial orientation, and cognitive maps. *Journal of Experimental Psychology: Human Perception and Performance, 3,* 590–598.

Krauss, R. A., & Glucksberg, S. (1969). The development of communication: Competence as a function of age. *Child Development, 40,* 255–266.

Kravitz, H., & Boehm, J. (1971). Rhythmic habit patterns in infancy: Their sequences, age of onset, and frequency. *Child Development, 42,* 399–413.

Krogman, W. M. (1970). Growth of head, face, trunk, and limbs in Philadelphia white and negro children of elementary and high school age. *Monographs of the Society for Research in Child Development, 35,* (3, Serial No. 136).

Kruper, J. C. (1985, April). *Fathers' and mothers' speech to infants*. Paper presented at the meeting of the Society for Research in Child Development, Toronto.

Kuczaj, S. A. (1985, April). *On the development of meanings and concepts*. Paper presented at the meeting of the Society for Research in Child Development, Toronto.

Kuczaj, S. A., & Brannick, N. (1979). Children's use of the *Wh* question modal auxiliary placement rule. *Journal of Experimental Child Psychology, 28,* 43–67.

Kuhn, D. (1980). *On the development of developmental psychology*. Unpublished manuscript, Harvard University, Cambridge, MA.

Labov, W. (1970). *The study of nonstandard English*. Urbana, IL: National Council of Teachers of English.

Ladd, G. W., & Emerson, E. S. (1984). Shared knowledge in children's friendships. *Developmental Psychology, 20,* 932–940.

Ladd, G. W., & Mars, K. T. (1985, April). *Reliability and validity of preschoolers' perceptions of peer behavior*. Paper presented at the meeting of the Society for Research in Child Development, Toronto.

Lahey, B. B., Hammer, D., Crumine, P. L., & Forehand, R. L. (1980). Birth order and sex interactions in child behavior problems. *Developmental Psychology, 16,* 608–615.

Lally, J. R., & Honig, A. S. (1977). *The family development research program* (Final report No. OCD–CB–100). Syracuse, NY: University of Syracuse.

Lamb, M. E. (1976). *The role of the father in child development*. New York: John Wiley.

Lamb, M. E. (1977a). The development of mother-infant and father-infant attachments in the second year of life. *Developmental Psychology, 13,* 637–648.

Lamb, M. E. (1977b). Father-infant and mother-infant interaction in the first year of life. *Child Development, 48,* 167–181.

Lamb, M. E. (1981). Fathers and child development: An integrative overview. In M. E. Lamb (Ed.), *The father's role in child development*. New York: John Wiley.

Lamb, M. E., Easterbrooks, M. A., & Holden, G. W. (1980). Reinforcement and punishment among preschoolers: Characteristics, effects, and coorelates. *Child Development, 51,* 1230–1236.

Lamb, M. E., Frodi, A. M., Hwang, P., Frodi, M., & Steinberg, J. (1983). Attitudes and behavior of traditional and nontraditional parents in Sweden. In R. Emde & R. Harmon (Eds.), *Attachment and affiliative systems*. New York: Plenum.

Lamb, M. E., & Roopnarine, J. L. (1979). Peer influences on sex-role development in preschoolers. *Child Development, 50,* 1219–1222.

REFERENCES

Landesman-Dwyer, S., & Sackett, G. P. (1983, April). *Prenatal nicotine exposure and sleep-walk patterns in infancy.* Paper presented at the meeting of Society for Research in Child Development, Detroit.

Lane, H. (1976). *The wild boy of Aveyron.* Cambridge, MA: Harvard University Press.

Langer, J. (1969). *Theories of development.* New York: Holt, Rinehart and Winston.

Lapsley, D. K. (1985). *On dialectics and developmental meta-theory: A critical appraisal.* Unpublished manuscript, Department of Psychology, University of Notre Dame, Notre Dame, IN.

Lapsley, D. K., Enright, R. D., & Serlin, R. C. (1986). Moral and social education. In J. Worrell & F. Danner (Eds.), *Adolescent development: Issues in education.* New York: Academic Press.

Lapsley, D. K., & Murphy, M. N. (1985). Another look at the theoretical assumptions of adolescent egocentrism. *Developmental Review, 5,* 201–217.

Lapsley, D. K., & Quintana, S. M. (1985). Integrative themes in social and developmental theories of self. In J. B. Pryor & J. Day (Eds.), *Social and developmental perspectives of social cognition.* New York: Springer-Verlag.

Lapsley, D. K., & Quintana, S. M. (in press). Recent approaches in children's elementary moral and social education. *Elementary School Guidance and Counseling Journal.*

Larson, M. E. (1973). Humbling cases for career counselors. *Phi Delta Kappan, 54,* 374.

Lasater, T. M., Briggs, J., Malone, P., Gilliom, C. F., & Weisburg, P. (1975, April). *The Birmingham model for parent education.* Paper presented at the meeting of the Society for Research in Child Development, Denver.

Laky, R. E., & Klein, R. E. (1979). The reactions of five-month-old infants to eye contact of the mother and of a stranger. *Merrill-Palmer Quarterly, 25,* 163–170.

Laycock, F. (1979). *Gifted children.* Glenview, IL: Scott, Foresman.

Lazar, L., & Darlington, R. (1982). Lasting effects of early education: A report from the Consortium for Longitudinal Studies. *Monographs of the Society for Research in Child Development, 17,* (2–3, Series No. 195).

Lazarus, R. S., & DeLongis, A. (1983). Psychological stress and coping in aging. *American Psychologist, 38,* 245–254.

Lecours, A. (1975). Myelogenetic correlates of the development of speech and language. In E. H. Lenneberg & E. Lenneberg (Eds.), *Foundations of language development.* New York: Academic Press.

Ledger, G. W., & Groff, R. A. (1985, April). *Working memory, M-space and metacognitive development in skilled and less-skilled readers.* Paper presented at the meeting of the Society for Research in Child Development, Toronto.

Lee, C. L. (1973, August). *Social encounters of infants: The beginnings of popularity.* Paper presented at the meeting of the International Society for the Study of Behavioral Development, Ann Arbor, MI.

Leg, R. G., & Bryden, M. P. (1979). Hemisphere differences in processing emotions and faces. *Brain and Language, 7,* 127–138.

Leiffer, A. D. (1973). *Television and the development of social behavior.* Paper presented at the meeting of the International Society for the Study of Behavioral Development, Ann Arbor, MI.

Leiffer, A. D., Gordon, N. J., & Graves, S. B. (1974). Children's television: More than entertainment. *Harvard Educational Review, 44,* 213–245.

Leiffer, A. D., Leiderman, P. H., Barnett, C. R., & Williams, J. A. (1972). Effects of mother–infant separation on maternal attachment behavior. *Child Development, 43,* 1203–1218.

Leigh, G. K. (1982). Kinship interaction over the family life span. *Journal of Marriage and the Family, 44,* 197–208.

Leler, H., Johnson, D. L., Kahn, A., Hines, R. P., & Torres, M. (1975, April). *The Houston model for parent education.* Paper presented at the meeting of the Society for Research in Child Development, Denver.

Lenneberg, E. H. (1962). Understanding language without the ability to speak: A case report. *Journal of Abnormal and Social Psychology, 65,* 419–425.

Lenneberg, E. H. (1967). *Biological foundations of language.* New York: John Wiley.

Lenneberg, E. H., Rebelsky, F. G., & Nichols, I. A. (1965). The vocalizations of infants born to deaf and hearing parents. *Human Development, 8,* 23–37.

Lepper, M., Greene, D., & Nisbett, R. E. (1973). Undermining children's intrinsic interest with extrinsic rewards. *Journal of Personality and Social Psychology, 28,* 129–137.

Lerner, R. (1982). Children and adolescents as producers of their own development. *Developmental Review, 2,* 342–370.

Lesser, G., Fifer, G., & Clark, D. (1965). Mental abilities of children from different social classes and cultural groups. *Monographs of the Society for Research in Child Development, 30* (Whole No. 102).

Lester, B. M., Hoffman, J., & Brazelton, T. B. (1985). The rhythmic structure of mother-infant interaction in term and preterm infants. *Child Development, 56,* 15–27.

Levin, J. (1976). What have we learned about maximizing what children learn? In J. Levin & V. Allen (Eds.), *Cognitive learning in children.* New York: Academic Press.

Levin, J. (1980). *The mnemonic '80s: Keywords in the classroom.* Theoretical paper No. 86. Wisconsin Research and Development Center for Individualized Schooling, Madison.

Levine, M. (1975). *A cognitive theory of learning research on hypothesis testing.* Hillsdale, NJ: Lawrence Erlbaum.

Levy, D. M., & Patrick, H. T. (1928). Relation of infantile convulsions, head-banging, and breath-holding to fainting and headaches (migraine) in the parents. *Archives of Neurology and Psychiatry, 19,* 865–887.

Levy, J., & Sperry, R. W. (1972). Lateral specialization of the human brain: Behavioral manifestations and possible evolutionary basis. In J. A. Kiger (Ed.), *The biology of behavior: Proceedings of the 32nd Annual Biology Colloquium.* Corvallis: Oregon State University Press.

Lewis, M. (1972). State as an infant-environment interaction: An analysis of mother-infant interaction as a function of sex. *Merrill-Palmer Quarterly, 18,* 95–121.

Lewis, M., & Brooks-Gunn, J. (1979). *Social cognition and the acquisition of the self*. New York: Plenum.

Lewis, M., & Cherry, L. (1977). Social behavior and language acquisition. In M. Lewis & L. Rosenblum (Eds.), *Interaction conversation and the development of language: The origins of behavior* (Vol. 5). New York: John Wiley.

Lewis, M., & Rosenblum, L. A. (Eds.) (1977). *Friendship and peer relations* (Vol. 4). New York: Plenum.

Lewkowicz, D. J. (1985). Bisensory response to temporal frequency in 4-month-old infants. *Developmental Psychology, 21*, 306–317.

Liberman, I. Y., Shankweiler, D., Liberman, A., & Fowler, C. (1977). Phonetic segmentation and reading in the beginning reader. In A. S. Reber & D. L. Scarborough (Eds.), *Toward a psychology of reading*. New York: John Wiley.

Liden, G., & Kankkunen, A. (1969). Visual reinforcement audiometry. *Acta Oto-Laryngologica, 67*, 281–292.

Lieberman, A. F. (1977). Preschoolers' competence with a peer: Relations with attachment and peer experience. *Child Development, 48*, 1277–1287.

Lipsett, L. P. (1979). Critical conditions in infancy: A psychological perspective. *American Psychologist, 34*, 973–980.

Lipsett, L. P., Engen, T., & Kaye, H. (1963). Developmental changes in the olfactory threshold of the neonate. *Child Development, 34*, 371–376.

Lipsett, L. P., Reilly, B. M., Butcher, M. J., & Greenwood, M. M. (1976). The stability and interrelationships of newborn sucking and heart rate. *Developmental Psychology, 9*, 305–310.

Livesley, W. J., & Bromley, D. B. (1973). *Person perception in childhood and adolescence*. New York: John Wiley.

Lockhart, R. S. (1984). What do infants remember? In M. Moscovitch (Ed.), *Infant memory: Its relation to normal and pathological memory in humans and other animals*. New York: Plenum.

Lockheed, M. (1985). Women, girls, and computers: A first look at the evidence. *Sex Roles, 13*, 115–122.

Locksley, A., & Colten, M. E. (1979). Psychological androgyny: A case of mistaken identity. *Journal of Personality and Social Psychology, 37*, 1017–1031.

Loehlin, J. C., & Nichols, R. C. (1976). *Heredity, environment, and personality: A study of 850 sets of twins*. Austin: University of Texas Press.

Logan, F. A. (1960). *Incentive: How the conditions of reinforcement affect the performance of rats*. New Haven: Yale University Press.

Long, T., & Long, L. (1983). *Latchkey children*. New York: Penguin.

Lorenz, K. Z. (1965). *Evolution and modification of behavior*. Chicago: University of Chicago Press.

Lovaas, O. I. (1977). *The autistic child: Language development through behavior modification*. New York: Halsted Press.

Lovaas, O. I., Koegel, R. L., & Schreibman, L. (1979). Stimulus overselectivity in autism: A review of research. *Psychological Bulletin, 86*, 1236–1254.

Lowrey, G. H. (1978). *Growth and development of children* (7th ed.). Chicago: Year Book Medical Publishers.

Lowy, L. (1981, August). *The older generation: What is due, what is owed?* Paper presented at the meeting of the American Psychological Association, Los Angeles.

Lucariello, J., & Nelson, J. (1985). Slot-filler categories as memory organizers for young children. *Developmental Psychology, 21*, 272–282.

Lundsteen, S. W., & Bernstein-Tarrow, N. B. (1981). *Guiding young children's learning*. New York: McGraw-Hill.

Luria, Z., & Herzog, E. (1985, April). *Gender segregation across and within settings*. Paper presented at the meeting of the Society for Research in Child Development, Toronto.

Lyle, J., & Hoffman, H. R. (1972). Children's use of television and other media. In E. A. Rubenstein, G. A. Comstock, & J. P. Murray (Eds.), *Television and social behavior* (Vol. 4). Washington, DC: U.S. Government Printing Office.

Maccoby, E. E. (1980). *Social development*. New York: Harcourt Brace Jovanovich.

Maccoby, E. E., & Jacklin, C. N. (1980). Sex differences in aggression: A rejoinder and reprise. *Child Development, 51*, 964–980.

Maccoby, E. E., & Martin, J. A. (1983). Socialization in the context of the family: Parent-child interaction. In P. H. Mussen (Ed.), *Handbook of child psychology* (4th ed., Vol. 4). New York: John Wiley.

Maccoby, E. E., & Masters, J. C. (1970). Attachment and dependency. In P. H. Mussen (Ed.), *Carmichael's manual of child psychology* (3rd ed., Vol. 2). New York: John Wiley.

Mackintosh, N. J. (1983). *Conditioning and associative learning*. New York: Oxford University Press.

Mahler, M. S. (1979a). *The selected papers of Margaret Mahler* (Vols. 1 and 2). New York: Jason Aronson.

Mahler, M. S. (1979b). *Separation-individuation*. New York: Jason Aronson.

Main, M. (1973). *Exploration, play, and cognitive functioning as related to child-mother attachment*. Unpublished doctoral dissertation, Johns Hopkins University, Baltimore.

Main, M., Kaplan, N., & Cassidy, J. (in press). Security in infancy, childhood, and adulthood: A move to the level of representation. *Monographs of the Society for Research in Child Development*.

Main, M., & Londerville, S. (1977, March). *Compliance and aggression in toddlerhood*. Paper presented at the meeting of the Society for Research in Child Development, New Orleans.

Mandler, J. M. (1979). Categorical and schematic organization in memory. In C. R. Puff (Ed.), *Memory organization and structure*. New York: Academic Press.

Mandler, J. M. (1983). Representation. In P. H. Mussen (Ed.), *Handbook of child psychology* (4th ed., Vol. 3). New York: John Wiley.

Mandler, J. M., & Robinson, C. A. (1978). Developmental changes in picture recognition. *Journal of Experimental Child Psychology, 26*, 122–136.

Mannarino, A. P. (1978). Friendship patterns and self-concept in preadolescent males. *Journal of Genetic Psychology, 133,* 105–110.

Mannarino, A. P. (1979). The relationship between friendship and altruism in preadolescent girls. *Psychiatry, 42,* 280–284.

Maratsos, M. P. (1983). Some current issues in the study of the acquisition of grammar. In P. H. Mussen (Ed.), *Handbook of child psychology* (4th ed.). New York: John Wiley.

Maratsos, M. P., & Chalkey, M. A. (1980). The internal language of childrens' syntax: The ontogenesis and representation of syntactic categories. In K. E. Nelson (Ed.), *Children's language* (Vol. 2). New York: Gardner Press.

Marcia, J. (1966). Development and validation of ego-identity status. *Journal of Personality and Social Psychology, 3,* 551–558.

Marcus, T. L., & Corsini, D. A. (1978). Parental expectation of preschool children as related to gender and socioeconomic status. *Child Development, 29,* 243–246.

Marjoribanks, K., Walberg, H. S., & Bargen, M. (1975). Mental abilities: Sibling constellations and social class correlates. *British Journal of Social and Clinical Psychology, 14,* 104–116.

Markus, H. (1977). Self-schemata and processing information about the self. *Journal of Personality and Social Psychology, 35,* 63–78.

Marr, D. B., & Sternberg, R. J. (1985, April). *Effects of contextual relevance on attention to novel information.* Paper presented at the meeting of the Society for Research in Child Development, Toronto.

Marshall, H. (1981). Open classroom: Has the term outlived its usefulness? *Review of Educational Research, 51,* 181–192.

Marshall, R. E., Porter, F. L., Rogers, A. G., Moore, J., Anderson, B., & Boxerman, S. B. (1982). Circumcision II. Effects upon mother–infant interaction. *Early Human Development, 7,* 367–374.

Maslow, A. H. (1970). *Motivation and personality* (2nd ed). New York: Harper & Row.

Masters, J. C., & Wellman, H. M. (1974). The study of human infant attachment: A procedural critique. *Psychological Bulletin, 81,* 218–237.

Matas, L., Arend, R. A., & Sroufe, L. A. (1978). Continuity in adaptation: Quality of attachment and later competence. *Child Development, 49,* 547–556.

Matheny, A. P., Dolan, R. S., & Wilson, R. S. (1976). Relation between twins' similarity: Testing an assumption. *Behavior Genetics, 6,* 343–351.

Maurer, D., Lewis, T. L., Cavanagh, P., & Anstis, S. (1985, April). *A new test of color vision for babies.* Paper presented at the meeting of the Society for Research in Child Development, Toronto.

Maurer, D., & Salapatek, P. (1976). Developmental changes in the scanning of faces by young infants. *Child Development, 47,* 523–527.

McCabe, A. E., & Moriarity, R. J. (1977, March). *A laboratory/field study of television violence and aggression in children's sports.* Paper presented at the meeting of the Society for Research in Child Development, New Orleans.

McCall, R. B. (1982). A hard look at stimulating and predicting development: The cases of bonding and screening infants. *Pediatrics in Review, 3,* 205–212.

McCall, R. B. (1985, April). *Discussion— Novelty as a source of developmental continuity in intelligence.* Paper presented at the meeting of the Society for Research in Child Development, Toronto.

McCall, R. B., Applebaum, M. I., & Hogarty, P. S. (1973). Developmental changes in mental performance. *Monographs of the Society for Research in Child Development, 38* (Serial No. 150).

McCandless, B. R. (1973). *Male caregivers in day care: Demonstration project.* Atlanta: Emory University.

McCandless, B. R., & Evans, E. (1973). *Children and youth.* New York: Holt, Rinehart & Winston.

McClelland, D. C. (1951). *Personality.* New York: Holt-Dryden.

McClelland, D. C. (1961). *The achieving society.* New York: Van Nostrand.

McClelland, D. C. (1973). Testing for competence rather than for "intelligence." *American Psychologist, 28,* 1–14.

McConaghy, M. J. (1979). Gender permanence and the genital basis of gender: Stages in the development of constancy of gender identity. *Child Development, 50,* 1223–1226.

McCord, J. (1980). Antecedents and correlates of vulnerability and resistance to psychopathology. In R. Zucker & A. Rabin (Eds.), *Further explorations in personality.* New York: John Wiley.

McCord, W., & McCord, J. (1959). *Origins of crime.* New York: Columbia University Press.

McFarlane, A. (1975). Olfaction in the development of social preference in the human neonate. In *Parent–infant interaction.* Amsterdam: CIBA Foundation Symposium 33, new series, ASP.

McGowan, J., & Gormly, J. (1976). Validation of personality traits: A multicriteria approach. *Journal of Personality and Social Psychology, 34,* 791–795.

McGraw, M. B. (1943). *The neuromuscular maturation of the human infant.* New York: Hafner.

McLaughlin, B. (1978). *Second-language acquisition in childhood.* Hillsdale, NJ: Lawrence Erlbaum.

McNeill, D. (1970). *The acquisition of language.* New York: Harper & Row.

McNemar, Q. (1942). *The revision of the Stanford-Binet Scale.* Boston: Houghton Mifflin.

Meacham, J. A. (1975). Patterns of memory ability in two cultures. *Developmental Psychology, 11,* 50–53.

Mead, G. H. (1934). *Mind, self, and society.* Chicago: University of Chicago Press.

Mead, M. (1978, December 30). The American family: An endangered species. *TV Guide.*

Mehler, J., Bertoncini, J., Barriere, M., & Jassik-Gerschenfeld, D. (1978). Infant recognition of mother's voice. *Perception, 7,* 491–497.

Meichenbaum, D. A. (1975). A self-instructional approach to stress management: A proposal for stress inoculation training. In C. Spielberger & I. Sarason (Eds.), *Stress and anxiety* (Vol. 1). Washington, DC: Hemisphere Publishing.

Meichenbaum, D. A. (1977). *Cognitive behavior modification.* New York: Plenum.

Meichenbaum, D., & Goodman, J. (1971). Training impulsive children to talk to themselves: A means of developing self-control. *Journal of Abnormal Psychology, 77,* 115–126.

Meilman, P. W. (1979). Cross-sectional age changes in ego identity status during adolescence. *Developmental Psychology, 15,* 230–231.

Meltzer, H. Y., & Stahl, S. M. (1976). The dopamine hypothesis of schizophrenia. *Schizophrenia Bulletin, 2,* 19–76.

Meltzoff, A. N. (1985). Immediate and deferred imitation in fourteen- and twenty-four-month-old infants. *Child Development, 56,* 62–72.

Mercer, J. R., & Lewis, J. F. (1978). *System of multicultural pluralistic assessment.* New York: Psychological Corporation.

Meredith, H. V. (1978). Research between 1960 and 1970 on the standing height of young children in different parts of the world. In H. W. Reese & L. P. Lipsitt (Eds.), *Advances in child development and behavior* (Vol. 12). New York: Academic Press.

Messinger, J. C. (1971). Sex and repression in an Irish folk community. In D. S. Marshall & R. C. Suggs (Eds.), *Human sexual behavior.* New York: Basic Books.

Milham, J., Widmayer, S., Bauer, C. R., & Peterson, L. (1983, April). *Predictory cognitive deficits for pre-term, low-birthweight infants.* Paper presented at the meeting of the Society for Research in Child Development, Detroit.

Mill, J. (1829). *An analysis of the phenomena of the human mind.*

Miller, G. A. (1981). *Language and speech.* San Francisco: W. H. Freeman.

Miller, M. M., & Reeves, B. B. (1976). Children's occupational sex-role stereotypes: The linkage between television content and perception. *Journal of Broadcasting, 20,* 35–50.

Miller, N., & Maruyama, G. (1976). Ordinal position and peer popularity. *Journal of Personality and Social Psychology, 33,* 123–131.

Mills, M., & Melhuish, E. (1974). Recognition of mother's voice in early infancy. *Nature, 252,* 123–124.

Milner, B. A. (1963). Effects of different brain lesions on card sorting. *Archives of Neurology, 9,* 90–100.

Minnett, A. M., Vandell, D. L., & Santrock, J. W. (1983). The effects of sibling status on sibling interactions: Influence of birth order, age spacing, sex of child, and sex of sibling. *Child Development, 54,* 1064–1072.

Minuchin, P. P., & Shapiro, E. K. (1983). The school as a context for social development. In P. H. Mussen (Ed.), *Handbook of child psychology* (4th ed., Vol. 4). New York: John Wiley.

Mischel, W. (1968). *Personality and assessment.* New York: John Wiley.

Mischel, W. (1970). Sex-typing and socialization. In P. H. Mussen (Ed.), *Carmichael's manual of child psychology* (3rd ed., Vol. 2). New York: John Wiley.

Mischel, W. (1973). Toward a cognitive social learning reconceptualization of personality. *Psychological Review, 80,* 252–283.

Mischel, W. (1974). Process in delay of gratification. In L. Berkowitz (Ed.), *Advances in experimental social psychology* (Vol. 7). New York: Academic Press.

Mischel, W. (1976). *Introduction to personality* (2nd ed.). New York: Holt, Rinehart & Winston.

Mischel, W. (1979). On the interface between cognition and personality: Beyond the person-situation debate. *American Psychologist, 34,* 740–754.

Mischel, W. (1983, August). *Convergences and challenges in the search for the person.* Invited address at the annual meeting of the American Psychological Association, Los Angeles.

Mischel, W. (1984). Convergences and challenges in the search for consistency. *American Psychologist, 39,* 351–364.

Mischel, W. (In press). The growth of insight into self-control principles. In S. R. Yussen (Ed.), *The growth of reflection.* New York: Academic Press.

Mischel, W., & Baker, N. (1975). Cognitive transformations of reward objects through instructions. *Journal of Personality and Social Psychology, 31,* 254–261.

Mischel, W., Ebbesen, E. B., & Zeiss, A. R. (1972). Cognitive and attentional mechanisms in delay of gratification. *Journal of Personality and Social Psychology, 21,* 204–218.

Mischel, W., & Mischel, H. (1975, April). *A cognitive social-learning analysis of moral development.* Paper presented at the meeting of the Society for Research in Child Development, Denver.

Mischel, W., & Patterson, C. J. (1976). Substantive and structural elements of effective plans for self-control. *Journal of Social and Personality Psychology, 34,* 942–950.

Mischel, W., Peake, P. K., & Zeiss, A. R. (1984). *Longitudinal studies of delay behavior.* Unpublished manuscript, Stanford University, Stanford, CA.

Mistry, J. J., & Lange, G. W. (1985). Children's organization and recall of information in scripted narratives. *Child Development, 56,* 953–961.

Mitchell, R. G., & Etches, P. (1977). Rhythmic habit patterns (stereotypies). *Developmental Medicine and Child Neurology, 19,* 545–550.

Mitteness, L. S., & Nydegger, C. N. (1982, October). *Dimensions of parent-child relations in adulthood.* Paper presented at the meeting of the Gerontological Society of America.

Mize, J. (1985, April). *Social skill training with preschool children: The effects of a cognitive-social learning approach.* Paper presented at the meeting of the Society for Research in Child Development, Toronto.

Moely, B. E., Olson, F. A., Halwes, T. G., & Flavell, J. H. (1969). Production deficiency in young childrens' clustered recall. *Developmental Psychology, 1,* 26–34.

Moerk, E. L. (1985, April). *The fuzzy set called imitations.* Paper presented at the meeting of the Society for Research in Child Development, Toronto.

Moerk, E. L., & Moerk, C. (1979). Quotations, imitations, and generalizations: Factual and methodological analyses. *International Journal of Behavioral Development, 2,* 43–72.

Molfese, D. L. (1972). *Cerebral asymmetry in infants, children, and adults: Auditory evoked responses to speech and noise stimuli.* Unpublished doctoral dissertation, Pennsylvania State University, University Park.

Molfese, D. L. (1973). Cerebral asymmetry in infants, children, and adults: Auditory evoked responses to speech and musical stimuli. *Journal of the Acoustical Society of America, 53,* 363.

Money, J. (1965). Psychosexual differentiation. In J. Money (Ed.), *Sex research, new developments*. New York: Holt, Rinehart & Winston.

Money, J. (1973). Biology = male/female destiny: A woman's view. *Contemporary Psychology, 18,* 603–604.

Monson, T. C., Hesley, J. W., & Chernick, L. (1982). Specifying personality traits can and cannot predict behavior: An alternative to abandoning the attempt to predict single-set criteria. *Journal of Personality and Social Psychology, 43,* 385–399.

Montemayor, R. (1982, October). *Parent-adolescent conflict*. Paper presented at the first biennial conference on adolescent research, Tucson.

Moore, J. M., Thompson, G., & Thompson, M. (1975). Auditory localization of infants as a function of reinforcement conditions. *Journal of Speech and Hearing Disorders, 40,* 29–34.

Moos, R. H., & Moos, B. S. (1978). Classroom social climate and student absences and grades. *Journal of Educational Psychology, 70,* 263–269.

Morais, J., Cary, L., Alegria, J., & Bertelson, P. (1979). Does awareness of speech as a sequence of phonemes arise spontaneously? *Cognition, 7,* 323–331.

Morgan, C. T., & King, R. A. (1971). *Introduction to psychology*. New York: McGraw-Hill.

Morgan, G. A., & Ricciuti, H. N. (1969). Infants' responses to strangers during the first year. In B. M. Foss (Ed.), *Determinants of infant behavior* (Vol. 4). London: Methuen.

Morgan, J. L. (1985, April). *Prosodic encoding of syntactic information in speech to young children*. Paper presented at the meeting of the Society for Research in Child Development, Toronto.

Morse, P. A. (1972). The discrimination of speech and nonspeech stimuli early in infancy. *Journal of Experimental Child Psychology, 14,* 477–492.

Mueller, E. (1979). (Toddlers + toys) = (An autonomous social system). In M. Lewis & L. A. Rosenblum (Eds.), *The child and its family*. New York: Plenum.

Mueller, E. (Discussant). (1985, April). *Early peer relations: Ten years of research*. Symposium presented at the meeting of the Society for Research in Child Development, Toronto.

Mueller, E., & Brenner, J. (1977). The origins of social skills and interaction among playgroup toddlers. *Child Development, 48,* 854–861.

Muir, D., Abraham, W., Forbes, B., & Harris, L. (1979). The ontogenesis of auditory localization response from birth to four months of age. *Canadian Journal of Psychology, 33,* 320–333.

Muir, D., Campbell, D., Low, J. A., Killen, H., Galbraith, R., & Karchmar, J. (1978, June). *Neonatal assessments of intrauterine growth in retarded, premature, and asphyxiated infants: Group differences and predictive value*. Paper presented at the meeting of the Canadian Psychological Association, Ottawa.

Murray, F. B. (1978, August). *Generation of educational practice from developmental theory*. Paper presented at the meeting of the American Psychological Association, Toronto.

Mussen, P. H., & Eisenberg-Berg, N. (1977). *Roots of caring, sharing, and helping*. San Francisco: W. H. Freeman.

Mussen, P. H., & Jones, M. C. (1958). The behavior-inferred motivations of late- and early-maturing boys. *Child Development, 29,* 61–67.

Myers, B. J. (1982). Early intervention using Brazelton training with middle-class mothers and fathers of newborns. *Child Development, 53,* 462–471.

N

National Education Association. (1974). *Today's changing roles: An approach to nonsexist teaching*. Minneapolis, MN: Author.

Neisser, U. (1967). *Cognitive psychology*. New York: Appleton-Century-Crofts.

Neisser, U. (1982). *Memory observed*. San Francisco: W. H. Freeman.

Nelson, K. E. (1973). Structure and strategy in learning to talk. *Monographs of the Society for Research in Child Development, 38* (Serial No. 149).

Nelson, K. E. (1975, April). *Facilitating syntax acquisition*. Paper presented at the meeting of the Eastern Psychological Association, New York.

Nelson, K. E. (1977). Cognitive development and the acquisition of concepts. In R. C. Anderson, R. J. Spiro, & W. E. Montague (Eds.), *Schooling and the acquisition of knowledge*. Hillsdale, NJ: Lawrence Erlbaum.

Nelson, K. E. (1978). How children represent knowledge of their world in and out of language: A preliminary report. In R. S. Siegler (Ed.), *Childrens' thinking: What develops?* Hillsdale, NJ: Lawrence Erlbaum.

Nelson, K. E. (1981). Social cognition as a script framework. In J. H. Flavell & L. Ross (Eds.), *Cognitive development: Frontiers and possible futures*. New York: Cambridge University Press.

Nelson, K. E. (1982). The syntagmatics and paradigmatics of conceptual representation. In S. Kuczaj (Ed.), *Language development: Language, thought and culture*. Hillsdale, NJ: Lawrence Erlbaum.

Nelson, K. E., Carskaddon, G., & Bonvillian, J. D. (1973). Syntax acquisition: Impact of experimental variation in adult verbal interaction with the child. *Child Development, 44,* 497–504.

Neugarten, B. L. (1980, February). Must everything be a mid-life crisis? *Prime Time*.

Newell, A., & Simon, H. A. (1972). *Human problem solving*. Englewood Cliffs, NJ: Prentice-Hall.

Newsom, C., Favell, J. E., & Rincover, A. (1983). Side effects of punishment. In S. Axelrod & J. Apsche, *The effects of punishment on behavior*. New York: Academic Press.

Nicholls, J. G. (1975). Causal attributions and other achievement-related cognitions: Effects of task outcomes, attainment value, and sex. *Journal of Personality and Social Psychology, 31,* 379–389.

Nickerson, E. T. (1975). *Intervention strategies for modifying sex stereotypes*. Paper presented at the annual convention of school psychologists, Atlanta.

Nicolich, L. (1977). Beyond sensorimotor intelligence: Assessment of symbolic maturity through analysis of pretend play. *Merrill-Palmer Quarterly, 23,* 89–99.

Niemark, E. D. (1982). Adolescent thought: Transition to formal operations. In B. B. Wolman (Ed.), *Handbook of developmental psychology*. Englewood Cliffs, NJ: Prentice-Hall.

Ninio, A., & Bruner, J. (1978). The achievement and antecedents of labeling. *Journal of Child Language, 5*, 1–15.

Norman, D. (1982). Commentary. In M. Hunt (Ed.), *The universe within*. New York: Simon & Schuster.

Nottelmann, E. D. (1982). *The interaction of physical maturity and school transition*. Paper presented at the meeting of the American Educational Research Association, New York.

Nottelmann, E. D., Susman, E. J., Inoff, G. E., Dorn, L. D., Cutler, G. B., Loriaux, D. L., & Chrousos, G. P. (1985, May). *Hormone level and adjustment and behavior during early adolescence*. Paper presented at the annual meeting of the American Association for the Advancement of Science, Los Angeles, CA.

Nucci, L. (1982). Conceptual development in the moral and conventional domains: Implications for values education. *Review of Educational Research, 52*, 93–122.

Nucci, L. (in press). Teaching children right from wrong: Education and the development of children's moral and conventional concepts. *Teacher Education Quarterly*.

Nucci, L., & Nucci, M. (1982). Children's responses to moral and social conventional transgressions in free-play settings. *Child Development, 53*, 1337–1342.

Nucci, L., & Turiel, E. (1978). Social interactions and the development of social concepts in preschool children. *Child Development, 49*, 400–407.

Nydegger, C. N. (1975, October). *Age and parental behavior*. Paper presented at the meeting of the Gerontological Society of America, Louisville, KY.

Nydegger, C. N. (1981, October). *The ripple effect of parental timing*. Paper presented at the meeting of the Gerontological Society of America.

O'Connor, M. J., Cohen, S., & Parmelee, A. H. (1984). Infant auditory discrimination in preterm and full-term infants as a predictor of 5-year intelligence. *Child Development, 20*, 159–165.

Oden, S. L., & Asher, S. R. (1975, April). *Coaching children in social skills for friendship making*. Paper presented at the meeting of the Society for Research in Child Development, Denver, CO.

Odling-Smee, F. J. (1978). The overshadowing of background stimuli by an informative CS in aversive Pavlovian conditioning with rats. *Animal Learning and Behavior, 6*, 43–51.

Odom, R. D. (1977, March). *The decalage from the perspective of a perceptual salience account of developmental change*. Paper presented at the meeting of the Society for Research in Child Development, New Orleans.

Offenbach, S. I. (1980). Children's learning as a function of hypothesis set size. *Child Development, 51*, 1050–1056.

O'Keefe, E. S. C., & Hyde, J. S. (1983). The development of occupational sex-role stereotypes: The effects of gender stability and age. *Sex Roles, 9*, 481–492.

Olson, G. M., & Strauss, M. S. (1984). The development of infant memory. In M. Moscovitch, *Infant memory: Its relation to normal and pathological memory in humans and other animals*. New York: Plenum.

Olweus, D. (1980). Bullying among choolboys. In R. Barnen (Ed.), *Children and violence*. Stockholm: Adaemic Litteratur.

Ortony, A. (1979). Beyond literal similarity. *Psychological Review, 86*, 161–180.

Overton, W. F., & Meehan, A. M. (1982). Individual differences in formal operational thought: Sex roles and learned helplessness. *Child Development, 53*, 1536–1543.

Owen, S. V., Froman, R. D., & Moscow, H. (1981). *Educational psychology*. Boston: Little, Brown.

Oyama, S. (1973). *A sensitive period for the acquisition of a second langue*. Unpublished doctorial dissertation, Harvard University, Cambridge, MA.

Paivio, A. (1971). *Imagery and verbal processes*. New York: Holt.

Pancake, V. R. (1985, April). *Continuity between mother-infant attachment and ongoing dyadic peer relationships in preschool*. Paper presented at the meeting of the Society for Research in Child Development, Toronto.

Paris, S. C., & Lindauer, B. K. (1976). The role of inferences in children's comprehension and memory for sentences. *Cognitive Psychology, 8*, 217–227.

Paris, S. G., Lindauer, B. K., & Cox, G. L. (1977). The development of inferential comprehension. *Child Development, 48*, 1728–1733.

Paris, S. G., & Lindauer, B. K. (1982). The development of cognitive skills during childhood. In B. B. Wolman (Ed.), *Handbook of developmental psychology*. Englewood Cliffs, NJ: Prentice-Hall.

Parke, R. D. (1972). Some effects of punishment on children's behavior. In W. W. Hartup (Ed.), *The young child* (Vol. 2). Washington, DC: National Association for the Education of Young Children.

Parke, R. D. (1974). Rules, roles, and resistance to deviation: Recent advances in punishment, discipline, and self-control. In A. Pick (Ed.), *Minnesota symposium on child psychology* (Vol. 8). Minneapolis: University of Minnesota Press.

Parke, R. D. (1976, September). *Child abuse: An overview of alternative models*. Paper presented at the meeting of the American Psychological Association, Washington, DC.

Parke, R. D. (1977). Some effects of punishment on children's behavior—revisited. In E. M. Hetherington & R. D. Parke (Eds.), *Readings in contemporary child psychology*. New York: McGraw-Hill.

Parke, R. D. (1981). *Fathers*. Cambridge, MA: Harvard University Press.

Parke, R. D., & Asher, S. R. (1983). Social and personality development. In M. R. Rosenzweig & L. W. Porter (Eds.), *Annual review of psychology* (Vol. 34). Palo Alto, CA: Annual Reviews.

Parke, R. D., & Collmer, C. W. (1976). Child abuse: An interdisciplinary analysis. In E. M. Hetherington (Ed.), *Review of child development research* (Vol. 5). Chicago: University of Chicago Press.

Parke, R. D., & Lewis, N. G. (1980). The family in context: A multilevel interactional analysis of child abuse. In R. W. Henderson (Ed.), *Parent-child interaction: Theory, research, and prospect.* New York: Academic Press.

Parke, R. D., Power, T. G., & Fisher, T. (1980). The adolescent father's impact on the mother and child. *Journal of Social Issues, 36,* 88–106.

Parke, R. D., & Sawin, D. B. (1980). The family in early infancy. In F. Pederson (Ed.), *The father-infant relationship: Observational studies in a family context.* New York: Praeger.

Parker, J., & Gottman, J. (1985, April). *Making friends with an extra-terrestrial: Conversational skills and friendship formation in young children.* Paper presented at the meeting of the Society for Research in Child Development, Toronto.

Parmalee, A. H., & Sigman, M. D. (1983). Perinatal brain development and behavior. In P. H. Mussen (Ed.), *Handbook of child psychology* (4th ed., Vol. 2). New York: John Wiley.

Parsons, J. E., Ruble, D. N., Hodges, K. L., & Small, A. W. (1976). Cognitive-developmental factors in emerging sex differences in achievement-related expectancies. *Journal of Social Issues, 32,* 47–61.

Parten, M. (1932). Social play among preschool children. *Journal of Abnormal and Social Psychology, 27,* 243–269.

Patten, B. (1933). *Human embryology.* New York: McGraw-Hill.

Patterson, G. R. (1977). Accelerating stimuli for two classes of coercive behaviors. *Journal of Abnormal Child Psychology, 5,* 335–350.

Patterson, G. R. (1979). A performance theory for coercive family interaction. In R. B. Cairns (Ed.), *The analysis of social interactions: Methods, issues, and illustrations.* Hillsdale, NJ: Lawrence Erlbaum.

Patterson, G. R. (1981). Mothers: The unacknowledged victims. *Monographs of the Society for Research in Child Development, 46,* (Whole No. 5).

Patterson, G. R. (1982). *Coercive family process.* Eugene, OR: Castalia Publications.

Patterson, G. R., & Hops, H. (1972). Coercion, a game for two: Intervention techniques for marital conflict. In R. E. Ulrich & P. Mountjoy (Eds.), *The experimental analysis of social behavior.* New York: Appleton-Century-Crofts.

Patterson, G. R., & Stouthmaer-Loeber, M. (1984). The correlation of family management practices and delinquency. *Child Development, 55,* 1299–1307.

Pavlov, I. P. (1927). *Conditioned reflexes* (F. V. Anrep, Trans. and Ed.). New York: Dover.

Pedersen, F. A., Anderson, B. J., & Cain, R. L. (1980). Parent-infant and husband-wife interactions observed at age five months. In F. A. Pedersen (Ed.), *The father-infant relationship: Observational studies in the family setting.* New York: Praeger.

Pepler, D. J., Abramovitch, R., & Corter, C. (1981). Sibling interaction in the home: A longitudinal study. *Child Development, 52,* 1344–1347.

Perloff, R. M., Brown, J. D., & Miller, M. M. (1972, August). *Mass media and sex-typing: Research perspectives and policy implications.* Paper presented at the meeting of the American Psychological Association, Toronto.

Peskin, H. (1967). Pubertal onset and ego functioning. *Journal of Abnormal Psychology, 72,* 1–15.

Petersen, A. C., & Taylor, B. (1980). The biological approach to adolescence. In J. Adelson (Ed.), *Handbook of adolescent psychology.* New York: John Wiley.

Peterson, P. E., Jeffrey, D. B., Bridgwater, C. A., & Dawson, B. (1985). How pronutrition television programming affects children's dietary habits. *Developmental Psychology, 20,* 55–63.

Peterson, P. L. (1977). Interactive effects of student anxiety, achievement orientation, and teacher behavior on student achievement and attitude. *Journal of Educational Psychology, 69,* 779–792.

Peterson, R. F., & Peterson, L. R. (1968). The use of positive reinforcement in the control of self-destructive behavior in a retarded boy. *Journal of Experimental Child Psychology, 69,* 779–792.

Phillips, J. L., Jr. (1975). *The origins of intellect: Piaget's theory* (2d ed.). New York: Freeman.

Piaget, J. (1932). *The moral judgment of the child.* New York: Harcourt, Brace & World.

Piaget, J. (1952a). Jean Piaget. In C. A. Murchison (Ed.), *A history of psychology in autobiography* (Vol. 4). Worcester, MA: Clark University Press.

Piaget, J. (1952b). *The origins of intelligence in children.* (M. Cook, Trans.). New York: International Universities Press.

Piaget, J. (1960). *The child's conception of the world.* Totowa, NJ: Littlefield, Adams. (Original work published 1926)

Piaget, J. (1962). *Play, dreams, and imitation in childhood.* New York: Norton.

Piaget, J. (1967). The mental development of the child. In D. Elkind (Ed.), *Six psychological studies by Piaget.* New York: Random House.

Piaget, J. (1970). Piaget's theory. In P. H. Mussen (Ed.), *Manual of child psychology* (3rd ed., Vol. 1). New York: John Wiley.

Piaget, J. (1971). *The construction of reality by the child.* New York: Ballantine. (Original work published 1954)

Piaget, J., & Inhelder, B. (1969). *The psychology of the child* (H. Weaver, Trans.). New York: Basic Books.

Piers, E. V., & Harris, D. B. (1964). Age and other correlates of self-concept in children. *Journal of Educational Psychology, 55,* 91–95.

Piontowski, D., & Calfee, R. (1979). Attention in the classroom. In G. Hale and M. Lewis (Eds.), *Attention and cognitive development.* New York: Plenum.

Platt, J. R., & Day, R. B. (1979). A hierarchical response-unit analysis of resistance to extinction following fixed-number and fixed consecutive-number reinforcement. *Journal of Experimental Psychology: Animal Behavior Processes, 5,* 307–320.

Pleck, J. H. (1975). Masculinity-femininity: Current and alternative paradigms. *Sex Roles, 1,* 161–178.

Pleck, J. H. (1979). Men's family work: Three perspectives and some new data. *The Family Coordinator, 28,* 481–488.

Plost, M., & Rosen, M. J. (1974). Effects of sex of career models on occupational preferences of adolescents. *AV Communication Review, 22,* 41–50.

Porteus, A. (1976). *Teacher-centered vs. student-centered instruction: Interactions with cognitive and motivational aptitudes.* Unpublished doctoral dissertation, Stanford University, Stanford, CA.

Posner, M. (1970). Abstraction and the process of recognition. In J. T. Spence & G. H. Bower (Eds.), *The psychology of learning and motivation* (Vol. 3). New York: Academic Press.

Postman, L. (1962). *Psychology in the making.* New York: Knopf.

Power, C. (1984). *Moral atmosphere.* Paper presented at the meeting of the American Educational Research Association, New Orleans.

Premack, A. J., & Premack, D. (1972). Teaching language to an ape. *Scientific American, 227,* 92–98.

Pressley, M. (1982). Elaboration and memory development. *Child Development, 53,* 296–309.

Pressley, M., & Levin, J. R. (1977). Task parameters affecting the efficacy of a visual imagery learning strategy in younger and older children. *Journal of Experimental Child Psychology, 24,* 53–59.

Pressley, M., & Levin, J. R. (1980). The development of mental imagery retrieval. *Child Development, 51,* 558–560.

Psathas, G. (1957). Ethnicity, social class, and adolescent independence. *American Sociological Review, 22,* 415–423.

Pulos, E., Teller, D. Y., & Buck, S. (1980). Infant color vision: A search for short wavelength-sensitive mechanisms by means of chromatic adaptation. *Vision Research, 20,* 485–493.

Purpura, D. P. (1974). Dendrite spine "dysgenesis" and mental retardation. *Science, 186,* 1126–1128.

Quadagno, D. M., Brisco, R., & Quadagno, J. S. (1977). Effect of perinatal gonadal hormones on selected nonsexual behavior patterns: A critical assessment of the nonhuman and human literature. *Psychological Bulletin, 84,* 62–80.

Quitkin, F., Rifkin, A., & Klein, D. F. (1976). Neurologic soft signs in schizophrenia and character disorders. *Archives of General Psychiatry, 33,* 845–853.

Rabinowitz, M., Valentine, K. M., & Mandler, J. M. (1981, September). *A developmental comparison of inferential processing: When adults don't always know best.* Paper presented at the meeting of the American Psychological Association, Los Angeles.

Radke-Yarrow, M., Zahn-Waxler, C., & Chapman, M. (1983). Children's prosocial dispositions and behavior. In P. H. Mussen (Ed.), *Handbook of child psychology* (4th ed., Vol. 4). New York: John Wiley.

Ramey, C. T., MacPhee, D., & Yeates, K. O. (1982). Preventing developmental retardation: A general systems model. In L. Bond & J. Joffe (Eds.), *Facilitating infant and early childhood development.* Hanover, NH: University Press of New England.

Rao, N. (1985, April). *Increasing social participation in pre-school social isolates.* Paper presented at the meeting of the Society for Research in Child Development, Toronto.

Rappaport, D. (1967). On the psychoanalytic theory of thinking. In M. M. Gill (Ed.), *The collected papers of David Rappaport.* New York: Basic Books.

Raven, J. C. (1960). *Guide to using the Standard Progressive Matrices.* London: Lewis.

Rebecca, M., Hefner, R., & Oleshansky, B. (1976). A model of sex role transcendence. *Journal of Social Issues, 32,* 197–206.

Reese, H. W. (1974). Cohort, age, and imagery in children's paired associate learning. *Child Development, 45,* 1176–1178.

Regan, J. W. (1971). Guilt, perceived injustice, and altruistic behavior. *Journal of Personality and Social Psychology, 18,* 124–132.

Reinisch, J. M., & Karow, W. G. (1977). Prenatal exposure to synthetic progestins and estrogens: Effects on human development. *Archives of Sexual Behavior, 6,* 257–288.

Rekers, G. A. (1979). Psychosexual and gender problems. In E. J. Mash & L. G. Terdal (Eds.), *Behavioral assessment of childhood disorders.* New York: Guilford Press.

Renshaw, P. D., and Asher, S. R. (1982). Social competence and peer status: The distinction between goals and strategies. In K. H. Rubin & H. S. Ross (Eds.), *Peer relationships and social skills in childhood.* New York: Springer.

Rescorla, R. A. (1967). Pavlovian conditioning and its proper control procedures. *Psychological Review, 74,* 71–80.

Rescorla, R. A., & Wagner, A. R. (1972). A theory of Pavlovian conditioning: Variations in the effectiveness of reinforcement and nonreinforcement. In A. Black & W. F. Prokasy (Eds.), *Classical conditioning II: Current research and theory.* New York: Appleton-Century-Crofts.

Rest, J. R. (1976). New approaches in the assessment of moral judgment. In T. Lickona (Ed.), *Moral development and behavior.* New York: Holt, Rinehart & Winston.

Rest, J. R. (1977, March). *Development in judging moral issues—A summary of research using the defining issues test.* Paper presented at the meeting of the Society for Research in Child Development, New Orleans.

Rest, J. R. (1983). Morality. In P. H. Mussen (Ed.), *Handbook of child psychology* (4th ed., Vol. 3). New York: John Wiley.

Rest, J. R., Turiel, E., & Kohlberg, L. (1969). Relations between level of moral judgment and preference and comprehension of the moral judgments of others. *Journal of Personality, 37,* 225–252.

Rheingold, H. L. (1969). The social and socializing infant. In D. A. Goslin (Ed.), *Handbook of socialization theory and research.* Chicago: Rand McNally.

Rheingold, H. L. (1973). Independent behavior in the human infant. In A. D. Pick (Ed.), *Minnesota Symposium of Child Psychology*. Minneapolis: University of Minnesota Press.

Rheingold, H. L., & Eckerman, C. O. (1970). The infant separates himself from his mother. *Science, 168*, 78–83.

Rheingold, H. L., & Samuels, H. R. (1969). Mainstreaming the positive behavior of infants by increased stimulation. *Developmental Psychology, 1*, 520–527.

Richards, R. A. (1976). A comparison of selected Guilford and Wallach-Kogan creativity thinking tests in conjunction with measures of intelligence. *Journal of Creative Behavior, 10*, 154–164.

Richardson, J. G., & Simpson, C. H. (1982). Children, gender, and social structure: An analysis of the contents of letters to Santa Claus. *Child Development, 53*, 429–436.

Ricks, M. (1983). *The origins of individual differences in competence: Attachment history and environmental support*. Unpublished doctoral dissertation, University of Massachusetts, Amherst.

Riegel, K. F. (1975). Adult life crisis: A dialectic interpretation of development. In N. Datan & L. H. Ginsberg (Eds.), *Life-span developmental psychology*. New York: Academic Press.

Ringness, T. A. (1975). *The affective domain in education*. Boston: Little, Brown.

Risley, T. R. (1978). The effects and side effects of punishing the autistic behaviors of a deviant child. *Journal of Applied Behavior Analysis, 1*, 21–34.

Risley, T. R., & Wolf, M. M. (1976). Establishing functional speech in echolalic children. *Behavior Research and Therapy, 5*, 73–88.

Robins, L. N. (1978). Sturdy childhood predictors of adult antisocial behavior: Replications from longitudinal studies. *Psychological medicine, 8*, 611–622.

Robinson, H. F. (1977). *Exploring teaching in early childhood education*. Boston: Allyn & Bacon.

Rock, I., Halper, F., & Clayton, T. (1972). The perception and recognition of complex figures. *Cognitive Psychology, 3*, 655–673.

Rode, S. S., Chang, P., Fisch, R. O., & Sroufe, L. A. (1981). Attachment patterns of infants separated at birth. *Developmental Psychology, 1*, 188–191.

Rodgers, J. L. (1984). Confluence effects: Not here, not now! *Developmental Psychology, 20*, 321–331.

Rogers, C. R. (1951). *Client-centered therapy*. Boston: Houghton Mifflin.

Rogers, T. (1981). A model of the self as an aspect of the human information-processing system. In N. Cantor & J. Kihlstrom (Eds.), *Cognition, social interaction, and personality*. Hillsdale, NJ: Lawrence Erlbaum.

Rogers, T., Kuiper, N., & Kierker, W. (1977). Self-reference and the encoding of personal information. *Journal of Personality and Social Psychology, 35*, 677–688.

Roper, R., & Hinde, R. A. (1978). Social behavior in a play group: Consistency and complexity. *Child Development, 45*, 920–927.

Rose, R. J., Harris, E. L., & Christian, J. C. (1979). Genetic variance in nonverbal intelligence: Data from kinships of identical twins. *Science, 205*, 1153–1155.

Rose, S. A., & Wallace, I. F. (1985). Visual recognition memory: A predictor of later cognitive functioning in preterms. *Child Development, 56*, 843–852.

Rosenblatt, D. (1977). Developmental trends in infant play. In B. Tizard & D. Harvey (Eds.), *The biology of play*. Philadelphia: Lippincott.

Rosenblith, J. F., & Sims-Knight, J. E. (1985). *In the beginning*. Monterey, CA: Brooks/Cole.

Rosenthal, R., & Jacobsen, L. (1968). *Pygmalion in the classroom*. New York: Holt, Rinehart & Winston.

Rosenthal, T. L., & Zimmerman, B. J. (1978). *Social learning and development*. New York: Academic Press.

Ross, A. O. (1974). *Psychological disorders of children: A behavioral approach to theory, research, and therapy*. New York: McGraw-Hill.

Rothbart, M. L. K. (1967). Birth order and mother-child interaction. *Dissertation Abstracts, 27*, 45–57.

Rovee-Collier, C. K. (1984). The ontogeny of learning and memory in human infancy. In R. Kail & N. E. Spear (Eds.), *Comparative perspectives on the development of memory*. Hillsdale, NJ: Lawrence Erlbaum.

Rovee-Collier, C. K., Sullivan, M. W., Enright, M., Lucas, D., & Fagen, J. (1980). Reactivation of infant memory. *Science, 208*, 1159–1161.

Rozin, P., Bressman, B., & Taft, M. (1974). Do children understand the basic relationship between speech and writing? The mow motorcycle test. *Journal of Reading Behavior, 6*, 327–334.

Rozin, P., & Gleitman, L. R. (1977). The structure and acquisition of reading II: The reading process and the acquisition of the alphabetic principle. In A. S. Reber & D. L. Scarborough (Eds.), *Toward a psychology of reading*. Hillsdale, NJ: Lawrence Erlbaum.

Rubenstein, J. L., Howes, C., & Boyle, P. (1981). A two year follow-up of infants in community based infant day care. *Journal of Child Psychology and Psychiatry, 22*, 209–218.

Rubin, K. H. (1973). Egocentrism in childhood: A unitary construct? *Child Development, 44*, 102–110.

Rubin, K. H. (1977). The social and cognitive value of preschool toys and activities. *Canadian Journal of Behavioural Science, 9*, 382–385.

Rubin, K. H. (1982). Nonsocial play in preschoolers: Necessary evil? *Child Development, 53*, 651–657.

Rubin, K. H., Fein, G. G., & Vanderberg, B. (1983). In P. H. Mussen (Ed.), *Handbook of Child Psychology* (4th ed., Vol. 4). New York: John Wiley.

Rubin, K. H., & Pepler, D. J. (1980). The relationship of child's play to social-cognitive development. In H. Foot, T. Chapman, & J. Smith (Eds.), *Friendship and childhood relationships*. London: John Wiley.

Rubin, K. H., & Schneider, F. W. (1973). The relationship between moral judgment, egocentrism, and altruistic behavior. *Child Development, 44*, 661–665.

Ruble, D. N., & Ruble, T. L. (1980). Sex stereotypes. In A. G. Miller (Ed.), *In the eye of the beholder: Contemporary issues in stereotyping*. New York: Holt, Rinehart & Winston.

Ruff, M. A., & Birch, H. G. (1974). Infant visual fixation: The effect of concentricity, curvilineavity, and the number of directions. *Journal of Experimental Psychology, 17*, 460–473.

Rutter, M. (1971). Parent-child separation: Psychological effects on the children. *Journal of Child Psychology and Psychiatry, 12*, 233–260.

Rutter, M. (Ed.). (1980). *Scientific foundations of developmental psychiatry*. London: Heinemann.

Rutter, M. (1983, April). *Influences from family and school*. Invited lecture presented at the meeting of the Society for Research in Child Development, Detroit.

Rutter, M. (in press). Statistical and personal interactions: Facets and perspectives. In D. Magnusson & V. Allen (Eds.), *Human development: An interactional perspective*. New York: Academic Press.

Rutter, M., & Garmezy, N. (1983). Developmental psychopathology. In P. H. Mussen (Ed.), *Handbook of child psychology* (4th ed., Vol. 4). New York: John Wiley.

Rutter, M., Maughan, B., Mortimore, P., & Ouston, J. (1979). *Fifteen thousand hours: Secondary schools and their effects on children*. Cambridge, MA: Harvard University Press.

Sagan, C. (1980). *Cosmos*. New York: Random House.

Sakabe, N., Arayama, T., & Suzuki, T. (1969). Human fetal evoked response to acoustic stimulation. *Acta Oto-Laryngologica, 252*, 29–36 (Suppl.).

Salapatek, P. (1975). Pattern perception in early infancy. In L. B. Cohen & P. Salapatek (Eds.), *Infant perception: From sensation to cognition* (vol. 1). Orlando, FL: Academic Press.

Salapatek, P., Bechtold, A. G., & Bushnell, B. W. (1976). Infant acuity as a function of viewing distance. *Child Development, 47*, 860–863.

Saltz, R. (1973). Effects of part-time "mothering" on IQ and SQ of young institutionalized children. *Child Development, 9*, 166–170.

Samuels, H. R. (1980). The effect of an older sibling on infant locomotor exploration of a new environment. *Child Development, 51*, 607–609.

Santrock, J. W. (1972). The relations of onset and type of father absence to cognitive development. *Child Development, 43*, 455–469.

Santrock, J. W. (1986). *Psychology: The science of mind and behavior*. Dubuque, IA: Wm. C. Brown.

Santrock, J. W., & Madison, T. D. (1985). Three research traditions in the study of adolescents from divorced families: Quasi-experimental, developmental; clinical; and family sociological. *Journal of Early Adolescence, 5*, 115–128.

Santrock, J. W., & Sitterle, K. A. (1985). The social and developmental worlds of children in divorced families. In D. C. Goldberg (Ed.), *Handbook of contemporary marriage and family*. Chicago: Dow-Jones-Irwin.

Santrock, J. W., Smith, P. C., & Bourbeau, P. (1976). Effects of group social comparison upon aggressive and regressive behavior in children. *Child Development, 47*, 831–837.

Santrock, J. W., & Warshak, R. A. (1979). Father custody and social development in boys and girls. *Journal of Social Issues, 35*, 112–125.

Santrock, J. W., & Warshak, R. A. (1986). Development, relationships, and legal/clinical considerations in father-custody families. In M. E. Lamb (Ed.), *The father's role: Applied perspectives*. New York: John Wiley.

Santrock, J. W., Warshak, R. A., Sitterle, K. A., Dozier, C., & Stephens, M. (1985, August). *The social development of children in stepparent families*. Paper presented at the meeting of the American Psychological Association, Los Angeles.

Santrock, J. W., & Yussen, S. R. (1981). *Childhood socialization/Social and personality development*. New York: Wiley.

Sapir, E. (1958). Language and environment. In D. G. Mandelbaum (Ed.), *Selected writings of Edward Sapir in language, culture, and personality*. Berkeley: University of California Press.

Sawin, D. B. (1979, March). *Assessing empathy in children: A search for an elusive construct*. Paper presented at the meeting of the Society for Research in Child Development, San Francisco.

Scarr, S. (1984, May). [Interview]. *Psychology Today*, pp. 59–63.

Scarr, S., & Kidd, K. K. (1983). Developmental behavior genetics. In P. H. Mussen (Ed.), *Handbook of child psychology* (4th ed., Vol. 2). New York: John Wiley.

Scarr, S., & Weinberg, R. A. (1976). IQ test performance of black children adopted by white families. *American Psychologist, 31*, 726–739.

Scarr, S., & Weinberg, R. A. (1980). Calling all camps! The war is over. *American Sociological Review, 45*, 859–865.

Schachter, S. (1959). *The psychology of affiliation*. Stanford, CA: Stanford University Press.

Schachter, S. (1963). Birth order, eminence, and higher education. *American Sociological Review, 28*, 757–767.

Schacter, D. L., & Moscovitch, M. (1984). Infants, amnesiacs, and dissociable memory systems. In M. Moscovitch (Ed.), *Infant memory: Its relation to normal and pathological memory in humans and other animals*. New York: Plenum.

Schaeffer, R. W. (1979). Human preferences for time dependent and response-dependent reinforcement schedules. *Bulletin of the Psychonomic Society, 14*, 293–296.

Schaffer, H. R., & Emerson, P. E. (1964). The development of social attachments in infancy. *Monographs of the Society for Research in Child Development, 29* (3, Serial No. 94).

Schaffer, R. (1977). *Mothering*. Cambridge, MA: Harvard University Press.

Schaie, K. W. (1965). A general model for the study of developmental problems. *Psychological Bulletin, 64*, 92–107.

Schank, R., & Abelson, R. (1976). *Scripts, plans, goals, and understanding*. Hillsdale, NJ: Lawrence Erlbaum.

Scheff, T. J. (1966). *Being mentally ill: A sociological theory*. Chicago: Aldine.

Schiff, A. R., & Knopf, I. J. (1985). The effects of task demands on attention allocation in children of different ages. *Child Development, 56*, 621–630.

Schildkraut, J. J., & Kety, S. S. (1967). Biogenic amines and emotion. *Science, 156*, 21–30.

Schneider, B. A., Trehub, S. E., & Bull, D. (1980). High-frequency sensitivity in infants. *Science, 207*, 1003–1004.

Schofield, A. T., & Vaughn-Jackson, P. (1913). *What a boy should know*. New York: Cassell.

Schramm, W., Lyle, J., & Parker, E. B. (1961). *Television in the lives of children*. Stanford, CA: Stanford University Press.

Schwartz, B. (1981, March). In pursuit of B. F. Skinner. *Swarthmore College Bulletin*, pp. 12–16.

Schwartz, K. (1978). Proximity to mother and wariness in infants associated with exploration of an unfamiliar object. *Dissertation Abstracts International, 38* (12B), 6204–6205.

Sears, R. R., (1977). Sources of life satisfactions of the Terman gifted men. *American Psychologist, 32*, 119–128.

Segal, N. L. (1985). Monozygotic and dizygotic twins: A comparative analysis of mental ability profiles. *Child Development, 56,* 1051–1058.

Seligman, M. E. P. (1975). *Learned helplessness.* San Francisco: W. H. Freeman.

Seligman, M. E. P., & Peterson, C. (in press). A learned helplessness perspective on childhood depression: Theory and research. In M. Rutter & C. E. Izard (Eds.), *Depression in childhood: Developmental perspectives.* New York: Guilford Press.

Selman, R. L. (1971). The relation of role-taking ability to the development of moral judgment in children. *Child Development, 42,* 79–91.

Selman, R. L. (1976). Social-cognitive understanding. In T. Lickona (Ed.), *Moral development and behavior.* New York: Holt, Rinehart & Winston.

Selman, R. L. (1980). *The growth of interpersonal understanding.* New York: Academic Press.

Selman, R. L., & Byrne, D. F. (1974). A structural-developmental analysis of levels of role taking in middle childhood. *Child Development, 45,* 803–806.

Selman, R. L., Newberger, C. M., & Jacquette, D. (1977, March). *Observing interpersonal reasoning in a clinic/educational setting: Toward the integration of development and clinical-child psychology.* Paper presented at the meeting of the Society for Research in Child Development, New Orleans.

Serbin, L. A., O'Leary, K. D., Kent, R. N., & Tonick, I. J. (1973). A comparison of teacher response to the preacademic and problem behavior of boys and girls. *Child Development, 44,* 796–804.

Sexton, M. A., & Geffen, G. (1979). Development of three strategies of attention in dichotic listening. *Developmental Psychology, 15,* 299–310.

Shantz, C. U. (1983). The development of social cognition. In P. H. Mussen (Ed.), *Handbook of child psychology* (4th ed., Vol. 3). New York: John Wiley.

Sharabany, R., Gershoni, R., & Hofman, J. E. (1981). Girlfriend, boyfriend: Age and sex differences in intimate friendship. *Developmental Psychology, 17,* 800–808.

Sharpe, L. W. (1976). The effects of a creative thinking program on intermediate-grade educationally handicapped children. *Journal of Creative Behavior, 10*(2), 138–145.

Shatz, M., & Gelman, R. (1973). The development of communication skills: Modifications in the speech of young children as a function of the listener. *Monographs of the Society for Research in Child Development, 38* (5, Serial No. 152).

Sheinhold, K., & Tenney, Y. J. (1982). Memory for a salient childhood event. In U. Neisser (Ed.), *Memory observed.* San Francisco: W. H. Freeman.

Sherif, M., Harvey, O. J., White, B. J., Hood, W. R., & Sherif, C. W. (1961). *Intergroup conflict and cooperation: The Robber's Cave experiment.* Norman, OK: Institute of Group Relations, University of Oklahoma.

Sherman, J. A. (1971). Imitation and language development. In H. W. Reese (Ed.), *Advances in child development and behavior* (Vol. 6), New York: Academic Press.

Shiffrin, R. M., & Schneider, W. (1977). Controlled and automatic human information processing. *Psychological Review, 84,* 127–190.

Short, E. (1985, April). *The relationship between children's memory performance and metacognitive knowledge: A developmental analysis of task-specific and general metamemory.* Paper presented at the meeting of the Society for Research in Child Development, Toronto.

Shucard, D. W., Shucard, J. L., & Cummins, K. R. (1979, March). *Auditory evoked potentials and sex related differences in brain development.* Paper presented at the biennial meeting of the Society for Research in Child Development, San Francisco.

Shuey, A. (1966). *The testing of Negro intelligence.* New York: Social Science Press.

Siegler, R. S. (1983). Information-processing approaches to development. In P. H. Mussen (Ed.), *Handbook of child psychology* (4th ed., Vol. 3). New York: John Wiley.

Siegler, R. S. (1984). Mechanisms of cognitive growth: Variation and selection. In R. J. Sternberg (Ed.), *Mechanisms of cognitive development.* San Francisco: W. H. Freeman.

Simmons, R. G., Blyth, D. A., & McKinney, K. L. (1983). The impact of puberty on adolescents: A longitudinal study. In J. Brooks-Gunn & A. C. Peterson (Eds.), *Girls at puberty: Biological and psychosocial perspectives.* New York: Plenum.

Simmons, R. G., Rosenberg, F., & Rosenberg, M. (1973). Disturbance in the self-image at adolescence. *American Sociological Review, 38,* 553–568.

Simpson, E. (1976). A holistic approach to moral development and behavior. In T. Lickona (Ed.), *Moral development and behavior.* New York: Holt, Rinehart & Winston.

Singh, J. A. L., & Zingg, R. M. (1942). *Wolf children and feral men.* New York: Harper & Row.

Sjolund, A. (1971). *The effect of day care institutions on children's development: An analysis of international research.* Copenhagen: The Danish National Institute of Social Research.

Skeels, H. (1966). Adult status of children with contrasting early life experiences. *Monograph of the Society for Research in Child Development, 31* (3, Serial No. 105).

Skinner, B. F. (1938). *The behavior of organisms.* New York: Appleton-Century-Crofts.

Skinner, B. F. (1957). *Verbal behavior.* New York: Appleton-Century-Crofts.

Skinner, B. F. (1971). *Beyond freedom and dignity.* New York: Knopf.

Slobin, D. (1972, July). Children and language: They learn the same all around the world. *Psychology Today,* pp. 71–76.

Slobin, D. (1973). Cognitive prerequisites for the development of grammar. In C. A. Ferguson & D. I. Slobin (Eds.), *Studies of child language development.* New York: Holt, Rinehart & Winston.

Smetana, J. (1983). Social-cognitive development: Domain distinctions and coordinations. *Developmental Review, 3,* 131–147.

Smetana, J. (1985). Preschool children's conceptions of transgressions: Effects of varying moral and conventional domain-related attributes. *Developmental Psychology, 21,* 18–29.

Smith, B. O., & Orlosky, D. E. (1975). *Socialization and schooling (basics of reform).* Bloomington, IN: Phi Delta Kappa.

Snarey, J. R., Reimer, J., & Kohlberg, L. (1985). Development of social-moral reasoning among Kibbutz adolescents: A longitudinal cross-sectional study. *Developmental Psychology, 21,* 3–17.

Snow, C. E. (1977). The development of conversation between mothers and babies. *Journal of Child Language, 4,* 1–22.

Snow, C. E. (1985, April). *Imitation as a cognitive mechanism: A discussion.* Paper presented at the meeting of the Society for Research in Child Development, Toronto.

Snow, R. E. (1971). Individual differences and instructional theory. *Educational Researcher, 6,* 11–15.

Sokolov, E. N. (1976). Learning and memory: Habituation as negative learning. In M. R. Rosenzwieg & E. L. Bennett (Eds.), *Thinking: Readings in cognitive science.* Cambridge: Cambridge University Press.

Solso, R. L. (1979). *Cognitive psychology.* New York: Harcourt Brace Jovanovich.

Song, M., & Ginsburg, H. P. (1985, April). *The development of informal and formal mathematical knowledge in Korean and American children.* Paper presented at the meeting of the Society for Research in Child Development, Toronto.

Sontag, L. W., & Wallace, R. F. (1935). The movement response of the human fetus to sound stimuli. *Child Development, 6,* 253–258.

Sophian, C. (1985). Perseveration and infants' search: A comparison of two- and three-location tasks. *Developmental Psychology, 21,* 187–194.

Spearman, C. E. (1927). *The abilities of man.* New York: Macmillan.

Spelke, E. S. (1979). Perceiving bimodally specified events in infancy. *Developmental Psychology, 15,* 626–636.

Spelke, E. S., & Born, W. S. (1982). *Perception of visual objects by 3-month-old infants.* Unpublished manuscript.

Spence, J. T., & Helmreich, R. (1972). The Attitudes Toward Women Scale: An objective instrument to measure the rights and roles of women in contemporary society. *JSAS Catalog of Selected Documents in Psychology, 2,* 66.

Spence, J. T., & Helmreich, R. L. (1978). *Masculinity and feminity: Their psychological dimensions.* Austin: University of Texas Press.

Spence, J. T., Helmreich, R. L., & Stapp, J. (1974). The personal attributes questionnaire: A measure of sex-role stereotypes and masculinity-femininity. *JSAS Catalog of Selected Documents in Psychology, 4,* 43.

Sperry, R. W. (1968). Hemisphere disconnection and unity in conscious awareness. *American Psychologist, 23,* 723–733.

Sperry, R. W. (1974). Lateral specialization in surgically separated hemispheres. In F. O. Schmitt & F. G. Worden (Eds.), *The neurosciences: Third study program.* Cambridge, MA: M.I.T. Press.

Sperry, R. W., & Gazzaniga, M. S. (1967). Language following surgical disconnection of the hemispheres. In C. H Milikan & F. L. Darley (Eds.), *Brain mechanisms underlying speech and language.* New York: Grune & Stratton.

Spitz, R. A. (1945). Hospitalism: An inquiry into the genesis of psychiatric conditions in early childhood. *Psychoanalytic Study of the Child, 1,* 53–74.

Sroufe, L. A. (1979). The coherence of individual development. *American Psychologist, 34,* 834–841.

Sroufe, L. A. (1985). Attachment classification from the perspective of infant-caregiver relationships and infant temperament. *Child Development, 56,* 1–14.

Sroufe, L. A., & Fleeson, J. (1985). Attachment and the construction of relationships. In W. W. Hartup and Z. Rubin (Eds.), *Relationships and development.* Hillsdale, NJ: Lawrence Erlbaum.

Sroufe, L. A., & Rutter, M. (1984). The domain of developmental psychopathology. *Child Development, 55,* 17–29.

Stallings, J. (1975). Implementation and child effects of teaching practices in Follow Through classrooms. *Monographs of the Society for Research in Child Development, 40* (Serial No. 163).

Stanley, J. C. (1977). Rationale of the study of mathematically precocious youth (SMPY) during its first five years of promoting educational acceleration. In Stanley, J. C., George, W. C., & Solano, C. H. (Eds.), *The gifted and creative: A fifty-year perspective.* Baltimore: The Johns Hopkins University Press.

Staub, E. (1971). A child in distress: The influence of age and the number of witnesses on children's attempts to help. *Journal of Personality and Social Psychology, 17,* 137–144.

Stein, A. H. (1972). Mass media and young children's development. In I. J. Gordon (Ed.), *Early childhood education.* Chicago: University of Chicago Press.

Stein, A. H., & Bailey, M. M. (1973). The socialization of achievement orientation in females. *Psychological Bulletin, 80,* 345–365.

Stein, M. (Ed.). (1972). *Changing sexist practices in the classroom.* Washington, DC: American Federation of Teachers.

Steinberg, L. D. (1980). *Understanding families with young adolescents.* Carrboro, NC: Center for Early Adolescence, University of North Carolina.

Steiner, J. E. (1979). Human facial expressions in response to taste and smell stimulation. In H. Reese and L. Lipsett (Eds.), *Advances in child development and behavior* (Vol. 13). New York: Academic Press.

Steinschneider, A., Lipton, E., & Richmond, J. (1966). Auditory sensitivity in the infant: Effect of intensity on cardiac and motor responsivity. *Child Development, 37,* 233–252.

Stern, D., Beebe, B., Jaffe, J., & Bennett, S. (1977). The infant's stimulus world during social interaction: A study of caregiver behaviors with particular reference to repetition and timing. In H. R. Schaffer (Ed.), *Studies in mother-infant interaction.* New York: Academic Press.

Stern, D. N., Spieker, S., & McKain, C. (1982). Intonation contours as signals in maternal speech to prelinguistic infants. *Developmental Psychology, 18,* 727–735.

Sternberg, R. J. (1977). *Intelligence, information processing, and analogical reasoning: The componential analysis of human abilities.* Hillsdale, NJ: Lawrence Erlbaum.

Sternberg, R. J. (Ed.). (1982). *Advances in the psychology of human intelligence.* Hillsdale, NJ: Lawrence Erlbaum.

Sternberg, R. J. (1984). Mechanisms of cognitive development: A componential approach. In R. J. Sternberg (Ed.), *Mechanisms of cognitive development.* San Francisco: W. H. Freeman.

Sternberg, R. J., & Davidson, J. E. (1983). Insight in the gifted. *Educational Psychologist, 18,* 52–58.

Steur, F. B., Applefield, J. M., & Smith, R. (1974). Televised aggression and interpersonal aggression among preschool children. *Journal of Experimental Psychology, 11,* 442–447.

Stevens, C. (1979, September). The neuron. *Scientific American,* p. 64.

Stevenson, H. W. (1972). *Children's learning.* New York: Appleton-Century-Crofts.

Stevenson, H. W. (1973). *The taxonomy of tasks.* Unpublished manuscript, University of Minnesota, St. Paul.

Stevenson, H. W. (1974, Fall). Reflections on the China visit. *Society for Research in Child Development Newsletter, 3.*

Stevenson, H. W. (1982). Influences of schooling on cognitive development. In D. A. Wagner & H. W. Stevenson (Eds.), *Cultural perspectives on child development.* San Francisco: W. H. Freeman.

Stevenson, H. W., Hale, G. A., Klein, R. E., & Miller, L. K. (1968). Interrelations and correlates in children's learning and problem solving. *Monographs of the Society for Research in Child Development, 33* (Serial No. 123).

Stevenson, H. W., Stigler, J. W., Lee, S., & Lucker, G. W. (1985). Cognitive performance and academic achievement of Japanese, Chinese, and American children. *Child Development, 56,* 718–734.

Stipek, D. J., & Hoffman, J. M. (1980). Children's achievement-related expectancies as a function of academic performance, histories and sex. *Journal of Educational Psychology, 72,* 861–865.

Stone, N. W., & Chesney, B. H. (1978). Attachment behaviors in handicapped infants. *Mental Retardation, 16,* 8–12.

Strauss, M. S., & Curtis, L. E. (1982). Infant perception of numerosity. *Child Development, 52,* 1146–1152.

Streissguth, A. P., Barr, H. M., & Martin, D. C. (1983). Maternal alcohol use and neonatal habituation assessed with the Brazelton Scale. *Child Development, 44,* 1109–1118.

Streissguth, A. P., Martin, D. C., Barr, H. M., Sandman, B. M., Kirchner, G. L., & Darby, B. L. (1984). Intra-uterine alcohol and nicotine exposure: Attention and reaction time in 4-year-old children. *Developmental Psychology, 20,* 533–541.

Stricker, L. J., Jacobs, P. I., & Kogan, N. (1974). Trait interrelations in implicit personality theories and questionnaire data. *Journal of Personality and Social Psychology, 29,* 198–207.

Sullivan, H. S. (1953). *The interpersonal theory of psychiatry.* New York: Norton.

Suomi, S. J., & Harlow, H. F. (1972). Social rehabilitation of isolate-reared monkeys. *Developmental Psychology, 6,* 487–496.

Suomi, S. J., Harlow, H. F., & Domek, C. J. (1970). Effect of repetitive infant-infant separation of young monkeys. *Journal of Abnormal Psychology, 76,* 161–172.

Sutton-Smith, B. (1973). *Child psychology.* New York: Appleton-Century-Crofts.

Sutton-Smith, B., & Rosenberg, B. G. (1970). *The sibling.* New York: Holt, Rinehart & Winston.

Suzuki, T., Kamijo, Y., & Kiuchi, S. (1964). Auditory tests of newborn infants. *Annals of Otology,* pp. 914–923.

Swadesh, M. (1971). *The origin and diversification of language* (J. Sherzer, Ed.). Chicago: Aldine-Atherton.

Szasz, T. (1961). *The myth of mental illness.* New York: Harper & Row.

Szasz, T. (1977). *Psychiatric slavery: When confinement and coercion masquerade as care.* New York: Free Press.

Tanner, J. M. (1966). Growth and physique in different populations of mankind. In P. T. Baker & J. S. Weiner (Eds.), *The biology of human adaptability.* Oxford: Clarendon.

Tanner, J. M. (1970). Physical growth. In P. H. Mussen (Ed.), *Carmichael's manual of child psychology* (Vol. 1). New York: John Wiley.

Tanner, J. M. (1973, September). Growing up. *Scientific American, 229,* p. 40.

Tanner, J. M. (1978). *Fetus into man: Physical growth from conception to maturity.* Cambridge, MA: Harvard University Press.

Tanner, J. M., Whitehouse, R. H., & Takaishi, M. (1966). Standards from birth to maturity for height, weight, height velocity, and weight velocity: British children, 1965. *Archives of Diseases in Childhood,* p. 41.

Tarpy, R. M., & Mayer, R. E. (1978). *Foundations of learning and memory.* Glenview, IL: Scott, Foresman.

Taylor, M. K., & Kogan, K. L. (1973). Effects of birth of a sibling on mother-child interactions. *Child Psychiatry and Human Development, 4,* 53–58.

Tedesco, N. S. (1974). Patterns in prime time. *Journal of Communication, 24,* 119–124.

Terman, L. M. (1925). *Genetic studies of genius: Mental and physical traits of a thousand gifted children* (Vol. 1). Stanford, CA: Stanford University Press.

Terman, L. M., & Oden, M. H. (1959). *Genetic studies of genius. The gifted at mid-life: Thirty-five years' follow-up of the superior child* (Vol. 5). Stanford, CA: Stanford University Press.

Terr, L. C. (1970). A family study of child abuse. *American Journal of Psychiatry, 223,* 102–109.

Terrace, H. (1979). *Nim.* New York: Knopf.

Thelen, E. (1979). Rhythmical stereotypies in normal human infants. *Animal Behavior, 27,* 699–715.

Thelen, E. (1981). Rhythmical behavior in infancy: An ethological perspective. *Developmental Psychology, 17,* 237–257.

Thelen, M. H., Frautschi, N. M., Fehrenback, P. A., & Kirkland, K. D. (1978). Imitation in the interest of social influence. *Developmental Psychology, 14,* 429–430.

Thelen, M. H., & Kirkland, K. D. (1976). On status and being imitated: Effects on reciprocal imitation and attraction. *Journal of Personality and Social Psychology, 33,* 691–697.

Thelen, M. H., Miller, D. J., Fehrenback, P. A., Frautschi, N. M., & Fishbein, M. D. (1980). Imitation during play as a means of social influence. *Child Development, 51,* 918–920.

Thomas, A., & Chess, S. (1977). *Temperament and development.* New York: Brunner/Mazel.

Thomas, A., Chess, S., & Birch, H. G. (1970). The origin of personality. *Scientific American, 223,* 102–109.

Thomas, E. A. C., & Martin, J. A. (1976). Analyses of parent-infant interaction. *Psychological Review, 83,* 141–156.

Thompson, G. G. (1944). The social and emotional development of pre-school children under two types of educational programs. *Psychological Monographs, 56* (5, Whole No. 258).

Thorndike, R. L. (1968). [Review of *Pygmalion in the classroom* by R. Rosenthal and L. Jacobsen]. *American Educational Research Journal, 5,* 708–711.

Thorndike, R. L. (1975). [Review of *Psychological testing of American minorities: Issues and consequences* by R. J. Samuda]. *Journal of Crosscultural Psychology, 7,* 123–125.

Thorndike, R. L., Hagen, E. P., & Sattler, J. M. (1985). *Stanford-Binet* (4th ed.). Chicago: Riverside Publishing.

Thorne, B. (1985, April). *Crossing the gender divide: What tomboys can teach us about processes of sex segregation.* Paper presented at the meeting of the Society for Research in Child Development, Toronto.

Thurstone, L. L. (1938). *Primary mental abilities. Psychometric Monographs* (No. 1).

Tieger, T. (1980). On the biological basis of sex differences in aggression. *Child Development, 51,* 943–963.

Tinbergen, N. (1969). *The study of instinct.* New York: Oxford University Press. (Originally published, 1951)

Tolman, E. C. (1932). *Purposive behavior in animals and man.* New York: Appleton-Century-Crofts.

Tolman, E. C., Ritchie, B. F., & Kalish, D. (1946). Studies in spatial learning: I. Orientation and short-cut. *Journal of Experimental Psychology, 36,* 13–24.

Tomasello, M., & Mannle, S. (1985). Pragmatics of sibling speech to one-year-olds. *Child Development, 56,* 911–917.

Toner, I. J., Holstein, R., & Hetherington, E. M. (1977). Reflection-impulsivity and self-control in preschool children. *Child Development, 48,* 239–245.

Torrance, E. P., & Torrance, P. (1972). Combining creative problem solving with creative expressive activities in the education of disadvantaged young people. *Journal of Creative Behavior, 6*(1), 1–10.

Trabasso, T. (1977). The role of memory as a system in making transitive references. In R. V. Kail, Jr., & J. W. Hagen (Eds.), *Perspectives on the development of memory and cognition.* Hillsdale, NJ: Lawrence Erlbaum.

Trehub, S. E., Bull, D., & Thorpe, L. A. (1984). Infants' perception of melodies: The role of melodic contour. *Child Development, 55,* 821–830.

Trehub, S. E., Schneider, B. A., & Endman, M. (1980). Developmental changes in infants' sensitivity to octave-band noises. *Journal of Experimental Child Psychology, 29,* 282–293.

Trickett, E., & Moos, R. (1974). Personal correlates of contrasting environments: Student satisfaction in high school classrooms. *American Journal of Community Psychology, 2,* 1–12.

Troll, L. E., & Bengston, V. L. (1982). Intergenerational relations through the life span. In B. B. Wolman (Ed.), *Handbook of developmental psychology.* Englewood Cliffs, NJ: Prentice-Hall.

Tryon, R. C. (1940). Genetic differences in maze-learning ability of rats. *Yearbook of the National Society for the Study of Education, 30,* 111–119.

Tuchman-Duplessis, H. (1975). Drug effects on the fetus. *Monographs on drugs* (Vol. 2). Sydney: ADIS Press.

Tulkin, S. R., & Kagan, J. (1971). Mother-child interaction in the first year of life. *Child Development, 43,* 31–41.

Tuma, N. B., & Hallinan, M. T. (1979). The effects of sex, race, and achievement on schoolchildren's friendships. *Social Forces, 57,* 1265–1285.

Turiel, E. (1966). An experimental test of the sequentiality of developmental stages in the child's moral judgments. *Journal of Personality and Social Psychology, 3,* 611–618.

Turiel, E. (1977). A critical analysis of Kohlberg's contributions to the study of moral thought. *Journal of Social Behavior, 7,* 41–63.

Turiel, E. (1978). Social regulations and domains of social concepts. In W. Damon (Ed.), *New directions for child development, Vol. 1: Social cognition.* San Francisco: Jossey-Bass.

Uddenberg, N. (1974). Reproductive adaptation in mother and daughter. *Acta Psychiatrica Scandanavia,* p. 254.

Underwood, B., & Moore, B. (1980). *Perspective taking and altruism.* Unpublished manuscript, University of Texas at Dallas, Richardson, TX.

Ungerer, J., Zelazo, P. R., Kearsley, R. B., & O'Leary, K. (1981). Developmental changes in the representation of objects in symbolic play from 18 to 34 months of age. *Child Development, 52,* 186–195.

USA Today, (October 16, 1984).

Uttal, D. H., Miller, K. J., & Stevenson, H. W. (1985, April). *Achievement in mathematics: Correlates of poor and excellent performance in American, Chinese, and American children.* Paper presented at the meeting of the Society for Research in Child Development, Toronto.

Uzgiris, I. C., & Hunt, J. M. (1972). *Toward ordinal scales of psychological development in infancy.* Unpublished manuscript, University of Illinois, Urbana.

Uzgiris, I. C., & Hunt, J. M. (1975). *Assessment in infancy: Ordinal scales of psychological development.* Urbana: University of Illinois Press.

Vandell, D. L. (1985, April). *Relationship between infant-peer and infant-mother interactions: What we have learned.* Paper presented at the meeting of the Society for Research in Child Development, Toronto.

Vandell, D. L., Wilson, K. S., & Buchanan, N. R. (1980). Peer interaction in the first year of life: An examination of its structure, content, and sensitivity to toys. *Child Development, 51,* 481–488.

Vandiver, R. (1972). *Sources and interrelation of premarital sexual standards and general liberality and conservatism.* Unpublished doctoral dissertation, Southern Illinois University, Carbondale.

Visher, E., & Visher, J. (1978). Common problems of stepparents and their spouses. *American Journal of Orthopsychiatry, 48,* 252–262.

Volterra, V., & Taeschner, T. (1978). The acquisition and development of language by bilingual children. *Journal of Child Language, 5,* 311–326.

Vurpillot, E. (1968). The development of scanning strategies and their relation to visual differentiation. *Journal of Experimental Child Psychology, 6,* 632–650.

Vygotsky, L. (1962). *Thought and language.* Cambridge, MA: MIT Press.

Vygotsky, L. S. (1978). Play and its role in the mental development of the child. *Soviet Psychology, 12,* 62–76.

Waddington, C. H. (1957). *The strategy of the genes.* London: Allen & Son.

Wagner, D. A. (1974). The development of short-term and incidental memory: A cross-cultural study. *Child Development, 45,* 389–396.

Walker, L. (1982). The sequentiality of Kohlberg's stages of moral development. *Child Development, 53,* 1330–1336.

Walker, L. (1984). Sex differences in the development of moral reasoning: A critical review. *Child Development, 55,* 677–691.

Walker-Andrews, A. S., & Lennon, E. M. (1985). Auditory-visual perception of changing distance by human infants. *Child Development, 56,* 544–548.

Wallach, M. A. (1973). Ideology, evidence, and creative research. *Contemporary Psychology, 18,* 162–164.

Wallach, M. A., & Kogan, N. (1965). *Modes of thinking in young children.* New York: Holt, Rinehart & Winston.

Wallerstein, J. (1982, July). *Children of divorce: Preliminary report of a ten-year follow-up.* Paper presented at the Tenth International Congress of the International Association for Child and Adolescent Psychiatry and Allied Professions, Dublin, Ireland.

Wallerstein, J. S., & Kelly, J. B. (1980). *Surviving the breakup.* New York: Basic Books.

Warden, D. A. (1976). The influence of context on childrens' use of identifying expressions and references. *British Journal of Psychology, 67,* 101–112.

Washburn, K. J., & Hakes, D. T. (1985, April). *Changes in children's semantic and syntactic acceptability judgments.* Paper presented at the meeting of the Society for Research in Child Development, Toronto.

Waterman, A. S., & Waterman, C. K. (1971). A longitudinal study of changes in ego identity status during the freshman year of college. *Developmental Psychology, 5,* 167–173.

Waters, E. (1978). The reliability and stability of individual differences in infant-mother attachment. *Child Development, 49,* 483–494.

Waters, E., & Sroufe, L. A. (1983). Social competence as a developmental construct. *Developmental Review, 3,* 79–97.

Waters, E., Wippman, J., & Sroufe, L. A. (1979). Attachment, positive affect, and competence in the peer group: Two studies in construct validation. *Child Development, 50,* 821–829.

Watson, J. B. (1913). Psychology as the behaviorist views it. *Psychological Review, 20,* 158–177.

Watson, J. B. (1924). *Behaviorism.* New York: Norton, 1924.

Watson, J. B. (1928). *Psychological care of infant and child.* New York: Norton.

Watson, J. B., & Raynor, R. (1920). Emotional reactions. *Journal of Experimental Psychology, 3,* 1–14.

Watson, M. W., & Fischer, K. W. (1977). A developmental sequence of age used in late infancy. *Child Development, 48,* 828–836.

Watson, M. W., & Fischer, K. W. (1980). Development of social roles in elicited and spontaneous behavior during the preschool years. *Developmental Psychology, 16,* 483–494.

Webb, P. A., & Abrahamson, A. A. (1976). Stages of egocentrism in children's use of "this" and "that": A different point of view. *Journal of Child Language, 3,* 349–367.

Wechsler, D. (1958). *The measurement and appraisal of adult intelligence* (4th ed.). Baltimore: Williams & Wilkins.

Weiner, B. (1974). *Achievement motivation and attribution theory.* Morristown, NJ: General Learning Press.

Weiner, I. B. (1980). Psychopathology in adolescence. In J. Adelson (Ed.), *Handbook of adolescent psychology.* New York: John Wiley.

Weiten, W. (1983). *Psychology applied to modern life.* Belmont, CA: Wadsworth.

Wellman, H. M., Ritter, R., & Flavell, J. H. (1985). Deliberate memory behavior in the delayed reactions of very young children. *Developmental Psychology, 11,* 780–787.

Werker, J. F., Gilbert, J. H. V., Humphrey, K., & Tees, R. C. (1981). Developmental aspects of cross-language speech perception. *Child Development, 52,* 349–355.

Werner, E. E., & Smith, R. S. (1982). *Vulnerable but not invincible: A longitudinal study of resilient children and youth.* New York: McGraw-Hill.

Werner, H., & Kaplan, B. (1963). *Symbol formation.* New York: John Wiley.

Wertheimer, M. (1961). Psychomotor coordination of auditory and visual space at birth. *Science, 134,* 1692.

West, D. J., & Farrington, D. P. (1977). *The delinquent way of life.* London: Heinemann Educational.

White House Conference on Children. Report of the committee on special classes. (1931). Gifted children. In *Special education: The handicapped and the gifted. Education and training. Section 3.* New York: Century, pp. 537–550.

Whitehurst, G. J. (1985, April). *The role of imitation in language learning by children with language delay.* Paper presented at the meeting of the Society for Research in Child Development, Toronto.

Whitehurst, G. J., Ironsmith, E. M., & Goldfein, M. (1974). Selective imitation of the passive construction through modeling. *Journal of Experimental Child Psychology, 17,* 288–302.

Whitehurst, G. J., & Vasta, R. (1975). Is language acquired through imitation? *Journal of Psycholinguistic Research, 4,* 37–58.

Whiting, B. B., & Whiting, J. W. M. (1975). *Children of six cultures: A psychocultural analysis.* Cambridge, MA: Harvard University Press.

Whorf, B. L. (1956). *Language, thought, and reality.* New York: John Wiley.

Widmayer, S., & Field, T. (1980). Effects of Brazelton demonstrations on early interactions of preterm infants and their teenage mothers. *Infant Behavior and Development, 3,* 79–89.

Wilkinson, L. C., Wilkinson, A. C., Spinelli, F., & Chiang, C. P. (1984). Metalinguistic knowledge of pragmatic rules in school-age children. *Child Development, 55,* 2130–2140.

Willemsen, E. (1979). *Understanding infancy.* San Francisco: W. H. Freeman.

Williams, J. (1979). Reading instruction today. *American Psychologist, 34,* 917–922.

Wilson, H. (1980). Parental supervision: A neglected aspect of delinquency. *British Journal of Social Work, 20,* 203–235.

Windle, W. F. (1940). *Physiology of the fetus. Origin and extent of function in prenatal life.* Philadelphia: Saunders.

Wingfield, A., & Sandoval, A. W. (1980). Perceptual processing for meaning. In L. W. Poon, J. L. Fozard, L. S. Cermak, D. Arenberg, & L. W. Thompson (Eds.), *New directions in memory and aging: Proceedings of the George Talland memorial conference.* Hillsdale, NJ: Erlbaum.

Witherspoon, R. (1980, November 22). Birth defects: A risk even before conception. *Dallas Morning News,* section C, p. 1.

Witryol, S. (1971). Incentives and learning in children. In H. W. Reese (Ed.), *Advances in child development and behavior* (Vol. 6). New York: Academic Press.

Wohlwill, J. F. (1973). *The study of behavioral development.* New York: Academic Press.

Wolff, P. H. (1967). The causes, control, and organization of behavior in the neonate. *Psychological Issues, 5,* 1–105.

Wolpe, J. (1963). Behavior therapy in complex neurotic states. *British Journal of Psychiatry, 110,* 28–34.

Wolpe, J., & Rachman, S. (1960). Psychoanalytic "evidence": A critique based on Freud's cases of Little Hans. *Journal of Nervous and Mental Disease, 130,* 135–148.

Worobey, J., & Belsky, J. (1982). Employing the Brazelton Scale to influence mothering: An experimental comparison of three strategies. *Developmental Psychology, 18,* 736–743.

Wright, J. C., & Huston, A. C. (1985, April). *Developmental changes in children's understanding of form and content.* Paper presented at the meeting of the Society for Research in Child Development, Toronto.

Wurster, R. M., & Griffiths, R. R. (1979). Human concurrent performances: Variation of reinforcer magnitude and rate of reinforcement. *Psychological Record, 29,* 341–354.

Wylie, R. C. (1974). *The self-concept.* Lincoln: University of Nebraska Press.

Wylie, R. C. (1979). *The self-concept: Theory and research on selected topics* (Vol. 2). Lincoln: University of Nebraska Press.

Yakovlev, P. I., & Lecours, A. (1967). The myelogenetic cycles of regional maturation of the brain. In A. Minkowski (Ed.), *Regional development of the brain in early life.* Oxford: Blackwell Scientific.

Yando, R. M., & Kagan, J. (1968). The effect of teacher tempo on the child. *Child Development, 39,* 27–34.

Yang, R. K., & Douthitt, T. C. (1974). Newborn responses to threshold tactile stimulation. *Child Development, 45,* 237–242.

Yarrow, L. J. (1964). Separation from parents during early childhood. In L. W. Hoffman & M. L. Hoffman (Eds.), *Review of child development research* (Vol. 1). New York: Russell Sage Foundation.

Yarrow, M. R., Campbell, J. D., & Burton, R. V. (1968). *Child rearing.* San Francisco: Jossey-Bass.

Yonas, A., Granrud, C. E., & Pettersen, L. (1985). Infants' sensitivity to relative size information for distance. *Developmental Psychology, 21,* 161–167.

Young, H. B., & Ferguson, L. R. (1981). *Puberty to manhood in Italy and the United States.* New York: Academic Press.

Yussen, S. R. (1977). Characteristics of moral dilemmas written by adolescents. *Developmental Psychology, 13,* 162–163.

Zahn-Waxler, C., Radke-Yarrow, M., & King, R. M. (1979). Childrearing and children's prosocial initiations toward victims of distress. *Child Development, 50,* 319–330.

Zajonc, R. B., & Markus, G. B. (1975). Birth order and intellectual development. *Psychological Review, 82,* 74–88.

Zajonc, R. B., Markus, H., & Markus, G. B. (1979). The birth order puzzle. *Journal of Personality and Social Psychology, 37,* 1325–1341.

Zamanhof, S., van Marthens, E., & Margolis, F. L. (1968). DNA (cell number) and protein in the neonatal brain: alteration by maternal dietary protein restriction. *Science, 160,* 322–323.

Zelniker, T., & Jeffrey, W. E. (1979). Attention and cognitive style in children. In G. Hale and M. Lewis (Eds.), *Attention and cognitive development.* New York: Plenum.

Zembar, M. J., & Naus, M. J. (1985, April). *The combined effects of knowledge base and mnemonic strategies on children's memory.* Paper presented at the meeting of the Society for Research in Child Development, Toronto.

Zenatti, A. (1969). Le developement genetique de la perception musicale. *Monographies Francaises de Psychologie* (Whole No. 17).

Zeskind, P. S. (1980). Adult responses to cries of low and high risk infants. *Infant Behavior and Development, 3,* 167–177.

Zigler, E. (1967). Familial mental retardation: A continuing dilemma. *Science, 155,* 292–298.

Zimmerman, B. J., & Rosenthal, T. L. (1974). Observational learning of rule-governed behavior by children. *Psychological Bulletin, 81,* 29–42.

CREDITS

CHAPTER 10

Opener: © Jean S. Buldain; **page 315:** Library of Congress/PHOTRI; **page 318:** © Legge & McGee Photo Enterprises; **page 320:** © James Marshall/Marshalplan; **page 323:** UPI/Bettmann Newsphotos; **page 328:** courtesy of Dr. Walter Mischel, Columbia University; **page 331:** © Steve Takatsuno; **page 333:** © Hildegard Adler; **page 338:** Harvard University News Office; **page 341:** © Will & Angie Rumpf; **page 343:** © Ron Byers; **page 346:** courtesy of Dr. Robert Hinde, MRC, Cambridge University; **page 349:** © James Shaffer; **page 355:** © Tom Lippert.

CHAPTER 11

Opener: © Ron Byers; **page 364:** © Hildegard Adler; **page 365:** © Norman Prince; **page 366:** © Michael Siluk; **page 368:** © Steve Takatsuno; **figure 11.1:** University of Wisconsin, Harlow Primate Laboratory; **page 374:** © James Shaffer; **page 378:** © Robert Eckert/EKM-Nepenthe; **page 382:** © Robert Pacheco/EKM-Nepenthe; **page 385:** © Gail B. Int Veldt; **page 388:** © Will & Angie Rumpf; **page 392:** © Michael Siluk/EKM-Nepenthe; **page 394:** © Hildegard Adler; **page 396:** © James Shaffer.

CHAPTER 12

Opener: © Brookins Photography; **page 404:** © Walter Imber; **page 406:** © Tom Lippert; **page 408:** © John Maher/EKM-Nepenthe; **page 412:** © Tom Ballard/EKM-Nepenthe; **page 418:** © James Marshall/Marshalplan; **page 419:** © Will & Angie Rumpf; **page 421:** © Kim Roberts Pedley; **pages 426, 427:** © James Shaffer; **page 434:** © James L. Reynolds; **page 437:** © Hildegard Adler; **page 438:** © Ron Byers; **page 440:** © John Maher/EKM-Nepenthe.

CHAPTER 13

Opener: © Tom Lippert; **page 453:** © Will & Angie Rumpf; **pages 455, 458:** © Ron Byers; **page 462:** © Mary Anne Compton; **page 466:** © Hildegard Adler; **page 469:** © Gail B. Int Veldt; **page 471:** © James Shaffer; **page 476:** © Steve Takatsuno; **page 479:** UPI/Bettmann Newsphotos; **page 480:** © Norman Prince.

CHAPTER 14

Opener: © Jean-Claude Lejeune; **page 490:** © Bob Coyle; **page 493:** © Robert Eckert/EKM-Nepenthe; **page 496:** © Legge & McGee Photo Enterprises; **page 497:** © David Kohli; **page 499:** © James Shaffer; **pages 501, 505:** © James L. Reynolds; **pages 508, 511:** © James Shaffer.

CHAPTER 15

Opener: © Norman Prince; **pages 518, 519:** © John Maher/EKM-Nepenthe; **page 524:** © James Shaffer; **page 528:** © Hildegard Adler; **page 529:** © Will & Angie Rumpf; **page 530:** © James Shaffer; **page 534:** © Presshuset/PHOTRI; **page 537:** © Brookins Photography; **page 539:** © Steve Takatsuno.

CHAPTER 16

Opener: © Tom Lippert; **page 551:** © A. Novak/PHOTRI; **page 553:** © Marla Murphy; **page 554:** © Kirk Kreutzig/Photographics; **page 556:** © Michael Siluk; **page 561:** © James Shaffer; **page 564:** © Cathy Cheney/EKM-Nepenthe; **page 566:** © Legge & McGee Photo Enterprises; **pages 569, 570:** © James Shaffer; **page 573:** © Steve Takatsuno.

ILLUSTRATIONS AND TEXT

CHAPTER 2

Figure 2.5: From Gottesman, I., "Genetic Aspects of Intellectual Behavior," in *Handbook of Mental Deficiency,* Norman R. Ellis, editor. © 1963 McGraw-Hill Book Company. Reprinted by permission of Norman R. Ellis. **Figure 2.6:** From *Psychology in the Making,* edited by Leo Postman. Copyright © 1962 Alfred A. Knopf, Inc., New York. Reprinted with permission of Random House, Inc. **Figure 2.10:** From Hole, John W., Jr., *Human Anatomy and Physiology,* 3d ed. © 1981, 1984 Wm. C. Brown Publishers, Dubuque, Iowa. All Rights Reserved. Reprinted by permission.

CHAPTER 3

Figure 3.3: From Patten, *Human Embryology.* © 1933 McGraw-Hill Book Company. Reprinted by permission of McGraw-Hill Book Company. **Figure 3.4:** From Thelen, Esther, "Rhythmical Behavior in Infancy: An Ethological Perspective," in *Developmental Psychology,* 17:237–257. Copyright 1981 by the American Psychological Association. Reprinted by permission of the author. **Figure 3.5:** From Petersen, A. C., and B. Taylor, "The biological approach to adolescence: biological change and physiological adaptation," in J. Adelson (ed.) *Handbook of Adolescent Psychology.* Copyright © 1980 John Wiley & Sons, Inc. Reprinted by permission of John Wiley & Sons, Inc. **Figure 3.6:** From Nottelmann, E. D., et al., "Hormone level and adjustment and behavior during early adolescence." Paper presented at the annual meeting of the American Association for the Advancement of Science, Los Angeles, CA. **Figure 3.7:** From Tanner, J. M., R. H. Whitehouse, and M. Takaishi, "Standards from birth to maturity for height, weight, height velocity, and weight velocity: British children 1965," in *Archives of Diseases in Childhood,* 1966, 41. Reprinted by permission. **Illustration, page 101:** From R. G. Simmons, D. A. Blyth, and K. L. McKinney in *Girls at Puberty: Biological and Psychosocial Perspectives,* (Eds. Jeanne Brooks-Gunn and Anne C. Petersen), New York: Plenum Press, 1983. Reprinted by permission.

CHAPTER 4

Figure 4.2: From Gibson, J. J., *The Ecological Approach to Visual Perception.* © 1979 Houghton Mifflin Company, Boston. Reprinted by permission. **Figure 4.4:** From Fantz, R. L., "Pattern discrimination and selective attention as determinants in infancy," in Aline H. Kidd and Jeanne L. Rivoire, *Perceptual Development in Children.* By permission of International Universities Press, Inc. Copyright 1966 by International Universities Press, Inc. **Figure 4.5:** From Banks, M. S., and Philip H. Salapatek, "Infant Visual Perception," in P. H. Mussen, ed., *Handbook of Child Psychology,* Vol. II. © 1983 John Wiley & Sons, Inc., New York. Reprinted by permission. **Figure 4.9:** From Carey, Susan, R. Diamond, and B. Woods, "The development of face recognition: A maturational component," in *Developmental Psychology,* 14, pp. 224–234. Copyright 1980 by the American Psychological Association. Reprinted by permission by the author. **Figure 4.10:** From Acredolo, L. P., "Development of spatial recognition in infancy," in *Developmental Psychology,* 14, pp. 224–234. Copyright 1978 by the American Psychological Association. Reprinted by permission of the author.

Figure 4.11: From Eimas, Peter D., et al., "Speech perception in infants," in *Science,* Vol. 171, pp. 303–306, Fig. 1, January 22, 1971. Copyright 1971 American Association for the Advancement of Science. Reprinted by permission of the publisher and the author.

CHAPTER 5

Figure 5.2: Adapted from *Learning and Behavior* by Paul Chance © 1979 by Wadsworth Publishing Company, Inc. Reprinted by permission of Wadsworth, Inc. **Figure 5.3:** From Morgan/King, *Introduction to Psychology.* © 1971 McGraw-Hill Book Company, New York. Reprinted by permission of McGraw-Hill Book Company. **Figure 5.6:** From Lepper, Mark R., D. Greene, and R. E. Nisbett, "Undermining Children's Intrinsic Interest with Extrinsic Rewards," in *Journal of Personality and Social Psychology,* p. 134. Copyright 1973 by the American Psychological Association. Reprinted by permission of the author. **Figure 5.7:** From Kirk, David L., *Biology Today,* 2d ed. © 1972, 1975 Random House, Inc., New York. Reprinted by permission. **Figure 5.8:** From Bandura, Albert, "Influence of models' reinforcement contingencies on the acquisition of imitative responses," in *Journal of Personality and Social Psychology,* 1, pp. 589–595. Copyright 1965 by the American Psychological Association. Reprinted by permission of the author.

CHAPTER 7

Figure 7.2: From Wingfield, A., A. W. Sandoval, "Perceptual processing for meaning," in L. W. Poon and J. L. Fozard, et al., (eds.), *New Directions in Memory and Aging: Proceedings of the George Talland Memorial Conference,* 1980. © 1980 by Lawrence Erlbaum Associates, Hillsdale, NJ. Reprinted by permission. **Figure 7.4:** From *Memory and Awareness* by R. Klatzky. W. H. Freeman and Company. Copyright © 1984. **Figure 7.5:** From Salapatek, Philip, "Pattern Perception in Early Infancy," in *Infant Perception: From Sensation to Cognition,* Vol. 1, L. B. Cohen and P. Salapatek, (eds.) Reprinted by permission of Academic Press, Orlando, and P. Salapatek. **Figure 7.6:** From Vurpillot, Eliane, "The Development of Scanning Strategies and Their Relation to Visual Differentiation," in *Journal of Experimental Psychology,* 6, pp. 632–650. Copyright 1968 Academic Press, Orlando. Reprinted by permission. **Figure 7.8:** From Dempster, Frank N., "Memory span: Sources of individual and developmental differences," in *Psychological Bulletin,* 1981, 89, 63–100. Copyright 1981 by the American Psychological Association. Reprinted by permission of the author. **Figure 7.9:** From Mandler, J. M., and C. A. Robinson, "Developmental changes in Picture Recognition," in *Journal of Experimental Psychology,* vol. 26, pp. 122–136. Copyright 1978 by the American Psychological Association. Reprinted by permission of the author. **Figure 7.10:** From Schank, R., and R. Abelson, *Scripts, Plans, Goals, and Understanding.* © 1976 Lawrence Erlbaum Associates, Hillsdale, NJ. Reprinted by permission.

CHAPTER 8

Figures 8.3 and 8.5: From *Language and Speech,* by G. A. Miller. W. H. Freeman and Company. Copyright © 1981. **Figure 8.4:** © *The Nobel Foundation* 1974. **Figure 8.7:** From R. Brown, C. Cazden, and U. Bellugi-Klima, in *Minnesota Symposium on Child Psychology,* Vol. 2, 1969, J. P. Hill, (ed.). © 1969 University of Minnesota Press, 2037 University Avenue, S.E., Minneapolis, Minnesota 55414. **Figure 8.8:** From *A Study of Writing,* Second Edition, by T. J. Gelb. Copyright © 1952 The University of Chicago Press. Reprinted by permission. **Figure 8.9:** From Rozin, P., and L. R. Gleitman, "The structure and acquisition of reading II: The reading process and the acquisition of the alphabetic principle," in A. S. Reber and D. L. Scarborough (eds.) *Toward a Psychology of Reading.* © 1977 by Lawrence Erlbaum Associates, Hillsdale, NJ. Reprinted by permission

CHAPTER 9

Figure 9.1: Adapted from Jerome M. Sattler, *Assessment of Children's Intelligence and Special Abilities,* Second Edition. Copyright © 1982 by Allyn and Bacon, Inc. Reprinted with permission. **Figure 9.2:** Sample items reproduced by permission from the *Differential Aptitude Tests.* Copyright 1972 by The Psychological Corporation, New York, N.Y. All rights reserved. **Figure 9.3:** From *The Nature of Human Intelligence* by J. P. Guilford. Copyright © 1967 by McGraw-Hill. Used with permission of McGraw-Hill Book Company. **Figure 9.4:** Item A5 from Raven's *Standard Progressive Matrices* reproduced by permission of J. C. Raven Limited. **Figure 9.5:** From Arthur R. Jensen, "How Much Can We Boost IQ and Scholastic Achievement," *Harvard Educational Review* 39, (1969): 50. Copyright © 1969 by President and Fellows of Harvard College. Reprinted by permission.

CHAPTER 10

Figure 10.1: From *Psychology: A Scientific Study of Human Behavior,* 5th ed. by L. S. Wrightsman, C. K. Sigelman, and F. H. Sanford. Copyright © 1961, 1965, 1970, 1975, 1979 by Wadsworth, Inc. Reprinted by permission of Brooks/Cole Publishing Company, Monterey, California 93940. **Figures 10.3 and 10.4:** From *Adjustment and Growth* by F. J. Bruno. Copyright © 1983 John Wiley & Sons, Inc. Reprinted by permission of the publisher. **Figure 10.6:** From Harris, F. R., M. M. Wolf, and D. M. Baer, "Effects of Adult Behavior," in *Young Children,* Vol. 20, No. 1, October 1964, p. 13. © 1964 National Association for the Education of Young Children. Reprinted by permission. **Figure 10.8:** Ulric Neisser, *Cognitive Psychology,* © 1967, pp. 17, 112. Adapted by permission of Prentice-Hall, Englewood Cliffs, New Jersey.

CHAPTER 11

Figure 11.2: From Harlow, H. F., and R. R. Zimmerman, "Affectional responses in the infant monkey," in *Science,* 130, pp. 421–432. Copyright 1959 American Association for the Advancement of Science. Reprinted by permission. **Figure 11.3:** From H. R. Schaffer and P. E. Emerson, "The Development of Social Attachments in Infancy," *Monographs of the Society for Research in Child Development* 29 (1964), Serial No. 94. © The Society for Research in Child Development. **Figure 11.5:** From E. E. Maccoby and J. A. Martin, "Socialization in the Context of the Family: Parent-Child Interaction," in P. H. Mussen (ed.), *Handbook of Child Psychology,* 4th ed., Vol. 4. Copyright © 1983 by John Wiley & Sons, Inc. Reprinted by permission of the publisher.

NAME INDEX

M

McAlpine, W., 83
McArthur, C. C., 562
McCabe, A., 442
McCall, R. B., 84, 289, 290
McCandless, B. R., 465
McClelland, D. C., 282, 283, 284, 451, 459
Maccoby, E. E., 84, 363, 367, 379, 381,
    409, 460, 470, 496, 505, 507, 516
McConaghy, M. J., 509
McCord, J., 567, 568
McCord, W., 567
McFarlane, A., 130, 131
MacFarlane, J. W., 288, 289
McGowan, J., 454
McGraw, M. B., 552
McKain, C., 127
McKinney, R. G., 101
McKinney, R. L., 101
Mackinnon, C. E., 384
Mackintosh, N. J., 143, 144
McLaughlin, B., 262
McNeill, D., 243
McNeill, H., 248
MacPhee, D., 429
McWhinney, B., 248
Madison, T. D., 388
Mahler, M. S., 354, 469, 475
Main, M., 373, 376, 395, 460
Maisel, E. B., 115
Mallor, O., 111
Malone, P., 292
Malone, S., 124
Malouf, R. E., 560
Mandler, J. M., 121, 208, 214, 218, 220
Mannarino, A. P., 414
Mannle, S., 257
Maratsos, M. P., 244, 248
Marcia, J., 479, 481
Marcus, T. L., 509
Margolis, F. L., 92
Marjoribanks, K., 294
Markman, E., 256
Markus, G. B., 294
Markus, H., 294, 467
Marr, D. B., 289
Mars, K. T., 411
Marshall, H., 432
Marshall, R. E., 132
Martin, D. C., 78
Martin, J. A., 84, 363, 381
Maruyama, G., 383
Maslow, A., 465
Masten, A. S., 564

Masters, J. C., 379, 409
Matas, L., 376, 377
Matheny, A. P., 53
Matthews, C. V., 298, 352
Maughan, B., 425
Maurer, D., 116, 204
May, M. A., 328
Mayer, R. E., 143
Meacham, J. A., 222
Mead, G. H., 474
Mead, M., 369
Mednick, S. A., 568
Mehler, J., 124
Meichenbaum, D. A., 162
Melhuish, E., 124
Mellman, P. W., 479, 480
Meltzer, H. Y., 60
Meltzoff, A., 172
Mendel, G., 45
Mendler, J. M., 212
Menlove, F. L., 334
Mercer, J. R., 285
Meredith, H. V., 90
Messinger, J. C., 349
Metcalf, D., 132
Meyer, C., 259
Milham, J., 81
Mill, J. S., 129
Miller, D. J., 159
Miller, G. A., 231, 239, 244, 246, 248, 256
Miller, K. J., 297
Miller, L. K., 282
Miller, M. M., 498, 500
Miller, N., 383
Mills, M., 124
Milner, B. A., 64
Minnett, A. M., 383
Minuchin, P. P., 436, 437, 540
Miranda, S., 115
Mischel, H., 334, 534
Mischel, W., 156, 161, 328, 329, 334, 336,
    451, 453, 454, 455, 456, 457, 460, 505,
    534
Mistry, J. J., 221
Mitchell, R. G., 87
Mitchell, S. K., 17
Mitteness, L. S., 367
Miura, I. T., 506
Mize, J., 411
Moely, B. E., 211
Moerk, C., 158
Moerk, E. L., 158, 239
Molfese, D. L., 244
Monahan, J., 556
Money, J., 491, 492, 493

Monson, T. C., 454
Montemayor, R., 394
Moore, B., 536
Moore, J. M., 124
Moos, B. S., 432
Moos, R. H., 432
Morais, J., 127
Morgan, C. T., 142
Morgan, J., 240
Moriarity, R., 442
Morse, P. A., 126
Mortimore, P., 425
Moscovitch, M., 208
Moscow, H., 301, 302
Moss, H., 463
Most, R., 422
Mueller, E., 405, 406
Muir, D., 124
Murphy, R. R., 340, 410
Murray, F., 186
Mussare, F., 560
Mussen, P. H., 100, 338, 538
Myers, B. J., 83

N

Naus, M. J., 214, 279
Neale, J. M., 300
Neisser, U., 24, 110, 216, 340, 341
Nelson, J., 220, 221
Nelson, K. E., 241, 251, 411
Neuberger, C. M., 402
Neugarten, B. L., 368
Neulinger, J., 383
Nevis, S., 115
Newell, A., 279
Newsom, C., 153
Nicholls, J. G., 508
Nichols, I. A., 249
Nichols, P. L., 294
Nichols, R. C., 51
Nicholson, J., 498
Nickerson, E. T., 502
Nicolich, L., 422
Ninio, A., 243
Nisbett, R. E., 152
Norman, D., 198
Norton-Ford, J. D., 162
Nottelmann, E. D., 96, 97, 437
Nucci, L., 530, 539
Nucci, M., 530
Nursten, J. P., 563
Nydegger, C. N., 367

SUBJECT INDEX

A

Abnormal behavior
  abused children, 556
  attentional dysfunction, 564
  childhood depression, 560–63
  childhood schizophrenia, 558–60
  continuity in disorders, 572–74, 576
    biological factors, 572
    early experiences and, 572–74
  developmental psychopathology, 551–52
  discontinuity in disorders, 575–76
  drug/alcohol use, 564–66
  eating problems, 552–53
    anorexia nervosa, 570–71
    bulimia, 570
  enuresis, 554
  infantile autism, 554–55, 559
  interactionist approach, 551
  juvenile delinquency, 566–69
  medical model, 550
  range in elementary school children, 557–58
  school phobia, 563–64
  sleeping problems, 553–54
  sociocultural model, 551
  statistical model, 550
  sudden infant death syndrome (SIDS), 552
  suicide, 569–70
  supernatural model, 549
  underachievement, 562–63
Abused children, 556
Accommodation
  Piaget's theory, 170, 192
  visual perception, 115
Acetylcholine, 60
Achievement, sex differences, 507–8
Action potentials, 58
Adaptation, Piaget's theory, 170
Adolescence
  anorexia nervosa, 570–71
  children's groups versus adolescents' groups, 416–17
  defense mechanisms in, 321
  depression, 574
    early experiences and, 574

divorce and, 388–89
drug/alcohol use, 564–66
identity development, 477–80
  college experiences in, 480
  identity versus identity confusion, 477
  modes of resolution, 479–80
juvenile delinquency, 566–69
moral development, 519, 523, 535
parent-adolescent conflicts, 393–94
parental changes during, 368
puberty, 96–101
  early/late maturation, 99–101
  endocrine system, 96–97
  height/weight in, 98
  sexual maturation, 98–99
self-development, 474–80
  cognitive strategies, 475
  differentiation in, 475
  independence, 475–77
  individuation in, 475
  parenting styles and, 476
  stability in, 475
sex-role development, 510–11
Adoption study, 50
Afferent nerves, 56
Aggression
  sex differences, 505, 507
  television viewing, 442
Ainsworth Strange Situation Test, 379
Alcohol use, 564–66
Alleles, 46
Altruism, 536–38
  development of, 536–38
  empathy and, 538
  perspective-taking skills, 538
  role-taking, 538
Anal stage, 319
Androgens, 96
Androgyny, 489–91, 502–3
  adjustment and, 489–90
  measurement of, 489–90
  parenting styles, 491
Animism, 182
  preoperational stage, 182
Anorexia nervosa, 570–71
Apgar scale, 83

Assimilation, Piaget's theory, 170, 192
Associative play, 419
Attachment, 369–80
  bonding, 83–84
  childhood depression and, 563
  cognitive developmental theory, 371
  day care and, 426
  definition of, 369–70
  development of, 372–73
  ethology, 371–72
  imprinting, 42
  individual differences, 373–75
  intergenerational effects, 395–96
  measurement of, 378–80
    Ainsworth procedure, 379
  psychoanalytic theory, 370
  relationships with others and, 375–78
  secure/insecure attachment, 374
  situational variables, 375
  socialization and, 376
  social learning theory, 370–71
Attention, 204–6. *See also* Memory
  definition of, 204
  divided attention task, 206
  externality effect, 204
  in infancy, 204
  orienting reflex, 204
  physiological changes and, 204
  selective attention task, 206
Attentional dysfunction, 564
Auditory perception, 123–27
  localization of sounds, 124
  music perception, 127
  prenatal hearing, 123–24
  speech perception, 124–27
  visual perception, relationship to, 128–29
  voice recognition, 124–25
Authoritarian parenting, 381
  adolescent autonomy and, 476
Authoritative parenting, 381
Autism, 554–55, 559
Automatic processes, information-processing approach, 201–2, 203
Autonomy versus shame/doubt, 324